PRINCIPLES OF
RISK MANAGEMENT AND INSURANCE

The Addison-Wesley Series in Finance

Berk/DeMarzo
Corporate Finance

Copeland/Weston/Shastri
*Financial Theory
and Corporate Policy*

Dufey/Giddy
Cases in International Finance

Eakins
*Finance: Investments,
Institutions, and Management*

Eiteman/Stonehill/Moffett
Multinational Business Finance

Gitman
Principles of Managerial Finance

Gitman
*Principles of Managerial Finance
—Brief Edition*

Gitman/Joehnk
Fundamentals of Investing

Gitman/Madura
Introduction to Finance

Hughes/MacDonald
*International Banking:
Text and Cases*

Madura
Personal Finance

Marthinsen
*Risk Takers: Uses and Abuses of
Financial Derivatives*

McDonald
Derivatives Markets

Megginson
Corporate Finance Theory

Melvin
International Money and Finance

Mishkin/Eakins
Financial Markets and Institutions

Moffett
Cases in International Finance

Moffett/Stonehill/Eiteman
*Fundamentals of
Multinational Finance*

Pennacchi
Theory of Asset Pricing

Rejda
*Principles of Risk Management
and Insurance*

Solnik/McLeavey
International Investments

Titman/Martin
*Valuation: The Art and Science of
Making Strategic Investments*

Principles of
RISK MANAGEMENT
AND INSURANCE

GEORGE E. REJDA

TENTH EDITION

PEARSON

Addison
Wesley

Boston   San Francisco   New York
London Toronto Sydney Tokyo Singapore Madrid
Mexico City Munich Paris Cape Town Hong Kong Montreal

Publisher: Greg Tobin
Editor in Chief: Denise Clinton
Senior Acquisitions Editor: Donna Battista
Director of Development: Kay Ueno
Assistant Editor: Allison Stendardi
Managing Editor: Nancy Fenton
Supplements Editor: Heather McNally
Media Producer: Bethany Tidd
Senior Marketing Manager: Roxanne Hoch
Rights and Permissions Advisor: Shannon Barbe
Senior Manufacturing Buyer: Carol Melville
Cover Design: Leslie Haimes
Production Coordination, Text Design, Art Studio, and Composition:
    Thompson Steele Inc.
Cover Photo: Photodisc Collection

ISBN 978-0-321-46857-4
ISBN 0-321-46857-0

3 4 5 6 7 8 9 10—CRW—10 09 08

CONTENTS

Preface   xvi

PART ONE   **BASIC CONCEPTS IN RISK MANAGEMENT AND INSURANCE**   1

CHAPTER 1   **RISK IN OUR SOCIETY**   2
Meaning of Risk   3
Chance of Loss   4
Peril and Hazard   5
Basic Categories of Risk   6
Types of Pure Risk   8
Burden of Risk on Society   11
Methods of Handling Risk   12

Summary 15 ▪ Key Concepts and Terms 15 ▪ Review Questions 16
Application Questions 16 ▪ Internet Resources 17 ▪ Selected References 17
Notes 17

Case Application   14

INSIGHT 1.1:   AT A GLANCE—THE ECONOMIC PROBLEM OF POOR HEALTH   10

CHAPTER 2   **INSURANCE AND RISK**   18
Definition of Insurance   19
Basic Characteristics of Insurance   19
Requirements of an Insurable Risk   21
Two Applications: The Risks of Fire and Unemployment   23
Adverse Selection and Insurance   24
Insurance and Gambling Compared   24
Insurance and Hedging Compared   25
Types of Insurance   25
Benefits of Insurance to Society   28
Costs of Insurance to Society   29

Summary 33 ▪ Key Concepts and Terms 34 ▪ Review Questions 34
Application Questions 35 ▪ Internet Resources 35 ▪ Selected References 36
Notes 36

Case Application   33

INSIGHT 2.1:   INSURANCE FRAUD HALL OF SHAME—SAMPLING OF OUTRAGEOUS CASES   30

INSIGHT 2.2:   DON'T THINK INSURANCE FRAUD IS COMMITTED ONLY BY HARDENED
CROOKS   32

Appendix   Basic Statistics and the Law of Large Numbers   38

CHAPTER 3   INTRODUCTION TO RISK MANAGEMENT   41

Meaning of Risk Management   42
Objectives of Risk Management   42
Steps in the Risk Management Process   43
Identifying Loss Exposures   44
Analyze the Loss Exposures   44
Select the Appropriate Techniques for Treating the Loss Exposures   45
Implement and Monitor the Risk Management Program   52
Benefits of Risk Management   53
Personal Risk Management   53

Summary 56 ▪ Key Concepts and Terms 57 ▪ Review Questions 57
Application Questions 58 ▪ Internet Resources 59 ▪ Selected References 59
Notes 59

Case Application   56

INSIGHT 3.1:   WHY DO FIRMS SELF-INSURE THEIR GROUP HEALTH INSURANCE PLANS?   49

INSIGHT 3.2:   SHOW ME THE MONEY—RISK MANAGER SALARIES RISE   54

CHAPTER 4   ADVANCED TOPICS IN RISK MANAGEMENT   61

The Changing Scope of Risk Management   62
Insurance Market Dynamics   65
Loss Forecasting   69
Financial Analysis in Risk Management Decision Making   72
Other Risk Management Tools   75

Summary 77 ▪ Key Concepts and Terms 78 ▪ Review Questions 78
Application Questions 78 ▪ Internet Resources 79 ▪ Selected References 80
Notes 80

Case Application   77

INSIGHT 4.1:   THE WEATHER (DERIVATIVES) REPORT   70

Appendix   Risk Management Application Problems   82

PART TWO   THE PRIVATE INSURANCE INDUSTRY   87

CHAPTER 5   TYPES OF INSURERS AND MARKETING SYSTEMS   88

Overview of Private Insurance in the Financial Services Industry   89
Types of Private Insurers   92
Agents and Brokers   98
Types of Marketing Systems   99
Group Insurance Marketing   102

Summary 103 ▪ Key Concepts and Terms 103 ▪ Review Questions 103
Application Questions 104 ▪ Internet Resources 104 ▪ Selected References 105
Notes 106

Case Application   102

INSIGHT 5.1:   HOLDING COMPANY SCHEMES: THE FEELING ISN'T MUTUAL   96

INSIGHT 5.2:   HOW MUCH DO INSURANCE AGENTS EARN?   99

CHAPTER 6   INSURANCE COMPANY OPERATIONS   107

Insurance Company Operations   108
Rate Making   108
Underwriting   109
Production   112
Claims Settlement   113
Reinsurance   115
Alternatives to Traditional Reinsurance   120
Investments   121
Other Insurance Company Functions   124

Summary 125 ▪ Key Concepts and Terms 126 ▪ Review Questions 126
Application Questions 126 ▪ Internet Resources 127 ▪ Selected References 128
Notes 128

Case Application   125

INSIGHT 6.1:   STIFFED BY YOUR INSURER? CHECK YOUR INSURER'S COMPLAINT
RECORD   115

INSIGHT 6.2:   NEW PROPOSALS FOR DEALING WITH MEGA-CATASTROPHES   121

CHAPTER 7   FINANCIAL OPERATIONS OF INSURERS   130

Property and Casualty Insurers   131
Life Insurance Companies   136
Rate Making in Property and Casualty Insurance   139
Rate Making in Life Insurance   143

Summary 144 ▪ Key Concepts and Terms 145 ▪ Review Questions 145
Application Questions 145 ▪ Internet Resources 146 ▪ Selected References 147
Notes 147

Case Application   143

INSIGHT 7.1:   PROFITABILITY OF INSURANCE INDUSTRY AND OTHER SELECTED
INDUSTRIES   137

CHAPTER 8   GOVERNMENT REGULATION OF INSURANCE   149

Reasons for Insurance Regulation   150
Historical Development of Insurance Regulation   151
Methods for Regulating Insurers   153
What Areas Are Regulated?   153
State Versus Federal Regulation   161
Current Problems and Issues in Insurance Regulation   163

Summary 169 ▪ Key Concepts and Terms 169 ▪ Review Questions 170
Application Questions 170 ▪ Internet Resources 171 ▪ Selected References 171
Notes 172

Case Application   168

INSIGHT 8.1:   2005 ANNUAL RANKING OF AUTOMOBILE INSURANCE COMPLAINTS
IN NEW YORK STATE (BASED ON 2004 DATA)   159

PART THREE   LEGAL PRINCIPLES IN RISK AND INSURANCE   173

CHAPTER 9   FUNDAMENTAL LEGAL PRINCIPLES   174
Principle of Indemnity   175
Principle of Insurable Interest   178
Principle of Subrogation   179
Principle of Utmost Good Faith   181
Requirements of an Insurance Contract   183
Distinct Legal Characteristics of Insurance Contracts   185
Law and the Insurance Agent   186

Summary 188 ▪ Key Concepts and Terms 189 ▪ Review Questions 190
Application Questions 190 ▪ Internet Resources 191 ▪ Selected References 191
Notes 191

Case Application   188

INSIGHT 9.1:   CORPORATION LACKING INSURABLE INTEREST AT TIME OF DEATH CAN RECEIVE
LIFE INSURANCE PROCEEDS   180

INSIGHT 9.2:   AUTO INSURER DENIES COVERAGE BECAUSE OF MATERIAL
MISREPRESENTATION   182

INSIGHT 9.3   INSURER VOIDS COVERAGE BECAUSE OF MISREPRESENTATIONS IN PROOF
OF LOSS   182

CHAPTER 10   ANALYSIS OF INSURANCE CONTRACTS   193
Basic Parts of an Insurance Contract   194
Definition of the "Insured"   197
Endorsements and Riders   198
Deductibles   198
Coinsurance   200
Coinsurance in Health Insurance   201
Other-Insurance Provisions   202

Summary 204 ▪ Key Concepts and Terms 204 ▪ Review Questions 205
Application Questions 205 ▪ Internet Resources 206 ▪ Selected References 206
Notes 207

Case Application   203

INSIGHT 10.1: WILL YOUR AUTO INSURANCE COVER YOU WHEN YOU DRIVE ANOTHER
PERSON'S CAR?   197

PART FOUR   LIFE AND HEALTH RISKS   209

CHAPTER 11   LIFE INSURANCE   210
Premature Death   211
Financial Impact of Premature Death on Different Types of Families   212
Amount of Life Insurance to Own   213
Types of Life Insurance   219
Variations of Whole Life Insurance   225
Other Types of Life Insurance   234

Summary 237 ▪ Key Concepts and Terms 239 ▪ Review Questions 239
Application Questions 239 ▪ Internet Resources 241 ▪ Selected References 242
Notes 242

Case Application   237

INSIGHT 11.1: 2001 CSO MORTALITY TABLE   222

INSIGHT 11.2: HOW GOOD IS CASH-VALUE LIFE INSURANCE AS AN INVESTMENT?   224

INSIGHT 11.3: VARIABLE UNIVERSAL LIFE INSURANCE: IS IT WORTH IT?   232

CHAPTER 12   LIFE INSURANCE CONTRACTUAL PROVISIONS   244
Life Insurance Contractual Provisions   245
Dividend Options   251
Nonforfeiture Options   253
Settlement Options   254
Additional Life Insurance Benefits   259

Summary 264 ▪ Key Concepts and Terms 264 ▪ Review Questions 265
Application Questions 265 ▪ Internet Resources 266 ▪ Selected References 267
Notes 267

Case Application   263

INSIGHT 12.1: IS THIS DEATH A SUICIDE?   247

INSIGHT 12.2: DON'T BE CONFUSED ABOUT DIVIDEND OPTIONS   252

INSIGHT 12.3: EXAMPLES OF LIFE SETTLEMENT CASES   262

CHAPTER 13   BUYING LIFE INSURANCE   268
Determining the Cost of Life Insurance   269
Rate of Return on Saving Component   273
Taxation of Life Insurance   275
Shopping for Life Insurance   277

Summary 280 ▪ Key Concepts and Terms 281 ▪ Review Questions 281
Application Questions 281 ▪ Internet Resources 282 ▪ Selected References 282
Notes 283

Case Application   280

INSIGHT 13.1: BE CAREFUL IN REPLACING AN EXISTING LIFE INSURANCE POLICY   273

Appendix   Calculation of Life Insurance Premiums   284

CHAPTER 14   ANNUITIES AND INDIVIDUAL RETIREMENT ACCOUNTS   290
Individual Annuities   291
Types of Annuities   292
Taxation of Individual Annuities   297
Individual Retirement Accounts   299

Summary 305 ▪ Key Concepts and Terms 306 ▪ Review Questions 306
Application Questions 306 ▪ Internet Resources 307 ▪ Selected References 307
Notes 307

Case Application 1   304

Case Application 2   304

INSIGHT 14.1: AT A GLANCE—ADVANTAGES OF AN IMMEDIATE ANNUITY   293

INSIGHT 14.2: TEN QUESTIONS TO ANSWER BEFORE YOU BUY A VARIABLE ANNUITY   298

INSIGHT 14.3: WILL YOU HAVE ENOUGH MONEY AT RETIREMENT? MONTE CARLO SIMULATIONS
CAN BE HELPFUL   303

CHAPTER 15   INDIVIDUAL HEALTH INSURANCE COVERAGES   309
Health-Care Problems in the United States   310
Individual Health Insurance Coverages   313
Hospital-Surgical Insurance   314
Major Medical Insurance   314
Health Savings Accounts   316
Long-Term-Care Insurance   319
Disability-Income Insurance   321
Individual Medical Expense Contractual Provisions   324
Shopping for Individual Health Insurance   326

Summary 330 ▪ Key Concepts and Terms 330 ▪ Review Questions 331
Application Questions 331 ▪ Internet Resources 332 ▪ Selected References 332
Notes 333

Case Application   329

INSIGHT 15.1: HEALTH SAVINGS ACCOUNTS ARE NOT AN EFFECTIVE WAY TO CONTROL
COSTS   318

INSIGHT 15.2: DON'T DELAY APPLYING FOR DISABILITY-INCOME INSURANCE   327

INSIGHT 15.3: STATE HIGH-RISK POOLS FOR THE UNINSURABLE   328

CHAPTER 16   EMPLOYEE BENEFITS: GROUP LIFE AND HEALTH
INSURANCE   334
Group Insurance   335
Group Life Insurance Plans   337
Group Medical Expense Insurance   340
Traditional Indemnity Plans   341
Managed Care Plans   343
Consumer-Driven Health Plans   349
Patients Bill of Rights   350
Group Medical Expense Contractual Provisions   351
Group Dental Insurance   352
Group Disability-Income Insurance   353
Cafeteria Plans   355

Summary 356 ▪ Key Concepts and Terms 357 ▪ Review Questions 358
Application Questions 358 ▪ Internet Resources 359 ▪ Selected References 360
Notes 360

Case Application   356

INSIGHT 16.1: CREDIT INSURANCE OVERCHARGES COST CONSUMERS BILLIONS OF DOLLARS
ANNUALLY   339

CHAPTER 17 EMPLOYEE BENEFITS: RETIREMENT PLANS   361
Fundamentals of Private Retirement Plans   362
Types of Qualified Retirement Plans   368
Defined-Contribution Plans   368
Defined-Benefit Plans   369
Section 401(k) Plans   371
Section 403(B) Plans   373
Profit-Sharing Plans   374
Retirement Plans for the Self-Employed   374
Simplified Employee Pension (SEP)   376
SIMPLE Retirement Plans   376
Funding Agency and Funding Instruments   377

Summary 378 ▪ Key Concepts and Terms 379 ▪ Review Questions 380
Application Questions 380 ▪ Internet Resources 381 ▪ Selected References 381
Notes 382

Case Application   378

INSIGHT 17.1: CHECK IT OUT—THE NEW ROTH 401(K) PLAN   373

INSIGHT 17.2: MAXIMUM TAX SAVINGS FOR A SOLE PROPRIETOR WITH A SELF-EMPLOYED 401(K)
PLAN   375

CHAPTER 18 SOCIAL INSURANCE   383
Social Insurance   384
Old-Age, Survivors, and Disability Insurance (OASDI)   386
Types of Benefits   387
Medicare   394
Unemployment Insurance   401
Workers Compensation   404

Summary 410 ▪ Key Concepts and Terms 410 ▪ Review Questions 411
Application Questions 411 ▪ Internet Resources 412 ▪ Selected References 413
Notes 413

Case Application   409

INSIGHT 18.1: WHEN IS THE RIGHT TIME TO DRAW SOCIAL SECURITY?   389

INSIGHT 18.2: PROPOSED CHANGES IN SOCIAL SECURITY—ESTIMATED IMPACT
ON ACTUARIAL DEFICIT   395

INSIGHT 18.3: AT A GLANCE—THE PROS AND CONS OF PERSONAL RETIREMENT ACCOUNTS UNDER
SOCIAL SECURITY   396

PART FIVE   PERSONAL PROPERTY AND LIABILITY RISKS   415

CHAPTER 19 THE LIABILITY RISK   416
Basis of Legal Liability   417
Law of Negligence   418
Imputed Negligence   420
Res Ipsa Loquitur   420
Specific Applications of the Law of Negligence   421

Current Tort Liability Problems   423

Summary 434 ▪ Key Concepts and Terms 435 ▪ Review Questions 435
Application Questions 435 ▪ Internet Resources 436 ▪ Selected References 437
Notes 437

Case Application   433

INSIGHT **19.1**: WHICH CITIES AND COUNTRIES ARE PERCEIVED AS "JUDICIAL HELLHOLES"?   **428**

INSIGHT **19.2**: STUDY SAYS WRONG-SITE SURGERY IS VERY RARE AND PREVENTABLE   **430**

INSIGHT **19.3**: MEDICAL ERRORS RANK WITH HIGHWAY ACCIDENTS AND BREAST CANCER AS A MAJOR
KILLER IN THE UNITED STATES   **431**

CHAPTER **20**   HOMEOWNERS INSURANCE, SECTION I   **439**
Homeowners Insurance   440
Analysis of Homeowners 3 Policy (Special Form)   441
Section I Coverages   445
Section I Perils Insured Against   451
Section I Exclusions   455
Section I Conditions   457
Section I and II Conditions   461

Summary 462 ▪ Key Concepts and Terms 463 ▪ Review Questions 463
Application Questions 464 ▪ Internet Resources 465 ▪ Selected References 466
Notes 466

Case Application   462

INSIGHT **20.1**: RENTERS INSURANCE: SHATTERING A FEW MYTHS   **444**

INSIGHT **20.2**: HURRICANE KATRINA—WINDSTORM AND FLOOD DAMAGE ANSWERS TO FREQUENTLY
ASKED QUESTIONS   **454**

INSIGHT **20.3**: THE BIG GAP BETWEEN REPLACEMENT COST AND ACTUAL CASH VALUE CAN EMPTY
YOUR WALLET   **458**

CHAPTER **21**   HOMEOWNERS INSURANCE, SECTION II   **467**
Personal Liability Insurance   468
Section II Exclusions   470
Section II Additional Coverages   474
Endorsements to a Homeowners Policy   476
Cost of Homeowners Insurance   478

Summary 486 ▪ Key Concepts and Terms 487 ▪ Review Questions 487
Application Questions 487 ▪ Internet Resources 489 ▪ Selected References 489
Notes 490

Case Application   486

INSIGHT **21.1**: DON'T LET YOUR DOG JEOPARDIZE YOUR HOMEOWNERS COVERAGE   **469**

INSIGHT **21.2**: IDENTITY THEFT INSURANCE CAN RESTORE YOUR GOOD NAME   **479**

Appendix   How to Save Money on a Homeowners Policy   491

CHAPTER **22**   AUTO INSURANCE   **494**
Overview of Personal Auto Policy   495
Part A: Liability Coverage   497

Part B: Medical Payments Coverage   500

Part C: Uninsured Motorists Coverage   502

Part D: Coverage for Damage to Your Auto   505

Part E: Duties After an Accident or Loss   512

Part F: General Provisions   513

Insuring Motorcycles and Other Vehicles   514

Summary 515 ▪ Key Concepts and Terms 515 ▪ Review Questions 515
Application Questions 516 ▪ Internet Resources 518 ▪ Selected References 518
Notes 519

Case Application   514

INSIGHT 22.1: THE TOP 10 REASONS TO PURCHASE THE RENTAL CAR COLLISION DAMAGE
        WAIVER (CDW)   508

INSIGHT 22.2: CRASH RISK IS FOUR TIMES HIGHER WHEN DRIVERS USE CELL PHONES,
        STUDY SAYS   510

CHAPTER 23   AUTO INSURANCE AND SOCIETY   520

Approaches for Compensating Auto Accident Victims   521

Auto Insurance for High-Risk Drivers   530

Cost of Auto Insurance   532

Shopping for Auto Insurance   536

Summary 540 ▪ Key Concepts and Terms 542 ▪ Review Questions 542
Application Questions 542 ▪ Internet Resources 543 ▪ Selected References 543
Notes 544

Case Application   541

INSIGHT 23.1: CLAIMS AGAINST ANOTHER DRIVER'S INSURANCE COMPANY   524

INSIGHT 23.2: INSURING YOUNG DRIVERS   534

CHAPTER 24   OTHER PROPERTY AND LIABILITY INSURANCE
        COVERAGES   545

ISO Dwelling Program   546

Mobilehome Insurance   547

Inland Marine Floaters   548

Watercraft Insurance   549

Government Property Insurance Programs   550

Title Insurance   555

Personal Umbrella Policy   556

Summary 560 ▪ Key Concepts and Terms 560 ▪ Review Questions 561
Application Questions 561 ▪ Internet Resources 562 ▪ Selected References 563
Notes 563

Case Application   559

INSIGHT 24.1: MYTHS AND FACTS ABOUT THE NATIONAL FLOOD INSURANCE PROGRAM
        (NFIP)   553

INSIGHT 24.2: EXAMPLES OF CLAIMS COVERED BY PERSONAL UMBRELLA POLICY   558

PART SIX   COMMERCIAL PROPERTY AND LIABILITY RISKS   565

CHAPTER 25   COMMERCIAL PROPERTY INSURANCE   566

ISO Commercial Property Program   567
Building and Personal Property Coverage Form   569
Causes-of-Loss Forms   572
Reporting Forms   574
Business Income Insurance   574
Other Commercial Property Coverages   577
Transportation Insurance   580
Businessowners Policy (BOP)   584

Summary 587 ▪ Key Concepts and Terms 588 ▪ Review Questions 588
Application Questions 589 ▪ Internet Resources 590 ▪ Selected References 591
Notes 591

Case Application   586

INSIGHT 25.1: EXAMPLES OF COVERAGE UNDER THE BUILDING AND PERSONAL PROPERTY COVERAGE
FORM   570

INSIGHT 25.2: ADVANTAGES OF THE SPECIAL CAUSES-OF-LOSS FORM   573

INSIGHT 25.3: EXAMPLES OF EQUIPMENT BREAKDOWN LOSSES   579

CHAPTER 26   COMMERCIAL LIABILITY INSURANCE   592

General Liability Loss Exposures   593
Commercial General Liability Policy   594
Employment-Related Practices Liability Insurance   600
Workers Compensation Insurance   601
Commercial Auto Insurance   604
Aircraft Insurance   606
Commercial Umbrella Policy   607
Businessowners Policy   609
Professional Liability Insurance   609
Directors and Officers Liability Insurance   611

Summary 612 ▪ Key Concepts and Terms 613 ▪ Review Questions 614
Application Questions 614 ▪ Internet Resources 615 ▪ Selected References 616
Notes 616

Case Application   612

INSIGHT 26.1: BASIC FACTS ABOUT WORKERS COMPENSATION   602

CHAPTER 27   CRIME INSURANCE AND SURETY BONDS   618

ISO Commercial Crime Insurance Program   619
Commercial Crime Coverage Form (Loss-Sustained Form)   620
Financial Institution Bonds   625
Surety Bonds   626

Summary 629 ▪ Key Concepts and Terms 630 ▪ Review Questions 630
Application Questions 630 ▪ Internet Resources 631 ▪ Selected References 631
Notes 632

Case Application   628

INSIGHT 27.1: TAKING HOME MORE THAN A PAYCHECK: EMPLOYEE THEFT COSTS U.S. EMPLOYERS $20 BILLION–$40 BILLION A YEAR   621

INSIGHT 27.2: FBI: 90% OF ORGANIZATIONS FACE COMPUTER ATTACK; 64% INCUR FINANCIAL LOSS   623

Appendix A   Homeowners 3 (Special Form)   633

Appendix B   Personal Auto Policy   656

Appendix C   Whole Life Insurance Policy with Riders   670

Appendix D   Flexible Premium (Universal) Life Insurance Policy   688

Glossary   708

Index   727

PREFACE

Since the last edition of *Principles of Risk Management and Insurance* appeared, several tragic events have occurred that clearly show the destructive presence of risk in the American economy. In August 2005, Americans watched in horror as Hurricane Katrina unleashed its fury and destruction on New Orleans, Louisiana, and surrounding states. Powerful winds and subsequent flooding caused billions of dollars of property damage and numerous deaths. Most of the city was flooded, and residents had to be evacuated. Because of an inadequate government response, the hurricane victims experienced intense human suffering, widespread dislocation, and the loss of numerous lives.

Fast forward to the present. New Orleans is slowly rebuilding; terrorists continue to kill innocent victims; and hurricanes, tornadoes, floods, and earthquakes continue their awesome destruction. To say that we live in a risky and dangerous world is an enormous understatement.

Likewise, the insurance industry has experienced rapid changes in the past three years. Some large brokerage firms have engaged in illegal bid-rigging schemes involving the payment of contingent commissions; many large insurers participated in the illegal arrangements. At the same time, some insurers employed questionable accounting practices that made their accounting statements and operating income appear better than was actually the case. A relatively large number of unauthorized insurance entities also operated in many states, which resulted in millions of dollars of unpaid claims. In addition, many angry hurricane victims have filed class action lawsuits against property insurers for denying or underpaying their hurricane claims; a large number of contested claims involved denial of flood-damage losses that were excluded under the homeowners policy. The Insurance Services Office (ISO) introduced a new 2005 Personal Auto Policy; ISO has also introduced a number of new commercial insur-

ance forms. As expected, the financial condition of Social Security and Medicare worsened, and the new Medicare Prescription Drug Program became operational. Finally, a number of congressional hearings examined the controversial issue of federal regulation of insurance rather than state regulation.

The tenth edition of *Principles of Risk Management and Insurance* discusses these changes and other changes as well. As in earlier editions, the text is designed for a beginning undergraduate course in risk management and insurance with no prerequisites. The tenth edition provides complete and current treatment of major risk management and insurance topics. Coverage includes a discussion of basic concepts of risk and insurance, introductory and advanced topics in risk management, functional and financial operations of insurers, legal principles, life and health insurance, property and liability insurance, employee benefits, and social insurance. Once again, the tenth edition places primary emphasis on insurance consumers and blends basic risk management and insurance principles with consumer considerations. As a user-friendly text, students can apply basic concepts immediately to their own personal risk management and insurance programs.

KEY FEATURES OF THE TENTH EDITION

Thoroughly revised and updated, the tenth edition provides an in-depth analysis of current industry issues and practices, which readers have come to expect from *Principles of Risk Management and Insurance*. Key features in the tenth edition include the following:

1. Major restructuring. Based on the comments of users and reviewers, the text has been restruc-

tured to meet the course needs of busy instructors. Major changes include the following:

- *Private insurance industry chapters moved forward.* Most instructors prefer to discuss the private insurance industry early in their courses. As such, the section on the private insurance industry, which appeared last in previous editions, has been moved closer to the front of the text to meet this request.

- *Life insurance chapters moved forward.* Many instructors prefer to teach life and health insurance first before covering property and liability insurance. As such, the section on life and health insurance has been moved forward in the text.

- *Commercial insurance chapters moved back.* Because of time constraints, most instructors spend little or no time discussing commercial property and liability insurance in a beginning course. Commercial lines are typically covered in an advanced course. As such, the section on commercial property and liability insurance has been moved back to the end of the text.

- *New chapter on financial operations.* Chapter 7 is a new chapter on the financial operations of insurers that discusses rate-making, reserves, and methods for determining the profitability of insurers.

Please note that each section in the text is a self-contained unit. Each section can be easily moved to a different part of a course to maintain continuity and to reflect the preferences of instructors. For instructors who prefer the previous sequence of chapters, a course syllabus can be easily changed to reflect the new arrangement. Most experienced instructors, however, prefer to cover only selected parts of the text. Those sections in the text that reflect the instructor's preferences can be easily selected.

2. More streamlined text. Many users have requested a shorter and more streamlined text. The tenth edition reflects this request. Two life insurance chapters have been condensed into one; the number of text pages has been reduced; discussion of dated insurance products has been eliminated; the number of appendices has been reduced; and unnecessary and redundant material has been deleted whenever possible.

3. New Insight boxes. *Insights* are valuable learning tools that provide real-world applications of concepts discussed in the chapter. Most insights in previous editions have been replaced by compelling new ones. Readers should look for these attention grabbers and others in the tenth edition:

- Don't think insurance fraud is committed only by hardened crooks

- Stiffed by your insurer? Check your insurer's complaint record

- Health savings accounts are not an effective way to control costs

- Check it out—the new Roth 401(k) plan

- Maximum tax savings for a sole proprietor with a self-employed 401(k) plan

- At a glance—the pros and cons of personal retirement accounts under Social Security

- Study says wrong-site surgery is very rare and preventable

- Hurricane Katrina—windstorm and flood damage, answers to frequently asked questions

- Don't let your dog jeopardize your homeowners coverage

- Crash risk is four times higher when drivers use cell phones, study says

4. Technical accuracy. As in previous editions, numerous experts have reviewed the text for technical accuracy, especially in areas where changes have occurred rapidly. The tenth edition offers technically accurate and up-to-date material.

5. Clarity in writing. Risk management and insurance topics can intimidate students if presented in an abstract or disjointed manner. Because readability is critical, the text presents principles and concepts directly and clearly, and strives to be the most user-friendly of introductory texts in risk management and insurance.

CONTENT CHANGES IN THE TENTH EDITION

All chapters have been thoroughly updated and revised. Timely content changes include the following:

1. Updated discussion of enterprise risk management. Chapter 4 has been updated to reflect new developments in enterprise risk management. The revised chapter includes a discussion of catastrophe modeling.

2. Updated discussion of government regulation. Chapter 8 discusses the latest developments in government regulation of the insurance industry. The chapter includes a discussion of the controversial and illegal bid-rigging schemes in the payment of contingent commissions, the use of illegal and misleading accounting methods by insurers, the sale of insurance by unauthorized entities, and other important regulatory issues.

3. Changes in life insurance. Chapter 11 discusses the fundamentals of life insurance. It is a condensation of two chapters that appeared in earlier editions. Chapter 13 discusses buying life insurance and now includes an appendix that has a brief explanation of life insurance rate making and legal reserves.

4. Annuities and individual retirement accounts. Chapter 14 now includes a discussion of Monte Carlo simulations to help investors determine how long their retirement funds will last during retirement.

5. Health savings accounts. Chapter 15 includes a thorough discussion of health savings accounts

and their potential for reducing the number of uninsured and for holding down the escalation in health-care costs.

6. Consumer-driven health plans. Chapter 16 discusses consumer-driven health plans as an employee benefit, which includes defined-contribution health plans and high-deductible health plans.

7. New retirement plans. Chapter 17 discusses the new Roth 401(k) plan for employees and the new self-employed 401(k) plan for one-owner business firms.

8. Pension Protection Act of 2006. Chapter 17 also discusses relevant provisions of the Pension Protection Act of 2006. This Act has an important impact on Section 401(k) plans and defined benefit pension plans.

9. Updated discussion on the financial condition of Social Security and Medicare. Chapter 18 discusses the current financial condition of Social Security and Medicare. It also includes a discussion of the new Medicare Prescription Drug Program that became operational in 2006.

10. Auto insurance. Chapter 22 has an in-depth discussion of the new 2005 Personal Auto Policy (PAP) designed by the Insurance Services Office (ISO).

11. Updated commercial lines chapters. Chapters 25, 26, and 27 have been updated to reflect revisions in the commercial lines forms by the Insurance Services Office (ISO). In 2006, ISO introduced a new businessowners policy (BOP), commercial crime coverage form, business auto coverage form, and other forms as well.

SUPPLEMENTS

The tenth edition contains a number of supplementary materials to help busy instructors save time and teach more effectively. The following supplements are available to qualified adopters.

Companion Web Site. As stated earlier, the tenth edition is accompanied by an Internet site at www.aw-bc.com/rejda that allows students to work through a variety of exercises and to take a self-assessment quiz after studying the chapter material. The Web site also provides an online syllabus builder that allows instructors to create a calendar of assignments for each class and to track student activity with an electronic grade book.

Instructor's Manual. Designed to reduce start-up costs and class preparation time, this comprehensive manual contains teaching notes; outlines; and answers to all end-of-chapter review, application, and case questions. Transparency masters that were included in the previous editions have been moved to the PowerPoint lecture slides.

Printed and Computerized Test Bank. Prepared by Professor Michael J. McNamara of Washington State University, this test bank enables instructors to construct objective exams quickly and easily. The test bank is available in Word, PDF, and TestGen formats. The easy-to-use TestGen software is a valuable test preparation tool that allows busy professors to view, edit, and add questions.

PowerPoint Presentation. Prepared by Professor Patricia Born of California State University, Northridge, this tool contains lecture notes expanded from the transparency masters of the previous edition. It also features the complete set of figures from the textbook. There are over 500 slides to aid in classroom presentation.

Study Guide. Also prepared by Michael J. McNamara, this study tool helps students analyze and internalize the topics learned in class. Every chapter includes an overview, learning objectives, outline, and extensive self-test with answers. The self-test section contains short answer, multiple choice, true/false, and case application questions which challenge students to apply the lessons covered in the tenth edition.

Instructor's Resource Disk. Fully compatible with Windows and Macintosh computers, this CD-ROM contains electronic files of every instructor supplement for the tenth edition. Files included are:

Microsoft Word and Adobe PDF files of the Instructor's Manual and Test Bank; Complete PowerPoint Lecture Slides; and the Computerized TestGen Test Bank. To order, contact your Sales Representative or go to http://www.aw-bc.com/irc to download all instructor resources at any time.

ACKNOWLEDGMENTS

A market-leading textbook is never written alone. I owe an enormous intellectual debt to many people for their kind and gracious assistance. Numerous educators, risk management experts, and industry personnel have taken time out of their busy schedules to review part or all of the tenth edition, to provide supplementary materials, to make valuable comments, to answer questions, or to provide other assistance. They include the following:

Burton T. Beam, Jr., The American College

Joseph M. Belth, Professor Emeritus, Indiana University

Steve Boe, Risk Management Department, Nike

Patricia Born, California State University, Northridge

Dave Christy, Agent, State Farm Insurance

Ann Costello, University of Hartford

Arthur L. Flitner, American Institute for Chartered Property Casualty Underwriters

Jane Francis, Consumer Affairs Division, Nebraska Department of Insurance

Lisa Gardner, Bradley University

Jack Gibson, International Risk Management Institute

Edward Graves, The American College

Mike Keyes, President and CEO, Oregon Mutual

Gen C. Lai, Washington State University

Jack Luff, Society of Actuaries

Jon Matthews, Central Carolina Community College

Michael J. McNamara, Washington State University

Cheryl D. Retzloff, LIMRA International

Jerry S. Rosenbloom, The Wharton School,
University of Pennsylvania

Kenn B. Tacchino, Widener University

A. Frank Thompson, University of Northern Iowa

Eric Wiening, Insurance and Risk Management/
Author-Educator, Consultant

Dennis Wheeler, Director of Product Development,
Blue Cross and Blue Shield of Nebraska

Millicent W. Workman, Research Analyst,
International Risk Management Institute, Inc.
(IRMI), and Editor, *Practical Risk Management*

Special thanks are due Professor Michael J.
McNamara of Washington State University for his
substantial contribution to the tenth edition. Professor McNamara wrote a new chapter on the financial

operations of insurers (Chapter 7) and revised Chapter 4 dealing with advanced topics in risk management. He also revised the test bank and the student
study guide, and reviewed each chapter for technical
accuracy. As a result, the tenth edition is a substantially improved product.

I would also like to thank Donna Battista at
Addison-Wesley for her substantive editorial comments, marketing insights, and technical suggestions.
Allison Stendardi at Addison-Wesley also deserves
recognition for her prompt assistance in responding
to the author's numerous requests.

Finally, the fundamental objective underlying
the tenth edition remains the same as in earlier editions—I have attempted to write an intellectually
stimulating and visually attractive textbook from
which students can learn and professors can teach.

George E. Rejda, Ph.D., CLU
Finance Department
College of Business Administration
University of Nebraska–Lincoln

PART ONE

BASIC CONCEPTS IN RISK MANAGEMENT AND INSURANCE

Chapter 1
Risk in Our Society

Chapter 2
Insurance and Risk

Chapter 3
Introduction to Risk Management

Chapter 4
Advanced Topics in Risk Management

CHAPTER 1

RISK IN OUR SOCIETY

*"When we take a risk, we are betting on an outcome that
will result from a decision we have made, though we do not
know for certain what the outcome will be."*

Peter L. Bernstein
Against the Gods, The Remarkable Story of Risk

LEARNING OBJECTIVES

After studying this chapter, you should be able to

◆ Explain the meaning of risk.

◆ Distinguish between pure risk, speculative risk, and enterprise risk.

◆ Identify the major pure risks that are associated with financial insecurity.

◆ Understand how risk is a burden to society.

◆ Explain the major methods of handling risk.

L ori, age 26, works as a waitress at an upscale restaurant in Dallas, Texas. After
the restaurant closed one evening, she drove home in a blinding rainstorm. A
drunk driver ran a red light, smashed head-on into Lori's car, and was instantly killed.
Lori was more fortunate. She lived but was unable to work for six months. During that
time, she incurred medical bills in excess of $100,000 and lost about $20,000 in tips
and wages. The restaurant did not provide any health or disability income insurance.

Lori's tragic accident shows that we live in a risky world. Other tragedies occur
daily. Terrorists and suicide bombers periodically kill and maim thousands of
bystanders throughout the world. Innocent children die as a result of gang drive-by
shootings. Motorists are killed or severely injured by drunk drivers. Homeowners lose
their homes and personal property because of fires, hurricanes, tornadoes, mudslides,
brush fires, and other natural disasters. Others incur catastrophic medical bills and
the loss of earnings because of heart attacks, stroke, cancer, or other disease. Still
others face financial ruin because they negligently injure someone and cannot pay a
liability judgment and other legal expenses.

This chapter discusses the nature and treatment of risk in our society. Topics
discussed include the meaning of risk, the major types of risk that threaten our
financial security, and the basic methods for handling risk.

MEANING OF RISK

There is no single definition of risk. Economists,
behavioral scientists, risk theorists, statisticians, and
actuaries each have their own concept of risk. However, risk traditionally has been defined in terms of
uncertainty. Based on this concept, **risk** *is defined
here as uncertainty concerning the occurrence of a
loss.*[1] For example, the risk of being killed in an
auto accident is present because uncertainty is present. The risk of lung cancer for smokers is present
because uncertainty is present. The risk of flunking
a college course is present because uncertainty is
present.

Although risk is defined as uncertainty in this
text, employees in the insurance industry often use
the term *risk* to identify the property or life being
insured. Thus, in the insurance industry, it is common to hear statements such as "that driver is a poor
risk" or "that building is an unacceptable risk."

Finally, when risk is defined as uncertainty, some
authors make a careful distinction between objective
risk and subjective risk.

Objective Risk

Objective risk (also called degree of risk) *is defined
as the relative variation of actual loss from expected
loss.* For example, assume that a property insurer has
10,000 houses insured over a long period and, on
average, 1 percent, or 100 houses, burn each year.
However, it would be rare for exactly 100 houses to
burn each year. In some years, as few as 90 houses
may burn; in other years, as many as 110 houses may
burn. Thus, there is a variation of 10 houses from the
expected number of 100, or a variation of 10 percent. This relative variation of actual loss from
expected loss is known as objective risk.

Objective risk declines as the number of exposures increases. More specifically, *objective risk varies
inversely with the square root of the number of cases
under observation.* In our previous example, 10,000
houses were insured, and objective risk was 10/100,
or 10 percent. Now assume that 1 million houses are
insured. The expected number of houses that will
burn is now 10,000, but the variation of actual loss
from expected loss is only 100. Objective risk is now

100/10,000, or 1 percent. Thus, as the square root of the number of houses increased from 100 in the first example to 1000 in the second example (10 times), objective risk declined to one-tenth of its former level.

Objective risk can be statistically calculated by some measure of dispersion, such as the standard deviation or the coefficient of variation. Because objective risk can be measured, it is an extremely useful concept for an insurer or a corporate risk manager. As the number of exposures increases, an insurer can predict its future loss experience more accurately because it can rely on the law of large numbers. The **law of large numbers** states that as the number of exposure units increases, the more closely the actual loss experience will approach the expected loss experience. For example, as the number of homes under observation increases, the greater is the degree of accuracy in predicting the proportion of homes that will burn. The law of large numbers is discussed in greater detail in Chapter 2.

Subjective Risk

Subjective risk *is defined as uncertainty based on a person's mental condition or state of mind.* For example, a customer who was drinking heavily in a bar may foolishly attempt to drive home. The driver may be uncertain whether he will arrive home safely without being arrested by the police for drunk driving. This mental uncertainty is called subjective risk.

The impact of subjective risk varies depending on the individual. Two persons in the same situation can have a different perception of risk, and their behavior may be altered accordingly. If an individual experiences great mental uncertainty concerning the occurrence of a loss, that person's behavior may be affected. High subjective risk often results in conservative and prudent behavior, while low subjective risk may result in less conservative behavior. For example, assume that a motorist previously arrested for drunk driving is aware that he has consumed too much alcohol. The driver may then compensate for the mental uncertainty by getting someone else to drive the car home or by taking a cab. Another driver in the same situation may perceive the risk of being arrested as slight. This second driver may drive in a more careless and reckless manner; a low subjective risk results in less conservative driving behavior.

CHANCE OF LOSS

Chance of loss is closely related to the concept of risk. **Chance of loss** *is defined as the probability that an event will occur.* Like risk, "probability" has both objective and subjective aspects.

Objective Probability

Objective probability *refers to the long-run relative frequency of an event based on the assumptions of an infinite number of observations and of no change in the underlying conditions.* Objective probabilities can be determined in two ways. First, they can be determined by deductive reasoning. These probabilities are called *a priori probabilities.* For example, the probability of getting a head from the toss of a perfectly balanced coin is 1/2 because there are two sides, and only one is a head. Likewise, the probability of rolling a 6 with a single die is 1/6, since there are six sides and only one side has six dots on it.

Second, objective probabilities can be determined by inductive reasoning, rather than by deduction. For example, the probability that a person age 21 will die before age 26 cannot be logically deduced. However, by a careful analysis of past mortality experience, life insurers can estimate the probability of death and sell a five-year term life insurance policy issued at age 21.

Subjective Probability

Subjective probability *is the individual's personal estimate of the chance of loss.* Subjective probability need not coincide with objective probability. For example, people who buy a lottery ticket on their birthday may believe it is their lucky day and overestimate the small chance of winning. A wide variety of factors can influence subjective probability, including a person's age, gender, intelligence, education, and the use of alcohol.

In addition, a person's estimate of a loss may differ from objective probability because there may be ambiguity in the way in which the probability is perceived. For example, assume that a slot machine in a casino requires a display of three lemons to win. The person playing the machine may perceive the probability of winning to be quite high. But if there are 10 symbols on each reel and only one is a lemon, the objective probability of hitting the jackpot with three lemons is quite small. Assuming that each reel spins independently of the others, the probability that all three will simultaneously show a lemon is the product of their individual probabilities ($1/10 \times 1/10 \times 1/10 = 1/1000$). This knowledge is advantageous to casino owners, who know that most gamblers are not trained statisticians and are therefore likely to overestimate the objective probabilities of winning.

Chance of Loss Distinguished from Risk

Chance of loss can be distinguished from objective risk. Chance of loss is the probability that an event that causes a loss will occur. Objective risk is the relative variation of actual loss from expected loss. *The chance of loss may be identical for two different groups, but objective risk may be quite different.* For example, assume that a property insurer has 10,000 homes insured in Los Angeles and 10,000 homes insured in Philadelphia and that the chance of a fire in each city is 1 percent. Thus, on average, 100 homes should burn annually in each city. However, if the annual variation in losses ranges from 75 to 125 in Philadelphia, but only from 90 to 110 in Los Angeles, objective risk is greater in Philadelphia even though the chance of loss in both cities is the same.

PERIL AND HAZARD

The terms *peril* and *hazard* should not be confused with the concept of risk discussed earlier.

Peril

Peril *is defined as the cause of loss.* If your house burns because of a fire, the peril, or cause of loss, is the fire. If your car is damaged in a collision with another car, collision is the peril, or cause of loss. Common perils that cause property damage include fire, lightning, windstorm, hail, tornadoes, earthquakes, theft, and burglary.

Hazard

A **hazard** *is a condition that creates or increases the chance of loss.* There are four major types of hazards:

- Physical hazard
- Moral hazard
- Morale hazard
- Legal hazard

Physical Hazard A physical hazard *is a physical condition that increases the chance of loss.* Examples of physical hazards include icy roads that increase the chance of an auto accident, defective wiring in a building that increases the chance of fire, and a defective lock on a door that increases the chance of theft.

Moral Hazard Moral hazard *is dishonesty or character defects in an individual that increase the frequency or severity of loss.* Examples of moral hazard include faking an accident to collect from an insurer, submitting a fraudulent claim, inflating the amount of a claim, and intentionally burning unsold merchandise that is insured. Murdering the insured to collect the life insurance proceeds is another important example of moral hazard.

Moral hazard is present in all forms of insurance, and it is difficult to control. Dishonest individuals often rationalize their actions on the grounds that "the insurer has plenty of money." This view is incorrect because the insurer can pay claims only by collecting premiums from other insureds. Because of moral hazard, premiums are higher for everyone.

Insurers attempt to control moral hazard by careful underwriting of applicants for insurance and by various policy provisions, such as deductibles, waiting periods, exclusions, and riders. These provisions are examined in Chapter 10.

Morale Hazard Some insurance authors draw a subtle distinction between moral hazard and morale hazard. Moral hazard refers to dishonesty by an insured that increases the frequency or severity of loss. **Morale hazard** *is carelessness or indifference to a loss because of the existence of insurance.* Some insureds are careless or indifferent to a loss because they have insurance. Examples of morale hazard include leaving car keys in an unlocked car, which increases the chance of theft; leaving a door unlocked that allows a burglar to enter; and changing lanes suddenly on a congested interstate highway without signaling. Careless acts like these increase the chance of loss.

Legal Hazard Legal hazard *refers to characteristics of the legal system or regulatory environment that increase the frequency or severity of losses.* Examples include adverse jury verdicts or large damage awards in liability lawsuits, statutes that require insurers to include coverage for certain benefits in health insurance plans, such as coverage for alcoholism; and regulatory action by state insurance departments that restrict the ability of insurers to withdraw from the state because of poor underwriting results.

BASIC CATEGORIES OF RISK

Risk can be classified into several distinct categories. The most important categories are the following:

- Pure and speculative risk
- Fundamental risk and particular risk
- Enterprise risk

Pure Risk and Speculative Risk

Pure risk *is defined as a situation in which there are only the possibilities of loss or no loss.* The only possible outcomes are adverse (loss) and neutral (no loss). Examples of pure risks include premature death, job-related accidents, catastrophic medical expenses, and damage to property from fire, lightning, flood, or earthquake.

Speculative risk *is defined as a situation in which either profit or loss is possible.* For example, if you purchase 100 shares of common stock, you would profit if the price of the stock increases but would lose if the price declines. Other examples of speculative risks include betting on a horse race, investing in real estate, and going into business for yourself. In these situations, both profit and loss are possible.

It is important to distinguish between pure and speculative risks for three reasons. First, private insurers typically insure only pure risks. With certain exceptions, private insurers generally do not insure speculative risks, and other techniques for dealing with speculative risk must be used. (One exception is that some insurers will insure institutional portfolio investments and municipal bonds against loss.)

Second, the law of large numbers can be applied more easily to pure risks than to speculative risks. The law of large numbers is important because it enables insurers to predict future loss experience. In con-

trast, it is generally more difficult to apply the law of large numbers to speculative risks to predict future loss experience. An exception is the speculative risk of gambling, where casino operators can apply the law of large numbers in a most efficient manner.

Finally, society may benefit from a speculative risk even though a loss occurs, but it is harmed if a pure risk is present and a loss occurs. For example, a firm may develop new technology for producing inexpensive computers. As a result, some competitors may be forced into bankruptcy. Despite the bankruptcy, society benefits because the computers are produced at a lower cost. However, society normally does not benefit when a loss from a pure risk occurs, such as a flood or earthquake that devastates an area.

Fundamental Risk and Particular Risk

A **fundamental risk** *is a risk that affects the entire economy or large numbers of persons or groups within the economy.* Examples include rapid inflation, cyclical unemployment, and war because large numbers of individuals are affected.

The risk of a natural disaster is another important fundamental risk. Hurricanes, tornadoes, earthquakes, floods, and forest and grass fires can result in billions of dollars of property damage losses and numerous deaths. In 2005, Hurricane Katrina destroyed a large part of New Orleans, Louisiana, and caused billions of property damage in Louisiana, Florida, Mississippi, and Texas. Hurricane Katrina was the largest single catastrophe in the history of the United States. Insured property damage losses exceeded the property damage to the World Trade Center caused by terrorists on September 11, 2001. Hurricanes Rita and Wilma caused additional property damage as well (see Exhibit 1.1).

More recently, the risk of a terrorist attack is rapidly emerging as a fundamental risk. Many countries have experienced a substantial increase in terrorism in recent years, resulting in substantial property damage and the loss of human lives. The terrorist attack in the United States on September 11, 2001, resulted in the loss of four commercial jets, destruction of the World Trade Center in New York City, substantial damage to the Pentagon, and thousands of dead or injured persons.

In contrast to a fundamental risk, a **particular risk** *is a risk that affects only individuals and not the*

EXHIBIT 1.1
**The 10 Most Costly Hurricanes in the United States
($ millions)**

Rank	Date	Location	Hurricane	Estimated insured loss[a]	
				Dollars When Occurred	In 2005 Dollars[b]
1	Aug. 25–29, 2005	AL, FL, GA, LA, MS, TN	Katrina	$40,600	$40,600
2	Aug. 23–24, 25–26, 1992	FL, LA, MS	Andrew	15,500	21,576
3	Oct. 24, 2005	FL	Wilma	10,300	10,300
4	Aug. 13–15, 2004	FL, NC, SC	Charley	7,475	7,728
5	Sep. 16–21, 2004	AL, FL, GA, OH, PA, NY, NC, 8 other states	Ivan	7,110	7,351
6	Sep. 17–18, 21–22, 1989	U.S. Virgin Islands, PR, GA, SC, NC, VA	Hugo	4,195	6,607
7	Sep. 20–26, 2005	AL, AR, FL, LA, MS, TN, TX	Rita	5,000	5,000
8	Sep. 5, 2004	FL, GA, SC, NC, NY	Frances	4,595	4,751
9	Sep. 15–25, 2004	PR, FL, PA, GA, SC, NY	Jeanne	3,440	3,557
10	Sep. 21–28, 1998	PR, U.S. Virgin Islands, AL, FL, LA, MS	Georges	2,900	3,475

[a]Property coverage only.
[b]Adjusted to 2005 dollars by the Insurance Information Institute.

SOURCE: ISO; Insurance Information Institute, *Insurance Factbook.*

entire community. Examples include car thefts, bank robberies, and dwelling fires. Only individuals experiencing such losses are affected, not the entire economy or large groups of people.

The distinction between a fundamental and a particular risk is important because government assistance may be necessary to insure a fundamental risk. Social insurance and government insurance programs, as well as government guarantees and subsidies, may be necessary to insure certain fundamental risks in the United States. For example, the risk of unemployment generally is not insurable by private insurers but can be insured publicly by state unemployment compensation programs. In addition, flood insurance subsidized by the federal government is available to business firms and individuals in flood-prone areas.

Enterprise Risk

Enterprise risk *is a term that encompasses all major risks faced by a business firm. Such risks include pure risk, speculative risk, strategic risk, operational risk, and financial risk.* We have already explained the meaning of pure and speculative risk. *Strategic*

risk refers to uncertainty regarding the firm's financial goals and objectives; for example, if a firm enters a new line of business, the line may be unprofitable. *Operational risk* results from the firm's business operations; for example, a bank that offers online banking services may incur losses if "hackers" break into the bank's computer.

Enterprise risk also includes financial risk, which is becoming more important in a commercial risk management program. **Financial risk** *refers to the uncertainty of loss because of adverse changes in commodity prices, interest rates, foreign exchange rates, and the value of money.* For example, a food company that agrees to deliver cereal at a fixed price to a supermarket in six months may lose money if grain prices rise. A bank with a large portfolio of Treasury bonds may incur losses if interest rates rise. Likewise, an American corporation doing business in Japan may lose money when Japanese yen is exchanged for American dollars.

Enterprise risk is becoming more important in commercial risk management, which is a process that organizations use to identify and treat major and minor risks. In the evolution of commercial risk management, some risk managers are now considering all types of risk in one program. **Enterprise risk management** *combines into a single unified treatment program all major risks faced by the firm.* As explained earlier, these risks include pure risk, speculative risk, strategic risk, operational risk, and financial risk. By packaging major risks into a single program, the firm can offset one risk against another. As a result, overall risk can be reduced. As long as all risks are not perfectly correlated, the combination of risks can reduce the firm's overall risk. In particular, if some risks are negatively correlated, overall risk can be significantly reduced. Chapter 4 discusses enterprise risk management in greater detail.

Treatment of financial risks typically requires the use of complex hedging techniques, financial derivatives, futures contracts, options, and other financial instruments. Some firms appoint a chief risk officer (CRO), such as the treasurer, to manage the firm's financial risks. Chapter 4 discusses financial risk management in greater detail.

TYPES OF PURE RISK

The preceding discussion shows several ways of classifying risk. However, in this text, we emphasize primarily the identification and treatment of pure risk. Major types of pure risk that can create great financial insecurity include (1) personal risks, (2) property risks, and (3) liability risks.

Personal Risks

Personal risks *are risks that directly affect an individual.* They involve the possibility of the loss or reduction of earned income, extra expenses, and the depletion of financial assets. There are four major personal risks:[2]

- Risk of premature death
- Risk of insufficient income during retirement
- Risk of poor health
- Risk of unemployment

Risk of Premature Death   **Premature death** *is defined as the death of a family head with unfulfilled financial obligations.* These obligations can include dependents to support, a mortgage to be paid off, or children to educate. If the surviving family members receive an insufficient amount of replacement income from other sources or have insufficient finan-

cial assets to replace the lost income, they may be financially insecure.

Premature death can cause financial problems only if the deceased has dependents to support or dies with unsatisfied financial obligations. Thus, the death of a child age seven is not "premature" in the economic sense.

There are at least four costs that result from the premature death of a family head. First, the human life value of the family head is lost forever. The **human life value** *is defined as the present value of the family's share of the deceased breadwinner's future earnings.* This loss can be substantial; the actual or potential human life value of most college graduates can easily exceed $500,000. Second, additional expenses may be incurred because of funeral expenses, uninsured medical bills, probate and estate settlement costs, and estate and inheritance taxes for larger estates. Third, because of insufficient income, some families may have trouble making ends meet or covering expenses. Finally, certain noneconomic costs are also incurred, including emotional grief, loss of a role model, and counseling and guidance for the children.

Risk of Insufficient Income During Retirement   The major risk associated with old age is insufficient income during retirement. The vast majority of workers in the United States retire before age 65. When they retire, they lose their earned income. Unless they have sufficient financial assets on which to draw, or have access to other sources of retirement income, such as Social Security or a private pension, they will be exposed to financial insecurity during retirement.

The majority of workers experience a substantial reduction in their money incomes when they retire, which can result in a reduced standard of living. *For example, according to the 2006 Current Population Survey, median money income for all households in the United States was $46,326 in 2005. In contrast, the median income for households with an aged householder 65 and older was only $26,036 in 2005, or about 44 percent less.*[3] This amount generally is insufficient for retired workers who have substantial additional expenses, such as high uninsured medical bills, high property taxes, or one or both spouses paying for the cost of long-term care in a nursing facility.

In addition, most workers are not saving enough for a comfortable retirement. During the next 15 years, millions of American workers will retire.

However, an alarming number of them will be financially unprepared for a comfortable retirement. According to a 2006 survey sponsored by the Employee Benefit Research Institute, the amounts saved for retirement are relatively small. *The survey found that 53 percent of all workers reported total savings and investments, excluding their homes, of less than $25,000. Only 12 percent reported saving $250,000 or more for retirement (see Exhibit 1.2).* In general, these amounts are relatively small and will not provide a comfortable retirement.

Risk of Poor Health   Poor health is another important personal risk. The risk of poor health includes both the payment of catastrophic medical bills and the loss of earned income. The costs of major surgery have increased substantially in recent years. For example, an open heart operation can cost more than $300,000, a kidney or heart transplant can cost more than $500,000, and the costs of a crippling accident requiring several major operations, plastic surgery, and rehabilitation can exceed $600,000. In addition, long-term care in a nursing home can cost $60,000 or more each year. Unless you have adequate health insurance, private savings and financial assets, or other sources of income to meet these expenditures, you may be financially insecure. Insight 1.1 discusses the economic problem of poor health in greater detail.

The loss of earned income is another major cause of financial insecurity if the disability is severe. In cases of long-term disability, there is a substantial loss of earned income, medical bills are incurred, employee benefits may be lost or reduced, savings are often depleted, and someone must take care of the disabled person.

Most workers seldom think about the financial consequences of long-term disability. The probability of becoming disabled before age 65 is much higher than is commonly believed, especially at younger ages. *Based on the interactive calculator of a national life insurer, the likelihood that a male, age 22, will become disabled for 90 days or longer before age 65 is 21 percent. The corresponding figure for a female, age 22, is 33 percent.*[4] Although disability for a specific individual cannot be predicted, the financial impact of total disability on savings, assets, and the ability to earn an income can be severe. In particular, the loss of earned income during a lengthy disability can be financially very devastating.

Risk of Unemployment   The risk of unemployment is another major threat to financial security. Unemployment can result from business cycle downswings, technological and structural changes in the economy, seasonal factors, and imperfections in the labor market.

Several important trends have aggravated the problem of unemployment. To hold down labor costs, large corporations have downsized, and their workforce has been permanently reduced; employers are increasingly hiring temporary or part-time workers to reduce labor costs; and millions of jobs have been lost to foreign nations because of outsourcing.

EXHIBIT 1.2
Reported Total Savings and Investments among Those Responding, by Age (not including value of primary residence or defined benefit plans)

	Worker Age Group					
	All Workers	Ages 25–34	Ages 35–44	Ages 45–54	Ages 55+	All Retirees
Less than $10,000	39%	54%	34%	31%	36%	30%
$10,000–$24,999	14	19	15	13	6	12
$25,000–$49,999	12	11	14	14	8	14
$50,000–$99,999	12	7	16	12	12	11
$100,000–$149,999	5	1	7	5	7	7
$150,000–$249,999	6	3	5	10	5	6
$250,000–$499,999	6	1	5	8	13	12
$500,000 or more	6	4	4	8	13	10

SOURCE: Employee Benefit Research Institute, "Will More of Us Be Working Forever? The 2006 Confidence Survey," *EBRI Issue Brief, No. 292,* Figure 3, April 2006.

INSIGHT 1.1

At a Glance—The Economic Problem of Poor Health

You might think that debt and despair are problems only of the uninsured. If so, think again. Millions of Americans face enormous health care costs and risk financial ruin. You may see your friends, coworkers, or neighbors try to recover from a painful illness or a car accident. What you probably don't see is how little their health insurance covers or how costly their medical bills are. Millions of Americans suffer from devastating financial burdens at the same time they face serious illness or injury. The middle class, those with college degrees, decent jobs, health insurance—the group of people who feel secure and well-protected—are at high, and often highest, risk of being left penniless when serious illness hits.

Millions of *insured* Americans are spending their life savings on health care
- **51 million** *insured* Americans spent more than one-tenth of their income on health care
- **10.7 million** *insured* Americans spent more than a quarter of their paycheck on health care
- **6.8 million** *insured* Americans spent more than one-third of their income on health care

People who can't afford out-of-pocket costs delay and skip needed health care
- **Almost one in five** Americans reported postponing seeking medical care
- Of these, **more than one in three** said the delay resulted in a temporary disability that included significant pain and suffering
- And **more than one in ten** said the delay caused a long-term disability

Those who *do* seek medical care are often ruined financially
- **Every 30 seconds,** an American files for bankruptcy after having a health problem
- **About half** of all personal bankruptcy cases are due to medical reasons
- Among those whose illness led to bankruptcy, **more than three in four** *had insurance* at the onset of the illness
- The majority of the medically bankrupt had been to college, had responsible jobs, and had been homeowners

Bankrupt families lose more than their assets
- **One in five** went without food
- **A third** had utilities shut off
- **Nearly two-thirds** skipped needed doctor or dentist visits

SOURCE: Adapted from Families USA, *Have Health Insurance? Think You're Well Protected? Think Again!* February 2005.

Regardless of the reason, unemployment can cause financial insecurity in at least three ways. First, workers lose their earned income and employee benefits. Unless there is adequate replacement income or past savings on which to draw, the unemployed worker will be financially insecure. Second, because of economic conditions, the worker may be able to work only part-time. The reduced income may be insufficient in terms of the worker's needs. Finally, if the duration of unemployment is extended over a long period, past savings and unemployment benefits may be exhausted.

Property Risks

Persons owning property are exposed to **property risks**—the risk of having property damaged or lost from numerous causes. Real estate and personal property can be damaged or destroyed because of fire, lightning, tornadoes, windstorms, and numerous other causes. There are two major types of loss associated with the destruction or theft of property: direct loss and indirect or consequential loss.

Direct Loss   A **direct loss** *is defined as a financial loss that results from the physical damage, destruction, or theft of the property.* For example, if you own a restaurant that is damaged by a fire, the physical damage to the restaurant is known as a direct loss.

Indirect or Consequential Loss   An **indirect loss** *is a financial loss that results indirectly from the occurrence of a direct physical damage or theft loss.* Thus, in addition to the physical damage loss, the restaurant would lose profits for several months while the restaurant is being rebuilt. The loss of profits would be a **consequential loss.** Other examples of a consequential loss are the loss of rents, the loss of the use of the building, the loss of a local market, and continuing expenses.

Extra expenses are another type of indirect, or consequential, loss. For example, suppose you own a newspaper, bank, or dairy. If a loss occurs, you must continue to operate regardless of cost; otherwise, you will lose customers to your competitors. It may be necessary to set up a temporary operation at some alternative location, and substantial extra expenses would then be incurred.

Liability Risks

Liability risks are another important type of pure risk that most persons face. Under our legal system, you can be held legally liable if you do something that results in bodily injury or property damage to someone else. A court of law may order you to pay substantial damages to the person you have injured.

The United States is a litigious society, and lawsuits are common. Motorists can be held legally liable for the negligent operation of their vehicles. Operators of boats and lake owners can be held legally liable because of bodily injury to boat occupants, swimmers, and water skiers. Business firms can be held legally liable for defective products that harm or injure customers; physicians, attorneys, accountants, engineers, and other professionals can be sued by patients and clients because of alleged acts of malpractice.

Liability risks are of great importance for several reasons. *First, there is no maximum upper limit with respect to the amount of the loss.* You can be sued for any amount. In contrast, if you own property, there is a maximum limit on the loss. For example, if your car has an actual cash value of $20,000, the maximum physical damage loss is $20,000. But if you are negligent and cause an accident that results in serious bodily injury to the other driver, you can be sued for any amount—$50,000, $500,000, or $1 million or more—by the person you have injured.

Second, a lien can be placed on your income and financial assets to satisfy a legal judgment. For example, assume that you injure someone, and a court of law orders you to pay damages to the injured party. If you cannot pay the judgment, a lien may be placed on your income and financial assets to satisfy the judgment. If you declare bankruptcy to avoid payment of the judgment, your credit rating will be impaired.

Finally, legal defense costs can be enormous. If you have no liability insurance, the cost of hiring an attorney to defend you can be staggering. If the suit goes to trial, attorney fees and other legal expenses can be substantial.

BURDEN OF RISK ON SOCIETY

The presence of risk results in certain undesirable social and economic effects. Risk entails three major burdens on society:

- The size of an emergency fund must be increased.
- Society is deprived of certain goods and services.
- Worry and fear are present.

Larger Emergency Fund

It is prudent to set aside funds for an emergency. However, in the absence of insurance, individuals and business firms would have to increase the size of their emergency fund to pay for unexpected losses. For example, assume you have purchased a $300,000 home and want to accumulate a fund for repairs if the home is damaged by fire, hail, windstorm, or some other peril. Without insurance, you would have to save at least $50,000 annually to build up an adequate fund within a relatively short period of time. Even then, an early loss could occur, and your emergency fund may be insufficient to pay the loss. If you are a middle-income wage earner, you would find such saving difficult. In any event, the higher the amount that must be saved, the more current consumption spending must be reduced, which results in a lower standard of living.

Loss of Certain Goods and Services

A second burden of risk is that society is deprived of certain goods and services. For example, because of the risk of a liability lawsuit, many corporations have discontinued manufacturing certain products. Numerous examples can be given. Some 250 companies in the world once manufactured childhood vaccines; today, only a small number of firms manufacture vaccines, due in part to the threat of liability suits. Other firms have discontinued the manufacture of certain products, including asbestos products, football helmets, silicone-gel breast implants, and certain birth-control devices because of fear of legal liability.

Worry and Fear

A final burden of risk is that worry and fear are present. Numerous examples can illustrate the mental unrest and fear caused by risk. Parents may be fearful if a teenage son or daughter departs on a skiing trip during a blinding snowstorm because the risk of being killed on an icy road is present. Some passengers in a commercial jet may become extremely nervous and fearful if the jet encounters severe turbulence during the flight. A college student who needs a grade of C in a course to graduate may enter the final examination room with a feeling of apprehension and fear.

METHODS OF HANDLING RISK

As we stressed earlier, risk is a burden not only to the individual but to society as well. Thus, it is important to examine some techniques for meeting the problem of risk. There are five major methods of handling risk:

- Avoidance
- Loss control
- Retention
- Noninsurance transfers
- Insurance

Avoidance

Avoidance is one method of handling risk. For example, you can avoid the risk of being mugged in a high-crime rate area by staying out of the area; you can avoid the risk of divorce by not marrying; and a business firm can avoid the risk of being sued for a defective product by not producing the product.

Not all risks should be avoided, however. For example, you can avoid the risk of death or disability in a plane crash by refusing to fly. But is this choice practical or desirable? The alternatives—driving or taking a bus or train—often are not appealing. Although the risk of a plane crash is present, the safety record of commercial airlines is excellent, and flying is a reasonable risk to assume.

Loss Control

Loss control is another important method for handling risk. Loss control consists of certain activities that reduce both the frequency and severity of losses. Thus, loss control has two major objectives: loss prevention and loss reduction.

Loss Prevention   Loss prevention aims at reducing the probability of loss so that the frequency of losses is reduced. Several examples of personal loss prevention can be given. Auto accidents can be reduced if motorists take a safe-driving course and drive defensively. The number of heart attacks can be reduced if individuals control their weight, stop smoking, and eat healthy diets.

Loss prevention is also important for business firms. For example, strict security measures at airports and aboard commercial flights can reduce acts of terrorism. Boiler explosions can be prevented by periodic inspections by safety engineers; occupational accidents can be reduced by the elimination of unsafe working conditions and by strong enforcement of safety rules; and fires can be prevented by forbidding workers to smoke in a building where highly flammable materials are used. In short, the goal of loss prevention is to prevent the loss from occurring.

Loss Reduction   Strict loss-prevention efforts can reduce the frequency of losses, yet some losses will inevitably occur. Thus, the second objective of loss control is to reduce the severity of a loss after it occurs. For example, a department store can install a sprinkler system so that a fire will be promptly extinguished, thereby reducing the severity of loss; a plant can be constructed with fire-resistant materials to minimize fire damage; fire doors and fire walls can be used to prevent a fire from spreading; and a community warning system can reduce the number of injuries and deaths from an approaching tornado.

From the viewpoint of society, loss control is highly desirable for two reasons. *First, the indirect costs of losses may be large, and in some instances can easily exceed the direct costs.* For example, a worker may be injured on the job. In addition to being responsible for the worker's medical expenses and a certain percentage of earnings (direct costs), the firm may incur sizable indirect costs: a machine may be damaged and must be repaired; the assembly line may have to be shut down; costs are incurred in training a new worker to replace the injured worker; and a contract may be canceled because goods are not shipped on time. By preventing the loss from occurring, both indirect costs and direct costs are reduced.

Second, the social costs of losses are reduced. For example, assume that the worker in the preceding example dies from the accident. Society is deprived forever of the goods and services the deceased worker could have produced. The worker's family loses its share of the worker's earnings and may experience considerable grief and financial insecurity. And the worker may personally experience great pain and suffering before dying. In short, these social costs can be reduced through an effective loss-control program.

Retention

Retention is a third method of handling risk. Retention means that an individual or a business firm retains all or part of a given risk. Risk retention can be active or passive.

Active Retention   Active risk retention means that an individual is consciously aware of the risk and deliberately plans to retain all or part of it. For example, a motorist may wish to retain the risk of a small collision loss by purchasing an auto insurance policy with a $500 or higher deductible. A homeowner may retain a small part of the risk of damage to the home by purchasing a homeowners policy with a substantial deductible. A business firm may deliberately retain the risk of petty thefts by employees, shoplifting, or the spoilage of perishable goods. In these cases, a conscious decision is made to retain part or all of a given risk.

Active risk retention is used for two major reasons. First, it can save money. Insurance may not be purchased at all, or it may be purchased with a deductible; either way, there is often substantial savings in the cost of insurance. Second, the risk may be deliberately retained because commercial insurance is either unavailable or unaffordable.

Passive Retention   Risk can also be retained passively. Certain risks may be unknowingly retained because of ignorance, indifference, or laziness. Pas-

sive retention is very dangerous if the risk retained has the potential for destroying you financially. For example, many workers with earned incomes are not insured against the risk of total and permanent disability. However, the adverse financial consequences of total and permanent disability generally are more severe than the financial consequences of premature death. Therefore, people who are not insured against this risk are using the technique of risk retention in a most dangerous and inappropriate manner.

In summary, risk retention is an important technique for handling risk, especially in a modern corporate risk management program, which will be discussed in Chapters 3 and 4. Risk retention, however, is appropriate primarily for high-frequency, low-severity risks where potential losses are relatively small. Except under unusual circumstances, risk retention should not be used to retain low-frequency, high-severity risks, such as the risk of catastrophic medical expenses, long-term disability, or legal liability.

Noninsurance Transfers

Noninsurance transfers are another technique for handling risk. The risk is transferred to a party other than an insurance company. A risk can be transferred by several methods, including:

- Transfer of risk by contracts
- Hedging price risks
- Incorporation of a business firm

Transfer of Risk by Contracts   Unwanted risks can be transferred by contracts. For example, the risk of a defective television or stereo set can be transferred to the retailer by purchasing a service contract, which makes the retailer responsible for all repairs after the warranty expires. The risk of a rent increase can be transferred to the landlord by a long-term lease. The risk of a price increase in construction costs can be transferred to the builder by having a guaranteed price in the contract.

Finally, a risk can be transferred by a **hold-harmless clause**. For example, if a manufacturer of scaffolds inserts a hold-harmless clause in a contract with a retailer, the retailer agrees to hold the manufacturer harmless in case a scaffold collapses and someone is injured.

Hedging Price Risks   Hedging price risks is another example of risk transfer. **Hedging** is a technique for transferring the risk of unfavorable price fluctuations to a speculator by purchasing and selling futures contracts on an organized exchange, such as the Chicago Board of Trade or New York Stock Exchange.

For example, the portfolio manager of a pension fund may hold a substantial position in long-term U.S. Treasury bonds. If interest rates rise, the value of the Treasury bonds will decline. To hedge that risk, the portfolio manager can sell U.S. Treasury bond futures. Assume that interest rates rise as expected, and bond prices decline. The value of the futures contract will also decline, which will enable the portfolio manager to make an offsetting purchase at a lower price. The profit obtained from closing out the futures position will partly or completely offset the decline in the market value of the Treasury bonds. Of course, interest rates do not always move as expected, so the hedge may not be perfect. Transaction costs also are incurred. However, by hedging, the portfolio manager has reduced the potential loss in bond prices if interest rates rise.

Incorporation of a Business Firm   Incorporation is another example of risk transfer. If a firm is a sole proprietorship, the owner's personal assets can be attached by creditors for satisfaction of debts. If a firm incorporates, personal assets cannot be attached by creditors for payment of the firm's debts. In essence, by incorporation, the liability of the stockholders is limited, and the risk of the firm having insufficient assets to pay business debts is shifted to the creditors.

Insurance

For most people, insurance is the most practical method for handling a major risk. Although private insurance has several characteristics, three major characteristics should be emphasized. First, *risk transfer* is used because a pure risk is transferred to the insurer. Second, the *pooling technique* is used to spread the losses of the few over the entire group so that average loss is substituted for actual loss. Finally, the risk may be reduced by application of the *law of large numbers* by which an insurer can predict future loss experience with greater accuracy. Each of these characteristics is treated in greater detail in Chapter 2.

CASE APPLICATION

Michael is a college senior who is majoring in marketing. He owns a high-mileage 1998 Ford that has a current market value of $2500. The current replacement value of his clothes, television set, stereo set, cell phone, and other personal property in a rented apartment totals $10,000. He wears disposable contact lenses, which cost $200 for a six-month supply. He also has a waterbed in his rented apartment that has leaked in the past. An avid runner, Michael runs five miles daily in a nearby public park that has the reputation of being extremely dangerous because of drug dealers, numerous assaults and muggings, and drive-by shootings. Michael's parents both work to help him pay his tuition.

For each of the following risks or loss exposures, identify an appropriate risk management technique that could have been used to deal with the exposure. Explain your answer.

a. Physical damage to the 1998 Ford because of a collision with another motorist
b. Liability lawsuit against Michael arising out of the negligent operation of his car
c. Total loss of clothes, television, stereo, and personal property because of a grease fire in the kitchen of his rented apartment
d. Disappearance of one contact lens
e. Waterbed leak that causes property damage to the apartment
f. Physical assault on Michael by gang members who are dealing drugs in the park where he runs
g. Loss of tuition assistance from Michael's father who is killed by a drunk driver in an auto accident

SUMMARY

- There is no single definition of risk. Risk traditionally has been defined as uncertainty concerning the occurrence of a loss.

- Objective risk is the relative variation of actual loss from expected loss. Subjective risk is uncertainty based on an individual's mental condition or state of mind.

- Chance of loss is defined as the probability that an event will occur; it is not the same thing as risk.

- Peril is defined as the cause of loss. Hazard is any condition that creates or increases the chance of loss.

- There are four major types of hazards. Physical hazard is a physical condition that increases the chance of loss. Moral hazard is dishonesty or character defects in an individual that increase the chance of loss. Morale hazard is carelessness or indifference to a loss because of the existence of insurance. Legal hazard refers to characteristics of the legal system or regulatory environment that increase the frequency or severity of losses.

- A pure risk is a risk where there are only the possibilities of loss or no loss. A speculative risk is a risk where either profit or loss is possible.

- A fundamental risk is a risk that affects the entire economy or large numbers of persons or groups within the economy, such as inflation, war, or recession. A particular risk is a risk that affects only the individual and not the entire community or country.

- Enterprise risk is a term that encompasses all major risks faced by a business firm. Enterprise risk management combines into a single unified treatment program all major risks faced by the firm. Such risks include pure risk, speculative risk, strategic risk, operational risk, and financial risk.

- Financial risk refers to the uncertainty of loss because of adverse changes in commodity prices, interest rates, foreign exchange rates, and the value of money.

- The following types of pure risk can threaten an individual's financial security:

  Personal risks

  Property risks

  Liability risks

- Personal risks are those risks that directly affect an individual. Major personal risks include the following:

  Risk of premature death

  Risk of insufficient income during retirement

  Risk of poor health

  Risk of unemployment

- A direct loss to property is a financial loss that results from the physical damage, destruction, or theft of the property.

- An indirect, or consequential, loss is a financial loss that results indirectly from the occurrence of a direct physical damage or theft loss. Examples of indirect losses are the loss of use of the property, loss of profits, loss of rents, and extra expenses.

- Liability risks are extremely important because there is no maximum upper limit on the amount of the loss; a lien can be placed on income and assets to satisfy a legal judgment; and substantial court costs and attorney fees may also be incurred.

- Risk entails three major burdens on society:

  The size of an emergency fund must be increased.

  Society is deprived of needed goods and services.

  Worry and fear are present.

- There are five major methods of handling risk:

  Avoidance

  Loss control

  Retention

  Noninsurance transfers

  Insurance

KEY CONCEPTS AND TERMS

Avoidance
Chance of loss
Direct loss
Enterprise risk
Enterprise risk
  management
Financial risk
Fundamental risk
Hazard
Hedging
Hold-harmless
  clause
Human life value
Incorporation

Indirect, or
  consequential loss
Law of large numbers
Legal hazard
Liability risks
Loss control
Moral hazard
Morale hazard
Noninsurance transfers
Objective probability
Objective risk
Particular risk
Peril
Personal risks

Physical hazard
Premature death
Property risks
Pure risk
Retention

Risk
Speculative risk
Subjective probability
Subjective risk

REVIEW QUESTIONS

1. a. Explain the meaning of risk.
   b. How does objective risk differ from subjective risk?

2. a. Define chance of loss.
   b. What is the difference between objective probability and subjective probability?

3. a. What is the difference between peril and hazard?
   b. Define physical hazard, moral hazard, morale hazard, and legal hazard.

4. a. Explain the difference between pure risk and speculative risk.
   b. How does fundamental risk differ from particular risk?

5. a. Explain the meaning of enterprise risk.
   b. What is financial risk?

6. a. What is enterprise risk management?
   b. How does enterprise risk management differ from traditional risk management?

7. List the major types of pure risk that are associated with great financial insecurity.

8. Describe the major social and economic burdens of risk on society.

9. Explain the difference between a direct loss and an indirect or consequential loss.

10. Briefly explain each of the following methods of handling risk. Give an example of each.
    a. Avoidance
    b. Loss control
    c. Retention
    d. Noninsurance transfers
    e. Insurance

APPLICATION QUESTIONS

1. Assume that the chance of loss is 3 percent for two different fleets of trucks. Explain how it is possible that objective risk for both fleets can be different even though the chance of loss is identical.

2. Several types of risk are present in the American economy. For each of the following, identify the type of risk that is present. Explain your answer.
   a. The Department of Homeland Security alerts the nation of a possible attack by terrorists .
   b. A house may be severely damaged in a fire.
   c. A family head may be totally disabled in a plant explosion.
   d. An investor purchases 100 shares of Microsoft stock.
   e. A river that periodically overflows may cause substantial property damage to thousands of homes in the floodplain.
   f. Home buyers may be faced with higher mortgage payments if the Federal Reserve raises interest rates at its next meeting.
   g. A worker on vacation plays the slot machines in a casino.

3. There are several techniques available for handling risk. For each of the following risks, identify an appropriate technique, or combination of techniques, that would be appropriate for dealing with the risk.
   a. A family head may die prematurely because of a heart attack.
   b. An individual's home may be totally destroyed in a hurricane.
   c. A new car may be severely damaged in an auto accident.
   d. A negligent motorist may be ordered to pay a substantial liability judgment to someone who is injured in an auto accident.
   e. A surgeon may be sued for medical malpractice.
   f. An individual may be forced to declare bankruptcy because he or she cannot pay catastrophic medical bills.

4. Andrew owns a gun shop in a high crime rate area. The store does not have a camera surveillance system. The high cost of burglary and theft insurance has substantially reduced his profits. A risk management consultant points out that several methods other than insurance can be used to handle the burglary and theft exposure. Identify and explain two noninsurance methods that could be used to deal with the burglary and theft exposure.

5. Risk managers use a number of methods for handling risk. For each of the following, what method for handling risk is used? Explain your answer.
   a. The decision not to carry earthquake insurance on a firm's main manufacturing plant

b. The installation of an automatic sprinkler system in a hotel

c. The decision not to produce a product that might result in a product liability lawsuit

d. Requiring retailers who sell the firm's product to sign an agreement releasing the firm from liability if the product injures someone.

INTERNET RESOURCES

■ The **American Risk and Insurance Association (ARIA)** is the premier professional association of risk management and insurance educators and professionals. ARIA is the publisher of *The Journal of Risk and Insurance* and *Risk Management and Insurance Review*. Links are provided to research, teaching, and other risk and insurance sites. Visit the site at

http://www.aria.org

■ The **Risk Theory Society** is an organization within the American Risk and Insurance Association that promotes research in risk theory and risk management. Papers are distributed in advance to the members and are discussed critically at its annual meeting. Visit the site at

http://www.aria.org/rts

■ The **Huebner Foundation and Geneva Association** act as an international clearinghouse for researchers and educators in insurance economics and risk management. The Huebner foundation at the University of Pennsylvania provides graduate fellowships to promising scholars in the areas of risk management and insurance education. The Geneva Association is an international organization that promotes research dealing with worldwide insurance activities. Visit the site at

http://www.huebnergeneva.org

■ The **Insurance Information Institute** is a trade association that provides consumers with information relating to property and casualty insurance coverages and current issues. Visit the site at

http://www.iii.org

■ **Society for Risk Analysis (SRA)** provides an open forum for all persons interested in risk analysis, including risk assessment, risk management, and policies related to risk. SRA considers threats from physical, chemical, and biological agents and from a variety of human activities and natural events. SRA is multidisciplinary and international. Visit the site at

http://www.sra.org

SELECTED REFERENCES

Bernstein, Peter L. *Against the Gods, The Remarkable Story of Risk*. New York: Wiley, 1996.

Employee Benefit Research Institute. "Will More of Us Be Working Forever? The 2006 Confidence Survey," *EBRI Issue Brief,* No 292, April 2006.

The I. I. I. Insurance Fact Book 2006. New York: Insurance Information Institute, 2006.

Rejda, George E. "Causes of Economic Insecurity." In *Social Insurance and Economic Security,* 6th ed. Upper Saddle River, NJ: Prentice-Hall, 1999, pp. 4–9.

Wiening, Eric A. *Foundations of Risk Management and Insurance,* 1st ed. Malvern, PA: American Institute for Chartered Property Casualty Underwriters/Insurance Institute of America, 2002, ch. 1.

NOTES

1. Risk has also been defined as (1) variability in future outcomes, (2) chance of loss, (3) possibility of an adverse deviation from a desired outcome that is expected or hoped for, (4) variation in possible outcomes that exist in a given situation, and (5) possibility that a sentient entity can incur a loss.

2. This section is based on George E. Rejda, *Social Insurance and Economic Security,* 6th ed. Upper Saddle River, NJ: Prentice-Hall, 1999, pp. 4–9.

3. U.S. Census Bureau, *Income, Poverty, and Health Insurance Coverage in the United States: 2005* (Washington, DC: U.S. Government Printing Office, 2006), Table 1.

4. Northwestern Mutual Financial Network at nmfn.com. Click on Learning Center and Calculators. Scroll down to "What Are the Odds?" for the interactive calendar that estimates the likelihood of being disabled for 90 days or longer before age 65.

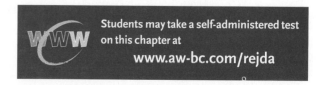
Students may take a self-administered test on this chapter at www.aw-bc.com/rejda

CHAPTER 2

INSURANCE AND RISK

"Insurance: An ingenious modern game of chance in which the player is permitted to enjoy the comfortable conviction that he is beating the man who keeps the table."

Ambrose Bierce

LEARNING OBJECTIVES

After studying this chapter, you should be able to

◆ Explain the basic characteristics of insurance.

◆ Explain the law of large numbers.

◆ Describe the requirements of an insurable risk from the viewpoint of a private insurer.

◆ Identify the major insurable and uninsurable risks in our society.

◆ Describe the major types of insurance.

◆ Explain the social benefits and social costs of insurance.

*P*enny, age 37, is a single parent who is employed as a beautician. She recently
experienced severe headaches and blurred vision. A medical exam revealed a
large brain tumor that required immediate surgery. The surgeon's fee, hospital bills,
and other expenses totaled $100,000. In addition, she could not work for almost
five months. Like many small business owners, Penny did not have any health
insurance or disability income insurance. Because of the lack of health insurance,
Penny experienced great financial insecurity and eventually had to declare
bankruptcy.

   Penny's unexpected surgery shows that poor health can cause serious financial
problems. In Chapter 1, we identified other major risks that can create financial
insecurity. For most people, insurance is the most important technique for handling
risk. Consequently, you should understand how insurance works. This chapter
discusses the basic characteristics of insurance, requirements of an insurable risk,
major lines of insurance, and social benefits and social costs of insurance.

DEFINITION OF INSURANCE

There is no single definition of insurance. Insurance can be defined from the viewpoint of several disciplines, including law, economics, history, actuarial science, risk theory, and sociology. But each possible definition will not be examined at this point. Instead, we will examine those common elements that are typically present in any insurance plan. However, before proceeding, a working definition of insurance—one that captures the essential characteristics of a true insurance plan—must be established.

   After careful study, the Commission on Insurance Terminology of the American Risk and Insurance Association has defined insurance as follows.[1] **Insurance** *is the pooling of fortuitous losses by transfer of such risks to insurers, who agree to indemnify insureds for such losses, to provide other pecuniary benefits on their occurrence, or to render services connected with the risk*. Although this lengthy definition may not be acceptable to all insurance scholars, it is useful for analyzing the common elements of a true insurance plan.

BASIC CHARACTERISTICS OF INSURANCE

Based on the preceding definition, an insurance plan or arrangement typically includes the following characteristics:

- Pooling of losses
- Payment of fortuitous losses
- Risk transfer
- Indemnification

Pooling of Losses

Pooling or the sharing of losses is the heart of insurance. **Pooling** *is the spreading of losses incurred by the few over the entire group, so that in the process, average loss is substituted for actual loss*. In addition, pooling involves the grouping of a large number of exposure units so that the law of large numbers can operate to provide a substantially accurate prediction of future losses. Ideally, there should be a large number of similar, but not necessarily identical, exposure units that are subject to the same perils.

Thus, pooling implies (1) the sharing of losses by the entire group, and (2) prediction of future losses with some accuracy based on the law of large numbers.

With respect to the first concept—loss sharing—consider this simple example. Assume that 1000 farmers in southeastern Nebraska agree that if any farmer's home is damaged or destroyed by a fire, the other members of the group will indemnify, or cover, the actual costs of the unlucky farmer who has a loss. Assume also that each home is worth $200,000, and, on average, one home burns each year. In the absence of insurance, the maximum loss to each farmer is $200,000 if the home should burn. However, by pooling the loss, it can be spread over the entire group, and if one farmer has a total loss, the maximum amount that each farmer must pay is only $200 ($200,000/1000). In effect, the pooling technique results in the substitution of an average loss of $200 for the actual loss of $200,000.

In addition, by pooling or combining the loss experience of a large number of exposure units, an insurer may be able to predict future losses with greater accuracy. From the viewpoint of the insurer, if future losses can be predicted, objective risk is reduced. Thus, another characteristic often found in many lines of insurance is risk reduction based on the law of large numbers.

The **law of large numbers** *states that the greater the number of exposures, the more closely will the actual results approach the probable results that are expected from an infinite number of exposures.*[2] For example, if you flip a balanced coin into the air, the *a priori* probability of getting a head is 0.5. If you flip the coin only ten times, you may get a head eight times. Although the observed probability of getting a head is 0.8, the true probability is still 0.5. If the coin were flipped 1 million times, however, the actual number of heads would be approximately 500,000. Thus, as the number of random tosses increases, the actual results approach the expected results.

A practical illustration of the law of large numbers is the National Safety Council's prediction of the number of motor vehicle deaths during a typical holiday weekend. Because millions of vehicles are on the road, the National Safety Council has been able to predict with some accuracy the number of motorists who will die during a typical Fourth of July weekend. For example, assume that 500 to 700 motorists are expected to die during a typical July 4

weekend. Although individual motorists cannot be identified, the actual number of deaths for the group of motorists as a whole can be predicted with some accuracy.

However, for most insurance lines, the actuary seldom knows the true probability and severity of loss. Therefore, estimates of both the average frequency and the average severity of loss must be based on previous loss experience. If there are a large number of exposure units, the actual loss experience of the past may be a good approximation of future losses. As noted in Chapter 1, objective risk varies inversely with the square root of the number of cases under observation: as the number of exposures increases, the relative variation of actual loss from expected loss will decline. Thus, the insurer can predict future losses with a greater degree of accuracy as the number of exposures increases. This concept is important because an insurer must charge a premium that will be adequate for paying all losses and expenses during the policy period. The lower the degree of objective risk, the more confidence an insurer has that the actual premium charged will be sufficient to pay all claims and expenses and provide a margin for profit.

A more rigorous statement of the law of large numbers can be found in the appendix at the end of this chapter.

Payment of Fortuitous Losses

A second characteristic of private insurance is the payment of fortuitous losses. A **fortuitous loss** *is one that is unforeseen and unexpected and occurs as a result of chance.* In other words, the loss must be accidental. The law of large numbers is based on the assumption that losses are accidental and occur randomly. For example, a person may slip on an icy sidewalk and break a leg. The loss would be fortuitous. Insurance policies do not cover intentional losses.

Risk Transfer

Risk transfer is another essential element of insurance. With the exception of self-insurance,[3] a true insurance plan always involves risk transfer. **Risk transfer** *means that a pure risk is transferred from the insured to the insurer, who typically is in a stronger financial position to pay the loss than the insured.*

From the viewpoint of the individual, pure risks that are typically transferred to insurers include the risk of premature death, poor health, disability, destruction and theft of property, and personal liability lawsuits.

Indemnification

A final characteristic of insurance is indemnification for losses. **Indemnification** *means that the insured is restored to his or her approximate financial position prior to the occurrence of the loss.* Thus, if your home burns in a fire, a homeowners policy will indemnify you or restore you to your previous position. If you are sued because of the negligent operation of an automobile, your auto liability insurance policy will pay those sums that you are legally obligated to pay. Similarly, if you become seriously disabled, a disability-income insurance policy will restore at least part of the lost wages.

REQUIREMENTS OF AN INSURABLE RISK

Insurers normally insure only pure risks. However, not all pure risks are insurable. Certain requirements usually must be fulfilled before a pure risk can be privately insured. From the viewpoint of the insurer, there are ideally six requirements of an **insurable risk.**

- There must be a large number of exposure units.
- The loss must be accidental and unintentional.
- The loss must be determinable and measurable.
- The loss should not be catastrophic.
- The chance of loss must be calculable.
- The premium must be economically feasible.

Large Number of Exposure Units

The first requirement of an insurable risk is a large number of exposure units. Ideally, there should be a large group of roughly similar, but not necessarily identical, exposure units that are subject to the same peril or group of perils. For example, a large number of frame dwellings in a city can be grouped together for purposes of providing property insurance on the dwellings.

The purpose of this first requirement is to enable the insurer to predict loss based on the law of large numbers. Loss data can be compiled over time, and losses for the group as a whole can be predicted with some accuracy. The loss costs can then be spread over all insureds in the underwriting class.

Accidental and Unintentional Loss

A second requirement is that the loss should be accidental and unintentional; ideally, the loss should be fortuitous and outside the insured's control. Thus, if an individual deliberately causes a loss, he or she should not be indemnified for the loss.

The requirement of an accidental and unintentional loss is necessary for two reasons. First, if intentional losses were paid, moral hazard would be substantially increased, and premiums would rise as a result. The substantial increase in premiums could result in relatively fewer persons purchasing the insurance, and the insurer might not have a sufficient number of exposure units to predict future losses.

Second, the loss should be accidental because the law of large numbers is based on the random occurrence of events. A deliberately caused loss is not a random event because the insured knows when the loss will occur. Thus, prediction of future experience may be highly inaccurate if a large number of intentional or nonrandom losses occur.

Determinable and Measurable Loss

A third requirement is that the loss should be both determinable and measurable. This means the loss should be definite as to cause, time, place, and amount. Life insurance in most cases meets this requirement easily. The cause and time of death can be readily determined in most cases, and if the person is insured, the face amount of the life insurance policy is the amount paid.

Some losses, however, are difficult to determine and measure. For example, under a disability-income policy, the insurer promises to pay a monthly benefit to the disabled person if the definition of disability stated in the policy is satisfied. Some dishonest claimants may deliberately fake sickness or injury to collect from the insurer. Even if the claim is legitimate, the insurer must still determine whether the insured satisfies the definition of disability stated in the policy. Sickness and disability are highly subjective, and the same event can affect two persons quite differently. For example, two accountants who are insured under separate disability-income contracts may be injured in an auto accident, and both may be classified as totally disabled. One accountant, however, may be stronger willed and more determined to return to work. If that accountant undergoes rehabilitation and returns to work, the disability-income benefits will terminate. Meanwhile, the other accountant would still continue to receive disability-income benefits according to the terms of the policy. In short, it is difficult to determine when a person is actually disabled. However, all losses ideally should be both determinable and measurable.

The basic purpose of this requirement is to enable an insurer to determine if the loss is covered under the policy, and if it is covered, how much should be paid. For example, assume that Shannon has an expensive fur coat that is insured under a homeowners policy. It makes a great deal of difference to the insurer if a thief breaks into her home and steals the coat, or the coat is missing because her husband stored it in a dry-cleaning establishment but forgot to tell her. The loss is covered in the first example but not in the second.

No Catastrophic Loss

The fourth requirement is that ideally the loss should not be catastrophic. This means that a large proportion of exposure units should not incur losses at the same time. As we stated earlier, pooling is the essence of insurance. If most or all of the exposure units in a certain class simultaneously incur a loss, then the pooling technique breaks down and becomes unworkable. Premiums must be increased to prohibitive levels, and the insurance technique is no longer a viable arrangement by which losses of the few are spread over the entire group.

Insurers ideally wish to avoid all catastrophic losses. In reality, however, this is impossible, because catastrophic losses periodically result from floods, hurricanes, tornadoes, earthquakes, forest fires, and other natural disasters. Catastrophic losses can also result from acts of terrorism.

Several approaches are available for meeting the problem of a catastrophic loss. First, reinsurance can be used by which insurance companies are indemnified by reinsurers for catastrophic losses. **Reinsurance** *is an arrangement by which the primary insurer that initially writes the insurance transfers to another insurer (called the reinsurer) part or all of the potential losses associated with such insurance.* The reinsurer is then responsible for the payment of its share of the loss. Reinsurance is discussed in greater detail in Chapter 6.

Second, insurers can avoid the concentration of risk by *dispersing their coverage over a large geographical area.* The concentration of loss exposures in a geographical area exposed to frequent floods, earthquakes, hurricanes, or other natural disasters can result in periodic catastrophic losses. If the loss exposures are geographically dispersed, the possibility of a catastrophic loss is reduced.

Finally, financial instruments are now available for dealing with catastrophic losses. These instruments include catastrophe bonds, which are designed to pay for a catastrophic loss. Catastrophe bonds are discussed in Chapter 6.

Calculable Chance of Loss

A fifth requirement is that the chance of loss should be calculable. The insurer must be able to calculate both the average frequency and the average severity of future losses with some accuracy. This requirement is necessary so that a proper premium can be charged that is sufficient to pay all claims and expenses and yield a profit during the policy period.

Certain losses, however, are difficult to insure because the chance of loss cannot be accurately estimated, and the potential for a catastrophic loss is present. For example, floods, wars, and cyclical unemployment occur on an irregular basis, and prediction of the average frequency and severity of losses is difficult. Thus, without government assistance, these losses are difficult for private carriers to insure.

Economically Feasible Premium

A final requirement is that the premium should be economically feasible. The insured must be able to pay the premium. In addition, for the insurance to be an attractive purchase, the premiums paid must be substantially less than the face value, or amount, of the policy.

To have an economically feasible premium, the chance of loss must be relatively low. One view is that if the chance of loss exceeds 40 percent, the cost of the policy will exceed the amount that the insurer must pay under the contract. For example, an insurer could issue a $1000 life insurance policy on a man age 99, but the pure premium would be about $980, and an additional amount for expenses would have to be added. The total premium would exceed the face amount of the insurance.[4]

Based on the preceding requirements, most personal risks, property risks, and liability risks can be privately insured, because the requirements of an insurable risk generally can be met. In contrast, *most market risks, financial risks, production risks, and political risks are difficult to insure by private insurers.*[5] These risks are speculative, and the requirements of an insurable risk discussed earlier are more difficult to meet. In addition, the potential of each risk to produce a catastrophe loss is great; this is especially true for political risks, such as the risk of war. Finally, calculation of a proper premium may be difficult because the chance of loss cannot be accurately estimated. For example, insurance that protects a retailer against loss because of a change in consumer tastes, such as a style change, generally is not available. Accurate loss data are not available, and there is no accurate way to calculate a premium. The premium charged may or may not be adequate to pay all losses and expenses. Since private insurers are in business to make a profit, certain risks are difficult to insure because of the possibility of substantial losses.

TWO APPLICATIONS: THE RISKS OF FIRE AND UNEMPLOYMENT

You will understand more clearly the requirements of an insurable risk if you can apply these requirements to a specific risk. For example, consider the risk of fire to a private dwelling. This risk can be privately insured because the requirements of an insurable risk are generally fulfilled (see Exhibit 2.1).

Consider next the risk of unemployment, which generally is not privately insurable at the present time. How well does the risk of unemployment meet the requirements of an insurable risk? As is evident in Exhibit 2.2, the risk of unemployment does not completely meet the requirements.

First, predicting unemployment is difficult because of the different types of unemployment and labor. There are professional, highly skilled, semi-skilled, unskilled, blue-collar, and white-collar workers. Moreover, unemployment rates vary significantly by occupation, age, gender, education, marital status, city, state, and by a host of other factors, including government programs and economic policies that frequently change. Also, the duration of unemployment varies widely among the different groups. In addition, because a large number of workers can become unemployed at the same time, a potential catastrophic loss is present. And because the different types of unemployment occur irregu-

EXHIBIT 2.1
Risk of Fire as an Insurable Risk

Requirements	Does the risk of fire satisfy the requirements?
1. Large number of exposure units	Yes. Numerous exposure units are present.
2. Accidental and unintentional loss	Yes. With the exception of arson, most fire losses are accidental and unintentional.
3. Determinable and measurable loss	Yes. If there is disagreement over the amount paid, a property insurance policy has provisions for resolving disputes.
4. No catastrophic loss	Yes. Although catastrophic fires have occurred, all exposure units normally do not burn at the same time.
5. Calculable chance of loss	Yes. Chance of fire can be calculated, and the average severity of a fire loss can be estimated in advance.
6. Economically feasible premium	Yes. Premium rate per $100 of fire insurance is relatively low.

EXHIBIT 2.2
Risk of Unemployment as an Insurable Risk

Requirements	Does the risk of unemployment satisfy the requirements?
1. Large number of exposure units	Not completely. Although there are a large number of employees, predicting unemployment is difficult because of the different types of unemployment and labor.
2. Accidental and unintentional loss	No. A large proportion of unemployment is due to individuals who voluntarily quit their jobs.
3. Determinable and measurable loss	Not completely. The level of unemployment can be determined, but the measurement of loss is difficult. Some unemployment is involuntary; however, some unemployment is voluntary.
4. No catastrophic loss	No. A severe national recession or depressed local business conditions could result in a catastrophic loss.
5. Calculable chance of loss	No. The different types of unemployment generally are too irregular to estimate the chance of loss accurately.
6. Economically feasible premium	No. Adverse selection, moral hazard, and the potential for a catastrophic loss could make the premium unaffordable.

larly, it is difficult to calculate the chance of loss accurately. For these reasons, the risk of unemployment generally is not privately insurable, but it can be insured by social insurance programs. Social insurance programs are discussed later in the chapter.

ADVERSE SELECTION AND INSURANCE

When insurance is sold, insurers must deal with the problem of adverse selection. **Adverse selection** *is the tendency of persons with a higher-than-average chance of loss to seek insurance at standard (average) rates, which if not controlled by underwriting, results in higher-than-expected loss levels.* For example, adverse selection can result from high-risk drivers who seek auto insurance at standard rates, from persons with serious health problems who seek life or health insurance at standard rates, and from business firms that have been repeatedly robbed or burglarized and seek crime insurance at standard rates. If the applicants for insurance with a higher-than-average chance of loss succeed in obtaining the coverage at standard rates, we say that the insurer is "adversely selected against." If not controlled by underwriting, adverse selection can result in higher-than-expected loss levels.

Adverse selection can be controlled by careful underwriting. **Underwriting** *refers to the process of selecting and classifying applicants for insurance.* Applicants who meet the underwriting standards are insured at standard or preferred rates. If the underwriting standards are not met, the insurance is denied or an extra premium must be paid. Insurers frequently sell insurance to applicants who have a higher-than-average chance of loss, but such applicants must pay higher premiums. The problem of adverse selection arises when applicants with a higher-than-average chance of loss succeed in obtaining the coverage at standard or average rates.

Policy provisions are also used to control adverse selection. Examples are the suicide clause in life insurance and the preexisting conditions clause in health insurance. These policy provisions are discussed in greater detail later in the text when specific insurance contracts are analyzed.

INSURANCE AND GAMBLING COMPARED

Insurance is often erroneously confused with gambling. There are two important differences between them. *First, gambling creates a new speculative risk, while insurance is a technique for handling an already existing pure risk*. Thus, if you bet $500 on a horse race, a new speculative risk is created, but if you pay $500 to an insurer for a homeowners policy that includes coverage for a fire, the risk of fire is already present. No new risk is created by the transaction.

The second difference between insurance and gambling is that gambling is socially unproductive, because the winner's gain comes at the expense of the loser. In contrast, insurance is always socially productive, because neither the insurer nor the insured is placed in a position where the gain of the winner comes at the expense of the loser. The insurer and the insured both have a common interest in the prevention of a loss. Both parties win if the loss does not occur. Moreover, frequent gambling transactions generally never restore the losers to their former financial position. In contrast, insurance contracts restore the insureds financially in whole or in part if a loss occurs.

INSURANCE AND HEDGING COMPARED

In Chapter 1, we discussed the concept of hedging, by which risk can be transferred to a speculator through purchase of a futures contract. An insurance contract, however, is not the same thing as hedging. Although both techniques are similar in that risk is transferred by a contract, and no new risk is created, there are some important differences between them. *First, an insurance transaction involves the transfer of insurable risks, because the requirements of an insurable risk generally can be met.* However, hedging is a technique for handling risks that are typically uninsurable, such as protection against a decline in the price of agricultural products and raw materials.

A second difference between insurance and hedging is that insurance can reduce the objective risk of an insurer by application of the law of large numbers. As the number of exposure units increases, the insurer's prediction of future losses improves, because the relative variation of actual loss from expected loss will decline. Thus, many insurance transactions reduce objective risk. In contrast, hedging typically involves only risk transfer, not risk reduction. The risk of adverse price fluctuations is transferred to speculators who believe they can make a profit because of superior knowledge of market

conditions. The risk is transferred, not reduced, and prediction of loss generally is not based on the law of large numbers.

TYPES OF INSURANCE

Insurance can be classified as either private or government insurance. Private insurance includes life and health insurance and property and liability insurance. Government insurance includes social insurance programs and all other government insurance plans. Thus, the major types of insurance, both private and public, can be classified as follows:

- Private insurance
    Life and health insurance
    Property and liability insurance
- Government insurance
    Social insurance
    Other government insurance

Private Insurance

Life and Health Insurance   At the end of 2004, 1179 life and health insurers were doing business in the United States.[6] **Life insurance** pays death benefits to designated beneficiaries when the insured dies. The benefits pay for funeral expenses, uninsured medical bills, estate taxes, and other expenses. The death proceeds can also provide periodic income payments to the deceased's beneficiary. In addition, life insurers sell group and individual retirement plans that pay retirement benefits. Life and health insurers also sell individual and group health insurance plans that cover medical expenses because of sickness or injury. Finally, both life and health insurers sell disability income plans that pay income benefits during a period of disability.

Property and Liability Insurance   In 2003, there were 2749 property and liability insurers in the United States.[7] **Property insurance** indemnifies property owners against the loss or damage of real or personal property caused by various perils, such as fire, lightning, windstorm, or tornado. **Liability insurance** covers the insured's legal liability arising out of property damage or bodily injury to others; legal defense costs are also paid.

EXHIBIT 2.3
Property and Casualty Insurance Coverages

1. Personal lines
   - Private passenger auto insurance
   - Homeowners insurance
   - Personal umbrella liability insurance
   - Boatowners insurance
2. Commercial lines
   - Fire and allied lines insurance
   - Commercial multiple-peril insurance
   - General liability insurance
   - Workers compensation insurance
   - Commercial auto insurance
   - Accident and health insurance
   - Inland marine and ocean marine insurance
   - Professional liability insurance
   - Equipment breakdown insurance (formerly called boiler and machinery insurance)
   - Fidelity and surety bonds
   - Crime insurance
   - Other miscellaneous lines

Property and liability insurance is also called property and casualty insurance. In practice, nonlife insurers typically use the term **property and casualty insurance** (rather than property and liability insurance) to describe the various coverages and operating results. **Casualty insurance** *is a broad field of insurance that covers whatever is not covered by fire, marine, and life insurance; casualty lines include auto, liability, burglary and theft, workers compensation, and health insurance.*

Exhibit 2.3 identifies the major property and casualty coverages sold today. The various coverages can be grouped into two major categories—personal lines and commercial lines. This division, however, is not completely precise and accurate because of the overlap of certain coverages. For example, although inland marine insurance is a commercial line, it also covers certain personal property, such as expensive jewelry and furs.

1. *Personal Lines.* **Personal lines** *refer to coverages that insure the real estate and personal property of individuals and families or provide protection against legal liability.* Major personal lines include the following:

- **Private passenger auto insurance** protects the insured against legal liability arising out of auto accidents that cause property damage or bodily injury to others. Auto insurance also includes physical damage insurance on a covered auto for damage or loss resulting from a collision, theft, or other perils.
- **Homeowners insurance** covers the dwelling, other structures, and personal property against loss or damage from numerous perils, including fire, lightning, windstorm, or tornado. The policy also includes theft coverage and personal liability insurance. A homeowners policy is a **multiple-line policy,** which refers to state legislation that allows insurers to write property and casualty lines in one policy.
- **Personal umbrella liability insurance** provides protection against a catastrophic lawsuit or judgment. Coverage applies on an excess basis after any underlying insurance coverages are exhausted. Policy limits typically range from $1 million to $10 million.
- **Boatowners insurance** covers the boats and watercraft of individuals and families. A boatowners policy combines into one policy physical damage insurance on the boat, liability insurance, medical expense insurance, and other coverages.

2. *Commercial Lines.* **Commercial lines** *refer to property and casualty coverages for business firms, nonprofit organizations, and government agencies.* Major commercial lines include the following:

- **Fire insurance** covers losses caused by fire and lightning; it is usually sold as part of a package policy, such as a commercial multiple-peril policy. **Allied lines** refer to coverages that are usually purchased with fire insurance, such as coverage for windstorm, hail, and vandalism. Indirect losses can also be covered, including the loss of business income, rents, and extra expenses.
- **Commercial multiple-peril insurance** is a package policy, which can be written to include property insurance, general liability insurance, business income insurance, equipment breakdown insurance, and crime insurance.
- **General liability insurance** covers the legal liability of business firms and other organizations

that arise out of property damage or bodily injury to others. Legal liability can arise out of the ownership of business property, sale or distribution of products, and manufacturing or contracting operations.

- **Workers compensation insurance** covers workers for a job-related accident or disease. The insurance pays for medical bills, disability income benefits, rehabilitation benefits, and death benefits to the dependents of an employee whose death is job related.
- **Commercial auto insurance** covers the legal liability of business firms arising out of the ownership or operation of business vehicles. It also includes physical damage insurance on covered business vehicles for damage or loss resulting from a collision, theft, or other perils.
- **Accident and health insurance** is also sold by property and casualty insurers. This line is similar to the health insurance coverages sold by life and health insurers.
- **Inland marine insurance** covers goods being shipped on land, which include imports, exports, domestic shipments, and means of transportation (for example, bridges, tunnels, and pipelines). Inland marine insurance also covers personal property such as fine art, jewelry, and furs.
- **Ocean marine insurance** covers ocean-going vessels and their cargo from loss or damage because of perils of the sea; contracts are also written to cover the legal liability of shippers and owners.
- **Professional liability insurance** provides protection against malpractice lawsuits or lawsuits that result from a substantial error or omission. Professional liability insurance covers the professional acts or omissions of physicians, surgeons, attorneys, accountants, and other professionals. For example, **medical malpractice insurance** covers physicians and other health-care providers for liability claims arising out of harm or injury to patients.
- **Equipment breakdown insurance** (also called **boiler and machinery insurance**) is a highly specialized line that covers losses due to the accidental breakdown of covered equipment. Such equipment includes steam boilers, air

conditioning and refrigeration equipment, and electrical generating equipment.

- **Fidelity bonds** cover loss caused by the dishonest or fraudulent acts of employees, such as embezzlement and the theft of money. **Surety bonds** provide for monetary compensation in the case of failure by bonded persons to perform certain acts, such as failure of a contractor to construct a building on time.
- **Crime insurance** covers the loss of property, money, and securities because of burglary, robbery, theft, and other crime perils.
- Other lines include **aircraft insurance,** which provides physical damage insurance on covered aircraft and liability coverage for legal liability arising out of the ownership or operation of aircraft. **Credit insurance** covers manufacturers and wholesalers against loss because an account receivable is uncollectible. **Financial guaranty insurance** guarantees the payment of principal and interest on debt instruments issued by the insured.

Government Insurance

Numerous government insurance programs are in operation at the present time. Government insurance can be divided into social insurance programs and other government insurance programs.

Social Insurance   Social insurance programs are government insurance programs with certain characteristics that distinguish them from other government insurance plans. These programs are financed entirely or in large part by mandatory contributions from employers, employees, or both, and not primarily by the general revenues of government. The contributions are usually earmarked for special trust funds; the benefits, in turn, are paid from these funds. In addition, the right to receive benefits is ordinarily derived from or linked to the recipient's past contributions or coverage under the program; the benefits and contributions generally vary among the beneficiaries according to their prior earnings, but the benefits are heavily weighted in favor of low-income groups. Moreover, most social insurance programs are compulsory. Covered workers and employers are required by law to pay contributions and participate in the programs. Finally, eligibility requirements and benefit rights are usually prescribed exactly by statute, leaving little room for administrative discretion in the award of benefits.[8]

Major social insurance programs in the United States include the following:

- Old-Age, Survivors, and Disability Insurance (Social Security)
- Medicare
- Unemployment insurance
- Workers compensation
- Compulsory temporary disability insurance
- Railroad Retirement Act
- Railroad Unemployment Insurance Act

Old-Age, Survivors, and Disability Insurance, commonly known as Social Security, is a massive income-maintenance program that provides retirement, survivor, and disability benefits to eligible individuals and families.

Medicare is part of the total Social Security program and covers the medical expenses of most people age 65 and older and certain disabled people younger than age 65.

Unemployment insurance programs provide weekly cash benefits to eligible workers who experience short-term involuntary unemployment. Regular state unemployment benefits are typically paid up to 26 weeks after certain eligibility requirements are met. Extended benefits also may be available to unemployed workers who exhaust their regular benefits.

As noted earlier, *workers compensation insurance* covers workers against a job-related accident or disease. Although workers compensation is a casualty line sold by private insurers, it is also an important form of social insurance. The social insurance aspects of workers compensation are discussed in Chapter 18.

In addition, *compulsory temporary disability insurance,* which exists in five states, Puerto Rico, and the railroad industry, provides for the partial replacement of wages that may be lost because of a temporary nonoccupational disability.[9] The *Railroad Retirement Act* provides retirement benefits, survivor benefits, and disability income benefits to railroad workers who meet certain eligibility requirements. Finally, the *Railroad Unemployment Insurance Act* provides unemployment and sickness benefits to railroad employees.

Other Government Insurance Programs Other government insurance programs exist at both the federal and state level. However, these programs do not have the distinguishing characteristics of social insurance programs. Important federal insurance programs include the Federal Employees Retirement System, the Civil Service Retirement System, various life insurance programs for veterans, pension termination insurance, insurance on checking and savings accounts in commercial banks and saving and loan associations (Federal Deposit Insurance Corporation), federal flood insurance, federal crop insurance, and numerous other programs.

Government insurance programs also exist at the state level. These programs include the Florida Hurricane Catastrophe Fund, the Wisconsin State Life Fund, title insurance programs in a few states, and the Maryland Automobile Insurance Fund. In addition, competitive and monopoly workers compensation funds are in operation in many states. Finally, the majority of states have special health insurance pools that make health insurance available to persons who are uninsurable or substandard in health.

BENEFITS OF INSURANCE TO SOCIETY

The major social and economic benefits of insurance include the following:

- Indemnification for loss
- Reduction of worry and fear
- Source of investment funds
- Loss prevention
- Enhancement of credit

Indemnification for Loss

Indemnification permits individuals and families to be restored to their former financial position after a loss occurs. As a result, they can maintain their financial security. Because insureds are restored either in part or in whole after a loss occurs, they are less likely to apply for public assistance or welfare benefits, or to seek financial assistance from relatives and friends.

Indemnification to business firms also permits firms to remain in business and employees to keep their jobs. Suppliers continue to receive orders, and customers can still receive the goods and services they desire. The community also benefits because its tax base is not eroded. In short, the indemnification function contributes greatly to family and business stability and therefore is one of the most important social and economic benefits of insurance.

Reduction of Worry and Fear

A second benefit of insurance is that worry and fear are reduced. This is true both before and after a loss. For example, if family heads have adequate amounts of life insurance, they are less likely to worry about the financial security of their dependents in the event of premature death; persons insured for long-term disability do not have to worry about the loss of earnings if a serious illness or accident occurs; and property owners who are insured enjoy greater peace of mind because they know they are covered if a loss occurs. Worry and fear are also reduced after a loss occurs, because the insureds know that they have insurance that will pay for the loss.

Source of Investment Funds

The insurance industry is an important source of funds for capital investment and accumulation. Premiums are collected in advance of the loss, and funds not needed to pay immediate losses and expenses can be loaned to business firms. These funds typically are invested in shopping centers, hospitals, factories, housing developments, and new machinery and equipment. The investments increase society's stock of capital goods, and promote economic growth and full employment. Insurers also invest in social investments, such as housing, nursing homes, and economic development projects. In addition, because the total supply of loanable funds is increased by the advance payment of insurance premiums, the cost of capital to business firms that borrow is lower than it would be in the absence of insurance.

Loss Prevention

Insurance companies are actively involved in numerous loss-prevention programs and also employ a wide variety of loss-prevention personnel, including safety engineers and specialists in fire prevention, occupational safety and health, and products liabil-

ity. Some important loss-prevention activities that property and casualty insurers strongly support include the following:

- Highway safety and reduction of automobile deaths
- Fire prevention
- Reduction of work-related injuries and disease
- Prevention of auto thefts
- Prevention and detection of arson losses
- Prevention of defective products that could injure the user
- Prevention of boiler explosions
- Educational programs on loss prevention

The loss-prevention activities reduce both direct and indirect, or consequential, losses. Society benefits, because both types of losses are reduced.

Enhancement of Credit

A final benefit is that insurance enhances a person's credit. Insurance makes a borrower a better credit risk because it guarantees the value of the borrower's collateral or gives greater assurance that the loan will be repaid. For example, when a house is purchased, the lending institution normally requires property insurance on the house before the mortgage loan is granted. The property insurance protects the lender's financial interest if the property is damaged or destroyed. Similarly, a business firm seeking a temporary loan for Christmas or seasonal business may be required to insure its inventories before the loan is made. If a new car is purchased and financed by a bank or other lending institution, physical damage insurance on the car may be required before the loan is made. Thus, insurance can enhance a person's credit.

COSTS OF INSURANCE TO SOCIETY

Although the insurance industry provides enormous social and economic benefits to society, the social costs of insurance must also be recognized. The major social costs of insurance include the following:

- Cost of doing business
- Fraudulent claims
- Inflated claims

INSIGHT 2.1

Insurance Fraud Hall of Shame—Sampling of Outrageous Cases

The Coalition Against Insurance Fraud has compiled a list of insurance fraud cases that are especially outrageous and shocking. The following is a sampling of the cases.

- **Surgeons cut rented patients no breaks.** More than 5000 people trooped through the Unity Outpatient Surgery center for a date with a scalpel. Most patients were immigrants from Latin countries, Vietnam, and other countries. They received colonoscopies, surgery for sweaty palms, and other procedures. *There was only one problem—the patients were healthy as horses.* Cash strapped and looking for a quick paycheck, the patients sold their bodies to crooked Southern California surgeons. Patients received $300–$1000 in cold cash plus other perks. The ringleader of the scam, Tam Vu Pham, paid recruiters handsomely to find patients. The surgeons operated on many of them and fraudulently billed insurers for more than $96 million in a massive "rent a patient" swindle. One healthy man had a circumcision, removal of his sweat glands, a nose operation, colonoscopy, and endoscopy. Pham pleaded guilty to criminal charges and faces up to 13 years in a California prison.

- **Getting to the root of dentist's con.** Amy Suda went to her dentist, Dr. Alreza Asgari, for routine tooth cleaning. Her previous dentist had given her a clean bill of health six months earlier. Asgari told her she needed a root canal, five cavities filled, and several wisdom teeth yanked. She had the work done; her mouth became infected; and she developed cysts and needed more surgery. Another patient, Joe Klein, had seven root canals done on healthy teeth. *Asgari subjected dozens of other patients to unnecessary root canals, cavity fillings, yanking of healthy teeth, and botched surgery.* He fraudulently billed insurers for more than $366,000 for the unnecessary dental work. Despite the diplomas plastered on his walls, it's unclear that Asgari even finished dental school. School officials at New York University say he only attended dental school. Asgari will spend up to five years in prison.

- **Cruise-ship conman walks plank.** Brian Calen claimed he lost the same right eye on three different luxury cruises and collected a small fortune in insurance money before investigators saw through his charade. He actually lost his sight 20 years ago when he was looking through a telescope on a cruise when the solar filter apparently fell off, and the sunlight blinded him. Calen kept taking cruises and claimed on several occasions that an unfortunate accident onboard had tragically cost him the sight in his right eye. He bilked insurers out of nearly $1.1 million. In one scam, Calen broke a champagne bottle and stuck glass shards into his right eye socket and claimed the bottle exploded and blinded him. Alert investigators discovered the grisly scam. Because of a plea bargain, Calen received five years of probation instead of hard time.

- **Blight of the living dead.** Clayton Daniels took a long, hard fall—it seemed. Police found his crumpled green Chevy at the base of a cliff, and his charred remains were in the front seat. Clayton's wife, Molly, tried to salve her seeming grief by claiming $110,000 in life insurance money. *There was only one problem. Clayton never died; the body wasn't his; and it wasn't even a man.* He and Molly had dug up the grave of an elderly woman and then stashed her corpse in the car and shoved it off the cliff. They wanted to fake Clayton's death to steal the life insurance money. Insurance investigators were suspicious. DNA evidence from the body revealed the body wasn't Clayton, and investigators found the scheme on Molly's computer. Molly received a 20-year sentence for insurance fraud, and 10 years for hindering Clayton's arrest. Clayton awaits trial on an arson charge.

- **Health scam creates healing feeling.** Pete Orr won more than 300 NASCAR races but lost his biggest race to cancer. Pete counted on his health-insurance provider TRG Marketing to help him heal and return to the track. But the firm was a fake and refused to pay more than $250,000 in medical bills. Likewise, Ginger Harpin had a brain tumor and piled up $75,000 in bills that TRG wouldn't pay. Rusty Baker killed himself rather than burden his family with his own medical bills that TRG wouldn't pay. TRG operators William Paul Crouse and Carmelo Zanfei stiffed more than 7200 trusting people, and used the victims' money to buy fancy houses and live swanky lifestyles. Angry victims complained to state insurance departments. Crouse and Zanfei were convicted in Florida and await sentencing.

- **Phony agents stalk trusting seniors.** Brian Shechtman's gang stalked more than 1200 trusting seniors in South Florida by going door-to-door, promising them low-cost supplemental health insurance. Instead, they secretly slipped the seniors expensive and unwanted life insurance without buying any health coverage. Seniors often discovered they were bilked when they submitted expensive medical claims, which, to their shock, weren't covered. Some seniors lost their homes and life savings after paying medical bills out of their own pockets. One 80-year-old woman with dementia forked over $18,000

INSIGHT 2.1 (continued)

Insurance Fraud Hall of Shame—Sampling of Outrageous Cases

for life insurance. After the seniors complained to Florida's chief financial officer who oversees insurance fraud, investigators finally busted Shechtman and his stooges. Prosecutors cut a plea deal because many victims had died or were mentally incapable or too ashamed to testify. Schechtman will serve two years in state prison.

- **Crime and courage at the Palomar.** Juan Ortiz torched the Palomar, his rickety old Hollywood, California, tenement for low-income residents. He wanted to collect the insurance money and avoid paying big money to fix code

violations. But the job was botched. Police believe Ortiz hired his brother to spread gasoline to start the blaze. However, a huge explosion erupted, and the building became a flaming inferno. Norma Galino leaned out of the window of the burning building, terrified. She handed her two children to firefighters as searing flames closed in on them. But Norma died just minutes later. She fell four stories onto the sidewalk below, dying instantly. Ortiz was convicted of insurance fraud.

SOURCE: Adaptation of *Insurance Fraud Hall of Shame 2005*, Coalition Against Insurance Fraud at http://insurancefraud.org/

Cost of Doing Business

One important cost is the cost of doing business. Insurers consume scarce economic resources—land, labor, capital, and business enterprise—in providing insurance to society. In financial terms, an expense loading must be added to the pure premium to cover the expenses incurred by insurance companies in their daily operations. An **expense loading** *is the amount needed to pay all expenses, including commissions, general administrative expenses, state premium taxes, acquisition expenses, and an allowance for contingencies and profit.* Sales and administrative expenses and state taxes and licensing fees for property and casualty insurers consume 28 cents of each premium dollar, whereas operating expenses of life insurers account for 14 percent of total expenditures.[10] As a result, total costs to society are increased. For example, assume that a small country with no property insurance has an average of $100 million of fire losses each year. Also assume that property insurance later becomes available, and the expense loading is 35 percent of losses. Thus, total costs to this country are increased to $135 million.

However, these additional costs can be justified for several reasons. First, from the insured's viewpoint, uncertainty concerning the payment of a covered loss is reduced because of insurance. Second, the costs of doing business are not necessarily wasteful, because insurers engage in a wide variety of loss-prevention activities. Finally, the insurance industry

provides jobs to millions of workers in the United States. However, because economic resources are used up in providing insurance to society, a real economic cost is incurred.

Fraudulent Claims

A second cost of insurance comes from the submission of fraudulent claims. Examples of fraudulent claims include the following:

- Auto accidents are faked or staged to collect benefits.
- Dishonest claimants fake slip-and-fall accidents.
- Phony burglaries, thefts, or acts of vandalism are reported to insurers.
- False health insurance claims are submitted to collect benefits.
- Dishonest policyowners take out life insurance policies on insureds who are later reported as having died.

The payment of such fraudulent claims results in higher premiums to all insureds. The existence of insurance also prompts some insureds to deliberately cause a loss so as to profit from insurance. These social costs fall directly on society.

Some types of insurance fraud are especially outrageous. The Coalition Against Insurance Fraud has established a "hall of shame" for insurance scams that are strikingly large, brazen, vicious, and in some cases, stupid (see Insight 2.1).

Inflated Claims

Another cost of insurance relates to the submission of inflated or "padded" claims. Although the loss is not intentionally caused by the insured, the dollar amount of the claim may exceed the actual financial loss. Examples of inflated claims include the following:

■ Attorneys for plaintiffs sue for high-liability judgments that exceed the true economic loss of the victim.

■ Insureds inflate the amount of damage in auto collision claims so that the insurance payments will cover the collision deductible.

■ Disabled persons often malinger to collect disability-income benefits for a longer duration.

■ Insureds exaggerate the amount and value of property stolen from a home or business.

Inflated claims must be recognized as an important social cost of insurance. Premiums must be increased to pay the additional losses. As a result,

INSIGHT 2.2

Don't Think Insurance Fraud Is Committed Only by Hardened Crooks

So, you think insurance faud is committed only by hardened crooks and large crime rings?

Actually, many normally honest people also commit fraud. Maybe even your church-going uncle . . . that helpful neighbor across the street . . . a friendly store owner downtown.

People sometimes "just fudge a bit" or tell "little white lies" when they apply for insurance or make a claim.

They may not even think this is real insurance fraud. "Heck, it's only a few dollars," or "Nobody's really being hurt," or "I've paid my premiums for years, and now it's my turn."

Well guess again. Try this quiz. If you check "yes" for any question, you may have committed insurance fraud.

Yes	or No	Have you ever knowingly:
❑	❑	said you drive fewer miles to work than you really do, when applying for auto coverage?
❑	❑	said you never use your car for work though you actually do, when applying for auto coverage?
❑	❑	said you park your car in a garage when you actually park it on the street, when applying for auto coverage?
❑	❑	said you live in a different location than you really do, when applying for auto coverage?
❑	❑	let a body shop pad your car repair bill to recoup your deductible when making an auto claim?
❑	❑	inflated the value of possessions stolen from your home or car when making a claim?
❑	❑	inflated the value of jewelry or other goods you lost when making a claim?
❑	❑	asked a repairman to pad a bill for damage to your home so you could recoup your deductible?
❑	❑	said your business has fewer employees than it really does, when you applied for workers compensation coverage?
❑	❑	said your employees have safer jobs than they really do, when you applied for workers compensation coverage?
❑	❑	fudged your medical history so you seem healthier on your life insurance application?
❑	❑	said you don't smoke even though you really do, when applying for life insurance coverage?
❑	❑	said an injury you received at home or while playing sports was work-related so you could collect workers compensation coverage?
❑	❑	stayed home even though you're healed, so you could keep collecting workers compensation?

Source: Reprinted with permission of the Coalition Against Insurance Fraud, www.insurancefraud.org

disposable income and the consumption of other goods and services are reduced.

Cost of Fraudulent and Inflated Claims

Another cost of insurance to society is the cost of fraudulent and inflated claims. This cost is huge. According to the Coalition Against Insurance Fraud, insurance fraud costs Americans at least $80 billion annually. *To put this number in proper perspective, this amount would pay the tuition for nearly 15.6 million students at America's four-year public universities for a year, or would pay the salaries of 2.2 million American workers for a year.*[11]

Lax Public Attitude Toward Insurance Fraud

A relatively high percentage of Americans have a lax attitude toward fraud. *Research by the Coalition Against Insurance Fraud showed that (1) two of three Americans tolerate insurance fraud to varying degrees; (2) two of five Americans want little or no punishment for insurance cheats; and (3) they blame the insurance industry for its fraud problems because they believe insurers are unfair.*[12]

Most Americans think insurance fraud is committed only by career criminals and large crime rings, such as auto-theft rings, chop shops, and dishonest doctors and lawyers. However, this restricted view of insurance fraud is incorrect. Many Americans who otherwise think they are basically honest often engage in a variety of actions that clearly fall within the category of insurance fraud (see Insight 2.2).

Although fraudulent and inflated claims must be recognized as a social cost of insurance, the economic benefits of insurance generally outweigh these costs. Insurance reduces worry and fear; the indemnification function contributes greatly to social and economic stability; financial security of individuals and firms is preserved; and from the perspective of insurers, objective risk in the economy is reduced. The social costs of insurance can be viewed as the sacrifice that society must make to obtain these benefits.

CASE APPLICATION

There are numerous definitions of insurance. Based on the definition of insurance stated in the text, indicate whether each of the following guarantees is considered insurance.

   a. A television set is guaranteed by the manufacturer against defects for 90 days.

   b. A new set of radial tires is guaranteed by the manufacturer against road defects for 50,000 miles.

   c. A builder of new homes gives a 10-year guarantee against structural defects in the home.

   d. A cosigner of a note agrees to pay the loan balance if the original debtor defaults on the payments.

   e. A large group of homeowners agrees to pay for losses to homes that burn during the year because of fire.

SUMMARY

■ There is no single definition of insurance. However, a typical insurance plan contains four elements:

    Pooling of losses

    Payment of fortuitous losses

    Risk transfer

    Indemnification

Pooling means that the losses of the few are spread over the group, and average loss is substituted for actual loss. Fortuitous losses are unforeseen and unexpected and occur as a result of chance. Risk transfer involves the transfer of a pure risk to an insurer. Indemnification means that the victim of a loss is restored in whole or in part by payment, repair, or replacement by the insurer.

- The law of large numbers states that the greater the number of exposures, the more likely the actual results will approach the expected results. The law of large numbers permits an insurer to estimate future losses with some accuracy.

- There are several ideal requirements of an insurable risk.

    There must be a large number of exposure units.

    The loss must be accidental and unintentional.

    The loss must be determinable and measurable.

    The loss should not be catastrophic.

    The chance of loss must be calculable.

    The premium must be economically feasible.

- Most personal risks, property risks, and liability risks can be privately insured, because the requirements of an insurable risk generally can be met. However, most market risks, financial risks, production risks, and political risks generally are difficult to insure privately.

- Adverse selection is the tendency of persons with a higher-than-average chance of loss to seek insurance at average rates, which, if not controlled by underwriting, results in higher-than-expected loss levels.

- Insurance is not the same as gambling. Gambling creates a new speculative risk, whereas insurance deals with an existing pure risk. Also, gambling is socially unproductive, because the winner's gain comes at the expense of the loser. Insurance is always socially productive because both the insured and insurer benefit if the loss does not occur.

- Insurance is not the same as hedging. Insurance involves the transfer of a pure risk, whereas hedging involves the transfer of a speculative risk. Also, insurance may reduce objective risk because of the law of large numbers. Hedging typically involves only risk transfer and not risk reduction.

- Insurance can be classified into private and government insurance. Private insurance consists of life and health insurance and property and liability insurance. Government insurance consists of social insurance and other government insurance programs.

- The major benefits of insurance to society are as follows:

    Indemnification for loss

    Reduction of worry and fear

    Source of investment funds

    Loss prevention

    Enhancement of credit

- Insurance imposes certain social costs to society, which include the following:

    Cost of doing business

    Fraudulent claims

    Inflated claims

KEY CONCEPTS AND TERMS

Adverse selection
Casualty insurance
Commercial lines
Expense loading
Fidelity bonds
Fortuitous loss
Indemnification
Inland marine insurance
Insurance
Law of large numbers
Life and health insurance
Multiple-line insurance
Ocean marine insurance
Personal lines
Pooling
Property and liability insurance
Reinsurance
Requirements of an insurable risk
Risk transfer
Social insurance
Surety bonds
Underwriting

REVIEW QUESTIONS

1. Explain each of the following characteristics of a typical insurance plan.
    a. Pooling of losses
    b. Payment of fortuitous losses
    c. Risk transfer
    d. Indemnification

2. Explain the law of large numbers.

3. Certain requirements ideally should be fulfilled before a pure risk can be privately insured. Explain the six requirements of an insurable risk.

4. Identify the approaches that insurers can use to deal with the problem of a catastrophic loss.

5. Why are most market risks, financial risks, production risks, and political risks considered difficult to insure by private insurers?

6. a. What is the meaning of adverse selection?
    b. Identify some methods that insurers use to control for adverse selection.

7. What are the two major differences between insurance and gambling?

8. What are the two major differences between insurance and hedging?

9. a. Identify the major fields of private insurance.
   b. Identify several property and casualty insurance coverages.

10. a. Explain the basic characteristics of social insurance programs.
    b. List the major social insurance programs in the United States.

APPLICATION QUESTIONS

1. Compare the risks of (i) fire with (ii) war in terms of how well they meet the requirements of an insurable risk.

2. a. Private insurers provide social and economic benefits to society. Explain the following benefits of insurance to society.
      (1) Indemnification for loss
      (2) Enhancement of credit
      (3) Source of funds for capital investment and accumulation
   b. Explain the major social and economic costs of insurance in the American economy.

3. Buildings in flood zones are difficult to insure by private insurers because the ideal requirements of an insurable risk are difficult to meet.
   a. Identify the ideal requirements of an insurable risk.
   b. Which of the requirements of an insurable risk are not met by the flood peril?

4. Private insurance provides numerous coverages that can be used to meet specific loss situations. For each of the following situations, identify a private insurance coverage that would provide the desired protection.
   a. Emily, age 28, is a single parent with two dependent children. She wants to make certain that funds are available for her children's education if she dies before her youngest child finishes college.
   b. Danielle, age 16, recently obtained her driver's license. Her parents want to make certain they are protected if Danielle negligently injures another motorist while driving a family car.
   c. Jacob, age 30, is married with two dependents. He wants his income to continue if he becomes totally disabled and unable to work.
   d. Tyler, age 35, recently purchased a house for $200,000 that is located in an area where tornadoes frequently occur. He wants to make certain that funds are available if the house is damaged or destroyed in a tornado.
   e. Nathan, age 40, owns an upscale furniture store. Nathan wants to be protected if a customer is injured while shopping in the store and sues him for the bodily injury.

INTERNET RESOURCES

■ The **American Insurance Association (AIA)** is an important trade and service organization for more than 400 insurers. The site lists available publications, position papers on important issues in property and casualty insurance, press releases, insurance-related links, and names of state insurance commissioners. Visit the site at
http://www.aiadc.org

■ The **Coalition Against Insurance Fraud** is an alliance of consumer, law enforcement, and insurance industry groups that attempt to reduce insurance fraud through public education and action. Numerous examples of fraudulent claims are listed. Visit this interesting site at
http://www.insurancefraud.org

■ The **Insurance Information Institute (III)** has an excellent site for obtaining information on property and casualty insurance. III provides timely consumer information on auto, homeowners, and business insurance, submission of claims and rebuilding after catastrophes, and ways to save money. The site contains background material and information for the news media, including television, newspapers, and radio. Visit this important site at
http://www.iii.org

■ **Insure.com** provides timely consumer information on new developments in auto, home, life, and health insurance. The site provides information on annuities, insurance company ratings, and state insurance regulations. The site also has a complaint finder, lawsuit library, links to other sites, and reader forums. It is an excellent source for background material. Visit the site at
http://www.insure.com

■ The **Insurance Journal** is a definitive online source of timely information on the property/casualty industry. A free online newsletter is available that provides breaking news on important developments in property and casualty insurance. Visit the site at

http://www.insurancejournal.com

■ The **Insurance Research Council (IRC)** is an independent, nonprofit research organization supported by leading property and casualty insurance companies and associations. IRC provides timely and reliable information based on extensive data collection and analyses and examines important public policy issues that affect insurers, customers, and the general public. IRC is devoted solely to research and communication of its research findings. Visit the site at

http://www.ircweb.org

■ **InsWeb** operates an online insurance marketplace that enables consumers to get quotes for numerous insurance products, including auto, homeowners, and renters insurance, term insurance, and individual health insurance. Overall, it is an excellent source of information for consumers. Visit the site at

http://www.insweb.com

■ The **National Association of Mutual Insurance Companies** is a trade association that represents mutual insurance companies involved in property and casualty insurance. Visit the site at

http://www.namic.org

SELECTED REFERENCES

Life Insurers Fact Book 2005. Washington, DC: American Council of Life Insurers, 2005.

The Financial Services Fact Book 2007, New York: Insurance Information Institute, 2007.

The I. I. I. Insurance Fact Book 2007. New York: Insurance Information Institute, 2007.

Wiening, Eric A. *Foundations of Risk Management and Insurance,* 1st ed. Malvern, PA: American Institute for Chartered Property Casualty Underwriters/Insurance Institute of America, 2002.

Wiening, Eric A., George E. Rejda, Constance M. Luthardt, and Cheryl L. Ferguson. *Personal Insurance,* 1st ed., 2002. Malvern, PA: American Institute for Chartered Property Casualty Underwriters/Insurance Institute of America, 2002.

NOTES

1. *Bulletin of the Commission on Insurance Terminology of the American Risk and Insurance Association,* (October 1965).
2. Robert I. Mehr and Sandra G. Gustavson, *Life Insurance: Theory and Practice,* 4th ed. (Plano, TX: Business Publications, 1987), p. 31.
3. Self-insurance is discussed in Chapter 3.
4. Robert I. Mehr, Emerson Cammack, and Terry Rose, *Principles of Insurance,* 8th ed. (Homewood, IL: Richard D. Irwin, 1985), pp. 36–37.
5. Market risks include the risks of adverse price changes in raw materials, general price level changes (inflation), changes in consumer tastes, new technology, and increased competition from competitors. Financial risks include the risks of adverse price changes in the price of securities, adverse changes in interest rates, and the inability to borrow on favorable terms. Production risks include shortages of raw materials, depletion of natural resources, and technical problems in production. Political risks include the risks of war, acts of terrorists, overthrow of government, adverse government regulations, and the nationalization of foreign plants by a hostile government.
6. *Life Insurers Fact Book 2005* (Washington, DC: American Council of Life Insurers, 2005), p. 1.
7. *The I. I. I. Insurance Fact Book 2006* (New York: Insurance Information Institute, 2006), p. v.
8. George E. Rejda, *Social Insurance and Economic Security,* 6th ed. (Upper Saddle River, NJ: Prentice-Hall, 1999), p. 11.
9. The five states are California, Hawaii, New Jersey, New York, and Rhode Island.
10. *The I. I. I. Insurance Fact Book 2006,* p. 18; *Life Insurers Fact Book 2005,* p. 63.
11. Coalition Against Insurance Fraud estimates.
12. Coalition Against Insurance Fraud at insurancefraud .org.

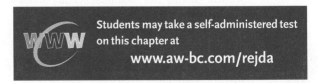

Students may take a self-administered test on this chapter at
www.aw-bc.com/rejda

APPENDIX

BASIC STATISTICS AND THE LAW OF LARGE NUMBERS*

The application of probability and statistics is crucial in the insurance industry. Insurance actuaries constantly face a tradeoff when determining the premium to charge for coverage: the premium must be high enough to cover expected losses and expenses, but low enough to remain competitive with premiums charged by other insurers. Actuaries apply statistical analysis to determine expected loss levels and expected deviations from these loss levels. Through the application of the law of large numbers, insurers reduce their risk of adverse outcomes.

In this appendix, we review some statistical concepts that are important to insurers, including probability, central tendency, and dispersion. Next, we examine the law of large numbers and how insurance companies apply it to reduce risk.

PROBABILITY AND STATISTICS

To determine expected losses, insurance actuaries apply probability and statistical analysis to given loss situations. The probability of an event is simply the long-run relative frequency of the event, given an infinite number of trials with no changes in the underlying conditions. The probability of some events can be determined without experimentation. For example, if a "fair" coin is flipped in the air, the probability the coin will come up "heads" is 50 percent, and the probability it will come up "tails" is also 50 percent. Other probabilities, such as the probability of dying during a specified year or the probability of being involved in an auto accident, can be estimated from past loss data.

A convenient way of summarizing events and probabilities is through a probability distribution. A probability distribution lists events that could occur and the corresponding probability of each event's occurrence. Probability distributions may be discrete, meaning that only distinct outcomes are possible, or continuous, meaning that any outcome over a range of outcomes could occur.[1]

Probability distributions are characterized by two important measures: central tendency and dispersion. Although there are several measures of central tendency, the measure most often employed is the mean (μ) or expected value (EV) of the distribution.[2] *The mean or expected value is found by multiplying each outcome by the probability of occurrence, and then summing the resulting products:*

$$\mu \text{ or } EV = \Sigma\, X_i P_i$$

*Prepared by Michael J. McNamara, Washington State University.

For example, assume that an actuary estimates the following probabilities of various losses for a certain risk:

Amount of Loss (X_i)		Probability of Loss (P_i)		$X_i P_i$
$ 0	×	.30	=	$ 0
$360	×	.50	=	$180
$600	×	.20	=	$120
		$\Sigma X_i P_i$	=	$300

Thus, we could say that the mean or expected loss given the probability distribution is $300.

Although the mean value indicates central tendency, it does not tell us anything about the riskiness or dispersion of the distribution. Consider a second probability-of-loss distribution:

Amount of Loss (X_i)		Probability of Loss (P_i)		$X_i P_i$
$225	×	.40	=	$ 90
$350	×	.60	=	$210
		$\Sigma X_i P_i$	=	$300

This distribution also has a mean loss value of $300. However, the first distribution is riskier because the range of possible outcomes is from $0 to $600. With the second distribution, the range of possible outcomes is only $125 ($350 − $225), so we are more certain about the outcome with the second distribution.

Two standard measures of dispersion are employed to characterize the variability or dispersion about the mean value. These measures are the variance (σ^2) and the standard deviation (σ). The variance of a probability distribution is the sum of the squared differences between the possible outcomes and the expected value, weighted by the probability of the outcomes:

$$\sigma^2 = \Sigma P_i (X_i - EV)^2$$

So the variance is the average squared deviation between the possible outcomes and the mean. Because the variance is in "squared units," it is necessary to take the square root of the variance so that the central tendency and dispersion measures are in the same units. The square root of the variance is the standard deviation. The variance and standard deviation of the first distribution are as follows:

$$\sigma^2 = .30(0 - 300)^2 + .50(360 - 300)^2$$
$$+ .20(600 - 300)^2$$
$$= 27,000 + 1,800 + 18,000$$
$$= 46,800$$

$$\sigma = \sqrt{46,800} = 216.33$$

For the second distribution, the variance and standard deviation are:

$$\sigma^2 = .40(225 - 300)^2 + .60(350 - 300)^2$$
$$= 2,250 + 1,500$$
$$= 3,750$$

$$\sigma = \sqrt{3,750} = 61.24$$

Thus, while the means of the two distributions are the same, the standard deviations are significantly different. *Higher standard deviations, relative to the mean, are associated with greater uncertainty of loss; therefore, risk is higher. Lower standard deviations, relative to the mean, are associated with less uncertainty of loss; therefore, risk is lower.*

The two probability distributions used in the discussion of central tendency and dispersion are "odd" in that only three and two possible outcomes, respectively, could occur. In addition, specific loss levels corresponding to the probabilities are assigned. In practice, estimating the frequency and severity of loss is difficult. Insurers can employ both actual loss data and theoretical loss distributions in estimating losses.[3]

LAW OF LARGE NUMBERS

Even if the characteristics of the population were known with certainty, insurers do not insure populations. Rather, they select a sample from the population and insure the sample. Obviously, the relationship between population parameters and the characteristics of the sample (mean and standard deviation) is important for insurers, since actual experience may vary significantly from the population parameters. The characteristics of the sampling distribution help to illustrate the law of large numbers, the mathematical foundation of insurance.

It can be shown that the average losses for a random sample of n exposure units will follow a normal distribution because of the Central Limit Theorem, which states:

> If you draw random samples of n observations from any population with mean μ_x and standard deviation σ_x, and n is sufficiently large, the distribution of sample means will be approximately normal, with the mean of the distribution equal to the mean of the population ($\mu_{\bar{x}} = \mu_x$), and the standard error of the sample mean ($\sigma_{\bar{x}}$) equal to the standard deviation of the population (σ_x) divided by the square root of n ($\sigma_{\bar{x}} = \sigma_x / \sqrt{n}$). This approximation becomes increasingly accurate as the sample size, n, increases.

The Central Limit Theorem has two important implications for insurers. First, it is clear that the sample distribution of means does not depend on the population distribution, provided n is sufficiently large. *In other words, regardless of the population distribution (bimodal, unimodal, symmetric, skewed right, skewed left, and so on), the distribution of sample means will approach the normal distribution as the sample size increases.* This result is shown in Exhibit A2.1.

The normal distribution is a symmetric, bell-shaped curve. It is defined by the mean and standard deviation of the distribution. About 68 percent of the distribution lies within one standard deviation of the mean, and about 95 percent of the distribution lies within two standard deviations of the mean. The normal curve has many statistical applications (hypothesis testing, confidence intervals, and so on), and is easy to use.

The second important implication of the Central Limit Theorem for insurers is that the standard error of the sample mean distribution declines as the sample size increases. Recall that the standard error is defined as

$$\sigma_{\bar{x}} = \sigma_x / \sqrt{n}$$

In other words, the standard error of the sample mean loss distribution is equal to the standard deviation of the population divided by the square root of the sample size. Because the population standard

Exhibit A2.1
Sampling Distribution Versus Sample Size

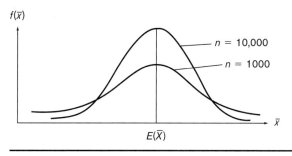

deviation is independent of the sample size, *the standard error of the sampling distribution, $\sigma_{\bar{x}}$, can be reduced by simply increasing the sample size.*

This result has important implications for insurers. For example, assume that an insurer would like to select a sample to insure from a population where the mean loss is $500 and the standard deviation is $350. As the insurer increases the number of units insured (n), the standard error of the sampling distribution ($\sigma_{\bar{x}}$) will decline. The standard error for various sample sizes is summarized here:

n	$\sigma_{\bar{x}}$
10	110.68
100	35.00
1,000	11.07
10,000	3.50
100,000	1.11

Thus as the sample size increases, the difference between actual results and expected results decreases. This result is shown graphically in Exhibit A2.2.

Exhibit A2.2
Standard Error of the Sampling Distribution Versus Sample Size

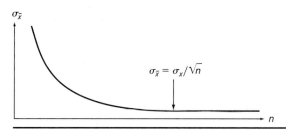

Obviously, when an insurer increases the size of the sample insured, underwriting risk (maximum insured losses) increases because more insured units could suffer a loss. The underwriting risk for an insurer is equal to the number of units insured multiplied by the standard error of the average loss distribution, $\sigma_{\bar{x}}$. Recalling that $\sigma_{\bar{x}}$ is equal to $\sigma_x / \sqrt{n}$, we can rewrite the expression for underwriting risk as:

$$n \times \sigma_{\bar{x}} = n \times \sigma_x / \sqrt{n} = \sqrt{n} \times \sigma_x$$

Thus, while underwriting risk increases with an increase in the sample size, it does not increase proportionately. Rather, it increases by the square root of the increase in the sample size.

Insurance companies are in the loss business—they expect some losses to occur. It is the deviation between actual losses and expected losses that is the major concern. By insuring large samples, insurers reduce their objective risk. There truly is "safety in numbers" for insurers.

NOTES

1. The number of runs scored in a baseball game is a discrete measure as partial runs cannot be scored. Speed and temperature are continuous measures as all values over the range of values can occur.
2. Other measures of central tendency are the median, which is the middle observation in a probability distribution, and the mode, which is the observation that occurs most often.
3. Introductory statistics texts discuss several popular theoretical distributions, such as the binomial and Poisson distributions, that can be used to estimate losses. Another popular distribution, the normal distribution, is discussed in the following section.

CHAPTER 3

INTRODUCTION TO RISK MANAGEMENT

"The essence of risk management lies in maximizing the areas where we have some control over the outcome while minimizing the areas where we have absolutely no control over the outcome . . ."

Peter L. Bernstein
Against the Gods: The Remarkable Story of Risk

LEARNING OBJECTIVES

After studying this chapter, you should be able to

◆ Define risk management and explain the objectives of risk management.

◆ Describe the steps in the risk management process.

◆ Explain the major risk control techniques, including
    Avoidance
    Loss prevention
    Loss reduction

◆ Explain the major risk-financing techniques, including
    Retention
    Noninsurance transfers
    Insurance

◆ Apply the principles of risk management to a personal risk management program.

Contemporary Homes is a large construction company that builds homes and apartment buildings in three states. In recent months, several employees have been injured on the job, and the theft of material and supplies from job sites has increased. The company's accountant recommended that the firm establish a risk management program to deal with these problems. Risk management is process that identifies the loss exposures faced by a firm and uses a number of methods, including insurance, to treat the loss exposures. After implementing the program, Contemporary Homes saw dramatic results. Job-related injuries declined; thefts of materials and supplies declined; and workers compensation premiums were reduced. The firm's profitability also increased.

Clearly, Contemporary Homes benefited from its risk management program. Other organizations have also recognized the merits of a formal risk management program. Today, risk management is widely used by corporations, small employers, nonprofit organizations, and state and local governments. Students can also benefit from a personal risk management program.

This chapter—the first of two dealing with risk management—discusses the fundamentals of traditional risk management. The following chapter discusses the newer forms of risk management that are rapidly emerging, including enterprise risk management and financial risk management. In this chapter, we discuss the meaning of risk management, objectives of risk management, steps in the risk management process, and the various techniques for treating loss exposures. The chapter concludes with a discussion of personal risk management.

MEANING OF RISK MANAGEMENT

Risk management *is a process that identifies loss exposures faced by an organization and selects the most appropriate techniques for treating such exposures.* Because the term "risk" is ambiguous and has different meanings, many risk managers use the term "loss exposure" to identify potential losses. A **loss exposure** *is any situation or circumstance in which a loss is possible, regardless of whether a loss occurs.* Examples of loss exposures include manufacturing plants that may be damaged in an earthquake or flood, defective products that may result in lawsuits against the company, the possible theft of company property because of inadequate security, and injuries to employees at work. In the past, risk managers generally considered only pure loss exposures faced by the firm. However, newer forms of risk management are emerging that consider both pure and speculative loss exposures faced by the firm. This chapter discusses only the traditional treatment of pure loss exposures. The newer forms of risk management—such as enterprise risk management—are discussed in Chapter 4.

OBJECTIVES OF RISK MANAGEMENT

Risk management has important objectives. These objectives can be classified as follows:[1]

- Pre-loss objectives
- Post-loss objectives

Pre-Loss Objectives

Important objectives before a loss occurs include economy, reduction of anxiety, and meeting legal obligations.

The first objective means that the firm should prepare for potential losses in the most economical way. This preparation involves an analysis of the cost of safety programs, insurance premiums paid, and the costs associated with the different techniques for handling losses.

The second objective is the reduction of anxiety. Certain loss exposures can cause greater worry and fear for the risk manager and key executives. For example, the threat of a catastrophic lawsuit from a defective product can cause greater anxiety than a small loss from a minor fire.

The final objective is to meet any legal obligations. For example, government regulations may require a firm to install safety devices to protect workers from harm, to dispose of hazardous waste materials properly, and to label consumer products appropriately. The risk manager must see that these legal obligations are met.

Post-Loss Objectives

Risk management also has certain objectives after a loss occurs. These objectives include survival, continued operation, stability of earnings, continued growth, and social responsibility.

The most important post-loss objective is survival of the firm. Survival means that after a loss occurs, the firm can resume at least partial operations within some reasonable time period.

The second post-loss objective is to continue operating. For some firms, the ability to operate after a loss is extremely important. For example, a public utility firm must continue to provide service. Banks, bakeries, dairies, and other competitive firms must continue to operate after a loss. Otherwise, business will be lost to competitors.

The third post-loss objective is stability of earnings. Earnings per share can be maintained if the firm continues to operate. However, a firm may incur substantial additional expenses to achieve this goal (such as operating at another location), and perfect stability of earnings may not be attained.

The fourth post-loss objective is continued growth of the firm. A company can grow by devel-

oping new products and markets or by acquiring or merging with other companies. The risk manager must therefore consider the effect that a loss will have on the firm's ability to grow.

Finally, the objective of social responsibility is to minimize the effects that a loss will have on other persons and on society. A severe loss can adversely affect employees, suppliers, creditors, and the community in general. For example, a severe loss that shuts down a plant in a small town for an extended period can cause considerable economic distress in the town.

STEPS IN THE RISK MANAGEMENT PROCESS

There are four steps in the risk management process (see Exhibit 3.1):

- Identify loss exposures
- Analyze the loss exposures
- Select appropriate techniques for treating the loss exposures
- Implement and monitor the risk management program

Each of these steps is discussed in some detail in the sections that follow.

EXHIBIT 3.1
Steps in the Risk Management Process

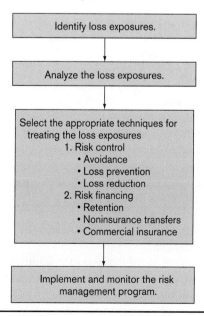

IDENTIFYING LOSS EXPOSURES

The first step in the risk management process is to identify all major and minor loss exposures. This step involves a painstaking analysis of all potential losses. Important loss exposures relate to the following:

1. Property loss exposures
   - Building, plants, other structures
   - Furniture, equipment, supplies
   - Computers, computer software, and data
   - Inventory
   - Accounts receivable, valuable papers and records
   - Company vehicles, planes, boats, mobile equipment
2. Liability loss exposures
   - Defective products
   - Environmental pollution (land, water, air, noise)
   - Sexual harassment of employees, discrimination against employees, wrongful termination
   - Premises and general liability loss exposures
   - Liability arising from company vehicles
   - Misuse of the Internet and e-mail transmissions
   - Directors' and officers' liability suits
3. Business income loss exposures
   - Loss of income from a covered loss
   - Continuing expenses after a loss
   - Extra expenses
   - Contingent business income losses
4. Human resources loss exposures
   - Death or disability of key employees
   - Retirement or unemployment
   - Job-related injuries or disease experienced by workers
5. Crime loss exposures
   - Holdups, robberies, burglaries
   - Employee theft and dishonesty
   - Fraud and embezzlement
   - Internet and computer crime exposures
   - Theft of intellectual property
6. Employee benefit loss exposures
   - Failure to comply with government regulations
   - Violation of fiduciary responsibilities
   - Group life and health and retirement plan exposures
   - Failure to pay promised benefits
7. Foreign loss exposures
   - Acts of terrorism
   - Plants, business property, inventory
   - Foreign currency risks
   - Kidnapping of key personnel
   - Political risks
8. Market reputation and public image of the company
9. Failure to comply with government laws and regulations

A risk manager has several sources of information that he or she can use to identify the preceding loss exposures. They include the following:

- *Risk analysis questionnaires.* Questionnaires require the risk manager to answer numerous questions that identify major and minor loss exposures.
- *Physical inspection.* A physical inspection of company plants and operations can identify major loss exposures.
- *Flowcharts.* Flowcharts that show the flow of production and delivery can reveal production bottlenecks where a loss can have severe financial consequences for the firm.
- *Financial statements.* Analysis of financial statements can identify the major assets that must be protected, loss of income exposures, and key customers and suppliers.
- *Historical loss data.* Historical and departmental loss data over time can be invaluable in identifying major loss exposures.

In addition, risk managers must keep abreast of industry trends and market changes that can create new loss exposures and cause concern. Major risk management issues include rising workers compensation costs, effects of mergers and consolidations by insurers and brokers, increasing litigation costs, financing risk through the capital markets, and repetitive motion injury claims. Protection of company assets and personnel against acts of terrorism is another important issue.

ANALYZE THE LOSS EXPOSURES

The second step in the risk management process is to analyze the loss exposures. This step involves an estimation of the frequency and severity of loss. **Loss**

frequency *refers to the probable number of losses that may occur during some given time period.* **Loss severity** *refers to the probable size of the losses that may occur.*

Once the risk manager estimates the frequency and severity of loss for each type of loss exposure, the various loss exposures can be ranked according to their relative importance. For example, a loss exposure with the potential for bankrupting the firm is much more important in a risk management program than an exposure with a small loss potential.

In addition, the relative frequency and severity of each loss exposure must be estimated so that the risk manager can select the most appropriate technique, or combination of techniques, for handling each exposure. For example, if certain losses occur regularly and are fairly predictable, they can be budgeted out of a firm's income and treated as a normal operating expense. If the annual loss experience of a certain type of exposure fluctuates widely, however, an entirely different approach is required.

Although the risk manager must consider both loss frequency and loss severity, severity is more important, because a single catastrophic loss could wipe out the firm. Therefore, the risk manager must also consider all losses that can result from a single event. Both the maximum possible loss and maximum probable loss must be estimated. The **maximum possible loss** *is the worst loss that could happen to the firm during its lifetime.* The **maximum probable loss** *is the worst loss that is likely to happen.* For example, if a plant is totally destroyed in a flood, the risk manager estimates that replacement cost, debris removal, demolition costs, and other costs will total $10 million. Thus, the maximum possible loss is $10 million. The risk manager also estimates that a flood causing more than $8 million of damage to the plant is so unlikely that such a flood would not occur more than once in 50 years. The risk manager may choose to ignore events that occur so infrequently. Thus, for this risk manager, the maximum probable loss is $8 million.

Catastrophic losses are difficult to predict because they occur infrequently. However, their potential impact on the firm must be given high priority. In contrast, certain losses, such as physical damage losses to cars and trucks, occur with greater frequency, are usually relatively small, and can be predicted with greater accuracy.

SELECT THE APPROPRIATE TECHNIQUES FOR TREATING THE LOSS EXPOSURES

The third step in the risk management process is to select the most appropriate technique, or combination of techniques, for treating the loss exposures. These techniques can be classified broadly as either risk control or risk financing.[2] **Risk control** *refers to techniques that reduce the frequency and severity of losses.* **Risk financing** *refers to techniques that provide for the funding of losses.* Many risk managers use a combination of techniques for treating each loss exposure.

Risk Control

As noted above, risk control is a generic term to describe techniques for reducing the frequency or severity of losses. Major risk-control techniques include the following:

- Avoidance
- Loss prevention
- Loss reduction

Avoidance Avoidance *means a certain loss exposure is never acquired, or an existing loss exposure is abandoned.* For example, flood losses can be avoided by not building a new plant in a floodplain. A pharmaceutical firm that markets a drug with dangerous side effects can withdraw the drug from the market to avoid possible legal liability.

The major advantage of avoidance is that the chance of loss is reduced to zero if the loss exposure is never acquired. In addition, if an existing loss exposure is abandoned, the chance of loss is reduced or eliminated because the activity or product that could produce a loss has been abandoned. Abandonment, however, may still leave the firm with a residual liability exposure from the sale of previous products.

Avoidance, however, has two major disadvantages. First, the firm may not be able to avoid all losses. For example, a company may not be able to avoid the premature death of a key executive. Second, it may not be feasible or practical to avoid the exposure. For example, a paint factory can avoid losses arising from the production of paint. Without paint production, however, the firm will not be in business.

Loss Prevention   Loss prevention *refers to measures that reduce the frequency of a particular loss.* For example, measures that reduce truck accidents include driver examinations, zero tolerance for alcohol or drug abuse, and strict enforcement of safety rules. Measures that reduce lawsuits from defective products include installation of safety features on hazardous products, placement of warning labels on dangerous products, and institution of quality-control checks.

Loss Reduction   Loss reduction *refers to measures that reduce the severity of a loss after it occurs.* Examples include installation of an automatic sprinkler system that promptly extinguishes a fire; segregation of exposure units so that a single loss cannot simultaneously damage all exposure units, such as having warehouses with inventories at different locations; rehabilitation of workers with job-related injuries; and limiting the amount of cash on the premises.

In conclusion, effective risk control techniques can significantly reduce the frequency and severity of claims, especially in workplace safety. *A study by one insurer found that for every $1 invested in workplace safety by employers, savings of $3 or more are possible.* [3] Effective safety programs reduce direct costs (payments to injured workers and health care providers) and indirect costs (such as overtime and lost productivity).

Risk Financing

As stated earlier, risk financing refers to techniques that provide for the funding of losses after they occur. Major risk-financing techniques include the following:

- Retention
- Noninsurance transfers
- Commercial insurance

Retention   Retention *means that the firm retains part or all of the losses that can result from a given loss.* Retention can be either active or passive. Active risk retention means that the firm is aware of the loss exposure and plans to retain part or all of it, such as collision losses to a fleet of company cars. Passive retention, however, is the failure to identify a loss exposure, failure to act, or forgetting to act. For example, a risk manager may fail to identify all company assets that could be damaged in an earthquake.

Retention can be effectively used in a risk management program under the following conditions:[4]

- *No other method of treatment is available.* Insurers may be unwilling to write a certain type of coverage, or the coverage may be too expensive. Also, noninsurance transfers may not be available. In addition, although loss prevention can reduce the frequency of loss, all losses cannot be eliminated. In these cases, retention is a residual method. If the exposure cannot be insured or transferred, then it must be retained.
- *The worst possible loss is not serious.* For example, physical damage losses to cars in a large firm's fleet will not bankrupt the firm if the cars are separated by wide distances and are not likely to be simultaneously damaged.
- *Losses are highly predictable.* Retention can be effectively used for workers compensation claims, physical damage losses to cars, and shoplifting losses. Based on past experience, the risk manager can estimate a probable range of frequency and severity of actual losses. If most losses fall within that range, they can be budgeted out of the firm's income.

Determining Retention Levels   If retention is used, the risk manager must determine the firm's **retention level**, *which is the dollar amount of losses that the firm will retain.* A financially strong firm can have a higher retention level than one whose financial position is weak.

Although a number of methods can be used to determine the retention level, only two methods are summarized here. First, a corporation can determine the maximum uninsured loss it can absorb without adversely affecting the company's earnings. One rough rule is that the maximum retention can be set at 5 percent of the company's annual earnings before taxes from current operations.

Second, a company can determine the maximum retention as a percentage of the firm's net working capital—for example, between 1 and 5 percent. Net working capital is the difference between a company's current assets and current liabilities. Although this method does not reflect the firm's overall financial position for absorbing a loss, it does measure the firm's ability to fund a loss.

Paying Losses   If retention is used, the risk manager must have some method for paying losses. The following methods are typically used:[5]

- *Current net income.* The firm can pay losses out of its current net income and treat losses as expenses for that year. A large number of losses could exceed current income, however, and other assets may have to be liquidated to pay losses.
- *Unfunded reserve.* An unfunded reserve is a bookkeeping account that is charged with actual or expected losses from a given exposure.
- *Funded reserve.* A funded reserve is the setting aside of liquid funds to pay losses. Funded reserves are not widely used by private employers, because the funds may yield a much higher rate of return by being used in the business. Also, contributions to a funded reserve are not income-tax deductible. Losses, however, are tax deductible when paid.

- *Credit line.* A credit line can be established with a bank, and borrowed funds may be used to pay losses as they occur. Interest must be paid on the loan, however, and loan repayments can aggravate any cash-flow problems a firm may have.

Captive Insurer   Losses can also be paid by a captive insurer. A **captive insurer** *is an insurer owned by a parent firm for the purpose of insuring the parent firm's loss exposures.* There are different types of captive insurers. A **single parent captive** (also called a **pure captive**) is an insurer owned by only one parent, such as a corporation. An **association or group captive** is an insurer owned by several parents. For example, corporations that belong to a trade association may own a captive insurer. Many captive insurers are located in the Caribbean because of a favorable regulatory climate, relatively low capital requirements, and low taxes.

In addition, captives are domiciled in the United States, especially in Vermont, Hawaii, and South Carolina. At least 19 states and jurisdictions in the United States have enacted specific captive laws and are actively seeking to attract captives by favorable regulation and legislation. There are about 5000 captives in existence today (see Exhibit 3.2).

EXHIBIT **3.2**
Growth in Captives over the Past Two Decades

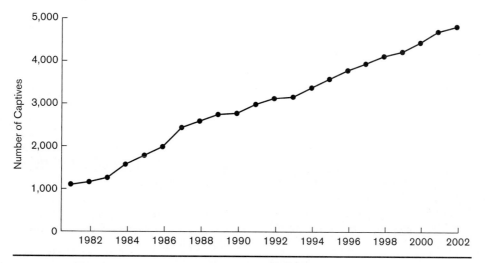

NOTE: Data are from *Captive Insurance Company Reports* and *Best's Captive Directory.*
SOURCE: Towers Perrin, *Captives 101: Managing Cost and Risk,* Exhibit 1, January 21, 2005.

Captive insurers are formed for several reasons, including the following:

- *Difficulty in obtaining insurance.* The parent firm may have difficulty obtaining certain types of insurance from commercial insurers, so it forms a captive insurer to obtain the coverage. This pattern is especially true for global firms that often cannot purchase certain coverages at reasonable rates from commercial insurers, including liability insurance, political risk insurance, and insurance against terrorist attacks.
- *Lower costs.* Forming a captive may reduce insurance costs because of lower operating expenses, avoidance of an agent's or broker's commission, and retention of interest earned on invested premiums and reserves that commercial insurers would otherwise receive. Also, the problem of wide fluctuations in commercial insurance premiums is avoided.
- *Easier access to a reinsurer.* A captive insurer has easier access to reinsurance, because reinsurers generally deal only with insurance companies, not with insureds.
- *Formation of a profit center.* A captive insurer can become a source of profit if it insures other parties as well as the parent firm and its subsidiaries.

Income Tax Treatment of Captives The Internal Revenue Service (IRS) earlier took the position that premiums paid to a *single parent captive (pure captive)* are not income-tax deductible. The IRS argued that there is no substantial transfer of risk from an economic family to an insurer, and that the premiums paid are similar to contributions to a self-insurance reserve, which are not deductible.

However, as a result of a number of complex court decisions and IRS rulings, premiums paid to captive insurers may be tax deductible under certain conditions. It is beyond the scope of the text to discuss in detail each of these rulings. However, according to Towers Perrin, Tillinghast, an actuarial consulting firm, premiums paid to captives are not income-tax deductible unless some or all of the following factors are present:[6]

- *The transaction is a bona fide insurance transaction, and the captive insurer takes some risk under a defensible business plan.*
- *The captive insurer's owner is organized such that subsidiaries, and not the parent, pay premiums to the captive insurer under a "brother–sister" relationship. (The term "brother–sister" refers to separate subsidiaries owned by the same parent, such as a captive insurer and an operating subsidiary.)*
- *The captive insurer writes a substantial amount of unrelated business. (If a captive insurer receives 30 percent or more of the premiums from unrelated third parties, many tax experts view this requirement as being met.) In addition, certain employee benefits are considered to be "unrelated business" if they are structured properly.*
- *Ownership of the captive insurer is structured so that the insureds are not the same as the shareholders.*

Finally, premiums paid to a *group captive* are usually income-tax deductible because the large number of insureds creates an essential element of insurance, which is the pooling of loss exposures over a large group.

Self-Insurance Our discussion of retention would not be complete without a brief discussion of self-insurance. The term self-insurance is commonly used by risk managers to describe aspects of their risk management programs. **Self-insurance** *is a special form of planned retention by which part or all of a given loss exposure is retained by the firm.* A better name for self-insurance is self-funding, which expresses more clearly the idea that losses are funded and paid for by the firm.

Self-insurance is widely used in workers compensation insurance. Self-insurance is also used by employers to provide group health, dental, vision, and prescription drug benefits to employees. Firms often self-insure their group health insurance benefits because they can save money and control health-care costs. There are other benefits of self-insurance as well (see Insight 3.1).

Finally, self-insured plans are typically protected by some type of stop-loss insurance that limits the employer's out-of-pocket costs once losses exceed certain limits.

Risk Retention Groups Federal legislation allows employers, trade groups, governmental units, and

INSIGHT 3.1

Why Do Firms Self-Insure Their Group Health Insurance Plans?

A self-insured group health insurance plan is one in which the employer assumes the financial risk for providing health insurance to its employees. In practical terms, self-insured employers pay out-of-pocket expenses as they are incurred instead of paying premiums to an insurance carrier, which is known as a fully-insured plan. Typically, a self-insured employer will set up a special trust fund to earmark money (corporate and employee contributions) to pay incurred claims.

Employers choose the self-insurance option for several reasons, including the following:

- *The employer can customize the plan to meet the specific health insurance needs of its workforce, as opposed to purchasing a "'one-size-fits-all" insurance policy.*
- *The employer maintains control over the health plan reserves, which maximizes interest income—income that*

would otherwise be earned by an insurance carrier from the investment of premium dollars.
- *The employer does not have to prepay for coverage, which improves cash flow.*
- *The employer is not subject to conflicting state health insurance regulations and mandated benefits, because self-insured health plans are regulated under federal law (Employee Retirement Income Act of 1974 or ERISA).*
- *The employer is not subject to state health insurance premium taxes, which generally are 2 to 3 percent of premiums.*
- *The employer is free to contract with health-care providers or network providers that best meet the health care needs of its employees.*

Source: Adapted from Self-Insured Institute of America, *Self-Insured Health Plans: Questions and Answers,* 2005.

other parties to form risk retention groups. A **risk retention group** *is a group captive that can write any type of liability coverage except employer liability, workers compensation, and personal lines.* For example, a group of physicians may find medical malpractice liability insurance difficult to obtain or too expensive to purchase. The physicians can form a risk retention group to insure their medical malpractice loss exposures.

Risk retention groups are exempt from many state insurance laws that apply to other insurers. Nevertheless, they must be licensed as a liability insurer in at least one state.

Advantages and Disadvantages of Retention The retention technique has both advantages and disadvantages in a risk management program.[7] The major advantages are as follows:

- *Save money*. The firm can save money in the long run if its actual losses are less than the loss component in a private insurer's premium.
- *Lower expenses*. The services provided by the insurer may be provided by the firm at a lower cost. Some expenses may be reduced, including

loss-adjustment expenses, general administrative expenses, commissions and brokerage fees, loss-control expenses, taxes and fees, and the insurer's profit.
- *Encourage loss prevention*. Because the exposure is retained, there may be a greater incentive for loss prevention.
- *Increase cash flow*. Cash flow may be increased, because the firm can use the funds that normally would be paid to the insurer at the beginning of the policy period.

The retention technique, however, has several disadvantages:

- *Possible higher losses*. The losses retained by the firm may be greater than the loss allowance in the insurance premium that is saved by not purchasing insurance. Also, in the short run, there may be great volatility in the firm's loss experience.
- *Possible higher expenses*. Expenses may actually be higher. Outside experts such as safety engineers may have to be hired. Insurers may be able to provide loss control and claim services less expensively.

■ *Possible higher taxes.* Income taxes may also be higher. The premiums paid to an insurer are immediately income-tax deductible. However, if retention is used, only the amounts paid out for losses are deductible, and the deduction cannot be taken until the losses are actually paid. Contributions to a funded reserve are not income-tax deductible.

Noninsurance Transfers   Noninsurance transfers are another risk-financing technique. **Noninsurance transfers** *are methods other than insurance by which a pure risk and its potential financial consequences are transferred to another party.* Examples of noninsurance transfers include contracts, leases, and hold-harmless agreements. For example, a company's contract with a construction firm to build a new plant can specify that the construction firm is responsible for any damage to the plant while it is being built. A firm's computer lease can specify that maintenance, repairs, and any physical damage loss to the computer are the responsibility of the computer firm. A firm may insert a hold-harmless clause in a contract, by which one party assumes legal liability on behalf of another party. Thus, a publishing firm may insert a hold-harmless clause in a contract, by which the author, not the publisher, is held legally liable if the publisher is sued for plagiarism.

In a risk management program, noninsurance transfers have several advantages:[8]

■ The risk manager can transfer some potential losses that are not commercially insurable.
■ Noninsurance transfers often cost less than insurance.
■ The potential loss may be shifted to someone who is in a better position to exercise loss control.

However, noninsurance transfers have several disadvantages:

■ The transfer of potential loss may fail because the contract language is ambiguous. Also, there may be no court precedents for the interpretation of a contract tailor-made to fit the situation.
■ If the party to whom the potential loss is transferred is unable to pay the loss, the firm is still responsible for the claim.
■ An insurer may not give credit for the transfers, and insurance costs may not always be reduced.

Insurance   Commercial insurance is also used in a risk management program. Insurance is appropriate for loss exposures that have a low probability of loss but the severity of loss is high.

If the risk manager uses insurance to treat certain loss exposures, five key areas must be emphasized:[9]

■ Selection of insurance coverages
■ Selection of an insurer
■ Negotiation of terms
■ Dissemination of information concerning insurance coverages
■ Periodic review of the program

First, the risk manager must select the insurance coverages needed. The coverages selected must be appropriate for insuring the major loss exposures identified in step one. To determine the coverages needed, the risk manager must have specialized knowledge of commercial property and liability insurance contracts. Commercial insurance is discussed in Chapters 25–27.

The risk manager must also determine if a deductible is needed and the size of the deductible. A **deductible** *is a provision by which a specified amount is subtracted from the loss payment otherwise payable to the insured.* A deductible is used to eliminate small claims and the administrative expense of adjusting these claims. As a result, substantial premium savings are possible. In essence, a deductible is a form of risk retention.

Most risk management programs combine the retention technique discussed earlier with commercial insurance. In determining the size of the deductible, the firm may decide to retain only a relatively small part of the maximum possible loss. The insurer normally adjusts any claims, and only losses in excess of the deductible are paid.

Another approach is to purchase **excess insurance**—*a plan in which the insurer does not participate in the loss until the actual loss exceeds the amount a firm has decided to retain.* A firm may be financially strong and may wish to retain a relatively larger proportion of the maximum possible loss. The retention limit may be set at the maximum probable loss (not maximum possible loss). For example, a retention limit of $1 million may be established for a single fire loss to a plant valued at $25 million. The $1 million would be viewed as the maximum probable loss. In the unlikely event of a total loss, the firm would absorb the first $1 million of loss, and the commercial insurer would pay the remaining $24 million.

Second, the risk manager must select an insurer or several insurers. Several important factors come into play here, including the financial strength of the insurer, risk management services provided by the insurer, and the cost and terms of protection. The insurer's financial strength is determined by the size of policyowners' surplus, underwriting and investment results, adequacy of reserves for outstanding liabilities, types of insurance written, and the quality of management. Several trade publications are available to the risk manager for determining the financial strength of a particular insurer. One of the most important rating agencies is the A. M. Best Company, which rates insurers based on their relative financial strength.

The risk manager must also consider the availability of risk management services in selecting a particular insurer. An insurance agent or broker can provide the desired information concerning the risk management services available from different insurers. These services include loss-control services, assistance in identifying loss exposures, and claim adjustment services.

The cost and terms of insurance protection must be considered as well. All other factors being equal, the risk manager would prefer to purchase insurance at the lowest possible price. Many risk managers will solicit competitive premium bids from several insurers to get the necessary protection and services at the lowest price.

Third, after the insurer or insurers are selected, the terms of the insurance contract must be negotiated. If printed policies, endorsements, and forms are used, the risk manager and insurer must agree on the documents that will form the basis of the contract. If a specially tailored **manuscript policy**[10] is written for the firm, the language and meaning of the contractual provisions must be clear to both parties. In any case, the various risk management services the insurer will provide must be clearly stated in the contract. Finally, if the firm is large, the premiums may be negotiable between the firm and insurer. In many cases, an agent or broker will be involved in the negotiations.

In addition, information concerning insurance coverages must be disseminated to others in the firm. The firm's employees and managers must be informed about the insurance coverages, the various records that must be kept, and the risk management services that the insurer will provide. Those persons responsible for reporting a loss must also be informed. The firm must comply with policy provisions concerning how notice of a claim is to be given and how the necessary proof of loss will be presented.

Finally, the insurance program must be periodically reviewed. This review is especially important when the firm has a change in business operations or is involved in a merger or acquisition of another firm. The review includes an analysis of agent and broker relationships, coverages needed, quality of loss control services provided, whether claims are paid promptly, and numerous other factors. Even the basic decision—whether to purchase insurance or retain the risk—must be reviewed periodically.

Advantages of Insurance   The use of commercial insurance in a risk management program has certain advantages:[11]

- The firm will be indemnified after a loss occurs. The firm can continue to operate and may experience little or no fluctuation in earnings.
- Uncertainty is reduced, which permits the firm to lengthen its planning horizon. Worry and fear are reduced for managers and employees, which should improve performance and productivity.
- Insurers can provide valuable risk management services, such as loss-control services, loss exposure analysis, and claims adjusting.
- Insurance premiums are income-tax deductible as a business expense.

Disadvantages of Insurance   The use of insurance also entails certain disadvantages and costs:

- The payment of premiums is a major cost, because the premium consists of a component to pay losses, an amount for expenses, and an allowance for profit and contingencies. There is also an opportunity cost. Under the retention technique discussed earlier, the premium could be invested or used in the business until needed to pay claims. If insurance is used, premiums must be paid in advance, and the opportunity to use the funds is forgone.

■ Considerable time and effort must be spent in negotiating the insurance coverages. An insurer or insurers must be selected, policy terms and premiums must be negotiated, and the firm must cooperate with the loss-control activities of the insurer.

■ The risk manager may have less incentive to follow a loss-control program, because the insurer will pay the claim if a loss occurs. Such a lax attitude toward loss control could increase the number of noninsured losses as well.

Which Method Should Be Used?

In determining the appropriate method or methods for handling losses, a matrix can be used that classifies the various loss exposures according to frequency and severity. This matrix can be useful in determining which risk management method should be used (see Exhibit 3.3).

The first loss exposure is characterized by both low frequency and low severity of loss. One example of this type of exposure would be the potential theft of office supplies. This type of exposure can be handled by retention, because the loss occurs infrequently and, when it does occur, it seldom causes financial harm.

The second type of exposure is more serious. Losses occur frequently, but severity is relatively low. Examples of this type of exposure include physical damage losses to automobiles, workers compensation claims, shoplifting, and food spoilage. Loss prevention should be used here to reduce the frequency of losses. In addition, because losses occur regularly and are predictable, the retention technique can also

be used. However, because small losses in the aggregate can reach sizable levels over a one-year period, excess insurance could also be purchased.

The third type of exposure can be met by insurance. As stated earlier, insurance is best suited for low-frequency, high-severity losses. High severity means that a catastrophic potential is present, while a low probability of loss indicates that the purchase of insurance is economically feasible. Examples of this type of exposure include fires, explosions, natural disasters, and liability lawsuits. The risk manager could also use a combination of retention and commercial insurance to deal with these exposures.

The fourth and most serious type of exposure is one characterized by both high frequency and high severity. This type of exposure is best handled by avoidance. For example, a truck driver with several convictions for drunk driving may apply for a job with a trucking company. If the driver is hired and injures or kills someone while under the influence of alcohol, the company would be faced with a catastrophic lawsuit. This exposure can be handled by avoidance. The driver should not be hired.

IMPLEMENT AND MONITOR THE RISK MANAGEMENT PROGRAM

At this point, we have discussed three of the four steps in the risk management process. The fourth step is to implement and monitor the risk management program. This step begins with a policy statement.

Risk Management Policy Statement

A **risk management policy statement** is necessary to have an effective risk management program. This statement outlines the risk management objectives of the firm, as well as company policy with respect to treatment of loss exposures. It also educates top-level executives in regard to the risk management process, gives the risk manager greater authority in the firm, and provides standards for judging the risk manager's performance.

In addition, a **risk management manual** may be developed and used in the program. The manual describes in some detail the risk management program of the firm and can be a very useful tool for

EXHIBIT 3.3
Risk Management Matrix

Type of Loss	Loss Frequency	Loss Severity	Appropriate Risk Management Technique
1	Low	Low	Retention
2	High	Low	Loss prevention and retention
3	Low	High	Insurance
4	High	High	Avoidance

training new employees who will be participating in the program. Writing the manual also forces the risk manager to state precisely his or her responsibilities, objectives, and available techniques.

Cooperation with Other Departments

The risk manager does not work alone. Other functional departments within the firm are extremely important in identifying pure loss exposures and methods for treating these exposures. These departments can cooperate in the risk management process in the following ways:

- *Accounting*. Internal accounting controls can reduce employee fraud and theft of cash.
- *Finance*. Information can be provided showing the effect that losses will have on the firm's balance sheet and profit and loss statement.
- *Marketing*. Accurate packaging and product-use information can prevent liability lawsuits. Safe distribution procedures can prevent accidents.
- *Production*. Quality control can prevent the production of defective goods and liability lawsuits. Effective safety programs in the plant can reduce injuries and accidents.
- *Human resources*. This department is responsible for employee benefit programs, retirement programs, safety programs, and the company's hiring, promotion, and dismissal policies.

This list indicates how the risk management process involves the entire firm. Indeed, without the active cooperation of the other departments, the risk management program will be a failure.

Periodic Review and Evaluation

To be effective, the risk management program must be periodically reviewed and evaluated to determine whether the objectives are being attained. In particular, risk management costs, safety programs, and loss-prevention programs must be carefully monitored. Loss records must also be examined to detect any changes in frequency and severity. Finally, the risk manager must determine whether the firm's overall risk management policies are being carried out, and whether the risk manager is receiving the cooperation of the other departments.

BENEFITS OF RISK MANAGEMENT

The previous discussion shows that the risk management process involves a complex and detailed analysis. Despite their complexities, however, an effective risk management program yields substantial benefits to the firm or organization. Major benefits include the following:

- The pre-loss and post-loss risk management objectives are more easily attainable.
- The cost of risk is reduced, which may increase the company's profits. The **cost of risk** is a risk management tool that measures certain costs. These costs include premiums paid, retained losses, loss control expenditures, outside risk management services, financial guarantees, internal administrative costs, and taxes, fees, and certain other expenses.
- Because the adverse financial impact of pure loss exposures is reduced, a firm may be able to enact an enterprise risk management program that treats both pure and speculative loss exposures.
- Society also benefits since both direct and indirect (consequential) losses are reduced. As a result, pain and suffering are reduced.

In conclusion, it is clear that risk managers are extremely important to the financial success of business firms in today's economy. In view of their importance, risk managers are paid relatively high salaries (see Insight 3.2).

PERSONAL RISK MANAGEMENT

The principles of corporate risk management are also applicable to a personal risk management program. **Personal risk management** *refers to the identification of pure risks faced by an individual or family, and to the selection of the most appropriate technique for treating such risks.* Personal risk management also considers other methods for handling risk in addition to insurance.

Steps in Personal Risk Management

A personal risk management program involves four steps: (1) identify loss exposures, (2) analyze the loss exposures, (3) select appropriate techniques for

INSIGHT 3.2

Show Me the Money—Risk Manager Salaries Rise

Risk managers saw healthy growth in their salaries and bonuses as the job market began heating up, but new challenges will require them to earn their extra pay, the profession's leading placement firm reports.

The "2004 Risk Management Compensation Survey" revealed an average salary of $162,352 among the 1609 risk managers queried. That represents a raise of 5.4 percent from 2003's average of $154,100, and 26 percent from the $128,626 posted in 2000.

The survey was conducted by Logic Associates Inc., the risk management field's leading recruitment service, and was co-sponsored by *National Underwriter.*

Once again, the survey found that "bigger is better" if you are a risk manager, as those working at the largest companies were clearly the best paid, getting higher salary and bonus payments than the overall average and much more lucrative deals than their peers at smaller firms.

How Do You Stack Up?

Average Risk Manager Compensation by Company Sales Volume

ON AVERAGE, RISK MANAGERS SAW THEIR SALARIES RISE 6.4 PERCENT last year to $162,352, while bonuses were up 8 percent to an average of $16,213. Over the past four years, the average risk manager's salary is 26 percent higher.

$ Sales Volume	2004 Avg. Salary	Pct. Change from 2003	Pct. Change from 2000	2004 Avg. Bonus	Pct. Change from 2003	Pct. Change from 2000	2004 Avg. Total Cash Compensation	Pct. Change from 2003	Pct. Change from 2000
0–200 Million	$93,010	4.7%	23%	$2,853	7.0%	14%	$95,863	4.7%	23%
201–500 Million	$107,599	5.8%	21%	$5,541	28.0%	54%	$113,140	6.7%	22%
501 Million–1 Billion	$119,620	4.9%	21%	$6,634	8.4%	31%	$126,254	5.0%	21%
1–2 Billion	$139,652	4.6%	21%	$10,943	9.7%	41%	$150,595	5.0%	22%
2–4 Billion	$159,851	4.0%	26%	$15,725	6.8%	42%	$175,576	4.3%	27%
4–7 Billion	$187,124	5.0%	26%	$22,321	12.5%	47%	$209,445	5.8%	28%
7–15 Billion	$226,123	5.6%	30%	$28,619	3.0%	38%	$254,742	5.3%	31%
Over 15 Billion	$265,835	7.0%	32%	$37,070	7.4%	39%	$302,905	7.0%	33%

SOURCE: Adapted from Sam Friedman, "Job Market Heating Up for Risk Managers," *National Underwriter,* Property & Casualty Edition, April 18, 2005, pp. 12–13.

treating the loss exposures, and (4) implement and review the program periodically.

Identify Loss Exposures   The first step is to identify all loss exposures that can cause serious financial problems. Serious financial losses can result from the following:

1. Personal loss exposures
   - Loss of earned income to the family because of the premature death of the family head
   - Insufficient income and financial assets during retirement
   - Catastrophic medical bills and the loss of earnings during an extended period of disability
   - Loss of earned income from unemployment
   - Identity theft

2. Property loss exposures
   - Direct physical damage to a home and personal property because of fire, lightning, windstorm, flood, earthquake, or other causes
   - Indirect losses resulting from a direct physical damage loss, including extra expenses, moving to another apartment or home during the period of reconstruction, loss of rents, and loss of use of the building or property
   - Theft of valuable personal property, including money and securities, jewelry and furs, paintings and fine art, cameras, computer equipment, coin and stamp collections, and antiques
   - Direct physical damage losses to cars, motorcycles, and other vehicles from a collision and other-than-collision losses

- Theft of cars, motorcycles, or other vehicles
3. Liability loss exposures
   - Legal liability arising out of personal acts that cause bodily injury or property damage to others
   - Legal liability arising out of libel, slander, defamation of character, and similar exposures
   - Legal liability arising out of the negligent operation of a car, motorcycle, boat, or recreational vehicle
   - Legal liability arising out of business or professional activities
   - Payment of attorney fees and other legal defense costs

Analyze the Loss Exposures   The second step is to analyze the loss exposures. The frequency and severity of potential losses should be estimated so that the most appropriate technique can be used to deal with the exposure. For example, the chance that your home will be totally destroyed by a fire, tornado, or hurricane is relatively small, but the severity of the loss can be catastrophic. Such losses should be insured because of their catastrophic potential. On the other hand, if loss frequency is high, but loss severity is low, such losses should not be insured (such as minor scratches and dents to your car). Other techniques such as retention are more appropriate for handling these types of small losses. For example, minor physical damage losses to your car can be retained by purchasing collision insurance with a deductible.

Select Appropriate Techniques for Treating the Loss Exposures   The third step is to select the most appropriate technique for treating each loss exposure. The major methods are avoidance, risk control, retention, noninsurance transfers, and insurance.

1. *Avoidance.* Avoidance is one method for treating a loss exposure. For example, you can avoid being mugged in a high-crime-rate area by staying out of the area. You can avoid the loss from the sale of a home in a depressed real estate market by renting instead of buying.
2. *Risk control.* Risk control refers to activities that reduce both the frequency and severity of loss. For example, you can reduce the chance of an auto accident by driving within the speed

limit, taking a safe driving course, and driving defensively. Car theft can be prevented by locking the car, removing the keys from the ignition, and installing anti-theft devices.

Risk control can also reduce the severity of a loss. For example, wearing a helmet reduces the severity of a head injury in a motorcycle accident. Wearing a seat belt reduces the severity of an injury in an auto accident. Having a fire extinguisher on the premises reduces the severity of a fire.

3. *Retention.* Retention means that you retain part or all of a loss if it should occur. As noted earlier, risk retention can be active or passive. Active risk retention means you are aware of the risk and plan to retain part or all of it. For example, you can retain small collision losses to your car by buying a collision insurance policy with a deductible. Likewise, you can retain part of a loss to your home or to personal property by buying a homeowners policy with a deductible.

Risk can also be retained passively because of ignorance, indifference, or laziness. This practice can be dangerous if the retained risk could result in a catastrophic loss. For example, many workers are not insured against the risk of long-term disability, even though the adverse financial consequences from a long-term permanent disability generally are more severe than the financial consequences of premature death. Thus, workers who are not insured against this risk are using risk retention in a most dangerous and inappropriate manner.

4. *Noninsurance transfers.* Noninsurance transfers are methods other than insurance by which a pure risk is transferred to a party other than an insurer. For example, the risk of damage to rental property can be transferred to the tenant by requiring a damage deposit and by inserting a provision in the lease holding the tenant responsible for damages. Likewise, the risk of a defective television set can be transferred to the retailer by purchasing an extended-warranty contract that makes the retailer responsible for labor and repairs after the warranty expires.

5. *Insurance.* In a personal risk management program, most people rely heavily on insurance as the major method for dealing with risk. The use of insurance in a personal risk management

program is discussed in greater detail later in the text when specific insurance contracts are analyzed.

Implement and Monitor the Program Periodically
The final step is to implement the personal risk management program and review the program peri-

odically. At least every two or three years, you should determine whether all major loss exposures are adequately covered. You should also review your program at major events in your life, such as a divorce, birth of a child, purchase of a home, change of jobs, or death of a spouse or family member.

CASE APPLICATION

City Bus Corporation provides school bus transportation to private and public schools in Lancaster County. City Bus owns 50 buses that are garaged in three different cities within the county. The firm faces competition from two larger bus companies that operate in the same area. Public school boards and private schools generally award contracts to the lowest bidder, but the level of service and overall performance are also considered.

a. Briefly describe the steps in the risk management process that should be followed by the risk manager of City Bus.

b. Identify the major loss exposures faced by City Bus.
c. For each of the loss exposures identified in (b), identify a risk management technique or combination of techniques that could be used to handle the exposure.
d. Describe several sources of funds for paying losses if retention is used in the risk management program.
e. Identify other departments in City Bus that would also be involved in the risk management program.

SUMMARY

- Risk management is a process to identify loss exposures faced by an organization or individual and to select the most appropriate techniques for treating such exposures.

- Risk management has several important objectives. Pre-loss objectives include the goals of economy, reduction of anxiety, and meeting legal obligations. Post-loss objectives include survival of the firm, continued operation, stability of earnings, continued growth, and social responsibility.

- There are four steps in the risk management process:
    Identify loss exposures.
    Analyze the loss exposures.
    Select appropriate techniques for treating the loss exposures.
    Implement and monitor the risk management program.

- Risk control refers to techniques that reduce the frequency and severity of losses. Major risk-control techniques include avoidance, loss prevention, and loss reduction.

- Risk financing refers to techniques that provide for the funding of losses after they occur. Major risk-financing techniques include retention, noninsurance transfers, and commercial insurance.

- Avoidance means that a loss exposure is never acquired or an existing loss exposure is abandoned. Loss prevention refers to measures that reduce the frequency of a particular loss. Loss reduction refers to measures that reduce the severity of a loss after it occurs.

- Retention means that the firm retains part or all of the losses that result from a given loss exposure. This technique can be used if no other method of treatment is available, the worst possible loss is not serious, and losses are highly predictable. Losses can be paid out of the firm's current net income; an unfunded or funded reserve can be established to pay losses; a credit line with a bank can provide funds to pay losses; or the firm can form a captive insurer.

- The advantages of retention are the saving of money on insurance premiums, lower expenses, greater incentive for loss prevention, and increased cash flow. Major disadvantages are possible higher losses that exceed the loss component in insurance premiums, possible higher expenses if loss-control and claims personnel must be hired, and possible higher taxes.

■ A captive insurer is an insurer that is owned and established by a parent firm for the purpose of insuring the parent firm's loss exposures. Captive insurers are often formed because of difficulty in obtaining insurance. They can also provide for lower costs; easier access to a reinsurer; and the formation of a profit center.

■ Self-insurance or self-funding is a special form of planned retention by which part or all of a given loss exposure is retained by the firm.

■ Noninsurance transfers are methods other than insurance by which a pure risk and its financial consequences are transferred to another party.

■ Noninsurance transfers have several advantages. The risk manager may be able to transfer some uninsurable exposures; noninsurance transfers may cost less than insurance; and the potential loss may be shifted to someone who is in a better position to exercise loss control.

■ Noninsurance transfers also have several disadvantages. The transfer of a potential loss may fail because the contract language is ambiguous; the firm is still responsible for the loss if the party to whom the potential loss is transferred is unable to pay the loss; and an insurer may not give sufficient premium credit for the transfers.

■ Commercial insurance can also be used in a risk management program. Use of insurance involves the selection of insurance coverages, selection of an insurer, negotiation of contract terms with the insurer, dissemination of information concerning the insurance coverages, and periodic review of the insurance program.

■ The major advantages of insurance include indemnification after a loss occurs, reduction in uncertainty, availability of valuable risk management services, and the income-tax deductibility of the premiums. The major disadvantages of insurance include the cost of insurance, time and effort that must be spent in negotiating for insurance, and a possible lax attitude toward loss control because of the existence of insurance.

■ A risk management program must be properly implemented and administered. This effort involves preparation of a risk management policy statement, close cooperation with other individuals and departments, and periodic review of the entire risk management program.

■ The principles of corporate risk management can also be applied to a personal risk management program.

KEY CONCEPTS AND TERMS

Association or group captive
Avoidance
Captive insurer
Cost of risk
Deductible
Excess insurance
Loss exposure
Loss frequency
Loss prevention
Loss reduction
Loss severity
Manuscript policy
Maximum possible loss
Maximum probable loss
Noninsurance transfers
Personal risk management
Retention
Retention level
Risk control
Risk financing
Risk management
Risk management manual
Risk management policy statement
Risk retention group
Self-insurance
Single parent captive (pure captive)

REVIEW QUESTIONS

1. What is the meaning of risk management?
2. Explain the objectives of risk management both before and after a loss occurs.
3. Describe the steps in the risk management process.
4. a. Identify the sources of information that a risk manager can use to identify loss exposures.
   b. What is the difference between the maximum possible loss and maximum probable loss?
5. a. Explain the meaning of risk control.
   b. Explain the following risk-control techniques.
      1. Avoidance
      2. Loss prevention
      3. Loss reduction
6. a. Explain the meaning of risk financing.
   b. Explain the following risk-financing techniques.
      1. Retention
      2. Noninsurance transfers
      3. Insurance
7. What conditions should be fulfilled before retention is used in a risk management program?

8. a. Define a captive insurer.
   b. Explain the advantages of a captive insurer in a risk management program.

9. a. What is self-insurance?
   b. What is a risk retention group?

10. a. Explain the advantages of using insurance in a risk management program.
    b. Explain the disadvantages of using insurance in a risk management program.

APPLICATION QUESTIONS

1. Scaffold Equipment manufactures and sells scaffolds and ladders that are used by construction firms. The products are sold directly to independent retailers in the United States. The company's risk manager knows that the company could be sued if a scaffold or ladder is defective, and someone is injured. Because the cost of products liability insurance has increased, the risk manager is considering other techniques to treat the company's loss exposures.
   a. Describe the steps in the risk management process.
   b. For each of the following risk management techniques, describe a specific action using that technique that may be helpful in dealing with the company's products liability exposure.
      (1) Avoidance
      (2) Loss prevention
      (3) Loss reduction
      (4) Noninsurance transfers

2. The Swift Corporation has 5000 sales representatives and employees in the United States who drive company cars. The company's risk manager has recommended to the firm's management that the company should implement a partial retention program for collision losses to company cars.
   a. Explain the advantages and disadvantages of a partial retention program to the Swift Corporation.
   b. Identify the factors that the Swift Corporation should consider before it adopts a partial retention program for collision losses to company cars.
   c. If a partial retention program is adopted, what are the various methods the Swift Corporation can use to pay for collision losses to company cars?
   d. Identify two *risk-control* measures that could be used in the company's partial retention program for collision losses.

3. Avoidance is a risk-control technique that can be used effectively in a risk management program.
   a. What is the major advantage of using the technique of avoidance in a risk management program?
   b. Is it possible or practical for a firm to avoid all potential losses? Explain your answer.

4. A risk management program must be implemented and periodically monitored to be effective. This step requires the preparation of a *risk management policy statement* and a *risk management manual*. The cooperation of other departments is also necessary.
   a. What benefits can the firm expect to receive from a well-prepared risk management policy statement?
   b. Identify several departments within a firm that are especially important in a risk management program.

5. Chris and Karen are married and own a three-bedroom home in a large Midwestern city. Their son, Christian, attends college away from home and lives in a fraternity house. Their daughter, Kelly, is a senior in high school. Chris is an accountant who works for a local accounting firm. Karen is a marketing analyst and is often away from home several days at a time. Kelly earns extra cash by babysitting on a regular basis.

   The family's home contains household furniture, personal property, a computer that Chris uses to prepare business tax returns on weekends, and a laptop computer that Karen uses while traveling. The Swifts also own three cars. Christian drives a 1998 Ford; Chris drives a 2005 Pontiac for both business and personal use; and Karen drives a 2007 Toyota and a rental car when she is traveling. Although the Swifts have owned their home for several years, they are considering moving because of the recent increase in violent crime in their neighborhood.
   a. Describe briefly the steps in the personal risk management process.
   b. Identify the major pure risks or pure loss exposures to which Chris and Karen are exposed with respect to each of the following:
      (1) Personal loss exposures
      (2) Property loss exposures
      (3) Liability loss exposures
   c. With respect to each of the loss exposures mentioned above, identify an appropriate personal risk management technique that could be used to treat the exposure.

INTERNET RESOURCES

- **Captive.com** disseminates information about captive insurers. The organization claims that its Web site enables risk managers, owners of captives, and anyone who has an interest in alternative risk transfer techniques to meet with colleagues, ask questions, and find needed resources. Visit the site at

  http://www.captive.com

- The **International Financial Risk Institute (IFRI)** provides financial risk management opportunities for senior risk practitioners, especially the chief risk officers of major financial institutions, and a forum to discuss and exchange ideas on the principles and practical application of financial risk management. Visit the site at

  http://riskinstitute.ch

- The **Nonprofit Risk Management Center** conducts research and education on risk management and insurance issues that are of special concern to nonprofit organizations. The organization provides technical assistance, a newsletter, easy-to-read publications, and workshops and conferences related to risk management and insurance. Visit the site at

  http://www.nonprofitrisk.org

- The **Public Risk Management Association** represents risk managers of state and local governmental units. The organization provides practical training and education for risk managers in the public sector and publishes a magazine, a newsletter, and detailed issue-specific publications. Visit the site at

  http://www.primacentral.org

- The **Risk and Insurance Management Society (RIMS)** is the premier professional association in the United States for risk managers and corporate buyers of insurance. RIMS provides a forum for the discussion of common risk management issues, supports loss-prevention activities, and makes known to insurers the insurance needs of its members. RIMS has local chapters in major cities and publishes *Risk Management* magazine. Visit the site at

  http://www.rims.org

- The **Self-Insurance Institute of America** is a national association that promotes self-insurance as an alternative method for financing losses. The organization publishes technical articles on self-insurance, holds educational conferences, and promotes the legislative and regulatory interests of the self-insurance industry at both the federal and state levels. Visit the site at

  http://www.siia.org

SELECTED REFERENCES

Baranoff, Etti G., Scott E. Harrington, and Gregory R. Niehaus. *Risk Assessment,* 1st ed. Malvern, PA: American Institute for Chartered Property Casualty Underwiters/Insurance Institute of America, 2005.

Elliott, Michael W. *Fundamentals of Risk Financing,* 1st ed. Malvern, PA: American Institute for Chartered Property Casualty Underwriters/Insurance Institute of America, 2002.

Harrington, Scott. E., and Gregory R. Niehaus. *Risk Management and Insurance,* 2nd ed. Boston, MA: Irwin/McGraw-Hill, 2004.

Head, George L., ed. *Essentials of Risk Control,* 3rd ed., vols. 1 and 2. Malvern, PA: Insurance Institute of America, 1995.

Head, George L., and Stephen Horn II. *Essentials of Risk Management,* 3rd ed., vols. 1 and 2. Malvern, PA: Insurance Institute of America, 1997.

Wiening, Eric A. *Foundations of Risk Management and Insurance.* Malvern, PA: American Institute for Chartered Property Casualty Underwriters/Insurance Institute of America, 2002.

Williams, C. Arthur, Jr., Michael L. Smith, and Peter C. Young. *Risk Management and Insurance,* 8th ed. Boston, MA: Irwin/McGraw-Hill, 1998.

NOTES

1. Robert I. Mehr and Bob A. Hedges, *Risk Management: Concepts and Applications* (Homewood, IL: Richard D. Irwin, 1974), chs. 1–2; see also Eric A. Wiening, *Foundations of Risk Management and Insurance* (Malvern, PA: American Society for Chartered Casualty Property Underwriters/Insurance Institute of America, 2002), ch. 3, and George L. Head and Stephen Horn II, *Essentials of Risk Management,* 3rd ed., vol. 1 (Malvern, PA: Insurance Institute of America, 1997), pp. 70–79.

2. This section is based on Head and Horn, pp. 36–44, and C. Arthur Williams, Jr., et al., *Principles of Risk*

Management and Insurance, 2nd ed., vol. 1 (Malvern, PA: American Institute for Property and Liability Underwriters, 1981), chs. 2–3.

3. See Caroline McDonald, "Workplace Safety Pays, Survey Shows," *National Underwriter,* Property & Casualty/Risk & Benefits Management Edition, September 17, 2001.
4. Williams et al., pp. 125–126.
5. Head and Horn, pp. 40–42.
6. Towers Perrin, Tillinghast, *Captives 101: Managing Cost and Risk,* January 21, 2005.
7. Williams et al., pp. 126–133.
8. Ibid., pp. 103–104.
9. Ibid., pp. 107–123, 146–151.
10. A manuscript policy is one specifically designed for a firm to meet its specific needs and requirements.
11. Williams et al., pp. 108–116.

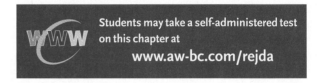

Students may take a self-administered test on this chapter at
www.aw-bc.com/rejda

CHAPTER 4

ADVANCED TOPICS IN RISK MANAGEMENT*

"The field of risk management is undergoing monumental change. Risk managers must understand financial markets and be able to effectively incorporate quantitative analysis and technology in their risk management programs."

Millicent Workman, CPCU,
Research Analyst, International Risk
Management Institute (IRMI), and
Editor, *Practical Risk Management*

LEARNING OBJECTIVES

After studying this chapter, you should be able to

◆ Explain the meaning of financial risk management and enterprise risk management.

◆ Describe the impact of the underwriting cycle and consolidation in the insurance industry on the practice of risk management.

◆ Explain the securitization of risk, including catastrophe bonds and weather options.

◆ Explain the methods that a risk manager employs to forecast losses.

◆ Show how financial analysis can be applied to risk management decision making.

◆ Describe other risk management tools that may be of assistance to risk managers.

*Prepared by Michael J. McNamara, Washington State University.

Susan Carley had experience in both insurance claims and underwriting when she accepted a staff position in the Risk Management Department of Northeast Petroleum Products (NPP) in 2002. NPP owns and operates a petroleum refinery and 72 service stations. The company also sells heating oil to more than 90,000 business and residential customers in the New England region and in two Canadian provinces.

Susan quickly became frustrated as NPP's risk manager was "old school," equating risk management with insurance management. Often risk management decisions were based on the whims of the risk manager rather than on sound financial analysis. Susan stayed with the company and began to work on her MBA, taking courses two nights a week. In addition to general business courses, Susan concentrated her efforts in statistics and finance. When NPP's risk manager retired earlier this year, Susan was offered the job as risk manager. Susan agreed to accept the position, provided she was given the latitude to make some major changes in the risk management program. She is interested, for example, in expanding the program beyond the traditional risks addressed by a risk management program. The chief financial officer is supportive and has encouraged Susan to make greater use of financial analysis in her decision making.

As discussed in Chapter 3, Susan's job as risk manager will involve more than simply purchasing insurance. She must identify the loss exposures faced by the company, analyze those exposures, select and implement a combination of risk treatment measures, and monitor the success of the risk management program.

This chapter builds on the discussion of risk management in Chapter 3 and discusses some advanced topics in risk management. Topics discussed include the changing scope of risk management, insurance market dynamics, loss forecasting, financial analysis in risk management decision making, and application of several risk management tools.

THE CHANGING SCOPE OF RISK MANAGEMENT

Traditionally, risk management was limited in scope to pure loss exposures, including property risks, liability risks, and personnel risks. An interesting trend emerged in the 1990s, however, as many businesses began to expand the scope of risk management to include speculative financial risks. Recently, some businesses have gone a step further, expanding their risk management programs to consider all risks faced by the organization.

Financial Risk Management

Business firms face a number of speculative financial risks. **Financial risk management** *refers to the* *identification, analysis, and treatment of speculative financial risks.* These risks include the following:

- Commodity price risk
- Interest rate risk
- Currency exchange rate risk

Commodity Price Risk   Commodity price risk *is the risk of losing money if the price of a commodity changes.* Producers and users of commodities face commodity price risks. For example, consider an agricultural operation that will have thousands of bushels of grain at harvest time. At harvest, the price of the commodity may have increased or decreased, depending on the supply and demand for grain. Because little storage is available for the crop, the grain must be sold at the current market price, even if that price is low. In a similar fashion, users and distributors of commodities face commodity price risks. Consider a cereal company that has promised to deliver 500,000 boxes of cereal at an agreed-upon price in six months. In the meantime, the price of grain—a commodity needed to produce the cereal—may increase or decrease, altering the profitability of the transaction. The first part of Exhibit 4.1 shows how futures contracts can be used to hedge a commodity price risk.[1]

Interest Rate Risk   Financial institutions are especially susceptible to interest rate risk. **Interest rate risk** *is the risk of loss caused by adverse interest rate movements.* For example, consider a bank that has loaned money at fixed interest rates to home purchasers under 15- and 30-year mortgages. If interest rates increase, the bank must pay higher interest rates on deposits while the mortgages are locked-in at lower interest rates. Similarly, a corporation might issue bonds at a time when interest rates are high. For the bonds to sell at their face value when issued, the coupon interest rate must equal the investor-required rate of return. If interest rates later decline, the company must still pay the higher coupon interest rate on the bonds.

Currency Exchange Rate Risk   The currency exchange rate is the value for which one nation's currency may be converted to another nation's currency. For example, one Canadian dollar might be worth the equivalent of two-thirds of one U.S. dollar.

At this currency exchange rate, one U.S. dollar may be converted to one and one-half Canadian dollars.

U.S. companies that have international operations (such as NPP's Canadian operations) are susceptible to currency exchange rate risk. **Currency exchange rate risk** *is the risk of loss of value caused by changes in the rate at which one nation's currency may be converted to another nation's currency.* For example, a U.S. company faces currency exchange rate risk when it agrees to accept a specified amount of foreign currency in the future as payment for goods sold or work performed. Likewise, U.S. companies with significant foreign operations face an earnings risk because of fluctuating exchange rates. When a U.S. company generates profits abroad, those gains must be translated back into U.S. dollars. When the U.S. dollar is strong (that is, when it has a high value relative to a foreign currency), the foreign currency purchases fewer U.S. dollars and the company's earnings therefore are lower. A weak U.S. dollar (that is, when it has a low value relative to a foreign currency) means that foreign profits can be exchanged for a larger number of U.S. dollars, and consequently the firm's earnings are higher.

Managing Financial Risks   The traditional separation of pure and speculative risks meant that different business departments addressed these risks. Pure risks were handled by the risk manager through risk retention, risk transfer, and loss control. Speculative risks were handled by the finance division through contractual provisions and capital market instruments. Examples of contractual provisions that address financial risks include call features on bonds that permit bonds with high coupon rates to be retired early and adjustable interest rate provisions on mortgages through which the interest rate varies with interest rates in the general economy. A variety of capital market approaches are also employed, including options contracts, forward contracts, futures contracts, and interest rate swaps.[2] The second part of Exhibit 4.1 shows how options can help to manage the risk of a decrease in the price of common stock.

During the 1990s, some businesses began taking a more holistic view of the pure and speculative risks faced by the organization, hoping to achieve cost savings and better risk treatment solutions by combining coverage for both types of risk. In 1997,

EXHIBIT 4.1
Managing Financial Risk—Two Examples

---

1. Hedging a Commodity Price Risk Using Futures Contracts

A corn grower estimates in May that his production will total 20,000 bushels of corn, with the harvest completed by December. Checking the price of futures contracts, he notices that the price of December corn is $2.90 per bushel. He would like to hedge the risk that the price of corn will be lower at harvest time and can do so by the appropriate use of futures contracts. Because corn futures contracts are traded in 5000 bushel units, he would sell four contracts in May totaling 20,000 bushels in the futures market. In December, he would buy back four contracts to offset his futures position. As demonstrated below, it doesn't matter whether the price of corn has increased or decreased by December. By using futures contracts and ignoring transaction expenses, he has locked in total revenue of $58,000.

If the market price of corn drops to $2.50 per bushel in December:

Revenue from sale of corn	20,000 × $2.50	=	$50,000
Sale of four contracts at $2.90 in May	58,000		
Purchase of four contracts at $2.50 in December	50,000		
Gain on futures transaction			8,000
Total revenue			$58,000

If the market price of corn increases to $3.00 per bushel in December:

Revenue from sale of corn	20,000 × $3.00	=	$60,000
Sale of four contracts at $2.90 in May	58,000		
Purchase of four contracts at $3.00 in December	60,000		
Loss on futures transaction			(2,000)
Total revenue			$58,000

2. Using Options to Protect Against Adverse Stock Price Movements

Options on stocks can be used to protect against adverse stock price movements. A call option gives the owner the right to buy 100 shares of stock at a given price during a specified period. A put option gives the owner the right to sell 100 shares of stock at a given price during a specified period. While there are many options strategies used to reduce risk, one simple alternative is discussed here: buying put options to protect against a decline in the price of stock that is already owned.

Consider someone who owns 100 shares of a stock priced at $43 per share. The owner may be concerned that the price of the stock will fall. At the same time, however, the owner may not wish to sell the stock as the sale would trigger taxation of a capital gain. In addition, the owner may believe that the price of the stock could increase. The stockholder could purchase a put option to offset a price decline.

Assume there is a put option available with a strike (exercise) price of $40. The owner of the stock could purchase the option. If the price of the stock increases, the stock owner has lost the purchase price of the option (called the premium), but the stock price has increased. But what if the price of the stock declines, say to $33 per share? In the absence of the put option, the stock owner has lost $10 ($43–$33) per share on paper. As owner of the put option, however, the stock holder has the right to sell 100 shares at $40 per share. Thus, the option is "in the money" by $7 per share ($40–$33) ignoring the option premium. The put option could be sold to offset the paper loss. Using put options in this way protects against losing money if the price of the stock declines.

Honeywell became the first company to enter into an "integrated risk program" with American International Group (AIG).[3] An **integrated risk program** *is a risk treatment technique that combines coverage for pure and speculative risks in the same contract.* At the time, Honeywell was generating more than one-third of its profits abroad. Its integrated risk program provided traditional property and casualty insurance, as well as coverage for currency exchange rate risk.

In recognition of the fact that they are treating these risks jointly, some organizations have created a new position. The **chief risk officer (CRO)** *is responsible for the treatment of pure and speculative risks faced by the organization.*[4] Combining responsibilities in one area permits treatment of the risks in a unified, and often more economical way. For example, the risk manager may be concerned about a large self-insured property claim. The financial manager may be concerned about losses caused by adverse changes in the exchange rate. Either loss, by itself, may not harm the organization if the company has a strong balance sheet. The occurrence of both losses, however, may damage the business more severely. An integrated risk management program can be designed to consider both contingencies by including a double-trigger option. A **double-trigger option** *is a provision that provides for payment only if two specified losses occur.* Thus payments would be made only if a large property claim and a large exchange rate loss occurred. The cost of such coverage is less than the cost of treating each risk separately.

Enterprise Risk Management

Encouraged by the success of financial risk management, some organizations are taking the next logical step. **Enterprise risk management** *is a comprehensive risk management program that addresses an organization's pure risks, speculative risks, strategic risks, and operational risks.* Pure and speculative risks were defined previously. *Strategic risk* refers to uncertainty regarding the organization's goals and objectives, and the organization's strengths, weaknesses, opportunities, and threats. *Operational risks* are risks that develop out of business operations, including such things as manufacturing products and providing services to customers. By packaging all of these risks in a single program, the corporation offsets one risk against another, and in the process reduces its overall risk. As long as the risks combined in the program do not exhibit perfect positive correlation, the combination of exposures reduces risk. Indeed, if some of the risks are negatively correlated, risk can be reduced significantly.

Consider NPP's operations, for example. During the summer, the company agrees to deliver heating oil in the fall at a specified price. Between summer and the delivery date, the price of heating oil may increase. Considering this risk only, Susan Carley

may decide to use heating oil futures contracts to hedge the company's price risk. NPP's other business operations, which include 72 service stations, provide a natural hedge position, however. If the price of fuel increases during the summer months, NPP will make money through its service station operations but lose money covering the promised heating oil delivery. Likewise, if the price of heating oil and gasoline falls between the summer and the fall, NPP will make money delivering heating oil at a price higher than the current market price of heating oil at a time when gasoline sales may not be as profitable.

To what extent have enterprise risk management (ERM) programs actually been adopted? Early studies estimated that 30 to 35 percent of U.S. and North American companies had adopted ERM.[5] Tillinghast-Towers Perrin conducted a number of studies of ERM adoption and practices across a wide spectrum of industries.[6] They found that 49 percent of the companies surveyed had fully (11 percent) or partially (38 percent) adopted ERM programs. Usage of ERM was most prominent in the financial services sector (the largest adopters being global insurers), followed by energy and mining, manufacturing, and telecommunications companies.

Organizations adopting ERM programs did so for several reasons. Among the reasons cited were: holistic treatment of risks facing the organization, advantage over competing businesses, positive impact upon revenues, reduction in earnings volatility, and compliance with corporate governance guidelines. Some barriers cited by survey respondents included: organization culture, turf battles, management's perception that ERM is not a priority, lack of a formal process, and deficiencies in intellectual capital and technology.

INSURANCE MARKET DYNAMICS

Chapter 3 discussed the various methods of dealing with risk. When property and liability loss exposures are not eliminated through risk avoidance, losses that occur must be financed in some other way. The risk manager must choose between two methods of funding losses: *risk retention* and *risk transfer.* Retained losses can be paid out of current earnings, from loss reserves, by borrowing, or by a captive insurance company. Risk transfer shifts the burden of paying for losses to another party, most often a property and liability insurance company. Decisions about whether to retain risks or to transfer them are influenced by conditions in the insurance marketplace. Three important factors influencing the insurance market are:

■ The underwriting cycle
■ Consolidation in the insurance industry
■ Securitization of risk

The Underwriting Cycle

For many years, a cyclical pattern has been observed in a number of underwriting results and profitability measures in the property and liability insurance industry. *This cyclical pattern in underwriting stringency, premium levels, and profitability is referred to as the* **underwriting cycle.** *Property and liability insurance markets fluctuate between periods of tight underwriting standards and high premiums, called a* **"hard" insurance market,** *and periods of loose underwriting standards and low premiums, called a* **"soft" insurance market.**

A number of measures can be used to ascertain the status of the underwriting cycle. Exhibit 4.2 shows the combined ratio for the property and liability insurance industry over time. The **combined ratio** *is the ratio of paid losses and loss adjustment expenses plus underwriting expenses to premiums.* If the combined ratio is greater than 1 (or 100 percent), underwriting operations are unprofitable. For example, the combined ratio of 107 for 2002 indicates that for every $1.00 that insurers collected in premiums, they paid out $1.07 in claims and expenses. If the combined ratio is less than 1 (or 100 percent), insurance companies are making money on underwriting operations.

EXHIBIT 4.2
Combined Ratio for All Lines of Property and Liability Insurance, 1956–2004*

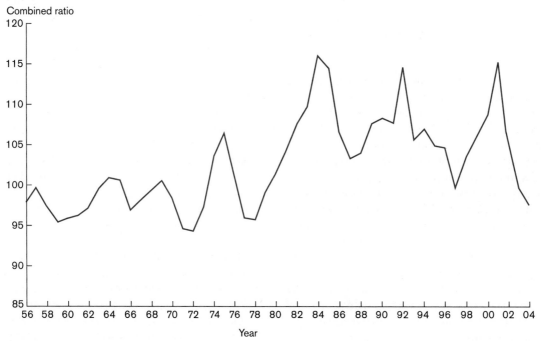

*Data from 1998–2002 include state funds.

SOURCE: *Best's Aggregates & Averages—Property/Casualty* (Oldwick, NJ: A.M. Best Company, 2005), p. 398.

Risk managers must consider current premium rates and underwriting standards when making their retention and transfer decisions. When the market is "soft," insurance can be purchased at favorable terms (for example, lower premiums, broader coverage, removal of exclusions). In a "hard" market, more retention is used because some insurance coverages are limited in availability or may not be affordable. The continued soft market of the late 1990s, for example, led some risk managers to purchase multiple-year insurance contracts in an effort to lock in favorable terms.

What causes these price fluctuations in property and liability insurance markets? Although a number of explanations have been offered,[7] two obvious factors affect property and liability insurance pricing and underwriting decisions:

- Insurance industry capacity
- Investment returns

Insurance Industry Capacity In the insurance industry, **capacity** *refers to the relative level of surplus.* **Surplus** *is the difference between an insurer's assets and its liabilities.* When the property and casualty insurance industry is in a strong surplus position, insurers can reduce premiums and loosen underwriting standards, because they have a cushion to draw on if underwriting results prove unfavorable. Given the flexibility of financial capital and the competitive nature of the insurance industry, other insurers often follow suit if one insurer takes this step. As competition intensifies, premiums are reduced further, and underwriting standards are applied less stringently. Underwriting losses begin to mount for insurers, because inadequate premiums have been charged. Underwriting losses reduce insurers' surplus, and at some point, premiums must be raised and underwriting standards tightened to restore the depleted surplus. These actions will lead to a return to profitable underwriting, which helps to replenish the surplus. When adequate surplus is restored, insurers once again are able to reduce premiums and loosen underwriting standards, causing the cycle to repeat.

External factors (such as earthquakes, hurricanes, and large liability awards) may also increase the level of claims, reducing surplus. The insurance market was hardening when the 9/11 terrorist attacks in 2001 occurred. Total insured losses from the attacks are estimated to be around $35 billion.[8]

The World Trade Center disaster produced what in the insurance industry is called a "clash loss." *A* **clash loss** *occurs when several lines of insurance simultaneously experience large losses.* The WTC disaster created large losses for life insurers, health insurers, and property and liability insurers.

The U.S. property and casualty insurance industry sustained a pre-tax operating loss of over $13 billion in 2001, and industry surplus declined by 8.5 percent that year.[9] While most of the 9/11 losses were paid by reinsurance companies, reinsurers passed the large losses back to primary companies through higher reinsurance rates. Primary insurers, in turn, increased the premiums paid by insurance purchasers. Increased premiums and tightened underwriting standards helped the industry return to underwriting profitability in 2003 and 2004, as shown in Exhibit 4.2. Improved underwriting results and investment returns helped the industry post surplus gains of 21.3 percent in 2003 and 13.6 percent in 2004. Industry surplus grew by over $110 billion between year-end 2002 and year-end 2004.

A second major shock to industry capacity occurred in 2005 with Hurricane Katrina. Estimated insured property losses totaled $40.6 billion (2005 dollars). Claims from Katrina and other hurricanes helped push the combined ratio to 100.9 in 2005.[10] Even with claims from Katrina and several other hurricanes, the property and casualty industry posted after-tax profits of $4.5 billion in 2005 and an increase in surplus for the year.[11]

Investment Returns Would you sell insurance if, for every dollar you collected in premiums, you expected to pay 78 cents in losses and 30 cents in expenses? That payout rate would lead to a loss of 8 cents per dollar of premiums collected. Property and casualty insurance companies can, and often do, sell coverages at an expected loss, hoping to offset underwriting losses with investment income. In reality, insurance companies are in two businesses: underwriting risks and investing premiums. If insurers expect favorable investment results, they can sell their insurance coverages at lower premium rates, hoping to offset underwriting losses with investment income. This practice is known as cash flow underwriting.

During the period from 1980 through 2002, the combined ratio for the property and casualty insurance industry exceeded 100 in every year except one

(1977). Insurers routinely lost money underwriting insurance during this period and relied on investment income to offset the underwriting losses. The high rate of return on the equity portion of property and casualty insurers' portfolios helped to fuel the prolonged soft market of the early and mid-1990s. Starting in 1999, however, investment returns fell for three consecutive years, reaching a low point in 2002 of 2.2 percent.[12] Investment income and the rate of return on invested assets rose to 8.3 percent in 2003 and 6.3 percent in 2004, reflecting an increase in short-term interest rates. Increased investment income, combined with underwriting profitability, produced the surplus growth discussed in the previous section.

Consolidation in the Insurance Industry

While changes were occurring in insurance product markets, changes were also occurring among the organizations operating in this sector of the economy. In the financial services industry, the consolidation trend is continuing. **Consolidation** *means the combining of business organizations through mergers and acquisitions.* A number of consolidation trends have changed the insurance marketplace for risk managers:

- Insurance company mergers and acquisitions
- Insurance brokerage mergers and acquisitions
- Cross-industry consolidations

Insurance Company Mergers and Acquisitions
Given the market structure of the property and liability insurance industry (numerous companies, relatively low barriers to entry given the flexibility of financial capital, and relatively homogenous products), insurance company consolidations do not have severe consequences for risk managers.[13] Risk managers may notice, however, that the marketplace is populated by fewer but larger, independent insurance organizations as a result of consolidation. An excellent recent example is the merger of Travelers Property Casualty Insurance Company and The St. Paul Companies in 2004, forming St. Paul Travelers.

Insurance Brokerage Mergers and Acquisitions
Unlike the consolidation of insurance companies, consolidation of insurance brokerages does have consequences for risk managers. **Insurance brokers** *are*

intermediaries who represent insurance purchasers. Insurance brokers offer an array of services to their clients, including attempting to place their clients' business with insurers. Clearly, a risk manager wants to obtain insurance coverages and related services under the most favorable financial terms available. Periodically, risk managers contact several insurance agents and insurance brokers in an effort to obtain competitive insurance coverage bids. The number of large, national insurance brokerages has declined significantly in recent years because of consolidation. For example, before the consolidation of recent years, a risk manager could obtain coverage bids from the Sedgwick Group, Johnson & Higgins, and Marsh & McLennan. As a result of consolidation, these three large, independent brokerages are now a single entity—Marsh and McLennan Companies, Inc. Other large insurance brokerages have merged with or been acquired by other insurance brokerages as well.[14]

Cross-Industry Consolidation Consolidation in the financial services arena is not limited to mergers between insurance companies or between insurance brokerages. Boundaries separating institutions with depository functions, institutions that underwrite risk, and securities businesses were enacted in Depression-era legislation. The divisions between banks, insurance companies, and securities firms began to blur in the 1990s. The U.S. Congress formally struck down the barriers with passage of the Financial Services Modernization Act of 1999 (also known by the names of the bill's sponsors, Gramm-Leach-Bliley). The 1998 merger between Citibank and Travelers, which created Citigroup, provides an excellent example of an integrated financial services company. The consolidated company included Citibank, Travelers Insurance Group, Smith Barney, and several other financial services operations. In 2002, Citigroup decided to spin off Travelers Insurance. A second example is the announcement in 2001 by Wells Fargo that it would acquire ACO Brokerage, parent firm of Acordia Inc., a large insurance brokerage. In addition to mergers and acquisitions between different types of financial institutions, some financial services companies are simply diversifying their operations by expanding into new sectors. State Farm Insurance, for example, has its own bank, offers mortgages, and sells mutual funds.

Securitization of Risk

Another important development in insurance and risk management is the accelerating use of securitization of risk. **Securitization of risk** *means that insurable risk is transferred to the capital markets through creation of a financial instrument, such as a catastrophe bond, futures contract, options contract, or other financial instrument.* The impact of risk securitization upon the insurance marketplace is an immediate increase in capacity for insurers and reinsurers. Rather than relying upon the capacity of insurers only, securitization provides access to the capital of many investors.

Insurers were among the first organizations to experiment with securitization. USAA Insurance Company, through a subsidiary, issued a catastrophe bond in 1997 to protect the company against catastrophic hurricane losses. **Catastrophe bonds** *are corporate bonds that permit the issuer to skip or defer scheduled payments if a catastrophic loss occurs.* Under the terms of the USAA bond, investors were paid principal and interest provided that hurricane losses during a time period did not exceed a specified level. Principal and interest would be lost, however, if hurricane claims exceeded a trigger point.[15]

Catastrophe bonds are not the only way in which risk can be securitized. The profitability of many businesses is determined, in large part, by weather conditions. Utility companies, agricultural enterprises, resorts, and other businesses face weather-related risk and uncertainty. More and more of these businesses are turning to the weather derivatives market, the fastest growing segment of the derivatives market, for assistance in managing this risk. *A* **weather option** *provides a payment if a specified weather contingency (e.g., temperatures higher or lower than normal) occurs.* To learn more about the weather derivatives market, see Insight 4.1.

LOSS FORECASTING

The risk manager must also identify the risks the organization faces, and then analyze the potential frequency and severity of these loss exposures. Although loss history provides valuable information, there is no guarantee that future losses will follow past loss trends. Risk managers can employ a number of techniques to assist in predicting loss levels, including the following:

- Probability analysis
- Regression analysis
- Forecasting based on loss distributions

Probability Analysis

Chance of loss is the probability that an adverse event will occur. The probability (P) of such an event is equal to the number of events likely to occur (X) divided by the number of exposure units (N). Thus, if a vehicle fleet has 500 vehicles and on average 100 vehicles suffer physical damage each year, the probability that a fleet vehicle will be damaged in any given year is:

$$P(\text{physical damage}) = 100/500 = .20 \text{ or } 20\%$$

Some probabilities of events can be easily deduced (for example, the probability that a fair coin will come up "heads" or "tails"). Other probabilities (for example, the probability that a male age 50 will die before reaching age 60) may be estimated from prior loss data.

The risk manager must also be concerned with the characteristics of the event being analyzed. Some events are **independent events**—*the occurrence does not affect the occurrence of another event.* For example, assume that a business has production facilities in Louisiana and Virginia, and that the probability of a fire at the Louisiana plant is 5 percent and that the probability of a fire at the Virginia plant is 4 percent. Obviously, the occurrence of one of these events does not influence the occurrence of the other event. If events are independent, the probability that they will occur together is the product of the individual probabilities. Thus, the probability that both production facilities will be damaged by fire is:

$$P(\text{fire at Louisiana plant})$$
$$\times P(\text{fire at Virginia plant}) = P(\text{fire at both plants})$$

$$= .04 \times .05 = .002 \text{ or } .2\%$$

Other events can be classified as **dependent events**—*the occurrence of one event affects the*

INSIGHT 4.1

The Weather (Derivatives) Report

Weather derivatives have come a long way since 1997 when a handful of American energy companies developed several dozen over-the-counter (OTC) contracts. Weather derivatives are traded on the Chicago Mercantile Exchange (CME), The London International Financial Futures Exchange, and the Helsinki Exchange, with futures and options exchanges in other countries also seriously considering this innovation.

Although the notional value of contracts written in the past year was down $1 million from the previous year, from April 2002 through March 2003, the number of contracts transacted worldwide nearly tripled according to the Weather Risk Management Association. This amounts to 11,756 contracts with a value of nearly $4.2 billion.

Originally targeted toward utilities to enable them to hedge against unseasonable weather, these derivatives are now used by farmers, resorts, casinos, the travel industry, manufacturers of seasonal equipment, underwriters, reinsurers, and any other sector with revenues subject to the vagaries of the weather.

Prior to the development of weather derivatives, businesses were unable to hedge against overall weather conditions. Some micro hedges existed, such as weather insurance (event insurance) and agricultural futures, but these are narrowly focused. Weather insurance hedges a *narrow window of time*, often one day. Agricultural futures hedge a tiny sector of the economy, such as soybeans. These micro hedges, even when aggregated, do not allow businesses to hedge against the risk of pervasively adverse weather conditions.

The impetus for the development of weather derivatives was the extreme warm winter of 1997 through 1998, when El Niño depressed the revenues of many utilities. An OTC market for weather options quickly emerged, but it proved ineffective due to lack of liquidity, an absence of price transparency, and the ever-present risk of counterparty default.

The embryonic OTC market for weather derivatives languished until 2001 when the Chicago Mercantile Exchange introduced exchange-traded weather derivatives (both futures and options) which created the liquidity, price transparency and counterparty certainty that the market needed to be viable. Later in the same year, the London International Financial Futures Exchange introduced weather futures that now allow Europeans to hedge against their respective weather conditions. In 2002, the Helsinki Exchange began trading weather futures to allow Scandinavian countries to hedge against their adverse weather conditions.

Currently, the weather derivatives market—which includes exchange-traded futures and options, as well as OTC contracts—is the fastest growing derivatives market in the world. In 2002, the CME alone traded $4.3 billion of weather derivatives contracts. Although this amount is just a fraction of the multitrillion-dollar derivatives market, it represents remarkable growth considering that 2002 was the first full year that CME offered such contracts.

What has caused such impressive growth? First, economists estimate that nearly 20 percent of the U.S. economy is directly or inversely affected by the weather. Such a percentage most likely applies to other developed economies, too, explaining the subsequent adoption of this contract by exchanges in England and Scandinavia.

Second, the exchanges are doing a good job of tooting their own horn. They heavily advertise this contract in applicable sectors so more and more firms are learning about and using this innovation. So far, ski lodges in the United States, pubs in the United Kingdom, restaurants and retail shops in Europe and golf courses in Japan have all used weather derivatives to hedge their revenue against the risk of adverse weather.

Finally, this growth is being fueled by new corporate governance codes, especially in the United States, which require companies to identify and hedge against foreseeable risks. Such regulation is especially applicable for utilities, which are publicly regulated.

Weather derivatives will continue to expand in Asia and Australia, as well as in the strongholds of Europe and the United States. This growth will likely develop from the latest movement toward smaller contracts, a broader spectrum of users, and a diversification in the types of weather protection acquired.

occurrence of the other. If two buildings are located close together, and one building catches on fire, the probability that the other building will burn is increased. For example, suppose that the individual probability of a fire loss at each building is 3 percent. The probability that the second building will have a fire given that the first building has a fire, however, may be 40 percent. Then what is the probability of two fires? This probability is a conditional probability that is equal to the probability of the first event multiplied by the probability of the second event given that the first event has occurred:

$$P(\text{fire at one bldg}) \times P \left(\begin{array}{c} \text{fire at second bldg} \\ \text{given fire at first bldg} \end{array} \right)$$

$$= P \text{ (both burn)}$$

$$.03 \times .40 = .012 \text{ or } 1.20\%$$

Events may also be mutually exclusive. *Events are* **mutually exclusive** *if the occurrence of one event precludes the occurrence of the second event.* For example, if a building is destroyed by fire, it cannot also be destroyed by flood. Mutually exclusive probabilities are additive. If the probability that a building will be destroyed by fire is 2 percent and the probability that the building will be destroyed by flood is 1 percent, then the probability the building will be destroyed by either fire or flood is:

$$P(\text{fire destroys bldg}) + P(\text{flood destroys bldg})$$

$$= P(\text{fire or flood destroys bldg})$$

$$.02 + .01 = .03 \text{ or } 3\%$$

If the independent events are not mutually exclusive, then more than one event could occur. Care must be taken not to "double-count" when determining the probability that at least one event will occur. For example, if the probability of minor fire damage is 4 percent and the probability of minor flood damage is 3 percent, then the probability of at least one of these events occurring is:

$$P(\text{minor fire}) + P(\text{minor flood})$$

$$- P(\text{minor fire and flood}) = P(\text{at least one event})$$

$$.04 + .03 - (.04) \times (.03) = .0688 \text{ or } 6.88\%$$

Assigning probabilities to individual and joint events and analyzing the probabilities can assist the risk manager in formulating a risk treatment plan.

Regression Analysis

Regression analysis is another method for forecasting losses. **Regression analysis** *characterizes the relationship between two or more variables and then uses this characterization to predict values of a variable.* One variable—the dependent variable—is hypothesized to be a function of one or more independent variables. It is not difficult to envision relationships that would be of interest to risk managers in which one variable is dependent upon another variable. For example, consider workers compensation claims. It is logical to hypothesize that the number of workers compensation claims should be positively related to some variable representing employment (for example, the number of employees, payroll, or hours worked). Likewise, we would expect the number of physical damage claims for a fleet of vehicles to increase as the size of the fleet increases or as the number of miles driven each year by fleet vehicles increases.

The first panel in Exhibit 4.3 provides data for a company's annual payroll in thousands of dollars and the corresponding number of workers compensation claims during the year. In the second panel of Exhibit 4.3, the number of claims is plotted against payroll. Regression analysis provides the coordinates of the line that best fits the points in the chart.[16] This line will minimize the sum of the squared deviations of the points from the line. Our hypothesized relationship is as follows:

$$\begin{array}{c} \text{Number of} \\ \text{workers} \\ \text{compensation} \\ \text{claims} \end{array} = B_0 + (B_1 \times \text{Payroll [in thousands]})$$

where B_0 is a constant and B_1 is the coefficient of the independent variable.

The regression results provided at the bottom of Exhibit 4.3 were obtained using spreadsheet software. The coefficient of determination, R-square, ranges from 0 to 1 and measures the model fit. An R-square value close to 1 indicates that the model does a good job of predicting Y values. By substituting the estimated payroll for next year (in thousands), the risk manager estimates that 509 workers compensation claims will occur in the next year.

Forecasting Based on Loss Distributions

Another useful tool for the risk manager is loss forecasting based on loss distributions. A **loss distribution** *is a probability distribution of losses that could occur.* Forecasting by using loss distributions works well if losses tend to follow a specified distribution

EXHIBIT 4.3
Relationship Between Payroll and Number of Workers Compensation Claims

Year	Payroll in thousands	Workers compensation claims
1995	$ 400	18
1996	520	26
1997	710	48
1998	840	96
1999	1200	110
2000	1500	150
2001	1630	228
2002	1980	250
2003	2300	260
2004	2900	300
2005	3400	325
2006	4000	412

Regression results: $Y = -6.1413 + .1074\ X$, $R^2 = .9519$

Predicted number of claims next year, if the payroll is $4.8 million:

$Y = -6.1413 + (.1074 \times 4800)$
$Y = 509.38$

and the sample size is large. Knowing the parameters that specify the loss distribution (for example, mean, standard deviation, and frequency of occurrence) enables the risk manager to estimate the number of events, severity, and confidence intervals. Many loss distributions can be employed, depending on the pattern of losses. The first section of the appendix at the end of this chapter discusses loss forecasting based on the normal distribution, a widely used distribution.

FINANCIAL ANALYSIS IN RISK MANAGEMENT DECISION MAKING

Risk managers must make a number of important decisions, including whether to retain or transfer loss exposures, which insurance coverage bid is best, and whether to invest in loss control projects. The risk manager's decisions are based on economics—weighing the costs and benefits of a course of action to see whether it is in the economic interests of the

company and its stockholders. Financial analysis can be applied to assist in risk management decision making. To make decisions involving cash flows in different time periods, the risk manager must employ time value of money analysis.

The Time Value of Money

Because risk management decisions will likely involve cash flows in different time periods, the time value of money must be considered. The **time value of money** *means that when valuing cash flows in different time periods, the interest-earning capacity of money must be taken into consideration.* A dollar received today is worth more than a dollar received one year from today, because the dollar received today can be invested immediately to earn interest. Therefore, when evaluating cash flows in different time periods, it is important to adjust dollar values to reflect the earning of interest.

A lengthy discourse on the time value of money is beyond the scope of this text.[17] Instead, we will limit our treatment to the valuation of single cash flows.

Suppose you open a bank account today and deposit $100. The value of the account today—the present value—is $100. Further assume that the bank is willing to pay 4 percent interest, compounded annually, on your account. What is the account balance one year from today? At that time, you would have your original $100, plus an additional 4 percent of $100, or $4 in interest:

$$\$100 + (\$100 \times .04) = \$104$$

Factoring, you would have

$$\$100 \times (1 + .04) = \$104$$

Thus, if you multiply the starting amount (the present value, or PV) by 1 plus the interest rate (i), it will give you the amount one year from today (the future value, or FV):

$$PV \times (1 + i) = FV$$

If you want to know the account balance after two years, simply multiply the balance at the end of the first year by 1 plus the interest rate. In this way, we arrive at the simple formula for the future value of a present amount:

$$PV\,(1 + i)^n = FV, \text{ where "}n\text{" is the number}$$
$$\text{of time periods}$$

In the second year, not only will you earn interest on the original deposit, but you will also earn interest on the $4 in interest you earned in the first period. *Because you are earning interest on interest (compound interest), the operation through which a present value is converted to a future value is called* **compounding.**

Compounding also works in reverse. Assume that you know the value of a future cash flow, but you want to know what the cash flow is worth today, adjusting for the time value of money. Dividing both sides of our compounding equation by $(1 + i)^n$ yields the following expression:

$$PV = \frac{FV}{(1 + i)^n}$$

Thus, if you want to know the present value of any future amount, divide the future amount by 1 plus the interest rate, raised to the number of periods. *This operation—bringing a future value back to present value—is called* **discounting.**

Financial Analysis Applications

In many instances, the time value of money can be applied in risk management decision making. We will consider two applications:

- Analyzing insurance coverage bids
- Loss-control investment decisions

Analyzing Insurance Coverage Bids   Assume that Susan Carley would like to purchase property insurance on a building. She is analyzing two insurance coverage bids. The bids are from comparable insurance companies, and the coverage amounts are the same. The premiums and deductibles, however, differ. Insurer A's coverage requires an annual premium of $90,000 with a $5000 per-claim deductible. Insurer B's coverage requires an annual premium of $35,000 with a $10,000 per-claim deductible. Susan is wondering whether the additional $55,000 in premiums is warranted to obtain the lower deductible. Using some of the loss forecasting methods just described, Susan predicts the following losses will occur:

Expected Number of Losses	Expected Size of Losses
12	$ 5000
6	$10,000
2	over $10,000
$n = 20$	

Which coverage bid should Susan select, based on the number of expected claims and the magnitude of these claims? For simplicity, assume that premiums are paid at the start of the year, losses and deductibles are paid at the end of the year, and 5 percent is the appropriate interest (discount) rate.

With Insurer A's bid, Susan's expected cash outflows in one year would be the first $5000 of 20 losses that are each $5000 or more, for a total of

$100,000 in deductibles. The present value of these payments is

$$PV = \frac{100,000}{(1 + .05)^1} = \$95,238$$

The present value of the total expected payments ($90,000 insurance premium at the start of the year plus the present value of the deductibles) would be $185,238.

With Insurer B's bid, Susan's expected cash outflows for deductibles at the end of the year would be

$$(\$5000 \times 12) + (\$10,000 \times 6)$$
$$+ (\$10,000 \times 2) = \$140,000$$

The present value of these deductible payments is

$$PV = \frac{140,000}{(1 + .05)^1} = \$133,333$$

The present value of the total expected payments ($35,000 insurance premium at the start of the year plus the present value of the deductibles) would be $168,333. Because the present values calculated represent the present values of cash outflows, Susan should select the bid from Insurer B, because it minimizes the present value of the cash outflows.

Loss-Control Investment Decisions Loss-control investments are undertaken in an effort to reduce the frequency and severity of losses. Such investments can be analyzed from a capital budgeting perspective by employing time value of money analysis. **Capital budgeting** *is a method of determining which capital investment projects a company should undertake.* Only those projects that benefit the organization financially should be accepted. If not enough capital is available to undertake all of the acceptable projects, then capital budgeting can assist the risk manager in determining the optimal set of projects to consider.

A number of capital budgeting techniques are available.[18] Methods that take into account time value of money, such as net present value (*NPV*) and internal rate of return (IRR), should be employed. The **net present value** *of a project is the sum of the present values of the future cash flows minus the cost of the project.*[19] The **internal rate of return** *on a*

project is the average annual rate of return provided by investing in the project. Cash flows are generated by increased revenues and reduced expenses. To calculate the NPV, the cash flows are discounted at an interest rate that considers the rate of return required by the organization's capital suppliers and the riskiness of the project. A positive net present value represents an increase in value for the firm; a negative net present value would decrease the value of the firm if the investment were made.

For example, Susan Carley has noticed a distressing trend in premises-related liability claims from several of NPP's service stations. Patrons claim to have been injured on the premises (for example, slip-and-fall injuries near gas pumps), and they have sued NPP for their injuries. Susan has decided to install camera surveillance systems at several of the "problem" service stations at a cost of $85,000 per system. She expects each surveillance system to generate an after-tax net cash flow of $40,000 per year for three years. The present value of $40,000 per year for three years discounted at the appropriate interest rate (we assume 8 percent) is $103,084. Therefore, the *NPV* of this project is

$$NPV = PV \text{ of future cash flows} - \text{Cost of project}$$
$$= \$103,084 - \$85,000 = \$18,084$$

As the project has a positive net present value, the investment is acceptable.

Alternatively, the project's internal rate of return could be determined and compared to the company's required rate of return on investment. The IRR is the interest rate that makes the net present value equal zero. In other words, when the IRR is used to discount the future cash flows back to time zero, the sum of the discounted cash flows is the cost of the project. For this project, the IRR is 19.44 percent. As 19.44 percent is greater than the required rate of return, 8 percent, the project is acceptable.

Although the cost of a project is usually known with some certainty, the future cash flows are merely estimates of the benefits that will be obtained by investing in the project. These benefits may come in the form of increased revenues, decreased expenses, or a combination of the two. Although some revenues and expenses associated with the project are easy to quantify, other values—

such as employee morale, reduced pain and suffering, public perceptions of the company, and lost productivity when a new worker is hired to replace an injured experienced worker—can prove difficult to measure.

OTHER RISK MANAGEMENT TOOLS

Our discussion of advanced risk management topics would not be complete without a brief discussion of some other risk management tools. We will divide our discussion into five parts:

- Risk management information systems (RMIS)
- Risk management intranets and Web sites
- Risk maps
- Value at risk (VAR) analysis
- Catastrophe modeling

Risk Management Information Systems (RMIS)

A key concern for risk managers is accurate and accessible risk management data. A **risk management information system (RMIS)** *is a computerized database that permits the risk manager to store and analyze risk management data and to use such data to predict and attempt to control future loss levels.* Risk management information systems may be of great assistance to risk managers in decision making. Such systems are marketed by a number of vendors, or they may be developed in-house.[20]

Risk management information systems have multiple uses. With regard to property exposures, the database may include a listing of a corporation's properties and the characteristics of those properties (construction, occupancy, protection, and exposure), property insurance policies, coverage terms, loss records, a log of fleet vehicles (including purchase dates, claims history, and maintenance records), and other data. On the liability side, the database may contain a listing of claims, the status of individual claims (pending, filed, in litigation, being appealed, or closed), historic claims, exposure bases (payroll, number of fleet vehicles, number of employees, and

so on), and liability insurance coverages and coverage terms.

Organizations with many employees often find risk management information systems of great assistance in tracking employees, especially in the area of workers compensation claims. For example, a business with production facilities across the country may self-insure its workers compensation program but hire a third party to administer the program. In addition to settling claims, the third party administrator (TPA) may provide detailed claims records to the company that become part of the company's database. Armed with these data, the risk manager can perform a number of analyses, such as examining the number of injuries incurred by geographic region, by type of injury or body part (for example, laceration or lower back injury), by job classification, and by employee identification number. Such an analysis may reveal, for example, that the injury rate is greater in the Southwest region or that a small number of employees account for a disproportionately high number of claims. In turn, the risk manager may use the results in measuring the effectiveness of loss-control investments and in targeting additional loss-control efforts. Accurate workers compensation records are also important if the business decides to purchase private insurance, because past performance must be documented to obtain lower premiums from insurers.

Risk Management Intranets and Web Sites

Some risk management departments have established their own Web sites, which include answers to "frequently asked questions" (FAQs) and a wealth of other information. In addition, some organizations have expanded the traditional risk management Web site into a risk management intranet. An **intranet** *is a Web site with search capabilities designed for a limited, internal audience.*[21] For example, a software company that sponsors trade shows at numerous venues each year might use a risk management intranet to make information available to interested parties within the company. Through the intranet, employees can obtain a list of procedures to follow (formulated by the risk management department) along with a set of forms that must be signed and filed before the event can be held (such as hold-harmless agreements).

Risk Maps

Some organizations have developed or are developing sophisticated "risk maps." **Risk maps** *are grids detailing the potential frequency and severity of risks faced by the organization.* Construction of these maps requires risk managers to analyze each risk that the organization faces before plotting it on the map. Use of risk maps varies from simply graphing the exposures to employing simulation analysis to estimate likely loss scenarios. In addition to property, liability, and personnel exposures, financial risks and other risks that fall under the broad umbrella of "enterprise risk" may be included on the risk map.[22]

Value at Risk (VAR) Analysis

A popular risk assessment technique in financial risk management is value at risk (VAR) analysis. **Value at risk (VAR)** *is the worst probable loss likely to occur in a given time period under regular market conditions at some level of confidence.* The concept is often applied to a portfolio of assets, such as a mutual fund or a pension fund, and is similar to the concept of "maximum probable loss" in traditional property and liability risk management.[23] For example, a mutual fund may have the following VAR characteristics: there is a 5 percent probability that the value of the portfolio may decline by $50,000 in any single trading day. In this case, the worst probable loss is $50,000, the time period is one trading day, and the level of confidence is 95 percent. Based on a VAR estimate, the risk level could be increased or decreased, depending on risk tolerance. Value at risk can also be employed to examine the risk of insolvency for insurers. VAR can be determined in a number of ways, including using historical data and running a computer simulation. While VAR is used in financial risk management, a growing number of organizations are considering financial risk under the broadened scope of risk management.

Catastrophe Modeling

Record-setting catastrophic losses occurred in the United States in 2005. Insured catastrophic losses were estimated to be $61.2 billion.[24] The bulk of these losses were attributable to Hurricane Katrina and four other hurricanes. These losses, on the heels of the tsunami disaster in late 2004 caused by an earthquake in the Indian Ocean, have focused greater attention on catastrophes and catastrophic losses.

Catastrophe modeling *is a computer-assisted method of estimating losses that could occur as a result of a catastrophic event.* Input variables include such factors as seismic data, meteorological data, historical losses, and values exposed to loss (e.g., structures, population, business income, etc.). The output from the computer analysis is an estimate of likely results from the occurrence of a catastrophic event, such as a category 5 hurricane or an earthquake of magnitude 7.8 on the Richter scale.

Catastrophe models are employed by insurers, brokers, ratings agencies, and large companies with exposure to catastrophic loss. An insurance company with hurricane exposure on the Eastern Seaboard or Gulf Coast, or earthquake exposure in California, may use catastrophe modeling to estimate possible aggregate losses from a disaster. Insurance brokerages, as a service to their customers, may offer catastrophe modeling services. Organizations that assess the financial viability of insurers, such as A. M. Best, use catastrophe models to determine risk potential and reserve adequacy. Some private companies also use catastrophe models in their risk management programs.

A number of organizations provide catastrophe modeling services, including RMS (Risk Management Solutions), AIR (Applied Insurance Resources, a subsidiary of the Insurance Services Office), EQUECAT (a subsidiary of ABS Group), and Impact Forecasting (a subsidiary of Aon Corporation). In addition to catastrophic losses caused by hurricanes and earthquakes, RMS also provides modeling for terrorism losses.

While catastrophe models are helpful tools, the models sometimes fail to forecast catastrophic events. In the wake of Hurricane Katrina, some insurers questioned the validity of the catastrophe models they employed.[25]

CASE APPLICATION

Great West States (GWS) is a railroad company operating in the Western United States. Juanita Salazar is risk manager of GWS. At the direction of the company's chief executive officer, she is searching for ways to handle the company's risks in a more economical way. The CEO stressed that Juanita should consider not only pure risks but also financial risks. Juanita discovered that a significant financial risk facing the organization is a commodity price risk—the risk of a significant increase in the price of fuel oil for the company's locomotives. A review of the company's income and expense statement showed that last year about 28 percent of its expenses were related to fuel oil.

Juanita was also asked to determine whether the installation of a new sprinkler system at the corporate headquarters building would be justified. The cost of the project would be $40,000. She estimates the project would provide an after-tax net cash flow of $25,000 per year for three years, with the first of these cash flows coming one year after investment in the project.

GWS is considering expanding its routes to include Colorado, New Mexico, Texas, and Oklahoma. The company is concerned about the number of derailments that might occur. Juanita ran a regression with "thousands of miles GWS locomotives traveled" as the independent variable and "number of derailments" as the dependent variable. Results of the regression are as follows:

$$Y = 2.31 + .022X$$

With the expansion, GWS trains will travel an estimated 640,000 miles next year.

a. With regard to the fuel oil price risk:
   (1) Discuss how Juanita could use futures contracts to hedge the price risk.
   (2) Discuss how a double-trigger, integrated risk management plan could be employed.
b. What is the net present value (NPV) of the sprinkler system project, assuming the rate of return required by GWS investors is 10 percent?
c. How many derailments should Juanita expect next year, assuming the regression results are reliable and GWS goes ahead with the expansion plan? (*Hint:* Be careful of scale factors when considering the independent variable.)

SUMMARY

- Financial risk management is the identification, analysis, and treatment of speculative financial risks. Such risks include commodity price risk, interest rate risk, and currency exchange rate risk.

- An integrated risk program is a risk treatment technique that combines coverage for pure and speculative risks within the same contract.

- Enterprise risk management is a comprehensive risk management program that addresses an organization's pure, speculative, strategic, and operational risks.

- A cyclical pattern—called the underwriting cycle—has been observed in underwriting stringency, premium levels, and profitability in the property and casualty insurance industry. In a "hard" insurance market, premiums are high and underwriting standards are tight. In a "soft" insurance market, premiums are low and underwriting standards are loose.

- Two important factors that affect property and casualty insurance company pricing and underwriting decisions are the level of capacity in the insurance industry and investment returns.

- The insurance industry has been experiencing consolidation through insurance company mergers and acquisitions, insurance brokerage mergers and acquisitions, and cross-industry consolidation.

- Insurers, reinsurers, and others are using securitization of risk to transfer risk to the capital markets through creation of a financial instrument, such as a catastrophe bond or a derivative.

- Risk managers can use a number of techniques to predict losses. These techniques include probability analysis, regression analysis, and forecasting by using loss distributions.

■ When analyzing events, the characteristics of the events must be considered. Events may be independent, dependent, or mutually exclusive.

■ Regression analysis is a method of characterizing the relationship that exists between two or more variables and then using the characterization as a predictor.

■ In analyzing cash flows in different periods, the time value of money must be considered.

■ Changing a present value into a future value is called compounding; determining the present value of a future amount is called discounting.

■ Risk managers can apply time value of money analysis in many situations, including insurance coverage bid analysis and loss-control investment analysis.

■ A risk management information system (RMIS) is a computerized database that permits risk managers to store and analyze risk management data and to use such data to predict future losses.

■ Risk managers may use Web sites, intranets, risk maps, value at risk (VAR) analysis, and catastrophe modeling in their risk management programs.

KEY CONCEPTS AND TERMS

Capacity
Capital budgeting
Catastrophe bond
Catastrophe modeling
Chief risk officer (CRO)
Clash loss
Combined ratio
Commodity price risk
Compounding
Consolidation
Currency exchange
 rate risk
Dependent events
Discounting
Double-trigger option
Enterprise risk
 management
Financial risk
 management

"Hard" insurance
 market
Independent events
Insurance brokers
Integrated risk program
Interest rate risk
Internal rate of return
 (IRR)
Intranet
Loss distribution
Mutually exclusive
 events
Net present value (NPV)
Regression analysis
Risk management
 information system
 (RMIS)
Risk maps
Securitization of risk

"Soft" insurance
 market
Surplus
Time value of money

Underwriting cycle
Value at risk (VAR)
 analysis
Weather option

REVIEW QUESTIONS

1. Name three speculative financial risks that may be considered by a risk manager.

2. How does enterprise risk management differ from traditional risk management?

3. What is the underwriting cycle? Differentiate between a "hard" and a "soft" insurance market.

4. What is meant by "consolidation" in the insurance industry?

5. How does securitization of risk increase capacity in the property and casualty insurance industry?

6. a. Why is loss forecasting necessary when making a decision about whether to retain or transfer loss exposures?
   b. What techniques can a risk manager use to predict future losses?

7. What is the danger of simply using past losses to estimate future losses?

8. Why is time value of money analysis used in risk management decision making?

9. What variables are difficult to quantify when analyzing investments in loss-control projects?

10. a. What is a risk management information system (RMIS)?
    b. How does a risk management Web site differ from a risk management intranet?

APPLICATION QUESTIONS

1. Integrated risk management programs are new to many risk managers and the insurance companies that offer such programs. What additional expertise, aside from knowledge of property and casualty insurance, must an insurance company possess to offer integrated risk management products?

2. A risk manager self-insured a property risk for one year. The following year, even though no losses had

occurred, the risk manager purchased property insurance to address the risk. What is the best explanation for the change in how the risk was handled, even though no losses had occurred?

3. Why do insurance brokerage mergers and acquisitions have a greater influence on corporate risk managers than do property and casualty insurance company mergers and acquisitions?

4. a. What would be the effect of ignoring the time value of money when making risk management decisions?
   b. What does the net present value of a loss control investment really represent to the owners of the organization?

5. During a "hard" insurance market, a manufacturing company decided to self-insure its workers compensation loss exposure. The company hired a third party to administer the workers compensation claims. Even though the risk was being self-insured, the risk manager insisted that the third-party administrator maintain meticulous records. When asked why such detailed records were necessary, the risk manager replied, "For story time with an insurance company next year." What did the risk manager mean?

INTERNET RESOURCES

- The **International Financial Risk Institute** provides a comprehensive introduction to financial risk management. This site educates readers on the most valuable official documents on this subject. Along with a risk management checklist, this site also includes a regulatory documents library, a collection of risk management case studies, and a risk management glossary. Visit the site at

  http://www.riskinstitute.ch

- The **Nonprofit Risk Management Center** conducts research and education on risk management and insurance issues that are of special concern to nonprofit organizations. The organization publishes a newsletter, easy-to-read publications, and informative briefs on frequently asked questions related to risk management and insurance. The organization also offers consulting services and risk audits. Visit the site at

  http://www.nonprofitrisk.org

- The **Public Risk Management Association** represents risk managers of state and local governmental units. The organization provides practical training and education for risk managers in the public sector; publishes a magazine, a newsletter, and detailed issue-specific publications; and provides cutting-edge updates on federal regulations and legislation. Visit the site at

  http://www.primacentral.org

- The **Risk and Insurance Management Society (RIMS)** is the premier professional association in the United States for risk managers and corporate buyers of insurance. RIMS provides a forum for the discussion of common risk management issues, supports loss-prevention activities, and makes known to insurers the insurance needs of its members. RIMS has local chapters in major cities and publishes *Risk Management* magazine. Visit the site at

  http://www.rims.org

- The **Self-Insurance Institute of America** is a national association that promotes self-insurance as an alternative method for financing losses. The organization publishes technical articles on self-insurance, holds educational conferences, and promotes the legislative and regulatory interests of self-insurance at both the federal and state levels. Visit the site at

  http://www.siia.org

- The **Casualty Actuarial Society (CAS)** promotes the application of actuarial science to property, casualty, and similar loss exposures. To learn more about the CAS, its research, and its publications, access the Web site at

  http://www.casact.org

- The **Insurance Information Institute (III)** is an excellent resource. The III provides a wealth of information about the property and casualty insurance industry, as well as reports on timely topics. The III also provides information on the financial services industry. Visit the site at

  http://www.iii.org

- Two industry education organizations provide professional designation programs in risk management. The **American Institute for CPCU** offers the "Associate in Risk Management" (ARM) designation. The **National Alliance for Insurance Education and Research** offers the "Certified Risk Manager" (CRM) designation. For information about these professional designations, visit the Web sites at

  http://aicpcu.org and http://scic.com

SELECTED REFERENCES

Adding Value Through Risk and Capital Management: An ERM Update of the Global Insurance Industry, Towers Perrin, Tillinghast, 2004, 40 pages.

Barton, Thomas L., William G. Shenkir, and Paul L. Walken. *Making Enterprise Risk Management Pay Off,* Prentice Hall, 2002.

Elliot, Michael W., *Capital Market Products for Risk Financing—An Educational Monograph with Exercises, 2000,* Center for the Advancement of Risk Management Education, American Institute for CPCU.

Enterprise Risk Management in the Insurance Industry— 2002 Benchmarking Survey Report, Tillinghast-Towers Perrin, 30 pages.

"ERM: Walking the Walk on Holistic Risk," *Risk Management Magazine,* September 2005. This edition includes three articles on enterprise risk management (ERM).

"Excellence in Risk Management II—A Qualitative Survey of Enterprise Risk Management Programs,"Marsh, September 2005.

Harrington, Scott E., and Gregory R. Niehaus. *Risk Management and Insurance,* 2nd ed. Boston, MA: Irwin/McGraw Hill, 2004.

Leimberg, Stephan R., Donald J. Riggin, Albert J. Howard, James W. Kallman, and Donald L. Schmidt. *The Tools & Techniques of Risk Management & Insurance,* The National Underwriter Company, 2002.

NOTES

1. A timely example is the use of futures contracts by Southwest Airlines. While other airlines were struggling with profitability because of soaring fuel costs, Southwest remained profitable. One of the main reasons for its profitability was the company's aggressive fuel hedging program. The company hedged 80 percent of its fuel costs in 2005 at $25 per-barrel oil, and 60 percent of its fuel cost in 2006 at $31 per-barrel oil. ("Southwest Airlines Beats," by Ross Snel, TheStreet.com, October 14, 2004.)

2. See an investments text for a detailed explanation of these capital market instruments.

3. As reported in "Who Needs Derivatives?" by Caroyln T. Geer, *Forbes Magazine,* April 21, 1997.

4. To learn more about the positioning, role and job of a chief risk officer (CRO), see "The Chief Risk Officer: What Does It Look Like and How Do You Get There?" *Risk Management,* September 2005, pp. 34–38; "Implementing Enterprise Risk Management: The Emerging Role of the Chief Risk Officer," International Risk Management Institute (IRMI), Inc., Web site January 2002; and "Rising Power of the Chief Risk Officer," by Des Dearlove, *Times on Line,* April 30, 2003.

5. Data reported by KPMG at the Third Annual Global Risk Management Summit and quoted in "ERM Advice for Pioneers," *Risk Management,* October 2001, p. 64; and "Enterprise Risk Management: Implementing New Solutions," The Economist Intelligence Unit (written in cooperation with MMC Enterprise Risk), 2001.

6. As discussed in "ERM Lessons Across Industries," by Jerry Miccolis of Tillinghast-Towers Perrin, March 2003. Miccolis draws upon data from three recent ERM surveys, including Tillinghast-Towers Perrin's "Enterprise Risk Management in the Insurance Industry, 2002 Benchmarking Survey Report." Also see "Adding Value through Risk and Capital Management: An ERM Update on the Global Insurance Industry," 2004, Tillinghast-Towers Perrin.

7. For a review of the literature on the causes of underwriting cycles, see Renbao Chen, Kie Ann Wong, and Hong Chew Lee, "Underwriting Cycles in Asia," *Journal of Risk and Insurance,* 1999, vol. 66, no. 1, pp. 29–47.

8. Insurance Information Institute, "The Ten Most Costly World Insurance Losses, 1970–2005." The $35 billion figure is for the World Trade Center and Pentagon attacks, in 2004 dollars.

9. Statistics presented in this paragraph are from *Best's Aggregates & Averages—Property/Casualty,* 2005, p. 88.

10. Insurance Information Institute, "The Ten Most Costly World Insurance Losses, 1970–2005" and "2006—First Quarter Results," by Robert Hartwig, Insurance Information Institute.

11. Insurance Information Institute, "Sound Risk Management and Strong Investment Results Enabled Insurance Industry to Weather Record Catastrophe Losses in 2005."

12. Investment return data quoted in this paragraph are from *Best's Aggregates & Averages—Property/Casualty,* 2005, p. 88.

13. Although the number of property and casualty insurers is decreasing due to consolidation, a study by the

Insurance Information Institute (III) showed the industry is still highly competitive. In 2004, the top four insurers wrote 29.9 percent of premiums. The next 45 insurers wrote 49.4 percent of premiums. In other words, 50 different insurers were responsible for approximately 79 percent of the premiums written.

14. For example, Acordia, Inc., the fifth largest insurance brokerage in the United States, acquired 16 insurance agencies and brokerages between January 2003 and April 2006.

15. For a discussion of the basics of risk securitization, see *Capital Market Products for Risk Financing—An Educational Monograph with Exercises* by Michael W. Elliot. This monograph was published in 2000 by the American Institute for CPCU's Center for the Advancement of Risk Management Education (CARME).

16. The line that best fits the data minimizes the sum of the squared deviations of the points from the line. Business statistics and econometrics textbooks provide a more detailed discussion of regression analysis.

17. Introductory business finance textbooks discuss the time value of money in greater detail. The time value of money calculations displayed here may also be performed using a financial calculator. Such calculators ease financial computations as the time value of money functions are preprogrammed.

18. Net present value and internal rate of return are discussed here. Some other methods are the payback method, discounted payback, and accounting rate of return. Net present value is preferred by many people because it employs the time value of money, uses the appropriate cash flow, and provides a dollars and cents answer that is easy to interpret.

19. The relevant cash flow measure captures increased revenues and decreased expenses. Depreciation is not subtracted directly as it is a noncash expense. Depreciation is considered, however, when determining the tax liability.

20. For a discussion of some criteria when selecting a Risk Management Information System (RMIS) see "Shopping for a New RMIS," by Ritza Vaughn, *Risk Management,* October 2003, pp. 12–16.

21. For a discussion of risk management intranets, see "Net Working," by Mark Dorn, *Risk Management,* June 1999, pp. 41–44.

22. For a discussion of risk mapping, see "Enhanced Risk Mapping," by Howard Kesternbaum, *Risk Management,* October 2001, pp. 40–46.

23. Value at risk is discussed in many contexts by many authors. For a representative discussion, see "Value-at-Risk: An Overview," by David M. Rowe and Arnold Miyamoto, *The Journal of Lending & Credit Risk Management,* February 1999, pp. 70–72; Chapter 2 of *Making Enterprise Risk Management Pay Off,* Thomas L. Barton, William G. Shenkir, and Paul L. Walker, 2002, Prentice Hall; and "Value at Risk (VAR): The New Benchmark for Managing Market Risk," Giuseppe Tardivo, *Journal of Financial Management and Analysis,* January 2002, pp. 16–26.

24. "Catastrophes: Insurance Issues," Insurance Information Institute, September 2006.

25. See, for example, "Catastrophe Model Angst Grows After Gulf Devastation," BestWire, October 31, 2005; and "Do Catastrophe Models Mislead," by Mark Jablonowski, *Risk Management Magazine,* July 2005, pp. 32–38.

Students may take a self-administered test on this chapter at
www.aw-bc.com/rejda

APPENDIX

RISK MANAGEMENT APPLICATION PROBLEMS

Risk managers need a number of skills to be successful. The ability to forecast losses, to apply time value of money analysis, and to use a variety of risk management tools is important. This appendix provides additional information on some quantitative aspects of risk management and some application problems. Solutions to the numbered application problems appear at the end of the appendix.

LOSS FORECASTING

Risk managers may employ probability distributions to assist in loss forecasting. Several distributions are available, including the normal, binomial, exponential, Poisson, and others. Selection of the distribution is often based upon loss history, especially when the number of losses is large. We will examine application of the normal distribution, which is used in many situations.

The normal distribution is a symmetric bell curve summarized by two parameters: the expected value and the standard deviation (m and s, respectively, in the discussion that follows). The area under the curve is equal to one, with 50 percent of the distribution on either side of the expected value. Based on the values of m and s, and an "Areas Under a Normal Curve" table (see Exhibit A4.1), the proba-

bility of any event (x) can be estimated based on the standard variate, z:

$$z = \frac{x - m}{s}$$

For example, assume that the number of weather-related property losses is normally distributed with a mean (m) equal to 16 and standard deviation (s) equal to 3. What is the probability that the number of weather-related property losses will be between 16 and 22? Substituting values into the formula, we can solve for the standard variate, z, which equals 2.00. The area corresponding to a standard variate of 2.00, according to Exhibit A4.1, is 0.4772. Therefore, the probability that between 16 and 22 weather-related losses will occur is almost 48 percent.

1. Assume the number of physical damage losses for a large fleet of vehicles is normally distributed with a mean of 400 and a standard deviation of 80. What is the probability that:

    a. More than 440 losses will occur?
    b. Between 320 and 480 losses will occur?
    c. Between 460 and 520 losses will occur?

The standard variate can also be used to determine "x values" corresponding to a given probability.

EXHIBIT A4.1
Areas Under the Normal Curve (One Tail)

z	.00	.01	.02	.03	.04	.05	.06	.07	.08	.09
0.0	.0000	.0040	.0080	.0120	.0160	.0199	.0239	.0279	.0319	.0359
0.1	.0398	.0438	.0478	.0517	.0557	.0596	.0636	.0675	.0714	.0753
0.2	.0793	.0832	.0871	.0910	.0948	.0987	.1026	.1064	.1103	.1141
0.3	.1179	.1217	.1255	.1293	.1331	.1368	.1406	.1443	.1480	.1517
0.4	.1554	.1591	.1628	.1664	.1700	.1736	.1772	.1808	.1844	.1879
0.5	.1915	.1950	.1985	.2019	.2054	.2088	.2123	.2157	.2190	.2224
0.6	.2257	.2291	.2324	.2357	.2389	.2422	.2454	.2486	.2517	.2549
0.7	.2580	.2611	.2642	.2673	.2704	.2734	.2764	.2794	.2823	.2852
0.8	.2881	.2910	.2939	.2967	.2995	.3023	.3051	.3078	.3106	.3133
0.9	.3159	.3186	.3212	.3238	.3264	.3289	.3315	.3340	.3365	.3389
1.0	.3413	.3438	.3461	.3485	.3508	.3531	.3554	.3577	.3599	.3621
1.1	.3643	.3665	.3686	.3708	.3729	.3749	.3770	.3790	.3810	.3830
1.2	.3849	.3869	.3888	.3907	.3925	.3944	.3962	.3980	.3997	.4015
1.3	.4032	.4049	.4066	.4082	.4099	.4115	.4131	.4147	.4162	.4177
1.4	.4192	.4207	.4222	.4236	.4251	.4265	.4279	.4292	.4306	.4319
1.5	.4332	.4345	.4357	.4370	.4382	.4394	.4406	.4418	.4429	.4441
1.6	.4452	.4463	.4474	.4484	.4495	.4505	.4515	.4525	.4535	.4545
1.7	.4554	.4564	.4573	.4582	.4591	.4599	.4608	.4616	.4625	.4633
1.8	.4641	.4649	.4656	.4664	.4671	.4678	.4686	.4693	.4699	.4706
1.9	.4713	.4719	.4726	.4732	.4738	.4744	.4750	.4756	.4761	.4767
2.0	.4772	.4778	.4783	.4788	.4793	.4798	.4803	.4808	.4812	.4817
2.1	.4821	.4826	.4830	.4834	.4838	.4842	.4846	.4850	.4854	.4857
2.2	.4861	.4864	.4868	.4871	.4875	.4878	.4881	.4884	.4887	.4890
2.3	.4893	.4896	.4898	.4901	.4904	.4906	.4909	.4911	.4913	.4916
2.4	.4918	.4920	.4922	.4925	.4927	.4929	.4931	.4932	.4934	.4936
2.5	.4938	.4940	.4941	.4943	.4945	.4946	.4948	.4949	.4951	.4952
2.6	.4953	.4955	.4956	.4957	.4959	.4960	.4961	.4962	.4963	.4964
2.7	.4965	.4966	.4967	.4968	.4969	.4970	.4971	.4972	.4973	.4974
2.8	.4974	.4975	.4976	.4977	.4977	.4978	.4979	.4979	.4980	.4981
2.9	.4981	.4982	.4982	.4983	.4984	.4984	.4985	.4985	.4986	.4986
3.0	.4987	.4987	.4987	.4988	.4988	.4989	.4989	.4989	.4990	.4990

Based on the previous information (normally-distributed losses, mean of 400, standard deviation of 80), above what number of physical damage claims do the highest 10 percent of x values fall? We know that the area to the right of the value of x is 10 percent. As the table shows probabilities between the expected value and x, we need to look in the table for a z value corresponding to .40. This z value is approximately 1.28. By substituting all of the known values back into our expression for z, we can solve for x:

$$1.28 = \frac{x - 400}{80}, x = (80 \times 1.28) + 400, x = 502.4$$

So 10 percent of all claims are above 502 claims.

TIME VALUE OF MONEY

The importance of the timing of cash flows and the interest-earning capacity of money was discussed in Chapter 4. Several additional time value of money/risk management examples are provided below for your consideration:

2. A sprinkler system for XYZ Company's production facility will cost $175,000. The project will provide net after-tax cash flows of $50,000 per year for five years. Assuming an interest (discount) rate of 6 percent, what is the net present value (NPV) of this project? What is the project's internal rate of return (IRR)? Do the NPV and IRR indicate this project is acceptable?

3. Under the terms of an out-of-court settlement in a class-action case, a pharmaceutical company must pay plaintiffs $500,000 per year for the next seven years, with the first payment one year from today. The company plans to create a funded claims reserve, and reserve assets can earn a 6 percent annual rate of return. What amount is needed to fully fund the reserve today, assuming the first annual disbursement to the plaintiffs is made one year from today?

4. Good-As-Gold (GAG), a canine obedience school, is being sued by the parents of a child who was injured by a dog in the custody of GAG. Two out-of-court settlements are under consideration. Under the first, GAG would pay the injured party $50,000 per year for 10 years, with the first payment one year from today. Under the second alternative, GAG would pay the injured party $50,000 today and $500,000 ten years from today. Which of these offers is best from GAG's perspective, assuming a 6 percent interest rate?

OTHER RISK MANAGEMENT APPLICATIONS

When losses are retained, an accurate forecast of the timing and magnitude of payments is needed to assure adequate financial resources will be on hand to pay claims. Consider the following example:

5. Harris Company began operations this year. The company retains property losses and estimates that property losses will be $100,000 this year. Property losses are expected to increase at a rate of 30 percent per year for the next two years. Harris expects to pay for 80 percent of property losses in the year the loss occurs, with the other 20 percent paid in the following year. How much in retained losses will Harris have to pay this year and in each of the next two years?

Property losses are easier to adjust and settle than are liability claims. In the case of liability losses, claims attributable to a specific year may not be reported until several years in the future. Once a claim is reported, there may be a lengthy process to determine whether the claim is valid and if damages should be awarded. And, of course, court decisions and damage awards may be appealed. The ability to forecast ultimate claims for various liability lines is an important skill for a risk manager. Consider the following two examples:

6. The Risk Manager of GBB Company has noted that GBB pays 40 percent (dollar value) of its general liability claims during the policy year. For the year just concluded, GBB paid $180,000 in new general liability claims. What total value of general liability claims should GBB expect for the year just concluded?

7. GBB Company has also noted that 30 percent of the product liability claims attributable to a policy year are actually filed during the policy year. For the year that just ended, a total of 24 product liability claims were filed. How many product liability claims should GBB expect, ultimately, to be attributable to the year that just ended?

Liability exposures often are described as having a "long tail," meaning that significant time can pass before all claims are reported, investigated, and settled. Loss development factors are multipliers that can be applied to claims settled to date to estimate what the ultimate claims for a period will equal.

8. Based on past workers compensation claims data, GBB's risk manager estimated loss development factors of 4.2 for year-end values one year ago, 3.4 for

year-end values two years ago, 2.3 for year-end values three years ago, 1.5 for year-end values four years ago, and 1.10 for year-end values five years ago. Workers compensation losses settled to date for the previous five years are:

5 Years Ago	4 Years Ago	3 Years Ago	2 Years Ago	Last Year
$450,000	$430,000	$400,000	$340,000	$300,000

Based on the loss development factors and claims settled to date, what are the ultimate workers compensation claims expected for each of the last five years?

Time value of money and probability are both important when insurable risk is securitized. An insurance company that faces catastrophe risk may issue catastrophe bonds. With catastrophe bonds, the probability of various loss contingencies must be considered when pricing the bond. Consider the following example:

9. An insurance company in Indonesia is concerned about catastrophic losses from an earthquake. In addition to reinsuring part of the exposure, the insurer decides to issue some dollar-denominated bonds to U.S. investors. The bonds will have a $1,000 maturity value, mature in 10 years, and provide a 12 percent annual interest (coupon) payment. The bond indenture specifies that if an earthquake registering between 6.0 and 7.5 on the Richter scale occurs in Indonesia in any year, only one-half of the annual interest will be paid; and if an earthquake exceeding 7.5 on the Richter scale occurs, no interest is payable.

Assume that seismologists estimate that the probability of a 6.0 to 7.5 earthquake in Indonesia in any year is 25 percent and the probability of an earthquake exceeding 7.5 is 5 percent in any given year. Further assume that the annual probabilities are independent (an earthquake in one year does not influence the probability of an earthquake in the following year).

If the investor-required rate of return for bonds of this degree of risk is 10 percent, what is the most an investor should be willing to pay for one of these newly issued catastrophe bonds?

SOLUTIONS

1. a. The z-value is: $(440 - 400)/80 = .50$. A z-value of .50 corresponds to an area of .1915. This value represents the area between 400 and 440. As the question asks for the probability of more than 440, the answer is the balance in the remainder of the tail: $.50 - .1915 = .3085$. So there is about a 31 percent probability that more than 440 losses will occur.

b. The question asks for the area one standard deviation above and one standard deviation below the mean. As the curve is symmetric, we can calculate one area, and multiply the value by two to get the total area. The z-value is: $(480 - 400)/80 = 1.00$. A z-value of 1.00 corresponds to an area of .3413. Multiplying this value by two, we get .6826. With a normal distribution, about 68 percent of the observations fall within one standard deviation of the mean.

c. We need to determine the area between 460 and 520. We can calculate the area between 400 and 520 first, and then subtract from this value the area between 400 and 460. The difference in areas should be the area between 460 and 520. The z-value for the first area is: $(520 - 400)/80 = 1.50$. This value corresponds to an area of .4332. The z-value for the second area is: $(460 - 400)/80 = .75$. This value corresponds to an area of .2734. The difference between these areas is .1598, so the probability of between 460 and 520 losses occurring is about 16 percent.

2. The present value of $50,000 per year for five years, assuming a 6 percent interest rate, is $210,618. Netting the present value of the future cash flows against the cost of the project, $175,000, produces a net present value (NPV) of $35,618. As the NPV is positive, the project is acceptable.

The internal rate of return is the interest rate that makes the present value of the future cash flows ($50,000 per year for five years) equal the cost of the project ($175,000). If the cash flows are equal, as in this case, the IRR can be determined easily using the annuity function on a financial calculator. The IRR of this project is 13.20 percent. As the project provides a rate of return exceeding the required rate of return, 6 percent, the project is acceptable. Note the NPV and IRR, properly applied, produce consistent capital-budgeting decisions.

3. The question is how much money would have to be placed in a claims reserve today so that at the end

of the year for the next seven years, $500,000 could be withdrawn from the account. The answer is simply the present value of $500,000 per year for seven years, assuming an interest rate of 6 percent. That value is $2,791,191.

4. The present value of $50,000 per year for 10 years is $368,004. The present value of the second alternative is $50,000 today plus the present value of $500,000 to be paid 10 years from today. This total is $329,197. As GAG would like to minimize the present value of its cash outflows, the second alternative is preferred. Note that the first alternative involves a lower cash outflow ($500,000 total dollars) than the second alternative ($550,000 total dollars). However, when adjusted for the timing of the cash flows, the second alternative is better.

5. Losses in year one are expected to be $100,000. Assuming a 30 percent growth rate, losses will be $130,000 in year two. Applying a 30 percent growth rate again, Harris Company should expect losses of $169,000 in year three. The loss payout pattern is 80 percent in the year of occurrence, with the balance paid out the following year. So:

Year 1 = $100,000 × .80 = $80,000

Year 2 = $130,000 × .80 + $100,000 × .20

= $124,000

Year 3 = $169,000 × .80 + $130,000 × .20

= $161,200

(Note that these figures have not been adjusted for the time value of money.)

6. GBB pays out 40 percent of the total ("x") during the policy year. If 40 percent of x is $180,000; then x must be $450,000.

7. Based on past experience, 30 percent of ultimate claims for policy year ("x") are filed during the policy year. If 30 percent of x is 24, then x must be 80 claims.

8. The earliest data are "seasoned"—in other words, as we get further away from the current year, there should be less adjustment needed. The more recent years have had less time to develop. Thus, additional claims are more likely to be reported for the recent years and the value of existing claims is likely to be understated. Applying the loss development factors provided to the current data, we have:

$450,000 × 1.10 = $495,000

for the year five years ago

$430,000 × 1.50 = $645,000

for the year four years ago

$400,000 × 2.30 = $920,000

for the year three years ago

$340,000 × 3.40 = $1,156,000

for the year two years ago

$300,000 × 4.20 = $1,260,000 for last year

9. The price of any financial security is equal to the present value (PV) of the future payments an investor will receive from owning the security, discounted at the appropriate interest rate. A regular 10-year corporate bond with a 12 percent annual coupon would provide 10 annual payments of $120 (.12 × $1,000) and $1,000 at maturity. For the catastrophe bond described, the annual interest payment is contingent upon whether an earthquake occurs. The expected value of the coupon payment is:

EV = .70 × $120 + .25 × $60 + .05 × ($0) = $99

The price of the bond is the present value of 10 annual expected payments of $99 plus the present value of $1000 at maturity:

Price = PV of 10 payments of $99 discounted at 10% + PV of $1,000 in 10 years discounted at 10%

Price = $608.31 + $385.54

= $993.85

PART TWO
The Private Insurance Industry

Chapter 5
Types of Insurers and Marketing Systems

Chapter 6
Insurance Company Operations

Chapter 7
Financial Operations of Insurers

Chapter 8
Government Regulation of Insurance

CHAPTER 5

TYPES OF INSURERS AND MARKETING SYSTEMS

"Insurers are increasingly using multiple distribution channels to sell their products."

Insurance Information Institute

LEARNING OBJECTIVES

After studying this chapter, you should be able to

◆ Describe the major types of private insurers, including the following:

Stock insurers	Lloyd's of London
Mutual insurers	Blue Cross and Blue Shield plans
Reciprocal exchanges	Health maintenance organizations

◆ Explain why some life insurers have demutualized or formed holding companies in recent years.

◆ Explain the difference between an agency building system and a nonbuilding agency system as life insurance marketing systems.

◆ Describe the direct response system for selling life insurance.

◆ Describe the different marketing systems in property and casualty insurance, including the following:

Independent agency system	Direct response system
Exclusive agency system	Mixed systems
Direct writer	

*R*ichard, age 25, is a senior at a large Southern university. The university recently sponsored a job fair for students seeking employment after graduation. Richard signed up for an interview with a large global insurer. He discovered that, in addition to insurance, insurers sell mutual funds and other investments; annuities; individual retirement accounts; 401(k) plans and other qualified retirement plans; and a wide variety of other financial products as well. He was surprised to hear that some insurers own banks, issue credit cards, and make real estate loans and home equity loans to individuals. Other insurers are subsidiaries of corporations that specialize in the sale of other products or services.

Thousands of life and health and property and casualty insurers are doing business in the United States today. As part of the financial services industry, private insurers have a profound impact on the American economy. Private insurers sell financial and insurance products that enable individuals, families, and business firms to attain a high degree of protection and economic security. The insurance industry also provides millions of jobs for workers and is an important source of capital to business firms. Indemnification for losses is one of the most important economic functions of insurers; insureds are restored completely or partially to their previous financial position, thereby maintaining their economic security.

This chapter discusses the role of private insurance companies in the financial services industry. Topics discussed include an overview of the financial services industry, the major types of private insurers, the major marketing methods for selling insurance, and the role of agents and brokers in the sales process.

OVERVIEW OF PRIVATE INSURANCE IN THE FINANCIAL SERVICES INDUSTRY

The financial services industry consists of thousands of financial institutions that provide financial products and services to the public. Financial institutions include commercial banks, savings and loan institutions, credit unions, life and health insurers, property and casualty insurers, mutual funds, securities brokers and dealers, private and state pension funds, various government-related financial institutions, finance companies, and other financial firms.

There are various ways of measuring the relative importance of private insurance in the financial services industry. One common method is to determine the percentage of industry assets held by each financial sector. Exhibit 5.1 shows the amount of assets held by various financial institutions at the end of 2005. The banking sector held 24 percent of the total assets; mutual funds and securities brokers and dealers accounted for 21 percent of the assets; and the insurance industry held 11 percent of the total assets. However, this figure is somewhat misleading and understates the relative financial importance of the insurance industry because private insurers also control a large amount of private pension assets (shown separately in Exhibit 5.1).

The financial services industry is changing rapidly. Two trends clearly stand out—consolidation and convergence of financial products and services. *Consolidation* means that the number of firms in the financial services industry has declined over time because of mergers and acquisitions. Because of competitive reasons, the number of commercial banks,

EXHIBIT 5.1
Assets of Financial Services Sectors by Industry, 2005
($ billions, end of year)

Sector	2005
Banking	
Commercial banking (1)	$9,236.0
Savings institutions (2)	1,788.7
Credit unions	685.5
Total	**$11,710.2**
Insurance	
Life insurance companies	$4,380.7
All other insurers	1,265.4
Total	**$5,646.1**
Securities	
Mutual and closed-end funds	$8,322.8
Securities broker/dealers (3)	2,144.1
Total	**$10,466.9**
Pensions	
Private pension funds (4)	$4,613.3
State and local government retirement funds	2,721.7
Federal government retirement funds	1,075.0
Total	**$8,410.0**
Government-related	
Government lending enterprises	$2,805.1
Federally-related mortgage pools	3,677.5
Total	**$6,482.6**
Other	
Finance companies	$1,334.6
Real estate investment trusts	354.6
Mortgage companies (5)	32.1
Asset-backed securities issuers	3,059.1
Funding corporations	1,488.0
Total	**$6,268.4**
Total All Sectors	**$48,984.2**

(1) Commercial banking includes U.S.-chartered commercial banks, foreign banking offices in the United States, bank holding companies, and banks in U.S.-affiliated areas.
(2) Savings institutions include savings and loan associations, mutual savings banks, and federal banks.
(3) Securities broker/dealers include investment banks.
(4) Private pension funds include defined benefit and defined contribution plans [including 401(k)s] and the Federal Employees Retirement Thrift Savings Plan.
(5) Data are for 1997 (latest data available)
NOTE: Data are from Board of Governors of the Federal Reserve System.

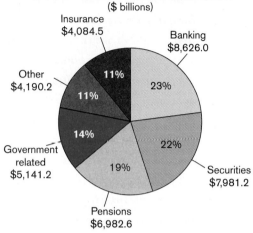

Assets of Financial Services Sectors, 2001
($ billions)

Insurance $4,084.5 — 11%
Banking $8,626.0 — 23%
Securities $7,981.2 — 22%
Pensions $6,982.6 — 19%
Government related $5,141.2 — 14%
Other $4,190.2 — 11%

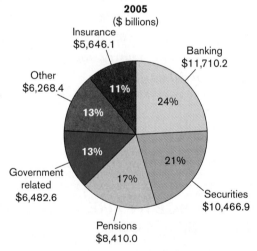

2005
($ billions)

Insurance $5,646.1 — 11%
Banking $11,710.2 — 24%
Securities $10,466.9 — 21%
Pensions $8,410.0 — 17%
Government related $6,482.6 — 13%
Other $6,268.4 — 13%

SOURCE: Insurance Information Institute, *The Financial Services Fact Book 2007*. See http://www.financialservicesfacts.org

securities dealers and brokerage firms, life and health insurers, and property and casualty insurers has declined significantly over time.

Convergence means that financial institutions can now sell a wide variety of financial products that earlier were outside their core business area. Because of the Financial Modernization Act of 1999, financial institutions, including insurers, can now compete in other financial markets that are outside their core business area. For example, many life insurers sell substantial amounts of life insurance and annuities through banks. Some insurers have established banks and savings institutions chartered by the Office of Thrift Supervision (OTS). Other insurers have established financial holding companies that allow them to engage in banking activities (see Exhibit 5.2).

EXHIBIT 5.2
Insurance Companies That Own OTS-Regulated Thrifts by Assets, 2005[a] ($000)

Insurance Company	Thrift Owned	State	Thrift Assets
Stichting Cumulatief Preferente[b]	ING Bank, FSB	DE	$53,128,800
United Services Automobile Assoc.	USAA Federal Savings Bank	TX	19,653,232
American Express Company	American Express Bank, FSB	UT	15,544,610
State Farm Mutual Auto Ins.	State Farm Bank, FSB	IL	12,218,679
American International Group	AIG Federal Savings Bank	DE	2,037,344
Principal Financial Group	Principal Bank	IO	1,265,143
ACACIA Life Insurance Company	Acacia Federal Savings Bank	VA	1,239,590
The Allstate Corporation	Allstate Bank	IL	1,000,266
Alfa Corporation	MidCountry Bank	IL	789,014
First American Corporation	First American Trust, FSB	CA	662,111
First Command Financial Plan	First Command Bank	TX	549,313
Prudential Financial Inc.	Prudential Bank & Trust, FSB	CT	546,590
FB Bancorp	Farm Bureau Bank, FSB	NV	433,842
Thrivent Financial for Lutherans	Thrivent Financial Bank	WI	416,595
New Jersey Manuf. Insurance	N.J.M. Bank, FSB	NJ	322,711
Illinois Mutual Life Insurance	Bankplus, FSB	IL	303,756
Grange Mutual Casualty Co.	The Grange Bank	OH	275,513
First Bancshares Inc.	First Home Savings Bank	MO	237,131
Ohio Farmers Insurance Co.	Westfield Bank, FSB	OH	222,238
American Sterling Corporation	American Sterling Bank	MO	195,392
Polish National Alliance of the US	Alliance FSB	IL	189,033
ACUITY	Acuity Bank	WI	180,948
Shelter Mutual Insurance Company	Shelter Financial Bank	MO	133,554
Nationwide Mutual Insurance	Nationwide Trust Company, FSB	OH	108,026
WR Berkley Corporation	InsurBanc	CT	93,822
Modern Woodmen of America	MWABank	IL	82,552
Donegal Mutual Insurance Co.	Province Bank FSB	PA	76,628
Guard Financial Group	Guard Security Bank	PA	75,667
Kansas City Life Insurance Co.	Generations Bank	MO	61,013
Western & Southern Fin. Group	Fort Washington Trust Company	OH	48,010
Country Life Insurance Company	Country Trust Bank	IL	28,802
Cuna Mutual Insurance Society	Members Trust Company	FL	23,469
New York Life Insurance Co.	New York Life Trust Company, FSB	NJ	20,618
Teachers Insurance and Annuity	TIAA-CREF Trust Company, FSB	MO	16,253
Massachusetts Mutual Life	The MassMutual Trust Company	CT	14,395
The Northwestern Mutual Life	Northwestern Mutual Trust Company	WI	12,006
AXA Assurances lard Mutuelle	Frontier Trust Company, FSB	ND	11,746
The Guardian Life Insurance	Guardian Trust Company, FSB	NY	7,078
The Auto Club Group	Auto Club Trust, FSB	MI	4,072
ACE Limited	INATrust, FSB	DE	3,412
Mennonite Mutual Aid Assoc.	MMA Trust Company	IN	3,074

[a] As of December 31, 2005. Regulated by the Office of Thrift Supervision.
[b] Non-U.S. parent.

NOTE: Data are from Office of Thrift Supervision, U.S. Department of the Treasury.

SOURCE: *The Financial Services Fact Book 2007.* See http://www.financialservicesfacts.org

TYPES OF PRIVATE INSURERS

A large number of private insurers are currently doing business in the United States. At the end of 2004, 1179 life and health insurers were doing business in the United States. These insurers sell a variety of life and health insurance products, annuities, mutual funds, pension plans, and related financial products. Exhibit 5.3 shows the top 20 U.S. life and health insurance groups and companies ranked by revenues and assets in 2005.

In 2003, 2749 property and casualty insurers were also doing business in the United States. These insurers sell property and casualty insurance and related lines, including inland marine coverages and surety and fidelity bonds. Exhibit 5.4 shows the top 20 U.S. property and casualty insurers ranked by revenues and assets in 2005.

There are various ways of classifying insurance companies. In terms of legal ownership and structure, the major types of private insurers can be classified as follows:

- Stock insurers
- Mutual insurers
- Reciprocal exchanges
- Lloyd's of London
- Blue Cross and Blue Shield plans
- Health maintenance organizations (HMOs)
- Other types of private insurers

Stock Insurers

A **stock insurer** *is a corporation owned by stockholders*. The objective is to earn profits for the stockholders. The stockholders elect a board of directors, who in turn appoint executive officers to manage the corporation. The board of directors has ultimate responsibility for the corporation's financial success. If the business is profitable, dividends can be declared and paid to the stockholders; the value of the stock may also increase. Likewise, the value of the stock may decline if the business is unprofitable.

A stock insurer cannot issue an assessable policy. An assessable policy permits the insurer to charge

Exhibit 5.3

Top Twenty U.S. Life/Health Insurance Groups and Companies by Revenues, 2005 ($ millions)

Rank	Group	Revenues	Assets
1	MetLife	$46,983	$481,645.0
2	Prudential Financial	31,708	417,776.0
3	New York Life Insurance	28,051	153,951.6
4	TIAA-CREF	25,917	399,160.8
5	Mass. Mutual Life Insurance	22,799	138,365.0
6	Northwestern Mutual	19,221	133,057.2
7	AFLAC	14,363	56,361.0
8	UnumProvident	10,437	51,866.8
9	Guardian Life of America	9,377	36,880.2
10	Principal Financial	9,010	127,035.0
11	Assurant	7,498	25,365.5
12	Thrivent Financial for Lutherans	6,190	54,932.1
13	Lincoln National	5,488	124,787.6
14	Pacific Life	4,840	86,977.2
15	Conseco	4,327	31,557.3
16	Western & Southern Financial	4,314	29,020.6
17	Jefferson-Pilot	4,220	36,078.3
18	Mutual of Omaha Insurance	4,051	16,441.3
19	Torchmark	3,126	14,768.9
20	Unitrin	3,048	9,198.3
NOTE: Data are from *Fortune.*			

SOURCE: Insurance Information Institute, *The Financial Services Fact Book 2007.* See http://www.financialservicesfacts.org

EXHIBIT 5.4

Top Twenty U.S. Property/Casualty Companies by Revenues, 2005 ($ millions)

Rank	Group	Revenues	Assets
1	American International Group	$108,905	$853,370.0
2	Berkshire Hathaway	81,663	198,325.0
3	State Farm Insurance Cos.	59,224	159,668.5
4	Allstate	35,383	156,072.0
5	Hartford Financial Services	27,083	285,557.0
6	St. Paul Travelers Cos.	24,365	113,187.0
7	Nationwide	21,832	158,258.0
8	Liberty Mutual Insurance Group	21,161	78,824.0
9	Loews (CNA)	15,363	70,675.6
10	Progressive	14,303	18,898.6
11	Chubb	14,082	48,060.7
12	USAA	11,980	51,037.9
13	Genworth Financial	10,504	105,292.0
14	Fidelity National Financial	9,669	11,104.6
15	First American Corp.	8,062	7,598.6
16	American Family Insurance Group	6,864	14,636.6
17	Safeco	6,351	14,887.0
18	Erie Insurance Group	5,104	13,056.6
19	Auto-Owners Insurance	5,014	11,728.6
20	W.R. Berkley	4,997	13,896.3

NOTE: Data are from *Fortune.*

SOURCE: Insurance Information Institute, *The Financial Services Fact Book 2007.* See http://www.financialservicesfacts.org

the policyowners additional premiums if losses are excessive. Instead, the stockholders must bear all losses. However, as noted earlier, stockholders also share in the profits when dividends are paid, or the stock appreciates in value, or both.

Mutual Insurers

A **mutual insurer** *is a corporation owned by the policyowners.* There are no stockholders. The policyowners elect a board of directors, who appoint executives to manage the corporation. Because relatively few policyowners bother to vote, the board of directors has effective management control of the company.

A mutual insurer may pay dividends to the policyowners or give a rate reduction in advance. In life insurance, a dividend is largely a refund of a redundant premium that can be paid if the mortality, investment, and operating experience are favorable. However, because the mortality and investment experience cannot be guaranteed, dividends legally cannot be guaranteed.

There are several types of mutual insurers, including the following:

- Advance premium mutual
- Assessment mutual
- Fraternal insurer

Advance Premium Mutual Most mutual insurers are advance premium mutuals. An **advance premium mutual** *is owned by the policyowners; there are no stockholders, and the insurer does not issue assessable policies.* Once the insurer's surplus (the difference between assets and liabilities) exceeds a certain amount, the states will not permit a mutual insurer to issue an assessable policy. The premiums charged are expected to be sufficient to pay all claims and expenses. Any additional costs because of poor experience are paid out of the company's surplus.

In life insurance, mutual insurers typically pay annual dividends to the policyowners. In property and casualty insurance, dividends to policyowners generally are not paid on a regular basis. Instead, such insurers may charge lower initial or renewal premiums that are closer to the actual amount needed for claims and expenses.

Assessment Mutual   An **assessment mutual** *has the right to assess policyowners an additional amount if the insurer's financial operations are unfavorable.* Relatively few assessment mutuals exist today, partly because of the practical problem of collecting the assessment. Those insurers still writing assessable policies are smaller insurers that operate in limited geographical areas, such as a state or county, and write only a limited number of insurance lines.

Fraternal Insurer   A **fraternal insurer** *is a mutual insurer that provides life and health insurance to members of a social or religious organization.* This type of insurer is also called a "fraternal benefit society." To qualify as a fraternal benefit society under the state's insurance code, the insurer must have some type of social or religious organization in existence. In addition, it must be a nonprofit entity that does not issue common stock; it must operate solely for the benefit of its members or beneficiaries; and it must have a representative form of government with a ritualistic form of work. Examples of fraternal insurers are the Knights of Columbus, Woodmen of the World Life Insurance Society, and Thrivent Financial for Lutherans.

Fraternal insurers sell only life and health insurance to their members. The assessment principle was used originally to pay death claims. Today, most fraternal insurers operate on the basis of the level premium method and legal reserve system that commercial life insurers use. Fraternal insurers also sell term life insurance. Because fraternal insurers are nonprofit or charitable organizations, they receive favorable tax treatment.

Changing Corporate Structure of Mutual Insurers
The corporate structure of mutual insurers—especially life insurers—is changing rapidly. Three trends are clearly evident:

1. *Increase in company mergers.* We noted earlier that the number of active life insurers has declined sharply in recent years. Most of the decline is due to company mergers and acquisitions. A merger means that one insurer is absorbed by another insurer or that two or more existing insurers are blended into an entirely new company. Mergers occur because insurers wish to reduce their operating costs and general overhead costs. They also occur because some insurers wish to acquire a line of new insurance, enter a new area of business, or become larger and benefit from economies of scale.

2. *Demutualization.* **Demutualization** *means that a mutual insurer is converted into a stock insurer.* Some mutual insurers have become stock insurers for the following reasons:[1]

   - The ability to raise new capital is increased.
   - Stock insurers have greater flexibility to expand by acquiring new companies or by diversification.
   - Stock options can be offered to attract and retain key executives and employees.
   - Conversion to a stock insurer may provide tax advantages.

   There are three principal methods by which a mutual insurer can convert to a stock insurer—pure conversion, merger, or bulk reinsurance (see Exhibit 5.5).[2] In a *pure conversion,* a mutual insurer amends its articles of incorporation and is reorganized as a stock insurer. In a *merger,* a mutual insurer and stock insurer are joined together as a single company, and the stock insurer is the surviving company. In *bulk reinsurance,* a mutual insurer cedes all of its assets and liabilities to a stock company, and the mutual insurer is then dissolved (see Exhibit 5.5).

3. *Mutual holding company.* Demutualization is cumbersome, expensive, and slow, and it requires the approval of regulatory authorities. As an alternative, many states have enacted legislation that allows a mutual insurer to form a holding company. A **holding company** *is a company that directly or indirectly controls an authorized insurer.* A mutual insurer is reorganized as a holding company that owns or acquires control of stock insurance companies that can issue common stock (see Exhibit 5.6). The mutual holding company would own at least 51 percent of the subsidiary stock insurer if the latter issues common stock.

EXHIBIT 5.5
Alternative Modes of Demutualization

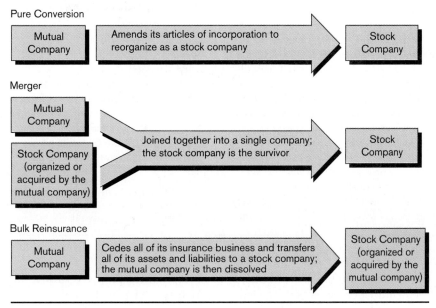

SOURCE: Reprinted with permission from HS323 Instructor Handbook, *Individual Life Insurance.* Copyright © 1998 by The American College. All Rights Reserved.

Mutual holding companies are highly controversial. Proponents argue that they offer numerous advantages:

- Insurers have an easier and less expensive way to raise new capital to expand or remain competitive.
- Insurers can enter new areas of insurance more easily, such as a life insurer acquiring a property and liability insurer.
- Stock options can be given to attract and retain key executives and employees.

Critics of mutual holding companies, however, argue that policyowners may be financially hurt by the change; the mutual holding structure could result in a reduction of dividends and other financial benefits to policyowners. Critics also argue that a conflict of interest may arise between top management and the policyowners. For example, top management may be given company stock or stock options for earning higher operating profits, which could result in lower dividends or higher premiums for policyowners (see Insight 5.1).

EXHIBIT 5.6
Mutual Holding Company Illustration

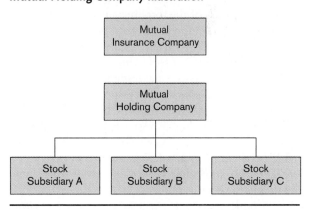

Lloyd's of London

Lloyd's of London is not an insurer, but is the world's leading insurance market that provides services and physical facilities for its members to write specialized lines of insurance. It is a meeting place where members of Lloyd's come together to pool

INSIGHT 5.1

Holding Company Schemes: The Feeling Isn't Mutual

Insurers wishing to preserve their mutual structure sometimes form a mutual holding company (MHC). An MHC is a corporation that allows insurance companies to sell stock for up to a 49 percent stake in the company *without* passing proceeds onto policyholders. MHCs are prohibited in some states, mainly because they give many stock options to senior management, coupled with a lack of accountability to shareholders. So, in effect, MHCs will give you obscure "membership interests" that don't really give you any options, because assets are transferred to the holding company and away from you. Policyholders get no voting rights in the new company. Although companies seeking to convert to MHCs often tell policyholders that the company will still be mutual after the conversion, in reality, policyholders lose a major advantage of the mutual structure: the lack of conflicts of interest between policyholders and stockholders.

Some smaller insurance companies have used subscription rights to demutualize. This is legal only in Pennsylvania and Illinois. Subscription rights allow policyholders to purchase stock at the initial public offering (IPO) price without paying a commission. Generally, access to IPOs is limited to large institutional investors, so proponents of subscription rights say policyholders have a rare opportunity to participate in the process.

SOURCE: Insure.com, Inc., a subsidiary of Quotesmith.com, Inc. Used with permission.

and spread risk. Membership in Lloyd's currently includes corporations, individual members (called Names), and Scottish limited partnerships. Lloyd's is also famous for insuring unusual exposure units, such as a prize for a hole-in-one at a golf tournament, or injury to a Kentucky Derby horse-race winner. These unusual exposures, however, account for only a small part of the total business.

Lloyd's of London has several important characteristics.[3] *First, Lloyd's technically is not an insurance company, but is a society of members (corporations and individuals) who underwrite insurance in syndicates.* Lloyd's by itself does not write insurance; the insurance is actually written by syndicates that belong to Lloyd's. In this respect, Lloyd's conceptually is similar to the New York Stock Exchange, which does not buy or sell securities, but provides a marketplace and other services to its members who buy and sell securities.

Second, as noted earlier, the insurance is written by the various syndicates that belong to Lloyd's. In early 2006, 62 syndicates were registered to conduct business at Lloyd's. Each syndicate is headed by a managing agent who manages the syndicate on behalf of the members who receive profits or bear losses in proportion to their share in the syndicate. The syndicates tend to specialize in marine, aviation, catastrophe, professional indemnity, and auto insurance coverages. Also, Lloyd's is a major player in the reinsur-

ance markets. As noted earlier, the unusual exposure units that have made Lloyd's famous account for only a small fraction of the total business. Likewise, life insurance accounts only for a small fraction of the total business and is limited to short-term contracts.

Third, new individual members or Names who belong to the various syndicates now have limited legal liability. Individual Names earlier had unlimited legal liability and pledged their personal fortune to pay their agreed-upon share of the insurance written as individuals. However, because of catastrophe asbestosis losses in the early 1990s, many Names could not pay their share of losses and declared bankruptcy. *As a result, no new Names with unlimited legal liability are admitted today.* Nevertheless, as of January 2006, 1497 individual Names still had unlimited legal liability, while 468 individual members had limited legal liability.[4] The importance of Names with unlimited legal liability will continue to decline as they slowly withdraw or die.

Another characteristic is that corporations with limited legal liability can join Lloyd's of London. To raise new capital, corporations are permitted to join Lloyd's. The infusion of new capital from corporations has substantially increased the ability of Lloyd's to write new business.

Individual members must also meet stringent financial requirements. Individual members are high net worth individuals. All premiums go into a premium trust fund, and withdrawals are allowed only for claims and expenses. Members must also deposit additional funds if premiums do not cover the claims, and the venture is a loss. A central guarantee fund is also available to pay claims if the members backing a policy go bankrupt and cannot meet their obligations.

Finally, Lloyd's is licensed only in a small number of jurisdictions in the United States. In the other states, Lloyd's must operate as a nonadmitted insurer. This means that a surplus lines broker or agent can place business with Lloyd's, but only if the insurance cannot be obtained from an admitted insurer in the state. Despite the lack of licensing, Lloyd's does a considerable amount of business in the United States. In particular, Lloyd's of London reinsures a large number of American insurers and is an important professional reinsurer.

Reciprocal Exchange

A reciprocal exchange is another type of private insurer. A **reciprocal exchange** *can be defined as an unincorporated mutual.* A reciprocal insurer has several distinct characteristics. *First, in its purest form, insurance is exchanged among the members; each member of the reciprocal insures the other members and, in turn, is insured by them.* Thus, there is an exchange of insurance promises—hence the name reciprocal exchange.

Second, a reciprocal is managed by an attorney-in-fact. The attorney-in-fact is usually a corporation that is authorized by the subscribers to seek new members, pay losses, collect premiums, handle reinsurance arrangements, invest the funds, and perform other administrative duties. However, the attorney-in-fact is not personally liable for the payment of claims and is not the insurer. The reciprocal exchange is the insurer.

Third, from a historical perspective, reciprocals can be classified as pure or modified. Historically, the reciprocals that operated earlier were of the pure type. A separate account was kept for each member. The account was credited with the member's premiums and share of investment earnings and debited for the member's share of losses and expenses. The balance in the account could be paid to a terminating member. Thus, in its purest form, insurance was provided "at cost" to the member.

Reciprocals today also can be of the modified type. In the modified form, a reciprocal is similar to an advance premium mutual. Individual accounts are not set up for each member to reflect the profit or losses of the reciprocal. In effect, the financial operations of the reciprocal are similar to a mutual insurer, with the exception of management by an attorney-in-fact.

Most reciprocals are relatively small and account for only a small percentage of the total property and liability insurance premiums written. In addition, most reciprocals specialize in a limited number of lines of insurance. However, a few reciprocals are multiple-line insurers that are large.

Blue Cross and Blue Shield Plans

Blue Cross and Blue Shield plans are another type of insurer organization. In most states, Blue Cross plans typically are organized as nonprofit, community-oriented prepayment plans that provide coverage primarily for hospital services. Blue Shield plans generally are nonprofit, prepayment plans that provide payment for physicians' and surgeons' fees and other medical services. In recent years, the majority of Blue Cross and Blue Shield plans have merged into single entities. However, a few separate Blue Cross plans and Blue Shield plans are still in operation.

Although most members are insured through group plans, individual and family coverages are also available. Blue Cross and Blue Shield plans also sponsor health maintenance organizations (HMOs) and preferred provider organizations (PPOs).

In the majority of states, Blue Cross and Blue Shield plans are nonprofit organizations that receive favorable tax treatment and are regulated under special legislation. However, to raise capital and become more competitive, a few Blue Cross and Blue Shield plans have converted to a for-profit status with stockholders and a board of directors. In addition, many nonprofit Blue Cross and Blue Shield plans own profit-seeking affiliates.

Health Maintenance Organizations

HMOs are organized plans of health care that provide comprehensive health-care services to their members. HMOs provide broad health-care services to a specified group for a fixed prepaid fee; cost control is emphasized; choice of health-care providers may be restricted; and less costly forms of treatment are often provided. The characteristics of HMOs will be discussed in greater detail in Chapter 16.

Other Private Insurers

In addition to the preceding, other types of private insurers merit a brief discussion. These include captive insurers and savings bank life insurance.

Captive Insurer   As noted in Chapter 3, a **captive insurer** *is an insurer owned by a parent firm for the purposes of insuring the parent firm's loss exposures.* There are different types of captive insurers. A *single parent captive* (also called a *pure captive)* is an insurer owned by one parent, such as a corporation. The captive can be an *association captive,* which is owned by several parents. For example, business firms that belong to a trade association may own a captive insurer.

Captive insurers are becoming more important in commercial property and casualty insurance, and about 5000 captives exist today. As noted in Chapter 3, captive insurers are formed because (1) a parent firm may have difficulty in obtaining insurance; (2) the parent's insurance costs may be lower; (3) a captive insurer makes access to reinsurers easier; (4) the captive insurer may be a source of profit to the parent if other parties are insured as well; and (5) there may be income-tax advantages to the parent under certain conditions. The characteristics of captives have already been discussed in Chapter 3, so additional treatment is not needed here.

Savings Bank Life Insurance   Savings Bank Life Insurance (SBLI) refers to life insurance that was sold originally by mutual savings banks in three states: Massachusetts, New York, and Connecticut. Today, SBLI is also sold to consumers over the phone or through Web sites in those states, and to consumers who reside in additional states as well, including Maine, New Hampshire, New Jersey, Pennsylvania, and Rhode Island. The objective of SBLI is to provide low-cost life insurance to consumers by holding down operating costs and the payment of high sales commissions to agents. SBLI is discussed in greater detail in Chapter 11.

AGENTS AND BROKERS

A successful sales force is the key to success in the financial services industry. Most insurance policies sold today are sold by agents and brokers.

Agents

When you buy insurance, you will probably purchase the insurance from an agent. An **agent** is someone who legally represents the principal and has the authority to act on the principal's behalf. An insurance agent receives authority to represent the insurer based on express authority, implied authority, and apparent authority. Express authority refers to the specific powers that the agent receives from the insurer. Implied authority means the agent has the authority to perform all incidental acts necessary to exercise the powers that are expressly given. Apparent authority is the authority the public reasonably believes the agent possesses based on the actions of the principal.[5] The principal is responsible for all acts of an agent whenever the agent is acting within the scope of express, implied, or apparent authority. This also includes wrongful and fraudulent acts, omissions, and misrepresentations so long as the agent is acting within the scope of the authority granted or implied by the principal.[6]

There is an important difference between a property and casualty insurance agent and a life insurance agent. A property and casualty agent has the power to bind the insurer immediately with respect to certain types of coverage. This relationship can be created by a *binder, which is temporary insurance until the policy is actually written.* Binders can be oral or written. For example, if you telephone an agent and request insurance on your motorcycle, the agent can make the insurance effective immediately. In contrast, a life insurance agent normally does not have the authority to bind the insurer. The agent is merely a soliciting agent who induces persons to apply for life insurance. The applicant for life insurance must be approved by the insurer before the insurance becomes effective.

Finally, many college students have an interest in insurance sales as a career. Insight 5.2 discusses the earnings of insurance agents and company-paid benefits.

INSIGHT 5.2

How Much Do Insurance Agents Earn?

According to the U.S. Department of Labor, the median annual earnings of wage and salary insurance sales agents were $41,720 in May 2004. The middle 50 percent earned between $29,980 and $66,160. The lowest 10 percent had earnings of $23,170 or less, while the highest 10 percent earned more than $108,800. Median annual earnings in May 2004 in the two industries employing the largest number of insurance sales agents were $42,010 for insurance carriers, and $41,840 for agencies, brokerages, and other insurance-related activities.

Many independent agents are paid by commission only, whereas sales workers who are employees of an agency or an insurance carrier may be paid in one of three ways—salary only, salary plus commission, or salary plus bonus. In general, commissions are the most common form of compensation, especially for experienced agents. The amount of the commission depends on the type and amount of insurance sold and on whether the transaction is a new policy or a renewal. Bonuses usually are awarded when agents meet their sales goals or when an agency meets its profit goals. Some agents involved with financial planning receive a fee for their services, rather than a commission.

Company-paid benefits to insurance sales agents usually include continuing education, training to qualify for licensing, group insurance plans, office space, and clerical support services. Some companies also may pay for automobile and transportation expenses, attendance at conventions and meetings, promotion and marketing expenses, and retirement plans. Independent agents working for insurance agencies receive fewer benefits, but their commissions may be higher to help them pay for marketing and other expenses.

Source: Excerpted from U.S. Department of Labor, Bureau of Labor Statistics, *Occupational Outlook Handbook,* 2006–07 edition.

Brokers

In contrast to an agent who represents the insurer, a **broker** *is someone who legally represents the insured.* A broker legally does not have the authority to bind the insurer. Instead, he or she can solicit or accept applications for insurance and then attempt to place the coverage with an appropriate insurer. But the insurance is not in force until the insurer accepts the business.

A broker is paid a commission from the insurers where the business is placed. Many brokers are also licensed as agents, so that they have the authority to bind their companies when acting as agents.

Brokers are extremely important in commercial property and casualty insurance. Large brokerage firms have knowledge of highly specialized insurance markets, provide risk management and loss-control services, and handle the accounts of large corporate insurance buyers.

Brokers are also important in the surplus lines markets. *Surplus lines refer to any type of insurance for which there is no available market within the state, and the coverage must be placed with a nonadmitted insurer.* A **nonadmitted insurer** *is an insurer not licensed to do business in the state.* A **sur-** **plus lines broker** *is a special type of broker who is licensed to place business with a nonadmitted insurer.* An individual may be unable to obtain the coverage from an admitted insurer because the loss exposure is too great, or the required amount of insurance is too large. A surplus lines broker has the authority to place the business with a surplus lines insurer if the coverage cannot be obtained in the state from an admitted company.

Finally, brokers are important in the area of employee benefits, especially for larger employers. Large employers often obtain their group life and medical expense coverages through brokers.

TYPES OF MARKETING SYSTEMS

Marketing systems refer to the various methods for selling insurance. Insurers employ actuaries, claims adjusters, underwriters, and other home office personnel, but unless insurance policies are profitably sold, the insurer's financial survival is unlikely. Thus, an efficient marketing system is essential to an insurance company's survival.

Life Insurance Marketing Systems

Marketing systems for the sale of life insurance have changed dramatically over time. Traditional methods for selling life insurance have been substantially modified, and new marketing models have emerged. The major life insurance marketing systems can be classified as follows.[7]

- Agency building system
- Nonbuilding agency system
- Direct response system

Agency Building System An **agency building system** is a system by which an insurer builds its own agency force by recruiting, financing, training, and supervising new agents. The new agents generally represent only the insurer.

Several types of agency building systems exist. Two basic types are the general agency system and managerial system.

- *General agency system.* Under the **general agency system,** the general agent is an independent contractor who represents only one insurer. The general agent is in charge of a territory and is responsible for recruiting, training, and motivating new agents. The general agent receives a commission based on the amount of business produced.

  Most insurers provide some financial assistance to the general agent. For example, the insurer may pay part or all of the expenses of hiring and training new agents, and it therefore has considerable control over the selection of agents and their training. The insurer may also provide an allowance for agency office expenses and other expenses.

- *Managerial system.* The **managerial system** is another type of agency building system. Under this system, branch offices are established in various areas. The branch manager is an employee of the company who has the responsibility for hiring and training new agents. In some companies, sales by the manager are not allowed or are discouraged; in other companies, sales are allowed but are usually not expected.

  The manager is paid a salary and commission based on the volume and quality of the insurance

sold and the number of productive agents hired. Under this system, the company pays the expenses of the branch office, including the financing of new agents.

Nonbuilding Agency System A **nonbuilding agency system** is a marketing system by which an insurer sells its products through established agents who are already engaged in selling life insurance. Under this system, an insurer enters into contracts with successful agents who agree to sell the insurer's products.

Examples of these nonbuilding agency systems abound. Only one of them—the personal-producing general agent—is discussed here.

Today, a considerable amount of new life insurance is sold by personal-producing general agents. A **personal-producing general agent** is a successful agent who is hired primarily to sell insurance under a contract that provides both direct and overriding commissions. A personal-producing general agent is an above-average salesperson or "super-producer" with a proven sales record. He or she is hired to sell insurance and not to recruit and train new agents. The personal-producing general agent usually receives higher commissions than the typical agent. In return, he or she is expected to sell a certain amount of insurance for a particular insurer. In addition, a personal-producing general agent may have contracts with more than one insurer. Finally, such agents typically pay their own expenses.

Direct Response System The **direct response system** is a marketing system by which life and health insurance is sold directly to customers without the services of an agent. Potential customers are solicited by television radio, mail, newspapers, and other media. Some insurers use *telemarketing* to sell their products. Many insurers also have Web sites through which life and health insurance can be sold directly to the customer.

The direct response system has several advantages to insurers. Insurers gain access to large markets; acquisition costs can be held down; and uncomplicated products can be sold effectively. One disadvantage, however, is that complex products are often difficult to sell because an agent's services may be required.

Property and Casualty Insurance Marketing Systems

The major methods for marketing property and casualty insurance include the following:

- Independent agency system
- Exclusive agency system
- Direct writer
- Direct response system
- Multiple distribution systems

Independent Agency System   The **independent agency system,** which is sometimes called the American agency system, has several basic characteristics. First, *the independent agency is a business firm that usually represents several unrelated insurers.* Agents are authorized to write business on behalf of these insurers and in turn are paid a commission based on the amount of business produced.

Second, the agency owns the *expirations or renewal rights to the business.* If a policy comes up for renewal, the agency can place the business with another insurer if it chooses to do so. Likewise, if the contract with an insurer is terminated, the agency can place the business with other insurers that the agency represents.

Third, the independent agent is *compensated by commissions that vary by line of insurance.* The commission rate on renewal business generally is the same as that paid on new business. If a lower renewal rate were paid, the insurer may lose business, because the agent would have a financial incentive to place the insurance with another insurer at the time of renewal.

In addition to selling, independent agents perform other functions. They are frequently authorized to adjust small claims. Larger agencies may also provide loss control services to their insureds, such as accident prevention and loss control engineers. Also, for some lines, the agency may bill the policyowners and collect the premiums. However, most insurers use *direct billing,* by which the policyowner is billed directly by the insurer. This is particularly true of personal lines of insurance, such as auto and homeowners.

Exclusive Agency System   *Under the* exclusive agency system, *the agent represents only one insurer or group of insurers under common ownership.* The agent may be prohibited by contract from representing other insurers.

Agents under the exclusive agency system do not usually own the expirations or renewal rights to the policies. There is some variation, however, in this regard. Some insurers do not give their agents any ownership rights in the expirations. Other insurers may grant limited ownership of expirations while the agency contract is in force, but this interest terminates when the agency contract is terminated.[8] In contrast, under the independent agency system, the agency has complete ownership of the expirations.

Another difference is the payment of commissions. Exclusive agency insurers generally pay a lower commission rate on renewal business than on new business. This approach results in a strong financial incentive for the agent to write new business and is one factor that helps explain the rapid growth of exclusive agency insurers. In contrast, as noted earlier, insurers using the independent agency system typically pay the same commission rate on new and renewal business.

Also, exclusive agency insurers provide strong support services to new agents. A new agent usually starts as an employee during a training period to learn the business. After the training period, the agent becomes an independent contractor who is then paid on a commission basis.

Direct Writer   A direct writer is often erroneously confused with an exclusive agency insurer. A **direct writer** *is an insurer in which the salesperson is an employee of the insurer, not an independent contractor.* The insurer pays all the selling expenses, including the employee's salary. Similar to exclusive agents, an employee of a direct writer usually represents only one insurer.

Employees of direct writers are usually compensated on a "salary plus" arrangement. Some companies pay a basic salary plus a commission directly related to the amount of insurance sold. Others pay a salary and a bonus that represent both selling and service activities of the employee.

Direct Response System   Like life and health insurers, property and casualty insurers also use the direct response system to sell insurance. As noted earlier, a direct response insurer sells directly to the public by television, telephone, mail, newspapers, and other media. Many property and casualty insurers also operate Web sites that provide information and premium quotes.

The direct response system is used primarily to sell personal lines of insurance, such as auto and homeowners insurance. It is not as useful in the marketing of commercial property and liability coverages because of complexity of contracts and rating considerations.

Multiple Distribution Systems The distinctions between the traditional marketing systems are breaking down as insurers search for new ways to sell insurance. To increase their profits, many property and casualty insurers use more than one distribution system to sell insurance. These systems are referred to as **multiple distribution systems.** For example, some insurers that have traditionally used the independent agency system now sell insurance directly to consumers over the Internet or by television and mail advertising. Other insurers that have used only exclusive agents (also called captive agents) in the past to sell insurance are now using independent agents as well. Other insurers are marketing property and casualty insurance through banks and to consumer groups through employers and through professional and business associations. The lines between the traditional distribution systems will continue to blur in the future as insurers develop new systems to sell insurance.

GROUP INSURANCE MARKETING

In addition to the preceding, many insurers use group marketing methods to sell individual insurance policies to members of a group. These groups include employers, labor unions, trade associations, and other groups. In particular, substantial amounts of new individual life insurance, annuities, long-term-care insurance, and other financial products are sold to employees in employer–employee groups. Employees pay for the insurance by payroll deduction. Workers no longer employed can keep their insurance in force by paying premiums directly to the insurer.

Some property and casualty insurers use mass merchandising plans to market their insurance. *Mass merchandising* is a plan for selling individually underwritten property and liability coverages to group members; auto and homeowners insurance are popular lines that are frequently used in such plans. As noted earlier, individual underwriting is used, and applicants must meet the insurer's underwriting standards. Rate discounts may be given because of a lower commission scale for agents and savings in administrative expenses. In addition, employees typically pay for the insurance by payroll deduction. Finally, employers do not usually contribute to the plans; any employer contributions result in taxable income to the employees.

CASE APPLICATION

Commercial Insurance is a large stock property and casualty insurer that specializes in the writing of commercial lines of insurance. The board of directors has appointed a committee to determine the feasibility of forming a new subsidiary insurer that would sell only personal lines of insurance, primarily homeowners and auto insurance. The new insurance company would have to meet certain management objectives. One member of the board of directors believes the new insurer should be legally organized as a mutual insurer. Assume you are an insurance consultant who is asked to serve on the committee. To what extent, if any, would each of the following objectives of the board of directors be met by formation of a mutual property and casualty insurer? Treat each objective separately.

a. Commercial Insurance must legally own the new insurer.

b. The new insurer should be able to sell common stock periodically in order to raise capital and expand into new markets.

c. The policies sold should pay dividends to the policyowners.

d. The new insurer should be licensed to do business in all states.

SUMMARY

- There are several basic types of insurers:

    Stock insurers

    Mutual insurers

    Lloyd's of London

    Reciprocal exchange

    Blue Cross and Blue Shield Plans

    Health maintenance organizations (HMOs)

    Captive insurers

    Savings bank life insurance

- An *agent* is someone who legally represents the insurer and has the authority to act on the insurer's behalf. In contrast, a *broker* is someone who legally represents the insured.

- *Surplus lines* refer to any type of insurance for which there is no available market within the state, and the coverage must be placed with a nonadmitted insurer. A *nonadmitted insurer* is a company not licensed to do business in the state. A *surplus lines broker* is a special type of broker who is licensed to place business with a nonadmitted insurer.

- In life insurance, several basic marketing methods are used:

    Agency building system

    Nonbuilding agency system

    Direct response system

- In property and casualty insurance, a number of marketing systems are used:

    Independent agency system

    Exclusive agency system

    Direct writer

    Direct response system

    Multiple distribution systems

- Many insurers use group insurance marketing methods to sell individual insurance policies to members of a group. Employees typically pay for the insurance by payroll deduction. Workers no longer employed can keep their insurance in force by paying premiums directly to the insurer.

KEY CONCEPTS AND TERMS

Advance premium mutual	Broker
Agency building system	Captive insurer
Agent	Contingent or profit-
Assessment mutual	sharing commission

Demutualization	Multiple distribution
Direct response system	systems
Direct writer	Mutual insurer
Exclusive agency system	Nonadmitted insurer
Expirations or renewal	Nonbuilding agency
rights to business	system
Fraternal insurer	Personal-producing
General agency system	general agent
Holding company	Reciprocal exchange
Independent agency system	Savings bank life insurance
Lloyd's of London	(SBLI)
Managerial system	Stock insurer
Mass merchandising	Surplus lines broker

REVIEW QUESTIONS

1. Describe the basic characteristics of stock insurers.

2. a. Describe the basic features of mutual insurers.
   b. Identify the major types of mutual insurers.

3. The corporate structure of mutual insurers is changing. Briefly describe three major trends that have an impact on the corporate structure of mutual insurers.

4. Explain the basic characteristics of Lloyd's of London.

5. Describe the basic characteristics of a reciprocal exchange.

6. Explain the legal distinction between an agent and a broker.

7. Briefly describe the basic characteristics of the following marketing systems in life and health insurance:
   a. Agency building system
   b. Nonbuilding agency system
   c. Direct response system

8. Briefly describe the basic characteristics of the following marketing systems in property and casualty insurance:
   a. Independent agency system
   b. Exclusive agency system
   c. Direct writer
   d. Direct response system
   e. Multiple distribution systems

9. Who owns the policy expirations or the renewal rights to the business under the independent agency system?

10. What is a mass-merchandising plan in property and liability insurance?

APPLICATION QUESTIONS

1. A group of investors are discussing the formation of a new property and casualty insurer. The proposed company would market a new homeowners policy that combines traditional homeowner coverages with unemployment benefits if the policyowner becomes involuntarily unemployed. Each investor would contribute at least $100,000 and would receive a proportionate interest in the company. In addition, the company would raise additional capital by selling ownership rights to other investors. Management wants to avoid the expense of hiring and training agents to sell the new policy and wants to sell the insurance directly to the public by selective advertising in personal finance magazines.
   a. Identify the type of insurance company that best fits the above description.
   b. Identify the marketing system that management is considering adopting.

2. Compare a stock insurer with a mutual insurer with respect to each of the following:
   a. Identification of the parties who legally own the company
   b. Right to assess policyowners additional premiums
   c. Right of policyowners to elect the board of directors

3. A luncheon speaker stated that "the number of life insurers has declined sharply during the past decade because of the increase in company mergers and acquisitions, demutualiztion of insurers, and formation of mutual holding companies."
   a. Why have mergers and acquisitions among insurers increased over time?
   b. What is the meaning of *demutualization?*
   c. Briefly explain the advantages of demutualization to a mutual life insurer.
   d. What is a mutual holding company?
   e. What are the advantages of a mutual holding company to an insurer?

4. A newspaper reporter wrote that "Lloyds of London is an association that provides physical facilities and services to the members for selling insurance. The insurance is underwritten by various syndicates who belong to Lloyd's." Describe Lloyd's of London with respect to each of the following:
   a. Liability of individual members and corporations
   b. Types of insurance written
   c. Financial safeguards to protect insureds

5. Property and casualty insurance can be marketed under different marketing systems. Compare the independent agency system with the exclusive agency system with respect to each of the following:
   a. Number of insurers represented
   b. Ownership of policy expirations
   c. Differences in the payment of commissions

INTERNET RESOURCES

- **The American College** is an accredited, nonprofit educational institution that provides graduate and undergraduate education, primarily on a distance learning basis, to people in the financial services field. The organization awards the professional Chartered Life Underwriter (CLU) designation, the Chartered Financial Consultant (ChFC) designation, and other professional designations. Visit the site at

  http://www.theamericancollege.edu

- The **American Council of Life Insurers (ACLI)** represents the life insurance industry on issues dealing with legislation and regulation. ACLI also publishes statistics on the life insurance industry in an annual fact book. Visit the site at

  http://www.acli.com

- The **American Institute for CPCU** is an independent, nonprofit organization that offers educational programs and professional certification to people in all segments of the property and casualty insurance business. The organization awards the professional CPCU designation and other designations. Visit the site at

  http://www.aicpcu.org

- The **American Insurance Association (AIA)** is an important trade association that represents property and casualty insurers. The site lists available publications, position papers on important issues in property and casualty insurance, press releases, insurance-related links, and names of state insurance commissioners. Visit the site at

http://www.aiadc.org

- The **Insurance Information Institute (III)** has an excellent site for obtaining information on the property and casualty insurance industry. It provides timely consumer information on auto, homeowners, and business insurance, and other types of property and casualty insurance. Visit the site at

http://www.iii.org

- The **Insurance Information Institute (III)** also publishes a fact book on the financial services industry. The publication has detailed information on the role of insurers in the financial services industry. Visit the site at

http://www.financialservicesfacts.org/financial

- The **Insurance Journal** is a definitive online source of timely information on the property/casualty industry. A free online newsletter is available that provides breaking news on important developments in property and casualty insurance. Visit the site at

http://www.insurancejournal.com

- **Insure.com** provides a considerable amount of timely information on the insurance industry. The stories reported are directed toward insurance consumers. Consumers can get premium quotes on life, health, auto, and homeowners insurance. Visit the site at

http://www.insure.com

- **InsWeb** offers insurance quotes from the nation's strongest insurers. You can obtain quotes for auto and homeowners insurance, term life insurance, individual health insurance, and other products as well. Visit the site at

http://www.insweb.com

- **LIMRA International, Inc.,** is the principal source of industry sales and marketing statistics in life insurance. Its site provides news and information about LIMRA and the financial services field, conducts research, and produces a wide range of publications. Visit the site at

http://www.limra.com

- **Lloyd's of London** provides a considerable amount of information about its history and chronology, global insurance operations, financial results, and key events on its Web site. The site also provides information to the news media. Visit the site at

http://www.lloyds.com

- The **National Association of Mutual Insurance Companies** is a trade association that represents mutual property and casualty insurance companies. Visit the site at

http://www.namic.org

- **Towers Perrin** is one of the world's largest actuarial and management consulting firms. The Tillinghast business of Towers Perrin provides a substantial amount of information on the insurance industry and advises other organizations on risk financing and self-insurance. Visit the site at

http://www.towersperrin.com

SELECTED REFERENCES

Black, Kenneth, Jr., and Harold D. Skipper, Jr. *Life Insurance,* 13th ed. Upper Saddle River, NJ: Prentice-Hall, 2000, chs. 23–24.

Carson, James M., Mark D. Forester, and Michael J. McNamara. "Changes in Ownership Structure: Theory and Evidence from Life Insurer Demutualizations," *Journal of Insurance Issues,* Vol. 21, No. 1 (1998), pp. 1–22.

Life Insurers Fact Book, 2005. Washington, DC: American Council of Life Insurers, 2005.

Myhr, Ann E., and James J. Markham. *Insurance Operations, Regulation, and Statutory Accounting,* 2nd ed. Malvern, PA: American Institute for Chartered Property Casualty Underwriters/Insurance Institute of America, 2004.

The Financial Services Fact Book 2007. New York: Insurance Information Institute, 2007.

The I.I.I. Insurance Fact Book 2007. New York: Insurance Information Institute, 2007.

Graves, Edward E., ed. *McGill's Life Insurance,* 6th ed. Bryn Mawr, PA: The American College, 2007.

Viswanathan, Krupa S., and J. David Cummins. "Ownership Structure Changes in the Insurance Industry: An Analysis of Demutualization," *Journal of Risk and Insurance,* Vol. 70, No. 3 (September 2003), pp. 401–437.

NOTES

1. Edward E. Graves, ed., *McGill's Life Insurance,* 5th ed. (Bryn Mawr, PA: The American College, 2004), pp. 600–601.
2. Ibid., pp. 602–604.
3. This section is based on *About Us,* Lloyd's of London at www.lloyds.com; and *Lloyd's of London,* Wikipedia, the free encyclopedia.
4. Wikipedia, the free encyclopedia.
5. Edward E. Graves, and Burke A. Christensen, *McGill's Legal Aspects of Life Insurance,* 4th ed. (Bryn Mawr, PA: The American College, 2004), pp. 124–127.
6. Ibid., p. 127.
7. Kenneth Black, Jr., and Harold D. Skipper, Jr., *Life and Health Insurance,* 13th ed. (Upper Saddle River, NJ: Prentice-Hall, 2000), pp. 603–613.
8. Ann E. Myhr, and James J. Markham, *Insurance Operations, Regulation, and Statutory Accounting,* 2nd ed. (Malvern, PA: American Institute for Chartered Property Casualty Underwriters/Insurance Institute of America, 2004), p. 3.13.

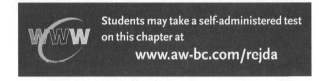

Students may take a self-administered test on this chapter at
www.aw-bc.com/rejda

CHAPTER 6

INSURANCE COMPANY OPERATIONS

"People who work for insurance companies do a lot more than sell insurance."

Insurance Information Institute

James, age 26, is a senior at a small liberal arts college in Connecticut. The college has a job placement office where recruiters interview students for possible employment. James has signed up for interviews with several insurance companies to learn about job opportunities in that industry. One recruiter explained that insurers hire new employees with a variety of educational backgrounds, and that a wide range of jobs exists in the industry today. James is surprised to learn of the wide range of employment opportunities in the insurance industry. Jobs exist in rate making, underwriting, sales, claims, finance, information technology, accounting, legal, and numerous other areas.

This chapter deals with these operational areas in the insurance industry. To make insurance available to the public, insurers must perform in a wide variety of specialized functions or operations. This chapter discusses the major functional operations of insurers.

INSURANCE COMPANY OPERATIONS

The most important insurance company operations consist of the following:

- Rate making
- Underwriting
- Production
- Claim settlement
- Reinsurance
- Investments

Insurers also engage in other operations, such as accounting, legal services, loss control, and data processing.

The sections that follow discuss each of these functional areas in some detail.

RATE MAKING

Rate making *refers to the pricing of insurance.* Insurance pricing differs considerably from the pricing of other products. When other products are sold, the company generally knows in advance what its costs of producing those products are, so that prices can be established to cover all costs and yield a profit. However, the insurance company does not know in advance what its actual costs are going to be. The total premiums charged for a given line of insurance may be inadequate for paying all claims and expenses during the policy period. It is only after the period of protection has expired that an insurer can determine its actual losses and expenses. Of course, the insurer hopes that the premium it charges plus investment income will be sufficient to pay all claims and expenses and yield a profit.

The person who determines rates and premiums is known as an **actuary.** An actuary is a highly skilled mathematician who is involved in all phases of insurance company operations, including planning, pricing, and research. In life insurance, the actuary studies important statistical data on births, deaths, marriages, disease, employment, retirement, and accidents. Based on this information, the actuary determines the premiums for life and health insurance policies. The objectives are to calculate premiums that will make the business profitable, enable the company to compete effectively with other insurers, and allow the company to pay claims and expenses as they occur. A life insurance actuary must also determine the legal reserves a company needs for future obligations.[1]

Professional certification as a life insurance actuary is attained by passing a series of examinations administered by the Society of Actuaries, which qualifies the actuary as a Fellow of the Society of Actuaries.

In property and casualty insurance, actuaries also determine the rates for different lines of insurance. Rates are based on the company's past loss experience and industry statistics. Statistics on hurricanes, tornadoes, fires, diseases, crime rates, traffic accidents, and the cost of living are also carefully analyzed. Many companies use their own loss data in establishing the rates. Other companies obtain loss data from advisory organizations, such as the Insurance Services Office (ISO). These organizations calculate historical or prospective loss costs that individual companies can use in calculating their own rates.

Actuaries in property and casualty insurance also determine the adequacy of loss reserves,[2] allocate expenses, and compile statistics for company management and for state regulatory officials.

To become a certified actuary in property and casualty insurance, actuarial science students must pass a series of examinations administered by the Casualty Actuarial Society. Successful completion of the examinations enables the actuary to become a Fellow of the Casualty Actuarial Society.

UNDERWRITING

Underwriting *refers to the process of selecting, classifying, and pricing applicants for insurance.* The underwriter is the person who decides to accept or reject an application. The fundamental objective of underwriting is to produce a profitable book of business. The underwriter constantly strives to select certain types of applicants and to reject others so as to obtain a profitable portfolio of business.

Statement of Underwriting Policy

Underwriting starts with a clear statement of underwriting policy. An insurer must establish an underwriting policy that is consistent with company objectives. The objective may be a large volume of business with a low profit margin or a smaller volume with a larger margin of profit. Classes of business that are acceptable, borderline, or prohibited must be clearly stated. The amounts of insurance that can be written on acceptable and borderline business must also be determined.

The insurer's underwriting policy is determined by top-level management in charge of underwriting.

The **line underwriters**—persons who make daily decisions concerning the acceptance or rejection of business—are expected to follow official company policy. The underwriting policy is stated in detail in an *underwriting guide* that specifies the lines of insurance to be written; territories to be developed; forms and rating plans to be used; acceptable, borderline, and prohibited business; amounts of insurance to be written; business that requires approval by a senior underwriter; and other underwriting details.

Basic Underwriting Principles

As noted earlier, the goal of underwriting is to produce a profitable volume of business. To achieve this goal, certain underwriting principles are followed. Three important principles are as follows:

- Selection of insureds according to the company's underwriting standards
- Proper balance within each rate classification
- Equity among policyowners

The first principle is that the underwriter must select prospective insureds according to the company's underwriting standards. This means that the underwriters should select only those insureds whose actual loss experience is not likely to exceed the loss experience assumed in the rating structure. For example, a property insurer may wish to insure only high-grade factories, and expects that its actual loss experience will be well below average. Underwriting standards are established with respect to eligible factories, and a rate is established based on a relatively low loss ratio.[3] Assume that the expected loss ratio is established at 70 percent, the ratio of losses plus loss adjustment expenses to earned premiums, and the rate is set accordingly. The underwriters ideally should insure only those factories that can meet stringent underwriting requirements, so that the actual loss ratio for the group will not exceed 70 percent.

The purpose of the underwriting standards is to reduce adverse selection against the insurer. There is an old saying in underwriting, "select or be selected against." *Adverse selection is the tendency of people with a higher-than-average chance of loss to seek insurance at standard (average) rates, which if not controlled by underwriting, will result in higher-than-expected loss levels.*

The second underwriting principle is to have a proper balance within each rate classification. This means that a below-average insured in an underwriting class should be offset by an above-average insured, so that on balance, the class or manual rate for the group as a whole will be adequate for paying all claims and expenses. For example, much of the underwriting today is **class underwriting,** especially for personal lines of insurance. Exposure units with similar loss-producing characteristics are grouped together and placed in the same underwriting class. Each exposure unit within the class is charged the same rate. However, all exposure units are not completely identical. Some will be above average for the class as a whole, while others will be below average. The underwriter must select a proper balance of insureds so that the class rate (average rate) will be adequate for paying all claims and expenses.

A final underwriting principle is equity among the policyowners. This means that equitable rates should be charged, and that each group of policyowners should pay its own way in terms of losses and expenses. Stated differently, one group of policyowners should not unduly subsidize another group. For example, a group of 20-year-old persons and a group of 80-year-old persons should not pay the same premium rate for individual life insurance. If identical rates were charged to both groups, younger persons would be subsidizing older persons, which would be inequitable. Once the younger persons became aware that they were being overcharged, they would seek other insurers whose classification systems are more equitable. The first insurer would then end up with a disproportionate number of older persons, and the underwriting results would be unprofitable. Thus, because of competition, there must be rate equity among the policyowners.

Steps in Underwriting

After the insurer's underwriting policy is established, it must be communicated to the sales force. Initial underwriting starts with the agent in the field.

Agent as First Underwriter This step is often called field underwriting. The agent is told what types of applicants are acceptable, borderline, or prohibited. For example, in auto insurance, an agent may be told

not to solicit applicants who have been convicted for drunk driving, who are single drivers under age 21, or who are young drivers who own high-powered sports cars. In property insurance, certain exposures, such as bowling alleys and restaurants, may have to be submitted to a company underwriter for approval.

In property and casualty insurance, the agent often has authority to bind the company immediately, subject to subsequent disapproval of the application and cancellation by a company underwriter. Thus, it is important that the agent follow company policy when soliciting applicants for insurance. To encourage submission of a book of profitable business, a *contingent or profit-sharing commission* may be paid based on the agent's premium volume and favorable loss experience.

In life insurance, the agent must also solicit applicants in accordance with the company's underwriting policy. The agent may be told not to solicit applicants who are active drug addicts or alcoholics, or work in hazardous occupations.

Sources of Underwriting Information The underwriter requires certain types of information in deciding whether to accept or reject an applicant for insurance. The type of information varies by type of insurance. In property insurance, both the physical features of the property and personal characteristics of the applicant must be considered. Physical features include the type of construction, occupancy of the building, quality of fire protection, and exposure from surrounding buildings.

With respect to personal characteristics of the applicant, information that reveals the presence of *moral hazard* is particularly important. The underwriter wants to screen out applicants who may intentionally cause a loss or inflate a claim. Thus, the applicant's present financial condition, past loss record, living habits, and moral character are especially important in the underwriting process.

Underwriting information can be obtained from a wide variety of sources. Important sources of information include the following:

- Application
- Agent's report
- Inspection report
- Physical inspection

- Physical examination and attending physician's report
- MIB report

The *application* is a basic source of underwriting information. It varies depending on the type of insurance. For example, in life insurance, the application will show the individual's age, gender, weight, occupation, personal and family health history, and any hazardous hobbies, such as skydiving.

An *agent's report* is another source of information. Most companies require the agent to give an evaluation of the prospective insured. For example, in life insurance, the agent may be asked to state how long he or she has known the applicant, to estimate the applicant's annual income and net worth, to judge whether the applicant plans to lapse or surrender existing life insurance, and to determine whether the application is the result of the agent's solicitation.

An *inspection report* may be required, especially if the underwriter suspects moral hazard. An outside firm investigates the applicant for insurance and makes a detailed report to the company. In life insurance, the report may include the applicant's present financial condition, drinking habits, marital status, amount of outstanding debts, delinquent bills, policy record, felony convictions, and additional information, such as whether the applicant has ever declared bankruptcy.

A *physical inspection* may also be required before an application for property and liability insurance is approved. The agent or company representative may physically inspect the property to be insured and then submit a report to the underwriter. For example, in workers compensation insurance, an inspection may reveal unsafe working conditions, such as dangerous machinery; violation of safety rules, such as not wearing goggles when a grinding machine is used; and an excessively dusty or toxic plant.

In life insurance, a *physical examination* will reveal whether the applicant is overweight, has high blood pressure, or has any abnormalities in the heart, respiratory system, urinary system, or other parts of the body. An *attending physician's report* may also be required, which is a report from a physician who has treated the applicant in the past.

A final source of underwriting information in life insurance is a **MIB (medical information bureau) report.** Companies that belong to this trade association report any health impairments, which are then recorded and made available to member companies. For example, if an applicant for life insurance has high blood pressure, this information would be recorded in the MIB files, which are coded and do not reveal the underwriting decision made by the submitting company.

Making an Underwriting Decision   After the underwriter evaluates the information, an underwriting decision must be made. There are three basic underwriting decisions with respect to an initial application for insurance:

- Accept the application
- Accept the application subject to certain restrictions or modifications
- Reject the application

First, the underwriter can accept the application and recommend that the policy be issued. A second option is to accept the application subject to certain restrictions or modifications. Several examples illustrate this second type of decision. Before a crime insurance policy is issued, the applicant may be required to place iron bars on windows or install an approved burglar alarm system; the applicant may be refused a homeowners policy and offered a more limited dwelling policy; a large deductible may be inserted in a property insurance policy; or a higher rate for life insurance may be charged if the applicant is substandard in health. If the applicant agrees to the modifications or restrictions, the policy is then issued.

The third decision is to reject the application. However, excessive and unjustified rejection of applications reduces the insurer's revenues and alienates the agents who solicited the business. If an application is rejected, the rejection should be based on a clear failure to meet the insurer's underwriting standards.

Many insurers now use computerized underwriting for certain personal lines of insurance that can be standardized, such as auto and homeowners insurance. As a result, underwriting decisions can be expedited.

Other Underwriting Considerations

Other factors are considered in underwriting. They include the following:

- *Rate adequacy and underwriting.* When rates are considered adequate for a class, insurers are more willing to underwrite new business. However, if rates are inadequate, prudent underwriting requires a more conservative approach to the acceptance of new business. If moral hazard is excessive, the business generally cannot be insured at any rate.

   In addition, in commercial property and casualty insurance, the underwriters have a considerable impact on the price of the product. A great deal of negotiation over price takes place between line underwriters and agents concerning the proper pricing of a commercial risk.

   Finally, the critical relationship between adequate rates and underwriting profits or losses results in periodic underwriting cycles in certain lines of insurance, such as commercial general liability and commercial multiperil insurance. If rates are adequate, underwriting profits are higher, and underwriting is more liberal. Conversely, when rates are inadequate, underwriting losses occur, and underwriting becomes more restrictive.
- *Reinsurance and underwriting.* Availability of reinsurance may result in more liberal underwriting. However, if reinsurance cannot be obtained on favorable terms, underwriting may be more restrictive.
- *Renewal underwriting.* In life insurance, policies are not cancelable. In property and casualty insurance, most policies can be canceled or not renewed. If the loss experience is unfavorable, the insurer may either cancel or not renew the policy. Most states have placed restrictions on the insurer's right to cancel.

PRODUCTION

The term **production** refers to the sales and marketing activities of insurers. Agents who sell insurance are frequently referred to as **producers**. This word is used because an insurance company can be legally chartered, personnel can be hired, and policy forms

printed, but no business is produced until a policy is sold. The key to the insurer's financial success is an effective sales force.

Agency Department

Life insurers have an agency or sales department. This department is responsible for recruiting and training new agents and for the supervision of general agents, branch office managers, and local agents.

Property and casualty insurers have marketing departments. To assist agents in the field, special agents may also be appointed. A *special agent* is a highly specialized technician who provides local agents in the field with technical help and assistance with their marketing problems. For example, a special agent may explain a new policy form or a special rating plan to agents in the field.

In addition to development of an effective sales force, an insurance company engages in a wide variety of marketing activities. These activities include the development of a marketing philosophy and the company's perception of its role in the marketplace; identification of short-run and long-run production goals; marketing research; development of new products to meet the changing needs of consumers and business firms; development of new marketing strategies; and advertising of the insurer's products.

Professionalism in Selling

The marketing of insurance has been characterized by a distinct trend toward professionalism in recent years. This means that the modern agent should be a competent professional who has a high degree of technical knowledge in a particular area of insurance and who also places the needs of his or her clients first. The professional agent identifies potential insureds, analyzes their insurance needs, and recommends a product to meet their needs. After the sale, the agent has the responsibility of providing follow-up service to clients to keep their insurance programs up-to-date. Finally, a professional agent abides by a code of ethics.

Several organizations have developed professional designation programs for agents and other personnel in the insurance industry. In life and health insurance, The American College has established the **Chartered Life Underwriter (CLU)** program. An individual must pass certain professional examinations to receive the CLU designation.

The American College also awards the **Chartered Financial Consultant (ChFC)** designation for professionals who are working in the financial services industry. To earn the ChFC designation, students must also pass professional examinations.

A similar professional program exists in property and casualty insurance. The American Institute for CPCU has established the **Chartered Property Casualty Underwriter (CPCU)** program. The CPCU program also requires an individual to pass professional examinations.

Other professionals are also important in the insurance industry. Many financial planners are also licensed as insurance agents. The **Certified Financial Planner (CFP)** designation is granted by the Certified Financial Planner Board of Standards, Inc. Many agents in property and liability insurance have been awarded the **Certified Insurance Counselor (CIC)** designation sponsored by the Society of Certified Insurance Counselors.

CLAIMS SETTLEMENT

Every insurance company has a claims division or department for adjusting claims. This section of the chapter examines the basic objectives in adjusting claims, the different types of claim adjustors, and the various steps in the claim-settlement process.

Basic Objectives in Claims Settlement

From the insurer's viewpoint, there are several basic objectives in settling claims.[4]

- Verification of a covered loss
- Fair and prompt payment of claims
- Personal assistance to the insured

The first objective in settling claims is to verify that a covered loss has occurred. This step involves determining whether a specific person or property is covered under the policy, and the extent of the coverage. This objective is discussed in greater detail later in the chapter.

The second objective is the fair and prompt payment of claims. If a valid claim is denied, the fundamental social and contractual purpose of protecting

the insured is defeated. Also, the insurer's reputation may be harmed, and the sales of new policies may be adversely affected. Fair payment means that the insurer should avoid excessive claim settlements and should resist the payment of fraudulent claims, because they will ultimately result in higher premiums. If the insurer follows a liberal claims policy, all policyowners will suffer because a rate increase will become necessary.

The states have passed laws that prohibit unfair claims practices. These laws are patterned after the National Association of Insurance Commissioners' Model Act. Some unfair claim practices prohibited by these laws include the following:[5]

- Refusing to pay claims without conducting a reasonable investigation.
- Not attempting in good faith to provide prompt, fair, and equitable settlements of claims in which liability has become reasonably clear.
- Compelling insureds or beneficiaries to institute lawsuits to recover amounts due under its policies by offering substantially less than the amounts ultimately recovered in suits brought by them.

A third objective is to provide personal assistance to the insured after a covered loss occurs. Aside from any contractual obligations, the insurer should also provide personal assistance after a loss occurs. For example, the claims adjustor could assist the agent in helping a family find temporary housing after a fire occurs.

Types of Claims Adjustors

The person who adjusts a claim is known as a **claims adjustor.** The major types of adjustors include the following:

- Agent
- Company adjustor
- Independent adjustor
- Adjustment bureau
- Public adjustor

An **insurance agent** often has authority to settle small first-party claims up to some maximum limit.[6] The insured submits the claim directly to the agent, who has the authority to pay up to some specified amount. This approach to claims settlement has several advantages: it is speedy, it reduces adjustment expenses, and it preserves the policy-owner's good will.

A **company adjustor** can settle a claim. The adjustor is usually a salaried employee who represents only one company. After notice of the loss is received, the company adjustor will investigate the claim, determine the amount of loss, and arrange for payment.

An **independent adjustor** can also be used to settle claims. An independent adjustor is a person who offers his or her services to insurance companies and is compensated by a fee. The company may use an independent adjustor in certain geographical areas where the volume of claims is too low to justify a branch office with full time adjustors. An independent adjustor may also be used in highly specialized areas where a company adjustor with the necessary technical skills and knowledge is not available.

An **adjustment bureau** can be used to settle claims. An adjustment bureau is an organization for adjusting claims that is supported by insurers that use its services. Claims personnel employed by an adjustment bureau are highly trained individuals who adjust claims on a full-time basis. An adjustment bureau is frequently used when a catastrophic loss, such as a hurricane, occurs in a given geographical area, and a large number of claims are submitted at the same time.

A **public adjustor** can be involved in settling a claim. *A public adjustor, however, represents the insured rather than the insurance company and is paid a fee based on the amount of the claim settlement.* A public adjustor may be employed by the insured if a complex loss situation occurs and technical assistance is needed, and also in those cases where the insured and insurer cannot resolve a dispute over a claim.

Steps in Settlement of a Claim

There are several important steps in settling a claim:

- Notice of loss must be given.
- The claim is investigated.
- A proof of loss may be required.
- A decision is made concerning payment.

Notice of Loss   The first step is to notify the insurer of a loss. A provision concerning notice of loss is usually stated in the policy. A typical provision requires the insured to give notice immediately or as soon as

possible after the loss has occurred. For example, the homeowners policy requires the insured to give immediate notice; a medical expense policy may require the insured to give notice within 30 days after the occurrence of a loss, or as soon afterward as is reasonably possible; and the personal auto policy requires that the insurer must be notified promptly of how, when, and where the accident or loss happened. The notice must also include the names and addresses of any injured persons and of witnesses.

Investigation of the Claim   After notice is received, the next step is to investigate the claim. An adjustor must determine that a covered loss has occurred and must also determine the amount of the loss. A series of questions must be answered before the claim is approved. The most important questions include the following:[7]

- Did the loss occur while the policy was in force?
- Does the policy cover the peril that caused the loss?
- Does the policy cover the property destroyed or damaged in the loss?
- Is the claimant entitled to recover?
- Did the loss occur at an insured location?
- Is the type of loss covered?
- Is the claim fraudulent?

The last question dealing with fraudulent claims is especially important. Insurance fraud is widespread, especially in auto and health insurance. Dishonest people frequently submit claims for bodily injuries that have never occurred.

Filing a Proof of Loss   An adjustor may require a proof of loss before the claim is paid. A proof of loss is a sworn statement by the insured that substantiates the loss. For example, under the homeowners policy, the insured may be required to file a proof of loss that indicates the time and cause of the loss, interest of the insured and others in the damaged property, other insurance that may cover the loss, and any change in title or occupancy of the property during the term of the policy.

Decision Concerning Payment   After the claim is investigated, the adjustor must make a decision concerning payment. There are three possible decisions. *The claim can be paid.* In most cases, the claim is paid promptly according to the terms of the policy. *The claim can be denied.* The adjustor may believe that the policy does not cover the loss or that the claim is fraudulent. Finally, the claim may be valid, but there may be a dispute between the insured and insurer over the amount to be paid. *In the case of a dispute, a policy provision may specify how the dispute is to be resolved.* For example, if a dispute concerning the value of lost or damaged property arises under the homeowners policy, both the insured and insurer select a competent appraiser. The two appraisers select an umpire. If the appraisers cannot agree on an umpire, a court will appoint one. An agreement by any two of the three is then binding on all parties.

When there is disagreement over the claim settlement, consumers may file a complaint with the state insurance department. Some states, however, do not provide complaint information on specific insurers. The National Association of Insurance Commissioners (NAIC) now has a Web site that permits consumers to check the complaint record of individual insurers (see Insight 6.1).

REINSURANCE

Reinsurance is another important insurance operation. This section discusses the meaning of reinsurance, the reasons for reinsurance, and the different types of reinsurance contracts.

Definitions

Reinsurance *is an arrangement by which the primary insurer that initially writes the insurance transfers to another insurer (called the reinsurer) part or all of the potential losses associated with such insurance.* The primary insurer that initially writes the business is called the **ceding company.** The insurer that accepts

---

INSIGHT 6.1

Stiffed by Your Insurer? Check Your Insurer's Complaint Record

Consumers often experience considerable frustration in their efforts to obtain accurate and timely information on complaints against specific insurers. Some state insurance departments provide detailed information on complaints and rank the insurers operating in the state based on a complaint index. However, not all states provide easily accessible complaint data to the public.

The National Association of Insurance Commissioners (NAIC) has a Web site that provides a wealth of information to consumers with respect to complaints against specific insurers. *Go to the NAIC Consumer Information Source at http://www.naic.org/cis/. Type in the company name, state, and business type. After locating the company, click on Closed Complaints.* Note that this Web site and address may change if the NAIC makes changes to its current site.

The information provided is based on closed consumer complaint reports. Four types of complaint data are available:
- *Complaint counts by state.* This source shows the total number of complaints in each state for a specific insurer. For example, one national insurer that advertises extensively on television received 2065 complaints from all persons in 2005.
- *Complaint counts by code.* This source shows the total number of complaints by type of coverage, reason the complaint was filed, and final decisions regarding the complaints.
- *Complaint ratio report.* This source is valuable because it compares a specific insurer with all insurers nationally using a single index number. This source compares the ratio of the insurer's market share of complaints to the insurer's market share of premiums for a specific policy type. For example, in 2005, the national median complaint ratio for private passenger auto insurance was 1.00. The above insurer received a score of 0.82, which was below the national median. The index score is also shown visually in a graph.
- *Complaint trend report.* This source shows whether complaints against the insurer are increasing or decreasing. The information presented shows the total number of complaints in the database for consecutive years with the percentage change in complaint counts between years. For example, the total number of complaints from all persons for the above insurer decreased from 2178 in 2004 to 2065 in 2005, or a decrease of 5 percent.

Information on complaints is especially valuable if you are shopping around for auto, homeowners, or health insurance and want to avoid insurers that have bad reputations for paying claims or for providing other services to policyowners.

part or all of the insurance from the ceding company is called the **reinsurer.** The amount of insurance retained by the ceding company for its own account is called the **retention limit** or **net retention.** The amount of the insurance ceded to the reinsurer is known as a **cession.** Finally, the reinsurer in turn may reinsure part or all of the risk with another insurer. This is known as a **retrocession.** In this case, the second reinsurer is called a **retrocessionaire.**

Reasons for Reinsurance

Reinsurance is used for several reasons. The most important reasons include the following:

- Increase underwriting capacity
- Stabilize profits
- Reduce the unearned premium reserve
- Provide protection against a catastrophic loss

Reinsurance also enables an insurer to retire from a territory or class of business and to obtain underwriting advice from the reinsurer.

Increase Underwriting Capacity Reinsurance can be used to increase the insurance company's underwriting capacity to write new business. The company may be asked to assume liability for losses in excess of its retention limit. Without reinsurance, the agent would have to place large amounts of insurance with several companies or not accept the risk. This is awkward and may create ill will on behalf of the policyowner. Reinsurance permits the primary company to issue a single policy in excess of its retention limit for the full amount of insurance.

Stabilize Profits Reinsurance is used to stabilize profits. An insurer may wish to avoid large fluctuations in annual financial results. Loss experience can fluctuate widely because of social and economic conditions, natural disasters, and chance. Reinsurance can be used to stabilize the effects of poor loss experience. For example, reinsurance may be used to cover a large exposure. If a large, unexpected loss occurs, the reinsurer would pay that portion of the loss in excess of some specified limit. Another arrangement would be to have the reinsurer reimburse the ceding insurer for losses that exceed a specified loss ratio during a given year. For example, an insurer may wish to stabilize its loss ratio at 70 per-

cent. The reinsurer then agrees to reimburse the ceding insurer for part or all the losses in excess of 70 percent up to some maximum limit.

Reduce the Unearned Premium Reserve Reinsurance can be used to reduce the unearned premium reserve. For some insurers, especially newer and smaller companies, the ability to write large amounts of new insurance may be restricted by the unearned premium reserve requirement. The **unearned premium reserve** *is a liability item on the insurer's balance sheet that represents the unearned portion of gross premiums on all outstanding policies at the time of valuation.* In effect, the unearned premium reserve reflects the fact that premiums are paid in advance, but the period of protection has not yet expired. As time goes on, part of the premium is considered earned, while the remainder is unearned. It is only after the period of protection has expired that the premium is fully earned.

As noted earlier, an insurer's ability to grow may be restricted by the unearned premium reserve requirement. This is because the entire gross premium must be placed in the unearned premium reserve when the policy is first written. The insurer also incurs relatively heavy first-year acquisition expenses in the form of commissions, state premium taxes, underwriting expenses, expenses in issuing the policy, and other expenses. In determining the size of the unearned premium reserve, there is no allowance for these first-year acquisition expenses, and the insurer must pay them out of its surplus. (Policyholders' surplus is the difference between assets and liabilities.[8])

For example, a one-year property insurance policy with an annual premium of $1200 may be written on January 1. The entire $1200 must be placed in the unearned premium reserve. At the end of each month, one-twelfth of the premium, or $100, is earned and the remainder is unearned. On December 31, the entire premium is fully earned. However, assume that first-year acquisition expenses are 30 percent of the gross premium, or $360. This amount will come out of the insurer's surplus up front. Thus, the more business it writes, the greater is the short-term drain on its surplus. A rapidly growing insurer's ability to write new business could eventually be impaired.

Reinsurance reduces the level of the unearned premium reserve required by law and temporarily increases the insurer's surplus position. As a result, the ratio of policyholders' surplus to net written premiums is improved, which permits the insurer to continue to grow.

Provide Protection Against a Catastrophic Loss Reinsurance also provides financial protection against a catastrophic loss. Insurers often experience catastrophic losses because of hurricanes and other natural disasters, industrial explosions, commercial airline disasters, and similar events. Reinsurance can provide considerable protection to the ceding company that experiences a catastrophic loss. The reinsurer pays part or all of the losses that exceed the ceding company's retention up to some specified maximum limit.

The tragic terrorist attacks on September 11, 2001, show clearly the importance of reinsurance to the insurance industry. Insured losses totaled about $36 billion (2005 dollars); however, reinsurers paid about two-thirds of the losses. Congress provided additional backup assistance by enacting the Terrorism Risk Insurance Act of 2002, which provides federal reinsurance to property and casualty insurers if future terrorist losses exceed certain levels (see Exhibit 6.1).

Another example of the importance of reinsurance is Hurricane Katrina. In 2005, Hurricane Katrina unleashed its fury on New Orleans, Louisiana, and surrounding states, which resulted in the largest single catastrophe in the history of the United States. Estimated insured property losses totaled $40.6 billion (2005 dollars); however, reinsurers are expected to pay about half of the losses, which will significantly reduce the losses incurred by primary insurers.

EXHIBIT **6.1**
Key Features of the Terrorism Risk Insurance Act of 2002

The Terrorism Risk Insurance Act (TRIA) was enacted in 2002. TRIA provides up to $100 billion in financial assistance to commercial property and casualty insurers for foreign terrorist losses that exceed certain thresholds. TRIA was scheduled to expire at the end of 2005. However, Congress enacted the Terrorism Risk Insurance Extension Act of 2005, which extended the program to the end of 2007. Key features of the revised law include the following:

- *Make terrorism insurance available.* Insurers must continue to make terrorism insurance available to clients until December 31,2007.

- *Program trigger.* A program trigger determines when federal funds are payable. For acts of terrorism occurring after March 31, 2006, the federal government is prohibited from making any payments unless aggregate insured losses for the industry exceed $50 million for the remainder of 2006 and $100 million in 2007.

- *Insurer deductible.* Insurer must meet a deductible. The deductible amount is based on a percentage of direct earned premiums for commercial property and casualty insurance premiums for the previous year. The insurer's deductible is 17.5 percent of direct earned premiums in 2006 and 20 percent in 2007.

- *Federal reinsurance quota share.* The federal government pays 90 percent of the amount of loss exceeding the deductible, and the insurer pays the remaining 10 percent. For 2007, the government pays only 85 percent of the amount exceeding the deductible, and the insurer pays the remaining 15 percent.

- *Industry retention and mandatory recoupment.* The industry must retain a certain amount of loss before federal assistance is available. This amount rises from $15 billion in 2005 to $25 billion in 2006 and $27.5 billion in 2007. The federal government recoups part of the loss payments by surcharges, which are paid by insurers and purchasers of commercial property and casualty insurance. The maximum surcharge that can be recouped from a policyholder is limited to 3 percent of the premium for the insurance policy covered by law.

- *Excluded coverages.* The new act excludes commercial auto insurance; burglary and theft insurance; surety insurance; professional liability insurance; and farm owners multi-peril insurance. Although the definition excludes professional liability insurance, it explicitly retains directors and officers liability insurance. Also excluded are federal crop insurance, federal flood insurance, private mortgage insurance, financial guaranty insurance, health and life insurance, medical malpractice insurance, and reinsurance or retrocessional reinsurance.

Other Reasons for Reinsurance   An insurer can also use reinsurance to retire from the business or from a given line of insurance or territory. Reinsurance permits the insurer's liabilities for existing insurance to be transferred to another carrier; thus, the policyowner's coverage remains undisturbed.

Finally, reinsurance allows an insurer to obtain the underwriting advice and assistance of the reinsurer. An insurer may wish to write a new line of insurance, but it may have little experience with respect to underwriting the line. The reinsurer can often provide valuable assistance with respect to rating, retention limits, policy coverages, and other underwriting details.

Types of Reinsurance

There are two principal forms of reinsurance: (1) facultative and (2) treaty.

Facultative Reinsurance   Facultative reinsurance *is an optional, case-by-case method that is used when the ceding company receives an application for insurance that exceeds its retention limit.* Before the policy is issued, the primary insurer shops around for reinsurance and contacts several reinsurers. The primary insurer is under no obligation to cede insurance, and the reinsurer is under no obligation to accept the insurance. But if a willing reinsurer can be found, the primary insurer and reinsurer can then enter into a valid contract.

Facultative reinsurance is frequently used when a large amount of insurance is desired. Before the application is accepted, the primary insurer determines whether reinsurance can be obtained. If it is available, the policy can then be written.

Facultative reinsurance has the advantage of flexibility, because a reinsurance contract can be arranged to fit any kind of case. It can increase the insurer's capacity to write large amounts of insurance. The reinsurance tends to stabilize the insurer's operations by shifting large losses to the reinsurer.

The major disadvantage of facultative reinsurance is uncertainty. The ceding insurer does not know in advance if a reinsurer will accept any part of the insurance. There is also a further disadvantage of delay, because the policy will not be issued until reinsurance is obtained. In times of bad loss experience, the reinsurance market tends to tighten, and the

avoidability and affordability of reinsurance may be a problem. Therefore, facultative reinsurance has the further disadvantage of being unreliable.

Treaty Reinsurance   Treaty reinsurance *means the primary insurer has agreed to cede insurance to the reinsurer, and the reinsurer has agreed to accept the business.* All business that falls within the scope of the agreement is automatically reinsured according to the terms of the treaty.

Treaty reinsurance has several advantages to the primary insurer. It is automatic, and no uncertainty or delay is involved. It is also economical, because it is not necessary to shop around for reinsurance before the policy is written.

Treaty reinsurance could be unprofitable to the reinsurer. The reinsurer generally has no knowledge about the individual applicant and must rely on the underwriting judgment of the primary insurer. The primary insurer may write bad business and then reinsure it. Also, the premium received by the reinsurer may be inadequate. Thus, if the primary insurer has a poor selection of risks or charges inadequate rates, the reinsurer could incur a loss. However, if the primary insurer consistently cedes unprofitable business to its reinsurers, the ceding insurer will find it difficult to operate because reinsurers will not want to do business with it.

There are several types of reinsurance treaties and arrangements, including the following:

- Quota-share treaty
- Surplus-share treaty
- Excess-of-loss treaty
- Reinsurance pool

Quote-Share Treaty   Under a **quota-share treaty,** the ceding insurer and reinsurer agree to share premiums and losses based on some proportion. *The ceding insurer's retention limit is stated as a percentage rather than as a dollar amount.* For example, Apex Fire Insurance and Geneva Re may enter into a quota-share treaty by which premiums and losses are shared 50 percent and 50 percent. Thus, if a $100,000 loss occurs, Apex Fire pays $100,000 to the insured but is reimbursed by Geneva Re for $50,000.

Premiums are also shared based on the same agreed-on percentages. However, the reinsurer pays a **ceding commission** to the primary insurer to help compensate for the expenses incurred in writing the business. Thus, in the previous example, Geneva Re would receive 50 percent of the premium less a ceding commission that is paid to Apex Fire.

The major advantage of quota-share reinsurance is that the primary insurer's unearned premium reserve is reduced. For smaller insurers and other insurers that wish to reduce the drain on surplus, a quota-share treaty can be especially effective. The principal disadvantage is that a large share of potentially profitable business is ceded to the reinsurer.

Surplus-Share Treaty   Under a **surplus-share treaty,** the reinsurer agrees to accept insurance in excess of the ceding insurer's retention limit, up to some maximum amount. *The retention limit is referred to as a line and is stated as a dollar amount.* If the amount of insurance on a given policy exceeds the retention limit, the excess insurance is ceded to the reinsurer up to some maximum limit. The primary insurer and reinsurer then share premiums and losses based on the fraction of total insurance retained by each party. Each party pays its respective share of any loss regardless of its size.

For example, assume that Apex Fire Insurance has a retention limit of $200,000 (called a line) for a single policy, and that four lines, or $800,000, are ceded to Geneva Re. Apex Fire now has a total underwriting capacity of $1 million on any single exposure. Assume that a $500,000 property insurance policy is issued. Apex Fire takes the first $200,000 of insurance, or two-fifths, and Geneva Re takes the remaining $300,000, or three-fifths. These fractions then determine the amount of loss paid by each party. If a $5000 loss occurs, Apex Fire pays $2000 (two-fifths), and Geneva Re pays the remaining $3000 (three-fifths). This arrangement can be summarized as follows:

Apex Fire	$ 200,000	(1 line)
Geneva Re	800,000	(4 lines)
Total underwriting capacity	$1,000,000	
$500,000 policy issued		
Apex Fire	$200,000	(2/5)
Geneva Re	$300,000	(3/5)
$5000 loss occurs		
Apex Fire	$2000	(2/5)
Geneva Re	$3000	(3/5)

Under a surplus-share treaty, premiums are also shared based on the fraction of total insurance retained by each party. However, the reinsurer pays a ceding commission to the primary insurer to help compensate for the acquisition expenses.

The principal advantage of a surplus-share treaty is that the primary insurer's underwriting capacity on any single exposure is increased. The major disadvantage is the increase in administrative expenses. The surplus-share treaty is more complex and requires greater record keeping.

Excess-of-Loss Treaty   An **excess-of-loss treaty** is designed largely for catastrophic protection. Losses in excess of the retention limit are paid by the reinsurer up to some maximum limit. The excess-of-loss treaty can be written to cover (1) a single exposure, (2) a single occurrence, such as a catastrophic loss from a tornado, or (3) excess losses when the primary insurer's cumulative losses exceed a certain amount during some stated time period, such as a year. For example, assume that Apex Fire Insurance wants protection for all windstorm losses in excess of $1 million. Assume that an excess-of-loss treaty is written with Franklin Re to cover single occurrences during a specified time period. Franklin Re agrees to pay all losses exceeding $1 million but only to a maximum of $10 million. If a $5 million hurricane loss occurs, Franklin Re would pay $4 million.

Reinsurance Pool   Reinsurance can also be provided by a reinsurance pool. A **reinsurance pool** *is an organization of insurers that underwrites insurance on a joint basis.* Reinsurance pools have been formed because a single insurer alone may not have the financial capacity to write large amounts of insurance, but the insurers as a group can combine their financial resources to obtain the necessary capacity. For example, the combined hull and liability loss exposures on a large commercial jet can exceed $500 million if the jet should crash. Such high limits are usually beyond the financial capability of a single insurer. However, a reinsurance pool for aviation insurance can provide the necessary capacity. Reinsurance pools also exist for nuclear energy exposures, oil refineries, marine insurance, insurance in foreign countries, and numerous other types of exposures.

The method for sharing losses and premiums varies depending on the type of reinsurance pool.

Pools work in two ways.[9] First, each pool member agrees to pay a certain percentage of every loss. For example, if one insurer has a policyowner that incurs a $500,000 loss, and there are 50 members in the pool, each insurer would pay 2 percent, or $10,000 of the loss, depending on the agreement.

A second arrangement is similar to the excess-of-loss reinsurance treaty. Each pool member is responsible for its own losses below a certain amount. Losses exceeding that amount are shared by all members in the pool.

ALTERNATIVES TO TRADITIONAL REINSURANCE

Some insurers and reinsurers are now using the capital markets as an alternative to traditional reinsurance. The financial capacity of the property and casualty industry to pay catastrophic losses from hurricanes, earthquakes, and other natural disasters is limited. Rather than rely solely on the limited financial capacity of the insurance industry to pay catastrophic claims, some insurers and reinsurers are using the capital markets to gain access to the capital of institutional investors. Having access to the capital markets substantially increases the funds available to pay catastrophe losses.

Securitization of Risk

There is an increasing use of the securitization of risk to obtain funds to pay for a catastrophe loss. **Securitization of risk** means *that an insurable risk is transferred to the capital markets through the creation of a financial instrument, such as a catastrophe bond, futures contract, options contract, or other financial instrument.* These instruments are also called risk-linked securities that transfer insurance-related risks to the capital markets. Insurers were among the first financial institutions to experiment with the securitization of risk.

Catastrophe Bonds

Catastrophe bonds are an excellent example of the securitization of risk. **Catastrophe bonds** *are corporate bonds that permit the issuer of the bond to skip or reduce scheduled interest payments if a catastrophic loss occurs.* The bonds are complex financial instruments issued by insurers and reinsurers and are designed to provide funds for catastrophe natural disaster losses. The bonds pay relatively high interest rates and help institutional investors to diversify their portfolios because natural disasters occur randomly and are not correlated with the stock market or other economic factors.

Catastrophe bonds are made available to institutional investors in the capital markets through an entity called a *special purpose reinsurance vehicle (SPRV),* which is specifically established for that purpose. The insurer purchases reinsurance from the SPRV and pays reinsurance premiums to the SPRV. The SPRV issues the catastrophe bonds, holds the premiums collected from insurers and the proceeds from the bond sales in a trust, and invests the funds in U.S. Treasuries or other high-quality assets. The bonds pay relatively high interest rates. *However, if a catastrophe loss occurs, the investors could forfeit the interest and even the principal, depending on how the bonds are structured.* The catastrophe bonds sold currently are indexed products where the loss of principal is based on formulas that consider the severity of a catastrophic loss and its location, such as earthquake losses in California, rather than on the actual losses experienced by the insurer.[10]

Catastrophe bonds are typically purchased by institutional investors seeking higher-yielding, fixed-income securities. The bonds generally are not available for direct purchase by individual retail investors. Insurers to date have transferred only a small portion of their catastrophe loss exposures to the capital markets. According to the Swiss Reinsurance Company, outstanding catastrophe bonds represent only about 0.5 percent of the worldwide catastrophe reinsurance coverage.[11]

According to the U.S. Government Accounting Office (GAO), there are several reasons that help explain the limited use of catastrophe bonds: (1) some insurers believe that the costs of issuing a catastrophe bond, which include high rates of return paid to investors and administrative costs, are significantly higher than the cost of traditional reinsurance; (2) certain statutory accounting standards that give credit on an insurer's balance sheet for traditional reinsurance purchases are currently not permitted for catastrophe bonds; and (3) some institutional investors perceive catastrophe bonds to be relatively illiquid.[12]

In conclusion, property and casualty insurers finance catastrophic losses in a number of ways. However, in recent years, catastrophic losses have reached astronomical levels that have threatened the financial solvency of some insurers. As a result, the insurance industry and public officials are currently considering several new proposals for the financing of mega-catastrophes (see Insight 6.2).

INVESTMENTS

The investment function is extremely important in the overall operations of insurance companies. Because premiums are paid in advance, they can be invested until needed to pay claims and expenses.

Life Insurance Investments

Assets held by life insurers have increased substantially over time. In 2004, U.S. life insurers held about $4.3 trillion in assets (see Exhibit 6.2). The funds available for investment are derived primarily from premium income, investment earnings, and maturing investments that must be reinvested.

A life insurer divides its assets into two accounts. The assets in the *general account* support the contractual obligations for guaranteed fixed dollar benefits, such as life insurance death benefits. The assets in the *separate account* support the liabilities for investment-risk products, such as variable annuities, variable life insurance, and private pension benefits.

State laws place restrictions on the types of assets in the general account. Because of the long-term nature of life insurance products, most investments

---

INSIGHT 6.2

New Proposals for Dealing with Mega-Catastrophes

Recent catastrophes have produced astronomically high losses. The terrorist attacks on September 11, 2001, caused about $36 billion (2005 dollars) in insured losses. In 2005, hurricane losses totalled $61.2 billion and were the highest on record. These huge losses have placed intense financial strain on property and casualty insurers. Several new proposals for the financing mega-catastrophes are summarized below.

- *Tax-deferred reserve.* The tax code would be amended to allow insurers to deduct contributions to a reserve before a catastrophe occurs. Funds would be accumulated on a tax-deferred basis and would be used to pay for a catastrophic loss. At present, contributions to a funded reserve prior to a loss are not income-tax deductible; losses, however, are tax deductible when paid.
- *National natural disaster pool.* A national natural disaster pool would be established to pay for mega-catastrophes. Part of the premium for commercial property and homeowners insurance would be ceded to a national pool and used to pay for natural disaster catastrophes. The funds would accumulate on a tax-free basis to speed accumulation. The pool would purchase reinsurance from the federal government; the federal government would also provide a line of credit.[a]

- *Regional natural disaster pools.* In this case, regional pools would be established in certain states. Part of the premium for commercial property and homeowners insurance would be ceded to the regional pool and used to finance mega-catastrophes in participating states. The funds would accumulate on a tax-free basis. The regional pool would purchase reinsurance from the federal government; the federal government would also provide a line of credit.[b]
- *Federal reinsurance pool.* Under this proposal, insurers would purchase federal reinsurance to pay for mega-catastrophe losses. Proponents argue that some natural disasters are privately uninsurable, and that the federal government already has considerable experience with the management and financing of major catastrophes through the federal flood insurance program. However, opponents argue that the private sector and free markets are more efficient in dealing with mega-catastrophes; private sector solutions will reduce the growth and influence of government in the insurance markets; and costs to taxpayers will increase under a federal program.

[a]Robert P. Hartwig, *Hurricane Season of 2005: Impacts on US P/C Insurance Markets in 2006 and Beyond,* Insurance Information Institute, December 7, 2005.
[b]Ibid.

EXHIBIT **6.2**
Growth of Life Insurers' Assets

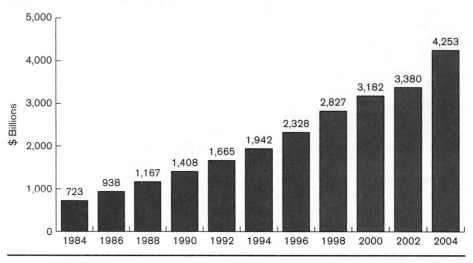

SOURCE: © ACLI, Reproduced with permission from ACLI. Further reproduction or distribution is prohibited without express consent from ACLI.

are in bonds, mortgages, and real estate; only a small percentage of the assets are invested in stocks. In contrast, state laws generally have fewer restrictions on the investment of assets in the separate account. As such, almost 80 percent of the assets in the sepa-

rate account were invested in stocks in 2004 (see Exhibit 6.3).

Life insurance investments have an important economic and social impact on the nation for several reasons. First, life insurance contracts are long-term,

EXHIBIT **6.3**
Asset Distribution of Life Insurers, 2004

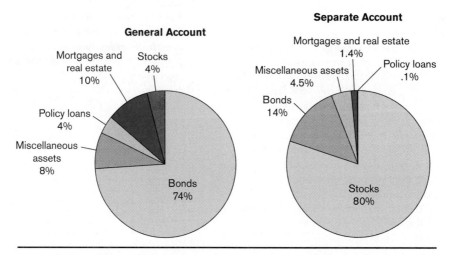

SOURCE: © ACLI, Reproduced with permission from ACLI. Further reproduction or distribution is prohibited without express consent from ACLI.

and the liabilities of life insurers extend over long periods of time, such as 50 or 60 years. Thus, safety of principal is a primary consideration. Consequently, as stated earlier, the majority of investments in the general account are in bonds.

Second, investment income is extremely important in reducing the cost of insurance to policyowners because the premiums can be invested and earn interest. The interest earned on investments is reflected in the payment of dividends to policyowners, which reduces the cost of life insurance.

Finally, life insurance premiums also are an important source of capital funds to the economy. These funds are invested in shopping centers, housing developments, office buildings, hospitals, new plants, and other economic and social ventures.

Property and Casualty Insurance Investments

In 2004, property and casualty insurance company investments totaled $1.06 trillion.[13] Most assets are invested in securities that can be quickly sold to pay claims if a major catastrophe occurs—primarily high-quality stocks and bonds rather than real estate (see Exhibit 6.4).

In addition, in 2004, net premiums written totaled $429 billion.[14] Premiums are typically paid in advance, so they can be invested until needed for claims and expenses.

Two important points must be stressed when the investments of property and casualty insurers are analyzed. *First, in contrast to life insurance, property*

EXHIBIT **6.4**
Investments, Property/Casualty Insurers, 2004

Investments by Type

Other 3.89%
Preferred stock 1.48%
Real estate 0.88%
Cash and short-term investments 8.54%
Common stock 18.47%
Bonds 66.74%

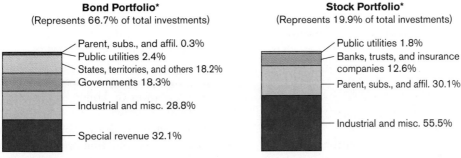

Bond Portfolio*
(Represents 66.7% of total investments)

- Parent, subs., and affil. 0.3%
- Public utilities 2.4%
- States, territories, and others 18.2%
- Governments 18.3%
- Industrial and misc. 28.8%
- Special revenue 32.1%

Stock Portfolio*
(Represents 19.9% of total investments)

- Public utilities 1.8%
- Banks, trusts, and insurance companies 12.6%
- Parent, subs., and affil. 30.1%
- Industrial and misc. 55.5%

*As of December 31, 2004.

NOTE: Data are from NAIC Annual Statement Database, via National Underwriter Insurance Data Services/Highline Data.

insurance contracts generally are short-term in nature. The policy period in most contracts is one year or less, and property claims are usually settled quickly. Also, in contrast to life insurance claims, which are generally fixed in amount, property insurance claim payments can vary widely depending on catastrophic losses, inflation, medical costs, construction costs, auto repair costs, economic conditions, and changing value judgments by society. For these reasons, the investment objective of liquidity is extremely important.

Second, investment income is extremely important in offsetting unfavorable underwriting experience. The investment of capital and surplus funds, along with the funds set aside for loss reserves and the unearned premium reserve, generate investment earnings that usually permit an insurer to continue its insurance operations despite an underwriting deficit.

OTHER INSURANCE COMPANY FUNCTIONS

Insurers also perform other functions. They include electronic data processing, accounting, legal, and loss-control services.

Electronic Data Processing

An important functional area is **electronic data processing (EDP).** Computers have revolutionized the insurance industry by speeding up the processing and storage of information and by eliminating many routine tasks. Computers are widely used in accounting, policy processing, premium notices, information retrieval, telecommunications, simulation studies, market analysis, training and education, sales, and policyowner services. Information can quickly be obtained on premium volume, claims, loss ratios, investments, and underwriting results.

Accounting

The **accounting department** is responsible for the financial accounting operations of an insurer. Accountants prepare financial statements, develop budgets, analyze the company's financial operations, and keep track of the millions of dollars that flow into and out of a typical company each year. Periodic reports are prepared dealing with premium income, operating expenses, claims, investment income, and dividends to policyowners. Accountants also prepare statutory annual statements that must be filed with state insurance departments. If the company is publicly traded, accountants must also prepare accounting statements based on Generally Accepted Accounting Principles (GAAP) for investors.

Legal Function

Another important function of insurance companies is the *legal function.* In life insurance, attorneys are widely used in advanced underwriting and estate planning. Attorneys also draft the legal language and policy provisions in insurance policies and review all new policies before they are marketed to the public. Other activities include providing legal assistance to actuarial personnel who testify at rate hearings; reviewing advertising and other published materials; providing general legal advice concerning taxation, marketing, investments, and insurance laws; and lobbying for legislation favorable to the insurance industry.

Attorneys must also keep abreast of the frequent changes in state and federal laws that affect the company and its policyowners. These include laws on consumerism, cost disclosure, affirmative action programs, truth in advertising, and similar legislation. Finally, attorneys must keep up with current court cases and legal precedents.

Loss-Control Services

Loss control is an important part of risk management, and a typical property and casualty insurer provides numerous loss-control services. These services include advice on alarm systems, automatic sprinkler systems, fire prevention, occupational safety and health, prevention of boiler explosions, and other loss-prevention activities. In addition, loss-control specialists can provide valuable advice on the construction of a new building or plant to make it safer and more resistive to damage, which can result in a substantial rate reduction. Loss-control specialists can also assist underwriters.

CASE APPLICATION

Reinsurance can be used by an insurer to solve several problems. Assume you are an insurance consultant who is asked to give recommendations concerning the type of reinsurance plan or arrangement to use. For each of the following situations, indicate the type of reinsurance plan or arrangement that the ceding insurer should use, and explain the reasons for your answer.

a. Company A is an established insurer and is primarily interested in having protection against a catastrophic loss arising out of a single occurrence.

b. Company B is a rapidly growing new company and desires a plan of reinsurance that will reduce the drain on its surplus from writing a large volume of new business.

c. Company C has received an application to write a $50 million life insurance policy on the life of the chief executive officer of a major corporation. Before the policy is issued, the underwriter wants to make certain that adequate reinsurance is available.

d. Company D would like to increase its underwriting capacity to underwrite new business.

SUMMARY

- Rate making refers to the pricing of insurance. Insurance rates are determined by actuaries.

- Underwriting refers to the process of selecting, classifying, and pricing applicants for insurance. There are several important underwriting principles:

    Selection of insureds according to the company's underwriting standards

    Proper balance within each rate classification

    Equity among policyowners

- In determining whether to accept or reject an applicant for insurance, underwriters have several sources of information. Important sources include the application, agent's report, inspection report, physical inspection, physical examination, attending physician's report, and the MIB report.

- Production refers to the sales and marketing activities of insurers. Agents who sell insurance are called producers.

- From the insurer's viewpoint, there are several basic objectives in settling claims:

    Verification of a covered loss

    Fair and prompt payment of claims

    Personal assistance to the insured

- The person who adjusts a claim is known as a claims adjustor. The major types of adjustors are as follows:

    Agent

    Company adjustor

    Independent adjustor

    Adjustment bureau

    Public adjustor

- Several steps are involved in settling a claim:

    Notice of loss must be given to the company.

    The claim is investigated by the company.

    A proof of loss may be required.

    A decision is made concerning payment.

- Reinsurance is used for several reasons:

    To increase the company's underwriting capacity

    To stabilize profits

    To reduce the unearned premium reserve

    To provide protection against a catastrophic loss

- With facultative reinsurance, the primary company shops around for reinsurance. The primary company is under no obligation to reinsure, and the reinsurer is under no obligation to accept the insurance. But if the primary company and reinsurer enter into a valid contract, it is known as facultative reinsurance. In contrast, under treaty reinsurance, if the business falls within the scope of the agreement, the primary company must cede insurance to the reinsurer, and the reinsurer must accept the ceded coverage.

- The most important types of automatic reinsurance treaties are as follows:

    Quota-share treaty

    Surplus-share treaty

    Excess-of-loss treaty

    Reinsurance pool

■ Other important insurance company operations include investments, accounting, legal services, loss-control services, and electronic data processing.

KEY CONCEPTS AND TERMS

Actuary
Adjustment bureau
Catastrophe bonds
Ceding commission
Ceding company
Certified Financial
  Planner (CFP)
Certified Insurance
  Counselor (CIC)
Cession
Chartered Financial
  Consultant (ChFC)
Chartered Life
  Underwriter (CLU)
Chartered Property
  Casualty Underwriter
  (CPCU)
Claims adjustor
Class underwriting
Company adjustor
Electronic data
  processing (EDP)
Excess-of-loss treaty
Facultative reinsurance
Independent adjustor

Line underwriter
Loss control
MIB report
Producers
Production
Public adjustor
Quota-share treaty
Rate making
Reinsurance
Reinsurance pool
Reinsurer
Retention limit (net
  retention)
Retrocession
Retrocessionaire
Securitization of risk
Surplus-share treaty
Treaty reinsurance
Underwriting
Unearned premium
  reserve

REVIEW QUESTIONS

1. How does rate making, or the pricing of insurance, differ from the pricing of other products?

2. a. Define the meaning of underwriting.
   b. Briefly explain the basic principles of underwriting.
   c. Identify the major sources of information available to underwriters.

3. Briefly describe the sales and marketing activities of insurers.

4. Explain the basic objectives in the settlement of claims.

5. Describe the steps involved in the settlement of a claim.

6. Briefly describe the following types of claims adjustors:
   a. Agent
   b. Company adjustor
   c. Independent adjustor
   d. Adjustment bureau
   e. Public adjustor

7. a. What is the meaning of reinsurance?
   b. Briefly explain the reasons for reinsurance.
   c. Explain the meaning of "securitization of risk."

8. Distinguish between facultative reinsurance and treaty reinsurance.

9. Briefly explain the following types of reinsurance treaties:
   a. Quota-share treaty
   b. Surplus-share treaty
   c. Excess-of-loss treaty
   d. Reinsurance pool

10. Briefly describe the following insurance company operations:
    a. Electronic data processing
    b. Accounting
    c. Legal services
    d. Loss control

APPLICATION QUESTIONS

1. Delta Insurance is a property insurer that enters into a surplus-share reinsurance treaty with Eversafe Re. Delta has a retention limit of $200,000 on any single building, and up to nine lines of insurance may be ceded to Eversafe. A building valued at $1,600,000 is insured with Delta. Shortly after the policy was issued, a severe windstorm caused a $800,000 loss to the building.
   a. How much of the loss will Delta pay?
   b. How much of the loss will Eversafe pay?
   c. What is the maximum amount of insurance that Delta can write on a single building? Explain your answer.

2. Liability Insurance Company writes a substantial amount of commercial liability insurance. A large construction company requests $100 million of liability insurance to cover its business operations. Liability Insurance has a reinsurance contract with Bermuda Re that enables the coverage to be written immediately. Under the terms of the contract, Liability Insurance pays 25 percent of the losses and retains 25 per-

cent of the premium. Bermuda Re pays 75 percent of the losses and receives 75 percent of the premium, less a ceding commission that is paid to Liability Insurance. Based on the preceding, answer the following questions.

a. What type of reinsurance contract best describes the reinsurance arrangement that Liability Insurance has with Bermuda Re?

b. If a $50 million covered loss occurs, how much will Bermuda Re have to pay? Explain your answer.

c. Why does Bermuda Re pay a ceding commission to Liability Insurance?

3. Property Insurance Company is a new property insurer. The company is growing rapidly because of a new homeowners policy that combines traditional homeowner coverages with insurance that pays off the mortgage if the insured dies or becomes totally disabled. Premiums written have increased substantially; new agents have been hired; and the company is considering expanding into additional states. However, its growth has been hampered by statutory accounting rules that require an insurer to write off immediately its first-year acquisition expenses but do not allow full recognition of premium income until the policy period has expired. In this case, explain how reinsurance will enable Property Insurance to continue to grow in an orderly fashion.

4. Richard lives in a sparsely populated county in northern Vermont. He owns and operates an adjustment bureau that adjusts property insurance claims in the area. Property insurers that market insurance in northern Vermont cannot afford to hire full-time claims adjustors for the area because it is not cost effective. A small property insurer contracts with Richard's company to adjust claims for homeowners who incur losses in the county where Richard lives. Richard's company is paid a fee for each claim that he adjusts and settles. What type of claims adjustor best describes Richard's company?

5. Felix is a property claims adjustor for a large property insurer. Janet is a policyowner who recently notified the company that the roof of her home incurred substantial hail damage because of a recent storm that caused severe property damage to homes in the area. Janet owns her home and is insured under a standard homeowners policy with no special endorsements. What questions should Felix ask before the claim is approved for payment by his company?

INTERNET RESOURCES

- The **American Institute for CPCU** is an independent, nonprofit organization that offers educational programs and professional certification to people in all segments of the property and casualty insurance business. The organization awards the professional CPCU designation and other designations. Visit the site at

  http://www.aicpcu.org

- The **American Council of Life Insurers (ACLI)** represents the life insurance industry on issues dealing with legislation and regulation. ACLI also publishes statistics on the life insurance industry in an annual fact book. Visit the site at

  http://www.acli.com

- **The American College** is an accredited, nonprofit educational institution that provides graduate and undergraduate education, primarily on a distance learning basis, to people in the financial services industry. The organization awards the professional Chartered Life Underwriter (CLU) designation, the Chartered Financial Consultant (ChFC) designation, and other professional designations. Visit the site at

  http://www.theamericancollege.edu

- The **American Insurance Association (AIA)** is an important trade association that represents property and casualty insurers. The site lists available publications, position papers on important issues in property and casualty insurance, press releases, insurance-related links, and names of state insurance commissioners. Visit the site at

  http://www.aiadc.org

- The **Insurance Information Institute (III)** has an excellent site for obtaining information on the property and liability insurance industry. It provides timely consumer information on auto, homeowners, and business insurance, and other types of property and liability insurance. Visit the site at

  http://www.iii.org

- The **Life Office Management Association (LOMA)** provides extensive information dealing with the management and operations of life insurers and financial services companies. Visit the site at

  http://www.loma.org

- **LIMRA International, Inc.,** is the principal source of industry sales and marketing statistics in life insurance. Its site provides news and information about LIMRA and the financial services field, conducts research, and publishes a wide range of publications. Visit the site at

  http://www.limra.com

- The **National Association of Insurance Commissioners (NAIC)** provides considerable information on complaints against specific insurers. Go to NAIC Consumer Information Source, type in the company name, state, and business type. After locating the company, click on Closed Complaints. Visit the site at

  http://www.naic.org/cis/

- The **National Association of Mutual Insurance Companies** is a trade association that represents mutual insurance companies in property and casualty insurance. Visit the site at

  http://www.namic.org

- **Towers Perrin** is one of the world's largest actuarial and management consulting firms. The Tillinghast division of Towers Perrin provides a substantial amount of information on the insurance industry and advises other organizations on risk financing and self-insurance. Visit the site at

  http://www.towersperrin.com

SELECTED REFERENCES

Black, Kenneth, Jr., and Harold D. Skipper, Jr. *Life Insurance,* 13th ed. Upper Saddle River, NJ: Prentice-Hall, 2000, chs. 25–26.

"Catastrophes: Insurance Issues," *Hot Topics & Issues Updates,* Insurance Information Institute, October 2006. This source is periodically updated.

Graves, Edward E., ed. *McGill's Life Insurance,* 6th ed. Bryn Mawr, PA: The American College, 2007.

Hartwig, Robert P. *Hurricane Season of 2005: Impacts on US P/C Insurance Markets 2006 and Beyond,* Insurance Information Institute, December 7, 2005.

Hubbard, R. Glenn, et al. "The Economic Effects of Federal Participation in Terrorism Risk," *Risk Management & Insurance Review,* Vol. 8, No. 2, September 2005, pp. 177–209.

Myhr, Ann E., and James J. Markham. *Insurance Operations, Regulation, and Statutory Accounting,* 2nd ed. Malvern, PA: American Institute for Chartered Property Casualty Underwriters/Insurance Institute of America, 2004.

Orsina, Miriam A., and Gene Stone. *Insurance Company Operations,* 2nd ed. Atlanta, GA: LOMA Education and Training, 2005.

"Reinsurance," *Hot Topics & Issues Updates,* Insurance Information Institute, July 2006. This source is periodically updated.

United States General Accounting Office. *Catastrophe Insurance Risk, The Role of Risk-Linked Securities and Factors Affecting Their Use,* GAO-02-941, September 2002.

United States General Accounting Office. *Catastrophe Insurance Risk, Status of Efforts to Securitize Natural Catastrophe and Terrorism Risk,* GAO-03-1033, September 2003.

Valverde, Jr., James L. *Managing Natural Disaster Risk. What Role Should the Federal Government Play?* Insurance Information Institute, January 2006.

Webb, Bernard L., et al. *Insurance Operations and Regulation,* 1st ed. Malvern, PA: American Institute for Chartered Property Casualty Underwriters/ Insurance Institute of America, 2002.

NOTES

1. A legal reserve is a liability item on a company's balance sheet that measures the insurer's obligations to its policyowners. State laws require a company to maintain policy reserves at a level that is sufficient to pay all policy obligations as they fall due.

2. In property and casualty insurance, a loss reserve is an estimated liability item that represents an amount for claims reported but not yet paid, claims in the process of settlement, and claims that have already occurred but have not been reported.

3. A loss ratio is the ratio of incurred losses and loss adjustment expenses to earned premiums. For example, if incurred losses and loss adjustment expenses are $70 and earned premiums are $100, the loss ratio is 0.70, or 70 percent.

4. For additional information on claims settlement, see Bernard L. Webb, et al. *Insurance Operations and*

Regulation, 1st ed. (American Institute for Chartered Property Casualty Underwriters/Insurance Institute of America, 2002), chs. 13–15.

5. Webb, et al., pp. 13.48–13.49.

6. A first-party claim is a claim submitted by the insured to the insurer, such as fire damage to property owned by the insured.

7. Robert I. Mehr, Emerson Cammack, and Terry Rose, *Principles of Insurance,* 8th ed. (Homewood, IL: Richard D. Irwin, 1985), pp. 616–617.

8. Technically, for a stock insurer, policyholders' surplus is the sum of capital stock (value of the contributions of original stockholders), plus surplus (the amount paid in by the organizers in excess of the par value of the stock), plus any retained earnings. In the case of a mutual insurer, there is no capital account. Policyholders' surplus is the excess of assets over liabilities.

9. *Sharing the Risk,* 3rd ed. (New York: Insurance Information Institute, 1989), pp. 119–120.

10. Insurance Information Institute, "Reinsurance," *Hot Topics & Issues Updates,* July 2006. This source is periodically updated.

11. Ibid.

12. U.S. General Accounting Office, *Catastrophe Insurance Risks, Status of Efforts to Securitize Natural Catastrophe and Terrorism Risk,* GAO-03-1033, September 2003.

13. *The I.I.I. Insurance Fact Book 2006* (New York: Insurance Information Institute, 2006), p. 24.

14. Ibid., p. 18.

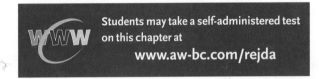

Students may take a self-administered test on this chapter at
www.aw-bc.com/rejda

CHAPTER 7

FINANCIAL OPERATIONS OF INSURERS*

"To manage an insurance enterprise successfully, you must understand the volatility inherent in each portfolio of risks and investments. Further, you must understand the impact that unexpected volatility has on the balance sheet, income statement, and cash flows."

Mike Keyes, President and CEO,
Oregon Mutual Insurance Company

LEARNING OBJECTIVES

After studying this chapter, you should be able to

◆ Understand the three major sections of the balance sheet for a property and casualty insurance company: assets, liabilities, and policyholders' surplus.

◆ Identify the sources of revenues and types of expenses incurred by a property and casualty insurance company.

◆ Explain how profitability is measured in the property and casualty insurance industry.

◆ Understand the balance sheet and income and expense statement of a life insurance company, and explain how profitability is measured in the life insurance industry.

◆ Explain the objectives of rate making in the property and casualty insurance industry and discuss the basic rate-making methods, including judgment rating, class rating, and merit rating.

---

*Prepared by Michael J. McNamara, Washington State University.

*N*ancy worked in the accounting department of a small manufacturing company. When the company downsized, Nancy lost her job. The home office of a property and casualty insurance company, ABC Insurance Company, is located in the city where Nancy lives. She applied for a job as a commercial insurance underwriting trainee and was hired by the company. She just completed her first year in the underwriting department.

Kyle is president of ABC Insurance Company. Recently he called a meeting for all home office employees to review the company's financial performance. Kyle stated, "For each dollar the company collected in premiums this past year, we paid 72 cents in claims and had 31 cents in expenses." "However," he added, "we were still profitable, and even though we had to increase our loss reserves, we were still able to increase surplus again this year."

Nancy was curious how the company made money given that they paid more in claims and expenses than they collected in premiums. She was also curious about the meaning of "loss reserves" and "surplus." She asked to see the company's financial statements and was surprised by what she saw. The statements were very different from the accounting statements she helped to prepare when she worked for the manufacturing company.

This chapter discusses the financial operations of insurers. Specific topics discussed are insurance company balance sheets, income statements, profitability measures, and rate-making methods.

In Chapter 2, the two sides of the private insurance industry, property and casualty insurance and life and health insurance, were discussed. The discussion of the financial operations of insurers is organized in the same way. First, we consider the financial statements for property and casualty insurance companies and for life insurance companies. Then, we discuss rate making in property and casualty insurance and in life insurance.

PROPERTY AND CASUALTY INSURERS

To understand the financial operations of an insurance company, it is necessary to examine the insurer's financial statements. Two important financial statements are the balance sheet and the income and expense statement.[1]

Balance Sheet

A **balance sheet** *is a summary of what a company owns (assets), what it owes (liabilities), and the difference between total assets and total liabilities (owners' equity).* A balance sheet shows these values at a specific point in time. This financial statement is called a balance sheet because the two sides of the financial statement must be equal:

Total assets = Total liabilities + Owners' equity

Exhibit 7.1 shows the balance sheet for the ABC Insurance Company at the end of 2006. Note

EXHIBIT **7.1**
ABC Insurance Company

ABC Insurance Company Balance Sheet December 31, 2006			
Assets:		Liabilities:	
Bonds	$250,000,000	Loss Reserves	$120,000,000
Common Stock	80,000,000	Unearned Premiums	101,000,000
Real Estate	20,000,000	Loss Adjustment Expenses	14,000,000
Cash & Short-term Investments	12,000,000	Commissions Payable	9,000,000
Mortgage-backed Securities	30,000,000	Other Liabilities	11,000,000
Total Invested Assets	$392,000,000	Total Liabilities	255,000,000
Premiums Receivable	29,600,000	Surplus and Capital	
Data Processing Equipment	400,000	Paid-in Surplus	16,000,000
Other Assets	18,000,000	Unassigned Surplus	169,000,000
Total Admitted Assets	$440,000,000	Total Liabilities and Surplus	$440,000,000

how the company's total assets equal the company's total liabilities plus owners' equity (policyholders' surplus).

Assets   The primary assets for an insurance company are its financial assets. An insurance company invests premium dollars and retained earnings in financial assets. Investments also provide an important source of income for an insurer. As with most insurance companies, ABC's primary investment holding is bonds. Other investments are in common and preferred stock, real estate, mortgage-backed securities, marketable securities, and cash/cash equivalents. The company's assets total $440 million.

Liabilities   While the assets of an insurance company are relatively straightforward, the liabilities are more complex. An insurer is required by law to maintain certain reserves on its balance sheet. Because premiums are paid in advance, but the period of protection extends into the future, an insurer must establish certain reserves to assure that premiums collected in advance will be available to pay future losses. A property and casualty insurer is required to maintain two principal types of financial reserves:

1. *Loss Reserves* The loss reserve is a large liability item on a property and casualty insurance company's

balance sheet. A loss reserve is the estimated cost of settling claims that have already occurred but that have not been paid as of the valuation date. More specifically, the **loss reserve** *is an estimated amount for (1) claims reported and adjusted but not yet paid, (2) claims reported and filed, but not yet adjusted, and (3) claims incurred but not yet reported to the company.* The loss reserve is especially important to a casualty insurer because bodily injury and property damage liability claims may take a long time to settle, especially if litigation is involved. In contrast, property insurance claims, such as auto collision and other physical damage claims and homeowners insurance claims, are settled more quickly; hence loss reserves are relatively small for property insurers. ABC's loss reserves are $120 million.

Loss reserves in property and casualty insurance can be classified as case reserves, reserves based on the loss ratio method, and reserves for incurred-but-not-reported claims.

Case reserves *are loss reserves that are established for each individual claim when it is reported.* Major methods of determining case reserves include the following: the judgment method, the average value method, and the tabular method.[2]

■ Under the *judgment method,* a claim reserve is established for each individual claim. The amount of the loss reserve can be based on the judgment of someone in the claims department or estimated using a computer program. Many insurers use computer programs that apply certain rules to calculate the size of the loss reserve. The details of an individual claim are entered, and a computer algorithm estimates the size of the required loss reserve.

- When the *average value method* is used, an average value is assigned to each claim. This method is used when the number of claims is large, and the average claim amount is relatively small. Loss reserves for auto physical damage claims are often based on this method.

- Under the *tabular value method,* loss reserves are determined for certain claims for which the amounts paid depend on life expectancy, duration of disability, remarriage of the beneficiary, and similar factors. This method is often used to establish loss reserves involving permanent disability, partial permanent disability, survivor benefits, and similar claims. The loss reserve is called a tabular reserve because the duration of the benefit period is based on data derived from mortality, morbidity, and remarriage tables.

The case reserves just discussed establish loss reserves for individual claims. In contrast, the **loss ratio method** *establishes aggregate loss reserves for a specific coverage line. Under the loss ratio method, a formula based on the expected loss ratio is used to estimate the loss reserve.* The expected loss ratio is multiplied by premiums earned during a specified time period. Loss and loss-adjustment expenses paid to date are then subtracted from the ultimate loss figure to determine the current loss reserve. The loss ratio method is required for certain lines of insurance, such as workers compensation, where the expected loss ratio ranges from 65 percent to 75 percent of earned premiums.

Many losses occur near the end of the accounting period but are not reported until the next period. The **incurred-but-not-reported (IBNR) reserve** *is a reserve that must be established for claims that have already occurred but have not yet been reported to the insurer.* For example, some accidents may occur on the final day of the accounting period. A loss

reserve is needed for these losses that will not be reported until the next accounting period.

2. *Unearned Premium Reserve* The **unearned premium reserve** *is a liability item that represents the unearned portion of gross premiums on all outstanding policies at the time of valuation.* An insurer is required by law to place the entire gross premium in the unearned premium reserve when the policy is first written, and to place renewal premiums in the same reserve. ABC Insurance Company's unearned premium reserve is $101 million.

The fundamental purpose of the unearned premium reserve is to pay for losses that occur during the policy period. Premiums are paid in advance, but the period of protection extends into the future. To assure policyowners that future losses will be paid, the unearned premium reserve is required.

The unearned premium reserve is also needed so that premium refunds can be paid to policyholders in the event of coverage cancellation. If the insurer cancels the policy, a full pro rata premium refund based on the unexpired portion of the policy term must be paid to the policyholder. Thus, the unearned premium reserve must be adequate so premium refunds can be made in the event of cancellation.

Finally, if the business is reinsured, the unearned premium reserve serves as the basis for determining the amount that must be paid to the reinsurer for carrying the reinsured policies until the end of their terms. In practice, however, the amount paid to the reinsurer may be considerably less than the unearned premium reserve as the reinsurer does not incur heavy first-year acquisition expenses in acquiring the reinsured policies.

Several methods can be used to calculate the unearned premium reserve. Only one method is described here. Under the **annual pro rata method,** it is assumed that the policies are written uniformly throughout the year. For purposes of determining the unearned premium reserve, it is assumed that all policies are written on July 1, which is the average issue date. Therefore, on December 31, the unearned premium reserve for all one-year policies is one-half of the premiums attributable to these policies. For two-year policies, the unearned premium reserve is three-fourths of the premium income, and for three-year policies, it is five-sixths of the premium income.

Several other liabilities merit mention. There are costs associated with paying reserved claims. ABC Insurance Company estimates that the **loss-adjustment expenses** to settle the reserved claims are $14 million. Other important liability items include commissions owed to agents selling ABC products and taxes owed to the government.

Policyholders' Surplus   Policyholders' surplus *is the difference between an insurance company's assets and liabilities.* It is not calculated directly—it is the "balancing" item on the balance sheet. If the insurer were to pay all of its liabilities from its assets, the amount remaining would be policyholders' surplus. ABC Insurance Company's paid-in capital and surplus total $185 million. This value is 42 percent of the company's total assets.

Surplus can be thought of as a cushion that can be drawn upon if liabilities are higher than expected. Recall that loss reserves are an estimate of future losses, but that actual losses could easily exceed that estimate. Obviously, the stronger an insurance company's surplus position, the greater is the security for its policyowners. Surplus represents the paid-in capital of investors plus retained income from insurance operations and investments over time. The level of surplus is also an important determinant of the amount of new business that an insurance company can write.[3]

Income and Expense Statement

The **income and expense statement** *summarizes revenues received and expenses paid over a specified period of time.* Exhibit 7.2 shows the income and expense statement for ABC Insurance Company for 2006.

Revenues   Revenues are cash inflows that the company can claim as income. *The two principal sources*

EXHIBIT 7.2
ABC Insurance Company

ABC Insurance Company Income and Expense Statement January 1, 2006–December 31, 2006		
Revenues:		
Premiums Written*	$206,000,000	
Premiums Earned		$205,000,000	
Investment Income:		
Interest	14,000,000	
Dividends	2,400,000	
Rental Income	600,000	
Gain on Sale of Securities	1,000,000	
Total Investment Income		18,000,000	
Total Revenues			$223,000,000
Expenses:		
Net Losses Incurred	133,600,000	
Loss Adjustment Expenses	14,000,000	
Total Losses and Loss Adj. Expenses		147,600,000	
Commissions	18,000,000	
Premium Taxes	5,050,000	
General Insurance Expenses	41,590,000	
Total Underwriting Expenses		64,640,000	
Total Expenses			212,240,000
Net Income Before Taxes			10,760,000
Federal Income Tax			3,260,000
Net Income			7,500,000

*Premiums written reflect coverage put in force during the accounting period.

of revenues for an insurance company are premiums and investment income. As noted in the discussion of the unearned premium reserve, premiums are not considered earned until the period of time for which the premiums were paid has passed. The premiums written that appear on the income and expense statement reflect the premiums for coverage that was placed on the books during the year. **Earned premiums** *represent the portion of the premiums for which insurance protection has been provided.* Insurance premiums are paid in advance for a specified period of protection. With the passage of time, an insurer "earns" the premium and can claim it as income under insurance accounting rules.

The second major source of income is investment income. Given the size of ABC's bond portfolio, it is not surprising that interest income is the major source of investment income. The company also received dividend income on the stocks owned and rental income on real estate the company owned. The company also sold some securities for more than the original purchase price, and realized a capital gain. The company's total revenues for 2006 were $223 million.

Expenses Partially offsetting the company's revenues were the company's expenses, which are cash outflows from the business. The major expenses for ABC Insurance Company were the cost of adjusting claims and paying the insured losses that occurred. The company paid $133.6 million in losses and $14 million in loss-adjustment expenses during 2006, for a total of $147.6 million.

Underwriting expenses are the other major category of expenses. These expenses consist of commissions that ABC paid agents for selling the company's products, premium taxes, and general insurance expenses. These items total $64.64 million in 2006. ABC Insurance Company's total expenses in 2006 were $212.24 million.

The company's taxable income (total revenues minus total expenses) was $10.76 million. The company paid $3.26 million in federal income taxes. The company's net income after taxes was $7.5 million. This money can be returned to stockholders through dividends or be used to increase the investment portfolio. If added to the investment portfolio, the company's total assets will increase relative to its total liabilities, and policyholders' surplus will rise.

Measuring Profit or Loss

One way of measuring the performance of an insurance company is to consider how the company did in its core business, underwriting risks.[4] A simple measure that can be used is the insurance company's loss ratio. The **loss ratio** *is the ratio of incurred losses and loss adjustment expenses to premiums earned.* The formula and the loss ratio for ABC Insurance Company are provided below:

$$\text{Loss ratio} = \frac{\text{Incurred losses} + \text{Loss adjustment expenses}}{\text{Premiums earned}}$$

$$= \frac{147,600,000}{205,000,000}$$

$$= .720$$

The loss ratio for individual coverage lines can be determined, as well as the overall loss ratio for the company. The loss ratio is often in the 65 percent to 75 percent range, but an insurer does not know at the beginning of the coverage period what the ultimate loss ratio will be.

A second important performance measure is the expense ratio. The **expense ratio** *is equal to the company's underwriting expenses divided by written premiums.* The ratio for ABC Insurance Company is

$$\text{Expense ratio} = \frac{\text{Underwriting expenses}}{\text{Premiums written}}$$

$$= \frac{64,640,000}{206,000,000}$$

$$= .314$$

As with the loss ratio, the expense ratio can be determined for individual coverage lines and in aggregate. Underwriting expenses include acquisition costs (commissions), general expenses, and underwriting costs. Some coverages, such as personal lines, are less costly to underwrite. Underwriting costs for large commercial accounts may be much higher. Obviously, a low expense ratio is preferred by insurers. Expense ratios are usually in the 25 percent to 40 percent range.

For an overall measure of underwriting performance, the combined ratio can be calculated. *The*

combined ratio *is the sum of the loss ratio and expense ratio.*[5] The combined ratio for ABC Insurance Company is 1.034:

Combined ratio = Loss ratio + Expense ratio

Combined ratio = .720 + .314 = 1.034

The combined ratio is one of the most common measures of underwriting profitability. *If the combined ratio exceeds 1 (or 100 percent), it indicates an underwriting loss. If the combined ratio is less than 1 (or 100 percent), it indicates an underwriting profit.* In the case of ABC Insurance Company, for every $100 in premiums the company collected, the company paid out $103.40 in claims and expenses.

At this point, it is important to recall the asset holdings of insurance companies. The investments an insurer makes in bonds, stocks, real estate, and other investments generate investment income. *A property and casualty insurance company can lose money on its underwriting operations, but still report positive net income if the investment income offsets the underwriting loss.* The **investment income ratio** *compares net investment income to earned premiums.* The formula and the ratio for the ABC Insurance Company are provided below:

$$\frac{\text{Investment}}{\text{income ratio}} = \frac{\text{Net investment income}}{\text{Earned premiums}}$$

$$= \frac{18,000,000}{205,000,000}$$

$$= .088$$

To determine the company's total performance (underwriting and investments), the overall operating ratio can be calculated. The **overall operating ratio** *is equal to the combined ratio minus the investment income ratio.* This ratio and the result for ABC are presented below:

$$\frac{\text{Overall}}{\text{operating ratio}} = \frac{\text{Combined}}{\text{ratio}} - \frac{\text{Investment}}{\text{income ratio}}$$

$$= 1.034 - .088$$

$$= .946 \text{ or } 94.6\%$$

At first glance, it may seem incorrect to subtract the investment income ratio. However, recall that a combined ratio in excess of 100 percent indicates an underwriting loss and that investment income will reduce or totally offset an underwriting loss. ABC Insurance Company's combined ratio was 103.4. The company's investment income ratio was 8.8 percent, producing an overall operating ratio of 94.6. An overall operating ratio of less than 100 indicates that the company, overall, was profitable. If the overall operating ratio exceeds 100, it means that investment income was not enough to offset the underwriting loss.

Recent Underwriting Results

As noted in Chapter 4, the combined ratio in the property and casualty insurance industry has only been less than 100 in three years between 1980 and 2004. Increased premium rates produced favorable underwriting results in 2003 and 2004.

Based on the conservative statutory formula method for determining underwriting profits, the property and casualty industry is not highly profitable. Even using Generally Accepted Accounting Principles (GAAP), the property and casualty insurance industry lagged other benchmarks. Insight 7.1 shows that from 1996 to 2005, a combined Fortune 500 index, a diversified financial index, and the commercial banks provided better returns in each year. The other two benchmarks provided, the life insurance industry and the utilities industry, outperformed property and casualty insurance companies in almost every year.

The estimated combined ratio for the property and casualty insurance industry for 2005 was 100.9, and the projected combined ratio for 2006 is 98.0.[6] The adverse results for 2005 were caused, in large part, by Hurricanes Katrina, Rita, Dennis, and Wilma.

LIFE INSURANCE COMPANIES

Balance Sheet

The balance sheet for a life insurance company is similar to the balance sheet of a property and casualty insurance company. The discussion that follows focuses on the major differences.

INSIGHT 7.1

Profitability of Insurance Industry and Other Selected Industries

Annual Rate of Return: Net Income After Taxes as a Percent of Equity, 1996 to 2005

| Year | Property/Casualty Insurance | | Life/ Health Insurance[d] | Selected Other Industries[a] | | | Fortune 500 Combined Industrials & Service[f] |
	Statutory Accounting[b]	GAAP Accounting[c]		Diversified Financial[e]	Commercial Banks	Electric and Gas Utilities	
1996	9.6%	9.3%	10.0%	18.5%	16.5%	11.5%	14.1%
1997	11.8	11.6	12.0	14.9	16.9	10.4	13.9
1998	9.2	8.5	11.0	19.8	16.0	10.2	13.4
1999	6.9	6.0	13.0	21.0	18.0	11.9	15.2
2000	6.8	5.9	10.0	21.3	16.7	11.8	14.6
2001	−1.8	−1.2	7.0	19.3	14.0	10.5	10.4
2002	3.3	2.2	1.0	19.5	17.3	7.9	10.2
2003	8.5	8.9	9.0	19.5	14.9	10.5	12.6
2004	9.3	9.4	11.0	15.0	15.5	10.5	13.9
2005	10.4	9.4	13.0	15.0	16.0	10.0	14.9

[a]Return on equity on a GAAP accounting basis, *Fortune*.
[b]Net income after taxes, divided by year-end policyholders' surplus. Calculated by the Insurance Information Institute from Highline Data. Statutory accounting is used by insurers when preparing the Annual Statements they submit to regulators.
[c]Return on average net worth, ISO.
[d]Return on equity on a GAAP accounting basis, *Fortune*. Combined stock and mutual companies as calculated by the Insurance Information Institute.
[e]Companies whose major source of revenue comes from providing diversified financial services. These companies are not specifically chartered as insurance companies, banks or savings institutions, or brokerage or securities companies, but they may earn revenue from these sources.
[f] *Fortune* 500 Combined Industrial and Service Businesses median return on equity.

SOURCE: Insurance Information Institute from the National Association of Insurance Commissioners (NAIC) Annual Statement Database, via HighlineData, LLC. Copyrighted Information. No portion of this work may be copied or redistributed without the express written permission of Highline Data, LLC.

Assets Like the property and casualty insurance companies discussed earlier, the assets of a life insurance company are primarily financial assets. However, there are three major differences between the assets of a property and casualty insurance company and the assets of a life insurance company. The first major difference is the average duration of the investments. The matching principle states that an organization should match the maturities of its sources and uses of funds. Most property and casualty insurance contracts are relatively short-term, often for one year or six months. Permanent life insurance contracts, however, may be in force for many years. As the matching principle suggests, life insurance company investments, on average, should be of longer duration than property and casualty insurance company investments. Note that life insurance companies invest more heavily in bonds, mortgages, and real estate than do property and casualty insurance companies. Property and casualty insurance companies place greater emphasis on liquidity, holding larger relative positions in cash and marketable securities.

The second major difference is created by the savings element in cash-value life insurance. Permanent life insurance policies develop a savings element over time called the cash value, which may be borrowed by the policyowner. When life insurance premiums are calculated, it is assumed that the life insurer will have the funds available to earn investment income. If a policyowner borrows the cash value, the life insurer must forgo the investment income that could have been earned on this money. Life insurance companies charge interest on life insurance policy loans, and this interest-bearing asset is called "contract loans" or "policy loans" on a life insurer's balance sheet. It can be thought of as an account receivable from the policyowner.

The third major difference in assets between a property and casualty insurer and a life insurance company is that a life insurance company may have separate account assets. To protect policyowners, state laws place limitations on a life insurance company's general investments. Separate account investments are not subject to these restrictions. Life insurers use separate accounts for assets backing interest-sensitive products, such as variable annuities, variable life insurance, and universal-variable life insurance.

Liabilities Policy reserves are the major liability item of life insurers. Under the level-premium method of funding cash-value life insurance, premiums paid during early years are higher than necessary to pay death claims, while those paid in later years are insufficient to pay death claims. The excess premiums collected in early years of the contract must be accounted for and held for future payment as a death claim to the policyowner's beneficiary. The excess premiums paid during the early years result in the creation of a policy reserve. *Policy reserves are a liability item on the balance sheet that must be offset by assets equal to that amount.* Policy reserves are considered a liability item because they represent an obligation of the insurer to pay future policy benefits. The policy reserves held by an insurer plus future premiums and future interest earnings will enable the insurer to pay all future policy benefits if the company's experience conforms to the actuarial assumptions used in calculating the reserve. Policy reserves are often called *legal reserves* because state insurance laws specify the minimum basis for calculating them. Reserves in life insurance are discussed in greater detail in the Appendix to Chapter 13.

Two other life insurance company reserves merit discussion—the reserve for amounts held on deposit and the asset valuation reserve (AVR).[7] The **reserve for amounts held on deposit** *is a liability that represents funds owed to policyholders and to beneficiaries.* Given the nature of the life insurance business, it is common for life insurers to hold funds on deposit for later payment to policyholders and beneficiaries. For example, a beneficiary may select a fixed-period or fixed-amount settlement option under a life insurance policy, or a policyholder may select the accumulate-at-interest dividend option.

As noted earlier, statutory accounting rules emphasizes the solvency of insurers. As such, the surplus position of a life insurer is crucial. The surplus, however, is determined in large part by the value of the assets the insurer holds. Given that the assets are largely financial assets, their values are subject to considerable fluctuation. The **asset valuation reserve** *is a statutory account designed to absorb asset value fluctuations not caused by changing interest rates.* The net effect of this reserve is to smooth the company's reported surplus over time.

Policyholders' Surplus As with property and casualty insurance companies, policyholders' surplus is the difference between a life insurer's total assets and total liabilities. Given the long-term nature of the life insurance industry, conservative long-term investments, and the absence of catastrophic losses in the life insurance industry, policyholders' surplus is less volatile in the life insurance industry than in the property and casualty insurance industry.

Income and Expense Statement

The income and expense statement for a life insurance company is similar to the statement reviewed earlier for a property and casualty insurance company. The major sources of revenues are premiums received for the various products sold (e.g., ordinary life insurance, group life insurance, annuities, and health insurance) and income from investments. As with property and casualty insurers, investment income can take the form of periodic cash flows (interest, dividends, and rental payments) and realized capital gains or losses.

Like a property and casualty insurance company, benefit payments are a major expense for a life insurance company. Benefit payments consist of death benefits paid to beneficiaries, annuity benefits paid to annuitants, matured endowments paid to policyowners, and benefits paid under health insurance policies (medical benefits and disability income payments). Those policyowners who choose to terminate their cash-value life insurance coverage are paid surrender benefits, another expense. Increased reserves, general insurance expenses, agents' commissions and licenses, premium taxes, and fees round out the list of important expenses.

A life insurer's net gain from operations before dividends and taxes is the insurer's total revenues less the insurer's total expenses. *A life insurer's* **net gain from operations** *(also called net income) equals total revenues less total expenses, policyowner dividends, and federal income taxes.*

Measuring Financial Performance

A number of measures can be used to gauge the financial performance of a life insurance company. For example, the measure displayed in Insight 7.1 is the rate of return on policyowners' surplus, similar to a return on equity (ROE) ratio. This measure is net gain from operations divided by policyowners' surplus. As illustrated in Insight 7.1, the profitability of life insurance companies is far less volatile than that of property and casualty insurers. The downturn in profitability from 2001–2003 reflects, in large part, low interest rates on invested assets.

RATE MAKING IN PROPERTY AND CASUALTY INSURANCE

Given the competitive nature of the insurance industry, rates charged by insurance companies are important. Before examining specific rate-making methods in property and casualty insurance, the objectives of rate making are discussed.

Objectives in Rate Making

Rate making, or insurance pricing, has several basic objectives. Because insurance rates, primarily property and casualty insurance rates, are regulated by the states, certain statutory and regulatory requirements must be met. Also, due to the overall goal of profitability, certain business objectives must be stressed. Thus, rate-making goals can be classified

into two categories: regulatory objectives and business objectives.

Regulatory Objectives The goal of insurance regulation is to protect the public. States enact rating laws that require insurance rates to meet certain standards. In general, rates charged by insurers must be adequate, not excessive, and not unfairly discriminatory.

The first regulatory requirement is that rates must be adequate. *This means the rates charged by insurers should be high enough to pay all losses and expenses.* If rates are inadequate, an insurer may become insolvent and unable to pay claims. As a result, policyowners, beneficiaries, and third-party claimants may be harmed. However, rate adequacy is complicated by the fact that an insurer does not know its actual costs when a policy is sold. The premium is paid up front, but it may not be sufficient to pay all claims and expenses during the policy period. It is only after the period of protection has expired that an insurer can determine its actual costs.

The second regulatory requirement is that rates must not be excessive. *This means that the rates should not be so high that policyholders are paying more than the actual value of their protection.* Exorbitant insurance prices are not in the public interest.

The third regulatory objective is that the rates must not be unfairly discriminatory. *This means that exposures that are similar with respect to losses and expenses should not be charged significantly different rates.*[8] For example, consider two men, both age 30, who live in the same neighborhood. Each owns a late-model sedan and has a clean driving record. If they purchase the same insurance coverage from the same insurer, they should not be charged different rates. However, if the loss exposures are substantially different, it is fair to charge different rates. Consider two other auto insurance buyers. The first is 45, he has a clean driving record, and he drives a four-year-old sedan. The second is 20 and he drives a new sports car. He has been arrested for speeding twice and for causing an accident by running a stop sign. It is fair, in this case, to charge the second man a higher rate for his coverage because of the higher probability of loss.

Business Objectives Insurers are also guided by certain business objectives in designing a rating system.

The rating system should meet all of these objectives: simplicity, responsiveness, stability, and encouragement of loss control.[9]

The rating system should be easy to understand so that producers can quote premiums with a minimum amount of time and expense. This is especially important in the personal lines market, where relatively small premiums do not justify a large amount of time and expense in the preparation of premium quotations. In addition, commercial insurance purchasers should understand how their premiums are determined so that they can take active steps to reduce their insurance costs.

Rates should be stable over short periods of time so that consumer satisfaction can be maintained. If rates change rapidly, insurance consumers may become irritated and dissatisfied. They may then look to government to control the rates or to enact a government insurance program.

Rates should also be responsive over time to changing loss exposures and changing economic conditions. To meet the objective of rate adequacy, the rates should increase when loss exposures increase. For example, as a city grows, auto insurance rates should increase to reflect greater traffic and increased frequency of auto accidents. Likewise, rates should reflect changing economic conditions. Thus, if inflation causes liability awards to increase, liability insurance rates should rise to reflect this trend.

Finally, the rating system should encourage loss-control activities. Loss-control efforts are designed to reduce the frequency and severity of losses. This point is important because loss control tends to keep insurance affordable. Profits are also stabilized. As you will see later, certain rating systems provide a strong financial incentive for the insured to engage in loss control.

Basic Rate-Making Definitions

You should be familiar with some basic terms that are widely used in rate making. A **rate** is the price per unit of insurance. An **exposure unit** is the unit of measurement used in insurance pricing. It varies by line of insurance. For example, in fire insurance, the exposure unit is $100 of coverage; in product liability, it is $1,000 of sales; and in auto collision insurance, it is one car-year, which is one car insured for a year.

The **pure premium** refers to that portion of the rate needed to pay losses and loss-adjustment expenses. The **loading** refers to the amount that must be added to the pure premium for other expenses, profit, and a margin for contingencies. The **gross rate** consists of the pure premium and a loading element. Finally, the **gross premium** paid by the insured consists of the gross rate multiplied by the number of exposure units. Thus, if the gross rate is 10 cents per $100 of property insurance, the gross premium for a $500,000 building would be $500.

Rate-Making Methods

There are three basic rate-making methods in property and casualty insurance: judgment, class, and merit rating. Merit rating, in turn, can be broken down into schedule rating, experience rating, and retrospective rating. Thus, the basic rating methods can be conveniently classified as follows:[10]

> Judgment rating
> Class rating
> Merit rating
> > Schedule rating
> > Experience rating
> > Retrospective rating

Judgment Rating Judgment rating *means that each exposure is individually evaluated, and the rate is determined largely by the judgment of the underwriter.* This method is used when the loss exposures are so diverse that a class rate cannot be calculated, or when credible loss statistics are not available.

Judgment rating is widely used in ocean marine insurance and in some lines of inland marine insurance. Because ocean-going vessels, ports, cargoes, and waters traveled are so diverse, some ocean marine rates are determined largely by the judgment of the underwriter.

Class Rating The second type of property and casualty rating is class rating. Most rates used today are class rates. **Class rating** *means that exposures with similar characteristics are placed in the same underwriting class, and each is charged the same rate.* The rate charged reflects the *average loss experience* for the class as a whole. Class rating is based on the assumption that future losses to insureds will be determined largely by the same set of factors. For example, major classification factors in homeowners insurance include construction material, age of the home, and protective devices (e.g., smoke detectors and fire extinguishers). Accordingly, newly constructed masonry homes with protective devices are not placed in the same underwriting class with older wood-frame homes that do not have protective devices.

The major advantage of class rating is that it is simple to apply. Also, premium quotations can be quickly obtained. As such, it is ideal for the personal lines market.

Class rating is also called *manual rating*. Class rating is widely used in homeowners insurance, private passenger auto insurance, workers compensation, and life and health insurance.

There are two basic methods for determining class rates: the **pure premium method** and the **loss ratio method.**

1. *Pure Premium Method* As stated earlier, the pure premium is that portion of the gross rate needed to pay losses and loss-adjustment expenses. *The pure premium can be determined by dividing the dollar amount of incurred losses and loss-adjustment expenses by the number of exposure units.* Incurred losses include all losses paid during the accounting period, plus amounts held as reserves for the future payment of losses that have already occurred during the same period. Thus, incurred losses include all losses that occur during the accounting period whether or not they have been paid by the end of the period. Loss-adjustment expenses are the expenses incurred by the company in adjusting losses during the same accounting period.

To illustrate how a pure premium can be derived, assume that in auto collision insurance, 500,000 autos in a given underwriting class generate incurred losses and loss-adjustment expenses of $33 million over a one-year period. The pure premium is $66. This can be illustrated by the following:

$$\text{Pure premium} = \frac{\text{Incurred losses and adjustment expenses}}{\text{Number of exposure units}}$$

$$= \frac{\$33,000,000}{500,000}$$

$$= \$66$$

The final step is to add a loading for expenses, underwriting profit, and a margin for contingencies. The expense loading is usually expressed as a percentage of the gross rate and is called the expense ratio. The final gross rate can be determined by dividing the pure premium by one minus the expense ratio. For example, if expenses are 40 percent of the gross rate, the final gross rate is $110. This can be illustrated by the following:[11]

$$\text{Gross rate} = \frac{\text{Pure premium}}{1 - \text{Expense ratio}}$$

$$= \frac{\$66}{1 - .40} = \$110$$

2. *Loss Ratio Method Under the loss ratio method, the actual loss ratio is compared with the expected loss ratio, and the rate is adjusted accordingly.* The actual loss ratio is the ratio of incurred losses and loss-adjustment expenses to earned premiums.[12] The expected loss ratio is the percentage of the premium that can be expected to be used to pay losses. For example, assume that a line of insurance has incurred losses and loss-adjustment expenses of $800,000 and earned premiums of $1 million. The actual loss ratio is 0.80 or 80 percent. If the expected loss ratio is 0.70 or 70 percent, the rate must be increased 14.3 percent. This can be illustrated by the following:

$$\text{Rate change} = \frac{A - E}{E}$$

where A = Actual loss ratio
E = Expected loss ratio

$$= \frac{0.80 - 0.70}{0.70}$$

$$= 0.143, \text{ or } 14.3\%$$

Merit Rating The third principal type of rating in property-casualty insurance is merit rating. **Merit rating** *is a rating plan by which class rates (manual* *rates) are adjusted upward or downward based on individual loss experience.* Merit rating is based on the assumption that the loss experience of a particular insured will differ substantially from the loss experience of other insureds. Thus, class rates are modified upward or downward depending on individual loss experience. There are three types of merit rating plans: schedule rating, experience rating, and retrospective rating.

1. *Schedule Rating Under a* **schedule rating** *plan, each exposure is individually rated. A basis rate is determined for each exposure, which is then modified by debits or credits for undesirable or desirable physical features.* Schedule rating is based on the assumption that certain physical characteristics of the insured's operations will influence the insured's future loss experience. Thus, the physical characteristics of the exposure to be insured are extremely important in schedule rating.

Schedule rating is used in commercial property insurance for large, complex structures, such as an industrial plant. Each building is individually rated based on several factors, including construction, occupancy, protection, exposure, and maintenance.

- *Construction* refers to the physical characteristics of the building. A building may be constructed with wood frame, brick, fire-resistive, or fireproof materials. A frame building is charged a higher rate than a brick building or fire-resistive building. Also, tall buildings and buildings with large open areas may receive debits because of the greater difficulty of extinguishing or containing a fire.

- *Occupancy* refers to the use of the building. The probability of a fire is greatly influenced by the use of the structure. For example, open flames and sparks from torches and welding equipment can quickly cause a fire. Also, if highly combustible materials or chemicals are stored in the building, a fire will be more difficult to contain.

- *Protection* refers to the quality of the city's water supply and fire department. It also includes protective devices installed in the insured building. Rate credits are given for a fire alarm system, security guard, fire doors, automatic sprinkler system, fire extinguishers, and similar protective devices.

- *Exposure* refers to the possibility that the insured building will be damaged or destroyed by a peril, such as fire that starts at an adjacent building and spreads to the insured building. The greater the exposure from surrounding buildings, the greater are the charges applied.

- *Maintenance* refers to the housekeeping and overall upkeep of the building. Debits are applied for poor housekeeping and maintenance. Thus, debits may be given for oily rags near a heat source or debris strewn on the grounds of the plant.

2. *Experience Rating Under* **experience rating,** *the class or manual rate is adjusted upward or downward based on past loss experience.* The most distinctive characteristic of experience rating is that *the insured's past loss experience is used to determine the premium for the next policy period.* The loss experience over the last three years is typically used to determine the premium for the next policy year. If the insured's loss experience is better than the average for the class as a whole, the class rate is reduced. If the loss experience is worse than the class average, the rate is increased. In determining the magnitude of the rate change, the actual loss experience is modified by a *credibility factor*[13] based on the volume of experience.

For example, assume that a retail firm has a general liability insurance policy that is experience rated. Annual premiums are $30,000, and the expected loss ratio is 30 percent. If the actual loss ratio over the years is 20 percent, and the credibility factor (C) is .29, the firm will receive a premium reduction of 9.7 percent. This reduction is illustrated below:

$$\text{Premium change} = \frac{A - E}{E} \times C$$

$$= \frac{.20 - .30}{.30} \times .29$$

$$= -9.7\%$$

Thus, the premium for the next policy period is $27,090. Obviously, experience rating provides a financial incentive to reduce losses, because premiums can be reduced by favorable loss experience.

Experience rating is generally limited to larger firms that generate a sufficiently high volume of premiums and more credible loss experience. Smaller firms are normally ineligible for experience rating. The rating system is frequently used in general liability insurance, workers compensation, commercial auto liability insurance, and group health insurance.

3. *Retrospective Rating Under a* **retrospective rating plan,** *the insured's loss experience during the current policy period determines the actual premium paid for that period.* Under this rating plan, a provisional premium is paid at the start of the policy period. At the end of the period, a final premium is calculated based on actual losses that occur during the policy period. There is a minimum and a maximum premium that must be paid. In practice, the actual premium paid generally will fall somewhere between the minimum and maximum premium, depending on the insured's loss experience during the current policy period.

Retrospective rating is widely used by large firms in workers compensation insurance, general liability insurance, auto liability and physical damage insurance, and burglary and glass insurance.

RATE MAKING IN LIFE INSURANCE

The discussion of rate making thus far has been limited to property and casualty insurance. Rate making is also important for life insurance companies, especially given the long-term nature of many life insurance contracts.

Life insurance actuaries use a mortality table or individual company experience to determine the probability of death at each attained age. The probability of death is multiplied by the amount the life insurer will have to pay if death occurs to determine the expected value of the death claims for each policy year. These annual expected values are then discounted back to the beginning of the policy period to determine the net single premium (NSP). The NSP is the present value of the future death benefit. Since most insureds pay life insurance premiums in installments, the NSP must be converted into a series of periodic level premiums to determine the net level premium. This is done through a mathematical adjustment that is discussed in the appendix to Chapter 13. After the net level premium is calculated, a loading for expenses is added to determine the gross premium. The Appendix to Chapter 13 discusses each of these steps in greater detail.

CASE APPLICATION

Carolyn is senior vice president of finance and chief actuary for Rock Solid Insurance Company (RSIC). Lonnie is double-majoring in finance and mathematics at State University. Lonnie applied for an internship with Rock Solid, and he is working for the company during the summer before the start of his senior year of college. Curious to learn what Lonnie knew about insurance company financial statements and rate-making, Carolyn prepared a quiz for Lonnie to take on his first day on the job. See if you can help Lonnie answer these questions.

1. At year-end last year, Rock Solid had total liabilities of $640 million and total assets of $900 million. What was the company's policyholders' surplus?

2. Explain how it is possible for Rock Solid to have $500 million in written premiums last year and $505 million in earned premiums last year.

3. Rock Solid's net underwriting result last year was a $540,000 loss. Explain how it is possible that Rock Solid was required to pay income taxes.

4. Rock Solid insures 50,000 wooden frame homes in one state. The company expects to pay $10 million in incurred losses and loss-adjustment expenses for insured property damage to these 50,000 homes. Based on this information, what is the pure premium rate?

5. The pure premium per unit of personal liability insurance for one group of prospective purchasers is $300. If Rock Solid wants to allow for a 40 percent expense ratio for this line of coverage, what gross rate per unit of coverage should be charged?

SUMMARY

- A balance sheet summarizes what a company owns (assets), what it owes (liabilities), and the difference between these two values (owners' equity).

- For an insurance company, the major assets are financial assets, which are investments in bonds, stocks, real estate, mortgage-backed securities, and marketable securities; as well as cash.

- An insurer's liabilities are called reserves. The loss reserve is the estimated cost of settling claims. Loss reserves in property and casualty insurance can be classified as case reserves, reserves established using the loss ratio method, and reserves for incurred-but-not-reported (IBNR) claims.

- Another important reserve for property and casualty insurers is the unearned premium reserve. This reserve equals the unearned portion of gross premiums for outstanding policies at the time of valuation.

- The difference between an insurer's total assets and total liabilities is called policyholders' surplus. Policyholders' surplus consists of paid-in capital at stock companies, plus retained profits from insurance operations and investments over time. Surplus represents a margin of safety for policyowners.

- The major sources of revenue for an insurance company are premiums and investment income. The major expenses are loss payments, loss-adjustment expenses, and other expenses including commissions, premium taxes, and general insurance company expenses.

- To determine an insurer's net income, total expenses are subtracted from total revenues. Policyholder dividends, if any, are deducted to determine taxable income, and federal income taxes are levied on taxable income.

- The loss ratio is the ratio of a property and casualty insurer's incurred losses and loss-adjustment expenses to earned premiums. The expense ratio is the ratio of the insurer's underwriting expenses to written premiums.

- The combined ratio is the sum of the loss ratio and the expense ratio. A combined ratio greater than 1 (or 100 percent) indicates an underwriting loss, and a combined ratio less than 1 (or 100 percent) indicates an underwriting profit.

- An insurance company can lose money from its underwriting operations and still be profitable if the investment income offsets the underwriting loss.

- The assets of life insurance companies tend to be of longer duration than the assets of property and casualty insurers. As a policyowner may borrow the cash value, life insurance premium loans are an asset for life insurers. Life insurers maintain separate accounts for the assets backing interest-sensitive products, such as variable annuities.

- The major liability item for a life insurance company is the policy reserve. Two other important reserves are the reserve for amounts held on deposit and the asset valuation reserve.

- A life insurer's net gain from operations equals total revenues, less total expenses, policyholder dividends, and federal income taxes.

- Insurance rates are regulated to make sure they are adequate, not excessive, and not unfairly discriminatory. Business objectives of rating systems include simplicity, responsiveness, stability, and encouragement of loss control.

- The rate is the price per unit of insurance and the exposure unit is the measurement base used. The pure premium is the portion of the premium needed to pay claims and loss adjustment expenses. The loading covers expenses, profit, and other contingencies. The gross rate is the sum of the pure premium and the loading element.

- Three major rating methods are used in property and casualty insurance: judgment, class, and merit rating.

- Judgment rating means that each exposure is individually evaluated, and the rate is determined largely by the underwriter's judgment.

- Class rating means that exposures with similar characteristics are placed in the same underwriting class, and each is charged the same rate. The rate charged reflects the average loss experience for the class as a whole. Most personal lines of insurance are class rated.

- Merit rating is a rating plan by which class rates are adjusted upward or downward based on individual loss experience. It is based on the assumption that the loss experience of an individual insured will differ substantially from the loss experience of other insureds.

- There are three principal types of merit rating plans:
  Schedule rating
  Experience rating
  Retrospective rating

- Under schedule rating, each exposure is individually rated, and debits and credits are applied based on the physical characteristics of the exposure to be insured. Experience rating means that the insured's past loss experience is used to determine the premium for the next policy period. Retrospective rating means the insured's loss experience during the current policy period determines the actual premium paid for that period.

- Life insurance rate makers determine the probability of loss payment in any given year, and based on this probability determine the expected value of the loss payment. These expected future payments are discounted back to the start of the coverage period to determine the net premium. A loading for expenses is added to determine the gross premium.

KEY CONCEPTS AND TERMS

Annual pro rata method
Asset valuation reserve
Balance sheet
Case reserves
Class rating (manual rating)
Combined ratio
Earned premiums
Expense ratio
Experience rating
Exposure unit
Gross premium
Gross rate
Income and expense statement
Incurred-but-not-reported (IBNR) reserve
Investment income ratio
Judgment rating
Loading
Loss-adjustment expenses
Loss ratio
Loss ratio method (loss reserves)
Loss ratio method (of rating)
Loss reserve
Merit rating
Net gain from operations
Overall operating ratio
Policyholders' surplus
Pure premium
Pure premium method (of rating)
Rate
Reserve for amounts held on deposit
Retrospective rating
Schedule rating
Unearned premium reserve

REVIEW QUESTIONS

1. a. What are the three major sections of a balance sheet?
   b. What is the balance sheet equation?

2. a. What types of assets appear on the balance sheet of an insurance company?
   b. Why are the liabilities of a property and casualty insurance company difficult to measure?

3. a. What are the two major sources of revenue for a property and casualty insurance company?
   b. What are the major expenses of a property and casualty insurance company?

4. a. How is the combined ratio of an insurance company calculated and what does the combined ratio measure?
   b. How is it possible for a property and casualty insurance company to be profitable if its combined ratio exceeds one (or 100 percent)?

5. Name three ways in which the assets of a life insurance company differ from the assets of a property and casualty insurance company.

6. What do the reserves on a life insurance company's balance sheet represent?

7. What are the major categories of expenses for a life insurance company?

8. a. What are the major regulatory objectives that must be satisfied in insurance rate making?
   b. What are the major business objectives?

9. In the context of rate making, explain the meaning of:
   a. rate
   b. exposure unit
   c. pure premium
   d. gross premium

10. Briefly describe the following methods for determining a class rate:
    a. pure premium method
    b. loss ratio method

11. Explain the following methods of merit rating:
    a. schedule rating
    b. experience rating
    c. retrospective rating

APPLICATION QUESTIONS

1. Based on the following information, determine the policyholders' surplus for XYZ Insurance Company:

Total invested assets	$50,000,000
Loss reserves	40,000,000
Total liabilities	70,000,000
Bonds	35,000,000
Unearned premium reserve	25,000,000
Total assets	90,000,000

2. Based on the following information, determine Mutual Life Insurance Company's gain from operations before income taxes and dividends to policyowners:

Total premium income	$20,000,000
Licenses, taxes, and fees	580,000
Death benefits paid	6,000,000
Net investment income	3,000,000
Commissions paid	5,900,000
General insurance expense	2,500,000
Surrender benefits paid	800,000
Annuity benefits paid	1,600,000

3. A large casualty insurer writes a substantial amount of private passenger auto insurance. An actuary analyzed claims data for a specific class of drivers for a recent one-year policy period. The claims data showed that the insurer paid out $30 million for incurred losses and loss-adjustment expenses for each 100,000 cars insured for one year. Based on the pure premium method, calculate the pure premium.

4. For last calendar year, a property insurer reported the following financial information for a specific line of insurance:

Premiums written	$25,000,000
Expenses incurred	5,000,000
Incurred losses and loss-adjustment expenses	14,000,000
Earned premiums	20,000,000

a. What was the insurer's loss ratio for this line of coverage?
b. Calculate the expense ratio for this line of coverage.
c. What was the combined ratio for this line of coverage?

5. a. Why are property and casualty insurance companies required to maintain loss reserves?
b. Briefly explain the following methods for determining loss reserves:
   (1) judgment method
   (2) average value method
   (3) tabular method
c. What is the incurred-but-not-reported (IBNR) loss reserve?

INTERNET RESOURCES

- The **American Academy of Actuaries** is a public policy and communications organization that represents actuaries in all practice specialties. The site provides timely studies on important insurance problems and issues. Visit the site at

  http://www.actuary.org

- The **American Council of Life Insurers** is a Washington DC–based trade association representing the interests of member companies. The council prepares *The Life Insurers Fact Book* annually, and this excellent resource is available online. Visit the site at

  http://www.acli.com

- The **American Society of Pension Actuaries** is an organization formed to educate pension actuaries, consultants, and other professionals in the employee benefits field. Visit the site at

  http://www.aspa.org

- The **Casualty Actuarial Society** is a professional organization that promotes education in actuarial science and provides statistics on property and casualty insurance. Visit the site at

  http://www.casact.org

- The **Conference of Consulting Actuaries** is an organization that consists of consulting actuaries in all disciplines. Visit the site at

  http://www.ccactuaries.org

- The **Insurance Information Institute** is a primary source for information, statistics, and analysis on topics in property and casualty insurance. Visit the site at

  http://www.iii.org

- **Insurance Journal,** the *Property Casualty Magazine,* is a free online journal that provides local and national news on the property and casualty insurance industry. Breaking news and current developments are sent daily to subscribers. Visit the site at

  http://www.insurancejournal.com

- The **Insurance Services Office (ISO)** provides statistical information, actuarial analysis and consulting, policy language, and related information to participants in the property and casualty insurance markets. Visit the site at

  http://www.iso.com

- The **Society of Actuaries** is a professional organization that educates and qualifies individuals to become actuaries, provides continuing education programs, and enforces a professional code of conduct. Membership is obtained by successful completion of a rigorous set of exams leading to the designation of Associate or Fellow in the Society. Visit the site at

http://www.soa.org

■ **Towers Perrin** is one of the world's largest actuarial and management consulting firms. The Tillinghast division of Towers Perrin provides a substantial amount of information on the insurance industry and advises other organizations on risk financing and self-insurance. Visit the site at

http://www.towersperrin.com

SELECTED REFERENCES

Black, Kenneth, Jr., and Harold D. Skipper, Jr. *Life Insurance,* 13th ed., Upper Saddle River, NJ: Prentice Hall, 2000, chs. 27–30.

Graves, Edward E., ed. *McGill's Life Insurance,* 6th ed., Bryn Mawr, PA: The American College, 2007.

The I.I.I. Insurance Fact Book, 2007. New York: Insurance Information Institute, 2007.

The Life Insurers Fact Book, 2005. Washington, DC: American Council of Life Insurers, 2005.

Myhr, Ann E., and James J. Markham. *Insurance Operations, Regulation, and Statutory Accounting,* 1st ed., Malvern, PA: American Institute for Chartered Property Casualty Underwriters / Insurance Institute of America, 2003.

Webb, Bernard L., et al. *Insurance Operations and Regulations,* 1st ed., Malvern, PA: American Institute for Chartered Property Casualty Underwriters/Insurance Institute of America, 2002.

Wiening, Eric A. *Foundations of Risk Management and Insurance,* 1st ed., Malvern, PA: American Institute for Chartered Property Casualty Underwriters/Insurance Institute of America, 2002.

NOTES

1. Simplified versions of the financial statements are presented in this chapter. In practice, the financial statements are more complex. Insurers are required to use statutory accounting rules for the financial statements prepared for regulators. Financial statements may also be prepared using Generally Accepted Accounting Principles (GAAP). Statutory accounting is conservative and emphasizes insurer solvency.

2. For a detailed discussion of loss reserves, see Bernard L. Webb, et al., *Insurance Operations and Regulation,* 1st ed. (Malvern, PA: American Institute for Chartered Property Casualty Underwriters/Insurance Institute of America, 2002), ch. 12.

3. Under statutory accounting, expenses are recognized immediately while premium income is earned over a period of time. An insurance company, therefore, is immediately placed in a negative position on any policy written as acquisition expenses must be charged immediately. Surplus can also be considered from a leverage perspective. Obviously, the more coverage written per dollar of surplus, the greater the policyowner leverage.

4. This section is based on Eric A. Wiening, *Foundations of Risk Management and Insurance,* 1st ed., Malvern, PA: American Institute for Chartered Property Casualty Underwriters/Insurance Institute of America, 2002. The author drew heavily on the material presented in ch. 5, especially pp. 5.21 through 5.26, in preparing this section.

5. The observant reader may note that the denominators in the loss ratio and the expense ratio are different—premiums earned for the loss ratio and premiums written for the expense ratio. This version of the combined ratio is called the "trade basis" combined ratio. A second version, the "statutory" combined ratio, uses earned premiums in both denominators. Although the statutory combined ratio is mathematically correct, the trade basis better matches income and expenses.

6. The combined ratio for 2005 was obtained from "2006–First Quarter Results" by Dr. Robert Hartwig, Insurance Information Institute. The projected combined ratio for 2006 was obtained from Dr. Robert Hartwig's "Special Report: Earlybird Forecast, 2006," Insurance Information Institute.

7. See Kenneth R. Black, Jr., and Harold D. Skipper, Jr., *Life Insurance,* 13th ed. (Upper Saddle River, NJ: Prentice Hall, 2000), pp. 914–915 for a discussion of these and other life insurer policy reserves.

8. Robert J. Gibbons, George E. Rejda, and Michael W. Elliott, *Insurance Perspectives* (Malvern, PA: American Institute for Chartered Property Casualty Underwriters, 1992), p. 119.

9. Bernard L. Webb, Connor M. Harrison, and James J. Markham, *Insurance Operations,* 2nd ed., Vol. 2 (Malvern, PA: American Institute for Chartered Property Casualty Underwriters, 1997), pp. 89–90.

10. The basic rate-making methods are discussed in some detail in Webb et al., Chs. 10 and 11. Also see Bernard L. Webb, J. J. Launie, Willis Park Rokes, and Norman A. Baglini, *Insurance Company Operations,* 3rd ed., Vol. 2 (Malvern, PA: American Institute for Property and Liability Underwrititers, 1984), chs. 9 and 10.

11. An equivalent method for determining the final rate is to divide the pure premium by the permissible loss ratio. The permissible loss ratio is the same at the expected loss ratio. If the expense ratio is .40, the permissible loss ratio is 1 − .40, or .60. Thus if the pure premium of $66 is divided by the permissible loss ratio of .60, the resulting gross rate is also $110.

$$\text{Gross rate} = \frac{\text{Pure premium}}{\text{Permissible loss ratio}} = \frac{\$66}{.60} = \$110$$

12. Earned premiums, as discussed earlier in the chapter, are premiums actually earned by a company during the accounting period, rather than the premiums written during the same period.

13. The credibility factor, C, refers to the statistical reliability of the data. It ranges from 0 to 1 and increases as the number of claims increases. If an actuary believes that the data are highly reliable and can accurately predict future losses, a credibility factor of 1 can be used. However, if the data are not completely reliable as a predictor of future losses, a credibility factor of less than 1 is used.

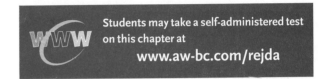

Students may take a self-administered test on this chapter at
www.aw-bc.com/rejda

CHAPTER 8

GOVERNMENT REGULATION OF INSURANCE

"There are serious shortcomings in state laws and regulatory activities with respect to protecting the interests of insurance consumers."

U.S. Government Accountability Office

LEARNING OBJECTIVES

After studying this chapter, you should be able to

◆ Explain the major reasons why insurers are regulated.

◆ Identify key legal cases and legislative acts that have had an important impact on insurance regulation.

◆ Identify the major areas that are regulated.

◆ Explain the objectives of rate regulation and the different types of rating laws.

◆ Explain the major arguments for and against state regulation of insurance.

*B*rittany, age 28, filled out an application for auto insurance and paid the agent $450 for the first premium. The application included collision coverage on her car. Shortly thereafter, Brittany was involved in an auto accident in which she was at fault, and her car was badly damaged. The insurer denied payment on the grounds that no auto policy was ever issued. A complaint to the state insurance department revealed that the agent did not remit the application and premium to the insurer. Further investigation revealed that the agent did not remit the premiums of other policyowners either. As a result, the state insurance department revoked the agent's license and fined the insurer for inadequate supervision of agents. The insurance department also recommended that the insurer pay for the damage to Brittany's car.

One important function of state insurance departments is to protect consumers. In the above case, the state insurance department helped Brittany resolve her claim dispute with the insurance company because of a dishonest agent. To protect consumers, the states regulate the market activities of insurers. Certain federal laws also apply to insurance.

This chapter discusses the fundamentals of insurance regulation. Topics covered include the reasons why insurers are regulated, the various methods for regulating insurers, and the specific areas that are regulated. The chapter concludes with a discussion of current issues in insurance regulation.

REASONS FOR INSURANCE REGULATION

Insurers are regulated by the states for several reasons, including the following:

- Maintain insurer solvency
- Compensate for inadequate consumer knowledge
- Ensure reasonable rates
- Make insurance available

Maintain Insurer Solvency

Insurance regulation is necessary to maintain the solvency of insurers. Solvency is important for several reasons. First, premiums are paid in advance, but the period of protection extends into the future. If an insurer goes bankrupt and a future claim is not paid, the insurance protection paid for in advance is worthless. Therefore, to ensure that claims will be paid, the financial strength of insurers must be carefully monitored.

A second reason for stressing solvency is that individuals can be exposed to great financial insecurity if insurers fail and claims are not paid. For example, if the insured's home is totally destroyed by a hurricane and the loss is not paid, he or she may be financially ruined. Thus, because of possible financial hardship to insureds, beneficiaries, and third-party claimants, regulation must stress insurer solvency.

Finally, when insurers become insolvent, certain social and economic costs are incurred. Examples include the loss of jobs by insurance company employees, a reduction in premium taxes paid to the states, and a "freeze" on the withdrawal of cash values by life insurance policyowners. These costs can be minimized if insolvencies are prevented.

Insurer solvency is an important issue that is discussed in greater detail later in the chapter.

Compensate for Inadequate Consumer Knowledge

Regulation is also necessary because of inadequate consumer knowledge. Insurance contracts are technical, legal documents that contain complex clauses and provisions. Without regulation, an unscrupulous insurer could draft a contract so restrictive and legalistic that it would be worthless.

Also, most consumers do not have sufficient information for comparing and determining the monetary value of different insurance contracts. It is difficult to compare dissimilar policies with different premiums because the necessary price and policy information is not readily available. For example, individual health insurance policies vary widely by cost, coverages, and benefits. The average consumer would find it difficult to evaluate a particular policy based on the premium alone.

Without good information, consumers cannot select the best insurance product. This failure can reduce the impact that consumers have on insurance markets as well as the competitive incentive of insurers to improve product quality and lower price. Thus, regulation is needed to produce the same market effect that results from knowledgeable consumers who are purchasing products in highly competitive markets.

Finally, some agents are unethical, and state licensing requirements are minimal. Thus, regulation is needed to protect consumers against unscrupulous agents.

Ensure Reasonable Rates

Regulation is also necessary to ensure reasonable rates. Rates should not be so high that consumers are being charged excessive prices. Nor should they be so low that the solvency of insurers is threatened. In most insurance markets, competition among insurers results in rates that are not excessive. Unfortunately, this result is not always the case. In some insurance markets with relatively small numbers of insurers, such as credit and title insurance, rate regulation is needed to protect consumers against excessive rates. Regulation also protects consumers against some insurers who may attempt to increase rates to exorbitant levels after a natural disaster occurs so as to recoup their underwriting losses.

Make Insurance Available

Another regulatory goal is to make insurance available to all persons who need it. Insurers are often unwilling to insure all applicants for a given type of insurance because of underwriting losses, inadequate rates, adverse selection, and a host of additional factors. However, the public interest may require regulators to take actions that expand private insurance markets so as to make insurance more readily available. If private insurers are unable or unwilling to supply the needed coverages, then government insurance programs may be necessary.

HISTORICAL DEVELOPMENT OF INSURANCE REGULATION

In this section, the development of insurance regulation by the states is briefly reviewed. You should pay careful attention to certain landmark legal decisions and legislative acts that have had a profound impact on insurance regulation.

Early Regulatory Efforts

Insurance regulation first began when state legislatures granted charters to new insurers, which authorized their formation and operation. The new insurers were initially subject to few regulatory controls. The charters required only that the companies issue periodic reports and provide public information concerning their financial conditions.

The creation of state insurance commissions was the next step in insurance regulation. In 1851, New Hampshire became the first state to create a separate insurance commission to regulate insurers. Other states followed suit. In 1859, New York created a separate administrative agency headed by a single superintendent who was given broad licensing and investigative powers. Thus, initial insurance regulation developed under the jurisdiction and supervision of the states.

Paul v. Virginia

The case of *Paul v. Virginia* in 1868 was a landmark legal decision that affirmed the right of the states to regulate insurance.[1] Samuel Paul was an agent in

Virginia who represented several New York insurers. Paul was fined for selling fire insurance in Virginia without a license. He appealed the case on the grounds that Virginia's law was unconstitutional. He argued that because insurance was interstate commerce, only the federal government had the right to regulate insurance under the commerce clause of the U.S. Constitution. The Supreme Court disagreed. The Court ruled that issuance of an insurance policy was not interstate commerce. Therefore, the insurance industry was not subject to the commerce clause of the Constitution. *Thus, the legal significance of Paul v. Virginia was that insurance was not interstate commerce, and that the states rather than the federal government had the right to regulate the insurance industry.*

South-Eastern Underwriters Association Case

The precedent set in *Paul v. Virginia,* which held that insurance is not interstate commerce, was overturned by the Supreme Court in 1944. The **South-Eastern Underwriters Association (SEUA)** was a cooperative rating bureau that was found guilty of price fixing and other violations of the Sherman Antitrust Act. *In the landmark case of U.S. v. South-Eastern Underwriters Association, the Supreme Court ruled that insurance was interstate commerce when conducted across state lines and was subject to federal regulation.*[2] The Court's decision that insurance was interstate commerce and subject to federal antitrust laws caused considerable turmoil for the industry and state regulators. The decision raised serious doubts concerning the legality of private rating bureaus, and the power of the states to regulate and tax the insurance industry.

McCarran-Ferguson Act

To resolve the confusion and doubt that existed after the SEUA decision, Congress passed the **McCarran-Ferguson Act** (Public Law 15) in 1945. *The McCarran-Ferguson Act states that continued regulation and taxation of the insurance industry by the states are in the public interest. It also states that federal antitrust laws apply to insurance only to the extent that the insurance industry is not regulated by state law.* Therefore, as long as state regulation is in effect, federal antitrust laws will not apply to insurance. However, the exemption from antitrust laws is not absolute. For example, the Sherman Act forbids any acts or agreements to boycott, coerce, or intimidate. In these areas, insurers are still subject to federal law.

At present, the states still have the primary responsibility for regulating insurance. However, Congress can repeal the McCarran-Ferguson Act, which would then give the federal government primary authority over the insurance industry. There have been strong pressures from some politicians and consumer groups to repeal the McCarran-Ferguson Act, but Congress to date has not done so. This important issue is discussed later in the chapter.

Financial Modernization Act of 1999

More recently, the **Financial Modernization Act of 1999** (also called the Gramm-Leach-Bliley Act) has had a significant impact on insurance regulation. The legislation changed federal law that earlier prevented banks, insurers, and investment firms from competing fully in other financial markets outside their core area. As a result, insurers can now buy banks; banks can underwrite insurance and sell securities; brokerage firms can sell insurance; and a company that wants to provide insurance, banking, and investment services through a single entity can form a new holding company for that purpose.

The legislation provides for several areas of regulation, which has produced additional complexity and some overlap into the regulatory process. State insurance departments continue to regulate the insurance industry and the insurance activities of other financial institutions; state and federal bank agencies regulate banks and thrifts; the Securities and Exchange Commission regulates the sale of securities; and the Federal Reserve has umbrella authority over bank affiliates that engage in risky activities such as underwriting insurance and developing real estate. As a result, regulation of the insurance industry has become more complex because of different levels of insurance at the state and federal level and the overlap of regulatory functions.

METHODS FOR REGULATING INSURERS

Three principal methods are used to regulate insurers: legislation, courts, and state insurance departments.

Legislation

All states have insurance laws that regulate the operations of insurers. These laws regulate (1) formation of insurance companies, (2) licensing of agents and brokers, (3) financial requirements for maintaining solvency, (4) insurance rates, (5) sales and claim practices, (6) taxation, and (7) rehabilitation or liquidation of insurers. Also, laws have been passed to protect the rights of consumers, such as laws restricting the right of insurers to terminate insurance contracts and laws making insurance more widely available.

Insurers are also subject to regulation by certain federal agencies and laws. Only a few are mentioned here. The Federal Trade Commission has authority to regulate mail-order insurers in those states where they are not licensed to do business. The Securities and Exchange Commission has issued regulations concerning the sale of variable annuities and variable life insurance and has jurisdiction over the sale of insurance company securities to the public. The Employee Retirement Income Security Act of 1974 (ERISA) applies to the private pension plans of insurers.

Courts

State and federal courts periodically hand down decisions concerning the constitutionality of state insurance laws, the interpretation of policy clauses and provisions, and the legality of administrative actions by state insurance departments. As such, the various court decisions can affect the market conduct and operations of insurers in an important way.

State Insurance Departments

All states, the District of Columbia, and U.S. territories have a separate insurance department or bureau. An insurance commissioner, who is elected or appointed by the governor, has the responsibility to administer state insurance laws. Through administrative rulings, the state insurance commissioner wields considerable power over insurers doing business in the state. The insurance commissioner has the power to hold hearings, issue cease-and-desist orders, and revoke or suspend an insurer's license to do business.

The state insurance commissioners belong to an important organization known as the **National Association of Insurance Commissioners (NAIC).** The NAIC, founded in 1871, meets periodically to discuss industry problems that might require legislation or regulation. The NAIC has drafted model laws in various areas and has recommended adoption of these proposals by state legislatures. Although the NAIC has no legal authority to force the states to adopt the recommendations, most states have accepted all or part of them.

WHAT AREAS ARE REGULATED?

Insurers are subject to numerous laws and regulations. The principal areas regulated include the following:

- Formation and licensing of insurers
- Solvency regulation
- Rate regulation
- Policy forms
- Sales practices and consumer protection

Formation and Licensing of Insurers

All states have requirements for the formation and licensing of insurers. A new insurer is typically formed by incorporation. The insurer receives a charter or certificate of incorporation from the state, which authorizes its formation and legal existence.

After being formed, insurers must be licensed to do business. The licensing requirements for insurers are more stringent than those imposed on other new firms. If the insurer is a capital stock insurer, it must meet certain minimum capital and surplus requirements, which vary by state and by line of insurance. A new mutual insurer must meet a minimum surplus requirement (rather than capital and surplus, as there are no stockholders), and other requirements.

A license can be issued to a domestic, foreign, or alien insurer. A **domestic insurer** is an insurer domiciled in the state; it must be licensed in the state as well as in other states where it does business. A **foreign insurer** is an out-of-state insurer that is chartered by another state; it must be licensed to do business in the state. An **alien insurer** is an insurer chartered by a foreign country. It must also meet certain licensing requirements to operate in the state.

Solvency Regulation

In addition to minimum capital and surplus requirements, insurers are subject to other financial regulations designed to maintain solvency.

Admitted Assets   An insurer must have sufficient assets to offset its liabilities. Only admitted assets can be shown on the insurer's balance sheet. **Admitted assets** *are assets that an insurer can show on its statutory balance sheet in determining its financial condition.* All other assets are nonadmitted assets.

Most assets are classified as admitted assets. These assets include cash, bonds, common and preferred stocks, mortgages, real estate, and other legal investments. Nonadmitted assets include premiums overdue by 90 or more days, office furniture and supplies, and certain investments or amounts that exceed statutory limits for certain types of securities. Nonadmitted assets are excluded because their liquidity is uncertain.

Reserves   Reserves *are liability items on an insurer's balance sheet and reflect obligations that must be met in the future.* The states have regulations for the calculation of reserves. The various methods for calculating reserves were discussed in Chapter 7.

Surplus   The surplus position is also carefully monitored. **Policyowners' surplus** *is the difference between an insurer's assets and its liabilities.* It is an item on the balance sheet that represents an insurer's net worth under statutory accounting principles.

In property and casualty insurance, policyowners' surplus is important for several reasons. First, the amount of new business an insurer can write is limited by the amount of policyowners' surplus. One

conservative rule is that a property insurer can safely write $2 of new net premiums for each $1 of policyowners' surplus. Second, policyowners' surplus is necessary to offset any substantial underwriting or investment losses. Finally, policyowners' surplus is required to offset any deficiency in loss reserves that may occur over time.

In life insurance, policyowners' surplus is less important because of the substantial safety margins in the calculation of premiums and dividends, conservative interest assumptions used in calculating legal reserves, conservative valuation of investments, greater stability in operations over time, and less likelihood of a catastrophic loss.

Risk-Based Capital   To reduce the risk of insolvency, life and health insurers must meet certain risk-based capital standards based on a model law developed by the NAIC. The NAIC has drafted a similar model law for property and casualty insurers. Only the standards for life insurers are discussed here.

Risk-based capital (RBC) *means that insurers must have a certain amount of capital, depending on the riskiness of their investments and insurance operations. Insurers are monitored by regulators based on how much capital they have relative to their risk-based capital requirements.* For example, insurers that invest in less-than-investment-grade corporate bonds ("junk bonds") must set aside more capital than if Treasury bonds were purchased.

The risk-based capital requirements in life insurance are based on a formula that considers four types of risk:

- *Asset risk.*   Asset risk is the risk of default of assets for affiliated investments; the parent company must hold an equivalent amount of risk-based capital that provides protection against the financial downturn of affiliates. The asset risk also represents the risk of default for bonds and other debt assets and a loss in market value for equity (common stock) assets.
- *Insurance risk.*   Insurance risk is the equivalent of underwriting risk and reflects the amount of surplus needed to pay excess claims because of random fluctuations and inaccurate pricing for future claim levels (risk of fluctuations in mortality experience).

- *Interest rate risk.* Interest rate risk reflects possible losses due to changing interest rates. The impact of interest rate changes is greatest on those products where the contractual guarantees favor the policyowners and where policyowners are likely to respond to changes in interest rates by withdrawing funds from the insurer. Examples include a decline in the market value of assets supporting contractual obligations because of a rise in interest rates, and liquidity problems caused by policyowners withdrawing funds because of changing interest rates.
- *Business risk.* Business risk represents the wide range of general business risks that life insurers face, such as guaranty fund assessments and insolvency because of bad management.

The NAIC requires a comparison of a company's total adjusted capital with the amount of required risk-based capital. *Total adjusted capital* is essentially the company's net worth (assets minus liabilities) with certain adjustments.

The model act requires certain regulatory and company actions that must be taken if an insurer's total adjusted capital falls below its RBC levels. The corrective action levels are summarized as follows:

Action Level	RBC Ratio	Required Action
No action	200% or higher	None
Company action level	150%–200%	Insurer must file a report with the regulator outlining the corrective actions to be taken.
Regulatory action level	100%–150%	Regulator must examine insurer; insurer must file an action plan.
Authorized control level	70%–100%	Regulator is authorized to take control of insurer.
Mandatory control level	Less than 70%	Regulator is required to take steps to place the insurer under control.

The effect of the RBC requirements is to raise the minimum amount of capital for many insurers and decrease the chance that a failing insurer will exhaust its capital before it can be seized by regulators. Thus, the overall result is to limit an insurer's financial risk and reduce the cost of insolvency. As a practical matter, the vast majority of insurers have total adjusted capital that exceeds their risk-based capital requirements.

Investments Insurance company investments are regulated with respect to types of investments, quality, and percentage of total assets or surplus that can be invested in different investments. The basic purpose of these regulations is to prevent insurers from making unsound investments that could threaten the company's solvency and harm the policyowners.

Life insurers typically invest in common and preferred stocks, bonds, mortgages, real estate, and policy loans. The laws generally place maximum limits on each type of investment based on a percentage of assets or surplus.

Property and casualty insurers invest in common and preferred stock, tax-free municipal and special revenue bonds, government and corporate bonds, cash, and other short-term investments. The percentage of assets invested in real estate is relatively small (slightly less than 1 percent in 2004). Most assets are invested in highly liquid securities—for example, high-quality stocks and bonds rather than real estate—that can be sold quickly to pay claims if a catastrophe loss occurs.

Dividend Policy In life insurance, the annual gain from operations can be distributed in the form of dividends to policyowners, or it can be added to the insurer's surplus for present and future needs. Many states limit the amount of surplus a participating life insurer can accumulate. The purpose of this limitation is to prevent life insurers from accumulating a substantial surplus at the expense of dividends to policyowners.

Reports and Examinations Annual reports and examinations are used to maintain insurer solvency. Each insurer must file an annual report with the state insurance department in states where it does business. The report provides detailed financial information to regulatory officials with respect to assets, liabilities, reserves, investments, claim payments, risk-based capital, and other information.

Insurance companies are also periodically examined by the states. Depending on the state, domestic insurers generally are examined one or more times every three to five years by the state insurance department. However, state regulations have the authority to conduct an examination at any time when considered necessary. Licensed out-of-state insurers are also periodically examined.

Liquidation of Insurers If an insurer is financially impaired, the state insurance department assumes control of the company. With proper management, the insurer may be successfully rehabilitated. If the insurer cannot be rehabilitated, it is liquidated according to the state's insurance code.

Most states have adopted the Insurers Supervision, Rehabilitation, and Liquidation Model Act drafted by the NAIC in 1977 or similar types of legislation. The act is designed to achieve uniformity among the states in the liquidation of assets and payment of claims of a defunct insurer and provides for a comprehensive system for rehabilitation and liquidation.

If an insurer becomes insolvent, some claims may still be unpaid. All states have **guaranty funds** that provide for the payment of unpaid claims of insolvent property and casualty insurers. In life insurance, all states have enacted guaranty laws and guaranty associations to pay the claims of policyowners of insolvent life and health insurers.

The **assessment method** is the major method used to raise the necessary funds to pay unpaid claims. Insurers are generally assessed after an insolvency occurs. New York is an exception because it maintains a permanent preassessment solvency fund, which assesses property and casualty insurers prior to any insolvency. A few states have preassessment funds for workers compensation. Insurers can recoup part or all of the assessments paid by special state premium tax credits, refunds from the state guaranty funds, and higher insurance premiums. The result is that taxpayers and the general public indirectly pay the claims of insolvent insurers.

The guaranty funds limit the amount that policyowners can collect if an insurer goes broke. For example, in life insurance, the guaranty fund may place a limit of $100,000 on cash values and $300,000 on the combined benefits from all policies. Some state funds also do not protect out-of-state residents when an insurer domiciled in the state goes broke.

Rate Regulation

Rate regulation is an important regulatory area. As noted in Chapter 7, property and casualty insurance rates must be adequate, not excessive, and not unfairly discriminatory. Rate regulation, however, is far from uniform. Some states have more than one rating law, depending on the type of insurance. The principal types of rating laws are the following:[3]

- Prior-approval laws
- Modified prior-approval law
- File-and-use law
- Use-and-file law
- Flex-rating law
- State-made rates
- Open competition

Prior-Approval Law Under a **prior-approval law,** rates must be filed and approved by the state insurance department before they can be used. In most states, if the rates are not disapproved within a certain period, such as 30 or 60 days, they are deemed to be approved.

Insurers have criticized prior-approval laws on several grounds. There is often considerable delay in obtaining a needed rate increase, because state insurance departments are often understaffed. The rate increase granted may be inadequate, and rate increases may be denied for political reasons. In addition, the statistical data required by the state insurance department to support a rate increase may not be readily available.

Modified Prior-Approval Law Under a **modified prior-approval law,** if the rate change is based solely on loss experience, the insurer must file the rates with the state insurance department, and the rates can be used immediately (i.e., file-and-use). However, if the rate change is based on a change in rate classifications or expense relationships, then prior approval of the rates is necessary (i.e., prior-approval). The insurance department can disapprove the rate filing at any time if the filing does not comply with the law.

File-and-Use Law   Under a **file-and-use law**, insurers are required only to file the rates with the state insurance department, and the rates can be used immediately. Regulatory authorities have the authority to disapprove the rates later if the filing violates state law. This type of law overcomes the problem of delay that exists under a prior-approval law.

Use-and-File Law   A variation of file-and-use is a **use-and-file law**. Under this law, insurers can put into effect immediately any rate changes, but the rates must be filed with the regulatory authorities within a certain period after first being used, such as 15 to 60 days.

Flex-Rating Law   Under a **flex-rating law**, prior approval of rates is required only if the rate increase or decrease exceeds a specified range. Rate changes of 5 to 10 percent are typically permitted without prior approval. The purpose of a flex-rating law is to allow insurers to make rate changes more rapidly in response to changing market conditions.

State-Made Rates   A small number of states have state-made rates that apply to specific lines of insurance. At the time of this writing, Massachusetts determines private passenger auto insurance rates; however, insurers are free to deviate from these rates with prior approval. However, Massachusetts is considering legislation that would allow flex-rating. In addition, in New Mexico, New York, and Texas, the state determines title insurance rates. In Florida, the state prescribes the maximum rate that title insurers can charge.[4]

Open Competition   Under this system, insurers are not required to file their rates with the state insurance department. However, insurers may be required to furnish rate schedules and supporting data to state officials. A fundamental assumption underlying open competition is that market forces will determine the price and availability of insurance rather than the discretionary acts of regulatory officials.

Commercial Lines Deregulation   Many states have passed legislation that exempts insurers from filing rates and policy forms for large commercial accounts with the state insurance department for approval. In most states, the legislation applies to commercial auto, general liability, and commercial property lines. Proponents of deregulation of commercial lines believe that insurers can design new products more quickly to meet the specific insurance needs of corporations; insurers can save money because rates and policy forms do not have to be filed for a commercial account with offices in several states; and risk managers can get specific coverages more quickly.

Life Insurance Rate Regulation   Life insurance rates are not directly regulated by the states.[5] Rate adequacy in life insurance is indirectly achieved by regulations that require legal reserves to be at least a minimum amount. Minimum legal reserve requirements indirectly affect the rates that must be charged to pay death claims and expenses.

Policy Forms

The regulation of policy forms is another important area of insurance regulation. Because insurance contracts are technical and complex, the state insurance commissioner has the authority to approve or disapprove new policy forms before the contracts are sold to the public. The purpose is to protect the public from misleading, deceptive, and unfair provisions.

Sales Practices and Consumer Protection

The sales practices of insurers are regulated by laws concerning the licensing of agents and brokers, and by laws prohibiting twisting, rebating, and unfair trade practices.

Licensing of Agents and Brokers   All states require agents and brokers to be licensed. Depending on the type of insurance sold, applicants must pass one or more written examinations. The purpose is to ensure that agents have knowledge of the state insurance laws and the contracts they intend to sell. If the agent is incompetent or dishonest, the state insurance commissioner has the authority to suspend or revoke the agent's license.

All states have legislation requiring the continuing education of agents. The continuing education requirements are designed to upgrade an agent's knowledge and skills.

Unfair Trade Practices   Insurance laws prohibit a wide variety of *unfair trade practices,* including misrepresentation, twisting, rebating, deceptive or false advertising, inequitable claim settlement, and unfair discrimination. The state insurance commissioner has the legal authority to stop insurers from engaging in unfair trade practices and deceptive advertising. Insurers can be fined, an injunction can be obtained, or, in serious cases, the insurer's license can be suspended or revoked.

Twisting   All states forbid twisting. **Twisting** *is the inducement of a policyowner to drop an existing policy and replace it with a new one that provides little or no economic benefit to the client.* Twisting laws apply largely to life insurance policies; the objective here is to prevent policyowners from being financially harmed by replacing one life insurance policy with another.

All states have replacement regulations so that policyowners can make an informed decision concerning the replacement of an existing life insurance policy. These laws are based on the premise that replacement of an existing life insurance policy generally is not in the policyowner's best interest. For example, a new front-end load for commissions and expenses must be paid; a new incontestable clause and suicide clause must be satisfied; and higher premiums based on the policyowner's higher attained age may have to be paid. *In some cases, however, switching policies can be financially justified.* However, deceptive sales practices by some agents of certain insurers have resulted in the replacement of life insurance policies that were financially harmful to the policyowners.

Rebating   The vast majority of states forbid rebating. **Rebating** *is giving an individual a premium reduction or some other financial advantage not stated in the policy as an inducement to purchase the policy.* One obvious example is a partial refund of the agent's commission to the policyowner. The basic purpose of antirebate laws is to ensure fair and equitable treatment of all policyowners by preventing

one insured from obtaining an unfair price advantage over another.

Consumer groups, however, believe that antirebating laws are harmful to consumers. Critics argue that (1) rebating will increase price competition and lower insurance rates; (2) present antirebating laws protect the incomes of agents rather than consumers; and (3) insurance purchasers are denied the right to negotiate price with insurance agents.

Complaint Division   State insurance departments typically have a complaint division or department for handling consumer complaints. The department will investigate the complaint and try to obtain a response from the alleged offending insurer or agency. Most consumer complaints involve claims. An insurer may refuse to pay a claim, or it may dispute the amount payable. Although state insurance departments respond to individual complaints, the departments generally lack direct authority to order insurers to pay disputed claims where factual questions are an issue. *However, you should phone or write your state insurance department if you feel you are being treated unfairly by your insurer or agent.* This is especially true for auto insurance disputes where certain insurers have significantly higher complaint ratios than others. For example, see Insight 8.1 for a discussion of the ranking of auto insurers in New York based on complaint ratios.

Publications and Brochures.   State insurance departments typically provide a wide variety of publications and brochures for consumers. The publications are also available on the insurance department's Web site. The publications provide considerable information on life, health, auto, homeowners, and long-term care insurance, and other insurance products as well. Many states also publish rate information on auto and homeowners insurance on the Internet so that consumers can make meaningful cost comparisons.

Taxation of Insurers

Insurers pay numerous local, state, and federal taxes. Two important taxes are the federal income tax and the state premium tax. Insurers pay federal income taxes based on complex formulas and rules established by federal legislation and the Internal Revenue Service. The states also require insurers to pay a premium tax on gross premiums received from policy-owners, such as 2 percent of the premium paid.

The primary purpose of the premium tax is to raise revenues for the states, not to provide funds for insurance regulation. Many state insurance depart-ments are underfunded and receive only a small fraction of the premium taxes collected. Critics of state regulation argue that if state regulation is to become more effective, more money must be devoted to insurance regulation.

INSIGHT 8.1

2005 Annual Ranking of Automobile Insurance Complaints in New York State (based on 2004 data)

The New York State Insurance Department makes available annual rankings of auto insurers doing business in New York. The rankings shown here are based on the complaint ratios of 48 insurance companies or groups of companies. The ratios are based on calendar year 2004 data.

The *complaint ratio* represents the number of private passenger auto insurance complaints upheld against an insurer in 2004, as a percentage of the insurer's average 2003–2004 private passenger auto insurance premiums in New York State. Insurers with the fewest upheld complaints per million dollars of premiums appear at the top of the list. *The best insurer with the lowest ratio is ranked first in the report; the worst insurer with the highest ratio is ranked last. The lower the ratio, the better is the insurer's performance. Insurers with the lowest and highest ratios for 2004 are shown below.* Data for 2002 and 2003 are shown for comparison purposes.

Lowest Complaint Ratios—Top 25

Company or Group	Complaint Ratio	Current Ranking*	2003 Ranking	2002 Ranking
American Modern	0.00	1	7	18
Electric	0.00	2	8	2
Amica	0.03	3	1	3
Amex Assurance	0.04	4	22	28
Preferred Mutual	0.04	5	4	7
USAA	0.06	6	2	4
National Grange	0.06	7	14	15
Harleysville	0.06	8	10	36
Country-Wide	0.06	9	25	37
Unitrin	0.07	10	17	26
Chubb	0.07	11	16	9
Response	0.08	12	11	10
Allianz	0.09	13	37	17
Eveready	0.09	14	13	43
Utica National	0.10	15	21	25
Progressive	0.10	16	19	22
Merchants Mutual	0.11	17	18	8
Central Services**	0.11	18	12	6
Fairfax Financial	0.11	19	43	***
State Farm	0.11	20	15	20
St. Paul Travelers	0.12	21	27	19
Nationwide	0.13	22	26	23
Liberty Mutual	0.13	23	20	31
Erie	0.13	24	3	5
Farm Family Casualty	0.14	25	29	32

*   Based on calendar year 2004 complaint data.

** In this report, the Central Services Group will be referred to as New York Central Mutual Fire Insurance Co. New York Central Mutual Fire writes over 99% of the group's private passenger auto business.

*** Insurer not ranked in that year due to low premium volume

INSIGHT 8.1 (continued)

2005 Annual Ranking of Automobile Insurance Complaints in New York State (based on 2004 data)

Worst Performers—Prior-Year Complaint Rankings of Bottom 10 New York State Private Passenger Auto Insurers

Company or Group	Complaint Ratio	Current Ranking*	2003 Ranking	2002 Ranking
Mercury Casualty	0.37	39	42	**
Lumbermens	0.39	40	41	27
White Mountains	0.45	41	36	16
Clarendon	0.65	42	46	50
Safeco	0.67	43	44	38
Tri-State Consumer	0.84	44	35	33
American Financial***	1.66	45	45	46
Long Island Insurance Co.	2.59	46	**	**
Infinity***	2.99	47	47	46
Empire Insurance Co.	6.45	48	49	49

*   Based on calendar year 2004 data.
**   Insurer not ranked in that year due to low premium volume
*** In 2003, some companies that were in the American Financial group in 2002 became part of the Infinity group, while
     others remained with the American Financial group. As a result, both American Financial and the Infinity group are ranked
     46th for 2002 in the above table.

Complaint Ratios of 10 Largest Private Passenger Auto Insurers New York State, 2004

Company or Group	Complaint Ratio	Current Ranking*	2003–2004 Average Premiums (in millions)	Market Share
Allstate	0.20	30	$1,784.5	16.7%
Berkshire-Hathaway (GEICO)	0.24	34	1,689.7	15.8
State Farm	0.11	20	1,288.9	12.1
Progressive	0.10	16	784.1	7.3
St. Paul Travelers	0.12	21	637.2	6.0
Liberty Mutual	0.13	23	613.1	5.7
AIG	0.22	33	386.8	3.6
New York Central Mutual**	0.11	18	374.1	3.5
Nationwide	0.13	22	319.9	3.0
White Mountains	0.45	41	315.6	3.0
Top 10			**$8,193.9**	**76.7%**
Total (all companies, incl. those with less than $10 million in premiums)			**$10,678.4**	**100.0%**

*   Based on calendar year 2004 data.
** a.k.a. Central Services Group.

SOURCE: Adapted from New York State Insurance Department, *2005 Annual Ranking of Automobile Insurance Complaints,* December 2005.

Most states also have **retaliatory tax laws** that affect premium taxes and other taxes. For example, assume that the premium tax is 2 percent in Nebraska and 3 percent in Iowa. If insurers domiciled in Nebraska are required to pay a 3 percent premium tax on business written in Iowa, then domestic insurers in Iowa doing business in Nebraska must also pay a 3 percent tax on business written in Nebraska even though Nebraska's rate is 2 percent. The purpose of a retaliatory tax law is to protect domestic insurers in the state from excessive taxation by other states where they do business.

STATE VERSUS FEDERAL REGULATION

Critics of state regulation argue that the McCarran-Ferguson Act should be repealed and replaced by federal regulation. Certain advantages are claimed for federal regulation.

Advantages of Federal Regulation

The following arguments are offered in support of federal regulation of insurance:

- *Uniformity of laws.* Federal regulation can provide greater uniformity of laws. Under state regulation, insurers doing business in more than one state must observe different state laws. Under federal regulation, the laws would be uniform.
- *Greater efficiency.* It is argued that federal regulation would be more efficient. Insurers doing business nationally would deal with only one federal agency rather than with numerous insurance departments. Also, the federal agency would be less likely to yield to industry pressures, especially those reflecting the views of local insurers. Federal regulation would also be less expensive to administer.
- *More competent regulators.* Federal regulation would attract higher-quality personnel who would do a superior job of regulating the insurance industry. The higher salaries and prestige would attract more highly talented and skilled individuals.

Advantages of State Regulation

Supporters of state regulation also offer convincing arguments for continued regulation of insurance by the states. The major advantages claimed for state regulation are as follows:

- *Greater responsiveness to local needs.* Local needs vary widely and state regulators can respond more quickly to local needs. In contrast, under federal regulation, "red tape" and government bureaucracy would result in considerable delay in solving problems at the local level.

- *Promotion of uniform laws by NAIC.* Proponents of state regulation argue that uniformity of laws can be achieved by the model laws and proposals of the NAIC. The NAIC also has a plan that puts the states on a time deadline to modernize state regulation. The states would have to meet certain modernization goals that cover market regulation, consumer protection, producer licensing, company licensing, and solvency regulation by certain specified dates.
- *Greater opportunity for innovation.* State regulation provides greater opportunities for innovation in regulation. An individual state can experiment, and if the innovation fails, only that state is affected. In contrast, poor federal legislation would affect all states.
- *Unknown consequences of federal regulation.* State regulation is already in existence, and its strengths and weaknesses are well known. In contrast, the consequences of federal regulation on consumers and the insurance industry are unknown.
- *Decentralization of political power.* State regulation results in a decentralization of political power. Federal regulation would result in further encroachment of the federal government on the economy and a corresponding dilution of states' rights.

Shortcomings of State Regulation

Congressional committees and the Government Accountability Office (GAO) have assessed the effectiveness of state regulation of insurance and have found serious shortcomings, including the following:

- *Inadequate protection against insolvency.* The insurance industry operates globally. Existing state regulation is considered inadequate for ensuring the solvency of insurers because many insurers depend on offshore companies to pay claims. Some reinsurers have refused to pay claims, and some offshore insurers have failed. Critics claim that state insurance departments do not have sufficient financial resources, legal authority, or determination to protect policyowners from mismanagement and fraud by some insurers here and abroad.

In addition, critics maintain that some property and casualty insurers have been licensed to do business when they were undercapitalized, and that state insurance departments have not carefully checked the background or monitored the activities of key executives who manage the companies. As a result, some insurers have become insolvent.

■ *Inadequate protection of consumers.* Critics argue that state insurance departments do not have systematic procedures for determining whether consumers are being treated properly with respect to claim payments, rate setting, and protection from unfair discrimination.

■ *Improvements needed in handling complaints.* Although many states prepare complaint ratios (ratio of complaints to premiums) for each company, the information may not be readily shared with the public.

■ *Inadequate market conduct examinations.* Market conduct examinations refer to insurance department examinations of consumer matters such as claims handling, underwriting, complaints, advertising, and other trade practices. Serious deficiencies have been found in many market conduct examination reports.

■ *Insurance availability.* Many states have not conducted current studies to determine whether property and liability insurance availability is a serious problem in their states.

■ *Regulators may be overly responsive to insurance industry.* State insurance departments are overly responsive to the insurance industry at the expense of consumers. Insurance regulation is not characterized by an "arm's-length" relationship between regulators and the regulated. Many state insurance commissioners were previously employed in the insurance industry, and many return to the industry after leaving office.

Repeal of the McCarran-Ferguson Act

As noted earlier, the McCarran-Ferguson Act gives the states primary responsibility for regulation of the insurance industry and also provides limited exemption from federal antitrust laws. Because of the shortcomings of state regulation, there is considerable public and political support for repeal of the McCarran-Ferguson Act.

Critics of state regulation present several arguments for repeal of the McCarran-Ferguson Act. They include the following:

■ *The insurance industry no longer needs broad antitrust exemption.* Critics argue that the "state action doctrine" has been fully developed and clarified by the Supreme Court. The state action doctrine defines certain activities required by state law that are exempt from federal antitrust activities. Because permissible actions of insurers have been clarified, exemption from the antitrust laws is no longer needed. In addition, it is argued that other industries are not exempt from antitrust laws, and the same should also be true for insurers.

■ *Federal regulation is needed because of the defects in state regulation.* Critics argue that federal minimum standards are needed to ensure nondiscrimination in insurance pricing, full availability of essential property and liability coverages, and elimination of unfair and excessive rate differentials among insureds.

However, many insurers and industry groups believe that repeal of the McCarran-Ferguson Act would be harmful to both the insurance industry and the public. They present the following arguments in support of their position:

■ *The insurance industry is already competitive.* More than 2700 property and casualty insurers and more than 1100 life insurers now compete for business.

■ *Small insurers would be harmed.* Smaller insurers would be unable to compete because they cannot develop accurate rates based on their limited loss and expense experience. Thus, smaller insurers may go out of business or be taken over by larger insurers. Hence a small number of large insurers will ultimately control the business, a result exactly opposite of that intended by repeal of the McCarran-Ferguson Act.

■ *Insurers may be prevented from developing common coverage forms.* This problem could lead to costly gaps in coverage for insurance buyers and increased litigation between insurers and policyowners. Also, it would be difficult for insureds to know what is covered and excluded if nonstandard forms are used.

- *Dual regulation may result from repeal of the McCarran-Ferguson Act.* However, the past record of federal regulation is poor. Federal regulators have done a poor job in regulating the savings and loan industry, which resulted in the insolvency of hundreds of thrifts with a cost to taxpayers of billions of dollars. Also, critics argue that federal regulation of railroads, airlines, and trucking has been destructive to competition. Federal regulation has also obstructed entry into an industry, entrenched the market power of large companies, and resulted in a cozy relationship between the regulators and the regulated.

CURRENT PROBLEMS AND ISSUES IN INSURANCE REGULATION

State insurance regulators face numerous problems and issues. Some timely issues include the following:

- Bid-rigging by brokerage firms
- Questionable accounting practices
- Unauthorized entities selling insurance
- Modernizing insurance regulation
- Insolvency of insurers
- Credit-based insurance scores

Bid-Rigging by Brokerage Firms

Brokers represent insureds who generally are corporations. Brokers have a fiduciary responsibility to place the business with reputable insurers that operate in their client's best interest. *However, in recent years, some large brokerage firms have engaged in illegal bid-rigging schemes involving contingent commissions that have been financially harmful to their clients.* Brokers receive commissions from insurers for the business placed with them. Some agents and brokers also receive contingent commissions based on premium volume, loss ratios, and other factors. Insurers pay contingent commissions to encourage agents and brokers to place the business with them. Thus, a broker has a strong financial incentive to place the business with the insurer that pays the highest contingent commission. In 2004, the attorney general of New York filed a civil complaint against

Marsh, Inc.—the world's largest risk management and insurance brokerage firm—and accused the firm of manipulating the insurance markets by rigged bids, false bids, price-fixing, and pressure tactics. Marsh was accused of increasing its contingent commission income by steering corporate clients to favored insurance companies that paid high contingent commissions. As a result, clients paid more for their insurance than was necessary. *Numerous large insurers also participated in the bid-rigging scheme,* which included the American International Group (AIG), ACE Ltd., Hartford, Munich American Risk Partners, and Universal Life Resources (ULR). Other brokerage firms, including AON, also engaged in illegal bid-rigging arrangements.

As a result of the civil complaint, Marsh discontinued the practice of receiving contingent commissions; greater transparency concerning commissions and sources of revenue are provided to clients; and several key executives resigned. The company also paid a large fine, which will be used to reimburse insureds. Because of the adverse publicity, large brokerage firms generally have discontinued the practice of receiving contingent commissions and are seeking other sources of income to make up for the lost revenue.

Questionable Accounting Practices

In recent years, some insurers have engaged in questionable accounting practices that make their accounting statements and operating income appear better than is actually the case. Detecting questionable accounting practices by insurers is a challenging problem for regulators. Because of limited staff and financial resources, it is often difficult for regulators to investigate and closely monitor the daily accounting transactions of insurers.

One example of a questionable accounting practice is the improper recording of transactions involving finite reinsurance. **Finite reinsurance** (also called **finite risk insurance**) is a complex reinsurance contract that transfers a limited amount of insurance risk to the reinsurer; total premiums paid to the reinsurer are very large and are close to the maximum coverage provided; potential claims are covered for a limited period, such as three years; and in many cases, the loss has already occurred, but its ultimate cost may not be known for some time (such as long-tail medical malpractice claims). Because total premiums are so large, the insurer or corporate client bears nearly all of the costs of a catastrophic loss. However, by spreading the premiums over several years, the insurer or client avoids taking a large financial hit immediately. Instead, the loss payments can be smoothed over a period of years, which reduces the variability in reported earnings and improves the insurer's apparent operating results.

In addition, in cases where liability losses have already occurred but will not be settled for some time in the future (such as asbestos liability claims), finite reinsurance allows the corporate client or insurer to take the liability off its books and improve its reported income.

The controversial problem in finite reinsurance is how to account for the transactions.[6] Unless a material amount of insurance risk is transferred, the transaction should not be booked as insurance but should be treated as a loan. The industry has adopted a rough rule of thumb; to be considered insurance, there must be at least a 10 percent chance of a 10 percent loss in the policy amount. Otherwise, the transaction is considered a loan, and the accounting is different. In one controversial case, the transaction was reversed; that is, the reinsurer transferred claims to the primary insurer to help the insurer increase its loss reserves. The American International Group (AIG) agreed to take over the obligation to pay up to $500 million in claims that General Re had already incurred. General Re is a reinsurer owned by Berkshire Hathaway. General Re paid AIG some $500 million in premiums paid by clients. In addition, AIG paid General Re a 5 million dollar fee for moving the liabilities to AIG's books. Although AIG seemed to be losing money, it booked the transaction as a $500 million increase in revenue and used that amount to increase its loss reserves to satisfy stockholders who believed that loss reserves were deficient. If the transaction were recorded as a loan, however, the $500 million in premiums could not be counted as additional reserves. In reality, the deal was an accounting gimmick that made the loss reserves of AIG appear larger than they actually were. In the eyes of federal officials, the transactions were designed to deceive regulators, stock analysts, and shareholders. Other questionable AIG accounting transactions forced the insurer to restate its earnings and reduce stockholders' equity, which caused

the price of its common stock to plummet. Finally, at the time of this writing, five former senior executives of Gen Re and AIG have been indicted in a criminal action by the Securities and Exchange Commission for sham reinsurance transactions and violation of federal securities laws; the executives have entered not-guilty pleas.

Because of recent abuses of finite reinsurance by several large insurers where little or no risk was transferred but the insurer's income was improved, the NAIC now requires greater disclosure of finite reinsurance contracts in the Annual Statement Blank that insurers must file with the state insurance department. The disclosures adopted for the 2005 annual statement require property and casualty insurers to report the contract terms and management objectives of finite reinsurance contracts in their annual financial statement. The CEO or CFO must also sign a statement that risk transfer has occurred and that there are no side agreements.[7] As such, state officials should be able to monitor finite reinsurance contracts more closely.

Unauthorized Entities Selling Insurance

Another serious regulatory problem is the sale of insurance by unauthorized entities (also called bogus entities or scams). *An unauthorized entity is an unlicensed insurer or bogus insurer not authorized by the state insurance department to sell insurance in the state.* In particular, the sale of health insurance by unauthorized entities to smaller employers is a serious problem. In their quest to purchase affordable health insurance, many smaller employers and individuals have purchased health insurance coverages from certain entities not authorized by state insurance departments to sell this coverage. *Although employers and individuals paid premiums, some or all of their claims were not paid.* A U.S. Government Accountability Office study identified 144 unauthorized entities that sold health insurance coverages in the states from 2000 through 2002. The unauthorized entities covered at least 15,000 employers and more than 250,000 policyowners, and at least $252 million in claims were not paid. At the time of the GAO survey in 2003, only 21 percent of the unpaid claims had been recovered.[8]

A typical scam involves recruitment of local insurance agents to sell health insurance. The health coverage is not approved by the state insurance department. The agents are told that the entity is regulated by federal law, not state law. In fact, the entity is operating illegally. Coverage is usually offered to applicants regardless of their health condition and at substantially lower premiums and better benefits than health plans sold by licensed insurers. Some scams involve the promotion of discount health cards as insurance. Although claims may be paid initially, the scam soon results in delayed payments and excuses for not paying. The result is that unsuspecting consumers and employers who thought they had coverage were personally liable for huge medical bills. Health-care providers also lost a considerable amount of money because of unpaid claims.

Regulators are responding to the problem in several ways. State officials issue cease-and-desist orders to stop the activities of unauthorized entities; state insurance departments issue public service announcements to television stations and the local news media to alert consumers and employers about bogus insurers; agents are fined for representing unauthorized entities; and the NAIC has created a special Web site (InsureUonline.org) that provides consumer information and links to state insurance departments and the NAIC complaint database.

Modernizing Insurance Regulation

Another important issue is the modernization of insurance regulation. As stated earlier, the insurance industry is regulated primarily by the states. Many critics believe the present system is cumbersome, unduly complex, costly, and anticompetitive, with considerable overlap and duplication. According to the American Council of Life Insurers (ACLI), to compete nationally, insurers must be licensed in all 50 states; obtain 50 separate regulatory approvals for each new product introduced; undergo annually more than 50 separate market-conduct examinations; and comply with 50 different sets of laws, rules, and administrative regulations.[9] Thus, the industry is in need of dire reform.

A number of reform proposals have been introduced by various groups. It is beyond the scope of the text to discuss each proposal in detail. Only two of them are discussed here: (1) an optional federal charter, and (2) the SMART Act.

Optional Federal Charter   The American Council of Life Insurers (ACLI) has proposed an optional federal charter for life insurers as an alternative to the present system. Under the proposal, life insurers would have the option of obtaining either a federal or state charter, depending on the insurer's specific needs and geographic scope of operations. Small local insurers may opt for a state charter, while large national insurers may prefer a federal charter. A major argument for a federal charter is that many new life insurance products sold today are investment products, and that life insurers are at a competitive disadvantage when they compete nationally with commercial banks and stock brokerage firms. Approval of new life insurance products may take as long as two years because of differences and inconsistencies in 50 state laws. In contrast, national commercial banks and stock brokerage firms can often develop and market new products in a shorter period. It is argued that a federal charter would enable large life insurers to speed up the development and approval of new products and make insurers more competitive at the national level.

Most industry trade associations and producer groups strongly oppose the ACLI proposal. Critics present two major arguments against a federal charter. First, there will be a dual system of insurance regulation, which will substantially increase the cost of insurance regulation. There will be at least two separate regulatory systems in each state—the present state system and a new federal system. The cost of regulation will increase because thousands of new federal employees must be hired; a mandatory federal charter may result in the loss of premium taxes to the states; and taxpayers and policyowners will have to pay more because of an additional layer of federal regulation.

Second, a new federal regulator would have the power to preempt state laws and may disagree with existing state laws that now affect policyowners and claimants under the present system. There are inconsistencies and differences in 50 state laws, which would make federal regulation difficult. Dual regulation may result in regulatory overlaps and confusion among policyowners and insurers as to which law should apply.

In addition, some consumer advocates believe that greater regulation of cash value products is needed at the state level to protect consumers, and that a federal charter may result in a "race to the bottom" to lower consumer protection standards if an insurer is chartered at the federal level.

In early 2006, a proposal for a federal charter was introduced in Congress (National Insurance Act of 2006, S. 2509). The bill would allow both insurers and producers to choose between regulation by state insurance departments or by a federal Office of National Insurance.

The SMART Act The SMART Act is another approach to insurance regulation. In 2004, Rep. Michael Oxley (R-OH) and Rep. Richard Baker (R-LA) released a draft of the State Modernization and Regulatory Transparency Act (SMART).[10] The proposed legislation addressed fifteen regulatory areas, including licensing, market conduct of insurers, life and health insurance, property/casualty insurance, and numerous other areas. The states would be required to comply with uniform standards, speed up the marketing of new products, and move toward a system of market-based rates. All states would be required to adopt flex rating, which allows insurers to increase rates if kept within a certain percentage range for the year. The licensing of insurers would be simplified by a single point-of-entry system; an insurer licensed to do business and in good standing in a model state could submit a uniform application to do business in other states as well. In addition, the states would develop standards and procedures for regulating the market conduct of insurers. Finally, a federal regulator would not monitor compliance with the law. Instead, a seven-member panel consisting of insurance commissioners and appointees from federal agencies would monitor the industry. However, because the panel would have no regulatory authority, federal courts would enforce compliance with the law.

The SMART Act is controversial. The National Association of Insurance Commissioners opposed the plan because of the federal preemption of state laws, federal supervision of state regulation, and complete rate deregulation for all states. The Consumer Federation of America also opposed the plan because there would be unprecedented federal intrusion into state insurance regulation, and millions of insurance consumers would be vulnerable to price gouging and abusive rating practices by insurers.

EXHIBIT 8.1
Insurance Company Insolvencies 1991–2004

Year	NAIC (Property/Casualty)	A. M. Best Co. (Property/Casualty)	NAIC (Life/Health)
1991	19	46	25
1992	29	56	12
1993	15	43	11
1994	11	31	8
1995	4	15	2
1996	6	11	4
1997	14 (13)*	34	4 (1)*
1998	4 (5)	18	2 (4)
1999	3 (3)	7	7 (4)
2000	9 (9)	30	4 (6)
2001	17 (7)	30	0 (3)
2002	12 (9)	38	1 (1)
2003	23 (6)**	—	(4)
2004 to March	18 (2)**	—	11 (2)
Total	238	359	116

* Single state insurers are in parentheses.
**Includes some insolvencies where single or multiple state is not identified.
SOURCE: Insurance Information Institute, "Insolvencies/Guaranty Funds," *Hot Topics & Insurance Issues,* April 2004. This source is periodically updated.

Insolvency of Insurers

Insolvency of insurers continues to be an important regulatory problem. According to the National Association of Insurance Commissioners (NAIC), 238 property and casualty insurers and 116 life and health insurers became insolvent between 1991 through March 2004 (see Exhibit 8.1). Insolvency numbers for property and casualty insurers by the A. M. Best Company are higher because it counts each company in a group separately.

More recently, despite Hurricane Katrina and other hurricanes in 2005, the number of property and casualty insurers that experience insolvency is relatively small. According to a Standard & Poor's report, the number of insolvent property and casualty insurers decreased from 13 in 2004 to 10 in 2005.[11]

Reasons for Insolvencies Insurers fail for several reasons. Major causes of failure include inadequate reserves for claims, inadequate rates, rapid growth and inadequate surplus, problems with affiliates, overstatement of assets, alleged fraud, failure of reinsurers to pay claims, mismanagement, and catastrophe losses.

When an insurer becomes insolvent or financially impaired, state regulators must take appropriate action. With proper management, the insurer may be rehabilitated. If rehabilitation is not feasible, the insurer may be involuntarily liquidated or acquired by a healthy insurer. Other possible regulatory actions include license revocation, cease-and-desist orders, and other actions that restrict an insurer's freedom to do business.

What happens to your policy or unpaid claim if your insurer becomes insolvent? Your policy may be sold to another insurer, and an unpaid claim may be paid by the state's guaranty fund. However, failure of a large insurer may result in delay of several years before all claims are paid, and claims may not be paid in full.

Methods of Ensuring Solvency   The principal methods of ensuring solvency are the following:

- *Financial requirements.* Insurers must meet certain financial requirements that vary among the states, such as minimum capital and surplus requirements, restrictions on investments, and valuation of loss reserves.
- *Risk-based capital standards.* As noted earlier, insurers must meet the risk-based capital standards based on a model law developed by the NAIC. The increased capital requirements help to prevent insolvency.
- *Annual financial statements.* Certain annual financial statements must be submitted to state insurance departments in a prescribed manner to provide information on premiums written, expenses, losses, investments, and other information. The financial statements are then reviewed by regulatory officials.
- *Field examinations.* State laws require that insurers generally must be examined every three to five years. The NAIC coordinates the examination of insurers that do business in several states.
- *Early warning system.* The NAIC administers an early warning system called the Insurance Regulatory Information System (IRIS). Financial ratios and other reports are developed based on

information in the annual statement. Based on a review of this information, insurers may be designated for immediate review or targeted for regulatory attention. The system, however, is not perfect. The financial ratios may not identify all troubled insurers. The system also has identified an increasing number of insurers, some of which do not require immediate regulatory attention.
- *FAST system.* The NAIC employs a solvency screening system called FAST (Financial Analysis Solvency Tracking) that prioritizes insurers for additional analysis. Different point values are assigned for the various ranges of financial ratio results. The points are then summed to determine a FAST score for each insurer. Based on their FAST scores, certain insurers are considered a priority for regulatory action.

Credit-Based Insurance Scores

Credit-based insurance scores are another important regulatory issue. An increasing number of insurers in auto and homeowners insurance are now using an applicant's credit record for purposes of underwriting and rating. The insurance score is derived from the applicant's credit history and is combined with other factors. Depending on the insurance score, the applicant may be denied insurance or placed in a higher rating class.

Insurance scoring based on the applicant's credit record is controversial. Proponents offer the following arguments:

- *There is a high correlation between an applicant's credit record and future claims experience.* Applicants with poor or marginal credit records are more likely to submit more auto or homeowners claims than applicants with good or superior credit records. Credit data enhance the ability of insurers to predict future claims experience with greater accuracy.
- *Insurers claim that underwriting and rating can be more objective and consistent.* Subjectivity and human bias in underwriting can be removed by automated underwriting based on objective insurance scores.
- *Most consumers have good credit records and benefit from credit scoring.* Consumers with

good credit records may qualify for lower rates or obtain coverage that might otherwise have been difficult to obtain.

Critics of insurance scores, however, present the following counterarguments:

- *The use of credit data in underwriting or rating discriminates against certain groups.* These groups include low-income people who are unable to obtain credit, the unemployed who fall behind in paying their bills, the sick and disabled who are late with their monthly credit card payments, and female-headed families with children who do not receive child-support payments, or the payments are late. In addition, the system discriminates against applicants for insurance who do not use credit but pay cash for their purchases.

  In rebuttal, proponents claim that credit-based insurance scores do not discriminate against certain groups because insurers do not use income, race, or ethnic background in the underwriting process. A Texas Department of Insurance study found that a strong relationship exists between credit scores and claims experience, and that there is no evidence of any disparate or unequal impact on any minority or socioeconomic group because income, race, or ethnic background are not considered in the underwriting process. As such, all identically situated individuals, regard-

less of differences in income, race, or ethnic background, would be charged exactly the same amount for auto or homeowners insurance under a rating plan that permits the use of credit data in personal lines underwriting.[12]
- *Credit reports are often wrong or contain errors that can harm insurance applicants.* Also, identity theft has increased, which could harm the ability of innocent victims to obtain insurance on favorable terms.
- *Insurance scoring is socially unacceptable.* An applicant for life insurance, for example, cannot be denied life insurance or charged higher premiums solely because of race. Some critics believe that the same argument should be applied to the use of credit records in underwriting.

To protect consumers, most states have enacted legislation that regulates the use of credit-based insurance scores. Typical laws require insurers to file an underwriting model that includes insurance scores with the state insurance department; the number of factors that can be used to calculate an insurance score may be limited; insurers are prohibited from penalizing consumers who do not use credit or have no credit history; insurers are usually prohibited from using insurance scores as the sole determinant in underwriting and rating; and insurers must inform consumers if credit information is used in underwriting or rating.[13]

CASE APPLICATION

Ashley is an actuary who is employed by the Nebraska Department of Insurance. Her duties include monitoring the financial position of insurance companies doing business in Nebraska. Based on an analysis of annual financial statements that insurers are required to submit, she discovered that Mutual Life Insurance has a risk-based capital ratio of 175 percent. Based on this information, answer the following questions.

a. What is the purpose of requiring insurers to meet risk-based capital requirements?
b. What regulatory action, if any, should the Nebraska Department of Insurance take with respect to Mutual Life Insurance?

c. Would your answer to part (b) change if the risk-based capital ratio for Mutual Life Insurance fell to 65 percent? Explain your answer.
d. Mutual Life Insurance has 25 percent of its assets invested in common stocks. Assume the stocks are sold, and the proceeds are invested in U.S. government bonds. What effect, if any, will this investment change have on the risk-based capital ratio of Mutual Life Insurance? Explain your answer.

SUMMARY

- The insurance industry is regulated for several reasons:

  To maintain insurer solvency

  To compensate for inadequate consumer knowledge

  To ensure reasonable rates

  To make insurance available

- The insurance industry is regulated primarily by the states. The McCarran-Ferguson Act states that continued regulation and taxation of the insurance industry by the states are in the public interest.

- Three principal methods are used to regulate the insurance industry:

  Legislation

  Courts

  State insurance departments

- The principal areas that are regulated include the following:

  Formation and licensing of insurers

  Solvency regulation

  Rate regulation

  Policy forms

  Sales practices and consumer protection

- Property and casualty insurance rates must be adequate, reasonable (not excessive), and not unfairly discriminatory. The principal types of rating laws are as follows:

  Prior-approval law

  Modified prior-approval law

  File-and-use law

  Use-and-file law

  Flex-rating law

  State-made rates

  Open competition

- Insurers must pay a state premium tax on gross premiums. The primary purpose is to raise revenues for the state, not to provide funds for insurance regulation.

- State versus federal regulation is an issue that has evoked considerable debate. The alleged advantages of federal regulation include the following:

  Uniformity of laws

  Greater efficiency

  More competent regulation

- The advantages of state regulation include the following:

  Greater responsiveness to local needs

  Promotion of uniform laws by the NAIC

  Greater opportunity for innovation

  Unknown consequences of federal regulation

  Decentralization of political power

- Critics argue that state regulation of insurance has serious shortcomings, including the following:

  Inadequate protection against insolvency

  Inadequate protection of consumers

  Improvements needed in handling complaints

  Inadequate market conduct examinations

  Insurance availability studies conducted only in a minority of states

  Regulators overly responsive to the insurance industry

- Several current issues in insurance regulation include the following:

  Bid-rigging by brokerage firms

  Questionable accounting practices

  Unauthorized entities selling insurance

  Modernizing insurance regulation

  Insolvency of insurers

  Credit-based insurance scores

KEY CONCEPTS AND TERMS

Admitted assets
Alien insurer
Assessment method
Credit-based insurance score
Domestic insurer
File-and-use law
Flex-rating law
Financial Modernization Act of 1999
Foreign insurer
Guaranty funds
McCarran-Ferguson Act
Modified prior-approval law
National Association of Insurance Commissioners (NAIC)
Open competition
Paul v. Virginia
Policyowners' surplus
Prior-approval law
Rebating
Reserves
Retaliatory tax laws
Risk-based capital (RBC)
South-Eastern Underwriters Association (SEUA)
Twisting
Use-and-file law

REVIEW QUESTIONS

1. Explain the reasons why the insurance industry is regulated.

2. Briefly explain the significance of the following legal cases and legislative acts with respect to insurance company regulation:
   a. *Paul v. Virginia*
   b. South-Eastern Underwriters Association Case
   c. McCarran-Ferguson Act
   d. Financial Modernization Act of 1999

3. Explain the principal methods for regulating insurance companies.

4. Identify the principal areas of insurance company operations that are regulated by the states.

5. Briefly describe the major types of rating laws.

6. Explain the following actions by agents that are prohibited by state law:
   a. Twisting
   b. Rebating

7. a. Explain the major arguments for federal regulation of the insurance industry.
   b. Explain the major arguments in support of state regulation of the insurance industry.
   c. Describe the shortcomings of state regulation.

8. a. Explain the major arguments for repeal of the McCarran-Ferguson Act.
   b. Explain the major arguments against repeal of the McCarran-Ferguson Act.

9. Identify the major techniques that regulators use to monitor insurance company solvency.

10. Describe the risk-based capital standards that insurers must meet.

APPLICATION QUESTIONS

1. The Financial Services Company is a large life insurer that sells annuity products to retired people. Company actuaries have designed a new annuity contract that combines lifetime annuity benefits with long-term care in a skilled nursing home. Financial Services wants to market the new annuity nationally in all 50 states. The company faces competition from a national commercial bank that is trying to sell a similar product to Social Security beneficiaries. The CEO of Financial Services believes that the new annuity product could be marketed more efficiently if the company had a fed-

eral charter. Several members of the board of directors, however, believe that a federal charter would be undesirable.
   a. What major regulatory obstacle does Financial Services face in trying to market the new annuity product in each state under the present system of state regulation?
   b. Assume that Financial Services has the option of obtaining a federal charter. Explain the advantages, if any, of a federal charter to Financial Services in their efforts to market the new annuity product.
   c. Explain the major arguments against federal charters.

2. Opal, age 75, has a $100,000 ordinary life insurance policy that has a cash value of $35,000. Opal is concerned about the cost of long-term care in a nursing home. A new agent of a national life insurer persuaded her to transfer the $35,000 into a deferred annuity. The agent told Opal that the annuity pays lifetime income benefits and also allows her to withdraw the $35,000 without penalty if she should enter a nursing home. After the policy was issued, Opal had ten days to change her mind. During the free-look period, a friend of Opal examined the policy. Analysis of the policy showed that only 10 percent of the cash value could be withdrawn each year without penalty. A 7 percent surrender charge would apply to any excess amounts withdrawn. In addition, the income payments were scheduled to start in 10 years when Opal attained age 85. Opal filed a complaint against the agent with the state insurance department. An investigation revealed that the agent had made similar misrepresentations to other clients.
   a. Based on the above facts, identify the illegal practice in which the agent engaged.
   b. What action can the state insurance department take against the dishonest agent?
   c. What action can the state insurance department take against the life insurer?

3. Although domiciled in Nebraska, Auto Insurance is licensed to sell auto insurance in 10 states. A different set of rates applies to each state. In five states, prior approval of rates is required. Two states have a file-and-use law, and the remaining three states have a flex-rating law. Auto Insurance has experienced poor underwriting results and needs to increase its rates.
   a. Explain how each of the above rating laws would apply to Auto Insurance.

b. Describe some possible problems that Auto Insurance may experience in trying to get its rates increased in a prior-approval state.

4. Janet, age 35, is divorced and has two preschool children. Janet earns only the federal minimum wage, and money is tight. Her former husband failed to make child-support payments for the past three months because he lost his job in a company merger. As a result, Janet fell behind in the payment of her bills and received several threatening letters from collection agencies. Janet believes that she can save money if she switched auto insurers. One auto insurer quoted her a rate that is substantially higher than the rate she is now paying. A company representative explained that Janet is being rated up because of her poor credit record. Janet is surprised because she has a good driving record and has not been involved in an accident within the last five years.

a. Explain the rationale for charging Janet a higher premium for auto insurance because of a poor credit record.

b. Explain the arguments against using credit-based insurance scores as a rating or underwriting factor in auto insurance.

INTERNET RESOURCES

■ The **Insurance Regulatory Examiners Society** is a nonprofit professional and educational association for insurance company examiners and other professionals working in insurance regulation. Visit the site at

http://www.go-ires.org

■ The **National Association of Insurance Commissioners (NAIC)** is an organization of state insurance commissioners that promotes uniformity in state insurance laws and recommends legislation to state legislatures. The Web site for each state insurance department can be accessed through the NAIC Web site. Visit the site at

http://www.naic.org

■ The **National Association of Insurance Commissioners (NAIC)** also provides considerable information on complaints against individual insurers. Go to the NAIC Consumer Information Source, type in the company name, state, and business type. After locating the company, click on "Closed Complaints." Visit the site at

http://www.naic.org/cis

■ The **National Conference of Insurance Guaranty Funds** is an advisory organization to state guaranty funds. It gathers and disseminates information regarding insurer insolvencies. Visit the site at

http://www.ncigf.org

■ The **National Conference of Insurance Legislators** is an organization of state legislators whose main area of public policy concern is insurance regulation and legislation. Visit the site at

http://www.ncoil.org

SELECTED REFERENCES

American Council of Life Insurers. *ACLI Releases Working Draft Proposal on Optional Federal Chartering,* News Release, April 13, 2001.

American Council of Life Insurers. *New Study Finds Significant Cost Savings Under Optional Federal Charter for Life Insurance,* News Release, August 2, 2005.

Belth, Joseph M., ed. "Eliot Spitzer and the Insurance Industry," *The Insurance Forum,* Vol. 32, No. 1, January 2005.

Consumer Federation of America. *Many State Legislators Involved with National Insurance Organization Have Close Ties to Insurance Industry,* Press Release, July 9, 2003.

CPCU Society's Connecticut Chapter. "The Federal Charter: A Primer," *CPCU eJOURNAL,* Vol. 57, No. 9, September 2004.

Hartwig, Robert P. *No Evidence of Disparate Impact in Texas Due to Use of Credit Information by Personal Lines Insurers.* New York: Insurance Information Institute, January 2005.

Insurance Information Institute. "Insolvencies/Guaranty Funds," *Hot Topics & Issues Updates.* New York: Insurance Information Institute, July 2006. This source is periodically updated.

Insurance Information Institute. "Credit Scoring," *Hot Topics & Issues Updates.* New York: Insurance Information Institute, July 2006. This source is periodically updated.

Insurance Information Institute. "Modernizing Insurance Regulation," *Hot Topics & Issues Updates.* New York: Insurance Information Institute, April 2006. This source is periodically updated.

Insurance Information Institute. "Overview of the Texas Credit Study: Texas Study Confirms That Credit

Scoring Accurately Assesses the Risk of Future Claims," *Hot Topics & Issues Updates*. New York: Insurance Information Institute (no date).

Insurance Information Institute. "Rates and Regulation," *Hot Topics & Insurance Issues*. New York: Insurance Information Institute, August 2006. This source is periodically updated.

Klein, Robert W. *A Regulator's Introduction to the Insurance Industry*. Kansas City, MO: NAIC Education and Research Foundation, 1999.

U.S. General Accounting Office. *Insurance Regulation, Common Standards and Improved Coordination Needed to Strengthen Market Regulation*, GAO-03-433, September 2003.

U.S. Government Accountability Office. *Private Health Insurance, Employers and Individuals Are Vulnerable to Unauthorized or Bogus Entities Selling Coverage*, GAO-04-312, February 2004.

NOTES

1. 8 Wall 168, 183 (1869).
2. 322 U.S. 533 (1944).
3. "Rates and Regulation," *Hot Topics & Issues Updates*, Insurance Information Institute, June 2006. This source is periodically updated.
4. Liam Pleven, "The Burden of Title Insurance," *The Wall Street Journal*, December 31, 2005–January 1, 2006, B 3.
5. There are certain exceptions. Maximum credit life insurance rates are regulated by the states.
6. This section is based on Insurance and Pensions, "Accounting for the Abuses at AIG," *Knowledge @Wharton*, April 20, 2005. See http://knowledge.wharton.upenn.edu/
7. "Regulators Approve Finite Reinsurance Disclosure Requirements," *Insurance Journal*. National News, October 17, 2005. See www.insurancejournal.com/.
8. U.S. Government Accountability Office, *Private Health Insurance, Employers and Individuals Are Vulnerable to Unauthorized or Bogus Entities Selling Coverage*, GAO-04-312, February 2004.
9. American Council of Life Insurers, *Regulatory Efficiency and Modernization*, 2004.
10. This section is based on "Modernizing Insurance Regulation," *Hot Topics & Issues Updates*, April 2006. This source is periodically updated.
11. "Insolvencies/Guaranty Funds," *Hot Topics & Issues Updates*, Insurance Information Institute, July 2006. This source is periodically updated.
12. Robert P. Hartwig, *No Evidence of Disparate Impact in Texas Due to Use of Credit Information by Personal Lines Insurers*. Insurance Information Institute, January 2005.
13. "Credit Scoring," *Hot Topics & Issues Updates*, Insurance Information Institute, July 2006. This source is periodically updated.

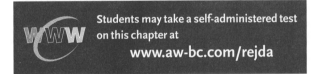

Students may take a self-administered test on this chapter at
www.aw-bc.com/rejda

PART THREE

LEGAL PRINCIPLES IN RISK AND INSURANCE

Chapter 9
Fundamental Legal Principles

Chapter 10
Analysis of Insurance Contracts

CHAPTER 9

FUNDAMENTAL LEGAL PRINCIPLES

"It is unfair to believe everything we hear about lawyers—some of it may not be true."

Gerald F. Lieberman

LEARNING OBJECTIVES

After studying this chapter, you should be able to

◆ Explain the fundamental legal principles that are reflected in insurance contracts, including
   principle of indemnity
   principle of insurable interest
   principle of subrogation
   principle of utmost good faith

◆ Explain how the legal concepts of representations, concealment, and warranty support the principle of utmost good faith.

◆ Describe the basic requirements for the formation of a valid insurance contract.

◆ Show how the nature of insurance contracts differs from that of other contracts.

◆ Explain the law of agency and how it affects the actions and duties of insurance agents.

*D*on, age 35, was recently released from a federal prison camp in Colorado after serving a five-year sentence for selling crack cocaine. When he applied for auto insurance in another state, he stated in the application that he had no driving offenses other than traffic tickets. In fact, Don had three convictions for driving under the influence of alcohol and had been involved in several auto accidents. The insurer issued the policy. Shortly thereafter, Don had another accident in which the other driver died. The family of the deceased sued Don for an unlawful death. The insurer denied liability for the claim because Don lied on the application and made several material misrepresentations. Don's introduction to insurance law was a costly lesson.

As Don discovered, insurance law can have substantial legal consequences for you after a loss occurs. When you buy insurance, you expect to be paid for a covered loss. Insurance law and contractual provisions determine whether you are covered and how much will be paid. Insurance contracts are complex legal documents that reflect both general rules of law and insurance law. Thus, you should have a clear understanding of the basic legal principles that underlie insurance contracts.

This chapter discusses the fundamental legal principles on which insurance contracts are based, legal requirements for a valid insurance contract, and legal characteristics of insurance contracts that distinguish them from other types of contracts. The chapter concludes with a discussion of the law of agency and its application to insurance agents.

PRINCIPLE OF INDEMNITY

The principle of indemnity is one of the most important principles in insurance. The **principle of indemnity** *states that the insurer agrees to pay no more than the actual amount of the loss; stated differently, the insured should not profit from a loss*. Most property and casualty insurance contracts are contracts of indemnity. If a covered loss occurs, the insurer should not pay more than the actual amount of the loss. A contract of indemnity does not mean that all covered losses are always paid in full. Because of deductibles, dollar limits on the amount paid, and other contractual provisions, the amount paid may be less than the actual loss.

The principle of indemnity has two fundamental purposes. *The first purpose is to prevent the insured from profiting from a loss*. For example, if Kristin's

home is insured for $200,000, and a partial loss of $50,000 occurs, the principle of indemnity would be violated if $200,000 were paid to her. She would be profiting from insurance.

The second purpose is to reduce moral hazard. If dishonest insureds could profit from a loss, they might deliberately cause losses with the intention of collecting the insurance. If the loss payment does not exceed the actual amount of the loss, the temptation to be dishonest is reduced.

Actual Cash Value

The concept of *actual cash value* supports the principle of indemnity. In property insurance, the basic method for indemnifying the insured is based on the actual cash value of the damaged property at the time of loss. The courts have used a number of methods to determine actual cash value, including the following:

- Replacement cost less depreciation
- Fair market value
- Broad evidence rule

Replacement Cost Less Depreciation Under this rule, **actual cash value** *is defined as replacement cost less depreciation.* This rule has been used traditionally to determine the actual cash value of property in property insurance. It takes into consideration both inflation and depreciation of property values over time. Replacement cost is the current cost of restoring the damaged property with new materials of like kind and quality. Depreciation is a deduction for physical wear and tear, age, and economic obsolescence.

For example, Sarah has a favorite couch that burns in a fire. Assume she bought the couch five years ago, the couch is 50 percent depreciated, and a similar couch today would cost $1000. Under the actual cash value rule, Sarah will collect $500 for the loss because the replacement cost is $1000, and depreciation is $500, or 50 percent. If she were paid the full replacement value of $1000, the principle of indemnity would be violated. She would be receiving the value of a new couch instead of one that was five years old. In short, the $500 payment represents indemnification for the loss of a five-year-old couch. This calculation can be summarized as follows:

$$\text{Replacement cost} = \$1000$$

$$\text{Depreciation} = \$500 \text{ (couch is 50 percent depreciated)}$$

$$\text{Actual cash value} = \text{Replacement cost} - \text{Depreciation}$$

$$\$500 = \$1000 - \$500$$

Fair Market Value Some courts have ruled that fair market value should be used to determine actual cash value of a loss. **Fair market value** *is the price a willing buyer would pay a willing seller in a free market.*

The fair market value of a building may be below its actual cash value based on replacement cost less depreciation. This difference is due to several factors, including a poor location, deteriorating neighborhood, or economic obsolescence of the building. For example, in major cities, large homes in older residential areas often have a market value well below replacement cost less depreciation. If a loss occurs, the fair market value may reflect more accurately the value of the loss. In one case, a building valued at $170,000 based on the actual cash value rule had a market value of only $65,000 when a loss occurred. The court ruled that the actual cash value of the property should be based on the fair market value of $65,000 rather than on $170,000.[1]

Broad Evidence Rule Many states use the broad evidence rule to determine the actual cash value of a loss. The **broad evidence rule** *means that the determination of actual cash value should include all relevant factors an expert would use to determine the value of the property.* Relevant factors include replacement cost less depreciation, fair market value, present value of expected income from the property, comparison sales of similar property, opinions of appraisers, and numerous other factors.

Although the actual cash value rule is used in property insurance, different methods are employed in other types of insurance. In liability insurance, the insurer pays up to the policy limit the amount of damages that the insured is legally obligated to pay because of bodily injury or property damage to another. In business income insurance, the amount paid is usually based on the loss of profits plus continuing expenses when the business is shut down because of a loss from a covered peril. In life insurance, the amount paid when the insured dies is the face value of the policy.

Exceptions to the Principle of Indemnity

There are several important exceptions to the principle of indemnity. They include the following:

- Valued policy
- Valued policy laws
- Replacement cost insurance
- Life insurance

Valued Policy A **valued policy** *is a policy that pays the face amount of insurance if a total loss occurs.* Valued policies typically are used to insure antiques, fine arts, rare paintings, and family heirlooms. Because of difficulty in determining the actual value of the property at the time of loss, the insured and insurer both agree on the value of the property when the policy is first issued. For example, you may have a valuable antique clock that was owned by your great-grandmother. Assume that the clock is worth $10,000 today and is insured for that amount. If the clock is totally destroyed in a fire, you would be paid $10,000—not the actual cash value. Because the amount paid may exceed the actual cash value, the principle of indemnity is violated.

Valued Policy Laws Valued policy laws are another exception to the principle of indemnity.[2] A **valued policy law** *is a law that exists in some states that requires payment of the face amount of insurance to the insured if a total loss to real property occurs from a peril specified in the law.* The specified perils to which a valued policy law applies vary among the states. Laws in some states cover only fire; other states cover fire, lightning, windstorm, and tornado; and some states include all insured perils. In addition, the laws generally apply only to real property, and the loss must be total. For example, a building insured for $200,000 may have an actual cash value of $175,000. If a total loss from a fire occurs, the face amount of $200,000 would be paid. Because the insured would be paid more than the actual cash value, the principle of indemnity would be violated.

The original purpose of a valued policy law was to protect the insured from an argument with the insurer if an agent had deliberately overinsured property so as to receive a higher commission. After a total loss, the insurer might offer less than the face amount for which the policyowner had paid premiums on the grounds that the building was overinsured. However, the importance of a valued policy law has declined over time because inflation in property values has made overinsurance less of a problem. Underinsurance is now the greater problem, because it results in both inadequate premiums for the insurer and inadequate protection for the insured.

Despite their reduced importance, valued policy laws can lead to overinsurance and an increase in moral hazard. Most buildings are not physically inspected before they are insured. If an insurer fails to inspect a building for valuation purposes, overinsurance and possible moral hazard may result. The insured may not be concerned about loss prevention, or may even deliberately cause a loss to collect the insurance proceeds. Although valued policy laws

provide a defense for the insurer when fraud is suspected, the burden of proof is on the insurer to prove fraudulent intent. Proving fraud is often difficult. For example, in an older case, a house advertised for sale at $1800 was insured for $10,000 under a fire insurance policy. About six months later, the house was totally destroyed by a fire. The insurer denied liability on the grounds of misrepresentation and fraud. An appeals court ordered the face amount of insurance to be paid, holding that nothing prevented the company from inspecting the property to determine its value. The insured's statement concerning the value of the house was an expression of opinion, not a representation of fact.[3]

Replacement Cost Insurance Replacement cost insurance is a third exception to the principle of indemnity. **Replacement cost insurance** *means there is no deduction for physical depreciation in determining the amount paid for a loss.* For example, assume that the roof on your home is 5 years old and has a useful life of 20 years. The roof is damaged by a tornado, and the current cost of replacement is $10,000. Under the actual cash value rule, you would receive only $7500 ($10,000 − $2500 = $7500). Under a replacement cost policy, you would receive the full $10,000 (less any applicable deductible). Because you receive the value of a brand-new roof instead of one that is 5 years old, the principle of indemnity is violated.

Replacement cost insurance is based on the recognition that payment of the actual cash value can still result in a substantial loss to the insured, because few persons budget for depreciation. In our example, you would have had to pay $2500 to restore the damaged roof, since it was one-fourth depreciated. To deal with this problem, replacement cost insurance can be purchased to insure homes, buildings, and business and personal property.

Life Insurance Life insurance is another exception to the principle of indemnity. A life insurance contract is not a contract of indemnity but is a valued policy that pays a stated sum to the beneficiary upon the insured's death. The indemnity principle is difficult to apply to life insurance for the obvious reason that the actual cash value rule (replacement cost less depreciation) is meaningless in determining the value of a human life. Moreover, to plan for personal and business purposes, such as the need to provide a specific amount of monthly income to the deceased's dependents, a certain amount of life insurance must be purchased before death occurs. For these reasons, a life insurance policy is another exception to the principle of indemnity.

PRINCIPLE OF INSURABLE INTEREST

The principle of insurable interest is another important legal principle. The **principle of insurable interest** *states that the insured must be in a position to lose financially if a covered loss occurs.* For example, you have an insurable interest in your car because you may lose financially if the car is damaged or stolen. You have an insurable interest in your personal property, such as a television set or computer, because you may lose financially if the property is damaged or destroyed.

Purposes of an Insurable Interest

To be legally enforceable, all insurance contracts must be supported by an insurable interest. Insurance contracts must be supported by an insurable interest for the following reasons.[4]

- To prevent gambling
- To reduce moral hazard
- To measure the amount of the insured's loss in property insurance

First, an insurable interest is necessary to prevent gambling. If an insurable interest were not required, the contract would be a gambling contract and would be against the public interest. For example, you could insure the property of another and hope for a loss to occur. You could similarly insure the life of another person and hope for an early death. These contracts clearly would be gambling contracts and would be against the public interest.

Second, an insurable interest reduces moral hazard. If an insurable interest were not required, a dishonest person could purchase a property insurance contract on someone else's property and then deliberately cause a loss to receive the proceeds. But if the insured stands to lose financially, nothing is gained

by causing the loss. Thus, moral hazard is reduced. In life insurance, an insurable interest requirement reduces the incentive to murder the insured for the purpose of collecting the proceeds.

Finally, in property insurance, an insurable interest measures the amount of the insured's loss. Most property insurance contracts are contracts of indemnity, and one measure of recovery is the insurable interest of the insured. If the loss payment cannot exceed the amount of one's insurable interest, the principle of indemnity is supported.

Examples of an Insurable Interest

Several examples of an insurable interest are discussed in this section. However, it is helpful at this point to distinguish between an insurable interest in property and casualty insurance and in life insurance.

Property and Casualty Insurance *Ownership of property* can support an insurable interest because owners of property will lose financially if their property is damaged or destroyed.

Potential legal liability can also support an insurable interest. For example, a dry-cleaning firm has an insurable interest in the property of the customers. The firm may be legally liable for damage to the customers' goods caused by the firm's negligence.

Secured creditors have an insurable interest as well. A commercial bank or mortgage company that lends money to buy a house has an insurable interest in the property. The property serves as collateral for the mortgage, so if the building is damaged, the collateral behind the loan is impaired. A bank that makes an inventory loan to a business firm has an insurable interest in the stock of goods, because the goods are collateral for the loan. However, the courts have ruled that unsecured or general creditors normally do not have an insurable interest in the debtor's property.[5]

Finally, a *contractual right* can support an insurable interest. Thus, a business firm that contracts to purchase goods from abroad on the condition that they arrive safely in the United States has an insurable interest in the goods because of the loss of profits if the merchandise does not arrive.

Life Insurance The question of an insurable interest does not arise when you purchase life insurance on your own life. The law considers the insurable interest requirement to be met whenever a person voluntarily purchases life insurance on his or her life. Thus, you can purchase as much life insurance as you can afford, subject of course to the insurer's underwriting rules concerning the maximum amount of insurance that can be written on any single life. Also, when you apply for life insurance on your own life, you can name anyone as beneficiary. The beneficiary is not required to have an insurable interest in your life.[6]

If you wish to purchase a life insurance policy on the life of another person, however, you must have an insurable interest in that person's life. Close family ties or marriage will satisfy the insurable interest requirement in life insurance. For example, a husband can purchase a life insurance policy on his wife and be named as beneficiary. Likewise, a wife can insure her husband and be named as beneficiary. A grandparent can purchase a life insurance policy on the life of a grandchild. However, remote family relationships will not support an insurable interest. For example, cousins cannot insure each other unless a pecuniary relationship is present.

If there is a **pecuniary (financial) interest,** the insurable interest requirement in life insurance can be met. Even when there is no relationship by blood or marriage, one person may be financially harmed by the death of another. For example, a corporation can insure the life of an outstanding salesperson, because the firm's profit may decline if the salesperson dies. One business partner can insure the life of the other partner and use the life insurance proceeds to purchase the deceased partner's interest if he or she dies.

When Must an Insurable Interest Exist?

In property insurance, the insurable interest must exist at the time of the loss. There are two reasons for this requirement. First, most property insurance contracts are contracts of indemnity. If an insurable interest does not exist at the time of loss, the insured would not incur any financial loss. Hence, the principle of indemnity would be violated if payment were made. For example, if Mark sells his home to Susan, and a fire occurs before the insurance on the home is canceled, Mark cannot collect because he no longer has an insurable interest in the property. Susan cannot collect either because she is not named as an insured under Mark's policy.

Second, you may not have an insurable interest in the property when the contract is first written but may expect to have an insurable interest in the future, at the time of possible loss. For example, in ocean marine insurance, it is common to insure a return cargo by a contract entered into prior to the ship's departure. However, the policy may not cover the goods until they are on board the ship as the insured's property. Although an insurable interest does not exist when the contract is first written, you can still collect if you have an insurable interest in the goods at the time of loss.

In contrast, in life insurance, the insurable interest requirement must be met only at the inception of the policy, not at the time of death. Life insurance is not a contract of indemnity but is a valued policy that pays a stated sum upon the insured's death. Because the beneficiary has only a legal claim to receive the policy proceeds, the beneficiary does not have to show that a financial loss has been incurred by the insured's death. For example, if Michelle takes out a policy on her husband's life and later gets a divorce, she is entitled to the policy proceeds upon the death of her former husband if she has kept the insurance in force. The insurable interest requirement must be met only at the inception of the contract (see Insight 9.1).

PRINCIPLE OF SUBROGATION

The principle of subrogation strongly supports the principle of indemnity. **Subrogation** *means substitution of the insurer in place of the insured for the purpose of claiming indemnity from a third person for a loss covered by insurance.*[7] *Stated differently, the insurer is entitled to recover from a negligent third party any loss payments made to the insured.* For example, assume that a negligent motorist fails to stop at a red light and smashes into Megan's car, causing damage in the amount of $5000. If she has collision insurance on her car, her company will pay the physical damage loss to the car (less any deductible) and then attempt to collect from the negligent motorist who caused the accident. Alternatively, Megan could attempt to collect directly from the negligent motorist for the damage to her car. Subrogation does not apply unless the insurer makes a loss payment. However, to the extent that a loss

INSIGHT 9.1

Corporation Lacking Insurable Interest at Time of Death Can Receive Life Insurance Proceeds

Legal Facts

A corporation purchased a $1 million life insurance policy on an officer who was a 20 percent stockholder in the company. Shortly thereafter, the officer sold his stock and resigned. Two years later he died. The insurer paid the death proceeds to the corporation. The personal representative of the deceased insured's estate claimed the insurable interest was only temporary and must continue until death. Is the corporation entitled to the policy proceeds even though it had no insurable interest at the time of death?

Court Decision

The court rejected the argument that the corporation's insurable interest must continue until death.[a] Its decision

reflects the principle that termination of an insurable interest before the policy matures does not affect the policyholder's right of recovery under a policy valid at its inception. The insurable interest requirement must be met only at the inception of the policy.

[a]*In re Al Zuni Trading*, 947 F.2d 1402 (1991).
SOURCE: Adapted from Buist M. Anderson, *Anderson on Life Insurance, 1992 Supplement* (Boston, MA: Little, Brown, 1992), p. 29. ©1992, Little, Brown and Company.

---

payment is made, the insured gives to the insurer any legal rights to collect damages from the negligent third party.

Purposes of Subrogation

Subrogation has three basic purposes. *First, subrogation prevents the insured from collecting twice for the same loss.* In the absence of subrogation, the insured could collect from the insurer and from the person who caused the loss. The principle of indemnity would be violated because the insured would be profiting from a loss.

Second, subrogation is used to hold the negligent person responsible for the loss. By exercising its subrogation rights, the insurer can collect from the negligent person who caused the loss.

Finally, subrogation helps to hold down insurance rates. Subrogation recoveries can be reflected in the rate-making process, which tends to hold rates below where they would be in the absence of subrogation.

Importance of Subrogation

You should keep in mind several important corollaries of the principle of subrogation.

1. *The general rule is that by exercising its subrogation rights, the insurer is entitled only to the amount it has paid under the policy.*[8] Some insureds may not be fully indemnified after a loss because of insufficient insurance, satisfaction of a deductible, or legal expenses in trying to recover from a negligent third party. Many policies, however, now have a provision that states how a subrogation recovery is to be shared between the insured and insurer.

In the absence of any policy provision, the courts have used different rules in determining how a subrogation recovery is to be shared. *One view is that the insured must be reimbursed in full for the loss; the insurer is then entitled to any remaining balance up to the insurer's interest, with any remainder going to the insured.*[9] For example, Andrew has a $200,000 home insured for only $160,000 under a homeowners policy. Assume that the house is totally destroyed in a fire because of faulty wiring by an electrician. The insurer would pay $160,000 to Andrew and then attempt to collect from the negligent electrician. After exercising its subrogation rights against the negligent electrician, assume that the insurer has a net recovery of $100,000 (after deduction of legal expenses). Andrew would receive $40,000, and the insurer can retain the balance of $60,000.

2. *The insured cannot impair the insurer's subrogation rights.* The insured cannot do anything after a loss that interferes with the insurer's right to proceed against a negligent third party. For example, if the insured waives the right to sue the negligent party, the right to collect from the insurer for the loss is also waived. This case could happen if the insured admits fault in an auto accident or attempts to settle a collision loss with the negligent driver without the insurer's consent. If the insurer's right to subrogate against the negligent motorist is adversely affected, the insured's right to collect from the insurer is forfeited.[10]

3. *Subrogation does not apply to life insurance and to most individual health insurance contracts.* Life insurance is not a contract of indemnity, and subrogation has relevance only for contracts of indemnity. Individual health insurance contracts usually do not contain subrogation clauses.[11]

4. *The insurer cannot subrogate against its own insureds.* If the insurer could recover a loss payment for a covered loss from an insured, the basic purpose of purchasing the insurance would be defeated.

PRINCIPLE OF UTMOST GOOD FAITH

An insurance contract is based on the **principle of utmost good faith**—*that is, a higher degree of honesty is imposed on both parties to an insurance contract than is imposed on parties to other contracts.* This principle has its historical roots in ocean marine insurance. An ocean marine underwriter had to place great faith in statements made by the applicant for insurance concerning the cargo to be shipped. The property to be insured may not have been visually inspected, and the contract may have been formed in a location far removed from the cargo and ship. Thus, the principle of utmost good faith imposed a high degree of honesty on the applicant for insurance.

The principle of utmost good faith is supported by three important legal doctrines: representations, concealment, and warranty.

Representations

Representations *are statements made by the applicant for insurance.* For example, if you apply for life insurance, you may be asked questions concerning your age, weight, height, occupation, state of health, family history, and other relevant questions. Your answers to these questions are called representations.

The legal significance of a representation is that the insurance contract is voidable at the insurer's option if the representation is (1) material, (2) false, and (3) relied on by the insurer.[12] **Material** *means that if the insurer knew the true facts, the policy would not have been issued, or it would have been issued on different terms. False* means that the statement is not true or is misleading. *Reliance* means that the insurer relies on the misrepresentation in issuing the policy at a specified premium.

For example, Joseph applies for life insurance and states in the application that he has not visited a doctor within the last five years. However, six months earlier, he had surgery for lung cancer. In this case, he has made a statement that is false, material, and relied on by the insurer. Therefore, the policy is voidable at the insurer's option. If Joseph dies shortly after the policy is issued, say three months, the company could contest the death claim on the basis of a material misrepresentation. Insight 9.2 provides an additional application of this legal principle.

If an applicant for insurance states an opinion or belief that later turns out to be wrong, the insurer must prove that the applicant spoke fraudulently and intended to deceive the company before it can deny payment of a claim. For example, assume that you are asked if you have high blood pressure when you apply for health insurance, and you answer "no" to the question. If the insurer later discovers you have high blood pressure, to deny payment of a claim, it must prove that you intended to deceive the company. Thus, a statement of opinion or belief must also be fraudulent before the insurer can refuse to pay a claim.

An **innocent misrepresentation** of a material fact, if relied on by the insurer, also makes the contract voidable. An innocent misrepresentation is one that is unintentional. A majority of court opinions have ruled that an innocent misrepresentation of a material fact makes the contract voidable.

INSIGHT 9.2

Auto Insurer Denies Coverage Because of Material Misrepresentation

Legal Facts

The insured misrepresented that she had no traffic violation convictions in the prior three-year period. After an accident, a check of her record revealed that she had two speeding tickets in that period. The insurer denied coverage.

Court Decision

State law regarding the voiding of insurance requires that the misrepresentation must be material and made with the intent to deceive. The insured claimed that she had forgotten about the two tickets, and therefore had no intent to deceive. The court ruled that it is unlikely she would forget both events. Decision is for the insurer.[a]

[a]*Benton v. Shelter Mutual Ins. Co.,* 550 So.2d 832 (La.App.2 Cir. 1989).

SOURCE: "Misrepresentations in Auto Coverage Applications," *FC & S Bulletins,* Miscellaneous Property section, Fire and Marine volume, October 1997, p. M.35.5.

Finally, the doctrine of material misrepresentations also applies to statements made by the insured after a loss occurs. If the insured submits a fraudulent proof of loss or misrepresents the value of the items damaged, the insurer has the right to void the coverage (see Insight 9.3).

Concealment

The doctrine of concealment also supports the principle of utmost good faith. A **concealment** *is intentional failure of the applicant for insurance to reveal a material fact to the insurer.* Concealment is the same thing as nondisclosure; that is, the applicant for insurance deliberately withholds material information from the insurer. The legal effect of a material concealment is the same as a misrepresentation—the contract is voidable at the insurer's option.

To deny a claim based on concealment, a nonmarine insurer must prove two things: (1) the concealed fact was known by the insured to be material, and (2) the insured intended to defraud the insurer.[13] For example, Joseph DeBellis applied for a life insurance policy on his life. Five months after the policy was issued, he was murdered. The death certificate named the deceased as Joseph DeLuca, his true name. The insurer denied payment on the grounds that Joseph had concealed a material fact by not

INSIGHT 9.3

Insurer Voids Coverage Because of Misrepresentations in Proof of Loss

Legal Facts

The insured experienced a burglary loss of $9000 and misrepresented the value of the items stolen. The insured provided receipts that showed a purchase price of $900 for a stereo set and $1500 for video equipment. The insurer proved that the stereo set cost only $400, and that the insured had not purchased the video equipment.

Court Decision

The court allowed the insurer to void coverage in its entirety. The court ruled that (1) insureds have an obligation to provide the insurer with true receipts, submit to an examination under oath, and provide a sworn proof of loss, and (2) the misrepresentations were material because they were made to mislead, discourage, or deflect the insurer's investigation of the claim.[a]

[a]*Passero v. Allstate Ins. Co.* 554 N.E.2d 384 (Ill. App. lst Dist. 1990).

SOURCE: "Misrepresentation in Proofs of Loss," *FC & S Bulletins,* Miscellaneous Property section, Fire and Marine volume, October 1997, p. M.35.5.

revealing his true identity and that he had an extensive criminal record. In finding for the insurer, the court held that intentional concealment of his true identity was material and breached the obligation of good faith.[14]

The doctrine of concealment is applied in a harsher manner in ocean marine insurance. An ocean marine insurer is not required to prove that the concealment is intentional. Applicants are required to reveal all material facts that pertain to the property to be insured. The applicant's lack of awareness of the materiality of the fact is of no consequence. Thus, an ocean marine insurer can successfully deny payment of a claim if it can show that the concealed fact is material.

Warranty

The doctrine of warranty also reflects the principle of utmost good faith. A **warranty** *is a statement that becomes part of the insurance contract and is guaranteed by the maker to be true in all respects.*[15] For example, in exchange for a reduced premium, a liquor store owner may warrant that an approved burglary and robbery alarm system will be operational at all times. A bank may warrant that a guard will be on the premises twenty-four hours a day. Likewise, a business firm may warrant that an automatic sprinkler system will be in working order throughout the term of the policy. A clause describing the warranty becomes part of the contract.

Based on the common law, in its strictest form, warranty is a harsh legal doctrine. Any breach of the warranty, even if minor or not material, allowed the insurer to deny payment of a claim. During the early days of insurance, statements made by the applicant for insurance were considered to be warranties. If the statement were untrue in any respect, even if not material, the insurer could deny payment of a claim based on a breach of warranty.

Because strict application of the warranty doctrine harmed many insureds, state legislatures and the courts have softened and modified the harsh common law doctrine of warranty over time. Some modifications of the warranty doctrine are summarized as follows:

- Statements made by applicants for insurance are considered to be representations and not war-

ranties. Thus, the insurer cannot deny liability for a claim if a misrepresentation is not material.
- Most courts will interpret a breach of warranty liberally in those cases where a minor breach affects the risk only temporarily or insignificantly.
- "Increase in hazard" statutes have been passed that state that the insurer cannot deny a claim unless the breach of warranty increases the hazard.
- Statutes have been passed that allow the insured to recover for a loss unless the breach of warranty actually contributed to the loss.

REQUIREMENTS OF AN INSURANCE CONTRACT

An insurance policy is based on the law of contracts. To be legally enforceable, an insurance contract must meet four basic requirements: offer and acceptance, consideration, competent parties, and legal purpose.

Offer and Acceptance

The first requirement of a binding insurance contract is that there must be an **offer and an acceptance** of its terms. In most cases, the applicant for insurance makes the offer, and the company accepts or rejects the offer. An agent merely solicits or invites the prospective insured to make an offer. The requirement of offer and acceptance can be examined in greater detail by making a careful distinction between property and casualty insurance, and life insurance.

In property and casualty insurance, the offer and acceptance can be oral or written. In the absence of specific legislation to the contrary, oral insurance contracts are valid. As a practical matter, most property and casualty insurance contracts are in written form. The applicant for insurance fills out the application and pays the first premium (or promises to pay the first premium). This step constitutes the offer. The agent then accepts the offer on behalf of the insurance company. In property and casualty insurance, agents typically have the power to bind their companies through use of a binder. A **binder** *is a temporary contract for insurance and can be either written or oral.* The binder obligates the company immediately prior to receipt of the application and issuance of the policy. Thus, the insurance contract can be effective immediately, because the agent accepts the offer on behalf of the company. This procedure is usually followed in personal lines of property and casualty insurance, including homeowners policies and auto insurance. However, in some cases, the agent is not authorized to bind the company, and the application must be sent to the company for approval. The company may then accept the offer and issue the policy or reject the application.

In life insurance, the procedures followed are different. A life insurance agent does not have the power to bind the insurer. Therefore, the application for life insurance is always in writing, and the applicant must be approved by the insurer before the life insurance is in force. The usual procedure is for the applicant to fill out the application and pay the first premium. A **conditional premium receipt** is then given to the applicant. The most common conditional receipt is the "insurability premium receipt." If the applicant is found insurable according to the insurer's normal underwriting standards, the life insurance becomes effective as of the date of the application. Some insurability receipts make the life insurance effective on the date of the application or the date of the medical exam, whichever is later.

For example, assume that Aaron applies for a $100,000 life insurance policy on Monday. He fills out the application, pays the first premium, and receives a conditional premium receipt from the agent. On Tuesday morning, he takes a physical examination, and on Tuesday afternoon, he is killed in a boating accident. The application and premium will still be forwarded to the insurer, as if he were still alive. If he is found insurable according to the insurer's underwriting rules, the life insurance is in force, and $100,000 will be paid to his beneficiary.

However, if the applicant for life insurance does not pay the first premium when the application is filled out, a different set of rules applies. Before the life insurance is in force, the policy must be issued and delivered to the applicant, the first premium must be paid, and the applicant must be in good health when the policy is delivered. Some insurers also require that there must be no interim medical treatment between submission of the application and delivery of the policy. These requirements are considered to be "conditions precedent"—in other words, they must be fulfilled before the life insurance is in force.[16]

Consideration

The second requirement of a valid insurance contract is **consideration**—the value that each party gives to the other. The insured's consideration is payment of the premium (or a promise to pay the premium) plus an agreement to abide by the conditions specified in the policy. The insurer's consideration is the promise to do certain things as specified in the contract. This promise can include paying for a loss from an insured peril, providing certain services, such as loss prevention and safety services, or defending the insured in a liability lawsuit.

Competent Parties

The third requirement of a valid insurance contract is that each party must be **legally competent.** *This means the parties must have legal capacity to enter into a binding contract.* Most adults are legally competent to enter into insurance contracts, but there are some exceptions. Insane persons, intoxicated persons, and corporations that act outside the scope of their authority cannot enter into enforceable insurance contracts. Minors generally lack full legal capacity to enter into a binding insurance contract. Such contracts usually are voidable by the minor, which means the minor can disaffirm the contract. However, most states have enacted laws that allow minors to enter into a valid life insurance contract at age 15 (age 18 in a few states).

The insurer must also be legally competent. Insurers generally must be licensed to sell insurance in the state, and the insurance sold must be within the scope of its charter or certificate of incorporation.

Legal Purpose

A final requirement is that the contract must be for a **legal purpose.** An insurance contract that encourages or promotes something illegal or immoral is contrary to the public interest and cannot be enforced. For example, a street pusher of heroin and other illegal drugs cannot purchase a property insurance policy that would cover seizure of the drugs by the police. This type of contract obviously is not enforceable because it would promote illegal activities that are contrary to the public interest.

DISTINCT LEGAL CHARACTERISTICS OF INSURANCE CONTRACTS

Insurance contracts have distinct legal characteristics that make them different from other legal contracts. Several distinctive legal characteristics have already been discussed. As we noted earlier, most property and casualty insurance contracts are contracts of indemnity; all insurance contracts must be supported by an insurable interest; and insurance contracts are based on utmost good faith. Other distinct legal characteristics are as follows:

- Aleatory contract
- Unilateral contract
- Conditional contract
- Personal contract
- Contract of adhesion

Aleatory Contract

An insurance contract is aleatory rather than commutative. An **aleatory contract** *is a contract where the values exchanged may not be equal but depend on an uncertain event.* Depending on chance, one party may receive a value out of proportion to the value that is given. For example, assume that Jessica pays a premium of $600 for $200,000 of homeowners insurance. If the home were totally destroyed by fire shortly thereafter, she would collect an amount that greatly exceeds the premium paid. On the other hand, a homeowner may faithfully pay premiums for many years and never have a loss.

In contrast, other commercial contracts are commutative. A **commutative contract** *is one in which the values exchanged by both parties are theoretically equal.* For example, the purchaser of real estate normally pays a price that is viewed to be equal to the value of the property.

Although the essence of an aleatory contract is chance, or the occurrence of some fortuitous event, an insurance contract is not a gambling contract. Gambling creates a new speculative risk that did not exist before the transaction. Insurance, however, is a technique for handling an already existing pure risk. Thus, although both gambling and insurance are aleatory in nature, an insurance contract is not a gambling contract because no new risk is created.

Unilateral Contract

An insurance contract is a unilateral contract. A **unilateral contract** *means that only one party makes a legally enforceable promise.* In this case, only the insurer makes a legally enforceable promise to pay a claim or provide other services to the insured. After the first premium is paid, and the insurance is in force, the insured cannot be legally forced to pay the premiums or to comply with the policy provisions. Although the insured must continue to pay the premiums to receive payment for a loss, he or she cannot be legally forced to do so. However, if the premiums are paid, the insurer must accept them and must continue to provide the protection promised under the contract.

In contrast, most commercial contracts are *bilateral* in nature. Each party makes a legally enforceable promise to the other party. If one party fails to perform, the other party can insist on performance or can sue for damages because of the breach of contract.

Conditional Contract

An insurance contract is a **conditional contract.** That is, the insurer's obligation to pay a claim depends on whether the insured or the beneficiary has complied with all policy conditions. **Conditions** *are provisions inserted in the policy that qualify or place limitations on the insurer's promise to perform.* The conditions section imposes certain duties on the insured if he or she wishes to collect for a loss. Although the insured is not compelled to abide by the policy conditions, he or she must do so to collect for an insured loss. The insurer is not obligated to pay a claim if the policy conditions are not met. For example, under a homeowners policy, the insured must give immediate notice of a loss. If the insured delays for an unreasonable period in reporting the loss, the insurer can refuse to pay the claim on the grounds that a policy condition has been violated.

Personal Contract

In property insurance, insurance is a **personal contract,** *which means the contract is between the insured and the insurer.* Strictly speaking, a property insurance contract does not insure property, but insures the owner of property against loss. The owner of the insured property is indemnified if the property is damaged or destroyed. Because the contract is personal, the applicant for insurance must be acceptable to the insurer and must meet certain underwriting standards regarding character, morals, and credit.

A property insurance contract normally cannot be assigned to another party without the insurer's consent. If property is sold to another person, the new owner may not be acceptable to the insurer. *Thus, the insurer's consent is required before a property insurance policy can be validly assigned to another party.* In practice, new property owners get their own insurance, so consent of the previous insurer is not required. In contrast, a life insurance policy can be freely assigned to anyone without the insurer's consent because the assignment does not usually alter the risk or increase the probability of death.

Conversely, a loss payment for a property loss can be assigned to another party without the insurer's consent. Although the insurer's consent is not required, the contract may require that the insurer be notified of the assignment of the proceeds to another party.

Contract of Adhesion

A **contract of adhesion** *means the insured must accept the entire contract, with all of its terms and conditions.* The insurer drafts and prints the policy, and the insured generally must accept the entire document and cannot insist that certain provisions be added or deleted or the contract rewritten to suit the insured. Although the contract can be altered by the addition of endorsements and riders or other forms, the contract is drafted by the insurer. To redress the imbalance that exists in such a situation, *the courts have ruled that any ambiguities or uncertainties in the contract are construed against the insurer.* If the policy is ambiguous, the insured gets the benefit of the doubt.

The general rule that ambiguities in insurance contracts are construed against the insurer is reinforced by the principle of reasonable expectations. The **principle of reasonable expectations** *states that an insured is entitled to coverage under a policy that he or she reasonably expects it to provide, and that to be effective, exclusions or qualifications must be conspicuous, plain, and clear.*[17] Some courts have ruled that insureds are entitled to the protection that they reasonably expect to have, and that technical restrictions in the contract should be clear and conspicuous. For example, in one case, a liability insurer refused to defend the insured on the grounds that the policy excluded intentional acts. The court ruled that the insurer was responsible for the defense costs. The insured had a reasonable expectation that defense costs were covered under the policy because the policy covered other types of intentional acts.[18]

LAW AND THE INSURANCE AGENT

An insurance contract normally is sold by an agent who represents the principal (the insurer). An agent is someone who has the authority to act on behalf of someone else. The principal (insurer) is the party for whom action is to be taken. Thus, if Patrick has the authority to solicit, create, or terminate an insurance contract on behalf of Apex Insurance, he would be the agent and Apex Insurance would be the principal.

General Rules of Agency

Important rules of law govern the actions of agents and their relationship to insureds. They include the following:[19]

- There is no presumption of an agency relationship.
- An agent must have authority to represent the principal.
- A principal is responsible for the acts of agents acting within the scope of their authority.

No Presumption of an Agency Relationship   There is no automatic presumption that one person legally can act as an agent for another. Some visible evidence of an agency relationship must exist. For example, a person who claims to be an agent for an auto insurer may collect premiums and then abscond with the funds. The auto insurer is not legally responsible for the person's actions if it has done nothing to create the impression that an agency relationship exists. However, if the person has a business card, rate data, and application blanks supplied by the insurer, then it can be presumed that a legitimate agent is acting on behalf of that insurer.

Authority to Represent the Principal An agent must be authorized to represent the principal. An agent's authority is derived from three sources: (1) express authority, (2) implied authority, and (3) apparent authority.

Express authority refers to powers specifically conferred on the agent. These powers are normally stated in the **agency agreement** between the agent and the principal. The agency agreement may also withhold certain powers. For example, a life insurance agent may be given the power to solicit applicants and arrange for physical examinations. Certain powers, however, such as the right to extend the time for payment of premiums or the right to alter contractual provisions in the policy, may be denied.

Agents also have **implied authority.** Implied authority refers to the authority of the agent to perform all incidental acts necessary to fulfill the purposes of the agency agreement. For example, an agent may have the express authority to deliver a life insurance policy to the client. It follows that the agent also has the implied power to collect the first premium.

Finally, an agent may bind the principal by **apparent authority.** If an agent acts with apparent authority to do certain things, and a third party is led to believe that the agent is acting within the scope of reasonable and appropriate authority, the principal can be bound by the agent's actions. Third parties have to show only that they have exercised due diligence in determining the agent's authority based on the agent's actual authority or conduct of the principal. For example, an agent for an auto insurer may frequently grant his or her clients an extension of time to pay overdue premiums. If the insurer has not expressly granted this right to the agent and has not taken any action to deal with the violation of company policy, it could not later deny liability for a loss on the grounds that the agent lacked authority to grant the time extension. The insurer first would have to notify all policyowners of the limitations on the agent's powers.

Principal Responsible for Acts of Agents A final rule of agency law is that the principal is responsible for all acts of agents when they are acting within the scope of their authority. This responsibility also includes fraudulent acts, omissions, and misrepresentations.

In addition, knowledge of the agent is presumed to be knowledge of the principal with respect to matters within the scope of the agency relationship. For example, if a life insurance agent knows that an applicant for life insurance is addicted to alcohol, this knowledge is imputed to the insurer even though the agent deliberately omits this information from the application. Thus, if the insurer issues the policy, it cannot later attack the validity of the policy on the grounds of alcohol addiction and the concealment of a material fact.

Waiver and Estoppel

The doctrines of waiver and estoppel have direct relevance to the law of agency and to the powers of insurance agents. The practical significance of these concepts is that an insurer legally may be required to pay a claim that it ordinarily would not have to pay.

Waiver *is defined as the voluntary relinquishment of a known legal right.* If the insurer voluntarily waives a legal right under the contract, it cannot later deny payment of a claim by the insured on the grounds that such a legal right was violated. For example, assume that an insurer receives an application for insurance at its home office, and that the application contains an incomplete or missing answer. Assume that the insurer does not contact the applicant for additional information, and the policy is issued. The insurer later could not deny payment of a claim on the basis of an incomplete application. In effect, the insurer has waived its requirement that the application be complete by issuing the policy.

The legal term *estoppel* was derived centuries ago from the English common law. **Estoppel** *occurs when a representation of fact made by one person to another person is reasonably relied on by that person to such an extent that it would be inequitable to allow the first person to deny the truth of the representation.*[20] Stated simply, if one person makes a statement of fact to another person who then reasonably relies on the statement to his or her detriment, the first person cannot later deny the statement was made. The law of estoppel is designed to prevent persons from changing their minds to the detriment of another party. For example, assume that an applicant for health insurance tells the agent of a health problem, and the agent assures the applicant that the health problem does have to be stated in the application. The insurer could be estopped from denying benefits on the grounds that this information was not included.[21]

CASE APPLICATION

Jeff is a book dealer who purchased a building from Richard. Jeff obtained a loan from the Gateway Bank to purchase the building, which held a mortgage on the building. Jeff planned to store his inventory of books in the building. He also planned to use part of the building for a fast-food restaurant. When Jeff applied for property insurance on the building, he did not tell the agent about the fast-food restaurant because premiums would be substantially higher. Eight months after the policy was issued, a fire occurred in the restaurant that caused substantial damage to the building.

  a. Do any of the following parties have an insurable interest in the building at the time of loss? Explain your answer.
    1. Jeff
    2. Richard
    3. Gateway Bank

  b. Richard told Jeff he could save money by taking over Richard's insurance instead of purchasing a new policy. Can Richard validly assign his existing property insurance policy to Jeff without notifying the insurer? Explain your answer.
  c. Could Jeff's insurer deny coverage for the fire loss based on a material concealment? Explain your answer.
  d. Investigation of the fire revealed that an electrician improperly wired an electrical outlet in the restaurant, which caused the fire. Explain how subrogation might apply in this case.

SUMMARY

- The principle of indemnity states that the insurer should not pay more than the actual amount of the loss; in other words, the insured should not profit from a covered loss.
- There are several exceptions to the principle of indemnity. These exceptions include a valued policy, valued policy laws, replacement cost insurance, and life insurance.
- The principle of insurable interest means that the insured must stand to lose financially if a loss occurs. All insurance contracts must be supported by an insurable interest to be legally enforceable. There are three purposes of the insurable interest requirement:

  To prevent gambling

  To reduce moral hazard

  To measure the amount of loss in property insurance

- In property and casualty insurance, the ownership of property, potential legal liability, secured creditors, and contractual rights can support the insurable interest requirement.
- In life insurance, the question of an insurable interest does not arise when a person purchases life insurance on his or her own life. If life insurance is purchased on the life of another person, there must be an insurable interest in that person's life. Close family ties, blood, marriage, or a pecuniary (financial) interest will satisfy the insurable interest requirement in life insurance.
- In property insurance, the insurable interest requirement must be met at the time of loss. In life insurance, the insurable interest requirement must be met only at the inception of the policy.
- The principle of subrogation means that the insurer is entitled to recover from a negligent third party any loss payments made to the insured. The purposes of subro-

gation are to prevent the insured from collecting twice for the same loss, to hold the negligent person responsible for the loss, and to hold down insurance rates.

- If the insurer exercises its subrogation rights, the insured generally must be fully restored before the insurer can retain any sums collected from the negligent third party. Also, the insured cannot do anything that might impair the insurer's subrogation rights. However, the insurer can waive its subrogation rights in the contract either before or after the loss. Finally, subrogation does not apply to life insurance contracts and to most individual health insurance contracts.

- The principle of utmost good faith means that a higher degree of honesty is imposed on both parties to an insurance contract than is imposed on parties to other contracts.

- The legal doctrines of representations, concealment, and warranty support the principle of utmost good faith. Representations are statements made by the applicant for insurance. The insurer can deny payment for a claim if the representation is material and false, and is relied on by the insurer in issuing the policy at a specified premium. In the case of statements of belief or opinion, the misrepresentation must also be fraudulent before the insurer can deny a claim. Concealment of a material fact has the same legal effect as a misrepresentation: the contract is voidable at the insurer's option.

- A warranty is a statement of fact or a promise made by the insured, which is part of the insurance contract and must be true if the insurer is to be liable under the contract. Based on common law, any breach of the warranty, even if slight, allows the insurer to deny payment of a claim. The harsh common law doctrine of a warranty, however, has been modified and softened by court decisions and statutes.

- To have a valid insurance contract, four requirements must be met:
    There must be an offer and acceptance.
    Consideration must be exchanged.
    The parties to the contract must be legally competent.
    The contract must be for a legal purpose.

- Insurance contracts have distinct legal characteristics. An insurance contract is an *aleatory contract* where the values exchanged may not be equal and depend on the occurrence of an uncertain event. An insurance contract is *unilateral* because only the insurer makes a legally enforceable promise. An insurance contract is *conditional* because the insurer's obligation to pay a claim depends on whether the insured or beneficiary has complied with all policy provisions. A property insurance contract is a *personal contract* between the insured and insurer and cannot be validly assigned to another party without the insurer's consent. A life insurance policy is freely assignable without the insurer's consent. Finally, insurance is a *contract of adhesion*, which means the insured must accept the entire contract, with all of its terms and conditions; if there is an ambiguity in the contract, it will be construed against the insurer.

- Three general rules of agency govern the actions of agents and their relationship to insureds:
    There is no presumption of an agency relationship.
    An agent must have the authority to represent the principal.
    A principal is responsible for the actions of agents acting within the scope of their authority.

- An agent can bind the principal based on express authority, implied authority, and apparent authority.

- Based on the legal doctrines of waiver and estoppel, an insurer may be required to pay a claim that it ordinarily would not have to pay.

KEY CONCEPTS AND TERMS

Actual cash value	Material fact
Agency agreement	Offer and acceptance
Aleatory contract	Pecuniary (financial)
Apparent authority	interest
Binder	Personal contract
Broad evidence rule	Principle of indemnity
Commutative contract	Principle of insurable
Concealment	interest
Conditional contract	Principle of reasonable
Conditions	expectations
Conditional premium	Principle of utmost good
receipt	faith
Consideration	Replacement cost
Contract of adhesion	insurance
Estoppel	Representations
Express authority	Subrogation
Fair market value	Unilateral contract
Implied authority	Valued policy
Innocent misrepresentation	Valued policy law
Legal purpose	Waiver
Legally competent parties	Warranty

REVIEW QUESTIONS

1. a. Explain the principle of indemnity.
   b. How is actual cash value calculated?
   c. How does the concept of actual cash value support the principle of indemnity?

2. a. What is a valued policy? Why is it used?
   b. What is a valued policy law?
   c. What is a replacement cost policy?

3. a. Explain the meaning of an insurable interest.
   b. Why is an insurable interest required in every insurance contract?

4. a. Explain the principle of subrogation.
   b. Why is subrogation used?

5. Explain the following legal doctrines:
   a. misrepresentation
   b. concealment
   c. warranty

6. List the four requirements that must be met to form a valid insurance contract.

7. Insurance contracts have certain legal characteristics that distinguish them from other contracts. Explain the following legal characteristics of insurance contracts.
   a. Aleatory contract
   b. Unilateral contract
   c. Conditional contract
   d. Personal contract
   e. Contract of adhesion

8. Explain the general rules of agency that govern the actions of agents and their relationship to insureds.

9. Identify three sources of authority that enable an agent to bind the principal.

10. Explain the meaning of:
    a. Waiver
    b. Estoppel

APPLICATION QUESTIONS

1. Jake borrowed $800,000 from the Gateway Bank to purchase a fishing boat. He keeps the boat at a dock owned by the Harbor Company. He uses the boat to earn income by fishing. Jake also has a contract with the White Shark Fishing Company to transport tuna from one port to another.
   a. Do any of the following parties have an insurable interest in Jake or his property? If an insurable interest exists, explain the extent of the interest.
   (1) Gateway Bank
   (2) Harbor Company
   (3) White Shark Fishing Company
   b. If Jake did not own the boat but operated it on behalf of the White Shark Fishing Company, would he have an insurable interest in the boat? Explain.

2. Ashley purchased a dining room set for $5000 and insured the furniture on an actual cash value basis. Three years later, the set was destroyed in a fire. At the time of loss, the property had depreciated in value by 50 percent. The replacement cost of a new dining room set at the time of loss was $6000. Ignoring any deductible, how much will Ashley collect from her insurer? Explain your answer.

3. Taylor purchased a 20-year-old house for $200,000. The house has an estimated useful life of 80 years. Taylor insured the house for $200,000. The replacement cost of a similar house with materials of like kind and quality is $240,000. The house is totally destroyed in a tornado.
   a. Based on the actual cash value rule, how much will Taylor collect from her insurer (ignore any deductible)?
   b. If the loss occurs in a state with a valued policy law, how much will Taylor collect from her insurer (ignore any deductible)?

4. Nicholas owns a laptop computer that was stolen. The laptop cost $2000 when it was purchased two years ago. A similar laptop computer today can be purchased for $1800. Assuming that the laptop was 50 percent depreciated at the time the theft occurred, what is the actual cash value of the loss?

5. Megan owns an antique table that has a current market value of $12,000. The table is specifically insured for $12,000 under a valued policy. The table is totally destroyed when a tornado touched down and damaged Megan's home. At the time of loss, the table had an estimated market value of $10,000. How much will Megan collect for the loss? Explain your answer.

6. A drunk driver ran a red light and smashed into Kristen's car. The cost to repair the car is $8000. She has collision insurance on her car with a $500 deductible.
   a. Can Kristen collect from both the negligent driver's insurer and her own insurer? Explain your answer.
   b. Explain how subrogation supports the principle of indemnity.

7. One requirement for the formation of a valid insurance contract is that the contract must be for a legal purpose.
   a. Identify three factors, other than the legal purpose requirement, that are essential to the formation of a binding insurance contract.
   b. Explain how each of the three requirements in part (a) is fulfilled when the applicant applies for an auto insurance policy.

8. Nicole is applying for a health insurance policy. She has a chronic liver ailment and other health problems. She honestly disclosed the true facts concerning her medical history to the insurance agent. However, the agent did not include all the facts in the application. Instead, the agent stated that he was going to cover the material facts in a separate letter to the insurance company's underwriting department. However, the agent did not furnish the material facts to the insurer, and the contract was issued as standard. A claim occurred shortly thereafter. After investigating the claim, the insurer denied payment. Nicole contends that the company should pay the claim because she answered honestly all questions that the agent asked.
   a. On what basis can the insurance company deny payment of the claim?
   b. What legal doctrines can Nicole use to support her argument that the claim should be paid?

INTERNET RESOURCES

■ **InsWeb** offers insurance quotes from the nation's strongest insurers. You can get quotes for auto insurance, homeowners insurance, term life insurance, individual health insurance, and other insurance lines as well. Visit the site at

http://www.insweb.com

■ **Lawyers.com** is an online source for identifying qualified legal counsel. The site contains consumer information on numerous legal topics, including insurance. Visit the site at

http://www.lawyers.com

■ The **Legal Information Institute** of Cornell University Law School provides detailed information on legal topics, including insurance law. Legal topics are listed alphabetically under "Law About . . ." Visit the site at

http://www.law.cornell.edu

■ **Nolo.com** is a leading source of self-help legal information for consumers, including topics on insurance law. The "Legal Encyclopedia" section contains several articles on insurance for consumers. Visit the site at

http://www.nolo.com

SELECTED REFERENCES

Anderson, Buist M. *Anderson on Life Insurance.* Boston: Little, Brown, 1991. See also *Anderson on Life Insurance, 1996 Supplement.*

Crawford, Muriel L. *Life and Health Insurance Law,* 8th ed. Boston, MA: Irwin/McGraw-Hill, 1998.

Fire, Casualty & Surety Bulletins. Fire and Marine volume. Erlanger, KY: National Underwriter Company. These bulletins contain interesting cases concerning the meaning of actual cash value, insurable interest, and other legal concepts.

Graves, Edward E., and Burke A. Christensen, eds. *McGill's Legal Aspects of Life Insurance*, 4th ed. Bryn Mawr, PA: The American College, 2004.

Keeton, Robert E., and Alan I. Widiss. *Insurance Law: A Guide to Fundamental Principles, Legal Doctrines, and Commercial Practices.* Student edition. St. Paul, MN: West Publishing, 1988.

Lorimer, James J., et al. *The Legal Environment of Insurance,* 4th ed., vols. 1 and 2. Malvern, PA: American Institute for Chartered Property and Liability Underwriters, 1993.

McGann, Diane M. *Life and Health Insurance Law.* Washington, DC: International Claim Association, 2005.

Wiening, Eric A. *Foundations of Risk Management and Insurance,* 1st ed. Malvern, PA: American Institute for CPCU/Insurance Institute of America, 2002, chs. 11–19.

Wiening, Eric A., and Donald S. Malecki. *Insurance Contract Analysis.* Malvern, PA: American Institute for Chartered Property Casualty Underwriters, 1992.

NOTES

1. *Jefferson Insurance Company of New York v. Superior Court of Alameda County,* 475 P. 2d 880 (1970).
2. Valued policy laws are in force in Arkansas, Florida, Georgia, Kansas, Louisiana, Minnesota, Mississippi, Missouri, Montana, Nebraska, New Hampshire, North Dakota, Ohio, South Carolina, South Dakota, Tennessee, Texas, West Virginia, and Wisconsin.

California also has a law that allows insureds to request a valued policy by paying for the insurance company's cost of inspection and property valuation. Iowa's law provides that the amount of insurance stated in a building insurance policy is *prima facie* evidence of the insurable value of the property on the date of the policy. Although Iowa's law is not a true valued policy law, it has the effect of shifting the burden of proof as to value of the building from the insured to the insurer in the settlement of claims.

3. *Gamel v. Continental Ins. Co.*, 463 S.W. 2d 590 (1971). For additional information concerning valued policy laws, the interested student should consult the *Fire, Casualty & Surety Bulletins*, Fire and Marine volume, Misc. Property section (Erlanger, KY: National Underwriter Company).

4. Edwin W. Patterson, *Essentials of Insurance Law*, 2nd ed. (New York: McGraw-Hill, 1957), pp. 109–111, 154–159.

5. Patterson, p. 114.

6. Buist M. Anderson, *Anderson on Life Insurance* (Boston: Little, Brown, 1991), p. 361.

7. Patterson, pp. 147–148.

8. James J. Lorimer et al., *The Legal Environment of Insurance*, 3rd ed., vol. 1 (Malvern, PA: American Institute for Property and Liability Underwriters, 1987), p. 376.

9. Lorimer et al., p. 377.

10. Patterson, p. 149.

11. Group health insurance contracts may contain subrogation clauses.

12. James J. Lorimer et al., *The Legal Environment of Insurance*, 4th ed., vol. 1 (Malvern, PA: American Institute for Chartered Property Casualty Underwriters, 1993), pp. 202–205.

13. Ibid., pp. 112–115.

14. Ibid., pp. 115–116.

15. Edward E. Graves and Burke A. Christensen, eds., *McGill's Legal Aspects of Life Insurance*, 4th ed. (Bryn Mawr, PA: The American College, 2004), p. 96.

16. Ibid., p. 46.

17. James J. Lorimer et al., *The Legal Environment of Insurance*, 3rd ed., vol. 1 (Malvern, PA: American Institute for Property and Liability Underwriters, 1987), pp. 402–403.

18. Ibid., p. 403.

19. Graves and Christensen, pp. 123–128.

20. Patterson, pp. 495–496.

21. Muriel L. Crawford, *Life & Health Insurance Law*, 8th ed. (Boston, MA: McGraw-Hill/Irwin, 1998), p. 107.

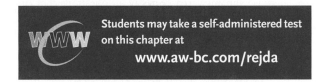

Students may take a self-administered test on this chapter at
www.aw-bc.com/rejda

CHAPTER 10

ANALYSIS OF INSURANCE CONTRACTS

"Let's kill all the lawyers."

William Shakespeare

LEARNING OBJECTIVES

After studying this chapter, you should be able to

◆ Identify the basic parts of any insurance contract.

◆ Explain the meaning of an "insured" in an insurance contract.

◆ Describe the common types of deductibles that appear in insurance contracts, including
    Straight deductible
    Calendar-year deductible

◆ Explain how coinsurance works in a property insurance contract.

◆ Show how coinsurance works in a health insurance contract.

◆ Explain how losses are paid when more than one insurance contract covers the same loss.

Kristi, age 30, is a physician's assistant in Oakland, CA. She purchased a home for $550,000. Shortly after she moved in, an earthquake occurred, and the home sustained a loss of $50,000. Kristi was upset when the claim adjustor told her that her homeowners policy would not cover the loss. Like most insureds, Kristi made the common mistake of not reading her homeowners policy before a loss occurred. As a result, she was not aware of the major policy exclusions, including the exclusion of earthquakes.

Kristi is not alone. Most people do not read or understand the contractual provisions that appear in their insurance policies. Individuals typically own several insurance policies, including auto and homeowners insurance as well as life and health insurance. These policies are complex legal documents that reflect the legal principles discussed in Chapter 9.

Although insurance contracts are not identical, they contain similar contractual provisions. This chapter discusses the basic parts of an insurance policy, the meaning of an "insured," endorsements and riders, deductibles, coinsurance, and other-insurance provisions. Grasping these topics will provide you with a foundation for a better understanding of specific insurance contracts discussed later in the text.

BASIC PARTS OF AN INSURANCE CONTRACT

Despite their complexities, insurance contracts generally can be divided into the following parts:

- Declarations
- Definitions
- Insuring agreement
- Exclusions
- Conditions
- Miscellaneous provisions

Although all insurance contracts do not necessarily contain all six parts in the order given here, such a classification provides a simple and convenient framework for analyzing most insurance contracts.

Declarations

The declarations section is the first part of an insurance contract. **Declarations** *are statements that provide information about the particular property or*

activity to be insured. Information contained in the declarations section is used for underwriting and rating purposes and for identification of the property or activity that is insured. The declarations section usually can be found on the first page of the policy or on a policy insert.

In property insurance, the declarations page typically contains information concerning the identification of the insurer, name of the insured, location of the property, period of protection, amount of insurance, amount of the premium, size of the deductible (if any), and other relevant information. In life insurance, although the first page of the policy technically is not called a declarations page, it contains the insured's name, age, premium amount, issue date, and policy number.

Definitions

Insurance contracts typically contain a page or section of definitions. Key words or phrases have quotation marks (". . .") around them or are in **boldface** type. For example, the insurer is frequently referred to as "we," "our," or "us." The named insured is referred to as "you" and "your." The purpose of the various definitions is to define clearly the meaning of key words or phrases so that coverage under the policy can be determined more easily.

Insuring Agreement

The insuring agreement is the heart of an insurance contract. The **insuring agreement** *summarizes the major promises of the insurer.* The insurer, in other words, agrees to do certain things, such as paying losses from covered perils, providing certain services (such as loss-prevention services), or agreeing to defend the insured in a liability lawsuit.

There are two basic forms of an insuring agreement in property insurance: (1) named-perils coverage and (2) "all-risks" coverage. *Under a* **named-perils policy,** *only those perils specifically named in the policy are covered.* If the peril is not named, it is not covered. For example, in the homeowners policy, personal property is covered for fire, lightning, windstorm, and certain other named perils. Only losses caused by these perils are covered. Flood damage is not covered because flood is not a listed peril.

Under an **"all-risks" policy,** *all losses are covered except those losses specifically excluded.* An "all-risks" policy is also called an **open-perils policy** and a **special coverage policy.** If the loss is not excluded, then it is covered. For example, the physical damage section of the personal auto policy covers losses to a covered auto. Thus, if a smoker burns a hole in the upholstery, or a bear in a national park damages the vinyl top of a covered auto, the losses would be covered because they are not excluded.

"All-risks" coverage is generally preferable to named-perils coverage, because the protection is broader with fewer gaps in coverage. If the loss is not excluded, then it is covered. In addition, a greater burden of proof is placed on the insurer to deny a claim. *To deny payment, the insurer must prove that the loss is excluded. In contrast, under a named-perils contract, the burden of proof is on the insured to show that the loss was caused by a named peril.*

Insurers and rating organizations generally have deleted the word *all* in their "all-risks" policy forms or are using special terminology. In the homeowners policy drafted by the Insurance Services Office, the phrase *"risk of direct physical loss to property"* is now used instead of the term *"all-risks."* However, this term is interpreted to mean that all losses to the described dwelling and other structures are covered except those losses specifically excluded. Likewise, the Insurance Services Office has drafted a *special-causes-of-loss form* that is used in commercial property insurance. Once again, this terminology is interpreted to mean that all losses are covered except those losses excluded. The deletion of any reference to "all-risks" is intended to avoid creating unreasonable expectations among policyowners that the policy covers all losses, even those losses that are specifically excluded.

Life insurance is another example of an "all-risks" policy. Most life insurance contracts cover all causes of death whether by accident or by disease. The major exclusions are suicide during the first two years of the contract; certain aviation hazard exclusions, such as military flying, crop dusting, or sports piloting; and in some contracts, death caused by war.

Exclusions

Exclusions are another basic part of any insurance contract. There are three major types of exclusions: excluded perils, excluded losses, and excluded property.

Excluded Perils   The contract may exclude certain perils, or causes of loss. In a homeowners policy, the perils of flood, earth movement, and nuclear radiation or radioactive contamination are specifically excluded. In the physical damage section of the personal auto policy, loss to a covered auto is specifically excluded if the car is used as a public taxi. In property and liability insurance, most insurance contracts exclude coverage for intentional acts.

Excluded Losses   Certain types of losses may be excluded. For example, in a homeowners policy, failure of an insured to protect the property from further damage after a loss occurs is excluded. In the personal liability section of a homeowners policy, a liability lawsuit arising out of the operation of an automobile is excluded. Professional liability losses are also excluded; a specific professional liability policy is needed to cover this exposure.

Excluded Property The contract may exclude or place limitations on the coverage of certain property. For example, in a homeowners policy, certain types of personal property are excluded, such as cars, planes, animals, birds, and fish.

Reasons for Exclusions Exclusions are necessary for the following reasons:[1]

- Some perils considered uninsurable
- Presence of extraordinary hazards
- Coverage provided by other contracts
- Moral hazard problems
- Coverage not needed by typical insureds

Exclusions are necessary because the peril may be considered uninsurable by commercial insurers. A given peril may depart substantially from the requirements of an insurable risk, as discussed in Chapter 2. For example, most property and casualty insurance contracts exclude losses for potential catastrophic events such as war or exposure to nuclear radiation. A health insurance contract may exclude losses within the direct control of the insured, such as an intentional, self-inflicted injury. Finally, predictable declines in the value of property, such as wear and tear and inherent vice, are not insurable. "Inherent vice" refers to the destruction or damage of property without any tangible external force, such as the tendency of fruit to rot and the tendency of diamonds to crack.

Exclusions are also used because extraordinary hazards are present. A hazard is a condition that increases the chance of loss or severity of loss. Because of an extraordinary increase in hazard, a loss may be excluded. For example, the premium for liability insurance under the personal auto policy is based on the assumption that the car is used for personal and recreational use and not as a taxi. The chance of an accident, and a resulting liability lawsuit, is much higher if the car is used as a taxi for hire. Therefore, to provide coverage for a taxi at the same premium rate for a family car could result in inadequate premiums for the insurer and unfair rate discrimination against other insureds who are not using their vehicles as a taxi.

Exclusions are also necessary because coverage can be better provided by other contracts. Exclusions are used to avoid duplication of coverage and to limit coverage to the policy best designed to pro-

vide it. For example, a car is excluded under a homeowners policy because it is covered under the personal auto policy and other auto insurance contracts. If both policies covered the loss, there would be unnecessary duplication.

In addition, certain property is excluded because of moral hazard or difficulty in determining and measuring the amount of loss. For example, homeowner contracts drafted by the Insurance Services Office limit the coverage of money to $200. If unlimited amounts of money were covered, fraudulent claims would increase. Also, loss-adjustment problems in determining the exact amount of the loss would also increase. Thus, because of moral hazard, exclusions are used.

Finally, exclusions are used because the coverage is not needed by the typical insured. For example, most homeowners do not own private planes. To cover aircraft as personal property under the homeowners policy would be grossly unfair to the vast majority of insureds who do not own planes because premiums would be substantially higher.

Conditions

Conditions are another important part of an insurance contract. **Conditions** *are provisions in the policy that qualify or place limitations on the insurer's promise to perform.* In effect, the conditions section imposes certain duties on the insured. If the policy conditions are not met, the insurer can refuse to pay the claim. Common policy conditions include notifying the insurer if a loss occurs, protecting the property after a loss, preparing an inventory of damaged personal property, and cooperating with the insurer in the event of a liability suit.

Miscellaneous Provisions

Insurance contracts also contain a number of miscellaneous provisions. In property and casualty insurance, miscellaneous provisions include cancellation, subrogation, requirements if a loss occurs, assignment of the policy, and other-insurance provisions. In life and health insurance, typical miscellaneous provisions include the grace period, reinstatement of a lapsed policy, and misstatement of age. Details of these provisions are discussed later in the text when specific insurance contracts are analyzed.

DEFINITION OF THE "INSURED"

Insurance contracts typically contain a definition of the "insured" under the policy. The contract must indicate the person or persons for whom the protection is provided. Several possibilities exist concerning the persons who are insured under the policy. First, some policies insure only *one person*. For example, in most life insurance contracts, only one person is specifically named as insured under the policy.

Second, the policy may contain a formal definition of the named insured. The **named insured** *is the person or persons named in the declarations section of the policy*. For example, in a homeowners policy, the named insured includes the person named in the declarations page and his or her spouse if a resident of the same household. Thus, Nicole may be the named insured under a homeowners policy. By definition, her husband is also included as a named insured as long as he resides in the same household.

The policy may also cover other parties even though they are not specifically named in the policy. For example, in addition to the named insured, a homeowners policy covers resident relatives of the named insured or spouse and any person under age 21 who is in the care of an insured, such as a foreign exchange student. The homeowners policy also covers resident relatives under age 24 who are full-time students and away from home. The personal auto policy covers the named insured and spouse, resident relatives, and any other person using the auto with the permission of the named insured (see Insight 10.1). In short, a contract may provide broad coverage with respect to the number of persons who are insured under the policy.

INSIGHT 10.1

Will Your Auto Insurance Cover You When You Drive Another Person's Car?

College students frequently drive cars that are owned by roommates or friends. Will your auto insurance cover you when you drive another person's car? Likewise, you may give permission to your roommate or friend to drive your car. Is your roommate or friend covered under your policy? To answer these questions, we must first examine the definition of an insured for liability coverage that appears in the 2005 Personal Auto Policy.

"Insured" as used in this Part means:[a]

1. You or any "family member for the ownership, maintenance or use of any auto or trailer."

2. Any person using "your covered auto."

3. For "your covered auto," any person or organization but only with respect to legal responsibility for acts or omissions of a person for whom coverage is afforded under this Part.

4. For any auto or "trailer," other than "your covered auto," any other person or organization but only with respect to legal responsibility for acts or omissions of you or any "family member" for whom coverage is afforded under this Part. This provision applies only if the person or organization does not own or hire the auto or "trailer."

For example, Chris and Karen Swift are the named insureds under the Personal Auto Policy that contains the above provision. Their son, Patrick, lives in a college dormitory during the school year while away from home. Although he does not live at home currently, he qualifies as a family member since the college stay is temporary, and he regards his parents' home as his permanent residence address.

Patrick drives a Honda titled in his parents' names. Because he is a family member, he clearly is an insured under the policy. What happens if Patrick allows his girlfriend to drive the Honda? Although she is not a family member, she nevertheless qualifies as "any person using your covered auto." Thus, the girlfriend is an insured.

What if Patrick occasionally drives his roommate's car? The car is not furnished for his regular use. Assuming Patrick is a family member under his parents' policy, he is insured while driving any car, including the roommate's car.

Finally, assume that Patrick is involved in an auto accident while delivering Thanksgiving food baskets for a local charity. The injured party sues both Patrick and the charitable organization. Patrick clearly is an insured and is covered. Is the charity also an "insured" under Patrick's policy? The answer is yes. The definition of insured extends coverage to any person or organization who is legally responsible for any acts or omissions by an insured. Thus, the charitable organization is considered an insured. Patrick's insurer must defend the charity in the suit.

[a]Insurance Services Office, 2005 Personal Auto Policy.

ENDORSEMENTS AND RIDERS

Insurance contracts frequently contain **endorsements and riders.** The terms *endorsements* and *riders* are often used interchangeably and mean the same thing. *In property and casualty insurance, an endorsement is a written provision that adds to, deletes from, or modifies the provisions in the original contract. In life and health insurance, a rider is a provision that amends or changes the original policy.*

There are numerous endorsements in property and casualty insurance that modify, extend, or delete provisions found in the original policy. For example, a homeowners policy excludes coverage for earthquakes. However, an earthquake endorsement can be added that covers damage from an earthquake or from earth movement.

In life and health insurance, numerous riders can be added that increase or decrease benefits, waive a condition of coverage present in the original policy, or amend the basic policy. For example, a waiver-of-premium rider can be added to a life insurance policy. If the insured becomes totally disabled, all future premiums are waived after an elimination period of six months, as long as the insured remains disabled according to the terms of the rider.

An endorsement attached to a the policy generally takes precedence over any conflicting terms in the policy. Also, many policies have endorsements that amend the policy to conform to a given state's law.

DEDUCTIBLES

A deductible is a common policy provision that requires the insured to pay part of the loss. A **deductible** *is a provision by which a specified amount is subtracted from the total loss payment that otherwise would be payable.* Deductibles typically are found in property, health, and auto insurance contracts. A deductible is not used in life insurance because the insured's death is always a total loss, and a deductible would simply reduce the face amount of insurance. Also, a deductible generally is not used in personal liability insurance because the insurer must provide a legal defense, even for a small claim. The insurer wants to be involved from the first dollar of loss so as to minimize its ultimate liability for a claim. Also, the premium reduction that would result from

a small deductible in personal types of third-party liability coverages would be relatively small.[2]

Purposes of Deductibles

Deductibles have several important purposes. They include the following:

- To eliminate small claims
- To reduce premiums
- To reduce moral and morale hazard

A deductible eliminates small claims that are expensive to handle and process. For example, an insurer can easily incur expenses of $500 or more in processing a $100 claim. Because a deductible eliminates small claims, the insurer's loss-adjustment expenses are reduced.

Deductibles are also used to reduce premiums paid by the insured. Because deductibles eliminate small claims, premiums can be substantially reduced. Insurance is not an appropriate technique for paying small losses that can be better budgeted out of personal or business income. Insurance should be used to cover large catastrophic events, such as medical expenses of $500,000 or more from an extended terminal illness. Insurance that protects against a catastrophic loss can be purchased more economically if deductibles are used. This concept of using insurance premiums to pay for large losses rather than for small losses is often called the **large-loss principle.** The objective is to cover large losses that can financially ruin an individual and exclude small losses that can be budgeted out of the person's income.

Other factors being equal, a large deductible is preferable to a small one. For example, many motorists with auto insurance have policies that contain a $250 deductible for collision losses instead of a $500 or larger deductible. They may not be aware of how expensive the extra insurance really is. For example, assume you can purchase collision insurance on your car with a $250 deductible with an annual premium of $900, while a policy with a $500 deductible has an annual premium of $800. If you select the $250 deductible over the $500 deductible, you have an additional $250 of collision insurance, but you must pay an additional $100 in annual premiums. Using a simple cost-benefit analysis, you are paying an additional $100 for an additional $250 of insurance, which is a relatively expensive increment of insurance. When analyzed in this manner, larger deductibles are preferable to smaller deductibles.

Finally, deductibles are used by insurers to reduce both moral and morale hazard. Some dishonest insureds may deliberately cause a loss in order to profit from insurance. Deductibles reduce moral hazard because the insured may not profit if a loss occurs.

Deductibles are also used to reduce morale hazard. Morale hazard is carelessness or indifference to a loss because of insurance, which increases the chance of loss. Deductibles encourage people to be more careful with respect to the protection of their property and prevention of a loss because the insured must bear a part of the loss.

Deductibles in Property Insurance

The following deductibles are commonly found in property insurance contracts:

- Straight deductible
- Aggregate deductible

Straight Deductible   With a **straight deductible,** *the insured must pay a certain number of dollars of loss before the insurer is required to make a payment.* Such a deductible typically applies to each loss. An example can be found in automobile collision insurance. For instance, assume that Ashley has collision insurance on her new Toyota, with a $500 deductible. If a collision loss is $7000, she would receive only $6500 and would have to pay the remaining $500 herself.

Aggregate Deductible   Commercial insurance contracts sometimes contain an aggregate deductible. An **aggregate deductible** means that all losses that occur during a specified time period, usually a policy year, are accumulated to satisfy the deductible amount. Once the deductible is satisfied, the insurer pays all future losses in full. For example, assume that the policy contains an aggregate deductible of $10,000. Also assume that losses of $1000 and $2000 occur, respectively, during the policy year. The insurer pays nothing because the deductible is not met. If a third loss of $8000 occurs during the same time period, the insurer would pay $1000. Any other losses occurring during the policy year would be paid in full.

Deductibles in Health Insurance

In health insurance, the deductible can be stated in terms of dollars or time. Deductibles in health insurance include the following:

- Calendar-year deductible
- Corridor deductible
- Elimination (waiting) period

Calendar-year Deductible   A **calendar-year deductible** *is a type of aggregate deductible that is found in basic medical expense and major medical insurance contracts.* Eligible medical expenses are accumulated during the calendar year, and once they exceed the deductible amount, the insurer must then pay the benefits promised under the contract. Once the deductible is satisfied during the calendar year, no additional deductibles are imposed on the insured.

Corridor Deductible   Employers with basic medical expense plans often wish to supplement the basic benefits with major medical benefits. A **corridor deductible** *is a deductible that can be used to integrate a basic medical expense plan with a supplemental major medical expense plan.* The corridor deductible must be satisfied before the major medical plan pays any benefits.

The corridor deductible applies only to eligible medical expenses that are not covered by the basic medical expense plan. For example, assume that Janet has $20,000 of covered medical expenses, of which $16,000 is paid by the basic medical expense plan. If the supplemental major medical plan has a $300 corridor deductible, Janet must pay $300. The supplemental plan will cover the remaining $3700 of expenses, subject to any limitations or coinsurance provisions that may apply.

Elimination (Waiting) Period   A deductible can also be expressed as an elimination period. An **elimination (waiting) period** *is a stated period of time at the beginning of a loss during which no insurance benefits are paid.* An elimination period is appropriate for a single loss that occurs over some time period, such as the loss of work earnings. Elimination periods are commonly used in disability-income contracts. For example, disability-income insurance contracts that replace part of a disabled worker's earnings typically have elimination periods of 30, 60, or 90 days, or even longer periods.

COINSURANCE

Coinsurance is a contractual provision that often appears in property insurance contracts. This is especially true of commercial property insurance contracts.

Nature of Coinsurance

A **coinsurance clause** *in a property insurance contract encourages the insured to insure the property to a stated percentage of its insurable value. If the co-insurance requirement is not met at the time of loss, the insured must share in the loss as a coinsurer.* The insurable value of the property is the actual cash value, replacement cost, or some other value described in the valuation clause of the policy. If the insured wants to collect in full for a partial loss, the coinsurance requirement must be satisfied. Otherwise, the insured will be penalized if a partial loss occurs.

A coinsurance formula is used to determine the amount paid for a covered loss. The coinsurance formula is as follows:

$$\frac{\text{Amount of insurance carried}}{\text{Amount of insurance required}} \times \text{Loss} = \frac{\text{Amount}}{\text{of recovery}}$$

For example, assume that a commercial building has an actual cash value of $1,000,000 and that the owner has insured it for only $600,000. If an 80 percent coinsurance clause is present in the policy, the required amount of insurance based on actual cash value is $800,000 (80% × $1,000,000). If a replacement cost policy is used, the required amount of insurance would be based on replacement cost. Thus, if a $100,000 loss occurs, only $75,000 will be paid by the insurer. This calculation can be illustrated as follows:

$$\frac{\$600,000}{\$800,000} \times \$100,000 = \$75,000$$

Since the insured has only three-fourths of the required amount of insurance in force at the time of loss, only three-fourths of the loss, or $75,000, will be paid. Because the coinsurance requirement is not met, the insured must absorb the remaining amount of the loss.

When applying the coinsurance formula, two additional points should be kept in mind. First, the amount paid can never exceed the amount of the actual loss even though the coinsurance formula produces such a result. This case could happen if the amount of insurance carried is greater than the minimum required amount of insurance. Second, the maximum amount paid for any loss is limited to the face amount of insurance.

Purpose of Coinsurance

The fundamental purpose of coinsurance is to achieve **equity in rating.** Most property insurance losses are partial rather than total losses. But if everyone insures only for the partial loss rather than for the total loss, the premium rate for each $100 of insurance would be higher. This rate would be inequitable to insureds who wish to insure their property to full value. For example, if everyone insures to full value, assume that the pure premium rate for fire insurance is 25 cents for each $100 of insurance, ignoring expenses and the profit allowance of the insurer (see Exhibit 10.1).

However, if each property owner insures only for a partial loss, the pure premium rate will increase from 25 cents per $100 of fire insurance to 40 cents per $100 (see Exhibit 10.2). This rate would be inequitable to property owners who want to insure their buildings to full value. If full coverage is desired, the insured would have to pay a higher rate of 40 cents, which we calculated earlier to be worth only 25 cents. This rate would be inequitable. *So, if the coinsurance requirement is met, the insured*

EXHIBIT **10.1**
Insurance to Full Value

Assume that 2000 buildings are valued at $200,000 each and are insured to full value for a total of $400 million of fire insurance. The following fire losses occur:

2 total losses	=	$ 400,000
30 partial losses at $20,000 each	=	$ 600,000
Total fire losses paid by insurer	=	$1,000,000
Pure premium rate	=	$\frac{\$1,000,000}{\$400,000,000}$
	=	25 cents per $100 of insurance

EXHIBIT 10.2
Insurance to Half Value

Assume that 2000 buildings are valued at $200,000 each and are insured to half value for a total of $200 million of fire insurance. The following fire losses occur:

2 total losses ($400,000)

Insurer pays only	=	$200,000
30 partial losses at $20,000 each	=	$600,000
Total fire losses paid by insurer	=	$800,000
Pure premium rate	=	$\dfrac{\$800,000}{\$200,000,000}$
	=	40 cents per $100 of insurance

receives a rate discount, and the policyowner who is underinsured is penalized through application of the coinsurance formula.

As an alternative to coinsurance, *graded rates* can be used, by which rate discounts are given as the amount of insurance to value is increased. However, this system requires an accurate appraisal of each property to determine the required amount of insurance, which would be extremely expensive for the insurer. In addition, the appraisal method is unsatisfactory if property values fluctuate widely during the policy period. For these reasons, the coinsurance formula, rather than a table of graded rates, is used to achieve equity in rating.

Coinsurance Problems

Some practical problems arise when a coinsurance clause is present in a contract. First, inflation can result in a serious coinsurance penalty if the amount of insurance is not periodically increased for inflation. The insured may be in compliance with the coinsurance clause when the policy first goes into effect; however, price inflation could increase the replacement cost of the property. The result is that the insured may not be carrying the required amount of insurance at the time of loss, and he or she will then be penalized if a loss occurs. Thus, if a coinsurance clause is present, the amount of insurance carried should be periodically evaluated to determine whether the coinsurance requirement is being met.

Second, the insured may incur a coinsurance penalty if property values fluctuate widely during the

policy period. For example, there may be a substantial increase in inventory values because of an unexpected arrival of a shipment of goods. If a loss occurs, the insured may not be carrying sufficient insurance to avoid a coinsurance penalty. One solution to this problem is an *agreed value coverage,* by which the insurer agrees in advance that the amount of insurance carried meets the coinsurance requirement. Another solution is a *reporting form,* by which property values are periodically reported to the insurer.

COINSURANCE IN HEALTH INSURANCE

Health insurance contracts frequently contain a coinsurance clause, which is technically called a **percentage participation clause.** In particular, major medical policies typically have a coinsurance provision that requires the insured to pay a certain percentage of covered medical expenses in excess of the deductible. A typical plan requires the insured to pay 20 or 25 percent of covered expenses in excess of the deductible. For example, assume that Megan has covered medical expenses in the amount of $50,500, and that she has a major medical policy with a $500 deductible and an 80-20 coinsurance clause. The insurer pays 80 percent of the bill in excess of the deductible, or $40,000, and Megan pays 20 percent, or $10,000 (plus the $500 deductible).

The purposes of coinsurance in health insurance are (1) to reduce premiums and (2) to prevent over-utilization of policy benefits. Because the insured pays part of the cost, premiums are reduced. In addition, the patient will not demand the most expensive medical services if he or she pays part of the cost.

OTHER-INSURANCE PROVISIONS

Other-insurance provisions typically are present in property and casualty insurance and health insurance contracts. These provisions apply when more than one contract covers the same loss. *The purpose of these provisions is to prevent profiting from insurance and violation of the principle of indemnity.* If the insured could collect the full amount of the loss from each insurer, there would be profiting from insurance and a substantial increase in moral hazard. Some dishonest insureds would deliberately cause a loss to collect multiple benefits.

Some important other-insurance provisions in property and liability insurance include (1) the pro rata liability clause, (2) contribution by equal shares, and (3) primary and excess insurance.

Pro Rata Liability

Pro rata liability is a generic term for a provision that applies when two or more policies of the same type cover the same insurable interest in the property. *Each insurer's share of the loss is based on the proportion that its insurance bears to the total amount of insurance on the property.* For example, assume that Jacob owns a building and wishes to insure it for $500,000. For underwriting reasons, insurers may limit the amount of insurance they will write on a given property. Assume that an agent places $300,000 of insurance with Company A, $100,000 with Company B, and $100,000 with Company C, for a total of $500,000. If a $100,000 loss occurs, each company will pay only its pro rata share of the loss (see Exhibit 10.3). Thus, Jacob would collect $100,000 for the loss, not $300,000.

The basic purpose of the pro rata liability clause is to preserve the principle of indemnity and to prevent profiting from insurance. In the preceding example, if the pro rata liability clause were not present, the insured would collect $100,000 from each insurer, or a total of $300,000 for a $100,000 loss.

Contribution by Equal Shares

Contribution by equal shares is another type of other-insurance provision that often appears in liability insurance contracts. Each insurer shares equally in

EXHIBIT 10.3
Pro Rata Liability Example

Company A	$\dfrac{\$300,000}{\$500,000}$	or .60 × $100,000 = $ 60,000
Company B	$\dfrac{\$100,000}{\$500,000}$	or .20 × $100,000 = $ 20,000
Company C	$\dfrac{\$100,000}{\$500,000}$	or .20 × $100,000 = $ 20,000
	Total loss payment	= $100,000

the loss until the share paid by each insurer equals the lowest limit of liability under any policy, or until the full amount of the loss is paid. For example, assume that the amount of insurance provided by Companies A, B, and C is $100,000, $200,000, and $300,000, respectively. If the loss is $150,000 each insurer pays an equal share, or $50,000 (see Exhibit 10.4).

However, if the loss were $500,000, how much would each insurer pay? In this case, each insurer would pay equal amounts until its policy limits are exhausted. The remaining insurers then continue to share equally in the remaining amount of the loss until each insurer has paid its policy limit in full, or until the full amount of the loss is paid. Thus, Company A would pay $100,000, Company B would pay $200,000, and Company C would pay $200,000 (see Exhibit 10.5). If the loss were $600,000, Company C would pay the remaining $100,000.

Primary and Excess Insurance

Primary and excess insurance is another type of other-insurance provision. The primary insurer pays first, and the excess insurer pays only after the policy limits under the primary policy are exhausted.

EXHIBIT 10.4
Contribution by Equal Shares (Example 1)

Amount of Loss = $150,000

	Amount of Insurance	*Contribution by Equal Shares*	*Total Paid*
Company A	$100,000	$50,000	$50,000
Company B	$200,000	$50,000	$50,000
Company C	$300,000	$50,000	$50,000

EXHIBIT 10.5
Contribution by Equal Shares (Example 2)

Amount of Loss = $500,000

	Amount of Insurance	Contribution by Equal Shares	Total Paid
Company A	$100,000	$100,000	$100,000
Company B	$200,000	$100,000 + $100,000	$200,000
Company C	$300,000	$100,000 + $100,000	$200,000

Auto insurance is an excellent example of primary and excess insurance. For example, assume that Bob occasionally drives Jill's car. Bob's policy has a liability insurance limit of $100,000 per person for bodily injury liability. Jill's policy has a limit of $50,000 per person for bodily injury liability. If Bob negligently injures another motorist while driving Jill's car, both policies will cover the loss. *The normal rule is that liability insurance on the borrowed car is primary and any other insurance is considered excess.* Thus, if a court orders Bob to pay damages of $75,000, Jill's policy is primary and pays the first $50,000. Bob's policy is excess and pays the remaining $25,000.

The **coordination-of-benefits provision** in group health insurance is another example of primary and excess coverage. This provision is designed to prevent overinsurance and the duplication of benefits if one person is covered under more than one group health insurance plan.

The majority of states have adopted part or all of the coordination-of-benefits provisions developed by the National Association of Insurance Commission-

ers (NAIC). The rules are complex, and only two of them are discussed here. *First, coverage as an employee is usually primary to coverage as a dependent.* For example, assume that Jack and Kelly McVay are both employed, and that each is insured as a dependent under the other's group health insurance plan. If Jack incurs covered medical expenses, his policy pays first as primary coverage. He then submits his unreimbursed expenses (such as the deductible and coinsurance payments) to Kelly's insurer. Kelly's coverage then applies as excess insurance. No more than 100 percent of the eligible medical expenses are paid under both plans.

Second, the birthday rule applies to dependents in families where the parents are married or are not separated. Under this rule, *the plan of the parent whose birthday occurs first during the year is primary.* For example, assume that Kelly's birthday is in January, and Jack's birthday is in July. If their daughter is hospitalized, Kelly's plan is primary. Jack's plan would be excess. The purpose of the birthday rule is to eliminate gender discrimination with respect to coverage of dependents.

CASE APPLICATION

Mike took his friend, Donna, out to dinner on her birthday. While driving Donna home, Mike became ill and asked Donna to drive. While driving Mike's car, Donna negligently injured another motorist when she failed to stop at a red light. Mike has an auto insurance policy with a liability insurance limit of $250,000 per person for bodily injury liability. Donna has a similar auto insurance policy with a liability limit of $100,000 per person.

a. If a court awards a liability judgment of $100,000 against Donna, how much, if any, will each insurer pay?

b. If the liability judgment is $300,000, how much, if any, will each insurer pay?

c. Assume that Mike cannot afford to pay the premium and lets his auto insurance policy lapse. At the time of the accident, he is uninsured. If the liability judgment against Donna is $100,000, how much, if any, will Donna's insurer pay?

SUMMARY

- Insurance contracts generally can be divided into the following parts:

    Declarations

    Definitions

    Insuring agreement

    Exclusions

    Conditions

    Miscellaneous provisions

- Declarations are statements concerning the property or activity to be insured.

- The definitions page or section defines the key words or phrases so that coverage under the policy can be determined more easily.

- The insuring agreement summarizes the promises of the insurer. There are two basic types of insuring agreements:

    Named-perils coverage

    "All-risks" coverage

- All policies contain one or more exclusions. There are three major types of exclusions:

    Excluded perils

    Excluded losses

    Excluded property

- Exclusions are necessary for several reasons. Certain perils are considered uninsurable by private insurers; extraordinary hazards may be present; coverage is provided by other contracts; moral hazard is present to a high degree; and coverage is not needed by the typical insured.

- Conditions are provisions that qualify or place limitations on the insurer's promise to perform. Conditions impose certain duties on the insured if he or she wishes to collect for a loss.

- Miscellaneous provisions in property and casualty insurance include cancellation, subrogation, requirements if a loss occurs, assignment of the policy, and other insurance provisions.

- The contract also contains a definition of "insured." The contract may cover only one person, or it may cover other persons as well even though they are not specifically named in the policy.

- An endorsement, or rider, is a written provision that adds to, deletes from, or modifies the provisions in the original contract. An endorsement or rider normally has precedence over any conflicting terms in the contract to which the endorsement is attached.

- A deductible requires the insured to pay part of the loss. A specified amount is subtracted from the total loss payment that otherwise would be payable. Deductibles are used to eliminate small claims, to reduce premiums, and to reduce moral and morale hazard. Examples of deductibles include a straight deductible, aggregate deductible, calendar-year deductible, corridor deductible, and elimination (waiting) period.

- A coinsurance clause in property insurance requires the insured to insure the property for a stated percentage of its insurable value at the time of loss. If the coinsurance requirement is not met at the time of loss, the insured must share in the loss as a coinsurer. The fundamental purpose of coinsurance is to achieve equity in rating.

- A coinsurance clause (percentage participation clause) is typically found in major medical policies. A typical provision requires the insurer to pay 80 percent of covered expenses in excess of the deductible and the insured to pay 20 percent.

- Other-insurance provisions are present in many insurance contracts. These provisions apply when more than one policy covers the same loss. The purpose of these provisions is to prevent profiting from insurance and violation of the principle of indemnity. Some important other-insurance provisions include the pro rata liability clause, contribution by equal shares, and primary and excess insurance.

KEY CONCEPTS AND TERMS

Aggregate deductible
"All-risks" policy
Calendar-year deductible
Coinsurance clause
Conditions
Contribution by equal shares
Coordination-of-benefits provision
Corridor deductible
Declarations
Deductible
Elimination (waiting) period
Endorsements and riders
Equity in rating
Exclusions
Insuring agreement

Large-loss principle
Named insured
Named-perils policy
Open-perils policy
Other-insurance
  provisions
Percentage participation
  clause (coinsurance)
Primary and excess
  insurance

Pro rata liability
Special coverage policy
Straight deductible

REVIEW QUESTIONS

1. Identify the basic parts of an insurance contract.

2. a. Describe the major types of exclusions typically found in insurance contracts.
   b. Why are exclusions used by insurers?

3. a. Define the term "conditions."
   b. Does the insurer have to pay an otherwise covered loss if the insured fails to comply with the policy conditions? Explain your answer.

4. a. What is the meaning of "named insured"?
   b. Can other parties be insured under a policy even though they are not specifically named? Explain your answer.

5. a. What is an endorsement or rider?
   b. If an endorsement conflicts with a policy provision, how is the problem resolved?

6. a. Describe the following types of deductibles:
      (i) straight deductible
      (ii) calendar-year deductible
      (iii) aggregate deductible
   b. Explain the purposes of deductibles in property insurance contracts.

7. a. Explain how a coinsurance clause in property insurance works.
   b. What is the fundamental purpose of a coinsurance clause?

8. Describe a typical coinsurance clause (percentage participation clause) in a major medical policy.

9. a. What is the purpose of other-insurance provisions?
   b. Give an example of the pro-rata liability clause.

10. Explain the meaning of primary insurance and excess insurance.

APPLICATION QUESTIONS

1. Michael owns a small plane that he flies on weekends. His agent informs him that aircraft are excluded as personal property under the homeowners policy. As an insured, he feels that his plane should be covered just like any other personal property he owns.
   a. Explain to Michael the rationale for excluding certain types of property, such as aircraft, under the homeowners policy.
   b. Explain some additional reasons why exclusions are present in insurance contracts.

2. a. A manufacturing firm incurred the following insured losses, in the order given, during the current policy year.

Loss	Amount of Loss
A	$ 2500
B	3500
C	10,000

   How much would the company's insurer pay for each loss if the policy contained the following type of deductible?
   (1) $1000 straight deductible
   (2) $15,000 annual aggregate deductible
   b. Explain the coordination-of-benefits provision that is typically found in group medical expense plans.

3. Stephanie owns a small warehouse that is insured for $200,000 under a commercial property insurance policy. The policy contains an 80 percent coinsurance clause. The warehouse sustained a $50,000 loss because of a fire in a storage area. The replacement cost of the warehouse at the time of loss is $500,000.
   a. What is the insurer's liability, if any, for this loss? Show your calculations.
   b. Assume that Stephanie carried $500,000 of property insurance on the warehouse at the time of loss. If the amount of loss is $10,000, how much will she collect?
   c. Explain the theory or rationale of coinsurance in a property insurance contract.

4. Andrew owns a commercial office building that is insured under three property insurance contracts. He has $100,000 of insurance from Company A, $200,000 from Company B, and $200,000 from Company C.

a. Assume that the pro rata liability provision appears in each contract. If a $100,000 loss occurs, how much will Andrew collect from each insurer? Explain your answer.

b. What is the purpose of the other-insurance provisions that are frequently found in insurance contracts?

5. Assume that a $300,000 liability claim is covered under two liability insurance contracts. Policy A has a $500,000 limit of liability for the claim, while Policy B has a $125,000 limit of liability. Both contracts provide for contribution by equal shares.

a. How much will each insurer contribute toward this claim? Explain your answer.

b. If the claim were only $50,000, how much would each insurer pay?

6. Ashley has a major medical health insurance policy with a $2 million lifetime limit. The policy has a $500 calendar year deductible and an 80-20 coinsurance clause (percentage participation clause). Ashley had outpatient surgery to remove a bunion on her foot and incurred medical bills of $10,000. How much will Ashley's insurer pay? How much will Ashley have to pay?

7. The Lincoln Saltdogs is a professional minor league baseball team in the American Association league. The clubhouse is insured for $300,000 under a commercial property insurance policy with an 80 percent coinsurance clause. The current replacement cost of the clubhouse is $500,000. After a playoff game for the league championship, a whirlpool tub for injured players shorted out, and a fire ensued. The clubhouse sustained a $40,000 fire loss. Ignoring any deductible, how much will the team's insurer pay for the loss?

INTERNET RESOURCES

■ The **New York State Insurance Department** publishes a number of consumer publications on basic insurance contracts that can be ordered online. The publications are helpful in understanding the various contractual provisions and coverages that appear in homeowners and auto insurance and other insurance contracts. Visit the site at

http://www.ins.state.ny.us

■ The **Office of the Commissioner of Insurance, State of Wisconsin** also makes available consumer publications on specific insurance contracts. These publications are helpful in understanding the contractual provisions and coverages that appear in life, health, auto, and homeowners insurance. Visit the site at

http://oci.wi.gov

■ The **Insurance Information Institute** publishes consumer materials dealing with property and liability insurance. The publications can help you understand the contractual provisions and coverages that appear in homeowners, auto, personal liability, and flood insurance, and other property and casualty insurance coverages. Visit the site at

http://www.iii.org

■ The **Texas Department of Insurance** provides a considerable amount of consumer information on auto, homeowners, life and health, and other types of insurance. Information on how to file a complaint against an insurer is also provided. Visit the site at

http://www.tdi.state.tx.us/index.html

SELECTED REFERENCES

Anderson, Buist M. *Anderson on Life Insurance.* Boston: Little, Brown, 1991. See also *Anderson on Life Insurance—1996 Supplement.*

Crawford, Muriel L. *Life and Health Insurance Law,* 8th ed. Boston: McGraw-Hill/Irwin, 1998.

Graves, Edward E., and Burke A. Christensen, eds. *McGill's Legal Aspects of Life Insurance,* 4th ed. Bryn Mawr, PA: The American College Press, 2004.

Keeton, Robert E., and Alan I. Widiss. *Insurance Law: A Guide to Fundamental Principles, Legal Doctrines, and Commercial Practices,* student edition. St. Paul, MN: West Publishing, 1988.

Lorimer, James J., et al. *The Legal Environment of Insurance,* 4th ed., vols. 1 and 2. Malvern, PA: American Institute for Property and Liability Underwriters, 1993.

McGann, Diane M. *Life and Health Insurance Law.* Washington, DC: International Claim Association, 2005.

Wiening, Eric A. *Foundations of Risk Management and Insurance*. Malvern, PA: American Society for CPCU/Insurance Institute of America, 2002, chs. 11–19.

Wiening, Eric A., and Donald S. Malecki. *Insurance Contract Analysis*. Malvern, PA: American Institute for Chartered Property Casualty Underwriters, 1992.

NOTES

1. C. Arthur Williams, Jr., George L. Head, Ronald C. Horn, and G. William Glendenning, *Principles of Risk Management and Insurance*, 2nd ed., vol. 2 (Malvern, PA: American Institute for Property Casualty Underwriters, 1981), pp. 52–56.

2. Ibid., pp. 200–201.

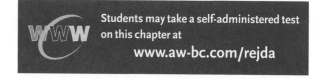

Students may take a self-administered test on this chapter at www.aw-bc.com/rejda

PART FOUR
LIFE AND HEALTH RISKS

Chapter 11
Life Insurance

Chapter 12
Life Insurance Contractual Provisions

Chapter 13
Buying Life Insurance

Chapter 14
Annuities and Individual Retirement Accounts

Chapter 15
Individual Health Insurance Coverages

Chapter 16
Employee Benefits: Group Life and Health Insurance

Chapter 17
Employee Benefits: Retirement Plans

Chapter 18
Social Insurance

CHAPTER 11

LIFE INSURANCE

"Death is one of the few things that can be done as easily lying down."

Woody Allen

"There are more dead people than living, and their numbers are increasing."

Eugene Ionesco

LEARNING OBJECTIVES

After studying this chapter, you should be able to:

◆ Explain the meaning of premature death.

◆ Describe the financial impact of premature death on the different types of families.

◆ Explain the needs approach for estimating the amount of life insurance to own.

◆ Describe the basic characteristics of term life insurance.

◆ Explain the basic characteristics of ordinary life insurance.

◆ Describe the following variations of whole life insurance:
   Variable life insurance
   Universal life insurance
   Variable universal life insurance

◆ Describe the basic characteristics of current assumption life insurance.

*J*eff, age 30, and Nicole, age 28, are married and have two preschool children. Nicole earns $50,000 annually as a registered nurse. Jeff earns $45,000 as a self-employed carpet layer. The couple has little savings, and both incomes are needed to maintain their standard of living. While carrying a heavy roll of carpet into a customer's house, Jeff died unexpectedly from a heart attack. At the time of his death, he was insured for only $25,000 under an individual life insurance policy. Can the family survive on the $25,000 left to them? Probably not. Although Social Security survivor benefits are payable, the monthly benefits are not large enough to replace all of his earnings. In addition, other financial factors must be considered, including funeral expenses, credit card debts, the remaining mortgage balance, and funding the children's college education. Clearly, $25,000 will not go far. Jeff's unexpected and untimely death will create economic insecurity for the surviving family members.

This chapter discusses the risk of premature death and how life insurance can alleviate the financial consequences of premature death. Topics covered include the meaning of premature death, the need for life insurance based on family type, determining the correct amount of life insurance to own, and a discussion of the major types of life insurance sold today.

PREMATURE DEATH

Meaning of Premature Death

Premature death *can be defined as the death of a family head with outstanding unfulfilled financial obligation,* such as dependents to support, children to educate, and a mortgage to pay off. Premature death can cause serious financial problems for the surviving family members because their share of the deceased family head's future earnings is lost forever. If replacement income from other sources is inadequate, or if the accumulated financial assets available to the family are also inadequate, the surviving family members will be exposed to great economic insecurity.

Costs of Premature Death

Certain costs are associated with premature death. First, the family's share of the deceased breadwinner's future earnings is lost forever. Second, additional expenses are incurred because of funeral expenses, uninsured medical bills, and estate settlement costs. Third, because of insufficient income, some families will experience a reduction in their standard of living. Finally, certain noneconomic costs are incurred, such as intense grief, loss of a parental role model, and counseling and guidance for the children.

Declining Problem of Premature Death

The economic problem of premature death has declined substantially over time because of an increase in life expectancy. Life expectancy is the average number of years of life remaining to a person at a particular age. *According to the Centers for Disease Control and Prevention, estimated average life expectancy* at birth *in the United States increased to a record 77.9 years in 2004, up from 77.5 years in 2003.*[1] Life expectancy has increased significantly over the past century because of substantial breakthroughs in medical science, rising real incomes and economic growth, and improvements in public health and sanitation.

Although life expectancy has increased, millions of Americans still die annually from three major causes of deaths: heart disease, cancer, and stroke.

Economic Justification for Life Insurance

The purchase of life insurance is economically justified if the insured has earned income, and others are dependent on those earnings for part or all of their financial support. If a family head dies prematurely with dependents to support and outstanding financial obligations, the surviving family members are exposed to great economic insecurity. Life insurance can be used to restore the family's share of the deceased breadwinner's earnings.

FINANCIAL IMPACT OF PREMATURE DEATH ON DIFFERENT TYPES OF FAMILIES

Single People

The number of single people has increased in recent years. Younger adults are postponing marriage, often beyond age 30, and many young and middle-aged adults are single again because of divorce. Premature death of single people with no dependents to support or other financial obligations is not likely to create a financial problem for others. Other than needing a modest amount of life insurance for funeral expenses and uninsured medical bills, this group does not need large amounts of life insurance. One exception is a single divorced parent who has child-support obligations. Premature death can create a serious financial problem for the surviving children.

Single-Parent Families

The number of single-parent families with children under age 18 has increased in recent years because of the large number of children born outside of marriage, divorce, legal separation, and death. Premature death of the single parent can cause great economic insecurity for the surviving children. *The need for large amounts of life insurance on the family head is great.* However, many single parents, especially families with female heads, have incomes below the

poverty line. Many of these families are simply too poor to purchase large amounts of insurance.

Two-Income Earners with Children

Families in which both spouses work outside the home have largely replaced the traditional family in which only one spouse is in the paid labor force. In two-income families with children, the death of one income earner can cause considerable economic insecurity for the surviving family members, because both incomes are necessary to maintain the family's standard of living. *Both income earners need substantial amounts of life insurance.* The life insurance can replace the lost earnings if one family head dies prematurely.

However, in two-income families without children, premature death of one income earner is not likely to cause economic insecurity for the surviving spouse. The need for large amounts of life insurance by income earners within this group is considerably less.

Traditional Families

Traditional families are families in which only one parent is in the labor force, and the other parent stays at home to take care of dependent children. *The working parent in the labor force needs substantial amounts of life insurance.* If the working spouse dies with an insufficient amount of life insurance, the family may have to adjust its standard of living downward.

In addition, the nonemployed spouse who is caring for dependent children also needs life insurance. The cost of child-care services can be a heavy financial burden to the working spouse if the nonemployed spouse dies prematurely.

Blended Families

A blended family is one in which a divorced spouse with children remarries, and the new spouse also has children. *The need for life insurance on both family heads is great.* Both spouses generally are in the labor force at the time of remarriage, and the death of one spouse may result in a reduction in the family's standard of living since the family's share of that income is lost.

Sandwiched Families

A sandwiched family is one in which a son or daughter with children provides financial support or other services to one or both parents. Thus, the son or daughter is "sandwiched" between the younger and older generations. *A working spouse in a sandwiched family needs a substantial amount of life insurance.* Premature death of a working spouse in a sandwiched family can result in the loss of financial support to both the surviving children and the aged parent(s).

Finally, in the family types discussed above, minor children are typically present who require financial support. Because parents usually support minor children, buying large amounts of life insurance on children is not recommended. *The major disadvantage in insuring minor children is that the family head may be inadequately insured.* Scarce premium dollars that could be used to increase the amount of life insurance on the family head are instead diverted to cover the children.

AMOUNT OF LIFE INSURANCE TO OWN

Once you determine that you need life insurance, the next step is to calculate the amount of life insurance to own. Some life insurers and financial planners recommend that insureds carry life insurance equal to some multiple of their earnings, such as six to ten times annual earnings. Such rules, however, are meaningless because they do not take into account that the need for life insurance varies widely depending on family size, income levels, existing financial assets, and financial goals.

Three approaches can be used to estimate the amount of life insurance to own:

- Human life value approach
- Needs approach
- Capital retention approach

Human Life Value Approach

As noted earlier, the family's share of the deceased breadwinner's earnings is lost forever if the family head dies prematurely. This loss is called the human life value. **Human life value** *can be defined as the present value of the family's share of the deceased breadwinner's future earnings.* It can be calculated by the following steps:

1. Estimate the individual's average annual earnings over his or her productive lifetime.
2. Deduct federal and state income taxes, Social Security taxes, life and health insurance premiums, and the costs of self-maintenance. The remaining amount is used to support the family.
3. Determine the number of years from the person's present age to the contemplated age of retirement.
4. Using a reasonable discount rate, determine the present value of the family's share of earnings for the period determined in step 3.

For example, assume that Richard, age 27, is married and has two children. He earns $50,000 annually and plans to retire at age 67. (For the sake of simplicity, assume that his earnings remain constant.) Of this amount, $20,000 is used for federal and state taxes, life and health insurance, and Richard's personal needs. The remaining $30,000 is used to support his family. This stream of future income is then discounted back to the present to determine Richard's human life value. Using a reasonable discount rate of 6 percent, the present value of $1 payable annually for 40 years is $15.05. Therefore, Richard has a human life value of $451,500 ($30,000 × $15.05 = $451,500). This amount represents the present value of the family's share of Richard's earnings that would be lost if he dies prematurely. As you can see, the human life has an enormous economic value when earning capacity is considered. The major advantage of the human life value concept is that it crudely measures the economic value of a human life.

However, the human life value approach has several limitations. First, other sources of income are ignored, such as Social Security survivor benefits. Second, in its simplest form, work earnings and expenses are assumed to be constant, and employee benefits are ignored. Third, the amount of money allocated to the family can quickly change because of divorce, birth of a child, or death of a family member. Also, the long run discount rate is critical; the human life value can be substantially increased by assuming a lower rate. Finally, the effects of inflation on earnings and expenses are ignored.

Needs Approach

The second method for estimating the amount of life insurance to own is the **needs approach.** The various family needs that must be met if the family head should die are analyzed, and the amount of money needed to meet these needs is determined. The total amount of existing life insurance and financial assets is then subtracted from the total amount needed. The difference, if any, is the amount of new life insurance that should be purchased. The most important family needs are the following:

- Estate clearance fund
- Income during the readjustment period
- Income during the dependency period
- Life income to the surviving spouse
- Special needs
    Mortgage redemption fund
    Educational fund
    Emergency fund
- Retirement needs

Estate Clearance Fund   An **estate clearance fund** or cleanup fund is needed immediately when the family head dies. Immediate cash is needed for burial expenses; uninsured medical bills; installment debts; estate administration expenses; and estate, inheritance, and income taxes.

Income During the Readjustment Period   The **readjustment period** is a one- or two-year period following the breadwinner's death. During this period, the family should receive approximately the same amount of income received while the family head was alive. The purpose of the readjustment period is to give the family time to adjust its living standard to a different level.

Income During the Dependency Period   The **dependency period** follows the readjustment period; it is the period until the youngest child reaches age 18. The family should receive income during this period so that the surviving spouse can remain at home, if necessary, to care for the children. The income needed during the dependency period is substantially reduced if the surviving spouse is already in the labor force and plans to continue working.

Life Income to the Surviving Spouse   Another important need is to provide life income to the surviving spouse, especially if he or she is older and has been out of the labor force for many years. Two income periods must be considered: (1) income during the blackout period, and (2) income to supplement Social Security benefits after the blackout period. The **blackout period** *refers to the period from the time that Social Security survivor benefits terminate to the time the benefits are resumed.* Social Security benefits to a surviving spouse terminate when the youngest child reaches age 16 and start again when the spouse attains age 60.

If a surviving spouse has a career and is already in the labor force, the need for life income is greatly reduced or even eliminated. However, this conclusion is not true for an older spouse under age 60 who has been out of the labor force for years, and for whom Social Security survivor benefits have temporarily terminated. The need for income during the blackout period is especially important for this group.

Special Needs   Families should also consider certain special needs, which include the following:

- *Mortgage redemption fund.* The amount of monthly income needed by surviving family members is greatly reduced when monthly mortgage payments or rent payments are not required.
- *Educational fund.* The family head may wish to provide an educational fund for the children. If the children plan to attend a private college or university, the cost will be considerably higher than at a public institution.
- *Emergency fund.* A family should also have an emergency fund. An unexpected event may occur that requires large amounts of cash, such as major dental work, home repairs, or a new car.

Retirement Needs   Because the family head may survive until retirement, the need for adequate retirement income should also be considered. Most retired workers are eligible for Social Security retirement benefits and may also be eligible for retirement benefits from their employer. If retirement income from these sources is inadequate, you can obtain additional income from cash-value life insurance, individual investments, a retirement annuity, or an individual retirement account (IRA).

Illustration of the Needs Approach

Exhibit 11.1 provides a worksheet that you can use to determine the amount of life insurance needed. The first part of the worksheet shows the amount needed to meet your various cash needs, income needs, and special needs. The second part analyzes your present financial assets for meeting these needs. The final part

determines the amount of additional life insurance needed, which is calculated by subtracting total assets from total needs. For example, Jennifer and Scott Smith are married and have a son, age 1. Jennifer, age 33, earns $60,000 annually as a marketing analyst for a large oil company. Scott, age 35, earns $40,000 as an elementary school teacher. Jennifer would like her family to be financially secure if she dies prematurely.

EXHIBIT **11.1**
How Much Life Insurance Do You Need?

What You Will Need	Jennifer Smith		Your Needs	
Cash needs				
Funeral costs	$ 15,000		$	
Uninsured medical bills	5,000			
Installment debts	12,000			
Probate costs	3,000			
Federal estate taxes	0			
State inheritance taxes	0			
Total estate clearance fund		$ 35,000		$
Income needs				
Readjustment period	24,000			
Dependency period	180,000			
Life income to surviving spouse	0			
Retirement income	0			
Total income needs		$ 204,000		$
Special needs				
Mortgage redemption fund	200,000			
Emergency fund	50,000			
College education fund	150,000			
Total special needs		$ 400,000		$
Total needs		$ 639,000		$

What You Have Today	Jennifer Smith		Your Assets	
Checking account and savings	$ 10,000		$	
Mutual funds and securities	35,000			
IRAs and Keogh plan	20,000			
Section 401(k) plan and employer savings plan	40,000			
Private pension death benefit	0			
Current life insurance	60,000			
Other financial assets	0			
Total assets		$ 165,000		$
Additional life insurance needed				
Total needs		$ 639,000		$
Less total assets		165,000		
Additional life insurance needed		$ 474,000		$

Cash Needs   Jennifer estimates that her family will need at least $15,000 for funeral expenses. Although Jennifer is insured under a group health insurance plan, certain medical services are excluded, and she must pay an annual deductible and coinsurance charges. Thus, she estimates that the family will need $5000 for uninsured medical expenses. She is also making monthly payments on a car loan and credit card debts. Installment debts currently total $12,000. In addition, she estimates that the cost of probating her will and attorney fees will be $3000, and that no federal estate taxes will be payable.

Income Needs   Jennifer also wants to provide monthly income to her family during the readjustment and dependency periods until her son reaches age 18. Jennifer and Scott's net take-home pay is approximately $6000 each month. Jennifer believes that her family can maintain its present standard of living if it receives 75 percent of that amount, or $4500 monthly. Thus, she wants the family to receive $4500 monthly for 17 years during the readjustment and dependency periods.

The family's need for $4500 per month is reduced if other sources of income are available. Scott's net take-home pay is about $2500 monthly. In addition, Scott and his son are eligible for Social Security survivor benefits. Scott's benefits are payable until his son reaches age 16, whereas his son's benefits are payable until age 18. In this example, we will assume that only the son will receive Social Security survivor benefits. Because Scott's earnings substantially exceed the maximum annual limit allowed under the Social Security earnings test, he will lose all of his Social Security survivor benefits. However, his son will continue to receive benefits until age 18. Jennifer's son will receive an estimated $1000 each month from Social Security until age 18. Thus, the family would receive a total of $3500 monthly from Scott's take-home pay and the son's Social Security benefit. Because their income goal is $4500 monthly, there is a monthly shortfall of $1000. Jennifer's family needs an additional $24,000 to provide monthly income of $1000 during the two-year readjustment period, and another $180,000 to provide monthly income for an additional 15 years during the dependency period. Thus, the family needs a total of $204,000 to meet the monthly goal of $4500 during the readjustment and dependency periods.

If Jennifer considers the time value of money, it will take less than $204,000 of life insurance to meet her income goal. Likewise, if she takes inflation into account, she must increase the amount of life insurance just to maintain the real purchasing power of the benefits. *However, she can ignore both present value and future inflation if she assumes that one offsets the other. Thus, in our example, we assume that the life insurance proceeds are invested at an interest rate equal to the rate of inflation.* Such an assumption builds into the program an automatic hedge against inflation that preserves the real purchasing power of the death benefit. In most cases, however, the death proceeds can be invested at a return exceeding the rate of inflation. The calculations are also simplified, and the use of present value tables and assumptions concerning future inflation rates are unnecessary.

In addition, Scott is currently in the labor force and plans to continue working if Jennifer should die. Thus, there is no need to provide additional income during the blackout period.

A final need to consider is retirement income. Scott will receive Social Security retirement benefits and a lifetime pension from the school district's retirement plan. He also has an individual retirement account (IRA) that will provide additional retirement income. Jennifer believes that Scott's total retirement income will be sufficient to meet his needs, so he does not need additional retirement income.

In summary, after considering Scott's take-home pay and Social Security survivor benefits, Jennifer determines that she will need an additional $204,000 to meet the income goal of $4500 monthly during the readjustment and dependency periods. Additional income during the blackout period is not needed.

Special Needs   Jennifer would like the mortgage to be paid off if she should die. The present mortgage balance is $200,000. She also wants to establish an emergency fund of $50,000 for the family and an educational fund of $150,000 for her son. Thus, her special needs total $400,000.

Determining the Amount of New Life Insurance Needed   The next step is to determine the amount of financial assets that can be used to satisfy her needs. Jennifer has a checking account and personal savings in the amount of $10,000. She owns several mutual funds and individual stocks with a current market value of $35,000. She has an individual retirement account with a current balance of $20,000, and $40,000 in a Section 401(k) plan sponsored by her employer. She is also insured for $60,000 under a group life insurance plan. Total financial assets available upon her death are $165,000.

Total family needs are $639,000, but her current financial assets are only $165,000. Thus, Jennifer needs an additional $474,000 of life insurance to protect her family.

The major advantage of the needs approach is that it is a reasonably accurate method for determining the amount of life insurance to own when specific family needs are recognized. The needs approach also considers other sources of income and financial assets. The major disadvantage, however, is that future projections over the insured's lifetime require numerous assumptions and the use of a computer. Dynamic programming models with changing assumptions are complex and usually are not needed by the typical insured.

Capital Retention Approach

Unlike the needs approach, which assumes liquidation of the life insurance proceeds, the capital retention approach preserves the capital needed to provide income to the family. The income-producing assets are then available for distribution later to the heirs.

The amount of life insurance needed based on the capital retention approach can be determined by the following steps:

- Prepare a personal balance sheet.
- Determine the amount of income-producing capital.
- Determine the amount of additional capital needed (if any).

Prepare a Personal Balance Sheet The first step is to prepare a personal balance sheet that lists all assets and liabilities. The balance sheet should include all death benefits from life insurance and from other sources. For example, Kevin, age 35, has a wife and two children, ages 3 and 5. Kevin earns $60,000 annually. If he should die, he wants his family to receive $40,000 annually. He also wants to establish an emergency fund and educational fund,

and pay off the mortgage, auto loan, and credit card balances. Kevin's personal balance sheet, including death benefits from life insurance and his pension plan, is as follows:

Assets

House	$225,000
Automobiles	20,000
Personal and household property	40,000
Securities and investments	60,000
Checking account	5,000
Individual and group life insurance	200,000
401(k) plan	70,000
Total	$620,000

Liabilities

Mortgage	$100,000
Auto loan	10,000
Credit cards	5,000
Total	$115,000

Determine the Amount of Income-Producing Capital The second step is to determine the amount of income-producing assets. This step is performed by subtracting the liabilities, cash needs, and non-income-producing capital from total assets. Kevin has $55,000 of capital that can produce income for the family. This amount is determined as follows:

Total assets		$620,000
Less:		
Mortgage payoff	$100,000	
Auto loan and credit card debts	15,000	
Final expenses	15,000	
Emergency fund	50,000	
Educational fund	100,000	
Non-income-producing capital (automobiles, personal and household property, value of home)	285,000	
Total deductions		565,000
Capital now available for income		$ 55,000

In the preceding illustration, the home is not an income-producing asset. Unless the home is sold or rented, it ordinarily does not produce cash income for the family. Thus, the home is considered to be part of *non-income-producing capital* that is subtracted from total assets to arrive at the amount of liquid assets that can produce income for the family.

Determine the Amount of Additional Capital Needed

The final step is to determine the amount of additional capital needed. This step involves a comparison of the income objective with other sources of income, such as Social Security survivor benefits. In Kevin's case, his family would have an income shortage of $23,700 annually based on his present financial situation. Assuming the liquid assets and life insurance proceeds can be invested to earn 6 percent annually, Kevin needs an additional $395,000 of life insurance to meet his financial goals. This calculation is summarized as follows:

Income objective for family	$ 40,000
Less:	
Income from capital now available ($55,000 × 6%)	−3,300
Social Security survivor benefits	−13,000
Income shortage	$ 23,700
Total new capital required ($23,700/.06)	$395,000

The capital retention approach has the advantages of simplicity, ease of understanding, and preservation of capital. In addition, investment income earned on the emergency and educational funds can be used as a partial hedge against inflation, or it can be accumulated to offset rising educational costs. The major disadvantage, however, is that a larger amount of life insurance is required to produce a given amount of income.

Interactive Calculators on the Internet

Many life insurers and premium quoting services have interactive calculators on their Web sites that calculate the amount of life insurance needed. You make assumptions about inflation, rates of return on the death proceeds, amount of income needed by the family, and certain other assumptions. However, the quality of the interactive calculators varies widely. Some calculators are extremely limited, and questions concerning the amount of accumulated assets and other sources of income are often ignored. Other calculators are more detailed and enable you to estimate more accurately the amount of life insurance needed.

In addition, depending on the type of calculator used, the amount of life insurance needed varies widely. *One study of 11 calculators produced recommendations ranging from $73,329 to $3.8 million for a male family head, age 35, and from $0 to $2.3 million for his spouse the same age.*[2] However, despite their limitations, the interactive calculators are worth checking out as a starting point for estimating the amount of life insurance needed.

Adequacy of Life Insurance for American Families

Most families own an insufficient amount of life insurance. A recent study by LIMRA International showed that the average amount of life insurance carried by households with any life insurance was $269,700 in 2004, which would replace only 3.6 years of household income. However, because averages are distorted by extreme values, the median amount is more realistic. *The median amount of life insurance per insured household was only $130,500, which would provide income to the survivors for a considerably shorter period. In addition, about one in five households (22 percent) had no life insurance at all.*[3]

The LIMRA study analyzed the reasons why people are underinsured. People delay buying life insurance for three major reasons:[4]

- *Although term insurance premiums have declined to historically low levels, consumers believe life insurance is too expensive to purchase.*
- *Consumers have difficulty in making correct decisions about the purchase of life insurance.*
- *Many consumers simply procrastinate and never get around to buying life insurance.*

Based on the above responses, it is clear that the life insurance industry must do a better job in educating consumers about the need for life insurance, the affordability of life insurance, and the correct amount of life insurance to own.

Opportunity Cost of Buying Life Insurance

The previous discussion shows that most family heads generally need substantial amounts of life insurance. However, this conclusion must be qualified by considering the opportunity cost of purchasing life insurance. Opportunity cost refers to what the insured gives up when life insurance is purchased. Since income is limited, the purchase of life insurance reduces the amount of discretionary income available for other high-priority needs. Many families today are heavily in debt and have little savings. Monthly payments on the mortgage, car loans, credit cards, utility costs, food, and taxes absorb most or all of an average family's income. Thus, after payment of other high priority expenses, many family heads have only a limited amount of discretionary income available to purchase life insurance. *As a result, the optimal amount of life insurance that should be purchased may not be possible.* However, as will be pointed out later, families with limited amounts of income to spend on life insurance can purchase inexpensive term insurance.

After determining the amount of insurance, the final step is to select the proper type of life insurance to purchase. The following section discusses the major types of life insurance that are sold today.

TYPES OF LIFE INSURANCE

From a generic viewpoint, life insurance policies can be classified as either **term insurance** or **cash-value life insurance.** Term insurance provides temporary protection, while cash-value life insurance has a savings component and builds cash values. Numerous variations and combinations of these two types of life insurance are available today.

Term Insurance

Term insurance has several basic characteristics.[5] First, the period of protection is temporary, such as 1, 5, 10, or 20 years. Unless the policy is renewed, the protection expires at the end of the period.

Most term insurance policies are **renewable,** which means that the policy can be renewed for additional periods without evidence of insurability. The premium is increased at each renewal date and is based on the insured's attained age. The purpose of the renewal provision is to protect the insurability of the insured. However, the renewal provision results in adverse selection against the insurer. Because premiums increase with age, insureds in good health

tend to drop their insurance, while those in poor health will continue to renew, regardless of the premium increase. To minimize adverse selection, many insurers have an age limitation beyond which renewal is not allowed, such as age 70 or 80. Some insurers, however, permit term policies to be renewed to age 95 or 99.

Most term insurance policies are also **convertible,** which means the term policy can be exchanged for a cash-value policy without evidence of insurability. There are two methods for converting a term policy. Under the *attained-age method,* the premium charged is based on the insured's attained age at the time of conversion. Under the *original-age method,* the premium charged is based on the insured's original age when the term insurance was first purchased. Most insurers offering the original-age method require the conversion to take place within a certain time period, such as five years, from the issue date of the term policy. The policyowner must also pay the difference between the premiums paid on the term policy and those that would have been paid on the new policy, with interest on the difference at a specified rate.[6] The purpose of the financial adjustment is to place the insurer in the same financial position it would have achieved if the policy had been issued at the original age. Because of the financial adjustment required, few term insurance policies are converted based on the original-age method.

Finally, term insurance policies have no cash-value or savings element. Although some long-term policies develop a small reserve, it is used up by the contract expiration date.

Types of Term Insurance A wide variety of term insurance products are sold today. They include the following:

- Yearly renewable term
- 5-, 10-, 15-, or 20-year term
- Term to age 65
- Decreasing term
- Reentry term
- Return of premium term insurance

Yearly renewable term insurance is issued for a one-year period, and the policyowner can renew for successive one-year periods to some stated age without evidence of insurability. Premiums increase with age at each renewal date. Most yearly renewable term policies also allow the policyowner to convert to a cash-value policy with no evidence of insurability.

Term insurance can also be issued for *5, 10, 15, or 20 years, or for longer periods*. The premiums paid during the term period are level, but they increase when the policy is renewed.

A *term to age 65 policy* provides protection to age 65, at which time the policy expires. The policy can be converted to a permanent plan of insurance, but the decision to convert must be exercised before age 65.

Decreasing term insurance is a form of term insurance where the face amount gradually declines each year. However, the premium is level throughout the period. In some policies, the premiums are structured so that the policy is fully paid for a few years before the coverage expires. For example, a 20-year decreasing term policy may require premium payments for 17 years. This method avoids paying a relatively large premium for only a small amount of insurance near the end of the term period.

Reentry term is a term insurance policy in which renewal premiums are based on select (lower) mortality rates if the insured can periodically demonstrate acceptable evidence of insurability. Select mortality rates are based on the mortality experience of recently insured lives. However, to remain on the low-rate schedule, the insured must periodically show that he or she is in good health and is still insurable. The rates are substantially increased if the insured cannot provide satisfactory evidence of insurability.

Return of premium term insurance is a newer product that returns the premiums at the end of the term period provided the insurance is still in force. Typical periods are 15, 20, 25, or 30 years. Depending on the insurer, there may be a partial refund if the insurance is not kept in force to the end of the period. The amount returned includes only base premiums and does not include any premiums for riders or substandard premiums.

Although this type of insurance is popular with consumers, it has several defects. The return of premiums suggests the insurance is free if the policy remains in force to the end of the term period; the protection is not free when the time value of money is considered. In addition, the insurance is expensive, which can result in a serious problem of underinsurance. For example, the annual premium by one insurer for a 15-year, $500,000 term insurance policy issued to a nonsmoking, preferred-risk male, age 32, is only $240. A return of premium policy would cost $985 annually, or 310 percent more. That same premium would buy more than $2 million of protection in the same company.

Uses of Term Insurance   Term insurance is appropriate in three situations. *First, if the amount of income that can be spent on life insurance is limited, term insurance can be effectively used*. Because of mortality improvements and keen price competition, term insurance rates have declined sharply in recent years. Substantial amounts of life insurance can be purchased for a relatively modest annual premium outlay (see Exhibit 11.2).

Second, term insurance is appropriate if the need for protection is temporary. For example, decreasing term insurance can be effectively used to pay off the mortgage if the family head dies prematurely.

Finally, term insurance can be used to guarantee future insurability. A person may desire large amounts of permanent insurance, but may be financially unable to purchase the needed protection today. Inexpensive term insurance can be purchased, which can be converted later into a permanent insurance policy without evidence of insurability.

Limitations of Term Insurance   Term insurance has two major limitations. *First, term insurance premiums increase with age at an increasing rate and eventually reach prohibitive levels*. Thus, term insurance is not suitable for individuals who need large amounts of life insurance beyond age 65 or 70.

Second, term insurance is inappropriate if you wish to save money for a specific need. Term insurance policies do not accumulate cash values. Thus, if you wish to save money for a child's college education or accumulate a fund for retirement, term insurance is inappropriate unless it is supplemented with an investment plan.

Decreasing term insurance also has several disadvantages. If you become uninsurable, you must convert the remaining insurance to a permanent plan to freeze the remaining amount of insurance. If the policy is not converted, the insurance protection continues to decline even though you are uninsurable. Moreover, decreasing term insurance does not provide for changing needs, such as birth of a child.

EXHIBIT 11.2
Examples of Term Life Insurance Premiums

$500,000 Term Life Insurance

Female Annual Premiums						Male Annual Premiums				
Age	10 Year	15 Year	20 Year	25 Year	30 Year	Age	10 Year	15 Year	20 Year	25 Year	30 Year
30	$ 140	$ 190	$ 225	$ 320	$ 365	30	$ 140	$ 195	$ 230	$ 320	$ 415
35	$ 145	$ 195	$ 230	$ 375	$ 415	35	$ 145	$ 195	$ 255	$ 375	$ 465
40	$ 195	$ 260	$ 315	$ 505	$ 525	40	$ 200	$ 260	$ 340	$ 560	$ 680
45	$ 295	$ 375	$ 480	$ 785	$ 825	45	$ 295	$ 455	$ 585	$ 855	$ 1,110
50	$ 435	$ 520	$ 665	$ 1,055	$ 1,095	50	$ 450	$ 690	$ 955	$ 1,390	$ 1,990
55	$ 645	$ 730	$1,070	$ 1,670	$ 2,700	55	$ 685	$1,025	$1,470	$ 2,765	$ 4,705
60	$ 950	$1,255	$1,745	$ 2,845	$ 6,170	60	$1,110	$1,710	$2,535	$ 5,735	$ 7,645
65	$1,550	$2,030	$3,130	$ 7,740	$ 7,950	65	$1,920	$3,360	$4,970	$10,045	$10,045
70	$2,425	$3,885	$5,845	$10,990	$10,990	70	$4,440	$5,555	$9,540	$13,140	$13,140

SOURCE: Insure.com

Nor does it provide an effective hedge against inflation. Because of inflation, the amount of life insurance in most families should be periodically increased just to maintain the real purchasing power of the original policy.

Whole Life Insurance

If the insured wants lifetime protection, term insurance is impractical because the coverage is temporary, and the premiums are prohibitive in cost at the older ages. In contrast, **whole life insurance** is a cash-value policy that provides lifetime protection. A stated amount is paid to a designated beneficiary when the insured dies, regardless of when the death occurs. Several types of whole life insurance are sold today. Some policies are traditional policies that have been widely sold in the past, whereas new variations of whole life insurance are constantly emerging.

Ordinary Life Insurance Ordinary life insurance *(also called continuous premium whole life and straight life) is a level-premium policy that provides lifetime protection to age 100.* If the insured is still alive at age 100, the face amount of insurance is paid to the policyowner at that time. The maturity date will rise to age 121 in the future. Because of improvements in longevity, companies are now adopting the newer 2001 mortality table to value their

legal reserve liabilities (discussed later). The maturity date will be age 121 for new ordinary life insurance policies sold where legal reserves are based on the 2001 mortality table. If the insured were to survive to age 121 (highly unlikely) the face amount of insurance would be paid a that time.

Ordinary life insurance has several basic characteristics. *First, as stated earlier, premiums are level throughout the premium-paying period.* As a result, the insured is actuarially overcharged during the early years and undercharged during the later years. The premiums paid during the early years are higher than is actuarially necessary to pay current death claims, whereas those paid in the later years are inadequate for paying death claims. *The excess premiums paid during the early years are accumulated at compound interest and are then used to supplement the inadequate premiums paid during the later years of the policy.* Because state law regulates the method of investing and accumulating the fund, it is referred to as a **legal reserve**. Technically, the legal reserve is a liability item that must be offset by sufficient financial assets. Otherwise, regulatory officials may declare the insurer to be insolvent. Insurers are required to calculate their minimum legal reserve liabilities according to certain standards. Many insurers now use the newer 2001 Commissioners Standard Ordinary (CSO) Mortality Table to value their legal reserve liabilities (see Insight 11.1). Its use is mandatory beginning in 2009.

INSIGHT 11.1

2001 CSO Mortality Table

The National Association of Insurance Commissioners (NAIC) requested the Society of Actuaries (SOA) and the American Academy of Actuaries to construct a new mortality table for use in the current statutory valuation of legal reserves. The SOA collected annual mortality data for 1990–1995 from 21 insurers that participated in the study. Supplemental data from other sources were also used, especially at the younger and older ages where mortality experience was scarce. The mortality experience was then projected to 2001 based on recent trends in mortality improvement. The actuaries also added an overall load of 15 percent as a mortality margin.

There are separate tables for smokers, nonsmokers, and a composite table that does not distinguish between smokers and nonsmokers for both males and females, for a total of six tables.

The 2001 CSO table reduces the statutory legal reserve requirements by approximately 20 percent. As a result, the new table will have a significant impact on basic reserves and tax reserves on new policies sold and on nonforfeiture or cash surrender requirements as well. The new table will also affect the guideline premiums paid by policyowners and maximum charges by insurers for the cost of insurance. Another possible impact is more competitive term insurance rates.

The majority of states have adopted the new table. The 2001 CSO table will be used as the minimum standard for all policies issued on or after January 1, 2009.

SOURCE: From Report of the American Academy of Actuaries' Commissioners' Standard Ordinary Task Force. Presented to the National Association of Insurance Commissioners' Life and Health Actuarial Task Force, June 2002.

Exhibit 11.3 shows the concept of the legal reserve under an ordinary life policy.[7] As the death rate increases with age, the legal reserve or savings component steadily increases, and the pure insurance portion called the net amount of risk steadily declines. The **net amount at risk** is the difference between the legal reserve and face amount of insurance. As a result of an increasing legal reserve and decreasing net amount of risk, the cost of the insurance can be kept within manageable

bounds at all ages, and the insurer can provide lifetime protection.[8]

A second characteristic is the accumulation of **cash-surrender values,** *which is the amount paid to a policyowner who surrenders the policy.* As noted earlier, under a system of level premiums, the policyowner overpays for the insurance protection during the early years, which results in a legal reserve and the accumulation of cash values.

Cash values should not be confused with the legal reserve. They are not the same thing and are computed separately. Because of the loading for expenses and high first-year acquisition expenses, cash values are initially below the legal reserve. However, the policyowner has the right to borrow the cash value or exercise one of the cash-surrender options. These options are discussed in Chapter 12.

Uses of Ordinary Life Insurance *An ordinary life policy is appropriate when lifetime protection is needed.* This means that the need for life insurance will continue beyond age 65 or 70. Some financial planners and consumer experts point out that the average person does not need large amounts of life insurance beyond age 65, because the need for life insurance declines with age. This view is an oversim-

EXHIBIT 11.3

Relationship Between the Net Amount at Risk and Legal Reserve (1980 CSO Mortality Table)

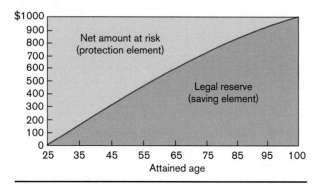

plification of a complex issue and can be misleading. Some persons may need substantial amounts of life insurance beyond age 65. For example, an estate clearance fund is still needed at the older ages; there may be a sizable estate tax problem if the estate is large; a divorce settlement may require the maintenance of a life insurance policy on a divorced spouse, regardless of age; and the policyowner may wish to leave a sizable bequest to a surviving spouse, children, or a charity, regardless of when death occurs. Because an ordinary life policy can provide lifetime protection, these objectives can be realized even though the insured dies at an advanced age.

Ordinary life insurance can also be used to save money. Some insureds wish to meet their protection and savings needs with an ordinary life policy. As stated earlier, ordinary life insurance builds cash values that can be obtained by surrendering the policy or by borrowing the cash value.

Substantial amounts of cash-value life insurance are sold today primarily as an investment and as a method to save money. Insight 11.2 discusses the investment merits of cash value life insurance in greater detail.

Limitation of Ordinary Life Insurance *The major limitation of ordinary life insurance is that some people are still underinsured after the policy is purchased.* Because of the savings feature, some persons may voluntarily purchase or be persuaded by a life insurance agent to purchase an ordinary life policy when term insurance would be a better choice. For example, assume that Mark, age 30, is married with two dependents to support. He estimates that he can spend only $500 annually on life insurance. Based on the rates of one insurer, this premium would purchase about $56,000 of ordinary life insurance. The same premium would purchase more than $600,000 of five-year term insurance from many insurers. It is difficult to justify the purchase of ordinary life insurance if it leaves the insured inadequately covered.

Limited-Payment Life Insurance A limited-payment policy is another type of traditional whole life insurance. The insurance is permanent, and the insured has lifetime protection. The premiums are level, but they are paid only for a certain period. For example, Shannon, age 25, may purchase a 20-year limited

payment policy in the amount of $25,000. After 20 years, the policy is completely paid up, and no additional premiums are required even though the coverage remains in force. A paid-up policy should not be confused with one that *matures*. A policy matures when the face amount is paid as a death claim or as an endowment. A policy is *paid-up* when no additional premium payments are required.

The most common limited-payment policies are for 10, 20, 25, or 30 years. A paid-up policy at age 65 or 70 is another form of limited-payment insurance. An extreme form of limited-payment life insurance is **single-premium whole life insurance,** which provides lifetime protection with a single premium. Because the premiums under a limited-payment policy are higher than those paid under an ordinary life policy, the cash values are also higher.

A limited-payment policy should be used with caution. It is extremely difficult for a person with a modest income to insure his or her life adequately with a limited-payment policy. Because of the relatively high premiums, the amount of permanent life insurance that can be purchased is substantially lower than if an ordinary life policy were purchased.

Endowment Insurance

Endowment insurance is another traditional form of life insurance. **Endowment insurance** pays the face amount of insurance if the insured dies within a specified period; if the insured survives to the end of the endowment period, the face amount is paid to the policyowner at that time. For example, if Stephanie, age 35, purchases a 20-year endowment policy and dies any time within the 20-year period, the face amount is paid to her beneficiary. If she survives to the end of the period, the face amount is paid to her.

At the present time, endowment insurance is relatively unimportant in terms of total life insurance in force. Endowment insurance accounts for less than 1 percent of the life insurance in force. Most new endowment policies cannot meet the tax definition of life insurance. If this definition is not met, the investment income credited to the cash surrender value is subject to current taxation. Thus, adverse tax consequences have discouraged the purchase of new endowment policies, and most life insurers have discontinued the sale of new endowment policies. Even so, many older endowment policies remain in

INSIGHT 11.2

How Good Is Cash-Value Life Insurance as an Investment?

Substantial amounts of cash-value life insurance are sold currently as an investment or tax shelter. Agents often cite the investment attributes of cash-value insurance, which include forced saving, safety of principal, favorable income tax treatment, liquidity, protection against claims of creditors, and a reasonable rate of return. Despite these alleged advantages, however, cash-value life insurance has two major defects as an appealing investment: (1) *the effective rate of return on the cash value is not disclosed to policyowners,* (2) *the loading for expenses when compared to competing investments is relatively high.*

One of the most important investment considerations is the rate of return earned on the investment. The annual total return (capital gains and dividends) on mutual funds and individual stocks can be easily determined and is readily available to investors. However, this is not true for cash-value life insurance. The problem is that part of the premium must be used to pay for the cost of the insurance protection, sales expenses, and administrative costs, while the remainder can be allocated to the cash value. Various techniques, such as the Linton Yield and the yearly-rate-of-return method by Professor Joseph Belth, are available for estimating the rate of return on the cash value after deducting the cost of insurance (see Chapter 13). However, these techniques are complex, and most policyowners are not aware of them and how they can be used. *Moreover, the life insurance industry has consistently opposed any legislation that would require the disclosure of the true effective annual rate of return on a cash-value policy.* Some policies, such as a universal life policy, quote a specific interest rate that is credited to the policy, such as a current interest rate of 5 percent. However, such rates are gross rates and do not reflect the true net rate of return after deductions for the cost of insurance and other policy expenses.

Is the rate of return on a cash-value policy reasonable? The Consumer Federation of America has analyzed more than 5000 cash-value policies for consumers and has issued several reports. One study of 57 cash-value policies shows negative rates of return during the early years. *The average rate of return on these policies was −90% in year one, −61.7% in year two, −22.3% in year three, and −1.2% in year four.*[a]

The annual rates of return are negative during the early years because there is little or no cash value in a policy because of relatively high first-year acquisition expenses and other continuing policy expenses.

Cash-value policies generally must be held for at least 15 years for the rate of return to become attractive. The same study shows the following average annual rates of return for the 57 policies over longer periods:

Years Policy Held	Average Annual Rate of Return
5	−14.5%
10	2.3%
15	5.1%
20	6.1%

The annual rate of return can be considered "reasonable" only if you are willing to hold the policy for at least 15 or 20 years. You will lose most or all of your money if you surrender the policy or let it lapse during the early years. The Consumer Federation of America estimates that about 25% of the policyowners who buy cash-value life insurance let the policies lapse in the first three years, and nearly 50% give up their policies in the first 10 years.[b] As a result, buyers of cash-value life insurance lose billions of dollars annually by terminating their policies prematurely.[c]

The second problem is that the expense loading is relatively high when compared to mutual funds and other investments. For example, variable universal life insurance is widely sold as an investment and tax shelter. The prospectus for one policy sold by a leading insurer shows that the loading for sales expenses for the first five years is 6.75% of the target premium. The target premium is the premium that keeps the policy in force for a specified number of years. In addition, state premium taxes and federal taxes are 3.25% of the premium. Thus, sales expenses and taxes are 10 percent of the target premiums paid for the first five policy years.

The same prospectus also shows various deductions from the cash value for policy expenses and investment management fees. These deductions include a monthly contract fee of $30; a monthly fee of 7 cents per $1000 of the policy face amount plus the face amount of any term insurance rider; a mortality and expense risk fee for certain mortality and expense guarantees; an investment management fee on the separate account in which the funds are invested; and other fees. The policy also has a deferred surrender charge that applies for the first 10 years. Finally, there is a monthly deduction for the cost of insurance. *As you can see, selling expenses, monthly fees, contract fees, surrender charges, and other expenses have a severe impact on the rate of return on cash-value life insurance policies.*

The Consumer Federation of America recommends that a new cash-value life insurance policy should be purchased as an investment only if (1) you are willing to hold the policy for at least 20 years, and (2) you have made maximum annual contributions to your employer's Section 401(k) plan or to your individual retirement account (IRA), which provide favorable income tax treatment at a much lower cost.

[a] James H. Hunt, *Analysis of Cash Value Life Insurance Policies,* Consumer Federation of America, July 1997.
[b] Ibid.
[c] Ibid.

force. Although endowment policies are no longer readily available in the United States, they are popular in many foreign countries.

VARIATIONS OF WHOLE LIFE INSURANCE

To remain competitive and to overcome the criticisms of traditional cash-value policies, insurers have developed a wide variety of whole life products that combine insurance protection with an investment component. Important variations of whole life insurance include the following:

- Variable life insurance
- Universal life insurance
- Variable universal life insurance
- Current assumption whole life insurance
- Indeterminate-premium whole life insurance

Variable Life Insurance

Variable life insurance *can be defined as a fixed-premium policy in which the death benefit and cash values vary according to the investment experience of a separate account maintained by the insurer.* The death benefit and cash surrender values will increase or decrease with the investment experience of the separate account. Although there are different policy designs, variable life policies have certain common features. They are summarized as follows:

- *A variable life policy is a permanent whole life contract with a fixed premium.* The premium is level and is guaranteed not to increase.
- *The entire reserve is held in a separate account and is invested in common stocks or other investments.* The policyowner has the option of investing the cash value in a variety of investments, such as a common stock fund, bond fund, balanced fund, money market fund, or international fund. If the investment experience is favorable, the face amount of insurance is increased. If the investment experience is poor, the amount of life insurance could be reduced, but it can never fall below the original face amount.
- *Cash surrender values are not guaranteed, and there are no minimum guaranteed cash values.*

The actual cash values depend on the investment experience. Thus, although the insurer bears the risk of excessive mortality and expenses, the policyowner bears the risk of poor investment results.

Universal Life Insurance

Universal life insurance is another important variation of whole life insurance. **Universal life insurance** (also called flexible premium life insurance) *can be defined as a flexible premium policy that provides protection under a contract that unbundles the protection and saving components.* Except for the first premium, the policyowner determines the amount and frequency of payments. The premiums, less explicit expense charges, are credited to a cash value account (also called an accumulation fund) from which monthly mortality charges are deducted and to which monthly interest is credited. In addition, universal life policies typically have a monthly deduction for administrative expenses.

Universal life insurance has certain characteristics, which include the following:[9]

- Unbundling of protection and saving component
- Two forms of universal life insurance
- Considerable flexibility
- Cash withdrawals permitted
- Favorable income-tax treatment

Unbundling of Component Parts A distinct characteristic of universal life insurance is the separation or unbundling of the protection component and the saving component. The policyowner receives an annual statement that shows the premiums paid, death benefit, and value of the cash-value account. The statement also shows the mortality charge and interest credited to the cash-value account.

- *Premiums.* As noted earlier, except for the first premium, the policyowner determines the frequency and amount of premium payments. Most policies have a *target premium,* which is a suggested level premium that will keep the policy in force for a specified number of years. However, the policyowner is not obligated to pay the target premium. Most policies also have a *no-lapse guarantee,* which guarantees that the policy will remain in force for a certain number of years, such as 15 or 20 years, if at least the minimum premium is paid. The minimum premium is specified in the policy and, depending on the insurer, may be less than or equal to the target premium.

- *Mortality charge.* A monthly mortality charge is deducted from the cash value account for the cost of the insurance protection. The cost of insurance is determined by multiplying the applicable monthly mortality rate by the net amount at risk (difference between the current death benefit and cash value). The policy contains a table that shows the maximum rate per $1000 of insurance that the company can charge. Most insurers charge less than the maximum rate. However, the insurer has the right to increase the current mortality charge up to the maximum guaranteed rate stated in the policy.
- *Expense charges.* Insurers typically deduct 5 to 10 percent of each premium for expenses. There is also a monthly fee for administrative expenses, such as $5 or $6. In addition, there is a relatively high surrender charge that applies if the policy is terminated during the early years. The surrender charge declines annually and disappears after a period of time, such as 10, 15, or 20 years. *As a result, the policyowner can lose a substantial amount of money if the policy is surrendered during the early years.* Finally, there is a charge for each partial cash withdrawal, such as $25.
- *Interest rate.* Interest earnings credited to the cash-value account depend on the interest rate. There are two rates of interest. The guaranteed cash value is credited with a contractually *guaranteed minimum interest rate,* such as 3 or 4 percent. The cash values, however, may be credited with a higher *current rate,* such as 4½ or 5 percent. The current rate is not guaranteed but changes periodically depending on market conditions and company experience.

If the policyowner borrows the cash value, the amount borrowed is usually credited with a lower rate of interest. The cash value representing the amount borrowed is credited with either the minimum interest rate or a rate 1 to 2 percent below the policy loan rate.

Two Forms of Universal Life Insurance There are two forms of universal life insurance (see Exhibit 11.4). *Option A pays a level death benefit during the early years.* As the cash value increases over time, the net amount at risk declines. However, the death benefit increases during the later years of the policy. If the death benefit did not increase, the policy would not meet the *corridor test* required by the Internal Revenue Code. As a result, the policy would not receive favorable income-tax treatment. The corridor test is a complex test that disqualifies a policy for favorable income-tax treatment if the cash values are excessive relative to the net amount at risk.

Option B provides for an increasing death benefit. The death benefit is equal to a constant net amount at risk plus the accumulated cash value. If the cash value increases over time, the death benefit will increase. Please note that an increasing death benefit each year is not guaranteed. The illustration of Option B in Exhibit 11.4 is based on the assumption that the policyowner pays at least the target premium and that the interest-rate assumptions are realized. In reality, the premiums paid by the policyowner may vary, and interest rates will change periodically. Thus, actual cash values will fluctuate and could even decline to zero, especially if premiums are discontinued and interest rates decline. As a result of fluctuations in the cash-value account, the death benefit will fluctuate and may not necessarily increase each year.

Considerable Flexibility Compared to traditional whole life products, universal life insurance provides considerable flexibility, which includes the following:

- The policyowner determines the frequency and amount of premium payments. Premiums can be discontinued if there is sufficient cash value to pay mortality costs and expenses.
- The death benefit can be increased or decreased. Evidence of insurability is required to increase the amount of insurance.
- The policy can be changed from a level death benefit to a death benefit equal to a specified face amount plus the policy cash value (with evidence of insurability).
- The policyowner can add cash to the policy at any time, subject to maximum guideline limits that govern the relationship between the cash value and the death benefit (tax law limitations).
- Policy loans are permitted at competitive interest rates.
- If the policy permits, additional insureds can be added.

EXHIBIT 11.4
Two Forms of Universal Life Insurance Death Benefits

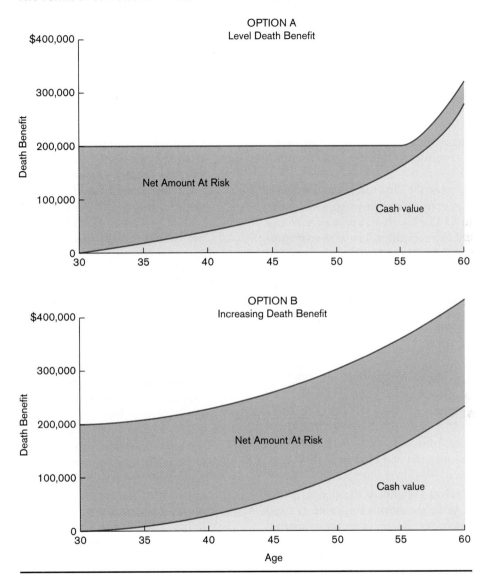

Cash Withdrawals Permitted   Part or all of the cash value can be withdrawn. Interest is not charged, but the death benefit is reduced by the amount of the withdrawal. Most insurers charge a fee for each cash withdrawal, such as $25. As noted earlier, policy loans are also permitted.

Favorable Income-Tax Treatment   Universal life insurance enjoys the same favorable federal income-tax treatment as traditional cash-value policies. The death benefit paid to a named beneficiary is normally received income-tax free. Interest credited to the cash-value account is not taxable to the policyowner in the year credited.

Universal Life Insurance Illustration   To illustrate how universal life insurance works, assume that Jason, age 25, buys a universal life policy with a level death benefit of $100,000. The annual planned premium is $445, which can be changed. For the sake of simplicity, assume that the mortality charge, expense charge, and crediting of interest are made annually. (However, in practice, there is a monthly deduction for mortality and expense charges and monthly crediting of interest.)

Each premium is subject to a 5 percent premium expense charge. The policy has a monthly administrative charge of $6. The policy provides for a maximum mortality charge, but the current mortality charge is only about two-thirds of the maximum rate. The policy has a guaranteed interest rate of 4.5 percent and a current interest rate of 5.5 percent that is not guaranteed.

When Jason pays the first premium of $445, there is a premium expense charge of approximately $22 (5 percent of $445). There is also an administrative charge of $72 ($6 monthly). The first-year mortality charge is $113 ($1.13 per $1000 of the specified $100,000 death benefit). The remaining $238 is credited with $13 of interest (5.5 percent on $238). Thus, the cash-value account at the end of the first year is $251. This calculation is summarized as follows:

Annual premium	$445
Less:	
Premium expense charges	−22
Administrative charges	−72
Mortality cost	−113
	$238
Interest at 5.5 percent	+13
Cash value account end of year	$251

However, if Jason surrenders the policy at the end of the first year, the surrender value is zero because of the surrender charge. A declining surrender charge applies if the policy is terminated within 16 years after the issue date. Exhibit 11.5 shows in greater detail the cash-value accumulation based on the guaranteed and current interest rates.

Limitations of Universal Life Universal life insurance has several limitations. Consumer experts point out the following limitations:[10]

- *Misleading rates of return.* The advertised rates of return on universal life insurance are misleading. For example, insurers may advertise current rates of interest of 4½ or 5 percent on universal life policies. *However, the advertised rates are gross rates and not net rates.* The advertised gross rate overstates the rate of return on the saving component because it does not reflect deductions for sales commissions, expenses, and the cost of the insurance protection. As a result of these deductions, the effective yearly return is substantially lower than the advertised rate and is often negative for several years after the policy is purchased.

- *Decline in interest rates.* Many earlier sales presentations showed sizable future cash values based on relatively high interest rates. However, interest rates have declined over time. *As a result, the earlier cash-value and premium-payment projections based on higher interest rates are misleading and invalid.* Actual cash values will be substantially less than the projected values based on higher interest rates when the policy was first sold.

- *Right to increase the mortality charge.* As stated earlier, insurers can increase the current mortality charge for the cost of insurance up to some maximum limit. Other expenses may be hidden in the mortality charge. If the insurer's expenses increase, the mortality charge could be increased to recoup these expenses. The increase may not be noticed or questioned because the insured may believe the increase is justified because he or she is getting older.

- *Lack of firm commitment to pay premiums.* Another limitation is that some policyowners do not have a firm commitment to pay premiums. As a result, the policy may lapse because of nonpayment of premiums. As stated earlier, premiums can be reduced or skipped in a universal life policy. However, at some point, money must be added to the account, or the policy will lapse.

Variable Universal Life Insurance

Variable universal life insurance is an important variation of whole life insurance. Most variable universal life policies are sold as investments or tax shelters.

Variable universal life insurance is similar to a universal life policy with two major exceptions:

- The policyowner determines how the premiums are invested, which provides considerable investment flexibility.

- The policy does not guarantee a minimum interest rate or minimum cash value. One exception,

Exhibit 11.5
$100,000 Universal Life Policy, Level Death Benefit, Male Age 25, Nonsmoker,
5.5 Percent Assumed Interest

Age	Year	Premium Outlay	Guaranteed Values			Nonguaranteed Projected Values		
			Death Benefit	Cash Value	Cash Surrender Value	Death Benefit	Cash Value	Cash Surrender Value
26	1	$445.00	$100,000	$222	$0	$100,000	$251	$0
27	2	445.00	100,000	454	0	100,000	516	0
28	3	445.00	100,000	698	140	100,000	796	238
29	4	445.00	100,000	953	395	100,000	1,092	534
30	5	445.00	100,000	1,219	661	100,000	1,392	834
31	6	445.00	100,000	1,498	991	100,000	1,709	1,202
32	7	445.00	100,000	1,788	1,331	100,000	2,041	1,584
33	8	445.00	100,000	2,079	1,673	100,000	2,393	1,987
34	9	445.00	100,000	2,383	2,028	100,000	2,764	2,409
35	10	445.00	100,000	2,689	2,385	100,000	3,143	2,839
36	11	445.00	100,000	2,994	2,740	100,000	3,542	3,288
37	12	445.00	100,000	3,300	3,097	100,000	3,964	3,761
38	13	445.00	100,000	3,609	3,457	100,000	4,396	4,244
39	14	445.00	100,000	3,919	3,818	100,000	4,853	4,752
40	15	445.00	100,000	4,232	4,181	100,000	5,323	5,272
41	16	445.00	100,000	4,557	4,557	100,000	5,832	5,832
42	17	445.00	100,000	4,872	4,872	100,000	6,369	6,369
43	18	445.00	100,000	5,190	5,190	100,000	6,924	6,924
44	19	445.00	100,000	5,495	5,495	100,000	7,509	7,509
45	20	445.00	100,000	5,790	5,790	100,000	8,114	8,114
46	21	445.00	100,000	6,069	6,069	100,000	8,739	8,739
47	22	445.00	100,000	6,325	6,325	100,000	9,376	9,376
48	23	445.00	100,000	6,568	6,568	100,000	10,025	10,025
49	24	445.00	100,000	6,785	6,785	100,000	10,687	10,687
50	25	445.00	100,000	6,976	6,976	100,000	11,363	11,363
51	26	445.00	100,000	7,133	7,133	100,000	12,052	12,052
52	27	445.00	100,000	7,242	7,242	100,000	12,729	12,729
53	28	445.00	100,000	7,280	7,280	100,000	13,390	13,390
54	29	445.00	100,000	7,241	7,241	100,000	14,033	14,033
55	30	445.00	100,000	7,106	7,106	100,000	14,668	14,668
56	31	445.00	100,000	6,866	6,866	100,000	15,282	15,282
57	32	445.00	100,000	6,498	6,498	100,000	15,873	15,873
58	33	445.00	100,000	5,981	5,981	100,000	16,445	16,445
59	34	445.00	100,000	5,282	5,282	100,000	16,989	16,989

Exʜɪʙɪᴛ **11.5** (continued)
$100,000 Universal Life Policy, Level Death Benefit, Male Age 25, Nonsmoker, 5.5 Percent Assumed Interest

			Guaranteed Values			Nonguaranteed Projected Values		
Age	Year	Premium Outlay	Death Benefit	Cash Value	Cash Surrender Value	Death Benefit	Cash Value	Cash Surrender Value
60	35	445.00	100,000	4,370	4,370	100,000	17,483	17,483
61	36	445.00	100,000	3,562	3,562	100,000	18,111	18,111
62	37	445.00	100,000	2,567	2,567	100,000	18,723	18,723
63	38	445.00	100,000	1,362	1,362	100,000	19,298	19,298
64	39	445.00	0*	0	0	100,000	19,839	19,839
65	40	445.00				100,000	20,322	20,322
66	41	445.00				100,000	20,819	20,819
67	42	445.00				100,000	21,233	21,233
68	43	445.00				100,000	21,570	21,570
69	44	445.00				100,000	21,824	21,824
70	45	445.00				100,000	21,951	21,951
71	46	445.00				100,000	21,915	21,915
72	47	445.00				100,000	21,721	21,721
73	48	445.00				100,000	21,327	21,327
74	49	445.00				100,000	20,695	20,695
75	50	445.00				100,000	19,772	19,772
76	51	445.00				100,000	18,478	18,478
77	52	445.00				100,000	16,780	16,780
78	53	445.00				100,000	14,574	14,574
79	54	445.00				100,000	11,770	11,770
80	55	445.00				100,000	8,215	8,215
81	56	445.00				100,000	3,685	3,685
82	57	445.00				0*	0	0

Nᴏᴛᴇ: This illustration assumes that the nonguaranteed projected values currently illustrated will continue unchanged for all years shown. This is not likely to occur, and actual results may be more or less favorable. Projected values are based on nonguaranteed elements that are subject to change. Guaranteed values are based on a guaranteed interest rate of 4.5 percent. Projected values are based on a current interest rate of 5.5 percent. Premiums are assumed to be paid at the beginning of the year. Benefits, cash values, and ages are shown at the end of the year.

*Coverage will terminate under current assumptions. Additional premiums would be required to continue coverage.

however, is that the policy may have a fixed-income account, which may guarantee a minimum interest rate on the account value.

Selection of Investments by Policyowner *A variable universal life policy allows the policyowner to*

invest the premiums in a wide variety of investments. The premiums are invested in one or more *separate accounts,* which are similar to mutual funds in their daily operations. Insurers typically have 10 or more separate accounts available. These accounts typically include a common stock fund, bond fund, balanced fund, international fund, real estate fund, money market fund, and other accounts. Some insurers also use the mutual funds of investment companies as subaccounts, such as mutual funds sold by Fidelity Investments and the Vanguard Group. The premiums purchase accumulation units, which reflect the value of the underlying investments.

The policyowner can switch out of the different funds without incurring an income-tax liability, such as switching out of a bond fund into a money market fund if interest rates rise.

No Minimum Interest Rate or Cash Value Guarantees
Unlike a universal life policy, *a variable universal life policy has no guaranteed minimum interest rate and no guaranteed minimum cash value.* When you buy a universal life policy, the cash value account earns a stated rate of interest determined by the insurer from time to time; there is also a minimum interest-rate guarantee. However, when you buy a variable universal life policy, you select one or more separate accounts, and the policy cash values reflect the value of these accounts. There is no minimum interest-rate or cash-value guarantee. However, as stated earlier, a fixed-income account may guarantee a minimum interest rate on the account value, such as 3 percent.

Relatively High Expense Charges
Variable universal life insurance policies have relatively high expense charges, which reduce the investment returns and erode the favorable tax treatment under the policy. Variable universal life insurance is typically sold as a tax shelter. Investment earnings are not currently taxable as income to the policyowner. If the policy stays in force until death, no federal income taxes are ever payable even if the separate account has sizable capital gains. However, according to the Consumer Federation of America, the various expense charges can more than offset the favorable income-tax treatment that variable universal life insurance now enjoys. A study of variable universal life policies by the Consumer Federation of America (CFA) showed the following charges:[11]

- *Front-end load.* Many policies have front-end loads for sales commissions and expenses, typically ranging from 5 percent to 11 percent.

- *Back-end surrender charge.* Policies purchased from agents typically have back-end surrender charges. The surrender charge usually exceeds the first-year premium and declines to zero over a 10- to 20-year period. Many policies have surrender charges that are level for the first five years, and then start to decline.
- *State premium taxes and federal taxes.* State premium taxes that vary by state and federal taxes average about 3 percent of premiums.
- *Investment management fees.* Deductions from the separate accounts are made daily for investment management fees. For the policies studied, investment management fees ranged from .20 percent to 1.62 percent.
- *Mortality and expense charges.* Mortality and expense (M&E) charges are also deducted for certain insurer guarantees. The variable universal life insurer guarantees the death benefit even though the stock market and other markets are declining; the insurer also guarantees future expense charges regardless of inflation. The CFA study showed that M&E charges ranged from .60 percent to .90 percent of the cash value.
- *Administrative costs.* Administrative costs are deducted monthly from the separate accounts, typically $5 to $10.

In addition to the above charges, there is a monthly deduction for the cost of insurance. The applicable mortality rate is multiplied by the net amount at risk (face amount minus the cash value) to determine the insurance charge.

Substantial Investment Risk
Variable universal life insurance is a risky type of life insurance to own. There is a substantial investment risk that falls entirely on the policyowner. Investment returns vary widely, depending on how the funds are invested. If the investment experience is poor, cash values can decline to zero. This is particularly important for policyowners who are making only minimum premium payments or have discontinued premium payments. If the premiums are invested largely in common stocks and the separate account declines sharply because of a severe stock market decline, the policyowner may have to pay additional premiums to keep the policy in force.

INSIGHT 11.3

Variable Universal Life Insurance: Is It Worth It?

A report prepared by the Consumer Federation of America's life insurance expert—actuary James H. Hunt, former Vermont insurance commissioner—addresses the question, is variable universal life insurance (VUL) worth it? The report's answer is that a VUL policy is extremely difficult to understand and comparison shop but can provide good value if intelligently purchased, held, and managed.

"Variable universal life insurance policies are so complex that they are difficult for most consumers to purchase intelligently," said Hunt. "Those seeking tax-sheltered investments should look first to 401(k)s or even to Roth IRAs," he added.

Variable universal life insurance combines features of term insurance and a mutual fund. It represents the most popular type of cash-value life insurance sold in recent years. In 2000, for example, variable life captured 57 percent of the market for new cash-value policies, as measured by premiums paid. And, well over 90 percent of these variable life premiums represented VUL policies worth $9 billion. While the decline in stock prices lowered VUL sales more recently, when these prices rebound so should VUL sales.

"Many consumers who, several years ago, replaced whole life policies by transferring policy values to VUL policies have lost billions of dollars," said Hunt. "On the other hand, those who are now replacing VUL policies with universal life policies could also lose billions of dollars if stock prices increase in the future," he added.

To help consumers evaluate new or existing VUL policies and other cash-value insurance policies, the nonprofit Consumer Federation offers a rate-of-return service provided by Hunt. In the past 15 years, Hunt has analyzed more than 5000 policies. The cost for the analysis is $65 for the first illustration and $50 for each additional illustration submitted at the same time.

High Charges May More than Offset Tax Benefits

As well as insurance protection, the main attraction of a VUL policy is providing a tax shelter—under current law, VUL investment earnings do not represent taxable income, and if the policy is held to death, no income taxes are ever assessed. The main cost of a VUL policy, however, which can more than offset the tax benefits, is an array of charges:

- Federal and state premium taxes that vary among states but average around 3 percent of premiums;
- M&E (mortality and expense) charges assessed against cash values that range, among policies studied, from 60 to 90 basis points (with 100 basis points equaling 1 percentage point);
- Investment management assets charges that vary, among policies studied, from 20 to 162 basis points; and
- Surrender charges that typically exceed the first year's premium and last from 10 to 15 years.

For consumers who bought VUL policies in recent years, the report recommends the following:

- Hold the policies at least through the surrender charge period;
- "Dollar cost average" through market weakness;

The Consumer Federation of America (CFA) believes variable universal life insurance policies are complex and difficult to understand. CFA recommends that consumers seeking tax-advantaged investments should first consider investing in a Section 401(k) plan or Roth IRA (see Insight 11.3). These retirement products are discussed later in the text.

Current Assumption Whole Life Insurance

Current assumption whole life insurance (also called interest-sensitive whole life) is a nonparticipating whole life policy in which the cash values are based on the insurer's current mortality, investment, and expense experience. A nonparticipating policy is a policy that does not pay dividends.

Common Features Although current assumption whole life products vary among insurers, they share some common features, summarized as follows:[12]

- *An accumulation account reflects the cash value under the policy.* The accumulation account is credited with the premiums paid less expenses and mortality charges plus interest based on current rates.
- *If the policy is surrendered, a surrender charge is deducted from the accumulation account.* A sur-

INSIGHT 11.3 (continued)

Variable Universal Life Insurance: Is It Worth It?

- Be informed about the level of asset charges on "name accounts" and consider changing to an index fund; and
- Never surrender a VUL policy with a loss without looking into a transfer of the loss in the policy—the excess of premiums over the surrender value—to a variable annuity.

When and How VUL Policies Should Be Purchased

The report recommends that consumers considering a VUL policy purchase should first compare an attractive VUL policy to a combination of term insurance and a low-cost mutual fund. In general, purchasing a VUL policy can make sense if one plans on taking substantial "tax-free" withdrawals or loans as retirement income and intends to maintain the policy until death. (And in general, VUL policies are more attractive than a combination of term insurance and a variable annuity, because the latter is expensive and its earnings will be taxable to someone, someday.)

Those wishing to purchase a VUL policy should look first to an insurer that deals directly with the public and charges no or low commissions. Low-load insurers include Ameritas (800-552-3553), USAA Life (800-531-8000), and TIAA-CREF (800-223-1200). The report notes that Ameritas is particularly attractive because it makes available the low-cost Vanguard separate accounts while allowing buyers to change their minds about investment purchases at minimum cost. TIAA-CREF policies also have very low asset charges.

When shopping for a VUL policy, the report specifically recommends that consumers:

- Decide on the amount of the premium you would like to pay and how frequently;
- Decide on the amount of insurance you would like to have and whether you want Option A or Option B. In seeking to maximize the tax-advantaged investment aspects of a policy, ask for the lowest Option B insurance amount that is not a Modified Endowment contract (MEC), and ask that Option A be illustrated beginning in policy year eight.
- Eliminate any riders, which usually offer poor value, such as a rider on your spouse. A term life rider on the insured person can be effective in lowering commission costs, but some term riders cost nearly double what careful shopping can achieve.
- Request an illustration at some hypothetical gross earnings rate, such as 8 percent. Specify that you would like the illustration to assume that 100 percent of your investment allocations be in the lowest cost, index account even if later you intend a different selection.
- Compare the columns of cash-surrender values among competing illustrations. In general, the higher the surrender values the better the policy.
- Read the full CFA report, which provides many examples of what different insurers charge for VUL policies as well as much analysis and advice.

SOURCE: Adapted from Consumer Federation of America, *New CFA Report Answers Question—Is Variable Universal Life Insurance Worth It?*, Press Release, February 24, 2003.

render charge that declines over time is deducted from the accumulation account to determine the net cash-surrender value.

- *A guaranteed interest rate and current interest rate are used to determine cash values.* The minimum cash values are based on the guaranteed interest rate, such as 3 or 4 percent. However, the accumulation account is credited with a higher interest rate based on current market conditions and company experience.
- *A fixed death benefit and maximum premium level at the time of issue are stated in the policy.* (However, under the low-premium version discussed next, both are subject to change.)

In addition to having the preceding characteristics, current assumption whole life products generally can be classified into two categories: (1) low-premium products and (2) high-premium products.

Low-Premium Products Under the low-premium version, the initial premium is substantially lower than the premium paid for a regular, nonparticipating whole life policy. The low premium is initially guaranteed only for a certain period, such as five years. However, after the initial guaranteed period expires, a *redetermination provision* allows the insurer to recalculate the premium based on the same or different actuarial assumptions with respect to mortality, interest, and expenses (hence, the name "current assumption whole life"). If the new premium is higher than the initial premium, the policyowner generally has the option of paying the higher premium and maintaining the same death benefit. Alternatively, the policyowner can continue to pay the lower premium, but the death benefit is reduced.

High-Premium Products Although premiums are higher under the second category, these policies typically contain a *vanishing premium provision* in which the premiums vanish after a certain time period, such as ten years. The premium vanishes when the accumulation account exceeds the net single premium needed to pay up the contract based on current interest and mortality costs.[13] *However, the policy remains paid up only if current interest and mortality experience remain unchanged or are more favorable than initially assumed.* If the accumulation account falls below the minimum cash surrender value, additional premiums are required.

Indeterminate-Premium Whole Life Insurance

An **indeterminate-premium whole life policy** *is a generic name for a nonparticipating policy that permits the insurer to adjust premiums based on anticipated future experience.* The maximum premium that can be charged is stated in the policy. The actual premium paid when the policy is issued is considerably lower and may be guaranteed for some initial period, such as three to five years. The intent is to have the actual premium paid reflect current market conditions. After the initial guaranteed period expires, the insurer can increase premiums up to the maximum limit if future anticipated experience with respect to mortality, investments, and expenses is expected to worsen. However, the premiums may not change if future experience is expected to be similar to past experience. Conversely, if future experience is expected to improve, then the insurer can further reduce the premiums if it desires to do so.

Exhibit 11.6 summarizes the basic characteristics of the major forms of life insurance. This chart helps to clarify the major types of life insurance and how they differ.

OTHER TYPES OF LIFE INSURANCE

A wide variety of additional life insurance products are sold today. Some policies are designed to meet special needs or have unique features. Others combine term insurance and cash-value life insurance to meet these needs.

Modified Life Insurance

A **modified life policy** is a whole life policy in which premiums are lower for the first three to five years and higher thereafter. The initial premium is slightly higher than for term insurance, but considerably lower than for an ordinary life policy issued at the same age.

The major advantage of a modified life policy is that insureds can purchase permanent insurance immediately even though they cannot afford the higher premiums for a regular whole life policy. Modified life insurance is particularly attractive to persons who expect that their incomes will increase in the future and that higher premiums will not be financially burdensome.

Preferred Risks

Most life insurers sell policies at lower rates to individuals known as **preferred risks.** These people are individuals whose mortality experience is expected to be lower than average. The policy is carefully underwritten and is sold only to individuals whose health history, weight, occupation, and habits indicate more favorable mortality than the average. The insurer may also require the purchase of a minimum amount of insurance, such as $100,000. If an individual qualifies for a preferred rate, substantial savings are possible.

A discount for nonsmokers is a current example of a preferred risk policy. Most insurers offer substantially lower rates to nonsmokers in recognition

EXHIBIT 11.6
Comparison of Major Life Insurance Contracts

	Term Insurance	Ordinary Life Insurance	Variable Life Insurance	Universal Life Insurance	Variable Universal Life Insurance	Current Assumption Whole Life Insurance
Death benefit paid	Level or decreasing death benefit	Level death benefit	Guaranteed minimum death benefit plus increased amount from favorable investment returns	Either level or an increasing death benefit	Either level or an increasing death benefit	Level death benefit
Cash value	No cash value	Guaranteed cash values	Cash value depends on investment performance (not guaranteed)	Guaranteed minimum cash value plus excess interest credited to the account	Cash value depends on investment performance (not guaranteed)	Guaranteed minimum cash value plus excess interest credited
Premiums paid	Premiums increase at each renewal	Level premiums	Fixed-level premiums	Flexible premiums	Flexible premiums	Premiums paid may vary based on insurer experience; guaranteed maximum premium
Policy loans	No	Yes	Yes	Yes	Yes	Yes
Partial withdrawal of cash value	No	No	No	Yes	Yes	Yes
Surrender charge	No	No explicit charge stated (reflected in cash values)	Yes	Yes	Yes	Yes

of the more favorable mortality that can be expected of this group.

Second-to-Die Life Insurance

Second-to-die life insurance (also called survivorship life) is a form of life insurance that insures two or more lives and pays the death benefit upon the death of the second or last insured. The insurance usually is whole life, but it can be term. Because the death proceeds are paid only upon the death of the second or last insured, the premiums are substantially lower than if two individual policies were issued.

Second-to-die life insurance is widely used at the present time in estate planning. As a result of an unlimited marital deduction, the deceased's entire estate can be left to a surviving spouse free of any federal estate tax. However, when the surviving spouse dies, a sizable state or federal estate tax may be due. A second-to-die policy would provide estate liquidity and the cash to pay estate taxes.

Savings Bank Life Insurance

Savings Bank Life Insurance (SBLI) is a type of life insurance that was sold originally by savings banks in Massachusetts, New York, and Connecticut. More recently, however, SBLI is also sold to consumers over the phone or through Web sites in those states, and in additional states as well. The objective of SBLI is to provide low-cost life insurance to consumers by holding down operating costs and payment of high sales commissions.

Maximum limits on the amount of life insurance on an individual's life have been substantially raised. In Massachusetts, the amount of term insurance on a single life ranges from $100,000 to $5 million. In addition, SBLI products in Massachusetts are sold directly to consumers in surrounding states, including Maine, New Hampshire, New Jersey, Pennsylvania, and Rhode Island.

In New York, savings bank life insurance was created in 1939. Recent legislation allowed savings bank life insurance to be sold by one mutual life insurance company. Established in 2000, the company is now called the SBLI USA Mutual Life Insurance Company. SBLI USA now sells to consumers in New York and other jurisdictions as well, including New Jersey, Pennsylvania, and Puerto Rico. Individual term insurance is available in amounts ranging from $100,000 to $1 million or more. Whole life insurance is also available in amounts ranging from $5000 to $1 million.

In Connecticut, substantial amounts of SBLI can also be purchased. An applicant can purchase up to $5 million of term insurance and up to $5 million in whole life.

Industrial Life Insurance

Historically, **industrial life insurance** was a class of life insurance that was issued in small amounts; premiums were payable weekly or monthly; and an agent of the company collected the premiums at the insured's home. More than nine out of ten policies were cash-value policies.

Today, industrial life insurance is also called **home service life insurance.** In most cases, home collections are no longer made. The policyowner remits the premiums to the agent or to the company. The amount of life insurance per policy generally ranges from $5000 to $25,000. Home service life insurance is relatively unimportant and accounts for less than 1 percent of all life insurance in force.

Group Life Insurance

Group life insurance is a type of insurance that provides life insurance on a group of people in a single master contract. Physical examinations are not required, and certificates of insurance are issued as evidence of insurance.

Group life insurance is important in terms of total life insurance in force. Most group life contracts provide term insurance coverage. In 2004, group life insurance accounted for 44 percent of all life insurance in force in the United States.[14] It is an important employee benefit provided by employers and will be discussed in greater detail in Chapter 16.

CASE APPLICATION

Sharon, age 28, is a single parent who earns $30,000 annually as a secretary at a local university. She is the sole support of her son, age 3. Sharon is concerned about the financial well-being of her son if she should die. Although she finds it difficult to save, she would like to start a savings program to send her son to college. She is currently renting an apartment but would like to own a home someday. A friend has told her that life insurance might be useful in her present situation. Sharon knows nothing about life insurance, and the amount of income available for life insurance is limited. Assume you are a financial planner who is asked to make recommendations concerning the type of life insurance that Sharon should buy. The following types of life insurance policies are available:

- Five-year renewable and convertible term
- Life-paid-up-at-age 65
- Ordinary life insurance
- Universal life insurance

a. Which of these policies would best meet the need for protection of Sharon's son if she should die prematurely? Explain your answer.
b. Which of these policies best meets the need to accumulate a college fund for Sharon's son? Explain your answer.
c. Which of these policies best meets the need to accumulate money for a down payment on a home? Explain your answer.
d. What major obstacle does Sharon face if she tries to meet all of her financial needs by purchasing cash-value life insurance?
e. Sharon decides to purchase the five-year term policy in the amount of $300,000. The policy has no cash value. Identify a basic characteristic of a typical term insurance policy that would help Sharon accumulate a fund for retirement.

SUMMARY

- Premature death means that a family head dies with outstanding unfulfilled financial obligations, such as dependents to support, children to educate, or a mortgage to pay off.

- At least four costs are associated with premature death:

    There is the loss of the human life value.

    Additional expenses may be incurred, such as funeral expenses, uninsured medical bills, and estate settlement costs.

    Because of insufficient income, some families may experience a reduction in their standard of living.

    Noneconomic costs are incurred, such as the emotional grief of the surviving dependents and the loss of a role model and guidance for the children.

- The purchase of life insurance can be economically justified if a person has an earning capacity, and someone is dependent on those earnings for at least part of his or her financial support.

- The financial impact of premature death varies by family type. Premature death can cause considerable economic insecurity if a family head dies in a single-parent family, in a family with two-income earners with children, or in a traditional, blended, or sandwiched family. In contrast, if a single person without dependents or an income earner in a two-income family without children dies, financial problems for the survivors are less likely to occur.

- The human life value is defined as the present value of the family's share of the deceased breadwinner's future earnings. This approach crudely measures the economic value of a human life.

- The needs approach can be used to determine the amount of life insurance to purchase. After considering other sources of income and financial assets, the various family needs are converted into specific amounts of life insurance. The most important family needs are as follows:

    Estate clearance fund

    Income during the readjustment period

Income during the dependency period

Life income to the surviving spouse

Special needs: mortgage redemption fund, education fund, emergency fund

Retirement needs

- The capital retention approach for estimating the amount of life insurance to purchase is based on the assumption that income-producing capital will be preserved and not liquidated.

- *Term insurance* provides temporary protection and is typically renewable and convertible without evidence of insurability. Term insurance is appropriate when income is limited, or when there are temporary needs. Because term insurance has no cash values, it cannot be used for retirement or savings purposes.

- There are several traditional forms of whole life insurance. *Ordinary life insurance* is a form of whole life insurance that provides lifetime protection. The premiums are level and are payable for life. The policy develops an investment or saving element called a cash-surrender value, which results from the overpayment of premiums during the early years. An ordinary life policy is appropriate when lifetime protection is desired or additional savings are desired.

- The legal reserve is a liability item for an insurer that reflects the excess premiums paid during the early years of the policy. The fundamental purpose of the legal reserve is to provide lifetime protection.

- Because a legal reserve is necessary for lifetime protection, cash values become available. Because the insured has paid more than is actuarially necessary during the early years of the policy, he or she should receive something back if the policy is surrendered.

- A *limited-payment policy* is another traditional form of whole life insurance. The insured also has lifetime protection, but the premiums are paid only for a limited period, such as 10, 20, or 30 years, or until age 65.

- *Endowment insurance* pays the face amount of insurance if the insured dies within a specified period. If the insured survives to the end of the endowment period, the face amount of insurance is paid to the policyowner at that time.

- *Variable life insurance* is a fixed-premium policy in which the death benefit and cash-surrender value vary according to the investment experience of a separate account maintained by the insurer. The entire reserve is held in a separate account and is invested in common stocks or other investments. The cash-surrender values are not guaranteed.

- *Universal life insurance* is another variation of whole life insurance. Conceptually, universal life can be viewed as a flexible-premium policy that provides lifetime protection under a contract that separates the protection and saving components. Universal life insurance has the following features:

Unbundling of protection, savings, and expense components

Two forms of universal life insurance

Considerable flexibility

Cash withdrawals permitted

Favorable income-tax treatment

- *Variable universal life insurance* is similar to universal life insurance with two major exceptions. First, the cash values can be invested in a wide variety of investments. Second, there is no minimum guaranteed interest rate, and the investment risk falls entirely on the policyowner.

- *Current assumption whole life insurance* is a nonparticipating whole life policy in which the cash values are based on the insurer's current mortality, investment, and expense experience. An accumulation account is credited with a current interest rate that changes over time.

- An *indeterminate-premium whole life policy* is a nonparticipating policy that permits the insurer to adjust premiums based on anticipated future experience. The initial premiums are guaranteed for a certain time period and can then be increased up to some maximum limit.

- A *modified life policy* is a whole life policy in which premiums are lower for the first three to five years and are higher thereafter.

- Many insurers sell policies with lower rates to preferred risks. The policies are carefully underwritten and sold only to individuals whose health history, weight, occupation, and habits indicate more favorable mortality than average. Minimum amounts of insurance must be purchased.

- *Second-to-die life insurance (survivorship life)* insures two or more lives and pays the death benefit upon the death of the second or last insured.

- *Savings bank life insurance* is sold in Massachusetts, New York, Connecticut, and other states. It is also sold directly to consumers over the phone or Internet.

- *Industrial life insurance* is a type of insurance in which the policies are sold in small amounts, and the premiums earlier were paid to an agent at the policyowner's home.

- *Group life insurance* provides life insurance on people in a group under a single master contract.

KEY CONCEPTS AND TERMS

Blackout period
Capital retention approach
Cash-surrender value
Cash-value life insurance
Convertible
Current assumption whole
  life insurance
Dependency period
Endowment insurance
Estate clearance fund
Group life insurance
Human life value
Indeterminate-premium
  whole life policy
Industrial (home service)
  life insurance
Legal reserve
Limited-payment policy
Modified life policy
Needs approach
Net amount at risk

Ordinary life insurance
Preferred risks
Premature death
Readjustment period
Reentry term
Renewable
Savings bank life
  insurance
Second-to-die life
  insurance
Single-premium whole life
  insurance
Term insurance
Universal life insurance
Variable life insurance
Variable universal life
  insurance
Whole life insurance

REVIEW QUESTIONS

1. a. Explain the meaning of premature death.
   b. Identify the costs associated with premature death.
   c. Explain the economic justification for the purchase of life insurance.

2. Explain the financial impact of premature death on the different types of families in the United States.

3. a. Define the human life value.
   b. Describe the steps in determining the human life value of a family head.

4. a. The needs approach is widely used for determining the amount of life insurance to purchase. Describe the following needs for a typical family head:
   1. Cash needs
   2. Income needs
   3. Special needs
   b. Explain the capital retention approach for determining the amount of life insurance to own.

5. a. Briefly explain the basic characteristics of term insurance policies.
   b. Identify the major types of term insurance policies sold today.
   c. Explain the situations that justify the purchase of term insurance.
   d. What are the major limitations of term insurance?

6. a. Briefly explain the basic characteristics of ordinary life policies.
   b. Why does an ordinary life insurance policy develop a legal reserve?
   c. Explain the situations that justify the purchase of ordinary life insurance.
   d. What is the major limitation of ordinary life insurance?

7. Describe the basic characteristics of variable life insurance.

8. a. Explain the basic characteristics of universal life policies.
   b. Explain the limitations of universal life insurance.

9. a. What is a variable universal life insurance policy?
   b. How does variable universal life insurance differ from a typical universal life insurance policy?
   c. Identify the various expense charges that policyowners must pay under a variable universal life insurance policy.

10. a. Describe the basic features of current assumption whole life insurance.
    b. What is a preferred risk policy?

APPLICATION QUESTIONS

1. Richard, age 45, is married with two children in high school. He estimates that his average annual earnings over the next 20 years will be $60,000. He estimates that one-third of his average annual earnings will be used to pay taxes, insurance premiums, and the costs

of self-maintenance. The remainder will be used to support his family. Richard wants to calculate his human life value and believes a 6 percent discount rate is appropriate. The present value of $1 payable for 20 years at a discount rate of 6 percent is $11.47. Calculate Richard's human life value.

2. a. The human life value is one method for estimating the amount of life insurance to own. Keeping all other factors unchanged, explain the effect, if any, of each of the following:

   (1) The discount rate used to calculate the human life value is increased.

   (2) The amount of average annual income going to the family is increased.

   (3) The period over which income is paid to the family is reduced.

   b. Explain the limitations of the human life value approach as a method for determining the amount of life insurance to own.

3. Kelly, age 35, is a single parent and has a one-year-old son. She earns $45,000 annually as a marketing analyst. Her employer provides group life insurance in the amount of twice the employee's salary. Kelly also participates in her employer's 401(k) plan. She has the following financial needs and objectives:

• Funeral costs and uninsured medical bills	$ 10,000
• Income support for her son, $2,000 monthly for 17 years	
• Pay off mortgage on home	150,000
• Pay off car loan and credit card debts	15,000
• College education fund for son	150,000

   Kelly has the following financial assets:

• Checking account	$ 2,000
• IRA account	8,000
• 401(k) plan	25,000
• Individual life insurance	25,000
• Group life insurance	90,000

   a. Ignoring the availability of Social Security survivor benefits, how much additional life insurance, if any, should Kelly purchase to meet her financial goals based on the needs approach? (Assume that the rate of return earned on the policy proceeds is equal to the rate of inflation.)

   b. How much additional life insurance, if any, is needed if estimated Social Security survivor benefits in the amount of $800 monthly are payable until her son attains age 18?

4. Janet, age 28, is married and has a son, age 3. She wants to determine how much life insurance she should own based on the capital retention approach. She would like to provide $30,000 each year before taxes to her family if she should die. She owns a house jointly with her husband that has a current market value of $250,000 and a mortgage balance of $100,000. She also owes $16,000 on a car loan and credit cards. She would like to have the mortgage, car loan, and credit card debts paid off if she should die. She has no investments, and her checking account balance is only $1,000. She owns an individual life insurance policy in the amount of $100,000 that her parents purchased for her when she was a baby. Estimated Social Security survivor benefits are $10,000 annually. Janet assumes the life insurance proceeds can be invested at 5 percent interest. Based on the capital retention approach, how much additional life insurance, if any, should Janet purchase to meet her financial goals?

5. Megan, age 32, is married and has a son, age 1. She recently purchased a cash-value life insurance policy that has the following characteristics:

   • The frequency and amount of premium payments are flexible.
   • The insurance and saving components are separate.
   • The interest rate credited to the policy is tied to current market conditions, but the policy guarantees a minimum interest rate.
   • The policy has a back-end surrender charge that declines to zero over some time period.

   Based on the above characteristics, what type of life insurance did Megan purchase? Explain your answer.

6. Todd, age 28, would like to save money for a comfortable retirement. He is considering purchasing a cash-value life insurance policy that has the following characteristics:

   • The premiums are invested in separate investment accounts selected by the policyowner.
   • Interest income and capital gains are not currently taxable to the policyowner.

- The frequency and amount of premium payments can be changed as financial circumstances change.
- A mortality and expense (M&E) charge is periodically deducted from the cash value account.

Based on the above characteristics, what type of life insurance is Todd considering purchasing? Explain your answer.

7. Life insurance policies have different characteristics. For each of the following, identify the life insurance policy that meets the description:
   a. A policy where the face amount of insurance increases if the investment results are favorable
   b. A policy that can be used to insure the human life value of an individual, age 35, at the lowest possible annual premium
   c. A policy that permits the policyowner to determine how the premiums are to be invested
   d. A policy that allows cash withdrawals for a down payment on a home or payment of college tuition for the children
   e. A policy that is sold to insureds whose mortality experience is expected to be lower than average
   f. A policy in which premiums are lower for the first three to five years and higher thereafter, which may appeal to insureds whose incomes are expected to increase
   g. A policy designed to pay estate taxes upon the death of the last surviving spouse

8. Richard, age 35, is married and has two children, ages 2 and 5. He is considering the purchase of additional life insurance. He has the following financial goals and objectives:

   - Pay off the mortgage on his home, which has 25 years remaining
   - Accumulation of a sizeable retirement fund
   - Payment of monthly income to the family if he should die
   - Withdrawal of funds from the policy when the children reach college age

   For each of the following life insurance policies, indicate which of the above financial goals, if any, could be met if the policy is purchased. Treat each policy separately.
   a. Decreasing term insurance
   b. Ordinary life insurance
   c. Universal life insurance
   d. Variable universal life insurance

INTERNET RESOURCES

- **A. M. Best Co.** is a major rating organization that rates the financial strength of insurance companies. The company also publishes periodicals, reports, and books relating to the insurance industry, including *Best's Review*. This publication provides considerable information about life insurance products and the insurance industry. Visit the site at

  http://www.ambest.com

- **The American College** offers professional certification and graduate degree programs in the financial services industry. It offers numerous programs and courses leading to the award of professional designations (CLU, ChFC, and others). Visit the site at

  http://www.theamericancollege.edu

- The **American Council of Life Insurers** represents the life insurance industry on issues dealing with legislation and regulation at the federal and state levels. The site provides consumer information on the uses and types of life insurance. Visit the site at

  http://www.acli.com

- The **Consumer Federation of America (CFA)** is a nonprofit organization that represents numerous consumer groups. This site is one of the best sources for obtaining meaningful consumer information about life insurance policies and other insurance products. CFA makes available a low-cost life insurance evaluation service by which individual life insurance policies can be evaluated for a small fee. Visit the site at

  http://www.consumerfed.org

- **INSWEB** provides timely information and premium quotes for life insurance as well as homeowners, auto, and other insurance products. Visit the site at

  http://www.insweb.com

- **Insure.com** provides up-to-date information, premium quotes, and other consumer information on life insurance. The site also provides news releases about events that affect the insurance industry. Visit the site at

  http://www.insure.com

- The **Life Office Management Association (LOMA)** provides extensive information dealing with the management and operations of life insurers and financial services companies. Visit the site at

http://www.loma.org

■ **LIMRA International, Inc.** is the principal source of life insurance sales and marketing statistics. The organization provides news and information about the financial services field, conducts research, and publishes a wide range of publications. Visit the site at

http://www.limra.com

■ The **National Association of Insurance Commissioners (NAIC)** has a link to all state insurance departments, which provide a considerable amount of consumer information on the types of life insurance discussed in this chapter. Click on "State Insurance Web Sites." For starters, check out New York, Wisconsin, and California. Visit the site at

http://www.naic.org

■ The **National Association of Insurance and Financial Advisors** represents sales professionals in life and health insurance and the financial services industry. The organization promotes ethical standards, supports legislation in the interest of policyowners and agents, and provides agent education seminars. Visit the site at

http://www.naifa.org

■ The **National Underwriter Company** publishes books and periodicals about life insurance products. The company publishes the *National Underwriter*, Life & Health/Financial Services edition, a weekly trade publication, which provides timely news about the life insurance industry. Visit the site at

www.nationalunderwriter.com

■ The **Society of Financial Service Professionals** represents individuals who have earned the professional Chartered Life Underwriter (CLU) and Chartered Financial Consultant (ChFC) designations. The site provides timely information on life insurance products. Visit the site at

www.financialpro.org

SELECTED REFERENCES

Black, Kenneth, Jr., and Harold D. Skipper, Jr. *Life Insurance*, 13th ed. Upper Saddle River, NJ: Prentice-Hall, 2000.

Elger, John F., "Calculating Life Insurance Need: Don't Let the Tools Fool You," *Journal of Financial Service Professionals*, vol. 57, no. 3 (May 2003).

Gokhale Jagadeesh and Laurence J. Kotlikoff, "The Adequacy of Life Insurance," *Research Dialogue*, Issue no. 72, New York: TIAA-CREF Institute, July 2002.

Graves, Edward E., ed. *McGill's Life Insurance*, 6th ed. Bryn Mawr, PA: The American College, 2007.

Mitchell, James O., "The Adequacy of Life Insurance Coverage in U.S. Households," *Journal of Financial Service Professionals*, vol. 57, no. 3 (May 2003).

Sevak, Purvi, et al. "The Economic Consequences of a Husband's Death: Evidence from the HRS and AHEAD," Social Security Bulletin, vol. 63, no. 2 (2003/2004).

Retzloff, Cheryl D. *Trends in Life Insurance Ownership among U.S. Households*. Windsor, CT: LIMRA International, 2005.

TIAA-CREF Institute, "The Adequacy of Life Insurance," *Quarterly* (Autumn 2002).

Todd, Jerry D. "Integrative Life Insurance Needs Analysis," *Journal of Financial Service Professionals,* vol. 58, no. 2 (March 2004).

NOTES

1. CDC National Center for Health Statistics, *Deaths: Preliminary Data for 2004*, Table 1.
2. John Elger, "Calculating Life Insurance Need: Don't Let the Tools Fool You," *Journal of Financial Service Professionals,* vol. 57, no. 3 (May 2003), Table 3, p. 40.
3. Cheryl D. Retzloff, *Trends in Life Insurance Ownership among U.S. Households,* (Windsor, CT: LIMRA International, 2005).
4. Ibid.
5. This section is based on Edward E. Graves, ed., *McGill's Life Insurance,* 5th ed. (Bryn Mawr, PA: The American College 2004), chs. 1–5; and Kenneth Black, Jr., and Harold D. Skipper, Jr., *Life Insurance,* 13th ed. (Upper Saddle River, NJ: Prentice-Hall, 2000), ch. 4.
6. Black and Skipper, p. 79.
7. This separation is only a theoretical concept. In practice, the death claim does not consist of two separate benefits that equal the face of the policy. Technically, an ordinary life policy is an undivided contract, and the death benefit is the face amount of insurance.

8. The *cost of insurance* is a technical term that is obtained by multiplying the net amount at risk by the death rate at the insured's attained age. Under the level-premium method, the cost of insurance can be kept within reasonable bounds at all ages.

9. This section is based on Graves, ch. 5; Black and Skipper, pp. 114–127; and Joseph M. Belth, ed., "The War Over Universal Life—Part 1," *Insurance Forum,* vol. 8, no. 11 (November 1981).

10. Limitations of universal life are discussed in Joseph M. Belth, ed. "Secondary Guarantees, Marketers, Actuaries, Regulators, and a Potential Financial Disaster for the Life Insurance Business," *Insurance Forum,* vol. 31, nos. 3 & 4 (March/April 2004); "Conseco's Assault on Universal Life Policyholders," *Insurance Forum,* vol. 30, no. 12 (December 2003); "The Likely Failure of a Universal Life Policy," *Insurance Forum,* vol. 28, no. 7 (July 2001); "The War Over Universal Life—Part 1," *Insurance Forum,* vol. 8, no. 11 (November 1981); and "The War Over Universal Life—Part 2," *Insurance Forum,* vol. 8, no. 12 (December 1981).

11. Consumer Federation of America, *New CFA Report Answers Question—Is Variable Universal Life Insurance Worth It?* February 24, 2003.

12. This section is based on Black and Skipper, pp. 97–101.

13. Ibid., p. 100.

14. *Life Insurers Fact Book 2005* (Washington, DC: American Council of Life Insurers, 2005), p. 88.

Students may take a self-administered test on this chapter at
www.aw-bc.com/rejda

CHAPTER 12

LIFE INSURANCE CONTRACTUAL PROVISIONS

"Few policyholders ever read a life insurance contract with any effort to understand its provisions."

Mehr and Gustavson,
Life Insurance: Theory and Practice

LEARNING OBJECTIVES

After studying this chapter, you should be able to

◆ Describe the following contractual provisions that appear in life insurance policies:
Incontestable clause
Suicide clause
Grace period provision

◆ Identify the dividend options that typically appear in participating life insurance policies.

◆ Explain the cash-surrender options (nonforfeiture options) that appear in cash-value policies.

◆ Describe the various settlement options for the payment of life insurance death benefits.

◆ Describe the following riders that can be added to a life insurance policy:
Waiver of premium   Cost-of-living rider
Guaranteed purchase option   Accelerated death benefits rider
Accidental death benefit rider

Mark, age 32, and Ashley, age 29, are married and have two small children. Ashley is the owner of a $300,000, 10-year term insurance policy, and Mark is named as beneficiary. The policy has been in force for three years. Ashley recently committed suicide because of breast cancer and severe depression. Mark is concerned that the insurer will not pay the death proceeds because Ashley caused her own death. Ashley's life insurance agent, however, assured him that the claim would be paid in full because the period for excluding suicide had expired.

In the above case, the payment of the death proceeds was affected by a provision in a life insurance policy dealing with suicide. Life insurance contracts contain dozens of contractual provisions that affect the insured and beneficiary and payment of the death proceeds. Some contractual provisions are mandatory and must be included in every life insurance policy. Other provisions are optional.

This chapter discusses some common life insurance contractual provisions. It is divided into three major parts. The first part discusses life insurance contractual provisions that can have important financial consequences for consumers. The second part analyzes the basic options that frequently appear in life insurance policies, including dividend options, nonforfeiture options, and settlement options. The final part discusses additional benefits and riders that can be added to a life insurance policy.

LIFE INSURANCE CONTRACTUAL PROVISIONS

Life insurance policies contain numerous contractual provisions. This section discusses the major contractual provisions that life insurance consumers should understand.

Ownership Clause

The owner of a life insurance policy can be the insured, the beneficiary, a trust, or another party. In most cases, the applicant, insured, and owner are the same person. Under the **ownership clause,** *the policyowner possesses all contractual rights in the policy while the insured is living.* These rights include naming and changing the beneficiary, surrendering the policy for its cash value, borrowing the cash value, receiving dividends, and electing settlement options. These rights generally can be exercised without the beneficiary's consent.

The policy also provides for a change of ownership. The policyowner can designate a new owner by filing an appropriate form with the company.

Entire-Contract Clause

The **entire-contract clause** *states that the life insurance policy and attached application constitute the entire contract between the parties.* All statements in the application are considered to be representations rather than warranties. No statement can be used by the insurer to void the policy unless it is a material misrepresentation and is part of the application. In addition, the insurer cannot change the policy terms unless the policyowner consents to the change.

There are two basic purposes of the entire-contract clause. First, it prevents the insurer from amending the policy without the knowledge or consent of the owner by changing its charter or bylaws. Second, it also protects the beneficiary. A statement made in connection with the application cannot be used by the insurer to deny a claim unless the statement is a material misrepresentation and is part of the application.

Incontestable Clause

The **incontestable clause** *states that the insurer cannot contest the policy after it has been in force two years during the insured's lifetime.* After the policy has been in force for two years during the insured's lifetime, the insurer cannot later contest a death claim on the basis of a material misrepresentation, concealment, or fraud when the policy was first issued. The insurer has two years in which to discover any irregularities in the contract. With few exceptions, if the insured dies, the death claim must be paid after the contestable period expires. For example, if Tony, age 25, applies for a life insurance policy, conceals the fact that he has high blood pressure, and dies within the two-year period, the insurer could contest the claim on the basis of a material concealment. But if he dies *after* expiration of the period, the insurer must pay the claim.

The purpose of the incontestable clause is to protect the beneficiary if the insurer tries to deny payment of the claim years after the policy was first issued. Because the insured is dead, he or she cannot refute the insurer's allegations. As a result, the beneficiary could be financially harmed if the claim is denied on the grounds of a material misrepresentation or concealment.

The incontestable clause is normally effective against fraud. If the insured makes a fraudulent misstatement to obtain the insurance, the company has two years to detect the fraud. Otherwise, the death claim must be paid. However, there are certain situations where the fraud is so outrageous that payment of the death claim would be against the public interest. In these cases, the insurer can contest the claim after the contestable period runs out. They include the following:[1]

- The beneficiary takes out a policy with the intent of murdering the insured.
- The applicant for insurance has someone else take a medical examination.
- An insurable interest does not exist at the inception of the policy.

Suicide Clause

Most life insurance policies contain a suicide clause. The **suicide clause** *states that if the insured commits suicide within two years after the policy is issued, the face amount of insurance will not be paid; there is only a refund of the premiums paid.* In some life insurance policies, suicide is excluded for only one year. If the insured commits suicide after the period expires, the policy proceeds are paid just like any other claim.

In legal terms, death is normally considered an unintentional act because of the strong instinct of self-preservation. Thus, there is a presumption against suicide. Consequently, the burden of proving suicide always rests on the insurer. To deny payment of the claim, the insurer must prove conclusively that the insured has committed suicide (see Insight 12.1).

The purpose of the suicide clause is to reduce adverse selection against the insurer. By having a suicide clause, the insurer has some protection against the individual who wishes to purchase life insurance with the intention of committing suicide.

Grace Period

A life insurance policy also contains a **grace period** *during which the policyowner has a period of 31 days to pay an overdue premium.* Universal life and other flexible-premium policies have longer grace periods, such as 61 days. The insurance remains in force during the grace period. If the insured dies within the grace period, the overdue premium is deducted from the policy proceeds.

The purpose of the grace period is to prevent the policy from lapsing by giving the policyowner additional time to pay an overdue premium. The policyowner may be temporarily short of funds or may have forgotten to pay the premium. In such cases, the grace period provides considerable financial flexibility.

Reinstatement Clause

A policy may lapse if the premium has not been paid by the end of the grace period, or if an automatic premium loan provision is not in effect. The **reinstatement provision** *permits the owner to reinstate a lapsed policy.* The following requirements must be fulfilled to reinstate a lapsed policy:

INSIGHT 12.1

Is This Death a Suicide?

Facts

A 20-year-old Marine served in a fighter squadron as a radar technician. He was familiar with .45-caliber semi-automatic pistols and had given instructions on their use. The Marine was a happy-go-lucky, cheerful person who sometimes tried to "shake up" his friends by placing a .45 to his head and pulling the trigger. One day when the Marine was apparently in good spirits, he suddenly put a pistol to his head, said "Here's to it" to a friend, and pulled the trigger. The gun fired, killing the Marine. The insurance company that insured him claimed the death was a suicide.

Decision

The death is not a suicide.

Reasoning

The company must prove that the death was intentional. The burden of proof was not met here (*Angelus v. Government Personnel Life Ins. Co.*, 321 P.2d 545 [Wash. 1958]).

SOURCE: *Business Law Text and Cases: The Legal Environment*, 3rd ed., by Frascona, Joseph L., ©1987. Reprinted by permission of Pearson Education, Inc., Upper Saddle River, NJ.

- Evidence of insurability is required.
- All overdue premiums plus interest must be paid from their respective due dates.
- Any policy loan must be repaid or reinstated, with interest from the due date of the overdue premium.
- The policy must not have been surrendered for its cash value.
- The policy must be reinstated within a certain period, typically three or five years from the date of lapse.

It may be advantageous for a policyowner to reinstate a lapsed policy rather than purchase a new one. First, the premium is lower because the reinstated policy was issued at an earlier age. Second, the acquisition expenses incurred in issuing the policy must be paid again under a new policy. Third, cash values and dividends are usually higher under the reinstated policy; the new policy may not develop any cash values until the end of the third year. Fourth, the incontestable period and suicide period under the old policy may have expired. Reinstatement of a lapsed policy does not reopen the suicide period, and a new incontestable period generally applies only to statements contained in the application for reinstatement. Statements contained in the original application cannot be contested after the original contestable period expires. Finally, the reinstated policy may contain more favorable policy provisions, such as a lower interest rate on policy loans.

A major disadvantage of reinstating a lapsed policy is that a substantial cash outlay is required if the policy lapsed several years earlier. Also, most life insurers have reduced premiums over time and have developed new products. As a result, it may cost less to purchase a new policy even though the insured is older when the new purchase is made. As a practical matter, most lapsed policies are not reinstated because of the required cash outlay.

Misstatement of Age or Sex Clause

Under the **misstatement of age or sex clause,** *if the insured's age or sex is misstated, the amount payable is the amount that the premiums paid would have purchased at the correct age and sex.* For example, assume that Troy, age 35, applies for a $20,000 ordinary life policy, but his age is incorrectly stated as age 34. If the premium is $20 per $1000 at age 35 and $19 per $1000 at age 34, the insurer will pay only 19/20 of the death proceeds. Thus, only $19,000 would be paid (19/20 × $20,000 = $19,000).

Beneficiary Designation

The beneficiary is the party named in the policy to receive the policy proceeds. The principal types of beneficiary designations are as follows:

- Primary and contingent beneficiary
- Revocable and irrevocable beneficiary
- Specific and class beneficiary

Primary and Contingent Beneficiary A **primary beneficiary** *is the beneficiary who is first entitled to receive the policy proceeds on the insured's death.* More than one party can be named primary beneficiary; however, the amount that each party receives must be specified.

A **contingent beneficiary** *is entitled to the proceeds if the primary beneficiary dies before the insured.* If the primary beneficiary dies before receiving the guaranteed number of payments under an installment settlement option, the remaining payments are paid to the contingent beneficiary.

In many families, the husband will name his wife primary beneficiary (and vice versa), and the children will be named as contingent beneficiaries. The legal problem in naming *minor children* as beneficiaries is that they lack the legal capacity to receive the policy proceeds directly. Most insurers will not pay the death proceeds directly to minor children.[2] Instead, they will require a guardian to receive the proceeds on the minor's behalf. If a court of law appoints a *guardian,* payment of the proceeds may be delayed and legal expenses will be incurred. One solution is to have a guardian named in the will who can legally receive the proceeds on the children's behalf. Another approach is to pay the proceeds to a *trustee* (such as a commercial bank with a trust department), which has the discretion and authority to use the funds for the children's welfare.

The insured's estate can be named as primary or contingent beneficiary. However, many financial planners do not recommend designation of the estate as beneficiary. The death proceeds may be subject to attorney fees and other probate expenses, federal estate taxes, state inheritance taxes, and claims of creditors. Payment of the proceeds may also be delayed until the estate is settled.

Revocable and Irrevocable Beneficiary Most beneficiary designations are revocable. A **revocable beneficiary** *means that the policyowner reserves the right to change the beneficiary designation without the beneficiary's consent.* The revocable beneficiary has only the expectation of benefits, and the policyowner can change the beneficiary whenever desired. All policy rights under the contract can be exercised without the consent of the revocable beneficiary.

In contrast, an **irrevocable beneficiary** *is one that cannot be changed without the beneficiary's consent.*

If the policyowner wishes to change the beneficiary designation, the irrevocable beneficiary must consent to the change. However, most policies today provide that the interest of a beneficiary, even an irrevocable beneficiary, terminates if the beneficiary dies before the insured. Thus, if the irrevocable beneficiary dies before the insured, all rights to the policy proceeds revert to the policyowner, who can then name a new beneficiary.

Specific and Class Beneficiary A **specific beneficiary** means the beneficiary is specifically named and identified. In contrast, under a **class beneficiary,** a specific person is not named but is a member of a group designated as beneficiary, such as "children of the insured." A class designation is appropriate whenever the insured wishes to divide the policy proceeds equally among members of a particular group.

Most insurers restrict the use of a class designation because of the problem of identifying members of the class. Although all insurers permit the designation of children as a class, they will not permit this designation to be used when the class members cannot be identified, or the relationship to the insured is remote. For example, the class designation "my children" means that all children of the insured share in the policy proceeds, whether legitimate, illegitimate, or adopted. But if "children of the insured" is used as the designation, the insured's children by any marriage would be included, but the spouse's children by a former marriage would be excluded. Thus, a class designation must be used with great care.

Change-of-Plan Provision

Life insurance policies may contain a **change-of-plan provision** that allows policyowners to exchange their present policies for different contracts. The purpose of this provision is to provide flexibility to the policyowner. The original policy may no longer be appropriate if family needs and financial objectives change.

If the change is to a *higher-premium policy,* such as changing from an ordinary life to a limited-payment policy, the policyowner must pay the difference in the policy reserve under the new policy and the policy reserve under the original policy. Evidence of insurability is not required, because the pure insurance protection (net amount at risk) is reduced.

The policyowner may also be allowed to change to a *lower-premium policy,* such as changing from a limited-payment policy to an ordinary life policy. In such a case, the insurer refunds the difference in cash values under the two policies to the policyowner. Evidence of insurability is required in this type of change, because the pure insurance protection is increased (higher net amount at risk).

Exclusions and Restrictions

A life insurance policy contains remarkably few exclusions and restrictions. *Suicide* is excluded only for the first two years. During a period of war, some insurers may insert a **war clause** in their policies, which excludes payment if the insured dies as a direct result of war. The purpose of the war clause is to reduce adverse selection against the insurer when large numbers of new insureds may be exposed to death during wartime.

In addition, **aviation exclusions** may be present in some policies. Most newly issued policies do not contain any exclusions with respect to aviation deaths, and aviation death claims are paid like any other claim. However, some insurers exclude aviation deaths other than as a fare-paying passenger on a regularly scheduled airline. Military aviation may also be excluded or be covered only by payment of an extra premium. In addition, a private pilot who does not meet certain flight standards may have an aviation exclusion rider inserted in the policy, or be charged a higher premium.

During the initial underwriting of the policy, the insurer may discover *certain undesirable activities or hobbies* of the insured. These activities may be excluded or covered only by payment of an extra premium. Some excluded activities are auto racing, skydiving, scuba diving, hang gliding, and travel or residence in a dangerous country.

Payment of Premiums

Life insurance premiums can be paid annually, semiannually, quarterly, or monthly. If the premium is paid other than annually, the policyowner must pay a carrying charge, which can be relatively expensive when the true rate of interest is calculated. For example, the semiannual premium may be 52 percent of the annual premium and so could be viewed

as a carrying charge of only 4 percent. However, the actual charge is 16.7 percent. Assume that your annual premium is $1000. You pay the semiannual premium of $520 and defer payment of $480. Six months later, the $480 and $40 carrying charge are due. This means that you are paying $40 for the use of $480 for six months, which is the equivalent of an annual percentage rate of 16.7 percent.[3]

Assignment Clause

A life insurance policy is freely assignable to another party. There are two types of assignments. *Under an* **absolute assignment,** *all ownership rights in the policy are transferred to a new owner.* For example, the policyowner may wish to donate a life insurance policy to a church, charity, or educational institution. This goal can be accomplished by an absolute assignment. The new owner can then exercise the ownership rights in the policy.

Under a **collateral assignment,** *the policyowner temporarily assigns a life insurance policy to a creditor as collateral for a loan. Only certain rights are transferred to the creditor to protect its interest, and the policyowner retains the remaining rights.* The party to whom the policy is assigned can receive the policy proceeds only to the extent of the loan; the balance of the proceeds is paid to the beneficiary.

In previous years, insurers typically used the American Bankers Association assignment form for a collateral assignment. However, as a result of numerous changes in state laws, the ABA form is no longer widely used. Instead, insurers generally use their own collateral assignment forms that are tailored to satisfy various state laws.

The purpose of the assignment clause is to protect the insurer from paying the policy proceeds twice if an unrecorded assignment is presented to the insurer after the death claim is paid to the beneficiary. If the insurer is not notified of the assignment, the proceeds are paid to the named beneficiary when the policy matures as a death claim or endowment. Under general rules of law, the insurer is relieved of any further obligation under the policy, even though a valid assignment is in existence at the insured's death. However, if the insurer is notified of the assignment, a new contract exists between the insurer and assignee (one who receives the assignment, such as a bank), and the insurer then recognizes the assignee's rights as being superior to the beneficiary's rights.

Policy Loan Provision

Cash-value life insurance contains a **policy loan provision** that allows the policyowner to borrow the cash value. The interest rate is stated in the policy. Older policies typically have a 5 or 6 percent loan rate. Newer policies typically have an 8 percent loan rate. However, all states permit insurers to charge a variable policy loan interest rate based on the National Association of Insurance Commissioner's model bill. If a variable interest rate is used, it can be based on Moody's composite yield on seasoned corporate bonds or some other index that is published regularly in the financial press. Another variable approach is a policy loan rate equal to the interest rate credited to the cash value plus a specified spread.[4]

On newly issued participating contracts, many insurers will reduce the dividend based on the amount of cash value borrowed. This step has the effect of indirectly increasing the effective interest rate on the policy loan. Under interest-sensitive policies, such as universal life and variable universal life, the current interest rate credited to the cash values that are borrowed is typically reduced, which again increases the effective interest rate on the loan.

Interest on a policy loan must either be paid annually or added to the outstanding loan if not paid. If the loan is not repaid by the time the policy matures as a death claim or endowment, the face amount of the policy is reduced by the amount of indebtedness. With the exception of a policy loan to pay a premium, the insurer can defer granting the loan for up to six months, but this is rarely done.

Persons who borrow their cash values often believe that they are paying interest on their own money. *This view is clearly incorrect. The cash value legally belongs to the insurer.* Although you have the contractual right to surrender or borrow the cash value, the cash value legally belongs to the insurer. Interest must be paid on the loan because the insurer assumes a certain interest rate when premiums, legal reserves, dividends, and surrender values are calculated. The insurer's assets must be invested in interest-bearing securities and other investments so that the contractual obligations can be met. *A policyowner must pay interest on the loan to offset the loss of interest to the insurer.* If the loan had not been granted, the insurer could have earned interest on the funds.

Notice, too, that policy loan provisions make it necessary for the insurer to keep some assets in lower-yielding, liquid investments to meet the demand for policy loans. Because these funds could have been invested in higher-yielding investments, policy-owners who borrow should pay interest because higher yields must be forsaken to maintain liquidity.

Advantages of Policy Loans The major advantage of a policy loan is the relatively low rate of interest that is paid. This is especially true for older contracts. The low policy loan rates of 5, 6, or 8 percent are substantially lower than credit card rates. There is also no credit check on the policyowner's ability to repay the loan; there is no fixed repayment schedule; and the policyowner has complete financial flexibility in determining the amount and frequency of loan repayments.

Disadvantages of Policy Loans The major disadvantage is that the policyowner is not legally required to repay the loan, and the policy could lapse if the total indebtedness exceeds the available cash value. Rather than repay the loan, the policyowner may let the policy lapse or may surrender the policy for any remaining cash value. Finally, if the loan has not been repaid by the time the policy matures, the face amount of insurance is reduced by the amount owed.

Automatic Premium Loan

The automatic premium loan provision can be added to most cash-value policies. *Under the* **automatic premium loan provision,** *an overdue premium is automatically borrowed from the cash value after the grace period expires, provided the policy has a loan value sufficient to pay the premium.* The policy continues in force just as before, but a premium loan is now outstanding. Interest is charged on the premium loan at the stated contractual rate. Premium payments can be resumed at any time without evidence of insurability.

The basic purpose of an automatic premium loan is to prevent the policy from lapsing because of nonpayment of premiums. The policyowner may be temporarily short of funds or may forget to pay the premium. Thus, the automatic premium loan provides considerable financial flexibility to the policyowner.

The automatic premium loan provision, however, has two major disadvantages. First, it may be overused. The policyowner may get into the habit of using the automatic premium loan provision too frequently. If the cash values are relatively modest and are habitually borrowed over an extended period, they could eventually be exhausted, and the contract would terminate. Second, the policy proceeds will be reduced if the premium loans are not repaid by the time of death.

DIVIDEND OPTIONS

Life insurance policies frequently contain dividend options. If the policy pays dividends, it is known as a **participating policy.** Both stock and mutual insurers issue participating policies, which gives the policyowner the right to share in the divisible surplus of the insurer. The dividend represents largely a refund of part of the gross premium if the insurer has favorable experience with respect to mortality, interest, and expenses. In contrast, a policy that does not pay dividends is known as a **nonparticipating policy.**

Policy dividends are derived from three principal sources: (1) the difference between expected and actual mortality experience; (2) excess interest earnings on the assets required to maintain legal reserves; and (3) the difference between expected and actual operating expenses. Because the dividends paid are determined by the insurer's actual operating experience, they cannot be guaranteed.

There are several ways in which dividends can be taken:

- Cash
- Reduction of premiums
- Dividend accumulations
- Paid-up additions
- Term insurance (fifth dividend option)

Cash

A dividend is usually payable after the policy has been in force for a stated period, typically one or two years. The policyowner receives a check equal to the dividend, usually on the anniversary date of the policy.

Reduction of Premiums

The dividend can be used to reduce the next premium coming due. The dividend notice will indicate the amount of the dividend, and the policyowner must then remit the difference between the premium and actual dividend paid. This option is appropriate whenever premium payments become financially burdensome. It can also be used if the policyowner has a substantial reduction in income and expenses must be reduced.

Dividend Accumulations

The dividend can be retained by the insurer and accumulated at interest. The policy guarantees a minimum interest rate such as 3 percent, but a higher rate may be paid based on current market conditions. The accumulated dividends generally can be withdrawn at any time. If not withdrawn, they are added to the amount paid when the policy matures as a death claim, or the contract is surrendered for its cash value. The dividend generally is not taxable for income-tax purposes. However, the interest income on the accumulated dividends is taxable income and must be reported annually for federal and state income-tax purposes. Thus, the accumulation option may be undesirable for policyowners who wish to minimize income taxes.

Paid-up Additions

Under the **paid-up additions option,** *the dividend is used to purchase a small amount of paid-up whole life insurance.* For example, assume that Paige, age 22, owns an ordinary life insurance policy. If a dividend of $50 were paid, about $200 of paid-up whole life insurance could be purchased.

The paid-up additions option has some favorable features. *First, the paid-up additions are purchased at net rates, not gross rates;* there is no loading for expenses. *Second, evidence of insurability is not required.* Thus, if the insured is substandard in health or is uninsurable, this option may be appealing, because additional amounts of life insurance can be purchased without demonstrating insurability.

One disadvantage, however, is that *paid-up additions are a form of single premium whole life insurance.* Consumer experts point out that rarely is a single premium policy appropriate for most insureds.

INSIGHT 12.2

Don't Be Confused About Dividend Options

Consumers may be confused concerning the best dividend option to select in a participating life insurance policy. In reality, there is no best dividend option. *The best dividend option is one that best meets your financial goals and objectives.* If money is tight and premiums are financially burdensome, dividends can be paid in cash or used to reduce premiums. If you are substandard in health or uninsurable, the paid-up additions option in a cash-value policy is attractive if you need additional insurance. The paid-up additions are purchased at net rates with no expense loading.

If you have a cash-value policy and wish to accumulate funds for retirement, the paid-up additions option is appropriate. The paid-up additions can also pay up a policy prior to retirement. Another advantage, according to the Consumer Federation of America, is that the interest rate credited to paid-up additions may be higher than the interest rate credited to accumulated dividends retained by the insurer under the interest option.[a]

If income-tax considerations are important, you should not use the dividend accumulations option. Although the dividends are not taxable, the interest earnings on the dividends are taxed as ordinary income. In this case, the paid-up additions option is more appropriate because the dividend becomes the legal reserve under the paid-up addition. Interest earnings credited to the legal reserve are not taxed as current income to the policyowner. Moreover, as stated earlier, the interest rate credited to paid-up additions may be higher than the interest rate credited to the accumulated dividends under the dividend accumulations option.

Finally, if you need more life insurance, you can use the fifth dividend option if it is available. In short, no single dividend option is best for all policyowners. Each policyowner should choose an option best suited to his or her financial situation.

[a]James H. Hunt, *Evaluating Cash Value Life Insurance Policies,* Consumer Federation of America, September 21, 2001.

For example, if a $100,000 ordinary life insurance policy is desired, the insured normally does not pay a single premium of $40,000 to obtain the protection. Consequently, why should a $40 dividend be used to buy a $100 paid-up addition? Because most people are underinsured, a better approach would be to use the dividends to purchase another policy if the applicant is insurable. A reasonable approach would be to accumulate the dividends either under the interest option or paid-up additions option for several years. The accumulated funds could then be used to purchase a new policy.

Term Insurance (Fifth Dividend Option)

Some insurers offer a fifth dividend option by which the dividend is used to purchase term insurance. Two forms of this option are typically used. *The dividend can be used to purchase one-year term insurance equal to the cash value of the basic policy, and the remainder of the dividend is then used to buy paid-up additions or is accumulated at interest.* This option may be appropriate if the policyowner regularly borrows the cash value. The face amount of the

policy would not be reduced by the amount of any outstanding loans at the time of death.

A second form of this option is to use the dividend to purchase yearly renewable term insurance. The actual amount of term insurance purchased depends on the amount of the dividend, the insured's attained age, and the insurer's term insurance rates. However, it is not uncommon for a $40 dividend to purchase $10,000 or more yearly renewable term insurance under this option. Unfortunately, this desirable option is offered by only a small proportion of companies.

Other Uses of Dividends

The dividends can also be used to convert a policy into a *paid-up contract.* If the paid-up option is used, the policy becomes paid up whenever the reserve value under the basic contract plus the reserve value of the paid-up additions or deposits equal the net single premium for a paid-up policy at the insured's attained age. For example, an ordinary life policy issued at age 25 could be paid up by age 48 by using this option.

The dividend can also be used to *mature a policy as an endowment*. When the reserve value under the basic policy plus the reserve value of the paid-up additions or deposits equal the face amount of insurance, the policy matures as an endowment. For example, a $50,000 ordinary life policy issued at age 25 would mature as an endowment at age 58 by using this option.[5]

Finally, keep in mind that the use of dividend options will vary among policyowners. There is no best dividend option. The best option to use is the one that best meets your financial goals and objectives (see Insight 12.2).

NONFORFEITURE OPTIONS

If a cash-value policy is purchased, the policyowner pays more than is actuarially necessary for the life insurance protection. Thus, the policyowner should get something back if the policy is surrendered. The payment to a withdrawing policyowner is known as a nonforfeiture value or cash-surrender value.

All states have standard **nonforfeiture laws** that require insurers to provide at least a minimum non-forfeiture value to policyowners who surrender their policies. There are three **nonforfeiture options** or cash-surrender options:

- Cash value
- Reduced paid-up insurance
- Extended term insurance

Cash Value

The policy can be surrendered for its cash value, at which time all benefits under the policy cease. A policy normally does not build any cash value until the end of the second or third year, although some policies have a small cash value at the end of the first year. The cash values are small during the early years because the relatively high first-year acquisition expenses incurred by the insurer in selling the policy have not yet been recovered. However, over a long period, the cash values accumulate to substantial amounts.

The insurer can delay payment of the cash value for six months if the policy is surrendered. This provision is required by law and is a carryover from the

Great Depression of the 1930s, when cash demands on life insurers were excessive. Insurers generally do not delay payment of the cash value.

The cash-surrender option can be used if the insured no longer needs life insurance. Although it is usually not advisable to surrender a policy for cash because other options may be more appropriate, there are circumstances where the cash-surrender option can be used. For example, if an insured is retired and no longer has any dependents to support, the need for substantial amounts of life insurance may be reduced. In such a case, the cash-surrender option could be used if cash is needed.

Reduced Paid-Up Insurance

Under the **reduced paid-up insurance** *option, the cash-surrender value is applied as a net single premium to purchase a reduced paid-up policy.* The amount of insurance purchased depends on the insured's attained age, the cash-surrender value, and the mortality and interest assumptions stated in the original contract. The reduced paid-up policy is the same as the original policy, but the face amount of insurance is reduced. If the original policy is participating, the reduced paid-up policy also pays dividends.

The reduced paid-up insurance option is appropriate if life insurance is still needed but the policy-owner does not wish to pay premiums. For example, assume that John has a $100,000 ordinary life policy that he purchased at age 37. He is now age 65 and wants to retire, but he does not want to pay premiums after retirement. The cash-surrender value can be used to purchase a reduced paid-up policy of about $77,300.

Extended Term Insurance

Under the **extended term insurance** *option, the net cash-surrender value is used as a net single premium to extend the full face amount of the policy (less any indebtedness) into the future as term insurance for a certain number of years and days.* In effect, the cash value is used to purchase a paid-up term insurance policy equal to the original face amount (less any indebtedness) for a limited period. The length of the term insurance protection is determined by the in-

EXHIBIT 12.1
Table of Guaranteed Values*

End of Policy Year	Cash Value	Alternatives to Cash Value			End of Policy Year
		Paid-Up Insurance or	Extended Insurance		
			Years	Days	
1	*****	***	**	***	1
2	*****	***	**	***	2
3	$400.00	$2,400	1	18	3
4	1,400.00	7,900	3	114	4
5	2,400.00	12,900	5	62	5
6	3,500.00	17,900	6	328	6
7	4,500.00	22,000	8	55	7
8	5,600.00	26,200	9	109	8
9	6,800.00	30,400	10	121	9
10	8,000.00	34,300	11	50	10
11	9,300.00	38,100	11	321	11
12	11,000.00	43,200	12	325	12
13	12,900.00	48,500	13	323	13
14	14,800.00	53,300	14	239	14
15	16,700.00	57,700	15	91	15
16	18,700.00	61,900	15	287	16
17	20,700.00	65,800	16	73	17
18	22,700.00	69,300	16	187	18
19	24,800.00	72,800	16	291	19
20	26,900.00	75,900	16	358	20
AGE 60	32,300.00	69,400	14	319	AGE 60
AGE 65	41,700.00	77,300	13	198	AGE 65

* This table assumes premiums have been paid to the end of the policy year shown. These values do not include any dividend accumulations, paid-up additions, or policy loans.

sured's attained age when the option is exercised, the net cash-surrender value, and the premium rates for extended term insurance. For example, in our earlier illustration, if John stopped paying premiums at age 65, the cash value would be sufficient to keep the $100,000 policy in force for another 13 years and 198 days. If he is still alive after that time, the policy is no longer in force.

If the policy lapses for nonpayment of premiums, and the policyowner has not elected another option, the extended term option automatically goes into effect in most policies. This means that many policies are still in force even though the policyowners mistakenly believe the policy is not in force because of nonpayment of premiums. However, if the automatic premium loan provision has been added to the policy, it has priority over the extended term option.

A whole life or endowment policy contains a table of guaranteed values that indicates the benefits under the three options at various ages.

Exhibit 12.1 illustrates the guaranteed values of one insurer for a $100,000 ordinary life policy issued to a male, age 37.

SETTLEMENT OPTIONS

Settlement options refer to the various ways that the policy proceeds can be paid. The policyowner can elect the settlement option prior to the insured's death, or the beneficiary may be granted that right. Most policies permit the cash-surrender value to be paid under the settlement options if the policy is surrendered. The most common settlement options are as follows:

- Cash
- Interest option
- Fixed-period option
- Fixed-amount option
- Life income options

Cash

When insureds die, cash may be needed immediately for funeral expenses and other expenses. The policy proceeds can be paid in a lump sum to a designated beneficiary or beneficiaries. Interest is paid on the policy proceeds from the date of death to the date of payment. The payment of interest is especially important in those cases where the life insurance proceeds are large, and the proceeds are paid several weeks or months after the insured's death. As a practical matter, most policy proceeds are paid in a lump sum within weeks following the insured's death.

Interest Option

Under the **interest option,** *the policy proceeds are retained by the insurer, and interest is periodically paid to the beneficiary.* The interest can be paid monthly, quarterly, semiannually, or annually. Most insurers guarantee a minimum interest rate on the policy proceeds retained under the interest option. If the policy is participating, a higher rate of interest is paid based on excess interest earnings. For example, an insurer may pay 4 percent on the proceeds even though the contractual rate is only 3 percent.

The beneficiary can be given withdrawal rights, by which part or all of the proceeds can be withdrawn. The beneficiary may also be given the right to change to another settlement option.

The interest option provides considerable flexibility, and it can be used in a wide variety of circumstances. In particular, it can be effectively used if the funds will not be needed until some later date. For example, educational funds could be retained at interest until the children are ready for college. Meanwhile, the interest income can supplement the family's income.

Fixed-Period Option

Under the **fixed-period (income for elected period) option,** *the policy proceeds are paid to a beneficiary over some fixed period of time.* Payments can be

Exhibit 12.2
Income for Elected Period (minimum monthly payment per $1000 of proceeds)

Years		Years		Years		Years	
1	$84.65	5	$18.12	9	$10.75	15	$7.10
2	43.05	6	15.35	10	9.83	20	5.75
3	29.19	7	13.38	11	9.09	25	4.96
4	22.27	8	11.90	12	8.46	30	4.45

made monthly, quarterly, semiannually, or annually. Both principal and interest are systematically liquidated under this option. If the primary beneficiary dies before receiving all payments, the remaining payments will be paid to a contingent beneficiary or to the primary beneficiary's estate.

Exhibit 12.2 illustrates the fixed-period option of one insurer for each $1000 of proceeds at a guaranteed interest rate of 3.5 percent. The length of the period determines the amount of each payment. If the fixed period is five years, a $100,000 policy would provide a monthly income of $1812. However, the monthly benefit would be only $983 if a 10-year period is elected.

The fixed-period option can be used in those situations where income is needed for a definite time period, such as during the readjustment, dependency, and blackout periods. The fixed-period option, however, should be used with caution. It is extremely inflexible. Partial withdrawals by the beneficiary normally are not allowed because of the administrative expense of recomputing the amount of the payment during the fixed period. However, many insurers will permit the beneficiary to withdraw the commuted value of the remaining payments in a lump sum.

Fixed-Amount Option

Under the **fixed-amount (income of elected amount) option,** *a fixed amount is periodically paid to the beneficiary.* The payments are made until both the principal and interest are exhausted. If excess interest is paid, the period is lengthened, but the amount of each payment is unchanged.

For example, assume that the death benefit is $50,000, the credited interest rate is 4 percent annually, and the desired monthly benefit is $3020. The actual monthly payout schedule would be calculated by the insurer. In this case, the beneficiary would receive $3020 monthly for 17 months. At that time, the principal and interest would be exhausted.

The fixed-amount option provides considerable flexibility. The beneficiary can be given limited or unlimited withdrawal rights and the right to switch the unpaid proceeds to another option. The beneficiary may also be allowed to increase or decrease the fixed amount. It is also possible to arrange a settlement agreement, by which the periodic payments can be increased at certain times, such as when grown children start college. Unless there is some compelling reason for using the fixed-period option, the fixed-amount option is recommended because of its greater flexibility.

Life Income Options

Death benefits can also be paid to the beneficiary under a life income option. The cash-surrender value can also be disbursed under a **life income option.** The major life income options are as follows.

Life Income   Some insurers include a straight life annuity option on their policies. *Under this option, installment payments are paid only while the beneficiary is alive and cease on the beneficiary's death.* Although this option provides the highest amount of installment income, there may be a substantial forfeiture of the proceeds if the beneficiary dies shortly after the payments start. Because there is no refund feature or guarantee of payments, other life income options are usually more desirable.

Life Income with Guaranteed Period   Under this option, the beneficiary receives a life income with a guaranteed period of payments. *If the primary beneficiary dies before receiving the guaranteed number of years of payments, the remaining payments are paid to a contingent beneficiary.* For example, assume that Megan is receiving $2000 monthly under a life income option, and the guaranteed period is 10 years. If Megan dies after receiving only one year of payments, the remaining nine years of payments will be paid to a contingent beneficiary or to her estate.

Exhibit 12.3 shows the life income option of one insurer with guaranteed periods ranging from 5 to 20 years for each $1000 of insurance proceeds. Females

receive lower periodic payments because of a longer life expectancy.

Life Income with Guaranteed Total Amount   Under this option, the beneficiary receives a lifetime income, and the total amount paid is guaranteed. *If the beneficiary dies before receiving installment payments equal to the total amount of insurance placed under the option, the payments continue until the total amount paid equals the total amount of insurance.* For example, assume that Laura has $100,000 of insurance paid to her as lifetime income under this option. If Laura dies after receiving only $10,000 in payments, the remaining $90,000 is paid in installments to another beneficiary or to her estate.

Exhibit 12.4 shows the life income-guaranteed total amount option of one insurer for each $1000 of life insurance proceeds. As noted earlier, females receive lower monthly payments because of a longer life expectancy.

Joint-and-Survivor Income   *Under this option, income payments are paid to two persons during their lifetimes, such as a husband and wife.* For example, Richard and Margo may be receiving $1200 monthly under a joint-and-survivor income annuity. If Richard dies, Margo continues to receive $1200 monthly during her lifetime. There are also variations of this option, such as a joint-and-two-thirds annuity or a joint-and-one-half annuity. Thus, the monthly income of $1200 would be reduced to $800 or $600 on the death of the first person.

Exhibit 12.5 illustrates the minimum monthly payment under the joint-and-survivor income option of one insurer for each $1000 of insurance proceeds. For example, if the insurance proceeds are $100,000, and a male and female beneficiary are both age 65, a monthly payment of $466 would be paid during the lifetime of both annuitants. However, the payments are guaranteed for 10 years.

Advantages of Settlement Options

The major advantages of settlement options are summarized as follows:

- *Periodic income is paid to the family.* Settlement options can restore part or all of the family's

EXHIBIT 12.3
Life Income with Guaranteed Period
(minimum monthly payment per $1000 of proceeds)

Payee's Adjusted Age	MALE Guaranteed Period				FEMALE Guaranteed Period			
	5 Yrs	10 Yrs	15 Yrs	20 Yrs	5 Yrs	10 Yrs	15 Yrs	20 Yrs
60	$5.14	$5.08	$4.98	$4.84	$4.68	$4.85	$4.61	$4.54
61	5.25	5.18	5.07	4.91	4.76	4.73	4.68	4.63
62	5.36	5.28	5.15	4.97	4.84	4.81	4.75	4.67
63	5.48	5.39	5.24	5.04	4.93	4.89	4.83	4.73
64	5.61	5.50	5.33	5.10	5.03	4.99	4.91	4.80
65	5.75	5.62	5.42	5.17	5.13	5.08	5.00	4.87
66	5.89	5.75	5.52	5.23	5.25	5.19	5.09	4.94
67	6.05	5.88	5.62	5.30	5.36	5.30	5.18	5.01
68	6.21	6.02	5.72	5.36	5.49	5.41	5.28	5.08
69	6.39	6.16	5.82	5.42	5.63	5.54	5.38	5.16
70	6.57	6.31	5.92	5.48	5.78	5.67	5.48	5.23
71	6.77	6.46	6.02	5.54	5.94	5.81	5.59	5.30
72	6.97	6.62	6.13	5.60	6.11	5.95	5.70	5.37
73	7.19	6.78	6.23	5.65	6.29	6.11	5.81	5.44
74	7.42	6.95	6.33	5.69	6.49	6.27	5.93	5.50
75	7.66	7.12	6.42	5.74	6.70	6.44	6.04	5.58
76	7.91	7.29	6.52	5.78	6.92	6.61	6.15	5.62
77	8.18	7.46	6.60	5.81	7.16	6.80	6.27	5.67
78	8.47	7.84	6.69	5.84	7.42	6.98	6.37	5.72
79	8.77	7.82	6.77	5.87	7.69	7.18	6.48	5.76
80	9.08	8.00	6.84	5.90	7.98	7.37	6.58	5.80
81	9.41	8.17	6.91	5.92	8.29	7.57	6.67	5.84
82	9.74	8.34	6.97	5.94	8.62	7.77	6.75	5.87
83	10.10	8.51	7.03	5.95	8.96	7.97	6.83	5.89
84	10.46	8.67	7.08	5.96	9.33	8.16	6.91	5.92
85 & over	10.84	8.82	7.13	5.97	9.71	8.34	6.97	5.94

NOTE: The payee's adjusted age reflects increases in longevity. To find the adjusted age, increase or decrease the payee's age at that time as follows:

1987–91	1992–98	1999–2006	2007–13	2014–20	2021–28	2029+
+3	+2	+1	0	−1	−2	−3

share of the deceased breadwinner's earnings. The financial security of the family can then be maintained.

- *Principal and interest are guaranteed.* The insurance company guarantees both principal and interest. There are no investment worries and administrative problems, because the funds are invested by the insurer.
- *Settlement options can be used in life insurance planning.* Life insurance can be programmed to meet the policyowner's needs and objectives.
- *An insurance windfall can create problems for the beneficiary.* The funds may be spent unwisely; bad investments may be made; and oth-

ers may try to get the funds. Many insurers now offer money market accounts for investment of the death proceeds so that beneficiaries are not forced to make immediate decisions concerning disposition of the funds.

Disadvantages of Settlement Options

The major disadvantages of settlement options are summarized as follows:

- *Higher yields often can be obtained elsewhere.* Interest rates offered by other financial institutions may be considerably higher.

EXHIBIT 12.4

Life Income with Guaranteed Total Amount
(minimum monthly payment per $1000 of proceeds)

Payee's Adjusted Age	Male	Female	Payee's Adjusted Age	Male	Female
60	$4.93	$4.57	73	$6.47	$5.87
61	5.02	4.64	74	6.84	6.01
62	5.11	4.71	75	6.81	6.17
63	5.20	4.79	76	7.00	6.34
64	5.30	4.87	77	7.19	6.51
65	5.40	4.96	78	7.40	6.70
66	5.52	5.05	79	7.62	6.90
67	5.63	5.14	80	7.85	7.11
68	5.75	5.25	81	8.09	7.33
69	5.88	5.36	82	8.35	7.57
70	6.02	5.47	83	8.61	7.81
71	6.16	5.60	84	8.89	8.07
72	6.31	5.73	85 & over	9.19	8.35

NOTE: The payee's adjusted age reflects increases in longevity. To find the adjusted age, increase or decrease the payee's age at that time as follows:

1987–91	1992–98	1999–2006	2007–13	2014–20	2021–28	2029+
+3	+2	+1	0	−1	−2	−3

EXHIBIT 12.5

Joint-and-Survivor Income Option 10-Year
Guaranteed Period (minimum monthly
payment per $1000 of proceeds)

Male Payee's Adjusted Age	Female Payee's Adjusted Age				
	60	65	70	75	80
60	$4.32	$4.50	$4.67	$4.82	$4.93
65	4.42	4.66	4.91	5.15	5.34
70	4.81	4.81	5.14	5.49	5.80
75	4.57	4.92	5.34	5.81	6.27
80	4.61	4.99	5.49	6.07	6.69

NOTE: The payee's adjusted age reflects increases in longevity. To find the adjusted age, increase or decrease the payee's age at that time as follows:

1987–91	1992–98	1999–2006	2007–13	2014–20	2021–28	2029+
+3	+2	+1	0	−1	−2	−3

- *The settlement agreement may be inflexible and restrictive.* The policyowner may have a settlement agreement that is too restrictive. The beneficiary may not have withdrawal rights or the right to change options. For example, the funds may be paid over a 20-year period under the fixed-period option with no right of withdrawal. An emergency may arise, but the beneficiary could not withdraw the funds.

- *Life income options have limited usefulness at the younger ages.* Life income options should rarely be used before age 65 or 70, which restricts their usefulness at the younger ages. If a life income option is elected at a young age, the income payments are substantially reduced. Also, using a life income option is the equivalent of purchasing a single-premium life annuity, which may be purchased at a lower cost from another insurer.

Use of a Trust

The policy proceeds can also be paid to a trustee, such as the trust department of a commercial bank. Under certain circumstances, it may be desirable to have the policy proceeds paid to a trustee rather than disbursed under the settlement options. This would be the case if the amount of insurance is substantial; if considerable flexibility and discretion in the amount and timing of payments are needed; if there are minor children or mentally handicapped adults who cannot manage their own financial affairs; or if the amounts paid must be periodically changed as the beneficiary's needs and desires change. These advantages are partly offset by the payment of a trustee's fee, and the investment results cannot be guaranteed.

ADDITIONAL LIFE INSURANCE BENEFITS

Other benefits can be added to a life insurance policy by the payment of an additional premium. These benefits provide valuable protection to the policyowner.

Waiver-of-Premium Provision

A **waiver-of-premium provision** can be added to a life insurance policy. In some policies, the waiver-of-premium provision is automatically included. Under this provision, if the insured becomes totally disabled from bodily injury or disease before some stated age, all premiums coming due during the period of disability are waived. During the period of disability, death benefits, cash values, and dividends continue as if the premiums had been paid.

Before any premiums are waived, the insured must meet the following requirements:

- Become disabled before some stated age, such as before age 60 or 65
- Be continuously disabled for six months (Some insurers have a shorter waiting period.)
- Satisfy the definition of total disability
- Furnish proof of disability satisfactory to the insurer

The insured must be totally disabled for premiums to be waived. Total disability is defined in the policy. In many current waiver-of-premium provisions, *total disability means that, because of disease or bodily injury, the insured cannot do any of the essential duties of his or her job, or of any job for which he or she is suited based on schooling, training, or experience.* If the insured can perform some but not all of these acts and duties, the disability is not considered to be total, and premiums will not be waived. If the insured is a minor and is going to school, premiums are waived if the minor is unable to attend school.

For example, assume that Professor Brown is a chemistry professor who has throat cancer. He cannot perform any of the essential duties of his job, which include teaching, research, and public service. As long as he remains totally disabled, all premiums are waived after a six-month elimination period. However, if he could work at another job for which he is suited based on his education, training, and experience, such as a research scientist for a chemical firm, he would not be considered totally disabled.

A second definition of total disability found in some policies is more liberal. Total disability is initially defined in terms of your own occupation. *For the first two years, total disability means the insured cannot work in the occupation that he or she had at the time the disability occurred.* After the initial period expires, the definition becomes stricter. *The insured is considered totally disabled only if he or she cannot work in an occupation for which he or she is qualified by education, training, and experience.* For example, assume that Dr. Pudwill is a dentist whose hand is severely injured in a hunting accident. For the first two years, he would be considered totally disabled, because he is unable to perform all duties of his occupation. Premiums during this initial period would be waived. However, after the initial period expires, if he could work in an occupation for which he is qualified by his education and training, he would not be considered totally disabled. Thus, if he could get a job as a research scientist or as a professor in a dental school, he would not be considered disabled. He would then have to resume premium payments.

Total disability can also be defined in terms of the loss of use of bodily members. For example, if Jason loses his eyesight in an explosion, or if both legs are paralyzed from some crippling disease, he would be considered totally disabled.

Before any premiums are waived, the insured must furnish satisfactory proof of disability to the insurer. The insurer may also require continuing proof of disability once each year. If satisfactory proof of disability is not furnished, no further premiums will be waived.

If you have adequate amounts of disability-income insurance, the waiver-of-premium rider is not needed. If you become disabled, the life insurance premiums could be treated like any other monthly expense that must be paid, such as housing, utilities, and food. However, most breadwinners are substantially underinsured against the risk of long-term disability. Thus, many financial planners recommend adding this provision to a life insurance policy, especially if the face amount of life insurance is large. During a period of long-term disability, premium payments can be financially burdensome. Because most persons are underinsured for disability-income benefits, waiver of premiums during a period in which income is reduced is highly desirable.

Guaranteed Purchase Option

The **guaranteed purchase option** *permits the policyowner to purchase additional amounts of life insurance at specified times in the future without evidence of insurability*. The guaranteed purchase option is also called the *guaranteed insurability option*. The purpose of the option is to guarantee the insured's future insurability. The insured may need additional life insurance in the future and may be unable to afford the additional insurance today. The guaranteed purchase option guarantees the purchase of specified amounts of life insurance in the future, even though the insured may become substandard in health or uninsurable.

Amount of Insurance The typical option allows the policyowner to purchase additional amounts of life insurance every three years up to some maximum age without evidence of insurability, such as age 46. In most cases, the additional insurance increases the face amount of the original policy. However, some insurers issue a new policy for each option exercised. For example, the guaranteed purchase option of one insurer allows additional purchases of life insurance

when the insured attains ages 25, 28, 31, 34, 37, 40, 43, and 46. The amount of life insurance that can be purchased at each option date is limited to the face amount of the basic policy subject to some minimum and maximum amount. For example, assume that Heather, age 22, purchases a $25,000 ordinary life policy with a guaranteed purchase option and becomes uninsurable after the policy is issued. Assuming that she elects to exercise each option, she would have the following amounts of insurance:

Age 22	$ 25,000 (basic policy)
	+
Age 25	$ 25,000
Age 28	25,000
Age 31	25,000
Age 34	25,000
Age 37	25,000
Age 40	25,000
Age 43	25,000
Age 46	25,000
Total insurance at age 46	$225,000

Although uninsurable, Heather has increased her insurance coverage from $25,000 to $225,000.

Advance Purchase Privilege Most insurers have some type of advance purchase privilege, by which an option can be immediately exercised on the occurrence of some event. If the insured marries, has a birth in the family, or legally adopts a child, an option can be immediately exercised prior to the next option due date. Some insurers will provide automatic term insurance for 90 days if the insured marries or a child is born. The insurance expires after 90 days unless the guaranteed insurability option is exercised.

If an option is exercised under the advance purchase privilege, the number of total options is not increased. If an option is exercised early, each new purchase eliminates the next regular option date. Finally, the policyowner typically has only 30 to 60 days to exercise an option. If the option expires without being used, it cannot be exercised at some later date. This provision protects the insurer from adverse selection.

Other Considerations An important consideration is whether the waiver-of-premium rider can be added to the new insurance without furnishing evidence of insurability. Insurer practices vary in this regard. The most liberal provision permits the waiver-of-premium rider to be added to the new insurance if the original policy contains such a provision. If premiums are being waived under the original policy, they are also waived for the new insurance. Thus, in our earlier example, if premiums are being waived under Heather's original policy of $25,000, the premiums for the new life insurance purchased will also be waived. A less liberal approach permits the disabled insured to purchase additional life insurance with each option, but not to waive the new premiums under the waiver-of premium rider.

Accidental Death Benefit Rider

The **accidental death benefit rider** (also known as **double indemnity**) *doubles the face amount of life insurance if death occurs as a result of an accident.* In some policies, the face amount is tripled. The cost of the rider is relatively low. For example, at one insurer, the rider costs $69 annually when added to a $100,000 policy issued to a male age 35. Thus, if the insured dies as a result of an accident, $200,000 will be paid.

Requirements for Collecting Benefits Before a double indemnity benefit is paid, several requirements must be satisfied:

- Death must be caused directly, and apart from any other cause, by accidental bodily injury.
- Death must occur within 90 days of the accident.
- Death must occur before some specified age, such as age 60, 65, or 70.

The first requirement is that accidental injury must be the direct cause of death. If death occurs from some other cause, such as disease, the double indemnity benefit is not paid. For example, assume that Sam is painting his two-story house. If the scaffold collapses and Sam is killed, a double indemnity benefit would be paid because the direct cause of death is an accidental bodily injury. However, if Sam died from a heart attack and fell from the scaffold, the double payment would not be made. In this case, heart disease is the direct cause of death, not accidental bodily injury.

The second requirement is that death must occur within 90 days of the accident. The purpose of this requirement is to establish the fact that accidental bodily injury is the proximate cause of death. However, because modern medical technology can prolong life for extended periods, many insurers are using longer time periods, such as 120, 180, or 365 days.

Finally, the accidental death must occur before some specified age. To limit their liability, insurers usually impose some age limitation. Coverage usually terminates on the policy anniversary date just after the insured reaches a certain age, such as 70.

Financial planners generally do not recommend purchase of the double indemnity rider. Although the cost is relatively low, there are three major objections to the rider. *First, the economic value of a human life is not doubled or tripled if death results from an accident.* Therefore, it is economically unsound to insure an accidental death more heavily than death from disease. *Second, most persons will die as a result of a disease and not from an accident.* Because most persons are underinsured, the premiums for the double indemnity rider could be better used to purchase an additional amount of life insurance, which would cover both accidental death and death from disease. *Finally, the insured may be deceived and believe that he or she has more insurance than is actually the case.* For example, a person with a $50,000 policy and a double indemnity rider may erroneously believe that he or she has $100,000 of life insurance.

Cost-of-Living Rider

The **cost-of-living rider** *allows the policyowner to purchase one-year term insurance equal to the percentage change in the consumer price index with no evidence of insurability.* The amount of term insurance changes each year and reflects the cumulative change in the consumer price index (CPI) from the issue date of the policy. However, insurers may limit the amount of insurance that can be purchased each year, such as a maximum of 10 percent of the policy face value. The policyowner pays the entire premium for the term insurance.

For example, assume that Luis, age 28, buys a $100,000 ordinary life insurance policy and that the CPI increases 5 percent during the first year. He would be allowed to purchase $5000 of one-year term insurance, and the total amount of insurance in force would be $105,000. The term insurance can be converted to a cash-value policy with no evidence of insurability.

Accelerated Death Benefits Rider

Many insurers now make available a living benefits rider that can be added to a life insurance policy. The **accelerated death benefits rider** *allows insureds who are terminally ill or who suffer from certain catastrophic diseases to collect part or all of their life insurance benefits before they die, primarily to pay for the medical care they require.* Benefits may also be payable if the insured is receiving long-term care in a nursing home or hospital.

Although accelerated death benefits riders are not uniform, they generally can be classified as follows:

- Terminal illness rider
- Catastrophic illness rider
- Long-term-care rider

The *terminal illness rider* allows terminally ill insureds with a limited life expectancy (24 months or less) to receive part or all of the policy proceeds. Insurers generally allow the rider to be added without an extra premium, but any lump sums advanced are discounted for interest to reflect the time value of money. The face amount of insurance, cash values if any, and premiums are reduced after the payment is made. For example, based on the rider of one insurer, Dr. Harry Crockett, age 59, who is terminally ill with cancer, requests 50 percent of his $100,000 term insurance policy. After the benefit is discounted for interest, he receives $46,296. After the payment is made, premiums are reduced 50 percent, and the face amount is reduced to $50,000.

The *catastrophic illness rider* allows insureds who have certain catastrophic diseases to collect part or all of the policy face amount. Covered diseases typically include AIDS, life-threatening cancer, coronary artery disease, kidney failure, and similar types of catastrophic diseases.

The *long-term-care rider* allows insureds who require long-term care to collect part of their life insurance prior to death. The rider may cover care in a skilled nursing facility, intermediate care facility, or

INSIGHT 12.3

Examples of Life Settlement Cases

Instead of letting a policy lapse without value or surrendering the policy for its cash value, the policyowner can sell the policy to a ready market of investors under certain conditions. A cash-value policy typically sells for a price that exceeds its cash-surrender value but is substantially less than the face amount of insurance. The insured generally must be age 65 or older, have a life expectancy of 15 years or less, and have deterioration in health since the policy was issued; the policy face amount must be at least $100,000, and the two-year contestable period has expired. The following are actual examples of life settlement cases:

- A 76-year-old man owned a policy with a face amount of $8 million and cash value of $795,000. Instead of surrendering the policy, he sold it for $2.3 million. If he had not sold the policy, he would have left more than $1.5 million on the table.[a]
- An 82-year-old woman owned a policy with a face amount of $5 million and a nominal cash surrender value of only

$2,500. She sold the policy for $900,000. Without the sale, she would have walked away from more than $698,000.[b]
- A 76-year-old man wanted to reduce the size of his estate by donating a $750,000 policy to a charity. The policy had a cash value of $142,189, which he could claim as a tax deduction. The charity would pay the premiums and receive the death benefit. His financial planner informed him about a life settlement as an alternative. As a result, the policyowner sold the policy for $225,000. The charity received cash immediately and was not burdened with premium payments. He was able to deduct an additional $82,811 for his gift.[c]

[a] Neil Alexander, "New Value in Old Policies," *Home Online Publications Journal of Accountancy* (October 2001).
[b] Ibid.
[c] *Examples of Life Settlement Cases* at www.life-settlementco.com.

custodial care facility. Some riders also cover certain types of home care. To illustrate, based on the rider of one insurer, a monthly benefit can be paid equal to 2 percent of the face amount of insurance up to a maximum of 50 percent of the face amount. Thus, if the face amount is $200,000, a monthly benefit of $4000 could be paid up to 25 months.

Viatical Settlement

People who are terminally ill often need large amounts of cash for medical bills, alternative medical treatment, living expenses, travel, and other purposes. As an alternative to the accelerated death benefit rider, terminally ill insureds may be able to sell their policies to private firms. A **viatical settlement** is the sale of a life insurance policy by a terminally ill insured to another party, typically to investors or investor groups who hope to profit by the insured's early death. The insured generally must have a life expectancy of 12 months or less. The policy is sold at a substantial discount, and the buyer continues to pay the premiums.

A life settlement is another version of a viatical settlement. A **life settlement** is the sale of a life insurance policy by a policyowner who no longer needs or wants the insurance. Life insurance purchased years ago may no longer be needed. For example, a corporation no longer needs life insurance on a key executive because he or she has retired; a couple divorces, and life insurance is dropped; the insured can no longer afford to pay prohibitively high premiums; the children are grown; estate-tax needs have changed; or the policy may be an under-performing policy with little cash value. Insight 12.3 provides examples of actual life settlements.

Viatical settlements and life settlements have their downside. The policies are sold to parties who do not have an insurable interest in the insured's life but instead acquire a financial interest in the insured's early death. As such, there may be an incentive to murder the insured. In addition, there are numerous cases of alleged and actual fraud committed against individual investors, life insurers, and policyowners. Finally, regulation of viatical and life settlements by state insurance departments may be inadequate.

CASE APPLICATION

Sonja, age 25, recently purchased a $100,000 ordinary life insurance policy on her life. The waiver-of-premium rider and guaranteed purchase option are attached to the policy. For each of the following situations, indicate the extent of the insurer's obligation, if any, to Sonja or to Sonja's beneficiary. Identify the appropriate policy provision or rider that applies in each case. Treat each event separately.

a. Sonja fails to pay the second annual premium due on January 1. She dies 15 days later.
b. Sonja commits suicide three years after the policy was purchased.
c. At Sonja's death, the life insurer discovers that Sonja deliberately lied about her age. Instead of being 25 years old, as she indicated, she was actually 26 years old at the time the policy was purchased.
d. Two years after the policy was purchased, Sonja is told that she has leukemia. She is uninsurable but would like to obtain additional life insurance.

e. Sonja is seriously injured in an auto accident. After six months, she is still unable to return to work. She has no income from her job, and the insurance premium payments are financially burdensome.
f. Sonja has a mentally disabled son. She wants to make certain that her son will have a continuous income after her death.
g. Sonja lets her policy lapse. After four years, she wants to reinstate the policy. Her health is fine. Point out to Sonja how she can reinstate her life insurance.
h. Sonja wants to retire and does not wish to pay the premiums on her policy. Indicate the various options that are available to her.
i. Ten years after the policy was purchased, Sonja is fired from her job. She is unemployed and is in desperate need of cash.
j. When Sonja applied for life insurance, she concealed the fact that she had high blood pressure. She dies five years later.

SUMMARY

- The *ownership clause* states that the policyowner possesses all contractual rights in the policy while the insured is living.

- The *entire-contract clause* states that the life insurance policy and attached application constitute the entire contract between the parties.

- The *incontestable clause* states that a life insurer cannot contest the policy after it has been in force two years during the insured's lifetime.

- The *suicide clause* states that if the insured commits suicide within two years after the policy is issued, the face amount is not paid. There is only a refund of the premiums paid.

- The *grace period* allows the policyowner a period of 31 days to pay an overdue premium. Universal life and other flexible premium policies have longer grace periods, such as 61 days. The insurance remains in force during the grace period.

- There are several types of beneficiary designations. A *primary beneficiary* is the party who is first entitled to receive the policy proceeds upon the insured's death. A *contingent beneficiary* is entitled to the proceeds if the primary beneficiary dies before the insured or dies before receiving the guaranteed number of payments under an installment settlement option. A *revocable beneficiary* designation means that the policyowner can change the beneficiary without the beneficiary's consent. An *irrevocable beneficiary* designation is one that cannot be changed without the beneficiary's consent.

- A *dividend* represents a refund of part of the gross premium if the experience of the company is favorable. Dividends paid to policyowners are not taxable and can be taken in several ways:

    Cash

    Reduction of premiums

    Dividend accumulations

    Paid-up additions

    Term insurance (in some companies)

- There are three *nonforfeiture* or cash-surrender options in cash-value contracts.

    Cash value

    Reduced paid-up insurance

    Extended term insurance

- The cash value can be borrowed under the policy loan provision. An automatic premium loan provision can also be added to the policy, by which an overdue premium is automatically borrowed from the cash value.

- *Settlement options* are the various ways that the policy proceeds can be paid. The most common settlement options are as follows:

    Cash

    Interest option

    Fixed-period option

    Fixed-amount option

    Life income options

- A *waiver-of-premium provision* can be added to a life insurance policy, by which all premiums coming due during a period of total disability are waived. Before any premiums are waived, the insured must meet the following requirements:

    Become disabled before some stated age, such as age 60 or 65

    Be continuously disabled for six months

    Satisfy the definition of total disability

    Furnish proof of disability satisfactory to the insurer

- The *guaranteed purchase option* permits the policyowner to purchase additional amounts of life insurance at specified times without evidence of insurability. The purpose of the option is to guarantee the insured's future insurability.

- The *accidental death benefit rider (double indemnity rider)* doubles the face amount of life insurance if death occurs as a result of an accident. Consumer experts generally do not recommend purchase of the double indemnity rider.

- The *cost-of-living rider* allows the policyowner to purchase one-year term insurance equal to the percentage change in the consumer price index with no evidence of insurability.

- The *accelerated death benefits rider* pays part or all of the life insurance death benefit to a terminally ill insured before death occurs to help pay for medical and other expenses.

KEY CONCEPTS AND TERMS

Absolute assignment	Accidental death benefit
Accelerated death benefits	rider (double
rider	indemnity)

Automatic premium loan
  provision
Aviation exclusion
Change-of-plan
  provision
Class beneficiary
Collateral assignment
Contingent beneficiary
Cost-of-living rider
Dividend accumulations
  option
Entire-contract clause
Extended term
  insurance
Fixed-amount option
Fixed-period option
Grace period
Guaranteed purchase
  option
Incontestable clause
Interest option
Irrevocable beneficiary
Life income options
Life settlement
Misstatement of age
  or sex clause

Nonforfeiture laws
Nonforfeiture options
Nonparticipating
  policy
Ownership clause
Paid-up additions
  option
Participating policy
Policy loan provision
Primary beneficiary
Reduced paid-up
  insurance
Reinstatement
  provision
Revocable beneficiary
Settlement options
Specific beneficiary
Suicide clause
Viatical settlement
Waiver-of-premium
  provision
War clause

REVIEW QUESTIONS

1. Briefly explain the following life insurance contractual provisions.
   a. Suicide clause
   b. Grace period
   c. Reinstatement clause

2. a. Describe the incontestable clause in a life insurance policy.
   b. What is the purpose of the incontestable clause?

3. a. Explain the requirements for reinstating a lapsed life insurance policy.
   b. What are the advantages and disadvantages of reinstating a lapsed life insurance policy?

4. Explain the following beneficiary designations.
   a. Primary and contingent beneficiary
   b. Revocable and irrevocable beneficiary
   c. Specific and class beneficiary

5. A life insurance policy is freely assignable to another party. Explain the following types of assignments:

   a. Absolute assignment
   b. Collateral assignment

6. a. Describe the policy loan provision that appears in a typical cash-value life insurance policy.
   b. Why is interest charged on a policy loan?
   c. List the advantages and disadvantages of a policy loan.

7. A life insurance policy that pays dividends is known as a participating policy.
   a. Identify the sources from which dividends can be paid.
   b. List the various dividend options in a typical life insurance policy.
   c. Can an insurer guarantee the payment of a dividend? Explain your answer.

8. All states have nonforfeiture laws that require the payment of a cash-surrender value when a cash-value policy is surrendered. Briefly explain the following nonforfeiture options that are found in a typical life insurance policy.
   a. Cash-value option
   b. Reduced paid-up insurance
   c. Extended term insurance

9. In addition to cash, life insurance death benefits can be paid under other settlement options. Briefly explain the following settlement options.
   a. Interest option
   b. Fixed-period option
   c. Fixed amount option
   d. Life income options

10. Explain the definition of total disability that is found in a typical waiver-of-premium provision.

APPLICATION QUESTIONS

1. Richard, age 35, owns an ordinary life insurance policy in the amount of $250,000. The policy is a participating policy that pays dividends. Richard has a number of financial goals and objectives. For each of the following situations, identify a dividend option that could be used to meet Richard's goals. Treat each situation separately.
   a. Richard finds the premium payments are financially burdensome. He wants to reduce his annual premium outlay.
   b. Richard has leukemia and is uninsurable. He needs additional life insurance protection.

c. Richard wants to accumulate additional cash for a comfortable retirement.

d. Richard would like to have a paid-up policy at the time of retirement.

e. Richard has substantial earned income that places him in a high marginal income-tax bracket. He wants the insurer to retain the dividends, but he does not want to pay income tax on the investment earnings.

2. Kathy, age 29, is married and has a son, age 3. She owns a $100,000 ordinary life insurance policy with a waiver-of-premium provision, guaranteed purchase option, and accelerated death benefits rider. Kathy has several financial goals and objectives for her family. For each of the following situations, identify an appropriate contractual provision or policy benefit that will enable Kathy to meet her financial goals. Treat each situation separately.

   a. If Kathy dies, she wants the policy proceeds to be paid in the form of monthly income to the family until her son attains age 18.

   b. Kathy is totally disabled in an auto accident when she failed to stop at a red light. After six months, she has not recovered and remains totally disabled. As a result, she cannot return to her former job or work in any occupation based on her previous training and experience. She finds that the premium payments for life insurance are financially burdensome.

   c. When she retires, Kathy would like to have the cash value in the policy paid to her in the form of lifetime income. She wants the payments to continue for at least 10 years.

   d. Kathy is terminally ill from a serious heart condition. Kathy's physician believes she will die within one year. Kathy has no savings and health insurance, and her medical bills are soaring. She needs $50,000 to pay all medical bills and other financial obligations.

   e. Three years after the policy was issued, Kathy was diagnosed with breast cancer. As a result, she is now uninsurable. She would like to purchase additional life insurance to protect her family.

3. Jim, age 32, purchased a $300,000 five-year renewable and convertible term insurance policy. In answering the health questions, Jim told the agent that he had not visited a doctor within the last five years. However, he had visited the doctor two

months earlier. The doctor told Jim that he had a severe heart problem. Jim did not reveal this information to the agent when he applied for life insurance. Jim died three years after the policy was purchased. At that time, the life insurer discovered the heart ailment. Explain the extent of the insurer's obligation, if any, with respect to payment of the death claim.

4. Additional riders and benefits often can be added to a life insurance policy to provide greater protection to the insured. Describe each of the following riders and options:

   a. Waiver-of-premium provision

   b. Guaranteed purchase option

   c. Double indemnity rider

   d. Cost-of-living rider

   e. Accelerated death benefits rider

INTERNET RESOURCES

- **Consumer Federation of America (CFA)** is a nonprofit organization that represents numerous consumer groups. This site is one of the best resources for obtaining meaningful consumer information about life insurance and other insurance products. CFA makes available a low-cost life insurance evaluation service by which individual life insurance policies can be evaluated for a small fee. Visit the site at

  http://www.consumerfed.org

- The **American Council of Life Insurers** represents the life insurance industry on issues dealing with legislation and regulation at the federal and state levels. The site provides consumer information on the purposes and types of life insurance. Visit the site at

  http://www.acli.com

- **INSWEB** provides timely information and premium quotes for life insurance as well as for homeowners, auto, and other insurance products. Visit the site at

  http://www.insweb.com

- **Insure.com** provides up-to-date information, premium quotes, and other consumer information on life insurance. The site also provides news releases about events that affect the insurance industry. Visit the site at

  http://www.insure.com

- **The National Underwriter Company** publishes books and other publications on life insurance products. The company publishes the *National Underwriter,* Life & Health/Financial Services edition, a weekly trade publication that provides news about the life insurance industry. Visit the site at

  http://www.nationalunderwriter.com

- The **National Association of Insurance Commissioners (NAIC)** has a link to all state insurance departments, which provide a considerable amount of consumer information on life insurance. Click on "State Insurance Web Sites." For starters, check out New York, Wisconsin, and California. Visit the site at

  http://www.naic.org

- The **Viatical Association of America** is a trade association that represents viatical settlement brokers and funding companies. A viatical settlement enables terminally ill individuals to obtain cash from their life insurance policies. Visit the site at

  http://www.viatical.org

SELECTED REFERENCES

Anderson, Buist M. *Anderson on Life Insurance.* Boston, MA: Little, Brown, 1991. See also the *September 1996 Supplement to Anderson on Life Insurance.*

Belth, Joseph M. *Life Insurance: A Consumer's Handbook,* 2nd ed. Bloomington, IN: Indiana University Press, 1985.

Black, Kenneth, Jr., and Harold D. Skipper, Jr. *Life Insurance,* 13th ed. Upper Saddle River, NJ: Prentice-Hall, 2000.

Crawford, Muriel L. *Life and Health Insurance Law,* 8th ed. Boston, MA: Irwin/McGraw-Hill, 1998.

Graves, Edward E., ed. *McGill's Life Insurance,* 6th ed. Bryn Mawr, PA: The American College, 2007.

Graves, Edward E., and Burke A. Christensen, eds. *McGill's Legal Aspects of Life Insurance,* 4th ed. Bryn Mawr, PA: The American College, 2004.

Wiening, Eric A., George E. Rejda, Constance M. Luthardt, and Cheryl L. Ferguson. *Personal Insurance,* 1st ed. Malvern, PA.: American Institute for Chartered Property Casualty Underwriters/ Insurance Institute of America, 2002.

NOTES

1. Edward E. Graves, ed., *McGill's Life Insurance,* 5th ed. (Bryn Mawr, PA: The American College, 2004), p. 747.
2. There are exceptions. In some states, minors can receive a limited amount of proceeds.
3. See Joseph M. Belth, ed., "Special Issue on Fractional Premiums," *Insurance Forum,* vol. 25, no. 12 (December 1998).
4. Graves, *McGill's Life Insurance,* p. 67.
5. Robert I. Mehr and Sandra G. Gustavson, *Life Insurance, Theory and Practice,* 4th ed. (Plano, TX: Business Publications, Inc., 1987), p. 206.

Students may take a self-administered test on this chapter at
www.aw-bc.com/rejda

CHAPTER 13

BUYING LIFE INSURANCE

"When you buy life insurance, it's relatively easy to compare first-year premium costs. But that figure tells you nothing about what the policy will cost over the long run."

Consumers Union

LEARNING OBJECTIVES

After studying this chapter, you should be able to

◆ Explain the defects in the traditional net cost method for determining the cost of life insurance.

◆ Explain the interest-adjusted surrender cost index and net payment cost index for determining the cost of life insurance.

◆ Explain the yearly rate-of-return method for determining the annual rate of return on the saving component in a life insurance policy.

◆ Describe the suggestions to follow when purchasing life insurance.

◆ Understand how life insurance premiums are calculated.

Julie, age 35, is a single parent with two preschool children. Her husband deserted her, and she receives no child support. Julie earns $28,000 annually as a nurse's aide in a community nursing home. She has no life insurance. Although money is tight, Julie would like to purchase some life insurance to protect her family. A life insurance agent recently met with her and presented several proposals. However, Julie does not know how to evaluate the various plans. Moreover, like most insurance consumers, she is unaware of the importance of performing a cost comparison of the different policies before buying life insurance.

This chapter is designed to answer the questions that Julie may have concerning the purchase of life insurance. Most consumers buy life insurance without much thought. They are often unaware of the huge cost variations among insurers and frequently purchase life insurance from the first agent who persuades them to buy. As a result, they may pay more than is necessary for their insurance protection. The purchase of a high-cost rather than a low-cost policy can cost thousands of dollars over a lifetime.

This chapter discusses the fundamentals of buying life insurance. Specific topics covered include the various methods for determining the cost of life insurance, the rate of return earned on the saving component of a cash-value policy, taxation of life insurance, and suggested guidelines for buying life insurance. The appendix to the chapter explains how life insurance premiums are calculated.

DETERMINING THE COST OF LIFE INSURANCE

The cost of life insurance is a complex subject. In general, cost can be viewed as the difference between what you pay for a life insurance policy and what you get back. If you pay premiums and get nothing back, the cost of the insurance equals the premiums paid. However, if you pay premiums and later get something back, such as the cash value and dividends, your cost will be reduced. Thus, in determining the cost of life insurance, four major factors must be considered: (1) annual premiums, (2) cash values, (3) dividends, and (4) time value of money. Two widely used cost methods that consider some or all of the preceding factors are the *traditional net cost method* and the *interest-adjusted cost method*. Al-though the following discussion is based on cash-value life insurance, the same cost methods can be used to determine the cost of term insurance.

Traditional Net Cost Method

From a historical perspective, life insurers previously used the **traditional net cost method** to illustrate the net cost of life insurance. Under this method, the annual premiums for some time period are added to-gether. Total expected dividends to be received dur-ing the same period and the cash value at the end of the period are then subtracted from the total premi-ums to determine the net cost of life insurance. For example, assume that the annual premium for a $10,000 ordinary life insurance policy issued to a female, age 20, is $132.10. Estimated dividends over

EXHIBIT 13.1
Traditional Net Cost Method

Total premiums for 20 years	$2642
Subtract dividends for 20 years	−599
Net premiums for 20 years	$2043
Subtract the cash value at the end of 20 years	−2294
Insurance cost for 20 years	−$251
Net cost per year (−$251 ÷ 20)	−$12.55
Net cost per $1000 per year (−$12.55 ÷ 10)	−$1.26

a 20-year period are $599, and the cash surrender value at the end of the twentieth year is $2294 (see Exhibit 13.1). The average cost per year is minus $12.55 (−$1.26 per $1000).

The traditional net cost method had several defects and was misleading. *The most glaring defect is that it did not consider the time value of money.* Interest that the policyowner could have earned on the premiums by investing elsewhere was not considered. In addition, the insurance illustration often showed the insurance to be free (to have a negative cost). This is contrary to common sense, because no insurer can provide free insurance and remain in business.

Interest-Adjusted Cost Method

The **interest-adjusted cost method** developed by the National Association of Insurance Commissioners is a more accurate measure of life insurance costs. *Under this method, the time value of money is taken into consideration by applying an interest factor to each element of cost.*

There are two principal types of interest-adjusted cost indexes, the *surrender cost index* and the *net payment cost index*. The surrender cost index is useful if you believe that you may surrender the policy at the end of 10 or 20 years, or some other time period. The net payment cost index is useful if you intend to keep your policy in force, and cash values are of secondary importance to you.

Surrender Cost Index The **surrender cost index** *measures the cost of life insurance if you surrender*

the policy at the end of some time period, such as 10 or 20 years (see Exhibit 13.2).

The annual premiums are accumulated at 5 percent interest, which recognizes the fact that the policyowner could have invested the premiums elsewhere. Although not shown, the annual dividends are also accumulated at 5 percent interest, which considers interest earnings on the dividends as well as the amount and timing of each dividend. Assume that the accumulated value of the dividends at the end of 20 years is $824. Using the same policy as before, the net premiums for 20 years adjusted for interest are $3762.

The next step is to subtract the cash value at the end of 20 years from the net premiums, which results in a total insurance cost of $1468. The policyowner pays this amount for the insurance protection for 20 years, after considering the time value of money.

The final step is to convert the total interest-adjusted cost for 20 years into an annual cost. This is done by dividing the total interest-adjusted cost by an *annuity due* factor of 34.719. This factor means that a $1 deposit at the *beginning* of each year at 5 percent interest will accumulate to $34.719 at the end of 20 years. By dividing the total interest-adjusted cost of

EXHIBIT 13.2
Surrender Cost Index

Total premiums for 20 years, each accumulated at 5%	$4586
Subtract dividends for 20 years, each accumulated at 5%	−824
Net premiums for 20 years	$3762
Subtract the cash value at the end of 20 years	−2294
Insurance cost for 20 years	$1468
Amount to which $1 deposited annually at the beginning of each year will accumulate to in 20 years at 5%	$34.719
Interest-adjusted cost per year ($1468 ÷ $34.719)	$42.28
Cost per $1000 per year ($42.28 ÷ 10)	$4.23

$1468 by $34.719, you end up with an annual interest-adjusted cost of $42.28, or $4.23 for each $1000 of insurance. As you can see, the interest-adjusted cost is positive, which means that it costs something to own life insurance when forgone interest is considered. In this case, the average annual cost is $42.28 if the policy is surrendered after 20 years.

Net Payment Cost Index The **net payment cost index** *measures the relative cost of a policy if death occurs at the end of some specified time period, such as 10 or 20 years. It is based on the assumption that you will not surrender the policy.* Therefore, it is the appropriate cost index to use if you intend to keep your life insurance in force.

The net payment cost index is calculated in a manner similar to the surrender cost index except that the cash value is not subtracted (see Exhibit 13.3).

If the policy is kept in force for 20 years, the policy has an annual cost of $108.36 ($10.84 per $1000) after interest is considered.

Substantial Cost Variation Among Insurers

There are enormous cost variations in cash-value life insurance based on the interest-adjusted cost indexes. Exhibit 13.4 shows the 10-year interest-adjusted costs for selected insurers for a $100,000 participating whole life policy issued to a male, age 35.

EXHIBIT 13.3
Net Payment Cost Index

Total premiums for 20 years, each accumulated at 5%	$4586
Subtract dividends for 20 years, each accumulated at 5%	−824
Insurance cost for 20 years	$3762
Amount to which $1 deposited annually at the beginning of each year will accumulate to in 20 years at 5%	$34.719
Interest-adjusted cost per year ($3762 ÷ $34.719)	$108.36
Cost per $1000 per year ($108.36 ÷ 10)	$10.84

In the interpretation of these indexes, the lower the index number, the less costly is the policy. As shown in Exhibit 13.4, the surrender cost index ranged from a low of $1.24 per $1000 for USAA Life to a high of $2.97 per $1000 for Massachusetts Mutual Life. The net payment cost index ranged from a low of $8.24 per $1000 for Manufacturers Life to a high of $10.47 for General American. *This wide variation in cost highlights the point stated earlier—you can save thousands of dollars over a long period by paying careful attention to the cost index when you shop for life insurance.*

Unfortunately, most consumers do not consider interest-adjusted cost data when they buy life insurance. Instead, they use premiums as a basis for comparing costs. However, using premiums alone provides an incomplete comparison. Interest-adjusted cost data will give you more accurate information about the expected cost of a policy.

Obtaining Cost Information

If you are solicited to buy life insurance, you can ask the agent to give you interest-adjusted cost data on the policy. Cost data can also be obtained by calling certain price quoting services at their toll-free numbers. In addition, cost data are available on the Internet (see Internet Resources). Finally, most policy illustrations include interest-adjusted cost data.

If you use interest-adjusted cost data, keep in mind the following points:

- *Shop for a policy and not an insurer.* Some insurers have excellent low-cost policies at certain ages and coverage amounts, but they are not as competitive at other ages and coverage amounts.
- *Compare only similar plans of insurance.* You should compare policies of the same type with the same benefits. Otherwise, the comparison can be misleading.
- *Ignore small variations in the cost index numbers.* Small cost differences can be offset by other policy features or by services that you can expect to get from an agent or insurer.
- *Cost indexes apply only to a new policy.* The cost data should not be used to determine

EXHIBIT **13.4**
Comparison of Interest-Adjusted Costs for Selected Companies

	Surrender Cost Index			Net Payment Index	
1	USAA Life	1.24	1	Manufacturers	8.24
2	Government Personnel Mut. Life	1.59	2	United Heritage Life	8.32
3	Country Life	1.74	3	John Hancock Mutual Life	8.71
4	Phoenix Home Life Mutual	1.92	4	Phoenix Home Life Mutual	9.08
5	Mutual Life of New York	2.10	5	Columbus Life	9.16
6	Columbian Mutual Life	2.35	6	State Farm	9.29
7	National Life Vermont	2.39	7	American Family Life	9.43
8	AmerUs Life	2.40	8	Country Life	9.55
9	John Hancock Mutual Life	2.47	8	Security Mutual of New York	9.55
10	Western-Southern Life	2.49	9	United Farm Family Life	9.57
11	Ohio National Life	2.51	10	Phoenix Home Life Mut. (Home Life)	9.65
12	Mutual Trust Life	2.54	11	Farm Family Life	9.66
12	Security Mutual of New York	2.54	12	Mutual Life of New York	9.82
13	Farm Family Life	2.56	13	Ohio National Life	9.83
13	Manufacturers Life	2.56	14	Berkshire Life	10.17
14	United Farm Family Life	2.60	15	New York Life	10.19
15	Penn Mutual Life	2.64	16	USAA Life	10.24
16	American Family Life	2.84	17	Farmers & Traders Life	10.28
17	State Farm	2.87	18	Knights of Columbus	10.40
18	Massachusetts Mutual Life	2.97	19	General American	10.47

NOTE: The indexes shown are the annual costs over a 10-year period for a $100,000 participating whole life policy issued to a male, age 35.
SOURCE: Copyrighted by A. M. Best Company. Used with permission.

whether to replace an existing policy with a new one. Other factors should be considered as well (see Insight 13.1).

■ *The type of policy you buy should not be based solely on a cost index.* You should buy the type of policy that best meets your needs, such as term, whole life, or some combination. Once you have decided on the type of policy, then compare costs.

NAIC Policy Illustration Model Regulation

Our discussion of life insurance costs would not be complete without a brief discussion of the Life Insurance Policy Illustration Model Regulation drafted by the National Association of Insurance Commissioners (NAIC).

The majority of states have adopted the model regulation. The model act requires insurers to present certain information to applicants for life insurance. The policy illustration contains a *narrative summary* that describes the basic characteristics of the policy, including how the policy functions, underwriting class, death benefit option, payment of premiums, and any riders. The narrative summary also describes the elements of the policy that are not guaranteed, federal tax guidelines for the policy, key definitions, and interest-adjusted cost data.

In addition, the policy illustration has a *numeric summary* that shows the premium outlay, value of the accumulation account, cash-surrender values, and death benefit. Three policy values must be provided based on (1) current interest rate credited to the policy, (2) guaranteed minimum interest rate under the policy, and (3) midpoint interest rate. The illustration also shows the number of years the insurance protection will remain in force under the three sets of interest assumptions. The applicant and agent must sign the illustration and indicate they have discussed and they understand that the nonguaranteed elements in the policy are subject to change and can be higher or lower than the values shown in the illustration.

Certain deceptive sales practices are prohibited in the illustration of policy values: insurers are prohibited from using anticipated gains from improvements in mortality in the sales illustration; the term "vanishing premium" cannot be used; and the values shown in the illustration must be justified by a self-support test.

Finally, the insurer must provide an annual report on the policy and notify the policyowners when a change occurs in the dividend scale or individual pricing elements that would negatively affect the policy values. The model regulation should reduce misunderstanding of policy values by policyowners and reduce deceptive sales practices by agents.

RATE OF RETURN ON SAVING COMPONENT

Another important consideration is the rate of return earned on the saving component of a traditional whole life insurance policy. Consumers normally do not know the annual rate of return they earn on the saving component in their policies. A consumer who buys a traditional cash-value policy with a low return can lose a considerable amount of money over the life of the policy through forgone interest. Thus, the annual rate of return you earn on the saving component is critical if you intend to invest money in a life insurance policy over a long period of time.

INSIGHT 13.1

Be Careful in Replacing an Existing Life Insurance Policy

Life Insurance Replacement

If you own a life insurance policy, you should be careful if you consider replacing it. Although the relative financial strength of the original company and the replacing company are important, you should consider other factors also, as described briefly below.

- *If you consider replacing a policy, your health and other items affecting eligibility should be reviewed.* You may not qualify for a new policy, or you may qualify only at high rates.
- *You should determine the cost of getting out of the original policy.* Many policies contain substantial surrender charges.
- *You should determine the cost of getting into the replacement policy.* Many policies involve substantial front-end expenses.
- *You should consider the tax implications of a replacement.* In some situations, the termination of a policy may trigger an income tax liability. It may be possible to defer the tax, but you should consult your tax adviser before you take action.
- *You should consider the incontestable clause.* If a policy is more than two years old, the company usually would be barred from voiding the policy because of what the company considers false statements made in the application. Thus the original policy may not be contestable, while a replacement policy may be contestable for two years.
- *You should also be aware of the suicide clause. Suicide usually is excluded during the first two years of a policy.* Thus the original policy may currently cover suicide, while a replacement policy may not cover suicide for two years.

If an individual advised you to replace a policy, try to find out how much compensation he or she will receive if you follow the advice. Some individuals who recommend replacement may be acting in a professional manner and may want to help reduce your expenses or avoid the problems that may arise if your original company gets into financial trouble. However, some individuals may descend on the policyowners of a financially troubled company like sharks who detect blood in the water. The fact that an individual receives compensation for selling a replacement policy does not necessarily mean that he or she is giving bad advice, but you should be on guard.

SOURCE: Adapted from Joseph M. Belth, ed. "Life Insurance Replacement," *The Insurance Forum*, vol. 33, no. 9 (September 2006), pp. 109–110.

Linton Yield

The **Linton yield** is one method that can be used to determine the rate of return on the saving portion of a cash-value policy. It was developed by M. Albert Linton, a well-known life insurance actuary. *In essence, the Linton yield is the average annual rate of return on a cash-value policy if it is held for a specified number of years.* It is based on the assumption that a cash-value policy can be viewed as a combination of insurance protection and a savings fund. To determine the average annual rate of return for a given period, it is first necessary to determine that part of the annual premium that is deposited in the savings fund. This amount can be determined by subtracting the cost of the insurance protection for that year from the annual premium (less any dividend). The balance of the premium is the amount that can be deposited into the savings fund. Thus, the average annual rate of return is the compound interest rate that is required to make the savings deposits equal the guaranteed cash value in the policy at the end of a specified period.

Calculation of the Linton yield is complex and requires specific information. Unfortunately, current rates of return based on the Linton yield are not readily available to consumers. However, an earlier Consumer Federation of America study of 109 cash-value policies based on the Linton yield showed that the annual rates of return vary widely. *The study showed that the average annual rates of return for the 109 policies ranged from a minus 87.9 percent for the first year to 8.2 percent for the twentieth year* (see Exhibit 13.5). The study concluded that consumers lose billions of dollars annually by terminating their policies early. The Consumer Federation of America recommends that consumers should not purchase a cash-value policy unless they plan to hold it for at least 20 years.

Annual rates of return based on the Linton yield are usually negative during the early years of the policy. These negative returns reflect the heavy first-year acquisition and administrative expenses when the policy is first sold. An agent receives a commission, and there may be a medical examiner's fee, an inspection report, and other expenses involved in issuing the policy. As a result of these expenses, most cash-value policies have little or no cash value at the end of the first year, and the cash values remain rela-

Exhibit 13.5

Average Annual Rates of Return for 109 Cash-Value Policies by Year of Policy

Year	Rate of Return (%)
1	−87.9
2	−54.9
3	−18.9
4	0.0
5	5.6
6	7.3
7	7.7
8	7.7
9	7.6
10	9.8
11	8.0
12	8.0
13	8.0
14	7.9
15	8.1
16	7.8
17	7.8
18	7.8
19	7.8
20	8.2

Source: Consumer Federation of America, *Rates of Return on Cash-Value Policies Vary Widely,* press release, July 16, 1997.

tively low during the early years. Thus, if you surrender the policy or allow it to lapse during the early years, you will lose a substantial amount of money.

Because current information on Linton yields is not readily available, this method has limited usefulness as a consumer tool. We must therefore consider other methods. The yearly rate-of-return method discussed next is a simple, but valuable methodology that can enable you to calculate the annual rate of return on the saving component in your policy.

Yearly Rate-of-Return Method

Professor Joseph M. Belth has developed the **yearly rate-of-return method** for calculating the yearly rate of return on the saving component of a cash-value policy.[1] The yearly rate of return is based on the following formula:

$$i = \frac{(CV + D) + (YPT)(DB - CV)(.001)}{(P + CVP)} - 1$$

where

i = yearly rate of return on the saving component, expressed as a decimal
CV = cash value at end of policy year
D = annual dividend
YPT = assumed yearly price per $1000 of protection (see benchmark prices in Exhibit 13.6)
DB = death benefit
P = annual premium
CVP = cash value at end of preceding policy year

The first expression in the numerator of the formula is the amount available in the policy at the end of the policy year. The second expression in the numerator is the assumed price of the protection component, which is determined by multiplying the amount of protection by an assumed price per $1000 of protection. Assumed prices per $1000 of protection for various ages are benchmarks derived from certain U.S. population death rates (see Exhibit 13.6). Finally, the expression in the denominator of the formula is the amount available in the policy at the beginning of the policy year.

For example, assume that Mark purchased a $100,000 participating ordinary life policy at age 35. He is now age 42 at the beginning of the eighth policy year. He would like to know the yearly rate of return on the saving component for the eighth year of the policy. The annual premium is $1500. The cash value in the policy is $7800 at the end of the seventh policy year and $9200 at the end of the eighth policy year. The eighth-year dividend is $400. Because Mark is age 42 at the beginning of the eighth policy year, the benchmark price is $4.00 per $1000 (see again Exhibit 13.6).

Based on the preceding information, the yearly rate of return for the eighth policy year is calculated as follows:

$$i = \frac{(9200 + 400) + (4)(100,000 - 9200)(.001)}{(1500 + 7800)} - 1$$

$$= \frac{(9600) + (4)((90,800)(.001)}{(9300)} - 1$$

$$= \frac{9600 + 363}{9300} - 1$$

$$= \frac{9963}{9300} - 1 = 1.071 - 1 = .071 = 7.1\%$$

The yearly rate of return for the eighth policy year is 7.1 percent, assuming that the yearly price per $1000 of protection is $4.

The major advantage of Belth's method is simplicity—you do not need a computer. The information needed can be obtained by referring to your policy and premium notice, or by contacting your agent or insurer.

TAXATION OF LIFE INSURANCE

Treatment of life insurance buying would be incomplete without a discussion of the taxation of life insurance. This section discusses briefly the taxation of life insurance.

EXHIBIT 13.6
Benchmark Prices

Age	Benchmark Price
Under 30	$ 1.50
30–34	2.00
35–39	3.00
40–44	4.00
45–49	6.50
50–54	10.00
55–59	15.00
60–64	25.00
65–69	35.00
70–74	50.00
75–79	80.00
80–84	125.00

NOTE: The benchmark prices are derived from certain U.S. population death rates. The benchmark figure for each five-year age bracket is close to the death rate per $1000 at the highest age in that bracket.

SOURCE: Adapted from Joseph M. Belth, *Life Insurance: A Consumer's Handbook*, 2nd ed. (Bloomington, IN: Indiana University Press, 1985), table 9, p. 84. Reprinted by permission of the author.

Federal Income Tax

Life insurance proceeds paid in a lump sum to a designated beneficiary are generally received income-tax free by the beneficiary. If the proceeds are periodically liquidated under a settlement option, the payments consist of both principal and interest. The principal is received income-tax free, but the interest is taxable as ordinary income.

Premiums paid for individual life insurance policies generally are not deductible for income-tax purposes. Dividends on life insurance policies are received income-tax free. However, interest on dividends retained under the interest option is taxable to the policyowner. If the dividends are used to buy paid-up additions, the cash value of the paid-up additions accumulates income-tax free unless the contract is terminated with a policy gain (discussed later). Thus, compared with the interest option, the paid-up additions option provides a small tax advantage.

In addition, the annual increase in cash value under a permanent life insurance policy is presently income-tax free. However, if the policy is surrendered for its cash value, any gain is taxable as ordinary income. If the cash value exceeds the premiums paid less any dividends, the excess is taxed as ordinary income.

Federal Estate Tax

If the insured has any ownership interest in the policy at the time of death, the entire proceeds are included in the gross estate of the insured for federal estate-tax purposes. Examples include the right to change the beneficiary, the right to borrow the cash value or surrender the policy, and the right to elect a settlement option. The proceeds are also included in the insured's gross estate if they are payable to the estate. They can be removed from the gross estate if the policyowner makes an *absolute assignment* of the policy to someone else and has no incidents of ownership in the policy at the time of death. However, if the assignment is made within three years of death, the proceeds will be included in the deceased's gross estate for federal estate-tax purposes.

A federal estate tax is payable if the decedent's taxable estate exceeds certain limits. After the tax-able estate is determined, a tentative tax is calculated. The tentative tax is reduced or eliminated by a tax credit called a *unified credit*. For individuals who die in 2006, the amount of the credit is $780,800, which eliminates the federal estate tax completely on taxable estates of $2,000,000 or less.

The amount of property exempt from taxation will increase in the future. For 2006–2008, the maximum exempt amount is $2,000,000. For 2009, the exempt amount will increase to $3,500,000. The estate tax will then be repealed in 2010. The following schedule shows the maximum exempt amounts in the future:

Year	Exempt Amount	Unified Credit
2006	2,000,000	780,800
2007	2,000,000	780,800
2008	2,000,000	780,800
2009	3,500,000	1,455,800
2010	Estate tax repealed	

In addition, federal estate-tax rates on taxable estates will decrease in the future and then will be eliminated. The highest federal estate-tax rates will decline according to the following schedule:

Year	Highest Estate Tax Rate (%)	On Amounts Over
2006	46	2,000,000
2007	45	1,500,000
2008	45	1,500,000
2009	45	1,500,000
2010	0	Estate tax repealed

Although the federal estate tax is repealed in 2010, the repeal is only for 2010 unless Congress acts to make repeal permanent. However, there is considerable opposition in Congress to complete repeal of the estate tax. At the time of this writing, legislation has been introduced that would gradually increase the federal estate tax exemption to $5 million per person and $10 million for a married couple. As a result, it is estimated that more than 99 percent of all estates would not pay any federal estate tax.

To determine whether a federal estate tax is payable, the gross estate must first be calculated. The *gross estate* includes the value of the property you own when you die, one-half of the value of the property owned jointly with your spouse, life insurance death proceeds in which the insured has any incidents of ownership, and certain other items. The gross estate can be reduced by certain deductions in determining the *taxable estate*. Allowable deductions include funeral and administrative expenses, claims against the estate, estate settlement and probate costs, charitable contributions, and certain other deductions.

In addition, the gross estate can be reduced by the *marital deduction,* which is a deduction of the value of the property included in the gross estate but passed on to the surviving spouse. This property is taxed later, when the surviving spouse dies. For example, assume that Richard dies in 2006 and has a gross estate of $3.2 million. He leaves $1 million of property outright to his spouse. Thus, the marital deduction is $1 million. Assume that debts, funeral expenses, and administrative costs total $200,000. The taxable estate is $2 million, and the tentative federal tax is $780,800. However, as a result of the unified credit of $780,800, the federal estate tax is zero (see Exhibit 13.7).

EXHIBIT 13.7
Calculating Federal Estate Taxes*

Gross estate		$3,200,000
Less:		
Debts	$150,000	
Administrative costs	30,000	
Funeral expenses	20,000	
		−200,000
Adjusted gross estate		$3,000,000
Less:		
Marital deduction		−1,000,000
Taxable estate		$2,000,000
Tentative tax		$ 780,800
Less:		
Applicable credit		780,800
Federal estate tax		$ 0

*Individual dies in 2006.

EXHIBIT 13.8
Shopping for Life Insurance

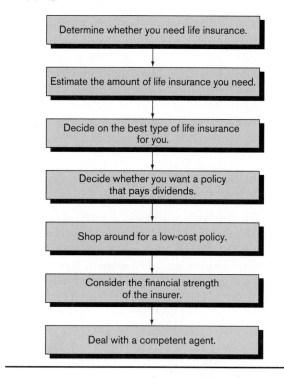

SHOPPING FOR LIFE INSURANCE

Developing a sound life insurance program involves seven steps, as illustrated in Exhibit 13.8 and discussed next.

Determine Whether You Need Life Insurance

The first step is to determine whether you need life insurance. If you are married or single with one or more dependents to support, you may need a substantial amount of life insurance. You may also need life insurance if you have a temporary need, such as paying off the mortgage on your home. In addition, if you have accumulated substantial assets, large amounts of life insurance may be needed to provide estate liquidity and to pay any state or federal estate taxes.

However, if you are single and no one is currently dependent on you for financial support, you do not need life insurance, other than a modest amount for burial purposes. The arguments for buying life insurance when you are young to protect your future insurability are not compelling. Even if your situation should change and you need life insurance in the future, *more than nine out of ten applicants for life insurance are accepted at standard or preferred rates.* Thus, it is a waste of money to buy life insurance when it is not needed.

Estimate the Amount of Life Insurance You Need

The needs approach is a practical method for determining the amount of life insurance to purchase. Persons with dependents often need surprisingly large amounts of life insurance. In determining the amount needed, you must consider your family's present and future financial needs, potential survivor benefits from Social Security, and other financial assets currently owned.

If you carry a sufficient amount of life insurance, it is unnecessary to purchase additional life insurance as supplemental coverage. These coverages are endless and include accidental death insurance from life insurers, accidental death and dismemberment insurance offered by commercial banks, credit life insurance on consumer loans, and life insurance sold by mail. In addition, flight insurance sold at airports is a bad buy for most consumers because commercial jets rarely crash.

Decide on the Best Type of Life Insurance for You

The next step is to select the best type of life insurance policy for you. *The best policy is the one that best meets your financial needs.* If the amount of money you can spend on life insurance is limited, or if you have a temporary need, consider only term insurance. If you need lifetime protection, consider ordinary life insurance or universal life insurance. If you believe that you cannot save money without being forced to do so, also consider ordinary life insurance or universal life insurance as a savings vehicle. However, remember that the an-

nual rates of return on cash-value policies can vary enormously.

Also, avoid purchasing a policy that you cannot afford. Many insureds let their policies lapse during the early years, especially cash-value policies. Because of a surrender charge, there is little or no cash value available during the early years if the policy is surrendered. *If you drop a cash-value policy after a few months or years, you will lose a substantial amount of money. Be sure you can afford the premium.*

Decide Whether You Want a Policy That Pays Dividends

In recent decades, participating life insurance policies that pay dividends generally have been better buys than nonparticipating policies because of high interest rates that permitted insurers to raise their dividends. However, interest rates have declined over time, and many insurers have reduced their dividends because excess interest earnings have declined. Thus, if you believe that interest rates will be higher in the future, you should consider a participating policy because excess interest has a powerful impact on dividends. However, if you believe that interest rates will remain at lower levels in the future, then consider a nonparticipating policy. Policies that do not pay dividends generally require a lower premium outlay.

You can ignore the above step if you are purchasing a variable life insurance, universal life insurance, or variable universal life insurance policy. These policies are nonparticipating and do not pay dividends.

Shop Around for a Low-Cost Policy

One of the most important suggestions is to shop carefully for a low-cost policy. There is enormous variation in the cost of life insurance. You should not purchase a life insurance policy from the first agent who approaches you. *Instead, you should compare the interest-adjusted cost of similar policies from several insurers before you buy.* Otherwise, you may be overpaying for the insurance protection. If you make a mistake and purchase a high-cost policy, this mistake can cost you thousands of extra dollars over your lifetime.

When you shop for a low-cost policy, you should also consider **low-load life insurance.** Some life insurers sell insurance directly to the public by using telephone representatives or fee-only financial planners. The major advantage is that marketing expenses for low-load policies are substantially lower than for policies sold by agents to the public. Two major low-load insurers that sell policies by phone are Ameritas Direct (800-689-6830) and USAA Life (800-531-8000).

Consider the Financial Strength of the Insurer

In addition to cost, you should consider the financial strength of the insurer issuing the policy. Some life insurers have become insolvent and have gone out of business. Although all states have state guaranty funds that pay the claims of insolvent life insurers, there are limits on the amount guaranteed. Although death claims are paid promptly, you may have to wait years before you can borrow or withdraw your cash value. Thus, it is important to buy life insurance only from financially sound insurers.

A number of rating organizations periodically grade and rate life insurers on their financial strength (see Exhibit 13.9). The companies are rated based on the amount of their capital and surplus, legal reserves, quality of investments, past profitability, competency of management, and numerous other factors. However, the various ratings are not always a reliable guide for consumers and can be confusing. There are wide variations in the grades given by the different rating agencies. Joseph M. Belth, a nationally known consumer expert in life insurance, recommends that an insurer should receive a high rating from at least two of the following four rating agencies before a policy is purchased. The following are considered high ratings for someone who is conservative:[2]

Best: A++, A+, A
Fitch: AAA, AA+, AA, AA−
Moody's: Aaa, Aa1, Aa2, Aa3
S&P: AAA, AA+, AA, AA−

Deal with a Competent Agent

You should also deal with a competent agent when you buy life insurance. Selling life insurance is a

EXHIBIT 13.9
Rating Categories for Major Rating Agencies

Rank Number	Ratings			
	Best	**Fitch**	**Moody's**	**S&P**
1	A++	AAA	Aaa	AAA
2	A+	AA+	Aa1	AA+
3	A	AA	Aa2	AA
4	A−	AA−	Aa3	AA−
5	B++	A+	A1	A+
6	B+	A	A2	A
7	B	A−	A3	A−
8	B−	BBB+	Baa1	BBB+
9	C++	BBB	Baa2	BBB
10	C+	BBB−	Baa3	BBB−
11	C	BB+	Ba1	BB+
12	C−	BB	Ba2	BB
13	D	BB−	Ba3	BB−
14	E	B+	B1	B+
15	F	B	B2	B
16		B−	B3	B−
17		CCC+	Caa1	CCC
18		CCC	Caa2	CC
19		CCC−	Caa3	R
20		CC	Ca	
21		C	C	

NOTE: The ratings in a given rank are not necessarily equivalent to one another.

SOURCE: Joseph M. Belth, ed., "Financial Strength of Insurance Companies," *The Insurance Forum*, vol. 33, no. 9 (September 20, 2006), p. 107. Reprinted with permission.

tough job, and only a relatively small proportion of new life insurance agents are successful.

Most new agents receive only a minimum amount of training before they are licensed to sell life insurance. New agents also are often placed under intense pressure to sell life insurance. Even mature agents are expected to sell a certain amount of insurance. As a result, some agents have engaged in deceptive sales practices by misrepresenting the insurance to clients or by recommending policies that maximize commissions rather than meeting the client's needs. Because of deceptive sales practices by agents, several major life insurers have been subject to heavy fines by state insurance departments and class action litigation by angry policyowners.

To reduce the possibility of receiving bad advice or being sold the wrong policy, you should consider the professional qualifications of the agent. An agent who is a **Chartered Life Underwriter (CLU)**,

Chartered Financial Consultant (ChFC), or Certified Financial Planner (CFP) should be technically competent to give proper advice. More importantly, agents who hold the preceding professional designations are expected to abide by a code of ethics that places their clients' interests above their own. Agents who are currently studying for these professional designations should also be considered.

CASE APPLICATION

A participating ordinary life policy in the amount of $10,000 is sold to an individual, age 35. The following cost data are given:

Annual premium	$230
Total dividends for 20 years	$1613
Cash value at end of 20 years	$3620
Accumulated value of the annual premiums at 5 percent for 20 years	$7985
Accumulated value of the dividends at 5 percent for 20 years	$2352

Amount to which $1 deposited annually at the beginning of each year will accumulate in 20 years at 5 percent $34.719

a. Based on this information, compute the annual net cost per $1000 of life insurance at the end of 20 years using the *traditional net cost method*.

b. Compute the annual *surrender cost index* per $1000 of life insurance at the end of 20 years.

c. Compute the annual *net payment cost index* per $1000 of life insurance at the end of 20 years.

SUMMARY

- There are enormous cost variations among similar life insurance policies. Purchase of a high-cost policy can cost thousands of extra dollars over the insured's lifetime for the same amount of insurance protection.

- The traditional net cost method for determining life insurance costs is defective because it ignores the time value of money, and the insurance is often shown to be free.

- The interest-adjusted method is a more accurate measure of life insurance costs. The time value of money is taken into consideration by applying an interest factor to each element of cost. If you are interested in surrendering the policy at the end of a certain period, the surrender cost index is the appropriate cost index to use. If you intend to keep your policy in force, the net payment cost index should be used.

- Annual rates-of-return data on the saving component in traditional cash-value life insurance policies are not readily available to consumers. However, the yearly rate-of-return method can be helpful to consumers in this regard.

- Life insurance death proceeds paid in a lump sum to a designated beneficiary are generally received income-tax free by the beneficiary. Premiums for individual life insurance are not income-tax deductible. If a policy is surrendered for its cash value, any gain is taxable as ordinary income. If the cash value exceeds the premiums paid less any dividends, the excess is taxed as ordinary income.

- If the insured has any ownership interest in the policy at the time of death, the entire proceeds are included in his or her gross estate for federal estate-tax purposes. A federal estate tax is payable if the decedent's taxable estate exceeds certain limits.

- Life insurance experts typically recommend several rules to follow when shopping for life insurance:
  Determine whether you need life insurance.
  Estimate the amount of life insurance you need.
  Decide on the best type of insurance for you.
  Decide whether you want a policy that pays dividends.
  Shop around for a low-cost policy.
  Consider the financial strength of the insurer.
  Deal with a competent agent.

KEY CONCEPTS AND TERMS

Certified Financial
  Planner (CFP)
Chartered Financial
  Consultant
  (ChFC)
Chartered Life
  Underwriter
  (CLU)
Interest-adjusted cost
  method
Linton yield
Low-load life
  insurance
Net payment cost
  index

Surrender cost index
Traditional net cost
  method
Yearly rate-of-return
  method

REVIEW QUESTIONS

1. Explain the basic defect in the traditional net cost method for determining the cost of life insurance.

2. a. Why is the interest-adjusted cost method a more accurate measure of the cost of life insurance?
   b. Briefly describe the surrender cost index as a method for determining the cost of life insurance.
   c. Briefly describe the net payment cost index as a method for determining the cost of life insurance.
   d. Where can you obtain interest-adjusted cost information?

3. Why is the rate of return on the saving component in most cash-value policies negative during the early years of the policy?

4. Briefly explain the Linton Yield as a method for determining the rate of return on the saving component of a cash-value policy.

5. Briefly explain the yearly rate-of-return method that policyowners can use to determine the rate of return on the saving component of a cash-value policy.

6. Explain the federal income-tax treatment of a cash-value policy with respect to each of the following:
   a. Payment of premiums
   b. Annual dividends
   c. Annual increase in the cash value
   d. Payment of death proceeds to a stated beneficiary

7. Explain the federal estate-tax treatment of life insurance death proceeds.

8. Describe the suggestions that consumers should follow when life insurance is purchased.

9. The states require life insurers to disclose certain policy information to applicants for life insurance. Describe the types of information that appear on a typical disclosure statement.

10. What is a low-load life insurance policy? Explain.

APPLICATION QUESTIONS

1. Nicole, age 25, is considering the purchase of a $20,000 participating ordinary life insurance policy. The annual premium is $248.60. Projected dividends over the first 20 years are $814. The cash value at the end of 20 years is $4314. If the premiums are invested at 5 percent interest, they will accumulate to $8631 at the end of 20 years. If the dividends are invested at 5 percent interest, they will accumulate to $1163 at the end of 20 years. A $1 deposit at the beginning of each year at 5 percent interest will accumulate to $34.719 at the end of 20 years.
   a. Based on the *traditional net cost method*, calculate the net cost per $1000 per year.
   b. Based on the *surrender cost index*, calculate the net cost per $1000 per year.
   c. Based on the *net payment cost index*, calculate the net cost per $1000 per year.

2. Todd, age 40, is considering the purchase of a $100,000 participating ordinary life insurance policy. The annual premium is $2280. Projected dividends over the first 20 years are $15,624. The cash value at the end of 20 years is $35,260. If the premiums are invested at 5 percent interest, they will grow to $79,159 at the end of 20 years. If the dividends are invested at 5 percent interest, they will accumulate to $24,400 at the end of 20 years. A $1 deposit at the beginning of each year at 5 percent interest will accumulate to $34.719 at the end of 20 years.
   a. Based on the *traditional net cost method*, calculate the net cost per $1000 per year.
   b. Based on the *surrender cost index*, calculate the net cost per $1000 per year.
   c. Based on the *net payment cost index*, calculate the net cost per $1000 per year.

3. John, age 52, is overweight, smokes, and had a mild heart attack five years ago. Ignoring the advice of his physician, he refuses to exercise, lose weight, and quit smoking. John owns a $25,000 participating ordinary life policy that he purchased 20 years ago. A life insurance agent approached John and proposed that he replace the older policy with a new life insurance policy. The agent claims the new policy is superior to the older policy that was purchased years ago. Despite John's health problems, the agent claims that John can get life insurance from his company. What factors should John consider before replacing the older policy with a new policy?

4. Allison is trying to complete her income-tax return. A number of questions have come up about life insurance. Explain the tax treatment of each of the following.

   a. Allison is the beneficiary named in her grandfather's life insurance policy. Her grandfather died this year and Allison received a lump-sum payment of $50,000. She wonders if she has to report the $50,000 as taxable income.

   b. Allison purchased a $100,000 cash value life insurance policy on her own life six years ago. This year, the cash value increased by $380. Allison wonders if the cash-value increase must be reported as taxable income. The policy remains in force.

   c. Allison's annual life insurance premium is $350. Allison itemizes her income-tax deductions. She wonders if her life insurance premium is a tax-deductible expense.

   d. Allison's ordinary life insurance policy is a participating policy. This year she received $120 in policyowner dividends. She wonders if she is required to report the $120 as taxable income.

INTERNET RESOURCES

- **Ameritas Direct** sells life insurance and annuities directly to consumers without traditional agents. Visit the site at

  http://www.ameritasdirect.com

- **Consumer Federation of America** makes available a low-cost life insurance evaluation service by which individ-

ual life insurance policies can be evaluated for a small fee. Visit the site at

http://www.consumerfed.org

- **Insure.com** provides premium quotes on life insurance and news releases about events that affect the insurance industry. Visit the site at

  http://www.insure.com

- **Insurance.com** is an online independent insurance agency that provides premium quotes on life insurance, health insurance, and other insurance products. Visit the site at

  http://www.insurance.com

- **Insweb** provides timely information and premium quotes for life insurance and other insurance products. Visit the site at

  http://www.insweb.com

- **QuickQuote** provides premium quotes on life insurance, health insurance, and numerous other insurance products. Visit the site at

  http://www.quickquote.com

- **Select Quote** monitors highly rated insurers that sell term life insurance. It claims that it makes only the strongest and competitively priced policies available to consumers. It also represents insurers that specialize in insuring people with different risks, such as a pilot, scuba diver, or diabetic. Visit the site at

  http://www.selectquote.com

- **Term4Sale** is considered to be one of the best consumer sites for obtaining term insurance quotes. Visit the site at

  http://www.term4sale.com

SELECTED REFERENCES

Belth, Joseph M., ed. "Financial Strength of Insurance Companies," *The Insurance Forum,* vol. 33, no. 9 (September 2006).

Belth, Joseph M. *Life Insurance: A Consumer's Handbook,* 2nd ed. Bloomington, IN: Indiana University Press, 1985.

Black, Kenneth, Jr., and Harold D. Skipper, Jr. *Life Insurance,* 13th ed. Upper Saddle River, NJ: Prentice-Hall, 2000.

Consumer Federation of America. *Rates of Return on Cash Value Life Insurance Policies Vary Widely, CFA Report Shows Why Consumers Lose Billions of Dollars Annually,* press release, July 16, 1997.

Graves, Edward E., ed. *McGill's Life Insurance,* 6th ed. Bryn Mawr, PA: The American College, 2007.

Hunt, James H. *Analysis of Cash Value Life Insurance Policies.* Washington, DC: Consumer Federation of America, July 1997.

Hunt, James H. *Evaluating Cash Value Life Insurance Policies.* Washington, DC: Consumer Federation of America, September 28, 2001.

Hunt, James H. *Variable Universal Life Insurance: Is It Worth It?* Washington, DC: Consumer Federation of America, February 2003.

Hunter, J. Robert, and James H. Hunt. *Term Life Insurance on the Internet: An Evaluation of On-Line Quotes.* Washington, DC: Consumer Federation of America, 2001.

NOTES

1. This section is based on Joseph M. Belth, *Life Insurance: A Consumer's Handbook,* 2nd ed. (Bloomington, IN: Indiana University Press, 1985), pp. 89–91, 208–209.

2. Joseph M. Belth, ed., "Financial Strength of Insurance Companies," vol. 33, no. 9 (September 2006), p. 108.

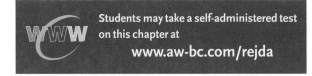

Students may take a self-administered test on this chapter at www.aw-bc.com/rejda

APPENDIX

CALCULATION OF LIFE INSURANCE PREMIUMS

Our discussion of life insurance would not be complete without a discussion of how life insurance premiums are calculated. This section discusses briefly the fundamentals of premium calculations and policy reserves of life insurers. [1]

Net Single Premium

Although most life insurance policies are not purchased with a single premium, the net single premium forms the foundation for the calculation of life insurance premiums. The **net single premium (NSP)** *is defined as the present value of the future death benefit.* It is that amount, which together with compound interest, will be sufficient to pay all death claims. In calculating the NSP, only mortality and investment income are considered. A loading for expenses will be considered later, when the gross premium is calculated.

The NSP is based on three basic assumptions: (1) premiums are paid at the beginning of the policy year, (2) death claims are paid at the end of the policy year, and (3) the death rate is uniform throughout the year.

Certain assumptions must also be made concerning the probability of death at each attained age.

Although life insurers generally develop their own mortality data, we will use selected data from the 2001 Commissioners Standard Ordinary (CSO) Mortality Table for male lives in our illustration. The 2001 CSO table shows mortality data from ages 0 to 120.

Finally, since premiums are paid at the beginning of the year and death claims are paid at the end of the year, the amounts needed for death claims can be discounted for interest. It is assumed that the amounts needed for death claims can be discounted annually at 5.5 percent compound interest.

Term Insurance The NSP for term insurance can be easily calculated. The period of protection is only for a specified period or to a stated age. The death benefit is paid if the insured dies within the specified period, but nothing is paid if the insured dies after the period of protection expires.

Yearly Renewable Term Insurance The NSP for yearly renewable term insurance is considered first. Assume that a $1000 yearly renewable term insurance policy is issued to a male, age 32. *The cost of each year's insurance is determined by multiplying the amount of insurance by the probability of death,* *which is then multiplied by the present value of $1 for the time period the funds are held.* By referring to the 2001 CSO mortality table for males in Exhibit A1, we see that out of 9,778,587 males alive at the beginning of age 32, 11,050 males will die during the year. Therefore, the probability that a male age 32 will die during the year is 11,050/9,778,587, or 0.00113. The amount of insurance is then multiplied by this fraction to determine the amount of money the insurer must have on hand from each policyowner at the end of the year to pay death claims. However, because premiums are paid in advance, and death claims at paid at the end of the year, the amount needed can be discounted for one year. From Exhibit A2, we see that the present value of $1 at 5.5 interest is .9479. Thus, if $1000 is multiplied by the probability of death at age 32, and the sum discounted for one year's interest, the resulting net single premium is $1.07. This calculation is summarized as follows:

$$\frac{Age\ 32,\ NSP}{\$1000 \times \dfrac{11,050}{9,778,587} \times .9479 = \$1.07}$$

If $1.07 is collected in advance from each of the 9,778,587 males who are alive at age 32, this amount together with compound interest will be sufficient to pay all death claims.

Exhibit A1
Commissioners 2001 Standard Ordinary (CSO) Table of Mortality, Male Lives (selected ages)

Age	Number Living at Beginning of Designated Year	Number Dying During Designated Year	Yearly Probability of Dying
30	9,800,822	11,173	0.00114
31	9,789,650	11,062	0.00113
32	9,778,587	11,050	0.00113
33	9,767,537	11,233	0.00115
34	9,756,305	11,512	0.00118
35	9,744,792	11,791	0.00121
36	9,733,001	12,458	0.00128
37	9,720,543	13,026	0.00134
38	9,707,517	13,979	0.00144
39	9,693,539	14,928	0.00154
40	9,678,610	15,970	0.00165

Source: Excerpted from 2001 C50 Composite Ultimate, Male, ANB.

Exhibit A2
Present Value of $1 at 5.5% Compound Interest

Number of Years	5.5%
1	0.9479
2	0.8985
3	0.8516
4	0.8072
5	0.7651
6	0.7252
7	0.6874
8	0.6516
9	0.6176
10	0.5854

Five-Year Term Insurance   In this case, the company must pay the death claim if the insured dies any time within the five-year period. However, death claims are paid at the end of the year in which they occur and not at the end of the five-year period. Thus, the cost of each year's mortality must be computed separately and then added together to determine the net single premium.

The cost of insurance for the first year is determined exactly as before, when we calculated the net single premium for yearly term insurance. Thus, we have the following equation:

$$\frac{Age\ 32,\ NSP,\ first\text{-}year\ insurance\ cost}{\$1000 \times \dfrac{11,050}{9,778,587} \times .9479 = \$1.07}$$

The next step is to determine the cost for the second year. Referring back to Exhibit A1, we see that at age 33, 11,233 males will die during the year. Thus, for the 9,778,587 males who are alive at age 32, the probability of dying during age 33 is 11,233/9,778,587. Note that the denominator does not change but remains the same for each probability calculation. Because the amount needed to pay second-year death claims will not be needed for two years, it can be discounted for two years. Thus, for the second year, we have the following calculation:

$$\frac{Age\ 33,\ NSP,\ second\text{-}year\ insurance\ cost}{\$1000 \times \dfrac{11,233}{9,778,587} \times .8985 = \$1.03}$$

EXHIBIT A3
Calculating the NSP for a Five-Year Term Insurance Policy, Male, Age 32

Age	Amount of Insurance	Probabiity of Death	Present Value of $1 at 5.5%	Cost of Insurance
32	$1000 $\times$ $\dfrac{11,050}{9,778,587}$	$\times$ .9479	=	$1.07 (year 1)
33	$1000 $\times$ $\dfrac{11,233}{9,778,587}$	$\times$ .8985	=	1.03 (year 2)
34	$1000 $\times$ $\dfrac{11,512}{9,778,587}$	$\times$ .8516	=	1.00 (year 3)
35	$1000 $\times$ $\dfrac{11,791}{9,778,587}$	$\times$ .8072	=	0.97 (year 4)
36	$1000 $\times$ $\dfrac{12,458}{9,778,587}$	$\times$ .7651	=	0.97 (year 5)
			NSP =	$5.04

For each of the remaining three years, we follow the same procedure (see Exhibit A3). If the insurer collects $5.04 in a single premium from each of the 9,778,587 males who are alive at age 32, that sum together with compound interest will be sufficient to pay all expected death claims during the five-year period.

Ordinary Life Insurance   In calculating the NSP for an ordinary life insurance policy, the same method used earlier for the five-year term policy is used except that the calculations are carried out each year to the end of the 2001 mortality table. If the remaining calculations are performed, the NSP for a $1000 ordinary life insurance policy issued to a male, age 32, would be $109.49.[2]

Net Annual Level Premium

If premiums are paid annually, the net annual level premium must be the mathematical equivalent of the NSP. The net annual level premium cannot be determined by simply dividing the NSP by the number of years of premium payments. Such a division would produce an inadequate premium for two reasons. First, the NSP is based on the assumption that premiums are paid at the beginning of the period. If premiums are paid in installments, and some insureds die early, there is a loss of future premiums. Second, installment payments result in the loss of interest income because of the smaller amounts invested.

The mathematical adjustment for the loss of premiums and interest is accomplished by dividing the NSP by the present value of an appropriate life annuity due of $1. More specifically, the **net annual level premium (NALP)** is *determined by dividing the present value of a life annuity due of $1(PVLAD) for the premium-paying period.* Thus, we obtain the following:

$$\text{NALP} = \frac{\text{NSP}}{\text{PVLAD of \$1 for the premium-paying period}}$$

If the annual premiums are paid for life, such as in an ordinary life policy, the premium is called a *whole life annuity due.* If the annual premiums are paid for only a temporary period, such as five-year term insurance, the premium is called a *temporary life annuity due.*

Term Insurance   Consider first the NALP for a five-year term insurance policy in the amount of $1000 issued to a male, age 32. Recall that the NSP for a five-year term insurance policy issued at age 32 is $5.04. This sum must be divided by the present value of a five-year *temporary life annuity due of $1.* For the first year, a $1 payment is due immediately. For the second year, the probability that a male age 32 will still be *alive* to pay the premium at age 33 must be determined. Referring back to Exhibit A1, 9,778,587 males are alive at age 32. Of this number,

9,767,537 are still alive at age 33. Thus, the probability of survival is 9,767,537/9,778,587. This fraction is multiplied by $1 and then discounted for one year's interest. Thus, the present value of the second payment is $0.95. Similar calculations are performed for the remaining three years. The calculations are summarized as follows:

$$
\begin{aligned}
\text{Age 32} \quad & \$1 \text{ due immediately} && \$1.00 \\[4pt]
\text{Age 33} \quad & \frac{9{,}767{,}537}{9\,778{,}587} \times \$1 \times .9479 = && 0.95 \\[4pt]
\text{Age 34} \quad & \frac{9{,}756{,}305}{9\,778{,}587} \times \$1 \times .8985 = && 0.90 \\[4pt]
\text{Age 35} \quad & \frac{9{,}744{,}792}{9\,778{,}587} \times \$1 \times .8516 = && 0.85 \\[4pt]
\text{Age 36} \quad & \frac{9{,}773{,}001}{9\,778{,}587} \times \$1 \times .8072 = && \underline{0.81} \\[6pt]
& \text{PVLAD of \$1} = && \$4.51
\end{aligned}
$$

The present value of a five-year temporary life annuity due of $1 at age 32 is $4.51. If the NSP of $5.04 is divided by $4.51, the net annual level premium is $1.12.

$$
\text{NALP} = \frac{\text{NSP}}{\text{PVLAD of \$1}} = \frac{\$5.04}{\$4.51} = \$1.12
$$

Ordinary Life Insurance   The net annual level premium for a $1000 ordinary life insurance policy issued to a male, age 32, is calculated in a similar manner. The same procedure is used except that the calculations are carried out to the end of the mortality table. If the calculations are performed, the present value of a whole life annuity due of $1 at age 32 is $17.08.[3] The NSP ($109.49) is then divided by the present value of a whole life annuity due at age 32 ($17.08), and the NALP is $6.41.

Gross Premium   The gross premium is determined by adding a loading allowance to the net annual level premium. The loading allowance must cover all operating expenses, provide a margin for contingencies, and, in the case of stock insurers, provide for a contribution to profits. If the policy is a participating policy, the loading must also reflect a margin for dividends.

POLICY RESERVES

Policy reserves, also known as legal reserves, are the major liability item of life insurers.[4] Under the level-premium method for paying premiums, premiums paid during the early years are higher than necessary to pay death claims, while those paid during the later years are insufficient to pay death claims. The excess premiums must be accounted for and held for future payment to the policyowners' beneficiaries. As such the excess premiums paid during the early years result in the creation of a policy reserve. *Policy reserves are a liability item on the insurer's balance sheet that must be offset by assets equal to that amount.* The policy reserves held by the insurer, plus future premiums and investment earnings, will enable the insurer to pay all policy benefits if the actual experience conforms to the actuarial assumptions used in calculating the reserve. Policy reserves are also called *legal reserves* because state law specifies the minimum basis for calculating them.

Purposes of the Reserve

The policy reserve has two purposes. *First, it is a formal recognition of the insurer's obligation to pay future claims.* The policy reserve plus future premiums and interest earnings must be sufficient to pay all future policy benefits.

Second, the reserve is a legal test of the insurer's solvency. The insurer must hold assets at least equal to its legal reserves and other liabilities. This requirement is a legal test of the insurer's ability to meet its present and future obligations to policyholders. As such, policy reserves should not be viewed as a fund. Rather, they are a liability item that must be offset by assets.

Definition of the Reserve

The **policy reserve** *can be defined as the difference between the present value of future benefits and the present value of future net premiums.* The net single premium is equal to the present value of future benefits. At the inception of the policy, the net single premium is also equal to the present value of future net premiums. The net single premium can be converted into a series of net level premiums without changing this relationship. However, once the first installment premium payment is made, this statement is no longer true. The present value of future benefits and the present value of future net premiums are no longer equal to each other. The present value of future benefits will increase over time, because the date of death is drawing closer, while the present value of future net premiums will decline, because fewer premiums will be paid. Thus, the difference between the two is the policy reserve.

This situation is illustrated in Exhibit A4, which shows the prospective reserve (defined later) for an ordinary life policy issued at age 45. At the inception of the policy, the net single premium is equal to the present value of future benefits and the present value of future net premiums.

The present value of future benefits increases over time, while the present value of future net premiums declines, and the reserve is the difference between them. Based on the older 1980 CSO mortality table for valuing legal reserves, the reserve for an ordinary life insurance policy continues to increase until it is equal to the policy face amount at age 100. If the insured is still alive at that time, the face amount is paid to the policyowner. However, the maturity date for new cash-value policies sold in the future will be age 121 as insurers switch over to the new 2001 CSO mortality table for valuation of their reserves. At the time of this writing, some insurers are now using this table to calculate their reserve liabilities. The 2001 CSO mortality table will be mandatory in 2009.

Types of Reserves

The reserve can be viewed either retrospectively or prospectively. If we refer to the past experience, the reserve is known as a retrospective reserve. The **retrospective reserve** *represents the net premiums collected by the insurer for a particular block of policies, plus interest earnings at an assumed rate, less the amounts paid out as death claims.*[5] Thus, the retrospective reserve is the excess of the net premiums accumulated at interest over the death claims paid out.

The reserve can also be viewed prospectively when we look to the future. The **prospective reserve** *is the difference between the present value of future benefits and the present value of future net premiums.* The retrospective and prospective methods are the mathematical equivalent of each other. Both methods will produce the same level of reserves at the end of any given year if the same set of actuarial assumptions is used.

Reserves can also be classified based on the time of valuation. At the time the reserves are valued, they can be classified as terminal, initial, and mean.

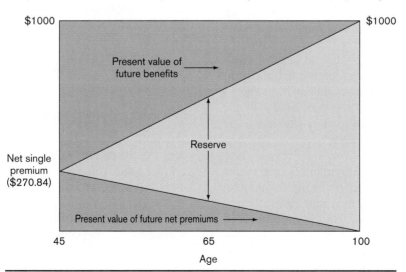

EXHIBIT A4
Prospective Reserve—Ordinary Life Insurance (1980 CSO mortality table)

A **terminal reserve** *is the reserve at the end of any given policy year*. It is used by companies to determine cash surrender values as well as the net amount at risk for purposes of determining dividends. The **initial reserve** *is the reserve at the beginning of any policy year*. It is equal to the preceding terminal reserve plus the net level annual premium for the current year. The initial reserve is also used by insurers to determine dividends. Finally, the **mean reserve** *is the average of the terminal and initial reserves*. It is used to indicate the insurer's reserve liabilities on its annual statement.

CASE APPLICATION

Assume that you are asked to explain how premiums in a life insurance policy are calculated. Based on the following information, answer the questions below.

a. Compute the net single premium for a five-year term insurance policy in the amount of $1000 issued to a male at age 30.

b. Compute the net annual level premium for the same policy as in part (a).

c. Is the net annual level premium the actual premium paid by the policyowner? Explain your answer.

Age at Beginning of Year	Number Living at Beginning of Designated Year	Number Dying During Designated Year	Present Value of $1 at 5.5%	
			Year	Factor
30	9,800,822	11,173	1	0.9479
31	9,789,650	11,062	2	0.8985
32	9,778,587	11,050	3	0.8516
33	9,767,537	11,233	4	0.8072
34	9,756,305	11,512	5	0.7651

NOTES

1. This section is based on Edward E. Graves, ed., *McGill's Life Insurance,* 5th ed. (Bryn Mawr, PA: The American College, 2004), chs. 11 and 13; and Kenneth Black, Jr., and Harold D. Skipper, Jr., *Life Insurance,* 13th ed. (Upper Saddle River, NJ: Prentice-Hall, 2000), pp. 714–727.

2. Graves, *McGill's Life Insurance,* 5th ed., p. 320.
3. Ibid., p. 332.
4. Life insurance reserves are discussed in detail in Graves, ch. 12, and Black and Skipper, ch. 29.
5. Graves, pp. 342–343.

CHAPTER 14

ANNUITIES AND INDIVIDUAL RETIREMENT ACCOUNTS

"Buy an annuity cheap, and make your life interesting to yourself and everybody else that watches the speculation."

Charles Dickens

Lori, age 27, is a registered nurse who is employed by a for-profit hospital in Los Angeles, California. Her annual salary is $60,000. She has several financial goals, which include saving for a comfortable retirement. Because she is a new employee, she is ineligible to participate in the hospital's retirement plan for one year. A financial planner recommended that Lori should establish an individual retirement account (Roth IRA). She could start saving immediately for retirement; the investment income would accumulate income-tax free; and the retirement distributions would be income-tax free. The planner pointed out that if Lori deposited $1000 quarterly into a Roth IRA for 40 years, and the IRA account earned an average annual return of 7 percent, she would have $869,854 in her account at age 67.

Like Lori, millions of workers dream of achieving financial independence and a comfortable retirement. Planning for a comfortable retirement should receive high priority in a personal risk management program. Retirement planning is especially important today because the proportion of older people in the population is increasing; the period of retirement for many workers is growing longer because of increased life expectancy; and studies show that many workers are not saving enough for a comfortable retirement.

This chapter discusses the timely topic of retirement planning and shows how annuities and IRAs can help ensure a comfortable retirement. Two major areas are emphasized. The first part discusses the annuity concept and the different types of annuities sold today. The second part discusses the characteristics of IRAs, including the traditional tax-deductible IRA and the Roth IRA.

INDIVIDUAL ANNUITIES

The vast majority of workers who retire today receive Social Security retirement benefits. Some workers also receive benefits from their employers' retirement plans. Individual annuities can also be purchased to provide additional retirement income. An annuity is a tax-deferred product. Although the premiums are paid with after-tax dollars, the investment income accumulates income-tax free and is not taxed until benefits are paid to the annuitant. The investment returns of tax-deferred compounding over long periods can be impressive (see Exhibit 14.1).

Annuity Principle

An **annuity** *can be defined as a periodic payment that continues for a fixed period or for the duration of a designated life or lives.* The person who receives the periodic payments or whose life governs the duration of payment is known as the **annuitant.**

An annuity is the opposite of life insurance. Life insurance creates an immediate estate and provides protection against dying too soon before financial assets can be accumulated. In contrast, an annuity provides protection against living too long and exhausting one's savings while the individual is

EXHIBIT **14.1**
Power of Tax-Deferred Growth

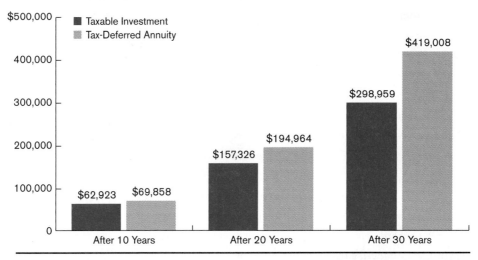

NOTE: The hypothetical example assumes a $5000 annual investment, a 6% annual rate of return, and a 31% combined federal and state tax bracket. Annual investments are made at the beginning of the year with after-tax dollars. Investment returns are credited at the end of the year and are taxed at that time. Chart balances shown are end-of-year balances.
SOURCE: Calculated from the Investment Growth Calculator, Fidelity Investments.

still alive. Thus, *the fundamental purpose of an annuity is to provide a lifetime income that cannot be outlived.* It protects against the loss of income because of excessive longevity and the exhaustion of savings.

Annuities are possible because the risk of excessive longevity is pooled by the group. Individuals acting alone cannot be certain that their savings will be sufficient during retirement. Some will die early before exhausting their savings, whereas others will still be alive after exhausting their principal. Although the insurance company cannot predict how long any particular member of the group will live, it can determine the approximate number of annuitants who will be alive at the end of each successive year. Thus, the company can calculate the amount that each person must contribute to the pool. Interest can be earned on the funds before they are paid out to the annuitants. Also, some annuitants will die early, and their unliquidated principal can be used to provide additional payments to annuitants who survive beyond their life expectancy. Thus, annuity payments consist of three sources: (1) premium payments, (2) interest earnings, and (3) the unliquidated principal of annuitants who die early. By pooling the

risk of excessive longevity, insurers can pay a lifetime income to annuitants that cannot be outlived.

Annuitants tend to be healthy individuals who generally live longer than most persons. Because of the higher life expectancy of annuitants, actuaries use special annuity tables to calculate annuity premiums.

TYPES OF ANNUITIES

Insurers sell a wide variety of individual annuities. For sake of convenience and understanding, the major annuities sold today can be classified as follows:

- Fixed annuity
- Variable annuity
- Equity-indexed annuity

Fixed Annuity

A **fixed annuity** pays periodic income payments that are guaranteed and fixed in amount. During the **accumulation period** prior to retirement, premiums are credited with interest. There are typically two interest rates: a guaranteed minimum interest rate and a current interest rate. The *guaranteed rate* is the minimum interest rate that will be credited to the fixed annuity, typically 1 percent to 3 percent. The *current rate* is higher and is based on current market conditions, such as 4 percent. The current rate is guaranteed only for a limited period, typically one to five years.

As an inducement to purchase the annuity, many insurers sell *bonus annuities,* which initially increase the amount of interest credited to the annuity. The bonus interest generally ranges from 3 percent to 4 percent of the amount deposited. For example, an investor who deposits $100,000 into an annuity with a 3 percent bonus would receive an additional $3000 of interest the first year. However, there is no such thing as a free lunch. The bonus is paid for by reduced renewal interest rates credited to the annuity in the future or by higher expense fees.

The **liquidation period** (also called the **payout period**) follows the accumulation period and refers to the period in which the funds are being paid to the annuitant. During the liquidation period, the accumulated cash can be *annuitized* or paid to the annuitant in the form of a guaranteed lifetime income. However, the periodic payments are fixed in amount and generally do not change. As a result, fixed annuities provide little or no protection against inflation.

Payment of Benefits   A fixed annuity can be purchased so that the income payments start immediately. This type of fixed annuity is called an immediate annuity. An **immediate annuity** *is one where the first payment is due one payment interval from the date of purchase.* For example, if the income is paid monthly, the first payment starts one month from the purchase date, or one year from the purchase date if the income is paid annually. Immediate annuities are typically purchased in a lump sum by people near retirement. An immediate annuity has the major advantage of a guaranteed lifetime income that cannot be outlived. There are other advantages as well (see Insight 14.1).

A fixed annuity can also be purchased that defers the income payments until some later date. A **deferred annuity** *provides income payments at some future date.* This type of annuity is essentially a plan for accumulating a sum of money prior to retirement on a tax-deferred basis. If the annuitant dies during the accumulation period prior to retirement, a death benefit is typically paid equal to the sum of the gross premiums paid or the cash value if higher. At the maturity date of the contract, the annuitant can receive the funds in a lump sum or have them paid out under one of the settlement options (discussed later).

A fixed annuity that defers the income payments until a future date can be purchased with a lump sum,

INSIGHT 14.1

At a Glance—Advantages of an Immediate Annuity

There are many advantages that immediate annuities can provide to the buyer. Here are just a few:

- **Security**   The annuity provides stable lifetime income, which can never be outlived or which may be guaranteed for a specified period.
- **Simplicity**   The annuitant does not have to manage his or her investments, watch markets, report interest or dividends.
- **High Returns**   The interest rates used by insurance companies to calculate immediate annuity income are generally higher than CD or Treasury rates, and because part of the principal is returned with each payment, greater amounts are received than would be provided by interest alone.

- **Preferred Tax Treatment**   It lets you postpone paying taxes on some of the earnings you've accrued in a "tax-deferred" annuity when rolled into an immediate annuity (only the portion attributable to interest is taxable income; the bulk of the payments are nontaxable return of principal).
- **Safety of Principal**   Funds are guaranteed to the assets of the insurer and are not subject to the fluctuations in the financial markets.

Source: Excerpted from *A Lesson in Immediate Annuities,* Immediate Annuities.com, 2005. Tel. 866-866-1999.

or the contract may permit flexible premium payments. A deferred annuity purchased with a lump sum is called a **single-premium deferred annuity**. In contrast, a **flexible-premium annuity** allows the annuity owner to vary the premium payments; there is no requirement that the owner must deposit a specified amount each year. Thus, the annuity owner has considerable flexibility in the payment of premiums.

Annuity Settlement Options The annuity owner has a choice of **annuity settlement options.** Cash can be withdrawn in a lump sum or in installments, or the funds can be annuitized and paid out as life income. As a practical matter, most annuities are not annuitized.

The following settlement options are typically available:

- *Cash option.* The funds can be withdrawn in a lump sum or in installments. The taxable portion of the distribution (discussed later) is subject to federal and state income taxes. The cash option also leads to adverse selection against the insurer because those in poor health will take cash rather than annuitize the funds.
- *Life annuity (no refund).* A **life annuity (no refund)** option provides a life income to the annuitant only while the annuitant is alive. *No additional payments are made after the annuitant dies.* This type of settlement option pays the highest amount of periodic income payments because it has no refund features. It is suitable for someone who needs maximum lifetime income and has no dependents or has provided for them through other means. However, because of the risk of forfeiting the unpaid principal if death occurs early, relatively few annuity owners elect this option.
- *Life annuity with guaranteed payments.* A **life annuity with guaranteed payments** (also called a **life annuity with period certain**) pays a life income to the annuitant with a certain number of guaranteed payments, such as 5, 10, 15, or 20 years. If the annuitant dies before receiving the guaranteed number of payments, the remaining payments are paid to a designated beneficiary. This option can be used by someone who needs lifetime income but who also wishes to provide income to the beneficiary in the event of an early

death. Because of the guaranteed payments, the periodic income payments are less than the income paid by a life annuity with no refund.
- *Installment refund option.* An **installment refund option** pays a life income to the annuitant. If the annuitant dies before receiving total income payments equal to the purchase price of the annuity, the payments continue to the beneficiary until they equal the purchase price. A **cash refund option** is another version of this option. If the annuitant dies before receiving total payments equal to the purchase price of the annuity, the balance is paid in a lump sum to the beneficiary.
- *Joint-and-survivor annuity.* A **joint-and-survivor annuity option** pays benefits based on the lives of two or more annuitants, such as a husband and wife or a brother and sister. The annuity income is paid until the last annuitant dies. Some contracts pay the full amount of the original income payments until the last survivor dies. Other plans pay only two-thirds or one-half of the original income after the first annuitant dies.

In addition to the above options, many insurers offer a fixed-annuity option that provides protection against inflation. An **inflation-indexed annuity option** provides periodic payments that are adjusted for inflation. However, because of the inflation protection, the initial monthly payment is less than the payment from a traditional fixed annuity. For example, based on the rates of one insurer, a 70-year-old male who purchases a $100,000 immediate annuity would receive lifetime income of $757 monthly. If indexed for inflation, however, the initial monthly payment would be about $569 or about 25 percent less.

Exhibit 14.2 provides examples of monthly income payments for a $250,000 immediate annuity issued to a male age 67.

Variable Annuity

A second type of annuity is a variable annuity. A **variable annuity** pays a lifetime income, but the income payments vary depending on common stock prices. *The fundamental purpose of a variable annuity is to provide an inflation hedge by maintaining the real purchasing power of the periodic payments during*

EXHIBIT 14.2
Examples of Monthly Income Annuity Payments from an Immediate Annuity, $250,000 Purchase Price, Male, Age 67

Annuity Settlement Option	Estimated Monthly Income
Life income with no refund	$1,865
Life income with 5 years guaranteed payments	1,841
Life income with 10 years guaranteed payments	1,782
Life income with 15 years guaranteed payments	1,698
Life income with 20 years guaranteed payments	1,603
Joint and survivor option[a]	1,582
Joint and survivor option with 20 years guaranteed	1,428

[a] Both annuitants are age 67. The survivor receives 100 percent of the monthly benefits.

SOURCE: Immediateannuities.com. Data shown are estimates for Nebraska as of September 2006.

retirement. It is based on the assumption of a positive correlation between the cost of living and common stock prices over the long run.

Basic Characteristics of a Variable Annuity Premiums are invested in a portfolio of common stocks or other investments that presumably will increase in value during a period of inflation. The premiums are used to purchase **accumulation units** during the period prior to retirement, and the value of each accumulation unit varies depending on common stock prices. For example, assume that the accumulation unit is initially valued at $1, and the annuitant makes a monthly premium payment of $100. During the first month, 100 accumulation units are purchased.[1] If common stock prices increase during the second month, and the accumulation unit rises to $1.10, about 91 accumulation units can be purchased. If the stock market declines during the third month, and the accumulation unit declines to $0.90, 111 accumulation units can be purchased. Thus, accumulation units are purchased over a long period of time in both rising and falling markets.

At retirement, the accumulation units are converted into **annuity units**. The number of annuity units remains constant during the liquidation period, but the value of each unit will change each month or year depending on the level of common stock prices. For example, at retirement, assume that the annuitant has 10,000 accumulation units. Assume that the accumulation units are converted into 100 annuity units.[2] As stated earlier, the number of annuity units remains constant, but the value of each unit will change over time. Assume that the annuity unit is initially valued at $10 when the annuitant retires. A monthly income of $1000 will be paid. During the second month, if the annuity unit increases in value to $10.10, the monthly income also increases to $1010. During the third month, if the annuity units decline in value to $9.90 because of a stock market decline, the monthly income is reduced to $990. Thus, the monthly income depends on the level of common stock prices.

Guaranteed Death Benefit Variable annuities typically provide a guaranteed death benefit that protects the principal against loss due to market declines. *The typical death benefit states that if the annuitant dies before retirement, the amount paid to the beneficiary will be the higher of two amounts: the amount invested in the contract or the value of the account at the time of death.* Thus, if the annuitant dies during a market decline, the beneficiary receives an amount at least equal to the total amount invested in the contract.

Some variable annuities go one step further and pay enhanced death benefits. Enhanced benefits either (1) guarantee the principal (contributions made) plus interest or (2) periodically adjust the value of the account to lock in investment gains. For example, the annuity may contain a *rising-floor death benefit* by which the death benefit is periodically reset. Thus, a 5 percent rising-floor benefit may be periodically reset so that the beneficiary will receive the principal plus 5 percent interest.

A second example is the *stepped-up benefit* by which the contract periodically locks in investment gains, such as every five years. For example, assume that $10,000 is invested in year 1, and the account is now worth $15,000 in year 5. The new death benefit is $15,000, even though the annuity owner has invested only $10,000.

Finally, an *enhanced earning benefit* is a type of death benefit that pays an additional amount for income taxes when the annuitant dies. The amount paid covers the income tax that heirs must pay on accumulated earnings in the annuity. For example, assume that $100,000 invested in a variable annuity grows to $200,000, and the annuitant dies. The designated beneficiary must pay an income tax on the $100,000 gain. The enhanced death benefit would pay an additional amount, such as 40 percent or $40,000, to help pay the income tax on the gain.

Fees and Expenses Variable annuity owners pay a number of fees and expenses. Some fees consist of investment management and administrative fees; other fees are insurance charges that pay for the guarantees and other services provided. In addition, most variable annuities have surrender charges.

Specifically, variable annuities typically contain the following fees and expenses:

- *Investment management charge*. This charge is a payment to the investment manager and asset-management company for the brokerage services and investment advice provided in the management of the investment portfolio.
- *Administrative charge*. This charge covers the paperwork, record keeping, and periodic reports to the annuity owner.
- *Mortality and expense risk charge*. This fee, called the "M&E" fee, pays for (1) the mortality risk associated with the guaranteed death benefit and excessive longevity; (2) a guarantee that annual expenses will not exceed a certain percentage of assets after the contract is issued; and (3) an allowance for profit.

- *Surrender charge*. Most annuities have a surrender charge if the annuity is surrendered during the early years of the contract. This charge helps to pay agents and brokers who sell variable annuities. It is usually a percentage of the account value and declines over time. The surrender charge is typically 7 percent of the account value for the first year, declining one percentage point for each year until it reaches zero for the eighth and later years. Most variable annuities permit partial withdrawals each year of as much as 10 percent of the account value without imposition of a surrender charge.

In addition to these charges, some annuities have a front-end load of 4 or 5 percent; the annuity may have an annual contract fee, such as $25 or $50; and there may be a charge if funds are transferred from one subaccount to another. *In the aggregate, total fees and expenses in most variable annuities are high and can easily exceed 2 percent of assets. As a result, long-run total returns may be significantly reduced in high-cost annuities.*

Some annuities, however, have relatively low annual expenses, and a small number do not have a surrender charge. Exhibit 14.3 shows the names and telephone numbers for a select group of low-cost variable annuities.

Equity-Indexed Annuity

An equity-indexed annuity offers the guarantees of a fixed annuity and limited participation in stock market gains. An **equity-indexed annuity** *is a fixed, deferred annuity that allows the annuity owner to participate in the growth of the stock market and*

Exhibit 14.3
Three Low-Cost Variable Annuities

Name	Total Annual Expenses	Sales Load	Surrender Charge	Minimum Investment	Telephone Number
Fidelity Personal Retirement Annuity	.35%[a]	None	None	$5000	800-544-4702
Vanguard Variable Annuity	.44%[b]	None	None	5000	800-522-5555
Lifetime Variable Select (TIAA-CREF)	.66%[c]	None	None	2500	800-223-1200

[a]VIP Index Fund.
[b]Vanguard Equity Index Portfolio. An annual fee of $25 applies to contracts less than $25,000.
[c]Stock Index Account.

also provides downside protection against the loss of principal and prior interest earnings if the annuity is held to term. Term periods typically range from one to ten years. The annuity value is linked to the performance of a stock market index, typically Standard and Poor's 500 Composite Stock Index. If the stock market rises, the annuity is credited with part of the gain in the index, which does not include the reinvestment of dividends. If the stock market declines, the annuity earns at least a minimum return, which typically is 3 percent on 90 percent of the principal invested.

The key elements of an equity-indexed annuity are (1) the participation rate, (2) the maximum cap rate, (3) the indexing method used, and (4) the guaranteed minimum value.

Participation Rate The *participation rate* is the percent of increase in the stock index credited to the contract. The insurer periodically determines the participation rate, which is subject to change. Participation rates typically range from 30 percent to 100 percent of the gain in the stock index. Investors may receive only part of the increase in the stock index (excluding the reinvestment of dividends). For example, if the participation rate is 70 percent and the stock index rises 9 percent during the measuring period, the index-linked interest rate credited to your annuity will be 6.3 percent (9% × 70% = 6.3%).

Maximum Cap Rate or Cap Some annuities have a maximum cap rate or upper limit on the index-linked interest rate credited to your annuity. The maximum cap rate is the maximum rate of interest the annuity will earn. In the earlier example, if the annuity has a maximum cap rate of 6 percent, the interest rate credited to the annuity would be only 6 percent, not 6.3 percent. Not all annuities have a maximum cap rate.

Indexing Method The *indexing method* refers to the method for crediting excess interest to the annuity. Insurers use several indexing methods for crediting interest, only one of which is discussed here. Under the *annual reset method* (also known as the *ratchet method*), interest earnings are calculated based on the annual change in the stock index; the index value starting point is also reset annually. Thus, if the stock index decreases during any con-

tract year, the decrease does not have to be recovered before any additional growth in the index will be credited to the contract.

Guaranteed Minimum Value Equity-indexed annuities with terms longer than one year have a guaranteed minimum value that provides downside protection against the loss of principal if the annuity is held to term. The most common minimum guarantee is 3 percent compounded on 90 percent of your initial deposit. *The result is a guaranteed minimum value at the end of the index period.* For example, if you deposit $100,000 in an equity-indexed annuity, 90 percent of that amount ($90,000) will earn a guaranteed rate of 3 percent compounded annually regardless of how the index performs. Thus, if you keep the annuity in force until the end of the index period, say seven years, you are guaranteed $110,689 in your account. However, because the minimum guarantee applies to only 90 percent of the single premium, an investor who surrenders the contract during the first three or four policy years may experience a loss of principal. If it is held to term, the principal is guaranteed against loss.

TAXATION OF INDIVIDUAL ANNUITIES

An individual annuity purchased from a commercial insurer is a nonqualified annuity. A *nonqualified annuity* is an annuity that does not meet the Internal Revenue Code requirements for employer benefits. As such, it does not qualify for most income-tax benefits that qualified employer retirement plans receive.

Premiums for individual annuities are not income-tax deductible and are paid with after-tax dollars. However, the investment income is tax deferred and accumulates free of current income taxes until the funds are actually distributed.

The taxable portion of any distribution is taxable as ordinary income. In addition, the taxable portion of a premature distribution before age 59½ is subject to a 10 percent penalty tax, with certain exceptions.[3]

The periodic annuity payments from an individual annuity are taxed according to the General Rule. Under this rule, the *net cost* of the annuity payments is recovered income-tax free over the payment

INSIGHT 14.2

Ten Questions to Answer Before You Buy a Variable Annuity

Variable annuities are a valuable retirement tool if used properly. However, variable annuities are not for everyone. Before you buy an annuity, you should answer the following questions:

- *What are the annual fees and expenses?* Most variable annuities have relatively high annual fees and expenses. According to Morningstar, the average variable annuity costs about 2.35% of plan assets each year. Other investments, especially no-load mutual funds, typically have lower annual expense charges. Before you buy, you should shop for an annuity with relatively low annual expenses.

- *Are you willing to be locked into the annuity for at least 15 years?* Most annuities have back-end surrender charges that extend over long periods, typically seven to ten years. You will lose a substantial amount of money if you surrender the annuity during the early years. Also, the favorable income tax advantages of a variable annuity require a long holding period of at least 15 years for the tax benefits to offset the high fees and expenses.

- *Have you made maximum annual contributions to your employer's 401(k) plan or other qualified retirement plan and to an individual retirement account?* Most employers make a partial matching contribution to qualified retirement plans, and you are passing up "free money" if you don't contribute the maximum allowed. Also, an IRA may have lower annual expense charges than a variable annuity.

- *Have you considered your tolerance for risk?* The value of your annuity depends on the investment experience of the underlying subaccounts. If the premiums are invested in a stock account, the value of your annuity can decline substantially in a severe market decline. Depending on your tolerance for risk, your "comfort" level may be adversely affected.

- *Are you willing to tolerate fluctuations in monthly income?* Variable annuity retirement benefits also fluctuate with the investment experience of the underlying subaccounts. If the funds are invested in a stock market account, a substantial market decline can be financially painful. Common stocks are also sensitive to interest rates. If interest rates rise because of inflationary expectations or a change in Federal Reserve monetary policy, your variable annuity benefits may decline.

- *Will you need the funds before age 59 1/2?* You should not buy a variable annuity if the funds will be needed before age 59 1/2. Cash withdrawals before age 59 1/2 generally are subject to a 10% federal tax penalty on the taxable portion of the distribution. You should have available cash to cover three to six months of living expenses, which reduces the need to withdraw funds from your annuity.

- *Is your combined federal and state income tax bracket at least 28 percent?* If you are in a lower tax bracket, high variable annuity fees and expenses can dilute the tax advantages of a deferred annuity.

- *Are you aware that capital gains are taxed as ordinary income when annuity distributions are made?* The taxable portion of a variable annuity distribution is taxed as ordinary income, which can be as high as 35% for 2006. In contrast, long-term capital gains in a taxable account are taxed currently at a maximum capital gains rate of 15 percent.

- *Are you aware that if you should die, your heirs will be taxed on the variable annuity earnings just as you would?* In contrast, mutual funds in a taxable account pass to the heirs free of income taxes because of a "stepped-up" cost basis. As a result, heirs don't pay income taxes on the accumulated gains.

- *Should you invest your IRA contributions in a variable annuity?* As a general rule, the answer is no. IRAs already receive favorable income-tax treatment. Investing IRA contributions in a variable annuity results in an unnecessary duplication of fees and expenses.

period. The amount of each payment that exceeds the net cost is taxable as ordinary income.

An exclusion ratio must be calculated to determine the nontaxable and taxable portions of the annuity payments. The **exclusion ratio** is determined by dividing the investment in the contract by the expected return:

$$\frac{\text{Investment in the contract}}{\text{Expected return}} = \text{Exclusion ratio}$$

The *investment in the contract (basis)* is the total cost of the annuity, which generally is the total amount of the premiums paid for the annuity less any nontaxable distributions previously received less the value of any refund features.[4] The *expected return* is the total amount that the annuitant can expect to receive under the contract. It is determined by multiplying the annual payments the annuitant will receive by the life expectancy of the annuitant, which is obtained from actuarial tables provided by the IRS.

As an example, assume that Ben, age 65, purchased an immediate annuity for $108,000 that pays a lifetime monthly income of $1000. The annuity has no refund features. Investment in the contract is $108,000. Based on the IRS actuarial table, Ben has a life expectancy of 20 years. Expected return is $240,000 (20 × 12 × $1000). The exclusion ratio is 0.45 ($108,000 ÷ $240,000). Each year, until the net cost is recovered, Ben receives $5400 tax free (45% × $12,000), and $6600, which is taxable. After the net cost is recovered, the total payment would be taxable.

In summary, annuities can be attractive to investors who have made maximum contributions to other tax-advantaged plans and who wish to save additional amounts on a tax-deferred basis. Also, because of the surrender charge, the investor should expect to remain invested for 10 or more years.

However, annuities are not for everyone, especially a variable annuity. You should not purchase a variable annuity if you will need the funds before age 59½; the period of investing is less than 15 years; and you have not made maximum annual contributions to other tax-advantaged plans, such as a Section 401(k) plan and an IRA. Other considerations are important as well (see Insight 14.2).

INDIVIDUAL RETIREMENT ACCOUNTS

An **individual retirement account (IRA)** allows workers with taxable compensation to make annual contributions to a retirement plan up to certain limits and receive favorable income-tax treatment.

There are two basic types of IRA plans:

- Traditional IRA
- Roth IRA

Traditional IRA

A **traditional IRA** is an IRA that allows workers to take a tax deduction for part or all of their IRA contributions. The investment income accumulates income-tax free on a tax-deferred basis, and the distributions are taxed as ordinary income.

Eligibility Requirements There are two eligibility requirements for establishing a traditional tax-deductible IRA. *First, the participant must have earned income during the year.* Earned income includes wages and salaries, bonuses, commissions, self-employment income, and taxable alimony and separate maintenance payments. However, earned income does not include investment income, pension or annuity income, Social Security, and rental income. For example, if a person receives only Social Security and investment income, he or she could not make an IRA contribution for that year.

Second, the participant must be under age 70½. No traditional IRA contributions are allowed for the tax year in which the participant attains age 70½ or any later year.

Annual Contribution Limits Changes in the tax code have substantially increased the annual contribution limits to an IRA plan. Special catch-up rules also allow older workers to make additional contributions. The catch-up provisions are designed to help older workers who have saved little or nothing for retirement.

For 2007, the maximum annual contribution is $4000 or 100 percent of earned compensation, whichever is less. Older workers age 50 and over can contribute an additional $1000, or a maximum of $5000. For 2008, the maximum annual contribution limit will increase to $5000. For workers age 50 or over, the maximum contribution limit will increase to $6000. After 2008, the annual IRA contribution limit will be indexed for inflation in increments of $500.

Income Tax Deduction of Traditional IRA Contributions Traditional IRA contributions may be (1) fully income-tax deductible, (2) partly deductible, or (3) not deductible at all. A full deduction is allowed in two general situations.

First, a worker who is not an active participant in an employer's retirement plan for any part of the year can make a fully deductible IRA contribution up to the annual maximum limit. As noted earlier, for 2007, the maximum tax-deductible IRA contribution is the lower of $4000 ($5000 if age 50 or older), or 100 percent of compensation.

Second, even if the worker is actively participating in the employer's retirement plan, the IRA contribution is fully or partly deductible if the worker's modified adjusted gross income is below certain thresholds. Modified adjusted gross income generally is the adjusted gross income figure shown on your tax return without taking into account the IRA deduction and certain other items.[5] For 2007, the annual threshold limits are $50,000–$60,000 for single taxpayers. For 2007, the annual threshold limits for married taxpayers are $80,000–$100,000. For example, a single worker with a modified adjusted gross income of $50,000 could deduct the entire IRA contribution. However, a single worker with a modified adjusted gross income of $55,000 could deduct only one-half of the IRA contribution.

Taxpayers with incomes that exceed the phase-out limits can contribute to a traditional IRA but cannot deduct their contributions. This type of IRA is called a **nondeductible IRA.** In such cases, a Roth IRA (discussed later) should be considered.

Spousal IRA   In many families, a married worker is an active participant in the employer's retirement plan, but the other spouse is not an active participant. A **spousal IRA** *allows a spouse who is not in the paid labor force or a low-earning spouse to make a fully deductible contribution to a traditional IRA up to the annual dollar limit even though the other spouse is covered under a retirement plan at work.* For 2006, the maximum annual IRA deduction for a spouse who is not an active participant is $4000, ($5000 if age 50 or older) even if the other spouse is covered under a retirement plan at work. Eligibility for a full deduction is limited to married couples with modified adjusted gross incomes of $150,000 or less (indexed for inflation). The tax deduction is phased out for married couples with modified adjusted gross incomes between $150,000 and $160,000 (indexed for inflation).

For example, Josh, age 35, is covered under a Section 401(k) retirement plan at work. His wife, Ashley, age 32, is a full-time homemaker. For 2006, their modified adjusted gross income is $125,000. For 2006, Ashley can make a tax-deductible IRA contribution of $4000 because she is not considered an active participant, and the couple's combined modified adjusted gross income is less than $150,000. However, Josh cannot make a tax-deductible contribution because his income exceeds the income threshold for active participants.

Tax Penalty for Premature Distributions   With certain exceptions, distributions from a traditional IRA before age 59½ are considered to be premature distributions. A 10 percent tax penalty must be paid on the amount of the distribution included in gross income. However, the penalty tax does not apply to distributions that result from any of the following:

- Death or disability of the individual
- Substantially equal payments paid over the life expectancy of the individual or the individual and his or her beneficiary
- Portions of any distributions treated as a return of nondeductible contributions
- Distributions used to pay for unreimbursed medical expenses in excess of 7½ percent of adjusted gross income
- Distributions to pay health insurance premiums for a worker separated from employment
- Distributions to pay for qualified education expenses
- Qualified acquisition costs for a first-time home buyer (maximum of $10,000)

Distributions from a traditional IRA must start no later than April 1 of the year following the calendar year in which the individual attains age 70½. The funds can be withdrawn in a lump sum or in installments. A minimum annual distribution requirement must be met. The minimum annual distribution payment is based on the life expectancy of the individual or the joint life expectancy of the individual and his or her beneficiary. The Internal Revenue Service (IRS) has developed life expectancy tables for purposes of determining the minimum annual distribution. If the distributions are less than the amount required by law, a 50 percent excise tax is imposed on the excess accumulation. The purpose of this requirement is to force participants in traditional IRAs to have the funds paid out over a reasonable period so that the federal government can collect taxes on the tax-deferred amounts.

Taxation of Distributions   Distributions from a traditional IRA are taxed as ordinary income, except for any nondeductible IRA contributions, which are received income-tax free. Part of the distribution is not taxable if nondeductible contributions are made. The other part is taxable and must be included in the taxpayer's income. A complex formula and an IRS worksheet must be used to compute the nontaxable and taxable portions of each distribution.

In addition, as noted earlier, a 10 percent tax penalty applies to premature distributions taken before age 59½.

Establishing a Traditional IRA Traditional IRAs can be established with a variety of financial organizations. You can set up an IRA with a bank, mutual fund, stock brokerage firm, or life insurer. Contributions to a traditional IRA can be made anytime during the year or up to the due date for filing a tax return, not including extensions.

There are two types of traditional IRAs: (1) an individual retirement account, and (2) an individual retirement annuity.

- *Individual Retirement Account.* An individual retirement account is a trust or custodial account set up for the exclusive benefit of the account holder or beneficiaries. The trustee or custodian must be a bank, a federally insured credit union, a savings and loan institution, or an entity approved by the IRS to act as trustee or custodian. Contributions must be in cash, except for rollover contributions (discussed later) that can be in the form of property other than cash. No part of the contributions can be used to purchase a life insurance policy. Likewise, IRA assets cannot be pledged as collateral for a loan.
- *Individual Retirement Annuity.* A traditional IRA can also be established by purchasing an individual retirement annuity from a life insurer. The annuity must meet certain requirements. The annuity owner's interest in the contract must be nonforfeitable. The contract must be nontransferable by the owner. In addition, the annuity must permit flexible premiums so that if earnings change, the IRA contributions can be changed as well. Contributions cannot exceed the annual maximum limit, and the distributions must begin by April 1 of the year following the year in which the annuity owner reaches age 70½.

IRA Investments IRA contributions can be invested in a variety of investments, including certificates of deposit, mutual funds, and individual stocks and bonds in a self-directed brokerage account. Contributions can also be invested in U.S. gold and silver coins and certain precious metals. However, the contributions cannot be invested in insurance contracts or collectibles, such as baseball cards or antiques.

IRA Rollover Account A *rollover* is a tax-free distribution of cash or other property from one retirement plan, which is then deposited into another retirement plan. The amount you roll over is tax free but generally becomes taxable when the new plan pays out that amount to you or to your beneficiary. For example, if you quit your job and receive a lump-sum distribution from your employer's qualified retirement plan, the funds can be rolled over or deposited into a special **IRA rollover account.** If you receive the funds directly, the employer must withhold 20 percent for federal income taxes. The withholding can be deferred, however, if the employer transfers the funds directly into the IRA rollover account.

Roth IRA

A **Roth IRA** is another type of IRA that provides substantial tax advantages. The annual contribution limits discussed earlier for a traditional IRA also apply to a Roth IRA.

The annual contributions to a Roth IRA are not tax deductible. However, the investment income accumulates income-tax free, and qualified distributions are not taxable if certain requirements are met. A qualified distribution is any distribution from a Roth IRA that (1) is made after a five-year holding period beginning with the first tax year for which a Roth contribution is made, and (2) is made for any of the following reasons:

- The individual is age 59½ or older.
- The individual is disabled.
- The distribution is paid to a beneficiary or to the estate after the individual's death.
- The distribution is used to pay qualified first-time home-buyer expenses (maximum of $10,000).

Unlike a traditional IRA, contributions to a Roth IRA can be made after age 70½, and the minimum distribution rules after attainment of age 70½ do not apply to Roth IRAs.

Income Limits For 2006, the maximum Roth IRA contribution is limited to single taxpayers with modified adjusted gross incomes of $95,000 or less, and to married couples filing jointly with modified adjusted gross incomes of $150,000 or less. Maximum annual Roth contributions are phased out for single taxpayers with modified adjusted gross incomes between $95,000 and $110,000, and for married couples filing jointly with modified adjusted gross incomes between $150,000 and $160,000. The income limits are indexed for inflation.

Conversion to a Roth IRA   A traditional IRA can be converted to a Roth IRA. Although the amount converted is taxed as ordinary income, qualified distributions from a Roth IRA are received income-tax free. The right to convert is limited to taxpayers with annual adjusted gross incomes of $100,000 or less. However, beginning in 2010, the $100,000 income limit on converting a traditional IRA to a Roth IRA will be eliminated. As such, wealthier taxpayers will be able to convert their traditional IRAs to a Roth IRA. Many investment firms provide interactive calculators on their Web sites to determine if conversion to a Roth IRA is financially desirable.

Adequacy of IRA Funds   The IRA assets can be paid out as income when the worker retires. However, unless a life annuity is purchased, the retiree faces the risk of still being alive after the IRA account is exhausted. The duration of benefit payments, however, depends on the rate of return on the invested assets after the worker retires and withdrawal rates. Because retired workers can spend 25 or 30 years in retirement, or even longer, financial planners generally recommend that the initial withdrawal rate should be limited to 4 to 5 percent of the IRA assets. Traditionally, tables have been prepared that show how long your IRA funds will last based on average rates of return on the invested assets and annual withdrawal rates (see Exhibit 14.4). The problem, however, is that *such tables assume that the average rate of return remains constant over the projection period*. In reality, this is incorrect because actual returns will vary significantly depending on fluctuations in the stock market, bond market, and other security markets. To deal with this problem, many financial planners now use Monte Carlo simulation techniques that give a more realistic outlook of the

EXHIBIT 14.4
How Long the Money Will Last (in years)

Withdrawal	Rate of Return											
	1%	2%	3%	4%	5%	6%	7%	8%	9%	10%	11%	12%
12%	7	8	8	8	8	9	9	10	10	11	12	13
11	8	8	9	9	9	10	10	11	12	13	14	15
10	9	9	10	10	10	11	12	13	14	15	17	19
9	10	10	11	11	12	13	14	15	16	18	21	26
8	11	11	12	13	14	15	16	18	20	24	30	*
7	12	13	14	15	16	18	20	22	27	36	*	*
6	14	15	16	18	19	22	25	31	44	*	*	
5	17	18	20	22	24	29	36	*	*	*		
4	20	22	25	28	33	42	*	*	*			
3	25	28	33	39	*	*	*	*				
2	35	40	50	*	*	*	*					
1	*	*	*	*	*	*						

NOTE: For example, if you have saved $700,000 for retirement and initially withdraw 4 percent of the money ($28,000), your money will last 42 years, assuming a 6 percent annual return. The table assumes that your initial withdrawal is increased each year to keep up with an inflation rate of 3 percent, the historical average.

SOURCE: Kiplinger's Personal Finance Website (www.kiplinger.com). © October 1, 1998. The Kiplinger Washington Editor's, Inc.

INSIGHT 14.3

Will You Have Enough Money at Retirement? Monte Carlo Simulations Can Be Helpful

T.Rowe Price has an interactive Retirement Income Calculator on its Web site (www.troweprice.com) that gives you a more realistic evaluation of the adequacy of your retirement funds. Instead of basing calculations on a single average rate of return over the entire retirement period, the Monte Carlo technique generates 500 computer simulations of what may happen hypothetically to your assets over a specified retirement period. Each simulation produces a financial result based on market upswings and downswings of various lengths and intensities, and different combinations of stocks, bonds, and short-term investments.

Projections based on a fixed annual rate of return over the entire retirement period can result in returns that are substantially different from the projected returns based on the Monte Carlo simulations. Theoretically, an 11% return one year and a 7% return the next year will average 9%, but the actual returns you experience may be quite different from the averages when it comes to real-world investing.

For example, assume that you have $100 to invest and that you will earn 10% each year. At the end of the first year, you will have $110 ($100 times 110%), and by the end of the second year, you will have $121 ($110 times 110%). But what happens if instead you lose 5% the first year and gain 25% in the second year? You still have an average return of 10%, but look at what happens to your financial position. *At the end of the first year, you will have only $95 ($100 times 95%), and by the end of the second year, you will have only $118.75 (instead of $121). The average return is the same in both cases, but the actual returns have produced different financial results.* Multiply these results by thousands of dollars over dozens of different market conditions, while factoring in regular annual withdrawals, and you can see how the differences pile up.

The box below illustrates one example of the Monte Carlo simulation technique based on the Retirement Income Calculator. A married male, age 67, with $500,000 of assets desires $3000 monthly to be paid over a 25-year retirement period with a success rate of 99%. Any simulation is considered a success if you have at least one dollar in your account at the end of the retirement period. A 99% success rate means you will have attained your goal in 495 of the 500 simulations. In the illustration, the desired income goal of $3000 monthly will not be met. The simulation results indicate that the monthly retirement withdrawal should not exceed $1750 to have a success rate of 99%.

Retirement Income Calculator

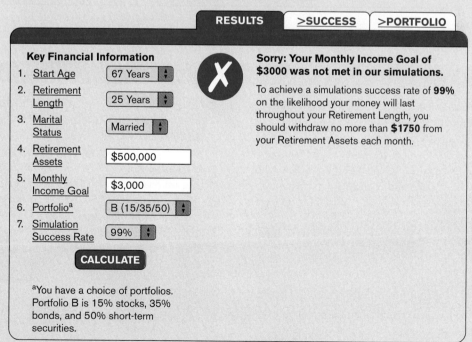

RESULTS   **>SUCCESS**   **>PORTFOLIO**

Key Financial Information

1. Start Age — 67 Years
2. Retirement Length — 25 Years
3. Marital Status — Married
4. Retirement Assets — $500,000
5. Monthly Income Goal — $3,000
6. Portfolio[a] — B (15/35/50)
7. Simulation Success Rate — 99%

CALCULATE

[a]You have a choice of portfolios. Portfolio B is 15% stocks, 35% bonds, and 50% short-term securities.

Sorry: Your Monthly Income Goal of $3000 was not met in our simulations.

To achieve a simulations success rate of **99%** on the likelihood your money will last throughout your Retirement Length, you should withdraw no more than **$1750** from your Retirement Assets each month.

SOURCE: Adapted from T. Rowe Price, "Tutorial," *Retirement Income Calculator.* Calculations are based on the Retirement Income Calculator.

future. These techniques simulate a wide variety of potential market outcomes that take into account fluctuations in market returns and different invest-

ment portfolios. Insight 14.3 provides an example of the Monte Carlo simulation technique of one financial planning investment firm.

CASE APPLICATION 1

Investors can invest in a wide variety of annuities and can also use different annuity settlement options to meet specific retirement needs. For each of the following retirement objectives, identify either (1) a specific annuity or (2) an annuity settlement option that can be used to meet the objective. Treat each situation separately.

a. James, age 35, is a sales representative and plans to retire at age 67. His monthly income varies. He would like to invest in an annuity that allows him to change the frequency and amount of premium payments.
b. Nancy, age 67, plans to retire in six months. She has $200,000 in a savings account. She would like to receive lifetime monthly income that is guaranteed.
c. Jennifer, age 63, plans to retire in 90 days. She has $100,000 to invest in an annuity and would like to receive lifetime monthly income to supplement her

Social Security benefits. However, she is concerned that she might die before she receives back the amount invested.
d. Fred, age 70, recently retired and has $50,000 to invest for additional income. He wants the retirement benefits to be protected against the risk of inflation.
e. Mary, age 75, is a widow with no dependents who needs additional retirement income. She has $25,000 to invest in an annuity. She wants to receive the maximum amount of monthly annuity income possible.
f. Kathy, age 32, would like to invest in the stock market, but she is conservative and risk averse. She would like to participate in any stock market gains, but she also wants her principal guaranteed against loss.

CASE APPLICATION 2

Scott and Allison are married and file a joint tax return. Scott is a graduate student who works part-time and earned $15,000 in 2007. He is not eligible to participate in his employer's retirement plan because he is a part-time worker. Allison is a high school teacher who earned $45,000 in 2007 and is an active participant in the school district's retirement plan. Assume you are a financial planner and the couple asks for your advice. Based on the preceding facts, answer each of the following questions.

a. Is Scott eligible to establish and deduct contributions to a traditional IRA? Explain your answer.
b. Is Allison eligible to establish and deduct contributions to a traditional IRA? Explain your answer.

c. Assume that Scott graduates and the couple's modified adjusted gross income is $120,000. Both Scott and Allison participate in their employers' retirement plans. Can either Scott or Allison, or both, establish a Roth IRA? Explain your answer.
d. Allison has a baby and withdraws from the labor force to raise the child. She is no longer an active participant in the school district's retirement plan. Scott receives a promotion and continues to participate in his employer's retirement plan. His annual salary is $110,000. Can Allison make a tax-deductible contribution to a traditional IRA? Explain your answer.
e. Explain to Scott and Allison the advantages of a Roth IRA over a traditional IRA.

SUMMARY

- An annuity provides periodic payments to an annuitant, which continue for either a fixed period or for the duration of a designated life or lives. The fundamental purpose of a life annuity is to provide lifetime income that cannot be outlived.

- A *fixed annuity* pays periodic income payments to an annuitant that are guaranteed and fixed in amount. A fixed annuity can be purchased so that the income payments start immediately, or the payments can be deferred to some later date. Deferred annuities typically provide for flexible premiums.

- Annuity settlement options typically include the following:

  Cash

  Life income (no refund)

  Life income with guaranteed payments

  Installment refund option

  Joint-and-survivor annuity option

- A *variable annuity* pays a lifetime income, but the income payments vary depending on the investment experience of the subaccount in which the premiums are invested. The purpose of this type of annuity is to provide an inflation hedge by maintaining the real purchasing power of the periodic payments.

- During the *accumulation period*, variable annuity premiums purchase accumulation units, which are then converted into *annuity units* at retirement. The number of annuity units remains constant during retirement, but the value of the annuity units changes periodically so that the income payments will change over time.

- Variable annuities typically pay a guaranteed death benefit if the annuitant dies before retirement. The typical death benefit is the higher of two amounts: the amount invested in the contract or the value of the account at the time of death.

- Variable annuities have numerous fees and charges. These charges include an investment management fee, a charge for administrative expenses, a management and expense risk charge for the guaranteed death benefit and other guarantees, and a surrender charge that declines over time. In the aggregate, total fees and expenses can be substantial.

- An *equity-indexed annuity* is a fixed, deferred annuity that allows the annuity owner to participate in the growth of the stock market. It also provides downside protection against the loss of principal and prior interest earnings if the annuity is held to term.

- The key elements of an equity-indexed annuity are (1) the participation rate, (2) the maximum cap rate, (3) the indexing method used, and (4) the guaranteed minimum value.

- An *exclusion ratio* is used to determine the nontaxable and taxable portions of the periodic annuity payments. The exclusion ratio is determined by dividing the investment in the contract by the expected return.

- The major types of IRAs are (1) a traditional IRA and (2) a Roth IRA.

- A *traditional IRA* allows workers to deduct part or all of their IRA contributions. The investment income accumulates income-tax free on a tax-deferred basis, and the distributions are taxed as ordinary income.

- To be eligible for a traditional IRA, the participant must have taxable compensation and be younger than age 70½.

- For 2007, the maximum annual IRA contribution for an individual worker is limited to $4000 ($5000 if age 50 or older) or 100 percent of earned income, whichever is less.

- IRA contributions to a traditional IRA are income-tax deductible if the participant (1) is not an active participant in an employer-sponsored retirement plan or (2) has taxable compensation below certain income thresholds.

- Distributions from a traditional IRA are taxed as ordinary income, except for any nondeductible IRA contributions, which are received income-tax free.

- With certain exceptions, distributions from a traditional IRA before age 59½ are considered to be a premature distribution. A 10 percent tax penalty must be paid on the amount of the distribution included in gross income.

- Distributions from a traditional IRA must start no later than April 1 of the year following the calendar year in which the individual attains age 70½.

- IRA contributions to a *Roth IRA* are not income-tax deductible. However, the investment income accumulates free of taxation, and qualified distributions are received income-tax free if certain requirements are met.

- A qualified distribution from a Roth IRA is any distribution that (1) is made after a five-year holding period beginning with the first tax year for which a Roth contribution is made, and (2) is paid when the individual attains age 59½, becomes disabled, dies, or is used to pay qualified first-time home-buyer expenses. Unlike a traditional IRA, contributions to a Roth IRA can be made after age 70½, and the minimum distribution rules after attainment of age 70½ do not apply.

KEY CONCEPTS AND TERMS

Accumulation period
Accumulation unit
Annuitant
Annuity
Annuity settlement
  options
Annuity unit
Cash refund option
Deferred annuity
Equity-indexed
  annuity
Exclusion ratio
Fixed annuity
Flexible-premium
  annuity
Immediate annuity
Individual retirement
  account (IRA)
Inflation-indexed annuity
  option
Installment refund
  option
IRA rollover account

Joint-and-survivor
  annuity option
Life annuity
  (no refund)
Life annuity with
  guaranteed payments
Liquidation period
Nondeductible IRA
Roth IRA
Single-premium
  deferred annuity
Spousal IRA
Traditional IRA
Variable annuity

REVIEW QUESTIONS

1. How does an annuity differ from life insurance?

2. Describe the major characteristics of a fixed annuity.

3. Identify the annuity settlement options that are typically found in a fixed annuity.

4. Describe the basic characteristics of a variable annuity.

5. Explain the major characteristics of an equity-indexed annuity.

6. Explain the eligibility requirements for a traditional IRA.

7. What are the annual contribution limits to an IRA?

8. Explain the basic characteristics of a traditional IRA.

9. Describe the major characteristics of a Roth IRA.

10. What is an IRA rollover?

APPLICATION QUESTIONS

1. Although both fixed and variable annuities can provide lifetime income to annuitants, they differ in important ways. Compare and contrast (1) a fixed annuity with (2) a variable annuity with respect to each of the following:
   a. Determining how the premiums are invested
   b. Stability of income payments after retirement
   c. Death benefits if the annuitant dies before retirement

2. An equity-indexed annuity and a variable annuity are both similar and different in many respects.
   a. Explain the major similarities between an equity-indexed annuity and a variable annuity.
   b. Identify the major differences between an equity-indexed annuity and a variable annuity.

3. Mario, age 65, purchased an immediate annuity for $120,000 that pays a lifetime monthly income of $1000. The annuity has no refund feature. Based on the IRS actuarial table, Mario has a life expectancy of 20 years. If Mario receives 12 monthly payments of $1000 the first year, how much taxable income must he report on his tax return?

4. Travis, age 25, graduated from college and obtained a position as a tax accountant. He is ineligible to participate in his employer's retirement plan for one year.
   a. Assume that Travis has a starting salary of $55,000 for 2007 and does not participate in the employer's retirement plan. Is Travis eligible to establish a traditional tax-deductible IRA? Explain your answer.
   b. Assume the same facts in (a). Is Travis eligible to establish a Roth IRA? Explain your answer.

5. A traditional IRA and a Roth IRA have both similarities and differences. Compare and contrast (1) a traditional IRA with (2) a Roth IRA with respect to each of the following:
   a. Income-tax treatment of IRA contributions and distributions
   b. Income limits for eligibility

c. Determining how the IRA contributions are invested

d. Eligibility, if any, of a spouse who is not in the paid labor force to make an IRA contribution

INTERNET RESOURCES

- **Annuity.com** provides annuity quotes online and timely information about fixed, equity-indexed, variable, and other tax-deferred annuities. Visit the site at

  http://www.annuity.com

- **Annuityshopper.com** provides online annuity rates for immediate annuities from major insurers. The site claims consumers can save thousands of dollars by shopping for immediate annuities through its service. Visit the site at

  http://www.annuityshopper.com

- **Charles Schwab** provides informative articles and information on retirement planning, annuities, and individual retirement accounts (IRAs). Visit the site at

  http://www.schwab.com

- **Fidelity Investments** offers timely information on retirement planning, annuities, and IRAs, including interactive calculators for making IRA decisions. Visit the site at

  http://www.fidelity.com

- **ImmediateAnnuities.com** claims it is the nation's leading annuity broker. The company helps consumers purchase safe and reliable life income annuities for their retirement. Visit the site at

  www.immediateannuities.com

- **Insure.com** provides timely information on annuities, IRAs, and other insurance products. Visit the site at

  http://www.insure.com

- The **Roth IRA Web site** is devoted to Roth IRAs and provides a considerable amount of consumer information on this type of IRA. The site provides links to articles, books, tapes, calculators, IRS documents, and a message board on Roth IRAs. Visit the site at

  http://www.rothira.com

- **TIAA-CREF** is an excellent source of accurate information on retirement planning, annuities, and IRAs. Visit the site at

  http://www.tiaa-cref.org

- The **Vanguard Group** provides timely information on variable annuities, IRAs, and retirement planning. Visit the site at

  http://www.vanguard.com

SELECTED REFERENCES

Black, Kenneth Jr., and Harold D. Skipper, Jr. *Life & Health Insurance,* 13th ed. Upper Saddle River, NJ: Prentice-Hall, 2000, ch. 8.

Graves, Edward E., ed. *McGill's Life Insurance,* 6th ed. Bryn Mawr, PA: The American College, 2007.

Kaster, Nicholas, and Glenn Sulzer. *Saving for the Future, Roth and Traditional IRAs.* Chicago, IL: CCH, Inc., 2002.

Leeuwenburg, Patsy, et al. *Annuity Principles and Products,* 2nd ed. Atlanta, GA: LOMA, 2004.

Littell, David A., and Kenn Beam Tacchino. *Planning for Retirement Needs,* 8th ed. Bryn Mawr, PA: The American College, 2006

Kaster, Nicholas, et al. *2006 U.S. Master Pension Guide.* Chicago, IL: CCH Inc., 2006.

NOTES

1. A deduction for administrative expenses and sales expenses is ignored.

2. The actual number of annuity units will depend on the market value of the account, attained age of the annuitant, number of guaranteed payments, conversion rates, assumed investment return, and other factors.

3. The 10 percent penalty tax does not apply to individuals who attain age $59\frac{1}{2}$ or become totally disabled; when the distribution is received by a beneficiary or estate after the individual dies; when the distribution is part of substantially equal payments paid over the life expectancy of the individual or individual and beneficiary; or when the distribution is from an annuity contract under a qualified personal injury settlement. Certain other exceptions also apply.

4. The procedure for determining the total cost of an annuity is complex. Total cost must be reduced by (1) any refunded premiums, rebates, dividends, or unrepaid loans that you received by the later of the annuity starting date or the date on which you received your first payment; (2) any additional premiums paid for double indemnity or disability payments; and (3) any other tax-free amounts you received under the contract or plan before the later of the dates specified in item 1. In addition, an adjustment must be made for any refund features in the annuity. The IRS provides worksheets for making these calculations.

5. Modified adjusted gross income is essentially the adjusted gross income figure shown on your tax return without taking into account any IRA deductions, student loan interest deduction, foreign earned income exclusion, foreign housing exclusion or deduction, exclusion of qualified bond interest, and exclusion of employer-paid adoption expenses.

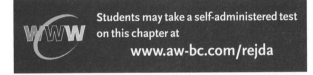

Students may take a self-administered test on this chapter at

www.aw-bc.com/rejda

CHAPTER 15

INDIVIDUAL HEALTH INSURANCE COVERAGES

"They had me on the operating table all day. They looked into my stomach, my gallbladder, they examined everything inside of me. Know what they decided? I need glasses."

Joe E. Lewis

LEARNING OBJECTIVES

After studying this chapter, you should be able to

◆ Explain the major health-care problems in the United States.

◆ Explain the basic characteristics of individual major medical insurance.

◆ Identify the basic characteristics of health savings accounts (HSA).

◆ Describe the key characteristics of long-term care insurance.

◆ Describe the major characteristics of disability-income insurance contracts.

◆ Describe the guidelines to follow when purchasing individual health insurance.

Jennifer, age 32, is a self-employed interior decorator who was diagnosed as having lung cancer that required immediate surgery. The surgeon's fee, hospital expenses, chemotherapy, and other medical bills totaled $100,000. Like many self-employed workers, Jennifer did not have any health insurance. In addition, she was unable to work for several months and did not have a disability-income insurance policy to restore her lost earnings. In short, because of the lack of health insurance, Jennifer was exposed to serious economic insecurity as result of the unexpected surgery.

As Jennifer's experience demonstrates, health insurance should be given high priority in any personal risk management program. If you are seriously ill or injured, you face two major problems: payment of your medical bills and the loss of earned income. A serious illness can result in catastrophic medical bills. Without proper protection, you may have to pay thousands of dollars out of your own pocket for medical bills. In addition, a lengthy disability can result in the loss of substantial amounts of earned income.

This chapter is the first of two chapters dealing with private health insurance. The discussion in Chapter 15 is limited to individual health and disability-income insurance coverages. Chapter 16 discusses the various group health insurance plans provided by employers. Although group health insurance accounts for more than 90 percent of the total medical expense premiums paid, a considerable amount of individual insurance is still sold today. Individual plans are especially important for individuals and families who are not covered by group insurance.

This chapter begins with a discussion of the health-care problems in the United States. The chapter also discusses individual health insurance coverages to deal with these problems. These coverages include hospital-surgical plans, major medical insurance, health savings accounts, long-term care insurance, and disability-income insurance. The chapter concludes with a discussion of guidelines to follow when individual health insurance is purchased.

HEALTH-CARE PROBLEMS IN THE UNITED STATES

The United States provides the highest quality health care in the world, and the health of Americans has improved remarkably. Despite major breakthroughs in medicine, the health-care delivery system is a source of considerable frustration. The present system has four major problems:

- Rising health care expenditures
- Large number of uninsured persons in the population
- Uneven quality of medical care
- Considerable waste and inefficiency

Rising Health-Care Expenditures

Total health care-expenditures in the United States have increased substantially over time and are out-stripping the growth in the economy. *According to the Centers for Medicare & Medicaid Services, estimated national health expenditures totaled $ 2.33 trillion in 2007, or 16.8 percent of the nation's gross domestic product. National health expenditures are projected to reach $4 trillion in 2015 or 20 percent of the gross domestic product.*[1] Thus, roughly one in six dollars of the nation's income is now spent on health care.

Rising health-care spending has a significant impact on the cost of health insurance, especially group health insurance. Group health insurance premiums are rising more rapidly than the overall infla-tion rate and increases in workers' earnings, which make it more difficult for employers to provide health insurance to their workers (see Exhibit 15.1).

Several factors account for the increase in health-care spending. According to the Blue Cross and Blue Shield Association, the key drivers of rising health-care costs currently are the following: [2]

- *Rising outpatient costs.* Outpatient costs are the fastest growing component of health-care costs. Together, outpatient and inpatient hospital ex-penditures accounted for over half of the growth in private health-care spending between 2002 and 2003.
- *Rising inpatient hospital costs.* Rising inpatient costs are due primarily to increased hospital expenses per inpatient stay. The rising costs per admission are partly the result of increased use

ExHIBIT **15.1**

Increases in Health Insurance Premiums Compared to Other Indicators, 1988–2005

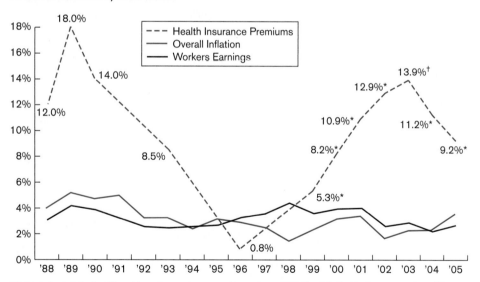

*Estimate is statistically different from the previous year shown at p < 0.05. No statistical tests were conducted for years prior to 1999.

†Estimate is statistically different from the previous year shown at p < 0.1. No statistical tests were conducted for years prior to 1999.

NOTE: Data are from KFF/HRET Survey of Employer-Sponsored Health Benefits, 1999–2005; KPMG Survey of Employer-Sponsored Health Benefits, 1993, 1996; The Health Insurance Association of America (HIAA), 1988, 1989, 1990; Bureau of Labor Statistics, Consumer Price Index, (U.S. City Average of Annual Inflation, April to April, 1988–2005; Bureau of Labor Statistics, Seasonally Adjusted Data from the Current Employment Statistics Survey, April to April, 1988–2005.

SOURCE: "Employer Health Benefits 2005 Annual Survey," (7315), The Henry J. Kaiser Family Foundation and Health Research and Educational Trust, September 2005. This information was reprinted with permission from the Henry J. Kaiser Family Foundation. The Kaiser Family Foundation, based in Menlo Park, California, is a nonprofit, private operating foundation focus-ing on the major helath care issues facing the nation and is not associated with Kaiser Permanente of Kaiser Industries.

of expensive technology, higher labor costs, and the consolidation of hospitals.

- *Rising cost of prescription drugs.* Prescription drugs are another major component of health-care costs. Pharmaceutical costs accounted for an estimated 12.2 percent of all health-care expenditures in 2005, up from 9.3 percent in 2000. The growth in pharmaceutical costs is due to inflation, introduction of new drugs, increased use of drugs, and changes in the therapeutic mix of drugs. Generic drugs, however, are a desirable offset to increases in drug costs.

- *Rising cost of physician services.* Physician services are the slowest growing component of health-care costs. However, physician costs account for about one-third of all health-care spending. Also, physicians are increasingly involved in ambulatory surgery centers and specialty hospitals.

Large Number of Uninsured Persons in the Population

Another serious problem is the large number of persons who are uninsured for health care. *According to the 2006 Current Population Survey, 46.6 million people, or 15.9 percent of the population, had no health insurance coverage in 2005, up from 15.6 percent in 2004.*[3] Groups with large numbers of uninsured persons include the following:[4]

- *Foreign born (33.6%)*
- *Hispanic origin (any race) (32.7%)*
- *Young adults, ages 18 to 24 (30.6%)*
- *Household income under $25,000 (24.4%)*
- *Blacks (19.6%)*
- *Asians (17.9%)*

In addition, many states have a high proportion of uninsured persons. Based on a three-year average, these states include Texas (24.6%), New Mexico (21.1%), Louisiana (18.7%), California (18.8%), and Oklahoma (19.5%).

Why are some people uninsured? One study of health-care costs by *USA Today*, Kaiser Family Foundation, and Harvard School of Public Health identified several reasons why adults have no health insurance. The major reason cited is affordability; health insurance is too expensive to purchase. Other reasons include refusal or denial of coverage, a belief that health insurance is not needed, and lack of knowledge on how to get health insurance (see Exhibit 15.2).

EXHIBIT 15.2
Reasons for Not Having Health Insurance

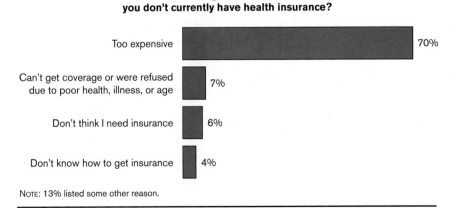

SOURCE: "Health Care Costs Survey," (7371), The USA Today/Kaiser Family Foundation/Harvard School of Public Health, August 2005. This information was reprinted with permission from the Henry J. Kaiser Family Foundation. The Kaiser Family Foundation, based in Menlo Park, California, is a nonprofit, private operating foundation focusing on the major helath care issues facing the nation and is not associated with Kaiser Permanente of Kaiser Industries.

Other reasons also explain why some people are uninsured. Many low-income people who are eligible for health-care coverage under the Medicaid program fail to sign up because they are not aware they are eligible. Some workers with relatively high incomes do not purchase health insurance because they view spending on health insurance as a low priority. Many younger people are healthy and believe that health insurance is unnecessary.

The sobering statistics show that large numbers of people in the United States are exposed to severe economic insecurity from poor health. Proposals for reducing the proportion of uninsured persons are endless and include universal health insurance; tax credits for workers to purchase health insurance; tax subsidies for small employers; state health insurance plans; expansion of Medicaid and Medicare; and numerous other proposals. It is beyond the scope of the text, however, to discuss these proposals in detail.

Uneven Quality of Medical Care

Another problem is that the quality of medical care varies widely depending on the physician, geographic location, and type of disease being treated. A report by the National Committee for Quality Assurance (NCQA) shows that there are "quality gaps" in the nation's health care system that prevent millions of patients from receiving the best medical care possible. The term "quality gap" means that millions of patients do not receive the care that medical science has shown to be effective in treating certain diseases, such as high blood pressure, diabetes, and smoking-related heart disease; stated differently, many doctors are not following the recommended guidelines in treating common ailments. As a result of the quality gap, the financial impact on the nation is severe. The NCQA concludes that quality gaps continue to result in 39,000–83,000 preventable deaths each year, between $2.8 billion and $4.2 billion in avoidable medical costs, up to 83 million sick days, and $13 billion in lost productivity.[5]

In addition, preventable in-hospital medical errors result in the deaths of thousands of patients each year. According to a HealthGrades study of 37 million patient records, an average of 195,000 people in the United States died from preventable hospi-

tal errors in each of the years 2000, 2001, and 2002. *According to HealthGrades, this number is the equivalent of the number of people who would die each year if 390 fully loaded jumbo jets crashed.*[6]

Waste and Inefficiency

A final problem is waste and inefficiency in the present system. The administrative costs of delivering health insurance benefits are excessively high; there is excessive paperwork by both health-care providers and insurers; claim forms are not uniform nationally; a considerable amount of medical care provided by physicians is considered inappropriate; defensive medicine by physicians often results in unnecessary tests and procedures; there is duplication of expensive technology in hospitals in many cities; and fraud and abuse by health-care providers are widespread.

INDIVIDUAL HEALTH INSURANCE COVERAGES

As stated earlier, most people with health insurance are covered under group health insurance plans. Group health insurance premiums account for more than 90 percent of all health insurance premiums. Chapter 16 discusses group health insurance coverages in some detail. However, individual coverages are also important. Millions of Americans are insured under individual medical expense plans. Some people are not employed and require individual coverage; workers retire and need supplemental health insurance; and college students frequently attain a limiting age under their parents' group health insurance plans and must obtain their own coverage. In addition, long-term-care insurance and disability-income insurance are important individual coverages that merit discussion. In this section, we discuss the following individual coverages:

- Hospital-surgical insurance
- Major medical insurance
- Health savings accounts
- Long-term care insurance
- Disability-income insurance

HOSPITAL-SURGICAL INSURANCE

Many older individual medical expense plans still in force are **hospital-surgical insurance** plans. These plans are also called basic plans because they cover routine medical expenses and are not designed to cover catastrophic losses. Lifetime aggregate limits are relatively low, such as $100,000. Maximum benefits for each illness are also relatively low, such as a maximum of $20,000 for each covered event. The types of medical expenses covered vary widely among insurers. Most policies cover the following:

- *Hospital expenses.* A typical policy covers *inpatient hospital expenses.* Some older plans pay actual room and board charges up to some maximum daily limit, such as $400 per day for a maximum of 365 days. Most insurers, however, have moved away from this approach. Newer plans cover the cost of a semiprivate room, subject to any deductible or coinsurance requirements.

  Individual plans also cover a variety of *miscellaneous hospital expenses,* such as X-rays, inpatient drugs, and laboratory tests. For example, the plan may pay 80 percent of the miscellaneous charges up to some maximum limit.
- *Surgical expenses.* Hospital-surgical plans also cover surgical expenses. Some older plans use a schedule approach by which common surgical procedures are listed in a schedule with a maximum dollar amount paid for each procedure. The current approach, however, is to reimburse surgeons on the basis of their usual **reasonable and customary charges.** Many insurers consider a fee to be reasonable and customary if it does not exceed the 80th or 90th percentile for a similar procedure performed by other surgeons in the same area. The insured must pay that portion of the fee that exceeds the upper limit.
- *Outpatient services.* Individual plans commonly cover certain *outpatient services,* such as emergency treatment within 72 hours of an injury; diagnostic X-rays, and lab expenses. The plans also have maximum limits on the amounts paid for outpatient services.
- *Physicians' visits.* Many plans provide coverage for physicians' visits, which pay for *nonsurgical treatment* provided by a physician to a patient while in the hospital. For example, a family physician may visit a patient who is hospitalized because of the flu.

At the present time, basic individual hospital-surgical plans have a limited presence in today's market and are relatively unimportant. Most basic plans still in existence are guaranteed renewable plans that do not permit an insurer to cancel. However, because of the rapid increase in health-care costs over time and low maximum benefits, relatively few individual basic plans are sold currently. Most new individual medical expense plans sold currently are major medical insurance plans.

MAJOR MEDICAL INSURANCE

Insureds often desire broader coverage than that provided by the basic coverages just discussed. **Major medical insurance** is designed to pay a high proportion of the covered expenses of a catastrophic illness or injury. A typical individual major medical policy has the following characteristics:

- Broad coverage
- High maximum limits
- Benefit period
- Deductible
- Coinsurance
- Exclusions

Broad Coverage

Major medical insurance provides broad coverage of all reasonable and necessary medical expenses and other related expenses from a covered illness or injury. The policy covers eligible expenses incurred while in the hospital, in the doctor's office, or at home. Eligible medical expenses include hospital room and board charges, miscellaneous hospital services and supplies, treatment by licensed physicians and surgeons, prescription drugs, durable medical equipment, and numerous other expenses.

High Maximum Limits

Major medical policies are written with high lifetime limits, such as $1 million, $2 million, $5 million, or some higher amount. Some plans have no maximum limits. High limits are necessary to meet the crushing financial burden of a major catastrophic illness or injury.

Benefit Period

The maximum amount paid under a major medical policy depends partly on the length of the benefit period. A **benefit period,** *such as three years, refers to the length of time that major medical benefits will be paid after the deductible is satisfied.* When the benefit period ends, the insured must then satisfy a new deductible to establish a new benefit period. For example, assume that Jennifer has a $1 million major medical expense policy with a $500 deductible and a three-year benefit period. Assume that she is severely injured in an auto accident and satisfies the deductible on the first day of her injury. A three-year benefit period for that illness is then established. At the end of three years, Jennifer must again satisfy a new deductible if the maximum amount of $1 million has not been paid.

The purpose of the benefit period is to provide a definite time period within which eligible medical expenses for a specific disease or injury must be incurred in order to be reimbursed under the policy.

Deductible

A major medical policy usually contains a deductible that must be satisfied before benefits are paid. The purpose of the deductible is to eliminate payment of small claims and the relatively high administrative expenses of processing small claims. By eliminating small claims, the insurer can provide high policy limits and still keep the premiums reasonable.

The following types of deductible provisions are commonly found in individual major medical policies:

- Calendar-year deductible
- Family deductible
- Common-accident provision

Most major medical policies have a calendar-year deductible. A **calendar-year deductible** *is an aggregate deductible that has to be satisfied only once during the calendar year.* All covered medical expenses incurred by the insured during the calendar

year can be applied toward the deductible. Once the deductible is met, no additional deductible has to be satisfied during the calendar year. To avoid paying two deductibles in a short period, most plans have a carryover provision. This provision means that unreimbursed medical expenses incurred during the last three months of the calendar year that are applied to this year's deductible can also be carried over and applied to next year's deductible.

The **family deductible** *specifies that medical expenses for all family members are accumulated for purposes of satisfying the deductible.* The accumulation period typically is one month, but a longer period could be used. For example, if medical expenses for the entire family exceed $500 during the month, the major medical policy starts to pay.

Individual major medical policies also contain a **common-accident provision.** *Only one deductible has to be satisfied if two or more family members are injured in a common accident, such as an auto accident.*

Coinsurance

Major medical policies contain a **coinsurance provision** *that requires the insured to pay a certain percentage of eligible medical expenses in excess of the deductible.* Coinsurance is also called a *percentage participation clause* in health insurance. A typical plan requires the insured to pay 20 percent or 25 percent of covered expenses in excess of the deductible. For example, assume that Megan has covered medical expenses in the amount of $10,500. She has a $1 million major medical policy with a $500 deductible and an 80-20 coinsurance provision. The insurer will pay $8000 of the total bill, and Megan will pay $2000 (plus the deductible). This is summarized as follows:

Covered expenses	$10,500
Less the deductible	−500
Remaining expenses	$10,000
80% paid by insurer	8000
20% paid by Megan	$ 2000

The purposes of the coinsurance clause are to reduce premiums and to prevent overutilization of policy benefits. Also, the insured is less likely to demand unnecessary medical services if he or she pays part of the cost.

Major medical policies also contain a **stop-loss limit** by which 100 percent of the eligible medical expenses are paid after the insured incurs a certain amount of out-of-pocket expenses, such as $2000. *The purpose of the stop-loss limit is to reduce the financial burden of a catastrophic loss.* For example, if Megan's covered medical expenses in excess of the deductible are $100,000 and the stop-limit is $2000, her major medical policy would pay $98,000. She would pay only $2000 (plus the deductible). Without the stop-limit, Megan would have to pay $20,000 (plus the deductible).

Exclusions

All major medical policies contain exclusions. Some common exclusions are as follows:

- Expenses caused by war or military conflict
- Elective cosmetic surgery
- Dental care, except as a result of an accident
- Eye and hearing examinations, eyeglasses, and hearing aids
- Pregnancy and childbirth, except complications of pregnancy (Maternity expenses can be covered by a rider.)
- Expenses covered by workers compensation and similar laws
- Services furnished by governmental agencies unless the patient has an obligation to pay
- Experimental surgery

To control cost, major medical plans typically contain **internal limits** for certain types of expenses. There may be annual or lifetime limits on the amount paid for certain diseases, such as alcoholism and drug addiction. For example, one plan limits inpatient coverage for alcoholism and drug addiction to no more than 45 days of treatment during any successive 12-month period.

Major Medical Insurance and Managed Care

Many individual major medical plans have incorporated elements of managed care into the plan design. Managed care is a generic term for medical expense plans that provide benefits to insureds in a cost-effective manner. For example, the plan may require precertification and approval for nonemergency admission into a hospital; certain types of surgery must be done on an outpatient basis, and an insured may be required to use a preferred provider or pay higher out-of-pocket costs for the benefits received. **Preferred providers** are physicians, hospitals, and other health-care providers who are part of a plan network and agree to provide medical services to plan members at discounted fees. Insureds who go outside the network for care must pay higher out-of-pocket costs for the care received.

HEALTH SAVINGS ACCOUNTS

Recent federal legislation allows all eligible persons under age 65 to establish health savings accounts and receive favorable income-tax treatment. A **health savings account (HSA)** *is a tax-exempt or custodial account established exclusively for the purpose of paying qualified medical expenses of the account beneficiary who is covered under a high-deductible health insurance plan.* Health savings accounts that receive favorable tax treatment have two components: (1) a high-deductible health insurance policy that covers catastrophic medical bills, and (2) an investment account from which the account holder can withdraw money tax-free for medical costs. These components are discussed below.

Eligibility Requirements To establish a qualified HSA and receive favorable tax treatment, you must meet certain requirements. First, you must be covered by a high-deductible health plan and must not be covered by any other comprehensive health plan that is not a qualified high-deductible plan. (This requirement does not apply to accident insurance, disability insurance, dental care, vision care, long-term care insurance, auto insurance, and certain other coverages.) Second, you must not be eligible for Medicare. Finally, you must not be claimed as a dependent on another person's tax return.

High-Deductible Health Plan The insurance is sold with a high deductible. For 2007, the *annual deductible* must be at least $1100 for an individual and $2200 for family coverage. The family deductible applies to the entire family and not to each family member. Qualified plans with higher annual deductibles are also available with reduced premiums. If the plan provides preventive services, such as a weight loss program, a deductible is not required. The deductible is indexed annually for inflation.

In addition, there is a maximum limit on annual *out-of-pocket expenses*. For 2007, annual out-of-pocket expenses, including the deductible and copayments, cannot exceed $5500 for an individual and $11,000 for a family. The out-of-pocket limits are adjusted annually for inflation. If the plan is a preferred provider organization (PPO), and you receive care outside the network, you will have higher out-of-pocket payments for deductibles and coinsurance.

The HSA may also have a *coinsurance requirement*. Although many HSA plans pay 100 percent of the covered expenses in excess of the deductible, some insureds prefer a lower premium plan with coinsurance. The coinsurance percentage is usually 20 percent of the covered costs in excess of the deductible up to some maximum annual limit. If you receive care outside the network, the coinsurance percentage is substantially higher, such as 40 percent.

Contribution Limits HSA contributions can be made by individuals, their employers, and family members. For 2007, total contributions for individual coverage are limited to the annual deductible but not to exceed $2850. Total contributions for family coverage are also limited to the annual deductible but not to exceed $5650. These amounts are adjusted annually for inflation. In addition, if you are between ages 55 and 65, you can make an additional catch-up contribution of $800, which will gradually increase to $1000 in 2009.

Favorable Tax Treatment The HSA investment account in a qualified plan receives favorable tax treatment. HSA contributions are income-tax deductible up to the annual limits described above. The tax deduction is "above the line," which means you do not have to itemize deductions on your tax return to deduct the contributions. *This means you are paying premiums with before-tax dollars.* In addition, investment earnings accumulate income-tax free, and distributions from the account are tax-free if used to pay for qualified medical expenses. However, distributions prior to age 65 for nonmedical purposes are subject to an income tax and a 10 percent tax

penalty. Once you attain age 65 or are covered under Medicare, you can no longer contribute to an HSA. However, you can still use the funds to pay for qualified medical expenses. If you are age 65 or older, you can also use the funds for nonmedical purposes, but the money used is taxable income.

Rationale for HSAs Proponents present numerous arguments for HSAs, which include the following:

- *If consumers have to pay for health care out of pocket, they will be more sensitive to health-care costs, will avoid unnecessary services, and will shop around for health care. As a result, health-care costs can be held down.*
- *Health insurance will be more affordable because of lower premiums, which will reduce the number of uninsured people.*
- *If medical bills are not incurred, money in the HSA account can be saved for retirement.*
- *Workers will still have health insurance if they change jobs or become unemployed.*

Critics of HSAs, however, present the following counterarguments:

- *The HSA tax breaks are geared toward people with higher incomes and are of limited value to low-income persons who are currently uninsured. A dollar deposited into an HSA will save 35 cents for someone in the 35 percent tax bracket but only 10 cents for a low-income person in the 10 percent tax bracket.*
- *Low income persons cannot afford to pay the high annual deductible until coverage begins and are unlikely to choose HSAs.*
- *HSAs are geared toward younger and healthier individuals who may decide not to join a traditional plan. However, unhealthy persons are more likely to remain in traditional plans. As a result, the pool of unhealthy workers may increase, which could increase premiums even more for individuals and employers who have traditional plans.*
- *HSAs will encourage insureds to forgo routine or preventive care. Good cost information often is not available.*
- *HSAs will not contain rising health care costs, and shopping for health care is not a reasonable option for most Americans (see Insight 15.1).*

INSIGHT 15.1

Health Savings Accounts Are
Not an Effective Way to Control Costs

Proponents of HSAs maintain that when consumers must spend money out of their own pockets on health care, they will avoid "unnecessary" health services and will shop for health-care bargains. In theory, this will create competition among health-care providers, forcing them to reduce their charges. This theory, however, is flawed. While consumers might end up buying less health care, it is doubtful that doctors and hospitals will reduce charges beyond the discounted rates insurance companies have already negotiated with them. In addition, even if consumers who spend their HSA dollars can successfully shop for health-care bargains (or forgo care), the amount saved would not be enough to affect system-wide health-care spending.

In reality, HSAs won't help contain rising health-care costs. Shopping for quality, affordable health care is simply not a reasonable option for the vast majority of Americans for a variety of reasons, including lack of knowledge, time, and available information. Instead, HSAs will encourage consumers to skip medical services, which could lead to catastrophic costs down the line. Instead of reducing overall costs, HSAs simply shift risk and costs from employers to workers.

- **Consumers lack the specialized knowledge required to choose among health care options.** Essential information about health-care quality and cost is unavailable to most consumers, so they will not have the information needed to make informed choices. Language barriers also present a barrier to shopping for care: about 45 million Americans have limited English proficiency. Most of those with limited English proficiency are Latino and Asian, and these numbers are increasing. Without the necessary information, consumers will not be able to protect their health while reducing the cost of their health care through "smart shopping."

- **Shopping for health care in not like shopping for a cheap television.** Electronics consumers may be willing to sacrifice quality for a cheaper price, but quality care is a necessity for every health-care consumer.

- **Individual consumers do not have the market clout to obtain the lowest prices.** A health-care consumer shopping for services would be treated as if he or she were uninsured. Without the negotiated discounts of a provider network, the uninsured can be charged more than twice as much as the insured for the same care.

- **HSAs may induce consumers to skip necessary services, leading to higher costs in the long run.** HSAs put consumers in the position of choosing between keeping money in their pockets or paying to see the doctor. Research has repeatedly shown that even modest increases in cost-sharing lead to consumers using fewer preventive and necessary services. Low-income people are even less likely to seek care if they must pay the full bill. When consumers wait until they are very sick to seek treatment, health-care costs rise significantly.

- **Rather than reduce costs, HSAs provide employers with a new way to pass additional costs on to workers.** Mercer Human Resource Consulting reports that, by 2006, nearly two-thirds of employers will contribute less than $500 to employees' HSAs. Of those employers, 39 percent will contribute nothing, leaving workers to meet high deductibles on their own. Rather than reducing costs, the burden will simply be shifted from employers to workers.

- **The savings that could result from consumer price sensitivity would be trivial compared to total health-care spending.** According to the Tax Policy Center, 95 percent of all medical expenditures from insured households would exceed HSA deductibles. People with chronic conditions account for the vast majority of total health-care spending. Consumers with chronic conditions have little in the way of flexibility to shop for cheaper care. Additionally, since there's no incentive for consumers to bargain hunt after they've reached their deductible, there's no reason to think HSAs will have a cost-cutting effect on 95 percent of medical spending. Ironically, the only way for HSAs to have a real effect on cost containment would be to drastically increase the minimum deductible so more households would face the pressure to save money.

Racial and ethnic minorities suffer disproportionately from chronic conditions and are thus less likely to benefit from HSAs. For example, African Americans and Latinos are twice as likely to suffer from diabetes as whites. Since racial and ethnic minorities are more likely to have acute or chronic conditions and are more likely to be low income, they are far less likely to benefit from HSA plans and far more likely to be harmed by high deductibles.

SOURCE: Excerpted from Families USA, *HSAs: Why High-Deductible Plans Are Not the Solution*, Issue Brief, January 2005.

LONG-TERM CARE INSURANCE

Long-term care insurance is another coverage that is rapidly growing in popularity. **Long-term care insurance** pays a daily or monthly benefit for medical or custodial care received in a nursing facility, in a hospital, or at home.

Chance of Entering a Nursing Home

Many older Americans will spend some time in a nursing home. *According to the National Association of Insurance Commissioners, about 44 percent of people attaining age 65 are expected to enter a nursing home at least once during their lifetime. Of those who enter a nursing home, about 53 percent will stay for one or more years.*[7] *The average length of time, however, for current residents is 2½ years.*[8]

The cost of long-term care in a nursing home is staggering. Most long-term facilities charge $60,000 to $90,000 or even more for each year of care. The Medicare program provides only limited assistance in paying for the cost of long-term care. The patient must require care in a skilled nursing facility, and only up to 100 days are covered. Custodial care is excluded altogether. In addition, most elderly are not initially eligible for long-term care under the Medicaid program, which is a welfare program that imposes strict eligibility requirements and a stringent means test. As a result, many older Americans have purchased long-term care policies to meet the crushing financial burden of an extended stay in a nursing facility.

Basic Characteristics

Most policies sold currently are tax-qualified to receive favorable income-tax treatment. Qualified policies generally have the following characteristics.[9]

Types of Policies   Long-term care policies generally can be classified into three major categories: (1) facility-only policies, (2) home health care only policies, and (3) comprehensive policies that combine care in a nursing facility and home health care into a single policy.

- A *facility-only policy* typically covers care in a nursing home, assisted-living facility, Alzheimer's facility, or hospice as long as the insured satisfies the benefit trigger (discussed later).
- A *home health care policy* covers care received outside of an institution and typically covers home health care, adult day care, and respite care. Respite care is a benefit that provides occasional full-time care to an insured who is receiving home health care services, which allows a caregiver to take a needed break.
- A *comprehensive policy* typically covers care in a nursing home, assisted living facility, and hospice and also makes available optional benefits for home health care and adult day care. All three types of policies generally provide for a care coordinator who evaluates the various options for providing care and recommends the most appropriate services for an insured.

Choice of Benefits   Purchasers of long-term care insurance have a choice of daily benefits, which typically range from $50 to $300 or more for each day of care. However, the daily benefit paid for home health care may be less than the benefits paid for nursing home care. Most policies are *reimbursement policies,* which reimburse the insured for actual charges up to some specified daily limit. For example, if the daily limit is $250 and actual charges are $200, the policy would pay only $200. Some policies, however, are *per diem* policies, which pay a fixed daily benefit amount regardless of the actual charges incurred. For example, if the daily limit is $300 and actual charges are $250, the policy would pay $300.

In addition, many insurers offer policies with *pooled benefits,* which provide a total dollar amount that can be used to pay for the different types of long-term care services. These policies usually have a daily, weekly, or monthly limit. For example, if the insured purchases a reimbursement policy with a daily benefit of $250 and a three-year benefit period, the pool of money would be $273,750. If actual daily charges are $250, the policy would pay benefits for a maximum of three years. However, if the daily cost of care is lower, the insured would receive benefits for more than three years.

Elimination Period   An **elimination period** is a waiting period during which time benefits are not paid. Elimination periods can range from zero to 365 days.

Common elimination periods are 30, 60, 100, or 180 days. A longer elimination period can substantially reduce premiums.

Eligibility for Benefits Tax-qualified policies have two *benefit triggers* that determine whether the insured is chronically ill and eligible for benefits. *The insured must meet only one of the two triggers to receive benefits.* The first trigger requires the insured to be unable to perform a certain number of **activities of daily living,** commonly called ADLs. The **ADLs** are eating, bathing, dressing, transferring from a bed to a chair, using the toilet, and maintaining continence. Benefits are paid if the insured cannot perform a certain number of ADLs listed in the policy without assistance from another person, such as two out of the six ADLs.

The second trigger is that the insured needs substantial supervision to be protected against threats to health and safety because of a *severe cognitive impairment.* For example, benefits can be triggered if the insured has a short- or long-term memory impairment; or becomes disoriented with respect to persons, place, time, or abstract reasoning; or has errors in judgment with respect to safety awareness.

Non-tax-qualified policies often have more liberal eligibility requirements and make benefits available if a *medical necessity trigger* is met. This means that benefits can be paid if a physician certifies that long-term care is needed even if the insured does not meet any of the benefit triggers described earlier. Also, nonqualified policies may have a different list of ADLs, and the insured may have to meet a smaller number of ADLs to qualify for benefits.

Inflation Protection Inflation can gradually erode the real purchasing power of the daily benefit. For example, a nursing home that charges $200 per day in 2007 might charge $350 or more for each day of care in 2021. Protection against inflation is especially important if the policy is purchased at a younger age.

Insurers use different methods to provide protection against inflation. One large insurer allows insureds to increase the daily benefit each year based on increases in the consumer price index (CPI). Evidence of insurability is not required, but premiums are increased accordingly. For example, if the daily benefit is $200, and the CPI increases 4 percent, the new daily benefit would be $208.

Another method is to automatically increase the initial daily benefit each year at some specified rate, such as 5 percent compounded over the life of the policy. Adding an automatic benefit increase to the policy is expensive and could easily double the annual premium in some cases.

Guaranteed Renewable Policy The policies sold currently are guaranteed renewable. Once issued, the policy cannot be canceled, but rates can be increased for the underwriting class in which the insured is placed.

Expensive Coverage Long-term care insurance is expensive, especially at the older ages. For example, a plan that costs $1,625 annually at age 50 will cost $3,100 at age 60 and $7,575 at age 70.[10]

Some insurance agents and financial planners recommend purchase of a long-term care policy at a younger age because premiums are lower. However, Consumers Union rejects that recommendation because of the lengthy period of premium payments before policy benefits may be needed. For example, assume that the insured purchases a long-term care policy at age 40 and pays a relatively modest annual premium of $685. The average age of admittance into a nursing home is age 83. Thus, the insured might pay premiums for more than 40 years before he or she knows whether the policy will be needed.[11] In addition, other important insurance needs, such as the need for disability income, should receive higher priority at the younger ages.

Nonforfeiture Benefits Most insurers offer *nonforfeiture benefits* as an optional benefit, which provides benefits if the insured lapses the policy. The most common nonforfeiture benefits are (1) a return of premium or (2) a shortened benefit period. Under a *return of premium* benefit, the policyowner receives cash, which is a percentage of the total premiums paid (excluding interest) after the policy lapses or death occurs. Under a *shortened benefit period,* coverage continues, but the benefit period or maximum dollar amount is reduced. A nonforfeiture benefit is expensive and can increase premiums by 20 percent to 100 percent.

If the insured does not purchase an optional non-forfeiture benefit, some states require that the policy include a provision called *contingent nonforfeiture benefits upon lapse,* which gives policyowners certain options if premiums rise by a specified percentage since the policy issue date. For example, if the policy is issued at age 70, and premiums rise 40 percent above the original premium, the insured has the option of decreasing the daily benefit or of converting to a paid-up policy with a shorter duration of benefits.

Taxation of Long-Term Care Insurance Long-term care insurance that meets certain requirements receives favorable income-tax treatment. The coverage can be an individual or group plan. Employer-paid premiums are deductible by the employer under a group plan and are not taxable to the employee.

Annual premiums paid by an individual for either individual or group coverage are deductible as medical expenses if the premiums paid plus other unreimbursed medical expenses exceed 7½ percent of the individual's adjusted gross income. However, certain annual limits apply. For 2007, the maximum annual deduction ranged from $290 for people age 40 or below to $3680 for people over age 70. These limits are indexed for inflation.

As noted earlier, most long-term care policies are written on a *reimbursement basis,* which reimburse the insured for actual expenses incurred up to the policy limits, and the benefits paid are income-tax free. However, some policies are written on a *per diem basis,* which pay the stated daily benefit regardless of actual expenses incurred if benefits are triggered. In this case, the tax-free benefits are limited to $260 daily (2007 limit). However, higher daily benefits are tax-free to the extent that long-term care expenses exceed that amount.

DISABILITY-INCOME INSURANCE

Disability-income insurance is another important form of individual health insurance. A serious disability can result in a substantial loss of work earnings. Unless you have replacement income from disability-income insurance, or income from other sources, you may be financially insecure. Many work-ers seldom think about the financial consequences of a long-term disability. However, the probability of becoming disabled before age 65 is much higher than is commonly believed, especially at the younger ages. *For example, based on the interactive calculator of a major national life insurer, the likelihood that a male, age 22, will become disabled for 90 days or more before age 65 is 21 percent. The corresponding figure for a female, age 22, is 33 percent.*[12] Although disability for a specific individual cannot be predicted, the financial impact of total disability on present savings, assets, and ability to earn an income can be devastating. In particular, the loss of earned income during an extended disability can be financially very painful.

Disability-income insurance provides income payments when the insured is unable to work because of sickness or injury. An individual policy pays monthly income benefits to an insured who becomes totally disabled from a sickness or accident. The amount of disability insurance you can buy is related to your earnings. To prevent overinsurance and to reduce moral hazard and malingering, most insurers limit the amount of insurance sold to no more than 60 to 80 percent of your gross earnings.

Meaning of Total Disability

The most important policy provision in a disability income policy is the meaning of "total disability." Most policies require the worker to be totally disabled to receive benefits.

Definitions of Total Disability There are several definitions of total disability. The most important include the following:

- Inability to perform all duties of the insured's own occupation
- Inability to perform the duties of any occupation for which the insured is reasonably fitted by education, training, and experience
- Inability to perform the duties of any gainful occupation
- Loss-of-income test

The most liberal definition defines total disability in terms of your own occupation. **Total disability** *is the complete inability of the insured to perform each and every duty of his or her own occupation.*

An example would be a surgeon whose hand is blown off in a hunting accident. The surgeon could no longer perform surgery and would be totally disabled under this definition.

The second definition is more restrictive. In this case, *total disability is the complete inability to perform the duties of any occupation for which the insured is reasonably fitted by education, training, and experience.* Thus, if the surgeon who lost a hand in a hunting accident could get a job as a professor in a medical school or as a research scientist, he or she would not be considered disabled because these occupations are consistent with the surgeon's training and experience.

The third definition is the most restrictive and is commonly used for hazardous occupations where a disability is likely to occur. *Total disability is defined as the inability to perform the duties of any gainful occupation.* The courts generally have interpreted this definition to mean that the person is totally disabled if he or she cannot work in any gainful occupation reasonably fitted by education, training, and experience.

Finally, some insurers use a loss-of-income test to determine if the insured is disabled. *You are considered disabled if your income is reduced as a result of a sickness or accident.* A disability-income policy containing this definition typically pays a percentage of the maximum monthly benefit equal to the percentage of earned income that is lost. For example, assume that Karen earns $5000 monthly and has a disability-income contract with a maximum monthly benefit of $3000. If Karen's work earnings are reduced to $2500 monthly because of the disability (50 percent), the policy pays $1500 monthly (50 percent of $3000).

Most insurers now combine the first two definitions. *For some initial period of disability—such as two years—total disability is defined in terms of the insured's own occupation. After the initial period of disability expires, the second definition is applied.* For example, Dr. Myron Pudwill is a dentist who can no longer practice because of arthritis in his hands. For the first two years, he would be considered totally disabled. However, after two years, if he could work as a dental supply representative or as an instructor in a dental school, he would no longer be considered disabled because he is reasonably fitted for these occupations by his education and training.

Finally, the policy may also contain a definition of *presumptive disability.* A total disability is presumed to exist if the insured suffers the total and irrecoverable loss of sight in both eyes, or the total loss or use of both hands, both feet, or one hand and one foot.

Partial Disability Some disability-income policies also pay partial disability benefits. **Partial disability** *is defined as the inability of the insured to perform one or more important duties of his or her occupation.* Partial disability benefits are paid at a reduced rate for a shorter period. Partial disability in most policies must follow a period of total disability. For example, a person may be totally disabled from an automobile accident. If the person recovers and goes back to work on a part-time basis to see if recovery is complete, partial disability benefits may be paid.

Residual Disability Newer policies frequently include a residual disability benefit, or this provision can be added as an additional benefit. **Residual disability** *means that a pro rata disability benefit is paid to an insured whose earned income is reduced because of an accident or sickness.* The typical residual disability provision has a time and duties test that considers both income and occupation. One common residual disability provision is as follows:[13]

1. You are not able to do one or more of your important daily business duties, or you are not able to do your usual daily business duties for as much time as it would normally take for you to do them.
2. Your loss of monthly income is at least 25 percent of your prior monthly income.
3. You are under the care and attendance of a physician.

However, some insurers use an alternative definition of residual disability that considers only the loss of earned income. In this definition, **residual disability** *means that you are engaged in your regular or another occupation, and your income is reduced because of an accident or sickness by at least 20 percent of your prior income.*

Finally, most insurers consider a loss of earned income in excess of 75 or 80 percent to be a loss of 100 percent, in which case the full monthly benefit for total disability is paid.

One major advantage of the residual disability definition is the payment of a partial benefit if the insured returns to work but earnings are reduced. For example, Jeff is a salesperson who earns $4000 monthly. He is seriously injured in an auto accident. When he returns to work, his earnings are only $3000 monthly, or a reduction of 25 percent. If his disability-income policy pays a monthly benefit of $2000 for total disability, a residual benefit of $500 is paid, and his total monthly income is $3500.

Benefit Period

The benefit period is the length of time that disability benefits are payable after the elimination period is met. The insured has a choice of benefit periods, such as 2, 5, 10 years, or up to age 65 or 70.

Most disabilities are relatively short. The majority of disabilities have durations of less than two years.[14] However, this fact does not mean that a two-year benefit period is adequate. The longer the disability lasts, the less likely the disabled person will recover. For example, a person who became disabled at age 22 and remains disabled for two years has a 41 percent chance of remaining disabled for at least five more years.[15] Thus, because of uncertainty concerning the duration of disability, you should elect a longer benefit period—ideally, one that pays benefits to age 65 or 70.

Elimination Period

Individual policies normally contain an elimination period (waiting period), during which time benefits are not paid. Insurers offer a range of elimination periods, such as 30, 60, 90, 180, or 365 days. Most insurers have stopped offering elimination periods that are shorter than 14 days, and elimination periods of 30 or more days are now the rule.

High-quality disability-income policies are expensive and can cost as much as 2 to 3 percent of your annual earnings. Increasing the elimination period from 30 to 90 days can substantially reduce the premiums. The majority of employers have sick leave or short-term disability plans that would provide some income during the longer elimination period. One disadvantage, however, is that a group disability-income plan is usually not convertible into an individual policy if the worker becomes unemployed.

Thus, group insurance is not a satisfactory substitute for a high-quality disability-income policy.

Finally, to make disability-income insurance more affordable, *some insurers sell policies with initially lower rates that gradually increase with age.* This approach is similar to term life insurance rates that increase as the insured gets older.

Waiver of Premium

Most policies automatically include a **waiver-of-premium** provision. If the insured is totally disabled for 90 days, future premiums will be waived as long as the insured remains disabled. In addition, there may be a refund of the premiums paid during the initial 90-day period. If the insured recovers from the disability, premium payments must be resumed.

Rehabilitation Provision

Disability-income policies typically include a rehabilitation provision. The insurer and insured may agree on a vocational rehabilitation program. To encourage rehabilitation, part or all of the disability-income benefits are paid during the training period. At the end of training, if the insured is still totally disabled, the benefits continue as before. But if the individual is fully rehabilitated and is capable of returning to work, the benefits will terminate. The costs of rehabilitation are usually paid by the company.

Accidental Death, Dismemberment, and Loss-of-Sight Benefits

Some disability-income policies pay accidental death, dismemberment, and loss-of-sight benefits in the event of an accident. The maximum amount paid, known as the principal sum, is based on a schedule. For example, the principal sum is paid for loss of both hands or both feet or sight of both eyes.

Optional Disability-Income Benefits

Several optional benefits can be added to a disability-income policy. They include the following:

- *Cost-of-living rider.* Under this option, the disability benefits are periodically adjusted for increases in the cost of living, usually measured by the consumer price index. Two limitations generally apply to the cost-of-living adjustment. First, the annual increase in benefits may be limited to a certain maximum percentage (such as 5 percent per year). Second, there may be a maximum limit on the overall increase in benefits (such as a 100 percent maximum increase in benefits). The rider is expensive and can increase the basic premium by 25 to 40 percent.

- *Option to purchase additional insurance.* Your income may increase, and you may need additional disability-income benefits. Under this option, the insured has the right to purchase additional disability-income benefits at specified times in the future with no evidence of insurability. The premium is generally based on the insured's age at the time the additional benefits are purchased.
- *Social Security rider.* Social Security disability benefits are difficult to obtain because of a strict definition of disability and stringent eligibility requirements. The Social Security rider pays you an additional amount if you are turned down for Social Security disability benefits.
- *Return of premium.* This rider pays back some of the premiums paid into the policy. For example, after 10 years, you would receive 80 per-cent of the premiums paid, less any claims. The option is controversial and is not recommended. Disability-income insurance is designed to provide income protection and should not be viewed as being similar to cash-value life insurance. The option is also expensive and can increase the already high cost of a policy by 30 to 100 percent.

INDIVIDUAL MEDICAL EXPENSE CONTRACTUAL PROVISIONS

All states have laws that require certain contractual provisions to appear in individual medical expense insurance contracts, while other provisions are optional. It is beyond the scope of this text to analyze in detail all contractual provisions. Instead, attention is focused on those provisions that are commonly found in newly issued medical expense contracts and are relevant to insurance consumers.

Renewal Provisions

A renewal provision refers to the length of time that an individual policy can remain in force. Renewal provisions include the following:[16]

- Optionally renewable
- Nonrenewable for stated reasons only
- Guaranteed renewable
- Noncancellable

Optionally Renewable This provision gives the insured the least protection with respect to continuation of coverage. Under an **optionally renewable policy,** *the insurer has the right to terminate a policy on any anniversary date, or in some cases, on a premium date.* The policy is renewable only with the consent of the insurer. Instead of nonrenewal, the insurer may specify the conditions that must be met before the policy is renewed. These conditions could include a policy amendment that excludes certain types of losses or injuries to certain parts of the body, or coverage for certain occurrences may be limited.

Nonrenewable for Stated Reasons Only This provision provides greater protection. The insurer may refuse to renew the coverage, but only for certain reasons stated in the policy, such as:

- The policyowner attains a certain age.
- The policyowner is no longer employed.
- The insurer decides to nonrenew all policies with the same form number as the policyowner's policy.

Guaranteed Renewable Most individual medical expense policies are guaranteed renewable. This type of renewal provision provides considerable protection to the insured. A **guaranteed renewable policy** *is one in which the insurer guarantees to renew the policy to some stated age. However, the insurer has the right to increase premium rates for the underwriting class in which the insured is placed.* The policy cannot be canceled, and renewal of the policy is at the insured's sole discretion.

Noncancellable A noncancellable policy provides the greatest protection to the insured. A **noncancellable policy** *is one that cannot be canceled. The insurer guarantees renewal of the policy to some* *stated age, and the premiums are guaranteed and cannot be increased during that period.* A noncancellable medical expense policy allows the insured to keep the insurance in force by the timely payment of premiums until at least age 50, or if the policy is issued after age 44, for at least five years from the issue date. Provided the insured pays the premiums on time, the insurer cannot cancel, refuse to renew, or increase premium rates stated in the policy, or unilaterally make any changes in the policy provisions.

The Health Insurance Portability and Accountability Act of 1996 now requires most new individual medical expense policies to be issued on a guaranteed renewable basis. Insurers are allowed to nonrenew such policies only under certain conditions, including nonpayment of premiums, fraud or misrepresentation, or discontinuation of the type of coverage provided by the policy.[17]

Preexisting-Conditions Clause

To control adverse selection, individual medical expense policies usually contain some type of **preexisting-conditions clause.** A preexisting condition is a physical or mental condition for which the insured received treatment or that existed during some specified time period prior to the effective date of the policy. Preexisting conditions are not covered until the policy has been in force for a specified period, such as two years, unless the condition is disclosed in the application and is not excluded by a rider.

The preexisting-conditions exclusion usually applies to health conditions not disclosed in the application. If the condition is disclosed in the application, it usually would be covered unless the insurer excludes the condition by attaching an exclusionary rider.

Many states have placed restrictions on the types of preexisting-conditions clauses that insurers can use. For example, a state may limit exclusions for a preexisting condition to 12 months, with a six-month look-back period (how far back the insurer can go to see whether the condition existed before the policy inception date).

In addition, the Health Insurance Portability and Accountability Act of 1996 (HIPPA) guarantees the availability of individual health insurance coverage with no preexisting-conditions limitations to certain individuals who have lost their group health insurance coverage. HIPPA is discussed in Chapter 16.

Notice of 10-Day Right to Examine Policy

If you are not satisfied with a medical expense policy, you have 10 days to return the policy after receiving it. The entire premium will be refunded, and the policy will be void.

Claims

A number of important provisions in an individual medical expense policy deal with claims. Under the *notice of claim provision,* you are required to give written notice to the insurer within 20 days after a covered loss occurs or as soon as is reasonably possible. Under the *claim forms provision,* the insurer is required to send you a claim form within 15 days after notice is received. Finally, under the *proof-of-loss provision,* you must send written proof of loss to the insurer within 90 days after a covered loss occurs. If it is not reasonably possible to provide proof of loss within 90 days, your claim will not be affected if the proof is sent as soon as possible. However, in any event, you must provide proof of loss within one year unless you are legally incapable of doing so.

Grace Period

A grace period is a required provision. The **grace period** *is a 31-day period after the premium due date to pay an overdue premium.* If the premium is paid after the due date but within the grace period, coverage is still in force.

Reinstatement

A medical expense policy has a reinstatement provision. If the premium is not paid within the grace period, the policy lapses. The **reinstatement provision** *permits the insured to reinstate a lapsed policy.* If the insured pays the premium to the insurance company or agent, and an application is not required, the policy is reinstated. However, if an application for reinstatement is required, the policy is reinstated only when the insurer approves the application. If the insurer has not previously notified the insured that the application for reinstatement has been denied, the policy is then automatically reinstated on the forty-fifth day following the date of the conditional receipt. The reinstated policy is subject to a 10-day waiting period for sickness, but accidents are covered immediately.

Time Limit on Certain Defenses

The time limit on certain defenses is a required provision and has the same effect as the incontestable clause in life insurance. The **time limit on certain defenses** *states that after the policy has been in force for two years, the insurer cannot void the policy or deny a claim on the basis of misstatements in the application, except for fraudulent misstatements.* After two years, the insurer could deny a claim if it could prove that the insured made a fraudulent misstatement when the policy was first issued.

SHOPPING FOR INDIVIDUAL HEALTH INSURANCE

High-quality individual health insurance plans are expensive. You should not waste money buying health insurance coverages that do not provide meaningful protection. Certain guidelines should be followed when you are purchasing health insurance (see Exhibit 15.3). They include the following:

- Insure for the catastrophic loss.
- Consider group health insurance first.
- Purchase a policy that has a preferred provider network.
- Don't ignore disability-income insurance.
- Avoid limited policies.
- Watch out for restrictive policy provisions and exclusions.
- Use deductibles and elimination periods to reduce premiums.

Insure for the Catastrophic Loss

The most important rule is to purchase health insurance that provides protection against a catastrophic loss that can destroy you financially. The cost of a serious illness or injury can prove ruinous. Open-heart surgery can cost more than $100,000; a kidney or heart transplant can cost more than $400,000; and the cost of a crippling auto accident requiring several major operations, plastic surgery, and rehabilitation can exceed $200,000. Unless you have adequate health insurance or financial assets to meet these expenditures, you will be financially insecure. The inability to pay for catastrophic medical bills is a major cause of personal bankruptcy. *Thus, you should purchase a high-quality individual major med-*

Exhibit 15.3
Guidelines for Health Insurance Shoppers

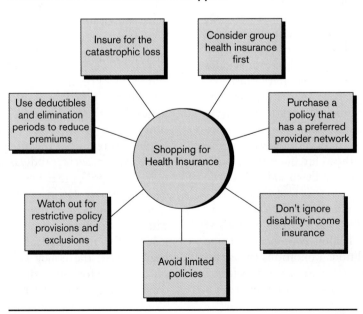

INSIGHT 15.2

Don't Delay Applying for Disability-Income Insurance

Applicants for disability-income insurance frequently have certain health impairments, such as lower back problems or arthritic knees, which may make them substandard or uninsurable for disability-income insurance but not for life insurance. As a result, the percentage of applicants for disability-income insurance who are classified as substandard or uninsurable is substantially higher than the percentage of applicants classified as substandard for life insurance. Typically, in life insurance, 3 to 5 percent of all applicants are classified as substandard and rated up because of health conditions. *In disability-income insurance, however, 15 to 25 percent of all appli-*

cants have health impairments that result in extra premiums, an exclusionary rider, or a combination of both. Moreover, in life insurance, only 1 to 3 percent of the applicants are considered uninsurable. *In contrast, in disability-income insurance, 5 to 10 percent of the applicants are considered uninsurable.*[a] These sobering statistics point out the advantage of applying for disability-income insurance when you are young and healthy, when fewer health impairments are present.

[a] Charles E. Soule, *Disability-Income Insurance, The Unique Risk*, 5th ed. Bryn Mawr, PA: The American College, 2002, p. 23.

ical policy or be covered under a group major medical plan. To limit your out-of-pocket expenses, make certain that the major medical policy has a stop-loss limit that requires the insurer to pay 100 percent of all covered expenses in excess of the stop-loss limit.

Consider Group Health Insurance First

In dealing with the risk of poor health, you should first consider whether group health insurance is available. You may be eligible to participate in a group health insurance plan sponsored by your employer or be a member of another group that offers group insurance.

Group health insurance is preferable to individual coverage for several reasons. First, employers frequently make available a number of group health insurance plans to their employees, ranging from traditional group indemnity plans to managed care plans, such as those involving health maintenance organizations (HMOs) and preferred provider organizations (PPOs). The various group indemnity plans have different deductible amounts, coinsurance requirements, and stop-loss limits. HMOs typically have no deductible or coinsurance requirements, or the amounts paid out-of-pocket are relatively low. Depending on your financial circumstances and need for protection, you can select the plan that best meets your needs and ability to pay.

Second, group health insurance is typically broader in coverage than individual protection and has fewer exclusions and restrictions. Also, there is

usually no individual underwriting in group health insurance.

Third, employers usually pay part of the monthly premiums, which makes the plan financially attractive to the employees and their families. Some employers pay the entire cost.

Finally, group health insurance plans provide substantial tax advantages to employees. The employer's contributions do not result in taxable income to the employee, and the employee's contributions can often be made with *before-tax dollars*. These tax advantages should not be ignored.

Purchase a Policy That Has a Preferred Provider Network

Another important suggestion is to shop for a policy that has a preferred provider network. Insurers frequently establish networks of health-care providers who agree to provide medical services to the insureds at discounted fees. Preferred providers include physicians, dentists, hospitals, pharmaceutical firms, and other health-care providers who are part of the network. If you see a preferred provider, your out-of-pocket cost will be substantially less than if you see a provider outside the network.

Don't Ignore Disability-Income Insurance

You should not ignore the importance of disability-income insurance in your health insurance program. A substantial amount of earned income is lost each

---

INSIGHT 15.3

State High-Risk Pools for the Uninsurable

The majority of states have special high-risk pools that provide health insurance to people who are medically uninsurable. Applicants must show they have been refused health insurance elsewhere before they are accepted. Two eligibility requirements are commonly imposed. First, the applicant must be a resident of the state. Second, the applicant must provide proof of one or more of the following: (1) be rejected by at least one insurer, (2) be currently insured under a plan with a higher premium than the pool premium, (3) be currently insured with a restrictive rider or rated policy, or (4) be offered a policy with a restrictive waiver or rider.

Major medical benefits are typically provided. A calendar-year deductible and 80 to 20 percent coinsurance are common. The plans typically have an annual stop-loss limit that caps annual out-of-pocket expenses.

The insurance is expensive, with maximum rates generally ranging from 125 to 400 percent of individual standard rates. Despite the high premiums, the pools have incurred

substantial underwriting losses. Health insurers doing business in a particular state are assessed their pro rata share of excess losses. In many states, the insurers can deduct all or part of the assessments from the state premium taxes paid. General revenue appropriations and taxes on tobacco and cigarettes are also used to fund excess losses in some states.

The major advantage of these pools is that they provide health insurance coverage to the medically uninsurable. The pools, however, are not a viable solution to the national problems of health insurance affordability and accessibility. They have incurred substantial underwriting deficits; the assessment method of funding such deficits is defective since the true cost is hidden and is shifted indirectly to taxpayers through premium tax offsets or to policyowners through higher premiums; only a small fraction of the medically uninsurable have obtained insurance through the pools; and high premiums make the insurance unaffordable to many applicants.

---

year because of sickness and injury, but not replaced by disability-income and sick-leave benefits.

You should consider purchasing an individual guaranteed renewable or noncancellable disability-income policy that will pay at least two-thirds of your earnings up to age 65 with an elimination period of 30 to 90 days. Even if you are covered under a group short-term or long-term disability-income plan, you should still consider an individual policy.

Finally, you should not delay in applying for disability-income insurance. As workers become older, they often develop health impairments that make them substandard or uninsurable for disability-income insurance but not necessarily for life insurance. As a result of strict underwriting, applicants for disability-income insurance are more likely to be considered substandard or uninsurable than in life insurance (see Insight 15.2).

Avoid Limited Policies

A **limited policy** covers only certain diseases or accidents, pays limited benefits, or places serious restrictions on the right to receive the benefits. A **hospital indemnity policy** is one example of a limited policy.

It pays a fixed daily or monthly benefit if you are admitted to a hospital. For example, the plan may pay $3000 monthly ($100 daily) if you are hospitalized; no health questions are asked, and the first month's premium is only $1. It sounds like a good deal, but in health insurance, there is no such thing as a "free lunch." The policy is limited. Most people will never collect benefits for an extended period. The average hospital stay for patients insured by private insurance is less than five days. Even if you are hospitalized for only five days, the benefit paid would be only $500. In addition, the policy covers you only while you remain in the hospital. If you recover at home, no payment is made.

A **cancer policy** is another example of a limited policy. If you are insured under a high-quality individual or group major medical policy, you do not need a cancer policy. Consumer experts argue that it is illogical to insure yourself more heavily against only one disease because you do not know how you will become disabled.

Accident-only policies should also be avoided because they are limited in coverage and benefits. A list of these policies is endless, but includes accident insurance offered by sponsors of credit cards, travel accident policies to cover you while on vacation, and airline accident policies sold over the counter or from vending machines in airports.

Watch Out for Restrictive Policy Provisions and Exclusions

If you are shopping for an individual policy, you should be aware of any restrictions on coverage that might apply. Two common restrictions are a preexisting-conditions clause and an **exclusionary rider.** An individual policy with a preexisting-conditions clause longer than one year should not be purchased. If possible, you should also avoid buying an individual policy in which an exclusionary rider appears. If you have been treated for certain diseases, such as cancer or heart disease, the insurer may add a rider to the policy that excludes the condition.

As a last resort, if you are uninsurable and cannot obtain either individual or group coverage, you may be eligible for coverage from a state high-risk pool for the uninsurable (see Insight 15.3). The majority of

states operate such high-risk pools. Information on enrolling is available from your state insurance department.

Use Deductibles and Elimination Periods to Reduce Premiums

High-quality individual health insurance coverages are expensive. A comprehensive major medical policy that covers the entire family can cost more than $10,000 annually. You can reduce your premiums by purchasing a policy with a substantial deductible. An annual deductible of $1000 or a higher amount will substantially reduce your premiums. Likewise, premiums for a disability-income policy can be substantially reduced by buying a policy with an elimination period of 90 days or longer.

Finally, you should contact more than one insurer before purchasing a policy. Although price is important, it should not be the only consideration. A low-premium policy may contain restrictive provisions, pay limited benefits, or reflect a restrictive claims policy.

CASE APPLICATION

Lorri, age 28, is a registered nurse who earns $4000 monthly working in a hospital. She is seriously injured in an automobile accident in which she is at fault and is expected to be unable to work for at least one year. She has a guaranteed renewable disability-income policy that pays $2800 monthly up to age 65 for accidents and sickness after a 90-day elimination period. A residual disability benefit is included in the policy. Lorri's policy contains the following provisions:

- *Total disability means:* (a) your inability during the first 24 months to perform substantially all of the important duties of your occupation; and you are not working at any gainful occupation; (b) after the first 24 months that benefits are payable, it means your inability to engage in any gainful occupation.
- *Gainful occupation means:* Any occupation or employment for wage or profit that is reasonably consistent with your education, training, and experience.

a. If Lorri is off work for one year because of the accident, indicate the extent, if any, of the insurer's obligation to pay disability benefits.

b. Assume that Lorri is disabled for one year, recovers, and returns to work part-time. If she earns $2000 monthly after returning to work, indicate the extent, if any, of the insurer's obligation to pay her disability benefits.

c. Assume that after two years, Lorri is unable to return to work as a full-time hospital nurse. A drug manufacturer offers her a job as a lab technician, which she accepts. Indicate the extent, if any, of the insurer's obligation to continue paying her disability benefits.

d. Following the accident, could Lorri's insurer cancel her policy or increase her premiums? Explain your answer.

SUMMARY

- The health-care delivery system in the United States has four major problems:

  Rising health-care expenditures

  Large number of uninsured in the population

  Uneven quality of medical care

  Waste and inefficiency

- Individual health insurance policies can generally be classified into the following categories:

  Hospital-surgical insurance

  Major medical insurance

  Health savings accounts

  Long-term care insurance

  Disability-income insurance

- Individual hospital-surgical policies typically cover hospital expenses, surgical expenses, outpatient diagnostic X-rays and lab expenses, and physician's in-hospital expenses.

- Major medical insurance is designed to cover the expenses of a catastrophic illness or injury. A typical major medical plan has certain characteristics:

  Broad coverage

  High maximum limits

  Benefit period

  Deductible

  Coinsurance

  Exclusions

- A health savings account is a high-deductible, major medical plan that receives favorable tax treatment. The contributions go into an investment account and are income-tax deductible; the investment income builds up income-tax free; and withdrawals are also income-tax free when used to pay for qualified medical expenses.

- Long-term care insurance pays a daily or monthly benefit for medical or custodial care in a nursing facility or at home.

- Disability-income policies provide for the periodic payment of income to an individual who is totally disabled. The benefits are paid after an elimination (waiting) period is satisfied. The insured generally has a choice of benefit periods. In addition, after 90 days, all premiums are waived if the insured is totally disabled.

- The definition of disability is stated in a disability-income policy. For some initial period, such as two years, total disability is typically defined as the inability to perform all duties of the insured's own occupation. After that time, total disability is defined as the inability to perform the duties of any occupation for which the insured is reasonably fitted by education, training, and experience.

- Health insurance policies contain certain contractual provisions. Some provisions are required by state law, while others are optional.

- A renewal provision refers to the length of time that an individual medical expense policy can remain in force. Renewal provisions include the following:

  Optionally renewable

  Nonrenewable for stated reasons only

  Guaranteed renewable

  Noncancellable

- Consumer experts recommend certain rules to follow when health insurance is purchased:

  Insure for the catastrophic loss.

  Consider group insurance first.

  Purchase a policy that has a preferred provider network.

  Don't ignore disability-income insurance.

  Avoid limited policies.

  Watch out for restrictive policy provisions and exclusions.

  Use deductibles and elimination periods to reduce premiums.

KEY CONCEPTS AND TERMS

Accident-only policy
Activities of daily living (ADLs)
Benefit period
Benefit triggers
Calendar-year deductible
Cancer policy
Coinsurance provision
Common-accident provision
Disability-income insurance
Elimination (waiting) period

Exclusionary rider
Family deductible
Grace period
Guaranteed renewable policy
Health savings accounts
Hospital indemnity policy
Internal limits
Limited policy
Long-term care insurance
Major medical insurance
Noncancellable policy
Nonrenewable for stated reasons only

Optionally renewable
  policy
Partial disability
Preexisting-conditions
  clause
Preferred provider
Reasonable and customary
  charges
Reinstatement
  provision
Residual disability

Schedule approach
Stop-loss limit
Time limit on certain
  defenses
Total disability
Waiver of premium
  provision

REVIEW QUESTIONS

1. What are the four major problems in health care in the United States?

2. a. Describe the basic characteristics of major medical insurance.
   b. Why are deductibles and coinsurance used in a major medical policy?

3. Briefly explain the major characteristics of a health savings account.

4. Briefly explain the basic characteristics of long-term care insurance.

5. a. Explain the various definitions of disability that are found in disability-income insurance.
   b. Briefly explain the following disability-income insurance provisions:
      (1) Residual disability
      (2) Benefit period
      (3) Elimination period
      (4) Waiver of premium

6. Identify the optional benefits that can be added to a disability-income policy.

7. Explain the following renewal provisions that appear in individual medical expense policies:
   a. Optionally renewable
   b. Nonrenewable for stated reasons only
   c. Guaranteed renewable
   d. Noncancellable

8. Explain the meaning of a preexisting condition.

9. Explain the time limit on certain defenses contractual provision.

10. Briefly describe the guidelines that consumers should follow when individual health insurance is purchased.

APPLICATION QUESTIONS

1. Brittany, age 28, purchased an individual major medical insurance policy with a lifetime limit of $1 million, a calendar-year deductible of $250, and an 80-20 percent coinsurance provision. Brittany had emergency surgery for an inflamed appendix. Covered medical expenses are $30,750. Brittany also lost $1000 in wages because she could not work for one week.
   a. What is the amount paid by the insurer? Explain.
   b. What is the amount paid by Brittany? Explain.
   c. Would your answer to (b) above change if Brittany's policy contained an annual stop-loss limit of $3000? Explain.

2. Fred and Janet and their two daughters, Kelly and Karen, are insured under an individual major medical policy that covers the entire family. The policy has a calendar-year deductible of $500 that applies to each covered person, an 80-20 percent coinsurance provision, and a common accident provision.
   a. Janet had gallbladder surgery and incurred covered medical expenses of $15,500. How much will Janet receive from her insurer?
   b. Fred, Kelly, and Karen were injured in the same bobsledding accident. Covered medical expenses are $2500 for George, $900 for Kelly, and $600 for Karen. How much of the loss will be paid by the insurer? Show your calculations.

3. Mark, age 25, is insured under an individual major medical policy with a lifetime limit of $2 million. The plan has a calendar-year deductible of $500, 80-20 percent coinsurance, and an annual stop-loss limit of $2000. Mark recently had outpatient arthroscopic surgery on his knee, which he injured in a skiing accident. The surgery was performed in an outpatient surgical center. Mark incurred the following medical expenses.

Outpatient X-rays and diagnostic tests	$700
Covered charges in the surgical center	9,800
Surgeon's fee	3,000
Outpatient prescription drugs	300
Physical therapy expenses	700

In addition, Mark could not work for two weeks and lost $2000 in earnings.
   a. Based on the above information, how much of the loss will be paid by the insurance company?
   b. If Mark's policy did not contain a stop-loss limit, how much will the insurance company pay? Show your calculations.

4. Jeff currently earns $3000 per month. He has an individual disability-income policy that will pay $2000 monthly if he is totally disabled. Disability is defined in terms of the worker's own occupation. The policy has a 30-day elimination period and also provides residual disability benefits. Benefits are payable until age 65.

   a. If Jeff is severely injured in an auto accident and cannot work for four months, how much will he collect under his policy?

   b. Assume Jeff returns to work but can only work part-time until he recovers completely. If he earns $200 monthly, what is the amount, if any, that Jeff can collect under his policy? Explain your answer.

INTERNET RESOURCES

- **America's Health Insurance Plans (AHIP)** is a national trade association that represents nearly 1300 member companies that provide health insurance coverage to more than 200 million Americans. The site provides considerable information on health-care issues in the United States. Visit the site at

  http://www.ahip.org/

- **eHealthInsurance.com** offers online applications for major medical insurance from several leading insurers. It allows you to shop privately for health insurance without sales pressure. Visit the site at

  http://www.ehealthinsurance.com

- **INSWEB** provides timely information and premium quotes for individual health insurance, small group health insurance, and Medicare supplement policies. Applicants fill out health forms, and the site provides quotes from multiple insurers. Visit the site at

  http://www.insweb.com

- **Insure.com** provides up-to-date information, premium quotes, and other consumer information on health insurance and other insurance products. The site also provides news releases about events that affect the insurance industry. Visit the site at

  http://www.insure.com

- The **National Association of Health Underwriters** is a professional association of health insurance professionals who sell and service medical expense, major medical, and disability-income insurance. Visit the site at

  http://www.nahu.org

- **QuickQuote** provides premium quotes on life insurance, health insurance, and numerous other insurance products. Visit the site at

  http://www.quickquote.com

- **The National Association of Insurance Commissioners (NAIC)** has a link to all state insurance departments, which provide a considerable amount of consumer information on the health insurance coverages discussed in this chapter. Click on "State Insurance Web sites." For starters, check out New York, Wisconsin, and California. Visit the site at

  http://www.naic.org

SELECTED REFERENCES

AHIP, America's Health Insurance Plans. *Guide to Long-Term Care Insurance*. Washington, DC, revised 2004.

AHIP, America's Health Insurance Plans. *Guide to Health Insurance*. Washington, DC, 2004.

AHIP, America's Health Insurance Plans. *Guide to Disability Income Insurance*. Washington, DC, 2004.

Beam, Burton T., Jr., and Thomas P. O'Hare. *Meeting the Financial Need of Long-Term Care,* 2nd ed. Bryn Mawr, PA: The American College, 2005.

Blue Cross and Blue Shield Association. *Medical Cost Reference Guide*. Chicago, IL., 2006.

ConsumerReports.org. *Do You Need Long-Term-Care Insurance?,* 2005.

Families, USA. *HSAs: Why High-Deductible Plans Are Not the Solution*. Washington, DC, Issue Brief, January 2005.

HealthGrades. *HealthGrades Quality Study, Third Annual Patient Safety in American Hospitals Study,* April 2006.

National Association of Health Underwriters. *A Primer on Health Savings Accounts for Consumers*. Arlington, VA, 2004.

National Association of Health Underwriters. *Consumer Guide to Health Savings Accounts (HSAs)*. Arlington, VA, 2004.

National Association of Insurance Commissioners. *A Shopper's Guide to Long-Term Care Insurance.* Kansas City, MO, 2006.

O'Hare, Thomas P. *Individual Medical Expense Insurance,* 3rd ed. Bryn Mawr, PA: The American College, 2004.

Rejda, George E. "Problem of Poor Health," in *Social Insurance and Economic Security,* 6th ed. Upper Saddle River, NJ: Prentice-Hall, 1999, ch. 8.

Soule, Charles E. *Disability Income Insurance: The Unique Risk,* 5th ed. Bryn Mawr, PA: The American College, 2002.

U.S. Census Bureau. *Income, Poverty, and Health Insurance Coverage in the United States: 2005,* Current Population Reports, P60-231, August 2006.

NOTES

1. Centers for Medicare & Medicaid Services, *National Health Expenditures Projections: 2005–2015,* Table 1.

2. Blue Cross and Blue Shield Association, *Medical Cost Reference Guide,* revised October 2004.

3. U.S. Bureau of the Census, *Income, Poverty, and Health Insurance Coverage in the United States: 2005,* Washington, DC (August 2006).

4. Ibid., Table 8.

5. National Committee for Quality Assurance, *The State of Health Care Quality: 2005* (Washington, DC: National Committee for Quality Assurance, 2005).

6. HealthGrades, *In-Hospital Deaths from Medical Errors at 195,000 per year. HealthGrades Study Finds,* Press Release, July 27, 2004.

7. *A Shopper's Guide to Long-Term-Care Insurance* (Kansas, City, MO: National Association of Insurance Commissioners, 2006).

8. Consumer Reports.org, *Do You Need Long-Term Care Insurance?* (2005).

9. This section is based on AHIP, America's Health Insurance Plans, *Guide to Long-Term Care Insurance,* revised edition, 2004; and Burton T. Beam, Jr., and Thomas P. O'Hare, *Meeting the Financial Need of Long-Term Care* (Bryn Mawr, PA: The American College 2005).

10. Consumer Reports.org, *Do You Need Long-Term Care Insurance?* (2005).

11. Ibid.

12. Northwestern Mutual Financial Network at nmfn.com. Click on "Learning Center and Calculators." Scroll down to "What are the Odds?" for the interactive calculator that estimates the likelihood of being disabled for 90 days or longer before age 65.

13. Kenneth Black, Jr., and Harold D. Skipper, Jr., *Life Insurance,* 13th ed. (Upper Saddle River, NJ: Prentice-Hall, 2000), pp. 157–158.

14. Edward E. Graves, ed., *McGill's Life Insurance,* 3rd ed. (Bryn Mawr, PA: The American College, 2000), p. 181.

15. Ibid., table 7-4, p. 170.

16. *The Health Insurance Primer: An Introduction to How Health Insurance Works* (Washington, DC: Health Insurance Association of America, 2000), pp. 83–84.

17. Ibid., p. 84.

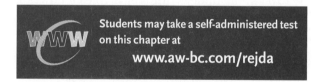

CHAPTER 16

EMPLOYEE BENEFITS: GROUP LIFE AND HEALTH INSURANCE

"Employee benefits are an extremely important part of almost everyone's financial security."

Jerry S. Rosenbloom
The Handbook of Employee Benefits

After studying this chapter, you should be able to

◆ Explain the underwriting principles followed in group insurance.

◆ Describe the basic characteristics of group term life insurance.

◆ Explain the major characteristics of the following group medical expense plans:
    Basic medical expense insurance
    Major medical insurance
    Dental insurance

◆ Describe the basic characteristics of the following managed care plans:
    Health maintenance organizations (HMOs)
    Preferred provider organizations (PPOs)
    Point of service plans (POS)

◆ Show how group short-term disability-income plans differ from group long-term disability plans.

◆ Describe the major characteristics of cafeteria plans.

*E*mployee benefits are very important in a personal risk management program. Employee benefits are employer-sponsored plans that pay benefits if a worker dies, becomes sick or disabled, or retires. The various benefits provide considerable financial security to employees and their families. They are also important in calculating total employee compensation. Although the starting salaries in many companies may be relatively low, generous employee benefits can substantially increase employees' total compensation packages. For example, David, age 26, is an English major who graduated from college and accepted an entry-level job with a national book publisher at an annual salary of $35,000. However, when employer contributions for life insurance, health and dental insurance, retirement, vacation, and other benefits are factored in, David's total annual compensation increases substantially to $42,000—an increase of 20 percent.

This chapter is the first of two chapters dealing with employee benefit plans. Chapter 16 is limited to employer-sponsored group life and health insurance plans. Retirement plans are discussed in Chapter 17. Topics discussed in this chapter include group life insurance, group medical expense plans, group dental insurance, group disability-income plans, and the Health Insurance Portability and Accountability Act. The chapter concludes with a discussion of cafeteria plans.

GROUP INSURANCE

Group insurance differs from individual insurance in several respects. *A distinctive characteristic is the coverage of many persons under one contract.* A master contract is formed between the insurer and the group policyowner for the benefit of the individual members. In most plans, the group policyowner is the employer. Employees receive a certificate of insurance that shows they are insured.

A second characteristic is that group insurance usually costs less than comparable insurance purchased individually. Employers usually pay part or all of the cost, which reduces or eliminates premium payments by the employees. In addition, administrative and marketing expenses are reduced as a result of mass distribution methods.

Another characteristic is that individual evidence of insurability is usually not required. Group selection of risks is used, not individual selection. The insurer is concerned with the insurability of the group as a whole rather than with the insurability of any single member within the group.

Finally, **experience rating** *is used in group insurance plans.* If the group is sufficiently large, the actual loss experience of the group is a major factor in determining the premiums charged.

Basic Underwriting Principles

Because individual evidence of insurability is usually not required, group insurers must observe certain underwriting principles so that the loss experience of the group is favorable. These principles are as follows:[1]

- Insurance incidental to the group
- Flow of persons through the group
- Automatic determination of benefits
- Minimum participation requirements
- Third-party sharing of cost
- Simple and efficient administration

Insurance Incidental to the Group   Insurance should be incidental to the group; that is, the group should not be formed for the sole purpose of obtaining insurance. This requirement is necessary to reduce adverse selection against the insurer. If the group is formed for the specific purpose of obtaining insurance, a disproportionate number of unhealthy persons would join the group to obtain low-cost insurance, and the loss experience would be unfavorable.

Flow of Persons Through the Group   Ideally, there should be a flow of younger persons into the group and a flow of older persons out of the group. Without a flow of younger persons into the group, the average age of the group will increase, and premium rates will likewise increase. Higher premiums may cause some younger and healthier members to drop out of the plan, while the older and unhealthy members will still remain, which would lead to still higher losses and increased rates. However, turnover of employees should not be so significant that administrative costs are high.

Automatic Determination of Benefits   Benefits should be automatically determined by some formula that precludes individual selection of insurance amounts. The amount of insurance can be based on earnings, position, length of service, or some combination of these factors. *The purpose of this requirement is to reduce adverse selection against the insurer.* If individual members were permitted to select the amount of insurance, unhealthy persons would likely select larger amounts, while healthier persons would likely select smaller amounts. The result would be a disproportionate amount of insurance on the impaired lives. However, many group insurance plans allow employees to select their own benefit levels up to certain maximum limits. If additional amounts of insurance are desired above the maximum allowed, evidence of insurability is usually required.

Minimum Participation Requirements   A minimum percentage of the eligible employees must participate in the plan. If the plan is a **noncontributory plan,** the premiums are paid entirely by the employer, and 100 percent of the eligible employees must be covered. If the plan is a **contributory plan,** the employee pays part or all of the cost and a large proportion of the eligible employees must elect to participate in the plan. In a contributory plan, it may be difficult to get 100 percent participation, so a lower percentage such as 50 to 75 percent is typically required.

There are two reasons for the minimum participation requirement. First, if a large proportion of eligible employees participate, adverse selection is reduced, because the possibility of insuring a large proportion of unhealthy lives is reduced. Second, if a high proportion of eligible members participate, the expense rate per insured member or per unit of insurance can be reduced.

Third-Party Sharing of Cost   Ideally, individual members should not pay the entire cost of their protection. In most groups, the employer pays part of the cost. A third-party sharing of cost avoids the problem of a substantial increase in premiums for older members. In a plan in which the members pay the entire cost, younger persons help pay for the insurance provided to older persons. Once they become aware of this fact, some younger persons may drop out of the plan and obtain their insurance more cheaply elsewhere. Older unhealthy members will still remain, causing premiums to increase even more. However, if the employer absorbs any increase in premiums because of adverse mortality experience, premiums paid by the employees can be kept fairly stable. In addition, a third-party sharing of cost makes the plan more attractive to individual members and encourages greater participation in the plan.

Simple and Efficient Administration   The group plan should be simple and efficiently administered. Premiums are collected from the employees by payroll deduction, which reduces the insurer's administrative expenses and keeps participation in the plan high.

Eligibility Requirements in Group Insurance

Insurers typically require that certain eligibility requirements must be satisfied before the insurance is in force. The eligibility requirements generally are designed to reduce adverse selection against the insurer.

Eligible Groups Eligible groups are determined by insurance company policy and state law. Eligible groups include individual employer groups, multiple-employer groups, labor unions, creditor-debtor groups, and miscellaneous groups, such as fraternities, sororities, and alumni groups.

Group insurers usually require the group to be a certain size before the group is insured. Traditionally, this size was ten members, but some insurers now insure groups with as few as two or three members. There are two reasons for a minimum-size requirement. First, the insurer has some protection against insuring a group that consists largely of substandard individuals, so that the financial impact of one impaired life on the loss experience of the group is reduced. Second, certain fixed expenses must be met regardless of the size of the group. The larger the group, the broader the base over which these expenses can be spread, and the lower the expense rate per unit of insurance.

Eligibility Requirements Before employees can participate in a group insurance plan, they must meet certain eligibility requirements, including the following:

- Be full-time employees
- Satisfy a probationary period
- Apply for insurance during the eligibility period
- Be actively at work when insurance becomes effective

Employers generally require the workers to be employed full-time before they can participate in the plan. A *full-time worker* is one who works the required number of hours established by the employer as a normal work week, which is at least 30 hours. However, some group plans today permit part-time workers to be covered. In some group insurance plans, new employees may have to satisfy a **probationary period,** which is a period of one to six months, before he or she can participate in the plan. The purpose of the probationary period is to eliminate transient workers who will be with the firm for only a short period. It is administratively expensive to maintain records and insure workers who will not be working permanently for the firm.

After the probationary period (if any) expires, the employee is eligible to participate in the plan. However, if the plan is contributory, the employee

must request coverage either before or during the eligibility period. The **eligibility period** is a period of time—typically 31 days—during which the employee can sign up for the insurance without furnishing evidence of insurability.

Finally, for group term and group disability-income insurance, employees typically are required to be actively at work on the day the insurance becomes effective. However, the situation is somewhat different for group health plans. The Health Insurance Portability and Accountability Act of 1996 (HIPPA) does not allow actively-at-work provisions to be included in group health plans, unless they do not apply to health conditions. Most group medical expense plans now use the term *commencement of employment* as an eligibility requirement. If employment does not commence until you show up for work, medical expense coverage does not begin until you actually show up for work. However, if you have an employment contract that states employment starts on a certain date, medical expense coverage will also start at that time (ignoring any probationary period requirement) even if you are not actively at work for health reasons.

GROUP LIFE INSURANCE PLANS

Group life insurance is a popular and relatively inexpensive employee benefit. At the end of 2004, $7.6 trillion of group life insurance was in force, which accounted for 44 percent of the total life insurance in force in the United States.[2]

The major types of group life insurance plans are the following:

- Group term life insurance
- Group accidental death and dismemberment insurance (AD&D)
- Group universal life insurance

Group Term Life Insurance

Group term life insurance is the most important form of group life insurance. More than 90 percent of the group life insurance in force is group term life insurance. The insurance provided is *yearly renewable* *term insurance,* which provides low-cost protection to the employees during their working years.

The amount of term insurance on an employee's life is typically one to five times the annual salary or earnings. The term insurance remains in force as long as the employee is part of the group. If the employee quits or is laid off, he or she has the right to convert the group term insurance to an individual cash-value policy within 31 days without evidence of insurability. However, the group term insurance normally cannot be converted into an individual term insurance policy.[3] As a practical matter, relatively few employees convert their group insurance because of the problem of cost and because group insurance will probably be provided by another employer. Those employees who do convert are usually substandard in health or uninsurable, which results in strong adverse selection against the insurer.

Most group plans allow a modest amount of life insurance to be written on the employee's spouse and dependent children. Because of state law and tax considerations, the amount of dependent life insurance is relatively low. The insurance on the spouse's life can be converted to an individual cash-value policy. Some states require that the conversion option should also apply to the insurance on the children.

Most employers provide a reduced amount of term insurance on retired employees. The amount of insurance may be a flat amount, such as $10,000, or it may be a percentage of the amount of insurance at the date of retirement, such as 50 percent.

Group term insurance has the major advantage of providing low-cost protection to employees that can be used to supplement individual life insurance policies. However, it has two major disadvantages. First, the insurance is temporary and terminates when the individual is no longer part of the group. Second, it is expensive for an older worker to convert to an individual policy after retirement.

Finally, group term life insurance is used by commercial banks and other lending institutions to insure the lives of debtors. Credit life insurance provides for the cancellation of any outstanding debt if the borrower dies. The lending institution is both the policyowner and beneficiary. The unpaid balance of the loan is paid to the creditor at the debtor's death. Many financial planners do not recommend the purchase of credit life insurance because of excessive

rates. Although the rates are regulated by the states, many debtors are overcharged for their protection (see Insight 16.1).

Group Accidental Death and Dismemberment (AD&D) Insurance

Many group life insurance plans also provide **group accidental death and dismemberment (AD&D) insurance** that pays additional benefits if the employee dies in an accident or incurs certain types of bodily injury. The AD&D benefit is some multiple of the group life insurance benefit, such as one or two times the insurance on the employee's life. The full AD&D benefit, called the *principal sum,* is paid if the employee dies in an accident. In addition, a percentage of the principal sum is paid for certain types of dismemberments, such as one-half the principal sum for the loss of a hand, foot, or eye because of accidental bodily injury.

Many plans also make available **voluntary accidental death and dismemberment insurance** in which employees can voluntarily purchase additional amounts of AD&D insurance. The employees normally pay the entire cost of the voluntary coverage.

Group Universal Life Insurance

In addition to group term life insurance, some employers make available **group universal life insurance** for their employees. These plans are similar to individual universal life insurance policies, but have some important differences. The major characteristics of group universal life plans are summarized as follows:[4]

- *Plan design.* Two approaches are used in the plan design. Under the first approach, there is only one plan. The employee who wants only term insurance pays only the mortality and expense charges. The employee who wants to accumulate cash values must pay higher premiums. Under the second approach, two plans are used—term insurance and universal life insurance. The employee who wants only term insurance pays into the term insurance plan. The employee who wants universal life insurance must pay higher premiums so that cash values are accumulated.

INSIGHT 16.1

Credit Insurance Overcharges Cost Consumers Billions of Dollars Annually

In 2000, consumers paid about $6 billion for credit insurance, but they would have paid only $3.5 billion if states had implemented the credit insurance rate standards of their insurance commissioners' own deliberative body, the National Association of Insurance Commissioners. *Consumers thereby paid $2.5 billion in overcharges in 2000—or 75 percent more than they should have had to pay.* For one of the coverages—credit unemployment insurance—the overcharge was 1000 percent.

Poor Value for Consumers

"In many states, credit life and credit disability insurance offers such poor value that consumers should not purchase it unless they are over age 50 or in poor health or both," said James Hunt, CFA's Life Actuary and coauthor of the report. "In most states, officials should lower maximum rates allowed, better enforce those rate caps, limit the sale of excessive amounts of credit life insurance and correct unfair refunds when debts are refinanced," said Hunt.

Consumer credit insurance is insurance sold in connection with a loan. The main coverages are credit life, credit disability, credit involuntary unemployment, credit leave of absence and credit property. Credit life insurance pays off the loan if the borrower dies, while credit disability, credit involuntary unemployment and credit leave of absence make the monthly loan payments in the event the borrower becomes disabled, involuntarily unemployed, or takes an approved family leave from work, respectively. Credit property pays to repair or replace property purchased (or pledged as collateral) with the loan.

Low Loss Ratio

The single most important measure of the reasonableness of credit insurance benefits in comparison to the cost is the *loss ratio*. The loss ratio is the ratio of benefits (also known as claims) paid by credit insurers to the premiums paid by consumers for the product. *The National Association of Insurance Commissioners (NAIC) model statutes and regulations for credit insurance specify a 60 percent minimum loss ratio. Yet, by 2000,*

the loss ratios for the major credit coverages were far below 60 percent.

- *In 2000, the loss ratio for all coverages combined was only 34.2 percent, down from 42.5 percent in 1995.*
- *The 2000 premium and loss ratios by coverage were*

Credit Life	$2.1 billion	40.7%
Credit Disability	$2.3 billion	46.1%
Credit Unemployment	$1.1 billion	5.8%
Credit Property	$0.5 billion	14.7%

- *Total premiums for the four major coverages have been around $6 billion a year for the past several years. If a 60 percent loss ratio standard had been enforced, consumers would have paid only $3.5 billion in 2000. Overcharges came to $2.5 billion, meaning that consumers paid 75 percent more premiums than they should have.*
- *The countrywide credit life loss ratio peaked at about 45 percent in 1993 and declined to less than 41 percent in 2000. The countrywide credit disability loss peaked in 1991 at about 59 percent and dropped to about 46 percent in 2000.*
- *From 1995 to 2000, while the amount of credit unemployment sold jumped from $600 million to $1.1 billion, the loss ratios dropped from a low of 18.2 percent to only 5.8 percent.*

Credit insurance is regulated by the states—typically by state insurance commissioners. In almost every state, the law empowers the insurance commissioner to disapprove credit life and credit disability insurance premiums if the benefits provided are not reasonable in relation to the premiums. Most states establish minimum loss ratios as the basis for this standard. *Yet, the report found that almost half the states were failing to enforce existing loss ratio standards.* And other states without loss ratio standards were failing to protect credit insurance consumers from excessive charges.

SOURCE: Adapted from *Credit Insurance Overcharges Hit $2.5 Billion Annually,* Consumer Federarion of America, press release, November 15, 2001.

The employee may be required to pay initial premiums equal to two or three times the cost of the pure insurance protection.
- *Amount of insurance.* Universal life insurance is issued on a guaranteed basis up to certain limits with no evidence of insurability. Employees gen-

erally select the amount of guaranteed coverage equal to some multiple of their salaries, such as one to five times their annual salary. Higher amounts of insurance require evidence of insurability, usually based on a simplified medical questionnaire.

- *Mortality and expense charges.* Most group universal life plans have guaranteed mortality charges for three years; after that time, the group is experience-rated. Expense charges must also be paid. These charges are generally lower than the expenses assessed against individual policies. Finally, there is a minimum interest rate guarantee on the cash values. Higher current rates are paid that change over time.
- *Premium flexibility.* Premiums can be reduced, increased, or even eliminated if the cash value is sufficient to pay current mortality and expense charges.
- *Loans and withdrawals.* Employees can make policy loans and withdrawals. The loan or withdrawal amount must be at least equal to a certain minimum amount, such as $250 or $500. The policy loan rate usually is based on some index, such as Moody's composite bond yield. Interest credited to the cash values on the amounts borrowed is also reduced, such as 2 percent less than Moody's composite bond yield.
- *Options at retirement.* The retired employee has the option of continuing the universal life coverage, and the insurer bills the retired employee directly. The employee also has the option of terminating the coverage and withdrawing the cash value; electing a settlement option for liquidation of the cash value in the form of annuity income; or decreasing the amount of pure insurance so that the cash value is sufficient to keep the policy in force with no additional premiums required.
- *Dependent coverage.* A term insurance rider can be added to cover dependents, such as $10,000 to $50,000 on the spouse and $5000 to $10,000 on each child.

GROUP MEDICAL EXPENSE INSURANCE

Group medical expense insurance is an employee benefit that pays the cost of hospital care, physicians' and surgeons' fees, and related medical expenses. These plans are extremely important in providing financial security to employees and their families. Group plans currently account for more than 90 percent of the total premiums paid for medical expense insurance.

Group medical expense insurance is available from a number of sources. Major sources include the following:

- Commercial insurers
- Blue Cross and Blue Shield plans
- Managed care organizations
- Self-insured plans by employers

Commercial Insurers

Commercial life and health insurers sell both individual and group medical expense plans. Some property and casualty insurers also sell medical expense coverages. Most individuals and families insured by commercial insurers are covered under group plans. The business is highly concentrated. Most of the business is written by a small number of insurers.

Commercial insurers also sponsor managed care plans that provide benefits to members in a cost-effective manner, including health maintenance organizations (HMOs) and preferred provider organizations (PPOs). Managed care plans are discussed in greater detail later in the chapter.

Blue Cross and Blue Shield Plans

Blue Cross and Blue Shield plans are medical expense plans that cover hospital expenses, physician's and surgeon's fees, ancillary charges, and other medical expenses. Major medical insurance is also available. The various plans sell individual, family, and group coverages. Most insureds are covered by group plans.

Blue Cross plans cover hospital expenses and other related expenses. The plans typically provide service benefits rather than cash benefits to the insured. Blue Cross plans typically pay for room and board and related services, and payment is made directly to the hospital rather than to the insured.

Blue Shield plans cover physicians' and surgeons' fees and related medical expenses. Most plans today write both Blue Cross and Blue Shield coverages. The joint plans offer both basic medical expense benefits and major medical insurance. Finally, like commercial insurers, Blue Cross and Blue Shield plans also sponsor managed care plans, including HMOs and PPOs.

In the majority of states, Blue Cross and Blue Shield plans are nonprofit organizations that receive favorable tax treatment and are regulated under special legislation. However, to raise capital and become more competitive, several Blue Cross and Blue Shield plans have converted to a for-profit status with stockholders and a board of directors. In addition, many nonprofit plans own for-profit affiliates.

Managed Care Organizations

Managed care organizations are another source of group medical expense benefits. Managed care organizations generally are for-profit organizations that make available managed care plans to employers. Managed care is a generic term for medical expense benefits that are provided to covered employees in a cost effective manner. There is great emphasis on controlling costs, and the care provided by physicians is carefully monitored.

Managed care organizations typically sponsor **health maintenance organizations (HMOs)** and other types of managed care plans. Health maintenance organizations (HMOs) are managed care plans that provide broad, comprehensive health care services to the members for a fixed prepaid fee. As stated earlier, there is great emphasis on controlling costs. HMOs and other managed care plans are discussed later in this chapter.

Self-Insured Plans by Employers

A large percentage of employers, especially larger employers, self-insure part or all of the health insurance benefits provided to their employees. **Self-insurance** (also called **self-funding**) *means that the employer pays part or all of the cost of providing health insurance to the employees.*

Self-insured plans are usually established with stop-loss insurance and an administrative services only contract. *Stop-loss insurance means that a commercial insurer will pay claims that exceed a certain dollar amount up to some maximum limit.* This arrangement protects employees when claims exceed a certain level.

An *administrative services only (ASO) contract is a contract between an employer and a commercial insurer (or other third party) in which the insurer provides only administrative services.* These services

can include plan design, claims processing, actuarial support, and record keeping.

Employers self-insure their medical expense plans for several reasons, including the following:

- *Under the Employee Retirement Income Security Act of 1974 (ERISA), self-insured plans generally are not subject to state regulation. Thus, a national employer does not have to comply with separate state laws.*
- *Costs may be reduced or increase less rapidly because of savings in state premium taxes, commissions, and the insurer's profit.*
- *The employer retains part or all of the funds needed to pay claims and earns interest until the claims are paid.*
- *Self-insured plans are exempt from state laws that require insured plans to offer certain state-mandated benefits.*

TRADITIONAL INDEMNITY PLANS

Group medical expense plans have changed dramatically over time. Older plans were called **traditional indemnity plans** or **fee-for-service plans.** Physicians were paid a fee for each covered service; insureds had considerable freedom in selecting their own physicians and other health-care providers; the plans paid cash indemnity benefits for covered services up to certain maximum limits; and cost-containment was not heavily stressed. However, newer indemnity plans have several cost-containment provisions, such as preadmission certification by which a covered person must be approved for admission into a hospital, and second opinions. In addition, traditional indemnity plans also use preferred provider networks to control costs. Preferred provider networks are discussed later in the chapter.

Traditional indemnity plans have declined in importance over time and covered only 3 percent of all covered employees in 2005. Today, managed care plans (discussed later) dominate the group medical expense market. However, despite their declining importance, two types of traditional indemnity plans merit a brief discussion: (1) basic medical expense insurance and (2) major medical insurance.

Basic Medical Expense Insurance

Basic medical expense insurance *is a generic name for group plans that provide only basic benefits.* The benefits are sufficient to pay routine medical expenses but generally are not designed to cover a catastrophic loss. Group basic medical expense plans typically provide the following benefits:

- Hospital expense insurance
- Surgical expense insurance
- Physicians' visits
- Miscellaneous benefits

Hospital expense insurance covers medical expenses incurred while in a hospital. Some older indemnity plans pay actual room and board charges up to some stated maximum, such as $500 per day. Newer plans typically pay **service benefits** in which the full cost of a semiprivate room is paid if the employee is hospitalized, subject to any deductible or coinsurance requirement. In addition to daily room and board benefits, most plans provide full or partial payment for miscellaneous hospital charges, such as drugs, X-rays, and operating room charges.

Surgical expense insurance is usually included in a basic plan to help pay surgeons' and physicians' fees for surgical operations. Several methods are used to compensate surgeons. Many older plans used a *schedule approach* in which the various surgical operations were listed in a schedule, and a maximum dollar amount was specified for each procedure.

Newer plans typically reimburse physicians on the basis of their **reasonable and customary charges.** A physician is paid his or her usual fee as long as it is considered reasonable and customary. Many insurers consider a fee to be reasonable and customary if it does not exceed the 85th or 90th percentile amount for a similar medical procedure performed by other physicians in the same area. However, insurers differ in how usual and customary fees are calculated. As a result, patients often must pay substantial amounts out-of-pocket because of "balance billing" by physicians for the remainder of the fee not paid by insurance.

Group basic medical expense plans also provide benefits for *physicians' visits* other than for surgery. Most plans cover physicians' visits only while the employee is hospitalized, but some plans cover office or home visits as well.

Finally, basic plans provide a wide variety of miscellaneous benefits. Depending on the plan, basic benefits may cover home health care visits by medical specialists, extended-care facility benefits, radiation therapy, diagnostic X-rays, CAT scans and magnetic resonance imaging (MRI), and supplemental accident benefits.

Basic medical expense plans have declined in importance over time. Most employers today provide broader and more comprehensive major medical benefits. However, some employers that provide only basic benefits may wish to supplement them with major medical benefits. We discuss group major medical insurance in the following sections.

Major Medical Insurance

Most employers with group health insurance plans typically provide major medical insurance to their employees. **Major medical insurance** is designed to pay a high proportion of the covered expenses of a catastrophic illness or injury. Major medical insurance can be written as a supplement to a basic medical expense plan, or it can be combined with a basic plan to form a comprehensive major medical policy.

Supplemental Major Medical Insurance Supplemental major medical insurance *is designed to supplement the benefits provided by a basic plan.* Some medical expenses are not covered under a basic plan, or the benefits paid may be exhausted under the basic plan. Medical expenses not covered under a basic plan may be eligible for reimbursement under the supplemental major medical plan.

Supplemental major medical insurance plans have characteristics similar to the individual major medical policies described in Chapter 15, but the benefits have much higher limits and are more comprehensive.

Most supplemental major medical plans have high lifetime limits, such as $1 million, $2 million, $5 million, or even higher limits. A few plans have no limits at all. These high limits reflect the rapid increase in medical costs over time.

A **coinsurance provision** of 80 percent is typically found in supplemental major medical plans. However, the coinsurance provision is modified by a

stop-loss limit, which places a dollar limit on the maximum amount that an individual must pay. Under a stop-loss provision, once the individual's annual out-of-pocket expenses exceed a certain amount, such as $2000, all remaining eligible medical expenses are paid in full.

A **corridor deductible** may be used to integrate a basic medical expense plan with a supplemental major medical plan. Before the supplemental major medical plan pays any benefits, a corridor deductible must be met. A *corridor deductible applies only to eligible medical expenses not covered by the basic medical expense plan.* As noted earlier, some medical expenses are not covered under a basic plan, or the expenses may be covered but the benefits paid by the basic plan are exhausted. These expenses may be eligible for reimbursement under the supplemental major medical plan, subject to a corridor deductible. This type of deductible can be illustrated by the following example:

Total medical expenses	$50,000
Paid by basic medical expense plan	40,000
Remaining medical expenses	$10,000
Corridor deductible paid by the insured	500
Balance of medical expenses to be paid	$9500
80 percent paid by supplemental major medical plan	7600
20 percent paid by the insured	$1900

Comprehensive Major Medical Insurance Many employers have comprehensive major medical plans for their employees. **Comprehensive major medical insurance** *is a combination of basic benefits and major medical insurance in one policy.* This type of plan is widely used by employers who want both basic benefits and major medical protection in a single policy. This type of plan is characterized by a deductible, such as $400 or $500; by high lifetime maximum limits of $1 million, $2 million, or some higher amount; and by coinsurance, such as 80–20 percent.

A **calendar-year deductible** is widely used in comprehensive major medical plans. The deductible has to be met only once during the calendar year. All covered medical expenses incurred by the insured during the year can be used to satisfy the deductible.

The deductible applies separately to the employee and each family member. However, to minimize the financial impact on the family, the major medical plan may contain a **family deductible provision.** Under this provision, additional deductibles for family members are waived if two or three separate deductibles have been satisfied by individual family members during the year.

In the previous discussion, major medical health insurance has been discussed as a traditional indemnity plan. However, major medical insurance is also used today in preferred provider organization (PPO) plans. A PPO plan is a managed care plan that is discussed in the following section.

MANAGED CARE PLANS

Employers and insurers have designed a variety of managed care plans to hold down the escalation in health care costs. **Managed care** *is a generic name for medical expense plans that provide covered services to the members in a cost-effective manner.* Under managed care plans, the employees' choice of physicians and hospitals may be limited to certain health care providers; cost control and cost reduction are heavily emphasized; utilization review is done at all levels; the quality of the care provided by physicians is carefully monitored and evaluated; health care providers share in the financial results through various risk-sharing techniques; and preventive care and healthy lifestyles are emphasized.

There are several types of managed care plans. They include the following:

- Health maintenance organizations (HMOs)
- Preferred provider organizations (PPOs)
- Point-of-service (POS) plans

Health Maintenance Organizations (HMOs)

A *health maintenance organization (HMO) is an organized system of health care that provides comprehensive services to its members for a fixed, prepaid fee.* Many employers sponsor HMOs that provide comprehensive medical services to covered employees.

Basic Characteristics HMOs have several basic characteristics that distinguish them from traditional group indemnity plans.

- *Organized health-care plan.* An HMO has the responsibility for organizing and delivering comprehensive health-care services to its members. The HMO owns or leases medical facilities, enters into agreements with hospitals and physicians to provide medical services, hires ancillary personnel, and has general managerial control over the various services provided.
- *Broad, comprehensive health services.* An HMO provides broad, comprehensive health-care services to the members. Most services generally are covered in full, with relatively few maximum limits on individual services. However, many HMOs limit the amount paid for the treatment of alcoholism and drug addiction. Covered services include hospital care, surgeons' and physicians' fees, maternity care, laboratory and X-ray services, outpatient, special-duty nursing, and numerous other services. Office visits to HMO physicians are covered either in full or at a nominal charge for each visit.
- *Restrictions on the choice of physician.* Traditional HMOs typically limit the choice of physicians and other health-care providers to providers who are part of the HMO network. However, as discussed later, some HMOs allow employees to select health-care providers outside of the plan network by payment of higher out-of-pocket costs. In addition, because HMOs operate in limited geographical areas, there may be limited coverage for medical care received outside of the area. HMOs typically cover only emergency medical treatment received outside of the geographical area of the HMO.
- *Payment of a fixed, prepaid fee.* HMO members pay a fixed, prepaid fee (usually monthly) for the medical services provided. High deductibles and coinsurance requirements are usually not emphasized. However, to control costs, many HMOs impose a coinsurance requirement for certain diseases, such as alcoholism and drug addiction. Some HMOs now impose an inpatient hospital deductible. In addition, there may be a nominal fee for certain services, such as $15 for an office visit.

- *Heavy emphasis on controlling costs.* HMOs place a heavy emphasis on controlling the cost of covered services. HMOs typically pay network physicians or medical groups a capitation fee. A **capitation fee** *is a method of payment by which a physician or hospital receives a fixed annual payment for each plan member regardless of the frequency or type of service provided.* As such, HMO providers have no financial incentive to provide unnecessary medical care because their financial compensation does not increase.

Some HMOs pay physicians a salary, which also holds down costs because the provider has no financial incentive to provide unnecessary services. HMOs also contract with specialists and other providers to provide certain medical services at negotiated fees. In addition, a **gatekeeper physician** generally controls access to an expensive specialist. A gatekeeper physician is a primary care physician who determines whether medical care from a specialist is necessary. However, some HMOs now allow patients to bypass the primary care physician and see a specialist directly. Finally, HMOs emphasize preventive care and healthy lifestyles, which also tend to hold down costs.

Types of HMOs There are several types of HMOs:

- *Staff model.* Under a staff model, physicians are employees of the HMO and are paid a salary and possibly an incentive bonus to hold down costs.
- *Group model.* Under a group model, physicians are employees of another group that has a contract with the HMO to provide medical services to its members. The HMO pays the group of physicians a monthly or annual capitation fee for each member. As stated earlier, a capitation fee is a fixed amount for each member regardless of the number of services provided. In return, the group agrees to provide all covered services to the members during the year. The group model typically has a closed panel of physicians that requires members to select physicians affiliated with the HMO.
- *Network model.* Under a network model, the HMO contracts with two or more independent group practices to provide medical services to

covered members. The HMO pays a fixed monthly fee for each member to the medical group. The medical group then decides how the fees will be distributed among the individual physicians.

- *Individual practice association plan (IPA).* A final type of HMO is an **individual practice association plan (IPA)**. An IPA is an open panel of physicians who work out of their own offices and treat patients on a fee-for-service basis. However, the individual physicians agree to treat HMO members at reduced fees. Physicians may be paid a capitation fee for each member or may be paid a reduced fee for treating each patient. In addition, to encourage cost containment, most IPAs have risk-sharing agreements with the participating physicians. Payments may be reduced if the plan experience is poor. A bonus is paid if the plan experience is better than expected.

Preferred Provider Organizations

A **preferred provider organization (PPO)** is a plan that contracts with health care providers to provide medical services to the members at reduced fees. The employer, insurer, or other group negotiates contracts with physicians, hospitals, and other providers of care to provide certain medical services to the plan members at discounted fees. To encourage patients to use PPO providers, deductibles and co-payment charges are reduced. In addition, the patient may be charged a lower fee for certain routine treatments, or offered increased benefits such as preventive health care services.

PPOs should not be confused with HMOs. There are three important differences.[5] *First, PPO providers typically do not provide medical care on a prepaid basis, but are paid on a fee-for-service basis as their services are used.* However, as stated earlier, the fees charged are below the provider's regular fee.

Second, unlike an HMO, patients are not required to use a preferred provider but have freedom of choice every time they need care. However, the patients have a financial incentive to use a preferred provider because the deductible and co-payment charges are reduced. In addition, if the health care provider's actual charge exceeds the negotiated fee, the provider absorbs the excess amount. Savings can

be substantial. For example, if a surgeon who participates in a PPO charges a normal fee of $4000 for a knee operation but the negotiated fee is only $3000, the patient does not have to pay the additional $1000. The surgeon absorbs this amount.

Finally, most PPOs do not use a gatekeeper physician, and employees do not have to get permission from a primary care physician to see a specialist.

PPOs offer the major advantage of controlling health care costs because provider fees are negotiated at a discount. PPOs also help physicians to build up their practice. Patients benefit because they pay less for their medical care. Enrollments in PPOs have increased rapidly over time and accounted for 61 percent of all employee enrollments in 2005.

Point-of-Service Plans

A **point-of-service (POS)** plan is another important type of managed care plan. A point-of-service (POS) plan is typically structured as an HMO, but members are allowed to go outside the network for medical care. *If patients see providers who are in the network, they pay little or nothing out of pocket, which is similar to an HMO. However, if the patients receive care from providers outside the network, the care is covered, but the patients must pay substantially higher deductibles and co-payments.* For example, a patient who sees a physician outside the network may be required to pay a $500 annual deductible and a coinsurance charge of 30 percent. If the patient sees a participating physician within the network, there is no additional charge.

The POS plan has the major advantage of preserving freedom of choice for plan members; it also eliminates the fear that plan members will not be able to see a physician or specialist of their choice. The major disadvantage is the substantially higher cost that a member must pay to see a provider outside the network.

Advantages of Managed Care Plans

Managed care plans have a number of advantages. Managed care plans generally have lower hospital and surgical utilization rates than traditional indemnity plans; plan members pay substantially lower out-of-pocket costs if they use network providers; and employees do not have to file claim forms.

EXHIBIT 16.1

Annual Change in Average Total Health Benefit Cost, 1988–2005, All Employers

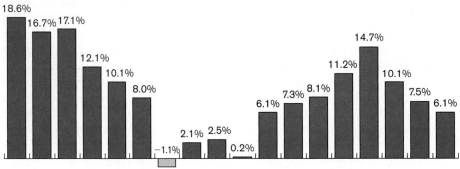

NOTE: Results for 1988–1998 are based on cost for active and retired employees combined. The change in cost from 1998–2005 is based on cost for active employees only.

SOURCE: Mercer Health & Benefits, *Health Benefit Cost Slows For a Third year, Rising Just 6.1% in 2005,* November 21, 2005.

In addition, heavy emphasis on cost control has reduced the annual rate of increase in health benefit costs for employers (see Exhibit 16.1). Although the rate of increase has slowed in recent years, it still substantially exceeds the rate of general inflation. However, on an absolute basis, total health benefit costs continue to increase. *According to Mercer Human Consulting, total health benefit cost per active employee increased from $6,679 in 2004 to $7,089 in 2005, or an increase of 6.1 percent (see Exhibit 16.2).* Costs are predicted to increase 6.7 percent in 2006.

EXHIBIT 16.2

Total Health Benefit Cost* Per Employee for Active Employees, 1994–2004

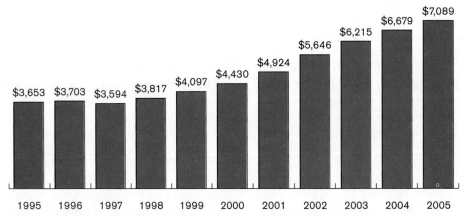

*Includes all medical, dental, and other health benefits for all covered employees and dependents. Includes employer and employee contributions.

SOURCE: Mercer Health & Benefits, *Health Benefit Cost Slows For a Third year, Rising Just 6.1% in 2005,* November 21, 2005.

According to Mercer Human Resource Consulting, employer health-care costs are rising for several reasons:[6] (1) the average age of the labor force is increasing, which results in higher medical costs as workers age; (2) new medical technology, such as genomics and new electronic diagnostic techniques, drive up health care costs; (3) mergers and acquisitions and general consolidation in the managed care industry have reduced competition; (4) health-care providers generally have more leverage in negotiating higher reimbursement rates than they had in the past; and (5) plan designs of the past decade have insulated employees from the true cost of medical care because their financial involvement generally is limited only to the payment of deductibles, copayments, or coinsurance charges. For example, many employees believe that a small copayment charge of $10, $20, or $30 is the true cost of a prescription drug when the actual cost may be 10 times higher. Cost insulation creates an environment in which employees have no incentive to hold down costs or reduce overutilization of plan benefits.

Disadvantages of Managed Care Plans

According to many critics, the major disadvantage of managed care plans is that the quality of care is being reduced because of the heavy emphasis on cost control. Critics argue that access to specialists may be delayed because some gatekeeper physicians do not promptly refer sick patients to specialists because of the additional cost to the plan; some patients who should be hospitalized are not admitted into a hospital; and certain diagnostic tests are not performed. In addition, critics agree that for-profit HMOs often skimp on preventive care to maximize profits.

Many physicians criticize managed care plans because of the restrictions placed on their freedom to treat patients. HMO physicians must often obtain approval from plan administrators or insurers before certain diagnostic tests or procedures can be given; they may have to argue for additional days of hospital coverage for patients who are too sick to be released; referral to a specialist may be denied or delayed; and prescription drugs may be limited only to certain drugs on an approved list. In addition, physicians argue that some HMOs impose a "gag rule" on the right of the doctor to discuss with patients alternative methods of treatment not approved by the HMO. Thus, many plan physicians believe the traditional doctor–patient relationship is being seriously compromised by outside third parties.

In addition, managed care plans commonly provide financial incentives to health-care providers to hold down costs, such as an incentive bonus based on the profitability of the plan. Critics argue that network physicians often have a financial conflict of interest between providing the highest-quality medical care to their patients and holding down costs to increase plan profits and the amount of their bonus.

Finally, many workers are unaware of the various restrictions and limitations in managed care plans, and state regulation of HMOs varies widely.

Although many physicians and patients are dissatisfied with managed care plans, studies show that the quality of health-care plans is improving. The National Committee for Quality Assurance (NCQA), a major accreditation organization, conducts an annual survey of managed care plans and rates the plans based on the quality of services provided. The 2005 survey showed that the quality of health care plans has improved significantly for millions of Americans over time.[7] Despite improvements, however, serious problems remain. The NCQA concluded that there are severe "quality gaps" in the nation's health-care system that prevent millions of patients from receiving the best medical care possible. The term "quality gap" means that health-care providers often fail to provide the recommended health-care services that medical science has shown to be effective in treating certain diseases. As a result of the failure to deliver recommended care, quality gaps cause an estimated 39,200 to 83,600 deaths each year (see Exhibit 16.3).

Current Developments in Managed Care Plans

Managed care plans are constantly changing. Two current developments that merit discussion are (1) declining HMO enrollments, and (2) current cost control strategies.

Declining HMO Enrollments   HMO enrollments grew steadily in the 1980s and early 1990s. *More recently, however, HMO enrollments declined from 33 percent of all covered workers in 2001 to 25 percent in 2005. Enrollments in traditional plans have*

EXHIBIT 16.3
Estimated Deaths Attributable to Failure to Deliver Recommended Care: Selected Measures/Conditions (U.S. population)

Measure	Avoidable Deaths
Beta-Blocker Treatment	800–1,200
Breast Cancer Screening	150–600
Controlling High Blood Pressure	12,000–32,000
Cervical Cancer Screening	650–850
Cholesterol Management (Control)	3,400–7,200
Diabetes Care–HbA1c Control	5,300–11,700
Smoking Cessation	8,300–13,200
Prenatal Care	1,000–1,750
Colorectal Cancer Screening	4,100–6,200
Flu Shots (65+)	3,500–7,500
Total	**39,200–83,600**

SOURCE: National Committee for Quality Assurance. *The State of Health Care Quality: 2005.* Washington, DC. National Committee for Quality Assurance, 2005: 10.

also declined dramatically since 1993 (see Exhibit 16.4). In contrast, enrollments in PPOs continue to increase. Consumer-driven health plans (discussed later) also made the charts in 2005.

Many employers have become dissatisfied with HMOs in recent years because of substantially higher HMO premiums and plan costs. In addition, traditional HMOs generally provide first dollar coverage

EXHIBIT 16.4
National Employee Enrollment, 1993–2005, Percent of All Covered Employees

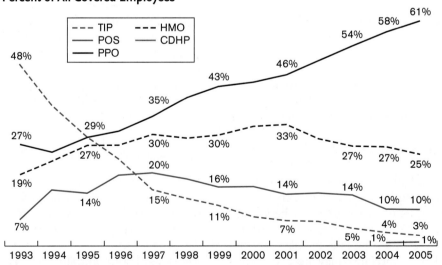

NOTE: PPO = Preferred Provider Organization; HMO = Health Maintenance Organization; POS = Point of Service; TIP = Traditional Indemnity Plan; CDHP = Consumer Directed Health Plan

SOURCE: Mercer Health & Benefits, *Health Benefit Cost Slows For a Third year, Rising Just 6.1% in 2005,* November 21, 2005.

or benefits with small copayments, which tend to insulate workers from the true cost of health care.

The decline in HMO enrollments is also due to employee dissatisfaction. Many employees are dissatisfied because of higher premiums, higher deductibles and copayment charges, and disruptions from network changes in physicians and health-care plans. Some physicians drop out of HMOs or their contracts are not renewed, while mergers in the managed care industry often cause changes in health-care plans. The result is employee dissatisfaction and withdrawal from the HMO.

Current Cost Control Measures To control costs, employers are employing a number of cost control measures, which include the following:

- *Increased cost sharing.* Employers continue to shift costs to employees by higher premiums, higher deductibles, higher coinsurance and co-payment charges, and higher maximum annual out-of-pocket expenses. More than one-third of small employers now have a deductible of $1000 or higher.[8]
- *Three-tier pricing for prescription drugs.* Under this pricing system, copayment charges vary depending on the drug used. For the first tier, if employees use less expensive generic drugs, the copayment charge is the lowest. For the second tier, if employees use a brand-name drug on an approved list (called a formulary), the copayment charge is higher. For the third tier, if employees use a brand name drug not included in the formulary, the copayment charge is even higher.

  Although three-tier pricing of prescription drugs is common, some group plans have added a fourth tier for very expensive drugs. Copayment or coinsurance charges are substantially higher for drugs in this category.
- *Tiered networks of health-care providers.* A tiered network is one in which employees receive a higher reimbursement rate or pay a lower copayment charge if they participate in a narrower network than that found in a typical PPO. The objective is to encourage patients to use less costly hospitals and doctors instead of more expensive providers.

- *Disease management programs.* Some diseases are chronic, such as asthma, diabetes, and heart disease. Many large employers have disease management programs that use network providers who provide counseling and preventive services for such diseases. Many employers also have Web sites that provide workers with information on self-care, health-care decision tools, and effective management of certain diseases.
- *Health risk assessments.* A *health risk assessment (HRA)* is an evaluation of the employee's health status based on information provided by the employee. This information includes health history, current medical condition, and current health habits. The information identifies employees who are potential participants in disease management programs. The HRA also provides suggestions for healthier lifestyles, improved health habits, and preventive care.
- *Health insurance for retired workers.* Health insurance coverage of employees who are not yet eligible for Medicare is expensive. Many employers have discontinued medical expense plans for retired workers. Other employers have increased premiums or have reduced benefits for pre-Medicare retirees who are now enrolled.

In addition to the above, some employers have introduced consumer-driven health plans that encourage employees to be more sensitive to health-care costs and to give them greater control over the spending of their health-care dollars. We discuss consumer-driven health plans in the following section.

CONSUMER-DRIVEN HEALTH PLANS

A **consumer-driven health plan** (CDHP) *is a generic term for an arrangement that gives employees a choice of health-care plans, which are designed to make employees more sensitive to health-care costs, to provide a financial incentive to avoid unnecessary care, and to seek out low-cost providers.*

There are a number of consumer-driven health plans available to employees. Two plans that merit a brief discussion are (1) defined contribution health plans, and (2) high deductible health plans.

Defined Contribution Health Plans

A **defined contribution health plan** is a generic term to describe an arrangement in which the employee has a choice of health-care plans, such as an HMO, PPO, or POS, and to which the employer contributes a fixed amount—hence the term, "defined contribution." If the employee selects a more expensive plan, he or she will incur greater out-of-pocket costs. For example, an employer may offer employees a choice of an HMO, PPO, or POS, and will contribute a maximum of $200 monthly to the plan. If the monthly premium for the HMO is $250, the employee pays a monthly premium of $50 However, if the PPO plan is more expensive and costs $300 monthly, the employee must pay a monthly premium of $100. Since the employer pays a fixed amount, the employee has a financial incentive to sign up for a less costly plan.

High-Deductible Health Plans

A **high-deductible health plan (HDHP)** is a consumer-driven health plan that consists of major medical health insurance with a high deductible and a health savings account (HSA). High-deductible plans in the group market are similar to the HSA plans for individuals discussed in Chapter 15. The employee is covered under a major medical plan with a high deductible, which is combined with a HSA from which the employee can withdraw money tax free to pay for medical costs. For 2007, the annual deductible must be at least $1100 for an individual and $2200 for family coverage. Maximum annual out-of-pocket expenses, including the deductible and copayments, cannot exceed $5500 for an individual and $11,000 for family coverage. In addition, although many high deductible plans pay 100 percent of the covered expenses in excess of the deductible, some plans have a coinsurance requirement. The coinsurance percentage is typically 20 percent and applies to all covered expenses in excess of the deductible up to some maximum annual out-of-pocket limit. Finally, investment earnings accumulate income-tax free, and distributions from the HSA are also tax free if used to pay for qualified medical expenses.

Because CDHPs can reduce employer costs, a growing number of employers now offer CDHPs to employees. Some 22 percent of large employers with

20,000 or more employees made these plans available to employees in 2005. In contrast, only 2 percent of smaller employers with 10 or more employees offered CDHPs to employees in 2005.[9] Although CDHPs can cut employer costs, some observers believe the quality of health care may be threatened. Because of high deductibles, some employees may postpone needed medical treatment or the purchase of life-enhancing prescription drugs.

PATIENTS' BILL OF RIGHTS

Because of dissatisfaction with managed care plans, federal legislation has been introduced that would protect the rights of patients in managed care plans. Legislation is considered necessary because of the denial of care and widespread dissatisfaction with managed care plans voiced by both patients and physicians.

Several proposals have been introduced. One proposal includes the following:

- Allows patients harmed by the denial of care the right to sue the managed care plan.
- Requires health plans to pay for emergency-room care even if the hospital is outside the network.
- Allows women to see obstetricians and gynecologists without prior approval and to designate them as primary-care physicians.
- Requires health plans to pay routine health-care costs associated with clinical trials.
- Defines "medical necessity" and prohibits plans from interfering with a doctor's care if the services provided are medically necessary.
- Requires health plans to pay for an overnight hospital stay for a patient who has a mastectomy if the doctor and patient want it.
- Allows patients who are pregnant or undergoing a plan of treatment the right to keep their doctors for 90 days even if the doctor leaves the network.
- Allows patients to appeal denials first through an internal process and then to outside experts.

Finally, it should be noted that most states already have laws that require health insurance plans to include most of the provisions contained in the various federal proposals (except for the right of consumers to sue health insurance plans directly).

GROUP MEDICAL EXPENSE CONTRACTUAL PROVISIONS

Group medical expense insurance plans contain numerous contractual provisions that can have a significant financial impact on the insured. Three important provisions deal with (1) preexisting conditions, (2) coordination of benefits, and (3) continuation of group health insurance.

Preexisting Conditions

Group medical expense plans often contain a **preexisting-conditions** provision that excludes coverage for a medical condition for a limited period after the worker enters the plan. The purposes of this provision are to reduce adverse selection against the insurer and to control employer costs.

In 1996, Congress enacted the **Health Insurance Portability and Accountability Act (HIPAA)**, which places restrictions on the right of insurers and employers to deny or limit coverage for preexisting conditions.

The following discussion summarizes the major provisions of the law dealing with preexisting conditions:

- Employer-sponsored group health insurance plans cannot exclude or limit coverage for a preexisting condition for more than 12 months (18 months for late enrollees). A *preexisting condition is defined as a medical condition diagnosed or treated during the previous six months.* A preexisting condition exclusion cannot be applied to pregnancy, newly born children, or adopted children.
- After the initial 12-month period expires, no new preexisting condition period can be imposed on workers who maintain continuous coverage with no more than a 63-day gap in coverage, even if the workers should change jobs or health-care plans.
- *Insurers and employers must give credit for previous coverage of less than 12 months with*

respect to any preexisting condition exclusion found in the new health plan. For example, a worker with a preexisting condition who was previously insured for eight months under a group plan when he or she changes jobs or health plans would face a maximum additional exclusion of four months for a preexisting condition, rather than the normal 12 months.
- Discrimination based on health status is prohibited. Employers that offer health insurance to employees and dependents cannot exclude, drop from coverage, or charge higher premiums based on health status. Health status is broadly defined to include the individual's medical condition; physical and mental illness; medical history; claims experience; evidence of insurability, including conditions arising out of acts of domestic violence; genetic information; and disability.
- The law also guarantees the availability of group health insurance to small employers. Commercial insurers, HMOs, and other groups issuing health insurance coverages are prohibited from denying coverage to firms that employ between 2 and 50 employees.

Because of limits on preexisting conditions and credit for previous and continuous coverage, employees will no longer be afraid to change jobs for fear of losing their group health insurance protection. As a result, they can change jobs and still be assured of health insurance coverage. Thus, the law makes the health insurance protection "portable."

However, portability does not mean that employees can take their present group health insurance benefits with them when they change jobs. **Portability** *means that when employees change jobs, the new employer or health plan must give them credit for previous and continuous health insurance coverage.* When the employees leave their present job, the insurer or employer must provide information showing how long they were covered while working at that job. The worker then presents this documentation to the new employer or health plan. If a worker has been covered for 12 months or more by a previous employer or health plan and does not have a gap in coverage of more than 63 days, the worker is eligible for coverage under the new employer's plan even though he or she has a preexisting condition.

Coordination of Benefits

Group medical insurance plans typically contain a **coordination-of-benefits provision,** which specifies the order of payment when an insured is covered under two or more group health insurance plans. Total recovery under all plans is limited to 100 percent of covered expenses. The purpose is to prevent overinsurance and duplication of benefits if an insured is covered by more than one plan.

The coordination-of-benefit provisions in most group plans are based on rules developed by the National Association of Insurance Commissioners (NAIC). These rules are complex and are beyond the scope of this text to discuss in detail. The following summarizes the major provisions based on the NAIC rules.

- *Coverage as an employee is usually primary to coverage as a dependent.* For example, Karen and Chris Swift both work, and each is insured as a dependent under the other's group medical insurance plan. If Karen incurs covered medical expenses, her plan pays first. She then submits any unreimbursed expenses (such as the deductible and coinsurance payments) to Chris's insurer for payment. No more than 100 percent of the eligible medical expenses are paid under both plans.
- With respect to dependent children, if the parents are married or are not separated, *the plan of the parent whose birthday occurs first during the year is primary; the plan of the parent with the later birthday is secondary.* For example, if Karen's birthday is in January and Chris's birthday is in July, Karen's plan would pay first if their son is hospitalized. Chris's plan would be secondary.
- If the parents of dependent children are not married, or are separated (regardless of whether they have ever been married), or are divorced, and there is no court decree specifying who is responsible for the child's health-care expenses, the following rules apply:
  - The plan of the parent who is awarded custody pays first.
  - The plan of the step-parent who is the spouse of the parent awarded custody pays second.
  - The plan of the parent without custody pays third.
  - The plan of the step-parent who is the spouse of the parent without custody pays last.

Continuation of Group Health Insurance

Employees often quit their jobs, are laid off, or are fired. If a qualifying event occurs that results in a loss of coverage, employees and covered dependents can elect to remain in the employer's health insurance plan for a limited period under the Consolidated Omnibus Budget Reconciliation Act of 1985 (also known as COBRA). The **COBRA law** applies to firms with 20 or more employees. *A qualifying event includes termination of employment for any reason (except gross misconduct), divorce or legal separation, death of the employee, and attainment of a maximum age by dependent children.* If the worker loses his or her job or no longer works the required number of hours, the terminated worker and his or her covered dependents can elect to remain in the employer's plan for as long as 18 months. However, the worker must pay 102 percent of the group insurance rate. If the worker dies or is divorced or legally separated or has a child who is no longer eligible for coverage, covered dependents have the right to remain in the group plan for up to three years.

After the period of protection under COBRA expires, some workers with preexisting conditions may be unable to obtain individual health insurance. The Health Insurance Portability and Accountability Act guarantees individual health insurance to eligible persons with no evidence of insurability if certain conditions are met. Eligible persons with health problems are guaranteed individual health insurance if they can meet the following requirements: (1) have employment-based health insurance for at least 18 months, (2) are ineligible for COBRA or have exhausted their COBRA coverage, and (3) are ineligible for coverage under any other employment-based health plan. The insurance provided is a guaranteed renewable policy.

GROUP DENTAL INSURANCE

Group dental insurance helps pay the cost of normal dental care and also covers damage to teeth from an accident. Dental insurance has the principal advantage of helping employees meet the costs of regular dental care. It also encourages insureds to see their dentists on a regular basis, thereby preventing or detecting dental problems before they become serious.

Benefits

Group dental insurance plans typically cover a wide variety of dental services, including X-rays, cleaning, fillings, extractions, inlays, bridgework and dentures, oral surgery, root canals, and orthodontia. In some plans, orthodontia benefits are excluded. Dentists are reimbursed on the basis of their reasonable and customary charges subject to any limitations on benefits stated in the plan. As discussed later, an annual deductible and coinsurance are used to control costs. However, the coinsurance requirements vary depending on the type of service provided. Dental services are typically grouped into different levels, with varying coinsurance requirements. To encourage routine dental care, coinsurance does not usually apply to diagnostic and preventive services (e.g., cleaning teeth), or the coinsurance percentage is lower. The following is an example of the classification of benefits and the reimbursement levels:[10]

- Type I. Diagnostic and preventive services: 100 percent
- Type II. Basic services, including anesthesia and basic restoration: 75 percent
- Major restoration, including endodontics, oral surgery, periodontics, and prosthodontics: 50 percent
- Type IV. Orthodontics: 50 percent

Cost Controls

To control costs and reduce adverse selection against the insurer when the plan is initially installed, several cost controls are used. They include the following:

- Deductibles and coinsurance
- Maximum limit on benefits
- Waiting periods
- Exclusions
- Predetermination-of-benefits provision

Most dental insurance plans use *deductibles* and **coinsurance** to control costs. The coinsurance percentage may vary depending on the type of service. To encourage regular visits to a dentist, many plans do not impose any coinsurance requirements for one or two routine dental examinations each year. However, fillings and oral surgery may be paid only at a rate of 80 percent, while the cost of orthodontia or dentures is may be paid at a lower rate of 50 percent.

Maximum limits on benefits are also used to control costs. There may be a maximum annual limit on the amount paid, such as $2000 during the calendar year. Another approach is to impose a lifetime maximum on certain types of dental services, such as a lifetime maximum of $5000 for dentures.

Waiting periods for certain types of services are used to control costs as well. For example, some plans do not cover dentures until the employee is insured for at least one year, and there may be only one replacement of dentures for each five-year period.

Certain *exclusions* are used to reduce costs. Common exclusions include cosmetic dental work, such as capping a tooth; replacement of lost or stolen dental devices, such as dentures or a space retainer; and benefits provided under a workers compensation or similar law.

A *predetermination-of-benefits provision* is also used to control costs. Under this provision, if the cost of dental treatment exceeds a certain amount, such as $300, the dentist submits a plan of treatment to the insurer. The insurer then specifies the services covered and how much the plan will pay. The employee is informed of the amount the plan will pay and then makes a decision on whether to proceed with the proposed plan of treatment.

Finally, it should be pointed out that, just as in medical expense insurance, there are dental HMOs, PPOs, and self-funded plans by employers that provide dental insurance to employees.

GROUP DISABILITY-INCOME INSURANCE

Group disability-income insurance pays weekly or monthly cash payments to employees who are disabled from accidents or illness. There are two basic types of plans: (1) short-term plans and (2) long-term plans.

Short-Term Plans

Many employers have short-term plans that pay disability benefits for relatively short periods ranging from 13 weeks to two years. The majority of short-term plans sold today pay benefits for a maximum period of 26 weeks. In addition, most plans have a short elimination period of one to seven days for sickness, while accidents are typically covered from the first day of disability. The elimination period reduces nuisance claims, holds down costs, and discourages malingering and excessive absenteeism.

Most short-term plans cover only **nonoccupational disability,** which means that an accident or illness must occur off the job. *Disability is usually defined in terms of the worker's own occupation. You are considered totally disabled if you are unable to perform all of the duties of your own occupation.* Partial disability is seldom covered under a group short-term plan; you must be totally disabled to qualify.

The amount of disability-income benefits is related to the worker's normal earnings and is typically equal to some percentage of weekly earnings, such as 50 to 70 percent. Thus, if Amy's weekly earnings are $600 and the plan replaces 70 percent of earnings, she would collect a maximum weekly benefit of $420 if she becomes disabled.

In addition, short-term plans have relatively few exclusions. As noted earlier, a disability that occurs on the job is usually not covered, because occupational disability is covered under a workers compensation law. Also, except for very small groups, preexisting conditions are covered immediately. Most plans also cover alcoholism, drug addiction, and nervous and mental disorders.

Long-Term Plans

Many employers also have long-term plans that pay benefits for longer periods, typically ranging from two years to age 65. However, if the disability occurs beyond age 65, benefits are paid for a limited period. For example, under the plan of one disability insurer, if the worker is younger than 60 at the time of disability, the maximum benefit period is to age 65. However, if a worker age 66 becomes disabled, the maximum benefit period is only 21 months.

A dual definition of disability is typically used to determine whether a worker is totally disabled. *For the first two years, you are considered disabled if you are unable to perform all of the duties of your own occupation. After two years, you are still considered disabled if you are unable to work in any occupation for which you are reasonably fitted by education, training, and experience.* In addition, in contrast to short-term plans, long-term plans typically cover both occupational and nonoccupational disability.

The disability-income benefits are usually paid monthly, and the maximum monthly benefits are substantially higher than the benefits paid by short-term plans. The maximum monthly benefit is generally limited to 50 to 70 percent of the employee's normal earnings. Most plans commonly pay maximum monthly benefits of $2000, $3000, $4000, or even higher amounts. A waiting period of three to six months is typically required before the benefits are payable.

To reduce malingering and moral hazard, other disability-income benefits are taken into consideration. If the disabled worker is also receiving Social Security or workers compensation benefits, the long-term disability benefit is reduced accordingly. However, many plans limit the reduction only to the amount of the initial Social Security disability benefit. Thus, if Social Security disability benefits are increased because of increases in the cost of living, the long-term disability-income benefit is not reduced further.

Some long-term plans have additional supplemental benefits. Under the *cost-of-living adjustment,* benefits paid to disabled employees are adjusted annually for increases in the cost of living. However, there may be a maximum limit on the percentage increase in benefits.

Under the *pension accrual benefit,* the plan makes a pension contribution so that the disabled employee's pension benefit remains intact. For example, if both Carlos and his employer contribute 6 percent of his salary into a pension plan, and Carlos becomes disabled, the plan would pay an amount equal to 12 percent of his monthly salary into the company's pension plan for as long as he remains disabled. Thus, Carlos would still receive his pension at the normal retirement age.

Finally, if the disabled worker dies, the plan may pay monthly *survivor income benefits* to an eligible surviving spouse or children for a limited period—

such as two years—following the disabled worker's death.

CAFETERIA PLANS

The final part of this chapter deals with cafeteria plans. **Cafeteria plans** *allow employees to select those employee benefits that best meet their specific needs.* Instead of a single benefits package that applies to all employees, cafeteria plans allow employees to select among the various group life, medical expense, disability, dental, and other plans that are offered. Cafeteria plans also allow employers to introduce new benefits to meet the specific needs of certain employees.

Although cafeteria plans vary among employers, they share certain common characteristics. First, in many plans, the employer gives each employee a certain number of dollars or credits that can be spent on the different benefits or taken as cash. If taken as cash, the employer's credits are taxed as income to the employee.

Second, many cafeteria plans are also *premium-conversion plans,* which is a generic name for a plan that allows employees to make their premium contributions for plan benefits with before-tax dollars. Premium-conversion plans are commonly used for group health and dental insurance. Employees elect to reduce their salaries, and the salary reduction is used to pay for plan benefits. In effect, employee premium contributions are paid with before-tax dollars. As a result, taxes are reduced, and disposable income is increased.

Third, cafeteria plans typically allow employees to establish flexible spending accounts. A **flexible spending account** *is an arrangement that permits employees to pay for certain unreimbursed medical expenses with before-tax dollars.* The employee agrees to a salary reduction, which is used to pay for certain expenses, permitted by the Internal Revenue Code, with before-tax dollars. These expenses include unreimbursed medical and dental expenses, plan deductibles, coinsurance charges, eyeglasses, hearing aids, cosmetic surgery, and other expenses not covered under a typical group plan. The Internal Revenue Service also issued a ruling that allows reimbursement for the purchase of over-the-counter pain drugs. One disadvantage, however, is that amounts in the flexible spending account not used by the employee by the end of the year are forfeited to the employer.

However, the Internal Revenue Service recently ruled that an employer could allow a grace period of up to 2½ months. However, the plan must be specifically designed to include this feature. Many plans have been amended to allow a grace period. However, because of administrative complexities, some employers have elected not to include a grace period in their plans. In addition, at the time of this writing, federal legislation has been introduced that would allow employees to carry over any unused funds up to $500 to the next plan year; workers would also have the option of moving the funds into a health savings account (HSA).

Many employers now provide debit cards that employees can use to pay for unreimbursed expenses out of their account balances. The debit card allows employees to be reimbursed immediately for their uncovered out-of-pocket expenses.

Finally, if the cafeteria plan meets certain requirements specified in the Internal Revenue Code, the employer's credits are not currently taxable to the employee.

Cafeteria plans have certain advantages, including the following:

- Employees can select those benefits that best meet their specific needs.
- Employees generally pay their share of the cost of benefits with before-tax dollars, which reduces taxes and increases take-home pay.
- Employers can more easily control rising employee benefit costs. For example, an employer may limit the number of benefit dollars or credits given to each employee or offer the employees a medical expense plan with a higher deductible.

Cafeteria plans also have certain disadvantages, including the following:

- The employer may incur higher initial development and administrative costs in establishing and managing a cafeteria plan rather than a traditional employee benefits plan.
- Administrative complexity is increased. The employee benefits manager must have knowledge of the details of a large number of plans and must be able to answer the specific questions of employees concerning these plans.

CASE APPLICATION

Karen Swift is president of an accounting firm that has ten employees. The only employee benefit provided by the firm is a paid two-week vacation for employees with one or more years of service. The firm's profits have substantially increased, and Karen would like to provide some additional benefits to the employees. Karen needs advice concerning the types of benefits to provide. Assume you are an employee benefits consultant. Based on the following considerations, answer the following questions:

a. Karen would like to provide life insurance for the employees equal to two times their salaries. She wants to minimize the cost of this benefit. What type of life insurance do you recommend?

b. Several employees have expressed an interest in having some life insurance in force on their lives

after retirement. Explain to Karen how employees can keep their life insurance after retirement.

c. Karen would also like to provide health insurance benefits to the employees. Identify the major types of group health insurance plans that she might consider.

d. Assume that Karen is considering both a preferred provider plan (PPO) and a health maintenance organization plan (HMO). Explain the major differences between these two plans to Karen.

e. Are there any other group insurance benefits that Karen should consider? Explain your answer.

f. Karen would like to give the employees a choice of benefits. Explain to Karen how this goal can be accomplished.

SUMMARY

- Group insurance provides benefits to a number of persons under a single master contract. Low-cost protection is provided, because the employer pays part or all of the premiums. Evidence of insurability is usually not required. Larger groups are subject to experience rating, by which the group's loss experience determines the premiums charged.

- Certain underwriting principles are followed in group insurance to obtain favorable loss experience:

  Insurance should be incidental to the group.

  There should be a flow of persons through the group.

  The benefits should be determined by some formula that precludes individual selection of insurance amounts.

  A minimum percentage of eligible employees should participate in the plan.

  There should be third-party sharing of costs.

  There should be simple and efficient administration of the plan.

- Most groups today are eligible for group insurance benefits. However, employees must meet certain eligibility requirements:

  Be full-time employees.

  Satisfy a probationary period in some plans.

  Apply for insurance during the eligibility period.

  Be actively at work when the insurance becomes effective.

- There are several types of group life insurance plans:

  Group term life insurance

  Group accidental death and dismemberment (AD&D) insurance

  Group universal life insurance

- Group medical expense plans are available from a number of sources, including:

  Commercial insurers

  Blue Cross and Blue Shield

  Health maintenance organizations (HMOs)

  Self-insured plans by employers

- Group basic medical expense insurance provides only basic benefits, which typically include:

  Hospital expense insurance

  Surgical expense insurance

  Physicians' visits insurance

  Coverage for miscellaneous benefits

- Group major medical insurance is designed to cover catastrophic losses. There are two basic types of group major medical plans:

  Supplemental major medical insurance

  Comprehensive major medical insurance

- Managed care is a generic name for a medical expense plan that provides necessary medical care in a cost-effective manner.

- A health maintenance organization (HMO) is a managed care plan that provides broad, comprehensive services to its members for a fixed, prepaid fee. A typical HMO has the following characteristics:

    Organized plan to deliver health services to the members

    Broad, comprehensive health services

    Restrictions on the choice of physician

    Payment of a fixed, prepaid fee

    Heavy emphasis on controlling costs

- A preferred provider organization (PPO) is a plan that contracts with health-care providers to provide certain medical services to its members at discounted fees. Members pay lower deductibles and coinsurance charges if preferred providers are used.

- A point-of-service (POS) plan is a managed care plan that allows members to receive medical care outside the network of preferred providers. However, the patient must pay substantially higher deductible and co-payment charges.

- A consumer-driven health plan (CDHP) is a generic term for a plan that gives employees a number of choices of health-care plans, which are designed to make employees more sensitive to health-care costs, to provide a financial incentive to avoid unnecessary care, and to seek out low-cost providers.

- Group medical expense plans contain certain contractual provisions that may have a financial impact on the insured. Major provisions include the following:

    Preexisting-conditions provision

    Coordination-of-benefits provision

    Continuation of group health insurance under the COBRA law

- Group dental insurance plans typically cover a wide variety of dental services. Dental services are typically grouped into different levels with varying coinsurance requirements. In many plans, coinsurance does not apply to diagnostic and preventive services, such as cleaning of teeth, or the coinsurance percentage is lower.

- Many employers provide disability-income benefits to covered employees. There are two basic types of plans:

    Short-term disability-income plans

    Long-term disability-income plans

- Cafeteria plans allow employees to select those benefits that best meet their specific needs. Flexible spending accounts in a cafeteria plan allow employees to pay for the benefits with before-tax dollars.

KEY CONCEPTS AND TERMS

Basic medical expense insurance

Blue Cross and Blue Shield plans

Cafeteria plans

Calendar-year deductible

Capitation fee

COBRA law

Coinsurance provision

Comprehensive major medical insurance

Consumer-driven health plans (CDHP)

Contributory plan

Coordination-of-benefits provision

Corridor deductible

Defined contribution health plan

Eligibility period

Experience rating

Family deductible provision

Flexible spending account

Gatekeeper physician

Group accidental death and dismemberment (AD&D) insurance

Group dental insurance

Group disability-income insurance

Group medical expense insurance

Group term life insurance

Group universal life insurance

Health Insurance Portability and Accountability Act (HIPAA)

Health maintenance organization (HMO)

Health savings account (HSA)

High-deductible health plan

Hospital expense insurance

Individual practice association (IPA) plan

Major medical insurance

Managed care

Master contract

Noncontributory plan

Nonoccupational disability

Point-of-service (POS) plan

Portability

Preexisting condition

Preferred provider organization (PPO)

Probationary period

Reasonable and customary charges

Self-insurance (self-funding)

Service benefits

Stop-loss limit

Supplemental major medical insurance

Surgical expense insurance

Traditional indemnity plans (fee-for-service)

Voluntary accidental death and dismemberment insurance

REVIEW QUESTIONS

1. Describe the basic underwriting principles that are followed in group insurance.

2. Explain the typical eligibility requirements that employees must meet in group insurance plans.

3. Briefly describe the following types of group life insurance plans:
   a. Group term life insurance
   b. Group accidental death and dismemberment insurance (AD&D)
   c. Group universal life insurance

4. a. Describe the major characteristics of Blue Cross and Blue Shield plans.
   b. Why do many employers self-insure (self-fund) their group medical expense plans?

5. a. Identify the benefits provided by basic medical expense plans.
   b. Briefly describe the major characteristics of the following group major medical insurance plans.
      1. Supplemental major medical insurance
      2. Comprehensive major medical insurance

6. a. What is a managed care plan?
   b. Briefly explain the basic characteristics of the following types of managed care plans:
      (1) Health maintenance organizations (HMOs)
      (2) Preferred provider organizations (PPOs)
      (3) Point-of-service (POS) plans
   c. What is a consumer-driven health plan (CDHP)?

7. The Health Insurance Portability and Accountability Act (HIPAA) places restrictions on the employer's right to deny or limit coverage for preexisting conditions.
   a. How is a preexisting condition defined under HIPAA?
   b. Describe the major provisions under HIPAA that deal with preexisting conditions.

8. Briefly explain each of the following group medical expense provisions:
   a. Coordination of benefits
   b. Continuation of group health insurance under the COBRA law

9. Briefly explain the basic characteristics of group dental insurance plans.

10. Briefly describe the major characteristics of the following group disability-income plans:
    a. Short-term disability-income plans
    b. Long-term disability-income plans

11. Describe the basic characteristics of cafeteria plans in an employee benefits program.

APPLICATION QUESTIONS

1. Group term life insurance and group universal life insurance have different characteristics and objectives. Compare (1) group term insurance with (2) group universal life insurance with respect to each of the following:
   a. Period of protection provided
   b. Right to continue the coverage after termination of employment
   c. Availability of employer contributions
   d. Right to obtain a policy loan

2. Margo, age 35, was severely injured in an auto accident. She is covered under her employer's preferred provider organization (PPO) plan. The plan provides major medical insurance with a $2 million lifetime limit, a calendar-year deductible of $300, a coinsurance requirement of 80-20 percent, and an annual stop-loss limit of $2,000. As a result of the accident, Margo incurred the following medical expenses:

Cost of ambulance to the hospital	$ 500
Hospital bill for a three-day stay	$15,300
Surgery for a broken leg	$ 5,000
Prescription drugs outside the hospital	$ 300
Physical therapy for the broken leg	$ 1,200

   In addition, Margo could not work for one month and lost $3000 in earnings.
   a. Based on the above, how much will Margo collect for her injury if she receives medical care from health care providers who are part of the PPO network?
   b. Assume that Margo's broken leg does not heal properly, and she needs another surgical operation. Margo would like a different surgeon with an outstanding professional reputation to perform the operation. The surgeon is not a member of the PPO network. Will Margo's plan pay for the surgery? Explain your answer.

3. Jane, age 28, and John, age 30, are married and have a son, age one. Jane is covered under her employer's group medical expense plan as an employee. Jane is also covered under John's plan as a dependent. The son is covered under both plans as a dependent.

Jane's birthday is January 10, while John's birthday is November 15. Both plans have the same coordination-of-benefits provision.

a. If Jane is hospitalized, which plan is primary? Which plan is excess?

b. If the son is hospitalized, which plan is primary? Which plan is excess?

c. Assume that the couple gets a divorce, and Jane is awarded custody of her son. A court decree states that John must provide health insurance on his son. If the son is hospitalized after the divorce, which plan is primary? Which plan is excess?

4. Jason, age 25, graduated from college and accepted a job as an accountant with a large employer. The company is subject to the Health Insurance Portability and Accountability Act (HIPAA) of 1996. The employer's group health insurance plan contains a provision that excludes preexisting conditions for 12 months. Jason had major surgery three months before he was hired in which a malignant tumor was removed from his lung. The surgeon explained that the risk of new tumors developing, although slight, was possible. Based on the preceding information, answer the following questions.

a. Six months after he was hired, Jason had surgery to have another malignant tumor removed from his lung. Does the group health insurance plan have to pay for the surgery? Explain your answer.

b. Would your answer to (a) above change if the second surgical operation occurred 18 months after Jason was hired? Explain your answer.

c. After working for the company for two years, Jason lost his job when his company merged with another firm. After six weeks, Jason found another job as an accountant. Jason enrolled in the new employer's group health insurance plan, which also excludes preexisting conditions for 12 months. The new employer is also subject to HIPAA. Assume that Jason must have his lungs x-rayed to detect any new tumors. Can the new group health insurance plan exclude coverage of the medical condition? Explain your answer.

5. Many employers have both group short-term and long-term disability-income plans. Compare (1) short-term plans with (2) long-term plans with respect to each of the following:

a. Definition of disability under the plan

b. Elimination period

c. Length of the benefit period

d. Offsets if other disability-income benefits are received

6. When group dental insurance plans are initially installed, the insurer is exposed to a high degree of adverse selection. Describe the various cost controls that can be incorporated into the dental plan to control for adverse selection.

INTERNET RESOURCES

- **America's Health Insurance Plans (AHIP)** is a national trade association that represents nearly 1300 member companies that provide health insurance coverage to more than 200 million Americans. The site provides considerable information on health-care issues in the United States. Visit the site at

  http://www.ahip.org

- **Blue Cross and Blue Shield** plans are nonprofit corporations that provide medical, hospital, and surgical benefits to plan members in specific geographical areas. The various plans account for a substantial portion of the group health insurance market. Visit the site at

  http://www.bcbs.com

- The **Employee Benefit Research Institute (EBRI)** is a nonprofit organization devoted exclusively to the dissemination of data, policy research, and educational material on economic security and employee benefits. Visit the site at

  http://www.ebri.org

- **Healthgrades.com** used a star system to rate hundreds of hospitals based on specific procedures. The stars range from a high of five to a low of one. Hospitals that have fewer complications for a specific procedure receive a higher grade. Information on physicians and nursing homes is also available. Visit the site at

  http://www.healthgrades.com

- The **International Foundation of Employee Benefit Plans** is a nonprofit educational organization that provides programs, publications, and research studies to individuals in the employee benefits field. The organization cosponsors the Certified Employee Benefit Specialist (CEBS) program. Visit the site at

  http://www.ifebp.org

■ **Medicare.gov** provides timely information on the Medicare program. The site also includes information on nursing homes and Medigap policies. Visit the site at

http://www.medicare.gov

■ The **Centers for Disease Control and Prevention (CDC)** is the leading federal agency for protecting the health and safety of people in the United States and abroad. CDC provides credible statistics to enhance health decisions and to promote good health. The CDC serves as the national focus for disease prevention and control, environmental health, and educational activities to improve health. Visit the site at

http://www.cdc.gov/nchs

■ The **National Committee for Quality Assurance (NCQA)** provides information to employers and consumers on the quality of their health-care plans. NCQA issues a report card on the quality of care provided and has an accreditation program for health-care plans. Visit the site at

http://www.ncqa.org

SELECTED REFERENCES

American Academy of Actuaries. *The Impact of Consumer-Driven Health Plans on Health Care Costs: A Closer Look at Plans with Health Reimbursement Accounts,* Public Policy Monograph, January 2004.

Beam, Burton T., Jr. *Group Benefits: Basic Concepts and Alternatives,* 11th ed. Bryn Mawr, PA: The American College, 2006.

Blue Cross and Blue Shield Association. *Medical Cost Reference Guide.* Chicago, IL, 2006.

Bos, Blaine, Mercer Human Resource Consulting. *National Survey of Employer-Sponsored Health Plans 2004,* November 2, 2004.

Kennedy, Deidre, et al. *2005 U.S. Master Employee Benefits Guide.* Chicago, IL: CCH Incorporated, 2005.

Lee, Thomas H., and Kinga Zapert. "Do High-Deductible Health Plans Threaten Quality of Care?" *New England Journal of Medicine,* Perspective, vol. 353: 1202–1204, no. 12, September 22, 2005.

Mercer Human Resource Consulting, *Health Benefit Cost Slows for a Third Year, Rising Just 6.1% in 2005,* November 21, 2005.

Rosenbloom, Jerry S. *The Handbook of Employee Benefits,* 6th ed. New York: McGraw-Hill, 2005.

The Kaiser Family Foundation and Health Research and Educational Trust. *Employer Health Benefits, 2005 Annual Survey* (2005).

The Kaiser Family Foundation and Health Research and Educational Trust. *Employer Health Benefits, 2005, Summary of Findings.*

The USA Today/Kaiser Family Foundation/Harvard School of Public Health. *Summary and Chartpack, Health Care Costs Survey,* August 2005.

NOTES

1. Burton T. Beam, Jr. *Group Benefits: Basic Concepts and Alternatives,* 11th ed. (Bryn Mawr, PA: The American College, 2006), ch. 4.
2. *Life Insurer's Fact Book, 2005* (Washington, DC: American Council of Life Insurers, 2005), p. 88.
3. In a few states, the terminating employee is allowed to purchase term insurance for a limited period (such as one year), after which he or she must convert to some form of cash-value life insurance.
4. Beam, ch. 5.
5. Beam, ch. 9.
6. See Blaine Bos, Mercer Human Resource Consulting, *National Survey of Employer-Sponsored Health Plans—2004,* November 12, 2004; and Blaine Bos, *2002 Mercer National Survey of Employer-Sponsored Health Plans,* Mercer Human Resource Consulting, 2002.
7. National Committee for Quality Assurance, *The State of Health Care Quality: 2005,* Washington, DC, 2005.
8. Mercer Human Resource Consulting, *National Survey of Employer-Sponsored Health Plans—2005,* November 2005.
9. Ibid.
10. Ronald L. Huling, "Dental Plan Design," in Jerry S. Rosenbloom, ed., *The Handbook of Employee Benefits,* 6th ed. (New York, NY: McGraw-Hill, 2005), p. 262.

Students may take a self-administered test on this chapter at
www.aw-bc.com/rejda

CHAPTER 17

EMPLOYEE BENEFITS: RETIREMENT PLANS

"Retirement at age 65 is ridiculous. When I was 65, I still had pimples."

George Burns

"When some fellers decide to retire, nobody knows the difference."

Kin Hubbard

LEARNING OBJECTIVES

After studying this chapter, you should be able to

◆ Explain the basic features of private retirement plans, including:
  Minimum age and service requirements
  Retirement ages
  Vesting rules

◆ Distinguish between defined-contribution and defined-benefit retirement plans.

◆ Describe the basic characteristics of Section 401(k) plans.

◆ Explain the major features of profit-sharing plans.

◆ Describe the basic characteristics of Keogh plans for the self-employed.

◆ Identify the major features of SIMPLE retirement plans for small employers.

ristin, age 28, is a marketing analyst for a large advertising agency. She earns $40,000 annually and recently became eligible to participate in the company's retirement plan. The company has a Section 401(k) retirement plan for eligible employees. Kristin has a number of questions about the plan, including the amount she can contribute, the amount contributed by the company, investment options, and the retirement age. She also wants to know whether she will receive anything if she should quit her job prior to retirement.

Like Kristin, many employees are bewildered by the complexities of private retirement plans. This chapter deals with the questions that Kristin and others may have concerning the basic features of private retirement plans. Although they are complicated, private retirement plans are extremely important in maintaining the worker's economic security during retirement. When added to Social Security retirement benefits, private retirement benefits enable retirees to attain a higher standard of living during retirement.

This chapter discusses the fundamentals of private retirement plans. It is divided into two major parts. The first part discusses the fundamentals of private retirement plans, including minimum age and service requirements, retirement ages, and vesting rules. The second part describes the major types of private retirement plans, including defined-contribution and defined-benefit plans, Section 401(k) plans, profit-sharing plans, and retirement plans for the self-employed.

FUNDAMENTALS OF PRIVATE RETIREMENT PLANS

Millions of workers participate in private retirement plans. These plans have an enormous social and economic impact on the nation. Retirement benefits increase the economic security of both individuals and families during retirement. Retirement contributions are also an important source of capital funds to the financial markets. These funds are invested in new plants, machinery, equipment, housing developments, shopping centers, and other worthwhile economic investments.

Federal legislation and the Internal Revenue Code have had a great influence on the design and growth of private retirement plans. The **Employee Retirement Income Security Act of 1974 (ERISA)** established minimum pension standards to protect the rights of covered workers.

More recently, the **Pension Protection Act of 2006** increases the funding obligations of employers, makes permanent the higher contribution limits that were scheduled to expire at the end of 2010, encourages automatic enrollment of employees in Section 401(k) plans and defined contribution plans, and contains numerous additional provisions that affect the design of private retirement plans.

The Internal Revenue Service (IRS) also exerts a significant influence on private retirement plans. The IRS continuously issues new rules and regulations that affect the design and growth of private retirement plans. The following discussion is based on current IRS requirements at the time of this writing.[1]

Favorable Income Tax Treatment

Private retirement plans that meet certain IRS requirements are called **qualified plans** and receive favorable income tax treatment. The employer's contributions are tax deductible up to certain limits as an ordinary business expense; the employer's contributions are not considered taxable income to the employees; the investment earnings on plan assets accumulate on a tax-deferred basis; and the pension benefits attributable to the employer's contributions are not taxed until the employee retires or receives the funds. The tax advantages of qualified plans to employees are substantial, especially if the employee starts early (see Exhibit 17.1).

Minimum Coverage Requirements

A qualified plan must benefit workers in general and not only **highly compensated employees.**[2] Certain **minimum coverage requirements** must be satisfied to receive favorable tax treatment. The coverage rules are complex and beyond the scope of the text to discuss in detail. However, to reduce discrimination in favor of highly compensated employees, a qualified retirement plan must meet one of the following tests:

- *Percentage test.* Under the percentage test, the plan must cover at least 70 percent of all non-highly compensated employees. This test is the easiest of the three tests to understand.
- *Ratio test.* Under the ratio test, the percentage of non-highly compensated employees covered under the plan must be at least 70 percent of the percentage of highly compensated employees who are covered. The following example meets the test:

| | Number of Employees | | |
	Total	Covered	Percent
Highly compensated employees	100	50	50%
Non-highly compensated employees	500	175	35
Total number of employees	600		
Ratio of percentages (35%/50%)			70

EXHIBIT 17.1
The Benefits of Starting Early in a Tax-Deferred Retirement Plan

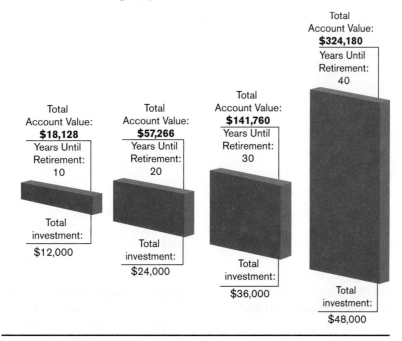

NOTE: This hypothetical example is based on a $100 monthly contribution to a tax-deferred retirement plan and an 8 percent rate of return compounded monthly. Your own plan account may earn more or less than this example and income taxes will be due when you withdraw funds from your account.

SOURCE: Fidelity Investments.

- *Average benefits test.* Under this test, two requirements must be met: (1) the plan must benefit a reasonable classification of employees and must not discriminate in favor of highly compensated employees, and (2) the average benefit for the non-highly compensated employees must be at least 70 percent of the average benefit provided to all highly compensated employees.

The minimum coverage tests typically come into play when an employer establishes a retirement plan for employees in one location (e.g., the Philadelphia office) but not in another location (e.g., the Boston office). The coverage tests are also important if an employer establishes a retirement plan for some workers based on job classification but not location.

Minimum Age and Service Requirements

Most pension plans have a **minimum age and service requirement** that must be met before employees can participate in the plan. *Under present law, all eligible employees who have attained age 21 and have completed one year of service must be allowed to participate in the plan.* One exception is that the plan can require two years of service if there is 100 percent immediate vesting (discussed later) upon entry into the plan.

For purposes of determining eligibility, a worker who works at least 1000 hours during an initial 12-month period after being hired earns one year of service. An hour of service is any hour for which the employee works or is entitled to be paid.

Retirement Ages

A typical pension plan has three retirement ages:

- Normal retirement age
- Early retirement age
- Deferred retirement age

Normal Retirement Age   The **normal retirement age** is the age that a worker can retire and receive a full, unreduced pension benefit. Age 65 is the normal retirement age in most plans. However, as a result of an amendment to the Age Discrimination in Employment Act, most employees cannot be forced to retire

at some stated mandatory retirement age. To remain qualified, with certain exceptions, private pension plans cannot impose a mandatory retirement age.

Early Retirement Age   An **early retirement age** is the earliest age that workers can retire and receive a retirement benefit. The majority of employees currently retire before age 65. For example, a typical plan may permit a worker with 10 years of service to retire at age 55.

In a defined benefit plan (discussed later), the retirement benefit is actuarially reduced for early retirement. The actuarial reduction is necessary for three reasons: (1) the worker's full benefit will not have accrued by the early retirement date; (2) the retirement benefit is paid over a longer period of time; and (3) early retirement benefits are paid to some workers who would have died before reaching the normal retirement age.

Deferred Retirement Age   The **deferred retirement age** is any age beyond the normal retirement age. A relatively small number of older employees continue working beyond the normal retirement age. However, under current law with certain exceptions, workers can defer retiring with no maximum age limit as long as they can do their jobs. Employees who continue working beyond the normal retirement age continue to accrue benefits under the plan.

Benefit Formulas

Qualified retirement plans are designed to pay retirement benefits, which, together with Social Security retirement benefits, will generally restore about 50 to 60 percent of the worker's gross earnings prior to retirement. A benefit formula is used to determine contributions or benefits.

Defined-Contribution Formulas   In a **defined-contribution formula,** *the contribution rate is fixed, but the retirement benefit is variable*. For example, both the employer and employee may contribute 6 percent of pay into the plan. Although the contribution rate is known, the retirement benefit will vary depending on the worker's current age, earnings, investment returns, and retirement age.

A fixed percentage of salary is typically used to determine the retirement contributions. For example, both the employee and employer may contribute 6 percent of salary into the plan. Each employee has an individual account, and the actual retirement benefit will depend on the value of the employee's account at retirement.

Defined-Benefit Formulas   In a **defined-benefit plan,** *the retirement benefit is known, but the contributions will vary depending on the amount needed to fund the desired benefit.* For example, assume a worker, age 50, is entitled to a retirement benefit at the normal retirement age equal to 50 percent of average pay for the highest three consecutive years of earnings. An actuary then determines the amount that must be contributed to produce the desired benefit.

In a defined-benefit plan, the benefit amount can be based on **career-average earnings,** which is an average of the worker's earnings while participating in the plan, or it can be based on **final average pay,** which generally is an average of the worker's earnings over a three- to five-year period prior to retirement.

When a new defined-benefit pension plan is installed, some older workers may be close to retirement. To pay more adequate retirement benefits, defined-benefit plans may give credit for service with the firm prior to the installation of the plan. The **past-service credits** provide additional pension benefits. The actual amount paid, however, will depend on the benefit formula used to determine benefits.

In a defined-benefit plan, numerous formulas can be used to determine the retirement benefit. They include the following:

- *Unit-benefit formula.* Under this formula, both earnings and years of service are considered. For example, the plan may pay a retirement benefit equal to 1 percent of the worker's final average pay multiplied by the number of years of service. Thus, a worker with a final average monthly salary of $4000 and 30 years of service would receive a monthly retirement benefit of $1200.
- *Flat percentage of annual earnings.* Under this formula, the retirement benefit is a fixed percentage of the worker's earnings, such as 25 to 50 percent. The benefit may be based on career-average earnings or on an average of final pay. This formula sometimes lowers the amount provided if the employee does not have the required amount of service. For example, a plan

may provide benefits equal to 50 percent of average final pay if the employee has 30 years of service. However, if the employee has only 20 years of service, he or she will receive only two-thirds of the benefit.

- *Flat dollar amount for each year of service.* Under this formula, a flat dollar amount is paid for each year of credited service. For example, the plan may pay $40 monthly at the normal retirement age for each year of credited service. If the employee has 30 years of credited service, the monthly pension is $1200. This formula is not widely used except in union-negotiated retirement plans.
- *Flat dollar amount for all employees.* This formula is sometimes used in collective bargaining plans by which a flat dollar amount is paid to all employees regardless of their earnings or years of service. Thus, the plan may pay $600 monthly to each worker who retires.

Years of service are extremely important in determining the total pension benefit. Frequent job changes and withdrawal from the labor force for extended periods can significantly reduce the size of the pension benefit. This is especially true for women who may have prolonged breaks in employment due to family considerations.

Vesting Provisions

Vesting *refers to the employee's right to the employer's contributions or benefits attributable to the contributions if employment terminates prior to retirement.* The employee is always entitled to the contributions he or she makes to the plan if employment terminates prior to retirement. However, the right to the employer's contributions, or benefits attributable to the contributions, depends on the extent to which vesting has been attained.

Qualified defined-benefit plans must meet one of the following **minimum vesting standards:**

- *Cliff vesting.* Under this rule, the employee must be 100 percent vested after five years of service.
- *Graded vesting.* Under this rule, the rate of vesting must meet or exceed the following minimum standard:

Years of Service	Percentage Vested
3	20%
4	40
5	60
6	80
7	100

However, all employer contributions to a qualified defined contribution or profit-sharing plan must vest at a faster rate. Faster vesting is designed to encourage greater participation by lower- and middle-income employees. Defined-contribution and profit-sharing plans must meet one of the following minimum vesting schedules:

- *Three-year cliff vesting.* Employer contributions must be 100 percent vested after three years.
- *Six-year graded vesting.* Employer contributions must meet or exceed the following vesting schedule:

Years of Service	Percentage Vested
1	0%
2	20
3	40
4	60
5	80
6	100

From the employer's viewpoint, the basic purpose of vesting is to reduce labor turnover. Employees have an incentive to remain with the firm until a vested status has been attained. In a defined-benefit plan, if employees terminate their employment before full vesting is attained, the forfeitures generally are used to reduce the employer's future pension contributions. However, in a defined-contribution plan, forfeitures can either be reallocated to the accounts of the remaining participants or used to reduce future employer contributions.

Limits on Contributions and Benefits

For 2007, under a *defined-contribution plan,* the maximum annual addition that can be made to an employee's account is limited to 100 percent of compensation, or $45,000, whichever is lower. This figure is indexed for inflation. Annual additions include all employer and employee contributions and any forfeitures allocated to the employee's account.

For 2007, *under a defined-benefit plan,* the maximum annual benefit is limited to 100 percent of the worker's average compensation for the three highest consecutive years of compensation, or $180,000, whichever is lower. This latter figure is indexed for inflation.

There is also a maximum limit on the annual compensation that can be counted when determining benefits and contributions under all plans. For 2007, the maximum annual compensation that can be counted in the contribution or benefit formula is $225,000 (indexed for inflation).

Participants in defined-benefit plans are protected against the loss of pension benefits up to certain limits if the pension plan should terminate. The **Pension Benefit Guaranty Corporation (PBGC)** is a federal corporation that guarantees the payment of vested or nonforfeitable benefits up to certain limits if a private pension plan is terminated. For plans terminated in 2006, the maximum guaranteed pension at age 65 is $3971.59 per month.

Employers must pay an annual premium for each covered employee. At the time of this writing, the PBGC has pension liabilities that substantially exceed its assets and is currently running a deficit. To deal with the problem, the Deficit Reduction Act of 2005 increased substantially the annual premiums employers must pay. In addition, the Pension Protection Act of 2006 requires pension plan sponsors to pay termination premiums of $1250 per participant for up to three years if they "dump" their pension liabilities on the PBGC, and then emerge from bankruptcy.

Early Distribution Penalty

A 10 percent tax penalty applies to funds withdrawn from a qualified plan before age 59½. The 10 percent penalty tax applies to the amount included in gross income. However, the early distribution penalty does not apply to distributions that are:

- Made after age 59½
- Made after the death or total and permanent disability of the employee
- Made after attaining age 55 and separation from service
- Made as part of a series of substantially equal payments paid over the worker's life expectancy or joint life expectancy of the worker and beneficiary after separation from service

- Distributions for certain medical expenses
- Payments to an alternate payee as a result of a qualified domestic relations order
- Payments made in connection with certain employee stock ownership plans (ESOPs)

Several additional exceptions to the early distribution penalty apply to individual retirement accounts (IRAs), simplified employee pensions (SEPs), and SIMPLE retirement plans (discussed later). The early distribution penalty does not apply to

- Distributions to pay for qualified education expenses
- Distributions to pay for a first-time home purchase ($10,000 limit)
- Distributions to pay health insurance premiums by an individual who is receiving unemployment insurance benefits

Minimum Distribution Requirements

Pension contributions cannot remain in the plan indefinitely. Plan distributions must start no later than April 1 of the calendar year following the year in which the individual attains age 70½. However, participants older than 70½ who are still working can delay receiving minimum distributions from a qualified retirement plan. The required beginning date of a participant who is still employed after age 70½ is April 1 of the calendar year that follows the calendar year in which he or she retires. *The preceding rule does not apply to individual retirement accounts (IRAs) and certain other qualified plans.*

Finally, the minimum distribution rules do not apply to Roth IRAs.

Funding of Pension Benefits

Qualified private pension plans use advance funding to finance the pension benefits. **Advance funding** *means the employer systematically and periodically sets aside funds prior to the employee's retirement.* This type of funding increases the security of benefits for the active employees because funds are periodically set aside prior to retirement, and the contributions and investment income receive favorable income-tax treatment.

Despite the emphasis on advance funding, many defined-benefit pension plans are seriously underfunded at the present time. To deal with the under-

funding problem, the Pension Protection Act of 2006 substantially increases the funding obligations of employers. The funding rules are complex and beyond the scope of the text to discuss in detail. In general, however, when the new rules are fully implemented, single-employer defined-benefit plans must meet a funding target of 100 percent of plan liabilities; funding shortfalls must be eliminated within seven years; plans that are severely underfunded (called "at-risk plans") must meet additional funding obligations; and plans that are less than 80 percent funded are prohibited from increasing benefits unless the benefits are paid for immediately. In addition, airlines have 10 to 17 years to meet the funding requirements. Finally, multi-employer defined-benefit plans must also meet certain minimum funding standards and follow new rules and regulations to ensure stronger funding.

Integration with Social Security

Many qualified private pension plans are integrated with Social Security. Because employers pay half of the total Old-Age, Survivors, and Disability Insurance (OASDI) payroll tax, they argue that OASDI retirement benefits should be considered in the calculation of private pension benefits. As a result, pension costs can be reduced. Also, integration provides a method for increasing pension benefits for highly compensated employees without increasing the cost of providing benefits to lower-paid employees.

The Internal Revenue Service has prescribed complex integration rules (called *permitted disparity rules*) that must be followed when a qualified retirement plan is integrated with OASDI. Only one integration rule—an *excess plan*—is discussed here. In a defined-contribution plan, the pension contribution rate can be higher for employees with earnings above a specified integration level than for employees with earnings below that level. The maximum integration level is the OASDI wage base. Thus, if the integration level is set at the OASDI wage base ($94,200 for 2006), highly compensated employees can receive an additional 5.7 percent of compensation in excess of the wage base, provided that the employer makes contributions at least equal to 5.7 percent of total compensation for all employees.

For example, the Smith Corporation has a defined-contribution pension plan that has a contribution rate of 6 percent of compensation, plus

5.7 percent of compensation in excess of the taxable OASDI wage base ($94,200 in 2006). The rule described above is met. Thus, if Kristin earns $200,000, the contribution made on her behalf will be $18,031 This amount is 6 percent of $200,000 ($12,000) plus 5.7 percent of $105,800 ($200,000 minus $94,200), or $6031.

If the employer cannot afford to contribute at least 5.7 percent of total compensation for all employees, the maximum disparity must be reduced. For example, if the contribution rate for all employees is 4 percent of total compensation, then an additional contribution of 4 percent of compensation in excess of the integration level can be made.

Finally, as noted earlier, the maximum integration level is the OASDI wage base. The integration level can be set lower, but this approach generally reduces the maximum disparity allowed.

Top-Heavy Plans

Special rules apply to top-heavy plans. A **top-heavy plan** is a retirement plan in which more than 60 percent of the plan assets are in accounts attributed to key employees. A plan is considered top-heavy if the present value of the cumulative accrued benefits for the key employees exceeds 60 percent of the present value of the cumulative accrued benefits under the plan for all covered employees. (Accrued benefits are measured in terms of benefits for defined-benefit plans and account balances for defined-contribution plans.)

A top-heavy plan must meet certain additional requirements to retain its qualified status. These requirements include the following:

- A special rapid vesting schedule must be used for nonkey employees (100 percent vesting after three years, or 20 percent after two years and 20 percent for each year thereafter).
- Certain minimum benefits or contributions must be provided for nonkey employees.

TYPES OF QUALIFIED RETIREMENT PLANS

A wide variety of qualified retirement plans are available today to meet the specific needs of employers. The most important include the following:

- Defined-contribution plans
- Defined-benefit plans
- Section 401(k) plans
- Section 403(b) plans
- Profit-sharing plans
- Retirement plans for the self-employed
- Simplified employee pension (SEP) plans
- SIMPLE retirement plans

The following sections discuss the basic characteristics of these plans.

DEFINED-CONTRIBUTION PLANS

As noted earlier, a **defined-contribution plan** is a retirement plan in which the contribution rate is fixed, but the actual retirement benefit varies, depending on the worker's age of entry into the plan, contribution rate, investment returns, and the age of normal retirement.

One example of a defined-contribution plan is a money purchase plan. A **money purchase plan** *is an arrangement in which each participant has an individual account, and the employer's contribution is a fixed percentage of the participant's compensation.* For example, the money purchase formula may specify an annual contribution by the employer of 10 percent of base pay to the employee's account. If the plan is contributory, both the employee and employer usually contribute at the same rate, such as 5 percent of base pay.

Defined-contribution plans are widely used by business firms today. Most new plans today are defined-contribution plans. One financial advantage to the firm is that past-service credits are not granted for service prior to the plan's inception date, which reduces the employer's cost. Defined-contribution plans are also widely used by nonprofit organizations and state and local governments, where pension costs must be budgeted as a percentage of payroll.

As stated earlier, each employee has an individual account, and the retirement contributions and investment income are credited to the account. The employee receives periodic statements that show the account value and investment returns. Amounts forfeited by employees who terminate their employment before they attain full vesting are used to reduce future employer contributions or are reallocated to the accounts of the remaining employees.

However, from the employee's perspective, a defined-contribution plan has several disadvantages. Retirement benefits can only be estimated; the benefit formula may produce an inadequate benefit if the worker enters the plan at an advanced age; and any investment losses must be borne by the employee. Also, some employees do not understand the factors to consider in choosing a particular investment, such as a stock fund, bond fund, money market fund, and other investment options.

In addition, because of fear and the desire to protect principal, some employees invest a large proportion of their retirement contributions in a **stable value fund.** This type of fund is a fixed-income fund that credits the contributions with a specified rate of interest but offers limited opportunities for the growth of principal. As a result, the retirement benefits may be inadequate.

DEFINED-BENEFIT PLANS

Traditional Defined-Benefit Plans

From a historical perspective, employers typically established defined-benefit plans that paid guaranteed benefits to retired workers. As noted earlier, a defined-benefit plan is a retirement plan in which the retirement benefit is known in advance, but the contributions vary depending on the amount needed to fund the desired benefit. Such plans typically pay benefits based on a *unit-benefit formula* that considers both earnings and years of participation in the plan. For example, the plan may provide a retirement benefit payable at the normal retirement age equal to 1.5 percent of final pay for each year of credited service. Assume Jennifer retires at age 65 and has 25 years of credited service and final pay of $50,000 based on an average of her three highest consecutive years of earnings. She would receive an annual lifetime pension of $18,750.

Defined-benefit retirement plans have the major advantages of guaranteeing the worker's retirement benefit; the retirement benefits reflect more accurately the effects of inflation because the benefits are usually based on a final-pay formula; the plans are usually noncontributory, which means that only the employer contributes to the plan; and the investment risk falls directly on the employer, not the employee.

In addition, defined-benefit plans favor workers who enter the plan at older ages because the employer must contribute a relatively larger amount for older workers than for younger workers.

Defined-benefit plans have declined in relative importance over the years. Because of actuarial considerations, defined-benefit plans are more complex and expensive to administer than defined contribution plans. Also, many defined-benefit plans have large unfunded past-service liabilities that are expensive to fund. In addition, many defined-benefit plans are inadequately funded at the present time, and many corporations have frozen their defined-benefit plans and are substituting some type of defined-contribution plan, which is less costly and easier to administer.

Cash-Balance Plans

Many employers have converted their traditional defined-benefit plans to a cash-balance plan. A **cash-balance plan** *is a defined-benefit plan in which the benefits are defined in terms of a hypothetical account balance; actual retirement benefits will depend on the value of the participant's account at retirement.*

In a typical cash-balance plan, the employer establishes "hypothetical accounts" for plan participants. The accounts are hypothetical because the contributions and interest credits are bookkeeping credits. Actual contributions are not allocated to the participants' accounts, and the accounts do not reflect actual investment gains or losses. The investment credits are also hypothetical and are based on an interest rate stated in the plan or on some external index.

Each year, the participants' accounts are credited with (1) a *pay credit,* such as 4 percent of compensation, and (2) an *interest credit,* such as 5 percent of the account balance. The interest credit can be based on a fixed rate or on a variable rate pegged to some index, such as a one-year Treasury bill rate. Investment gains and losses on the plan's assets do not directly affect the benefits promised to the participants. Thus, the employer bears the investment risks and realizes any investment gains. For example, assume that the employer makes a contribution of 4 percent of pay each year to the participants' accounts. If James earns $50,000 annually, his "account" is credited with $2000. Each year, his account balance will be credited with a stated interest rate, such as 5 percent. At retirement, James can elect to receive a life annuity that will pay him a life income. Instead of an annuity, the cash-balance plan may allow him to elect a lump-sum payment equal to the account balance, which can then be rolled over into an IRA.

Many employers have converted traditional defined-benefit plans into cash-balance plans in an effort to hold down pension costs. Also, younger workers benefit because they can understand the plan better; benefits accrue at a faster pace than under a traditional defined-benefit plan; and the benefits are portable for workers who leave before retirement age.

On the downside, however, critics argue that the switch to a cash-balance plan can reduce expected benefits for older workers by 20 to 40 percent. When the conversion occurs, plan benefits are "frozen," which means that earned benefits do not continue to grow. However, under a defined-benefit plan, a large

part of the initial retirement benefit is earned during the last three-to-five years prior to retirement. When benefits are frozen, the worker's pension grows only from the annual interest and wage credits under the cash-balance plan. As a result, the initial retirement benefit for an older worker may be substantially less than if the defined-benefit formula had remained in place. The cash-balance plan may also contain a "wear away" provision under which participants with large pre-conversion benefits may not accrue any new benefits for a period of time after the conversion occurs. As a result, many older workers believe that cash-balance plans are discriminatory because the cash-balance formula produces a retirement benefit that is substantially lower than the defined-benefit formula. This can be illustrated by Exhibit 17.2, which shows that a worker, age 55, at the time of conversion receives a substantially lower benefit under a cash-balance formula as compared to a younger worker, age 35.

ExHIBIT 17.2
How Conversion to a Cash-Balance Plan Potentially Lowers Annuity Benefits

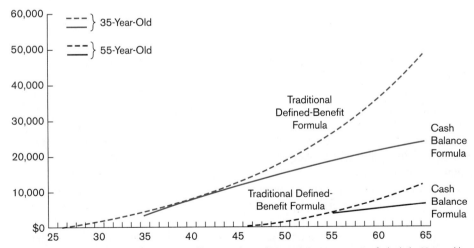

NOTE: Model results are based on the assumption of $40,000 salary and 10-year tenure at conversion for both the 35-year-old and the 55-year-old worker at conversion.

SOURCE: United States General Accounting Office, *Private Pensions, Implication of Conversion to Cash Balance Plans*, GAO/HEHS-00-185 (September 2000), Figure 4, p. 26

The Pension Protection Act of 2006 clarifies the status of cash-balance plans, which makes it easier for employers to establish such plans. The legislation also contains a number of provisions that provide greater protection to older workers when a conversion occurs. The legislation (1) restricts the use of wear away provisions in a plan conversion, (2) provides that no inference of age discrimination arises if the benefits are of equal present value regardless of the participants' ages, (3) requires the adoption of a three-year cliff vesting schedule, and (4) imposes interest-crediting limitations.[3]

SECTION 401(K) PLANS

Section 401(k) plans are becoming increasingly popular among employees as a tax-deferred saving plan. A **Section 401(k) plan** *is a qualified cash or deferred arrangement (CODA) that allows eligible employees the option of putting money into the plan or receiving the funds as cash.* Plan contributions are not currently taxable as income to plan participants.

A Section 401(k) plan can be a qualified profit-sharing plan, savings or thrift plan, or stock bonus plan. A plan can be established that includes both employer and employee contributions, or the employee contributions alone.

In a typical plan, both the employer and employees contribute, and the employer matches part or all of the employee's contributions. For example, for each dollar contributed by the employee, the employer may contribute 25 or 50 cents, or some higher amount.

Most plans allow the employees to determine how the funds are invested. Employees typically have a choice of investments, such as a common stock mutual fund, bond fund, fixed-income fund, and other funds.

Many plans also allow the contributions to be invested in company stock. However, it is risky to invest a large proportion of 401(k) funds in the company's stock. For example, thousands of Enron employees who invested a large part of their 401(k) contributions in Enron Corporation stock lost substantial amounts of money when the company declared bankruptcy in late 2001. The workers lost not only their jobs but also a major part of their retirement savings.

Annual Limit on Elective Deferrals

Eligible employees can voluntarily elect to have their salaries reduced if they participate in a Section 401(k) plan. The salary reduction is technically called an "elective deferral." The amount of salary deferred is then invested in the employer's Section 401(k) plan. The amounts deferred accumulate free of current income taxes until the funds are withdrawn. However, Social Security taxes must be paid on the contributions to the plan. The funds are taxed as ordinary income when withdrawals are made.

For 2007, the maximum limit on elective deferrals in a Section 401(k) plan is $15,500 for workers under age 50. Workers who are age 50 or older before the end of the plan year can make an additional catch-up contribution of $5,000. The maximum dollar limits are indexed for inflation in increments of $500.

Actual Deferral Percentage Test

To prevent discrimination in favor of highly compensated employees in a Section 401(k) plan, an **actual deferral percentage (ADP) test** must be satisfied. That is, the actual percentage of salary deferred for highly compensated employees is subject to certain limitations. In general, the eligible employees are divided into two groups: (1) highly compensated employees, and (2) other eligible employees. The percentage of salary deferred for each employee is totaled and then averaged to get an ADP for each group. The ADPs of both groups are then compared. The rules for calculating the ADPs are complex and beyond the scope of this text to discuss in detail. However, Exhibit 17.3 shows the permissible ADPs for highly compensated employees based on these rules. For example, if the non-highly compensated group has an ADP of 6 percent, the ADP for the highly compensated group is limited to 8 percent for favorable tax treatment.

Limitations on Distributions

As noted earlier, a 10 percent penalty tax applies to an early distribution of funds before age 59½ with certain exceptions. Exceptions include death or disability of the employee, payments that are part of a life or joint life annuity payout, separation from

EXHIBIT **17.3**
Permissible Actual Deferral Percentages (ADPs) for
Highly Compensated Employees (HCE)

ADP for Non-HCE	ADP for HCE
1%	2%
2	4
3	5
4	6
5	7
6	8
7	9
8	10
9	11.25
10	12.50
11	13.75
12	15

SOURCE: Nicholas Kaster et al., *2006 U.S Master Pension Guide* (Chicago, IL: CCH Incorporated, 2006), p. 894.

service after age 55, payments for medical expenses deductible under the Internal Revenue Code, and payments to a qualified payee under a qualified domestic relations order.

The plan may permit the withdrawal of funds for a hardship withdrawal. The IRS recognizes four reasons for a hardship withdrawal:

- Certain unreimbursable medical expenses
- Purchase of a primary residence
- Payments for post-secondary education expenses
- Payments to prevent eviction or foreclosure on your home

The 10 percent penalty tax still applies to a hardship withdrawal. However, 401(k) plans typically have a *loan provision* that allows funds to be borrowed without a tax penalty.

Despite the substantial tax penalties for a premature distribution, many employees often use their 401(k) funds and other retirement funds for purposes other than retirement, such as spending the funds outright, paying off debts, or buying a home. Employees who take money out of their retirement plans early

will receive a substantially lower amount of income during retirement. As a result, they may be exposed to serious financial insecurity during retirement.

Recent Legislation

The new Pension Protection Act of 2006 contains a number of provisions that affect Section 401(k) plans and other defined contribution plans. Some important provisions are summarized as follows:

- *Higher contribution limits made permanent.* The new law makes permanent the higher contribution limits that were scheduled to expire at the end of 2010.
- *Automatic enrollment.* To encourage greater employee participation, the legislation encourages employers to automatically enroll eligible workers in Section 401(k) plans or defined contribution plans. Workers have the right to elect out of the plan.
- *Investment advice.* The plan provider that administers the 401(k) plan is allowed to provide investment advice to participating workers on how to invest the funds. The investment advice must be based on a computer model approved by an independent third party.
- *Sale of company stock.* Employers often make contributions to a 401(k) plan or other defined-contribution plan with company stock. Some workers invest too heavily in company stock and are financially harmed if the company fails. The legislation places limits on the length of time that employers can require participants to hold company stock before it can be sold. If an employer makes a matching contribution with company stock, you can sell it after three years of service. If you already have three years of service and acquired company stock before the new law became effective, you can sell one-third of the stock in each of the next three years. However, any new company stock that you acquire after the law goes into effect can be sold at any time.

In summary, a 401(k) plan should play an important role in your retirement plans. You should also consider new retirement options as they become available. Beginning in 2006, employers will have

INSIGHT 17.1

Check It Out—The New Roth 401(k) Plan

Beginning in 2006, employers have the option of allowing employees to invest in a new Roth 401(k) plan. In a traditional 401(k) plan, you make contributions with before-tax dollars, and distributions are taxed as ordinary income. *In a Roth 401(k), you make contributions with after-tax dollars, and qualified distributions at retirement are received income-tax free.* Investment earnings also accumulate on a tax-free basis. Distributions from the Roth 401(k) are income-tax free if you are at least age 59$1/2$, and the account is held for at least five years. However, with certain exceptions, there is a 10 percent tax penalty under both plans if you withdraw funds before age 59$1/2$.

There are no income limitations. Employees at all income levels can contribute to a Roth 401(k). For 2007, if you are under age 50, you can contribute a maximum of $15,500 into the plan. If you are age 50 or older, you can contribute an additional $5000. You can split the contributions between a traditional 401(k) and a Roth 401(k), but your contributions to both accounts cannot exceed the maximum annual limits. If your employer makes a matching contribution, it is made with before-tax money and must go into the traditional 401(k) plan.

Another advantage is that funds in a Roth 401(k) can be rolled over into a Roth IRA, which has no minimum distribution requirements at age 70$1/2$. As a result, larger sums can be bequeathed to heirs on a tax-free basis.

Which is better retirement option—a traditional 401(k) or Roth 401(k)? The investment results depend on a number of key factors, which include your tax bracket before and after retirement, the length of time the funds are invested, and whether you spend or save the immediate tax savings from a traditional 401(k).

According to a *Wall Street Journal* study, most workers may be better off financially with a Roth 401(k), especially if the funds are invested over a long period.[a] For example, assume that you earn $100,000 annually, receive a 3% annual raise, contribute 6% of salary into the plan, and are in the 28% tax bracket before and after retirement; annual investment returns average 8$1/2$%; and the immediate tax savings under a traditional 401(k) plan are invested and not spent. The following shows how much you would have after 10 years and 35 years:[b]

Years	Traditional 401(k)	Tax Savings	Total	Roth 401(k)	Percent Gain
10	$ 141,155	$ 48,228	$ 189,383	$ 196,049	3.5%
35	1,085,025	212,927	1,297,953	1,506,979	16.1

If you make a more realistic assumption that the immediate tax savings under a traditional 401(k) are spent and not saved, the superiority of the Roth 401(k) would be significantly greater.

[a] Karen Hube, "New kid in town, traditional 401(k)s have a new partner: Roth 401(k)s. Here's why they might work for you," *Wall Street Journal,* September 26, 2005, pp. R6–R7.

[b] Adapted from Ibid., p. R7.

the option of offering a new Roth 40l(k) plan that has tax advantages similar to the Roth IRA discussed in Chapter 14. Insight 17.1 discusses the new **Roth 401(k) plan.**

SECTION 403(B) PLANS

Section 403(b) plans are retirement plans designed for employees of public educational systems and tax-exempt organizations, such as hospitals, nonprofit groups, and churches. These plans are also known as **tax-sheltered annuities (TSA).** Under the plan, eligible employees voluntarily elect to reduce their salaries by a fixed amount. The salary reduction is called an "elective deferral," which is then invested in the 403(b) plan. Employers may make a matching contribution, such as 50 cents for each dollar contributed by the employee by salary reduction. For example, if Kathy earns $3000 monthly and elects to defer $200 monthly, only $2800 is subject to income taxes. The $200 salary reduction plus any employer contributions are then invested in the 403(b) plan.

A 403(b) plan can be funded by purchasing an annuity from an insurance company or by investing in mutual funds. If an annuity is used, the employer must purchase the annuity, and the employee's rights under the contract must be nonforfeitable. *Nonforfeitable* means that the amounts contributed by the employer cannot be taken away from the employee. Employee salary reductions are always nonforfeitable. In addition, the annuity must nontransferable. *Nontransferable* means the annuity contract cannot be sold, assigned, or pledged as collateral for a loan.

Current law places a maximum annual dollar limit on elective deferrals under a 403(b) plan. For 2007, the maximum limit on elective deferrals for workers under age 50 is $15,500. Employees age 50 and older can make an additional catch-up contribution of $5000. The above limits are adjusted for increases in the cost-of-living.

Finally, beginning in 2006, employers have the option of allowing employees to invest in a new **Roth 403(b) plan.** A Roth 403(b) plan is similar to the Roth 401(k) plan discussed earlier. Contributions to the plan are made with after-tax dollars; investment earnings accumulate on a tax-free basis; and qualified distributions at retirement are received income-tax free.

PROFIT-SHARING PLANS

Many employers have profit-sharing plans to provide retirement income to eligible employees. A **profit-sharing plan** *is a defined-contribution plan in which the employer's contributions are typically based on the firm's profits.* However, there is no requirement that the employer must actually earn a profit to contribute to the plan.

Employers establish profit-sharing plans for several reasons. Eligible employees are encouraged to work more efficiently; the employer's cost is not affected by the age or number of employees; and there is greater flexibility in employer contributions. If there are no profits, there are no contributions.

The profit-sharing contributions can be discretionary—based on an amount determined annually by the board of directors—or they can be based on a formula, such as a certain percentage of profits above a certain level. There are annual limits, however, on the amount that can be contributed into an em-

ployee's account. *For 2007, the maximum employer tax-deductible contribution is limited to 25 percent of the employee's compensation or $45,000, whichever is less.*

The profit-sharing funds are typically distributed to the employees at retirement, death, disability, or termination of employment (only the vested portion), or after a fixed number of years (at least two years). Amounts forfeited by employees who leave the company before they attain full vesting are reallocated to the accounts of the remaining participants.

A 10 percent tax penalty applies to a distribution to a participant younger than age 59½. To avoid the tax penalty, many plans have loan provisions that permit employees to borrow from their accounts.

RETIREMENT PLANS FOR THE SELF-EMPLOYED

Sole proprietors and partners can establish qualified retirement plans and enjoy most of the favorable tax advantages now available to participants in qualified corporate pension plans. Retirement plans for the owners of unincorporated business firms are commonly called **Keogh plans.** The contributions to the plan are income-tax deductible up to certain limits, and the investment income accumulates on a tax-deferred basis. The amounts deposited and the investment earnings are not taxed until the funds are distributed.

With certain exceptions, the same rules that apply to qualified corporate pension plans now apply to retirement plans for the self-employed.

Limits on Contributions and Benefits

For 2007, if the Keogh plan is a defined-contribution plan, the maximum annual contribution by a self-employed individual is limited to 25 percent of compensation or $45,000, whichever is lower. However, for purposes of determining the amount that can be contributed, self-employment net earnings must be reduced by (1) one-half of the Social Security self-employment tax and (2) the actual contributions into the plan. This latter adjustment presents a problem because the amount of the Keogh deduction and the amount of net earnings are dependent on each other. Fortunately, the IRS has prepared a worksheet to help you make the correct calculation. *However, for our purposes here, the maximum annual contribution into a defined-contribution Keogh plan is limited to 20 percent of net earnings after subtracting one-half of the Social Security self-employment tax.* If the 20 percent figure is used, the resulting amount is exactly equal to 25 percent of compensation after the two adjustments are made.

For example, after deducting one-half of the Social Security payroll tax, Shannon has net self-employment earnings of $50,000. She can make a maximum tax-deductible contribution of $10,000 into the plan, which reduces her taxable earnings to $40,000. This amount is exactly equal to 25 percent of her net income after the contribution is made ($10,000/$40,000 = 25%).

For 2007, if the Keogh plan is *a defined-benefit plan*, a self-employed individual can fund for a maximum annual benefit equal to 100 percent of average compensation for the three highest consecutive years of compensation, or $180,000, whichever is lower. This latter figure is indexed for inflation.

For example, assume that Nancy, age 50, establishes a defined-benefit plan that will provide a retirement benefit equal to 50 percent of her net income at age 65. If average net income for the three highest consecutive years is $50,000, she can fund for a maximum annual benefit of $25,000. An actuary then determines the amount that she can contribute annually into the plan to reach that goal. In this case, based on 7 percent interest and certain actuarial assumptions, Nancy could contribute $10,847 annually into the plan.

Other Requirements

Certain other requirements must also be met, including the following:

- All employees at least age 21 and with one year of service must be included in the plan. A two-year waiting period can be required if the plan provides for full and immediate vesting upon entry.
- Certain annual reports must be filed with the IRS.
- A 10 percent tax penalty applies to the withdrawal of funds prior to age 59½ (except for certain distributions as noted earlier).
- Plan distributions must start no later than April 1 of the year following the calendar year in which the self-employed person attains age 70½.
- If the plan is top-heavy, the special top-heavy rules discussed earlier must also be met.

INSIGHT 17.2

Maximum Tax Savings for a Sole Proprietor with a Self-Employed 401(k) Plan

The self-employed 401(k) plan combines a profit-sharing plan with a 401(k) plan. *The plan is limited to self-employed individuals or business owners with no employees other than a spouse, which includes sole proprietors, partnerships, corporations, and "S" corporations.* Taxable income is reduced by the contributions into the plan. Investment income also accumulates income-tax free. For 2007, a self-employed 401(k) plan allows a maximum annual contribution of 25 percent of compensation (20 percent of net self-employment income for the owner) into the plan. In addition, for 2007, a self-employed 401(k) plan allows you to make a salary deferral up to $15,500, which also reduces taxable income. If you are age 50 or older, for 2007, you can make an additional catch-up salary deferral of $5000. However, total profit-sharing contributions and salary deferrals for an individual under age 50 cannot exceed $45,000 for 2007.

Example: Taylor, age 35, is a freelance writer. In 2007, her net self-employment income is $50,000. She can contribute 20 percent or $10,000 into her self-employed 401(k) plan. She can also elect a salary deferral of $15,500. As a result, taxable income is reduced from $50,000 to $24,500. She has tax-sheltered 51 percent of her net earnings.

In addition to the Keogh plans just discussed, small business owners have a number of additional retirement plans available to them. One of the most attractive is a **self-employed 401(k) plan** (also called a solo 401(k) plan), which combines a profit-sharing plan with an individual 401k) plan. The tax savings are significant, especially for sole proprietors (see Insight 17.2).

SIMPLIFIED EMPLOYEE PENSION (SEP)

A **simplified employee pension (SEP)** is a retirement plan in which the employer contributes to an IRA established for each eligible employee; however, the annual contribution limits are substantially higher. SEP plans are popular with smaller employers because the amount of required paperwork is minimal.

In one type of plan, called a **SEP-IRA,** the employer contributes to an IRA owned by each employee. The SEP-IRA must cover all qualifying employees who are at least age 21, have worked for the employer in at least three of the immediately preceding five years, and have received at least $500 (indexed limit for 2007) from the employer in compensation during the tax year.

For 2007, the maximum annual tax-deductible employer contribution to a SEP-IRA is limited to 25 percent of the employee's compensation, or $45,000, whichever is less. There is full and immediate vesting of all employer contributions under the plan.

SIMPLE RETIREMENT PLANS

Smaller employers are eligible to establish a Savings Incentive Match Plan for Employees, or SIMPLE for short. The **SIMPLE retirement plan** is limited to employers that employ 100 or fewer eligible employees and do not maintain another qualified plan. Under a SIMPLE plan, smaller employers are exempt from most nondiscrimination and administrative rules that apply to qualified plans. A SIMPLE plan can be structured either as an IRA or as a 401(k)

plan. Only the IRA arrangement is discussed here (SIMPLE-IRA).

Eligible Employees

All employees who have earned at least $5000 from the employer during any two previous years and who are reasonably expected to earn at least $5000 during the current year must be allowed to participate in a SIMPLE plan. Self-employed individuals can also participate.

Employee Contributions

For 2007, eligible employees can elect to contribute up to 100 percent of compensation up to a maximum of $10,500. Participants age 50 and older in 2007 can elect an additional catch-up contribution of $2500. The amount elected by the employee can be expressed as a percentage of compensation or as a specific dollar amount.

Employer Contributions

Employers can choose between two options and can switch options each year if certain notification requirements are met:

- *Matching option.* The employer matches the employee's contributions on a dollar-for-dollar basis up to 3 percent of the employee's compensation but not to exceed $10,500 for 2007.
- *Nonelective contribution option.* The employer must contribute 2 percent of compensation for each eligible employee but not to exceed $4500 for 2007. (For 2007, the maximum compensation for determining contributions is $225,000.) The contribution must be made regardless of whether the employee participates or not.

If employers elect the matching option, they can reduce the matching contribution to 1 percent of compensation provided the employees are notified within a reasonable time before the 60-day election period during which employees can decide whether to participate in the plan. The employer is allowed to contribute at the lower rate for any two years during a five-year period ending with that year. The option to contribute at a lower matching rate is especially helpful to firms that are strapped for cash during lean years.

All contributions go into an IRA account and are fully and immediately vested. Withdrawals of funds by SIMPLE participants under age 59½ are subject to a 10 percent tax penalty. However, withdrawals during the first two years of participation are subject to a stiff 25 percent tax penalty.

FUNDING AGENCY AND FUNDING INSTRUMENTS

An employer must select a funding agency when a pension plan is established. A **funding agency** *is a financial institution that provides for the accumulation or administration of the funds that will be used to pay pension benefits.* If the funding agency is a commercial bank or individual trustee, the plan is called a *trust-fund plan.* If the funding agency is a life insurer, the plan is called an *insured plan.* If both funding agencies are used, the plan is called a *split-funded combination plan.*

The employer must select a funding instrument to fund the pension plan. A **funding instrument** *is a trust agreement or insurance contract that states the terms under which the funding agency will accumulate, administer, and disburse the pension funds.* Funding instruments that are widely used today include the following: [4]

- Trust-fund plan
- Separate investment account
- Guaranteed investment contract (GIC)
- Investment guarantee contract

Trust-Fund Plan

Most private pension plan assets are invested in trust-fund plans. Under a **trust-fund plan,** all contributions are deposited with a trustee, who invests the funds according to the trust agreement between the employer and trustee. The trustee can be a commercial bank or individual trustee. Annuities are not purchased when the employees retire, and the pension benefits are paid directly out of the fund. The

trustee does not guarantee the adequacy of the fund. In addition, there are no guarantees of principal and interest rates when a defined-benefit plan is used. A consulting actuary periodically determines the adequacy of the fund.

Separate Investment Account

A separate investment account is a group pension product with a life insurance company. Under a **separate investment account,** the plan administrator can invest in one or more of the separate accounts offered by the insurer. The pension contributions can be invested in stock funds, bond funds, and similar investments. The assets in the separate account are segregated from the insurer's general investment account and are not subject to claims by the insurer's creditors. Separate accounts are popular because they permit the plan administrator to invest in a wide variety of investments, including common stocks.

Guaranteed Investment Contract (GIC)

A **guaranteed investment contract** (**GIC**) is an arrangement in which the insurer guarantees the interest rate for a number of years on a lump-sum deposit. The insurer also guarantees the principal against loss. Guaranteed investment contracts are popular with employers because of interest rate guarantees and protection against the loss of principal. Guaranteed investment contracts are sometimes used to fund the fixed-income option in a defined contribution retirement plan, such as a 401(k) plan. In addition, most guaranteed investment contracts make annuity options or other payment options available, but the employer is not required to use these options.

Investment Guarantee Contract

An **investment guarantee contract** is a group pension product that is similar to a GIC. The major difference, however, is that the insurer receives the pension funds over a number of years, such as five years, and the guaranteed interest rate for the later years is only a projected rate; if the actual returns are higher, the pension funds receive the higher rate. This type of funding vehicle may be appealing to employers who expect interest rates to rise in the future.

CASE APPLICATION

Richard, age 40, is the owner of Auto Repair, Inc. Because of a competitive labor market, he wants to establish a retirement plan for his employees. He is considering several retirement plans, including (1) a *defined-contribution plan*, (2) a *Section 401(k) plan*, and (3) a *SEP-IRA*. Assume you are a financial planner and Richard asks for your advice. Answer the following questions.

a. Explain to Richard the advantages and disadvantages of each of the three retirement plans.
b. Michael, age 28, is a mechanic for Auto Repair who earned $50,000 in 2007. Assume that the firm establishes a defined-contribution plan with a contribution rate of 6 percent of compensation by both the employee and employer. For 2007, what is the maximum tax-deductible contribution the firm can make to Michael's account?
c. Susan, the company's office manager, is 28 years old, and earns $35,000. She has worked for the

company for three years. Can Richard exclude her from participating in the defined-contribution plan to hold down pension costs? Explain your answer.
d. Assume Auto Repair selects a Section 401(k) plan. The plan allows participants to defer 6 percent of their salary up to an annual maximum limit ($15,500 for 2007 for participants under age 50). The employer makes a matching contribution of 50 cents for each dollar contributed. James, age 25, is a mechanic who has decided to defer only 3 percent of his salary because of substantial personal debts. What advice would you give to James?
e. Richard's wife, Maria, age 35, is self-employed as a freelance writer. After deducting half of the Social Security self-employment payroll tax, she has a net income of $50,000 for the current tax year. What is the maximum tax-deductible contribution Maria can make to a defined-contribution Keogh plan?

SUMMARY

- Qualified retirement plans receive favorable income-tax treatment. Employer contributions are tax-deductible and not considered taxable income to employees; investment earnings accumulate income-tax free; and pension benefits attributable to the employer's contributions are not taxed until the employee retires or receives the funds.

- Under the tax law, qualified pension plans must meet certain minimum coverage requirements, which are designed to reduce discrimination in favor of highly compensated employees.

- To meet the minimum coverage requirement, a retirement plan must satisfy one of the following tests:

    Percentage test

    Ratio test

    Average benefit test

- All employees who are at least age 21 and have one year of service must be allowed to participate in a qualified retirement plan.

- A retirement plan has a normal retirement age, an early retirement age, and a deferred retirement age. Most em-

ployees cannot be forced to retire at some mandatory retirement age. Benefits generally continue to accrue for employees who work beyond the normal retirement age.

- The benefits in a defined-benefit plan are typically based on the following benefit formulas:

    Unit-benefit formula

    Flat percentage of annual earnings

    Flat dollar amount for each year of service

    Flat dollar amount for all employees

- Vesting refers to the employee's right to the employer's contributions or benefits attributable to the contributions if employment terminates prior to retirement. Qualified retirement plans must meet certain minimum vesting standards.

- For 2007, under a *defined-contribution plan*, the maximum annual addition to an employee's account is limited to 100 percent of compensation, or $45,000, whichever is lower.

- For 2007, under a *defined-benefit plan*, the maximum annual benefit is limited to 100 percent of the worker's average compensation for the three highest consecutive years of compensation, or $180,000, whichever is lower.

- A *defined-contribution plan* is a retirement plan in which the contribution rate is fixed, but the actual retirement benefit varies, depending on the worker's age of entry into the plan, contribution rate, investment returns, and the age of normal retirement.

- A *defined-benefit plan* is a retirement plan in which the retirement benefit is known, but the contributions vary depending on the amount needed to fund the desired benefit. Defined-benefit plans typically pay benefits based on a unit-benefit formula that considers both earnings and years of participation in the plan.

- A *cash-balance plan* is a defined-benefit plan in which the benefits are defined in terms of a hypothetical account balance. The participant's account is credited with a pay credit and an interest credit. Actual retirement benefits will depend on the value of the participant's account at retirement.

- A *Section 401(k) plan* is a qualified cash or deferred arrangement (CODA) that allows eligible employees the option of putting money into the plan or receiving the funds as cash. The employee typically agrees to a salary reduction, which reduces the employee's taxable income. For 2007, the maximum salary reduction is limited to $15,500 for participants under age 50. Participants age 50 and older can make a catch-up contribution of $5000. These limits are indexed for inflation. The contributions deposited in the plan accumulate income-tax free until the funds are withdrawn.

- A *Section 403(b) plan* is a retirement plan for employees of public schools and tax-exempt organizations. This plan is also called a *tax-sheltered annuity.* Eligible employees can voluntarily elect to reduce their salaries by a fixed amount, which is then invested in the plan. For 2007, the maximum elective deferral for workers under age 50 is $15,500. Participants age 50 and older can make a catch-up contribution of $5000.

- A *profit-sharing plan* is a defined-contribution plan in which the employer's contributions are typically based on the firm's profits.

- A self-employed individual can establish a *Keogh plan* and receive favorable federal income-tax treatment. The contributions to the plan are income-tax deductible, and the investment income accumulates on a tax-deferred basis.

- A *simplified employee pension (SEP)* is a retirement plan in which the employer contributes to an individual retirement account (IRA) established for each eligible employee. For 2007, the maximum annual tax-deductible employer contribution to a SEP-IRA is limited to 25 percent of the employee's compensation, or $45,000, whichever is less. There is full and immediate vesting of all employer contributions under the plan.

- Under a *SIMPLE plan,* for 2007, eligible employees can elect to contribute up to $10,500. Employees age 50 and older can make an additional catch-up contribution of $2500. The maximum annual contribution limit will increase in the future. The employer has the option of either matching the employee's contributions on a dollar-for-dollar basis up to 3 percent of compensation, or making a nonelective contribution of 2 percent of compensation for all eligible employees.

- The major types of funding instruments to fund a pension plan are as follows:
  - Trust-fund plan
  - Separate investment account
  - Guaranteed investment contract (GIC)
  - Investment guarantee contract

KEY CONCEPTS AND TERMS

Actual deferral percentage (ADP) test
Advance funding
Average benefit test
Career-average earnings
Cash-balance plan
Deferred retirement age
Defined-benefit plan
Defined-contribution formula
Defined-contribution plan
Early retirement age
Employee Retirement Income Security Act of 1974 (ERISA)
Final average pay
Funding agency
Funding instrument
Guaranteed investment contract (GIC)
Highly compensated employees
Investment guarantee contract
Keogh plans
Minimum age and service requirement
Minimum coverage requirements
Minimum vesting standards
Money purchase plan
Normal retirement age
Past-service credits
Pension Benefit Guaranty Corporation (PBGC)
Pension Protection Act of 2006
Profit-sharing plan
Qualified plan
Roth 401(k) plan

Roth 403(b) plan
Section 401(k) plan
Section 403(b) plan
Self-employed 401(k)
  plan
Separate investment
  account
SEP-IRA
SIMPLE retirement plan
Simplified employee
  pension (SEP)

Top-heavy plan
Trust-fund plans
Vesting

REVIEW QUESTIONS

1. a. What are the federal income-tax advantages to employers in a qualified retirement plan?
   b. What are the federal income-tax advantages to employees in a qualified retirement plan?

2. A qualified retirement plan must meet certain minimum coverage requirements to receive favorable income-tax treatment. Explain the ratio test, which satisfies the minimum coverage requirement.

3. Explain the following retirement ages in a typical qualified retirement plan:
   a. Early retirement age
   b. Normal retirement age
   c. Deferred retirement age

4. Briefly explain the basic characteristics of a defined-contribution retirement plan.

5. a. Briefly explain the basic characteristics of a traditional defined-benefit retirement plan.
   b. What is a cash-balance retirement plan?

6. a. Describe the basic characteristics of a Section 401(k) plan.
   b. Describe the basic characteristics of a Section 403(b) plan (also called a tax-sheltered annuity).

7. Explain the major characteristics of a profit-sharing plan.

8. Describe the basic features of a Keogh plan for the self-employed.

9. Briefly explain the major characteristics of a simplified employee pension (SEP).

10. Briefly explain the basic characteristics of a SIMPLE retirement plan.

APPLICATION QUESTIONS

1. Qualified retirement plans must meet certain requirements to receive favorable federal income-tax treatment. Briefly explain each of the following:
   a. Minimum age and service requirements
   b. Vesting provisions
   c. Limitations on contributions and benefits
   d. Early distribution tax penalty

2. Fine Furniture has 1000 employees who are eligible to participate in the firm's defined-contribution retirement plan. Of this number, 100 employees are considered highly compensated, and 900 employees are non-highly compensated employees. The retirement plan covers all highly compensated employees. What is the minimum number of non-highly compensated employees who must be covered under the plan in order to satisfy the ratio test?

3. A national labor union representing pipeline construction workers has a defined-benefit pension plan for its members. Ron, age 65, is a heavy equipment operator who wants to retire. He has been a member of the union for 30 years. The pension plan has a unit-benefit formula, which provides a retirement benefit equal to 1.5 percent of the worker's final average compensation for each year of credited service. Final average compensation is based on the worker's highest three years of earnings. Ron's final average compensation is $70,000. How much will Ron receive each month when he retires?

4. Scott, age 35, is the owner of a local retail firm that sells carpets and other floor coverings. The company employs five people. One employee is a college student who works only part-time. The student earned $4000 last year, and his earnings are expected to be the same this year. Assume that Scott installs a SIMPLE retirement plan. For 2007, the plan permits eligible employees under age 50 to contribute a maximum of $10,500 into the plan. Employees age 50 and older can make an additional catch-up contribution of $2500. The company also makes a matching contribution into the plan. Based on this information, answer the following questions.
   a. Does Scott have to include the part-time student in the SIMPLE plan? Explain your answer.
   b. One employee who earns $40,000 elects to contribute $10,500 into the plan. What is the amount of the company's contribution?

c. If the company experiences financial problems in a business recession, can Scott reduce the company's contributions to the plan? Explain your answer.

5. Brandon, age 26, is a self-employed carpenter. One month ago, Brandon hired his brother, age 20, to help in the business because of a local housing boom. Brandon wants to accumulate a retirement fund and decides to adopt a Keogh plan to fund his retirement. Brandon's gross earnings are $120,000. After deducting allowable business deductions and one-half of the Social Security self-employment payroll tax, Brandon's net earnings are $80,000.
    a. What is the maximum tax-deductible contribution Brandon can make to the Keogh plan?
    b. Does Brandon have to include his brother in his Keogh plan? Explain your answer.

6. An employer must select a funding agency and a funding instrument when a pension plan is established.
    a. What is a funding agency?
    b. Briefly describe each of the following funding instruments:
        (1) Trust-fund plan
        (2) Separate investment account
    c. What is a guaranteed investment contract (GIC)?

INTERNET RESOURCES

■ The **American Benefits Council** is an organization that represents plan sponsors and technical professionals in the employee benefits field. The site provides an analysis of proposed legislation affecting private pension plans and other employee benefits. Visit the site at

http://www.appwp.org

■ The **Employee Benefit Research Institute (EBRI)** is a nonprofit organization that makes available research studies and notes on qualified retirement plans. Visit the site at

http://www.ebri.org

■ **Fidelity Investments** provides a substantial amount of timely information on retirement planning and qualified retirement plans, including 401(k) plans. Visit its 401(k) site at

http://www.401k.com

■ The **Pension Benefit Guaranty Corporation** is a federal corporation that protects the retirement benefits of workers in defined-benefit pension plans. The site provides timely information on defined-benefit pension plans. Visit the site at

http://www.pbgc.gov

■ The **Employee Benefits Security Administration (EBSA)** is an agency of the U.S. Department of Labor that provides information and statistics on qualified retirement plans. Visit the site at

http://www.dol.gov/ebsa

■ **Charles Schwab** provides informative articles and information on retirement planning, annuities, and individual retirement accounts (IRAs). Visit the site at

http://www.schwab.com

■ **The Vanguard Group** provides timely information on retirement planning, variable annuities, and IRAs. Visit the site at

http://www.vanguard.com

■ **TIAA-CREF** has an excellent site that provides a considerable amount of information on retirement planning and retirement options. Visit the site at

http://www.tiaa-cref.org

SELECTED REFERENCES

Commerce Clearing House. *Law, Explanation and Analysis, Economic Growth, and Tax Relief Reconciliation Act of 2001.* Chicago, IL: CCH Inc., 2001.

Deloitte. Global Employer Rewards. *Securing Retirement, An Overview of the Pension Protection Act of 2006,* August 3, 2006.

Deloitte. Global Employer Rewards. *Securing the Future: Defined Benefit Plans and the Pension Protection Act 2006.*

Kaster, Nicholas, et al. *2006 U.S. Master Pension Guide,* Chicago, IL: CCH Inc., 2006.

Littell, David A., and Kenn Beam Tacchino. *Planning for Retirement Needs,* 8th ed. Bryn Mawr, PA: The American College, 2006.

McGill, Dan M., and Donald S. Grubbs, Jr. *Fundamentals of Private Pensions,* 6th ed. Homewood, IL: Irwin, 1989.

Rosenbloom, Jerry S., ed. *The Handbook of Employee Benefits,* 6th ed. New York: McGraw-Hill, 2005.

NOTES

1. This chapter is based on Nicholas Kaster, et al., *2006 U.S. Master Pension Guide* (Chicago, IL: CCH Inc., 2006); and David A. Littell and Kenn Beam Tacchino, *Planning for Retirement Needs,* 8th ed. (Bryn Mawr, PA: The American College, 2006). IRS documents for taxpayers were also used.

2. For 2007, highly compensated employees are employees who (1) owned 5 percent of the company at any time during the year or preceding year or (2) had compensation from the employer in excess of $100,000 (indexed for inflation) during the preceding year, and if the employer elects, were in the top-paid group of employees for the preceding year (that is, the highest 20 percent of employees based on compensation).

3. Preston, Gates, Ellis LLP: Publications. *Pension Protection Act of 2006 Contains Far-Reaching Reforms for Retirement Plans,* August 11, 2006.

4. David A. Littell and Kenn Beam Tacchino, *Planning for Retirement Needs*, 8th ed. (Bryn Mawr, PA: The American College, 2006), ch. 12.

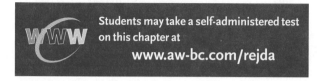

CHAPTER 18

SOCIAL INSURANCE

"Economic security is one of the unfulfilled needs of humans. Social security programs have been designed to aid people in their quest for economic security."

Robert J. Myers
Social Security, 4th ed.

LEARNING OBJECTIVES

After studying this chapter, you should be able to

◆ Explain the reasons why social insurance programs are established.

◆ Describe the basic characteristics of social insurance programs.

◆ Identify the major benefits provided by the Old-Age, Survivors, and Disability Insurance (OASDI) program.

◆ Identify the major benefits under the Medicare program.

◆ Describe the basic objectives and important provisions of state unemployment insurance programs.

◆ Explain the basic objectives and major provisions of workers compensation programs.

S ocial insurance programs are compulsory government insurance programs with certain characteristics that distinguish them from private insurance and other government insurance programs. The various programs provide a safety net against the financial insecurity that can result from premature death, unemployment, poor health, job-related disabilities, and old age. Social insurance programs are especially valuable to workers and families with low incomes. For example, Carlos, age 30, died unexpectedly from pancreatic cancer in early 2006. He left behind a wife and daughter, age 1. At the time of his death, Carlos had annual covered earnings of $20,000 under Social Security. As a result, his wife and daughter received monthly Social Security survivor benefits of approximately $1318, which enabled them to maintain at least a minimum standard of living.[1]

This chapter discusses the major social insurance programs in the United States. The programs discussed include the Social Security program (OASDI), Medicare, state unemployment insurance programs, and workers compensation programs.

SOCIAL INSURANCE

Reasons for Social Insurance

Although the United States has a highly developed system of private insurance, social insurance programs are necessary for several reasons.

- *Social insurance programs are enacted to solve complex social problems.* A social problem affects most or all of society and is so serious that direct government intervention is necessary. For example, the Social Security program came into existence because of the Great Depression of the 1930s, when massive unemployment required a direct government attack on economic insecurity.
- *Social insurance programs are necessary because certain risks are difficult to insure privately.* For example, unemployment is difficult to insure privately because it does not completely meet the requirements of an insurable risk. However, the risk of unemployment can be insured by state unemployment insurance programs.
- *Social insurance programs provide a base of economic security to the population.* Social insurance programs provide a layer of financial protection to most persons against the long-term

financial consequences of premature death, old age, occupational and nonoccupational disability, and unemployment.

Basic Characteristics of Social Insurance

Social insurance programs in the United States have certain characteristics that distinguish them from other government insurance programs:[2]

- Compulsory programs
- Floor of income
- Emphasis on social adequacy rather than individual equity
- Benefits loosely related to earnings
- Benefits prescribed by law
- No means test
- Full funding unnecessary
- Financially self-supporting

Compulsory Programs With few exceptions, social insurance programs are compulsory. A compulsory program has two major advantages. First, the goal of providing a floor of income to the population can be achieved more easily. Second, adverse selection is reduced, because both healthy and unhealthy lives are covered.

Floor of Income Social insurance programs are generally designed to provide only a floor of income with respect to the risks that are covered. Most persons are expected to supplement social insurance benefits with their own personal program of savings, investments, and private insurance.

The concept of a floor of income is difficult to define. One extreme view is that the floor of income should be so low as to be virtually nonexistent. Another extreme view is that the social insurance benefit by itself should be high enough to provide a comfortable standard of living, so that private insurance benefits would be unnecessary. A more realistic view is that social insurance benefits, when combined with other income and financial assets, should be sufficient for most persons to maintain a reasonable standard of living. Any group whose basic needs are still unmet would be provided for by supplemental public assistance (welfare) benefits.

Social Adequacy Rather Than Individual Equity Social insurance programs pay benefits based largely on social adequacy rather than on individual equity. Social adequacy *means that the benefits paid should provide a certain standard of living to all contributors. This means that the benefits paid are heavily weighted in favor of certain groups, such as low-income persons, large families, and the presently retired aged.* In technical terms, the actuarial value of the benefits received by these groups exceeds the actuarial value of their contributions. In contrast, the individual equity principle is followed in private insurance. **Individual equity** *means that contributors receive benefits directly related to their contributions; the actuarial value of the benefits is closely related to the actuarial value of the contributions.*

The basic purpose of the social adequacy principle is to provide a floor of income to all covered persons. If low-income persons received social insurance benefits actuarially equal to the value of their tax contributions (individual equity principle), the benefits paid would be so low that the basic objective of providing a floor of income to everyone would not be achieved.

Benefits Loosely Related to Earnings Social insurance benefits are loosely related to the worker's earnings. The higher the worker's covered earnings, the greater will be the benefits. The relationship between

higher earnings and higher benefits is loose and disproportionate, but it does exist. Thus, some consideration is given to individual equity.

Benefits Prescribed by Law Social insurance programs are prescribed by law. The benefits or benefit formulas, as well as the eligibility requirements, are established by law. In addition, the administration or supervision of the program is performed by government.

No Means Test Social insurance benefits are paid as a matter of right without any demonstration of need. A formal means test is not required. A **means test** is used in public assistance—welfare applicants must show that their income and financial assets are below certain levels as a condition of benefit eligibility. By contrast, applicants for social insurance benefits have a statutory right to the benefits if they fulfill certain eligibility requirements.

Full Funding Unnecessary For example, the Social Security program is not fully funded. A **fully funded program** means that the accumulated OASDI trust fund assets plus the present value of future contributions will be sufficient to discharge all liabilities over the valuation period. Social Security actuaries make cost estimates over a 75-year projection period and even beyond. According to the 2006 Board of Trustees report, the present value of the unfunded obligations from 2006 through the infinite horizon is $13.4 trillion. (Infinite horizon means that the current OASDI program and the demographic and most economic trends used for the 75-year projection period continue indefinitely.) However, the combined OASDI trust fund balance at the end of 2005 totaled only $1858.7 billion.[3] To be fully funded, a substantially higher trust fund balance would be required.

A fully funded Social Security program is unnecessary for several reasons. First, because the program will operate indefinitely and not terminate in the predictable future, full funding is unnecessary. Second, because the Social Security program is compulsory, new workers will always enter the program and pay taxes to support it. Third, the federal government can use its taxing and borrowing powers to raise additional revenues if the program has financial problems. Finally, from an economic viewpoint, full funding would require substantially higher Social

386 CHAPTER 18 / SOCIAL INSURANCE

Security taxes, which would be deflationary and cause substantial unemployment. In contrast, private pension plans must emphasize full funding, because private pension plans can terminate.

Financially Self-Supporting Social insurance programs in the United States are designed to be financially self-supporting. This means the programs should be almost completely financed from the earmarked contributions of covered employees, employers, and the self-employed, and interest on the trust-fund investments.

OLD-AGE, SURVIVORS, AND DISABILITY INSURANCE (OASDI)

The Old-Age, Survivors, and Disability Insurance (OASDI) program, commonly known as **Social Security,** is the most important social insurance program in the United States. Social Security was enacted into law as a result of the Social Security Act of 1935. More than nine out of ten workers are working in occupations covered by Social Security, and about one in six persons receives a monthly cash benefit.

Covered Occupations

The following groups are covered under the Social Security program:

- *Employees in private firms.* Virtually all private-sector employees are covered under the program at the present time.
- *Federal civilian employees.* Federal civilian employees hired after 1983 are covered on a compulsory basis. However, federal civilian employees hired before 1984 are covered only for Hospital Insurance under Medicare but not for OASDI.
- *State and local government employees.* State and local government employees can be covered by a voluntary agreement between the state and the federal government. The majority of state and local government employees are now covered. However, state and local government employees hired after March 1986 are covered for Hospital Insurance (HI) under the Medicare program and must pay the Hospital Insurance tax.

After July 1, 1991, all state and local government employees who are not participating in a public retirement system are covered on a compulsory basis. However, students employed in public schools, colleges, and universities can be excluded.

- *Employees of nonprofit organizations.* All employees of nonprofit charitable, educational, and religious organizations are covered if they are paid at least $100 during the year.
- *Self-employment.* Self-employed persons are covered if their net annual earnings are $400 or more.
- *Domestic employment in private homes.* Domestic employees are covered only if they earn $1500 or more in 2006.
- *Other groups.* Ministers are covered on a self-employment basis unless they elect out because of conscience or religious principles. U.S. military personnel are covered on a compulsory basis. Finally, railroad workers subject to the Railroad Retirement Act are not required to pay OASDI taxes directly. However, because of certain coordinating provisions, railroad employees are, in reality, covered compulsorily for OASDI and HI under Medicare.

Determination of Insured Status

Before you or your family can receive benefits, you must have credit for a certain amount of work in covered employment. Credits can be earned anytime during the year. For 2007, you receive one **credit** (also called a **quarter of coverage**) for each $1000 of covered earnings. A maximum of four credits can be earned each year. The amount of covered earnings required to earn one credit will automatically increase each year as average wages in the national economy rise.

To become eligible for the various benefits, you must attain an insured status. There are three types of insured status:

- Fully insured
- Currently insured
- Disability insured

Retirement benefits require a fully insured status. Survivor benefits require either a fully insured or currently insured status, although certain survivor benefits require a fully insured status. Disability benefits require a disability-insured status.

Fully Insured   To be eligible for retirement benefits, you must be fully insured. You are **fully insured** for retirement benefits if you have 40 credits. However, for people born before 1929, fewer credits are required.

Currently Insured   You are **currently insured** if you have earned at least 6 credits during the last 13 calendar quarters ending with the quarter of death, disability, or entitlement to retirement benefits.

Disability Insured   The number of credits required to be **disability insured** depends on your age when you become disabled. The following rules apply if you are under age 31:

- If you become disabled before age 24, you generally need 1½ years of work (six credits) in the three years before you became disabled.
- For ages 24 through 30, you generally need credits for half of the time between age 21 and the time you became disabled. For example, a worker disabled at age 27 needs credit for three years of work out of the past six years.
- If you are disabled at age 31 or older, you generally need at least 20 credits in the 10 years before you became disabled. At least 20 credits must be earned during the past 10 years immediately before you became disabled. The following table shows how many credits you would need at selected ages:

Disabled at Age	Credits Needed	Years of Work
31 through 42	20	5
44	22	5½
46	24	6
48	26	6½
50	28	7
52	30	7½
54	32	8
56	34	8½
58	36	9
60	38	9½
62 or older	40	10

Finally, blind persons are required only to have a fully insured status. They are not required to meet the recent-work test requirement that applies to other disability applicants.

TYPES OF BENEFITS

The total program consists of Social Security (OASDI) and Medicare. The OASDI program pays monthly retirement, survivor, and disability benefits to eligible beneficiaries. The Medicare program covers the medical expenses of almost all persons aged 65 and older and certain disabled beneficiaries younger than age 65. We discuss only OASDI cash benefits at this point; Medicare is covered later in the chapter.

Retirement Benefits

Social Security retirement benefits are an important source of income for most retired workers. Without these benefits, poverty and economic insecurity among the aged would be substantially increased.

Full Retirement Age   For persons born in 1937 or earlier, the **full retirement age** for unreduced benefits is age 65. However, the full retirement age will gradually increase in the future to age 67 to improve the financial solvency of the OASDI program and to allow for the increase in life expectancy (see Exhibit 18.1).

Early Retirement Age   Workers and their spouses can retire as early as age 62 with actuarially reduced benefits (see Exhibit 18.1).

The actuarial reduction in benefits for early retirement at age 62 will gradually increase to 30 percent in the future when the higher full retirement age provisions become fully effective.

At the present time, more than half of the OASDI beneficiaries apply for retirement benefits before the full retirement age. Is it desirable to receive retirement benefits early? This is a complex question and depends on your need for retirement income, state of health, life expectancy, whether you are still working in the labor force, and whether you have other assets that yield income. Insight 18.1 discusses this issue in greater detail.

EXHIBIT **18.1**
Social Security Full Retirement Age and Reduction in Benefits by Age

No matter what your full retirement age (also called "normal retirement age") is, you may start receiving benefits as early as age 62.

Year of Birth[a]	Full Retirement Age	Age 62 Reduction Months[b]	Monthly % Reduction	Total % Reduction at Age 62
1937 or earlier	65	36	.555	20.00
1938	65 and 2 months	38	.548	20.83
1939	65 and 4 months	40	.541	21.67
1940	65 and 6 months	42	.535	22.50
1941	65 and 8 months	44	.530	23.33
1942	65 and 10 months	46	.525	24.17
1943–1954	66	48	.520	25.00
1955	66 and 2 months	50	.516	25.84
1956	66 and 4 months	52	.512	26.66
1957	66 and 6 months	54	.509	27.50
1958	66 and 8 months	56	.505	28.33
1959	66 and 10 months	58	.502	29.17
1960 and later	67	60	.500	30.00

[a] If you were born on January 1, you should refer to the previous year.
[b] If you were born on the first of the month, the benefit is figured as if your birthday were in the previous month.
SOURCE: Social Security Administration.

Monthly Retirement Benefits Monthly retirement benefits can be paid to retired workers and their dependents. Eligible persons include the following:

- *Retired worker.* Monthly retirement benefits can be paid at the full retirement age to a fully insured worker. Reduced benefits can be paid as early as age 62.
- *Spouse of a retired worker.* The spouse of a retired worker can also receive monthly benefits if she or he is at least age 62 and has been married to the retired worker for at least one year. A divorced spouse is also eligible for benefits based on the retired worker's earnings if she or he is at least age 62, and the marriage lasted at least 10 years.
- *Unmarried children younger than age 18.* Monthly benefits can also be paid to unmarried children of a retired worker who are younger than age 18 (or 19 if full-time elementary or high school students).

- *Unmarried disabled children.* Unmarried disabled children age 18 or older are also eligible for benefits based on the retired worker's earnings if they were severely disabled before age 22 and continue to remain disabled.
- *Spouse with dependent children younger than age 16.* A spouse at any age can receive a monthly benefit if the spouse is caring for an eligible child younger than age 16 (or is caring for a child of any age who was disabled before age 22) who is receiving a benefit based on the retired worker's earnings. The mother's or father's benefit terminates when the youngest child attains age 16 (unless the mother or father is caring for a child disabled before age 22).

Retirement Benefit Amount The monthly retirement benefit is based on the worker's **primary insurance amount (PIA),** which is the monthly amount paid to a retired worker at the full retirement age or

INSIGHT 18.1

When Is the Right Time to Draw Social Security?

If you're like most Americans, your monthly Social Security check could represent a significant chunk of your annual retirement income. According to the Vanguard Center for Retirement Research, even the wealthiest 40% of retirees depend on Social Security for a third of their retirement income, on average.

Given the importance of this income stream, you'll want to take great care as you decide when to start receiving benefits. The amount you receive every month will depend to a large extent on whether you apply for benefits at age 62, at your full retirement age (65 to 67, depending on your birth year), or up to age 70.

Your monthly benefit at age 62 could be as much as 25% less than your "full" benefit at age 66. And if you delay your first payment until age 70, your monthly benefit could be almost 40% higher than your full benefit. These differences apply to all of you payments throughout your life.

Does It Pay to Delay?

If you knew for certain how long you would live, and if your only concern was to receive as much as possible from Social Security during your lifetime, deciding when to start receiving payments would be easy.

As the table below indicates, if you knew you wouldn't live past age 75, you would want to collect your first benefit at age 62. If you could count on living to age 80, however, you might want to wait until full retirement age to begin collecting. The advantage of delaying your benefit until age 70 eventually exceeds the advantage of starting at age 62—but not until sometime between ages 80 and 85.

Of course, you don't know how long you'll live. The National Center for Health Statistics says that, on average, Americans who are 65 years old live to about age 83 (age 81.6 for men and 84.5 for women). You can estimate your longevity to some extent by considering your current state of health and your family medical history. But these are not definite indicators as to when you should apply for Social Security.

So when is the best time to receiving Social Security? The correct answer is there's no ideal age. Or, to be more precise, it varies from person to person and is often apparent only in hindsight. *Ultimately, your decision will likely hinge on whether you need extra income at age 62 or thereafter, and on the state of your health.*

Postponing Social Security Benefits Can Pay Off—In the Long Run

If you begin collecting Social Security benefits at	And your monthly benefit* is	By age 75, you would have received	By age 80, you would have received	By age 85, you would have received	By age 90, you would have received
Age 62	$1,200	$187,200	$259,200	$331,200	$403,200
Age 66	$1,600	$172,800	$268,800	$364,800	$460,800
Age 70	$2,200	$132,000	$264,000	$396,000	$528,000

*The sample benefits used in the table are based on Social Security Administration estimates for an individual with an income of $60,000 who qualifies for full benefits at age 66 in 2017. All amounts are in constant 2005 dollars and do not include potential earnings from reinvestment. Actual income will include increases in benefits based on inflation.

to a disabled worker. The PIA, in turn, is based on the worker's **average indexed monthly earnings (AIME),** which is a method that updates the worker's earnings based on increases in the average wage in the national economy. The indexing of covered wages results in a relatively constant replacement rate so that workers retiring today and in the future will have about the same proportion of their work earnings replaced by OASDI benefits.

Earnings are indexed by taking into account changes in average wages in the national economy since the worker actually earned the money. The indexing year is the second year before the worker reaches age 62, becomes disabled, or dies, whichever occurs first. For example, assume that Vicki is a registered nurse who retired at age 62 in 2006. The critical year for setting the index factor is the second year before she attained age 62 (2004). To illustrate the method for one year, assume that Vicki's actual earnings in 1966 were $4889. If her actual earnings in 1966 are multiplied by the index factor for that year (7.2187), her indexed earnings for 1966 are $35,292. This procedure is carried out for each year during the measurement period, except that actual dollar amounts are counted for and after the indexing year. The index factors change each year as average wages in the national economy change.

For persons born after 1928, the highest 35 years of indexed earnings are used to calculate the worker's AIME for retirement benefits. (For those born earlier, fewer years are counted.) The AIME is then used to determine the worker's primary insurance amount. A weighted benefit formula is used, which weights the benefits heavily in favor of low-income groups. This weighting reflects the social adequacy principle discussed earlier.

Exhibit 18.2 provides examples of monthly OASDI retirement benefits for selected beneficiary designations.

Delayed Retirement Some workers delay their retirement and work beyond the full retirement age. If you continue working, you can increase your future Social Security benefits in two ways. First, each addi-

EXHIBIT 18.2

Examples of Monthly OASDI Retirement Benefits at the Full Retirement Age (FRA)

The following table shows *approximate* monthly benefits at FRA for you and your spouse. It is assumed that you have worked steadily since age 22 and received average pay raises throughout your working career. It is also assumed that your earnings, and the general level of wages and salaries in the country, will stay the same until you retire. This way, *the table shows the value of your benefits in today's dollars.*

Your spouse may, instead, quality for a higher retirement benefit based on her or his own work record.

Your Age in 2006	Who Receives Benefits	Your Present Annual Earnings					
		$20,000	$35,000	$50,000	$65,000	$80,000	$94,200 and Up
65	You	$882	$1,257	$1,631	$1,809	$1,943	$2,053
	Spouse	441	628	815	904	971	1,026
64	You	874	1,246	1,618	1,796	1,935	2,048
	Spouse	437	623	809	898	967	1,024
63	You	874	1,247	1,620	1,802	1,951	2,074
	Spouse	437	623	810	901	975	1,037
62	You	877	1,249	1,622	1,809	1,963	2,090
	Spouse	438	624	811	904	981	1,045
61	You	878	1,252	1,625	1,811	1,970	2,103
	Spouse	439	626	812	905	985	1,051
55	You	885	1,264	1,643	1,822	2,000	2,162
	Spouse	442	632	821	911	1,000	1,081
50	You	891	1,275	1,651	1,831	2,011	2,182
	Spouse	445	637	825	915	1,005	1,091
45	You	898	1,287	1,660	1,842	2,024	2,203
	Spouse	449	643	830	921	1,012	1,101
40	You	904	1,297	1,667	1,851	2,035	2,216
	Spouse	452	648	833	925	1,017	1,108
35	You	910	1,308	1,674	1,860	2,047	2,226
	Spouse	455	654	837	930	1,023	1,113
30	You	913	1,313	1,677	1,865	2,052	2,230
	Spouse	456	656	838	932	1,026	1,115

SOURCE: Donna A. Clements and Robert J. Myers, *2006 Guide to Social Security and Medicare Overview* (Louisville, KY: Mercer Human Resource Consulting, November 2005), p. 12.

tional year of work adds another year of earnings to your Social Security earnings record. Higher lifetime earnings may result in higher benefits when you retire.

Second, a **delayed retirement credit** is available if you delay receiving retirement benefits beyond the full retirement age. Your primary insurance amount will be increased by a certain percentage from the time you reach the full retirement age until you start receiving benefits, or until you reach age 70. The percentage increase varies depending on the year of birth. For example, for workers born in 1943 or later, the primary insurance amount is increased 8 percent per year (prorated monthly) for each year of delay beyond the full retirement age.

Automatic Cost-of-Living Adjustment The cash benefits are automatically adjusted each year for changes in the cost of living, which maintains the real purchasing power of the monthly benefits during periods of inflation. Whenever the consumer price index for all urban wage earners and clerical workers on a quarterly basis increases from the third quarter of the previous year to the third quarter of the present year, the benefits are automatically increased by the same percentage for the December benefits (payable in January). The cost-of-living increase for benefits payable in January 2007 was 3.3 percent.

Earnings Test The OASDI program has an **earnings test (retirement test)** that can result in a reduction or loss of monthly benefits for workers with earned incomes above certain annual limits. The earnings test applies to the following:

- *Beneficiary under the full retirement age*. If a beneficiary is under the full retirement age, $1 in benefits will be deducted for each $2 of earnings in excess of the annual limit. For 2007, the annual limit is $12,960. The annual limit is increased annually based on increases in average wages in the national economy.
- *Calendar year in which the beneficiary attains the full retirement age*. The earnings test is liberalized for this age group. In the calendar year in which the beneficiary attains the full retirement age, $1 in benefits will be deducted for each $3 of earnings above the annual limit. For 2007, the annual limit is $34,440. *However, only earn-*

ings before the month in which the beneficiary attains the full retirement age are counted. For example, assume that Jason attains the full retirement age in July 2007. During the first six months of 2007, Jason earned $37,440. Because his earnings are $3000 over the annual limit, he will lose $1000 in benefits.

The annual limit for this age group will increase in the future based on increases in average wages in the national economy.

- *Earnings test eliminated after attainment of the full retirement age*. The earnings test does not apply in and after the month the beneficiary attains the full retirement age. *Beneficiaries who have attained the full retirement age or beyond can earn any amount and receive full OASDI benefits.* As an alternative, beneficiaries who continue working beyond the full retirement age can elect to receive a delayed retirement credit instead of monthly cash benefits.

The earnings test does not apply to investment income, dividends, interest, rents, or annuity payments. The purpose of this exception is to encourage private savings and investments to supplement OASDI benefits.

Survivor Benefits

Survivor benefits can be paid to the dependents of a deceased worker who is either fully or currently insured. For certain survivor benefits, a fully insured status is required.

Social Security survivor benefits provide a substantial amount of financial protection to families in terms of private life insurance equivalents. For an average family, the survivor benefits are equivalent to a $354,000 life insurance policy.[4] However, the benefits are paid monthly and not in a lump sum.

- *Unmarried children younger than age 18*. Survivor benefits can be paid to unmarried children younger than age 18 (younger than 19 if full-time elementary or high school students).
- *Unmarried disabled children*. Unmarried children age 18 or older who become severely disabled before age 22 are eligible for survivor benefits based on the deceased parent's earnings.
- *Surviving spouse with children younger than age 16*. A widow, widower, or surviving divorced

spouse is entitled to a monthly benefit if she or he is caring for an eligible child who is younger than age 16 (or who is disabled before age 22) and is receiving a benefit based on the deceased worker's earnings. The benefits terminate for the surviving spouse when the youngest child reaches age 16, or the disabled child dies, marries, or is no longer disabled.

- *Surviving spouse age 60 or older.* A surviving spouse age 60 or older is also eligible for survivor benefits. The deceased worker must be fully insured. A surviving divorced spouse age 60 or older is also eligible for survivor benefits if the marriage lasted at least 10 years.
- *Disabled widow or widower, ages 50 through 59.* A disabled widow, widower, or surviving divorced spouse who is age 50 or older can receive survivor benefits under certain conditions. The person must be disabled at the time of the worker's death or become disabled no later than seven years after the mother's or father's benefits end. The deceased must be fully insured.
- *Dependent parents.* Dependent parents age 62 and older can also receive survivor benefits based on the deceased's earnings. The deceased worker must be fully insured.
- *Lump-sum death benefit.* A lump-sum death benefit of $255 can be paid when a worker dies. The benefit, however, can be paid only if there is an eligible surviving widow, widower, or entitled child.

Disability Benefits

Disability income benefits can be paid to disabled workers who meet certain eligibility requirements. The benefits provide considerable protection against the loss of income during a long-term disability. Social Security disability benefits for an average family are equivalent to a private disability insurance policy worth over $233,000.[5]

To be eligible for benefits, a disabled worker must meet the following eligibility requirements:

- Be disability insured
- Meet a five-month waiting period
- Satisfy the definition of disability

A disabled worker must be disability insured and must also meet a five-month waiting period. Benefits begin after a waiting period of five full calendar months. Therefore, the first payment is for the sixth full month of disability.

The definition of disability stated in the law must also be met. A strict definition of disability is used in the program: *The worker must have a physical or mental condition that prevents him or her from doing any substantial gainful activity and is expected to last (or has lasted) at least 12 months or is expected to result in death.* The impairment must be so severe that the worker is prevented from doing any substantial gainful work in the national economy. In determining whether a person can do substantial gainful work, his or her age, education, training, and work experience can be taken into consideration. If the disabled person cannot work at his or her own occupation but can engage in other substantial gainful work, the disability claim will not be allowed.

The major groups eligible to receive OASDI disability-income benefits are as follows:

- *Disabled worker.* A disabled worker under the full retirement age receives a benefit equal to 100 percent of the primary insurance amount. The worker must meet the definition of disability, be disability insured, and satisfy a full five-month waiting period.
- *Spouse of a disabled worker.* Benefits can be paid to the spouse of a disabled worker at any age if she or he is caring for a child younger than age 16 or a child who became disabled before age 22 and is receiving benefits based on the disabled worker's earnings. If no eligible children are present, the spouse must be at least age 62 to receive benefits.
- *Unmarried children younger than age 18.* Disability benefits can be paid to unmarried children younger than age 18 (or younger than 19 if a full-time elementary or high school student).
- *Unmarried disabled children.* Unmarried children age 18 or older who became severely disabled before age 22 are also eligible for benefits, based on the disabled worker's earnings.

Taxation of OASDI Benefits

Some beneficiaries who receive monthly cash benefits must pay an income tax on part of the benefits. The amount of benefits subject to taxation depends on your combined income. *Combined income* (also called *provisional income*) is the sum of your adjusted gross income, plus tax-free interest, plus one-half of your Social Security benefits. If your combined income exceeds certain dollar thresholds, some benefits are taxable.

If you file a federal tax return as an individual and your combined income is between $25,000 and $34,000, up to 50 percent of the benefits are subject to taxation. If your combined income exceeds $34,000, up to 85 percent of your benefits are subject to taxation.

If you are married and file a joint tax return and have a combined income between $32,000 and $44,000, up to 50 percent of the benefits are subject to taxation. If your combined income exceeds $44,000, up to 85 percent of the benefits are subject to taxation.

For married taxpayers who file separate tax returns and have lived together anytime during the year, the dollar threshold is zero. If not living together, you are considered to be a single person.

The Social Security Administration will send you a form each year that shows the amount of Social Security benefits received. The Internal Revenue Service has prepared a detailed worksheet to determine the amount of benefits, if any, to include in your taxable income.

Financing Social Security Benefits

Social Security benefits are financed by a payroll tax paid by employees, employers, and the self-employed; interest income on the trust fund investments; and by revenues derived from the taxation of part of the monthly cash benefits.

In 2007, a worker paid a payroll tax of 6.2 percent on covered earnings up to a maximum of $97,500. The maximum taxable earnings base will automatically increase in the future if wages in the national economy increase. In addition, a worker pays a Medicare tax of 1.45 percent on all earned income, including earnings that exceed the OASDI wage base. The employee's contribution is matched by an identical contribution from the employer.

The self-employed pay a tax rate that is twice the employee rate. However the self-employed are allowed certain deductions, which reduce the effective tax rate.

Long-Range OASDI Actuarial Deficit It has always been the intent of Congress that the OASDI program should be actuarially sound. Although the present program is currently running an annual surplus, the program will experience a serious long-range actuarial deficit in the years ahead. Based on the intermediate cost estimate in the 2006 Board of Trustees Report, the OASDI trust funds will experience serious financial problems in the future. The annual cost of OASDI benefits represents 4.2 percent of the gross domestic product (GDP) in 2005 and is projected to increase to 6.12 percent of GDP in 2030. *The projected 75-year actuarial deficit in the combined Old-Age and Survivors Insurance (OASI) and Disability Insurance (DI) trust funds is 2.02 percent of taxable payroll, up from 1.92 percent in last year's report. The program continues to fail a long-range test of close financial balance by a wide margin. Projected OASDI tax income will begin to fall short of outlays in 2017 and will be sufficient to finance only 74 percent of the scheduled annual benefits by 2040, when the combined OASDI trust fund is projected to be exhausted.*[6]

Reducing the Long-Range Deficit Reducing the long-range deficit will require some hard choices. Based on the 2006 Board of Trustees Report, the Social Security program can be actuarially balanced over the next 75 years in various ways, *which include an immediate increase of 16 percent in payroll tax revenues or an immediate reduction in benefits of 13 percent, or some combination of the two. Greater adjustment in scheduled benefits and revenues will be required if the changes are delayed or gradually phased in.*[7]

The deficit can be reduced or eliminated by (1) increasing payroll taxes, (2) decreasing benefits, (3) using general revenues of the federal government to pay benefits, or (4) by some combination of each. Proposed changes include the following:

- Use "progressive indexing" to determine benefits. For purposes of determining the worker's average monthly indexed earnings, a price index rather than a wage index would be used, which results in substantial cost savings. However, the indexing method for lower income groups would still be based on a wage index, as is now the case. As covered earnings increase, a combination of wage and price indexing would be used. For up-per income groups, the indexing method would be based solely on a price index. The overall re-sult would be a substantial reduction in the long-range deficit.

- Move up scheduled increases in the full retire-ment age, or increase it beyond age 67.
- Reduce benefits for future retirees across the board.
- Increase the OASDI taxable wage earnings base to cover a larger percentage of earnings.
- All OASDI benefits would be subject to the fed-eral income tax (instead of a maximum of 85 percent as is now the case).
- Extend OASDI coverage on a compulsory basis to all new state and local government employees.
- Increase the number of years used in calculating retirement benefits from 35 to 38.
- Invest part of the trust fund assets in private investments, such as common stock.

In addition, the general revenues of the federal government could be used to fund part of the pro-gram. However, the federal budget is currently run-ning a large deficit because of the war in Iraq, disas-ter payments for Hurricane Katrina and other natu-ral disasters, recent federal income-tax cuts, and excessive spending by Congress. Thus, increased reliance on general revenue financing to reduce the long-range deficit is unlikely.

The American Academy of Actuaries has de-signed a Social Security game that allows you to make hypothetical changes in the Social Security program and see the impact of such changes on the long-range actuarial deficit (see Insight 18.2).

Voluntary Personal Retirement Accounts The cur-rent debate over reducing the long-range actuarial deficit also includes proposals that would create voluntary personal retirement accounts. One pro-posal would allow younger workers to divert two full percentage points from the OASDI payroll tax into voluntary personal retirement accounts. The tax contributions would be invested in a common stock fund or other approved investments. At re-tirement, the worker would receive benefits from the individual account and from traditional Social Security benefits. If the worker died before retire-ment, the deceased worker's spouse or beneficiary would inherit the assets.

Voluntary retirement accounts are controversial. Insight 18.3 summarizes the major arguments for and against personal retirement accounts.

MEDICARE

Medicare is an important part of the total Social Security program that covers the medical expenses of most persons age 65 and older. Medicare also covers disabled persons younger than age 65 who have been entitled to disability benefits for at least 24 months. In addition, the program covers persons younger than age 65 who need long-term kidney dialysis treatment or a kidney transplant.

The Medicare program is complex and contro-versial. The present program also includes prescrip-tion drug plans and health-care plans of private insurers. Medicare currently has a bewildering array of plans, which include the following:

- The Original Medicare Plan
- Medicare Advantage Plans
- Other Medicare Health Plans
- Medicare Prescription Drug Plans

The following section discusses the major provisions in each of these plans.

The Original Medicare Plan

Beneficiaries can elect the Original Medicare Plan, which is the traditional plan run by the federal gov-ernment that provides Part A and Part B benefits. Beneficiaries can elect any provider that accepts Medicare patients. Medicare pays its share of the bill, and the beneficiary pays the balance. Some serv-ices are not covered.

Hospital Insurance Hospital Insurance (also called **Medicare Part A**) provides coverage for inpatient hospital stays and other benefits as well. Part A ben-efits include the following:

- *Inpatient hospital care.* Inpatient care in a hospi-tal is covered for up to 90 days for each benefit period. A *benefit period* starts when the patient first enters the hospital and ends when the patient has been out of the hospital or skilled nursing facility for 60 consecutive days. For the first 60

INSIGHT 18.2

Proposed Changes in Social Security—Estimated Impact on Long-Range Actuarial Deficit

There are no easy solutions for saving Social Security. The long-range actuarial deficit can be eliminated by increasing revenues, reducing benefits, or both. The American Academy of Actuaries has an interactive program on its Web site (www.actuary.org/socialsecurity) that allows you to make hypothetical changes in the Social Security program. The pro-

gram then shows the estimated change in the long-range actuarial deficit based on the Board of Trustees Reports. Also shown are arguments for and against the proposed change. One major advantage is that you can propose changes that are consistent with your political, economic, and ideological beliefs. The following are examples of the proposed changes:

	Reduction in Long-Range Deficit
Benefit Reductions	
• Accelerate the increase in the retirement age to 67, then keep adjusting as needed.	36%
• Reduce the cost-of-living adjustment (COLA) by 1/2 percentage point.	42
• Reduce benefits by 5 percent for future retirees.	32
• Curb benefits for those earning more than $20,000 annually before retirement.	70
Revenue Increases	
• Raise the payroll tax on workers and employers by 1/2 percentage point each.	51
• Raise the annual earning cap to $118,000.	26
• Tax Social Security benefits like pension benefits.	20
• Include new state and local government workers.	11
Investing in the Private Sector	
• Invest 40 percent of the trust fund in stocks and other private-sector investments.	50
• Create personal retirement accounts. (Divert 1 percentage point of the payroll tax to private accounts.)	0

Source: Adapted from American Academy of Actuaries, *The Social Security Game*, www.actuary.org/socialsecurity/game/html

days, Medicare pays all covered costs except for an initial inpatient hospital deductible ($992 in 2007). The deductible is paid only once during the benefit period no matter how many times the patient is hospitalized. For the 61st through 90th day, Medicare pays all covered costs except for a daily coinsurance charge ($248 in 2007). If the patient is still hospitalized after 90 days, a *lifetime reserve* of 60 additional days is available. Lifetime reserve days are subject to a daily coinsurance charge ($496 in 2007). The inpatient hospital deductible and coinsurance charges are adjusted annually to reflect changes in hospital costs.

■ *Skilled nursing facility care.* Inpatient care in a skilled nursing facility is covered up to maximum of 100 days in a benefit period. The first

20 days of covered services are paid in full. For the next 80 days, the patient must pay a daily coinsurance charge ($124 in 2007). To be eligible for coverage, the patient must be hospitalized first for at least three days and must require skilled nursing care. Intermediate care and custodial care are not covered.

■ *Home health care.* Health-care services in the patient's home are covered if the patient requires skilled care and meets certain conditions. Covered services include part-time or intermittent skilled nursing care, home health-aide services, physical therapy, occupational therapy, and speech-language services that are ordered by the patient's doctor and provided by a Medicare-certified home health-care agency. Also covered are medical social services, durable medical

INSIGHT 18.3

At a Glance—The Pros and Cons of Personal Retirement Accounts under Social Security

Workers under a certain age, such as age 50, could voluntarily invest part of the OASDI payroll tax into a personal retirement account. At retirement, workers would receive benefits from their individual accounts and from traditional OASDI benefits. Under one proposal, future OASDI retirement benefits for all workers would be reduced. For workers with private accounts, benefits would be reduced further to reflect the payroll taxes diverted into personal accounts. The major arguments for such accounts are summarized as follows:

- *A worker would own real financial assets that can be passed on to the heirs.* This reinforces the concept of an ownership society.
- *Low-income workers would have an opportunity to save and accumulate funds.* The working poor cannot easily save under the present system.
- *The unequal distribution of wealth in the United States would be reduced.* Income inequality in the United States has increased over time.
- *Higher investment returns can be obtained than under the present system.* The real rate of return for many workers under the present system is under 2 percent.
- *Personal accounts would create a pension plan for workers who are not covered by private pensions.* Fewer than half of the workers currently participate in an employer-sponsored retirement plan.

The arguments against personal retirement accounts are summarized as follows:

- *Personal accounts alone do nothing to reduce the long-range deficit.* Other structural changes in the program are also necessary.
- *Massive federal borrowing would be necessary to finance the transition costs of moving to a new system.* As a result, the federal debt will be substantially increased.
- *Risk of economic insecurity during retirement may increase if the stock market crashes shortly before retirement.* The principle of a guaranteed safety net under the OASDI program would be violated. In addition, the OASDI program is one of the relatively small number of defined-benefit retirement plans still in existence.
- *The potential impact on survivor and disability income benefits has largely been ignored.* Survivor and disability benefits may be lower if the stock market declines just before you die or become disabled.
- *The administrative cost to private firms who would service millions of small accounts may be disproportionately high.* The present OASDI program has relatively low administrative costs.

equipment, medical supplies, and other services. No cost-sharing provisions apply to covered services, but the patient must pay 20 percent of the Medicare-approved amount for durable medical equipment.

- *Hospice care.* Hospice care is available for beneficiaries with a terminal illness. Benefits include drugs for pain relief and symptom control, medical and support services from a Medicare-approved hospice, and other services not otherwise covered by Medicare. Hospice care is usually given in the patient's home. However, short-term hospital and inpatient respite care are covered when necessary. Respite care is care given to a hospice patient so that the usual caregiver can rest for a short period.
- *Blood transfusions.* Part A also pays for the cost of inpatient blood transfusions in a hospital or

skilled nursing facility during a covered stay. The first three pints of blood are not covered. The patient then pays 20 percent of the Medicare-approved amount for additional pints of blood (unless donated to replace what is used).

Hospitals are reimbursed for inpatient services under a prospective payment system. Hospital care is classified into **diagnosis-related groups (DRGs),** and a flat amount is paid for each type of care depending on the diagnosis group in which the case is placed. Thus, a flat, uniform amount is paid to each hospital for the same type of care or treatment. However, the amount paid varies among different geographical locations and by urban and rural facilities.

The purpose of the DRG system is to create a financial incentive to encourage hospitals to operate more efficiently. Hospitals can keep the payment amounts that exceed their costs, but they must absorb any costs in excess of the DRG flat amounts.

Medical Insurance   Medical Insurance (also called Medicare Part B) is a voluntary program that covers physicians' fees and related medical services. Beneficiaries who are covered under Part A on the basis of their covered earnings are automatically covered under Part B unless they voluntarily decline the coverage.

Part B pays for certain services that are medically necessary. Covered services include the following:

- *Physician services and other services.* Part B covers physician services and other services, which include outpatient medical and surgical services and supplies, diagnostic tests, ambulatory surgery center fees for approved procedures, and durable medical equipment. Part B also covers a second and sometimes a third medical opinion, outpatient mental health care, and outpatient occupational and physical therapy, including speech-language services.
- *Clinical laboratory services.* These services include blood tests, urinalysis, some screening tests, and additional services.
- *Home health care.* Part B also provides home health-care services. These services are similar to those provided by Part A.
- *Outpatient hospital services.* Part B covers hospital services and supplies received as an outpatient as part of a doctor's care.
- *Blood.* Part B covers pints of blood received as a patient or as part of a Part B covered service. Coverage is similar to the blood coverage provided under Part A.

Part B has numerous exclusions, including most dental care, dentures, routine foot care, and hearing aids. Eyeglasses are covered only if the patient needs corrective lenses after a cataract operation. Routine physical exams are not covered except for a one-time physical exam within the first six months of coverage under Part B.

Amount Paid by Part B   The beneficiary must meet an annual Part B deductible ($131 in 2007), which is indexed to the growth in Part B spending. *Part B then pays 80 percent of the Medicare-approved amount for most physician services, outpatient therapy, preventive services, and durable medical equipment.* Most outpatient mental health services are reimbursed only at a rate of 50 percent. However, there is no charge for home health-care services, clinical laboratory services, and flu shots.

Medical payments to physicians are made on an assigned or nonassigned basis. By accepting an assignment, a physician agrees to accept the Medicare-approved amount as payment in full. The patient is not liable for any additional out-of-pocket costs other than the calendar-year deductible and coinsurance payments. However, physicians who do not accept an assignment of a Medicare claim cannot charge more than 15 percent above the allowable charge. Many physicians refuse to accept new Medicare patients because the Medicare-approved payments are often less than the physician's actual cost of treatment.

Part B Monthly Premiums   Beneficiaries with Part B coverage pay monthly premiums, which are supplemented by the federal government out of its general revenues. Under previous law, all Part B beneficiaries paid only 25 percent of the cost of the program, and the federal government paid the rest. Beginning in 2007, however, Part B premiums will be means tested based on modified adjusted gross income, and upper-income beneficiaries will pay substantially more than 25 percent of the cost. The income reported two years earlier on the beneficiary's federal income tax return will determine the Part B premiums paid. For example, the premium paid in 2007 is based on the 2005 federal income tax return. The income threshold for married couples is twice the individual threshold limit. The chart below shows the Part B monthly premiums based on income for 2007. These amounts will change each year.

You pay	If your yearly income is	
	Single	Married
$93.50	$80,000 or less	$160,000 or less
$105.80	$80,001–$100,000	$160,001–$200,000
$124.40	$100,001–$150,000	$200,001–$300,000
$142.90	$150,001–$200,000	$300,001–$400,000
$161.40	Above $200,000	Above $400,000

The means testing of Part B premiums based on income represents a significant departure from a basic social insurance principle, which is the payment of benefits to eligible applicants without a formal means test. Public assistance and other welfare programs require applicants to meet a means test before the benefits are paid, and the benefit amount is related to the applicant's income. The current Medicare law introduces a welfare element into the Part B program because Part B premiums for some beneficiaries will increase because of their incomes. As a result, the social insurance character of Part B will be diluted when the new means test becomes operational.

Financing of Medicare

Hospital Insurance (Part A) is financed by a payroll tax paid by covered employees, employers, and the self-employed, plus a relatively small amount of general revenues. As stated earlier, the payroll tax for covered employees and employers is 1.45 percent on all covered earnings, even those that exceed the maximum Social Security earnings base. Medical Insurance (Part B) is financed by monthly premiums and the general revenues of the federal government.

Medicare Financial Crisis   Medicare Part A has serious financial problems. *The 2006 Board of Trustees Report shows that the projected 75-year actuarial deficit in the Hospital Insurance Trust Fund (HI) is now 3.51 percent of taxable payroll, up from 3.09 percent in last year's report.* The HI trust fund is projected to be exhausted by 2018. HI could be brought into actuarial balance over the next 75 years by an immediate increase of 121 percent in program income or an immediate 51 percent reduction in program outlays, or some combination of the two. Greater adjustments will be required if the changes are delayed or phased in gradually.[8]

The unsatisfactory financial condition is due to several factors, including an increase in the number of Medicare beneficiaries, inflation in hospital costs exceeding the overall rate of inflation, fraud and abuse by health-care providers, increased home health-care costs, and an inefficient and inflationary fee-for-service method of reimbursement.

To hold down Medicare costs, Congress earlier reduced payments to hospitals and physicians, placed spending limits on specified services, placed limits on fee increases paid to physicians, implemented the diagnosis-related group method in which flat amounts are paid to hospitals for each specific case, and introduced other cost-reduction measures as well. Despite these efforts, however, Medicare costs continue to increase. The current law contains provisions that will allow private plans to compete with the Medicare program (discussed later). One major objective is to stimulate competition so that, hopefully, the escalation in Medicare costs can be slowed.

Medicare Advantage Plans

Medicare Advantage Plans (Part C) are private health plans that are part of the Medicare program. Beneficiaries can elect to be covered under such plans instead of the Original Medicare Plan. Beneficiaries generally receive all Medicare-covered health-care services, and the plan may also include coverage for prescription drugs. Medicare pays a set monthly amount to the private plan, which is paid whether or not a beneficiary uses any services. Most plans generally provide extra benefits and have lower copayments than the Original Medicare Plan. However, beneficiaries may be required to see physicians who belong to the plan or go to certain hospitals to receive covered services.

Medicare Advantage plans include the following:

- Medicare HMOs
- Medicare PPOs
- Medicare Special Needs Plans
- Medicare Private Fee-for-Service Plans
- Medicare Medical Savings Account Plans

Medicare Health Maintenance Organization (HMO) Plans   Medicare HMOs are managed care plans operated by private insurers. Managed care is a generic term to describe a plan where health care is carefully monitored, and there is great emphasis on controlling costs. Patients generally must receive care from doctors and hospitals that are part of the network. However, beneficiaries are covered for emergency or urgently needed care outside of the service area of the HMO. Some Medicare HMOs have a point-of-service option that allows patients to see providers who are not part of the plan network, but they must pay higher out-of-pocket costs for the services provided.

Medicare Preferred Provider Organization (PPO) Plans   Beneficiaries also have the option of receiving care from a Medicare PPO. In addition to covered Medicare services, the PPO may provide additional benefits, such as coverage for prescription drugs.

Members generally can see any doctor or provider that accepts Medicare patients. In most PPO plans, members receive care from providers that belong to the plan network. However, members are free to use providers that are outside the network, but they must pay higher out-of-pocket costs. Plan members do not need a referral from a primary-care doctor to see a specialist.

Finally, beginning in 2006, *regional PPOs* will be available in most areas. Unlike local PPOs, which service individual counties, regional PPOs will service an entire region, such as a state or multi-state area.

Medicare Special Needs Plans This is a special type of plan that provides more focused care for specific groups of people, such as those who reside in nursing homes, or those who are covered under both Medicare and Medicaid, or those with certain chronic or disabling conditions. For example, a special needs plan may exist for beneficiaries with diabetes that has health-care providers with experience in treating diabetes; the plan may also provide education, nutrition, and exercise programs to control diabetes.

Medicare Private Fee-for-Service Plans These plans are fee-for-service plans offered by private companies. A fee is charged for each service provided. *A distinctive feature is that the private company, rather than Medicare, decides how much it will pay and the amounts members must pay for the services provided.* Members can go to any Medicare-approved doctor or hospital that accepts the terms of the plan's payments. The plan may provide extra benefits not covered under the Original Medicare Plan, such as extra days in the hospital.

Medicare Medical Savings Account Plans Medicare Medical Savings Account Plans may also be available. These plans are similar to health savings accounts discussed in Chapter 15 and have two parts. The first part is a Medicare Advantage plan with a high annual deductible. The plan does not pay covered costs until the beneficiary meets the annual deductible, which varies by plan. The second part is a Medical Savings Account into which Medicare deposits money that the beneficiary can use to pay health-care costs.

Other Medicare Health Plans

Other Medicare health plans are not part of Medicare Advantage but are still part of the total Medicare program. These plans include (1) Medicare Cost Plans in which members receive care from primary-care doctors and hospitals that are part of the network but can also receive care from non-network providers, in which case the services would be covered under the Original Medicare Plan, but the members must pay the Part A and Part B co-insurance and deductibles; (2) demonstration projects that test and evaluate recommendations for improving Medicare; and (3) PACE (programs of all-inclusive care for the elderly) that combine medical, social, and long-term-care services for the frail elderly.

Medicare Prescription Drug Plans

Medicare Prescription Drug Coverage (Part D) is a relatively new benefit, which became effective in 2006. Coverage for prescription drugs is now available to all Medicare beneficiaries. Numerous plans are available. Beneficiaries select a specific prescription drug plan and pay monthly premiums. Premiums and deductibles are reduced or waived for beneficiaries with limited incomes and resources. The monthly premium is not affected by health status or number of prescriptions used.

Beneficiaries who are covered under the Original Medicare Plan can add prescription drug coverage to their benefits by joining a stand-alone Medicare Prescription Drug Plan that covers only prescription drugs. Alternatively, beneficiaries can join a Medicare Advantage Plan or other Medicare health plan that provides prescription drug coverage in addition to covered Medicare services. Beneficiaries who are now covered for prescription drugs under the group plans of former employers or labor unions can elect to remain in their present plan.

Cost of Prescription Drug Coverage Beneficiaries pay part of the cost, and Medicare pays part of the cost. Monthly premiums vary depending on the plan selected. In 2006, the average monthly premium for the private plans was about $25.

All prescription drug plans must provide at least **standard coverage,** which Medicare has established.

The cost-sharing provisions for the various plans are complex and are summarized below:

- *Annual deductible.* You must meet an annual deductible. For 2007, no plan can have a deductible that exceeds $265. The deductible changes each year.
- *Copayment or coinsurance charge.* After the annual deductible is met, you must meet a copayment or coinsurance charge. This is the amount you must pay for your prescription after meeting the deductible. In some plans, you pay the same copayment amount (fixed amount) or coinsurance charge (a percentage of the cost) for each prescription filled. In other plans, there may be different levels or tiers with different costs, such as generic drugs that cost less than brand names. Some brand names may also have a lower copayment charge than other brand names. For 2007, maximum copayment or coinsurance charges for all prescription drugs are limited to $2400. This limit also changes each year.
- *Coverage gap.* Medicare drug plans have a *coverage gap* (also called a "donut hole"). This means that after you have paid a certain amount out of pocket for covered drugs (not to exceed $3850 in 2007), you must pay 100 percent of the cost of your drugs while you are in the coverage gap. This amount does not include the monthly premium you must continue to pay. In 2007, the most you have to pay out of pocket while in the coverage gap is $3051.25. Once you have reached your plan's out-of-pocket limit, you will have *catastrophe coverage.* You would pay only a small coinsurance amount (such as 5 percent of the drug cost) or a small copayment (such as $5.35) for each prescription filled for the remainder of the calendar year. If you are a low-income beneficiary, you will not have a coverage gap. However, you generally will have to pay a small copayment or coinsurance charge.

For 2007, Exhibit 18.3 shows how these provisions work under current law.

Financial Help for Low-Income Beneficiaries The Medicare prescription program provides financial help for beneficiaries with limited incomes and financial resources. Depending on the amount of annual income and financial resources, the monthly premiums and yearly deductible are reduced or waived. However, low-income beneficiaries must pay a small copayment charge for each prescription filled. To qualify, a single person must have an annual income below $14,700, and financial resources cannot exceed $11,500. A married couple living together must have an annual income below $19,800, and financial resources must be less than $23,000. The figures shown are for 2006 and will increase in the future.

EXHIBIT 18.3
**Example of Cost-Sharing Provisions
Under Medicare Prescription Drug Coverage (2007)**

The example below shows calendar year costs for covered drugs in a plan that meets Medicare's standards in 2007: Mr. Jones joins the ABC Prescription Drug Plan. His coverage begins on January 1, 2007. He pays the plan a monthly premium throughout the year, even during his coverage gap. He doesn't get "extra help."			
1. Yearly Deductible →	**2. Copayment/ Coinsurance** →	**3. Coverage Gap ("donut hole")** →	**4. Catastrophic Coverage**
Mr. Jones pays the first $265 of his drug costs.	Mr. Jones pays a copayment or coinsurance amount, and his plan pays its share for each drug until his total drug costs (including his deductible) reach $2400.	Mr. Jones pays **everything** until he has spent $3850 out-of-pocket ($3051.25 while in the coverage gap; not including the drug plan's premium). Even though he is paying everything, he gets a discount because he belongs to a Medicare drug plan.	Once Mr. Jones has spent $3850 out-of-pocket for the year, his coverage gap ends. He only pays a small coinsurance (like 5%) or a small copayment (like $2.15 or $5.35) for each prescription until the end of the year.

SOURCE: Medicare.gov/

Other Provisions Current law also contains additional provisions that deal with prescription drugs. Other provisions are designed to encourage private plans to compete with Medicare. Some important provisions that merit a brief discussion include the following:

- *Importing drugs from foreign countries.* Importing drugs from foreign countries is not allowed. However, drugs could be imported from Canada if the Department of Health and Human Services (HHS) certifies that the drugs are safe, something that HHS has refused to do at the time of this writing.
- *Prohibiting federal government to negotiate drug prices.* The federal government is prohibited from using its purchasing power to negotiate lower drug prices with pharmaceutical firms.
- *Role of private firms.* Private firms will administer the program on a regional basis. The new law provides substantial subsidies to private insurers to encourage them to participate in the program, which includes PPOs and private-fee-for-service plans.
- *Competition from private plans.* Beginning in 2010, the original Medicare plan will face competition from private plans in a demonstration project in six metropolitan areas. The demonstration project will last six years. The areas selected must have at least two private plans that enroll at least 25 percent of the Medicare beneficiaries. For beneficiaries who remain in the Original Medicare Plan, premium increases are limited to a maximum of 5 percent annually and are waived for low-income beneficiaries. The federal government will provide a backup drug plan in any region that does not have at least one private health plan and one stand-alone drug plan.

Medigap Insurance

Because of numerous exclusions, deductibles, cost-sharing provisions, and limitations on approved charges, Medicare does not pay all medical expenses. As a result, most Medicare beneficiaries either have post-retirement health benefits from their former employers or have purchased a Medigap policy or Medicare supplement policy that pays part or all of the covered charges not paid by Medicare.

Medigap policies are sold by private insurers and are strictly regulated by federal law. There are 12 standard policies, each of which offers a different combination of benefits. The basic policy has a core package of benefits. The remaining policies have a different combination of benefits. Each policy has a letter designation ranging from A through L. Insurers are not allowed to change the various combinations of benefits or the letter designations.

Insurers must provide an open enrollment period of six months from the date the applicant first enrolls in Medicare Part B and is age 65 or older. Applicants cannot be turned down or charged higher premiums because of poor health if they buy a policy during that period. Once the Medigap open enrollment period ends, beneficiaries may not be able to buy a policy of their choice but may have to accept whatever an insurer is willing to provide.

UNEMPLOYMENT INSURANCE

Unemployment insurance programs are federal-state programs that pay weekly cash benefits to workers who are involuntarily unemployed. Each state has its own unemployment insurance program. The various state programs arose out of the unemployment insurance provisions of the Social Security Act of 1935.

Unemployment insurance has several basic objectives:

- Provide cash income during involuntary unemployment
- Help unemployed workers find jobs
- Encourage employers to stabilize employment
- Help stabilize the economy

Weekly cash benefits are paid to unemployed workers during periods of **short-term involuntary unemployment,** thus helping them maintain their economic security. A second objective is to help unemployed workers find jobs; applicants for benefits must register for work at local employment offices, and officials provide assistance in finding suitable jobs. A third objective is to encourage employers to stabilize their employment through experience rating (discussed later). Finally, unemployment benefits help stabilize the economy during recessionary periods.

Coverage

Most private firms, state and local governments, and nonprofit organizations are covered for unemployment benefits. A *private firm* is subject to the federal unemployment tax if it employs one or more employees in each of at least 20 weeks during the calendar year (or preceding calendar year), or it pays wages of $1500 or more during a calendar quarter of either year. Most jobs in *state and local government* are also covered for unemployment insurance benefits. However, state and local governments are not required to pay the federal unemployment tax but instead may elect to reimburse the system for the benefits paid to government employees. In addition, *nonprofit charitable, educational, or religious organizations* are covered if they employ four or more workers for at least one day in each of 20 different weeks during the current or prior year. A nonprofit organization has the right either to pay the unemployment tax or to reimburse the states for the benefits paid.

Agricultural firms are covered if they have a quarterly payroll of at least $20,000 or employ ten or more workers in at least 20 weeks during the current or prior year. *Domestic employment* in a private household is covered if the employer pays domestic wages of $1000 or more in a calendar quarter during the current or prior year.

Eligibility Requirements

An unemployed worker must meet the following eligibility requirements to receive benefits:

- Have qualifying wages and employment during the base year
- Be able and available for work
- Actively seek work
- Be free from disqualification
- Serve a one-week waiting period

The applicant must earn qualifying wages of a specified amount during his or her base year. In most states, the base year is the first four of the last five calendar quarters preceding the unemployed worker's claim for benefits. Most states also require employment in at least two calendar quarters during the base year. The purpose of this requirement is to limit benefits to workers with a current attachment to the labor force.

The applicant must be physically and mentally capable of working and must be available for work. The claimant must register for work at a public employment office and actively seek work.

The applicant must not be disqualified from receiving benefits. Disqualifying acts include voluntarily quitting his or her job without good cause, direct participation in a labor dispute, being discharged for misconduct, or refusing suitable work.

Finally, a one-week waiting period must be satisfied in most states. The waiting period eliminates short-term claims, holds down costs, and provides time to obtain the claimant's wage record and process the claim.

Benefits

A weekly cash benefit is paid for each week of total unemployment. The benefit paid varies with the worker's past wages, within certain minimum and maximum dollar amounts. Most states use a formula that pays weekly benefits based on a fraction of the worker's high quarter wages. For example, a fraction of $\frac{1}{26}$ results in the payment of benefits equal to 50 percent of the worker's full-time wage in the highest quarter (subject to minimum and maximum amounts). For instance, assume that Jennifer earns $400 weekly or $5200 during her highest quarter. Applying the fraction of $\frac{1}{26}$ to this amount produces a weekly unemployment benefit of $200, or 50 percent of her full-time weekly wage. Several states also pay a dependent's allowance for certain dependents.

During the fourth quarter of calendar year 2005, the average weekly benefit amount ranged from $109 in Puerto Rico to $360 in Massachusetts. The average weekly benefit for the United States was $263 during the same period.[9] In virtually all jurisdictions, the maximum duration of regular benefits is limited to 26 weeks.

During periods of high unemployment, some workers exhaust their regular unemployment benefits. A permanent federal-state program of extended benefits pays additional benefits to unemployed workers who exhaust their regular benefits during periods of high unemployment in individual states. Under the **extended-benefits program**, claimants can receive up to 13 additional weeks of benefits or one-half the total amount of regular benefits, whichever is less. There is an overall limit of 39 weeks for both regular and extended benefits. The costs of the extended benefits are shared equally by the federal government and the states.

Financing

State unemployment insurance programs are financed largely by payroll taxes paid by employers on the covered wages of employees. Three states also require minimal employee contributions. All tax contributions are deposited in the Federal Unemployment Trust Fund. Each state has a separate account, which is credited with the unemployment-tax contributions and the state's share of investment income. Unemployment benefits are paid out of each state's account.

For 2006, covered employers paid a federal payroll tax of 6.2 percent on the first $7000 of annual wages paid to each covered employee. Employers can credit toward the federal tax any contributions paid under an approved unemployment insurance program and any tax savings under an approved experience-rating plan. The total employer credit is limited to a maximum of 5.4 percent. The remaining 0.8 percent is paid to the federal government and used for state and federal administrative expenses, for financing the federal government's share of the extended-benefits program, and for maintaining a loan fund from which states can temporarily borrow when their accounts are depleted.

Because of a desire to strengthen their unemployment reserves and maintain fund solvency, the majority of states have a taxable wage base that exceeds $7000.

Experience rating is also used, by which firms with favorable employment records pay reduced tax rates. The major argument in support of experience rating is that firms have a financial incentive to stabilize their employment. However, some cyclical and seasonal firms have little control over their employment, and experience rating provides little financial incentive for them to stabilize employment. Also, labor unions are opposed to experience rating, because some business firms may resist benefit increases and contest some valid claims.

Problems and Issues

State unemployment insurance programs have numerous problems and issues. Some important problems are summarized as follows:

- *Decline in the proportion of total unemployed who receive benefits.* Only a relatively small proportion of the total unemployed receive state unemployment insurance benefits at any time. Exhibit 18.4 shows the proportion of the total unemployed who file for or collect regular state unemployment benefits, commonly called the recipiency rate. Although the recipiency rate increased during the 2000–2001 recession, it has declined to slightly above 40 percent since that time. However, it is still below the higher levels of the 1950s and 1960s when more than 50 percent of the total unemployed received unemployment benefits.

  According to the Advisory Council on Unemployment Compensation, the decline in recipiency rates is due to: (1) tighter eligibility requirements and more restrictive policy changes at both the state and federal level, (2) a decline in the percentage of unionized workers for whom unemployment insurance claims historically have been high, (3) a decline in the proportion of workers employed in the manufacturing sector in which claim rates also have been high, and (4) the increasing percentage of the unemployed who live in states in which the receipt of unemployment benefits is below the national average.[10]

- *Inadequate unemployment trust fund balances.* Many states have relatively low trust fund balances for paying benefits. During previous recessions, many states found their trust fund balances inadequate for paying benefits because of higher unemployment and a longer duration of payments. States can borrow from their federal unemployment account if their trust fund balances decline to a level where benefit obligations cannot be met.

  One widely used measure to estimate the adequacy of a state's unemployment trust account is known as an average high-cost multiple. The *average high-cost multiple* is a measure of solvency and indicates how many years a state can pay unemployment benefits if it paid benefits equivalent to the average amount paid out during the three highest-cost 12-month periods during the previous 20 years, without collecting any additional revenue. The Interstate Commission of Employment Security Administrators has recommended an average high-cost multiple of 1.5. This means that a state would have enough

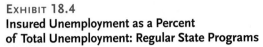

EXHIBIT 18.4

Insured Unemployment as a Percent of Total Unemployment: Regular State Programs

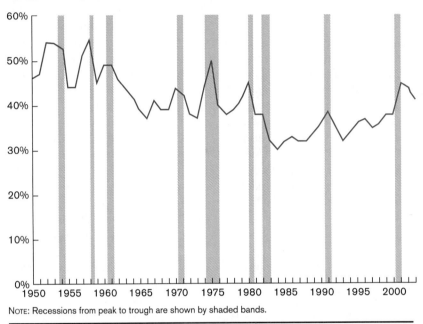

NOTE: Recessions from peak to trough are shown by shaded bands.

SOURCE: U.S. Department of Labor, Employment Training Administration, *Unemployment Insurance Chartbook*, Chart A.12, updated April 2, 2004.

money in its trust fund account to pay benefits for 1.5 years at a rate equivalent to the average amount paid out during the previous three worst 12-month periods without the benefit of any revenue inflow. *However, in calendar 2003, only seven jurisdictions had an average high-cost multiple of 1.5 or higher. Only 15 jurisdictions met a less severe standard of 1.0. The average for the United States was only .41 (see Exhibit 18.5).* New Mexico had the highest average high-cost multiple, while Illinois, Minnesota, Missouri, and New York had outstanding loans and negative trust fund balances.

■ *High Exhaustion Rates During Recessions.* Another important issue is the relatively high percentage of claimants who exhaust their regular state unemployment benefits during business recessions. Because of the limited duration of unemployment benefits, many claimants exhaust their regular benefits during business recessions and are still unemployed.

The exhaustion rate represents the proportion of claimants who collect all of their regular

state unemployment benefits to which they are entitled. Exhibit 18.6 shows that exhaustion rates have increased during each of last five business recessions. In addition, the exhaustion rate often remains relatively high during periods of economic recovery and low unemployment. *For example, during 2003, a period of economic recovery, the exhaustion rate exceeded 40 percent (see Exhibit 18.6).* Claimants who are still unemployed after exhausting their regular benefits often experience considerable economic insecurity.

WORKERS COMPENSATION

Workers compensation is a social insurance program that provides medical care, cash benefits, and rehabilitation services to workers who are disabled from job-related accidents or disease. The benefits are extremely important in reducing the economic insecurity that may result from a job-related disability.

ᴇxʜɪʙɪᴛ **18.5**

Average High-Cost Multiple by State (calendar year 2003)

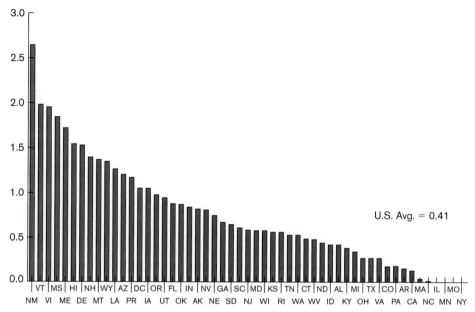

Nᴏᴛᴇ: The average high-cost multiple measures solvency and indicates the number of years a state could pay benefits if it were to pay an amount equivalent to the average amount paid out during the three highest-cost 12-month periods in the previous 20 years, without collecting any additional revenue.

Sᴏᴜʀᴄᴇ: U.S. Department of Labor, Employment Training Administration, *Unemployment Insurance Chartbook,* Chart B.3, updated April 2, 2004.

Development of Workers Compensation

Under the *common law of industrial accidents,* dating back to 1837, workers injured on the job had to sue their employers and prove negligence before they could collect damages. However, an employer could use three common law defenses to defeat lawsuits from injured workers:

- Contributory negligence doctrine
- Fellow-servant doctrine
- Assumption-of-risk doctrine

Under the **contributory negligence doctrine,** an injured worker could not collect damages if he or she contributed in any way to the injury. Under the **fellow-servant doctrine,** the injured worker could not collect if the injury resulted from the negligence of a fellow worker. And under the **assumption-of-risk doctrine,** the injured worker could not collect if he or she had advance knowledge of the dangers inherent in a particular occupation and still chose to work

in that occupation. As a result of the harsh common law, relatively few disabled workers collected adequate amounts for their injuries.

The enactment of *employer liability laws* between 1885 and 1910 was the next step in the development of workers compensation. These laws reduced the effectiveness of the common law defenses, improved the legal position of injured workers, and required employers to provide safe working conditions for their employees. However, injured workers were still required to sue their employers and prove negligence before they could collect for their injuries.

Finally, the states passed *workers compensation laws* as a solution to the growing problem of work-related accidents. In 1908, the federal government passed a workers compensation law covering certain federal employees, and by 1920, most states had passed similar laws. All states today have workers compensation laws.

Workers compensation is based on the fundamental principle of **liability without fault.** *The*

EXHIBIT **18.6**
**Exhaustion Rates: Proportion of Claimants Who Collect Their Full Entitlement
to State Unemployment Insurance Benefits**

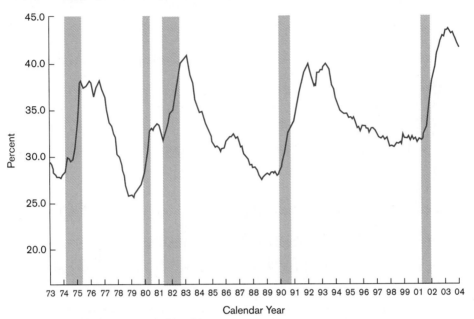

NOTE: Recessions from peak to trough are shown by shaded bands.

SOURCE: U.S. Department of Labor,Employment Training Administration, *Unemployment Insurance Chartbook,* Chart A.8,
updated April 2, 2004.

*employer is held absolutely liable for job-related in-
juries or disease suffered by the workers, regardless of
who is at fault.* Disabled workers are paid for their
injuries according to a schedule of benefits established
by law. The workers are not required to sue their
employers to collect benefits. The laws provide for the
prompt payment of benefits to disabled workers
regardless of fault and with a minimum of legal for-
mality. The costs of workers compensation benefits
are therefore considered to be a normal cost of production, which is included in the price of the product.

Objectives of Workers Compensation

State workers compensation laws have several basic
objectives:

- Broad coverage of employees for job-related ac-
  cidents and disease
- Substantial protection against the loss of income
- Sufficient medical care and rehabilitation services

- Encouragement of safety
- Reduction in litigation

A *fundamental objective is to provide broad
coverage of employees for job-related accidents and
disease.* That is, workers compensation laws should
cover the vast majority of occupations or job-related
accidents and disease.

A *second objective is to provide substantial protection against the loss of income.* The cash benefits
are designed to restore a substantial proportion of
the disabled worker's lost earnings, so that the disabled worker's previous standard of living can be
maintained.

A *third objective is to provide sufficient medical
care and rehabilitation services to injured workers.*
Workers compensation laws require employers to
pay hospital, surgical, and other medical costs incurred by injured workers. Also, the laws provide for
rehabilitation services to disabled employees so they
can be restored to productive employment.

Another objective is to encourage firms to reduce job-related accidents and to develop effective safety programs. Experience rating is used to encourage firms to reduce job-related accidents and disease, because firms with superior accident records pay relatively lower workers compensation premiums.

Finally, workers compensation laws are designed to reduce litigation. The benefits are paid promptly to disabled workers without requiring them to sue their employers. The objective is to reduce or eliminate the payment of legal fees to attorneys, and time-consuming and expensive trials and appeals.

Complying with the Law

All states except Texas have compulsory laws that require covered employers to provide specified benefits to workers who become disabled from a job-related accident or disease. Employers can comply with state law by purchasing a workers compensation policy, by self-insuring, or by obtaining insurance from a monopoly or competitive state fund.

Most firms purchase a workers compensation policy from a private insurer. The policy pays the benefits that the employer must legally provide to workers who have a job-related accident or disease.

Self-insurance is allowed in most states. Many large firms self-insure their workers compensation losses to save money. In addition, group self-insurance is often available to smaller firms that pool their risks and liabilities.

Finally, workers compensation insurance can be purchased from a state fund in certain states. In some jurisdictions, covered employers generally must purchase workers compensation insurance from a **monopoly state fund** or self-insure the risk. Other states have a **competitive state fund** that competes with private insurers.[11]

Covered Occupations

Although most occupations are covered by workers compensation laws, certain occupations are excluded or have incomplete coverage. Because of the nature of the work, most states exclude or provide incomplete coverage for farm workers, domestic servants, and casual employees. Some states have numerical exemptions, by which small firms with fewer than a specified number of employees (typi-

cally three to five) are not required to provide workers compensation benefits. However, employers can voluntarily cover employees in an exempted class.

Eligibility Requirements

Two principal eligibility requirements must be met to receive workers compensation benefits. First, the disabled person must work in a covered occupation. Second, the worker must have a job-related accident or disease. *This means the injury or disease must arise out of and in the course of employment.* The courts have gradually broadened the meaning of this term over time. The following situations are usually covered under a typical workers compensation law:

- An employee who travels is injured while engaging in activities that benefit the employer.
- The employee is injured while performing specified duties at a specified location.
- The employee is on the premises and is injured going to the work area.
- The employee has a heart attack while lifting some heavy materials while at work.

Workers Compensation Benefits

Workers compensation laws provide four principal benefits:

- Unlimited medical care
- Disability income
- Death benefits
- Rehabilitation services

Unlimited Medical Care   Medical care generally is covered in full in virtually all states with no time or monetary limitations. However, some states have special provisions that limit the amounts paid for certain medical procedures.

Medical care is expensive. To hold down medical costs, many states allow employers to use managed care arrangements to treat injured employees. The use of health maintenance organizations (HMOs) and preferred provider organizations (PPOs) has also increased over time.

Disability Income   Disability-income benefits can be paid after the disabled worker satisfies a waiting period that usually ranges from three to seven days.

If the injured worker is still disabled after a certain number of days or weeks, most states pay disability benefits retroactively to the date of injury.

The weekly cash benefit is based on a percentage of the injured worker's average weekly wage, typically two-thirds, and the degree of disability. There are four classifications of disability: (1) temporary total, (2) permanent total, (3) temporary partial, and (4) permanent partial. Temporary total disability claims are the most common and account for the majority of all cash claims. For example, a worker in Nebraska may break a leg and be totally disabled for three months. After a one-week waiting period, the disabled worker would receive two-thirds of his or her weekly wage up to a weekly maximum of $600 (2006).

Death Benefits   Death benefits can be paid to eligible survivors if the worker dies as a result of a job-related accident or disease. Two types of benefits are paid. First, a burial allowance is paid. Second, weekly income benefits can be paid to eligible surviving dependents. The weekly benefit is based on a proportion of the deceased worker's wages (typically two-thirds) and is usually paid to a surviving spouse for life or until she or he remarries. Upon remarriage, the widow or widower typically gets one or two years of payments in a lump sum. A weekly benefit can also be paid to each dependent child until a specified age, such as age 18 or later.

Rehabilitation Services   All states provide rehabilitation services to restore disabled workers to productive employment. In addition to weekly disability benefits, workers who are being rehabilitated are compensated for board and room, travel, books, and equipment. Training allowances may also be paid in some states.

Problems and Issues

Workers compensation programs have numerous problems and issues. Three problems that merit a brief discussion are as follows: [12]

- *Continued threat of terrorist attacks.* Workers compensation insurers still face the risk of terrorist attacks. Estimated claim costs for future acts of terrorism could cost insurers anywhere from $300,000 to $1 million per employee, depending on the state. Employers with a high concentration of employees in a single building in large metropolitan areas, such as New York City, are especially vulnerable and are considered high risk. Because of possible catastrophe losses, all but the largest insurers are limiting coverage, which is forcing some employers to self-insure more of the exposure or deal with several insurers to obtain the desired coverage.

- *Rising costs of medical care.* Workers compensation claim costs have two components: payments for lost income (called indemnity payments) and payments for medical care. In recent years, the average claim cost for workers compensation medical care has risen more rapidly than indemnity payments and now accounts for more than 50 percent of total claim costs (see Exhibit 18.7).

  The cost of medical care in workers compensation has also increased more rapidly than the consumer price index (CPI) for medical care. This is due partly to the increased use of newer and more expensive prescription drugs to treat injured workers and to the significant increase in the utilization and cost of hospital services, especially critical care services and the use of MRI (magnetic resonance imaging) tests. [13]

- *Attorney involvement in claims.* Although a fundamental objective of workers compensation is to pay injured workers promptly without lawsuits, attorneys are frequently involved in the settlement of claims. In most states, attorneys are involved in only 5 to 10 percent of all workers compensation claims; however, in cases involving seriously injured workers, attorneys are involved in about one-third of the claims. Although attorney involvement increases claim costs by 12 to 15 percent, injured claimants must pay attorney fees, so there is generally no net gain in actual benefits received.[14]

  Attorney involvement is due to (1) suits by injured workers who are dissatisfied with their workers compensation awards and then sue for higher amounts; (2) denial of claims by some employers, which results in lawsuits by the injured workers; and (3) court decisions that have eroded the **exclusive remedy doctrine.** This doctrine states that workers compensation benefits should

**Workers Compensation Average Claim Cost,
Medical vs. Indemnity, 1994 and 2004**

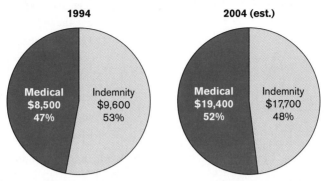

NOTE: Data for 1994 are from *2004 State of the Line: Analysis of Workers' Compensation Results,* National Council on Compensation Insurance Inc. Data for 2004 are from Sedgwick CMS Business Intelligence Unite estimate, Sedgwick CMS 2004–2005 Report & Outlook.

SOURCE: Reprinted from *Risk & Insurance* ® July 2005. Copyright 2006. All Rights Reserved.

be the sole and exclusive remedy for injured workers; workers have a statutory right to receive benefits without proving negligence, but in turn, they give up the right to sue the employer. This doctrine has been eroded by court decisions in recent years. As a result, injured employees often can receive both workers compensation benefits and a tort damage award based on negligence.

CASE APPLICATION

Sam, age 35, and Kathy, age 33, are married and have a son, age 1. Sam is employed as an accountant and earns $60,000 annually. Kathy is an associate professor of finance at a large university and earns $120,000 annually. Both are currently and fully insured under the OASDI program. Assume you are a financial planner who is asked to give them advice concerning OASDI and other social insurance programs. Answer each of the following questions based on the following situations. Treat each situation separately.

a. Sam is killed instantly in an automobile accident. To what extent, if any, would the surviving family members be eligible to receive OASDI survivor benefits?

b. Kathy has laryngitis that damaged her vocal cords. As a result, she can no longer teach. She is offered a research position in the business research bureau of the university where she is employed. To what extent, if any, would Kathy be eligible to receive OASDI disability benefits?

c. A deranged student fired a pistol at Kathy because she gave him a grade of D+. As a result, Kathy was seriously injured and is expected to be off work for at least one year while she is recovering. To what extent, if any, would existing social insurance programs in the United States provide income during the period of temporary disability?

d. Sam would like to retire at age 62 and still work part-time as an accountant. He has been informed that the OASDI earnings test would be relevant in his case. Explain how the earnings test might affect his decision to work part-time after retirement.

e. Sam resigned from his job to find a higher-paying position. Explain whether Sam could receive unemployment insurance benefits during the period of temporary unemployment before he finds a new job.

SUMMARY

- Social insurance programs are compulsory insurance programs with certain characteristics that distinguish them from other government insurance programs. Social insurance programs in the United States have the following characteristics:

    Compulsory programs

    Floor of income

    Emphasis on social adequacy rather than individual equity

    Benefits loosely related to earnings

    Benefits prescribed by law

    No means test

    Full funding unnecessary

    Financially self-supporting

- The Old-Age, Survivors, and Disability Insurance (OASDI) program, commonly called Social Security, is the most important social insurance program in the United States. The program pays monthly cash benefits to eligible beneficiaries who retire or become disabled. The program also pays survivor benefits to eligible surviving family members.

- Medicare currently has numerous plans, which include (1) the Original Medicare Plan, (2) Medicare Advantage Plans, (3) Other Medicare Health Plans, and (4) Medicare Prescription Drug Plans.

- Unemployment insurance programs are federal-state programs that pay weekly cash benefits to workers who are involuntarily unemployed. Unemployment insurance programs have several objectives:

    Provide cash income to unemployed workers during periods of involuntary unemployment

    Help unemployed workers find jobs

    Encourage employers to stabilize employment

    Help stabilize the economy

- Unemployed workers must meet certain eligibility requirements to receive weekly cash benefits:

    Have qualifying wages and employment during the base year

    Be able and available for work

    Actively seek work

    Be free from disqualification

    Serve a one-week waiting period in most states

- Workers compensation is a social insurance program that provides medical care, cash benefits, and rehabilitation services to workers who become disabled from job-related accidents or disease. Workers compensation laws have the following objectives:

    Broad coverage of employees for job-related injuries and disease

    Substantial protection against the loss of income

    Sufficient medical care and rehabilitation services

    Encouragement of safety

    Reduction in litigation

- Workers compensation laws typically pay the following benefits:

    Unlimited medical care

    Weekly disability-income benefits

    Death benefits to survivors

    Rehabilitation services

KEY CONCEPTS AND TERMS

Assumption-of-risk doctrine
Average indexed monthly earnings (AIME)
Competitive state fund
Contributory negligence doctrine
Credit (quarter of coverage)
Currently insured
Diagnosis-related groups (DRGs)
Disability insured
Earnings test (retirement test)
Exclusive remedy doctrine
Experience rating
Extended-benefits program
Fellow-servant doctrine
Full retirement age
Fully funded program
Fully insured
Hospital Insurance (Medicare Part A)
Individual equity
Liability without fault
Means (needs) test
Medical Insurance (Medicare Part B)
Medicare Advantage Plans
Medicare Prescription Drug Coverage
Medigap policy
Monopoly state fund
Original Medicare Plan
Primary insurance amount (PIA)
Short-term involuntary unemployment
Social adequacy
Social Security (OASDI)
Unemployment insurance
Workers compensation

REVIEW QUESTIONS

1. Explain the reasons for social insurance programs in the United States.

2. Describe the basic characteristics of social insurance programs.

3. The OASDI program has several types of insured status. Briefly explain the meaning of the following:
   a. Fully insured
   b. Currently insured
   c. Disability insured

4. The OASDI program provides several major benefits. Briefly describe each of the following:
   a. Retirement benefits
   b. Survivor benefits
   c. Disability benefits

5. Explain the definition of disability used in the OASDI program.

6. a. The Original Medicare Plan provides several benefits. Identify the major benefits that are available under each of the following:
   (1) Hospital Insurance (Medicare Part A)
   (2) Medical Insurance (Medicare Part B)
   b. Briefly describe the major choices available to Medicare beneficiaries under Medicare Advantage Plans.
   c. Briefly describe the Medicare Prescription Drug Coverage program

7. Explain the basic objectives of state unemployment insurance programs.

8. Explain the eligibility requirements for receiving unemployment insurance benefits.

9. Describe the basic objectives of workers compensation laws.

10. Identify the major benefits provided under a typical workers compensation law.

APPLICATION QUESTIONS

1. The OASDI program provides retirement benefits to covered employees and their dependents.
   a. Briefly describe the eligibility requirements for OASDI retirement benefits.
   b. Explain whether each of the following persons would be eligible for OASDI retirement benefits based on the retired worker's earnings record. Treat each item separately.
      (1) A retired worker's unmarried son, age 25, who became totally disabled at age 15 because of an auto accident.
      (2) A spouse, age 63, of a retired worker who is no longer caring for an unmarried child under age 18.
      (3) A retired worker's spouse, age 45, who is caring for the 12-year-old daughter of the retired worker
      (4) A divorced spouse, age 55, who was married to a retired worker for six years.

2. The OASDI program pays survivor benefits to eligible family members based on the deceased worker's earnings record.
   a. Describe the eligibility requirements for OASDI survivor benefits.
   b. Explain whether each of the following persons would be eligible for OASDI survivor benefits based on the deceased worker's earnings record. Treat each item separately.
      (1) A surviving spouse, age 35, who is caring for an unmarried child under age 16.
      (2) A son, age 19, who is attending college full-time.
      (3) A surviving spouse, age 55, who has no children under age 16 in her care.
      (4) A surviving spouse, age 60, who has been out of the labor force for several years.
      (5) A dependent parent, age 80, who was receiving financial help from the deceased worker.

3. The OASDI program pays disability benefits to a disabled worker and eligible family members.
   a. Describe the eligibility requirements for OASDI disability benefits.
   b. Explain whether each of the following persons would be eligible for disability-income benefits. In each case, assume that the disabled worker is disability-insured. Treat each item separately.
      (1) A worker, age 22, who is injured in an auto accident and is expected to return to work within three months.
      (2) The disabled worker's spouse, age 25, who is caring for a dependent child under age 16; the disabled worker is currently receiving benefits.
      (3) The disabled worker's daughter, age 16, who is attending high school full-time.

(4) A university professor, age 50, who can no longer teach because of chronic laryngitis but can work as a research scientist for a drug company.

(5) A worker, age 40, with a crushed foot who expects to be off work for at least one year.

4. The Original Medicare Plan consists of Hospital Insurance (Medicare Part A) and Medical Insurance (Medicare Part B). For each of the following losses, indicate whether the loss is covered under Medicare Part A or Medicare Part B. (Ignore any deductible or coinsurance requirements. Treat each event separately.)

a. Mary, age 66, is hospitalized for five days because of a heart attack.

b. John, age 62, has prostate cancer and visits his family doctor for treatment.

c. Marion, age 80, is a patient in a skilled nursing facility. She has been confined to the nursing home for more than two years.

d. Don, age 72, has a hearing impairment and obtains a hearing aid from a local firm.

e. Sarah, age 68, has a speech impairment and is confined to her home because of a stroke. A licensed speech therapist visits her in the home and provides services to restore her speech.

f. Fred, age 78, has an arthritic hip that makes it painful to walk and needs surgery to have the hip replaced.

g. Michael, age 65, is covered under the Original Medicare Plan. His spouse, age 62, has cancer and requires chemotherapy.

5. A critic of state unemployment insurance programs stated that "unemployment insurance programs are designed to maintain economic security for unemployed workers, but several critical problems must be resolved."

a. What type of unemployment is covered under a typical state unemployment insurance program?

b. Describe some situations that may disqualify a worker for unemployment benefits.

c. Why has the proportion of unemployed workers who receive unemployment benefits declined over time?

6. Workers compensation laws provide considerable financial protection to workers who have a job-related accident or disease.

a. Explain the fundamental legal principle on which workers compensation laws are based.

b. List the various ways that covered employers can comply with the state's workers compensation law.

c. Explain the eligibility requirements for collecting workers compensation benefits.

d. Explain why lawsuits by injured employees against their employers have increased in many states.

INTERNET RESOURCES

■ The **Employment and Training Administration (ETA)** is a federal agency in the U.S. Department of Labor that provides detailed information and data on state unemployment compensation programs. Visit the site at

http://www.doleta.gov

■ The **Centers for Medicare & Medicaid Services (CMS)**, which is part of the U.S. Department of Health and Human Services, administers the Medicare program. CMS provides timely information and data on the Medicare program to consumers, health-care professionals, and the media, including actuarial cost estimates for the program. Visit the site at

http://www.cms.hhs.gov

■ **Medicare.gov** is the official government site for people on Medicare. The site provides information on the basics of Medicare, nursing homes, participating physicians, Medicare publications, and prescription drug assistance programs. Visit the site at

http://www.medicare.gov

■ The **National Academy of Social Insurance** is a professional organization that attempts to improve public understanding of social insurance programs. It publishes timely and important research studies on Social Security and Medicare. Visit the site at

http://www.nasi.org

■ The **National Council on Compensation Insurance Holdings, Inc.** develops and administers rating plans and systems for workers compensation insurance. Visit the site at

http://www.ncci.com

■ The **Office of the Chief Actuary** in the Social Security Administration provides actuarial cost estimates of the

OASDI program and determines the annual cost-of-living adjustments in benefits. The site provides a number of timely publications. Visit the site at

http://www.ssa.gov/OACT

■ The **Social Security Administration (SSA)** is an independent federal agency that administers the Social Security program. Its Web site provides current information on OASDI retirement, survivor, and disability benefits and recent changes in the program. Visit the site at

http://www.socialsecurity.gov

■ The **Social Security Advisory Board** is an independent, bipartisan board that advises the president and members of Congress on matters relating to Social Security. Its Web site provides timely and relevant reports dealing with Social Security. Visit the site at

http://www.ssab.gov

■ The **Workers Compensation Research Institute** is an independent, not-for-profit research organization providing high-quality, objective information about public policy issues involving workers compensation systems. Visit the site at

http://www.wcrinet.org/

SELECTED REFERENCES

2006 Guide to Social Security and Medicare. Louisville, KY: William M. Mercer, November 2005.

Burton, Jr., John F. "Workers' Compensation," in Jerry S. Rosenbloom, ed., *The Handbook of Employee Benefits,* 6th ed. New York: The McGraw Hill Companies, 2005, ch 23.

Diamond, Peter A. "The Public Pension Reform Debate in the United States and International Experience," *Risk Management & Insurance Review,* vol. 9, no. 1 (Spring 2006), pp. 9–35.

Insurance Information Institute. "Workers Compensation," *Hot Topics & Issues Updates,* October 2006. This source is periodically updated.

Medicare and You 2007. Baltimore, Maryland: Centers for Medicare & Medicaid Services, 2007.

Myers, Robert J. "Social Security and Medicare," in Jerry S. Rosenbloom, ed., *The Handbook of Employee Benefits,* 6th ed. New York: The McGraw Hill Companies, 2005, ch. 22.

National Academy of Social Insurance. *Reporters' Social Security and Medicare Source* at www.nasi.org. This is an online source that is continually updated whenever new changes in legislation or actuarial projections are published.

Rejda, George E. *Social Insurance and Economic Security,* 6th ed. Upper Saddle River, NJ: Prentice-Hall, 1999.

———. "Fundamentals of Unemployment Compensation Programs," in Jerry S. Rosenbloom, ed., *The Handbook of Employee Benefits,* 6th ed. New York: The McGraw-Hill Companies, 2005, ch. 24.

Social Security Advisory Board. *Social Security: Why Action Should Be Taken Soon.* Washington, DC, September 2005.

Social Security and Medicare Board of Trustees. *Status of the Social Security and Medicare Programs: A Summary of the 2006 Annual Reports,* Washington, DC, March 2006.

U.S. Congress, House, Committee on Ways and Means. *2005 Green Book, Background Material and Data on Programs within the Jurisdiction of the Committee on Ways and Means.* Washington, DC, U.S. Government Printing Office, 2005.

U.S. Department of Labor, Employment Standards Administration, Office of Workers' Compensation Programs. *State Workers' Compensation Laws, List of Benefit Tables,* 2005.

NOTES

1. Calculated from "Monthly Survivor Benefits in 2006," *2006 Guide to Social Security and Medicare Overview,* 34th ed. (Louisville, KY: Mercer Human Resource Consulting, November 2005), p. 41.
2. George E. Rejda, *Social Insurance and Economic Security,* 6th ed. (Upper Saddle River, NJ: Prentice-Hall, 1999), pp. 18–25, chs. 5 and 6.
3. *The 2006 Annual Report of the Board of Trustees of the Federal Old-Age and Survivors Insurance and Disability Insurance Trust Funds.* (Washington DC: U.S. Government Printing Office, 2006,) pp. 37, 58–60.
4. Social Security Administration.
5. Ibid.
6. Data cited are from Social Security and Medicare Board of Trustees, *Status of Social Security and Medicare Programs, A Summary of the 2006 Annual Reports,* 2006.

7. Ibid.

8. Ibid.

9. Data obtained from U.S. Department of Labor, Employment and Training Division.

10. *Advisory Council on Unemployment Compensation, Report and Recommendations* (Washington, DC: Advisory Council on Unemployment Compensation, 1994), pp. 31–32.

11. As of January 1, 2005, exclusive or monopoly funds existed in North Dakota, Ohio, Washington, West Virginia, and Wyoming. In West Virginia, the exclusive fund converted to a private, for-profit employers' mutual insurance company, effective January 1, 2006. On July 1, 2008, the market for workers compensation in West Virginia will open to all qualified private carriers. Competitive state funds exist in Arizona, California, Colorado, Hawaii, Idaho, Illinois, Kentucky, Louisiana, Maine, Maryland, Minnesota, Montana, New Mexico, New York, Oklahoma, Oregon, Pennsylvania, Texas, and Utah.

12. This section is based on Insurance Information Institute, "Workers Compensation," *Hot Topics & Issues Updates,* October 2006. This source is periodically updated.

13. Ibid.

14. Ibid.

PART FIVE
PERSONAL PROPERTY AND LIABILITY RISKS

Chapter 19
The Liability Risk

Chapter 20
Homeowners Insurance, Section I

Chapter 21
Homeowners Insurance, Section II

Chapter 22
Auto Insurance

Chapter 23
Auto Insurance and Society

Chapter 24
Other Property and Liability
Insurance Coverages

CHAPTER 19

THE LIABILITY RISK

"I was never ruined but twice, once when I lost a lawsuit and once when I won one."

Voltaire

LEARNING OBJECTIVES

After studying this chapter, you should be able to

◆ Define negligence and explain the elements of a negligent act.

◆ Explain the following legal defenses that can be used in a lawsuit:
   Contributory negligence
   Comparative negligence
   Assumption of risk
   Last clear chance rule

◆ Apply the law of negligence to specific liability situations.

◆ Explain the defects in the current tort liability system and the proposals for tort reform.

◆ Explain the following tort liability problems:
   Medical malpractice crisis
   Corporate fraud and lax corporate governance
   Increase in asbestos lawsuits

Shania, age 38, lives in a high-crime-rate area in Omaha, Nebraska. She has three large Rottweiler dogs in her back yard for protection. She was fined earlier by the city because she allowed the dogs to run free without a leash, which frightened the neighbors. One afternoon, the dogs escaped because Shania carelessly left the gate open. Without provocation, the dogs attacked a 10-year-old boy who later died from the mauling. The parents of the deceased child sued Shania for a wrongful death and were awarded damages of $300,000. Shania could not pay the judgment against her and was forced to declare bankruptcy.

Shania experienced the legal effects of being negligent in a financially painful manner. Like Shania, other people often face similar liability situations. Motorists are sued because of the negligent operation of their vehicles when someone is killed or injured. Corporations are sued because of defective products that injure others, aggressive accounting practices and accounting fraud that result in investor losses, insider trading, violation of security laws, and inadequate oversight of management. Physicians, attorneys, accountants, engineers, and other professionals are sued for malpractice, negligence, and incompetence. Governmental and charitable institutions are sued because they no longer enjoy complete immunity from lawsuits. Thus, the liability risk is extremely important to people who wish to avoid or minimize potential losses.

This chapter discusses the law of negligence and the tort liability system in the United States. This knowledge forms the foundation for an understanding of liability insurance discussed later in the text. Specific topics discussed include the law of negligence, elements of a negligent act, application of the law of negligence to specific liability situations, and current tort liability problems.

BASIS OF LEGAL LIABILITY

Each person has certain legal rights. A **legal wrong** *is a violation of a person's legal rights, or a failure to perform a legal duty owed to a certain person or to society as a whole.*

There are three broad classes of legal wrongs. A *crime* is a legal wrong against society that is punishable by fines, imprisonment, or death. A *breach of contract* is another class of legal wrongs. Finally, a **tort** is a legal wrong for which the law allows a remedy in the form of money damages. The person who is injured or harmed (called the **plaintiff** or *claimant*) by the actions of another person (called the *defendant* or **tortfeasor**) can sue for damages.

Torts generally can be classified into three categories:

- Intentional torts
- Strict liability (absolute liability)
- Negligence

Intentional Torts

Legal liability can arise from an intentional act or omission that results in harm or injury to another person or damage to the person's property. Examples of intentional torts include assault, battery, trespass, false imprisonment, fraud, libel, slander, and patent or copyright infringement.

Strict Liability

Because the potential harm to an individual or society is so great, some people may be held liable for the harm or injury done to others even though negligence cannot be proven. **Strict liability** *means that liability is imposed regardless of negligence or fault.* Strict liability is also referred to as **absolute liability.** Some common situations in which strict liability applies include the following:

- Blasting operations that injure another person
- Manufacturing of explosives
- Owning wild or dangerous animals
- Crop spraying by airplanes
- Occupational injury and disease of employees under a workers compensation law

Negligence

Negligence is another type of tort that can result in substantial liability. Because negligence is so important in liability insurance, it merits special attention.

LAW OF NEGLIGENCE

Negligence *typically is defined as the failure to exercise the standard of care required by law to protect others from an unreasonable risk of harm.* The meaning of the term standard of care is based on the care required of a reasonably prudent person. In other words, your actions are compared with the actions of a reasonably prudent person under the same circumstances. If your conduct and behavior are below the standard of care required of a reasonably prudent person, you may be found negligent.

The standard of care required by law is not the same for each wrongful act. Its meaning is complex and depends on the age and knowledge of the parties involved; court interpretations over time; skill, knowledge, and judgment of the claimant and tortfeasor; seriousness of the harm; and a host of additional factors.

Elements of Negligence

To collect damages, the injured person must show that the tortfeasor is guilty of negligence. There are four essential **elements of negligence.**

- Existence of a legal duty
- Failure to perform that duty
- Damage or injury to the claimant
- Proximate cause relationship between the negligent act and the infliction of damages

Existence of a Legal Duty *The first requirement is the existence of a legal duty to protect others from harm.* For example, a motorist has a legal duty to stop at a red light and to drive an auto safely within the speed limits. A manufacturer has a legal duty to produce a safe product. A physician has a legal duty to inquire about allergies before prescribing a drug.

If there is no legal duty imposed by law, you cannot be held liable. For example, you may be a champion swimmer, but you have no legal obligation to dive into a swimming pool to save a two-year-old child from drowning. Nor do you have a legal obligation to stop and pick up a hitchhiker at night when the temperature is 30 degrees below zero. To be guilty of negligence, there must first be a legal duty or obligation to protect others from harm.

Failure to Perform That Duty *The second requirement is the failure to perform the legal duty required by law:* that is, you fail to comply with the standard of care to protect others from harm. Your actions would be compared with the actions of a reasonably prudent person under similar circumstances. If your conduct falls short of this standard, the second requirement would be satisfied.

The defendant's conduct can be either a positive or negative act. Driving at high speeds in a residential area or running a red light are examples of positive acts that a reasonably prudent person would not do. A negative act is simply the failure to act: you fail to do something that a reasonably prudent person would have done. For example, if you injure someone because you failed to repair the faulty brakes on your car, you could be found guilty of negligence.

Damage or Injury *The third requirement is damage or injury to the claimant.* The injured person must show damage or injury as a result of the action or inaction of the alleged tortfeasor. For example, a speeding motorist may run a red light, smash into your car, and seriously injure you. Because you are injured and your car is damaged, the third requirement of negligence has been satisfied.

The dollar amount of the award for damages depends on several factors. The law recognizes the following types of damages, which are expressed in monetary terms:

- Compensatory damages (special damages and general damages)
- Punitive damages

Compensatory damages are awards that compensate injured victims for the losses actually incurred. Compensatory damages include both special damages and general damages. **Special damages** are awards for losses that can be determined and documented, such as medical expenses, lost earnings, or property damage. **General damages** are awards for losses that cannot be specifically measured or itemized, such as compensation for pain and suffering, disfigurement, or loss of companionship of a spouse.

Punitive damages are awards designed to punish people and organizations so that others are deterred from committing the same wrongful act. Awards for punitive damages are often several times the amount awarded for compensatory damages.

Proximate Cause Relationship   The final requirement is that a proximate cause relationship must exist. A **proximate cause** *is a cause unbroken by any new and independent cause, which produces an event that otherwise would not have occurred.* That is, there must be an unbroken chain of events between the negligent act and the infliction of damages. For example, a drunk driver who runs a red light and kills another motorist would meet the proximate cause requirement.

Defenses Against Negligence

Certain legal defenses can defeat a claim for damages. Some important legal defenses include the following:

- Contributory negligence
- Comparative negligence
- Last clear chance rule
- Assumption of risk

Contributory Negligence   A few jurisdictions have contributory negligence laws.[1] Contributory negligence *means that if the injured person's conduct falls below the standard of care required for his or her protection, and such conduct contributed to the injury, the injured person cannot collect damages.* Thus, under strict application of common law, if you contributed in any way to your own injury, you cannot collect damages. For example, if a motorist on an expressway suddenly slows down without signaling and is rear-ended by another driver, the failure to signal could constitute contributory negligence. The first motorist cannot collect damages for injuries if contributory negligence is established.

Comparative Negligence   Because of the harshness of contributory negligence laws if strictly applied, most states have enacted some type of comparative negligence law. Such laws allow an injured person to recover damages even though he or she has contributed to the injury. Under a **comparative negligence law,** if both the plaintiff (injured person) and the defendant contribute to the plaintiff's injury, the financial burden of the injury is shared by both parties according to their respective degrees of fault.

Comparative negligence laws are not uniform among the states. The major types of comparative negligence laws can be classified as follows:[2]

- Pure rule
- 49 percent rule
- 50 percent rule

Under the *pure rule,* you can collect damages for your injury even if you are negligent, but your award is reduced proportionately. For example, if you are 60 percent responsible for an auto accident and your actual damages are $10,000, your award is reduced by 60 percent to $4000.

Under the *49 percent rule,* you can recover reduced damages only if your negligence is less than the negligence of the other party. This rule means you can recover from the other party only if you are 49 percent or less at fault.

Under the *50 percent rule,* you can recover reduced damages only if your negligence is not greater than the negligence of the other party. This rule means you can recover only if you are not more than 50 percent at fault. You should not confuse the 50 percent rule with the 49 percent rule discussed earlier. Unlike the 49 percent rule, the 50 percent rule allows both parties to recover damages when both parties are equally at fault. However, each party's recovery would be limited to 50 percent of his or her actual damages.

Last Clear Chance Rule Another statutory modification of the contributory negligence doctrine is known as the **last clear chance rule,** *which states that a plaintiff who is endangered by his or her own negligence can still recover damages from the defendant if the defendant has a last clear chance to avoid the accident but fails to do so.* For example, a jaywalker who walks against a red light is breaking the law. But if a motorist has a last clear chance to avoid hitting the jaywalker and fails to do so, the injured jaywalker can recover damages for the injury.

Assumption of Risk The **assumption of risk** doctrine is another defense that can be used to defeat a claim for damages. *Under this doctrine, a person who understands and recognizes the danger inherent in a particular activity cannot recover damages in the event of an injury.* In effect, the assumption of risk bars recovery for damages even though another person's negligence causes the injury. For example, assume you are teaching a friend with a severe vision impairment to drive a car, and he negligently crashes into a telephone post and injures you. He could use the assumption of risk doctrine as a legal defense if you sue for damages.

Many states have eliminated the assumption of risk as a separate defense. Formerly, assumption of risk was an affirmative defense available to defendants. However, in most jurisdictions currently, assumption of risk has been subsumed or incorporated within the state's comparative negligence or contributory negligence law.

IMPUTED NEGLIGENCE

Imputed negligence *means that under certain conditions, the negligence of one person can be attributed to another.* Several examples can illustrate this principle. First, an *employer–employee relationship* may exist where the employee is acting on behalf of the employer. The negligent act of an employee can be imputed to the employer. Therefore, if you are driving a car to deliver a package for your employer and negligently injure another motorist, your employer could be held liable for your actions.

Second, many states have some type of **vicarious liability law,** by which a motorist's negligence is imputed to the vehicle's owner. For example, if the driver is acting as an agent for the owner of the vehicle, the owner can be held legally liable. Thus, if Jeff drives Lisa's car to a dry cleaner to pick up a garment, Lisa could be held legally liable if Jeff should injure someone while driving the car.

Third, under the **family purpose doctrine,** the owner of an automobile can be held liable for the negligent acts committed by immediate family members while they are operating the family car. Thus, if Shannon, age 16, negligently injures another motorist while driving her father's car and is sued for $100,000, her father could be held liable.

In addition, imputed negligence may arise out of a *joint business venture.* For example, two brothers may be partners in a business. One brother may negligently injure a customer with a company car, and the injured person sues for damages. Both partners could be held liable for the injury.

A **dram shop law** is a final example of imputed negligence. Under such a law, a business that sells liquor can be held liable for damages that may result from the sale of liquor. For example, assume that a bar owner continues to serve a customer who is drunk, and that after the bar closes, the customer injures three people while driving home. The bar owner could be held legally liable for the injuries.

RES IPSA LOQUITUR

An important modification of the law of negligence is the doctrine of **res ipsa loquitur,** meaning "the thing speaks for itself." *Under this doctrine, the very fact that the injury or damage occurs establishes a presumption of negligence on behalf of the defendant. It is then up to the defendant to refute the presumption of negligence.* That is, the accident or injury normally would not have occurred if the defendant had not been careless. Examples of the doctrine of *res ipsa loquitur* include the following:

- A dentist extracts the wrong tooth.
- A surgeon leaves a surgical sponge in the patient's abdomen.
- A surgical operation is performed on the wrong patient.

To apply the doctrine of *res ipsa loquitur,* the following requirements must be met:

- The event is one that normally does not occur in the absence of negligence.
- The defendant has exclusive control over the instrumentality causing the accident.
- The injured party has not contributed to the accident in any way.

SPECIFIC APPLICATIONS OF THE LAW OF NEGLIGENCE

Property Owners

Property owners have a legal obligation to protect others from harm. However, the standard of care owed to others depends upon the situation. Three groups traditionally have been recognized: (1) trespasser, (2) licensee, and (3) invitee.[3] However, as will be discussed later, a number of jurisdictions have abolished or modified these common law classifications.

Trespasser A **trespasser** *is a person who enters or remains on the owner's property without the owner's consent.* In general, the trespasser takes the property as he or she finds it. The property owner does not have any obligation to the trespasser to keep the land in reasonably safe condition. However, the property owner cannot deliberately injure the trespasser or set a trap that would injure the trespasser. The duty to refrain from injuring the trespasser or from setting a trap to injure that person is sometimes referred to as the *duty of slight care.*

Licensee A **licensee** *is a person who enters or remains on the premises with the occupant's expressed or implied permission.* Examples of licensees include door-to-door salespersons, solicitors for charitable or religious organizations, police officers and firefighters when they are on the property to perform

their duties, and social guests in almost all jurisdictions. A licensee takes the premises as he or she finds them. However, the property owner or occupant is required to warn the licensee of any unsafe condition or activity on the premises, which is not apparent or open, but there is no obligation to inspect the premises for the benefit of the licensee.

Invitee An **invitee** *is a person who is invited onto the premises for the benefit of the occupant.* Examples of invitees include business customers in a store, mail carriers, and garbage collectors. In addition to warning the invitee of any dangerous condition, the occupant has an obligation to inspect the premises and to eliminate any dangerous condition revealed by the inspection. For example, a store escalator may be faulty. The customers must be warned about the unsafe escalator (perhaps by a sign) and prevented from using it. The faulty escalator must be repaired; otherwise, customers in the store could be injured, and the owner would be liable.

Many jurisdictions have abolished either partly or completely the preceding common law classifications with respect to the degree of care owed to visitors. According to the Nebraska Supreme Court, the majority of states and the District of Columbia have either reconsidered the traditional common law classification scheme or have abolished some or all of the categories.[4]

Attractive Nuisance Doctrine

An **attractive nuisance** *is a condition that can attract and injure children.* Under the attractive nuisance doctrine, the occupants of land are liable for the injuries of children who may be attracted by some dangerous condition, feature, or article. This doctrine is based on the principles that children may not be able to recognize the danger involved and may be injured, and that it is in the best interest of society to protect them rather than protect the owner's right to the land. Thus, the possessor of the land must keep the premises in a safe condition and use ordinary care to protect the trespassing children from harm.[5]

Several examples can illustrate the attractive nuisance doctrine, by which the occupant or owner can be held liable:

- A homeowner carelessly leaves a ladder standing on the side of the house. A small child climbs the ladder and falls off the roof breaking both legs.
- A homeowner has a miniature house for the children. A neighbor's child attempts to enter through an unlocked window, which falls on her neck and strangles her.
- A building contractor carelessly leaves the keys in a tractor. While driving the tractor, two small boys are seriously injured when the tractor overturns.

Owners and Operators of Automobiles

The owner of an automobile who drives in a careless and irresponsible manner can be held liable for property damage or bodily injury sustained by another person. There is no single rule of law that can be applied in this situation. The legal liability of the owner who is also the operator has been modified over time by court decisions, comparative negligence laws, the last clear chance rule, no-fault auto insurance laws (see Chapter 23), and a host of additional factors. However, the laws in all states clearly require the owner of an automobile to exercise reasonable care while operating the automobile.

With respect to the liability of the owner who is not the operator, the general rule is that the owner is not liable for the negligent acts of operators. But there are exceptions to this general principle. In all states the owner can be held liable for an operator's negligence if an *agency relationship* exists. As stated earlier, if your friend drives your car on a business errand for you and injures someone, you can be held liable. In addition, under the *family purpose doctrine* discussed earlier, the owner of an automobile can be held liable for the negligent operation of the vehicle by an immediate family member.

Governmental Liability

Based on the common law, federal, state, and local governments could not be sued unless the government gave its consent. The immunity from lawsuits was based on the doctrine of **sovereign immunity,** meaning that the king or queen can do no wrong. This doctrine, however, has been significantly modified over time by both statutory law and court decisions.

A governmental unit can be held liable if it is negligent in the performance of a **proprietary function.** Proprietary functions of government typically include the operation of water plants; electrical, transportation, and telephone systems; municipal auditoriums; and similar money-making activities. Thus, if some seats collapse at a rock concert in a city auditorium, the city can be sued and held liable for injuries to spectators. With respect to **governmental functions**—for example, the planning of a sewer system—immunity from lawsuits has also been eroded. Today, governmental entities can be sued in almost every aspect of governmental activity, including false arrest, failure to meet certain standards of care, and failure to arrest.

Charitable Institutions

At one time, charitable institutions were generally immune from lawsuits. This immunity has gradually been eliminated by state law and court decisions. The trend today is to hold charities responsible for acts of negligence. This is particularly true with respect to commercial activities. For example, a hospital operated by a religious order can be sued for malpractice, and a church sponsoring a dance, carnival, or bingo game can be held liable for injuries to participants.

Employer and Employee Relationships

Under the doctrine of **respondeat superior,** an employer can be held liable for the negligent acts of employees while they are acting on the employer's behalf. Thus, if a sales clerk in a sporting goods store carelessly drops a barbell set on a customer's toe, the owner of the store can be held liable.

For an employer to be held liable for the negligent acts of the employees, two requirements must be fulfilled. *First, the worker's legal status must be that of an employee.* A person typically is considered an employee if he or she is given detailed instructions on how to do a job, is furnished tools or supplies by the employer, and is paid a wage or salary at regular intervals. *Second, the employee must be acting within the scope of employment when the negligent act occurred.* That is, the employee must be engaged in the type of work that he or she is employed to perform. There is no simple test to determine whether the tort is committed within the scope of employment. Numerous factors are considered, including whether the act is authorized by the employer, whether the act is one commonly performed by the employee, and whether the act is intended to advance the employer's interests.[6]

Parents and Children

Under the earlier common law, parents usually were not responsible for their children's torts. Children who reached the age of reason were responsible for their own wrongful acts. However, there are several exceptions to this general principle. *First, a parent can be held liable if a child uses a dangerous weapon, such as a gun or knife, to injure someone.* For example, if a 10-year-old child is permitted to play with a loaded revolver, and someone is thereby injured or killed, the parents can be held responsible. *Second, the parent can be legally liable if the child is acting as an agent for the parent.* For example, if a son or daughter is employed in the family business, the parents can be held liable for any injury to a customer caused by the child's actions. *Third, if a family car is operated by a minor child, the parents can be held liable under the family purpose doctrine discussed earlier.* In addition, property damage and vandalism by children have increased over time, especially by teenagers. *Most states have passed laws that hold the parents liable for the willful and malicious acts of children that result in property damage to others.* For example, Nebraska has a parental liability law that holds the parents liable for the willful and intentional destruction of property by minor children.

Animals

Owners of wild animals are held strictly liable (absolute liability) for the injuries of others even if the animals are domesticated. For example, an owner of an exotic pet such as a tiger is strictly liable if the pet escapes and injures someone even if the owner uses due care in keeping the animal restrained.

In addition, depending on the state, strict liability may also be imposed on the owners of ordinary house dogs. Until recently, dog owners were liable for dog bites and other injuries only if the injured person could prove that the owner knew the dog was dangerous. If the dog had never bitten anyone previously, the dog owner usually was not liable. *However, in about 30 states and the District of Columbia, the injured person has to show only that the dog caused the injury; in such cases, the dog owner is liable based on the doctrine of strict liability.*[7]

CURRENT TORT LIABILITY PROBLEMS

Certain tort liability problems have emerged that create serious problems for risk managers, business firms, physicians, and liability insurers. Timely liability problems that merit discussion include the following:

- Defective tort liability system
- Medical malpractice crisis
- Corporate fraud and lax corporate governance
- Increase in asbestos law suits

Defective Tort Liability System

Critics charge that the present tort liability system in the United States has numerous defects that reduce its effectiveness in compensating injured victims. Major defects include the following:

- Rising tort liability costs
- Inefficiency in compensating injured victims
- Uncertainty of legal outcomes
- Higher jury awards
- Long delays in settling lawsuits

Rising Tort Liability Costs Critics claim that the present system is costly and that tort costs are rising rapidly. The number of lawsuits has increased over time, and the legal costs of settling these lawsuits are enormous. The tort system in the United States reached a record $260 billion in 2004, which is equivalent to a tax of $886 per person, or $41 more than in 2003 (see Exhibit 19.1). These costs include (1) incurred losses, which reflect losses paid or expected to be paid to third parties, and the collective change in loss reserves for incurred claims; (2) legal defense costs, which include defense costs, claim investigation, and general claim-handling costs; and

EXHIBIT **19.1**

Tort Costs in the United States, 1990–2004 ($ billions)

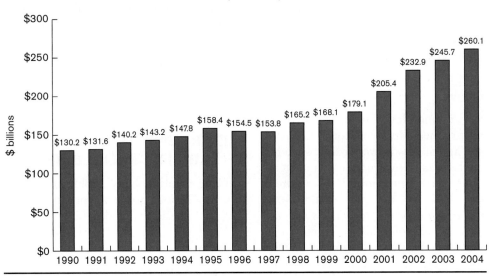

SOURCE: Data are from Towers Perrin Tillinghast, *U.S. Tort Costs and Cross-Border Perspectives: 2005 Update,* Appendix IA (2006).

(3) administrative expenses, which reflect expenses, other than defense costs, incurred by insurers or self-insurers in the administration of tort claims.

In addition, tort costs continue to rise more rapidly than the nation's gross domestic product (see Exhibit 19.2) and are expected to continue rising in the future. *Tort costs in the United States are expected to increase to an estimated $314 billion in 2007, or 2.3 percent of the nation's gross domestic product.*[8] Tort costs are substantially higher in the United States than in other industrialized countries, which make it more difficult for American companies to compete in the global markets.

Several factors help explain the substantial increase in tort costs over time. These factors include (1) social inflation that results in juries and judges being desensitized to the value of the dollar when damages are awarded, (2) aggressive and creative litigation strategies by plaintiffs' attorneys to maximize awards, (3) rising medical costs that increase the costs of personal injury claims, (4) abuses in class action lawsuits and the definition of a "class," (5) actions by the states and courts in striking down portions of state tort reform legislation, (6) an increase in the number and size of stockholder lawsuits against boards of directors and company offi-

cers because of corporate fraud, greed, illegal manipulation of earnings, and accounting scandals, (7) a deep pocket syndrome in which some plaintiffs' attorneys deliberately go after defendants who can pay large settlements, and (8) exploitation of high verdict cases by the media.[9] In addition, tort costs have increased because of an upward adjustment of liabilities tied to asbestos claims (discussed later).

Inefficiency in Compensating Injured Victims Critics argue that the present system is inefficient in compensating injured victims. The number of class action lawsuits has increased over time. However, critics charge that plaintiffs often receive relatively small amounts for their injuries or doubtful benefits (such as coupons to buy the defendant's product), while attorneys receive a disproportionate share of the settlement.

In addition, *critics argue the present system is inefficient because injured victims receive less than half of each tort dollar paid.* A Tillinghast study found that out of each dollar spent on liability claims, injured victims received only 22 cents for their actual economic loss (such as medical bills and loss of earnings) and another 24 cents for noneconomic loss (such as pain and suffering). The remain-

Exhibit **19.2**
**Growth in Tort Costs vs. GDP Since 1950
(ratio to 1950 levels)**

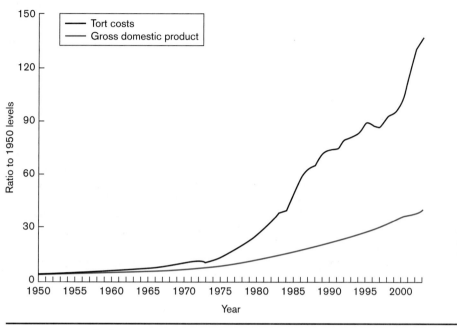

Exhibit **19.2**
**Growth in Tort Costs vs. GDP Since 1950
(ratio to 1950 levels)**

Source: Towers Perrin Tillinghast, *U.S. Tort Costs: 2004 Update,* January 2005, p. 2.

ing 54 cents paid for claimants' attorneys, defense costs, and administrative costs (see Exhibit 19.3).

Uncertainty of Legal Outcomes   Critics argue that because of changing legal doctrines, there is considerable uncertainty in predicting legal outcomes. The result is considerable confusion for insurers, employers, risk managers, government officials, and taxpayers.

For example, an injured party at one time had to prove that the other party was at fault to collect damages. Today, emphasis is on providing the injured party with some form of legal redress, regardless of blame. Thus, critics argue that the ability to pay is more important today than determining who is at fault, and that the burden of paying injured persons falls heavily on insurers, wealthy people, corporations, and others with "deep pockets."

As a result of the uncertainty in legal outcomes, property and casualty insurers often must pay tort liability claims that they did not envision paying when the coverage was first written.

Exhibit **19.3**
Where the Tort Dollar Goes, 2002[a]

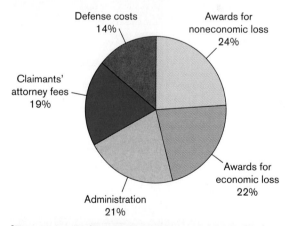

[a]First-party benefits (the cost of legal defense and claims handling), benefits paid to third parties (claimants and plaintiffs) or their attorneys, and administrative (overhead) costs. Includes costs associated with all claims, including those settled out of court.

Note: Data are from Tillinghast-Towers Perrin.

Source: Insurance Information Institute, *The I.I.I. Insurance Fact Book, 2005,* p. 131.

Higher Jury Awards   Critics also argue that jury awards for certain types of lawsuits continue to increase. These cases include motor vehicle liability, premises liability, wrongful death, medical malpractice, and products liability. Exhibit 19.4 shows the increase in both median and average jury awards between 1997 and 2003.

Higher jury awards and out-of-court settlements result in premium increases for liability insurance, which increase the cost of doing business. As a result, many firms, especially those that have already been sued, are purchasing higher liability insurance limits, which also increases the cost of goods and services to consumers (see Exhibit 19.5).

Finally, the likelihood of a catastrophic award varies drastically by venue. Some states are perceived to treat defendants fairly and equitably, while certain other states are perceived to have expensive legal systems. Moreover, at the county level, tort reform advocates view certain counties as "judicial hell-holes" because the counties are perceived to be drastically unfair to corporate defendants and insurers (see Insight 19.1).

Long Delays in Settling Lawsuits   The tort system is also marred by long delays in settling lawsuits. Cases take months or even years to settle. In 1950, only 20 civil trials in the federal courts lasted longer than 20 days. By 1981, the number of comparable lengthy trials had increased ninefold. More recent studies show that lengthy delays are still a problem. The National Center for State Courts found that the median processing time in 1989 for all tort cases in 25 urban trial courts studied was 441 days. According to Jury Verdict Research, between 1997 and 2003, it took an average of 38 months from the time of the incident for a trial to begin in motor vehicle accidents and 52 months in medical malpractice cases.[10]

A considerable amount of time involves a pretrial examination of the facts, such as interviews, depositions, and requests for documents. Repeated requests for documents can be time-consuming and expensive during the discovery stage of a suit. Moreover, attorneys frequently use delaying tactics during the discovery stage as an economic weapon against opponents. The overall result is a substantial increase in delay and cost.

EXHIBIT 19.4
Median and Average Jury Awards, 1997 and 2003 ($000)

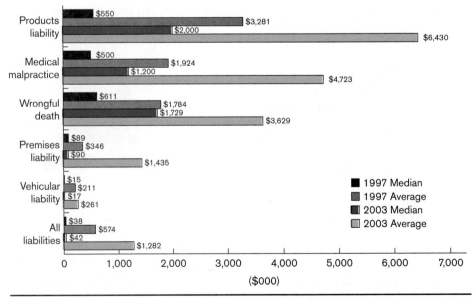

SOURCE: *Current Award Trends in Personal Injury.* Copyright 2005 by LRP Publications, 747 Dresher Road, P.O. Box 980, Horsham, PA 19044-0980. All Rights Reserved.

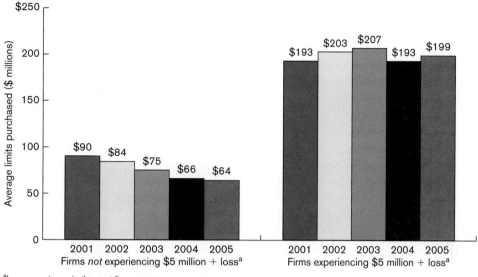

EXHIBIT **19.5**
U.S. Average Liability Limits Relative to Loss Experience, 2001–2005

Firms *not* experiencing $5 million + loss[a]

Firms experiencing $5 million + loss[a]

[a]Loss experience in the past five years.

SOURCE: *2005 Limits of Liability Report*, © Marsh Inc.

Tort Reform   Various tort-reform proposals have been enacted into law or are being considered by both the federal government and the states.

1. **Federal Tort Reform** The following summarizes recent actions of Congress dealing with tort reform at the federal level:

   ■ In 2005, Congress enacted the *Class Action Fairness Act,* which moves class action suits of more than $5 million from the state to federal courts. The act is intended to reduce venue shopping by plaintiffs' attorneys who seek jurisdictions where their clients are likely to win large awards.
   ■ At the time of this writing, the House has passed the *Protection of Lawful Commerce in Arms Act* that protects gun manufacturers and sellers of guns from lawsuits based on the criminal use of their products.
   ■ At the time of this writing, the House also has approved the *Personal Responsibility in Food Consumption Act* (also called the "cheeseburger bill"). The bill protects food companies

and fast-food restaurants from lawsuits by overweight customers and other parties that seek to hold restaurants and food companies liable for weight gain or obesity.
   ■ In 2005, the House also passed the *Lawsuit Abuse Reduction Act,* which imposes sanctions against attorneys who file frivolous suits.

2. **State Tort Reform** Most states have enacted or are considering some type of tort-reform legislation to deal with the problems discussed earlier. Some important state tort reforms include the following:[11]

   ■ *Capping noneconomic damages, such as pain and suffering.* Many states have enacted legislation that places a maximum limit on noneconomic damages, such as compensation for pain and suffering. Reform measures may include all tort suits or only specific suits, such as medical malpractice.
   ■ *Reinstating the state-of-the art defense.* This proposal has relevance with respect to products liability suits. If the product conformed to

INSIGHT 19.1

Which Cities and Counties Are Perceived as "Judicial Hellholes"?

Some plaintiff attorneys are notorious for "forum shopping." That is, they prefer to file suits in those jurisdictions where legal outcomes are favorable for their clients. Conversely, defendants in civil cases prefer jurisdictions where the legal outcomes are likely to favor them.

The likelihood that a defendant will have to pay a catastrophic award varies drastically by venue. Some states are kinder to defendants than others. The U.S. Chamber of Commerce ranked the liability systems in 50 states perceived to be the most equitable based on several factors, including fairness, jury predictability, treatment of class action suits, and punitive damages. The top ten states in 2003 perceived to be the most equitable were:

1. Delaware
2. Nebraska
3. North Dakota
4. Virginia
5. Iowa
6. Indiana
7. Minnesota
8. South Dakota
9. Wyoming
10. Idaho

The bottom states ranked 41–50 with the most expensive legal systems were:

41. Hawaii
42. Florida
43. Arkansas
44. Texas
45. California
46. Illinois
47. Louisiana
48. Alabama
49. West Virginia
50. Mississippi*

At the city and county level, some jurisdictions are perceived to be so drastically unfair to corporate defendants and liability insurers that they are called "judicial hellholes" by tort-reform advocates. Given the history of damages awarded to plaintiffs in these jurisdictions, they are probably the last place on earth in which a corporation would want to defend a liability suit. These include:

- Madison County, Illinois
- St. Claire County, Illinois
- Hampton County, South Carolina
- West Virginia (entire state)
- Jefferson County, Texas
- Orleans Parish, Louisiana
- South Florida
- Philadelphia, Pennsylvania
- Los Angeles County, California

In some counties, there are more plaintiffs in asbestos-related lawsuits than there are residents.

*Tort reform legislation in Mississippi should improve future rankings.
Source: Data from David Dial, et al., "Tort Excess 2005: The Necessity for Reform from a Policy, Legal and Risk Management Perspective," *Hot Topics & Insurance Issues.*

the prevailing state of the art at the time it was manufactured, it would not be considered a defective product today.

- *Restricting punitive damage awards.* Punitive damages were originally intended to punish defendants for egregious conduct and to deter others from engaging in the same behavior. However, in many cases, awards for punitive damages are so large that they bear little relationship to the compensatory damages awarded by the courts. More than half of the states have passed laws that limit the imposition of punitive damages. Other states are considering legislation that would limit the maximum amount that could be paid for punitive damages or restrict the imposition of punitive damages to certain types of cases.

- *Modifying the collateral source rule.* Under the **collateral source rule,** *the defendant cannot introduce any evidence that shows the injured party has received compensation from other collateral sources.* For example, a delivery driver who is injured in a rear-end collision may be able to collect medical expenses from the negligent driver. However, job-related medical expenses are also covered under a state's workers compensation law. Therefore, the injured driver might "double dip" and receive a total amount that exceeds the medical bills. The collateral source rule would be modified so that recovery from other sources could be considered in determining the amount of damages. About one-third of the states have enacted laws that would alter this rule. The effect would be to reduce the size of the damages awarded.

- *Modifying the **joint and several liability rule**. Under this rule, several people may be responsible for the injury, but a defendant who is only slightly responsible may be required to pay the full amount of damages.* This could happen if one defendant had substantial financial assets ("deep pockets"), and the other defendants had few or no assets. Under tort reform, the joint and several liability rule would be modified. For example, many states now prohibit application of the joint and several liability rule to noneconomic damages, such as pain and suffering.

- *Alternative dispute resolution (ADR) techniques.* Another proposal is to use alternative dispute resolution (ADR) techniques to resolve legal disputes. *An ADR is a technique for resolving a legal dispute without litigation.* For example, **arbitration** is a technique by which parties in a dispute agree to be bound by the decision of an independent third party. **Mediation** is a technique by which a neutral third party tries to arrange a settlement without resorting to litigation. To reduce lawsuits between insurers and consumers over claims, many states now use binding arbitration or formal mediation to resolve disputes.

- *Restrictions on obesity lawsuits.* Consumers love hamburgers, cheeseburgers, fries, and similar high-calorie foods, which they often purchase from fast-food restaurants. Undesirable weight gains have resulted in a number of lawsuits against fast-food restaurants. As stated earlier, federal legislation has been introduced that would place restrictions on obesity lawsuits. Likewise, at the state level, at least 10 states have enacted laws that generally exempt manufacturers, distributors, sellers, and advertisers of food from civil liability when plaintiffs claim that weight gains or other health problems are due to the long-run consumption of such food.

Effectiveness of State Tort Reform Proposals   To determine the effectiveness of tort reform legislation, the Congressional Budget Office (CBO) reviewed nine empirical research studies dealing with tort reform. The studies analyzed the effects of tort reform legislation, including caps on damages, modifications to joint-and-several liability, and changes in the collateral-source rule. Some major conclusions are the following:[12]

- *The most consistent finding in the studies reviewed was that caps on damages reduced the number of lawsuits filed, the value of the awards, and insurance costs.*

- *Four studies examined the effects of modifying the joint-and-several liability rule. The results were mixed. One study found no effect. Another study found no effect on the number of lawsuits filed after enactment of the reform but a significant surge in cases before the reform took effect. A third study found an increase in the value of noneconomic awards but found no other significant effects. The final study provided evidence that joint-and-several liability reform was a factor in reducing insurers' losses in the mid-1980s.*

- *Two studies separately analyzed the impact of reform of the collateral-source rule. One study found that both economic and noneconomic damages were reduced. The other study found that discretionary collateral-rule offsets (considered by the judge's discretion) led to increased profitability for insurers.*

CBO, however, urged caution in interpreting the above results. First, data were limited, and the findings were not sufficiently consistent to be considered conclusive. Second, some studies were limited because they analyzed only specific types of torts, such as bodily injury claims in auto accidents, which made generalizations difficult. Finally, various tort reform measures may be enacted as a package, which makes it difficult for policymakers to separate the effects of the different types of tort reform.

Medical Malpractice Crisis

Medical malpractice is one of the most important liability issues today. Medical malpractice occurs when a negligent act or omission by a physician or

---

INSIGHT 19.2

Study Says Wrong-Site Surgery Is Very Rare and Preventable

Wrong-site surgery—including surgery on the wrong organ or limb, at the wrong site on the spine, or the wrong person—is extremely rare and major injury from it even rarer, according to a study supported by Health and Human Services' Agency for Healthcare Research and Quality.

Researchers led by Mary R. Kwaan, M.D., M.P.H., Brigham and Women's Hospital, and Harvard School of Public Health in Boston estimate that a wrong-site surgery serious enough to result in a report to insurance risk managers or in a lawsuit would occur approximately once every 5 to 10 years at a single large hospital.

The study was published in the April 2006 issue of *Archives of Surgery*. The study assessed all wrong-site surgeries reported to a large medical malpractice insurer between 1985 and 2004 and found that the number of wrong-site surgeries conducted on limbs or organs other than the spine occurred once in every 112,994 operations. Forty cases of wrong-site surgery were identified among 1,153 malpractice claims and 259 instances of insurance loss related to surgical

care. Twenty-five of the cases were non-spine wrong-site surgeries, with the remainder involving surgery of the spine.

"The good news is that wrong-site surgery is extremely rare, and major injury from it even less common," said AHRQ Director Carolyn M. Clancy, M. D. "The less good news is that although site-verification protocols offer some protection against such errors, they are not foolproof. We have a lot more to do to ensure that wrong-site surgery never happens."

The Study examined site-verification protocols at 25 hospitals as a means to prevent wrong-site surgery from occurring. Available medical records for 13 of the 25 non-spine wrong-site surgery cases show that injury was temporary and minor in 10 of the cases. Researchers conclude that following the Joint Commission on Accreditation of Healthcare Organizations Universal Protocol for Preventing Wrong Site, Wrong Procedure, Wrong Person Surgery might have prevented eight of the cases.

Source: Excerpted from "Study Says Wrong-Site Surgery is Very Rare and Preventable," *Insurance Journal*, National News, April 17, 2006.

---

other health-care professional results in injury or harm to the patient. For example, a physician who prescribes the wrong drug that causes a patient's death could be guilty of medical negligence. A surgeon who amputates the wrong leg is another example of medical malpractice. However, a recent study concluded that surgery on the wrong organ or limb is extremely rare (see Insight 19.2).

An unfavorable medical outcome alone does not necessarily mean the physician is negligent. To determine liability, the patient must show that the doctor deviated from the generally accepted standards of practice in this particular case. In addition, if the standard of care was not followed, the patient must show that this failure caused the injury. The physician's negligence must cause injury or harm to the patient. Even if the physician makes the wrong diagnosis, fails to treat the illness or injury properly, or prescribes the wrong drug, there is no case unless the negligence actually caused the injury or worsened the condition.

Rising Medical Malpractice Tort Costs   Medical malpractice tort costs have increased over time and continue to rise. Medical malpractice tort costs totaled $28.7 billion in 2004, up from $26.5 billion

in 2003. Since 1975, medical malpractice costs have increased at an annual rate of 11.7 percent versus 9 percent for all other tort costs.[13]

The medical malpractice crisis has had a severe financial impact on health care providers and insurers. Malpractice insurance premiums are substantial; some physicians pay $100,000 or more annually for coverage. Many physicians have abandoned high-risk areas, such as obstetrics, gynecology, and neurosurgery. Groups of physicians have staged protests and walkouts in certain parts of the country. Malpractice insurers have incurred heavy underwriting losses, and several malpractice insurers have withdrawn from the medical malpractice market. Finally, some physicians have formed physician-owned insurance companies because malpractice insurance is too costly or not available.

Reasons for Medical Malpractice Crisis   There is no single reason that explains the medical malpractice crisis in the United States. Two major factors, however, are the following:

- *Many malpractice suits are due to medical errors by health-care providers, especially errors in hospitals that result in the death of patients.* A study by the Institute of Medicine estimates that medical errors may cause 44,000 to 98,000 deaths each year, which exceed the number of people who die each year from motor vehicle accidents or from breast cancer (see Insight 19.3). A more recent study by HealthGrades estimates that an average of 195,000 people in the United States died from preventable hospital errors in each of the years 2000, 2001, and 2002.[14] This latter figure is the equivalent of the number of people who would die each year if 390 fully loaded jumbo jets crashed.

- As stated earlier, *many insurers have experienced significant underwriting losses,* which have resulted in substantial increases in medical malpractice premiums for certain medical specialties. Also, legal defense costs incurred by insurers to defend malpractice suits are relatively high even when the health care provider wins. One measure of underwriting profit or loss is the **combined ratio,** which is the percentage of each premium dollar an insurer spends on claims and expenses. When the combined ratio is over 100, the insurer has an underwriting loss. *According to the National Underwriter Data Services, the medical malpractice combined ratio was 109.2 in 2004. This means that malpractice insurers paid out $109 in losses and expenses for each*

$100 of medical malpractice premiums collected. However, the underwriting results show a significant improvement from 2003, when the combined ratio was139.0.[15]

In addition, other factors have contributed to the medical malpractice problem, including the following:

- *People are more litigious than in the past.*
- *The media has made more people aware of the vulnerability of physicians to malpractice suits.*
- *The intimate relationship between patients and physicians that existed in the past has been lost.*
- *Physicians and other medical experts will now testify against physicians in malpractice cases.*
- *Physicians accuse attorneys of filing malpractice suits because of the high fees that attorneys can collect if they win.*
- *Some state medical boards are reluctant to discipline their own members.*
- *There is growing resentment against large for profit health-care firms and managed care plans.*

Regardless of the reason, the majority of medical malpractice plaintiffs appear to lose if the case goes to a jury. According to Jury Verdict Research, *the medical malpractice plaintiff recovery rate overall in 2003 was only 36 percent.*[16]

INSIGHT 19.3

Medical Errors Rank with Highway Accidents and Breast Cancer as a Major Killer in the United States

Many malpractice suits are due to medical errors that result in the death of patients. The Institute of Medicine estimates that medical errors may cause 44,000 to 98,000 deaths each year. Even using the lower estimate, the Institute of Medicine claims that more people die in a given year as a result of medical errors than from motor vehicle accidents, breast cancer, or AIDS.[a]

Opportunities for mistakes and errors result from a number of factors, including the following:[b]

- Medication errors in prescribing and dispensing drugs, both in and out of the hospital
- More care and increasingly complex care that is provided in ambulatory settings, such as outpatient surgical centers, clinics, and physician offices

- Decentralized and fragmented health-care delivery system, such as frequent referral of patients to multiple health-care providers, none of whom has access to complete information about the patient
- Few demands for improvements in patient safety by group purchasers of health care

The Institute of Medicine believes that a large percentage of adverse effects from medical errors can be prevented by a greater emphasis on patient safety.

[a] Linda T. Kohn, Janet M. Corrigan, and Molla S. Donaldson, eds., "Executive Summary," *To Err Is Human, Building a Safer Health System* (Washington, DC: National Academy Press, 2000).
[b] Ibid.

Approaches to Medical Malpractice Crisis Several approaches have been taken to help solve the medical malpractice problem. They include the following:

- *Place caps on noneconomic damages.* At least 25 states have enacted laws that place caps on the amount paid for noneconomic damages, such as compensation for pain and suffering.
- *Arbitration panels.* Some states have formed arbitration panels to resolve disputes between physicians and patients.
- *Attorney fees.* Limitations would be placed on contingent fees charged by attorneys.
- *Shorter period for filing suits.* The period for filing suits against physicians would be shortened, such as within three years of the injury.
- *More effective medical review boards.* State review boards would be upgraded so that problem physicians could be identified more easily. Physicians cited by review boards would have to undergo retraining.
- *Training programs to reduce medical errors.* Training programs to reduce medical errors would be intensified, especially in the use of new technology.
- *Emphasize risk management.* Risk management principles would be emphasized to reduce loss frequency and severity. For example, anesthesiologists earlier developed certain practice standards to reduce claims. The causes of most claims were identified, and standards were developed to avoid them. As a result, anesthesiologists experienced a significant reduction in malpractice claims and a corresponding reduction in malpractice premiums. Other risk management techniques include the requirement that physicians study medical malpractice prevention as part of the licensing requirement; increasing the number of states that require mandatory reporting of medical errors; and encouraging physicians to use new health technology, such as writing prescriptions for drugs with electronic equipment.

Corporate Fraud and Lax Corporate Governance

Another liability issue is the problem of corporate fraud and lax corporate governance. In recent years, many large corporations have used dishonest or aggressive accounting practices to inflate stated earnings and profits; other companies have concealed or misstated certain accounting transactions. When these practices were discovered, earnings were revised downward, and shareholders lost millions of dollars. Because of class action suits by angry stockholders, employees, and investors, several large corporations have been forced into bankruptcy, including Enron, WorldCom, and Global Crossing. Thousands of employees have lost their jobs and a large part of their retirement savings as well. In addition, the Securities and Exchange Commission has indicted numerous company officials in different industries for securities fraud, illegal accounting practices, destruction of company records, and obstruction of justice. Some company officials pleaded guilty and are now serving lengthy federal prison sentences.

Boards of directors are also attacked for lax corporate governance and inadequate oversight of management. Boards are criticized because of the disconnect between the boards and audit committees, poor internal controls and accountability, excessive executive salaries and loans, undisclosed CEO and director financial arrangements, compromising of auditors and lawyers, and unclear disclosure of complex financial transactions (such as off-balance-sheet transactions and the use of derivatives). Critics claim that many board members are mere figureheads who are on the board because of their names or national visibility; that board members may not understand complex financial transactions that often involve mathematical formulas, derivatives, and hedging techniques; and that board members often serve on multiple boards and cannot devote the time necessary to understand and scrutinize the actions of management.

To deal with the problem, in 2002 Congress enacted the bipartisan *Sarbanes-Oxley Act* corporate accountability law. The law is designed to expose and punish acts of corruption, restore confidence in corporate America, and protect small investors. The law requires the company's CEO and CFO to swear to the accuracy of the quarterly and annual financial reports; makes it generally unlawful for an accounting firm to provide major nonaudit services to a company while auditing the company's books; prohibits companies from retaliating against stock market analysts who criticize them; requires companies to disclose whether the board of directors' audit committee has at least one member who is a financial expert; and makes tampering with company records a crime with increased criminal penalties for mail and wire fraud.

Corporate fraud and greed also have had a significant financial impact on *directors and officers liability insurance* (D&O). D&O insurance covers directors and company officers for their wrongful acts and for deceptive statements that result in lawsuits against the company. Chapter 26 discusses D&O insurance in greater detail.

Increase in Asbestos Lawsuits

A critical liability problem is the significant increase in the number and cost of asbestos lawsuits over time. Exposure to materials containing asbestos can cause lung cancer and other respiratory diseases. Because the disease has a long latency period, it can take as long as 40 years for someone exposed to asbestos to be diagnosed with an asbestos-related disease.

The first asbestos suit was filed in 1966. By the end of 2000, more than 600,000 people had filed claims for asbestos-related personal injuries, and more than 6000 companies were named as defendants.[17] Many of these companies are no longer in business. One reason for the increase in suits is the increased number of claimants who file claims against more than one company. Many claimants who have signs of exposure but not a debilitating disease file multiple claims because they fear if they later develop an asbestos-related disease, the company responsible may be bankrupt because of

asbestos claims. The claims are not confined to a single industry, but include both traditional industries and new industries.

A major problem is the sharp escalation in asbestos costs over time. Total insured losses for asbestos lawsuits are enormous and are at least $122 billion. Total future costs are expected to reach $200 billion.

Solving the asbestos problem is not easy. Some proposals to resolve the problem include the following:[18]

- *Establish a national trust fund to pay claimants.* At the time of this writing, Congress is considering legislation that would establish a national trust fund to pay claimants. Defendant companies and their insurers would contribute to the fund, which would compensate asbestos victims over several decades based on clearly defined medical criteria. A trust fund would ensure finality to the problem.
- *Establish clear medical criteria for determining loss.* The criteria would include requiring the manifestation of an asbestos-related disease before a claim is filed.
- *Create a single venue for asbestos litigation.* The objective is to eliminate "forum shopping" by plaintiff's attorneys who seek the most favorable jurisdiction to try the case.
- *Cap legal fees.* Legal fees would be capped in asbestos cases, such as a sliding scale for attorney fees.

CASE APPLICATION

Michael went deer hunting with Ed. After seeing bushes move, Michael quickly fired his rifle at what he thought was a deer. However, Ed caused the movement in the bushes and was seriously injured by the bullet. Ed survived and later sued Michael on the grounds that "Michael 's negligence was the proximate cause of the injury."

a. Based on the above facts, is Michael guilty of negligence? Your answer must include a definition of negligence and the essential elements of negligence.

b. Michael's attorney believes that if contributory negligence could be established, it would greatly

influence the outcome of the case. Do you agree with Michael's attorney? Your answer must include a definition of contributory negligence.

c. If Michael can establish comparative negligence on the part of Ed, would the outcome of the case be changed? Explain your answer.

d. Assume that Michael and Ed are hunting on farmland without obtaining permission from the owner. If Michael fell into a marshy pond covered by weeds and injured his back, would the property owner be liable for damages? Explain your answer.

SUMMARY

- A tort is a legal wrong for which the law allows a remedy in the form of money damages. There are three categories of torts: intentional torts, strict liability, and negligence.

- Negligence is defined as the failure to exercise the standard of care required by law to protect others from an unreasonable risk of harm. There are four elements of negligence:

   Existence of a legal duty

   Failure to perform that duty

   Damages or injury to the claimant

   Proximate cause relationship

- *Contributory negligence* means that if the injured person's conduct falls below the standard of care required for his or her protection, and such conduct contributed to the injury, the injured person cannot collect damages. Under a *comparative negligence law,* the injured person can collect, but the award for damages is reduced. Under the *last clear chance rule,* a plaintiff who is endangered by his or her own negligence can still recover damages from the defendant if the defendant has a last clear chance to avoid the accident but fails to do so. Under the *assumption of risk doctrine,* a person who understands and recognizes the danger inherent in a particular activity cannot recover damages in the event of injury.

- Under certain conditions, the negligence of one person can be imputed to another. Imputed negligence may arise from an employer–employee relationship, vicarious liability law, family purpose doctrine, joint business venture, or a dram shop law.

- Under the doctrine of *res ipsa loquitur* (the thing speaks for itself), the very fact that the injury or damage occurs establishes a presumption of negligence on behalf of the defendant.

- The standard of care required by law varies with the situation. Specific liability situations can involve property owners, attractive nuisances, owners and operators of automobiles, governmental units and charitable institutions, employers and employees, parents and children, and the owners of animals.

- Tort reform advocates claim that the present tort liability system in the United States has the following defects:

   Rising tort liability costs

   Inefficiency in compensating injured victims

   Uncertainty of legal outcomes

   Higher jury awards

   Long delays in settling lawsuits

- Some state tort reform proposals include the following:

   Capping noneconomic damages, such as pain and suffering

   Reinstating the state-of-the art defense

   Restricting punitive damage awards

   Modifying the collateral source rule

   Modifying the joint and several liability rule

   Alternative dispute resolution (ADR) techniques

   Restrictions on obesity lawsuits

- The medical malpractice crisis is due to several factors. These causes include medical errors by health-care providers, large underwriting losses by insurers that result in substantial premium increases for malpractice insurance, increased willingness of patients to sue physicians, exploitation of malpractice suits by the media, loss of the intimate relationship between physicians and patients that existed in the past, increased willingness of physicians and medical experts to testify against other physicians, increased tendency for attorneys to file malpractice suits because of potentially high fees, and the ineffectiveness or reluctance of some state medical boards to discipline physicians.

- Corporate fraud and lax corporate governance are important tort liability issues. Many corporations have been sued because of dishonest or aggressive accounting practices that inflate stated earnings and profits, concealment or misstatement of certain accounting transactions that have resulted in enormous investor losses, violation of security laws, destruction of company records, and obstruction of justice.

- Boards of directors have been sued because of lax corporate governance and inadequate oversight of management.

- The number of asbestos lawsuits has increased substantially over time. Some proposals to deal with asbestos claims include the establishment of a national trust fund to pay claimants over several decades, requiring evidence of an asbestos-related disease before a claim can be filed, creation of a single venue for asbestos litigation to eliminate "forum shopping," and placing a cap on legal fees.

KEY CONCEPTS AND TERMS

Alternative dispute
 resolution (ADR)
 techniques
Arbitration
Assumption of risk
Attractive nuisance
Collateral source rule
Combined ratio
Comparative negligence
 law
Compensatory damages
Contributory negligence
 law
Dram shop law
Elements of negligence
Family purpose doctrine
General damages
Governmental function
Imputed negligence
Invitee
Joint and several liability
 rule
Joint underwriting
 association (JUA)
Last clear chance rule

Legal wrong
Licensee
Mediation
Negligence
Plaintiff
Proprietary function
Proximate cause
Punitive damages
Res ipsa loquitur
Respondeat superior
Sovereign immunity
Special damages
Strict liability (absolute
 liability)
Tort
Tortfeasor
Trespasser
Vicarious liability law

REVIEW QUESTIONS

1. a. Define the meaning of negligence.
   b. Explain the four elements of negligence.
2. What is the meaning of strict liability?
3. Explain the following types of damages:
   a. Compensatory damages (special damages and general damages)
   b. Punitive damages
4. Describe the following legal defenses that can be used by defendants who are accused of negligence:
   a. Contributory negligence
   b. Comparative negligence
   c. Last clear chance rule
   d. Assumption of risk doctrine

5. Explain the meaning of imputed negligence.
6. Explain the meaning of *res ipsa loquitur.*
7. Briefly describe the standard of care to protect others from harm for each of the following liability situations:
   a. Property owners
   b. An attractive nuisance
   c. Owners and operators of automobiles
   d. Governmental units and charitable institutions
   e. Employers and employees
   f. Parents and children
   g. Owners of animals
8. a. Explain the major defects in the tort liability system in the United States.
   b. Identify several proposals for tort reform in the United States.
9. a. Explain the reasons for the medical malpractice crisis in the United States.
   b. Identify several proposals for dealing with the medical malpractice problem in the United States.
10. Briefly explain the following tort liability problems:
    a. Corporate fraud and lax corporate governance
    b. Increase in asbestos suits

APPLICATION QUESTIONS

1. Smith Construction is building a warehouse for Raymond. The construction firm routinely leaves certain construction equipment at the building site overnight and on weekends. Late one night, Fred, age 10, began playing on some of Smith's construction equipment. Fred accidentally released the brakes of a tractor on which he was playing, and the tractor rolled down a hill and smashed into the building under construction. Fred was severely injured in the accident. Fred's parents sue both Smith Construction and Raymond for the injury.
   a. Based on the elements of negligence, describe the requirements that must be met for Smith Construction to be held liable for negligence.
   b. Describe the various classes of persons that are recognized by the law with respect to entering upon the property of another. In which class of persons would Fred belong?
   c. What other legal doctrine is applicable in this case because of Fred's age? Explain your answer.

2. a. Parkway Distributors is a wholesale firm that employs several outside salespersons. Emily, a salesperson employed by Parkway Distributors, was involved in an accident with another motorist while she was using her car to make regular sales calls for Parkway Distributors. Emily and the motorist are seriously injured in the accident. The motorist sues both Emily and Parkway Distributors for the injury based on negligence.

   (1) Describe the requirements that the motorist must establish to show that Emily is guilty of negligence.

   (2) On what legal basis might Parkway Distributors be held legally liable for the injury to the motorist? Explain your answer.

   b. Tom asks his girlfriend, Megan, to go to a supermarket and purchase some steaks for dinner. While driving Tom's car to the supermarket, Megan ran a stop sign and seriously injured a pedestrian. Does Tom have any legal liability for the injury? Explain your answer.

3. Whirlwind Mowers manufactures and sells power lawn mowers to the public and distributes the products through its own dealers. Andrew is a homeowner who has purchased a power mower from an authorized dealer on the basis of the dealer's recommendation that "the mower is the best one available to do the job." Andrew was cutting his lawn when the mower blade flew off and seriously injured his leg.

   a. Andrew sues Whirlwind Mowers and asks damages based on negligence in producing the power mower. Is Whirlwind Mowers guilty of negligence? Explain your answer.

   b. The doctrine of *res ipsa loquitur* can often be applied to cases of this type. Show how this doctrine can be applied to this case. Your answer must include a definition of *res ipsa loquitur*.

   c. Explain the various types of damages that Andrew might receive if Whirlwind Mowers is found guilty of negligence.

4. Mathew was involved in an auto accident. He was judged to be 40 percent at fault in the accident, and the other party was judged to be 60 percent at fault. Mathew's actual damages were $50,000. Under a pure comparative negligence law, how much, if any, will Mathew receive for his injury?

5. Dr. Jones is an orthopedic surgeon. One patient required arthroscopic surgery on his right knee because of cartilage damage. When the patient awoke from surgery, he was surprised to see bandages on both knees. He was told that Dr. Jones made an incision on the wrong knee, realized his mistake, and then proceeded with the surgery on the correct knee. In this case, Dr. Jones is presumed to be negligent under which legal doctrine?

6. Sarah is a college student who was late for class. She tried to cross the street in the middle of the block instead of at the intersection corner where a traffic light was in operation. A motorist hit her. Although Sarah placed herself in danger, she may be able to collect for her injuries if she can show that the motorist had an opportunity to avoid hitting her but failed to do so. Identify the legal rule that might apply in Sarah's case.

7. Elizabeth was injured in a work-related auto accident. She sued the other driver for her injuries, and the case went to court. While questioning Elizabeth, the defendant's attorney asked her if her injuries were paid under the company's group health insurance plan. Elizabeth's attorney immediately objected to the question. The judge ruled that the question was improper and instructed the jury to disregard the question. Based on the judge's reaction to the question, identify the legal rule that is in force in the jurisdiction where the trial took place.

8. Daniel believes that a chemical company is responsible for contaminating some land that he owns. He files suit against the chemical company. Rather than have the case go to court, the chemical company's attorney suggests arbitration to resolve the legal dispute. Explain how arbitration would work in this case.

INTERNET RESOURCES

■ **FreeAdvice.com** is a leading legal site for consumers and small businesses. The site provides general legal information to help people understand their legal rights on numerous legal topics but is not a substitute for an attorney. Visit the site at

   http://www.freeadvice.com

- **Nolo.com** is a leading source of self-help legal information for consumers, including topics dealing with personal injury law. Visit the site at

  http://www.nolo.com

- The **Legal Information Institute** of Cornell Law School provides detailed information on torts, personal injury, and products liability law. Legal topics are listed alphabetically under "Law About . . ." Click on "Insurance" for various topics and statutes dealing with insurance law. Related links are also given. Visit the site at

  http://www.law.cornell.edu

- The **RAND Institute for Civil Justice** publishes numerous high-quality research studies that make recommendations for improving the civil justice system in the United States. Several studies examine many of the liability issues discussed in this chapter. Visit the site at

  http://www.rand.org/icj/

SELECTED REFERENCES

Congress of the United States, Congressional Budget Office. *The Effects of Tort Reform: Evidence from the States,* (June 2004).

Dial, David, et al. *Tort Excess 2005: The Necessity for Reform from a Policy, Legal and Risk Management Perspective,* Insurance Information Institute, 2005.

Hartwig, Robert P. *Liability Trends, Issues and Jury Verdicts: Impact on Insurance Liability and Excess Casualty Markets,* Insurance Information Institute, October 2003.

Insurance Information Institute, "Litigiousness, Insurers' Legal Defense Costs," *Facts and Statistics,* (no date).

Jury Verdict Research, *Jury Verdict Research Releases Medical Malpractice Study: Yearly Analyses Show an Upward Trend in Median Awards for Personal Injury Cases,* JVR News Release, June 22, 2005.

Kolbe, Philip T., Nancy A. Mardis, and Michael J. McNamara. "Bodily Injury Liability and Residential Property Values: Canine Risks," *Real Estate Law Journal,* vol. 34, no. 1, (Summer 2005), pp. 43–59.

"Liability System," *Hot Topics & Issues Updates,* Insurance Information Institute, August 2006. This source is periodically updated.

Lorimer, James J., et al. *The Legal Environment of Insurance,* 4th ed., vol. 2. Malvern, PA: American Institute for Chartered Property Casualty Underwriters, 1993.

"Medical Malpractice," *Hot Topics & Issues Updates,* Insurance Information Institute, August 2006. This source is periodically updated.

The I.I.I. Insurance Fact Book 2006. New York: Insurance Information Institute, 2006.

Towers-Perrin Tillinghast, *U.S. Tort Costs and Cross-Border Perspectives: 2005 Update,* (2006).

NOTES

1. According to the American Tort Reform Association, the District of Columbia, Alabama, Maryland, North Carolina, and Virginia still have contributory negligence doctrines in effect. See "The Liability System," *Hot Topics & Issues Updates,* Insurance Information Institute, August 2006. This source is periodically updated.

2. James J. Lorimer et al., *The Legal Environment of Insurance,* 4th ed., vol. 2 (Malvern, PA: America Institute for Property and Liability Underwriters, 1993), pp. 18–19.

3. This section is based on Donald J. Hirsch, *Casualty Claim Practice,* 6th ed. (Burr Ridge, IL: Irwin, 1996), pp. 58–62.

4. *Opinion of the Supreme Court of Nebraska, Case Title, Roger W. Heins, Appellant, v. Webster County, Nebraska, doing business as Webster County Hospital, Appellee.* Filed August 23, 1996, No. S-94-713.

5. Lorimer et al., p. 30.

6. Lorimer et al., p. 132.

7. Northeast Louisiana Chapter of the Society of CPCU, "Liability Concerns of Dog Owners and Their Insurers," *CPCU Journal,* vol. 45, no. 3 (September 1992), p. 184.

8. Towers-Perrin Tillinghast, *U.S. Tort Costs and Cross-Border Perspectives: 2005 Update,* (2006).

9. David Dial et al., *Tort Excess 2005: The Necessity for Reform from a Policy, Legal and Risk Management Perspective,* Insurance Information Institute, 2005.

10. Insurance Information Institute, "Liability System," *Hot Topics & Issues Updates,* November 2005. This source is periodically updated.

11. This section is based on David Dial, et al., *Tort Excess 2005: The Necessity for Reform from a Policy, Legal and Risk Management Perspective,* Insurance Information Institute, 2005.

12. Congress of the United States, Congressional Budget Office, *The Effects of Tort Reform: Evidence from the States,* (June 2004).

13. Towers-Perrin Tillinghast, *U.S. Tort Costs and Cross-Border Perspectives: 2005 Update,* (2006).

14. HealthGrades, *In-Hospital Deaths from Medical Errors at 195,000 per Year, HealthGrades Study Finds,* Press Release, July 27, 2004.

15. Insurance Information Institute, "Medical Malpractice," *Hot Topics & Issues Updates,* August 2006. This source is periodically updated.

16. Jury Verdict Research, *Jury Verdict Research Releases Medical Malpractice Study: Yearly Analyses Show an Upward Trend in Median Awards for Personal Injury Cases,* JVR News Release, June 22, 2005.

17. *The I.I.I. Fact Book 2003* (New York: Insurance Information Institute, 2003), p. 114.

18. David Dial et al., *Tort Excess 2005: The Necessity for Reform from a Policy, Legal and Risk Management Perspective* (New York: Insurance Information Institute, 2005).

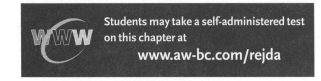

Students may take a self-administered test on this chapter at
www.aw-bc.com/rejda

CHAPTER 20

HOMEOWNERS INSURANCE, SECTION I

"There's no place like home, after the other places close."

English Proverb

LEARNING OBJECTIVES

After studying this chapter, you should be able to

◆ Identify the major homeowners policies for homeowners, condominium owners, and renters.

◆ Explain the major provisions in Section I of the Homeowners 3 policy, including
  Section I property coverages
  Section I perils insured against
  Section I exclusions

◆ Given a specific property loss situation, explain whether the Homeowners 3 policy would cover the loss.

◆ Explain the insured's duties after a loss occurs.

◆ Explain and give an illustration of the loss settlement provision in the Homeowners 3 policy.

*C*hris, age 42, and Karen, age 38, are married and live in New Orleans, Louisiana. In August 2005, Hurricane Katrina—the worst natural disaster in the history of the United States— struck the city with awesome destruction and violence. Powerful winds and subsequent flooding caused billions of dollars of property damage and the loss of numerous lives. Most of the city was flooded, and the residents had to be evacuated. Damage to the couple's home and personal possessions totaled about $150,000. Flooding caused about $50,000 of that damage, and flood damage was not covered by the couple's homeowners insurance. As a result, their goal of financial security received a serious setback.

Although a homeowners policy provides considerable protection, the experience of Chris and Karen shows that not all property losses are covered. In this chapter, we discuss the major homeowners policies that are sold today to insure homes, condominiums, and personal property. We also discuss the various limitations and exclusions that appear in current homeowners and renters policies.

Each homeowners policy is divided into two major sections. Section I covers the property of the insured, which can include a home or condominium, other structures, and personal property. Section II provides personal liability insurance and also covers medical payments to others. This chapter discusses the Section I provisions. The Section II provisions are discussed in Chapter 21.

HOMEOWNERS INSURANCE

Homeowners insurance contracts were first introduced in the 1950s. Since that time, they have been revised several times. In this chapter, we discuss the homeowners forms drafted by the Insurance Services Office (ISO).[1]

ISO forms are widely used throughout the United States. Some insurers, however, use the homeowners forms designed by the American Association of Insurance Services (AAIS), which is an advisory organization similar to ISO. Other insurers use their own forms, which differ slightly from the ISO forms.

Eligible Dwellings

A homeowners policy on a private dwelling is designed for the owner-occupants of a one-, two-, three-, or four-family dwelling used exclusively for private residential purposes (although certain business occupancies are permitted, such as a home day care business and offices for business or professional purposes). A one-family dwelling may not be occupied by more than one additional family or more than two roomers or boarders. Separate homeowners forms are written for renters and condominium owners.

Overview of Homeowners Policies

The following forms are used in the current ISO homeowners program:

- HO-2 (broad form)
- HO-3 (special form)
- HO-4 (contents broad form)
- HO-5 (comprehensive form)
- HO-6 (unit-owners form)
- HO-8 (modified coverage form)

Homeowners 2 (Broad Form)   Homeowners 2 *is a named-perils policy that insures the dwelling, other structures, and personal property against loss from certain listed perils.* Covered perils include fire, lightning, windstorm, hail, explosion, and other perils. A complete list of covered perils can be found in Exhibit 20.1. HO-2 also covers the additional living expenses or fair rental value in the event a covered loss makes the dwelling uninhabitable.

Homeowners 3 (Special Form)   Homeowners 3 *insures the dwelling and other structures against risk of direct physical loss to property.* This means that all direct physical losses to the dwelling and other structures are covered, except those losses specifically excluded. Losses to the dwelling and other structures are paid on the basis of full replacement cost with no deduction for depreciation if certain conditions (discussed later) are met.

Personal property is covered for the same broad form perils listed in HO-2. Homeowners 3 is a popular and widely used form that is discussed in greater detail later in this chapter.

Homeowners 4 (Contents Broad Form)   Homeowners 4 *is designed for tenants who rent apartments, houses, or rooms.* Homeowners 4 covers the tenant's personal property against loss or damage and also provides personal liability insurance. Personal property is covered for the same named perils listed in Homeowners 2. In addition, 10 percent of the insurance on personal property can be applied to cover any additions or alterations to the building made by the insured. Most renters need a homeowners policy (see Insight 20.1).

Homeowners 5 (Comprehensive Form)   *The HO-5 form insures the dwelling, other structures, and personal property against the risk of direct physical loss to property.* This provision means that all direct physical losses are covered except those losses specifically excluded. Unlike the other homeowners forms that cover personal property only for certain named perils, HO-5 insures personal property for all direct physical losses except those losses specifically excluded.

Homeowners 6 (Unit-Owners Form)   Homeowners 6 *is designed for the owners of condominium units and cooperative apartments.* The condominium association carries insurance on the building and other property owned in common by the owners of the different units. Homeowners 6 covers the personal property of the unit owner for the same named perils listed in Homeowners 2. In addition, there is a minimum of $5000 of insurance on the condominium unit that covers certain property, such as built-in appliances, carpets, additional kitchen cabinets, and wallpaper.

Homeowners 8 (Modified Coverage Form)   Homeowners 8 *is a modified coverage form that covers loss to the dwelling and other structures on the basis of repair cost, which is the amount required to repair or replace damaged property using common construction materials and methods.* Payment is not based on replacement cost. In some states, actual cash value is used to determine the amount payable.

The HO-8 policy is designed for an older home whose replacement cost substantially exceeds its market value. For example, an older home with a replacement cost of $300,000 may have a market value of only $200,000. Insurers will not insure a home for replacement cost when its current market value is substantially lower. Thus, to make homeowners coverage available for older homes and to reduce moral hazard, the HO-8 form has been developed.

The HO-8 policy provides only limited coverage for the theft of personal property. Theft coverage is limited to a maximum of $1000 per occurrence and applies only to losses that occur on the residence premises.

Exhibit 20.1 compares the various homeowners forms, basic coverages, and insured perils.

ANALYSIS OF HOMEOWNERS 3 POLICY (SPECIAL FORM)

In the remainder of this chapter, we examine the major provisions that appear in Section I in the Homeowners 3 policy (special form). As you study this section, you may find it helpful to refer to the Homeowners 3 policy in Appendix A at the end of the text.

EXHIBIT **20.1**
Comparison of ISO Homeowners Coverages

Coverage	HO-2 (broad form)	HO-3 (special form)	HO-4 (contents broad form)
		Section I Coverages	
A. Dwelling	Minimum varies by company.	Minimum varies by company.	Not applicable
B. Other structures	10% of A	10% of A	Not applicable
C. Personal property	50% of A	50% of A	Minimum amount varies.
D. Loss of use	30% of A	30% of A	30% of C
Covered perils	Fire or lightning Windstorm or hail Explosion Riot or civil commotion Aircraft Vehicles Smoke Vandalism or malicious mischief Theft Falling objects Weight of ice, snow, or sleet Accidental discharge or overflow of water or steam Sudden and accidental tearing apart, cracking, burning, or bulging of a steam, hot water, air conditioning, or automatic fire protective sprinkler system, or from within a household appliance Freezing of a plumbing, heating, air conditioning, or automatic fire sprinkler system, or of a household appliance Sudden and accidental damage from artificially generated electrical current Volcanic eruption	Dwelling and other structures are covered against risk of direct physical loss to property. All losses are covered except those losses specifically excluded. Personal property is covered for the same perils as HO-2.	Same perils as HO-2 for personal property
		Section II Coverages[a]	
E. Personal liability	$100,000	$100,000	$100,000
F. Medical payments to others	$1000 per person	$1000 per person	$1000 per person

[a] Minimum amounts can be increased.

Exнiвiт **20.1** (continued)
Comparison of ISO Homeowners Coverages

HO-5 (comprehensive form)	HO-6 (unit-owners form)	HO-8 (modified coverage form)
	Section I Coverages	
Minimum varies by company.	$5000 minimum.	Minimum varies by company.
10% of A	Included in Coverage A	10% of A
50% of A	Minimum amount varies.	50% of A
30% of A	50% of C	10% of A
Dwelling and other structures are covered against risk of direct physical loss to property. All direct physical losses are covered except those losses specifically excluded. Personal property is covered against risk of direct physical loss to property. All direct physical losses are covered except those losses specifically excluded.	Same perils as HO-2 for personal property	Fire or lightning Windstorm or hail Explosion Riot or civil commotion Aircraft Vehicles Smoke Vandalism or malicious mischief Theft (applies only to loss on the residence premises up to a maximum of $1000) Volcanic eruption
	Section II Coverages[a]	
$100,000	$100,000	$100,000
$1000 per person	$1000 per person	$1000 per person

INSIGHT 20.1

Renters Insurance: Shattering a Few Myths

Introduction

Many renters overlook or underestimate their insurance needs because they believe only "homeowners" need insurance. However, just as most of us would not think of owning an automobile without auto insurance, renters need protection for their personal possessions and from liability. Even the smallest apartment can easily contain personal property worth thousands of dollars. And all of us are at risk for liability.

Common Renting Myths

- **MYTH #1** *Insurance is too expensive.* Some renters fail to insure their personal possessions because they believe insurance is too expensive, but renters insurance is typically available for as little as $100 a year.

- **MYTH #2** *My landlord's insurance protects me.* Many renters think they are protected under their landlord's policy. However, the property owner's insurance covers the building itself and seldom a tenant's possessions. Clarify this with your landlord before signing a lease.

- **MYTH #3** *The landlord is liable if someone trips in my apartment and gets injured.* Again, the owner's policy may specifically exclude liability for something that occurs within your rented residence. You could be held liable for injury to another person or damage to another's property if the incident occurred within your residence.

A Look at Premiums

Renters insurance, because you are not insuring a building, is surprisingly inexpensive. Of course, like all property protection policies, the value of the property to be insured and other risk factors are weighed by the insurance company to determine your premium. As with your automobile insurance, your renters deductible is the amount you agree to pay in the event of a loss. For example, if your $2,000 stereo is stolen from your home, and you have a deductible of $250, the insurance company would pay you $1,750, which is $2,000 minus your deductible.

Coverage for All

Renters insurance offers the same general personal property coverage and liability protection as a homeowners policy. Property insurance covers the cost of repairing or replacing personal property that has been damaged, destroyed, or stolen. Your property is covered both within your home and when you are traveling.

You also receive liability protection. If someone suffers an injury or damage to their property because of something you did or did not do, you could be liable. If, for example, your grandmother's oak dresser dents the walls in your apartment's lobby while you are carrying it into the building, you could be held liable. Likewise, if a fire starts in your apartment and spreads throughout the building, and you are deemed at fault, you could be held liable for damage to the entire building.

In addition most renters policies include coverage for additional living expenses (also called 'loss-of-use" coverage) if you are forced by fire or other damage to temporarily live elsewhere.

Alteration for a Better Fit

Most policies limit the amount of reimbursement for theft of valuable items, such as jewelry, furs, silverware, and guns. If you have some particularly valuable items in these categories, you may need to purchase additional coverage called a "floater." These types of policies cover each item individually and are usually quite inexpensive.

Other additions to your renters insurance that add or change the policy's provisions are called endorsements. Some endorsements extend the number of risks insured against, some cover property otherwise excluded, and some increase the amount the insurer will pay for a covered loss.

Also, it is important to note that the standard policy excludes damage from earthquakes and floods, so talk to your insurance agent about coverage for these incidents.

What It's All Worth

If your property does get damaged, destroyed or stolen, the insurance company will use one of two ways to determine its value:

- **Actual Cash Value** This is the replacement cost of the item minus depreciation. For example, a new couch may cost $1,000. If your 5-year-old couch is damaged in a fire, its value might have depreciated 50%. Therefore, the amount of your coverage for it would be $500.
- **Replacement Coverage** This is the cost of replacing an item without deducting for depreciation. So today's cost for a couch similar to the 5-year-old couch damaged by fire would determine the amount of compensation. If the couch still costs $1,000 today, that would be the amount of your coverage.

You can select which type of coverage you would prefer. Having replacement coverage adds only about 10% to 15% to the cost of the premium and may well be worth this slight increase.

INSIGHT 20.1 (continued)

Renters Insurance: Shattering a Few Myths

A Final Note

At least once during a lifetime most people will rent a home. Paying rent instead of a mortgage payment does not make your personal possessions any less valuable.

Should your belongings be damaged or destroyed, or should someone suffer an injury in your home, renters insur-

ance can offer the peace of mind of knowing that you are protected.

SOURCE: Adapted from *Renters Insurance: Shattering a Few Myths*, Independent Insurance Agents of America.

Persons Insured

Certain words and phrases are defined in the policy. One of the most important is the meaning of the term "insured." The following persons are considered insureds under the policy:

- *Named insured and spouse.* The named insured is the person or persons named in the declarations page of the policy. The named insured under the policy is also referred to as "you." Coverage also applies to the spouse of the named insured if she or he is a resident of the same household.
- *Resident relatives.* Resident relatives residing in the named insured's household are insureds under the policy. Thus, children or other relatives residing in the named insured's household are covered under the named insured's policy.
- *Other persons under age 21.* Other persons under age 21 who are in the care of the named insured or resident relative are considered insureds under the policy. Examples are a foster child, a ward of the court, or a foreign exchange student.
- *Full-time student away from home.* The definition of "insured" includes a full-time student away from home who was a resident of the named insured's household before moving out to attend school, provided the student is under age 24 and a relative of the named insured, or is under age 21 and in the care of the named insured or a resident relative.

In addition to the above, the definition of "insured" includes the following persons under the Section II coverages:

- *Any person legally responsible for covered animals or watercraft.* For example, if you leave your dog with a neighbor, and the dog bites someone, the neighbor has liability coverage under your policy. However, coverage does not apply to a person or organization having custody of animals or watercraft for business purposes, such as an operator of a dog kennel or boat marina.
- *With respect to a motor vehicle covered by the policy, coverage applies to persons employed by the named insured or by other insureds as defined above while working for the insured.* For example, if an employee mows your lawn with a riding mower that you own and someone is injured, he or she has liability coverage under your policy.

SECTION I COVERAGES

There are four basic coverages and several additional coverages in Section I of the Homeowners 3 policy:

- Coverage A: Dwelling
- Coverage B: Other structures
- Coverage C: Personal property
- Coverage D: Loss of use
- Additional coverages

Coverage A: Dwelling

Coverage A covers the dwelling on the residence premises as well as any structure attached to the dwelling. Thus, the home and an attached garage or carport would be insured under this section. Materials and supplies intended for construction or repair of the dwelling or other structures are also covered here.

Coverage A specifically excludes land. Thus, if the land on which the dwelling is located is damaged from an insured peril—such as an airplane crash—the land is not covered.

Coverage B: Other Structures

Coverage B insures other structures on the residence premises that are separated from the dwelling by clear space. This coverage includes a detached garage, tool shed, or horse stable. Structures connected to the dwelling only by a fence, utility line, or other similar connection are considered to be other structures.

The amount of insurance under Coverage B is based on the amount of insurance on the dwelling (Coverage A). Under the HO-3 policy, 10 percent of the insurance on the dwelling applies as additional insurance to the other structures. For example, if the home is insured for $300,000, the other structures are covered for $30,000.

Coverage B has several important exclusions. Land damage is excluded. Also, with the exception of a private garage, there is no coverage if the other structure is rented to someone who is not a tenant of the dwelling. For example, assume that Todd owns and occupies a home that has a horse stable on the premises. If Todd rents the horse stable to another person, he would have no coverage if the stable burns in a fire.

In addition, other structures from which a business is conducted are not covered. Thus, if Charles operates an auto repair business in a detached garage, the garage is not covered if it is damaged in a tornado.

Finally, other structures used to store business property are excluded. However, the current form will cover a structure that contains business property owned by the insured or tenant of the dwelling, provided such property does not include gaseous or liquid fuel, other than fuel in a permanently installed fuel tank in a vehicle parked in the structure. For example, if a professional painter stores ladders in a storage shed on his own premises, the shed would be covered as long as it does not contain gaseous or liquid fuel (other than fuel in a parked vehicle).

Coverage C: Personal Property

Personal property owned or used by an insured is covered anywhere in the world. This provision also includes borrowed property. In addition, after a loss and at the named insured's request, the insurance can be extended to cover the personal property of a guest or resident employee while the property is in any residence occupied by an insured. For example, if you invite a guest to dinner in your home and the guest's coat burns in a fire, the loss can be covered under your policy.

The amount of insurance on personal property is equal to 50 percent of the insurance on the dwelling. That amount can be increased. For example, if Eric's home is insured for $300,000, an additional $150,000 of insurance applies to personal property. The full amount of insurance on personal property applies both on and off the premises anywhere in the world. *One exception is that if personal property is usually located at another residence, such as a cabin or vacation home, the off-premises coverage is limited to 10 percent of Coverage C, or $1000, whichever is greater.* For example, assume that Eric has $150,000 of insurance on his personal property. He could take that property on an extended trip to Europe and have coverage up to a maximum of $150,000 while it is off the premises. Assume by contrast that Eric owns a cabin or summer home on a river, and that furniture and fishing gear are normally kept there the entire year. In this case, a maximum of $15,000 (10% × $150,000) would apply to the loss of personal property at that location.

The 10 percent limitation does not apply to personal property that is moved from the residence premises because the residence premises is being repaired or remodeled and is not a fit place in which to live or store property. For example, the 10 percent limitation does not apply to personal property located at a residence temporarily occupied by an insured while the residence premises is undergoing repair or remodeling and is not a fit place in which to live.

The limitation also does not apply to personal property in a newly acquired principal residence for 30 days from the time the named insured begins to move the property there. The amount of insurance under Coverage C applies in full to such personal property during the 30-day period. However, the

EXHIBIT **20.2**
Special Limits of Liability

Type of Property	Amount
1. Money, bank notes, bullion, gold, silver, platinum, coins, medals, stored value cards, and smart cards	$200
2. Securities, valuable papers, manuscripts, personal records, passports, tickets, and stamps	$1500
3. Watercraft of all types	$1500
4. Trailers not used with watercraft of all types	$1500
5. Theft of jewelry, watches, furs, and precious and semiprecious stones	$1500
6. Theft of firearms and related equipment	$2500
7. Theft of silverware, goldware, platinumware, and pewterware	$2500
8. Property on the residence premises used primarily for business purposes	$2500
9. Property away from the residence premises used primarily for business purposes (except adaptable electronic equipment described in 10 and 11 below)	$500
10. Electronic apparatus, while in or upon a motor vehicle, but only if the apparatus is equipped to be operated by power from the motor vehicle's electrical system while still capable of being operated by other power sources	$1500
11. Electronic apparatus used primarily for business *while away from the premises and not in or upon a motor vehicle*. The apparatus must be equipped to be operated by power from the motor vehicle's electrical system while still capable of being operated by other power sources.	$1500

insurer must be notified within 30 days for full protection to continue.

Special Limits of Liability Because of moral hazard and loss-adjustment problems, and a desire by the insurer to limit its liability, certain types of property have maximum dollar limits on the amount paid for any loss (see Exhibit 20.2).

The $200 limit on money includes coin collections. If you have a valuable coin collection, it should be scheduled and insured for a specific amount of insurance. A **schedule** *is a list of covered property with specific amounts of insurance.* A valuable stamp collection should also be insured separately because there is a $1500 limit on stamps.

Coverage on watercraft of all types is limited to $1500, including trailers, furnishings, equipment, and outboard motors. A boat with a value in excess of this limit should be insured separately.

The theft of jewelry and furs is limited to a maximum of $1500. Expensive jewelry and furs should be scheduled and specifically insured. In addition, there is a $2500 limit on the theft of firearms and a $2500 limit on the theft of silverware, goldware, platinumware, and pewterware. Thus, a valuable silverware collection should be specifically insured based on the current value of the collection. Note that the limits on jewelry and furs, guns, silverware, and goldware apply only to the theft peril. The full amount of insurance applies to losses from other covered perils.

Property used primarily for business purposes is limited to $2500 on the premises and $500 away from the premises. However, the $500 limit does not apply to adaptable electronic apparatus.

The homeowners policy provides $1500 of coverage on portable electronic apparatus used in motor vehicles that can also be operated independently from other power sources, such as certain portable television sets, cellular phones, fax machines, and CD players. *The limitation applies to electronic apparatus while in or upon a motor vehicle but only if the apparatus is equipped to be operated by power from the motor vehicle's electrical system while still capable of being operated by other power sources.* The limit applies to electronic equipment used either for personal or business use while in or upon a motor vehicle.

Finally, there is a $1500 limit on electronic apparatus used primarily for business while away from the residence premises and not in or upon a motor vehicle. The apparatus must be equipped to be operated by power from the motor vehicle's electrical system while still capable of being operated by other power sources. For example, a laptop computer with auto adapter used primarily for business purposes is covered up to $1500 if it is stolen while you are on a business trip.

Property Not Covered   Certain types of property are excluded under Coverage C. The following property is not covered.

1. *Articles separately described and specifically insured.* Coverage C does not cover articles separately described and specifically insured under either the homeowners policy or some other policy. The intent here is to avoid duplicate coverage. Thus, if jewelry or furs are specifically insured, Coverage C of the homeowners policy will not contribute toward the loss.

2. *Animals, birds, and fish.* Pets are excluded because they are difficult to value. Specialized coverages can be used to cover high-value animals, such as thoroughbred horses and pedigreed dogs.

3. *Motor vehicles.* Motor vehicles and their accessories and equipment are specifically excluded. Thus, cars, motorcycles, and motorscooters are ex-

cluded under the policy. Likewise, the theft of a car battery or wheel covers from the car would not be covered.

The exclusion also applies to electronic equipment and accessories designed to be operated solely by power from the electrical system of a motor vehicle, but only while the property is in or upon the motor vehicle. Accessories include antennas, tapes, wires, discs, and similar property that can be used with the electronic equipment while in or upon the vehicle. Thus, the theft of stereo tapes, CD discs, and similar property is excluded from coverage. You should remember that the exclusion of electronic equipment and accessories applies only while the property is in or upon the vehicle. A stereo tape or CB radio that is removed from the vehicle and taken into the house would be covered under the homeowners policy.

Finally, motor vehicles not required to be registered for use on public roads that are used solely to service the insured residence or designed to assist the handicapped are exempt from the exclusion. Thus, a garden tractor, riding lawn mower, or electric wheelchair would normally be covered under the policy.

4. *Aircraft and parts.* Aircraft and parts are specifically excluded. However, the policy does cover hobby or model aircraft not used or designed to carry people or cargo.

5. *Hovercraft and parts.* Hovercraft and parts are also excluded. A hovercraft is a self-propelled vehicle that generates a cushion of air on which to move.

6. *Property of roomers, boarders, and other tenants.* Property of roomers and boarders who are not related to an insured is excluded. Thus, if the insured rents a room to a student, the student's property is not covered under the insured's homeowners policy. However, the property of roomers, boarders, and tenants related to an insured is covered.

7. *Property in a regularly rented apartment.* Property in an apartment regularly rented or being held for rental to others by an insured is specifically excluded. However, as discussed later, the homeowners policy provides some coverage for landlord's furnishings in an apartment on the residence premises that is regularly rented or held for rental.

8. *Property rented or held for rental to others off the residence premises.* Property away from the residence premises that is rented to others is specifically excluded. For example, if Jennifer owns a bike rental business, the bicycles are not covered under Jennifer's homeowners policy.

9. *Business records.* The homeowners policy excludes business data stored in books of account, drawings or other paper records, or in computers and related equipment. The overall effect of this exclusion is to eliminate coverage for the expense of reproducing business records.

10. *Credit cards, electronic fund transfer cards, or access devices.* Coverage of personal property does not include credit cards, electronic fund transfer cards, or access devices. There is some coverage for the unauthorized use of such cards under Additional Coverages (discussed later).

11. *Water or steam.* The homeowners policy excludes coverage of water or steam as personal property. Thus, water or steam delivered through a public water main or from the insured's own well is now excluded. Also, water in a swimming pool is not covered either.

Coverage D: Loss of Use

Coverage D provides protection when the residence premises cannot be used because of a covered loss. The amount of additional insurance under this coverage is 30 percent of the amount of insurance on the dwelling (Coverage A). Three benefits are provided: *additional living expense, fair rental value, and prohibited use.*

Additional Living Expense   If a covered loss makes the residence premises not fit to live in, the company pays the additional living expenses that the insured may incur as a result of the loss. **Additional living expense** *is the increase in living expenses actually incurred by the insured to maintain the family's normal standard of living.* For example, assume that Heather's home is damaged by a fire. If she rents a furnished apartment for three months at $800 per month, the additional living expense of $2400 would be covered.

Fair Rental Value   The fair rental value is also paid when part of the premises is rented to others. **Fair rental value** *means the rental value of that part of the residence premises rented to others or held for rental less any expenses that do not continue while the premises are not fit to live in.* For example, Heather may rent a room to a student for a monthly rent of $200. If the home is uninhabitable after a fire, and it takes three months to rebuild, Heather would receive $600 for the loss of rents (less any expenses that do not continue). This payment would be in addition to the payment under the additional living expense coverage described earlier.

Prohibited Use   Loss-of-use coverage also includes prohibited use losses. Even if the covered home is not damaged, a civil authority may prohibit the insured from using the premises because of direct damage to neighboring premises from an insured peril. The additional living expenses and fair rental value can be paid for up to two weeks. For example, Heather may be ordered out of her home by a fire marshal because the house next door is unstable after an explosion occurred. Her additional living expenses and fair rental value loss would be covered for up to two weeks.

Additional Coverages

In addition to basic Coverages A, B, C, and D, the HO-3 policy provides several additional coverages.

Debris Removal   The homeowners policy pays the reasonable expense of removing the debris of covered property damaged by an insured peril. Debris removal also pays the cost of removing volcanic ash or dust from a volcanic eruption that causes a direct loss to a building or property inside a building.

The cost of removing debris is included in the policy limit that applies to the damaged property. However, if the actual damage plus the cost of removal exceed the policy limit, an additional 5 percent of the amount of insurance is available for debris removal. For example, assume that a detached garage is covered for $30,000, and a total loss from a fire occurs. If the entire $30,000 is needed to rebuild the garage, up to an additional $1500 is also available for debris removal.

In addition, the homeowners policy covers the removal of trees owned by the named insured felled by windstorm or hail, or by the weight of ice, snow, or sleet. Coverage also applies to the removal of a neighbor's tree felled by a Coverage C peril. Coverage applies provided the tree (1) damages a covered structure, or (2) blocks a driveway and prevents a motor vehicle required to be registered for road use from entering or leaving the residence premises, or (3) blocks and prevents use of a ramp or access fixture designed to assist a handicapped person to enter and leave the dwelling. The maximum paid is limited to $1000 regardless of the number of fallen trees. No more than $500 of that limit is paid for the removal of any one tree.

Reasonable Repairs The policy pays the reasonable cost of necessary repairs incurred by the insured to protect the property from further damage after a covered loss occurs. For example, a broken picture window may have to be temporarily boarded up immediately after a severe windstorm to protect personal property from further damage.

Trees, Shrubs, and Other Plants The homeowners policy covers trees, shrubs, plants, or lawns on the residence premises against loss from a limited number of perils. *Coverage is provided only for fire, lightning, explosion, riot, civil commotion, aircraft, vehicles not owned or operated by a resident of the premises, vandalism, malicious mischief, or theft.* Note that *windstorm* is not listed. If an expensive tree is blown over in a severe windstorm, the cost of replacing the tree is not covered.

The maximum limit for a loss under this coverage is 5 percent of the insurance that covers the dwelling. However, no more than $500 of that limit can be applied to any single tree, plant, or shrub (but not lawns).

Fire Department Service Charge The insurer will pay up to $500 if the named insured is liable by a contract or agreement for a fire department charge when firefighters from another municipality are called to protect covered property from an insured peril. A deductible does not apply to this coverage.

Property Removal If property is removed from the premises because it is endangered by an insured peril, direct loss from any cause is covered for a maximum of 30 days while the property is removed. Thus, furniture being moved and stored in a public warehouse because of a fire in the home is covered for a direct loss from any cause for a maximum of 30 days. For example, if an earthquake occurred and damaged the furniture stored in a warehouse after the fire, the loss caused by the otherwise excluded earthquake would be covered.

Credit Card, Electronic Fund Transfer Card or Access Device, Forgery, and Counterfeit Money If credit cards are stolen or lost and used in an unauthorized manner, any loss to the insured is covered up to a maximum of $500. Likewise, loss that results from the theft or unauthorized use of an insured's electronic fund transfer card is covered. If a forged or altered check results in a loss to the insured, it is also covered. If the insured accepts counterfeit money in good faith, that loss is covered, too. A deductible does not apply to this coverage.

Loss Assessment The insurer pays up to $1000 for any loss assessment charged against the named insured by a corporation or association of property owners because of the direct loss to property collectively owned by all members. For example, property owners in a subdivision may belong to a homeowners association that collectively owns a clubhouse, swimming pool, tennis courts, fences, and a sign at the entrance to the subdivision. Assume that a tornado completely destroys the clubhouse. If the homeowners association insurance policy does not cover the entire loss, each property owner may be assessed his or her share of the loss. HO-3 will pay up to $1000 the loss assessment charge that otherwise the property owner would have to pay.

Collapse Collapse of a building is covered as an additional coverage. The policy defines collapse as an abrupt falling down or caving in of a building or any part of a building with the result that the building or part of the building cannot be occupied for its intended use.

Collapse of a building (or any part of a building) is covered only if the loss is caused by any of the following:

- Perils insured against in Coverage C
- Hidden decay, unless known to the insured prior to collapse

- Hidden insects or vermin damage, unless known to the insured prior to collapse
- Weight of contents, equipment, animals, or people
- Weight of rain that collects on a roof
- Use of defective materials or methods in construction, remodeling, or renovation if the collapse occurs during the course of construction, remodeling, or renovation

Glass or Safety Glazing Material   The policy covers the breakage of glass or safety glazing material that is part of a covered building, storm door, or storm window. Damage to covered property from the glass or safety glazing material is also covered. For example, if a baseball breaks a storm window, the glass damage is covered. If the shattering of glass causes damage to a lamp near the window, the lamp damage also would be covered.

Landlord's Furnishings   The homeowners policy will pay up to $2500 for loss to the named insured's appliances, carpets, and other household furnishings in each apartment on the residence premises that is regularly rented out or held for rental by an insured. The coverage applies to all losses caused by the perils insured against (Coverage C perils), with the exception of theft. For example, Susan has a furnished apartment on the second floor of her house that is rented to students. The appliances, carpets, and furniture inside the apartment are covered up to $2500.

Ordinance or Law   Many communities have building codes that may increase the cost of repairing or reconstructing a damaged building. For example, a new ordinance may require the use of copper pipes rather than galvanized or plastic pipes when the pipes must be replaced after a loss.

The named insured can apply up to 10 percent of the amount of insurance under Coverage A to cover the increased costs of construction or repair because of some ordinance or law. If higher amounts of insurance are desired, an endorsement can be added to the policy. The coverage provided is additional insurance.

Grave Markers   Grave markers, including mausoleums, are covered for up to $5000 for loss caused by a peril insured against under Coverage C.

Deductible   A deductible of $250 applies to each covered loss. The deductible can be increased to reduce premiums. Increasing the deductible to $500 can reduce premiums by up to 12 percent; a $1000 deductible can reduce premiums by up to 25 percent. The deductible does not apply to a fire department service charge or to losses involving credit cards, ATM cards, forgery, or counterfeit money.

Eighteen states and the District of Columbia have hurricane deductibles. In states that are vulnerable to catastrophes, insurers can use *percentage deductibles* rather than dollar deductibles to limit their exposure to catastrophe losses from natural disasters, such as hurricanes, windstorms, or hail. *Depending on the state and insurer, percentage deductibles for windstorm and hail losses, which may be mandatory in some coastal areas of a state, vary from 1 percent to 15 percent of the limit of insurance on the dwelling.*[2] For example, if a house is insured for $200,000 with a 2 percent windstorm deductible, the first $4000 of loss must be paid by the policyowner. Depending on the state, policyholders may be given a "buy back option," which requires payment of a higher premium to have a traditional dollar deductible.

SECTION I PERILS INSURED AGAINST

In this section, we discuss the various perils, or causes of loss, to covered property.

Dwelling and Other Structures

The dwelling and other structures are insured against "risk of direct physical loss to property." *This means that all direct physical losses are covered except certain losses specifically excluded.* If a loss to the dwelling or other structure is not excluded, the loss is covered under the policy.

Excluded Losses   Certain types of losses to the dwelling and other structures, however, are specifically excluded. They include the following:

1. *Collapse.* Losses involving collapse are specifically excluded, except those collapse losses covered under "additional coverages" discussed earlier.

2. *Freezing.* Freezing of a plumbing, heating, air conditioning, or automatic fire protection sprinkler system, or household appliance is not covered unless the named insured uses reasonable care to maintain heat in the building, or the water supply is shut off and drained.

   However, if the building has an automatic sprinkler system, the insured is required to use reasonable care to continue the water supply and maintain heat in the building for the coverage to apply.

3. *Fences, pavement, patio, and similar structures.* Damage to a fence, pavement, patio, swimming pool, foundation, and similar structures is not covered if the damage is caused by freezing and thawing, or from the pressure or weight of water or ice.

4. *Dwelling under construction.* Theft to a dwelling under construction, or of materials and supplies used in construction, is not covered until the dwelling is both completed and occupied.

5. *Vandalism and malicious mischief.* Damage from vandalism, malicious mischief, or the breakage of glass and safety-glazing materials is not covered if the dwelling is vacant for more than 60 consecutive days immediately before the loss.

6. *Mold, fungus, or dry rot.* Loss to the dwelling or other structures from mold, fungus, or dry rot is excluded. However, an undetected loss—mold, fungus, or dry rot within the walls, ceilings, or beneath the floor caused by the accidental discharge of water or steam from a plumbing, heating, air conditioning, household appliance, or fire sprinkler system—is covered under the policy. In addition, loss from the discharge or overflow of water from a storm drain, water, or sewer pipe off the residence premises is covered as well.

7. *Other exclusions.* The following causes of loss are also excluded:
   - Wear and tear, marring, deterioration
   - Mechanical breakdown, latent defect, inherent vice (tendency of property to decompose)
   - Smog, rust or other corrosion, or dry rot
   - Smoke from agricultural smudging or industrial operations
   - Discharge, seepage, or release or escape of pollutants unless the discharge or release is caused by a Coverage C peril

   - Settling, cracking, shrinking, bulging, or expansion of pavements, patios, foundations, walls, floors, roofs, or ceilings
   - Birds, vermin, rodents, or insects
   - Animals owned or kept by an insured

Personal Property

Personal property (Coverage C) is covered on a named-perils basis. The policy pays for direct physical loss to personal property from the perils discussed in the following section.

Fire or Lightning The homeowners policy covers a direct physical loss to property from fire or lightning. Direct physical loss means that fire or lightning is the proximate cause of the loss. **Proximate cause** *means there is an unbroken chain of events between the occurrence of a covered peril and damage or destruction of the property.* For example, assume a fire starts in the bedroom of your home. Firefighters spray water in the other rooms to keep the fire from spreading, and the water causes considerable damage to your books, furniture, and drapes. The entire loss is covered, including the water damage, because fire is the proximate cause of loss.

What is a fire? The homeowners policy does not define a fire; however, various court decisions have clarified its meaning. Two requirements must be met. *First, there must be combustion or rapid oxidation that causes a flame or at least a glow.* Thus, scorching, heating, and charring that occur without a flame or glow are not covered. For example, a garment accidentally scorched by an iron is not covered because there is no flame or glow.

Second, the fire must be hostile or unfriendly. A hostile fire is outside its normal confines. A friendly fire is intentionally started and is exactly where it is supposed to be. For example, the glow at the end of a lit cigar would be a friendly fire. However, if the burning ashes fell on a couch causing a fire, the fire would be hostile, and the loss would be covered.

A homeowners policy also covers the peril of lightning. For example, the cost of rebuilding a chimney damaged by lightning would be covered, even if no fire occurs.

Windstorm or Hail Windstorm or hail damage is also covered. However, damage to the interior of the building and its contents because of rain, snow, sand, or dust is not covered unless there is an opening in the roof or wall caused by wind or hail that allows the elements to enter. For example, if a window is left open, rain damage to a sofa is not covered under the HO-3 policy. But if the wind or hail should break the window, allowing rain to enter through the opening, the water damage to personal property inside the room would be covered.

An important exclusion applies to boats. Boats and related equipment are covered only while inside a fully enclosed building. For example, if a boat is stored in the driveway of the home and is damaged by a windstorm, the loss is not covered.

Although the homeowners policy covers windstorm and hail damage, damage from floods is specifically excluded. In 2005, Hurricane Katrina caused severe windstorm and flood damage in New Orleans, Louisiana, which led to numerous disputes regarding covered and excluded damage. To clarify the coverage provided by the homeowners policy, the Insurance Information Institute has provided answers to frequently asked questions to assist homeowners who have experienced both windstorm and flood damage (see Insight 20.2).

Explosion Broad coverage is provided for damage caused by an explosion. Any type of explosion loss is covered, such as a furnace explosion that damages personal property.

Riot or Civil Commotion Damage to personal property from a riot or civil commotion is covered. Each state defines the meaning of a riot. It is usually defined as an assembly of three or more persons who commit a lawful or unlawful act in a violent or tumultuous manner, to the terror or disturbance of others. Civil commotion is a large or sustained riot that involves an uprising of the citizens.

Aircraft Aircraft damage, including damage from self-propelled missiles and spacecraft, is covered. For example, if a commercial jet crashes into your residence, damage to your personal property is covered. Likewise, if a self-propelled missile from a nearby military base goes astray, the property is covered against loss.

Vehicles Property damage from vehicles is covered. For example, if your suitcase, clothes, and camera

are damaged in an auto accident, the loss is covered. Likewise, if you carelessly back out of the garage and run over your bicycle, the loss is covered.

Smoke Sudden and accidental damage from smoke is covered, including emissions of smoke or fumes from a furnace or related equipment. For example, if the fireplace malfunctions and smoke pours into the family room, any smoke damage to the furniture, rugs, or drapes is covered. However, smoke damage from agricultural smudging or industrial operations is specifically excluded.

Vandalism or Malicious Mischief If someone intentionally damages your personal property, the loss is covered.

Theft Theft losses are covered, including the attempted theft and the loss of property when it is likely that the property has been stolen.

Although coverage of theft is fairly broad, there are several exclusions. They include the following:

1. *Theft by an insured is excluded.* For example, if Danielle, age 16, steals $100 from her mother's purse before running away from home, the theft is not covered.
2. *Theft in or to a dwelling under construction,* or of materials and supplies used in the construction of a dwelling, is not covered until the dwelling is completed and occupied.
3. *Theft from any part of the premises rented to someone other than an insured is not covered.* For example, if the insured rents a room to a student, the theft of a radio owned by the insured and located inside the room would not be covered.

Several important exclusions also apply when the theft occurs away from the residence premises. They include the following:

1. *Temporary residence.* If property is located at any other residence owned, rented to, or occupied by an insured, the loss is not covered unless an insured is temporarily residing there. For example, Brian owns a cabin on the river. Theft of property inside the cabin is not covered unless Brian is temporarily residing there. He is not required to be physically present in the residence at the time of loss, but he must be temporarily

INSIGHT 20.2

Hurricane Katrina—Windstorm and Flood Damage Answers to Frequently Asked Questions

To assist property owners who experienced both windstorm and flood losses from Hurricane Katrina and other hurricanes, the Insurance Information Institute has provided clarifying information on the coverage provided by the homeowners policy. The questions and answers below deal specifically with windstorm and flood losses:

Q: Are losses from flood covered under homeowners, renters and business insurance policies?
A: In general, homeowners insurance policies do not cover losses in the event of a flood. Flood insurance for homeowners, renters, and businesses is readily available through the Federal Emergency Management Agency's (FEMA) National Flood Insurance Program (NFIP). It is sold via the more than 80 participating insurance companies that write and service policies through a special arrangement with the Federal Insurance Mitigation Association (FIMA), as well as through thousands of insurance agents nationwide.

Q: If my home was damaged or destroyed by one of the hurricanes, will my homeowners insurance company pay to have it rebuilt?
A: The typical homeowners policy covers damage due to wind, wind-driven rain and fire (including arson), theft (including looting), vandalism, and damage to your home caused by fallen trees. So if your home has been damaged or destroyed by windstorm damage or by any of these named perils, your homeowners insurance company will pay to have your home repaired or rebuilt up to the limits of your policy. Most homeowners policies also cover damage to other structures on the premises, such as a garage or a tool shed.

You are covered for flood if you purchased flood insurance from the federal government's National Flood Insurance Program, a division of the Federal Emergency Management

Agency (FEMA). The coverage has been readily available at affordable prices from the federal government since 1968.

Flood losses have never been covered under any homeowners insurance policy.

Q: Does my homeowners insurance provide any coverage for water damage from a hurricane?
A: Rain entering through wind-damaged windows, doors, or a hole in a wall or the roof, resulting in standing water or puddles, is considered windstorm—rather than flood—damage and is covered by your homeowners policy. The NFIP flood insurance policy only covers damage caused by the general condition of flooding typically caused by storm surge, wave wash, tidal waves, or the overflow of any body of water over normally dry land areas. Buildings that sustain this type of damage usually have a watermark, showing how high the water rose before it subsided.

Q: How will insurers distinguish between wind and flood damage when settling the claim?
A: Generally speaking, wind damage is covered under a homeowners insurance policy, and flood damage is covered under a flood insurance policy issued by the National Flood Insurance Program (NFIP). It is not unusual for flooding to accompany a hurricane. The insurance industry has many years of experience settling claims with different causes of loss. Each claim will be evaluated on a case-by-case basis. Seasoned insurance adjusters will utilize NFIP guidelines in apportioning losses between a flood insurance policy and a homeowners insurance policy.

Source: Excerpted from Hurricane Insurance Information Center, "Hurricane FAQs," Insurance Information Institute, 2005.

---

living or residing there. For example, if he is fishing at the river when the theft occurs, the loss would be covered.

In addition, *theft of personal property of an insured student while at a residence away from home is covered if the student has been there any time during the 60 days immediately preceding the loss*. For example, assume you are attending

college and are temporarily living away from home. If your television set is stolen from your college residence, the loss is covered by your parent's HO-3 policy if you have been there any time during the 60-day period preceding the loss.

2. *Watercraft.* Theft of a boat, its furnishings, equipment, and outboard motor is excluded if the theft occurs away from the premises.

3. *Trailers and campers.* Theft of trailers or campers away from the premises is not covered. Trailers and campers can be covered under the personal auto policy, which is discussed in Chapter 22.

Falling Objects   Damage to personal property from falling objects is covered. However, loss to property inside the building is not covered unless the roof or outside wall of the building is first damaged by the falling object. For example, if a mirror on a stand falls and breaks, the loss is not covered. But if the mirror falls and breaks because the exterior of the dwelling is first damaged by a falling tree, the loss would be covered.

Weight of Ice, Snow, or Sleet   Damage to indoor personal property resulting from the weight of ice, snow, or sleet is covered. For example, if the weight of snow causes the roof to sag, any damage to the personal property inside the dwelling would be covered.

Accidental Discharge or Overflow of Water or Steam
If loss results from an accidental discharge or overflow of water or steam from a plumbing, heating, air conditioning, or automatic fire protective sprinkler system, or from a household appliance, the property damage is covered. For example, if an automatic dishwasher malfunctions and floods the kitchen, water damage to personal property, such as an area rug, would be covered. However, the cost of repairing the system or appliance from which the water or steam escapes is not covered.

Sudden and Accidental Tearing Apart, Cracking, Burning, or Bulging of a Steam, Hot Water, Air Conditioning, or Automatic Fire Protective Sprinkler System, or Appliance for Heating Water   If any of these perils cause damage to personal property, the loss is covered. For example, damage to personal property from a hot water heater that suddenly cracks is covered.

Freezing of a Plumbing, Heating, Air Conditioning, or Automatic Fire Protective Sprinkler System, or Household Appliance   Freezing is not covered unless the insured used reasonable care to maintain heat in the building, or shuts off the water supply and drains the system.

However, if there is an automatic sprinkler system in the building, the insured must use reasonable care to continue the water supply and maintain heat for coverage to apply.

Sudden and Accidental Damage from an Artificially Generated Electrical Current   For example, an electrical power surge that causes an electric clothes dryer to burn out would be covered. However, loss to tubes, transistors, or electronic components that are part of appliances, computers, or home entertainment units is specifically excluded. Thus, a television picture tube that burns out is not covered.

Volcanic Eruption   Loss resulting from a volcanic eruption is also covered. However, losses caused by earthquakes, land shock waves, or tremors are excluded.

SECTION I EXCLUSIONS

In addition to the specific exclusions previously discussed, several general exclusions appear in the policy.

Ordinance or Law

With the exception of the ordinance or law coverage described earlier under the additional coverages section, and glass replacement as required by law, the policy excludes loss due to any ordinance or law. However, as we noted earlier, if the amount of insurance provided under the additional coverages section is inadequate, higher amounts can be obtained by an endorsement to the policy.

Earth Movement

Property damage from earth movement is excluded. This includes damage from an earthquake, shock waves from a volcanic eruption, landslide, mudslide or mudflow, subsidence or sinkholes, or earth sinking or shifting. However, an ensuing loss caused by fire or explosion is covered. An earthquake endorsement can be added to the policy.

Water Damage

Property damage from certain water losses is specifically excluded. The following types of water damage losses are not covered:

- Floods, surface water, waves, tidal water, and overflow or spray from a body of water
- Water or water-borne material that backs up through sewers or drains or overflows from a sump pump
- Water or water-borne material below the surface of the ground that exerts pressure on or seeps through a building, sidewalk, driveway, foundation, swimming pool, or other structure

Power Failure

There is no coverage for loss caused by the failure of power or other utility service if the failure takes place off the residence premises. For example, if the contents of a freezer thaw and spoil because of the failure of an electrical power plant 15 miles away, the loss is not covered. However, if the power failure is caused by an insured peril on the residence premises, any resulting loss is covered. Thus, if lightning strikes the home and power is interrupted on the premises, the spoilage of food in a freezer is covered.

Neglect

If the insured neglects to use all reasonable means to save and preserve the property at or after the time of loss, the loss is not covered. For example, a broken picture window may have to be boarded up after a windstorm to protect personal property in the room from wind or rain damage.

War

Property damage from war is specifically excluded. War is excluded in nearly all property insurance contracts.

Nuclear Hazard

Nuclear hazard losses are excluded, including nuclear reaction, radiation, or radioactive contamination. For example, if a radiation leak from a nuclear power plant contaminates your property, the loss is not covered.

Intentional Loss

An intentional loss is excluded. An intentional loss is a loss arising out of any act the insured commits or conspires to commit with the intent to cause a loss. For example, if the insured arranges to have his home burned to collect the claim payment, the loss is not covered.

Governmental Action

Loss due to governmental action is also excluded. Governmental action refers to the destruction, confiscation, or seizure of property by any governmental or public authority. For example, if the house and cash of a drug dealer are seized by drug enforcement officials, the loss would not be covered. However, the exclusion does not apply to acts ordered by a government or public authority to prevent the spread of a fire.

Weather Conditions

This exclusion applies only to weather conditions that contribute to a loss that would otherwise be excluded. For example, landslide damage caused by excessive rain and heavy winds is excluded under this provision. Likewise, flooding or earth movement caused by excessive rain is excluded. However, damage to a house caused solely by windstorm or hail would be covered.

Acts or Decisions

This exclusion applies to losses that result from the failure to act by any person, group, organization, or government body. For example, if a governmental unit fails to develop a plan to control flood losses, property damage from a flood that resulted from failure to develop a plan would not be covered.

Faulty, Inadequate, or Defective Planning and Design

Also excluded are losses that result from faulty or defective planning, zoning, design, workmanship, materials, or maintenance. For example, a completed house that pulls away from the foundation because of faulty design would not be covered.

SECTION I CONDITIONS

Section I in the homeowners policy contains numerous conditions. The most important are discussed here.

Insurable Interest and Limit of Liability

If more than one party has an insurable interest in the property, the insurer's liability for any one loss is limited to each insured's insurable interest at the time of loss but not to exceed the maximum amount of insurance.

Duties After a Loss

The insured must perform certain duties after a loss occurs. The insurer has the right to deny coverage for a loss if the insured does not comply with his or her duties and such failure is prejudicial to the insurer. The following duties are required:

- *Give prompt notice.* The insured must give prompt notice to the insurer or an agent of the insurer. In case of a theft, the police must be notified as well. The card company must also be notified in case of loss or theft of a credit or ATM card.
- *Protect the property.* The insured must protect the property from further damage, make reasonable and necessary repairs to protect the property, and keep an accurate record of the repair expenses.
- *Prepare an inventory of damaged personal property.* The inventory must show in detail the quantity, description, actual cash value, and the amount of loss. Taking an inventory of your property before a loss occurs is highly advisable.
- *Exhibit the damaged property.* The insured may be required to show the damaged property to the insurer as often as is reasonably required. The insured may also be required to submit to questions under oath without any other insured being present and sign a sworn statement.
- *File a proof of loss within 60 days after the insurer's request.* The proof of loss must include

the time and cause of loss, interest of the insured and all others in the property, all liens on the property, other insurance covering the loss, and other relevant information.

Loss Settlement

This section of the homeowners policy deals with the payment of losses. You should know how losses are paid under a homeowners policy.

Personal Property   Covered losses to personal property are paid on the basis of *actual cash value* at the time of loss but not to exceed the amount necessary to repair or replace the property. Losses to carpets, domestic appliances, awnings, and outdoor antennas and outdoor equipment are also paid on an actual cash value basis. In addition, losses to structures that are not buildings, as well as grave markers, are paid on an actual cash value basis.

Personal property can be insured for replacement cost by adding a replacement cost endorsement to the policy. Under this endorsement, there is no deduction for depreciation in determining the amount paid for a loss to personal property. You should consider insuring your personal property on the basis of replacement cost. Otherwise, if a loss occurs, you could pay a substantial amount of money out of pocket (see Insight 20.3).

Dwelling and Other Structures   Covered losses to the dwelling and other structures are paid on the basis of replacement cost with no deduction for depreciation. Replacement cost insurance on the dwelling is one of the most valuable features in a homeowners policy. If the amount of insurance carried is equal to at least 80 percent of the replacement cost of the damaged building at the time of loss, full replacement cost is paid up to the limits of the policy with no deduction for depreciation. **Replacement cost** *is the amount necessary to repair or replace the dwelling with material of like kind and quality at current prices.* For example, assume that a home has a current replacement value of $250,000 and is insured for $200,000. If the home is damaged by a tornado, and repairs cost $50,000, the full $50,000 is paid with no deduction for depreciation. If the home is totally destroyed, however, the maximum amount paid for the damage to

INSIGHT 20.3

The Big Gap Between Replacement Cost and Actual Cash Value Can Empty Your Wallet

If you own personal property, you should consider the big gap between replacement cost and actual cash value. *You could pay a large amount out of pocket because of depreciation if the loss payment is based on actual cash value.* The table below, based on the depreciation schedule of a large property and casualty insurer, shows that the insured would receive $7790 (less the deductible) based on *replacement cost* compared with only $3967 based on *actual cash value.* Actual cash value is replacement cost less depreciation.

Item	Age	Replacement Cost	Depreciation	Actual Cash Value
Television set	5 years	$ 900	$ 450	$ 450
Sofa	4 years	1500	600	900
Draperies	2 years	2000	400	1600
5 women's dresses	4 years	500	400	100
3 pairs of men's shoes	2 years	200	133	67
3 end tables	15 years	1200	900	300
Refrigerator	10 years	800	560	240
Area rug	New	200	0	200
Cosmetics	6 months	200	180	20
Kitchen dishes	4 years	250	200	50
30 cans food	New	40	0	40
Total		$7790	$3823	$3967

NOTE: The above hypothetical losses show the effect of depreciation, which is based on age and condition of the property; the older the item, the greater is the amount of depreciation.

the building is the face amount of the policy—in this case, $200,000.

A different set of rules applies if the amount of insurance is less than 80 percent of the replacement cost at the time of loss. Stated simply, if the insurance carried is less than 80 percent of the replacement cost, the insured receives the *larger* of the following two amounts:

(1) Actual cash value of that part of the building damaged

or

(2) $\dfrac{\text{Amount of insurance carried}}{80\% \times \text{Replacement cost}} \times \text{Loss}$

For example, assume that a dwelling has a replacement cost of $250,000, but is insured for only

$150,000. The roof of the house is 10 years old and has a useful life of 20 years, so it is 50 percent depreciated. Assume that the roof is severely damaged by a tornado, and the replacement cost of a new roof is $20,000. Ignoring the deductible, the insured receives the larger of the following two amounts:

(1) Actual cash value = $20,000 − $10,000

   = $10,000

(2) $\dfrac{\$150,000}{80\% \times \$250,000} \times \$20,000 = \$15,000$

The insured receives $15,000 for the loss. The entire loss would have been paid if the insured had carried at least $200,000 of insurance.

With the exception of losses that are both less than 5 percent of the amount of insurance and less than $2500, the insured must actually repair or replace the property to receive full replacement cost. Otherwise, the loss is paid on the basis of actual cash value. However, the insured can submit a claim for the actual cash value and then collect an additional amount when the actual repair or replacement is completed, provided the additional claim is made within 180 days after the loss.

Extended and Guaranteed Replacement Cost A home may be damaged beyond repair in a major catastrophe, such as a hurricane or tornado. Also, there may be a shortage of lumber and other building materials after a catastrophe occurs, which can substantially increase the cost of rebuilding. Insuring your home for only 80 percent of replacement cost will not provide complete protection. Some insurers make available an **extended replacement cost endorsement,** which pays up to an extra 20 percent or more above the policy limits, depending on the insurer. The insured agrees to insure the dwelling for full replacement cost and must also notify the insurer if alterations or remodeling increase the value of the dwelling.

A few insurers offer a **guaranteed replacement cost** policy. The insured agrees to insure the home to 100 percent of its estimated replacement cost rather than 80 percent. *If a total loss occurs, the insurer agrees to replace the home exactly as it was before the loss even if the replacement cost exceeds the amount of insurance stated in the policy.* For example, if the home is insured for $400,000 and it costs $500,000 to restore the home to its previous condition, the insurer will pay $500,000. Because of underappraising the value of the home by some insurance agents, price gouging by some contractors because of a shortage of building materials, inflation, and fraud in some cases, guaranteed replacement cost policies are rapidly disappearing.

Loss to a Pair or Set

In the event of **loss to a pair or set,** *the insurer can elect either to repair or replace any part of the pair or set or to pay the difference between the actual cash value of the property before and after the loss.* For example, assume that Kathy has a set of three matching wall decorations hanging on the wall in her living room, and one of the decorations is badly damaged in a fire. The insurer can elect either to replace or repair the damaged wall decoration or to pay the difference in the actual cash value of the entire set before and after the loss.

Appraisal Clause

The **appraisal clause** *is used when the insured and insurer agree that the loss is covered, but the amount of the loss is in dispute.* Either party can demand that the dispute be resolved by an appraisal. Each party selects a competent and impartial appraiser. The appraisers then select an umpire. If they cannot agree on an umpire after 15 days, a judge in a court of record will appoint one. If the appraisers fail to agree on the amount of the loss, only their differences are submitted to the umpire. An agreement in writing by any two of the three is then binding on both parties. Each party pays the fee of his or her appraiser, and the umpire's fee is shared equally by both parties.

Other Insurance and Service Agreement

If other insurance covers a Section I loss, the insurer will pay only the proportion of the loss that its limit of liability bears to the total amount of insurance covering the loss. The pro rata liability clause was explained in Chapter 10.

The pro rata clause does not apply to articles of personal property that are separately described and specifically insured by other insurance. In such cases, as stated in Coverage C (property not covered), personal property that is separately described and specifically insured is not covered by the homeowners policy.

Finally, many homeowners purchase home warranty contracts or appliance service agreements that guarantee the repair or replacement of defective parts if certain conditions are met. The homeowners policy is excess over any amount payable under a home warranty or service agreement.

Suit Against the Insurer

No legal action can be brought against the insurer unless all policy provisions have been complied with, and legal action is started within two years after the loss occurs.

Insurer's Option

After giving written notice to the insured, the insurer has the right to repair or replace any part of the damaged property with like property. For example, assume that a television set is stolen. By giving written notice, the insurer can replace the stolen TV with a similar item rather than paying cash. Insurers often can purchase television sets, stereos, and other types of property from wholesale distributors at a lower cost than the insured would pay in the retail market. By exercising the replacement option, an insurer can meet its contractual obligation for a covered loss, but its loss settlement costs can be reduced.

Loss Payment

The insurer is required to make a loss payment directly to the named insured unless some other person is named in the policy or is legally entitled to receive the loss payment. In many homeowners contracts, a mortgagee (lender) is named in the policy, which allows the mortgagee to receive a loss payment to the extent of its insurable interest. A legal representative of the insured is also entitled to receive a loss payment. For example, if Angela dies before receiving payment for a covered loss, the loss payment is made to the executor of her estate.

Abandonment of Property

The insurer is not obligated to accept any property abandoned by the insured after a loss occurs. The insurer has the option of paying for the damaged property in full and then taking the damaged property as salvage, or the insurer can elect to have the property repaired. However, the decision to exercise these options belongs to the insurer. For example, assume your personal property is insured for $50,000. A fire occurs, and the salvage value of the property after the loss is $10,000. The insurer can pay you $40,000, or it can take the damaged property and pay you $50,000. However, you cannot abandon the property to the insurer and demand payment of $50,000.

Mortgage Clause

The **mortgage clause** is designed to protect the mortgagee's insurable interest. The mortgagee usually is a savings and loan institution, commercial bank, or other lending institution that makes a loan to the mortgagor (home buyer) so that the property can be purchased. The property serves as collateral for the mortgage loan. If the property is damaged or destroyed, the collateral securing the loan is impaired, and the loan might not be repaid.

The mortgagee's insurable interest in the property can be protected by the mortgage clause that is part of the homeowner policy. *Under this provision, if the mortgagee is named in the policy, the mortgagee is entitled to receive a loss payment from the insurer to the extent of its interest, regardless of any policy violation by the insured.* For example, if Troy intentionally sets fire to his house, the loss is not covered because the fire is intentional. However, the mortgagee's insurable interest in the property is still protected. The loss payment would be paid to the mortgagee to the extent of the mortgagee's interest. The mortgagee is also entitled to a 10-day cancellation notice if the insurer decides to cancel.

In exchange for the guarantee of payment, the mortgage clause imposes certain obligations on the mortgagee. They are as follows:

- To notify the insurer of any change in ownership, occupancy, or substantial change in risk of which the mortgagee is aware
- To pay any premium due if the insured neglects to pay the premium
- To provide a proof-of-loss statement if the insured fails to do so
- To give subrogation rights to the insurer in those cases where the insurer denies liability to the insured but must make a loss payment to the mortgagee

Policy Period

The policy period begins and ends at 12:01 A.M. standard time on the dates specified in the policy period. Only losses that occur during the policy period are covered.

Concealment or Fraud

The policy states that no insured is covered if any insured intentionally conceals or misrepresents any material fact, engages in fraudulent conduct, or makes false statements relating to the insurance. The provision applies both before and after a loss.

SECTION I AND II CONDITIONS

The homeowners policy contains several common conditions that apply to both Sections I and II. They are summarized as follows:

- *Liberalization Clause.* If the insurer broadens the coverage it offers without charging a higher premium within 60 days before inception of the policy or during the policy period, the broadened coverage applies immediately to the present policy. However, the liberalization clause does not apply to changes that are implemented with a general program revision that includes both a broadening and restriction of coverage.
- *Waiver or Change of Policy Provisions.* A waiver or change in any policy provision must be approved in writing by the insurer to be valid.
- *Cancellation.* The insured can cancel at any time by returning the policy or by notifying the insurer in writing when the cancellation is to become effective.

  The insurer can cancel under the following conditions:

  1. The premium is not paid. The insured must be given at least 10 days' written notice of cancellation.
  2. A new policy can be canceled for any reason if it has been in force for less than 60 days and is not a renewal policy. The insured must be given at least 10 days' notice of cancellation.
  3. If the policy has been in force for 60 or more days or is a renewal policy, the insurer can cancel if there is a material misrepresentation of fact that would have caused the insurer not to issue the policy, or if the risk has increased substantially after the policy was issued. The insured must be given at least 30 days' notice of cancellation.
  4. If the policy is written for a period longer than one year, it can be canceled for any reason on the anniversary date by giving the insured at least 30 days' notice of cancellation.

     State law may specify the conditions under which insurers can cancel or non-renew a policy. Whenever there is a conflict between state law and any policy provision, state law has priority over the policy provision. This is handled by an amendatory endorsement to the policy that makes the policy conform to state law.

- *Nonrenewal of the Policy.* The insurer has the right not to renew the policy when it expires. The insured must be given at least 30 days' notice before the expiration date if the policy is not renewed.
- *Assignment of the Policy.* The homeowners policy cannot be assigned to another party without the insurer's written consent. Thus, if Richard sells his home to Michelle, he cannot validly assign his homeowners policy to Michelle unless the insurer agrees to the assignment. As a practical matter, the new owner usually buys his or her own policy. The homeowners policy is a personal contract between the insured and insurer. The assignment provision allows the insurer to select its own insureds and provides some protection against moral hazard and adverse selection. However, after a loss occurs, the loss payment can be freely assigned to another party without the insurer's consent. The party who receives the payment does not become a new insured, and the risk to the insurer is not increased.
- *Subrogation.* A general principle is that an insured cannot unilaterally waive the insurer's right of subrogation against a third party who caused the loss without jeopardizing coverage under the policy. However, the homeowners policy contains an important exception to this general principle. The subrogation clause allows the insured to waive in writing, before a loss occurs, all rights of recovery against any person. For example, assume that Jerome lives in one unit of a duplex and rents out the other unit. The lease may state that Jerome as landlord waives his right of recovery against the tenant if the tenant should negligently cause a loss (such as a fire). The waiver would protect the tenant against a subrogation recovery by Jerome's insurer if the tenant should cause a loss. To be effective, however, the waiver must be in writing before a loss occurs.

  If the right of recovery is not waived, the insurer may require the insured to assign all rights of recovery against a third party to the extent of the loss payment. This provision allows the insurer to exercise its subrogation rights against a negligent third party who caused the loss.

■ *Death of Named Insured or Spouse.* If the named insured or resident spouse dies, coverage is extended to the legal representative of the

deceased but only with respect to the premises and property of the deceased. Coverage also continues for resident relatives who are insured under the policy at the time of the named insured or spouse's death.

CASE APPLICATION

Jack and Jane are married and own a home insured for $150,000 under an unendorsed HO-3 policy. The replacement cost of the home is $250,000. Personal property is insured for $75,000. Jane has jewelry valued at $10,000. Jack has a coin collection valued at $15,000 and a motorboat valued at $20,000.

a. Assume you are a financial planner who is asked to evaluate the couple's HO-3 policy. Based on the above facts, do you believe that their present coverages are adequate? If not, make several recommendations for improving the coverage.

b. A fire damaged one bedroom. The actual cash value of the loss is $10,000. The cost of repairs is $16,000. How much will the insurer pay for the loss?

c. A burglar broke into the home and stole a new television set, jewelry, and several paintings. The actual

cash value of the stolen property is $4000. The cost of replacing the property is $9000. In addition, the coin collection was taken. Indicate the extent, if any, to which an unendorsed HO-3 policy will cover the preceding losses.

d. Assume that Jack and Jane have a disagreement with their insurer concerning the value of the above losses. How would the dispute be resolved under their HO-3 policy?

e. Assume that Jane operates an accounting business from her home. Her home business office contains a computer used solely for business, office furniture, file cabinets, and other business personal property. Explain whether her HO-3 policy would cover business personal property used in a home business.

SUMMARY

■ The homeowners policy can be used to cover the dwelling, other structures, personal property, additional living expenses, personal liability claims, and medical payments to others.

■ Section I provides coverage on the dwelling, other structures, personal property, loss-of-use benefits, and additional coverages. Section II provides personal liability insurance to the insured and also covers the medical expenses of others who may be injured while on the insured premises or by some act of the insured or by an animal owned by the insured.

■ The HO-2 policy (broad form) covers the dwelling, other structures, and personal property against loss on a named-perils basis.

■ The HO-3 policy (special form) covers the dwelling and other structures against risk of direct physical loss to the described property. All losses to the dwelling and other structures are covered except those losses specifi-

cally excluded. Personal property is covered on a named-perils basis.

■ The HO-4 policy (contents broad form) is designed for renters. HO-4 covers the personal property of tenants on a named-perils basis and also provides personal liability insurance.

■ The HO-5 policy (comprehensive form) insures the dwelling, other structures, and personal property against the risk of direct physical loss to property. All direct physical losses are covered except those losses specifically excluded.

■ The HO-6 policy (unit-owners form) is designed for condominium owners. HO-6 covers the personal property of the insured on a named-perils basis. There is also a minimum of $5000 of insurance on the condominium unit that covers certain property, such as alterations, fixtures, and improvements.

■ The HO-8 policy (modified coverage form) is designed for older homes. Losses to the dwelling and other structures are paid on the basis of repair cost, which is the amount required to repair or replace the property using common construction materials and methods. Losses are not paid based on replacement cost.

- The conditions section imposes certain duties on the insured after a loss to covered property occurs. The insured must give immediate notice of the loss; the property must be protected from further damage; the insured must prepare an inventory of the damaged personal property and may be required to show the damaged property to the insurer as often as is reasonably required; and proof of loss must be filed within 60 days after the insurer's request.

- The replacement cost provision is one of the most valuable features of the homeowners policy. Losses to the dwelling and other structures are paid on the basis of replacement cost if the insured carries insurance at least equal to 80 percent of the replacement cost at the time of loss. Losses to personal property are paid on the basis of actual cash value. However, an endorsement can be added that covers personal property on a replacement cost basis.

- The mortgage clause provides protection to the mortgagee. The mortgagee is entitled to receive a loss payment from the insurer regardless of any policy violation by the insured.

KEY CONCEPTS AND TERMS

Additional living expense
Appraisal clause
Extended replacement cost endorsement
Fair rental value
Guaranteed replacement cost
Homeowners 2 (broad form)
Homeowners 3 (special form)
Homeowners 4 (contents broad form)
Homeowners 5 (comprehensive form)
Homeowners 6 (unit-owners form)
Homeowners 8 (modified coverage form)
Liberalization clause
Loss to a pair or set
Mortgage clause
Proximate cause
Replacement cost
Schedule

REVIEW QUESTIONS

1. Identify the basic types of homeowners policies that are used today.

2. Identify the persons who are insured under a homeowners policy.

3. The Section I property coverages provide different types of coverages to an insured. For each of the following coverages, briefly describe the type of coverage provided, and give an example of a loss that would be covered.
   a. Coverage A—Dwelling
   b. Coverage B—Other Structures
   c. Coverage C—Personal Property
   d. Coverage D—Loss of Use
   e. Additional Coverages

4. a. Briefly describe the special limits of liability that apply to certain types of personal property.
   b. Why are these special limits used?

5. a. Coverage A and Coverage B under a Homeowners 3 policy insure the dwelling and other structures against "risk of direct physical loss." Explain the meaning of this phase.
   b. Coverage C under a Homeowners 3 policy covers personal property on a named-perils basis. List the various perils that are covered.

6. List the major exclusions that are found in Section I of the Homeowners 3 policy.

7. Briefly describe the duties imposed on the insured under a homeowners policy after a property loss occurs.

8. The Section I Conditions section of the Homeowners 3 policy deals with the payment of losses to an insured.
   a. How is the amount paid for a covered loss to personal property determined?
   b. How is the amount paid for a covered loss to the dwelling and other structures determined?

9. a. Describe the extended replacement cost endorsement that can be added to a Homeowners 3 policy.
   b. What is a guaranteed replacement cost policy?

10. A home buyer may obtain a mortgage loan to purchase a house. Explain briefly how the mortgage clause protects the insurable interest of the lending institution (mortgagee).

APPLICATION QUESTIONS

1. Heather owns a home with a replacement cost of $400,000 that is insured under a Homeowners 3 policy for $280,000. The roof was badly damaged in a severe windstorm, and it will cost $20,000 to repair the roof. The actual cash value of the loss is $10,000. Ignoring any deductible, how much will Heather collect from the insurer?

2. Michelle purchased a Homeowners 3 policy with no special endorsements to cover her home and personal property. A fire occurred and destroyed a wide screen television. Heather paid $4000 for the TV new, and it was 25 percent depreciated when the fire occurred. The replacement cost of a similar television is $5000. Ignoring any deductible, how much will Michelle collect for the loss?

3. Tom and Cindy Jones insured their home and personal property under an unendorsed Homeowners 3 policy. The home has a current replacement cost of $300,000. The policy contains the following limits:

Coverage A	$240,000
Coverage B	24,000
Coverage C	120,000
Coverage D	72,000

The home was badly damaged in a fire, and the family was forced to live in a motel for 60 days while their home was being rebuilt. Undamaged personal property was stored in a rental unit during the period of reconstruction. What dollar amount, if any, is payable under their Homeowners 3 policy for the following (ignore any deductible)?

a. Three bedrooms were totally destroyed in the fire. The replacement cost of restoring the bedrooms is $80,000. The actual cash value of the loss is $50,000.
b. Monthly mortgage payment of $1500 on their home
c. Rental of motel room at $100 daily for 60 days
d. Meals eaten in the motel restaurant for 60 days at an average cost of $60 daily (food costs at home average $20 daily)
e. Rent for storing undamaged furniture in a rental unit while the home is being rebuilt, $200 monthly

4. Megan has her home and personal property insured under an unendorsed Homeowners 3 (special form)

policy. Indicate whether each of the following losses is covered. If the loss is not covered, explain why it is not covered.

a. Megan carelessly spills a can of paint while painting a bedroom. A wall-to-wall carpet that is part of the bedroom is badly damaged and must be replaced.
b. Water backs up from a clogged drainpipe, floods the basement, and damages some books stored in a box.
c. Megan's house is totally destroyed in a tornado. Her valuable Doberman Pinscher dog is killed in the tornado.
d. During a freeze, fire pots from a nearby orange grove emit dense smoke that settles on Megan's freshly painted house.
e. Megan is on vacation, and a thief breaks into her hotel and steals a suitcase containing jewelry, money, clothes, and an airline ticket.
f. Megan's son is playing baseball in the yard. A line drive shatters the living room window.
g. A garbage truck accidentally backs into the garage door and shatters it.
h. Defective wiring causes a fire in the attic. Damage to the house is extensive. Megan is forced to move into a furnished apartment for three months while the house is being rebuilt.
i. Megan's son, age 20, is attending college but is home for Christmas. A stereo set is stolen from his dormitory room during his absence.
j. During the winter, heavy snow damages part of the front lawn, and the sod must be replaced.
k. During a windstorm, an elm tree in Megan's yard is blown over.
l. Carpeting is damaged from the overflow of water from a bathtub because Megan left the water running while answering the telephone.
m. The home is badly damaged in a severe earthquake. As a result of the earthquake, the front lawn has a three-foot crack and is now uneven.
n. An icemaker in the refrigerator breaks and water seeps into the flooring and carpets, causing considerable damage to the dwelling.

5. James has his home and personal property insured under a Homeowners 3 (special form) policy. The dwelling is insured for $120,000. The replacement cost of the home is $200,000. Indicate the extent to

which each of the following losses would be covered under James's Homeowners 3 policy. (Ignore the deductible.)

a. Lightning strikes the roof of the house and severely damages it. The actual cash value of the damaged roof is $10,000, and it will cost $16,000 to replace the damaged portion.

b. A living room window is broken in a hailstorm. The drapes are water stained and must be replaced. The actual cash value of the damaged drapes is $400. Replacement cost is $600.

c. The water heater explodes and damages some household contents. The actual cash value of the damaged property is $2000, and the cost of replacing the property is $3200.

6. Sarah owns a valuable diamond ring that has been in her family for generations. She is told by an appraiser that the ring has a current market value of $50,000. She feels that the ring is adequately insured because she owns a Homeowners 3 (special form) policy. Is Sarah correct in her thinking? If not, how would you advise her concerning proper protection of the ring?

7. Paul has his home and its contents insured under a Homeowners 3 (special form) policy. He carries $160,000 of insurance on the home, which has a replacement cost of $200,000. Explain the extent to which each of the following losses is covered. (Ignore the deductible.) If Paul's policy does not cover the loss or inadequately covers any of these losses, show how full coverage can be obtained.

a. Paul's stamp collection, which is valued at $5000, is stolen from his home.

b. Teenage vandals break into Paul's home and destroy a painting that has a market value of $1000.

c. A motorboat stored in the driveway of Paul's home is badly damaged during a hailstorm. The actual cash value of the damaged portion is $8000, and its replacement cost is $20,000.

8. Craig owns a home with a replacement cost of $200,000 that is subject to a $100,000 mortgage held by First Federal as the mortgagee. Craig has the home insured for $160,000 under the HO-3 policy, and First Federal is named as mortgagee under the Mortgage Clause. Assume there is a covered fire loss to the dwelling in the amount of $50,000. To whom would the loss be paid? Explain your answer.

INTERNET RESOURCES

- The **Insurance Information Institute** provides timely information on homeowners insurance and other personal property insurance coverages. Articles on homeowners insurance and other property and liability coverages can be accessed directly online. Visit the site at

  http://www.iii.org

- **Insure.com** provides up-to-date information, premium quotes, and other consumer information on homeowners insurance. In addition, the site includes timely information and news releases about events that affect the insurance industry. Visit the site at

  http://www.insure.com

- **Insurance.com** provides premium quotes on a variety of insurance products, including homeowners and renters insurance, auto insurance, life insurance, and health insurance. You can even get quotes on pet insurance. Visit the site at

  http://www.insurance.com

- **INSWEB** provides premium quotes on homeowners, auto, and other insurance products. You can comparison shop from your computer. The site also provides articles from industry, consumer, and regulatory groups. Visit the site at

  http://www.insweb.com

- The **International Risk Management Institute (IRMI)** is an online source that provides valuable information about personal lines and commercial lines. The site provides timely articles on a wide range of risk management and insurance topics and offers a number of free e-mail newsletters. Visit the site at

  http://www.irmi.com

- The **National Association of Insurance Commissioners (NAIC)** has a link to all state insurance departments, which provide a considerable amount of consumer information on homeowners insurance. Click on "State Insurance Web Sites." For starters, check out New York, Wisconsin, and California. Visit the site at

  http://www.naic.org

- **Quicken.com** provides timely information on homeowners, condominium, renters, and auto insurance.

The site also provides premium quotes for homeowners, auto, and life insurance, as well as other personal insurance lines. Visit the site at

http://www.quicken.com/insurance

SELECTED REFERENCES

"Catastrophes: Insurance Issues," *Hot Topics & Issues Updates,* Insurance Information Institute, August 2006. This source is periodically updated.

Fire, Casualty & Surety Bulletins, Personal Lines volume, Dwelling section. Erlanger, KY: National Underwriter Company. The bulletins are updated monthly.

Hamilton, Karen L., and Cheryl L. Ferguson. *Personal Risk Management and Property-Liability Insurance,* First Edition. Malvern, PA: American Institute for Chartered Property Casualty Underwriters/Insurance Institute of America, 2002.

Hartwig, Robert P. *The Use of Credit Information as an Underwriting Tool in Personal Lines Insurance: Analysis of Evidence and Benefits.* Insurance Information Institute, PowerPoint presentation, October 22, 2003.

International Risk Management Institute (IRMI). IRMI .com is an online source that provides information on personal lines and commercial lines. The site provides timely articles on a wide range of risk management and insurance topics and offers a number of free e-mail newsletters.

Richard, Diane W. *Homeowners Coverage Guide,* 2nd ed. Cincinnati, OH: The National Underwriter Company, 2002.

Wiening, Eric A., George E. Rejda, Constance M. Luthardt, and Cheryl L. Ferguson. *Personal Insurance,* 1st ed. Malvern, PA: American Institute for Chartered Property Casualty Underwriters/Insurance Institute of America, 2002.

NOTES

1. The discussion of homeowners insurance in this chapter is based on the *Fire, Casualty & Surety Bulletins,* Personal Lines volume, Dwelling section (Erlanger, KY: National Underwriter Company); and the copyrighted homeowners forms drafted by the Insurance Services Office (ISO). The ISO forms and various policy provisions are used with the permission of ISO.
2. "Catastrophes: Insurance Issues," *Hot Topics & Issues Updates,* (New York: Insurance Information Institute, August 2006). This topic is periodically updated.

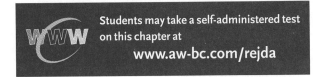

Students may take a self-administered test on this chapter at
www.aw-bc.com/rejda

CHAPTER 21

HOMEOWNERS INSURANCE, SECTION II

"How to win in court: If the law is on your side, pound on the law; if the facts are on your side, pound on the facts; if neither is on your side, pound on the table."

Unknown

LEARNING OBJECTIVES

After studying this chapter, you should be able to

◆ Explain the personal liability coverage found in Section II of the homeowners policy.

◆ Explain the medical payments to others coverage found in Section II of the homeowners policy.

◆ Identify the major exclusions that apply to the Section II coverages in the homeowners policy.

◆ Explain the following endorsements that can be added to a homeowners policy:
   Inflation guard endorsement
   Personal property replacement cost endorsement

◆ Explain the suggestions that consumers should follow when shopping for a homeowners policy.

Jeff, age 26, graduated from college and accepted a job with a public relations firm in San Francisco, California. He was anxious to start work so that he could pay off his student loans. He rented an apartment and carelessly started a grease fire when he was grilling hamburgers on the deck to his apartment. His apartment and two adjacent apartments were severely damaged. The management company sued Jeff for the fire loss and was awarded damages of $200,000. Jeff did not own a homeowners policy, which would have paid a large part of the loss. His goal of early repayment of student loans received a serious setback.

Jeff learned in a painful way the value of personal liability insurance. This chapter discusses the important provisions that appear in Section II of a homeowners policy. Section II provides personal liability insurance to the named insured and his or her family members and also covers the medical expenses of others who are injured by personal acts of an insured or by an animal owned by an insured.

The chapter also discusses several endorsements that can be added to a homeowners policy to broaden the coverages. It concludes with a discussion of important suggestions to follow when you shop for a homeowners policy.

PERSONAL LIABILITY INSURANCE

Personal liability insurance protects the named insured and family members against legal liability arising out of their personal acts. The insurer will provide a legal defense and pay those sums that an insured is legally obligated to pay up to the policy limit.[1] With the major exceptions of legal liability arising out of the negligent operation of an automobile, and business and professional liability, most personal acts are covered.

The various homeowner forms designed by the Insurance Services Office (ISO) contain the same Section II coverages. The following section discusses the major provisions in Section II.

Insuring Agreements

The Section II liability coverages in the homeowners policy provide the following two coverages:

- Coverage E: Personal liability, $100,000 per occurrence

- Coverage F: Medical payments to others, $1000 per person

Higher limits are available for a small additional premium.

Coverage E: Personal Liability Personal liability *insurance protects an insured when a claim or suit for damages is brought because of bodily injury or property damage allegedly caused by an insured's negligence.* If you are liable for damages, the insurer will pay up to the policy limits those sums that you are legally obligated to pay. Damages also include any prejudgment interest awarded against you.

The minimum amount of liability insurance is $100,000 for each occurrence. The insurance amount is a single limit that applies to both bodily injury and property damage liability on a per-occurrence basis. **Occurrence** *is defined as an accident, including continuous or repeated exposure to substantially the same general harmful conditions, which results in bodily injury or property damage during the policy period.* An occurrence can be a sudden accident, or it can be a gradual series of incidents that occur over time.

INSIGHT 21.1

Don't Let Your Dog Jeopardize Your Homeowners Coverage

Is your dog your best friend? Not when your homeowners policy is concerned. More than 4.7 million people annually are bitten by dogs, and an estimated 800,000 injuries require medical attention. You could be liable if your dog bites someone. *In 2005, dog-bite claims accounted for about 15 percent of the liability claims dollars paid out under homeowners insurance policies; the average dog-bite claim was $21,200.* The majority of dog bites occurred on the owner's property.

Insurers are limiting their exposure. Most insurers cover homeowners and renters with dogs. However, once your dog bites someone, the situation changes. *Your insurer may exclude dog bites from future coverage, charge a higher premium, nonrenew the homeowners policy, or suggest you find a new home for the dog.* Some insurers require dog owners to sign liability waivers for dog bites; other insurers charge higher premiums for biting breeds, such as Rottweilers and Pit Bulls. Some insurers will provide coverage if you take the dog to a behavior modification class, or you restrain the dog with a muzzle, chain, or cage.

Your liability as a dog owner. If your dog bites someone, are you legally liable? It depends on the state. There are three types of laws that impose liability:

- *Dog-bite statute.* In this case, you are automatically liable for any injury or property damage your dog causes without provocation. You are liable based on the doctrine of strict liability. The majority of states have this type of law.
- *One-bite rule.* In this case, you are responsible for an injury caused by your dog if you know that the dog can cause that type of injury (e.g., has bitten someone in the past). In this case, the victim must prove that the owner knew the dog was dangerous.
- *Negligence laws.* You are liable if the injury occurs because you were unreasonably careless or negligent in controlling the dog.

In most states, you are not liable to trespassers who are injured by your dog.

SOURCE: Adapted from "Dog Bite Liability," Insurance Information Institute, *Hot Topics & Issues Updates*, April 2006.

The insurer also agrees to provide a legal defense even if the suit is groundless, false, or fraudulent. The insurer has the right to investigate and settle the claim or suit either by defending you in a court of law or by settling out of court. As a practical matter, most personal liability suits are settled out of court. The insurer must defend you and cannot offer or tender its policy limits to be relieved of its duty to defend. Unless the claim is settled for a lesser amount, defense coverage continues until the policy limits are exhausted by payment of a judgment or settlement.

Personal liability coverage is broad. The following examples illustrate the types of losses covered:

- Your dog bites a small child; dog bites account for a large percentage of all homeowners liability claims (see Insight 21.1).
- While burning leaves in the yard, you accidentally set fire to your neighbor's house.
- A guest in your home trips on a torn carpet and sues you for bodily injury.
- You are shopping and carelessly break an expensive Chinese vase.

Personal liability insurance is based on legal liability. Before the insurer will pay any sums for damages, you must be legally liable. In contrast, medical payments to others, discussed next, is not based on negligence or legal liability.

Coverage F: Medical Payments to Others   This coverage is a mini-accident policy that is part of a homeowners policy. Medical payments to others is not based on legal liability. The insured is not required to be legally liable for coverage to apply. In contrast, personal liability coverage discussed earlier requires the insured to be legally liable for the coverage to apply.

Medical payments to others *pays the reasonable medical expenses of another person who is accidentally injured while on an insured location, or by the activities of an insured, resident employee, or animal owned by or in the care of an insured.* This coverage can be illustrated by the following examples:

- A guest slips in your home and breaks an arm. Reasonable medical expenses are paid up to the policy limits.

- A neighbor's child falls off a swing in your backyard and is injured. The child's medical expenses are covered up to the policy limits.
- You are playing golf and accidentally injure another golfer.
- Your dog bites a neighbor. The neighbor's medical expenses are paid up to the policy limits.

The insurer will pay for necessary medical expenses incurred or medically ascertained within three years from the date of the accident. The medical expenses covered are the reasonable charges for medical and surgical procedures, X-rays, dental care, ambulances, hospital stays, professional nursing, prosthetic devices, and funeral services.

Medical payments coverage does not apply to you or to regular residents of your household, other than a residence employee. For example, a swing set in your backyard may collapse, and your daughter and a neighbor's child are injured. Only the medical expenses of the neighbor's child are covered. An exception is a residence employee who is injured on the premises. For example, a babysitter may burn her hand while cooking lunch for your children. Her medical expenses would be covered under the policy, unless the state's workers compensation law applies to the loss.

With respect to the medical expenses of others, the policy states the situations under which coverage applies. Medical payments to others applies only to the following persons and situations:

- To a person on the insured location (discussed later) with the insured's permission
- To a person off the insured location, if the bodily injury
  - Arises out of a condition on the insured location or the ways immediately adjoining
  - Is caused by activities of an insured
  - Is caused by a residence employee in the course of employment by an insured
  - Is caused by an animal owned by or in the care of an insured

Medical payments to others cover the medical expenses of a person who is accidentally injured while on an insured location with the permission of an insured. *Insured locations* include the following:

- Residence premises shown in the declarations
- Any other residence acquired during the policy period, such as a summer home
- Rented garage or storage unit
- Nonowned premises where the insured is temporarily residing, such as a motel room
- Vacant land other than farmland
- Land owned or rented to an insured on which a residence is being built for an insured
- Cemetery plots or burial plots
- Part of a premises occasionally rented to an insured for nonbusiness purposes, such as a hall rented for a wedding reception

Medical payments to others also covers injuries away from an insured location if the injury arises out of a condition on the insured location or ways immediately adjoining, or is caused by activities of the insured, by a resident employee in the course of employment by an insured, or by an animal owned or in the care of an insured. For example, coverage applies to a pedestrian who trips or falls on an icy sidewalk or street adjacent to the premises. Coverage also applies if an insured accidentally injures another player while playing basketball. Likewise, if a babysitter takes your children to a public park and accidentally injures another child, coverage applies.

SECTION II EXCLUSIONS

The Section II coverages contain numerous exclusions. Some exclusions apply to both personal liability (Coverage E) and medical payments to others (Coverage F). Others apply separately to Coverage E and Coverage F.

Exclusions That Apply to Both Coverage E and Coverage F

The following section discusses several exclusions that apply to both Coverage E and Coverage F.

Motor Vehicle Liability   Legal liability arising out of motor vehicles is not covered if the involved vehicle is:

- Registered for use on public roads or property
- Not registered for use on public roads or property but such registration is required by law or government regulation

- Used in an organized race or speed contest
- Rented to others
- Used to carry persons or cargo for a charge
- Used for any business purpose, except for a motorized golf cart while on a golfing facility

Thus, liability arising out of cars, trucks, motorcycles, mopeds, and motorbikes is not covered. In addition, if you are towing a boat trailer, horse trailer, or rental trailer, coverage does not apply. Coverage can be obtained by purchasing an auto insurance policy.

Certain vehicles, however, are exceptions to the preceding exclusion, and therefore, coverage applies. The preceding exclusion of motor vehicles does not apply to the following:

- *The vehicle is in dead storage on a insured location.* For example, an unlicensed car may be on blocks in the insured's garage. A liability claim arising out of dead storage of the car is covered if the car is not subject to motor vehicle registration.
- *The vehicle is used solely to service an insured's residence.* For example, if a riding lawn mower is used solely at the insured's residence, coverage applies if an insured injures someone while using the mower.
- *The vehicle is designed to assist the handicapped.* For example, if a handicapped person injures someone while operating a motorized wheelchair, coverage applies.
- *The vehicle is designed for recreational use off public roads and is not owned by the insured, or it is owned by the insured, and the occurrence takes place on an insured location.* For example, property damage caused by the insured while operating a rented all-terrain vehicle (ATV) would be covered. Also, an owned ATV used on an insured location would be covered.
- *A motorized golf cart owned by an insured is also covered.* The cart must be designed to carry no more than four people and must have a maximum speed of no more than 25 miles per hour. Coverage applies if the cart is on a golfing facility and is used to play golf or some other recreational activity allowed by the facility. Coverage also applies if the cart is used to travel to and from an area where motor vehicles or golf carts are parked or stored, or is used to cross public

roads at designated points to access the facility. Finally, coverage applies at a private residential community, including its roads upon which a motorized golf cart can legally travel, which is subject to the authority of property owner's association and contains the insured's residence. Thus, if an insured has a home in a private residential community that has a golf course and injures someone while driving the golf cart to the facility, coverage would apply.

Watercraft Liability The Section II coverages exclude watercraft liability if the boat is used in an organized race or speed contest (except sailboats or a predicted log cruise), rented to others, used to carry people or cargo for a fee, or used for any business purpose.

Certain watercraft are exceptions to the preceding exclusion, and therefore coverage applies. Exhibit 21.1 indicates the types of watercraft covered under a homeowners policy and an example of each type.

Aircraft Liability The Section II coverages exclude aircraft liability. An aircraft is any device used or designed to carry people or cargo in flight, such as an airplane, helicopter, glider, or hot air balloon. However, the exclusion does not apply to model or hobby aircraft not used or designed to carry people or cargo.

Hovercraft Liability The homeowners policy excludes coverage for hovercraft liability. A hovercraft is defined as a self-propelled motorized ground effect vehicle and includes flarecraft and air cushion vehicles.

Expected or Intentional Injury The Section II coverages do not apply to bodily injury or property damage that is expected or intended by an insured. For example, suppose a softball player intentionally hits the umpire with a bat, and it is clear that the player intended to injure the umpire. Any claim or suit for damages would not be covered.

The exclusion does not apply to bodily injury that results from the use of reasonable force by an insured to protect persons or property. Thus, if Mark injures a mugger who is trying to rob him, any resulting suit for damages would be covered.

EXHIBIT 21.1

Watercraft Exposures Covered by Section II of the HO-3 Policy

Covered Watercraft Liability Exposures	Examples
1. Watercraft that are stored	A 30-foot sailboat stored out of the water at a marina for the winter
2. Sailboats (with or without auxiliary power) shorter than 26 feet	A 17-foot catamaran owned by the insured
3. Sailboats (with or without auxiliary power) longer than 26 feet *not owned by or rented to* an insured	A 32-foot sailboat the insured borrowed from her brother for a vacation
4. Inboard or inboard-outdrive watercraft with engines of 50 horsepower or less that are *not owned by* an insured	A 50-horsepower inboard motor boat borrowed from a neighbor
5. Inboard or inboard-outdrive watercraft of more than 50 horsepower *not owned by or rented to* an insured	A 150-horsepower inboard motor boat borrowed from a neighbor
6. Watercraft with one or more outboard engines or motors with 25 total horsepower or less	A fishing boat with 15-horsepower motor, owned by the insured
7. Watercraft with one or more outboard engines or motors with more than 25 total horsepower that are *not owned* by an insured	A boat with 75-horsepower outboard motor, borrowed from a friend
8. Watercraft with outboard engines or motors of more than 25 total horsepower owned by an insured if acquired during the policy period. If the insured acquires such watercraft before policy period, they are covered only if the insured: • declares them at the policy inception, or • reports the intention to insure them within 45 days of acquiring them	A new boat with 100-horsepower outboard motor purchased by the insured after the effective date of the policy

SOURCE: Eric A. Wiening, George E. Rejda, Constance M. Luthardt, and Cheryl L. Ferguson, *Personal Insurance*, 1st ed. Malvern, PA.: American Institute for Chartered Property Casualty Underwriters/Insurance Institute of America, 2002, Exhibit 6-3, p. 6.12.

Business Activities Liability arising out of a business activity is excluded. A business is defined as a trade, profession, or occupation that the insured engages in on a full-time, part-time, or occasional basis. It also includes any other activity engaged in for money or other compensation. For example, if you operate a beauty shop in your home and carelessly burn a customer with a hair dryer, a lawsuit by the customer is not covered.

Certain activities, however, are not subject to the business exclusion:

- Activities for which no insured received more than $2000 in total compensation for the 12 months prior to the policy period

- Volunteer activities for which no money is received except for expenses
- Providing home care services without compensation, other than the mutual exchange of such services
- Providing home day care services to a relative

For example, a garage sale not conducted as a regular business, volunteer work for a local church, and babysitting by a grandmother for her grandchildren would be covered.

In addition, legal liability arising out of the rental of any part of the premises is excluded. For example, if you own a twelveplex apartment house that is rented to students, liability claims arising out of ownership of the apartment building are not covered.

There are several exceptions to the rental exclusion. First, if a house is occasionally rented and used only as a residence, coverage applies. For example, if a professor rents out his or her home while on sabbatical leave, coverage will still apply.

Coverage also applies if part of the residence is rented to others. For example, assume that you live in a duplex and rent the other unit to a single family. Liability coverage still applies if the renting family does not take in more than two roomers or boarders.

Coverage also applies if part of the insured residence is rented and used as an office, school, studio, or private garage. For example, if a room above a garage is rented to an artist who uses the room as a studio, the insured still has coverage for claims arising out of the rental.

Finally, coverage also applies to an insured under age 21 who is involved in a part-time or occasional self-employed business with no employees. For example, teenagers are covered while delivering newspapers on a bicycle, washing cars, cutting lawns, or babysitting.

Professional Services Legal liability arising out of professional services is excluded. Physicians and dentists are not covered for malpractice claims under the homeowners policy. Also, attorneys, accountants, nurses, architects, engineers, and other professionals are not covered for legal liability for rendering or failing to render professional services. The loss exposures involving professional activities are substantially different from those faced by the typical homeowner. For this reason, a professional liability policy is necessary to cover professional activities. Professional liability insurance is examined in greater detail in Chapter 26.

Uninsured Locations Liability arising out of the ownership or rental of a premises that is not an "insured location" is also excluded. The meaning of "insured location" has already been explained. Examples of uninsured locations would be farmland owned or rented by an insured, a principal or secondary residence owned by an insured other than the named insured or spouse, and land owned by the insured on which a 12-unit apartment is being built.

War Section II coverages exclude war, undeclared war, civil war, insurrection, rebellion, and other hostile military acts. The homeowners contracts also exclude liability arising out of the discharge of a nuclear weapon even if accidental.

Communicable Disease Exclusion Liability arising out of the transmission of a communicable disease by an insured is excluded under both personal liability insurance and medical payments to others. The exclusion applies to all communicable diseases and is not limited only to sexually transmitted diseases.

Sexual Molestation, Corporal Punishment, or Physical or Mental Abuse The homeowners policy excludes bodily injury or property damage liability arising out of sexual molestation, corporal punishment, or physical or mental abuse.

Controlled Substance Exclusion Liability arising out of the use, sale, manufacture, delivery, transfer, or possession of a controlled substance is specifically excluded. Controlled substances include methamphetamine, cocaine, LSD, marijuana, and all narcotic drugs. The exclusion does not apply to the legitimate use of prescription drugs by a person who is following the orders of a licensed physician.

Exclusions That Apply Only to Coverage E

Several exclusions apply only to Coverage E (personal liability).

Contractual Liability Contractual liability *means that an insured agrees to assume the legal liability of another party by a written or oral contract.* The policy excludes the following contractual liability exposures:

- *Liability of an insured for any loss assessment* charged against the insured as a member of any association, corporation, or community of property owners. However, an additional coverage (discussed later) provides $1000 of coverage for a loss assessment if certain conditions are met.
- *Liability under any contract or agreement is excluded.* However, the exclusion does not apply to written contracts that (1) directly relate to the

ownership, maintenance, or use of an insured location, or (2) where the liability of others is assumed by the insured prior to an occurrence. Thus, there would be coverage for liability assumed under a written lease, an equipment rental agreement if the equipment is used to maintain the residence premises, or other written contracts where legal liability of a nonbusiness nature is assumed by an insured prior to an occurrence.

Property Owned by the Insured   *Property damage to property owned by the insured is also excluded.* Thus, if a teenage son accidentally breaks some furniture, the parents' claim for damages against their son would not be covered.

Property in the Care of the Insured   *Damage to property rented to, occupied or used by, or in the care of the insured is not covered.* For example, if you damage an apartment that you are renting, a lawsuit by the landlord seeking reimbursement for the damage would not be covered.

The exclusion does not apply to property damage caused by fire, smoke, or explosion. For example, if you rent an apartment and carelessly start a fire, you can be held liable for the damage. In such a case, the homeowners policy would cover the property damage to the apartment up to the policy's liability limit.

Workers Compensation   *There is no coverage for bodily injury to any person who is eligible to receive benefits provided by the named insured under a workers compensation, nonoccupational disability, or occupational disease law.* This is true if the workers compensation benefits are either mandatory or voluntary. In some states, domestic workers must be covered for workers compensation benefits by their employers; in other states, the coverage is voluntary.

Nuclear Energy   *The homeowners policy excludes liability arising out of nuclear energy.* If any insured is involved in a nuclear incident, any resulting liability is not covered by the homeowners policy.

Bodily Injury to an Insured   *There is no coverage for bodily injury to the named insured or to any insured as defined in the policy.* For example, if one spouse

accidentally trips and injures the other spouse, the injured spouse cannot collect damages.

Exclusions That Apply Only to Coverage F

A final set of exclusions applies only to Coverage F (medical payments to others).

Injury to a Resident Employee Off an Insured Location   *If an injury to a resident employee occurs off an insured location and does not arise out of or in the course of employment by an insured, medical payments coverage does not apply.* For example, if Tanya is employed by the insured as a cook and is injured in a car accident on her way home, her medical expenses are not covered.

Workers Compensation   This exclusion is similar to the workers compensation exclusion discussed earlier under personal liability insurance. *Medical payments coverage does not apply to any person who is eligible to receive benefits provided by the named insured under a workers compensation, nonoccupational disability, or occupational disease law.* The injured employee's medical expenses should be covered by workers compensation insurance.

Nuclear Energy   *Medical payments coverage does not cover any person for bodily injury that results from nuclear reaction, radiation, or radioactive contamination.*

Persons Regularly Residing on the Insured Location   *Medical payments coverage does not cover injury to any person (other than a residence employee of an insured) who regularly resides on any part of the insured location.* Thus, a tenant injured in a household accident cannot receive payment for medical expenses. The intent here is to minimize collusion among household members.

SECTION II ADDITIONAL COVERAGES

A homeowners policy automatically includes several additional coverages, including coverage for claim expenses, first-aid expenses, damage to property of others, and loss-assessment charges.

Claim Expenses

Claim expenses are paid as an additional coverage. The insurer pays the court costs, attorney fees, and other legal expenses incurred in providing a legal defense. The claim expenses are paid in addition to the policy limits for liability damages.

The insurer also pays the premiums on bonds required in a suit defended by the insurer. For example, a judgment may be appealed, and if an appeal bond is required, the insurer pays the premium.

Reasonable expenses incurred by the insured at the insurer's request to assist in the investigation and defense of a claim or suit are also paid. This obligation includes payment for the actual loss of earnings up to $250 per day. Finally, interest on a judgment that accrues after the judgment is awarded, but before payment is made, is also paid by the insurer.

First-Aid Expenses

The insurer pays any **first-aid expenses** incurred by the insured for bodily injury covered under the policy. For example, a guest may slip in your home and break a leg. If you call an ambulance to take the injured person to the hospital and are later billed for $600 by the ambulance company, this amount would be paid as a first-aid expense.

Damage to Property of Others

Damage to property of others *pays up to $1000 per occurrence for property damage caused by an insured*. The damaged property is valued on the basis of replacement cost. This coverage can be illustrated by the following examples:

- A son, age 10, accidentally breaks a neighbor's window while playing softball.
- At a party, you carelessly burn a hole in the owner's carpet with your cigarette.
- You borrow your neighbor's lawn mower and accidentally damage the blade by striking a rock.

The insured is not required to be legally liable for coverage to apply. The loss is paid even when there is no legal obligation to do so.

The purpose of this coverage is to preserve personal friendships and keep peace in the neighbor-

hood. Also, in many states, the parents are held responsible for the property damage caused by a young child. If this coverage were not provided, the person whose property is damaged would have to file a claim for damages against the insured who caused the damage.

A maximum of $1000 is paid under this coverage. Amounts in excess of this limit are paid only by proving negligence and legal liability by the person who caused the damage.

Damage to property of others also contains a specific set of exclusions. The major ones are summarized as follows:

- *Property Covered Under Section I.* Property damage is excluded to the extent of any amount recoverable under Section I of the policy.
- *Intentional Property Damage by an Insured Age 13 or Older.* If the property damage is intentionally caused by an insured, age 13 or older, coverage does not apply. This exclusion is relevant to teenage vandalism, which is a serious national problem. Thus, if a teenager damages a plate-glass window with a slingshot, deliberately knocks over a mailbox, or maliciously damages a tree, the parents' policy will not cover the property damage.
- *Property Owned by an Insured.* Property damage to property owned by an insured is also excluded. For example, if a son damages some power tools owned by his parents, the damage would not be covered. However, coverage does apply if the property is rented. Thus, if you rent a portable television set and accidentally drop it, the damage is covered.
- *Property Owned by or Rented to a Tenant.* Coverage does not apply to property owned by or rented to a tenant of an insured or to a resident in the named insured's household.
- *Business Liability.* Property damage arising out of a business engaged in by an insured is excluded. Thus, if you operate a lawn-maintenance business and accidentally cut down a shrub while mowing a customer's lawn, the damage is not covered.
- *Act or Omission in Connection with the Premises.* Property damage caused by an act or omission in connection with a premises owned, rented, or controlled by the insured, other than

an insured location, is not covered. For example, without an endorsement, farmland owned by the insured is not covered under the homeowners policy. Thus, if the insured should accidentally damage the tractor of the tenant who is farming the land, coverage does not apply.

- *Motor Vehicles, Aircraft, Watercraft, or Hovercraft*. Property damage that results from the ownership, maintenance, or use of a motor vehicle, aircraft, watercraft, or hovercraft is not covered. For example, if you run over a neighbor's 10-speed bicycle with your auto, the loss is not covered.

Loss Assessment

The homeowners policy provides coverage of $1000 for certain loss assessments. Higher limits are available by endorsement. For example, assume that you belong to a homeowners association that rents a hall for a monthly meeting. Someone is injured at one of the meetings and is awarded a judgment of $110,000. If the association's liability policy has policy limits of only $100,000, the $10,000 balance will be split among the association members and each member would be assessed a portion of the $10,000 balance. The homeowners policy would pay your loss-assessment charge up to $1000. This amount can be increased by an endorsement.

ENDORSEMENTS TO A HOMEOWNERS POLICY

Some property owners have special needs or desire broader coverage than that provided by a standard homeowners policy. Numerous endorsements can be added to a homeowners policy to meet individual needs, including the following:

- Inflation guard endorsement
- Earthquake endorsement
- Personal property replacement cost loss settlement endorsement
- Scheduled personal property endorsement (with agreed value loss settlement)
- Personal injury endorsement
- Watercraft endorsement
- Home business insurance coverage endorsement

Inflation Guard Endorsement

Many homeowners are underinsured because inflation has increased the replacement cost of their home. If a loss occurs and you do not carry insurance at least equal to 80 percent of the replacement cost of the dwelling, you will be penalized because the full replacement cost will not be paid.

To deal with inflation, you should add an **inflation guard endorsement** to your homeowners policy if it is not included by your insurer. The inflation guard endorsement is designed for use with the ISO homeowner forms and provides for an annual pro rata increase in the limits of insurance under Coverages A, B, C, and D. The percentage increase is selected by the insured, such as 4 percent or 6 percent. For example, if the policyowner selects a 6 percent inflation guard endorsement, the various limits are increased by 6 percent annually. This specified annual percentage increase is prorated throughout the policy year. Thus, a house originally insured for $300,000 would be covered for $309,000 at the end of six months.

Earthquake Endorsement

An **earthquake endorsement** can be added that covers earthquakes, landslides, volcanic eruption, and earth movement. A single earthquake is defined as all earthquake shocks that occur within a 72-hour period. A deductible must be satisfied. The base deductible is 5 percent of the limit that applies *either* to the dwelling (Coverage A) or to personal property (Coverage C), whichever is greater. There is a minimum deductible of $250. The deductible can be increased with a reduction in premiums. There is no other deductible that applies to an earthquake loss. The deductible does not apply to Coverage D (loss of use) and to additional coverages. In some states where earthquakes occur frequently, or the risk of an earthquake is high, higher deductibles of 10 to 20 percent are typically used.

Although earthquakes can cause catastrophic losses, most property owners in earthquake zones do not have earthquake insurance. Insurers in California selling homeowners insurance must offer earthquake insurance on new policies, but the majority of homeowners do not carry earthquake insurance. The major reasons for their reluctance to purchase earthquake coverage are high cost, high deductibles, a mistaken belief that earthquakes will not occur, and the belief that the federal government will provide disaster relief.

In California, earthquake coverage is also available through the California Earthquake Authority (CEA). The CEA is a privately financed, publicly managed entity that offers residential earthquake insurance to California homeowners, renters, condominium owners, and mobilehome owners. Fifteen private insurers participate in the arrangement. Structural damage to a home is subject to a deductible of 15 percent of the amount of insurance on the dwelling; however, a 10 percent deductible is available if the homeowner pays a higher premium. As stated earlier, most homeowners do not carry earthquake coverage. According to the Insurance Information Institute, only about 13 percent of homeowners in California purchase earthquake insurance.[2]

Personal Property Replacement Cost Loss Settlement Endorsement

An unendorsed homeowners policy covers losses to personal property on the basis of actual cash value. However, a **personal property replacement cost loss settlement endorsement** can be added to the policy. *Under the endorsement, claims are paid on the basis of replacement cost with no deduction for depreciation.* The endorsement applies to personal property, awnings, carpets, domestic appliances, and outdoor equipment.

The replacement cost endorsement for personal property has several important limitations. The amount paid is limited to the *smallest* of the following amounts:

- Replacement cost at the time of loss
- Full repair cost
- Coverage C limit, if applicable
- Any special dollar limits in the policy (such as theft limits on jewelry, furs, and silverware)
- For loss to any item, the limit of liability that applies to the item

If the cost to repair or replace exceeds $500, the property must actually be repaired or replaced to receive replacement cost. Otherwise, only the actual cash value is paid.

The replacement cost endorsement excludes certain types of property, such as antiques, fine arts, and similar property; collector's items and souvenirs; property that is not in good or workable condition; and obsolete property stored or not used.

As a general rule, you should consider adding the replacement cost endorsement for personal property to your homeowners policy. You usually cannot find used property that replaces exactly the property lost. Also, because of depreciation, the amount paid for a loss based on actual cash value policy is substantially less than that payable based on replacement cost. Most insureds typically are unaware of the big difference between replacement cost and actual cash value.

Scheduled Personal Property Endorsement (with Agreed Value Loss Settlement)

The homeowners policy has limits on the amounts paid for certain personal property losses. Also, insureds may desire broader coverage than the homeowners policy provides. If you own valuable jewelry, furs, silverware, cameras, musical instruments, fine arts, antiques, or a stamp or coin collection, you can list the property in a schedule and insure it for a specific amount agreed to by the insurer.

Under the **scheduled personal property endorsement (with agreed valued loss settlement)**, the insurer agrees to pay the stated amount for a scheduled item if a total loss occurs. The endorsement insures property against risks of direct physical loss, which means the property is insured on an "all risks," or "open perils" basis. *All direct physical losses to scheduled property are covered except those losses specifically excluded.* For example, if a diamond ring insured for $25,000 is stolen; the amount paid is $25,000. Likewise, if a grand piano insured for $75,000 is damaged beyond repair in a tornado; the amount paid is $75,000.

Personal Injury Endorsement

The homeowners policy only covers legal liability arising out of bodily injury or property damage to someone else. Personal injury coverage, which should not be confused with bodily injury coverage, can be added to the homeowners policy as an endorsement.

Personal injury means legal liability arising out of the following:

- False arrest, detention, or imprisonment
- Malicious prosecution
- Wrongful eviction, wrongful entry, or invasion of the right of private occupancy of a room, dwelling, or premises
- Oral or written publication of material that slanders a person or organization, or an organization's products or services
- Oral or written publication of material that violates a person's right to privacy

For example, if you have a person arrested who is later found innocent, or if you make false statements that damage a person's reputation, you may be liable for damages. These losses are not covered under a homeowners policy but would be covered by the personal injury endorsement.

Watercraft Endorsement

The **watercraft endorsement** covers watercraft that are otherwise excluded under the homeowners policy. The endorsement provides liability and medical payments coverage on any inboard or inboard-out-drive powered watercraft; sailing vessels 26 feet or more in length; and watercraft powered by one or more outboard motors exceeding 25 total horse-power.

Home Business Insurance Coverage Endorsement

A growing number of home owners operate a business out of their homes. A standard homeowners policy provides only limited coverage on business property, and legal liability arising out of a business operation is excluded. A **home business insurance coverage endorsement** can be added that covers both business property and legal liability arising out of a home-based business. This type of endorsement increases the coverage on business property on the residence premises from $2500 to the Coverage C limit on personal property. Coverage on business property away from the premises is increased from $500 to $5000. The endorsement also provides coverage for accounts receivable, valuable papers and records, and the loss of business income and extra expenses when loss from an insured peril causes the business to be suspended.

The home business insurance endorsement covers business liability loss exposures that are normally found in a commercial package policy for a business firm. Liability coverage includes (1) bodily injury and property damage liability, (2) personal and advertising injury, and (3) products and completed operations exposures associated with the home business. These coverages are discussed in Chapter 26.

In addition to the preceding endorsements, dozens of additional endorsements are available to meet the specific needs of homeowners. One new endorsement provides coverage for *identity theft*. Some insurers now include this coverage in their homeowner policies. Others sell the coverage either as a separate policy or as an endorsement to a homeowners or renters policy (see Insight 21.2).

COST OF HOMEOWNERS INSURANCE

As an informed consumer, you should understand how the cost of a homeowners policy is determined. Also, certain underwriting factors determine if an applicant for a homeowners policy is acceptable for insurance. Major rating and underwriting factors include the following:

- Construction
- Location
- Fire-protection class
- Construction costs
- Age of home
- Type of policy
- Deductible amount
- Insurance score
- CLUE report

Construction

Construction of the home is an extremely important rating factor. The more fire-resistant the home is, the lower the rate. Thus, wooden homes cost more to insure than brick homes. However, earthquake insurance costs are substantially less for wooden homes.

INSIGHT 21.2

Identity Theft Insurance Can Restore Your Good Name

Identity theft occurs when a thief uses your name, driver's license, Social Security number, ATM account number, credit card number, or other identification for fraudulent purposes. The number of identity theft victims is much higher than originally believed. According to a recent survey by Chubb Group of Insurance Companies, 20 percent of the respondents have been a victim of identity fraud or theft.[a]

Consumers whose identities are stolen can spend months or even years and thousands of dollars trying to restore their good name and credit record. Victims may lose job opportunities, be refused loans for education, housing, cars, or even be arrested for crimes they didn't commit. Victims often experience humiliation, anger, and frustration as they try to reclaim their identities and clean up their credit records. The following is a typical example of identity theft reported to the Federal Trade Commission: [b]

> I first was notified that someone had used my Social Security number for their taxes in February 2004. I also found that this person opened a checking account, cable and utility accounts, and a cell phone account in my name. I'm still trying to clear up everything and just received my income tax refund after waiting four to five months. Trying to work and get all this cleared up is very stressful.

Identity theft insurance reimburses crime victims for the cost of restoring their identity and cleaning up their credit record. Insureds are reimbursed for lost wages, phone calls, notary and certified mailing costs, attorney fees with the prior consent of the insurer, and other specified expenses. Some insurers now include the coverage in their homeowners policies. Others make it available as a separate policy or as an endorsement to a homeowners policy. Coverage varies depending upon the insurer. One company provides expense reimbursement limits from $500 up to $25,000 per covered person to restore a victim's credit history. The following expenses are covered:

- Lost wages up to a certain limit because of time off to deal with identity theft
- Loan reapplication fees to reapply for loans turned down because of erroneous credit information that reflects the identity theft
- Phone charges for calling financial institutions, business firms, and law enforcement agencies to discuss the identity theft
- Certified mail and notary costs for completing and delivering fraud affidavits
- Attorney fees incurred with the insurer's prior consent because of the cost of defending suits brought incorrectly by business firms and collection agencies, removing criminal or civil judgments wrongly entered against the insured, and challenging information on a credit report.

Finally, it should be noted that identity theft insurance covers only expenses incurred and not any dollar amount that the thief may steal.

[a] "Survey: One in Five Americans Have Been Victims of Identity Fraud," www.insurancejournal.com, National News, July 8, 2005.
[b] Consumer complaint to the FTC, July 8, 2004.

Location

Location of the home is another important rating factor. For rating purposes, the loss experience of each rating territory is determined. Insureds who reside in territories with high losses from fires, storms, natural disasters, or crime must pay higher rates than insureds who reside in low-loss territories.

Fire-Protection Class

The fire-protection class affects the rates charged. The Insurance Services Office (ISO) rates the quality of public fire departments from one to ten. A lower number results in a lower rate. Accessibility of the home to the fire department and water supply and fire hydrants is also important. Homes in rural areas generally have higher rates than homes in large cities.

Construction Costs

Construction costs have a significant effect on rates. The costs of labor and materials vary widely in the United States. The higher the cost of repairing or rebuilding your home, the higher your premium is likely to be.

Type of Policy

The type of policy is extremely important in determining the total premium. The Homeowners 3 policy (special form) is more expensive than the Homeowners 2 policy (broad form) because the coverage is broader. The Homeowners 5 policy (comprehensive form) is the most expensive contract because the dwelling, other structures, and personal property are covered on an "all risks" or "open perils" basis. All direct physical damage losses are covered except those losses specifically excluded.

Deductible Amount

The deductible amount has an important effect on cost. The higher the deductible, the lower the premium. A flat $250 deductible applies to all covered losses. The deductible can be increased with a reduction in premiums. The deductible does not apply to a fire department service charge, coverage for credit or ATM cards, scheduled property that is specifically insured, and the personal liability coverages under Section II.

Insurance Score

Many insurers also use the applicant's *credit record* for purposes of underwriting and rating. The applicant's credit record is used to determine an insurance score. An **insurance score** *is a credit-based score that is highly predictive of future claim costs.* Insurance scores predict the average claim behavior for a group of insureds with essentially the same credit history. Insureds as a group with poor credit and low insurance scores generally file more homeowners claims than insureds with good credit and higher insurance scores.

Several credit organizations calculate insurance scores for insurers. One of the most important is the Fair Isaac Corporation (FICO) which calculates insurance scores for insurers. The majority of consumers have good credit records.

Insurers claim there is a strong and statistically significant relationship between insurance scores and underwriting experience. The lower the insurance score, the more likely insureds as a group are likely to file homeowners claims. Actuarial studies generally support this conclusion. For example, one study

by Tillinghast Towers-Perrin, a major actuarial consulting firm, examined the relationship between insurance scores and loss ratios (cost of claims filed relative to the premiums collected). Tillinghast reviewed nine samples of data from eight insurers. The study showed that in eight out of nine samples, the probability that a statistically significant correlation exists between insurance scores and loss ratios exceeded 99 percent. *That is, insureds with low insurance scores, as a group, accounted for a high proportion of the dollars paid out in claims.* Exhibit 21.2 shows the insurance scores and relative performance for three insurers from the Tillinghast study. As insurance scores decline, claimants as a group tend to file more claims.

A more recent study by the Texas Department of Insurance confirms the strong correlation between credit scores and loss ratios. The Texas study analyzed the relationship between credit scores and average loss ratios. *The study showed that the loss ratios for homeowners insurance for people with the worst credit scores are triple that of people with the best credit scores (see Exhibit 21.3).*

CLUE Report

For purposes of underwriting and rating, insurers also use reports that reveal the prior claim history of a home. CheckPoint is a commercial firm that prepares Comprehensive Loss Underwriting Exchange (CLUE) reports for insurers that show the claims history on homes that insurers are asked to insure. CLUE is a database that contains up to five years of information on property claims, which includes the date of loss, type of loss, and amounts paid.

The use of CLUE reports is controversial. Critics claim that insurers are terrified of rising losses from mold claims and water damage and do not wish to insure homes that have experienced such losses. Also, some homebuyers have found it difficult to obtain homeowners insurance because the CLUE report indicated a history of previous claims on the home they would like to purchase. Likewise, some homeowners selling their homes may not get the best price if the home has been rejected by several insurers because of previous claims.

However, in rebuttal, insurers claim they can rate more accurately based on claim history by using CLUE reports in their underwriting. Also, insurers

Exhibit 21.2
Tillinghast Towers-Perrin Study: Relationship between Insurance Scores and Loss Ratio Relativities for Three Homeowners Insurers

Homeowners Company A

Source: Tillinghast Towers-Perrin

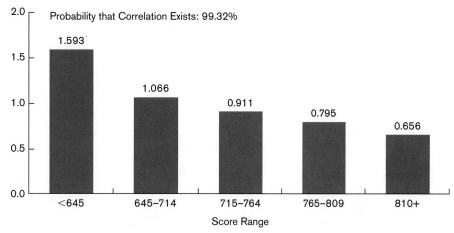

Homeowners Company B

Source: Tillinghast Towers-Perrin

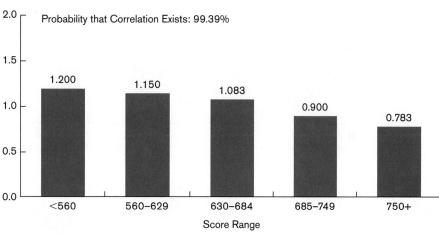

Homeowners Company C

Source: Tillinghast Towers-Perrin

Source: Excerpted from Robert P. Hartwig and Claire Wilkinson, *The Use of Credit Information in Personal Lines Insurance Underwriting,* Insurance Issues Series (New York: Insurance Information Institute, June 2003), vol. 1, no. 2, Exhibits 8, 9, 10.

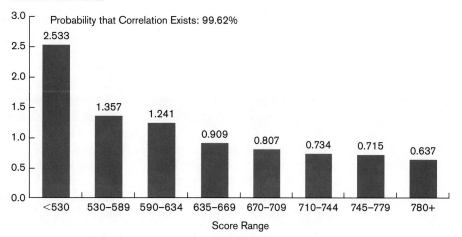

Exhibit **21.3**

Homeowners: New Texas Study Confirms Strong Correlation Between Credit Score and Loss Performance

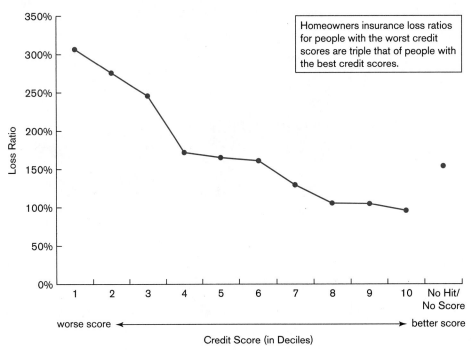

Homeowners insurance loss ratios for people with the worst credit scores are triple that of people with the best credit scores.

Loss Ratio (y-axis)

Credit Score (in Deciles) (x-axis, 1 through 10, No Hit/No Score)

worse score ← → better score

NOTE: 1. Data incorporate losses from all perils, including water damage, wind, and hail.
   2. Data are from *Use of Credit Information by Insurers in Texas*, Texas Department of Insurance, December 30, 2004.

SOURCE: Robert P. Hartwig, Insurance Information Institute, *No Evidence of Disparate Impact in Texas Due to Use of Credit Information by Personal Lines Insurers*, Insurance Information Institute, January 2005.

can detect fraudulent claims more easily and the filing of numerous claims by some homeowners.

Suggestions for Buying a Homeowners Policy

As a careful insurance consumer, you should remember certain suggestions when purchasing a homeowners policy (see Exhibit 21.4).

Carry Adequate Insurance The first suggestion is to carry adequate amounts of property insurance on both your home and personal property. This consideration is particularly important if a room is added or home improvements are made because the value of the home may be substantially increased. The home must be insured for at least 80 percent of its replacement cost to avoid a penalty if a partial loss occurs. *However, you should seriously consider insuring your home for 100 percent of its replacement cost.* Few homeowners can afford an additional out-of-pocket payment equal to 20 percent of replacement cost if a total loss occurs.

Add Necessary Endorsements Certain endorsements may be necessary depending on your needs, local property conditions, or high values for certain types of personal property. To deal with inflation, you should add an *inflation guard endorsement* to your homeowners policy if your insurer does not include it. An *earthquake endorsement* is desirable if you live in an earthquake zone. The *personal property replacement cost endorsement* is also desirable because you are indemnified on the basis of replacement cost with no deduction for depreciation. In addition, if you own valuable property, such as jewelry, furs, fine art, or a valuable coin or stamp col-

EXHIBIT 21.4
Tips for Buying a Homeowners Policy

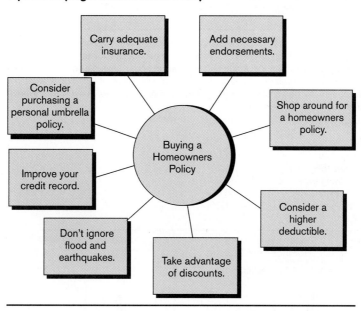

lection, you should add the *scheduled personal property endorsement* to your policy. Each item is listed and specifically insured for a certain amount.

Shop Around for a Homeowners Policy   Another important suggestion is to shop around for a homeowners policy. Because considerable price variation occurs among insurers, you can often reduce your homeowners premium by shopping around. Consequently, it pays to get a premium quote from several insurers before you buy a homeowners policy. Several Internet sites provide premium quotes (see Internet Resources). Some states also publish shoppers' guides to assist consumers who purchase homeowners policies. These guides indicate the wide variation in premiums charged by insurers. For example, Exhibit 21.5 shows the annual premiums for an HO-3 policy for selected cities in Wisconsin by zip code based on a survey by the Office of the Commissioner of Insurance. In Madison, Wisconsin, annual premiums for a dwelling insured for $150,000 under an HO-3 policy ranged from $223 (Auto-Owners Ins. Co.) to $660 (Milwaukee Mutual), *or 196 percent more.* In Milwaukee, Wisconsin, annual premiums for a similar policy ranged from $310 (Wilson Mutual) to $911 (State Farm Fire and Casualty), *or 194 percent more.* Clearly, it pays to shop around.

Consider a Higher Deductible   Another suggestion for reducing premiums is to purchase a policy with a higher deductible. The standard homeowners deductible is $250. *A higher deductible can substantially reduce your premiums.* You can usually get a discount of 10 percent with a $500 deductible and a 20 to 30 percent discount with a $1000 deductible. For example, Patrick has a $1000 deductible in his homeowners policy instead of the standard $250, which saves him $180 annually. In other words, Patrick saves $180 each year but loses only $750 in coverage. That additional $750 is very expensive coverage.

Take Advantage of Discounts   When you shop for a homeowners policy, you should inquire whether you are eligible for any discounts or credits, which can further reduce your premiums. Insurers offer a wide variety of discounts based on numerous factors, including age of the home, fire and smoke alarms, sprinkler system, dead-bolt locks, and fire extinguishers.

The appendix to this chapter provides additional suggestions for reducing the cost of a homeowners policy.

Don't Ignore Flood and Earthquakes   The homeowners policy covers hurricanes, tornadoes, wind-

EXHIBIT 21.5
Homeowners Annual Insurance Premiums
Effective January 1, 2006

Example: A 20-year-old frame house equipped with dead-bolt locks and smoke/fire detectors is insured for $150,000 under an HO-3 policy. Protection against loss to personal property in the building is 75% of the coverage on the dwelling and is covered on a replacement cost basis. Personal property on the premises is protected against loss due to theft in an amount equal to the personal property coverage. Off-premises theft losses are covered for 10% of the personal property amount.

Coverage and Limits:

Dwelling	$150,000
Contents	112,000
Off-premises theft	11,250
Additional living expenses	30,000
Personal liability	300,000
Medical payments	1,000
Deductible	500

Refer to Footnote	Companies Writing Homeowners Policies	City of Madison (53704)	City of Milwaukee (53704)
(1)	ACUITY, A Mutual Ins. Co.	$460	$536
(2)	Allstate Property & Casualty Ins. Co.	393	419
(3)	American Family Mutual Ins. Co.	579	774
(4)	Auto-Owners Ins. Co.	223	314
(5)	Badger Mutual Ins. Co.	363	415
(6)	Cincinnati Ins. Co.	279	311
(7)	Fire Insurance Exchange	404	662
(8)	General Casualty Co. of Wisconsin	396	772
(9)	Germantown Mutual Ins. Co.	445	476
(10)	Milwaukee Mutual Ins. Co.	660	677
(11)	Rural Mutual Ins. Co.	352	450
(12)	Safeco Ins. Co. of America	297	328
(13)	SECURA Ins. Co.	611	780
(14)	Sentry Ins., A Mutual Co.	300	471
(15)	State Farm Fire and Casualty Co.	526	911
(16)	West Bend Mutual Ins. Co.	250	322
(17)	Wilson Mutual Ins. Co.	310	310
	Wisconsin Mutual Ins. Co.	329	367

(1) ACUITY HO-3 provides 50% of dwelling coverage ($75,000) for additional living expenses. Additional discounts may be available.

(2) Town class 1–4; Rating group 1A; Age of home discount; Protective device discount (also assumes fire extinguisher).

(3) Rates reflect town classes 1–7.

(4) Rates effective January 11, 2005. Rates quoted using protection class 1–5. Multi-policy discount, mature discount age 65+ and new home discounts applied. Personal property quoted as replacement cost coverage. Insurance score superior (65–69). Rates quoted with $500/$1,000 wind/hail deductible.

(5) Rates quoted for Preferred Program using protection class 1–8. Additional living expense coverage is unlimited.

(6) Applied 0–3 loss credit; Personal property is included at 75% of Coverage A (home). Additional living expense is actual loss sustained.

(7) Special form policy quoted. Personal property limit $113,000 automatically included. Additional living expense limit $75,000 (50% of dwelling) automatically included. Non-smoker, auto/home and home security discounts applied. Off-premises theft limit $11,300 (10% of personal property) at secondary residence only, otherwise limit is $113,000. FPRA score "G" applied.

(8) Preferred Program quoted. Coverage C (personal property) is 80% of Coverage A (home) or $120,000. Insurance Bureau Score not available.

Eᴄ̨ʜɪʙɪᴛ **21.5** (ᴄᴏɴᴛ'ᴅ)
**Homeowners Annual Insurance Premiums
Effective January 1, 2006**

(9) Additional living expenses is quoted using 40% of Coverage (A) home.

(10) Protection class 1–6; Select tier.

(11) Preferred coverage form quoted. Additional discounts/surcharges may be applicable.

(12) HO-3 is no longer available for new business. Premium quoted using HO-33. Company has minimum deductible of $1,000 in these listed territories, except in city of Milwaukee a $500 deductible is used. Assumptions for risk were no prior claims in last 5 years, protection class of 3, part of an account with active auto policy, and good or above average credit. In addition, additional living expenses are automatically included either to shortest time to repair/replace or maximum of 12 months.

(13) Additional discounts may be available.

(14) Additional living expenses coverage is 25% of Coverage A (home) not 20%. Used the city of Superior for Douglas County. Used the city of Wausau for Marathon County. Used the city of Waukesha for Waukesha County.

(15) Premium quoted using $500 deductible. Premium includes $63,750 in contents on a replacement cost basis. Premium includes $2,500 for jewelry and furs theft coverage ($1,500 per item). Additional living expense coverage equals actual loss sustained within 24 months. Up to 30% discount for homes with newer utilities. Other discounts available such as home/auto, claim free, home alert, automatic sprinklers. An additional 20% of the dwelling coverage amount applies for the dwelling if insured to 100% replacement cost.

(16) Rates shown are for Home & Highway Personal Package program. Rates include $5,000 medical payments and maximum financial stability discount.

(17) Premier Homeowner Program, protection class 1–6. Coverage C (personal property) is automatically 70% of Coverage A (home), so the premium includes a charge to increase to 75%. Medical payments of $2,000 and personal injury automatically included. Auto/home discount applied. Insurance Score discount given–discount varies based on the Insurance Score.

Sᴏᴜʀᴄᴇ: Excerpted from *Consumer's Guide to Homeowner's Insurance (2006)*, State of Wisconsin, Office of the Commissioner of Insurance.

storms, and fire losses. However, floods and earthquakes are specifically excluded. Although federal flood insurance is available, and an earthquake endorsement can be added to the homeowners policy, most property owners are not insured against these two perils. If you reside in a flood or earthquake zone, you should seriously consider covering such perils in your personal risk management program. Otherwise, you stand to lose a substantial amount of money if a flood or earthquake occurs. For example, in 2005, Hurricane Katrina caused flooding in more than 80 percent of the city of New Orleans, which resulted in billions of property damage losses. Most homeowners did not carry flood insurance and experienced severe financial problems as a result.

Improve Your Credit Record   Another important suggestion is to improve your credit record. As noted

earlier, many insurers use an applicant's credit record and insurance score for purposes of underwriting and rating. Applicants with good or superior credit records may be able to purchase a homeowners policy more cheaply than applicants with poor credit records. A good credit record can also result in lower interest rates on mortgage loans, auto loans, and credit cards.

Consider Purchasing a Personal Umbrella Policy   A basic homeowners policy provides only $100,000 of personal liability insurance, which is insufficient in the event of a catastrophic liability loss. A **personal umbrella policy** provides an additional $1 million to $10 million of liability insurance after the underlying coverage is exhausted. It also covers liability arising out of personal injury, including coverage for libel, slander, and defamation of character. The homeowners policy does not cover personal injury without an endorsement. Also, in addition to coverage on your home and personal activities, the personal umbrella policy provides excess liability insurance on your cars, boats, and recreational vehicles. The personal umbrella policy is explained in greater detail in Chapter 24.

CASE APPLICATION

Lucia and her husband, Geraldo, recently purchased a home for $250,000. The home is insured under an HO-3 policy for $250,000 with no endorsements attached. The home is located in an area where property values have increased steadily over the years. Lucia collects antiques for a hobby. Geraldo has a stamp collection that contains several rare stamps. The couple also owns a 30-foot sailboat that they use on weekends.

a. Assume you are a risk management consultant who has been asked to evaluate the couple's HO-3 policy. Identify three endorsements that Lucia and Geraldo may wish to purchase to modify their HO-3 policy.

b. Explain how the above HO-3 policy would be modified by each endorsement identified in your answer to (a) above.

c. For each of the following losses, indicate whether Section II of the homeowners policy would provide full coverage for the loss. If full coverage would not be provided, explain why.

(1) Lucia entertains members of a local garden club in her home and serves the guests a buffet luncheon. Two guests become seriously ill and sue Lucia, alleging she had served them contaminated food. The court awards each guest damages of $60,000.

(2) Geraldo is an architect. The roof of a new addition to a client's home collapses. The client alleges that the roof collapsed because of Geraldo's faulty design. The cost of rebuilding is $40,000. The client seeks to recover that amount from Geraldo.

(3) During a visit to a friend's home, Lucia accidentally breaks a figurine that she picked up to admire. The figurine has a value of $475. The friend is seeking damages from Lucia.

SUMMARY

- Section II of the homeowners policy protects the named insured, resident relatives, and other persons for legal liability arising out of their personal acts.

- Insured locations include the residence premises described in the declarations, other residences acquired during the policy period, a residence where the insured is temporarily residing, vacant land other than farmland, cemetery or burial plots, land on which a residence is being built, and occasional rental of a premises for other than business purposes.

- Personal liability insurance (Coverage E) protects the insured against a claim or suit for damages because of bodily injury or property damage caused by the insured's negligence. The company will defend the insured and pay out those sums that the insured is legally obligated to pay up to the policy limits.

- Medical payments to others (Coverage F) pays the reasonable medical expenses of another person who may be accidentally injured on the premises, or by the activities of an insured, resident employee, or animal owned by or in the care of an insured. It is not necessary to prove negligence and establish legal liability before the medical expenses are paid. The coverage does not apply to injuries of the named insured and regular residents of the household, other than residence employees.

- Section II also provides four additional coverages: (1) claim expenses, (2) first-aid expenses, (3) damage to property of others, and (4) coverage for a loss-assessment charge.

- Numerous endorsements can be added to a homeowners policy to meet individual needs, including the following:

  Inflation guard endorsement

  Earthquake endorsement

Personal property replacement cost loss settlement endorsement

Scheduled personal property endorsement (with agreed value loss settlement)

Personal injury endorsement

Watercraft endorsement

Home business insurance coverage endorsement

- The cost of a homeowners policy depends on numerous factors. These include construction, location, fire-protection class, construction costs, age of the home, type of policy, deductible amount, insurer, insurance score, and CLUE report.

- Certain suggestions should be followed when shopping for a homeowners policy:

  Carry adequate insurance.

  Add necessary endorsements.

  Shop around for a homeowners policy.

  Consider a higher deductible.

  Take advantage of discounts.

  Don't ignore floods and earthquakes.

  Improve your credit record.

  Consider purchasing a personal umbrella policy.

KEY CONCEPTS AND TERMS

Claim expenses
Contractual liability
Damage to property of others
Earthquake endorsement
First-aid expenses
Home business insurance coverage endorsement
Inflation guard endorsement
Insurance score
Medical payments to others
Occurrence
Personal injury endorsement
Personal liability
Personal property replacement cost loss settlement endorsement
Personal umbrella policy
Scheduled personal property endorsement (with agreed value loss settlement)
Watercraft endorsement

REVIEW QUESTIONS

1. What is the meaning of an *occurrence* under Section II of the homeowners policy?

2. Briefly explain the personal liability coverage (Coverage E) in Section II of the homeowners policy.

3. a. Briefly explain the coverage for medical payments to others (Coverage F) in Section II of the homeowners policy.
   b. Identify the people who are covered for medical payments to others (Coverage F) in the homeowners policy.

4. Personal liability (Coverage E) and medical payments to others (Coverage F) provide protection to insureds at various insured locations. Identify the insured locations under Section II in the homeowners policy.

5. List the major exclusions that apply to personal liability (Coverage E) and medical payments to others (Coverage F) in the homeowners policy.

6. Section II of the homeowners policy provides several additional coverages. One additional coverage is called *damage to the property of others*. Briefly describe this coverage.

7. Briefly describe the following endorsements that can be added to a homeowners policy:
   a. Earthquake endorsement
   b. Inflation guard endorsement
   c. Personal property replacement cost loss settlement endorsement.
   d. Scheduled personal property endorsement (with agreed value loss settlement)

8. Homeowners insurance premiums are based on a number of factors. Identify the major factors that determine the cost of a homeowners policy.

9. Many insurers now use insurance scores in the underwriting and rating of a homeowners policy.
   a. What is an insurance score?
   b. Why do insurers use insurance scores in underwriting and rating?

10. Briefly explain the suggestions that consumers should follow when shopping for a homeowners policy.

APPLICATION QUESTIONS

1. Indicate whether the following losses are covered under Section II of the homeowners policy. Assume there are no special endorsements. Give reasons for your answers.

a. The insured's dog bites a neighbor's child and also chews up the neighbor's coat.

b. The insured accidentally injures another player while playing softball.

c. A guest slips on a waxed kitchen floor and breaks an arm.

d. A neighbor's child falls off a swing in the insured's yard and breaks an arm.

e. The insured accidentally falls on an icy sidewalk and breaks a leg.

f. While driving to the supermarket, the insured injures another motorist with the automobile.

g. A ward of the court, age 10, in the care of the insured, deliberately breaks a neighbor's window.

h. The insured paints houses for a living. A can of paint accidentally falls onto a customer's roof and discolors it.

i. The insured falls asleep while smoking a cigarette in a rented hotel room, and the room is badly damaged by the fire.

j. The insured borrows a camera, and it is stolen from a motel room while the insured is on vacation.

2. Joseph is the named insured under a Homeowners 3 policy (special form) with a liability limit of $100,000 per occurrence and a $1000 limit for medical payments to others. For each of the following situations, explain whether the loss is covered under Section II of Joseph's homeowners policy.

   a. Joseph is a self-employed accountant who works in his home. One of Joseph's clients sues him for negligence in the preparation of a tax return and is awarded a $3000 judgment against him.

   b. Joseph's 25-year-old son, who recently married and now lives in his own apartment, negligently kills another hunter in a hunting accident. The son is sued for $1 million in a wrongful-death accident.

3. Martha rents an apartment and is the named insured under a Homeowners 4 policy (contents broad form) with a liability limit of $100,000 per occurrence and $1000 medical payments. For each of the following situations, indicate to what extent, if any, the loss is covered under Section II of Martha's homeowners policy. Assume there are no special endorsements, and each situation is an independent event.

   a. Martha attends a party at a friend's house. She accidentally burns a hole in the living room couch with her cigarette. It will cost $500 to repair the damaged couch.

   b. Martha rents a snowmobile at a ski resort and accidentally collides with a skier. Martha is sued for $200,000 by the injured skier.

4. Explain whether each of the following losses would be covered under Section II in the homeowners policy. If the exposure is not covered, explain how coverage can be obtained.

   a. The insured owns a restaurant in a large city. The insured is sued by several customers who allege they became seriously ill from a contaminated banana cream pie served at the restaurant.

   b. While operating a 30-foot sailboat, the insured injures a swimmer.

   c. The insured is sued by his ex-wife, who alleges her reputation has been ruined because the insured lied about her relationship with another man.

5. Jerry and Lois Gower own and operate the Gower Painting Co. The couple is insured under a Homeowners 3 policy with no special endorsements. The policy has a $100,000 per occurrence limit for personal liability and a $1000 limit for medical payments to others. For each of the following situations, indicate to what extent, if any, the loss is covered under Section II of their homeowners policy.

   a. Jerry left a ladder standing against a house that he was painting. When Jerry went to lunch, a small child, age 7, climbed the ladder and was seriously injured when the ladder collapsed. Jerry is sued by the child's parents for $200,000.

   b. Lois accidentally fell off the roof of a second story house that she was painting and injured her leg. She incurred medical expenses of $3000.

   c. The couple's daughter, Jennifer, age 22, attends college at a large Midwestern university. While playing softball, Jennifer made a hard slide into second base and accidentally injured the opposing player. The injured player claims Jennifer intended to injure her and sues Jennifer for $50,000.

   d. Lois has a basset hound, Huey, for a pet. Huey is a friendly, docile dog and loves people. One morning, Lois carelessly left the backyard gate open, and Huey escaped from the fenced yard. A neighbor tried to catch the dog, and Huey bit him on the hand and leg. The neighbor incurred medical bills of $800. Lois is later sued by the neighbor for $50,000 when the dog bite became infected and did not heal.

   e. Jerry is playing golf with a friend who is riding in a golf cart that he is operating. The cart overturned when Jerry carelessly ran into a wooded area on the outside of the fairway and hit a tree. Jerry's friend is seriously injured and sues Jerry for $150,000.

INTERNET RESOURCES

- The **Insurance Information Institute** provides timely information on homeowners insurance and other personal property insurance coverages. Articles on homeowners insurance and other property and liability coverages can be accessed directly online. Visit the site at

  http://www.iii.org

- **Insure.com** provides news, premium quotes, and other consumer information on homeowners insurance. The site also provides news releases about events that affect the insurance industry. Visit the site at

  http://www.insure.com

- **Insurance.com** provides premium quotes on a variety of insurance products, including homeowners and renters insurance, auto insurance, life insurance, and health insurance. You can even get quotes on pet insurance. Visit the site at

  http://www.insurance.com

- **INSWEB** provides premium quotes on homeowners, auto, and other insurance products. You can comparison shop from your computer. In addition, the site provides information and articles from industry, consumer, and regulatory groups. Visit the site at

  http://www.insweb.com

- The **International Risk Management Institute (IRMI)** is an online source that provides valuable information about personal lines and commercial lines. The site provides timely articles on a wide range of risk management and insurance topics and offers a number of free e-mail newsletters. Visit the site at

  http://www.irmi.com

- **Quicken.com** provides timely information on homeowners, condominium, renters, and auto insurance. The site also provides premium quotes for homeowners, auto, and life insurance, as well as other personal insurance lines. Visit the site at

  http://www.quicken.com/insurance

SELECTED REFERENCES

"CLUE Claims Databases," *Hot Topics & Issues Updates,* Insurance Information Institute, April 2006. This source is periodically updated.

"Catastrophes: Insurance Issues," *Hot Topics & Issues Updates,* Insurance Information Institute, October 2006. This source is periodically updated.

"Earthquakes: Risk and Insurance Issues," *Hot Topics & Issues Updates,* Insurance Information Institute, September 2006. This source is periodically updated.

Fair, Isaac Corporation. *Predictiveness of Credit History for Insurance Loss Relativities,* A Fair Isaac Paper, October 1999.

Fire, Casualty & Surety Bulletins, Personal Lines volume, Dwelling section. Erlanger, KY: National Underwriter Company. The bulletins are updated monthly.

Hamilton, Karen L., and Cheryl L. Ferguson. *Personal Risk Management and Property-Liability Insurance,* 1st ed. Malvern, PA.: American Institute for Chartered Property Casualty Underwriters/Insurance Institute of America, 2002.

Hartwig, Robert P., *No Evidence of Disparate Impact in Texas Due to Use of Credit Information by Personal Lines Insurers.* Insurance Information Institute, January 2005.

Hartwig, Robert P., and Claire Wilkinson. *The Use of Credit Information in Personal Lines Insurance Underwriting.* New York: Insurance Information Institute, Insurance Issues Series, vol. 1, no. 2, June 2003.

International Risk Management Institute (IRMI). IRMI.com is an online source that provides information on personal lines and commercial lines. The site provides timely articles on a wide range of risk management and insurance topics and offers a number of free e-mail newsletters.

Lee, Diana, et al. "Give Us Some Credit: The Use of Credit Information in Insurance Underwriting and Rating," *Risk Management & Insurance Review,* vol. 8, no. 1, Spring 2005.

Richardson, Diane W. *Homeowners Coverage Guide,* 2nd ed. Cincinnati, OH: The National Underwriter Company, 2002.

Wiening, Eric A., George E. Rejda, Constance M. Luthardt, and Cheryl L. Ferguson. *Personal Insurance,* 1st ed. Malvern, PA.: American Institute for Chartered Property Casualty Underwriters/ Insurance Institute of America, 2002.

NOTES

1. The discussion of Section II liability coverages in this chapter is based largely on the *Fire, Casualty & Surety Bulletins*, Personal Lines volume, Dwelling section (Erlanger, KY: National Underwriter Company); and the copyrighted HO-3 policy and subsequent coverage modifications drafted by the Insurance Services Office (ISO). The HO-3 policy and various policy provisions are used with the permission of ISO.

2. "Earthquakes: Risk and Insurance issues," *Hot Topics & Issues Updates,* September 2006. This topic is periodically updated.

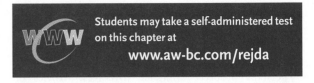

Students may take a self-administered test on this chapter at
www.aw-bc.com/rejda

APPENDIX

HOW TO SAVE MONEY ON A HOMEOWNERS POLICY*

The price you pay for your homeowners insurance can vary by hundreds of dollars depending on the size of your house and the insurance company from which you buy your policy. Here are 12 steps you can take to save money.

1. **Shop around.** Prices vary from company to company, so it pays to shop around. Get quotes from several companies. You can call the companies directly or access information on the Internet. The state insurance department may also provide comparisons of prices charged by major insurers.

   You buy insurance to protect you financially and provide peace of mind. It is important to pick a company that is financially stable. Check the financial health of insurance companies by examining the ratings assigned by rating services, such as A. M. Best (http://www.ambest.com) and Standard & Poor's (http://www.standardand poors.com/ratings).

   Get quotes from different types of insurance companies. Some sell through exclusive agents. These agencies have the same name as the insurance company. Some sell through independent agents who offer policies from several insurance companies. Others do not use agents. They sell directly to consumers over the phone or via the Internet.

   But don't shop price alone. You want a company that answers your questions and handles claims fairly and efficiently. Ask friends and relatives for their recommendations. Contact your state insurance department to find out whether it makes available consumer complaint ratios by company.

2. **Raise your deductible.** The higher your deductible, the more money you save on your premium. Consider a deductible of at least $500. If you can afford to raise it to $1000, you may save as much as 25 percent.

   If you live in a disaster-prone area, your insurance policy may have a separate deductible for damage from major disasters. If you live near the East Coast, you may have a separate windstorm deductible; if you live in a state vulnerable to hail storms, you may have a separate deductible for hail; and if you live in an earthquake-prone area, your earthquake endorsement has a deductible.

*This appendix is adapted from "How Can I Save Money?" Insurance Information Institute.

3. **Buy your home and auto policies from the same insurer.** Most companies that sell homeowners insurance also sell auto and umbrella liability insurance. An umbrella liability policy will give you extra liability coverage. Some insurance companies will reduce your premium by 5 percent to 15 percent if you buy two or more insurance policies from them. But make certain this combined price is lower than buying individual coverages from different companies.

4. **Make your home more disaster-resistant.** Find out from your insurance agent or company representative what you can do to make your home more resistant to windstorms and other natural disasters. You may be able to save on premiums by adding storm shutters and shatter-proof glass, reinforcing your roof, or buying stronger roofing materials. Older homes can be retrofitted to make them better able to withstand earthquakes. In addition, consider modernizing your heating, plumbing, and electrical systems to reduce the risk of fire and water damage.

5. **Don't confuse what you paid for your house with rebuilding costs.** The land under your house isn't at risk from theft, windstorm, fire, and the other perils covered in your homeowners policy. So don't include its value in deciding how much homeowners insurance to buy. If you do, you'll pay a higher premium than you should.

6. **Ask about discounts for home security devices.** You can usually get discounts of at least 5 percent for a smoke detector, burglar alarm, or dead-bolt locks. Some companies may cut your premiums by as much as 15 percent or 20 percent if you install a sophisticated sprinkler system and a fire and burglar alarm that rings at the police, fire, or other monitoring stations. These systems aren't cheap, and not every system qualifies for a discount. Before you buy one, find out what kind your insurer recommends, how much the device would cost, and how much you'd save on premiums.

7. **Seek out other discounts.** Many companies offer discounts, but they don't all offer the same discount or the same amount of discount in all states. Ask your agent or company representative about discounts available to you. For example, if you're at least 55 years old and retired, you may qualify for a discount of up to 10 percent at some companies. If you've completely modernized your plumbing or electrical system recently, some companies may also provide a price break.

8. **See if you can get group coverage.** Does your employer administer a group insurance program? Check to see if a homeowners policy is available and is a better deal than you can find elsewhere. In addition, professional, alumni, and business groups may offer an insurance package at a reduced price.

9. **Stay with the same insurer.** If you've been insured with the same company for several years, you may receive a discount for being a long-term policyowner. Some insurers will reduce premiums by 5 percent if you stay with them for three to five years and by 10 percent if you're a policyowner for six years or more. To ensure you're getting a good deal, periodically compare this price with the prices of policies from other insurers.

10. **Review policy limits and the value of your possessions annually.** You want your policy to cover any major purchases or additions to your home. But you don't want to spend money for coverage you don't need. If your five-year-old fur coat is no longer worth the $5000 you paid for it, you'll want to reduce or cancel your floater (extra insurance for items whose full value is not covered by standard homeowners policies) and pocket the premium savings.

11. **Look for private insurance if you are in a government plan.** If you live in a high-risk area—one that is especially vulnerable to coastal storms, fires, or crime—and you've been buying your homeowners insurance through a government plan, find out from insurance agents, company representatives, or your state department of insurance which insurance companies might be interested in your business. You may find there are steps you can take that will allow you to buy insurance at a lower price in the private market.

12. **When you're buying a home, consider the cost of homeowners insurance.** The price you pay for homeowners insurance depends in part on the cost of rebuilding your home and the likelihood that it will be damaged by natural disasters or destroyed by fire. You may pay less if you buy a house close to a fire hydrant or in a community that has a professional rather than a volunteer fire department. Premiums may be lower if your home's electrical, heating, and plumbing systems are less than 10 years old. If you live in the East, consider a brick home because it's more wind-resistant. If you live in an earthquake-prone area, look for a wooden frame house because it is more likely to withstand this type of disaster. Choosing wisely could cut your premiums by 5 percent to 15 percent.

Remember that flood insurance and earthquake damage are not covered by a standard homeowners policy. If you buy a house in a flood-prone area, you'll have to pay for a flood insurance policy that costs an average of $400 a year. The Federal Emergency Management Agency provides useful information on flood insurance on its Web site (http://www.fema.gov/business/nfip). A separate earthquake policy is available from most insurance companies. The cost of the coverage will depend on the likelihood of earthquakes in your area and the construction features of your home.

If you have questions about insurance for any of your possessions, be sure to ask your agent or company representative. For example, if you run a business out of your home, be sure you have adequate coverage. Most homeowners policies cover business equipment in the home, but only up to $2500 and they offer no business liability insurance.

CHAPTER 22

AUTO INSURANCE

"A careful driver is one who honks his horn when he goes through a red light."

Henry Morgan

LEARNING OBJECTIVES

After studying this chapter, you should be able to

◆ Identify the parties that are insured for liability coverage under the Personal Auto Policy (PAP).

◆ Describe the liability coverage in the PAP.

◆ Explain the medical payments coverage in the PAP.

◆ Describe the uninsured motorists coverage in the PAP.

◆ Explain the coverage for damage to your auto in the PAP.

◆ Explain the duties imposed on the insured after an accident or loss.

*M*organ, age 22, overslept and was rushing to an early morning class at a local university. While driving at a high rate of speed on a crowded expressway, she lost control of her car and smashed into another vehicle. The other driver was seriously injured, and his car was wrecked beyond repair. Although Morgan was not hurt, her car was badly damaged. She received a citation from the police for reckless driving. Morgan reported the accident to her insurer, who subsequently settled the bodily injury and property damage claim with the injured driver.

Morgan's auto policy protected her against the financial consequences of her negligent act. Her insurer also paid for the physical damage to her car less a modest deductible. Auto insurance provides similar protection to millions of motorists. It is one of the most important coverages to emphasize in a personal risk management program. Legal liability arising out of an auto accident can reach catastrophic levels; medical expenses and physical damage to an expensive car can be substantial; and noneconomic costs may also be incurred, including pain and suffering and the unexpected death of a family member.

This chapter discusses the major provisions of the *Personal Auto Policy (PAP)* drafted by the Insurance Services Office (ISO). The PAP policy is widely used throughout the United States. Some insurers, such as State Farm and Allstate, have designed their own forms that differ somewhat from the PAP form, but the differences are relatively minor.

OVERVIEW OF PERSONAL AUTO POLICY

In this section, we discuss the major provisions of the 2005 Personal Auto Policy (PAP) drafted by the Insurance Services Office (ISO).[1] The 2005 PAP is widely used throughout the United States and replaces the older 1998 form.

Eligible Vehicles

Only certain types of vehicles are eligible for coverage under the PAP. An eligible vehicle is a four-wheel motor vehicle owned by the insured or leased by the insured for at least six continuous months. Thus, a private passenger auto, station wagon, or sport utility vehicle owned by the insured is eligible for coverage.

A pickup or van is eligible for coverage if the vehicle has a Gross Vehicle Weight Rating of 10,000 pounds or less and is not used for the delivery and transportation of goods and materials. The limitation on use does not apply if (1) such use is incidental to the named insured's business of installing, maintaining, or repairing furnishings or equipment (such as a plumber who transports work tools and supplies in a van) or (2) the vehicle is used in ranching or farming.

Your Covered Auto

An extremely important provision is the definition of **your covered auto.** Four classes of vehicles are considered to be covered autos:

- Any vehicle shown in the declarations
- A newly acquired auto

- A trailer owned by the named insured
- A temporary substitute vehicle

Any Vehicle Shown in the Declarations Any vehicle shown on the declarations page is a covered auto. Covered autos include a private passenger auto, station wagon, sport utility vehicle, pickup, or van owned by the named insured. A vehicle listed in the declarations that is leased for at least six months is a covered auto as well.

Newly Acquired Auto A newly acquired private passenger auto, pickup, or van is a covered auto if it is acquired by the named insured during the policy period. As stated earlier, a pickup or van must (1) have a Gross Vehicle Weight Rate of 10,000 pounds or less, and (2) must not be used to transport business materials unless the materials are incidental to the named insured's business, and that business is installing, maintaining, or repairing furnishing or equipment, or is used in farming or ranching.

With respect to liability coverage, medical payments coverage, and uninsured motorists coverage, coverage begins automatically on the date you become the owner. If the coverages on all listed vehicles are not the same, you receive the broadest coverage provided for any vehicle shown in the declarations.

If the vehicle you acquire is an *additional vehicle,* you are automatically covered for 14 days, but you must notify the insurer within 14 days after you become the owner for coverage to continue. If the vehicle you acquire is a *replacement vehicle,* you are automatically covered until the policy expires; you are not required to notify the insurer. A replacement vehicle is one that replaces a vehicle shown in the declarations. As a result, liability coverage, medical payments coverage, and uninsured motorists coverage apply automatically to a replacement vehicle without first having to notify the insurer.

With respect to coverage for damage to your auto, however, a different set of rules applies. The PAP contains notification provisions that apply separately to collision coverage and other-than-collision coverage. *If the declarations page indicates that collision coverage applies to at least one auto, the newly acquired auto is automatically covered on the date of ownership, but you must notify the insurer within 14 days after you become the owner for collision coverage to continue.* The lowest deductible on any vehicle shown in the declarations applies to the newly acquired auto. A similar notification provision applies separately to other-than-collision coverage.

The time requirement for notifying the insurer is reduced if there is no collision coverage on any vehicle. *If the declarations page does not indicate collision coverage for at least one auto, a newly acquired auto is automatically insured for collision coverage for only four days.* You must notify the insurer within four days after you become the owner for collision coverage to continue. If a loss occurs before you notify the insurer, a $500 collision deductible must be met. A similar notification provision applies separately to other-than-collision coverage.

Trailer Owned by the Named Insured A trailer owned by the named insured is also a covered auto. A trailer is a vehicle designed to be pulled by a private passenger auto, pickup, or van and also includes a farm wagon or farm implement while being towed by such vehicles. For example, you may be pulling a boat trailer that overturns and injures another motorist. The liability coverage in the PAP would cover the loss.

Temporary Substitute Vehicle A temporary substitute vehicle is also a covered auto. A **temporary substitute vehicle** is a nonowned auto or trailer that you are temporarily using because of mechanical breakdown, repair, servicing, loss, or destruction of a covered vehicle. For example, if you drive a loaner car furnished by a repair shop or drive a friend's car while your car is in the garage for repairs, your PAP covers the nonowned vehicle.

Summary of PAP Coverages

The PAP consists of a declarations page, a definitions page, and the following six parts:

- Part A: Liability Coverage
- Part B: Medical Payments Coverage
- Part C: Uninsured Motorists Coverage
- Part D: Coverage for Damage to Your Auto
- Part E: Duties after an Accident or Loss
- Part F: General Provisions

PART A: LIABILITY COVERAGE

Liability coverage (Part A) is the most important part of the PAP. It protects a covered person against a suit or claim arising out of the ownership or operation of a covered vehicle.

Insuring Agreement

In the insuring agreement, the insurer agrees to pay any damages for bodily injury or property damage for which any insured is legally responsible because of an auto accident. The PAP is typically written with split limits. **Split limits** *mean that the amounts of insurance for bodily injury liability and property damage liability are stated separately.* For example, split limits of $250,000/$500,000/$100,000 mean that you have bodily injury liability coverage of $250,000 for each person and a maximum of $500,000 of bodily injury coverage for each accident. You also have $100,000 of property damage liability coverage. (Practitioners frequently refer to such limits as 250/500/100.)

Liability coverage can also be written with a single limit by adding an appropriate endorsement to the policy. A **single limit** *applies to both bodily injury and property damage liability: the total amount of insurance applies to the entire accident without a separate limit for each person.* For example, a single limit of $500,000 would apply to both bodily injury and property damage liability.

The amount paid as damages includes any prejudgment interest awarded against the insured. Many states allow plaintiffs (injured persons) to receive interest on the judgment from the time the suit is entered to the time the judgment is determined. Any prejudgment interest is considered part of the damages awarded and is subject to the policy limit of liability.

The insurer also agrees to defend you and pay all legal defense costs. The defense costs are paid in addition to the policy limits. *However, the insurer's duty to settle or defend the claim ends when the limit of liability has been exhausted by payment of judgments or settlements.* This provision means that the insurer cannot deposit the policy limits into an escrow account and walk away without first defending the insured. The obligation to defend ends when the policy limits are exhausted by payment of a judgment against the insured or settlement with a claimant. The duty to defend also ends if the claim is settled for less than the policy limits.

In addition, the insurer has no obligation to defend any claim not covered by the policy. For example, if you intentionally cause bodily injury or property damage and are sued, the insurer has no obligation to defend you because intentional acts are specifically excluded.

Insured Persons

The following four groups are insured under the liability section of the PAP:

- The named insured and any resident family member
- Any person using the named insured's covered auto
- Any person or organization legally responsible for any insured's use of a covered auto on behalf of that person or organization
- Any person or organization legally responsible for the named insured's or family members' use of any auto or trailer (other than a covered auto or one owned by that person or organization)

First, the named insured and resident family members are insured for liability coverage. The named insured also includes a spouse if a resident of the same household. In recognition of the widespread divorce and separation found today, the PAP provides coverage for 90 days to a spouse who no longer resides in the named insured's household and is not listed as a named insured in the policy. If a spouse ceases to be a resident of the same household and is not listed as a named insured, the spouse is covered for 90 days following the change in residency, or until the spouse obtains a separate PAP or the policy period ends, whichever occurs first. If both spouses are named in the declarations as named insureds in the same PAP, the policy covers both spouses even though one spouse no longer resides in the same residence.

For example, Jennifer and James are married and live in the same residence. Jennifer is the named insured under her PAP policy. Assume that James is not listed as a named insured in her policy. He is still considered a named insured because he is Jennifer's husband. If the couple separates and James moves into another apartment, he is covered for 90 days under Jennifer's policy, or until he purchases his own policy, if earlier. However, if both were named insureds under the same PAP, James would continue to be covered as a named insured until the policy expires, or until he purchases his own policy, if earlier.

A family member is a person related to the named insured by blood, marriage, or adoption who resides in the same household, including a ward of the court or foster child. *Thus, the husband, wife, and children are covered while using any auto, owned or non-owned.* If the children are attending college and are temporarily away from home, they are still covered under their parents' policy.

Second, any other person using the named insured's covered auto is also insured provided that person can establish a reasonable belief that permission to use the covered auto exists. For example, John may have permitted his girlfriend, Susan, to drive his car several times over the past six months. If Susan takes John's car without his express permission, she is covered under his policy as long as she can show a reasonable belief that John would have given her permission to use the car.

Third, coverage also applies to any person or organization legally responsible for any insured's use of a covered auto on behalf of that person or organization. For example, if Mark drives his car on an errand for his employer and injures someone, the employer is covered for any resulting suit or claim against the employee.

Finally, coverage applies to any person or organization legally responsible for the named insured's or family members' use of any auto or trailer (other than a covered auto or one owned by the person or organization). For example, Mark may borrow the car of a fellow worker to mail a package for his employer. If Mark injures someone while driving that car, the employer is also covered for any suit or claim against the employee. However, the PAP does not extend coverage to the employer when the named insured is using an auto owned by the employer. So if Mark is driving to the post office in a company car, the employer is not insured under Mark's PAP.

Supplementary Payments

In addition to the policy limits and a legal defense, certain **supplementary payments** can be paid. They include the following:

- Up to $250 for the cost of a bail bond
- Premiums on appeal bonds and bonds to release attachments
- Interest accruing after a judgment
- Up to $200 daily for the loss of earnings
- Other reasonable expenses

Premiums on a bail bond can be paid up to $250 because of an auto accident that results in property damage or bodily injury. However, payment is not made for a traffic violation such as a speeding ticket except if an accident occurs. For example, assume Richard is drunk and injures another motorist in an auto accident. If he is arrested, and bail is set at $2500, the insurer will pay the bail bond premium up to a maximum of $250.

Premiums on an appeal bond and a bond to release an attachment of property in any suit defended by the insurer are also paid as supplementary payments. If interest accrues after a judgment is awarded, the interest is also paid as a supplementary payment. Any prejudgment interest, however, is part of the liability limits.

The insurer will also pay up to $200 daily for the loss of earnings (but not other income) due to attendance at a hearing or trial at the company's request.

Finally, other reasonable expenses incurred at the insurer's request are paid. For example, you may be a defendant in a trial and be requested to testify. If you have meal or transportation expenses, they would be paid as a supplemental payment.

Exclusions

A lengthy list of exclusions applies to the liability coverage under the PAP. They are summarized as follows:

1. *Intentional injury or damage.* Intentional bodily injury or property damage is specifically excluded. For example, a driver changes lanes suddenly without signaling and cuts sharply in front of Richard's car. Richard is enraged and deliberately rams the vehicle. The intentional property damage to the other driver's car is not cov-

ered by Richard's PAP. Unfortunately, "road rage" is widespread nationally and is responsible for numerous motor vehicle deaths.

2. *Property owned or transported.* Liability coverage is not provided to any person for damage to property owned or being transported by that person. For example, the suitcase and camera belonging to a friend may be damaged in an auto accident while you and your friend are on vacation together. The damage would not be covered by your PAP.

3. *Property rented, used, or in the insured's care.* Damage to property rented to, used by, or in the care of the insured is not covered. For example, if you rent some skis that are damaged in an auto accident, the property damage is not covered. The exclusion, however, does not apply to property damage to a residence or private garage. For example, if you rent a house and carelessly back into a partly opened garage door, the property damage to the door would be covered.

4. *Bodily injury to an employee.* Bodily injury to an employee of the insured who is injured during the course of employment is also excluded. The intent here is to cover the employee's injury under a workers compensation law. However, a domestic employee injured during the course of employment would be covered if workers compensation benefits are not required or available.

5. *Use as a public or livery conveyance.* Another exclusion is liability arising out of the ownership or operation of a vehicle while it is being used as a public or livery conveyance. The intent here is to exclude coverage if the insured makes the vehicle available for hire to the general public. However, the exclusion does not apply to a share-the-expense carpool.

6. *Vehicles used in the auto business.* If a person is employed or engaged in the auto business, liability arising out of the operation of vehicles in the auto business is excluded. The auto business refers to the selling, repairing, servicing, storing, or parking of vehicles designed for use mainly on public highways. It also includes road testing and delivery. For example, assume you take your car to a garage for repairs. If a mechanic has an accident and injures someone while road testing your car, your PAP liability coverage

does not protect the mechanic. (However, if you are sued because you are the car owner, you are covered.) The intent of this exclusion is to exclude loss exposures that should be covered under the auto repair firm's liability policy, such as a garage policy.

The preceding exclusion does not apply to the operation, ownership, or use of a covered auto by the named insured, by any resident family member, or by any partner, agent, or employee of the named insured or family member. For example, if an auto mechanic has an accident while driving his or her own car to pick up a repair part, the mechanic's PAP would cover the loss.

7. *Other business vehicles.* Liability coverage does not apply to any vehicle maintained or used in any other business (other than farming or ranching). This exclusion is similar to the preceding auto business exclusion except it applies to all other business use with certain exceptions. The intent here is to exclude liability coverage for commercial vehicles and trucks that are used in a business. For example, if you drive a city bus or operate a large cement truck, your PAP liability coverage does not apply.

The exclusion does not apply to an owned or nonowned private passenger auto, pickup, or van. Thus, you are covered if you drive your car on company business.

8. *Using a vehicle without reasonable belief of permission.* If a person uses a vehicle without a reasonable belief that he or she has permission to do so, the liability coverage does not apply. The exclusion does not apply to a family member who is using a covered auto owned by the named insured.

9. *Nuclear energy exclusion.* Liability of insureds who are covered under special nuclear energy contracts is also excluded.

10. *Vehicle with fewer than four wheels.* Liability coverage does not apply to any vehicle that has fewer than four wheels or is designed for use mainly off public roads. Thus, motorcycles, mopeds, motorscooters, minibikes, and trail bikes are excluded. However, the exclusion does not apply if the vehicle is being used in a medical emergency or to any *nonowned* golf cart. For example, if you rent a golf cart and injure another golfer, liability coverage applies.

11. *Vehicle furnished or made available for the named insured's regular use.* Liability coverage excludes a vehicle other than a covered auto that is owned by, furnished, or made available for the named insured's regular use. You can occasionally drive another person's car and still have coverage under your policy. *However, if the nonowned auto is driven regularly or is furnished or made available for your regular use, your PAP liability coverage does not apply.* For example, if your employer furnishes you with a car, or if a car is available for your regular use in a company carpool, the liability coverage does not apply. The key point is not how frequently you drive someone else's car, but whether it is furnished or made available for your regular use.

    For an additional premium, the **extended nonowned coverage endorsement** can be added to the PAP that covers the insured while operating a nonowned auto on a regular basis.

12. *Vehicle owned by, furnished, or made available for the regular use of any family member.* This exclusion is similar to the preceding exclusion. However, it does not apply to the named insured and spouse. For example, if Mary borrows a car owned and insured by her son who lives with her, the liability coverage under Mary's PAP would cover her while driving the son's car.

13. *Racing vehicle.* Liability coverage does not apply to any vehicle while it is located inside a racing facility for the purpose of competing in or preparing for a prearranged racing or speed contest.

Limit of Liability

As noted earlier, the PAP is typically written with split limits. That is, the amounts of insurance for bodily injury liability and property damage liability are stated separately. The maximum amount paid for bodily injury to each person is the amount shown in the declarations. Subject to that limit for each person, the maximum amount paid for bodily injury to all persons resulting from any one auto accident is the amount shown in the declarations. The maximum amount paid for property damage resulting from any one auto accident is also shown in the declarations.

Out-of-State Coverage

An important provision applies if the accident occurs in a state other than where the covered auto is principally garaged. If the accident occurs in a state that has a financial responsibility law with higher liability limits than the limits shown in the declarations, the PAP automatically provides the higher specified limits.

Likewise, if the state has a compulsory insurance or similar law that requires a nonresident to have insurance whenever he or she uses a vehicle in that state, the PAP provides the required minimum amounts and types of coverage.

Other Insurance

In some cases, more than one liability policy covers a loss. If other applicable liability insurance applies to an *owned vehicle,* the insurer pays only its pro rata share of the loss. The insurer's share is the proportion that its limit of liability bears to the total applicable limits of liability under all policies. However, if the insurance applies to a *nonowned vehicle,* the insurer's insurance is excess over any other collectible insurance (see Exhibit 22.2).

PART B: MEDICAL PAYMENTS COVERAGE

Medical payments coverage is frequently included in the PAP. Medical payments are paid without regard to fault.

Insuring Agreement

Under this provision, the company will pay all reasonable medical and funeral expenses incurred by an insured for services rendered within three years from the date of the accident. Covered expenses include medical, surgical, X-ray, dental, and funeral expenses. The benefit limits typically range from $1000 to $10,000 per person and apply to each insured who is injured in the accident.

Medical payments coverage is not based on fault. Thus, if you are injured in an auto accident and are at fault, medical payments can still be paid to you and to other injured passengers in the car.

Exhibit 22.2
Primary and Excess Insurance

Ken is the named insured and borrows Karen's car with her permission. Ken has $50,000 of liability insurance and Karen has a $100,000 limit. Both policies will cover any loss. Ken negligently injures another motorist and must pay damages of $125,000. *The rule is that insurance on the borrowed car is primary, and other insurance is excess.*

Each company pays as follows:

Karen's insurer (primary)	$100,000
Ken's insurer (excess)	25,000
Total	$125,000

Insured Persons

Two groups are insured for medical payments coverage:

- Named insured and family members
- Other persons while occupying a covered auto

The named insured and family members are covered if they are injured while occupying any motor vehicle or are injured as pedestrians when struck by a motor vehicle designed for use mainly on public roads. For example, if the parents and children are injured in an auto accident while on vacation, their medical expenses are covered up to the policy limits. If the named insured or any family member is struck by a motor vehicle or trailer while walking, his or her medical expenses are also paid. However, if you are injured by a farm tractor, snowmobile, or bulldozer, your injury is not covered, because these vehicles are not designed for use mainly on public roads.

Other persons are also covered for their medical expenses while occupying a covered auto. For example, if you own your car and are the named insured, all passengers in your car are covered for their medical expenses under your policy. However, if you are operating a *nonowned vehicle,* other passengers in the car (other than family members) are not covered for their medical expenses under your policy. The intent here is to have other passengers in the nonowned vehicle seek protection under their own insurance or under the medical expense coverage that applies to the nonowned vehicle.

Exclusions

Medical payments coverage has numerous exclusions. They are summarized as follows:

1. *Motorized vehicle with fewer than four wheels.* Bodily injury while occupying a motorized vehicle with fewer than four wheels is excluded.
2. *Public or livery conveyance.* When a covered auto is used as a public or livery conveyance, the medical payments coverage does not apply. The exclusion does not apply to a share-the-expense carpool.
3. *Using the vehicle as a residence.* Coverage does not apply if the injury occurs while the vehicle is being used as a residence or premises. For example, if you own and occupy a camper trailer as a residence in a campground while on vacation, medical expense coverage does not apply if you burn yourself while cooking on a stove in the trailer.
4. *Injury occurring during course of employment.* Coverage does not apply if the injury occurs during the course of employment, and workers compensation benefits are required or available.
5. *Vehicle furnished or made available for the named insured's regular use.* Coverage does not apply to any injury sustained while occupying or when struck by a vehicle (other than a covered auto) that is owned by the named insured or is furnished or made available for the named insured's regular use. The intent here is to avoid providing "free" medical payments coverage on an owned or regularly used car not described in the policy.
6. *Vehicle furnished or made available for the regular use of any family member.* A similar exclusion applies to any vehicle (other than a covered auto) that is owned by any family member or is furnished or made available for the regular use of any family member. The exclusion does not apply to the named insured and spouse. For example, if a son living at home owns a car that is not insured for medical payments coverage, and the parents are injured while occupying the son's car, the parent's medical expenses would be covered under their policy.
7. *Using a vehicle without a reasonable belief of permission.* Coverage does not apply if the

injury occurs while occupying a vehicle without a reasonable belief of being entitled to do so. The exclusion does not apply to a family member who is using a covered auto owned by the named insured.

8. *Vehicle used in the business of an insured.* Coverage does not apply to any injury sustained while occupying a vehicle when it is being used in the business of an insured. The intent here is to exclude medical payments coverage for non-owned trucks and commercial vehicles used in the business of an insured person. The exclusion does not apply to a private passenger auto, to a pickup or van, or to a trailer used with any of the preceding vehicles.

9. *Nuclear weapon, radiation, or war.* Bodily injury from a nuclear weapon, nuclear radiation, or war is not covered.

10. *Racing vehicle.* Coverage does not apply to a bodily injury sustained while occupying a vehicle located inside a racing facility for the purpose of competing in or preparing for a pre-arranged racing or speed contest.

Other Insurance

If other auto medical payments insurance applies to an *owned vehicle,* the insurer pays its pro rata share of the loss based on the proportion that its limits bear to the total applicable limits.

However, medical payments coverage is excess with respect to a *nonowned vehicle.* For example, assume that Kim is driving her car and picks up Patti for lunch. Kim loses control of the car and hits a tree, and Patti is injured. Patti's medical bills are $6000. Kim has $2000 of medical expenses coverage, and Patti has $5000. Kim's insurer pays the first $2000 as primary insurer, and Patti's insurer pays the remaining $4000 as excess insurance.

PART C: UNINSURED MOTORISTS COVERAGE

Some motorists are irresponsible and drive without liability insurance. Across the United States, if someone is injured in an auto accident, the chances are about one in seven that the at-fault driver is unin-

sured. According to a recent Insurance Research Council (IRS) study, the estimated percentage of uninsured motorists increased nationally from 12.7 percent in 1999 to 14.6 percent in 2004.[2] However, there is wide variation among the states. The IRC study showed that the estimated percentage of uninsured drivers ranged from 26 percent in Mississippi to 4 percent in Maine.[3]

The **uninsured motorists coverage** pays for the bodily injury (and property damage in some states) caused by an uninsured motorist, by a hit-and-run driver, or by a negligent driver whose insurance company is insolvent.

Insuring Agreement

The insurer agrees to pay compensatory damages that an insured is legally entitled to receive from the owner or operator of an uninsured motor vehicle because of bodily injury caused by an accident. Damages include medical bills, lost wages, and compensation for a permanent disfigurement resulting from the accident. Several important points must be emphasized with respect to this coverage.

1. *The coverage applies only if the uninsured motorist is legally liable.* If the uninsured motorist is not liable, the insurer will not pay for the bodily injury.

2. *The insurer's maximum limit of liability for any single accident is the amount shown in the declarations.* You cannot receive duplicate payments for the same elements of loss under the uninsured motorists coverage and Part A (liability coverage) or Part B (medical payments coverage) of the policy, or any underinsured motorists coverage provided by the policy. Also, you cannot receive a duplicate payment for any element of loss for which payment has been made by or on behalf of persons or organizations legally responsible for the accident. Finally, the insurer will not pay you for any part of a loss if you are entitled to be paid for that part of the loss under a workers compensation or disability benefits law.

3. *The claim is subject to arbitration if the insured and insurer disagree over the amount of damages or whether the insured is entitled to receive any damages.* However, both the insured and insurer must agree to arbitration. Under this

provision, each party selects an arbitrator. The two arbitrators select a third arbitrator. A decision by two of the three arbitrators is binding on all parties. However, the decision is binding only if the damages awarded do not exceed the state's minimum financial responsibility law limits.

4. *Some states also include coverage for property damage from an uninsured motorist in their uninsured motorists law.* In these states, if an uninsured driver runs a red light and smashes into your car, the property damage to the car would be covered under the uninsured motorists coverage, subject to any applicable deductible.

There is considerable variation among the states that include property damage coverage in their uninsured motorists law. In some states, property damage coverage is an optional coverage that is purchased separately from the regular uninsured motorists coverage. In other states, both bodily injury and property damage coverages are included together in the uninsured motorists coverage; however, the insured may have the option of waiving the coverage if it is not desired. Finally, the property damage is subject to a deductible.

Insured Persons

Three groups are insured under the uninsured motorists coverage:

- The named insured and his or her family members
- Any other person while occupying a covered auto
- Any person legally entitled to recover damages

First, the named insured and his or her family members are covered if they are injured by an uninsured motorist. Second, any other person who is injured while occupying a covered auto is also insured; the coverage applies only if the individual is occupying a covered auto. Finally, any person legally entitled to recover damages is insured. An individual may not be physically involved in the accident but may be entitled to recover damages from the person or organization legally responsible for the bodily injury of the insured person. For example, if the named insured is killed by an uninsured motorist,

the surviving spouse could still collect damages under the uninsured motorists coverage.

Uninsured Vehicles

An extremely important provision defines an uninsured motor vehicle. Four groups of vehicles are considered to be uninsured vehicles:

1. An uninsured vehicle is a motor vehicle or trailer for which no bodily injury liability insurance policy or bond applies at the time of the accident.
2. A bodily injury liability policy or bond may be in force on a vehicle. However, the amount of insurance on that vehicle may be less than the amount required by the state's financial responsibility law in the state where the named insured's covered auto is principally garaged. This vehicle is also considered to be an uninsured motor vehicle.
3. A hit-and-run vehicle is also considered to be an uninsured vehicle. Thus, if the named insured or any family member is struck by a hit-and-run driver while occupying a covered auto or a non-owned auto, or while walking, the uninsured motorists coverage will pay for the injury.
4. Another uninsured vehicle is one to which a bodily injury liability policy applies at the time of the accident, but the insurer or bonding company denies coverage or becomes insolvent. For example, if you have a valid claim against a negligent driver, but his or her insurer becomes insolvent before the claim is paid, your uninsured motorists coverage would pay the claim.

Exclusions

The uninsured motorists coverage has several general exclusions, summarized as follows:

1. *No uninsured motorists coverage on vehicle.* Coverage does not apply to an insured while occupying or when struck by a motor vehicle owned by that insured, which is not insured for coverage under this policy.
2. *Primary coverage under another policy.* Family members are not covered while they are occupying a vehicle owned by the named insured,

which is insured for uninsured motorists' coverage on a primary basis under another policy. The intent here is to have such family members seek protection under the policy insuring the vehicle that they are occupying.

3. *Settling a claim without the insurer's consent.* If an insured or legal representative settles a bodily injury claim without the insurer's consent, and the settlement prejudices the insurer's right to recover a loss payment, the uninsured motorist coverage does not apply. The purpose of this exclusion is to protect the insurer's subrogation rights.

4. *Using the vehicle as a public or livery conveyance.* If an insured occupies a covered auto when it is being used as a public or livery conveyance, coverage does not apply. The exclusion does not apply to a share-the-expense carpool.

5. *No reasonable belief of permission.* Coverage does not apply to any insured who is using a vehicle without a reasonable belief that he or she is entitled to do so. This exclusion does not apply to a family member who is using a covered auto owned by the named insured.

6. *No benefit to workers compensation insurer.* The uninsured motorists coverage cannot directly or indirectly benefit a workers compensation insurer or self-insurer. A workers compensation insurer may have a legal right of action against a third party who has injured an employee. If an uninsured driver injures an employee who receives workers compensation benefits, the workers compensation insurer could sue the uninsured driver or attempt to make a claim under the injured employee's uninsured motorists coverage. This exclusion prevents the uninsured motorists coverage from providing benefits to the workers compensation insurer.

7. *No punitive damages.* The PAP excludes payment for punitive or exemplary damages under the uninsured motorists coverage.

Other Insurance

The PAP contains a number of complex provisions that apply when more than one uninsured motorist coverage provision applies to the loss. These provisions are summarized as follows:

- The maximum amount paid is limited to the highest limit of any of the policies that provide uninsured motorists coverage.
- If an insurer provides uninsured motorist coverage on a *vehicle not owned by the named insured, the insurance provided is excess over any collectible insurance providing insurance on a primary basis.* For example, Jeffrey has an uninsured motorist coverage limit of $25,000, and Ashley has an uninsured motorist coverage limit of $50,000. If Jeffrey is injured by an uninsured driver while occupying Ashley's car and has bodily injuries of $60,000, Ashley's policy is primary and pays $50,000. Jeffrey's insurer pays the remaining $10,000 as excess insurance.
- When the named insured's policy and the other policy provide uninsured motorists coverage on a *primary basis,* each policy pays its pro rata share of the loss. Each insurer's share is the proportion that its limit of liability bears to the total of all applicable limits of liability for coverage provided on a primary basis.
- When the named insured's policy and the other policy provide uninsured motorists coverage on an *excess basis,* each policy also pays its pro rata share of the loss. Each insurer's share is the proportion that its limit of liability bears to the total of all applicable limits of liability for coverage provided on an excess basis.

Underinsured Motorists Coverage

Underinsured motorists coverage can be added to the PAP to provide more complete protection. Underinsured motorists coverage applies when a negligent third-party driver carries liability insurance, but the limits carried are less than the insured's actual damages for bodily injury.

An underinsured vehicle is defined as a vehicle to which a liability policy or bond applies at the time of the accident, but the liability limits carried are less than the limits provided by the insured's underinsured motorists coverage. The maximum amount paid for bodily injury under the coverage varies among the states. *In general, the maximum amount paid is the underinsured motorist's coverage limit stated in the policy less the amount paid by the negli-*

gent driver's insurer. For example, assume that Kristen adds the underinsured motorists coverage to her policy in the amount of $100,000. She is injured by a negligent driver who has liability limits of $25,000/$50,000, which satisfy the state's minimum required bodily injury limits. If her bodily injury damages are $100,000, she would receive only $25,000 from the negligent driver's insurer, because that amount is the driver's applicable limit of liability. However, she would receive another $75,000 from her insurer under her underinsured motorists coverage.

However, assume that Kristen's bodily injury damages are $125,000. The maximum amount she would collect under the underinsured motorists coverage is still only $75,000, which is the difference between the $100,000 limit under her underinsured motorists coverage and the $25,000 collected from the negligent driver's insurer (see preceding rule). To collect the full amount of her injury, Kristen should have carried limits of at least $125,000.

Underinsured motorist coverage endorsements are not uniform among the states. In some states, the underinsured motorists coverage can be added as an endorsement to the PAP to complement the coverage provided by the uninsured motorists coverage. In other states, a single endorsement provides both uninsured and underinsured coverage and replaces the uninsured motorist coverage that is part of the standard PAP. In addition, some states make the underinsured motorists coverage mandatory, while other states make it optional. Finally, the available or required limits for the underinsured motorists coverage also vary by state.

PART D: COVERAGE FOR DAMAGE TO YOUR AUTO

Part D (**coverage for damage to your auto**) provides coverage for the damage or theft of an auto.

Insuring Agreement

The insurer agrees to pay for any direct and accidental loss to a covered auto or any nonowned auto as defined in the insuring agreement, including their equipment, less any deductible. If two autos insured under the same policy are damaged in the same accident, only one deductible must be met. If the deductible amounts are different, the higher deductible will apply. *Two optional coverages are available: (1) collision coverage and (2) other-than-collision coverage (also called comprehensive).* A collision loss is covered only if the declarations page indicates that collision coverage is provided for that auto. Likewise, coverage for an other-than-collision loss is in force only if the declarations page indicates that other-than-collision coverage is provided for that auto.

Collision Loss   Collision *is defined as the upset of your covered auto or nonowned auto or its impact with another vehicle or object.* The following are examples of a collision loss:

- You lose control of your car on an icy street, and it overturns.
- Your car hits another car, a telephone pole, a tree, or a building.
- Your car is parked, and you find the rear fender dented when you return.
- You open your car door in a parking lot, and the door is damaged when it hits the vehicle parked next to you.

Collision losses are paid regardless of fault. If you cause the accident, your insurer will pay for the damage to your car, less any deductible. If the other driver damages your car, you can either collect from the negligent driver (or from his or her insurer), or look to your insurer to pay the claim. If you collect from your own insurer, you must give up subrogation rights to your insurer, who will then attempt to collect from the negligent party who caused the accident. If the entire amount of the loss is recovered, your insurer will refund the deductible.

Other-Than-Collision Loss   The PAP can be written to cover an **other-than-collision loss**. The PAP distinguishes between a collision and an other-than-collision loss. This distinction is important because some car owners do not wish to pay for collision coverage on their cars. Also, the deductibles under the two coverages may be different. Other-than-collision coverage is frequently written with a lower deductible.

Loss from any of the following perils is considered to be an other-than-collision loss:

- Missiles or falling objects
- Fire
- Theft or larceny
- Explosion or earthquake
- Windstorm
- Hail, water, or flood
- Malicious mischief or vandalism
- Riot or civil commotion
- Contact with a bird or animal
- Glass breakage

These perils are self-explanatory, but a few comments are in order. Theft of the vehicle is covered, including the theft of equipment, such as wheel covers, tires, or a stereo. Theft of an air bag from a covered vehicle parked on the street is also covered.

Colliding with a bird or animal is not a collision loss. Thus, if you hit a bird or deer with your car, the physical damage to the car is considered to be an other-than-collision loss.

Finally, if glass breakage is caused by a collision, you can elect to have it covered as a collision loss. This distinction is important because both coverages (collision loss and other-than-collision loss) are written with deductibles. Without this qualification, you would have to pay two deductibles if the car has both body damage and glass breakage in the same accident. By treating glass breakage as part of the collision loss, only the collision deductible must be satisfied.

Nonowned Auto The Part D coverages also apply to a nonowned auto. As defined in Part D, a **nonowned auto** *is a private passenger auto, pickup, van, or trailer not owned by or furnished or made available for the regular use of the named insured or family member, while it is in the custody of or is being operated by the named insured or family member.* For example, if Tyler borrows Mike's car, Tyler's collision coverage and other-than-collision coverage on his car apply to the borrowed car. However, Tyler's insurance is excess over any physical damage insurance on the borrowed car.

The Part D coverages apply only if the nonowned auto is not furnished or made available for the regular use of the named insured or family member. You can occasionally drive a borrowed automobile, and your physical damage insurance will cover the borrowed vehicle. *However, if the vehicle is driven on a regular basis or is furnished or made available for your regular use, the Part D coverages do not apply.* The key point here is not how frequently you drive a nonowned auto, but whether the vehicle is furnished or made available for your regular use.

The Part D coverages also apply to a temporary substitute vehicle, which is also considered in Part D to be a nonowned auto. A temporary substitute vehicle is a nonowned auto or trailer that is used as a temporary replacement for a covered auto that is out of normal use because of its breakdown, repair, servicing, loss, or destruction. *Thus, the Part D coverages that apply to a covered auto also apply to a temporary substitute vehicle for that auto.* For example, if your car is in the shop for repairs, and you are furnished a loaner car, your physical damage insurance also applies to the loaner car.

If you have an accident while operating a nonowned auto, the PAP provides the broadest physical damage coverage applicable to any covered auto shown in the declarations. For example, assume that you own two cars. One vehicle is insured for both a collision loss and an other-than-collision loss, and the other is insured only for an other-than-collision loss. If you drive a nonowned auto, the borrowed vehicle is covered for both collision and other-than-collision losses.

Collision Damage Waiver (CDW) on Rental Cars
Our discussion of collision insurance on nonowned cars would not be complete without a brief discussion of the collision damage waiver (CDW) on rental cars. This coverage is sometimes called a loss damage waiver (LDW). When you rent a car and check the CDW box, you are relieved of financial responsibility if the rental car is damaged or stolen. However, the rental agreement contains numerous restrictions. The CDW may be void even when checked if you cause an accident by speeding, driving while intoxicated, or driving on unpaved roads. The CDW is expensive and can easily increase the daily rental cost by $15, $20, or some higher amount.

Should you purchase the CDW if you rent a car? Many consumer experts say the CDW is not needed if (1) you carry collision and comprehensive insurance on your own car because the coverages also apply to the rental car, and (2) certain credit cards cover the physical damage or theft of a rental car on an excess basis if the card is used to rent the car.

The preceding view that the CDW may be unnecessary is not uniform among all financial advisors. In particular, the Independent Insurance Agents & Brokers of America, an association of independent property/casualty insurance agents and brokers, says consumers in general should purchase the CDW, at least for short-term rentals. Because of numerous restrictive provisions in the rental agreement, incomplete protection under the PAP, and credit card limitations, the organization believes consumers generally should buy the CDW even if it is costly (see Insight 22.1)

Deductible   The collision coverage is typically written with a straight deductible of $250, $500, or some higher amount. Coverage for other-than-collision losses is also normally written with a deductible. Deductibles are designed to prevent small claims, hold down premiums, and encourage the insured to be careful in protecting the car from damage or theft.

Transportation Expenses

Part D also pays for temporary transportation expenses. The insurer will pay, without application of a deductible, up to $20 daily to a maximum of $600 for temporary transportation expenses incurred by the insured because of loss to a covered auto. Payments can be made for a train, bus, taxi, rental car, or other transportation expense. *Payments are made for other-than-collision losses only if the declarations indicate that other-than-collision coverage is provided on that auto. Likewise, payments are made for collision losses only if the declarations indicate that collision coverage is provided for that auto.*

The coverage also includes payment of any expenses for which the insured is legally responsible because of loss to a nonowned auto, such as the loss of daily rent on a rental car.

Finally, if the loss is caused by the total theft of a covered auto or nonowned auto, expenses incurred during the first 48 hours after the theft occurred are not covered. If the loss is caused by a peril other than theft, expenses incurred during the first 24 hours after the auto has been withdrawn from use are not covered.

Coverage for *towing and labor costs* can be added by an endorsement. This coverage pays for towing and labor costs if a covered auto or nonowned auto breaks down, provided the labor is performed at the place of breakdown. The maximum amount paid is $25, $50, or $75 for each breakdown depending on the amount of insurance purchased. For example, if you call a repair truck because your car fails to start, the labor costs and any towing costs will be paid up to the policy limits. Labor costs, however, are covered only for work done at the place of the breakdown. The cost of repairs at a service station or garage is not covered.

Exclusions

Numerous exclusions apply to the Part D coverages, summarized as follows:

1. *Use as a public or livery conveyance.* Loss to a covered auto or any nonowned auto is excluded while the vehicle is being used as a public or livery conveyance. Again, the exclusion does not apply to a share-the-expense carpool.
2. *Damage from wear and tear, freezing, and mechanical or electrical breakdown.* There is no coverage for any damage due to wear and tear, freezing, mechanical or electrical breakdown, or road damage to tires. The intent here is to exclude the normal maintenance cost of operating an auto. However, the exclusion does not apply to the total theft of a covered auto or any nonowned auto. For example, if a stolen car is recovered but the electrical system is damaged by a thief who hot-wired the car, the loss is covered.
3. *Radioactive contamination or war.* Damage from radioactive contamination or war is excluded.
4. *Electronic equipment.* The 2005 PAP expands coverage of certain types of electronic equipment. New cars often include electronic equipment such as navigational systems, video entertainment systems, and Internet access systems. Because the electronic equipment is permanently attached to the vehicle, insureds expect that the PAP will cover such equipment.

INSIGHT 22.1

The Top 10 Reasons to Purchase the Rental Car Collision Damage Waiver (CDW)

It has been debated for years whether or not a person renting a vehicle should purchase the collision (or loss) damage waiver from the rental company. *Our recommendation is that consumers, in general, **should** purchase the CDW/LDW, at least for short-term rentals. Our reasons are given below.*

- **Loss Valuation.** The personal auto policy (PAP) covers the lesser of the actual cash value of the vehicle or the amount necessary to repair or replace the damaged property. However, the rental agreement may contractually obligate you to reimburse the rental company for the full value of the vehicle. Also, the PAP also does not pay for any *betterment* (increased value of new parts replacing old ones) of the vehicle, nor any *diminution* of value (if the market value of the vehicle after repairs is less than that before the accident).

- **Loss Settlement.** As implied above, there may be disagreement over the value of the vehicle or the amount charged for labor and materials to repair it. The insurance company has the right to "... *inspect and appraise the damaged property before its repair or disposal.*" However, the rental company, unlike you, is not contractually obligated to the insurer—it may choose to make the repairs immediately, potentially resulting in a lack of PAP coverage because of failure to comply with this contractual condition. In any case, purchase of the CDW usually allows the renter to walk away without the headaches involved in adjusting an auto claim.

- **Loss Payment.** The rental agreement may require immediate reimbursement for damages, and it is customary practice for the rental company to charge your credit card. This can create a significant debt, *max* out the card's credit limit (perhaps shortening a vacation or business trip), or result in litigation.

- **Loss Damage Waivers (LDW).** Rental agreements often make the renter responsible for *any* loss in value beyond normal wear and tear, regardless of the cause and regardless of fault. In order for your PAP to respond, you must insure at least one vehicle for both collision and other-than-collision (often called *comprehensive*) coverage. If not, your policy will not respond to the rental car damage and loss of use claims.

- **Indirect Losses.** You most likely will be responsible for the rental company's loss of rental income on the damaged unit. Your policy has limited coverage for these charges.

- **Administrative Expenses.** The rental contract may make the insured liable for various *administrative* or loss-related expenses such as towing (e.g., one insured was charged for a 230-mile tow), appraisal, claims adjustment, and storage. Some of these expenses may not be covered by the PAP.

- **Other Insurance.** The PAP says that it is excess over: (1) any coverage provided by the owner of the auto, (2) any other applicable physical damage insurance, and (3) any other source of recovery applicable to the loss, such as travel policies or credit card coverages. The potential controversy over who pays what is obvious and can result in litigation. In addition, keep in mind that many states have statutes, proprietary policy forms, and/or case law precedents that may govern rental car exposures.

- **Excluded Vehicles & Territories.** The PAP normally does not provide physical damage coverage for motorcycles, mopeds, motor homes, or other vehicles that are not private passenger autos, pickups, vans, or trailers. In addition, use of covered vehicles is limited to the U.S., its territories and possessions, Puerto Rico, and Canada (the rental agreement may also exclude operation outside a specific geographical area).

- **Excluded Uses & Drivers.** The PAP may have limitations on use of vehicles that are not otherwise excluded by the rental agreement CDW or LDW. Also, the PAP may include an exclusionary endorsement for certain drivers or may apply only to designated individuals—the CDW will probably also only apply to certain individuals, but operators for which no PAP coverage is available may be afforded protection under the rental agreement by adding them as designated drivers.

- **Additional and/or Future Costs.** The PAP will include a deductible in the range of $100–$500 or higher. In addition, payment for damage to a rental car may result in a significant premium increase (if not nonrenewal) via surcharges or loss of credits.

Although most CDW/LDW fees are considered outrageous, if not unconscionable, **we advise you to purchase the CDW/LDW for short-term rentals.** If anything, this will give you peace of mind while on vacation or business, and it could save you from a lot of inconvenience and lost time and money.

SOURCE: "Virtual University," © Independent Insurance Agents & Brokers of America, Inc.

Coverage of electronic equipment is somewhat complicated. The 2005 PAP first excludes loss to electronic equipment that reproduces, receives, or transmits audio, visual, or data signals. The policy provides examples of excluded equipment, including but not limited, to the following:

- Radios and stereos
- Tape decks
- Compact disc systems
- Navigation systems
- Internet access systems
- Personal computer
- Video entertainment systems
- Telephones
- Televisions
- Two-way mobile radios
- Scanners
- Citizens band radios

However, the above exclusion does not apply to electronic equipment that is permanently installed in a covered auto or nonowned auto. Thus, there is coverage of such equipment if the equipment is permanently installed in the vehicle. Note that a car telephone must be permanently installed for coverage to apply. Thus, a portable cell phone that many people use while driving would not be covered.

Safety experts believe that drivers can be easily distracted while using a cell phone, which increases the chance of an auto accident. The extent to which the use of cell phones contributes to auto accidents is controversial. However, new research studies suggest that using a cell phone while driving can be extremely dangerous (see Insight 22.2).

5. *Tapes, records, and discs.* Loss to stereo tapes, records, discs, or other media designed for use with the electronic equipment described previously is also excluded. An endorsement can be added to the PAP to cover excluded tapes, records, and discs.

6. *Government destruction or confiscation.* The PAP excludes total loss to a covered auto or nonowned auto due to destruction or confiscation by a governmental or civil authority. For example, if a federal drug agency confiscates a drug dealer's car, the loss would not be covered.

7. *Trailer, camper body, or motor home.* The PAP excludes loss to a trailer, camper body, or motor home not shown in the declarations. This exclusion also applies to facilities and equipment, such as cooking, dining, plumbing or refrigeration equipment, and awnings or cabanas. For example, damage to a stove or refrigerator is not covered.

The exclusion does not apply to a nonowned trailer. Likewise, it does not apply to a trailer or camper body acquired during the policy period provided that you notify the insurer within 14 days after you become the owner.

8. *Loss to a nonowned auto used without reasonable belief of permission.* Loss to a nonowned auto is not covered when it is used by the named insured or his or her family member without a reasonable belief of permission.

9. *Radar detection equipment.* Equipment for the detection or location of radar or laser is excluded. This exclusion is justified on the basis that radar detection equipment circumvents state and federal speed laws.

10. *Custom furnishings or equipment.* Loss to customized furnishings or equipment in or upon a pickup or van is not covered. Such furnishings or equipment include special carpeting, furniture or bars, height-extending roofs, and custom murals or paintings.

11. *Nonowned auto used in the auto business.* Loss to a nonowned auto maintained or used by someone engaged in the business of selling, repairing, servicing, storing, or parking vehicles designed for use on public highways is specifically excluded. For example, if a mechanic damages a customer's car while road testing it, the loss is not covered under the mechanic's PAP. Instead, this business loss exposure should be covered under a commercial garage policy.

12. *Racing vehicle.* Loss to a covered auto or nonowned auto is not covered while it is located inside a racing facility for the purpose of competing in or preparing for a prearranged racing or speed contest.

13. *Rental car.* Loss to or loss of use of a vehicle rented by the named insured or family member is not covered if a state law or rental agreement precludes the car rental agency from recovering from the named insured or family member.

INSIGHT 22.2

Crash Risk Is Four Times Higher When Drivers Use Cell Phones, Study Says

Common sense as well as experience tell us that handling and dialing cell phones while driving compromise safety, and evidence is accumulating that phone conversations also increase crash risk.

New research from the Insurance Institute for Highway Safety quantifies the added risk—*drivers using phones are four times as likely to get into crashes serious enough to injure themselves.*

The increased risk was estimated by comparing phone use within 10 minutes before an actual crash occurred with use by the same driver during the prior week. Subjects were drivers treated in hospital emergency rooms for injuries suffered in crashes from April 2002 to July 2004.

The study, "Role of cellular phones in motor vehicle crashes resulting in hospital attendance" by S. McEvoy et al., is published in the *British Medical Journal,* available at bmj.com.

"The main finding of a fourfold increase in injury crash risk was consistent across groups of drivers," said Anne McCartt, Institute vice president for research and an author of the study. "Male and female drivers experienced about the same increase in risk from using a phone. So did drivers older and younger than 30 and drivers using hand-held and hands-free phones."

Weather wasn't a factor in the crashes, almost 75 percent of which occurred in clear conditions. Eighty-nine percent of the crashes involved other vehicles. More than half of the injured drivers reported that their crashes occurred within 10 minutes of the start of the trip.

The study was conducted in the Western Australian city of Perth. The Institute first tried to conduct this research in the United States, but U.S. phone companies were unwilling to make customers' billing records available, even with permission from the drivers. Phone records could be obtained in Australia, and the researchers got a high rate of cooperation among drivers who had been in crashes.

Another reason for conducting the study in Australia was to estimate crash risk in a jurisdiction where hand-held phone use is banned. It has been illegal while driving in Western Australia since July 2001. Still one-third of the drivers said their calls had been placed on hand-held phones.

Hands-Free Versus Hand-Held

The results suggest that banning hand-held phone use won't necessarily enhance safety if drivers simply switch to hands-free phones. Injury crash risk didn't differ from one type of reported phone use to the other.

"This isn't intuitive. You'd think using a hands-free phone would be less distracting, so it wouldn't increase crash risk as much as using a hand-held phone. But we found that either phone type increased the risk, "McCartt said. "This could be because the so-called hands-free phones that are in common use today aren't really hands-free. We didn't have sufficient data to compare the different types of hands-free phones, such as those that are fully voice activated."

Evidence of Risk Is Mounting

The findings of the Institute study, based on the experience of about 500 drivers, are consistent with 1997 research that showed phone use was associated with a fourfold increase in the risk of property damage crash. This Canadian study also used cell phone billing records to establish the increase in risk. The Institute's new study is the second to use phone records and the first to estimate whether and how much phone use increases the risk of an injury crash.

Taken together, the two studies confirm that the distractions associated with phone use contribute significantly to crashes. Other studies have been published about cell phone use while driving, but most have been small-scale and have involved simulated or instrumented driving, not the actual experience of drivers on the road. When researchers have tried to assess the effects of phone use on real-world crashes, they usually have relied on police reports for information. But such reports aren't reliable because, without witnesses, police cannot determine whether a crash-involved driver was using a phone.

SOURCE: "Crash Risk Is Four Times Higher When Drivers Use Cell Phones, Study Says," *Insurance Journal,* National News, July 12, 2005. © Wells Publishing, Inc.

Limit of Liability

The amount paid for a physical damage loss to a covered vehicle is the lower of (1) actual cash value of the damaged or stolen property, or (2) amount necessary to replace the property with other property of like kind and quality. If the cost of repairs exceeds the vehicle's actual cash value, the vehicle may be declared a total loss, and the amount paid is the actual cash value less the deductible. In practice, insurers declare a vehicle to be a total loss if the estimated cost of repairs plus the salvage value exceeds the actual cash value of the car.

For a partial loss, such as a smashed fender, only the amount necessary to repair or replace the damaged property with property of like kind and quality will be paid. A car can be repaired with parts manufactured by the original equipment manufacturer (*OEM*) or with generic auto parts (also called *after market parts*). Some policyholders believe that generic auto parts are of lower quality than OEM parts, which has resulted in a number of lawsuits against auto insurers. However, in 2005, the Illinois Supreme Court ruled that insurers are free to use generic auto parts to repair damaged cars and trucks, which are often less expensive than OEM parts.

Most states now require insurers to notify policyowners when generic auto parts are used to repair the vehicle. Insurance company practices differ in this regard. In some cases, policyowners can pay the difference between OEM parts and generic parts and have the vehicle repaired with OEM parts. Some auto insurers offer policyowners a choice between OEM parts and generic parts by an endorsement to the policy. Some insurers always use OEM parts, while others use OEM parts for repairing new or late model cars. You should call your agent and inquire about the claim settlement practices of your company so you know what to expect if your car is damaged.

The PAP also has limits on the amount paid for certain losses. Loss to a nonowned trailer is limited to $1500. Loss to equipment designed for the reproduction of sound, which is installed in locations not used by the auto manufacturer for such equipment, is limited to $1000.

Betterment If the value of the vehicle is increased after repairs are completed (such as repainting the entire car when only one fender and door are damaged), the insurer will not pay for the **betterment** or increase in value.

Diminution in Value A car damaged in an auto accident may have a reduced market or resale value. In recent years, many insureds have requested payment for the loss in market value. The Insurance Services Office has prepared a clarifying endorsement that insurers can add to the policy. The endorsement

states that any loss in market or resale value (also called **diminution in value**) from a direct and accidental physical damage loss to a covered auto is not covered.

Finally, many consumers obtain new cars on a lease arrangement. The value of a new car declines substantially during the first year because of depreciation. Also, the collision deductible on a leased car may be $500 or even higher. If a leased car is totaled in an accident shortly after purchase, the amount paid by the insurer may be substantially less than the payoff amount of the lease. As a result, you could owe a bank or other financial institution hundreds or even thousands of dollars. This risk can be handled by **gap insurance,** *which pays the difference between the amount your insurer pays for a totaled car and the amount owed on the lease or loan.*

You normally do not buy a gap policy when you lease a car. The dealer typically buys a master policy from an insurer and includes the cost in the monthly lease payment. You should check with the car dealer before you lease the car.

ISO also has an endorsement that can be added to the PAP that bridges the gap between the amount paid by Part D and the amount owed to the lessor or lender.

Payment of Loss

The insurer has the option of paying for a physical damage loss in money (including any sales tax) or repairing or replacing the damaged or stolen property. If the car or its equipment is stolen, the insurer will pay the expense of returning the stolen car to the named insured and will also pay for any damage resulting from the theft. The insurer also has the right to keep all or part of the recovered stolen property at an agreed or appraised value.

Other Sources of Recovery

If other insurance covers a physical damage loss, the insurer pays only its pro rata share. The insurer's share is the proportion that its limit of liability bears to the total of all applicable limits.

With respect to a nonowned auto (including a temporary substitute), the Part D coverages are excess over any other collectible source of recovery. *Thus, any physical damage insurance on the borrowed car is primary, and your physical damage insurance is excess.* If you borrow a car and damage it, the owner's physical damage insurance (if any) applies first, and your collision insurance is excess, subject to any deductible. For example, assume that you borrow a friend's car and damage it in an accident. The owner's collision deductible is $500, and your collision deductible is $250. If repairs to the borrowed car are $2000, the owner's PAP pays $1500 ($2000 − $500), and your PAP pays $250 ($500 − $250). The remaining $250 of loss would have to be paid either by the owner or by you. In short, if the owner's collision deductible is larger than your deductible, your insurer pays the difference between the two deductibles.

Appraisal Provision

The PAP contains an **appraisal provision** for handling disputes over the amount of a physical damage loss. This provision is particularly important in the case of damage to a low-mileage car or to a car in above-average condition. The insured may claim that the car is worth more than the amount stated in the various publications of car prices that auto dealers use. To resolve the dispute, either party can demand an appraisal of the loss. Each party selects a competent and impartial appraiser. The two appraisers then select an umpire. Each appraiser states separately the actual cash value of the car and the amount of the loss. If the appraisers fail to agree, they submit their differences to the umpire. A decision by any two parties is binding on all. Each party pays his or her appraiser, and the umpire's expenses are shared equally. Finally, by agreeing to an appraisal, the insurer does not waive any rights under the policy.

PART E: DUTIES AFTER AN ACCIDENT OR LOSS

You should know what to do if you have an accident or loss. Some obligations are based on common sense, while others are required by law and by the provisions of the PAP. You should first determine if anyone is hurt. If someone is injured, an ambulance should be called immediately. If there are bodily

injuries, or the property damage exceeds a certain amount (such as $200), you must notify the police in most jurisdictions. You should give the other driver your name, address, and the name of your agent and insurer and request the same information from him or her. You should also get the name and address of any witnesses.

You should not admit fault. The question of who caused the accident will be determined by the insurers involved or by a court of law.

After the accident occurs, you are required to perform certain duties. The 2005 PAP states specifically that the insurer has no duty to provide coverage if you fail to comply with certain listed duties. However, the insurer can deny coverage only if failure to comply is prejudicial (harmful) to the insurer. Many courts have held that the insured's failure to comply with every duty may not harm the insurer's position or interest. The 2005 PAP recognizes this principle and states that the insurer is relieved of its obligation to provide coverage only if failure to comply with the listed duties is prejudicial to the insurer.

You are required to notify your company or agent promptly of the accident. Failure to report the accident promptly to your insurer could jeopardize your coverage if you are later sued by the other driver. In addition, you must cooperate with the insurer in the investigation and settlement of a claim. You must send to the insurer copies of any legal papers or notices received in connection with the accident. If you are claiming benefits under the uninsured motorists, underinsured motorists, or medical payments coverages, you may be required to take a physical examination at the insurer's expense. You must also authorize your insurer to obtain medical reports and other pertinent records. Finally, you must submit a proof of loss at the insurer's request.

Some additional duties are imposed on you if you are seeking benefits under the uninsured motorists coverage. The police must be notified if a hit-and-run driver is involved. Also, if you bring a lawsuit against the uninsured driver, you must send copies of the legal papers to your insurer.

If your car is damaged, and you are seeking indemnification under Coverage D, other duties are imposed on you. You must take reasonable steps to protect the vehicle from further damage; your insurer will pay for any expense involved. You must also permit the insurer to inspect and appraise the car before it is repaired.

PART F: GENERAL PROVISIONS

This section contains a number of general provisions. Only two of them are discussed here.

Policy Period and Territory

The PAP provides coverage only in the United States, its territories or possessions, Puerto Rico, and Canada. The policy also provides coverage while a covered auto is being transported between the ports of the United States, Puerto Rico, or Canada. For example, if you rent a car while vacationing in England, Germany, or Mexico, you are not covered. Additional auto insurance must be purchased to be covered while driving in foreign countries. If you intend to drive in Mexico, you should first obtain liability insurance from a Mexican insurer. A motorist from the United States who has not purchased insurance from a Mexican insurer could be detained in jail after an accident, have his or her automobile impounded, and be subject to other penalties as well.

Termination

An important provision applies to termination of the insurance by either the insured or insurer. There are four parts to this provision:

- Cancellation
- Nonrenewal
- Automatic termination
- Other termination provisions

All states place restrictions on the insurer's right to cancel or nonrenew an auto insurance policy. Many states, however, have laws that differ from the termination provisions contained in the PAP. In such cases, an endorsement is added to the PAP to make the auto policy conform to state law.

Cancellation   The named insured can cancel at any time by returning the policy to the insurer or by giving advance written notice of the effective date of **cancellation.**

The insurer also has the right of cancellation. If the policy has been in force for *fewer than 60 days*, the insurer can cancel by sending a cancellation notice to the named insured. At least 10 days' notice must be given if the cancellation is for nonpayment of premiums and at least 20 days' notice is required in all other cases. Thus, the insurer has 60 days to investigate a new insured to determine whether he or she is acceptable.

After the policy has been in force for 60 days, or it is a renewal or continuation policy, the insurer can cancel for only three reasons: (1) the premium has not been paid, (2) the driver's license of any insured has been suspended or revoked during the policy period, or (3) the policy was obtained through material misrepresentation.

Nonrenewal   The insurer may also discontinue coverage by not renewing the policy when it comes up for renewal. If the insurer decides not to renew, the named insured must be given at least 20 days' notice before the end of the policy period.

Automatic Termination   If the insurer decides to renew the policy, an automatic termination provision becomes effective. This means that if the named insured does not accept the insurer's offer to renew, the policy automatically terminates at the end of the current policy period. Thus, once the insurer bills the named insured for another period, the insured must pay the premium, or the policy automatically terminates on its expiration date. However, some insurers may provide a short grace period to pay an overdue renewal premium.

Finally, if other insurance is obtained on a covered auto, the PAP insurance on that auto automatically terminates on the day the other insurance becomes effective.

Other Termination Provisions   Many states place additional restrictions on the insurer's right to cancel or not renew an auto policy. If state law requires a longer period of advance notice to the named insured or modifies any termination provision, the PAP is modified to comply with those requirements. Also, if the policy is canceled, the named insured is entitled to any premium refund; however, making or offering to make a premium refund is not a condition for cancellation. Finally, the effective date of cancellation stated in the cancellation notice is the end of the policy period.

INSURING MOTORCYCLES AND OTHER VEHICLES

The PAP excludes coverage for motorcycles, mopeds, and similar vehicles. However, a **miscellaneous-type vehicle endorsement** can be added to the PAP to insure motorcycles, mopeds, motorscooters, golf carts, motor homes, dune buggies, and similar vehicles. One exception is a snowmobile, which requires a separate endorsement to the PAP. The miscellaneous-type vehicle endorsement can be used to provide the same coverages found in the PAP.

You should be aware of several points if the miscellaneous-type vehicle endorsement is added to the PAP. First, the liability coverage does not apply to a nonowned vehicle. Although other persons are covered while operating your motorcycle with your permission, the liability coverage does not apply if you operate a nonowned motorcycle (other than as a temporary substitute vehicle).

Second, a passenger hazard exclusion can be elected, which excludes liability for bodily injury to any passenger on the motorcycle. When the exclusion is used, the insured pays a lower premium. For example, if a passenger on your motorcycle is thrown off and is injured, the liability coverage on the motorcycle does not apply.

Finally, the amount paid for any physical damage losses to the motorcycle is limited to the lowest of (1) the stated amount shown in the endorsement, (2) the actual cash value, or (3) the amount necessary to repair or replace the property (less any deductible).

CASE APPLICATION

Kim, age 20, is a college student who recently purchased her first car from a friend who had financial problems. The vehicle is a high-mileage 1996 Toyota Tercel with a current market value of $2000. Assume you are a financial planner and Kim asks your advice concerning the various coverages in the PAP.

a. Briefly describe the major coverages that are available in the PAP.
b. Which of the available coverages in (a) should Kim purchase? Justify your answer.
c. Which of the available coverages in (a) should Kim not purchase? Justify your answer.
d. Assume that Kim purchases the PAP coverages that you have recommended. To what extent, if any, would Kim's insurance cover the following situations?
  (1) Danielle, Kim's roommate, borrows Kim's car with her permission and injures another motorist. Danielle is at fault.
  (2) Kim is driving under the influence of alcohol and is involved in an accident where another motorist is seriously injured.
  (3) During the football season, Kim charges a fee to transport fans from a local bar to the football stadium. Several passengers are injured when Kim suddenly changes lanes without signaling and hits another car.
  (4) Kim drives her boyfriend's car on a regular basis. While driving the boyfriend's car, she is involved in an accident in which another motorist is injured. Kim is at fault.
  (5) Kim rents a car in England where she is participating in a summer study program. The car is stolen from a dormitory parking lot.
e. Kim also owns a motorcycle. To what extent, if any, does Kim's PAP cover the motorcycle?

SUMMARY

- The Personal Auto Policy (PAP) consists of a declarations page, a definitions page, and six major parts:
    - Part A: Liability Coverage
    - Part B: Medical Payments Coverage
    - Part C: Uninsured Motorists Coverage
    - Part D: Coverage for Damage to Your Auto
    - Part E: Duties After an Accident or Loss
    - Part F: General Provisions

- Liability coverage protects the insured from bodily injury and property damage liability arising out of the negligent operation of an auto or trailer.

- A covered auto includes any vehicle shown in the declarations; newly acquired vehicles; a trailer owned by the insured; and a temporary substitute auto.

- Insured persons include the named insured and spouse, resident family members, other persons using a covered auto if a reasonable belief that permission to use the vehicle exists, and any person or organization legally responsible for the acts of a covered person.

- Medical payments coverage pays all reasonable medical, dental, and funeral expenses incurred by an insured person for services rendered within three years from the date of the accident.

- Uninsured motorists coverage pays for the bodily injury of a covered person caused by an uninsured motorist, a hit-and-run driver, or a negligent driver whose insurer is insolvent.

- Underinsured motorists coverage can be added as an endorsement to the PAP. The coverage applies when a negligent driver carries liability insurance, but the liability limits carried are less than the limit provided by the underinsured motorists coverage.

- Coverage for damage to your auto pays for a direct physical loss to a covered auto or nonowned auto less any deductible. A collision loss or other-than-collision loss is covered only if the declarations page indicates that such coverages are in effect.

- Certain duties are imposed on the insured after an accident occurs. A person seeking coverage must cooperate with the insurer in the investigation and settlement of a claim and send to the insurer copies of any legal papers or notices received in connection with the accident.

- After the policy has been in force for 60 days, or it is a renewal or continuation policy, the insurer can cancel the policy only if the premium has not been paid, the driver's license of an insured has been suspended or revoked during the policy period, or the policy was obtained through material misrepresentation. The insurer can also discontinue coverage by not renewing the policy. If the insurer decides not to renew the policy when it comes up for renewal, the named insured must be given at least 20 days' notice of its intention not to renew.

- Motorcycles and mopeds can be insured by adding the miscellaneous-type vehicle endorsement to the personal auto policy.

KEY CONCEPTS AND TERMS

Appraisal provision
Betterment
Cancellation
Collision
Coverage for damage to your auto
Diminution in value
Extended nonowned coverage endorsement
Gap insurance
Liability coverage
Medical payments coverage
Miscellaneous-type vehicle endorsement
Nonowned auto
Nonrenewal
Other-than-collision loss
Personal Auto Policy (PAP)
Single limit
Split limits
Supplementary payments
Temporary substitute vehicle
Underinsured motorists coverage
Uninsured motorists coverage
Your covered auto

REVIEW QUESTIONS

1. The Personal Auto Policy (PAP) contains several coverages that meet the insurance needs of typical insureds. For each of the following coverages, briefly describe the type of coverage provided, and give an example of a loss that would be covered.
    a. Part A: Liability Coverage
    b. Part B: Medical Payments Coverage
    c. Part C: Uninsured Motorists Coverage
    d. Part D: Coverage for Damage to Your Auto

2. The PAP provides coverage for *your covered auto*. Identify the four classes of vehicles that are considered to be covered autos.

3. The PAP provides liability coverage to four groups. Identify the four groups of persons or parties who can be insured under the PAP.

4. In addition to the policy limits and a legal defense, the PAP provides for certain supplementary payments. Briefly describe the supplementary payments that can be paid under the liability section of the PAP.

5. a. List the major exclusions that apply to liability coverage (Part A) in the PAP.
   b. List the major exclusions that apply to medical payments coverage (Part B) in the PAP.

6. Describe the major features of the uninsured motorists coverage (Part C) in the PAP.

7. Coverage for Damage to Your Auto (Part D) in the PAP provides for two optional coverages: (1) collision coverage, and (2) other-than-collision coverage.
   a. What is a collision loss? Explain your answer.
   b. What is other-than-a-collision loss? Explain your answer.
   c. List the major exclusions that apply to Coverage for Damage to Your Auto (Part D).

8. Coverage for Damage to Your Auto (Part D) in the PAP also covers the insured while driving a nonowned auto.
   a. Define the meaning of a nonowned auto.
   b. If the insured drives a nonowned auto on a regular basis, does the insured's PAP provide coverage? Explain your answer.

9. Explain the duties imposed on the insured after an accident or loss occurs.

10. Does the PAP cover you if you are driving a vehicle in a foreign country? Explain your answer.

APPLICATION QUESTIONS

1. Fred has a PAP with the following coverages:

   Liability coverages: $100,000/$300,000/$50,000
   Medical payments coverage: $5000 each person
   Uninsured motorists coverage: $25,000 each person
   Collision loss: $250 deductible
   Other-than-collision loss: $100 deductible

   With respect to each of the following situations, indicate whether the loss is covered and the amount payable, if any, under the policy. Assume that each situation is a separate event.
   a. Fred's son, age 16, is driving a family car, runs a red light, and kills a pedestrian. The family of the deceased pedestrian sue for $500,000.
   b. Fred borrows a friend's car to go to the supermarket. He fails to stop at a red light and negligently smashes into another motorist. The other driver's car, valued at $15,000, is totally destroyed. In addition, repairs to the friend's car are $5000.
   c. Fred's daughter, Heather, attends college in another state and drives a family auto. Heather lets her boyfriend drive the car, and he negligently injures another motorist. The boyfriend is sued for $50,000.
   d. Fred's wife is driving a family car in a snowstorm. She loses control of the car on an icy street and smashes into the foundation of a house. The property damage to the house is $30,000. The damage to the family car is $8000. Fred's wife has medical expenses of $5000.
   e. Fred is walking across a street and is struck by a motorist who fails to stop. He has bodily injuries in the amount of $15,000.
   f. Fred's car is being repaired for faulty brakes. While road testing the car, a mechanic injures another motorist and is sued for $50,000.
   g. Fred's car hits a cow crossing a highway. The cost of repairing the car is $2500.
   h. A thief breaks a car window and steals a camera and golf clubs locked in the car. It will cost $400 to replace the damaged window. The stolen property is valued at $500.
   i. Fred's wife goes shopping at a supermarket. When she returns, she finds that the left rear fender has been damaged by another driver who did not leave a name. The cost of repairing the car is $2000.
   j. Fred works for a construction company. While driving a large cement truck, he negligently injures another motorist. The injured motorist sues Fred for $25,000.
   k. Fred's son drives a family car on a date. He gets drunk, and his girlfriend drives him home. The girlfriend negligently injures another motorist who has bodily injuries in the amount of $200,000.
   l. Stereo tapes valued at $500 are stolen from Fred's car. The car was locked when the theft occurred.

m. While driving a rented golf cart, Fred accidentally injures another golfer with the cart.

2. Karen is the named insured under a PAP that provides coverage for bodily injury and property damage liability, medical payments, and the uninsured motorists coverage. For each of the following situations, briefly explain whether the claim is covered by Karen's PAP.

a. Karen ran into a telephone pole and submitted a medical expense claim for Jason, a passenger in Karen 's car at the time of the accident.

b. Karen allowed Scott to use her car. While operating Karen's car, Scott damaged Gray's car in an accident caused by Scott's negligence. Karen is sued by Gray for damages.

c. Karen's husband ran over a bicycle while driving a friend's car. The owner of the bicycle demands that Karen's husband pay for the damage.

d. In a fit of anger, Karen deliberately ran over the wagon of a neighbor's child that had been left in Karen's driveway after repeated requests that the wagon be left elsewhere. The child's parents seek reimbursement.

3. Janet has a PAP with the following coverages:

Liability coverages: $100,000/$300,000/$50,000
Medical payment coverage: $5000 each person
Uninsured motorists coverage: $25,000 each person
Collision loss: $250 deductible
Other-than-collision loss: $100 deductible
Towing and labor cost coverage: $75 each disablement

To what extent, if any, is each of the following losses covered under Janet's PAP? Treat each event separately.

a. Janet rents a car while on vacation. She is involved in an accident with another motorist when she fails to yield the right of way. The injured motorist is awarded a judgment of $100,000. The rental agency carries only liability limits of $30,000 on the rental car. The rental agency carries no collision insurance on its cars and is seeking $15,000 from Janet for repairs to the rental car.

b. Janet borrows her friend's car with permission. She is in an accident with another motorist in which she is at fault. The cost of repairing the friend's car is $5000. The friend's auto policy has a $500 deductible for collision losses and $100 for other-than-collision losses.

c. Janet is employed as a salesperson and is furnished a company car. She is involved in an accident with another motorist while driving the company car during business hours. The injured motorist claims Janet is at fault and sues her for $100,000. Damage to the company car amounts to $5000.

d. Janet's car will not start because of a defective battery. A wrecker tows the car to a service station where the battery is replaced. Towing charges are $60. The cost of replacing the battery is $100.

4. Michael was driving a neighbor's pickup truck to get a load of firewood. A child darted out between two parked cars and ran into the street in front of the truck. In an unsuccessful attempt to avoid hitting the child, Michael lost control of the vehicle and hit a telephone pole. The child was critically injured, the pickup truck was badly damaged, and the telephone pole collapsed. Michael has liability coverage and collision coverage under his PAP. The neighbor also has a PAP with liability coverage and collision coverage on the pickup.

a. If Michael is found guilty of negligence, which insurer will pay first for the bodily injuries to the child and the property damage to the telephone pole? Explain.

b. Which insurer will pay for the physical damage to the neighbor's pickup? Explain.

5. Pablo traded in his 2000 Ford for a new Ford. One week later, he hit an oily spot in the road on his way to work and skidded into a parked car. The 2000 Ford was insured under the PAP with full coverage, including a $250 deductible for a collision loss. At the time of the accident, Pablo had not notified his insurer of the trade-in. The physical damage to the parked car was $8000. Damage to Pablo's car was $5000. Will Pablo's PAP cover either or both of these losses? Explain.

6. James, age 18, lives at home and occasionally drives the car of his friend, Mary. Mary carries $300,000 of liability insurance on her car under a PAP. James is also insured under his mother's PAP, which provides $500,000 of liability coverage. Assume that James has an accident while using Mary's car and is found to be legally liable in the amount of $400,000. How much, if any, will each policy pay? Explain your answer.

7. Patrick has a PAP with liability limits of $50,000/$100,000/$25,000. Patrick failed to stop at a red light

and hit a van. The van sustained damages of $15,000. Three passengers in the van were injured and incurred the following bodily injuries:

Passenger A, $15,000
Passenger B, $60,000
Passenger C, $10,000

Patrick was also injured and incurred medical bills of $10,000. His car sustained damages of $10,000. Because of his injury, Patrick was unable to work and lost $5000 in wages. How much will Patrick's insurer pay under the liability coverage (Part A) section of his PAP? Explain your answer.

INTERNET RESOURCES

- **All Quotes Insurance.Com** uses the power of technology to find solutions to your insurance needs. The database contains hundreds of qualified insurance providers that provide competitive quotes. You can get quotes on auto, homeowners, life, health, disability income and other insurance products. Visit the site at

  www.allquotesinsurance.com

- The **Insurance Research Council (IRC),** a division of the American Institute for CPCU, provides the insurance industry and the public with timely research studies that are relevant to public policy issues dealing with risk and insurance. Visit the site at

  http://www.ircweb.org

- The **RAND Institute for Civil Justice** is an organization within the RAND Corporation that conducts independent, objective research and analysis concerning the civil justice system. Many research studies deal with auto insurance and the insurance industry. Visit the site at

  http://www.rand.org/icj/

- **GEICO DIRECT** sells auto insurance directly over the phone (800-861-8380). The company claims that a 15-minute call can save you 15 percent or more on auto insurance rates. GEICO DIRECT also has a Web site that provides similar premium quotes online. Visit the site at

  http://www.geico.com

- The **Insurance Information Institute** provides timely information on auto insurance and other personal property insurance coverages. Numerous consumer brochures and articles on auto insurance and other property and liability coverages can be accessed directly online. Visit the site at

  http://www.iii.org

- **Insure.com** provides premium quotes for auto insurance, homeowners insurance, and other insurance products. The site also provides timely information and news releases about auto insurance and events that affect the insurance industry. Visit the site at

  http://www.insure.com

- **INSWEB** provides premium quotes for auto, homeowners, and other insurance products. You can comparison shop from your computer. In addition, the site has a learning center and provides information and articles from industry, consumer, and regulating groups. Visit the site at

  http://www.insweb.com

- The **International Risk Management Institute (IRMI)** is an online source that provides valuable information about personal lines and commercial lines. The site provides timely articles on a wide range of risk management and insurance topics and offers a number of free e-mail newsletters. Visit the site at

  http://www.irmi.com

- The **Progressive Casualty Insurance Company** has a user-friendly site that gives auto insurance quotes for most states. Progressive claims its rates are highly competitive. Progressive also provides comparison rates from other insurers. Visit the site at

  http://www.progressive.com

- The **National Association of Insurance Commissioners (NAIC)** has a link to all state insurance departments, which provide a considerable amount of consumer information on auto insurance. On the home page, click on "State Insurance Web Sites." For starters, check out New York, Wisconsin, and California. Visit the site at

  http://www.naic.org

SELECTED REFERENCES

"Cell Phones and Driving," *Hot Topics & Issues Updates,* Insurance Information Institute, July 2006. This source is periodically updated.

Fire, Casualty & Surety Bulletins, Personal Lines volume, Personal Auto section. Erlanger, KY: National Underwriter Company. The bulletins are updated monthly.

Hamilton, Karen L., and Cheryl L. Ferguson. *Personal Risk Management and Property-Liability Insurance,* 1st ed. Malvern, PA.: American Institute for Chartered Property Casualty Underwriters/Insurance Institute of America, 2002.

Hartwig, Robert P., and Claire Wilkinson. *The Use of Credit Information in Personal Lines Insurance Underwriting,* Insurance Information Institute, Insurance Issues Series, vol. 1, no. 2, June 2003.

International Risk Management Institute (IRMI). IRMI.com is an online source that provides information on personal lines and commercial lines. The site provides timely articles on a wide range of risk management and insurance topics and offers a number of free e-mail newsletters.

Wiening, Eric A., George E. Rejda, Constance M. Luthardt, and Cheryl L. Ferguson. *Personal Insurance,* 1st ed. Malvern, PA.: American Institute for Chartered Property Casualty Underwriters/Insurance Institute of America, 2002.

Wiening, Eric A., and David D. Thamann. *Personal Auto, Personal Lines Coverage Guide,* 2nd ed. Erlanger, KY: The National Underwriter Company, 2005.

NOTES

1. The material in this chapter is based on *Fire, Casualty & Surety Bulletins*, Personal Lines volume, Personal Auto section (Erlanger, KY: National Underwriter Company); and the 2005 edition of the Personal Auto Policy (copyrighted) by the Insurance Services Office. The Personal Auto Policy is used with the permission of the Insurance Services Office.
2. Insurance Research Council, *IRC Study Estimates More Than 14% of Drivers Are Uninsured,* News Release, June 28, 2006.
3. Ibid.

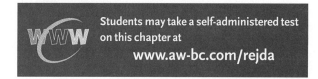
Students may take a self-administered test on this chapter at www.aw-bc.com/rejda

CHAPTER 23

AUTO INSURANCE AND SOCIETY

"The current system of paying for auto injuries suffers from two fundamental problems: premiums are too high and victims with serious injuries rarely receive full compensation."

Joint Economic Committee, 105th Congress

LEARNING OBJECTIVES

After studying this chapter, you should be able to

◆ Describe each of the following approaches for compensating auto accident victims:
Financial responsibility laws
Compulsory insurance laws
Unsatisfied judgment fund
Uninsured motorists coverage
Low-cost auto insurance
"No pay, No play laws"

◆ Explain the meaning of no-fault auto insurance and the rationale for no-fault insurance laws.

◆ Describe each of the following methods for providing auto insurance to high-risk drivers:
Auto insurance plan
Joint underwriting association (JUA)
Reinsurance facility

◆ Identify the major factors that determine the cost of auto insurance to consumers.

◆ Explain the suggestions that consumers should follow in shopping for auto insurance.

A shley, age 24, graduated from college with an accounting degree and accepted a job with a public accounting firm in Chicago, Illinois. Shortly after she moved to Chicago, a drunk driver ran a red light and smashed into her car. Ashley was seriously injured, and her car was damaged beyond repair. Ashley incurred medical bills in excess of $50,000 and was unable to work for three months. When she tried to collect damages from the negligent driver, she discovered that the driver was uninsured and unemployed and had a lengthy history of alcohol abuse. In short, Ashley had to eat the loss.

Ashley had an unfortunate and costly introduction to the auto insurance reparations system. Each year, millions of motorists are injured or killed in auto accidents in the United States. Society then has the problem of compensating these victims for their bodily injuries and property damage caused by negligent drivers. Society also has the burden of providing auto insurance to irresponsible drivers, including drunk drivers, high-risk drivers, and drivers who habitually break traffic laws. Society must also deal with the problem of compensating innocent accident victims who are injured by uninsured drivers.

This chapter discusses the preceding problems in depth. Four areas are emphasized: (1) the various approaches for compensating auto accident victims, (2) no-fault auto insurance as an alternative to the tort liability system, (3) methods for providing auto insurance to high-risk drivers, and (4) suggestions for buying auto insurance.

APPROACHES FOR COMPENSATING AUTO ACCIDENT VICTIMS

In many cases, innocent persons who are injured in auto accidents are unable to recover financial damages from the negligent motorists who injured them. Although accident victims may have bodily injuries or suffer property damage, they may recover nothing or receive less than full indemnification. To deal with this problem, the states use a number of approaches to provide some protection to accident victims from irresponsible and reckless drivers. They include the following:[1]

- Financial responsibility laws
- Compulsory insurance laws
- Unsatisfied judgment funds
- Uninsured motorists coverage
- Low-cost auto insurance
- "No pay, no play" laws
- No-fault auto insurance

Financial Responsibility Laws

All states have enacted some type of financial responsibility law or compulsory insurance law that requires motorists to furnish proof of financial responsibility up to certain minimum dollar limits. A **financial responsibility law** *does not require proof of financial responsibility until after the driver has his or her first accident or until after conviction for certain offenses, such as driving under the influence of alcohol.* Proof of financial responsibility is typically required under the following circumstances:

- After an accident involving bodily injury or property damage over a certain amount
- Upon failure to pay a final judgment resulting from an auto accident

■ Following a conviction for certain offenses, such as drunk driving or reckless driving

Under these conditions, if a motorist cannot demonstrate that he or she meets the state's financial responsibility law requirements, the state can revoke or suspend the motorist's driving privileges.

Evidence of financial responsibility can be provided by producing evidence of an auto liability insurance policy with at least certain minimum limits, such as $25,000/$50,000/$25,000.[2] Other ways in which the financial responsibility law can be satisfied are by posting a bond, by depositing securities or money in the amount required by law, or by showing that the person is a qualified self-insurer. Exhibit 23.1 shows the minimum liability insurance limits for the various states. The first two figures refer to bodily injury liability, and the third figure refers to property damage liability. For example, 20/40/10 means bodily injury coverage of $20,000 per person, $40,000 per accident, and $10,000 for property damage.

Although financial responsibility laws provide some protection against irresponsible motorists, they have two major defects:

■ *There is no guarantee that all accident victims will be paid.* The accident victim may not be paid if he or she is injured by an uninsured driver, hit-and-run driver, or driver of a stolen car. An irresponsible motorist often drives without a license, so the law fails to achieve the objective of getting the irresponsible driver off the road.
■ *Accident victims may not be fully indemnified for their injuries.* Most financial responsibility laws require only minimum liability insurance limits, which are relatively low. If the bodily injury exceeds the minimum limit, the accident victim may not be fully compensated.

Compulsory Insurance Laws

Liability insurance is compulsory in most states and the District of Columbia. A **compulsory insurance law** *requires motorists to carry at least a minimum amount of liability insurance before the vehicle can be licensed or registered.*

Some people believe that compulsory insurance laws provide greater protection against uninsured drivers because motorists must provide evidence of financial responsibility before an accident occurs.

However, recent studies by various groups conclude that compulsory insurance laws generally are ineffective in reducing the percentage of uninsured drivers. Critics of compulsory insurance laws cite the following defects:

■ *In general, there is no correlation between compulsory insurances laws and the number of uninsured vehicles on the highway.* There will always be part of the population that chooses to drive without insurance. That percentage is not precisely known and varies among the states. This group either takes a chance or pursues fraudulent compliance measures.[3]
■ *According to the Property Casualty Insurers Association of America, mandatory auto insurance does not reduce the number of uninsured drivers.* Unlicensed and uninsured drivers are involved in more than 20 percent of the fatal crashes on America's highways. Compulsory insurance laws do not prevent drivers from owning or operating a vehicle.[4]
■ *Many states have computer reporting systems to track uninsured motorists. Evidence suggests that reporting systems have not effectively met their major objective of identifying and tracking uninsured drivers.* Reporting programs are costly, difficult to implement, hard to maintain, and place a financial burden on insured drivers.[5]

Finally, you may be involved in an auto accident where the other driver is at fault but is in compliance with the state's financial responsibility or compulsory insurance law. You can file a claim against the negligent driver or his or her insurer for any bodily injury or physical damage to your car. These claims are called "third-party" claims. A third-party claim against another driver's insurer is a common source of complaint to state insurance departments. Insight 23.1 discusses some common questions and answers about third-party claims prepared by the Texas Department of Insurance. Although some answers refer specifically to Texas law, they are relevant to drivers in other states as well.

Unsatisfied Judgment Funds

Five states—Maryland, Michigan, New Jersey, New York, and North Dakota—have established unsatisfied judgment funds for compensating in-

EXHIBIT 23.1
Table of Limits, Financial Responsibility and Compulsory Insurance Laws

---

Split or Single Limits

The laws of all states express the requirement in terms of *split limits.* For example, if the chart shows "25/50/10," the law requires that the policy provide at least $25,000 for bodily injury to each person, $50,000 for all bodily injury, and $10,000 for property damage for each accident.

The insurance laws of some states also state the requirement in terms of a *combined single limit.* For example, if the chart shows "15/30/10 or 40," the law provides that a policy with a combined single limit of at least $40,000 will also satisfy the requirement. A combined single limit of $40,000 means that the insurance will pay up to $40,000 for all bodily injury and property damage arising out of each accident. The required limits for the Canadian provinces are expressed as combined single limits only.

Required Limits, by State

State	Limit	State	Limit
Alabama	20/40/10 or 50	Newfoundland	200
Alaska	20/100/25 or 125	New Hampshire	25/50/25
Alberta	200	New Jersey	15/30/5
Arizona	15/30/10 or 40	New Mexico	25/50/10
Arkansas	25/50/25	New York	25/50/10
British Columbia	200	Northwest Territories	200
California	15/30/5	North Carolina	30/60/25
Colorado	25/50/15	North Dakota	25/50/25
Connecticut	20/40/10	Nova Scotia	200
Delaware	15/30/5	Nunavut	200
District of Columbia	25/50/5	Ohio	12.5/25/7.5
Florida	10/20/10 or 30	Oklahoma	25/50/25
Georgia	25/50/25	Ontario	200
Hawaii	20/40/10	Oregon	25/50/10
Idaho	25/50/15	Pennsylvania	15/30/5
Illinois	20/40/15	Prince Edward Island	200
Indiana	25/50/10	Puerto Rico	No F. R. Requirement
Iowa	20/40/15	Quebec	50**
Kansas	25/50/10	Rhode Island	25/50/25
Kentucky	25/50/10 or 60	Saskatchewan	200
Louisiana	10/20/10	South Carolina	15/30/10
Maine	50/100/25	South Dakota	25/50/25
Manitoba	200	Tennessee	25/50/10 or 60
Maryland	20/40/15	Texas	20/40/15
Massachusetts	15/40/5	Utah	25/50/15 or 65
Michigan	20/40/10	Vermont	25/50/10
Minnesota	30/60/10	Virginia	25/50/20
Mississippi	25/50/25	Washington	25/50/10
Missouri	25/50/10	West Virginia	20/40/10
Montana	25/50/10	Wisconsin	25/50/10
Nebraska	20/50/25	Wyoming	25/50/20
Nevada	15/30/10	Yukon	200
New Brunswick	200		

** Because Quebec has a complete no-fault system for bodily injury, the minimum limit applies only to property damage within Quebec and combined bodily injury and property damage outside Quebec.

SOURCE: *Fire Casualty & Surety Bulletins,* Personal Lines volume, Personal Auto section (Erlanger, KY: National Underwriter Company), May 2006, p. D2.2.

nocent accident victims. An **unsatisfied judgment fund** *is a state fund for compensating auto accident victims who have exhausted all other means of recovery.* These funds have certain common characteristics:[6]

- The accident victim must obtain a judgment against the negligent motorist and must show that the judgment cannot be collected.
- The maximum amount paid by the fund generally is limited to the state's compulsory insurance

INSIGHT 23.1

Claims Against Another Driver's Insurance Company

"Third-Party" claims against another driver's auto insurance company are a common source of complaints and inquiries to the Texas Department of Insurance (TDI).

A third-party claim occurs when another driver causes an accident and you look to his or her liability insurance to pay your auto repair, medical, and other expenses. An auto liability policy obligates the insurance company to pay any amounts for which its policyholder is legally responsible as a result of an accident, up to the dollar limits of the policy.

Here are answers to some frequently asked questions about third-party claims:

Q How long does the other driver's insurance company have to pay my claim?
A There are no specific legal limits. A company is legally required to act in good faith and pay third-party claims promptly and fairly when liability is reasonably clear.

Q Must the other driver's insurer pay for a rental car while mine is being fixed?
A Yes. However, Texas courts have held that there is no such obligation if your car was "totaled" and is being replaced instead of repaired.

Q The other driver's company wants me to sign a release. How long can I delay?
A Don't sign until you are satisfied with your total settlement. You have two years after the accident to either settle your claim or file a lawsuit.

Q Can the other driver's insurance company delay paying for my car repairs to pressure me into signing a release on my injury claim?
A No. Texas law prohibits this unfair tactic. If it occurs, you have the right to file a formal complaint with TDI.

Q How much can I claim for pain and suffering?
A There is no set formula for this. It is determined on a case-by-case bases.

Q Can the at-fault driver's insurance company tell me where to get my car fixed?
A No. Texas law prohibits companies from dictating a particular car-repair shop or requiring parts of a particular brand, type, age, or condition.

Q The other driver claims he didn't cause our accident. I have two witnesses who say he did. The police did not investigate. What can I do?
A Make sure the other driver's insurance company and your insurers know about these witnesses and encourage the companies to take the witnesses' statements.

Q The other driver's insurance adjuster has submitted an estimate lower than the estimates I got from two different body shops. What are my options?
A You can challenge the adjuster's estimate by comparing it with the body shops' estimates. If you can't get satisfaction and you believe the company is treating you unfairly, you can file a complaint with TDI.

Q My car was totaled, and the other driver's insurance company based its offer on a "market survey." Do I have to accept the offer?
A A market survey involves checking newspaper ads, used car lots, auto trade magazines, and dealerships for the average price of cars like yours in your area. You don't have to accept the offer. You can do your own survey and present it to the company for negotiation.

Q The other driver's insurer offered to pay $35 a day for a rental car while my car is being fixed. But my car is a luxury model. Is $35 all the company is obligated to pay?
A The company must pay for the "loss of use" of your damaged car. That means paying a reasonable amount for a rental. There is no specific limit.

Source: Excerpted from "Claims Against Another Driver's Insurance Company," Saving Money on Your Insurance by the Commissioner of Insurance. Texas Department of Insurance. http://www.tdi.state.tx.us/commish/columns/cc1102.html

law. The amount paid may also be reduced by collateral sources of recovery, such as workers compensation benefits.

■ The negligent driver is not relieved of legal responsibility when the fund makes a payment to the accident victim. Negligent drivers must

repay the fund or lose their driver's license until the fund is reimbursed for the payments.

The method of financing benefits varies from state to state. Funds can be obtained by charging a fee to each motorist, by assessing insurers based on the amount of auto liability insurance written in the state, by assessing the uninsured motorists in the state, and by surcharging drivers with convictions for moving vehicle violations.

Uninsured Motorists Coverage

Uninsured motorists coverage is another approach for compensating injured auto accident victims. The injured person's insurer agrees to pay the accident victim who has a bodily injury (or property damage in some states) caused by an uninsured motorist, by a hit-and-run driver, or by a negligent driver whose insurer is insolvent.

Uninsured motorists coverage has the following advantages.

- *Motorists have some protection against an uninsured driver.* Many states require the coverage to be mandatorily included in all auto liability insurance policies sold within the state. In other states, coverage is included in the policy unless the insured voluntarily declines the protection by signing a written waiver.
- *Claim settlement is faster and more efficient than a tort liability lawsuit.* Although the accident victim must establish negligence by the uninsured driver, it is not necessary to sue the negligent driver and win a judgment.

Uninsured motorist's coverage, however, has several defects as a technique for compensating injured auto accident victims. They include the following:

- *Unless higher limits are purchased, the maximum amount paid is limited to the state's financial responsibility or compulsory insurance law requirement.* The minimum limits are relatively low. Thus, the accident victim may not be fully compensated for his or her loss.
- *The injured person must establish that the uninsured motorist is legally liable for the accident.* This task may be difficult in some cases and expensive if an attorney must be hired.
- *Property damage is not covered in many states.* Unless you have collision coverage, you would collect nothing for any property damage to your car caused by an uninsured motorist in those states.

Low-Cost Auto Insurance

As stated earlier, compulsory insurance laws generally have not been effective in reducing the number of uninsured drivers. A few states have enacted new laws to deal with the problem. Many drivers are uninsured because of the high cost of auto insurance. **Low-cost auto insurance** provides minimum amounts of liability insurance at reduced rates to motorists who cannot afford regular insurance or have limited financial assets to protect.

In 2000, California enacted a pilot program that initially provided low-cost auto insurance to low-income drivers in Los Angeles and San Francisco who could meet certain eligibility requirements. However, in 2006, the program was expanded to allow eligible drivers in 16 counties to participate as well. To qualify, the applicant must be a good driver; family income must be under a certain level; and the value of an insured vehicle cannot exceed $20,000. The bodily injury liability limits are $10,000 per person, $20,000 per accident, and $3000 for property damage for each accident. Medical payments coverage and uninsured motorists coverage are available as optional coverages. However, physical damage coverage is not available.

The program does not appear to be effective in increasing the number of insured drivers. Low-income drivers have few assets to protect, and many drivers still find auto insurance too expensive to purchase. Only about 25,000 low-cost policies were written as of May 2006. [7]

New Jersey offers motorists three choices: (1) Standard Policy, (2) Basic Policy, and (3) Dollar-a-Day policy. Most New Jersey drivers select the *Standard Policy,* which provides a number of different coverage options and the opportunity to purchase additional protection. [8] The *Basic Policy* is a limited and less expensive policy and is designed for drivers with few family responsibilities or financial assets to protect, such as younger drivers who are just starting jobs and cannot afford more comprehensive coverage. The Basic Policy is a no-fault coverage (discussed later) that provides $15,000 in personal injury protection, up to $250,000 for permanent and significant injury, and $5000 in property damage liability. Policyowners also have the option to purchase $10,000 of bodily injury liability insurance. Uninsured motorists and underinsured motorists coverages are not available. Collision insurance and comprehensive insurance are available as an option from some insurers.

Finally, the *Dollar-a-Day policy* is limited to Medicaid recipients and costs $360 annually or $365 if purchased in two six-month payments. The policy provides up to $15,000 for emergency care, up to $250,000 for treatment of serious brain and spinal cord injuries, and a $10,000 death benefit. Part of the premium goes into a pool for uninsured drivers, which reduces the financial burden on drivers who carry insurance.

"No Pay, No Play" Laws

Another approach is enactment of **"no pay, no play" laws,** which prohibit uninsured motorists from suing negligent drivers for noneconomic damages, such as compensation for pain and suffering. Some states are considering the proposal as a method for reducing the number of uninsured drivers. A few states have enacted such laws. In Michigan, uninsured drivers who are 50 percent or more at fault cannot collect noneconomic damages in an auto accident. California prohibits suits by both uninsured drivers and drunk drivers. Louisiana requires uninsured drivers to pay the first $10,000 of out-of-pocket medical expenses and the first $10,000 in property damage before uninsured drivers can sue the other party. New Jersey prohibits uninsured drivers, drunk drivers, and motorists who commit intentional acts from filing lawsuits for economic and noneconomic damages. In addition, Iowa's law prohibits motorists from collecting noneconomic damages for injuries resulting from the accident if the motorist used the vehicle to commit a felony.

No-Fault Auto Insurance

No-fault auto insurance is another method for compensating injured accident victims. Because of dissatisfaction and defects in the traditional tort liability system, about half of the states, the District of Columbia, and Puerto Rico currently have some type of no-fault law in effect.

Definition of No-Fault Insurance No-fault auto insurance *means that after an auto accident involv-*

ing a bodily injury, each party collects from his or her own insurer regardless of fault. It is not necessary to determine who is at fault and prove negligence before a loss payment is made. Regardless of who caused the accident, each party collects from his or her own insurer.

In addition, a true no-fault law places some restriction on the right to sue the negligent driver who caused the accident. If a bodily injury claim is below a certain **monetary threshold** (such as $5000), an injured motorist would not be permitted to sue but instead would collect from his or her own insurer. However, if the bodily injury claim exceeds the threshold amount, the injured person has the right to sue the negligent driver for damages. If the negligent driver is insured, the negligent driver's insurance company will usually cover the loss.

In some states, a verbal rather than monetary threshold is used. A **verbal threshold** *means that a suit for damages is allowed only in serious cases, such as those involving death, dismemberment, disfigurement, or permanent loss of a bodily member or function.* Thus, if the injured person has a less severe injury than those listed, the injured person would not be permitted to sue but instead would collect from his or her insurer.

Basic Characteristics of No-Fault Plans No-fault plans vary widely among the states with respect to the type of law, benefits provided, and restrictions on the right to sue.[9]

1. *Types of no-fault plans.* Several types of no-fault plans and proposals exist. They include the following:

- Pure no-fault plan
- Modified no-fault plan
- Add-on plan
- Choice no-fault plan

Under a **pure no-fault plan,** *accident victims could not sue at all, regardless of the amount of the claim, and no payments would be made for pain and suffering.* In effect, the tort liability system would be abolished, because accident victims could not sue for damages. Instead, injured persons would receive unlimited medical benefits and lost wages from their insurers. No state has enacted a pure no-fault plan at this time.

Under a **modified no-fault plan,** *an injured person has the right to sue a negligent driver only if the bodily injury claim exceeds the dollar or verbal threshold.* Otherwise, the accident victim collects from his or her own insurer. Thus, modified no-fault plans only partially restrict the right to sue.

An **add-on plan** *pays benefits to an accident victim without regard to fault, and the injured person still has the right to sue the negligent driver who caused the accident.* This plan also includes the right to sue for pain and suffering. Because the injured person retains the right to sue, add-on plans are not true no-fault laws.

Three states (Kentucky, New Jersey, and Pennsylvania) have **choice no-fault plans.** Under such laws, motorists can elect to be covered under the state's no-fault law and pay lower premiums, or they can retain the right to sue under the tort liability system and pay higher premiums.

Slightly more than half of the jurisdictions with no-fault laws have enacted modified plans where restrictions are placed on the right to sue. The remainder have add-on plans or choice no-fault laws. As noted earlier, no state has enacted a pure no-fault plan, and three states have choice no-fault laws.

2. *No-fault benefits.* No-fault benefits are provided by adding an endorsement to an auto insurance policy. The endorsement is typically called "personal injury protection coverage (PIP)" which describes the no-fault benefits. Benefits are restricted to the injured person's *economic loss,* such as medical expenses, a percentage of lost wages, and certain other expenses. The injured person can sue for *noneconomic loss* (such as pain and suffering and inconvenience) only if the dollar threshold is exceeded or the verbal threshold is met.

The following benefits are typically provided:

- Medical expenses
- Loss of earnings
- Essential services expenses
- Funeral expenses
- Survivors' loss benefits

Medical expenses are paid usually up to some maximum limit. Michigan has no dollar limit on medical benefits. Rehabilitation expenses incurred by an injured accident victim are also paid.

Payments are made for the loss of earnings. The no-fault benefits are typically limited to a stated percentage of the disabled person's weekly or monthly earnings, with a maximum limit in terms of dollar amount and duration.

Benefits are also paid for **essential services expenses** *ordinarily performed by the injured person.* Examples include housework, cooking, lawn mowing, and house repairs.

Funeral expenses are paid up to some dollar limit. In some states, funeral expenses are included as part of the medical expense limit. In other states, funeral expenses are a separate benefit.

Survivors' loss benefits *are payable to eligible survivors, such as a surviving spouse and dependent children.* The survivors typically receive periodic income payments or a lump sum to compensate them for the death of a covered person.

A number of states also require that **optional no-fault benefits** above the prescribed minimums be made available. Likewise, many states require insurers to offer **optional deductibles** that may be used to restrict or eliminate certain no-fault coverages.

3. *Right to sue.* In those states with add-on plans, there are no restrictions on the right to sue. The accident victim can receive first-party no-fault benefits from his or her insurer and still sue the negligent driver for damages.

All states permit a lawsuit in the event of a serious injury. A serious injury typically is an injury that results in death, dismemberment, disfigurement, bone fracture, permanent loss of a bodily function or organ, or permanent disability. Under these circumstances, the injured person can sue for damages, including payment for pain and suffering.

In those states with modified no-fault laws, the right to sue is restricted. In general, the accident victim can sue the negligent driver for general damages, including pain and suffering, only if a dollar or verbal threshold is met.

Finally, the three states with choice no-fault laws allow motorists to elect coverage under the state's no-fault law with lower premiums and restrictions on lawsuits or, alternatively, to retain the right to sue under the tort liability system with higher premiums.

4. *Exclusion of property damage.* With the exception of Michigan, no-fault laws cover only bodily

injury and not property damage. Thus, if a negligent driver smashed into your car, you would still be permitted to sue for the property damage to your car. It is argued that a lawsuit for property damage does not normally result in long court delays, expensive legal fees, and defects similar to those now found in bodily injury lawsuits. Also, the size of a property damage claim settlement is relatively small when compared to bodily injury liability settlements.

Arguments for No-Fault Laws Proponents of no-fault laws argue that an alternative system is needed because of defects in the present tort liability system. These defects include the following:

- *Difficulty in determining fault.* Critics argue that auto accidents occur suddenly and unexpectedly, and determination of fault is often difficult. Under a no-fault law, it is not necessary to determine fault. Each party collects from his or her insurer if the bodily injury claim is below a certain dollar threshold or does not meet the description of a verbal threshold.
- *Inequity in claim payments.* Under the present system, small claims are often overpaid, whereas serious claims may be underpaid. As a result, auto accident victims with serious injuries often recover less than the full amount of their economic losses.
- *High transactions costs and attorney fees.* Critics also argue that the present tort system incurs high transactions costs and attorney fees. More than half of the tort dollars moving through the traditional tort system never reach injured victims. We noted in Chapter 19 that attorney fees, legal defense costs, and administrative costs account for 54 percent of each tort dollar paid. In contrast, injured victims receive only 22 cents for their actual economic loss (such as medical bills and lost earnings) and another 24 cents for noneconomic loss (such as pain and suffering). Thus, the present system is flawed by high transaction costs and attorney fees.
- *Fraudulent and inflated claims.* The present system is flawed because of fraudulent and inflated claims. Two types of abuse are present. First, explicit fraud occurs, including staged auto accidents, fake claims, and collusion among doctors,

attorneys, and chiropractors. Second, the present system encourages injured victims to inflate their claims above their actual losses to increase their damage awards. Because payments for noneconomic losses (pain and suffering) are difficult to calculate, one rule of thumb is to calculate such losses as two to three times the claimant's economic losses (medical bills and lost wages). *When pain and suffering awards are based on a multiple of medical expenses and wage loss, claimants have a powerful incentive to inflate their claims.*
- *Delay in payments.* Under the present system, many claims are not paid promptly because of the time consumed by investigation, negotiation, and waiting for a court date. Moreover, hiring an attorney does not necessarily speed up payment. An Insurance Research Council (IRC) study of auto accident victims showed that claimants without attorneys received payments significantly more quickly than claimants with attorneys. *Among claimants without an attorney, 62 percent of those who filed with their own insurer, and 40 percent of those who filed with another insurer, settled their claims within three months. In contrast, among claimants who hired an attorney, only 29 percent of those who filed with their own insurer, and 8 percent of those who filed with another insurer, settled their claims in less than three months.*[10]

Arguments Against No-Fault Laws Supporters of the present system argue that no-fault laws are also defective. Major arguments against no-fault laws include the following:

- *Defects of the negligence system are exaggerated.* A large proportion of fatal crashes and serious accidents involve alcohol where fault can usually be determined without difficulty. Also, the fact that most claims are settled out of court suggests that the present system is working fairly well.
- *Claims of efficiency and premium savings are exaggerated.* Predictions of greater efficiency and premium savings from no-fault laws are exaggerated and unreliable. In many states with no-fault laws, premiums have increased more rapidly than in tort liability states.

- *Court delays are not universal.* Court delays are a problem only in certain large metropolitan areas, and delays can be reduced by providing more adequate courts and improved procedures. The courts are burdened because of an increase in the number of divorce cases, drug and other criminal cases, and other types of civil suits.
- *Safe drivers may be penalized.* A no-fault plan can penalize safe drivers and provide a bonus for irresponsible motorists who cause accidents. The rating system may inequitably allocate accident costs to the drivers who are not at fault, and their premiums may go up as a result.
- *There is no payment for pain and suffering.* Plaintiff attorneys argue that the true cost to the accident victim cannot be measured only by the actual dollar amount of medical expenses and loss of wages. Pain and suffering should also be considered in determining the amount of damages.
- *The tort liability system needs only to be reformed.* This reform could be accomplished by increasing the number of judges and courtrooms, limiting the fees of attorneys, and using arbitration rather than the courts to settle small cases.

Evaluation of No-Fault Laws   Some states have repealed their no-fault laws because relatively low monetary thresholds have increased the number of lawsuits. Other states have changed their plans over time. A study of no-fault plans by the Institute for Civil Justice provides valuable information concerning the effectiveness of no-fault plans. The major conclusions are as follows:[11]

- *No-fault plans reduce transaction costs (attorney fees and claim processing costs).* All no-fault plans reduce transaction costs. However, a no-fault plan that absolutely banned compensation for noneconomic loss would eliminate about three-fourths of the transaction costs. Alternative plans that allow some access to the liability system would reduce transaction costs by 20 to 40 percent, depending on the plan design.
- *No-fault plans match the compensation received for an injury more closely with the economic loss sustained.* No-fault plans increase the fraction of economic loss that is compensated and reduce the amount paid for noneconomic loss. Economic loss includes medical bills, lost wages, and other losses measured in monetary terms. Injured people with smaller claims tend to recover amounts that approximate their medical costs and lost wages. However, seriously injured people recover a larger share of their losses because they can collect both no-fault benefits and liability compensation.
- *No-fault plans eliminate compensation for noneconomic loss, such as pain and suffering, for injured people below the threshold.* Noneconomic losses include pain and suffering, disfigurement, and other losses not measured in monetary terms.
- *No-fault plans generally pay benefits more quickly.* On average, no-fault plans pay benefits to injured people about two months faster than under the traditional system.
- *No-fault plans can yield substantial savings over the traditional system, or such plans can increase costs depending on the plan design.* Under different no-fault alternatives, total injury coverage costs may decrease. Such costs, however, may be higher under no-fault plans, depending on the threshold and level of no-fault benefits. This is especially true in states that have relatively low dollar thresholds. Whether a particular no-fault plan will reduce total injury costs will depend on the provisions in the plan and plan design.
- *On the negative side, fraudulent claims have been a problem in several states.* Fraudulent claims arise out of staged accidents, use of runners, excessive use of medical diagnostic tests, phony pain clinics, and corrupt physicians, lawyers, and chiropractors. In particular, fraudulent no-fault claims earlier were a major problem in New York. According to the Insurance Research Council, one in four PIP claims in New York included an element of fraud.[12] To reduce fraud, New York enacted regulations that shortened the time period for reporting an accident and the submission of medical bills. As a result, fraudulent claims have declined significantly.

AUTO INSURANCE FOR HIGH-RISK DRIVERS

Some drivers have difficulty obtaining auto insurance through normal market channels. This group includes younger drivers who account for a disproportionate number of auto accidents, drivers with poor driving records, and drivers with one or more convictions for drunk driving. These drivers can obtain auto insurance in the **shared market** (also called the **residual market**). The shared market refers to plans in which auto insurers participate to make insurance available to drivers who are unable to obtain coverage in the standard markets.

High-risk drivers who have difficulty in obtaining auto insurance in the standard markets can purchase the insurance from a number of sources. They include the following:

- Automobile insurance plan
- Joint underwriting association (JUA)
- Reinsurance facility
- Maryland Automobile Insurance Fund
- Specialty insurers

Automobile Insurance Plan

Most states have an **automobile insurance plan** (also called an **assigned risk plan**) that makes auto insurance available to motorists who are unable to obtain insurance in the voluntary market. Under such a plan, all auto insurers in the state are assigned their proportionate share of high-risk drivers based on the total volume of auto insurance premiums written in the state. For example, if insurer A writes 5 percent of the auto insurance premiums in the state, insurer A must accept 5 percent of the high-risk applicants in the automobile insurance plan (see Exhibit 23.2). The premiums charged, however, are substantially higher than those charged in the voluntary markets. It is not uncommon for high-risk drivers to pay two or three times the standard premium.

The major advantage of automobile insurance plans is that a high-risk driver generally has at least one source for obtaining liability insurance. Thus, the social objective of protecting innocent accident victims is at least partially met. Nevertheless, such plans have several disadvantages, which include the following:

- *Despite higher premiums paid by high-risk drivers, auto insurance plans have incurred substantial underwriting losses.* Thus, good drivers in the voluntary markets are subsidizing the substandard drivers.
- *High premiums may cause many high-risk drivers to go uninsured.* This effect is the exact opposite of what the plans are intended to accomplish.
- *Many drivers who are "clean risks" with no driving convictions are arbitrarily placed in the plans.* This can happen when poor territorial loss experience or inadequate rate increases granted by regulatory officials cause insurers to restrict the writing of auto insurance in a given territory or state in the standard markets.

Joint Underwriting Association

A few states have established joint underwriting associations to make auto insurance available to high-risk drivers. A **joint underwriting association (JUA)** is an organization of auto insurers operating in the state in which high-risk business is placed in a common pool, and each company pays its pro rata share of pool losses and expenses. The JUA influences the design of the high-risk auto policy and sets the rates that are charged. All underwriting losses are proportionately shared by the companies based on premiums written in the state.

A limited number of insurance companies are designated as servicing insurers to administer the high-risk JUA business. Each agent or broker is assigned a company that provides claim services and other services to the policyowners. Although only a limited number of large insurers are servicing insurers, all insurers share in the underwriting losses, as noted earlier.

Reinsurance Facility

A few states have established a **reinsurance facility** (or **pool**) for placing high-risk drivers. Under this arrangement, the insurance company must accept all applicants for insurance, both good and bad drivers.

EXHIBIT 23.2
Example of an Automobile Insurance Plan (Generalized)

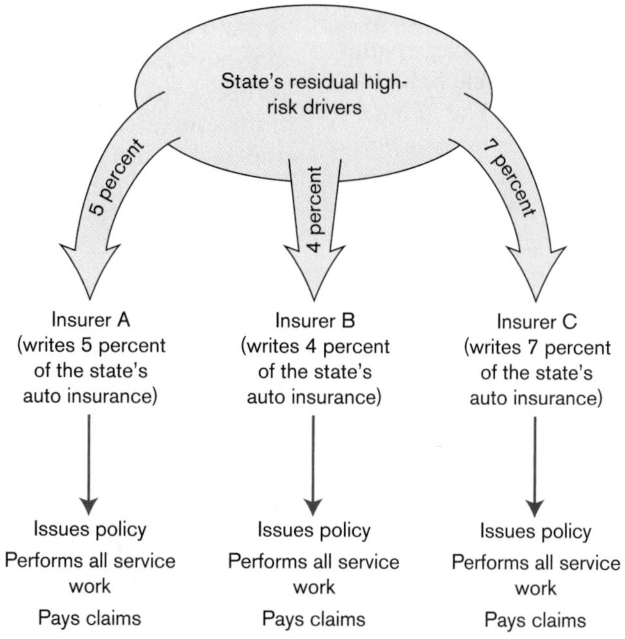
State's residual high-risk drivers
5 percent
4 percent
7 percent
Insurer A (writes 5 percent of the state's auto insurance)
Insurer B (writes 4 percent of the state's auto insurance)
Insurer C (writes 7 percent of the state's auto insurance)
Issues policy
Performs all service work
Pays claims
Issues policy
Performs all service work
Pays claims
Issues policy
Performs all service work
Pays claims

SOURCE: Adapted from Karen L. Hamilton and Cheryl L. Ferguson, *Personal Risk Management and Property-Liability Insurance,* 1st ed. (Malvern, PA: American Institute for Chartered Property Casualty Underwriters/Insurance Institute of America, 2002), Exhibit 9-5, p. 9.37.

If the applicant is considered a high-risk driver, the insurer has the option of placing the driver in the reinsurance pool. Although the high-risk driver is in the reinsurance pool, the original insurer services the policy. Underwriting losses in the reinsurance facility are shared by all auto insurers in the state.

Maryland Automobile Insurance Fund

The **Maryland Automobile Insurance Fund** is a state fund that makes auto insurance available to Maryland motorists who are unable to obtain insurance in the voluntary markets. The state fund came into existence because of high rates charged by private insurers, large numbers of motorists who had been placed in the assigned risk plan, and difficulties experienced by high-risk drivers in obtaining insurance. The fund provides insurance only to drivers who have been canceled or refused insurance by private insurers.

Specialty Insurers

Specialty insurers are insurers that specialize in insuring motorists with poor driving records. These insurers typically insure drivers who have been canceled or refused insurance, teenage drivers, and drivers convicted of drunk driving. The premiums are substantially higher than premiums paid in the standard markets. The actual premium paid is based on the individual's driving record, typically over the past three years. The higher the number of chargeable accidents or moving vehicle traffic violations, the higher the premium charged. The liability insurance limits are at least equal to the financial responsibility law requirement in the state, and many insurers offer higher limits on an optional basis. In addition, because the drivers have a high probability of being involved in an accident, medical payments coverage often has relatively low limits, and collision insurance may require a high deductible.

COST OF AUTO INSURANCE

Auto insurance is expensive. Auto insurers have substantially increased their rates over time because of rising medical costs, higher motor vehicle repair costs, soaring jury awards in motor vehicle liability cases, and insurance fraud and abuse. You should be aware of the factors that determine auto insurance premiums and what you can do to reduce your premiums.

The major rating factors for determining private passenger auto premiums are as follows:

- Territory
- Age, gender, and marital status
- Use of the auto
- Driver education
- Good student discount
- Number and types of cars
- Individual driving record
- Insurance score

Territory

A base rate for liability insurance is first established, determined largely by the territory where the auto is principally used and garaged. Each state is divided into rating territories—for example, a large city, a part of a city, a suburb, or a rural area. Claims data are compiled for each territory in determining the basic rate. Thus, a city driver normally pays a higher rate than a rural driver because of the higher number of auto accidents in congested cities. In particular, auto insurance premiums are substantially higher in certain large cities because of the higher density of traffic, increased likelihood of theft and vandalism, and higher incidence of fraud. Exhibit 23.3 shows average auto insurance premiums for the five most expensive and five least expensive cities in 2006.

Age, Gender, and Marital Status

Age, gender, and marital status are important in determining the total premium. Most states permit these factors to be used in determining premiums.

Age is an extremely important rating factor because young drivers account for a disproportionate number of auto accidents. In 2004, drivers under age 25 accounted for 13 percent of all licensed drivers. However, this group accounted for 29 percent of the drivers in all accidents and 25 percent of all fatal accidents (see Exhibit 23.4). Drivers over age 65 are also involved in a high percentage of fatal accidents (see Exhibit 23.5).

Gender is also relevant. Insurers generally charge female drivers lower rates than males, but the rate gap is narrowing, especially at the younger ages. In recent years, female drivers have experienced

EXHIBIT 23.3

Top Five Most Expensive and Least Expensive Cities for Automobile Insurance, 2006*

Most Expensive Cities			Least Expensive Cities		
Rank	City	Average Auto Premiums	Rank	City	Average Auto Premiums
1	Detroit, MI	$5,894	1	Roanoke, VA	$912
2	Philadelphia, PA	4,440	2	Wapakoneta, OH	980
3	Newark, NJ	3,977	3	Chattanooga, TN	1,040
4	Los Angeles, CA	3,430	4	Green Bay, WI	1,042
5	New York City, NY	3,303	5	Raleigh, NC	1,057

* As of February, 2006. Assumes $100/$300/$50 liability limits, collision and comprehensive with $500 deductibles, $2,000 medical, and $100/$300 uninsured coverage.

NOTE: Data are from Runzheimer International.

SOURCE: Insurance Information Institute.

EXHIBIT 23.4
Accidents by Age of Drivers, 2004

Accidents by Age of Drivers, 2004

Age Group	Number of Drivers	Percent of Total	Drivers in Fatal Accidents	Percent of Total	Drivers in All Accidents	Percent of Total
Under 20	9,369,000	4.7%	6,900	11.0%	2,690,000	14.0%
20 to 24	16,907,000	8.5	9,000	14.5	2,940,000	15.3
25 to 34	36,040,000	18.2	11,400	18.1	3,950,000	20.6
35 to 44	40,609,000	20.5	10,400	16.5	3,580,000	18.6
45 to 54	38,944,000	19.7	9,800	15.6	2,980,000	15.5
55 to 64	27,424,000	13.8	6,200	5.8	1,650,000	8.6
65 to 74	16,226,000	8.2	4,000	6.3	820,000	4.3
Over 74	12,581,000	6.4	5,300	8.4	590,000	3.1
Total	**198,100,000**	**100.0%**	**63,000**	**100.0%**	**19,200,000**	**100.0%**

NOTE: Percent of total columns may not add due to rounding; driver columns do not add because drivers under the age of 16 are not included.

SOURCE: Insurance Information Institute from the National Safety Council.

higher accident rates than male drivers. However, male drivers are involved in a higher proportion of accidents where someone is killed.[13]

Marital status is also important for some age groups, because young married male drivers tend to have relatively fewer accidents than unmarried male drivers in the same age category.

Certain credits and rate discounts may be allowed with respect to the rating factor of age. A premium credit may be given if a youthful driver of a family car is attending a school or college more than 100 miles away from home and does not have a car at school. Also, female drivers ages 30 through 64 may be eligible for a rate discount if they are the only drivers in their households. Older drivers are also eligible for rate discounts from many insurers.

When teenagers are added to the parent's policy, auto insurance premiums soar. Discounts are

EXHIBIT 23.5
Motor Vehicle Deaths per 100,000 Persons by Age, 2004

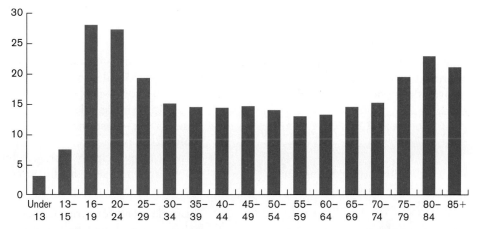

NOTE: Data are from U.S. Department of Transportation, National Highway Traffic Safety Administration.

SOURCE: *The I.I.I. Insurance Fact Book* (New York, NY: Insurance Information Institute, 2006), p. 117.

INSIGHT 23.2

Insuring Young Drivers

It's a Question that many parents dread hearing, "Mom, Dad, can I borrow the keys?"

If you're the parent of a new driver, be prepared. Your auto insurance bill will likely increase—and stay that way—until the young driver is out on his or her own. Male drivers under the age of 25 and unmarried female drivers under the age of 21 pay the highest rates for auto insurance coverage. But there are some things you can do to help control these costs.

One way to keep auto insurance costs in check is to ask your agent about available discounts. One of the most common is a discount for drivers' education. Most insurance companies offer a 10 percent driver training credit for teenagers who complete a driver education course. That discount is also available to parents—or any driver—who complete a state-approved drivers' safety course. An additional 5 percent discount is offered to drivers who complete an approved drug and alcohol awareness course.

While all regulated insurance companies are required to offer the driver education discount, there are other discounts that vary from company to company. Some insurance companies offer optional discounts based on the type of car insured and the kind of safety features it has. Ask your insurance agent whether the company offers a discount for students with good grades. And if your child is in college and does not have access to a car, be sure to tell the agent. You may be eligible for additional savings through a "student away at school discount."

Once your teenager begins driving, tell the insurance company as soon as possible. The parents' auto insurance

policy covers all drivers in the household, including children, even if they are not specifically named on the policy. If you don't notify the company, and it later finds out that you have a teenage driver, you will likely be billed for the additional premium you should have been paying. Your insurance company cannot refuse to renew your policy simply because a child in your house has reached driving age.

The rules regarding driver classification and assignment of vehicles are complex and address a variety of situations. Generally, if a teenager is the "principle driver" of an automobile, his or her rate will be determined on the basis of that vehicle. If not, the teenage driver is assigned to the vehicle that produces the highest rate, usually the most expensive. Be sure to discuss that issue with your agent.

You may also want to consider raising the amount of your deductible, or dropping physical damage coverage, if your son or daughter is driving an older car.

The auto insurance market is fairly competitive so one of the best ways to save money is to do some comparison shopping. Companies charge significantly different rates for the same coverage. Consumers should get quotes from several companies regarding their family's auto and driver situation.

SOURCE: Excerpted from "Insuring Young Drivers," *Saving Money on Your Insurance* by the Commissioner of Insurance. Texas Department of Insurance. http://www.tdi.state.tx.us/commish/columns/cc1003.html

especially important in such cases, especially discounts for an approved safe-driver course, and if available, an approved drug and alcohol awareness course (see Insight 23.2).

Use of the Auto

Use of the auto is another important rating factor. Insurers classify vehicles on the basis of how the car is driven, such as the following:

- Pleasure use—not used in business or customarily driven to work, unless the one-way mileage to work is under 3 miles

- Drive to work—not used in business, but is driven 3 to 15 miles to work each day
- Drive to work—not used in business, but is driven 15 or more miles each way
- Business use—customarily used in business or professional pursuits
- Farm use—principally garaged on a farm or ranch, and not used in any other business or driven to school or work

A car classified for farm use has the lowest rating factor, followed next by pleasure use of the car. Driving the car to work or using it for business purposes requires a higher rating factor.

Driver Education

If a youthful operator successfully completes an approved driver education course, he or she can receive a driver training credit, such as 10 or 15 percent. The rate credit is based on the premise that driver education courses for teenage drivers can reduce accidents.

Good Student Discount

A **good student discount** can also reduce premiums. The cost reduction is based on the premise that good students are better drivers; the psychological makeup and intellectual capacity of the superior student also contribute to the safer operation of an auto; and a superior student will probably spend more time studying and less time driving.

To qualify for the discount, the individual must be a full-time student in high school or college, be at least age 16, and meet one of the following:

- Rank in the upper 20 percent of the class
- Have a B average, or the equivalent
- Have at least a 3.0 average
- Be on the dean's list or honor roll

A school official must sign a form indicating that the student has met one of the scholastic requirements.

Number and Types of Cars

A **multicar discount** is available if the insured owns two or more cars. This discount is based on the assumption that two cars owned by the same person will not be driven as frequently as only one car owned by that person or family.

The year, make, and model also affect the cost of physical damage insurance on the car. As the car gets older, premiums for physical damage insurance decline.

Also, the cost of repairs is an important rating factor for physical damage insurance. New cars are rated based on susceptibility to damage and cost of repairs. Cars that are damage-resistant and relatively easy to repair generally have lower rates.

Individual Driving Record

Many insurers have **safe driver plans** where the premiums paid are based in large part on the individual driving records of the insured and vehicle operators who live with the insured. Drivers who have clean driving records qualify for lower rates than drivers who have poor records. A clean driving record means that the driver has not been involved in any accident where he or she is at fault and has not been convicted of a serious traffic violation in the last three years.

Points are assessed for accidents and traffic violations, and rate surcharges are applied accordingly. Points are charged for a conviction of drunk driving, failure to stop and report an accident, homicide or assault involving an auto, driving on a suspended or revoked driver's license, and other offenses. The actual premium paid is based on the total number of accumulated points.

Most insurers impose a surcharge for a chargeable accident that exceeds a given amount, such as $500. The surcharge generally lasts three years. For example, the base premium may be surcharged 10 percent for the first accident and 25 percent for the second.

Insurance Score

Another important rating factor is an insurance score based on the applicant's credit record. *An* **insurance score** *is a credit-based score that proponents claim is highly predictive of future claim costs.* An insurance score is a statistical analysis of an individual's credit record that indicates the likelihood of filing an insurance claim within a specified future time period. The insurance score is based on an individual's credit history and is then combined with other rating factors for purposes of underwriting and rating. Insurers claim there is a high correlation between insurance scores and the likelihood of an auto accident. As a group, drivers with poor credit tend to file relatively more claims than drivers with good credit; conversely, drivers with good credit tend to file relatively fewer claims. Actuarial studies generally support this conclusion. For example, a study by the Casualty Actuarial Society shows that drivers with the worst credit (category A) had the highest loss ratio (see Exhibit 23.6). Another study by the Texas Department of Insurance shows that drivers with good credit are involved in fewer accidents than drivers with poor credit (see Exhibit 23.7).

EXHIBIT 23.6
**Casualty Actuarial Society Credit Study,
Personal Automobile Loss Ratio by Category**

Category	Earned Premium	Incurred Loss	Loss Ratio
A	$74,279	$75,333	101.4%
B	158,922	124,723	78.5%
C	69,043	47,681	69.1%
D	91,746	52,688	57.4%
Total	**$393,990**	**$300,425**	**76.3%**

Category A – Unacceptable Credit Rating
Category B – No established credit history (or does not meet the definition of A, C or D)
Category C – Good Credit Rating
Category D – Excellent Credit Rating

NOTE: Data are from Casualty Actuarial Society.

SOURCE: Excerpted from Robert P. Hartwig and Claire Wilkinson, *The Use of Credit Information in Personal Lines Insurance Underwriting,* Insurance Issues Series (New York: Insurance Information Institute, June 2003), vol. 1, no. 2, exhibit 13.

Credit organizations, such as Fair Isaac and ChoicePoint, calculate insurance scores for auto insurers based on the applicant's credit history. A mathematical formula assigns weights to various credit factors and then summarizes the results in a three digit number. The formulas used to calculate insurance scores are proprietary, but typically include late payments, outstanding debt, past due amounts, public records, payment patterns, and similar credit factors.

SHOPPING FOR AUTO INSURANCE

As a careful insurance consumer, you should remember certain suggestions when you buy auto insurance (see Exhibit 23.8).

Carry Adequate Liability Insurance

The most important rule in purchasing auto insurance is to carry adequate liability insurance. If you carry minimum limits to satisfy the state's financial or compulsory insurance law, such as $25,000/$50,000/$25,000, you are seriously underinsured.

Even if you carry higher limits of $100,000/$300,000/$50,000, you are still underinsured in a bad accident where you are at fault. A negligent driver who is underinsured could have a deficiency judgment filed against him or her, under which both present and future income and assets could be attached to satisfy the judgment. You can avoid this problem by carrying adequate liability limits.

You should also consider purchasing a personal umbrella policy, which will provide another $1 million to $10 million of liability insurance on your car on an excess basis after the underlying insurance limit is exhausted. The personal umbrella policy is discussed in Chapter 24.

Carry Higher Deductibles

Another important suggestion is to carry higher deductibles for collision and other-than-collision losses (also called comprehensive). Many insureds have $250 deductibles. Increasing the deductible from $250 to $500, however, will reduce your collision and comprehensive cost by 15 to 30 percent. If you can afford an expensive car with a market value of $30,000 or more, you might even consider a $1000 collision deductible.

EXHIBIT **23.7**

New Texas Study Shows People with Good Credit Involved in Far Fewer Accidents; Personal Automobile Insurer Group B, Claim Frequency vs. Credit Score

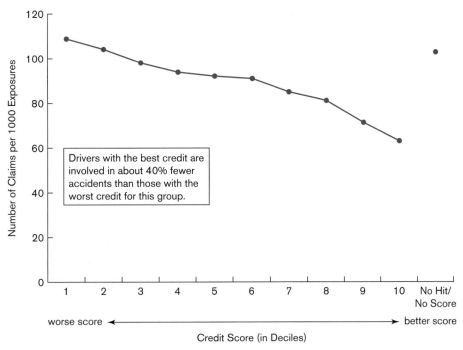

NOTES: 1. Includes BI (bodily injury) and PD (property damage).
2. Data are from *Use of Credit Information by Insurers in Texas,* Texas Department of Insurance, December 30, 2004.

SOURCE: Robert P. Hartwig, Insurance Information Institute, *No Evidence of Disparate Impact in Texas Due to Use of Credit Information by Personal Lines Insurers,* Insurance Information Institute, January 2005.

Drop Collision Insurance on Older Vehicles

You should consider dropping collision insurance on your car if it is an older model with a low market value. The cost of repairs after an accident will often exceed the value of an older car, but the insurer will pay no more than its current market value (less the deductible). One rough rule of thumb is that when a standard auto (such as a Chevrolet, Ford, or Dodge) is more than six years old, you should drop the physical damage insurance on the car.

Shop Around for Auto Insurance

Another important suggestion is to shop carefully for auto insurance. There is intense price competition among insurers. Contact several insurers and com-

pare premiums. Many state insurance departments publish shoppers' guides to help insurance consumers make better purchase decisions. State insurance departments also have Web sites that provide information on auto insurance rates in different cities within the state. For example, Exhibit 23.9 compares the rates of 15 insurers that write 76 percent of the coverage in Nebraska for six different classes of drivers in southeast and southwest Omaha. As you can see, rates among insurers vary widely for the same coverages. The savings by shopping around and comparing rates can be substantial.

Take Advantage of Discounts

When shopping for auto insurance, you should determine whether you are eligible for one or more discounts. All insurers do not offer the same discounts,

EXHIBIT 23.8
Tips for Buying Auto Insurance

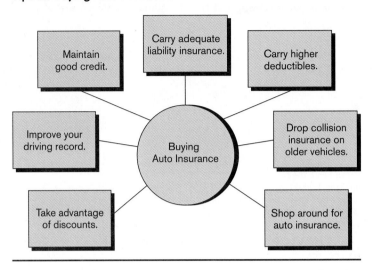

and certain discounts are not available in all states. Common discounts include the following:

- *Multicar discount*—10 to 15 percent
- *No accidents in three years*—5 to 10 percent
- *Drivers over age 50*—5 to 15 percent
- *Defensive driving course*—5 to 10 percent
- *Antitheft device*—5 to 50 percent discount for comprehensive (other-than-collision)
- *Antilock brakes*—5 to 10 percent
- *Good student discount*—5 to 25 percent
- *Auto and homeowners policy with same insurer*—5 to 15 percent
- *College student away from home without a car*—10 to 40 percent

Improve Your Driving Record

If you are a high-risk driver and are paying exorbitant premiums, improving your driving record will substantially reduce your premiums. In the meantime, you should consider other alternatives. Although physical damage insurance on a new or late-model car can easily double the premiums for a high-risk driver, an older car can be driven without collision insurance. You might also consider riding a motorcycle or bicycle or using mass transit. Nevertheless, there is no substitute for a good driving record.

To maintain a good driving record, you should not drive after you have been drinking alcohol. Impaired drivers account for a relatively high proportion of auto accidents in which someone is seriously injured or killed. A conviction for driving under the influence (DUI) can have a devastating effect on the premiums you are charged. Premiums can easily double or triple after a DUI conviction.

Maintain Good Credit

Another important suggestion is to maintain good credit. As noted earlier, many auto insurers use an applicant's credit record for purposes to underwriting or rating. Applicants with good or superior credit records may be able to purchase auto insurance at lower rates than applicants with poor credit records. A good credit record can also result in lower interest rates on credit cards and mortgage loans and higher credit limits. If your credit history is poor, clean it up if you wish to pay lower premiums.

EXHIBIT **23.9**
Auto Insurance Premiums for Omaha, Nebraska (Six-Month Premiums)

Type of Car and Coverage Limits		
	2005 Toyota Camry LE 4-Door	
Liability Limits of:	$100,000/$300,000	Bodily Injury
	$100,000	Property Damage
	$5,000	Medical Payments
	$100,000/$300,000	Underinsured Motorist
	$100,000/$300,000	Uninsured Motorist
	$250	Collision Deductible
	$100	Comprehensive Deductible

Hypothetical Drivers

Example 1: 17-year-old single male, principal driver, pleasure use, driving fewer than 12,000 miles annually, lives with parents. No violations or accidents in the last three years.

Example 2: 17-year-old single female, principal driver, pleasure use, driving fewer than 12,000 miles annually, lives with parents. No violations or accidents in the last three years.

Example 3: 21-year-old single male, principal driver, pleasure use, driving fewer than 12,000 miles annually, student, rents apartment. No violations or accidents in the last three years.

Example 4: 21-year-old single female, principal driver, pleasure use, driving fewer than 12,000 miles annually, student, rents apartment. No violations or accidents in the last three years.

Example 5: 44-year-old married female, principal driver, pleasure use, driving fewer than 12,000 miles annually, employed 10+ years, owns home 15+ years. No violations or accidents in the last three years.

Example 6: 65-year-old married male, principal driver, pleasure use, driving fewer than 12,000 miles annually, employed 10+ years, owns home 15+ years. No violations or accidents in the last three years.

	Premiums: Southeast Omaha					
	Example 1	Example 2	Example 3	Example 4	Example 5	Example 6
Company	17-yr-old Single Male	17-yr-old Single Female	21-yr-old Single Male	21-yr-old Single Female	44-yr-old Married Female	65-yr-old Married Male
Allstate Fire & Casualty Ins. Co.	$1,399	$1,088	$ 867	$ 726	$ 508	$ 484
American Family Mutual Ins. Co.	1,385	988	1,054	745	332	302
American Standard Ins. Co. of Wisconsin	2,139	1,651	1,864	1,269	604	551
Farm Bureau Mutual Ins. Co.[a]	1,758	1,338	907	817	584	528
Farmers Insurance Exchange[b]	4,889	3,415	3,274	2,426	1,630	1,419
Farmers Mutual Ins. Co. of Nebraska	1,612	1,139	859	714	461	414
Motor Club Ins. Association	2,417	1,732	1,732	1,258	665	601
Nationwide Affinity Ins. Co.	2,533	1,873	1,594	1,260	674	593
Nationwide Agribusiness Ins. Co.	2,652	1,961	1,669	1,319	705	621
Progressive Direct Ins. Co.	4,151	3,131	1,765	1,284	788	773
Progressive Northern Ins. Co.	3,814	3,112	853	626	811	769
Shelter Mutual Ins. Co.	2,487	1,646	1,507	1,128	665	523
State Farm Fire & Casualty Co.	2,013	1,482	1,148	918	516	450
State Farm Mutual Auto Ins. Co.	1,851	1,362	1,055	844	474	413
United Services Automobile Assn.	1,733	1,031	915	694	495	472

EXHIBIT **23.9** (continued)
Auto Insurance Premiums for Omaha, Nebraska (Six-Month Premiums)

	Premiums: Southwest Omaha					
	Example 1	Example 2	Example 3	Example 4	Example 5	Example 6
Company	17-yr-old Single Male	17-yr-old Single Female	21-yr-old Single Male	21-yr-old Single Female	44-yr-old Married Female	65-yr-old Married Male
Allied Fire & Casualty Ins. Co.	$1,154	$ 900	$ 714	$ 600	$ 422	$ 404
American Family Mutual Ins. Co.	1,385	988	1,054	745	332	302
American Standard Ins. Co. of Wisconsin	2,139	1,651	1,864	1,269	604	551
Farm Bureau Mutual Ins. Co.[a]	1,437	1,095	740	668	476	430
Farmers Insurance Exchange[b]	3,177	222	2,126	1,581	1,066	930
Farmers Mutual Ins. Co. of Nebraska	1,612	1,139	859	714	461	414
Motor Club Ins. Association	2,258	1,618	1,618	1,175	622	563
Nationwide Affinity Ins. Co.	2,362	1,756	1,474	1,172	620	548
Nationwide Agribusiness Ins. Co.	2,473	1,839	1,543	1,227	650	574
Progressive Direct Ins. Co.	3,681	2,783	1,557	1,138	701	687
Progressive Northern Ins. Co.	3,454	3,841	764	569	744	705
Shelter Mutual Ins. Co.	1,997	1,323	1,211	908	537	423
State Farm Fire & Cas. Co.	1,664	1,226	951	761	429	374
State Farm Mutual Auto Ins. Co.	1,528	1,125	873	699	394	343
United Services Automobile Assn.	1,628	965	861	654	467	446

[a] Rates quoted do not include a membership fee.
[b] The collision deductible was changed from $250 to $200 because the company does not offer a $250 deductible
 All quotes are based on a neutral ("no hit") credit score, if applicable. Rates are as of August 1, 2006.
SOURCE: *Nebraska Department of Insurance Auto Rate Guide* (2006).

SUMMARY

- Financial responsibility laws require motorists to show proof of financial responsibility after an accident involving bodily injury or property damage over a certain amount, for conviction of certain offenses, and for failure to pay a final judgment resulting from an auto accident. Most motorists meet the financial responsibility law requirements by carrying auto liability insurance limits of a certain amount.

- Compulsory insurance laws require motorists to carry auto liability insurance at least equal to a certain amount before the vehicle can be licensed or registered.

- Five states have unsatisfied judgment funds to compensate accident victims who have exhausted all other means of recovery. The accident victim must obtain a judgment against the negligent driver who caused the accident and show that the judgment cannot be collected.

- Uninsured motorists coverage is another approach for compensating auto accident victims. Uninsured motorists coverage compensates the accident victim who has a bodily injury caused by an uninsured motorist, by a hit-and-run driver, or by a negligent driver whose company is insolvent.

- No-fault auto insurance means that after an auto accident involving a bodily injury, each party collects from his or her own insurer, regardless of fault. There are several types of no-fault plans and no-fault proposals: pure no-fault plan; modified no-fault plan; add-on plan; and choice no-fault plan.

CASE APPLICATION

Paige, age 26, has purchased a new Ford sedan. She has a clean driving record. Collision coverage on the car in a small midwestern city where she lives would cost approximately $630 every six months with a $100 deductible, $566 with a $250 deductible, $492 with a $500 deductible, and $368 with a $1000 deductible. The state has a compulsory insurance law that requires minimum liability limits of $25,000/$50,000/$25,000. Paige would like to purchase collision insurance with a $100 deductible because the out-of-pocket cost to repair her car in an accident where she is at fault would be relatively small. She also would like to purchase only minimum liability limits, because she has few financial assets to protect. Paige is also concerned that she might be seriously injured by a driver who has no insurance.

Assume that Paige asks your advice concerning her auto insurance coverages. Based on the above facts, answer the following questions.

a. Paige wants to know why auto insurance costs so much. Explain to her the factors that determine auto insurance rates.
b. Do you recommend that Paige purchase collision insurance with a $100 deductible? Explain your answer.
c. Do you agree with Paige that only minimum liability limits should be purchased because she has few financial assets to protect? Explain your answer.
d. Assume that Paige adds the uninsured motorist coverage to her policy. Would she be completely protected against the financial consequences of a bodily injury caused by an uninsured driver? Explain your answer.
e. Paige would like to reduce her auto premiums because her monthly car payments are high. Explain to Paige the various methods for reducing or holding down auto insurance premiums.

- The arguments for no-fault auto insurance laws are summarized as follows:
    - Difficulty in determining fault
    - Inequity in claim payments
    - High transaction costs and attorney fees
    - Fraudulent and excessive claims
    - Delay in payments
- The arguments against no-fault auto insurance laws are summarized as follows:
    - Defects of the negligence system are exaggerated.
    - Claims of efficiency and premium savings are exaggerated.
    - Court delays are not universal.
    - Safe drivers may be penalized.
    - There is no payment for pain and suffering.
    - The tort liability system needs to be reformed instead.
- Several approaches are used to provide auto insurance to high-risk drivers:
    - Automobile insurance plan
    - Joint underwriting association (JUA)
    - Reinsurance facility

    - Maryland Automobile Insurance Fund
    - Specialty insurers
- The premium charged for auto insurance is a function of numerous variables, including:
    - Territory
    - Age, gender, and marital status
    - Use of the auto
    - Driver education
    - Good student discount
    - Number and types of cars
    - Individual driving record
    - Insurance score
- Consumer experts suggest several rules to follow when shopping for auto insurance:
    - Carry adequate liability insurance.
    - Carry higher deductibles.
    - Drop collision insurance on older vehicles.
    - Shop around for auto insurance.
    - Take advantage of discounts.
    - Improve your driving record.
    - Maintain good credit.

KEY CONCEPTS AND TERMS

Add-on plan
Assigned risk plan
Automobile insurance plan
Choice no-fault plan
Compulsory insurance law
Essential services expenses
Financial responsibility
 law
Good student discount
Insurance score
Joint underwriting
 association (JUA)
Low-cost auto insurance
Maryland Automobile
 Insurance Fund
Modified no-fault plan
Monetary threshold
Multicar discount
No-fault auto insurance

"No pay, no play" laws
Optional deductibles
Optional no-fault
 benefits
Pure no-fault plan
Reinsurance facility (or
 pool)
Safe driver plans
Shared market (residual
 market)
Specialty insurers
Survivors' loss benefits
Uninsured motorists
 coverage
Unsatisfied judgment
 fund
Verbal threshold

REVIEW QUESTIONS

1. a. What is a financial responsibility law?
   b. What is a compulsory insurance law?

2. a. Describe the characteristics of unsatisfied judgment funds.
   b. How are unsatisfied judgment funds financed?

3. a. Describe the characteristics of a low-cost auto insurance plan.
   b. What is a "no pay, no play" law?

4. a. Explain the meaning of no-fault auto insurance.
   b. What is the difference between a monetary threshold and a verbal threshold?
   c. Describe the major types of no-fault laws.
   d. List the arguments for and against no-fault auto insurance.

5. Describe the characteristics of automobile insurance plans.

6. What is a joint underwriting association (JUA)?

7. Describe the characteristics of a reinsurance facility.

8. Describe the characteristics of specialty insurers.

9. a. Identify the factors that determine the premiums charged for auto insurance.

   b. Explain the significance of an applicant's credit score in auto insurance underwriting and rating.

10. Explain the suggestions that consumers should follow when shopping for an auto insurance policy.

APPLICATION QUESTIONS

1. All states have financial responsibility or compulsory insurance laws that require motorists to carry at least minimum amounts of auto liability insurance.
   a. What are the various ways in which proof of financial responsibility can be satisfied in a state with a financial responsibility law?
   b. Does a financial responsibility law or compulsory insurance law guarantee that injured auto accident victims will be adequately compensated for their injuries? Explain your answer.
   c. How effective are compulsory insurance laws in reducing the problem of uninsured drivers?

2. Uninsured motorists coverage is another approach to the problem of uninsured drivers.
   a. Explain the advantages of the uninsured motorists coverage in meeting the problem of uninsured drivers.
   b. Explain the defects of the uninsured motorists coverage as a technique for compensating people who are injured by uninsured drivers.

3. Some states have passed some type of no-fault auto insurance laws to compensate injured auto accident victims.
   a. Describe the no-fault benefits that are typically paid in a state with a no-fault law.
   b. Why have no-fault auto insurance laws been enacted into law?
   c. Explain the arguments against no-fault auto insurance laws.
   d. How well have no-fault auto insurance laws worked? Explain your answer.

4. Society has the problem of providing auto insurance to high-risk drivers, including irresponsible drivers, drunk drivers, and drivers who habitually break traffic laws. An automobile insurance plan (assigned risk plan) is one approach to the problem of providing auto insurance to high-risk drivers.
   a. What is an automobile insurance plan?
   b. Describe the eligibility requirements for obtaining insurance from an automobile insurance plan.

c. Explain the process for assigning high-risk drivers to individual insurers.

d. Explain the disadvantages of automobile insurance plans.

INTERNET RESOURCES

■ **All Quotes Insurance.Com** uses the power of technology to find solutions to your insurance needs. The database contains hundreds of qualified insurance providers that provide competitive quotes. You can get quotes on auto, homeowners, life, health, disability income and other insurance products. Visit the site at

www.allquotesinsurance.com

■ **The Insurance Research Council (IRC),** a division of the American Institute for CPCU, provides the insurance industry and the public with timely research studies that are relevant to public policy issues dealing with risk and insurance. Visit the site at

http://www.ircweb.org

■ The **RAND Institute for Civil Justice** is an organization within the RAND Corporation that conducts independent, objective research and analysis concerning the civil justice system. Many research studies deal with auto insurance and the insurance industry. Visit the site at

http://www.rand.org/centers/icj/

■ **GEICO DIRECT** sells auto insurance directly over the phone (800-861-8380). The company claims that a 15-minute call can save you 15 percent or more on auto insurance rates. GEICO DIRECT's Web site provides similar premium quotes online. Visit the site at

http://www.geico.com

■ The **Insurance Information Institute** provides timely information on auto insurance and other personal property and liability insurance coverages. Numerous consumer brochures and articles on auto insurance and other property and liability coverages can be accessed directly online. Visit the site at

http://www.iii.org

■ **Insure.com** provides premium quotes for auto insurance, homeowners insurance, and other insurance products. The site also provides timely information and news releases about auto insurance and events that affect the insurance industry. Visit the site at

http://www.insure.com

■ **INSWEB** provides premium quotes for auto, homeowners, and other insurance products. In addition, the site has a learning center and provides information and articles from consumer, industry, and regulatory groups. Visit the site at

http://www.insweb.com

■ The **International Risk Management Institute (IRMI)** is an online source that provides valuable information about personal lines and commercial lines. The site provides timely articles on a wide range of risk management and insurance topics and offers a number of free e-mail newsletters. Visit the site at

http://www.irmi.com

■ The **Progressive Casualty Insurance Company** has a user-friendly site that provides auto insurance quotes. Progressive claims its rates are highly competitive. Progressive also provides comparison rates from other insurers. Visit the site at

http://www.progressive.com

SELECTED REFERENCES

Abrahamse, Allan, and Stephen Carrol. "The Effects of a Choice Auto Insurance Plan on Insurance Costs and Compensation." *CPCU Journal,* vol. 51, no. 1 (Spring 1998), pp. 19–39.

Carrol, Stephen J., and James S. Kakalik. "No-Fault Approaches to Compensating Auto Accident Victims." *The Journal of Risk and Insurance,* vol. 60, no. 2 (June 1993), pp. 265–287.

————. *No-Fault Automobile Insurance: A Policy Perspective.* Santa Monica, CA: RAND, Institute for Civil Justice, 1991.

Carrol, Stephen J., James S. Kakalik, Nicholas M. Pace, and John L. Adams. *No-Fault Approaches to Compensating People Injured in Automobile Accidents.* Santa Monica, CA: RAND, Institute for Civil Justice, 1991.

"Compulsory Auto Insurance," *Hot Topics & Issues Updates,* Insurance Information Institute, September 2006. This source is periodically updated.

Fire, Casualty & Surety Bulletins, Personal Lines volume, Personal Auto section. Erlanger, KY: National Underwriter Company. The bulletins are updated monthly.

Hartwig, Robert P. *New York PIP Insurance Update: Is New York's No-Fault Crisis Solved?* Insurance Information Institute, June 2, 2005.

Hartwig, Robert P. *No Evidence of Disparate Impact in Texas Due to Use of Credit Information by Personal Lines Insurers,* Insurance Information Institute, January 2005.

International Risk Management Institute (IRMI). IRMI .com is an online source that provides information on personal lines and commercial lines. The site provides timely articles on a wide range of risk management and insurance topics and offers a number of free e-mail newsletters.

Kinzler, Peter, *"Issue Analysis, Auto Insurance Reform Options: How to Change State Tort and No-Fault Laws to Reduce Premiums and Increase Consumer Choice,"* National Association of Mutual Insurance Companies, August 2006.

National Association of Insurance Commissioners. *Uninsured Motorists: A Growing Problem for Consumers, An NAIC White Paper,* Prepared by the NAIC Property and Casualty Insurance Committee, Draft Date, December 6, 2005.

"No-Fault Auto Insurance." *Hot Topics & Issues Updates.* New York: Insurance Information Institute, October 2006. This source is periodically updated.

Schmidt, Joan T., and Jia-Hsing Yeh. "An Economic Analysis of Auto Compensation Systems: Choice Experiences from New Jersey and Pennsylvania." *The Journal of Risk & Insurance,* vol. 70, no. 4 (December 2003), pp. 601–628.

Wiening, Eric A., and David D. Thamann. *Personal Auto, Personal Lines Coverage Guide,* 2nd ed. Erlanger, KY: The National Underwriter Company, 2005.

Wiening, Eric A., George E. Rejda, Constance M. Luthardt, and Cheryl L. Ferguson. *Personal Insurance,* 1st ed. Malvern, PA.: American Institute for Chartered Property Casualty Underwriters/Insurance Institute of America, 2002.

NOTES

1. A complete discussion of these laws can be found in *Fire, Casualty & Surety Bulletins,* Personal Lines volume, Personal Auto section (Erlanger, KY: National Underwriter Company). Discussion of financial responsibility laws is based on this source.

2. The first two figures refer to bodily injury liability limits, and the third figure refers to property damage liability. The liability limits apply to each accident.

3. American Association of Motor Vehicle Administrators (AAMVA), *The Financial Responsibility and Insurance Committee Resource Guide,* March 2005.

4. "Mandatory Auto Insurance Insurance Does Not Reduce Number of Uninsured Drivers, Says Insurer Trade Group," www.insurancejournal.com, national news, July 25, 2004.

5. Insurance Industry Committee on Motor Vehicle Identification, *Online Insurance Verification, Using Web Services to Verify Auto Insurance Coverage,* March 15, 2004.

6. Eric A. Wiening, et al., *Personal Insurance,* 1st ed. (Malvern, PA: American Institute for Chartered Property Casualty Underwriters/Insurance Institute of America, 2002), pp.2.8–2.10.

7. See "Compulsory Auto Insurance," *Hot Topics & Issues Updates,* Insurance Information Institute, September 2006. This source is periodically updated.

8. New Jersey Department of Banking and Insurance, *New Jersey Auto Insurance Buyer's Guide* (no date).

9. This section is based on "No-Fault Automobile Insurance," in *Fire, Casualty & Surety Bulletins,* Personal Lines volume, Personal Auto section (Erlanger, KY: National Underwriter Company). The bulletins are updated monthly.

10. Insurance Research Council, *Auto Injury Victims Who Hire an Attorney Are Less Likely to Be Satisfied with Their Total Payment: Findings from a New IRC Study,* news release, August 19, 2004.

11. Stephen J. Carrol, et al., *No-Fault Approaches to Compensating People Injured in Automobile Accidents* (Santa Monica, CA: RAND, Institute for Civil Justice, 1991), pp. xvi, 43.

12. "No-Fault Auto Insurance." *Hot Topics & Issues Updates.* New York: Insurance Information Institute, October 2006. This source is periodically updated.

13. *The I.I.I. Insurance Fact Book 2006* (New York: Insurance Information Institute, 2006), p. 117–118.

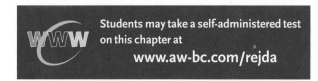

Students may take a self-administered test on this chapter at **www.aw-bc.com/rejda**

CHAPTER 24

OTHER PROPERTY AND LIABILITY INSURANCE COVERAGES

"Variety is the very spice of life."

William Cowper,
Olney Hymns (1779)

LEARNING OBJECTIVES

After studying this chapter, you should be able to

◆ Describe the following ISO dwelling forms:
   Dwelling Property 1 (basic form)
   Dwelling Property 2 (broad form)
   Dwelling Property 3 (special form)

◆ Explain how a mobilehome can be insured.

◆ Identify the types of property that can be insured under a personal articles floater.

◆ Explain how recreational boats can be insured.

◆ Explain the basic provisions of the national flood insurance program.

◆ Describe the basic characteristics of title insurance.

◆ Explain the major characteristics of a personal umbrella policy.

Josh, age 28, loves the outdoors and is an avid fisherman. He recently purchased a new boat with a 350-horsepower engine for $35,000. However, his insurance agent explained that Josh's homeowners policy would only pay a maximum of $1500 for a covered physical damage loss, and that personal liability coverage under the homeowners policy would not apply. The agent suggested that the boat should be insured under a separate policy. Josh wisely took his agent's advice and insured the boat under a separate boat owner's policy.

Josh had a specialized need for insurance that required a separate policy. Likewise, some property owners have special needs that require special insurance coverages. This chapter discusses several property and liability insurance coverages designed to meet specific needs. Topics discussed include the Insurance Services Office (ISO) dwelling program, mobilehome insurance, inland marine floaters, insurance on boats, title insurance, and national flood insurance. The chapter concludes with a discussion of the personal umbrella policy.

ISO DWELLING PROGRAM

Although the majority of homeowners are insured under a homeowners policy, certain dwellings are ineligible for coverage under a homeowners policy. For example, if the home is not occupied by the owner but is rented to a tenant, the property owner is ineligible for a homeowners policy. Also, some property owners do not need a homeowners policy, or they may want a less costly policy. Most of these homes can be insured under a dwelling policy drafted by the Insurance Services Office (ISO).

The ISO dwelling forms are narrower in coverage than the current homeowners forms. One major difference is that the dwelling forms do not include coverage for theft or for personal liability insurance without appropriate endorsements. In contrast, the homeowners forms automatically include theft coverage and personal liability insurance as part of a standard policy.

The current ISO dwelling program includes the following forms:[1]

- Dwelling Property 1—Basic Form
- Dwelling Property 2—Broad Form
- Dwelling Property 3—Special Form

Dwelling Property 1 (Basic Form)

The basic form provides coverages similar to the homeowners policies discussed in Chapter 20. Coverage A insures the dwelling shown in the declarations; materials and supplies located on or next to the described location used to construct or repair the dwelling; and if not otherwise covered in the policy, building equipment and outdoor equipment used to service the described location.

Coverage B covers other structures set apart from the dwelling by clear space, such as a detached garage or storage shed.

Coverage C covers the personal property of the named insured and resident family members while the property is on the described location. Up to 10 percent of the Coverage C limit can be applied to cover personal property anywhere else in the world.

Coverage D covers the fair rental value if a loss makes part of the dwelling rented to others unfit for normal use. A maximum of 20 percent of the insurance on the dwelling can be applied to cover the loss of rents, subject to a maximum monthly limit of one-twelfth of that amount.

Finally, Coverage E can be added as an endorsement to the basic form, which provides coverage for additional living expenses.

The basic form covers only a limited number of perils that apply to both the dwelling and personal property. Coverage for fire, lightning, and internal explosion can be purchased alone. For an additional premium, extended perils coverage and coverage for vandalism and malicious mischief can be added to the policy. Thus, the basic form can provide coverage for the following named perils:

- *Fire or lightning*
- *Internal explosion*
- *Windstorm or hail*
- *Explosion*
- *Riot or civil commotion*
- *Aircraft*
- *Vehicles*
- *Smoke*
- *Volcanic eruption*
- *Vandalism or malicious mischief*

All covered property losses are paid on an actual cash value basis. However, for losses to the dwelling and other structures, some states require that a modified loss settlement endorsement appear in the policy. Under this endorsement, if the building is repaired or replaced at the same site within 180 days of the loss, the insurer pays the lesser of (1) the limit of liability, or (2) the amount actually spent to repair or replace using common construction materials and methods. If the insured elects not to repair or replace the building, the insurer pays the lowest of the limit of liability, the market value, or the amount it would cost to repair or replace.

Dwelling Property 2 (Broad Form)

The broad form provides broader coverage than the basic form. Covered losses to the dwelling and other structures are indemnified on the basis of *replacement cost* rather than actual cash value. The replacement cost provisions are similar to those found in the homeowner contracts. The broad form also includes a new benefit for additional living expense (Coverage E). If a covered loss makes the property unfit for normal use, the additional increase in living expenses is paid.

The broad form includes all of the perils listed in the basic form plus the following additional perils:

- *Damage by burglars*
- *Falling objects*
- *Weight of ice, snow, or sleet*
- *Accidental discharge or overflow of water or steam*
- *Explosion of a steam or hot water heating system, an air conditioning or automatic fire protective sprinkler system, or an appliance for heating water*
- *Freezing of a plumbing, heating, air conditioning or automatic fire protective sprinkler system, or household appliance*
- *Sudden and accidental damage from an artificially generated electrical current*
- *Volcanic eruption*

Dwelling Property 3 (Special Form)

The special form provides the broadest coverage in the ISO dwelling program. The dwelling and other structures are insured against risk of direct loss to covered property. This means that coverage is provided on an "all risks" or "open perils" basis. *All direct physical losses to the dwelling and other structures are covered except those losses specifically excluded.* However, personal property is covered for the same named perils found in the broad form discussed earlier.

Endorsements to the Dwelling Program

Several endorsements can be added to a dwelling form, depending on the needs and desires of the property owner. They include *theft coverage*, which can be written on a limited or broad basis by an endorsement. Personal liability insurance is also available by adding a *personal liability supplement* to the policy, which provides personal liability insurance similar to the liability coverage found in the homeowners policy.

MOBILEHOME INSURANCE

Mobilehomes generally cost less than conventional housing. Because of cost, some families have purchased mobilehomes as an alternative to conventional housing. Mobilehomes are also purchased as a vacation home or second home.

Under the ISO program, **mobilehome insurance** is written by adding an endorsement to either a Homeowners 2 or Homeowners 3 policy, which tailors the homeowners policy to meet the special characteristics of mobilehomes. A number of specialty insurers also write a mobilehome insurance based on their own forms tailored to mobilehome exposures. The following discussion of mobilehome insurance is based on the ISO program.[2]

Eligibility

An eligible mobilehome typically must be at least 10 feet wide and 40 feet long, must be capable of being towed on its own chassis, and must be designed for year-round living. These requirements are imposed to eliminate coverage for camper trailers pulled by autos and insured under auto insurance policies.

Coverages

Coverages on a mobilehome are similar to those found in a homeowners policy. Coverage A insures mobilehomes on a *replacement cost basis*. Coverage A also insures floor coverings, household appliances, dressers, cabinets, and other built-in furniture when installed on a permanent basis.

Some mobilehomes have depreciated to the point where replacement cost coverage is inappropriate. In such cases, an optional actual cash value endorsement can be added.

Coverage B insures other structures and is 10 percent of Coverage A, with a minimum limit of $2000. Coverage C insures unscheduled personal property and is 40 percent of Coverage A. Finally, coverage D provides for loss-of-use coverage and is 30 percent of the Coverage A limit.

An additional coverage pays up to $500 for the cost incurred in transporting the mobile home to a safe place to avoid damage when it is endangered by a covered peril, such as a forest fire. No deductible applies to this coverage. The $500 limit can be increased to a higher limit by an endorsement.

Finally, Coverages E and F provide for comprehensive personal liability insurance and medical payments to others. This coverage is similar to the coverage provided in the homeowner contracts.

INLAND MARINE FLOATERS

Many people own certain types of valuable personal property—such as jewelry, furs, and cameras—that are frequently moved from one location to another. This property can be insured by an appropriate inland marine floater. An **inland marine floater** *is a policy that provides broad and comprehensive protection on property frequently moved from one location to another.*

Basic Characteristics of Inland Marine Floaters

Although inland marine floaters are not uniform, they have certain common characteristics:[3]

- *Coverage can be tailored to the specific type of personal property to be insured.* For example, under a personal articles floater, several types of property can be insured, such as jewelry, coins, or stamps. The insured can select the appropriate coverages needed.
- *Desired amounts of insurance can be selected.* The homeowners policy has several limits on personal property. For example, there is a $200 limit on money and coins, a $1500 limit on stamp collections, and a $2500 limit for the theft of silverware or goldware. Higher limits are available through a floater policy.
- *Broader and more comprehensive coverage can be obtained.* For example, a personal articles floater insures against risks of direct physical loss to covered property. Consequently, all direct physical losses are covered except those losses specifically excluded.
- *Most floaters cover insured property anywhere in the world.* This protection is especially valuable for global travelers.
- *Inland marine floaters are often written without a deductible.*

Personal Articles Floater

The **personal articles floater (PAF)** is an inland marine floater that provides comprehensive protection on valuable personal property.[4] The coverage can be added as an endorsement to a homeowners policy, or it can be written separately as a stand-alone contract. When written as a separate contract, the PAF insures certain optional classes of personal property on an "all-risks" or "open perils" basis. *All direct physical losses are covered except certain losses specifically excluded.*

The classes of personal property that can be covered include the following:

- *Jewelry.* Because of moral hazard, insurance on jewelry is underwritten carefully. Each item is described with a specific amount of insurance.
- *Furs.* Each item is listed separately with a specific amount of insurance.
- *Cameras.* Most photographic equipment can be covered under the PAF. Each item must be individually described and valued.
- *Musical instruments.* Musical instruments, cases, amplifying equipment, and similar articles can also be covered. Instruments played for pay are not covered unless a higher premium is paid.
- *Silverware.* The PAF can also be written to cover silverware and goldware.
- *Golfer's equipment.* Golf clubs and equipment are covered anywhere in the world. Golfer's clothes in a locker are also covered when the insured is playing golf.
- *Fine arts.* Fine arts include paintings, etchings, lithographs, antique furniture, rare books, rare glass, bric-a-brac, and manuscripts.
- *Stamp and coin collections.* Stamp and coin collections can be insured on a *blanket basis;* the stamps or coins are not described, and the insurance applies to the entire collection. The amount paid is the market value of the stamps and coins at the time of loss, with a $1000 maximum limit on any unscheduled coin collection and a $250 maximum limit on any single stamp or coin.

However, if the stamps or coins are valuable, they can be individually *scheduled.* The agreed value amount is then the amount paid if a loss occurs.

Scheduled Personal Property Endorsement

Coverage provided by a PAF can be added to a homeowners policy by use of a **scheduled personal property endorsement.** The endorsement provides essentially the same coverages provided by the free-standing personal articles floater.

WATERCRAFT INSURANCE

Millions of Americans own or operate boats for pleasure and recreation. The homeowners policy, however, provides only limited coverage of boats. Coverage on a boat, its equipment, and boat trailer is limited to $1500. Direct loss from windstorm or hail is covered only if the boat is inside a fully enclosed building. Theft of the boat or its equipment away from the premises is excluded. Also, boats are covered for only a limited number of named (broad form) perils, and more comprehensive protection may be desired. Finally, legal liability arising out of the operation or ownership of larger boats is not covered under the homeowners policy. For these reasons, boat owners often purchase separate insurance contracts that provide broader protection.[5]

Insurance on recreational boats generally can be classified into two categories:

- Boatowners package policy
- Yacht insurance

Boatowners Package Policy

Many insurers have designed a **boatowners package policy** that combines physical damage insurance on the boat, medical expense insurance, liability insurance, and other coverages into one policy. Although the package policies are not uniform, they have certain common characteristics.

Physical Damage Coverage A boatowners policy provides physical damage insurance on the boat on an "all-risks" or "open perils" basis. *All direct physical losses are covered except certain losses specifically excluded.* Thus, if the boat collides with another boat, is stranded on a reef, or is damaged by heavy winds, the loss is covered. Certain exclusions apply, including wear and tear, gradual deterioration, mechanical breakdown, use of the boat for commercial purposes, and use of the boat (except sailboats in some policies) in any race or speed contest.

Liability Coverage The insured is covered for property damage and bodily injury liability arising out of the negligent ownership or operation of the boat. For example, if an operator carelessly damages another boat, swamps another boat, or accidentally injures some swimmers, the loss is covered. Certain exclusions apply, including intentional injury, use of the boat for commercial purposes, and use of the boat (sailboats sometimes excepted) in any race or speed test.

Medical Expense Coverage   This coverage is similar to that found in auto insurance contracts. The coverage pays the reasonable and necessary medical expenses of a covered person who is injured while in the boat or while boarding or leaving the boat. Most policies impose a limit of one to three years during which time the medical expenses must be incurred. In addition, many policies cover the medical expenses of waterskiers who are injured while being towed. If not covered, coverage can be obtained by an endorsement to the policy.

Uninsured Boaters Coverage   Some boatowners policies have an optional uninsured boaters coverage for bodily injury caused by an uninsured boater, which is similar to the uninsured motorists coverage in auto insurance.

Yacht Insurance

Yacht insurance is designed for larger boats, such as cabin cruisers, inboard motorboats, and sailboats over 26 feet in length. Yacht policies are not standard, but certain coverages typically appear in all policies. The following section summarizes the major provisions of a yacht policy of one insurer.

Property Damage   This coverage insures the yacht and its equipment for property damage on an "all-risks" or "open perils" basis. The policy covers accidental direct physical loss or damage to the yacht except certain losses specifically excluded. Thus, if the yacht is damaged or sinks because of heavy seas, high winds, or collision with another vessel, the loss is covered. Exclusions include wear and tear; weathering; damage from insects, mold, animals, and marine life; marring, scratching, denting, and blistering; and freezing or extremes of temperature. A deductible applies to property damage losses.

Liability Coverage   Liability coverage insures the legal liability of an insured arising out of the owner-

ship, operation, or maintenance of the yacht. For example, collision with another boat or damage to a dock or marina would be covered. The coverage also includes the cost of raising, removing, or destroying a sunken or wrecked yacht.

Medical Payments Coverage   This coverage pays for necessary and reasonable medical expenses because of accidental bodily injury. Covered expenses include medical, hospital, ambulance, professional nursing, and funeral costs.

Uninsured Boaters Coverage   This coverage pays the bodily injury damages up to the policy limit that the insured is legally entitled to recover from an uninsured owner or operator of another yacht.

Other Coverages   The policy may also include additional coverages. These coverages include coverage for legal liability incurred by the insured to maritime workers who are injured in the course of employment and who are covered under the U.S. Longshoremen's and Harbor Workers' Compensation Act; physical damage insurance on a vessel trailer listed in the declarations; and coverage for personal property while aboard the yacht. Personal property includes clothing, personal effects, fishing gear, and sports equipment, but not money, jewelry, traveler's checks, or other valuables.

GOVERNMENT PROPERTY INSURANCE PROGRAMS

Government insurance programs are often necessary because certain perils are difficult to insure privately, and coverage may not be available at affordable premiums from private insurers. Two government insurance programs merit a brief discussion:

- National Flood Insurance Program
- FAIR plans

National Flood Insurance Program

Buildings in flood zones are difficult to insure privately because the ideal requirements of an insurable risk discussed in Chapter 2 are not easily met. The exposure units in flood zones are not independent of each other, and the potential for a catastrophic loss is present. Thus, premiums for private flood insurance in flood-prone areas would be too high for most insureds to pay. Also, adverse selection is a problem because only property owners in flood zones are likely to seek protection. For these reasons, financial assistance from the federal government is needed.

Because of increasing flood losses and the escalating costs of disaster relief to the taxpayers, Congress created the **National Flood Insurance Program** (**NFIP**) in 1968.[6] The purposes of the legislation are to reduce flood damage in communities by floodplain management ordinances and to provide flood insurance to property owners.

Flood insurance can be purchased from agents or brokers who represent private insurers. Agents or brokers who are not affiliated with private insurers can also write federal flood insurance directly with the NFIP.

Most flood insurance policies are written with private insurers. Under the *write-your-own program* enacted in 1983, private insurers sell federal flood insurance under their own names, collect the premiums, and receive an expense allowance for policies written and claims paid. The federal government is responsible for all underwriting losses. The NFIP is self-supporting for the average historical loss year, which means that unless a widespread disaster occurs, claims and operating expenses are paid by flood insurance premiums, not by the taxpayers. However, at the time of this writing, the federal flood insurance program is not financially self-supporting. Hurricane Katrina and other hurricanes in 2005 resulted in the payment of billions of dollars for flood damage losses that accompanied the hurricanes. At the time of this writing, legislation has been introduced that will substantially increase the borrowing authority of the National Flood Insurance Program to pay claims.

Federal law requires individuals to purchase flood insurance if they have federal guaranteed financing to build, buy, refinance, or repair structures located in special flood zones in the participating community. This financing requirement includes federal FHA and VA loans as well as most conventional mortgage loans.

Eligibility Requirements   Most buildings and their contents can be covered by flood insurance if the community agrees to adopt and enforce sound flood control and land use measures.

When a community joins the program, it is provided with a flood hazard boundary map that shows the general area of flood losses, and residents are allowed to purchase limited amounts of insurance at subsidized rates under the emergency portion of the program.

A flood insurance rate map is then prepared that divides the community into specific zones to determine the probability of flooding in each zone. When this map is prepared, and the community agrees to adopt more stringent flood control and land use measures, the community enters the regular phase of the program. Higher amounts of flood insurance can then be purchased.

Definition of Flood   In the Standard Flood Insurance Policy, flood is defined, in part, as:

> *A general and temporary condition of partial or complete inundation of two or more acres of normally dry land area or of two or more properties (at least one of which is your property) from overflow of inland or tidal waters, from unusual and rapid accumulation or runoff of surface waters from any source, or from mudflow.*

For example, flood damage caused by an overflow of rivers, streams, or other bodies of water, by abnormally high waves, or by severe storms is covered. Note that the accumulation or runoff of surface water can come from any source, such as melting snow, ice, or heavy rain. If the flooding causes damage from mudflow, the loss is also covered.

Amounts of Insurance   Under the *emergency program*, maximum coverage on single-family dwellings is limited to $35,000 on the building and $10,000 on the contents. For other residential and nonresidential buildings, maximum coverage is limited to $100,000 on the building and $100,000 on the contents (see Exhibit 24.1).

Under the *regular program*, maximum coverage on single-family dwellings is limited to $250,000 on the building and $100,000 on the contents. Commercial structures can be insured up to a limit of $500,000 on the building and $500,000 on the contents.

EXHIBIT 24.1
**Amount of Federal Flood Insurance under the Emergency
and Regular Programs**

Building Coverage	Emergency Program	Regular Program
Single-family dwelling*	$ 35,000*	$250,000
Other residential*	35,000*	250,000
Other residential	100,000*	250,000
Non-residential	100,000*	500,000
Contents Coverage		
Residential	$ 10,000	$100,000
Nonresidential including Small Business	100,000	500,000

*Under the Emergency Program, higher limits of building coverage are available in Alaska, Hawaii, the U.S. Virgin Islands, and Guam.
SOURCE: Federal Emergency Management Agency (FEMA).

Single family dwellings and residential condominium buildings can be indemnified on a *replacement cost* basis if certain conditions are met. The insured must carry insurance equal to 80 percent of the replacement cost of the dwelling at the time of loss, or the maximum amount of insurance available at the inception of the policy, whichever is less. If the amount of insurance carried is less than 80 percent of the full replacement cost at the time of loss, the amount paid is subject to a coinsurance penalty. Losses to contents are always adjusted on an actual cash value basis (replacement cost less depreciation).

Waiting Period   With certain exceptions, there is a 30-day waiting period for new applications and for endorsements to increase the amount of insurance on existing policies. Without a waiting period, property owners in flood zones could delay purchasing insurance until an imminent flood threatens their property.

Deductible   A $500 deductible applies separately to both the building and contents. Higher deductibles are available with a saving in premiums.

Premiums   The cost of the protection is relatively low. The preferred risk policy is available for slightly more than $100 annually. The average flood insurance policy costs about $400 annually and is less expensive than interest on federal disaster loans.

There are numerous misconceptions and myths about the federal flood insurance program. In-

sight 24.1 discusses some common misunderstandings about the program.

Critical Flood Insurance Problems   According to the U.S. Government Accountability Office (GAO), the federal flood insurance program faces several critical problems. Two important problems are summarized as follows:[7]

- *Reducing losses from policy subsidies and repetitive loss properties.* According to the GAO, the program is not actuarially sound because (1) a large number of policies are heavily subsidized, and (2) many buildings in flood zones incur repeated losses. About 29 percent of the NFIP policies are subsidized by the federal government. As a result of these subsidies, some policyholders pay premiums that are only 35–40 percent of the actuarially correct premium. In addition, properties that experience repeated flooding constitute a significant drain on NFIP resources. These properties generally pay subsidized rates and account for about 1 percent of the properties insured under the program, but account for 25 to 30 percent of all claim losses.[8]
- *Low level of participation.* Another current problem is the low level of participation by property owners who reside in flood zones. The GAO estimates that less than half of the eligible properties participate in the flood insurance program. Moreover, the extent of noncompliance with the

INSIGHT 24.1

Myths and Facts about the National Flood Insurance Program (NFIP)

To clear up misconceptions about National Flood Insurance, the NFIP has compiled the following list of common myths about the program:

1. **MYTH:** *You can't buy flood insurance if you are located in a high-flood-risk area.*
   FACT: You can buy National Flood Insurance no matter where you live if your community participates in the NFIP, except in Coastal Barrier Resources System (CBRS) areas. The program was created in 1968 to provide flood insurance to people who live in areas with the greatest risk of flooding, called Special Flood Hazard Areas (SFHAs). In fact, under the National Flood Insurance Act, lenders must require borrowers whose property is located within an SFHA to purchase flood insurance as a condition of receiving a federally regulated mortgage loan. There is an exemption for conventional loans on properties within CBRS areas.

2. **MYTH:** *You can't buy flood insurance immediately before or during a flood.*
   FACT: You can purchase flood coverage at any time. There is a 30-day waiting period after you've applied and paid the premium before the policy is effective, with the following exceptions: 1) If the initial purchase of flood insurance is in connection with the making, increasing, extending, or renewing of a loan, there is no waiting period. The coverage becomes effective at the time of the loan, provided application and payment of premium is made at or prior to loan closing. 2) If the initial purchase of flood insurance is made during the 13-month period following the effective date of a revised flood map for a community, there is a one-day waiting period. This only applies where the Flood Insurance Rate Map (FIRM) is revised to show the building to be in an SFHA when it had not been in an SFHA.
   The policy does not cover a "loss in progress," defined by the NFIP as a loss occurring as of 12:01 AM on the first day of the policy term. In addition, you cannot increase the amount of insurance coverage you have during a loss in progress.

3. **MYTH:** *Homeowners insurance policies cover flooding.*
   FACT: Unfortunately, many homeowners do not find out until it is too late that their homeowners policies do not cover flooding. National Flood Insurance protects your most valuable assets—your home and belongings.

4. **MYTH:** *Flood insurance is only available for homeowners.*
   FACT: Flood insurance is available to protect homes, condominiums, apartments, and nonresidential buildings, including commercial structures. A maximum of $250,000 of building coverage is available for single-family residential buildings; $250,000 per unit for residential condominiums. The limit for contents coverage on all residential buildings is $100,000, which is also available to renters.
   Commercial structures can be insured to a limit of $500,000 for the building and $500,000 for the contents.

5. **MYTH:** *You can't buy flood insurance if your property has been flooded.*
   FACT: You are still eligible to purchase flood insurance after your home, apartment, or business has been flooded, provided that your community is participating in the NFIP.

6. **MYTH:** *Only residents of high-flood-risk zones need to insure their property.*
   FACT: Even if you live in an area that is not flood prone, it's advisable to have flood insurance. Between 20 percent and 25 percent of the NFIP's claims come from outside high-flood-risk areas. The NFIP's Preferred Risk Policy, available for just over $100 per year, is designed for residential properties located in low- to moderate-flood-risk zones.

7. **MYTH:** *National Flood Insurance can only be purchased through the NFIP directly.*
   FACT: NFIP flood insurance is sold through private insurance companies and agents, and is backed by the federal government.

8. **MYTH:** *The NFIP does not offer any type of basement coverage.*
   FACT: Yes it does. The NFIP defines a basement as any area of a build with a floor that is below ground level on all sides. While flood insurance does not cover basement improvements, such as finished walls, floors or ceilings, or personal belongings that may be kept in a basement, such as furniture and other contents, it does cover structural elements, essential equipment, and other basic items normally located in a basement. Many of these items are covered under building coverage, and some are covered under contents coverage. The NFIP encourages

INSIGHT 24.1 (continued)

Myths and Facts about the National Flood Insurance Program (NFIP)

people to purchase both building and contents coverage for the broadest protection.

The following items are covered under building coverage, as long as they are connected to a power source and installed in their functioning location:

- Sump pumps
- Oil tanks and the oil in them, natural gas tanks and the gas in them.
- Well water tanks and pumps, cisterns, and the water in them
- Pumps and/or tanks used in conjunction with solar energy
- Furnaces, hot water heater, air conditioners, and heat pumps
- Electrical junction and circuit breaker boxes and required utility connections
- Foundation elements
- Stairways, staircases, elevators, and dumbwaiters
- Unpainted drywalls and ceilings, including fiberglass insulation
- Cleanup

The following items are covered under contents coverage:

- Clothes washers
- Clothes dryers
- Food freezers and the food in them

9. **MYTH**: *Federal disaster assistance will pay for flood damage.*
    FACT: Before a community is eligible for disaster assistance, it must be declared a federal disaster area. Federal disaster assistance declarations are issued in less than 50% of flooding incidents. The premium for an NFIP policy, averaging about $400 a year, is less expensive than interest on federal disaster loans.

    Furthermore, if you are uninsured and receive federal disaster assistance after a flood, you must purchase flood insurance to remain eligible for future disaster relief.

10. **MYTH**: *The NFIP encourages coastal development.*
    FACT: One of the NFIP's primary objectives is to guide development away from high-flood-risk areas. NFIP regulations minimize the impact of structures that are built in SFHAs by requiring them not to cause obstructions to the natural flow of floodwaters. Also, as a condition of community participation in the NFIP, those structures built within SFHAs must adhere to strict floodplain management regulations.

In addition, the Coastal Barrier Resources Act (CBRA) of 1982 relies on the NFIP to discourage building in fragile coastal areas by prohibiting the sale of flood insurance in designated CBRA areas. While the NFIP does not prohibit property owners from building along coastal areas, any federal financial assistance, including federally backed flood insurance, is prohibited. However, CBRA does not prohibit privately financed development or insurance.

11. **MYTH**: *The NFIP does not cover flooding resulting from hurricanes or the overflow of rivers or tidal waters.*
    FACT: The NFIP defines covered flooding as a general and temporary condition during which the surface of normally dry land is partially or completely inundated. Two properties in the area or two or more acres must be affected. Flooding can be caused by:

- The overflow of inland or tidal waters, or
- The unusual and rapid accumulation of runoff of surface waters from any source, such as heavy rainfall, or
- Mudslides, i.e., mudflows, caused by flooding, that could be described as a river of liquid and flowing mud, and
- The collapse or destabilization of land along the shore of a lake or other body of water, resulting from erosion or the effect of waves, or water currents exceeding normal, cyclical levels.

12. **MYTH**: *Wind-driven rain is considered flooding.*
    FACT: No, it isn't. Rain entering through wind-damaged windows, doors or a hole in a wall or the roof, resulting in standing water or puddles, is considered windstorm— rather than flood—damage. National Flood Insurance only covers damage caused by the general condition of flooding (defined above), typically caused by storm surge, wave wash, tidal waves, or the overflow of any body of water over normally dry land areas. Buildings that sustain this type of damage usually have a watermark, showing how high the water rose before it subsided. Although the Standard Flood Insurance Policy (SFIP) specifically excludes wind and hail damage, most homeowners policies provide such coverage.

SOURCE: Adapted from Federal Emergency Management Agency, "Myths and Facts about the NFIP," modified April 4, 2006

mandatory purchase requirement by property owners in flood zones is unknown.[9]

Some reasons given for the low participation rate include the following:[10]

— Homeowners fail to comprehend their vulnerability to flooding because of misperception concerning the probability of a flood occurring.
— Many property owners believe they live outside of floodplains.
— Low-income residents may not be able to afford flood insurance.
— Property owners believe federal assistance will be available if a flood occurs.

At the time of this writing, legislation has been introduced that would make the federal flood insurance program more attractive to property owners and increase participation rates. The proposed changes include the following:

— Reducing the waiting period from 30 to 15 days
— Higher maximum coverage limits
— Coverage for additional living expenses
— Optional replacement cost coverage for contents
— Optional finished basement coverage
— Optional business interruption coverage
— Increasing the amount the NFIP can borrow to pay claims
— Updating of flood maps and elevation standards

FAIR Plans

During the 1960s, major riots occurred in many cities in the United States, resulting in millions of dollars in property damage. Subsequently, many property owners in riot-prone areas were unable to obtain property insurance at affordable premiums. This problem resulted in the creation of **FAIR plans** (Fair Access to Insurance Requirements), which were enacted into law as a result of the Urban Property and Reinsurance Act of 1968. *The basic purpose of a FAIR plan is to make property insurance available to urban property owners who are unable to obtain coverage in the standard markets.* FAIR plans typically provide coverage for fire and extended-coverage perils, vandalism, and malicious mischief. FAIR

plans have been established in 32 states and the District of Columbia.

In addition, seven states have beach and windstorm plans that are in operation along the Atlantic and Gulf Coast seaboard, where property is highly vulnerable to damage from severe windstorms and hurricanes.[11]

Each state with a FAIR plan has a pool or syndicate that provides basic property insurance to persons who cannot obtain insurance in the standard markets. The pools or syndicates are operated by private insurers. Each insurer in the pool or syndicate is assessed its proportionate share of losses and expenses based on the proportion of property insurance premiums written in the state.

FAIR plan premiums are higher than premiums paid in the standard market. However, basic insurance is made available where coverage otherwise would not exist. All FAIR plans cover fire, vandalism, riot, and windstorm. About a dozen states provide some type of homeowners policy, which includes personal liability coverage. The FAIR plan in California covers brush fires.

Before a building is insured under a FAIR plan, it must meet certain underwriting standards. If these standards are met, a policy is issued. If the building is substandard, the property owner must make certain improvements that reduce the risk of fire, theft, or water damage, such as upgrading the electrical wiring, heating, or plumbing systems, repairing the roof, or improving security. If the property owner does not correct the conditions that make the home prone to losses, the FAIR plan administrator may deny coverage.

TITLE INSURANCE

Our discussion of property insurance coverages would not be complete without a brief description of title insurance. **Title insurance** *protects the owner of property or the lender of money for the purchase of property against any unknown defects in the title to the property under consideration.* Defects to a clear title can result from an invalid will, incorrect description of the property, defective probate of a will, undisclosed liens, easements, and numerous other legal defects that occurred sometime in the past. Without a clear title, the owner could lose the property to someone with a superior claim or incur other losses because of an unknown lien, unmarketability of the title, and attorney expenses. Title insurance is designed to provide protection against these losses.

Any liens, encumbrances, or easements against real estate are normally recorded in a courthouse in the area where the property is located. This information is recorded in a legal document known as an *abstract,* which is a history of ownership and title to the property. When real estate is purchased, the purchaser may hire an attorney to search the abstract to determine whether there are any defects to a clear title to the property. However, the purchaser is not fully protected by this method, because there may be an unknown lien, encumbrance, or other title defect not recorded in the abstract. The owner could still incur a loss despite a diligent and careful title search. Thus, the owner needs a stronger guarantee that he or she will be indemnified if a loss occurs. Title insurance can provide that guarantee.

Title insurance policies have certain characteristics that distinguish them from other contracts:

- *The policy provides protection against title defects that have occurred in the past, prior to the effective date of the policy.*
- *The policy is written by the insurer based on the assumption that no losses will occur.* Any known title defects or facts that have a bearing on the title are listed in the policy and excluded from coverage.
- *The premium is paid only once when the policy is issued.* No additional premiums are required.
- *The policy term runs indefinitely into the future.* As long as the title defect occurred before the issue date of the policy, any insured loss is covered, no matter when it is discovered in the future.
- *If a loss occurs, the insured is indemnified in dollar amounts up to the policy limits.* The policy does not guarantee possession by the owner, removal of any title defects, or a legal remedy against known defects.

The policy limit is usually the purchase price of the property. If the property appreciates in value over the years, the homeowner could be underinsured at the time of loss. This consideration is especially important in those areas where inflation in housing prices is occurring.

PERSONAL UMBRELLA POLICY

Personal liability claims occasionally reach catastrophic levels and can exceed the liability limits of a homeowners or auto insurance policy. For example, catastrophic losses can result from a chain-reaction accident on an icy highway where cars collide and several people are killed or injured; a boating accident in which a boat is swamped by another boat and several people are injured or drown; or a defamation-of-character lawsuit by someone who claims that his or her reputation is ruined.

The **personal umbrella policy** *provides protection against a catastrophic lawsuit or judgment.* Most insurers write this coverage in amounts ranging from $1 million to $10 million. Coverage is broad and covers catastrophic liability loss exposures arising out of the home, cars, boats, recreational vehicles, sports, and other personal activities.

Basic Characteristics

Although personal umbrella policies differ among insurers, they share several common characteristics, including the following:[12]

- Excess liability insurance
- Broad coverage
- Self-insured retention or deductible
- Reasonable cost

Excess Liability Insurance *The personal umbrella policy provides excess liability insurance over underlying insurance contracts that apply.* The umbrella policy pays only after the underlying insurance limits are exhausted. The insured is required to carry certain minimum amounts of liability insurance on the underlying contracts. Although the required amounts vary among insurers, the amounts shown in Exhibit 24.2 are typical.

If the required amounts of underlying insurance are not maintained, the umbrella insurer pays only the amount that it would have paid had the underlying insurance been kept in force.

Broad Coverage *The umbrella policy provides broad coverage of personal liability loss exposures.* The policy covers bodily injury and property damage liability, as well as personal injury. **Personal injury**

EXHIBIT **24.2**
**Typical Underlying Coverage Amounts Required
to Qualify for a Personal Umbrella Policy**

Auto liability insurance	$250,000 / $500,000 / $50,000 or $500,000 single limit
Personal liability insurance (separate contract or homeowners policy)	$100,000 or $300,000
Large watercraft	$500,000

typically includes false arrest, detention, or imprisonment; malicious prosecution; wrongful eviction or wrongful entry; libel, slander, and defamation of character; and oral or written publication of material that violates a person's right to privacy.

The umbrella policy also covers certain losses not covered by any underlying contract after a self-insured retention or deductible is met. In addition to the policy limits, most umbrella policies pay legal defense costs as well.

Self-Insured Retention   The umbrella policy typically contains a self-insured retention or deductible. The **self-insured retention,** *or deductible, applies only to losses covered by the umbrella policy but not by any underlying contract.* The self-insured retention is typically $250 but can be higher. Examples of claims not covered by the underlying contracts but insured under an umbrella policy include libel, slander, defamation of character, and a variety of additional claims (see Insight 24.2).

To illustrate, assume that Andrea has a $1 million personal umbrella policy and an auto insurance policy with limits of $250,000 per person and $500,000 per accident for bodily injury liability. If she negligently injures another motorist and must pay damages of $650,000, the auto policy pays the first $250,000. The umbrella policy pays the remaining $400,000, because the underlying limit of $250,000 per person under the auto policy has been exhausted. The self-insured retention does not apply here.

Now assume that Andrea is sued by her ex-husband for defamation of character and must pay damages of $50,000. If there is no underlying coverage and the self-insured retention is $250, her umbrella policy would pay $49,750. The self-insured retention must be paid by Andrea in this case.

Reasonable Cost   An umbrella policy is reasonable in cost. The actual cost depends on several variables, including the number of cars, boats, and motorcycles to be covered. For most families, the annual premium for a $1 million umbrella policy is less than $350.

ISO Personal Umbrella Policy

In 1998, the Insurance Services Office (ISO) introduced a standard personal umbrella policy. Member companies can use the ISO policy or develop their own umbrella policy. The following discussion summarizes the basic characteristics of the ISO policy.

Persons Insured   The ISO umbrella policy covers the following people:

- *Named insured and spouse if a resident of the same household*
- *Resident relatives, including a ward of the court or foster child*
- *Household residents younger than age 21 in the care of the named insured or an insured age 21 or older*
- *Any person using an auto, recreational motor vehicle, or watercraft that is owned by the named insured and covered under the umbrella policy*
- *Any other person or organization legally responsible for the named insured or family member while using an auto or recreational motor vehicle covered under the policy. For example, if James does volunteer work and negligently injures another motorist while delivering food baskets for a local church, the church is also covered.*

INSIGHT 24.2

Examples of Claims Covered by Personal Umbrella Policy

The following are examples of claims covered by personal umbrella insurance:

- The mast on a boat broke and seriously injured a guest on the boat. The amount of the judgment that exceeded the limit of the insured's watercraft policy was paid by the insured's personal umbrella insurer.

- The insured caused an accident involving a school bus and injured several children. The resulting judgments resulted in damages that far exceeded the insured's personal auto policy (PAP) liability limit. The insured's personal umbrella policy covered the amount in excess of the PAP limit up to the umbrella liability limit.

- The insured slandered two police officers. Although the insured's homeowners policy did not cover this loss, the insured's personal umbrella policy provided protection.

- The insured rented a car in France and was involved in a serious accident. Personal umbrella coverage responded

to the loss, although the PAP coverage did not apply because the accident occurred overseas.

- The insured's son rented a motorcycle and was involved in a serious accident. The underlying automobile and homeowners contracts did not cover the resulting third-party claim, but the personal umbrella policy covered the loss.

Although in the first two examples, the claims were covered under the boat and auto policies, the umbrella policy covered amounts over and above the limits on these policies (subject to its limit). In the last three examples, the personal umbrella policy provided broader coverage than that of the homeowners or auto policies and thus provided the only liability coverage available to the insured.

Source: Eric A. Weining, George E. Rejda, Constance M. Luthardt, and Cheryl L. Ferguson, *Personal Insurance*, 1st ed., (Malvern, PA.: American Institute for Chartered Property Casualty Underwriters/Insurance Institute of America, 2002), pp 9.14–9.15

Coverages The umbrella policy pays for damages in excess of the retained limit for bodily injury, property damage, or personal injury for which the insured is legally liable because of a covered loss. The **retained limit** is (1) the total limits of the underlying insurance or any other insurance available to an insured, or (2) the deductible stated in the declarations if the loss is covered by the umbrella policy but not by any underlying insurance or other insurance.

In addition to the liability limit, the policy pays legal defense costs; expenses incurred by the insurer while defending the suit; premiums on any required bonds; reasonable expenses incurred by an insured at the insurer's request, including the loss of earnings up to $250 daily; and interest on any unpaid judgment.

Exclusions The ISO policy contains numerous exclusions. Major exclusions include the following:

- *Expected or intentional injury.* Expected or intentional injury is excluded. However, the exclusion does not apply to intentional bodily injury resulting from reasonable force to protect people or property, such as acting in self defense against an intruder who is breaking into your home.

- *Certain personal injury losses.* The policy excludes coverage for certain personal injury losses, such as libel and slander that the insured knows to be false or which occurred prior to the policy's inception. It also excludes criminal acts and acts committed against an employee, such as discrimination in hiring, firing, or promotion.

- *Rental of the premises.* With certain exceptions, the ISO policy excludes liability arising out of rental of the residence premises to someone else. This exclusion does not apply to the occasional rental of the residence premises, such as a professor who goes on a sabbatical leave and rents out his or her home for six months. The exclusion also does not apply if part of the residence premises is rented as an office, school, studio, or private garage.

- *Business liability.* The policy excludes liability arising out of business activities by the insured. This exclusion does not apply to an insured who performs civic or public activities without compensation other than reimbursement for expenses, such as a Girl or Boy Scout leader. Likewise, it does not apply to minors younger than age 18 (21 if a full-time student) who are self-employed, such as delivering newspapers, mowing lawns, baby-sitting, or removing snow.

■ *Professional services.* The policy excludes liability arising out of the rendering of or failure to render professional services.

■ *Aircraft, watercraft, and recreational vehicles.* The policy excludes liability arising out of the ownership or use of aircraft, except model or hobby aircraft. Also excluded are activities involving watercraft or recreational motor vehicles unless coverage is provided by underlying insurance.

■ *No reasonable belief.* The ISO personal umbrella policy excludes coverage for a person using an auto, recreational motor vehicle, or watercraft without a reasonable belief that he or she is entitled to do so. This exclusion does not apply to a family member who uses a vehicle owned by the named insured, such as a teenager who drives a family car without first getting permission.

■ *Vehicles used in racing.* The policy excludes the use of autos, recreational motor vehicles, or watercraft in a prearranged race or speed contest. The exclusion does not apply to sailboats or to watercraft involved in predicted log cruises.

■ *Communicable disease, sexual molestation, or use of a controlled substance.* The policy excludes liability arising out of the transmission of a communicable disease; sexual molestation; corporal punishment; physical or mental abuse; or the use or sale of a controlled substance, such as methamphetamine, cocaine, marijuana, and narcotic drugs (except prescription drugs).

■ *Directors and officers.* The ISO policy excludes acts or omissions of an insured as an officer or member of a board of directors. This exclusion does not apply to nonprofit organizations in which the insured receives no compensation other than reimbursement for expenses.

■ *Care, custody, and control.* The policy excludes coverage for damage to property rented to, used by, or in the care, custody, and control of the insured to the extent that the insured is required by contract to provide insurance for such property. The exclusion does not apply to property damage caused by fire, smoke, or explosion.

In addition, the ISO personal umbrella policy excludes liability arising out of bodily injury to the named insured or any family member; damage to property owned by an insured; bodily injury to any person eligible to receive workers compensation benefits; and liability arising out of the escape of fuel from a fuel system, absorption or inhalation of lead, or lead contamination.

CASE APPLICATION

Fred purchased an older house near a river. Although the house needs major repairs, it will be his major residence. The river overflows periodically, which has caused substantial damage to several homes in the area. Fred lives alone, but he keeps two German shepherd dogs on the premises as watchdogs. He also has a small 15-horsepower boat, which is used for fishing.

An insurance agent has informed Fred that the house cannot be insured under a Homeowners 3 (HO-3) policy because the house did not meet the underwriting requirements. The agent stated he would try to get the underwriter to approve a Dwelling Property 3 policy (DP-3) or a Dwelling Property 1 policy (DP-1). As a last resort, the agent stated that coverage might be available through the state's FAIR plan.

a. Assume you are a risk management consultant. Identify the major loss exposures that Fred faces.

b. Explain the major differences among the HO-3, DP-3, and DP-1 policies discussed by the agent.

c. To what extent will each of the coverage alternatives discussed by the agent cover the loss exposures identified in (a)?

d. Assume that Fred obtains a DP-3 policy. Do you recommend that he also purchase the personal liability supplement? Explain.

e. Assume that Fred obtains a DP-1 policy. Do you recommend that he also purchase flood insurance through the National Flood Insurance Program? Explain.

SUMMARY

- The ISO dwelling program is designed for dwellings that are ineligible for coverage under a homeowners policy and for persons who do not want or need a homeowners policy.

- The *Dwelling Property 1 policy* is a basic form that provides coverage for a limited number of named perils. The *Dwelling Property 2 policy* is a broad form that includes all perils covered under the basic form and some additional perils. The *Dwelling Property 3 policy* is a special form that covers the dwelling and other structures against risks of direct loss to property. All direct physical losses are covered except for those losses specifically excluded; personal property is covered on a named-perils basis.

- A mobilehome can be insured by an endorsement to a Homeowners 2 or Homeowners 3 policy. Thus, the coverages on a mobilehome are similar to those found in homeowner contracts.

- An *inland marine floater* provides broad and comprehensive protection on personal property that is frequently moved from one location to another. Although inland marine floaters are not uniform, they share certain common characteristics. Insurance can be tailored to the specific types of personal property to be insured; desired amounts of insurance and type of coverage can be selected; broader and more comprehensive coverage can be obtained; most floaters cover insured property anywhere in the world; and floaters are often written without a deductible.

- A *personal articles floater (PAF)* insures certain optional classes of personal property on an "all-risks" or "open perils" basis. All direct physical losses are covered except certain losses specifically excluded. The classes are jewelry, furs, cameras, musical instruments, silverware, golfer's equipment, fine arts, postage stamps, and coin collections. Individual items are listed and insured for specific amounts.

- A *scheduled personal property endorsement* is an endorsement that can be added to the homeowners policy that provides essentially the same coverages provided by a personal articles floater.

- Insurance on recreational boats generally can be divided into two categories. A *boatowners package policy* combines physical damage insurance, medical expense insurance, liability insurance, and other coverages into one contract. *Yacht insurance* is designed for larger boats such as cabin cruisers and inboard motorboats. Yacht insurance provides physical damage insurance on the boat and equipment, liability insurance, medical payments insurance, and other coverages.

- The flood peril is difficult to insure privately because of the problems of a catastrophic loss, prohibitively high premiums, and adverse selection. Federal flood insurance is available to cover buildings and personal property in flood zones.

- Under the *write-your-own program,* private insurers write flood insurance, collect premiums, and pay claims. They are then reimbursed for any losses by the federal government.

- *FAIR plans* provide basic property insurance to individuals who are unable to obtain coverage in the normal markets. If the property meets certain underwriting standards, it can be insured at standard or surcharged rates. In some cases, the owner may be required to make certain improvements in the property before the policy is issued.

- *Title insurance* protects the owner of property or secured lender against any unknown defects in the title to the property.

- A *personal umbrella policy* is designed to provide protection against a catastrophic lawsuit or judgment. The major features of a personal umbrella policy are as follows:

   The policy provides excess liability insurance over basic underlying insurance contracts.

   Coverage is broad and includes protection against certain losses not covered by the underlying contracts.

   A self-insured retention must be met for certain losses covered by the umbrella policy but not by any underlying contract.

   The umbrella policy is reasonable in cost.

KEY CONCEPTS AND TERMS

Boatowners package policy
Dwelling Property 1 (basic form)
Dwelling Property 2 (broad form)
Dwelling Property 3 (special form)
FAIR plans
Flood
Inland marine floater
Mobilehome insurance
National Flood Insurance Program (NFIP)
Personal articles floater (PAF)

Personal injury

Personal umbrella policy

Retained limit

Self-insured retention

Title insurance

Yacht insurance

REVIEW QUESTIONS

1. The ISO dwelling program has several forms. Describe the characteristics of each of the following:
   a. Dwelling Property 1 (basic form)
   b. Dwelling Property 2 (broad form)
   c. Dwelling Property 3 (special form)

2. Explain how personal liability insurance can be added to a dwelling policy.

3. Describe the basic characteristics of inland marine floaters.

4. A personal articles floater (PAF) provides comprehensive protection for valuable personal property. Give three examples of property that might require coverage under a PAF instead of a standard homeowners policy.

5. Identify the coverages found in a typical boatowners package policy.

6. Why are buildings in flood zones difficult to insure by private insurers?

7. The National Flood Insurance Program (NFIP) has numerous provisions. Briefly explain each of the following:
   a. Write-your-own program
   b. Meaning of a flood
   c. Waiting period

8. What is the purpose of a FAIR plan?

9. Describe the basic characteristics of title insurance.

10. Briefly explain the basic characteristics of a personal umbrella policy.

APPLICATION QUESTIONS

1. Pedro owns a sixplex apartment building and lives in one unit. The building is insured under the Dwelling Property 1 (basic form) policy for $320,000. The replacement cost of the building is $400,000. Explain to what extent, if any, Pedro will recover for the following losses:
   a. A fire occurs in one of the apartments because of defective wiring. The actual cash value of the damage is $20,000, and the replacement cost is $24,000.
   b. The tenants move out because the apartment is unfit for normal living. It will take three months to restore the apartment to its former condition. The apartment is normally rented for $900 monthly.
   c. A tenant's personal property is damaged in the fire. The actual cash value of the damaged property is $5000, and its replacement cost is $7000.

2. Mathew owns a mobilehome that is insured by an endorsement to a Homeowners 3 policy. Explain to what extent, if at all, this policy would pay for each of the following losses:
   a. A severe windstorm damages the roof of the mobilehome.
   b. A built-in range and oven are also damaged in the storm.
   c. A window air conditioner is badly damaged in the storm.
   d. Mathew must move to a furnished apartment for three months while the mobilehome is being repaired.

3. Morgan has an outboard motorboat insured under a boatowners package policy. Indicate whether each of the following losses would be covered under Morgan's policy. If the loss is not covered, or not completely covered, explain why.
   a. Morgan's boat was badly damaged when it struck a log floating in the water.
   b. An occupant in Morgan's boat was injured and incurred medical expenses when the boat struck a concrete abutment.
   c. The motor was stolen when the boat was docked at a marina.
   d. A small child in Morgan's boat was not wearing a life jacket. The child fell overboard and drowned. The child's parents have sued Morgan.

4. Dan has a personal umbrella policy with a $1 million limit. The self-insured retention is $250. Dan has a homeowners policy with no special endorsement and an auto insurance policy. The policies have the following liability limits:

   Homeowners policy: $300,000
   Personal auto policy: $250,000/$500,000/$50,000

   The liability limits meet the umbrella insurer's requirements with respect to the minimum amounts of liability insurance on the underlying contracts. Indicate whether each of the following losses would be covered under Dan's personal umbrella policy. If the loss is not covered, or not covered fully, explain why.

a. Dan coaches a Little League baseball team. A team member sitting behind third base was struck in the face by a line drive and lost the sight in one eye. Dan is sued by the parents, who allege that his coaching and supervision are inadequate. The team member is awarded damages of $1 million.

b. Dan is a member of the board of directors for the local YMCA. Dan is sued by a YMCA member who was seriously injured when a trampoline collapsed. The injured member is awarded damages of $500,000.

c. Dan accuses a male teenager, age 14, of stealing his racing bike valued at $2000. The police arrest the youth and book him. The police later arrest the actual thief and recover the bicycle. Dan is sued by the youth's parents for false arrest. The teenager is awarded damages of $100,000.

d. Dan fails to stop at a red light, and his car strikes another motorist. The injured motorist is awarded damages of $200,000.

5. Lori has a personal umbrella policy with a $1 million limit. The self-insured retention is $250. Lori has a homeowners policy with no special endorsement and an auto insurance policy. The policies have the following liability limits:

Homeowners policy: $300,000
Personal auto policy: $250,000/$500,000/ $50,000

The liability limits meet the umbrella insurer's requirements with respect to the minimum amounts of liability insurance on the underlying contracts. Indicate the amount, if any, that would be paid by Lori's umbrella policy for each of the following losses.

a. Lori's dog bites a small child. The parents sue Lori and are awarded damages of $25,000.

b. Lori failed to stop at a red light, and her car hit a school bus. Two children are severely injured. A court awards each child damages in the amount of $350,000.

c. Lori is a volunteer for a local nonprofit charity. While being interviewed on television with other guests, Lori called one of the guests a "bag lady." The guest sues Lori for defamation of character and is awarded damages of $25,000.

d. Lori is a member of the board of directors for a local bank. She receives an annual fee of $50,000 for her service as a board member. She is also a

member of the board's audit committee. The shareholders sue Lori and other board members for not discovering several fraudulent accounting transactions that caused millions of dollars of losses to the shareholders. A court awards the shareholders damages of $5 million.

INTERNET RESOURCES

■ The **Federal Emergency Management Agency (FEMA)** provides valuable consumer information about the National Flood Insurance Program. Check out this site at

http://www.fema.gov/business/nfip

■ The **Insurance Information Institute (III)** provides valuable consumer information on a number of property and liability insurance contracts for individuals and families. A timely feature is "Hot Topics & Issues Updates." The III sponsors a site at

http://www.iii.org

■ Another site with useful information about home, auto, and other property and liability insurance coverages is sponsored by the **Independent Insurance Agents & Brokers of America.** You can find this site at

http://www.independentagent.com

■ **Insure.com** provides consumers with information on a variety of insurance products, including homeowners and auto insurance. Check out this interesting site at

http://www.insure.com

■ **INSWEB** provides premium quotes for auto, homeowners, and other insurance products. The site has a learning center and provides information and articles from consumer, industry, and regulatory groups. Visit the site at

http://www.insweb.com

■ The **National Association of Insurance Commissioners (NAIC)** has a link to all state insurance departments, which provide a considerable amount of consumer information for auto, homeowners, and other personal insurance coverages. Click on "State Insurance Web Sites." For starters, check out New York, Wisconsin, and California. Visit the site at

http://www.naic.org

SELECTED REFERENCES

Chesebrough, John R., and George E. Rejda. "Personal Umbrella Liability Insurance—A Critical Analysis." *CPCU Journal,* vol. 48, no. 2 (June 1995), pp. 98–104.

Fire, Casualty & Surety Bulletins. Fire and Marine volume and Casualty and Surety volume. Erlanger, KY: National Underwriter Company. See also the Personal Lines volume and Guide to Policies I volume. The bulletins are published monthly.

"Personal Umbrella Liability Policy." *The CPCU Handbook of Insurance Policies,* 6th ed. Malvern, PA: American Institute for CPCU, 2005, pp. 104–110.

Hamilton, Karen L., and Cheryl L. Ferguson. *Personal Risk Management and Property-Liability Insurance,* 1st ed. Malvern, PA.: American Institute for Chartered Property Casualty Underwriters/Insurance Institute of America, 2002.

Hartwig, Robert P., and Claire Wilkinson. *The National Flood Insurance Program,* Insurance Information Institute, October 2005.

Wiening, Eric A., George E. Rejda, Constance M. Luthardt, and Cheryl L. Ferguson. *Personal Insurance,* 1st ed. Malvern, PA.: American Institute for Chartered Property Casualty Underwriters/Insurance Institute of America, 2002.

NOTES

1. The ISO dwelling program is described in detail in *Fire, Casualty & Surety Bulletins,* Personal Lines volume, Dwelling section. The dwelling property forms by the Insurance Services Office were also used by the author in preparing this section.

2. For a detailed explanation of mobilehomes, see "Mobilehome Insurance," *Fire, Casualty & Surety Bulletins,* Personal Lines volume, Dwelling section.

3. Eric A. Wiening, George E. Rejda, Constance M. Luthardt, and Cheryl L. Ferguson, *Personal Insurance,* 1st ed. (Malvern, PA.: American Institute for Chartered Property Casualty Underwriters/Insurance Institute of America, 2002), p. 9.4.

4. Discussion of the personal articles floater is based on *Fire, Casualty & Surety Bulletins,* Personal Lines volume, Misc. Personal section.

5. Insurance on recreational boats is based on *Fire, Casualty & Surety Bulletins,* Companies and Coverages volume, Aircraft-Marine section; and the yacht policy discussed in the *CPCU Handbook of Insurance Policies,* 6th ed. (Malvern, PA: American Institute for Chartered Property Casualty Underwriters/Insurance Institute of America, 2005), pp. 78–84.

6. Current details of the federal flood insurance program can be found in the *Fire, Casualty & Surety Bulletins,* Fire and Marine volume, Catastrophe section. See also, Federal Emergency Management Agency, *Flood Insurance* at http://www.fema.gov/business/nfip/

7. GAO, *Federal Emergency Management Agency: Challenges Facing the National Flood Insurance Program,* Statement of William O. Jenkins Jr., Director, Homeland Security and Justice Issues, GAO-06-174T (Washington, DC: October 18, 2005).

8. Ibid.

9. Ibid.

10. United States Senate, Republican Policy Committee, *National Flood Insurance: Crisis and Renewal,* March 14, 2006.

11. FAIR plans exist in Arkansas (rural), California, Connecticut, Delaware, District of Columbia, Florida (Citizens Property Insurance Corporation), Georgia, Hawaii, Illinois, Indiana, Iowa, Kansas, Kentucky, Louisiana (Citizens), Maryland, Massachusetts, Michigan, Minnesota, Mississippi (rural), Missouri, New Jersey, New Mexico, New York, North Carolina, Ohio, Oregon, Pennsylvania, Rhode Island, Virginia, Washington, West Virginia, and Wisconsin. Beach and windstorm plans exist in Alabama, Florida, Louisiana, Mississippi, North Carolina, South Carolina, and Texas.

12. Discussion of the personal umbrella policy is based on John R. Chesebrough and George E. Rejda, "Personal Umbrella Liability Insurance—A Critical Analysis," *CPCU Journal,* vol. 48, no. 2 (June 1995), pp. 98–104; "Personal Umbrella Liability Insurance," in *Fire, Casualty & Surety Bulletins,* Companies and Coverage volume, Personal Packages section (Erlanger, KY: National Underwriter Company); and "Personal Umbrella Liability Policy," *The CPCU Handbook of Insurance Policies,* 6th ed. (Malvern, PA: American Institute for Chartered Property Casualty Underwriters/Insurance Institute of America, 2005), pp. 104–110.

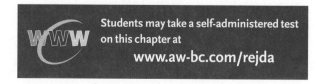

Students may take a self-administered test on this chapter at
www.aw-bc.com/rejda

PART SIX
COMMERCIAL PROPERTY AND LIABILITY RISKS

Chapter 25
Commercial Property Insurance

Chapter 26
Commercial Liability Insurance

Chapter 27
Crime Insurance and Surety Bonds

CHAPTER 25

COMMERCIAL PROPERTY INSURANCE

"Protecting the company assets in the event of a loss is a key function of the risk manager's job. Commercial property insurance is the primary technique for financing the risks associated with damage or destruction of these assets."

Rebecca A. McQuade
Director of Risk Management, PACCAR Inc

After studying this chapter, you should be able to

◆ Explain the basic provisions in the building and personal property coverage form, including

Covered property	Optional coverages
Additional coverages	Extensions of coverage

◆ Identify the causes of loss that are covered under the following forms:

Causes-of-loss basic form	Causes-of-loss special form
Causes-of-loss broad form	

◆ Explain how a business income loss is determined under the business income (and extra expense) coverage form.

◆ Explain what is covered by each of the following ocean marine policies, including

Hull insurance	Protection and indemnity (P&I) insurance
Cargo insurance	Freight insurance

◆ Identify the types of property that can be covered by an inland marine insurance policy.

◆ Describe the major provisions in a businessowners policy (BOP), including

Coverages provided	Optional coverages
Additional coverages	

S al is the owner and general manager of Sal's Pizza, which owns five retail pizza restaurants in three Midwestern cities. The business is highly profitable because of the high-quality pizza that the restaurants serve. Recently, an oven in one restaurant overheated, which caused a severe fire and extensive property damage. When Sal called his insurance agent to report the fire, the agent stated that the property damage to the restaurant was fully covered except for a small deductible. Sal was also relieved to hear that the insurance on the business would cover a large part of the business income lost during the restoration period.

Like Sal's Pizza, other business firms own valuable commercial real estate; business personal property, such as office furniture, computers, machinery, and supplies; and inventories of finished products. This property can be damaged or destroyed if a loss occurs. In addition, firms may experience a substantial loss of business income and incur sizable extra expenses in the event of a loss.

This chapter discusses commercial property insurance, with emphasis on the commercial property insurance program developed by the Insurance Services Office (ISO). More specifically, the chapter discusses the commercial package policy, the building and personal property coverage form, business income insurance, and other property coverages. The chapter also discusses ocean marine insurance and inland marine insurance, which cover transportation and other commercial risks. The chapter concludes with an analysis of the ISO businessowners policy, which is designed for small- to medium-sized business firms.

ISO COMMERCIAL PROPERTY PROGRAM

The Insurance Services Office (ISO) has designed a commercial property program that makes available package policies tailored to meet the specific needs of business firms, such as a **commercial package policy (CPP)**. *A package policy is one that combines two or more coverages into a single policy.* If both property and liability insurance coverages are combined into a single policy, it is also known as a *multiple-line policy*. In contrast, a policy that provides only one type of coverage is known as a *monoline policy*.

When compared with individual policies, a package policy has several advantages. There are fewer gaps in coverage; insureds pay relatively lower premiums because individual policies are not purchased; savings in insurer expenses can be passed on to the policyowner; and the insured has the convenience of a single policy.

This section discusses the format of the commercial package policy, which is widely used by business firms. The CPP can be used to insure motels, hotels, apartment houses, office buildings, retail stores, churches and schools, processing firms such as dry cleaners, manufacturing firms, and a wide variety of other commercial firms. The CPP can be specifically tailored to cover most property and liability loss exposures in a single policy, with the major exceptions of professional liability, workers compensation, and surety bonds.

Under the ISO program, each commercial package policy contains (1) a common policy declarations page, (2) a common policy conditions page, and (3) two or more coverage parts.[1] Exhibit 25.1 shows in greater detail the various parts of a commercial package policy.

EXHIBIT 25.1
Components of the ISO Commercial Package Policy (CPP)

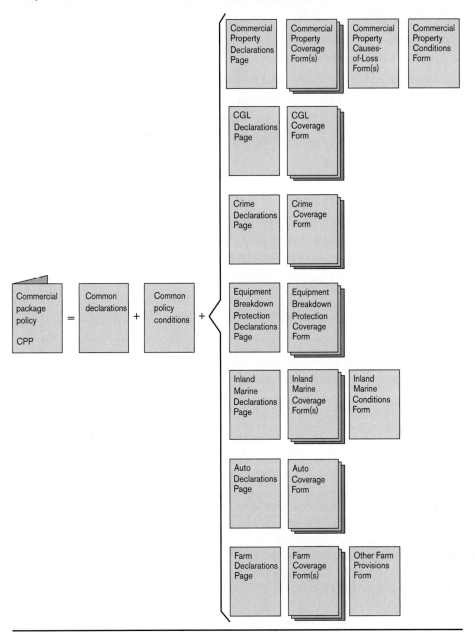

SOURCE: Arthur L. Flitner and Jerome Trupin, *Commercial Insurance,* 1st ed. (Malvern, PA: American Institute for CPCU/Insurance Institute of America, 2002), p. 1.11.

Common Policy Declarations

Each commercial package policy contains a *common policy declarations page* that shows the name and address of the insured, policy period, description of the insured property, a list of coverage parts that apply, and the premium amount.

Common Policy Conditions

Each commercial package policy also contains a *common policy conditions page* that applies to all commercial lines of insurance. The common conditions are summarized as follows:

- *Cancellation.* Either party can cancel by giving the other party advance notice. The insurer can cancel by giving notice of cancellation for non-payment of premiums at least 10 days in advance and 30 days in advance for any other reason. If the insurer cancels, a pro rata refund of the premium is made. If the insured cancels, the refund may be less than pro rata.
- *Changes.* Any changes in the policy can be made only by an endorsement issued by the insurer.
- *Examination of books and records.* The insurer has the right to audit the insured's books and records any time during the policy period and up to three years after the policy period ends.
- *Inspections and surveys.* The insurer has the right to make inspections and surveys that relate to insurability of the property and premiums to be charged.
- *Premiums.* More than one party may be named as an insured in the declarations page. The *first named insured* in the declarations is the party responsible for the payment of premiums.
- *Transfer of rights and duties.* The insured's rights and duties under the policy cannot be transferred without the insurer's written consent. One exception is that the rights and duties can be transferred to a legal representative if an individual named insured should die.

Coverage Parts

Each commercial package policy contains two or more of the following *coverage parts:*

- Commercial property
- Commercial general liability

- Commercial crime
- Equipment breakdown
- Inland marine coverage form(s)
- Auto
- Farm

Each coverage part, in turn, contains (1) its own declarations page that applies to that coverage, (2) the specific conditions that apply to that coverage part, (3) coverage forms that describe the various coverages provided, and (4) where applicable, a causes-of-loss form that describes the various perils that are covered.

BUILDING AND PERSONAL PROPERTY COVERAGE FORM

The **building and personal property coverage form** is a commercial property coverage part that is widely used to cover a direct physical damage loss to commercial buildings and business personal property.

Covered Property

The insured selects the property to be covered. Covered property can include the following:

- Building
- Named insured's business personal property
- Personal property of others in the care, custody, or control of the named insured

For coverage to apply, the declarations page must show a limit of insurance for that category. Depending on its needs, a business firm can elect one or all three coverages (see Insight 25.1).

Building   The form covers the building described in the declarations and includes any completed additions and fixtures and permanently installed machinery and equipment. Certain outdoor fixtures are also covered, such as light poles, flagpoles, and mailboxes. Finally, equipment used to maintain or service the building (such as fire-extinguishing equipment, appliances for cooking and dishwashing, floor buffers, and vacuum cleaners) is also covered.

Business Personal Property   Business personal property of the named insured inside or on the building or

INSIGHT 25.1

Examples of Coverage Under the Building and Personal Property Coverage Form

The building and personal property coverage form can be used to cover a building, business personal property, and personal property of others. Most business firms do not require coverage in all three categories. Depending on its needs, a firm can elect only those coverages desired.

Examples

1. Worldwide Realty, Inc., is the owner of a building rented to others. It has purchased coverage for the building only.
2. Sue Brown, doing business as Sue's Leather Restoring, operates in Worldwide Realty's building. Sue has no need for building insurance because she is a tenant. She has purchased coverage for her own business personal property and for the personal property of others in her care, custody, or control.

3. Smith and Jones, LLP, a law firm operating in Worldwide Realty's building, has purchased coverage only for its own business personal property because it does not have an insurable interest in the building and does not have any personal property of others in its possession.
4. City Laundry, Inc., a commercial laundry, owns and occupies the building adjacent to Worldwide Realty's building. City Laundry has purchased coverage for the building, its business personal property, and the personal property of others in its care, custody, or control.

SOURCE: Adapted from Jerome Trupin and Arthur L. Flitner, *Commercial Property Risk Management and Insurance*, 6th ed., vol. 1 (Malvern, PA: American Institute for CPCU, 2001), pp. 3.6–3.7.

within 100 feet of the premises is also covered. It includes furniture and fixtures; computer systems, machinery and equipment; stock or inventory; and all other personal property owned by the insured and used in the insured's business.

In addition, the insured's interest in the personal property of others is covered to the extent of labor, materials, and other charges. For example, a machine shop may repair a piece of machinery owned by a customer. If parts and labor are $1000 and the machinery is damaged from an insured peril before it is delivered to the customer, the insured's interest of $1000 is covered.

The insured's use interest in improvements and betterments as a tenant is also covered as business personal property. Improvements and betterments include fixtures, alterations, installations, or additions that are made part of the building at the insured's expense and cannot be removed legally. An example of an improvement is the installation of a new air conditioning unit by an insured who leases a building to open a new bar and restaurant.

Finally, business personal property includes leased personal property that the insured has a contractual obligation to insure. An example would be leased computer equipment for which the insured is required to provide insurance.

Personal Property of Others Personal property of others in the care, custody, or control of the named insured is also covered. For example, if a tornado destroys a machine shop and equipment belonging to customers is damaged, the loss would be covered.

Additional Coverages Several additional coverages are provided, summarized as follows:

- *Debris removal.* The cost of debris removal is paid up to certain limits specified in the policy. Debris removal coverage does not apply to the cost of extracting pollutants from land or water.
- *Preservation of property.* If property is moved to another location for safekeeping because of a covered loss, any direct physical loss or damage to the property while being moved or while stored at the other location is covered. Coverage applies only if the loss or damage occurs within 30 days after the property is first moved.
- *Fire department service charge.* A maximum of $1000 can be paid for a fire department service charge. No deductible applies to this coverage.
- *Pollutant cleanup and removal.* The insurer also pays the cost to clean up and remove pollutants from land or water at the described premises if the release or discharge of the pollutants results

from a covered cause of loss. The maximum paid is limited to $10,000 during each separate 12-month policy period.

- *Increased cost of construction.* Another additional coverage is the increased cost of construction because of an ordinance or law. The additional coverage applies only to buildings insured on a replacement cost basis. The maximum amount of additional insurance that applies to each described building insured under this form is $10,000, or 5 percent of the limit of insurance that applies to that building, whichever is less.
- *Electronic data.* The policy pays the cost to replace or restore electronic data destroyed or corrupted by a covered cause of loss, including CDs, floppy disks, hard drives, and similar equipment. Covered causes of loss include damage caused by a computer virus except if caused by an employee or leased employee. The maximum paid is $2500 during any policy year.

Extensions of Coverage   If a coinsurance requirement of 80 percent or higher is shown in the declarations, or a value-reporting period symbol is shown on the declarations page, the insurance can be extended to cover other property. The extensions of coverage are summarized as follows:

- *Newly acquired or constructed property.* Insurance on the building is extended to cover new buildings while being built on the described premises and to newly acquired buildings at other locations. The insurance applies for a maximum period of 30 days and is limited to a maximum of $250,000 for each building. In addition, the insurance on business personal property ($100,000 maximum) can be applied to business personal property at newly acquired locations. This insurance also applies for a maximum period of 30 days.
- *Personal effects and property of others.* Insurance on business personal property can be extended to cover the personal effects of the named insured, officers, partners, or employees. However, the extension does not apply to theft. The extension also applies to personal property of others in the named insured's care, custody, or control. The maximum paid is limited to $2500.

- *Valuable papers and records (other than electronic data).* Insurance on business personal property can also be extended to cover the costs of researching, replacing, or restoring lost information on lost or damaged valuable papers and records. The maximum paid is limited to $2500 at each described premises.
- *Property off the premises.* Covered property that is temporarily at a location not owned, leased, or operated by the insured is covered up to $10,000. The extension of coverage does not apply to property in or on a vehicle or to property in the care, custody, or control of salespersons. However, if the property is in the care, custody, or control of salespersons at a trade show, fair, or exhibition, the extension of coverage will apply.
- *Outdoor property.* Outdoor fences, radio and television antennas, detached signs, and trees, plants, and shrubs are covered up to a maximum of $1000, but not more than $250 for any single tree, shrub, or plant. The insurance applies only to losses caused by fire, lightning, explosion, riot or civil commotion, or aircraft.
- *Nonowned detached trailers.* Coverage can also be extended to nonowned detached trailers under certain circumstances. The trailer must be used in the business and in the insured's care, custody, and control; the insured must also have a contractual obligation to pay for any loss or damage to the trailer. However, coverage ceases if the trailer is attached to any motor vehicle whether in motion or not. For example, a construction company may rent a trailer that is used as a temporary office while at a worksite; coverage applies as long as the trailer is not attached to any motorized vehicle. The maximum paid under this extension is $5000.

Other Provisions

Numerous additional provisions are included in the building and personal property coverage form, but it is beyond the scope of this text to discuss each of them. Several important provisions, however, are summarized here.

Deductible   A standard deductible of $250 applies to each occurrence. Higher deductible amounts are available. Only one deductible must be satisfied if several buildings or different types of business personal property are damaged in the same occurrence.

Coinsurance   If a coinsurance percentage is stated in the declarations, the coinsurance requirement must be met to avoid a coinsurance penalty. To reduce misunderstanding and confusion, the form contains several excellent examples of how coinsurance works.

Optional Coverages   Three optional coverages are preprinted in the form, which eliminates the need for separate endorsements.

- *Agreed value.* If the coinsurance requirement is not met, the insured incurs a coinsurance penalty. To avoid a coinsurance penalty, the agreed value option can be used. This option suspends the coinsurance clause while the agreed value option is in force. For losses to be paid in full, the amount of insurance carried must equal the agreed value. For example, if the agreed value is $100,000, and the limit of insurance is $100,000, all covered losses will be paid in full (minus the deductible) up to the limit of insurance. However, if the amount of insurance carried is $75,000, only three-fourths of a covered loss will be paid.
- *Inflation guard.* This option automatically increases the amount of insurance by an annual percentage shown in the declarations.
- *Replacement cost.* Under the replacement cost option, there is no deduction for depreciation if a loss occurs. However, this option does not apply to the property of others; contents of a residence; manuscripts; works of art, antiques, and similar property; and stock (unless designated in the declarations). Replacement cost insurance generally is recommended when buildings and their contents are insured. Otherwise, the loss is paid on an actual cash-value basis.
- *Extension of replacement cost.* Another optional coverage is the extension of replacement cost to personal property of others in the named insured's care, custody, or control.

CAUSES-OF-LOSS FORMS

A *causes-of-loss form* must be added to the policy to have a complete contract. Insureds can select one of the following forms:

- Causes-of-loss basic form
- Causes-of-loss broad form
- Causes-of-loss special form

Causes-of-Loss Basic Form

The **causes-of-loss basic form** provides coverage for 11 basic causes of loss to covered property:

- Fire
- Lightning
- Explosion
- Windstorm or hail
- Smoke
- Aircraft or vehicles
- Riot or civil commotion
- Vandalism
- Sprinkler leakage
- Sinkhole collapse
- Volcanic action

Causes-of-Loss Broad Form

The **causes-of-loss broad form** includes all causes of loss covered by the basic form plus several additional causes:

- Falling objects
- Weight of snow, ice, or sleet
- Water damage

The broad form also covers collapse of a building as an additional coverage. Collapse is covered only if caused by the following:

- Certain specified causes of loss
- Hidden decay
- Hidden insect or vermin damage
- Weight of people or personal property
- Weight of rain that collects on a roof
- Use of defective materials or methods in construction or remodeling if collapse occurs during the course of construction or remodeling

Causes-of-Loss Special Form

The **causes-of-loss special form** insures against "risks of direct physical loss" (formerly called "all-risks"). *That is, all direct physical damage losses to insured property are covered unless specifically excluded or limited in the form itself.* Important exclusions include loss due to the enforcement of an ordinance or law, flood, earth movement, and mold. The burden of proof falls on the insurer to show that the loss is not covered because of a specific exclusion or limitation that applies. In addition, collapse is included as an additional coverage.

The special form provides for three additional extensions of coverage. First, personal property in transit is covered for certain causes of loss while the property is in or on a motor vehicle owned, leased, or operated by the insured. The maximum paid is $5000.

Second, if the damage results from a covered water damage loss or from other liquids, the cost of tearing out and replacing part of the building or structure to repair the leaking water system or appliance is covered.

Finally, the special form covers glass damage as an additional extension of coverage. The insurer will pay for the cost of boarding up openings if repair or replacement of the damaged glass is delayed. The insurer will also pay the expense of removing or replacing obstructions when glass that is part of the building is being repaired or replaced. The cost of removing or replacing window displays, however, is not covered.

Because of its advantages, most risk managers prefer the special form (see Insight 25.2).

INSIGHT 25.2

Advantages of the Special Causes-of-Loss Form

The special causes-of-loss form insurance provides coverage for risks of direct physical loss to covered property. *The burden of proof as to coverage falls on the insurer—not the insured.* As long as the insured can demonstrate that a direct physical loss has occurred to covered property, the cause of loss is presumed to be covered unless the *insurer* can prove that an exclusion applies.

In contrast, the basic and broad forms place the burden of proof on the insured. Unless the *insured* can prove that one of the named perils caused the loss, the insurer has no obligation to pay. Which party has the burden of proof can make a major difference when the cause of loss is not entirely clear.

Insured and students of insurance sometimes ask for examples of "all-risks" type losses that would not be covered under a broad form. Some examples include the following:

- *Theft.* Because many types of theft are not excluded, those that are not excluded are covered.
- *Friendly fire.* The named peril "fire" is generally held to mean only *hostile fire.* No such limitation applies to the special form and most other "all-risks" forms because they do not exclude damage by friendly fire. Although court decisions are eroding the doctrine of friendly fire, an insured that has suffered a loss caused by a friendly fire might have to institute a lawsuit to prevail under a named perils policy.
- *Vehicle damage.* The aircraft or vehicles peril of the basic and broad forms contains a contact requirement. However, vehicles can harm property without making contact with the damaged property. The special form covers damage by vehicles whether or not direct physical contact occurs. It also covers damage caused by vehicles regardless of whether the insured owns or operates the damage-causing vehicle. The basic and broad forms exclude coverage when the vehicle is owned by the insured or operated in the course of the insured's business.
- *Water damage caused by ice dam.* When melting snow or ice backs up under roof shingles (usually because gutters are clogged with ice, a phenomenon referred to as "ice damming"), the resulting water damage is covered by the special form but not by the basic form or the broad form.

These examples help to illustrate the breadth of "all-risks" coverage. **The key point is this: A cause of loss that is not specifically excluded is covered.**

Another advantage is the relatively small additional premium charged for special form coverage instead of broad form coverage. The vast majority of risk managers and experienced insurance producers therefore prefer the special form.

SOURCE: Adapted from Jerome Trupin and Arthur L. Flitner, *Commercial Property Risk Management and Insurance*, 6th ed., vol. 1 (Malvern, PA: American Institute for CPCU, 2001), pp. 5.30–5.31.

REPORTING FORMS

Some business firms have wide fluctuations in the value of business personal property during the policy period, especially in the value of inventories held for sale. A **reporting form** requires the insured to report periodically the value of insured business personal property. The major advantage of the reporting form is that premiums are based on the actual value of the covered property if the insured reports accurately rather than on the limit of insurance, which may be greater than the value of the covered property on hand.

Under the ISO commercial property program, the *value reporting form* is used to insure fluctuations in business personal property. An advance premium is paid at the inception of the policy based on the limit of insurance. The final premium is determined at the end of the policy period based on the values reported. The insured has the option of reporting daily, weekly, monthly, quarterly, or at the end of the policy year. As long as the insured reports the correct values, the full amount of the loss is covered (subject to the policy limit and deductible) even if the value of the property on hand exceeds the value reported at the last reporting date. For example, assume that the insured correctly reports business personal property of $1 million at the last reporting date. Before the next reporting date, the value of covered property increases to $5 million. If a total loss occurs, the loss is covered in full up to the policy limit (less a deductible).

If the insured is dishonest or careless and underreports, he or she will be penalized if a loss occurs. *If the insured underreports the property values at a location, and a loss occurs at that location, recovery is limited to the proportion that the last value reported bears to the correct value that should have been reported.* For example, if the actual value of business personal property on hand, including inventory, is $500,000, and the insured reports only $400,000, only four-fifths of any loss will be paid (less the deductible).

BUSINESS INCOME INSURANCE

Business firms often experience an indirect loss as a result of a direct physical damage loss to covered property, such as the loss of profits, rents, or extra expenses during the period of restoration. **Business income insurance** (formerly called *business interruption insurance*) is designed to cover the loss of business income, expenses that continue during the shutdown period, and extra expenses because of loss from a covered peril.

Two basic ISO forms are used to insure business income losses:[2]

- Business income (and extra expense) coverage form
- Extra expense coverage form

Business Income (and Extra Expense) Coverage Form

The **business income (and extra expense) coverage form** is used to cover the loss of business income whether the income is derived from retail or service operations, manufacturing, or rents. When a firm has a business income loss, profits are lost, and certain expenses may still continue, such as rent, interest, insurance premiums, and some salaries. The form covers both the loss of business income and extra expenses that result from a physical damage loss to covered property.

Loss of Business Income   The business income and extra expense coverage form covers the loss of business income due to the suspension of operations during the period of restoration. The suspension of operations must result from the direct physical loss or damage to property caused by an insured peril at the described premises. The insured perils are listed in the causes-of-loss form attached to the policy. *Business income is defined as the net profit or loss before income taxes that would have been earned, and continuing normal operating expenses, including payroll.* The business income loss is the difference between expected net income if the loss did not occur and actual net income after the loss. For example, assume that a retail shoe store has a fire and experiences a reduction in its net income during a three-month rebuilding period. Based on past and projected future earnings, the firm expected to earn net income of $75,000 during the three-month period if the loss did not occur. However, because of limited operations following the loss, actual net income was only $25,000. The business income loss is $50,000 ($75,000 − $25,000).

Consider a second example. In this case, the firm has no earnings during the shutdown period but has continuing expenses. Assume that Sal's Pizza is totally destroyed in a tornado, and it will take six months to rebuild. Based on past earnings and projected future income, Sal expected to earn a net income of $100,000 during the six-month period if the loss did not occur. During the shutdown period, however, there were no revenues, and Sal had continuing expenses of $10,000. As a result, the firm experienced a net loss of $10,000. As in the previous example, actual net income is subtracted from expected net income to determine the business income loss. In this case, the business income loss is $110,000, calculated as $100,000 − (−$10,000). The loss payment covers the net income that would have been earned if the loss had not occurred and continuing expenses during the shutdown period.

Extra Expenses   The business income (and extra expense) coverage form also covers extra expenses. **Extra expenses** are the necessary expenses incurred by the firm during the period of restoration that would not have been incurred if the loss had not taken place. Examples of covered expenses are the cost of relocating temporarily to another location, increased rent at another location, and the rental of substitute equipment.

Additional Coverages   The business income form provides several additional coverages, summarized as follows:

- *Action of civil authority.* Loss of business income and extra expenses caused by action of a civil authority that prohibits access to the described premises because of a covered cause of loss are also paid. The coverage for business income begins 72 hours after the time of that action and continues for up to three consecutive weeks after the coverage begins.
- *Alterations and new buildings.* The loss of business income as a result of a direct physical damage loss to a new building on the premises (whether completed or under construction) is covered. The loss of business income because of alterations or additions to existing buildings is covered as well.

- *Extended business income.* A business that reopens may experience reduced earnings after the repairs are completed, and additional time may be needed to rebuild a customer base. For example, a restaurant that reopens after a fire may need time to attract former customers back. The extended business income provision covers the reduction in earnings for a limited period after the business reopens. The extended period begins on the date the property is repaired and operations are resumed and ends after 30 consecutive days or when business income returns to normal, whichever occurs first.
- *Interruption of computer operations.* Coverage also applies to the suspension of operations caused by an interruption of computer operations from a covered cause of loss. For example, business operations may be temporarily suspended because a "hacker" breaks into the company's computer system, causing it to crash. The maximum paid is $2500 during any policy year.

Coinsurance   The business income coverage form can be purchased with coinsurance of 50, 60, 70, 80, 90, 100, or 125 percent. *The basis for coinsurance is the sum of net income that would have been earned and continuing normal operating expenses, including payroll, for the 12 months following the inception of the policy or the last anniversary date, whichever is later.* This sum is then multiplied by the coinsurance percentage to determine the required amount of insurance. For example, assume that net income and operating expenses for the 12 months of the current policy term are $400,000, and that the coinsurance percentage is 50 percent; the required amount of insurance would be $200,000.

The actual coinsurance percentage selected depends on the length of time it takes to resume operations, and on the period of time during which most of the business is done. If the firm expects to be shut down for more than one year, the 125 percent option should be selected. If the firm expects to be shut down for no more than six months and business is uniform throughout the year, a coinsurance percentage of 50 percent should be selected. However, when seasonal peak periods are considered, this percentage may be inadequate, because 50 percent of the firm's business may not occur within a consecutive six-month period. Thus, when business income is seasonal or has peak periods, a coinsurance percentage higher than 50 percent is advisable to provide greater protection during a prolonged shutdown period that continues during the peak period.

Ordinary payroll is covered under the business income coverage form unless it is excluded by an endorsement to the policy. The endorsement can exclude ordinary payroll, or it can be covered for a limited period, such as 90 days. Limiting or excluding ordinary payroll reduces the premium.

Optional Coverages The business income form also has coverages that can be activated by an appropriate entry on the declarations page. The optional coverages are summarized as follows:

- *Maximum period of indemnity*. This optional coverage eliminates coinsurance and pays for the loss of business income for a maximum period of 120 days. The amount paid cannot exceed the policy limit. This option can be used by smaller firms that will not be shut down for more than 120 days if a loss occurs.
- *Monthly limit of indemnity*. This optional coverage eliminates coinsurance and limits the maximum monthly amount that will be paid for each consecutive 30-day period to a fraction of the policy limit. The fractions are one-third, one-fourth, and one-sixth. For example, if the fraction selected is one-third, and the policy limit is $120,000, the maximum paid for each consecutive 30-day period is $40,000.
- *Business income agreed value*. This option suspends the coinsurance clause and places no limit on the monthly amount paid, provided that the agreed amount of business income insurance is carried. The agreed amount is the coinsurance percentage (50 percent or higher) multiplied by an estimate of net income and operating expenses for the 12 months of the policy period.
- *Extended period of indemnity*. This option extends the recovery period following completion of repairs from 30 days to a longer period stated in the declarations. The extended period of indemnity can be up to two years. This option is advantageous for those firms that need a longer recovery period to recapture old business and resume normal operations.

Extra Expense Coverage Form

Certain firms such as banks, newspapers, and dairies must continue to operate after a loss occurs; otherwise, customers will be lost to competitors. The **extra expense coverage form** is a separate form that can be used to cover the extra expenses incurred by the firm in continuing operations during a period of restoration. The extra expense form does not cover the loss of business income because of the interruption of operations. However, the additional expenses to continue operating are covered, subject to certain limits stated in the declarations on the amount of insurance that can be used. A common limitation is 40 percent, 80 percent, and 100 percent. A maximum of 40 percent can be paid when the recovery period is 30 days or less, 80 percent when the recovery period is longer than 30 days but does not exceed 60 days, and 100 percent when the recovery period is longer than 60 days.

Business Income from Dependent Properties

Some firms depend on a single supplier for raw materials and supplies or on a single customer to purchase most or all of the firm's products. The insured's business may incur a loss because of property damage incurred by the sole supplier or customer. An appropriate endorsement can be added to a business income policy that covers loss of income at the insured's location that results from direct damage to property at other locations.

There are four types of dependent properties situations for which this coverage may be needed.[3]

- *Contributing location*. A contributing location is a location that furnishes materials or services to the insured. For example, the insured may depend on one supplier for raw materials. If the supplier's factory is damaged, the insured's business may be forced to shut down.
- *Recipient location*. A recipient location is a location that purchases the insured's products or services. For example, a specialized cheese manufacturer may sell most of its cheese production to a resort hotel. If the hotel is closed because of fire, the cheese factory may have to shut down.
- *Manufacturing location*. A manufacturing location is a location that manufactures products for

delivery to the insured's customers. If the manufacturer's plant is damaged, the products cannot be delivered, and the insured would incur a loss.

- *Leader location.* A leader location is a location that attracts customers to the insured's place of business. For example, a major department store in a shopping center may have a fire. As a result, smaller stores in the shopping center may experience a decline in sales.

OTHER COMMERCIAL PROPERTY COVERAGES

The building and personal property coverage form discussed earlier is designed to meet the commercial property insurance needs of most business firms. However, many firms have certain needs that require the use of specialized coverages, which include the following:

- Builders risk insurance
- Condominium insurance
- Equipment breakdown insurance
- Difference in conditions (DIC) insurance

Builders Risk Insurance

A building under construction is exposed to numerous perils, especially the peril of fire. Under the simplified commercial property program by ISO, the **builders risk coverage form** can be used to insure buildings under construction. This form can be used to cover the insurable interest of a general contractor, subcontractor, or building owner.

Under the builders risk coverage form, insurance is purchased equal to the *full value* of the completed building. Because the building is substantially overinsured during the initial stages of construction, the rate charged is adjusted to reflect the average value exposed.

If desired, a *builders risk reporting form* can be attached as an endorsement, which requires the builder to report monthly the value of the building under construction. The initial premium reflects the value of the building at the inception of the policy period and not the completed value of the building. As construction progresses, the amount of insurance on the building is increased based on the reported values. The premiums are adjusted during the policy period based on the values reported by the builder.

Condominium Association Coverage Form

Owners of individual condominium units have a common interest in the building, which includes the exterior walls, the roof, and the plumbing, heating, and air conditioning systems. However, property insurance on the building and common elements of other condominium property is purchased in the name of the condominium owners association (named insured).

The **condominium association coverage form** covers the following types of property:

- Building
- Named insured's business personal property
- Personal property of others

The form covers the condominium building and equipment used to maintain or service the building, such as fire extinguishing equipment and outdoor furniture. If required by the condominium association agreement, the form also covers fixtures, improvements and alterations that are part of the building, and appliances within individual units (such as a dishwasher or stove).

The form also covers the named insured's business personal property. The named insured is the condominium owners association. One example of business personal property is equipment in a condominium health club, such as treadmills, weights, stationary bikes, and similar equipment. Another example is furniture in a community clubhouse.

Finally, the condominium association form covers personal property of others in the named insured's care, custody, and control. For example, if the association leases several riding lawn mowers, snowblowers, and other equipment to maintain the grounds, the equipment is covered.

Condominium Commercial Unit-Owners Coverage Form

Business or professional firms may own individual units in a commercial condominium. For example, a physician, dentist, or business firm may own individual office space in a commercial office building that is legally organized as a condominium.

The condominium commercial unit-owners coverage form is used to insure only the owners of commercial condominium units. Owners of residential condominium units normally insure their personal property under the Homeowners 6 policy (unit-owner form).

The **condominium commercial unit-owners coverage form** covers the following categories of property:

- Business personal property of the unit owner
- Personal property of others in the named insured's care, custody, or control

Business personal property includes the following:

- Furniture
- Fixtures and improvements that are part of the building and owned by the unit owner
- Machinery and equipment
- Stock
- All other personal property owned by the unit owner and used in the business
- Labor, materials, or services furnished by the unit owner on personal property of others
- Leased personal property that the unit owner has a contractual obligation to insure

The condominium form also covers the personal property of others in the care, custody, or control of the unit owner. The personal property must be in or on the building described in the declarations or within 100 feet of the described premises if in the open or in a vehicle.

Equipment Breakdown Insurance

Equipment breakdown insurance (formerly known as *boiler and machinery insurance*) covers losses due to the accidental breakdown of covered equipment. Such equipment includes steam boilers; air conditioning and refrigeration equipment; electrical generating equipment; pumps, compressors, turbines, and engines; machinery used in manufacturing; and computer equipment.

The causes-of-loss forms discussed earlier exclude steam boiler explosions, electrical breakdown, and mechanical breakdown. The **equipment breakdown protection coverage form** can be used to pro-

vide such coverage. Coverage can be written separately as a monoline policy, or it can be part of a commercial package policy.

Covered Cause of Loss The covered cause of loss is a breakdown to covered equipment. A *breakdown* is a direct physical loss that causes damage to covered equipment. *Covered equipment* refers to the boiler, machinery, or electrical or mechanical equipment insured under the policy, including communication equipment and computer equipment. Covered equipment also includes equipment owned by a public or private utility used solely to support utility services to the premises. Insight 25.3 gives examples of covered equipment breakdown losses.

Coverages Provided The current ISO form contains numerous coverages that can be included or omitted depending on the needs of the business firm. A specific coverage is in force if the declarations page indicates either a limit of insurance, or if the word "INCLUDED" is shown for the coverage. If neither is indicated, there is no coverage for that benefit.

- *Property damage.* The form pays for direct damage to covered property located at the premises described in the declarations. Covered property is property owned by the insured or property in the insured's care, custody, or control for which the insured is legally liable.
- *Expediting expenses.* Expediting expenses are the reasonable extra costs the insured must pay to make temporary repairs or to expedite the permanent repair or replacement of the damaged property. For example, the extra transportation charges to speed up delivery of a replacement part would be covered.
- *Business income and extra expense–extra expense only.* This coverage pays for the loss of business income and extra expenses. Business income refers to the loss of business income and extra expenses incurred during the period of restoration. However, if shown in the declarations, only extra expenses can be covered. For example, a firm may have its own power plant and an emergency standby connection with an outside public utility firm in case power is interrupted because of a covered loss. The extra costs of the outside power would be covered.

INSIGHT 25.3

Examples of Equipment Breakdown Losses

Steam boiler explosions can cause extensive damage not only to the boiler itself but to the building that houses it. In one case, a heating boiler in a telephone company switching office exploded and tore through the roof, leaving the building looking as if it had been struck by a military missile.

Boilers can sustain serious damage as a result of a malfunction even when they don't explode. Severe overheating of a boiler in a factory, caused by low-water conditions in the boiler, resulted in damage to the furnace tubes and a portion of the rear tube sheet. The physical damage loss was $27,000, and the business income loss was $30,000.

Although boiler explosions provided the original impetus for equipment breakdown coverage, other types of equipment can suffer serious damage in many other ways.

- A short circuit in the aluminum bus (an electrical conductor) in an apartment building caused extensive damage to the building's electrical cables and wiring. Residents were temporarily relocated. The physical damage loss was $120,000, and the extra expense loss was $72,000.

- The rotating cylinder door assembly of a 400-pound commercial washing machine opened during the extract cycle, damaging the basket and inner and outer shells. The cost to repair the physical damage amounted to $61,000.
- A portion of an air conditioning compressor became detached and fell into the evaporator, puncturing several tubes. The cooling water from the tubes contaminated the refrigerant and caused severe damage to the driving motor windings. The loss amounted to $45,000.
- Voltage fluctuation caused two terminal boards in an office building's phone computer to short-circuit. The resulting loss amounted to $52,000.

SOURCE: Arthur L. Flitner and Jerome Trupin, *Commercial Insurance*, 1st ed (Malvern, PA: American Institute for Chartered Property Casualty Underwriters/Insurance Institute of America, 2002), p 6.4. Originally adapted with permission from *Whistle Stop*, a publication of The Hartford Steam Boiler Inspection and Insurance Company, Hartford, CT. Reprinted here with permission of The Hartford Steam Boiler Inspection and Insurance Company.

- *Spoilage damage*. This coverage pays for spoilage damage to raw materials, property in process, or finished products. For example, the loss of refrigeration in a meatpacking plant that results in the spoilage of meat would be covered.
- *Utility interruption*. This coverage extends the protection provided by the business income and extra expense coverages. For example, if a power generator owned by a local public utility has a mechanical failure, and the insured firm loses power and must shut down its business operations, the resulting loss of business income would be covered. However, the insured must select a waiting period—such as 12 hours—before coverage applies.
- *Newly acquired premises*. Coverage automatically applies to newly acquired premises leased or purchased. The insured is required to notify the insurer of the newly acquired premises as soon as practicable.
- *Ordinance or law coverage*. This coverage pays for the increase in loss that results from an ordinance or law regulating the demolition, construction, repair, or use of the building. The form

describes in detail what losses will be paid or not paid because of some ordinance or law.
- *Errors and omissions*. If the insured has made an unintentional error or mistake in describing the property or premises to be insured, the loss or damage will still be covered.
- *Brands and labels*. If there is a loss to covered property, the insurer may take any part of the property at an agreed or appraised value. This coverage allows the insured to stamp the word *salvage* on the merchandise or to remove the brand or label from the damaged merchandise at the insurer's expense. The insurer pays the reasonable cost provided the total cost of the activity and the value of the damaged property do not exceed the limit of insurance for such coverage.
- *Contingent business income and extra expense— extra expense only coverage*. This coverage extends the firm's business income coverage to insure the loss of income that results from a breakdown at a nonowned premises critical to the firm's operation. For example, assume that the insured does business in a shopping mall and that the entire mall is blacked out because of a

short circuit in an electrical generator in another store. As a result, the firm must shut down and loses sales. The loss of income would be covered.

Difference in Conditions Insurance

Difference in conditions (DIC) insurance is an "all-risks" policy that covers other perils not insured by basic property insurance contracts.[4] DIC insurance is written as a separate contract to supplement the coverage provided by the underlying contracts. As such, it excludes perils covered by the underlying contracts (such as fire and extended coverage perils, vandalism and malicious mischief, and sprinkler leakage). However, most other insurable perils are covered. The policy can also be written to include coverage for flood, earthquake, and building collapse. A substantial deductible must be satisfied for losses not covered by the underlying contracts.

DIC insurance has two major advantages. First, it can be used to fill gaps in coverage. Many large multinational corporations use a DIC policy to insure their overseas property. Many foreign countries require property insurance to be purchased locally; if the local coverage is inadequate, a DIC policy can fill the gap in coverage.

Second, DIC insurance can be used to insure unusual and catastrophic exposures that are not covered by the underlying contracts. Some unusual losses that have been paid include the following:[5]

- An accident caused molasses to spill into a machine. The cost to clean the machine was $38,000.
- Dust collected on a roof, solidified, and the weight caused the roof to collapse.
- A city water main broke, which flooded the basement of an industrial plant, causing hundreds of thousands of dollars of damage.

TRANSPORTATION INSURANCE

Billions of dollars of goods are shipped by business firms each year. These goods are exposed to damage or loss from numerous transportation perils. The goods can be protected by ocean marine and inland marine contracts. **Ocean marine insurance** *provides protection for goods transported over water.* All types of oceangoing vessels and their cargo can be insured by ocean marine contracts; the legal liability of ship owners and cargo owners can also be insured.

Inland marine insurance *provides protection for goods shipped on land.* It includes insurance on imports and exports, domestic shipments, and means of transportation such as bridges and tunnels. In addition, inland marine insurance can be used to insure fine arts, jewelry, furs, and other property.[6]

Ocean Marine Insurance

Ocean marine insurance is one of the oldest forms of transportation insurance. Ocean marine contracts are complex, reflecting maritime law, trade customs, and court interpretations of the various policy provisions.

There are several types of ocean marine contracts. Some basic coverages include the following:

- **Hull insurance** *covers physical damage to the ship or vessel.* It is similar to collision insurance that covers physical damage to an automobile caused by a collision. Hull insurance is always written with a deductible. In addition, it contains a **collision liability clause** (also called a **running down clause**) that covers the owner's legal liability if the ship collides with another vessel or damages its cargo. However, the running down clause does not cover legal liability arising out of injury or death to other persons, damage to piers and docks, and personal injury and death of crew members.
- **Cargo insurance** *covers the shipper of the goods if the goods are damaged or lost.* The policy can be written to cover a single shipment. If regular shipments are made, an open-cargo policy can be used that insures the goods automatically when a shipment is made. The shipper is required to report periodically the shipments that are made. The open-cargo policy has no expiration date and remains in force until it is canceled.
- **Protection and indemnity (P&I) insurance** *is usually written as a separate contract that provides comprehensive liability insurance for property damage or bodily injury to third parties.* P&I insurance protects the ship owner for damage caused by the ship to piers, docks, and harbor installations, damage to the ship's cargo,

illness or injury to the passengers or crew, and fines and penalties.

- **Freight insurance** *indemnifies the ship owner for the loss of earnings if the goods are damaged or lost and are not delivered.*

Basic Concepts in Ocean Marine Insurance

Ocean marine insurance is based on certain fundamental concepts. The following section discusses these concepts and related contractual provisions.

Implied Warranties Ocean marine contracts contain three implied warranties:

- Seaworthy vessel
- No deviation from planned course
- Legal purpose

The ship owner implicitly warrants that the vessel is seaworthy, which means that the ship is properly constructed, maintained, and equipped for the voyage to be undertaken.

The warranty of no deviation means that the ship cannot deviate from its original course. However, an intentional deviation is permitted in the event of an unavoidable accident, to avoid bad weather, to save the life of an individual on board, or to rescue persons from some other vessel.

The warranty of legal purpose means that the voyage should not be for some illegal venture, such as smuggling drugs into a country.

The implied warranties described above are subject to numerous exceptions and qualifications. Discussion of the various exceptions, however, is beyond the scope of the text.

Covered Perils An ocean marine policy provides broad coverage for certain specified perils, including **perils of the sea,** such as damage or loss from bad weather, high waves, collision, sinking, and stranding. Other covered perils include loss from fire, enemies, pirates, thieves, jettison (throwing goods overboard to save the ship), barratry (fraud by the master or crew at the expense of the ship or cargo owners), and similar perils.

Ocean marine insurance can also be written on an "all-risks" basis. All unexpected and fortuitous losses are covered except those losses specifically excluded.

Common exclusions are losses due to delay, war, inherent vice (tendency of certain types of property to decompose), and strikes, riots, or civil commotion.

Particular Average In marine insurance, the word *average* refers to a partial loss. A **particular average** *is a loss that falls entirely on a particular interest,* as contrasted with a general average, a loss that falls on all parties to the voyage. Under the *free-of-particular-average clause* (FPA), partial losses are not covered unless the loss is caused by certain perils, such as stranding, sinking, burning, or collision of the vessel.

The FPA clause can be written with a percentage, such as 3 percent. If the loss exceeds the stated percentage, the entire loss is payable. For example, if cargo is insured for $100,000, a partial loss under $3000 falls entirely on the insured; if the loss is $3000 or more, the insurer pays the loss in full.

General Average A **general average** *is a loss incurred for the common good and consequently is shared by all parties to the venture.* For example, if a ship damaged by heavy waves is in danger of sinking, part of the cargo may be jettisoned to save the ship. The loss falls on all parties to the voyage: the ship owner, cargo owners, and freight interests. In this context, *freight* refers to the revenue that a cargo ship earns. Each party must pay its share of the loss based on the proportion that its interest bears to the total value in the venture. For example, assume that the captain must jettison $1 million of steel to save the ship. Also assume that the various interests are as follows:

Value of steel	$ 2 million
Value of other cargo	3 million
Value of ship and freight	+15 million
Total	$20 million

The owner of the steel would absorb 2/20 of the loss, or $100,000. The owners of the other cargo would pay 3/20 of the loss, or $150,000. Finally, the ship and freight interests would pay 15/20 of the loss, or $750,000.

Certain conditions must be satisfied to have a general average loss:[7]

- *Imminent peril.* There must be an imminent peril to all interests in the venture—ship, cargo, and freight.

- *Voluntary.* The sacrifice must be voluntary, and the special expense incurred must be reasonable.
- *Preservation of at least part of the value.* The effort must be successful. At least part of the value must be saved.
- *Free from fault.* Any party that claims a general average contribution from other interests in the voyage must be free from fault with respect to the risk that threatens the venture.

Inland Marine Insurance

Inland marine insurance grew out of ocean marine insurance. Ocean marine insurance first covered property from the point of embarkation to the place where the goods landed. As commerce and trade developed, goods had to be shipped over land as well. Inland marine insurance developed in the 1920s to cover property being transported over land, means of transportation such as bridges and tunnels, and property of a mobile nature.

Nationwide Marine Definition

As inland marine insurance developed, conflicts arose between fire insurers and marine insurers. To resolve the confusion and conflict, the companies drafted a **nationwide marine definition** in 1933 to define the property that marine insurers could write. The definition was approved by the National Association of Insurance Commissioners (NAIC) and was later revised and broadened in 1953. In 1976, the NAIC drafted a new definition of marine insurance that has been adopted by most states. At present, marine insurance can be written on the following types of property:

- Imports
- Exports
- Domestic shipments
- Means of transportation and communication
- Personal property floater risks
- Commercial property floater risks

Major Classes of Inland Marine Insurance

Commercial property that can be insured by inland marine contracts can be classified into the following categories:

- Domestic goods in transit
- Property held by bailees

- Mobile equipment and property
- Property of certain dealers
- Means of transportation and communication

Domestic Goods in Transit   Domestic goods may be shipped by a common carrier, such as a trucking company, railroad, or airline, or by the company's own trucks. The goods can be damaged because of fire, lightning, flood, earthquake, or other perils. They can also be damaged from the collision, derailment, or overturn of the transportation vehicle. These losses can be insured by an inland marine policy.

Although a common carrier is legally liable for safe delivery of the goods, liability does not extend to all losses. For example, a common carrier is not responsible for losses due to acts of God (such as a tornado), acts of public authority, acts of public enemies (war), improper packaging by the shipper, and inherent vice.

In addition, shipping charges are reduced if the shipper agrees to limit the carrier's liability for the goods at less than their full value (called a *released bill of lading*). Consequently, the shipper can save money by agreeing to a released bill of lading and then purchase insurance to cover the shipment.

Property Held by Bailees   Inland marine insurance can be used to insure property held by a bailee. A **bailee** *is someone who has temporary possession of property that belongs to another.* Examples of bailees are dry cleaners, laundries, and television repair shops. Under common law, bailees are legally liable for damage to customers' property only if they or their employees are negligent. However, to ensure customer goodwill, many bailees purchase bailees customers insurance that covers the damage or loss to customers' property while in the bailee's possession regardless of fault, normally from certain named perils.

Mobile Equipment and Property   Inland marine property floaters can be used to cover property that is frequently moved from one location to another, such as a tractor, crane, or bulldozer. Also, plumbing, heating, or air conditioning equipment can be covered while being transported to a job site or while being installed.

In addition, a property floater policy can be used to insure certain other types of property, such as fine arts, livestock, theatrical property, computers, and signs.

Property of Certain Dealers

Inland marine insurance is also used to insure the property of certain dealers. Specialized inland marine policies or inland marine "block" policies are used to insure the property of jewelers, furriers, and dealers in diamonds, fine art, cameras, and musical instruments, and other dealers. Most policies provide coverage on an "all-risks" basis.

Means of Transportation and Communication

Means of transportation and communication refers to property at a fixed location that is used in transportation or communication. Inland marine insurance can be used to cover bridges, tunnels, piers, docks, wharves, pipelines, power transmission lines, radio and television towers, outdoor cranes, and similar equipment for loading, unloading, or transporting. For example, a bridge may be damaged by a flood, an ice jam, or a ship that collides with it; a television tower or power line may be blown over in a windstorm; or a fire may start in a tunnel when a gasoline truck overturns and explodes. These losses can be insured under inland marine contracts.

The commercial property loss exposures just described can be insured by a wide variety of inland marine contracts. For purposes of regulation, inland marine contracts are classified into two categories: (1) *filed forms* and (2) *nonfiled forms*. With filed forms, the policy forms and rates are filed with the state insurance department. Filed forms are typically used in situations where there are a large number of potential insureds and the loss exposures are reasonably homogeneous.

In contrast, nonfiled forms refer to policy forms and rates that are not filed with the state insurance department. Nonfiled forms are used in situations where the insured has specialized or unique needs, the number of potential insureds is relatively small, and the loss exposures are diverse.[8]

Filed Inland Marine Forms

Under the ISO simplified commercial inland marine program, the various policy forms and rates are filed with the state insurance department.

Numerous forms can be used in the ISO commercial inland marine insurance program. The major forms are summarized here:

- The **accounts receivable coverage form** indemnifies the firm if it is unable to collect outstanding customer balances because of damage or destruction of the records. A firm may incur a sizable loss if its accounts receivable records are lost because of a fire, theft, or other peril, and the amount owned by customers cannot be collected.
- The **camera and musical instrument dealers coverage form** is used to cover stock in trade consisting principally of cameras or musical instruments and related equipment and accessories. The property of others in the insured's care, custody, or control is also covered.
- The **commercial articles coverage form** covers photographic equipment and musical instruments that are used commercially by photographers, professional musicians, motion picture producers, production companies, and other persons.
- The **equipment dealers form** covers the stock in trade of dealers in agricultural implements and construction equipment. The form can also be extended to cover furniture, fixtures, office supplies, and machinery used in the business.
- The **film coverage form** covers exposed motion picture film as well as magnetic or video tapes.
- The **floor plan coverage form** refers to a financing plan in which the dealer borrows money to buy merchandise to display and sell, but the title is held by the lending institution or manufacturer. The form can be used to cover the interest of the dealer, the lending institution, or both. The property covered is the merchandise that is financed.
- The **jewelers block coverage form** covers jewelry, watches, and precious stones of retail and wholesale jewelers, jewelry manufacturers, and diamond wholesalers.
- The **mail coverage form** covers securities in transit by first-class mail, registered or certified mail, or express mail. It is designed for stock brokerage firms, banks, and other financial institutions that ship securities by mail.
- The **physicians and surgeons equipment coverage form** covers the medical, surgical, or dental

equipment of physicians and dentists, including furniture, fixtures, and improvements.

- The **signs coverage form** covers neon, mechanical, and electrical signs. Each covered sign must be scheduled.

- The **theatrical property coverage form** covers costumes, stage scenery, and similar property used in theatrical productions. For example, a Broadway show may be presented in another city, which requires the shipment of stage props and scenery to that city. The theatrical property can be covered under this form.

- The **valuable papers and records coverage form** covers loss to valuable papers and records, such as student transcripts at a university, plans and blueprints of an architectural firm, and prescription records in a drugstore. The form covers the cost of reconstructing the damaged or destroyed records. It can also be used to insure the loss of irreplaceable records, such as a rare manuscript.

Nonfiled Inland Marine Forms

Nonfiled forms are also available to meet the specialized or unique needs of commercial firms. Only a few of them are discussed here.

Shipment of Goods   As noted earlier, inland marine insurance can be used to cover the domestic shipment of goods. An **annual transit policy** can be used by manufacturers, wholesalers, and retailers to cover the shipment of goods on public trucks, railroads, and coastal vessels. Both outgoing and incoming shipments can be insured. Although these forms are not standardized, they have similar characteristics. They can be written either on an "all-risks" or a named-perils basis.

Although a transit policy provides broad coverage, it contains certain exclusions. The policy can be written to cover the theft of an entire shipment, but pilferage of the goods generally is not covered. Other common exclusions are losses from strikes, riots or civil commotion, leakage and breakage (unless caused by an insured peril), marring, scratching, dampness, molding, and rotting.

A **trip transit policy** is used by firms and individuals to cover a single shipment. For example, an electrical transformer worth thousands of dollars that is shipped from an Eastern factory to the West Coast or the household goods of executives who are transferred can be insured under a variation of the trip transit policy.

Bailee Forms   As stated earlier, a bailee is someone who has temporary possession of property that belongs to others. A *bailees liability policy* can be used to cover the firm's liability for the property of customers, such as clothes in a laundry. A bailees liability policy, however, covers the loss only if the firm is legally liable. In contrast, a *bailees customers policy* can be used to cover the loss or damage to the property of others regardless of legal liability. A bailees customers policy generally is designed for firms that hold the property of others that have high value, such as fur coats. A covered loss is paid regardless of legal liability, and the goodwill of customers is maintained.

Business Floaters   A **business floater** is an inland marine policy that covers property that frequently moves (floats) from one location to another. Numerous business floaters are available. For example, a *contractors equipment floater* can be used to insure the property of contractors, such as bulldozers, tractors, cranes, earthmovers, and scaffolding equipment. A *garment contractors floater* covers garments and parts of garments that are sent by a garment manufacturer for processing to outside firms, such as buttonhole makers, pleaters, or embroiderers.

Means of Transportation and Communication   Inland marine contracts can be used to cover bridges, tunnels, towers, pipelines, power lines, and similar property. For example, a toll bridge lost revenues because a ship ran into a bridge pylon, forcing the bridge to close. A business income policy can be written to cover this exposure.

This type of property can be insured either on a risk-of-direct-physical-loss basis or on a named-perils basis, depending on the specific needs of the insured.

BUSINESSOWNERS POLICY (BOP)

A **businessowners policy (BOP)** is a package policy specifically designed for small- to medium-sized retail stores, office buildings, apartment buildings, and similar firms. There are different BOP policies on the market today. In this section, we discuss the BOP designed by the Insurance Services Office (ISO). The ISO form provides both property and liability insurance in one policy. The following section discusses only the property insurance coverages; the liability insurance coverages are discussed in the following chapter.[9]

Eligible Business Firms

A BOP can be written to cover buildings and business personal property of the owners of apartments and residential condominium associations; office and office condominium associations; retail establishments; and eligible mercantile, service, or processing firms such as appliance firms, beauty parlors, and photocopy services. BOP coverage is also available for certain contractors, "limited-cooking" restaurants, and convenience stores.

Certain business firms are ineligible for a BOP because the loss exposures are outside those contemplated for the average small- to medium-sized firm. They include auto repair or service stations; automobile dealers, motorcycles, or mobilehomes; parking lots; bars; places of amusement such as a bowling alley; and banks and financial institutions.

BOP Coverages

The current ISO version of the BOP is a *special form,* which insures property on an "all risks" or "open perils" basis; all losses are covered except those losses specifically excluded. However, if desired, named-perils coverage is available by an endorsement to the policy; only those perils named in the policy are covered.

The present BOP form is a self-contained policy that incorporates the property coverages, liability coverages, and policy conditions into one contract. The following discussion summarizes the basic characteristics of the ISO form.

1. *Buildings.* The BOP covers the buildings that are described in the declarations, including completed additions, fixtures and outdoor fixtures, and permanently installed machinery and equipment. The building coverage also includes personal property in apartments or rooms furnished by the named insured as a landlord, and personal property owned by the named insured to maintain or service the premises, such as fire-extinguishing equipment and refrig-

erating and dishwashing appliances. The limit of insurance on the building is automatically increased each year by a stated percentage shown in the declarations to keep pace with inflation.

2. *Business personal property.* Business personal property is also covered. It includes property owned by the named insured used in the business; property of others in the insured's care, custody, and control; tenant's improvements and betterments; and leased personal property for which the named insured has a contractual responsibility to insure. Business personal property also includes exterior building glass if the named insured is a tenant, and no limit of insurance is shown in the declarations. The glass must be owned by the named insured or in the insured's care, custody, and control. A peak season provision provides for a temporary increase of 25 percent of the amount of insurance when inventory values are at their peak.

In addition, business personal property at newly acquired locations is covered for a maximum of $100,000 for 30 days at each premises. This provision provides automatic protection until the BOP can be endorsed to cover the new location. Business personal property in transit or temporarily away from the insured location is covered up to a maximum of $10,000.

3. *Covered causes of loss.* The latest edition of the BOP insures property against "risks of direct physical loss," which means that all direct physical losses are covered unless specifically excluded or limited in the form itself.

The BOP can also be issued on a named perils basis by an endorsement. Covered causes of loss include fire, lightning, explosion, windstorm or hail, smoke, aircraft or vehicles, riot or civil commotion, vandalism, sprinkler leakage, sinkhole collapse, volcanic action, and certain transportation perils. The named perils endorsement also includes an optional coverage for burglary and robbery.

4. *Additional coverages.* The BOP includes several additional coverages that might be needed by the typical businessowner:

- Debris removal
- Preservation of covered property after a loss occurs

- Fire department service charge
- Collapse
- Water damage, other liquids, powder or molten material damage
- Business income, extended business income, and extra expense
- Pollutant cleanup and removal
- Loss of business income and extra expense because of action by a civil authority
- Money orders and counterfeit money ($1000 maximum)
- Forgery and alteration losses ($2500 maximum)
- Increased cost of construction because of an ordinance or law ($10,000 maximum for each described building insured on a replacement cost basis)
- Business income from dependent properties ($5000 maximum)
- Glass expenses incurred to put up temporary plates or board up openings if repair or replacement of damaged glass is delayed
- Fire extinguisher systems recharge expense ($5000 maximum in any one occurrence)
- Replacing or restoring electronic data destroyed or corrupted by a covered cause of loss ($10,000 maximum)
- Interruption of computer operations ($10,000 maximum)

- Limited coverage for "fungi," wet or dry rot, and bacteria ($15,000 maximum)

5. *Optional coverages.* The BOP provides several optional coverages to meet the specialized needs of businessowners by payment of an additional premium:

- Outdoor signs
- Money and securities
- Employee dishonesty
- Mechanical breakdown

6. *Deductible.* A standard deductible of $500 per occurrence applies to all property coverages. Optional deductibles of $250, $1000, and $2500 are also available. The deductible does not apply, however, to the fire department service charge, business income losses, extra expenses, action by a civil authority, and recharge expense for a fire extinguisher system.

7. *Business liability insurance.* The businessowners policy also has business liability coverage similar to the commercial general liability policy (CGL). The businessowner is insured for bodily injury and property damage liability, and advertising and personal injury liability. Medical expense insurance is also provided. Commercial general liability insurance is discussed in Chapter 26.

CASE APPLICATION

Kimberly owns and operates a tennis shop in a resort area. The business is seasonal. A large part of the annual revenues are due to sales in June, July, and August. Kimberly keeps the shop open during the remaining months of the year, but the inventory carried during those months is reduced. During the summer months, the amount of inventory on hand is substantially increased. Kimberly has the business insured under the special form businessowners policy (BOP) with no special endorsements attached.

   a. Assume you are a risk management consultant. Identify the major loss exposures that Kimberly faces.

   b. Assume that a covered loss occurs in July, which damages part of the inventory. Does the BOP pro-

vide any protection for the increase in inventory during the summer months? Explain your answer.

   c. Kimberly plans to hire an additional employee during the summer months when sales are increasing. She is concerned about possible employee theft and dishonesty. Explain to Kimberly how this loss exposure can be handled under the BOP.

   d. A fire damaged the building. As a result, Kimberly incurred a business income loss because the business was closed for three months.

   e. Vandals broke the exterior glass window to the business, which caused substantial damage to the building.

SUMMARY

- Under the ISO commercial property insurance program, a commercial package policy (CPP) contains a common declarations page, a common policy conditions page, and two or more coverage parts. Each coverage part, in turn, has its own declarations page, relevant policy conditions, coverage forms, and a causes of loss form.

- A *commercial package policy* combines two or more coverage parts into a single policy. When compared with individual policies, a package policy has fewer gaps in coverage; premiums are relatively lower because individual policies are not purchased; savings in insurer expenses can be passed on to the policyholder; and the insured has the convenience of a single policy.

- The coverage parts available under the ISO commercial property program include the following:

    Commercial property coverage form(s)

    Commercial general liability coverage form

    Crime coverage form

    Equipment breakdown protection coverage form

    Inland marine coverage form(s)

    Auto coverage form

    Farm coverage form(s)

- The *building and personal property coverage form* can be used to insure the commercial building, business personal property, and personal property of others in the care and custody of the insured.

- Under the ISO commercial property insurance program, a causes-of-loss form must be added to a commercial policy to form a complete contract. There are three causes-of-loss forms:

    Causes-of-loss basic form

    Causes-of-loss broad form

    Causes-of-loss special form

- The *business income (and extra expense) coverage form* covers the loss of business income due to the suspension of business operations because of a covered loss. Business income is the net profit or loss before income taxes that would have been earned if the loss had not occurred, and continuing normal operating expenses, including payroll. Extra expenses incurred as a result of a loss are also covered.

- The *extra expense coverage form* covers only the extra expenses incurred by the firm in continuing operations during the period of restoration. Loss of profits is not covered.

- Certain miscellaneous commercial coverages are important to business firms that have unique or specialized needs, including builders risk insurance, condominium insurance, equipment breakdown protection insurance, and difference in conditions insurance.

- Ocean marine insurance can be classified into four categories that reflect the various insurable interests:

    Hull insurance

    Cargo insurance

    Protection and indemnity (P&I) insurance

    Freight insurance

- A particular average in ocean marine insurance is a loss that falls entirely on a particular interest, as contrasted with a general average that falls on all parties to the voyage.

- Inland marine contracts are used to insure the following classes of commercial property:

    Domestic goods in transit

    Property held by bailees

    Mobile equipment and property

    Property of certain dealers

    Means of transportation and communication

- For purposes of regulation, inland marine contracts are classified into filed forms and nonfiled forms. Filed forms are policy forms and rates that are filed with the state insurance department. Nonfiled forms are not filed with the state insurance department.

- Filed inland marine forms include the following:

    Accounts receivable coverage form

    Camera and musical instrument dealers
        coverage form

    Commercial articles coverage form

    Equipment dealers form

    Film coverage form

    Floor plan coverage form

    Jewelers block coverage form

    Mail coverage form

    Physicians and surgeons equipment
        coverage form

    Signs coverage form

Theatrical property coverage form

Valuable papers and records coverage form

- Nonfiled inland marine forms include the following:

    Annual transit policy

    Trip transit policy

    Bailee forms

    Business floaters

    Means of transportation and communication

- A *businessowners policy* is a package policy for small-to medium-sized business firms. It covers the building, business personal property, loss of business income, extra expenses, and business liability exposures. Optional coverages are available for outdoor signs, money and securities, employee dishonesty, and mechanical breakdown.

KEY CONCEPTS AND TERMS

Annual transit policy
Bailee
Builders risk coverage
   form
Building and personal
   property coverage
   form
Business floater
Business income (and
   extra expense) coverage
   form
Business income
   insurance
Businessowners policy
   (BOP)
Cargo insurance
Causes-of-loss forms
   (basic, broad,
   special)
Collision liability clause
   (running down
   clause)
Commercial package
   policy (CPP)
Condominium association
   coverage form
Condominium commercial
   unit-owners coverage
   form

Difference in conditions
   (DIC) insurance
Equipment breakdown
   protection coverage
   form
Extra expense coverage
   form
Freight insurance
General average
Hull insurance
Implied warranties
Inland marine
   insurance
Means of transportation
   and communication
Nationwide marine
   definition
Ocean marine insurance
Package policy
Particular average
Perils of the sea
Protection and indemnity
   (P&I) insurance
Reporting form
Trip transit policy

REVIEW QUESTIONS

1. a. What is a package policy?
   b. Explain the advantages of a commercial package policy to a business firm as compared to the purchase of separate policies.

2. Identify the causes of loss that are covered under the following forms:
   a. Causes-of-loss basic form
   b. Causes-of-loss broad form
   c. Causes-of-loss special form

3. Explain the following provisions in the *building and personal property coverage form*:
   a. Covered property
   b. Additional coverages
   c. Optional coverages

4. The *business income (and extra expense) coverage form* contains a number of policy provisions. Explain the following provisions:
   a. Business income loss
   b. Coverage of extra expenses

5. Briefly describe the following commercial property insurance coverages:
   a. Builders risk insurance
   b. Condominium insurance
   c. Equipment breakdown insurance
   d. Difference in conditions (DIC) insurance

6. Explain the following ocean marine insurance coverages:
   a. Hull insurance
   b. Cargo insurance
   c. Protection and indemnity (P&I) insurance
   d. Freight insurance

7. a. What is the difference between a particular average loss and a general average loss in ocean marine insurance?
   b. What conditions must be fulfilled to have a general average loss?

8. Identify the major types of commercial property that can be insured under an inland marine insurance policy.

9. Briefly describe the following inland marine coverages:
   a. Accounts receivable coverage form
   b. Valuable papers and records coverage form
   c. Bailees customer policy

10. A *businessowners policy* (BOP) contains a number of coverages. Explain the following:

a. Coverage of buildings
b. Coverage of business personal property
c. Covered causes of loss
d. Additional coverages provided by the BOP

APPLICATION QUESTIONS

1. Michael owns a television repair shop that is insured under a commercial package policy. The policy includes the *building and personal property coverage form* and the *causes-of-loss broad form*. The declarations page indicates that coverage applies to both the building and the named insured's business property. Explain whether or not the following losses would be covered under his policy.
   a. A fire occurs on the premises, and the building is badly damaged.
   b. A burglar steals some money and securities from an unlocked safe.
   c. A business computer and fax machine are damaged by vandals who break into the shop after business hours.
   d. A tornado touched down near the store. Several television sets of customers in the shop for repair were damaged in the storm.

2. Never-Die Battery manufactures batteries for industrial and consumer use. The company purchased a commercial package policy (CPP) to cover its property exposures. In addition to common policy conditions and declarations, the policy contains a *building and personal property coverage form and an equipment breakdown protection coverage form*. The policy also contains the *causes-of-loss broad form*. With respect to each of the following losses, indicate whether or not the loss is covered.
   a. An explosion occurred that damaged the building where finished batteries are stored.
   b. Because of the explosion, the company incurred expenses for special delivery of replacement parts for machines used to manufacture the batteries.
   c. The explosion injured several employees who received emergency treatment at a local hospital.
   d. An automatic sprinkler system accidentally discharged in the finished goods building. Some recently manufactured batteries were ruined because of water damage and corrosion.

3. Ashley owns a retail shoe store that is insured for $120,000 under the *business income (and extra*

expense) coverage form. Because of a fire, Ashley was forced to close the store for three months. Based on past and projected future earnings, Ashley expected the store to earn a net income of $30,000 during the three-month shutdown period if the loss had not occurred. During the shutdown period, there were no revenues, and Ashley had continuing expenses of $10,000. How much will Ashley recover for the business income loss? Explain your answer.

4. a. Janet is the risk manager of Daily News, a daily publication in a highly competitive market. She wants to be certain that the newspaper will continue to be published if the company's printing facilities are damaged or destroyed by a covered cause of loss. What type of insurance can Janet purchase to cover the added cost of continuing to print the paper after a physical damage loss has occurred?
   b. James opened a book store in a mall. His store was located between a theater and a department store. James counts on the theater and department store to generate walk-in business for his store. James knows that if either of the other businesses closes, his store would incur a substantial financial loss. What type of insurance can James purchase to cover this type of loss exposure?

5. The *Mary Queen,* an ocean-going oil tanker, negligently collided with a large freighter. The *Mary Queen* is insured by an ocean marine hull insurance policy with a running down clause. For each of the following losses, explain whether the ocean marine coverage would apply to the loss.
   a. Damage to the *Mary Queen*
   b. Damage to the freighter
   c. Death or injury to the crew members on the freighter

6. An Ocean Transfer cargo ship was forced to jettison some cargo in a severe ocean storm. The various interests in the voyage at the time the property was jettisoned are the following:

Value of the ship	$4.0 million
Value of iron ore	$2.0 million
Value of lumber and wood chips	$2.0 million

Assume the captain must jettison iron ore valued at $800,000. What is the amount that Ocean Transfer must pay under the principle of a general average loss? Explain your answer.

7. The value of business personal property at Jennifer's business fluctuates periodically, which is due largely to fluctuations in the value of inventory on hand. Jennifer's property insurance policy requires the periodic reporting of business personal property. The limit of insurance is $500,000. Jennifer believes she can save money by underreporting the value of inventory. Last period, she reported only $200,000 when the actual value was $400,000. Shortly after filing the last report, the value of the inventory increased to $500,000. The inventory was totally destroyed when a fire occurred. Ignoring any deductible, what is the amount that Jennifer's insurer will pay? Explain your answer.

8. Richard owns and operates a small furniture store. In addition to Richard, the firm employs two sales representatives. Richard's agent advises him that the store can be insured under a *businessowners policy* (BOP). Identify the various loss exposures to Richard's furniture store that can be covered by a businessowners policy.

INTERNET RESOURCES

- **A. M. Best Company** is an organization that rates insurers and publishes books and periodicals relating to the insurance industry, including property and liability insurance. Visit the site at

  http://www.ambest.com

- The **American Association of Insurance Services** is an insurance organization that develops policy forms, manual rules, and rating information used by more than 600 property and casualty insurers in the United States. Visit the site at

  http://www.aaisonline. com

- The **American Insurance Association** is a trade and service organization for property and liability insurers that provides a forum for discussing problems as well as safety, promotional, and legislative issues. Visit the site at

  http://www.aiadc.org

- The **Independent Insurance Agents & Brokers of America** sponsors a site that provides a considerable amount of information on commercial property and liability insurance. The site is designed for agents, risk managers, and consumers. Visit the site at

  http://www.independentagent.com

- The **Insurance Institute for Highway Safety/Highway Loss Data Institute** is a nonprofit organization that compiles, processes, and provides the public with insurance data on human and economic losses resulting from highway accidents. Visit the site at

  http://www.iihs.org

- The **Insurance Information Institute** is a primary source of information, analysis, and referral on subjects dealing with property and liability insurance. Visit the site at

  http://www.iii.org

- The **Inland Marine Underwriters Association** provides a forum for discussing common problems encountered by inland marine insurers. Visit the site at

  http://www.imua.org

- The **Insurance Services Office (ISO)** provides statistical information, actuarial analysis, policy language, and technical information to participants in property and liability insurance markets. ISO has drafted a considerable number of commercial property forms, as discussed in this chapter. Visit the site at

  http://www.iso.com

- The **Insurance Research Council** is a division of the American Institute for CPCU. It provides the public and the insurance industry with timely research information relating to property and liability insurance. Visit the site at

  http://www.ircweb.org

- The **Property Casualty Insurers Association of America— PCI** is the nation's premier trade association of property and casualty insurers. Established in 2004 by a merger of the Alliance of American Insurers (Alliance) and the National Association of Independent Insurers (NAII), PCI advocates the public policy position of its members on important issues and provides members with targeted industry information. Visit the site at

  http://www.pciaa.net/sitehome.nsf/main

- The **Risk and Insurance Management Society (RIMS)** is the premier organization of corporate risk managers that makes known to insurers the insurance needs of business and industry, supports loss prevention, and provides a forum for discussing common objectives and problems. RIMS also publishes *Risk Management Magazine.* Visit the site at

http://www.rims.org

SELECTED REFERENCES

Commercial Insurance Fact Book 2006. New York: Insurance Information Institute, 2006.

Fire, Casualty & Surety Bulletins, Fire and Marine volume. Erlanger, KY: National Underwriter Company. The various commercial coverages are discussed in the Commercial Property section, Business Income section, Inland Marine section, and Boiler & Machinery section.

Flitner, Arthur L., and Arthur E. Brunck. *Ocean Marine Insurance,* 2nd ed., vols. 1 and 2. Malvern, PA: Insurance Institute of America, 1992.

Flitner, Arthur L., and Jerome Trupin. *Commercial Insurance,* 1st ed., 5th printing. Malvern, PA: American Institute for Chartered Property Casualty Underwriters/ Insurance Institute of America, March 2005.

The CPCU Handbook of Insurance Policies, 6th ed. Malvern, PA: American Institute for CPCU/Insurance Institute of America, 2005.

Trupin, Jerome, and Arthur L. Flitner. *Commercial Property Risk Management and Insurance,* 7th ed. Malvern, PA: American Institute for CPCU/Insurance Institute of America, 2003.

NOTES

1. This chapter is based on *Fire, Casualty & Surety Bulletins,* Fire and Marine volume, Commercial Property section (Erlanger, KY: National Underwriter Company); Arthur L. Flitner and Jerome Trupin, *Commercial Insurance,* 1st ed., 5th printing (Malvern, PA: American Institute for Chartered Property Casualty Underwriters/Insurance Institute of America, March 2005); Jerome Trupin and Arthur L. Flitner, *Commercial Property Risk Management and Insurance,* 6th ed., (Malvern, PA: American Institute for Chartered Property Casualty Underwriters/Insurance Institute of America, 2001); and *The CPCU Handbook of Insurance Policies,* 6th ed. (Malvern, PA: American Institute for Chartered Property Casualty Underwriters/Insurance Institute of America, 2005). The author also drew on the various copyrighted commercial property and liability forms of the Insurance Services Office (ISO). The forms are used with the permission of ISO.

2. This section is based on *Fire, Casualty & Surety Bulletins,* Fire and Marine volume, Business Income section (Erlanger: KY: National Underwriter Company); and Flitner and Trupin, ch. 4.

3. Flitner and Trupin , p. 4.22.

4. DIC insurance is discussed in detail in Trupin and Flitner, *Commercial Property Risk Management and Insurance,* 6th ed., pp. 7.24–7.30.

5. William H. Rodda et al., *Commercial Property Risk Management and Insurance,* 2nd ed., vol. 1 (Malvern: PA: American Institute for Property and Liability Underwriters, 1983), pp. 221–222.

6. Transportation insurance is discussed in detail in *Fire, Casualty & Surety Bulletins,* Fire and Marine volume, Inland Marine section; Trupin and Flitner, ch. 10; and Philip Gordis, *Property and Casualty Insurance,* 33rd ed. (Indianapolis, IN: Rough Notes Co., 1995), chs. 16 and 20. The author drew on these sources in preparing this section.

7. Gordis, pp. 336–337.

8. Flitner and Trupin, p. 7.9

9. The businessowners policy is discussed in *Fire, Casualty & Surety Bulletins,* Fire and Marine volume, Commercial Property section; Flitner and Trupin, ch. 11.

Students may take a self-administered test on this chapter at www.aw-bc.com/rejda

CHAPTER 26

COMMERCIAL LIABILITY INSURANCE

"The litigious nature of American society is a risk that can impact a company's bottom line. Liability insurance is a key tool for managing this risk."

William B. Hedrick,
Senior Vice President, Marsh USA, Inc.

David, age 38, is the owner of Modern Electric, which specializes in the installation of new electrical systems that conserve energy. The firm employs five electricians. On one residential job, a company electrician improperly installed an electrical outlet, which shorted out and caused a major fire in a new house under construction. The property damage exceeded $50,000. David is fearful that the company may be sued for the property damage. When David reported the loss to his insurance agent, the agent assured David that the company's general liability policy would cover any liability suits arising out of the incident.

In the above case, David's company faced a possible lawsuit for the property damage caused by an employee. Business firms today often operate in highly competitive markets where suits for bodily injury and property damage are common. The suits range from small nuisance claims to multimillion-dollar demands. Firms are sued because of defective products, injuries to customers, damage to others' property, pollution of the environment, sexual harassment, discrimination against employees, and numerous other reasons. Commercial liability insurance can provide firms with the protection needed to deal with these loss exposures.

This chapter discusses the major liability loss exposures of business firms and the commercial coverages available for insuring these exposures. Topics covered include the commercial general liability (CGL) policy, the employment practices liability policy, workers compensation and employers liability policy, and other commercial liability coverages.

GENERAL LIABILITY LOSS EXPOSURES

General liability refers to legal liability arising out of business operations other than auto or aviation accidents and employee injuries. A business firm typically purchases a commercial general liability (CGL) policy to cover its general liability loss exposures. Important general liability loss exposures include the following:

- Premises and operations liability
- Products liability
- Completed operations liability
- Contractual liability
- Contingent liability

Premises and Operations Liability

Legal liability can arise out of the *ownership and maintenance of the premises* where the firm does business. Firms are legally required to maintain the premises in a safe condition and are responsible for the actions of their employees. Customers in a store legally are considered to be *invitees*, and the highest degree of care is owed to them. The customers must be warned and protected against any dangerous condition on the premises. For example, a firm may be held liable if a customer slips on a wet floor and breaks a leg.

Legal liability can also arise out of the firm's operations, either on or off the premises. For example, employees unloading lumber in a lumberyard may accidentally damage a customer's truck, or a construction worker on a high-rise building may carelessly drop a tool that injures a pedestrian.

Products Liability

Products liability *refers to the legal liability of manufacturers, wholesalers, and retailers to persons who are injured or incur property damage from defective products.* Firms can be successfully sued on the basis of negligence, breach of warranty, and strict liability. These topics were discussed earlier in Chapter 19, and additional treatment is not needed here.

Completed Operations Liability

Completed operations liability *refers to liability arising out of faulty work performed away from the premises after the work or operation is completed.* Contractors, plumbers, electricians, repair shops, and similar firms can be held liable for bodily injuries and property damage to others after their work is completed. When the work is in progress, it is part of the operations exposure. However, after the work is completed, it is a completed operations exposure. For example, a hot water tank may explode if it is improperly installed, or ductwork in a supermarket may collapse and injure a customer because of improper installation.

A general liability policy provides coverage for both products liability and completed operations. Both products liability and completed operations loss exposures are now included in a definition called **products-completed operations hazard.** *The policy covers liability losses that occur away from the premises and arise out of the insured's product or work after the insured has relinquished possession of the product or the work has been completed.* For example, assume that a gas furnace is improperly installed, and an explosion occurs one month later. The installer's liability is insured under the products-completed operations coverage.

Contractual Liability

Contractual liability *means that the business firm agrees by a written or oral contract to assume the legal liability of another party.* For example, a manufacturing firm rents a building, and the lease specifies that the building owner is to be held harmless for any liability arising out of use of the building. Thus, by a written lease, the manufacturing firm assumes some potential legal liability that ordinarily would be the owner's responsibility.

Contingent Liability

Contingent liability *refers to liability arising out of work done by independent contractors.* As a general rule, business firms are not legally liable for work done by independent contractors. However, a firm can be held liable if (1) the activity is illegal, (2) the situation or type of work does not permit delegation of authority, or (3) the work done by the independent contractor is inherently dangerous.[1] For example, a general contractor may hire a subcontractor to perform a blasting operation. If someone is injured by the blast, the general contractor can be held liable even though the subcontractor is primarily responsible.

Other Liability Loss Exposures

Because of various exclusions, CGL policies do not cover all liability loss exposures of business firms. Other important loss exposures include (1) liability arising out of the ownership or use of autos, aircraft, or watercraft; (2) occupational injury or disease to employees; (3) suits by employees alleging sexual harassment, discrimination, failure to hire or promote, and other employment-related practices; (4) professional liability; and (5) directors and officers liability. Specialized coverages are available for insuring these exposures. We discuss these coverages later in the chapter.

COMMERCIAL GENERAL LIABILITY POLICY

The **commercial general liability (CGL) policy** is widely used by business firms to cover their general liability loss exposures. The CGL policy has two coverage forms: an occurrence form and a claims-made form. The following section discusses both forms of the CGL policy drafted by the Insurance Services Office (ISO).[2] Discussion is based on the latest version of the CGL (December 2004 edition).

Overview of the CGL Occurrence Policy

The CGL occurrence policy can be written alone or as part of a commercial package policy. The occurrence form contains five major sections:

- Section I—Coverages
  Coverage A: Bodily injury and property damage liability
  Coverage B: Personal and advertising injury liability
  Coverage C: Medical payments
  Supplementary payments: Coverages A and B
- Section II—Who Is an Insured?
- Section III—Limits of Insurance
- Section IV—Commercial General Liability Conditions
- Section V—Definitions

Section I—Coverages

Section I provides coverage for bodily injury and property damage liability, personal and advertising injury liability, medical payments, and certain supplementary payments.

Coverage A: Bodily Injury and Property Damage Liability The insurer agrees to pay on behalf of the insured all sums up to the policy limits that the insured is legally obligated to pay because of **bodily injury or property damage** to which the insurance applies. The bodily injury or property damage must be caused by an occurrence. An **occurrence** *is defined as an accident, including continuous or repeated exposure to substantially the same general harmful conditions.* For example, an explosion occurs in a store, and several customers are injured, or a meat company processes a batch of contaminated hamburger, and over a period of time several persons become violently ill. These incidents would be considered occurrences and would be covered by the CGL.

In addition, the current CGL policy contains a provision for a known loss. Under this provision, coverage does not apply when a loss is known or is apparent before the policy's inception date, such as a loss in progress. Bodily injury or property damage is covered only if (1) it is caused by an occurrence during the policy period, and (2) no insured or employee authorized to receive notice of an occurrence or claim knew prior to the policy inception date that the bodily injury or property damage had occurred in whole or in part. For example, if an insured knew that prior to the policy period, actions by the firm were causing bodily injury or property damage, any bodily injury or property damage claims arising out of the known occurrence would not be covered.

Defense Costs The insurer also pays legal defense costs. The insurer has the right to investigate a claim or suit and settle it at its discretion. The insurer's duty to defend ends when the applicable limits of insurance are paid out in a judgment or settlement. Legal defense costs are generally paid in addition to the policy limits. The insurer has a vested interest in making certain that the suit is defended properly.

Exclusions A lengthy list of exclusions applies to both bodily injury and property damage liability. Major exclusions include the following:

- *Expected or intended injury.* Bodily injury or property damage that is expected or intended by the insured is not covered. However, the exclusion does not apply to bodily injury that results from the use of reasonable force to protect persons or property.
- *Contractual liability.* The policy excludes liability assumed by a contract or agreement. However, the exclusion does not apply to liability that the insured would have in the absence of the contract or agreement. The exclusion also does not apply to liability assumed under an *insured contract.* An insured contract refers to a lease of the premises, a sidetrack agreement, an easement or license agreement, an obligation to indemnify a municipality, an elevator maintenance agreement, or a tort liability assumption (liability imposed by law in the absence of any contract or agreement) for bodily injury and property damage.
- *Liquor liability.* The exclusion applies only to firms in the business of manufacturing, distributing, selling, serving, or furnishing alcohol. For example, if a bartender continues to serve a drunken customer who injures another person, the bar owner is not covered for any claim or suit. However, the liquor exclusion does not

apply to firms that are not in the liquor business. For example, an insured that serves drinks at a company-sponsored party would be covered. Coverage can be obtained by firms in the liquor manufacturing and distribution business by adding the liquor liability coverage form to the policy.

- *Workers compensation.* Any legal obligation of the insured to pay benefits under a workers compensation law or similar law is excluded.
- *Employers liability.* The policy excludes liability for bodily injury to an employee arising out of and in the course of employment. It also excludes a claim by a spouse or close relative who is seeking damages as a result of a job-related injury to an employee of the insured. For example, a suit by a spouse who seeks damages for the loss of consortium (loss of companionship, affection, and comfort) following a work-related injury is not covered.
- *Pollution exclusion.* Chemical, manufacturing, and other firms may pollute the environment with smoke, fumes, acids, toxic chemicals, waste materials, and other pollutants. Leaking underground storage tanks can also damage the environment. The CGL policy excludes bodily injury or property damage arising out of the discharge or seepage of pollutants. The exclusion also applies to cleanup costs incurred because of a government order. There are several exceptions to the pollution exclusion, which go beyond the scope of the text to discuss. Pollution coverage can be obtained by a pollution endorsement or by adding a separate pollution liability coverage form to the policy
- *Aircraft, auto, and watercraft exclusion.* Liability arising out of the ownership or operation of aircraft, autos, and watercraft is specifically excluded. The intent here is to exclude legal liability that should be covered by other policies. The exclusion does not apply to watercraft while ashore on premises owned or rented by the insured and to nonowned watercraft less than 26 feet in length and not used to carry people or property for a fee. In addition, the exclusion does not apply to bodily injury to customers resulting from parking autos on the premises or next to the premises, which is important for firms that park the cars of cus-

tomers. However, physical damage to the car being parked is not covered because of the care, custody, or control exclusion (discussed later).

- *Mobile equipment.* Mobile equipment is not covered when the equipment is (a) being transported by an insured's auto or (b) used in or in preparation for any racing, speed, or demolition contest, or in any stunting activity. For example, a bulldozer is excluded while being transported to a job site on a trailer.
- *War.* Bodily injury or property damage due to war is specifically excluded. War is defined to include civil war, insurrection, rebellion, or revolution.
- *Damage to property.* The CGL policy excludes property owned, rented, or occupied by the insured, premises that the insured sells or abandons, property loaned to the named insured, and personal property in the insured's care, custody, or control. Other excluded losses are property damage to that particular part of real property on which the insured, contractors, or subcontractors are working and part of any property that must be restored, repaired, or replaced because the insured's work is performed incorrectly.
- *Property damage to the insured's product.* The policy excludes **property damage to the insured's product** if the damage results from a defect in the product. For example, a defective hot water tank may explode. The damage to the tank itself is not covered. However, the insured's liability for the explosion damage to other property would be covered under the manufacturer's liability policy.
- *Property damage to the insured's work.* The policy also excludes **property damage to the insured's work** that is included in the "products-completed operations hazard." The insured's work refers to the work or operations of the insured as well as material, parts, and equipment used in the work. For example, an employee of a heating contractor may improperly install a gas furnace that later explodes after it was installed. Although the property damage to the customer's building is covered, the value of the employee's work is specifically excluded. The exclusion does not apply if the work is performed by a subcontractor on behalf of the insured.

- *Property damage to impaired property*. The policy also excludes **property damage to impaired property** that is not physically damaged. If property is impaired because of a defect in the insured's product or work, or failure to perform, the loss is not covered. Impaired property is tangible property that cannot be used or is less useful because (1) it incorporates the insured's product or work, or (2) the insured fails to perform the terms of a contract or agreement, and (3) the property can be restored to use by correction of the insured's product or work or fulfillment of the contract. For example, assume that the insured manufactures airplane parts, and a faulty part causes several jets to be grounded. The planes are considered impaired property. The loss of use of the jets is not covered by the insured's CGL policy.
- *Recall of products*. Damages and expenses arising out of the recall of defective products are also excluded. In recent years, firms have incurred substantial losses in recalling defective products such as autos, drugs, or food products. The CGL specifically excludes such losses.
- *Personal and advertising injury*. Coverage A does not apply to bodily injury arising out of personal and advertising injury. For example, Coverage A would not apply to a customer who is falsely arrested for shoplifting and later submits a claim that he or she was physically injured in the same incident. (However, there would be coverage for the incident under Coverage B—Personal and Advertising Injury Liability.)
- *Electronic data*. The CGL excludes damages arising out of the loss, loss of use, damage, corruption, inability to access, or inability to manipulate electronic data. The CGL excludes liability for electronic data, which is not considered tangible property for purposes of property damage liability insurance.

Fire Damage Coverage   The final provision under Coverage A is a statement that certain exclusions in the preceding list (technically exclusions c. through n.) do not apply to fire damage to premises rented to the named insured or temporarily occupied by the named insured with the permission of the owner. This coverage is also known as **fire legal liability coverage.** A separate limit of insurance applies to this coverage. For example, assume that the named insured rents a building, and an employee negligently starts a fire. We noted earlier that legal liability arising out of property rented to or occupied by the named insured would not be covered. However, the exclusion does not apply to fire damage coverage. Thus, if the named insured is sued by the landlord for the fire damage, he or she has coverage under the CGL policy.

Coverage B: Personal and Advertising Injury Liability
Under this coverage, the insurer agrees to pay those sums that the insured is legally obligated to pay as damages because of personal and advertising injury. This term is defined in the policy and includes the following:

- False arrest, detention, or imprisonment
- Malicious prosecution
- Wrongful eviction or entry
- Oral or written publication that slanders or libels
- Oral or written publication that violates a person's right to privacy
- Use of another's advertising idea in your advertisement
- Infringing upon another's copyright, slogan, or trade dress (total image and appearance of a product, including graphics, size, and shape)

For example, if a customer is falsely arrested for stealing, coverage applies if the firm is sued. Likewise, if a marketing manager uses an ad based on advertising ideas owned by an outside ad agency, coverage applies if the firm is sued.

Coverage C: Medical Payments   Medical payments cover the medical expenses of persons who are injured in an accident on the premises or on ways next to the premises, or as a result of the insured's operations. The medical expenses must be incurred within one year of the accident and are paid without regard to legal liability. For example, if a customer falls on a slippery floor in a supermarket, the medical expenses are covered up to the policy limits.

The insured does not have to be legally liable for medical payments coverage to apply. The insurance limit for this coverage is relatively low in comparison with the limits for Coverage A and Coverage B.

Supplementary Payments: Coverages A and B Certain supplementary payments are included under Coverages A and B in addition to the policy limits:

- All expenses incurred by the insurer
- Up to $250 for the cost of a bail bond because of an accident or traffic violation arising out of the use of a vehicle to which the insurance applies
- Cost of bonds to release attachments
- Actual loss of earnings by the insured up to $250 a day because of time off from work
- All costs taxed against the insured in the suit such as court costs
- Prejudgment interest
- All interest that accrues after entry of the judgment (postjudgment interest)

Section II—Who Is an Insured?

The CGL policy can be used to insure a variety of individuals and organizations. If designated in the declarations, insureds include the following:

- Owner and spouse if a sole proprietorship
- Partners, members, and their spouses if a partnership or joint venture
- Members and managers if a limited liability company
- Officers, directors, and stockholders if a corporation

- A trust and trustees, but only with respect to their duties as trustees

The following are also insured under the policy:

- Volunteer workers, but only while performing duties related to the named insured's business
- Employees acting within the scope of their employment
- Any person or organization acting as a real estate manager
- A legal representative if the named insured should die
- Any newly acquired or formed organization, other than a partnership, joint venture, or limited liability company

Section III—Limits of Insurance

The limits of insurance state the maximum amount that the insurer will pay regardless of the number of insureds, claims made or suits brought, or persons or organization making such claims or bringing suits. Several limits apply (see Exhibit 26.1).

1. *General aggregate limit.* This limit is the maximum amount that the insurer will pay for the sum of the following: damages under Coverage A (except bodily injury and property damage included in the "products-completed operations

EXHIBIT 26.1
Illustration of the CGL Limits of Insurance

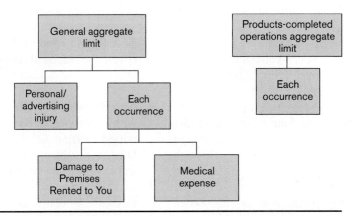

SOURCE: Adapted with permission from International Risk Management Institute, Inc. *Commercial Liability Insurance*, vol. 1, p. IV.E 14. Copyright 1994.

hazard"); damages under Coverage B; and medical expenses under Coverage C.

2. *Products-completed operations aggregate limit.* This limit is the maximum amount that the insurer will pay under Coverage A because of bodily injury and property damage included in the "products-completed operations hazard."

3. *Personal and advertising injury limit.* This limit is the maximum amount that the insurer will pay under Coverage B for personal injury and advertising injury.

4. *Each-occurrence limit.* This limit is the maximum amount that the insurer will pay for the sum of all damages under Coverage A and the medical expenses under Coverage C arising out of any one occurrence.

5. *Damage to rented premises.* This limit is the maximum amount that the insurer will pay for damages under Coverage A for property damage to rented premises from a single fire.

6. *Medical expense limit.* This limit is the maximum amount that the insurer will pay under medical expenses because of a bodily injury sustained by any one person.

Section IV—Commercial General Liability Conditions

This section states the various conditions that apply to the general liability coverage form. The conditions include provisions dealing with bankruptcy; duties in the event of an occurrence, claim, or suit; legal action against the insurer; other insurance; premium audit; and numerous additional conditions. However, space limitations preclude a discussion of these conditions here.

Section V—Definitions

This section in the CGL policy defines more precisely the various terms used in the policy. Numerous definitions are stated in some detail. However, space limitations preclude a discussion of these definitions here.

Overview of the CGL Claims-Made Policy

The Insurance Services Office (ISO) also offers a claims-made policy, which is similar to the occurrence policy with the major exceptions of payment of claims on a claims-made basis, inclusion of an extended reporting period (Section V), and moving the definitions to Section VI.

Meaning of "Claims-Made" An occurrence policy is one that covers claims arising out of occurrences that take place during the policy period, regardless of when the claim is made. In contrast, the **claims-made policy** *covers only claims that are first reported during the policy period, provided the event occurred after the retroactive date (if any) stated in the policy.* The retroactive date is an extremely important concept that is discussed later.

To illustrate the difference between the two concepts, assume a building contractor purchased an occurrence policy three years ago, and the policy has been kept in force up to the present time. The contractor replaces the occurrence policy with a claims-made policy. If the contractor were sued because of a defect in a building constructed three years earlier, the occurrence policy would cover the claim. However, assuming no retroactive coverage, the claims-made policy would not cover the loss because it occurred prior to the inception date of the policy.

Rationale for Claims-Made Policies Insurers have developed claims-made policies as an alternative to occurrence policies because of the problem of **long-tail claims.** The long-tail refers to a relatively small number of claims that are reported years after the policy was first written. Under an occurrence policy, the insurer that provided coverage when the incident occurred was responsible for the claim. As a result, insurers had to pay claims on policies that expired years earlier. This problem made it difficult for actuaries to estimate accurately the correct premiums to charge and the correct loss reserve to establish for incurred but not yet reported (IBNR) claims. Under a claims-made policy, premiums, losses, and loss reserves can be estimated with greater accuracy.

Retroactive Date A claims-made policy can be written to cover events that occur prior to the inception of the policy. Coverage will depend on the retroactive date, if any, inserted in the policy. To be covered, the occurrence must take place after the retroactive date, and the claim must be reported during the current policy term. If the occurrence takes place before the retroactive date, the claims-made policy will not respond.

For example, assume that the retroactive date is the date of the original claims-made policy. The issue date of the original claims-made policy is January 1, 2004. The most recent claims-made policy is issued on January 1, 2007. The insured would be covered for all occurrences that take place after January 1, 2004, and are reported during the current policy period.

Extended Reporting Periods   The claims-made policy also contains a provision that extends the period for reporting claims. *The purpose is to provide coverage under an expired claims-made policy for claims first reported after the policy expires.* The extended reporting period does not extend the period of protection. To be covered, the injury must occur after the retroactive date but before the end of the policy period. Injuries that occur before the retroactive date or after the policy expires are not covered.

The **basic extended reporting period** is automatically provided without an extra charge whenever one of the following occurs:

- The policy is canceled or not renewed.
- The insurer renews or replaces the policy with a retroactive date that is later than the retroactive date in the original policy.
- The claims-made policy is replaced with an occurrence policy.

The basic extended reporting period provides for two separate reporting periods or "tails." The first tail is a five-year period after the policy expires; the second tail is a 60-day period after the expiration date.

The five-year tail applies to claims arising out of an occurrence reported to the company during the policy period or no later than 60 days after the end of the policy period. (However, the occurrence must take place during the policy period or after the retroactive date.) For example, assume that a customer in a supermarket slips and falls on a wet floor during the policy period. The insured reports the occurrence promptly to the company, but no actual claim is made against the insured during the policy period. Any resulting claim arising out of that reported occurrence is covered by the expired policy if the claim is made before the end of the five-year period.

The second tail of 60 days applies to all other claims; these claims result from occurrences that take place during the policy period (or after the retroactive date), but are not reported to the insurer during the policy period. Coverage applies if the occurrence is reported to the insurer within 60 days after the policy expires. For example, referring back to our earlier example, the insured may have been unaware that the customer fell, so the incident was not reported to the company. However, if a claim is made against the insured after the policy expires, coverage applies if the occurrence is reported to the insurer within 60 days after the expiration date.

If the insured wants a longer reporting period after the policy expires, the supplemental extended reporting period can be added by an endorsement and payment of an additional premium. The insured must request the endorsement in writing within 60 days after the policy expires.

EMPLOYMENT-RELATED PRACTICES LIABILITY INSURANCE

Employers are frequently sued by employees and potential employees because of wrongful termination, discrimination, sexual harassment, failure to promote, failure to hire, and other employment-related practices. In recent years, the number of such suits has increased substantially, and the median awards for damages have also increased. The median award increased from $114,248 in 1995 to $218,133 in 2004, or a sharp increase of 91 percent.[3] General liability insurance policies typically exclude or offer limited protection against liability arising out of the employment practices of employers. Many insurers now offer a separate policy or have specific endorsements to deal with these exposures.

ISO makes available an **employment-related practices liability coverage form,** which deals with employment practices loss exposures. The following discussion is based on the ISO form.

Insuring Agreement

Under the ISO form, the insurer agrees to pay damages resulting from an "injury" to which the insurance applies. An *injury,* as defined in the policy, is an injury to an employee arising out of one or more of the following offenses:

- Demotion or failure to promote, negative evaluation, reassignment or discipline of an employee, wrongful refusal to employ
- Wrongful termination of employment, wrongful denial of training or deprivation of career opportunity, breach of employment contract
- Negligent hiring or supervision
- Retaliatory action against employees
- Coercing an employee to commit an unlawful act or omission
- Work related harassment
- Employment-related libel, slander, invasion of privacy, defamation or humiliation
- Other work-related verbal, physical, mental, or emotional abuse, such as discrimination based on race, age, or gender.

Co-Payment

The ISO form includes a co-payment provision that requires the insured to pay part of the damages and legal defense costs up to some maximum limit. For example, assume that the co-payment percentage is 20 percent, and the maximum co-payment charge is $25,000. If actual damages and legal defense costs amount to $100,000, the insured would pay $20,000. If the actual claim is $200,000, the insured would pay a maximum of $25,000.

Legal Defense

The ISO form also provides for a legal defense; however, legal defense costs are included as part of the policy limit. Payment of legal defense costs reduces the amount of insurance available to pay damages.

Note that a claim cannot be settled without the insured's consent. This provision is designed to protect the employer's image and reputation. However, if the insurer works out a settlement with a claimant but the employer refuses to settle, any final settlement above the initial settlement is the employer's responsibility.

Exclusions

The ISO form contains a number of exclusions, which include the following:

- Criminal, fraudulent, or malicious acts
- Contractual liability
- Workers compensation and similar laws
- Violation of laws applicable to employers, such as the Age Discrimination in Employment Act, and the Family and Medical Leave Act of 1993
- Strikes and lockouts of employees

Because of the growing number of sexual harassment suits filed in recent years, interest in employment practices liability insurance is increasing. Most insurers will check an employer's program on sexual harassment very carefully before writing such insurance.

WORKERS COMPENSATION INSURANCE

Millions of workers are injured or become sick each year because of job-related accidents and disease. All states have workers compensation laws that provide benefits to workers who have a job-related injury or occupational disease. Employers can meet their legal obligations to injured workers by purchasing a workers compensation policy, by self-insurance, or by purchasing the coverage from a competitive or monopolistic state fund in some states.

As stated in Chapter 18, workers compensation insurance provides medical care, cash benefits, survivor benefits, and rehabilitation services to workers who are injured or die from job-related accidents or disease. The benefits paid are based on the principle of **liability without fault.** *The employer is held absolutely liable for job-related accidents and disease regardless of fault.* Workers receive benefits according to state law and are not required to sue their employers to receive benefits. The benefits are extremely important to workers who are injured or die as a result of job-related accidents or disease. Insight 26.1 provides some basic facts about workers compensation laws.

This section discusses the current version of the **workers compensation and employers liability insurance policy** drafted by the National Council on Compensation Insurance.[4] The historical development of workers compensation as a form of social insurance was treated earlier in Chapter 18.

INSIGHT 26.1

Basic Facts about Workers Compensation

Workers compensation benefits are payable to workers injured on the job and survivors of workers injured on the job. Workers compensation is the "exclusive remedy" for providing compensation for such injuries or fatalities. To qualify for workers compensation benefits, the injury or fatality must arise out of and in the course of employment. Background and facts about workers compensation:

- It is the nation's oldest social insurance program.
- It is a state-based program that protects injured workers and their survivors against the financial consequences of work-related accidents, disease, and deaths.
- The percentage of the workforce eligible to receive workers compensation benefits is estimated at 97%.
- Workers compensation does not exclude any type of treatment or service. The only coverage criteria are that the injury, illness, or death is work-related, and that the treatment or service provided is reasonable and necessary.
- Generally, employers are mandated by law to provide workers compensation coverage for their employees.
- Workers compensation is financed by employers, either through self-insurance or, more commonly, by securing insurance with an insurer licensed to write workers compensation insurance.

Although state workers compensation programs and laws differ, common features include:

- All state workers compensation laws require payment of all reasonable and necessary medical treatment, at no cost to the worker, with no co-payments or deductibles for as long as necessary to rehabilitate the injured worker, even for life.
- All workers compensation laws also provide tax-free benefits for lost wages, typically at two-thirds of a worker's wage.
- The duration, and sometimes the level of wage loss benefits depends on whether there is any permanent injury and, if so, the extent of permanency.
- All workers compensation laws also provide benefits for the survivors and dependents of workers whose deaths were work-related; these benefits continue for the life of the surviving spouse or until remarriage.
- Dependency benefits are usually provided until at least age 18 but sometimes longer, as in the case of a dependent who's attending college or another educational institution.

SOURCE: Excerpted from American Insurance Association, "Protecting Workers Compensation from Terrorism," *AIA Advocate*, February 10, 2003.

The workers compensation and employers liability policy provides the following coverages:

- Part One: Workers Compensation Insurance
- Part Two: Employers Liability Insurance
- Part Three: Other-States Insurance

Part One: Workers Compensation Insurance

Part One refers to **workers compensation insurance.** Under this section, the insurer agrees to pay all workers compensation benefits and other benefits that the employer must legally provide to covered employees who have a job-related injury or an occupational disease. There are no policy limits for Part One. The insurer instead pays all benefits required by the workers compensation law of any state listed in the declarations.

Under certain conditions, the employer is responsible for payments made by the insurer that exceed regular workers compensation benefits. These

situations generally involve fines or penalties associated with intentional misconduct by the employer. The employer must reimburse the insurer for any payments that exceed regular workers compensation benefits because of the following:

- Serious and willful misconduct by the employer
- Knowingly employing workers in violation of law
- Failure to comply with a health or safety regulation
- Discharge, coercion, or discrimination against any employee in violation of the workers compensation law

Part Two: Employers Liability Insurance

Part Two refers to **employers liability insurance,** which covers employers against lawsuits by employees who are injured in the course of employment, but whose injuries (or disease) are not compensable under the state's workers compensation law. This part is similar to other liability insurance policies where negligence must be established before the insurer is legally obligated to pay.

Employers liability insurance is needed for several reasons. First, a few states do not require workers compensation insurance for smaller employers with fewer than a certain number of employees, such as three or fewer. In such cases, an employer can be covered under the employers liability section if an employee with a work-related injury or disease sues for damages.

Second, an injury or disease that occurs on the job or at the work place may not be considered work related, and, therefore, would not be covered under the state's workers compensation law. However, the injured employee may still believe that the employer should be held accountable, and the employer would be covered if sued.

Third, some state workers compensation laws permit lawsuits by spouses and dependents for the *loss of consortium*. The employer would be covered under Part Two in such a case.

Finally, some employers are confronted with lawsuits because of *third-party over cases*. An injured employee may sue a negligent third party, and the third party, in turn, sues the employer for contributory negligence. The lawsuit would be covered under Part Two (unless the employer assumed the liability of the third party, in which case it may be covered by the employer's CGL policy). For example, assume that a machine is defective, and its operator is injured. In addition to the payment of workers compensation benefits, the state may allow the injured employee to sue the negligent third party. If the injured employee sues the manufacturer of the defective machine, the manufacturer, in turn, could sue the employer for failure to provide proper operating instructions or failure to enforce safety rules. The employer would be covered in such cases.

The employers liability section of the ISO policy also contains several exclusions. Major exclusions include:

- Liability assumed under contract
- Punitive damages because of a bodily injury to an employee who is hired in violation of the law
- Bodily injury to an employee employed in violation of the law

- Obligations imposed on the employer because of a workers compensation, occupational disease, unemployment compensation, or disability benefits law
- Intentional bodily injury caused by the employer
- Bodily injury outside the United States or Canada
- Damages resulting from coercion, demotion, evaluation, reassignment, harassment, discrimination, or termination of any employee
- Bodily injury to any person subject to the Longshore and Harbor Workers Compensation Act
- Bodily injury to any person subject to the Federal Employers Liability Act
- Bodily injury to a master or crew member of any vessel
- Fines or penalties because of violation or federal or state law
- Damages payable under the Migrant and Seasonal Agricultural Worker Protection Act

Part Three: Other-States Insurance

Part Three of the workers compensation and employers liability policy provides **other-states insurance**. Workers compensation coverage (Part One) applies only to those states listed on the information page (declarations page) of the policy. However, the employer may face a workers compensation claim under the law of another state. This possibility could arise if an employee is injured while on a business trip in a state that was not considered when the workers compensation policy was first written, or if the law of a particular state is broadened so that employees are now covered under that state's workers compensation law. Also, the employer's operations may be expanded in a particular state, which brings the employees under the state's workers compensation law.

Other-states insurance applies only if one or more states are shown on the information page of the policy. The information page is the equivalent of a declarations page. *In such cases, if the employer begins work in any of the states listed, the policy applies as if that state were listed in the policy for workers compensation purposes.* Thus, the employer has coverage for any workers compensation benefits that it may have to make under that state's workers compensation law.

In summary, workers compensation insurance is an important commercial coverage that provides considerable economic security to workers who are disabled by a job-related accident or disease. Weekly cash benefits are paid during the period of disability; medical care is unlimited; rehabilitation services and survivor benefits are also available.

In addition, because of experience rating and loss prevention programs, workers compensation programs promote occupational safety and health.

COMMERCIAL AUTO INSURANCE

Legal liability arising out of the ownership and use of cars, trucks, and trailers is another important loss exposure for many firms. This section examines several commercial auto coverages that can be used to meet this exposure.[5]

Business Auto Coverage Form

The ISO **business auto coverage form** (2006 edition) is widely used by business firms to insure their commercial auto exposures. Firms have considerable flexibility with respect to the autos that can be covered. There are 10 numerical classifications, each of which is referred to as a symbol:

1. Any auto
2. Owned autos only
3. Owned private passenger autos only
4. Owned autos other than private passenger autos only
5. Owned autos subject to no-fault plans
6. Owned autos subject to a compulsory uninsured motorists law
7. Specifically described autos
8. Hired autos only
9. Nonowned autos only
19. Mobile equipment subject to compulsory or financial responsibility or other motor vehicle insurance law only

If one or more of the symbols 1 through 6 or 19 are selected, there is automatic coverage on newly acquired autos that the named insured acquires during the policy period. If symbol 7 is used, newly acquired autos are covered only if two conditions are met: (1) the insurer must already cover all autos that the named insured owns for the coverage provided, or the new auto must replace an auto that the named insured previously owned that had such coverage, and (2) the named insured informs the insurer within 30 days after acquisition that he or she wants the auto insured for that coverage.

Liability Insurance Coverage An insured is covered for a bodily injury or property damage claim to which the insurance applies, which is caused by an accident that results from the ownership, maintenance, or use of a covered auto. For example, if an employee drives a company car during the course of employment and injures another motorist, the employer has coverage for any resulting lawsuit. The employee has coverage as well.

The insuring agreement also provides limited coverage for pollution losses. The business auto coverage form has a broad pollution exclusion that excludes liability coverage for almost all pollution losses. However, there are limited exceptions. The insurer will pay all covered pollution cost or expense to which the insurance applies. To be covered, the pollution cost or expense must be caused by an accident that results from the ownership, maintenance, or use of a covered auto. However, the pollution cost or expense is covered only if there is either bodily injury or property damage to which the insurance applies, which is caused by the same accident. For example, a company employee driving a company car may negligently smash into an oil truck on a crowded expressway, which causes the truck to overturn spilling oil over the environment. The cleanup cost that the insured might have to pay is covered.

Finally, the insurer agrees to defend any insured and pay all legal defense costs. Defense costs are in addition to the policy limit. The duty to defend or settle ends when the limit of insurance is exhausted by the payment of judgments or settlements.

Physical Damage Coverage Three physical damage coverages are available to insure covered autos against damage or loss, summarized as follows:

- *Comprehensive coverage.* The insurer will pay for loss to a covered auto or its equipment from any cause except the covered auto's collision with another object or its overturn.
- *Specified causes-of-loss coverage.* As an alternative to comprehensive coverage, only losses from certain specified perils are covered: fire, lightning, or explosion; theft; windstorm, hail, or earthquake; flood; mischief or vandalism; or the sinking, burning, collision, or derailment of any conveyance transporting the covered auto.
- *Collision coverage.* Loss caused by the covered auto's collision with another object or its overturn is covered under this provision.

Coverage for towing and labor costs can be added if desired. The insurer will pay towing and labor costs up to the limit shown in the declarations each time a covered auto of the private passenger type is disabled. However, the labor must be performed at the place of disablement.

In addition, if a damaged covered auto has comprehensive coverage, the coverage applies to glass breakage, to loss caused by hitting a bird or animal, and to loss caused by falling objects or missiles. If glass breakage results from a collision, the insured can elect to have it covered as a collision loss. Without this option, the insured would have to meet two deductibles if both glass breakage and body damage result from the same collision. By treating glass breakage as part of the collision loss, only the collision deductible must be satisfied.

The insurer will also pay up to $20 per day (after 48 hours) up to a maximum of $600 for transportation expenses incurred by the insured because of the total theft of a covered auto of the private passenger type. The coverage applies only to covered autos that are insured for either comprehensive or specified causes-of-loss coverage.

Garage Coverage Form

The **garage coverage form** is a specialized form for auto dealers. Auto dealers include both franchised auto dealers (such as a Chevrolet or Toyota dealer) and nonfranchised dealers (such as a used car dealer).[6] The major coverages include liability coverage, garagekeepers coverage, and physical damage coverage.

Liability Coverage The insurer agrees to pay all sums that an insured must legally pay as damages because of bodily injury or property damage to which this insurance applies caused by an accident in the course of garage operations. *Garage operations* are defined to include garage business locations, autos covered under the form, and all operations necessary or incidental to a garage business. As such, the liability section includes coverage for premises and operations liability, auto liability, incidental contractual liability, and products and completed operations.

The insured has a choice of autos that can be covered, and numerical symbols are used to denote the covered autos, an approach similar to the business auto policy.

The liability section of the garage policy contains numerous exclusions. Because of space constraints, only two of them are discussed here. *First, damage to the property of others in the insured's care, custody, or control is excluded.* Thus, damage to a customer's car on an automobile servicing hoist, or damage to a customer's car while it is being road tested by a mechanic, would not be covered. These common exposures can be covered by adding garagekeepers coverage to the policy.

Second, there is no coverage for property damage to any of the insured's products if the product is defective at the time it is sold. For example, assume that a dealer sells a tire that has a hidden defect. The defective tire later blows out, and the car is damaged in a collision. This exclusion eliminates coverage for the defective tire, but the property damage caused by the defective tire would be covered. The intent of this exclusion is to cover property damage or bodily injury caused by a defective product but not any damage to the product itself.

Garagekeepers Coverage As noted earlier, the garage coverage form excludes coverage for property of others in the care, custody, or control of the insured. Adding garagekeepers coverage to the policy can eliminate this exclusion. The insurer agrees to pay all sums the insured must legally pay as damages for loss to a customer's car left in the insured's care while the insured is attending, servicing, repairing, parking, or storing the vehicle in its garage operations.

Three coverages are available: (1) comprehensive coverage, (2) specified causes of loss coverage, and

(3) collision coverage. These coverages apply only if the insured is legally liable for the loss. For example, if a customer's car were stolen because the dealer carelessly left the garage door unlocked, the loss would be covered. In contrast, if a customer's car were damaged by a tornado, the loss would not be covered because the insured could not be held liable for a tornado. It is possible, however, to broaden the coverage on customers' autos without regard to legal liability by payment of an additional premium. This approach is called direct coverage, which indemnifies customers for their losses even though the garage has no legal liability to do so. The insured checks a box on the declarations page to activate the option.

Physical Damage Coverage   Physical damage insurance on covered autos can also be included in the garage policy. The following three coverages are available:

- *Comprehensive coverage.* The insurer will pay for a loss from any cause except for the covered auto's collision with another object or its overturn.
- *Specified causes of loss coverage.* Covered perils are fire, lightning or explosion, theft, windstorm, hail, earthquake, flood, mischief or vandalism, and the sinking, burning, collision, or derailment of any conveyance transporting the covered auto.
- *Collision coverage.* Loss caused by the covered auto's collision with another object or its overturn is covered under this provision.

AIRCRAFT INSURANCE

Major commercial airlines own fleets of expensive jets, and the liability exposure is enormous. Occasionally, a commercial jet will crash accidentally because of mechanical or human error, killing hundreds of passengers and causing extensive property damage to surrounding buildings. Legal liability losses arising out of the crash of a fully loaded jet airliner can be catastrophic. In addition, many firms own aircraft used for company business. Company planes sometimes crash, resulting in death or bodily

injury to the passengers, as well as death or injury to people on the ground and substantial property damage to surrounding buildings where the crash occurs. Finally, thousands of Americans own or operate small planes, which may crash because of mechanical problems, pilot error, or inexperience.

Most states apply the common-law rules of negligence to aviation accidents. However, some states have absolute or strict liability laws that hold the owners or operators of aircraft absolutely liable for aviation accidents. As a result of international treaties and agreements among countries, absolute liability is also imposed on commercial airlines for aviation accidents that occur during international flights.

Aircraft Insurers

Aircraft insurance is highly specialized and is underwritten by a relatively small number of insurer organizations. Most of the domestic aviation market is accounted for by two multicompany aviation pools: United States Aircraft Insurance Group (USAIG) and Associated Aviation Underwriters (AAU). Both pools underwrite and manage aviation insurance on behalf of the individual insurers that belong to the pool. The two pools account for most of the aviation insurance that is written for commercial airlines, aircraft manufacturers, and large domestic airports.

Aircraft Insurance for Private Business and Pleasure Aircraft

AAU offers a policy designed for the owners and operators of private business and pleasure aircraft. The policy provides physical damage coverage for damage to the aircraft and liability coverage for property damage and bodily injury arising out of the ownership or use of the insured aircraft.[7]

Physical Damage Coverages   A plane on the ground can be damaged by wind, fire, collapse, theft, vandalism, or other perils. While taxiing, the plane can collide with vehicles, buildings, or other aircraft. The most severe exposure is present when the plane is in flight. A plane can collide with another plane; it can be struck by lightning or damaged by turbulent winds; or it can experience mechanical difficulties

COMMERCIAL UMBRELLA POLICY **607**

from a fire or explosion. Planes can also be damaged or destroyed by acts of terrorism.

Physical damage insurance provides coverage for direct damage to the aircraft. The insured has a choice of physical damage coverages. There are three insuring agreements for physical damage to the aircraft:

- *"All-risks" basis.* All physical damage losses to the aircraft, including disappearance, are covered except those losses excluded.
- *"All-risks" basis, not in flight.* The aircraft is covered on an "all-risks" basis only when it is on the ground and not in flight. Fire or explosion following a crash is not covered.
- *"All-risks" basis, not in motion.* The aircraft is covered on an "all-risks" basis only when it is standing still. Fire or explosion after a crash is not covered.

Although aircraft can be covered on an "all-risks" basis, certain exclusions apply. Excluded losses include damage to tires (unless caused by fire, theft, or vandalism), wear and tear, deterioration, mechanical or electrical breakdown, and failure of installed equipment. However, these exclusions do not apply if such physical damage is coincident with and results from the same cause as other loss covered by the policy.

Liability Coverages Three liability coverages are available—bodily injury liability, passenger bodily injury liability, and property damage liability. Separate limits typically apply to each coverage; however, liability insurance for all three coverages can be written as a single limit if desired. In addition, coverage also applies to bodily injury and property damage arising out of the maintenance or use of the premises where the aircraft is stored or parked.

Liability coverage contains several important exclusions. Excluded losses are liability assumed in a contract, workers compensation, and damage to property in the insured's care, custody, and control (except personal effects of passengers up to $3000 and damage to an aircraft hangar or its contents up to $25,000). Also excluded are damage or injury from noise, such as sonic boom, interference with the quiet enjoyment of property, and pollution losses.

COMMERCIAL UMBRELLA POLICY

Because firms are often sued for large amounts, they may seek protection against catastrophic loss exposures not adequately insured under general liability policies. A **commercial umbrella policy** can provide protection against catastrophic liability judgments that might otherwise bankrupt a firm.

Most insurers that write commercial umbrella policies use their own forms. However, the Insurance Services Office (ISO) has designed a standard umbrella policy for commercial firms. The following discussion summarizes the major provisions in the ISO **commercial liability umbrella coverage form.**[8]

Coverages

The ISO commercial umbrella policy pays the ultimate net loss in excess of the retained limit for bodily injury, property damage, and personal and advertising injury to which the insurance applies. The **ultimate net loss** *is the total sum the insured is legally obligated to pay as damages.* The **retained limit** *refers to (1) the available limits of underlying insurance listed in the declarations, or (2) the self-insurance retention, whichever applies.*

If the loss is covered by both an underlying insurance contract and the umbrella policy, the umbrella policy pays only after the underlying limits are exhausted. For example, assume that an umbrella policy has a limit of $5 million. Assume also that the underlying limit under a commercial general liability (CGL) policy is $1 million for each occurrence, and a judgment against the insured amounts to $3 million. The underlying insurance would pay $1 million, and the umbrella policy would pay the remaining $2 million.

If the loss is not covered by any underlying insurance but is covered by the umbrella policy, the insured must satisfy a **self-insured retention (SIR).** The SIR can range from $500 for small firms to $1 million or more for large corporations. For example, assume that a firm's SIR amount is $25,000. A customer in the firm's store who is falsely accused and arrested for shoplifting wins a judgment against the insured in the amount of $100,000. If the loss is not covered by any underlying policy, the insured would pay $25,000. The umbrella policy would pay the remaining $75,000.

Legal defense costs are also paid when the underlying insurance does not provide coverage, or the underlying limits are exhausted.

Required Underlying Coverages

Insureds are required to carry certain minimum amounts of liability insurance before the umbrella insurer will pay any claims. The following underlying coverages and limits are typically required:

Commercial general liability insurance

$1,000,000 (each occurrence)
$2,000,000 (general aggregate)
$2,000,000 (products and completed-operations aggregate)

Business auto liability insurance

$1,000,000 (combined single limit)

Employers liability insurance

$500,000 (bodily injury per accident)
$500,000 (bodily injury by disease per employee)
$500,000 (disease aggregate)

The commercial umbrella policy applies when the loss exceeds the underlying limits.

Exclusions

The ISO commercial umbrella form contains a lengthy list of exclusions. Under bodily injury and property damage liability, losses arising out of the following are excluded:

- Expected or intended injury
- Contractual liability (with certain exceptions)
- Liquor liability
- Any obligation of the insured under a workers compensation or similar law
- Any obligation of the insured under the Employees Retirement Income Security Act (ERISA)

- Any auto that is not a covered auto
- Bodily injury to an employee in the course of employment
- Liability arising out of employment-related practices
- Pollution
- Liability arising out of aircraft or watercraft unless provided by underlying insurance
- Racing activities
- War
- Property in the insured's care, custody, or control
- Damage to your product
- Damage to your work
- Damage to impaired property or property not physically impaired
- Recall of products, work, or impaired property
- Bodily injury arising out of personal and advertising injury
- Liability arising out of professional services
- Electronic data

A lengthy set of exclusions also applies to personal and advertising injury liability. Under personal and advertising injury, claims arising out of the following are not covered:

- Acts caused by or at the direction of the insured with the knowledge that the act would violate the rights of another
- Oral or written publication of material that the insured knows to be false
- Oral or written publication of material whose first publication occurred before the policy period
- Criminal acts of the insured
- Breach of contract except an implied contract to use someone else's idea in your ad
- Failure of the product to perform as stated in the ad
- Wrong description of the price or products
- Infringement of copyright or patent
- An insured whose business is advertising, broadcasting, publishing, or telecasting
- Electronic chatrooms or bulletin boards
- Unauthorized use of another's name or product
- Pollutants
- Employment-related practices, such as failure to hire, harassment, and humiliation
- Professional services

BUSINESSOWNERS POLICY

The ISO businessowners policy (BOP) discussed in Chapter 25 also provides general liability insurance to business firms. The liability coverage is written on an occurrence basis, and, with certain exceptions, it is similar to the commercial general liability coverage (CGL) form discussed earlier.[9] The following discussion is based on the ISO form.

Business Liability

Business liability coverage pays those sums the insured becomes legally obligated to pay as damages because of bodily injury, property damage (including fire damage to rented premises), or personal and advertising injury. For example, if an escalator in a clothing store is defective and a customer is injured, the loss would be covered. Likewise, if a customer in the clothing store is erroneously arrested for shoplifting, any suit for wrongful arrest would be covered.

Medical Expenses

Coverage for medical expenses is also provided. The insured does not have to be legally liable, and medical expenses are paid up to the policy limit regardless of fault. The medical expenses must result from a bodily injury caused by an accident on the premises owned or occupied by the named insured, or on ways next to the premises, or from business operations. Medical bills must be incurred and reported to the insurer within one year from the date of the accident. For example, if a customer slips on a wet floor in a supermarket and is injured, the medical expenses are paid without regard to legal liability up to the medical expense limit.

Legal Defense

The insurer pays the legal costs of defending the insured. The legal costs are paid in addition to the amount that the insurer is legally obligated to pay as damages on the insured's behalf. The duty to defend applies only to claims covered under the policy and ends when the applicable limit of insurance is paid out as judgments, settlements, or medical expenses.

The definition of an insured also includes employees while they are acting in the scope of their employment. This provision protects a negligent employee who might be named in the lawsuit along with the employer.

Exclusions

In general, the BOP business liability coverage exclusions are similar to those in the CGL policy. One important difference, however, deals with professional liability. Although the BOP excludes professional liability, a pharmacist's professional liability endorsement is available to a retail druggist or drugstore. In addition, professional liability endorsements are available for barbers, beauticians, funeral directors, optical and hearing aid establishments, printers, and veterinarians.

PROFESSIONAL LIABILITY INSURANCE

Lawsuits against physicians, attorneys, engineers, and other professionals are common. This section briefly discusses professional liability insurance that provides protection against malpractice lawsuits or lawsuits involving a substantial error or omission.

Physicians Professional Liability Insurance

Professional liability insurance forms are not uniform, and insurers typically use their own forms. Professional liability insurance for physicians can be illustrated by a discussion of the **physicians, surgeons, and dentists professional liability coverage form** drafted by ISO.[10]

- *There are two insuring agreements.* Coverage A covers the individual liability of each person named as an insured on the declaration page. Under Coverage A, the insurer agrees to pay all sums that the insured is legally obligated to pay as damages because of injury to which the insurance applies. The injury must be caused by a medical incident. A *medical incident* is any act or omission that arises out of the providing or failure to provide medical or dental services by the insured, or by any person acting under the personal direction and supervision of the insured. For example, if Dr. Smith operates on a patient and the patient is paralyzed after the operation, any resulting malpractice lawsuit would be covered. Likewise, if the office nurse gives a wrong shot to a patient, and the patient is harmed, Dr. Smith has liability coverage for the incident. However, the nurse is typically not included as an insured under the physician's policy but must secure his or her own professional liability policy. Thus, the nurse is not covered under Dr. Smith's policy for the medical incident unless an endorsement is added to the policy.

Coverage B is an insuring agreement that applies to group liability, which refers to liability arising out of a partnership, limited liability company, association, or professional corporation. For example, if a physician insured under Coverage A is a partner in a medical group, the physician is not insured under Coverage A for any acts of malpractice committed by other partners. Coverage B is required to cover this exposure.

- *Liability is not restricted to accidental acts of the physician or surgeon.* In many cases the physician or surgeon deliberately intends to do a certain act; however, the professional diagnosis or the performance of the act may be faulty, and the patient is injured. For example, Dr. Smith may intend to operate on a patient by using a certain surgical procedure. If the patient is harmed or injured by the operation, Dr. Smith would still be covered for his willful, intentional act to operate in a certain way.

- *There is a maximum limit per medical incident and an aggregate limit for each coverage.* For example, a patient and the patient's family may file separate claims against a physician for damages arising out of the same medical incident. Under current forms, the per-medical-incident limit is the maximum that would be paid for both claims. The aggregate limit is the maximum amount that would be paid as damages during any policy year.

- *Current forms permit the insurer to settle the claim without the physician's or surgeon's consent.* Payment of a claim could be viewed as an admission of guilt. Older forms required the insurer to obtain the physician's consent before a claim could be settled. However, current forms permit the insurer to settle without the physician's consent because an occasional claim

against a physician in certain high-risk categories is not viewed as being overly detrimental to his or her character.

- *An extended reporting period endorsement can be added.* A physician with a claims-made policy may retire, change insurers, or drop the malpractice insurance. To protect the physician, an extended reporting period endorsement can be added, which covers future claims arising out of incidents that occurred during the period in which the claims-made policy was in force.

- *Professional liability insurance is not a substitute for other necessary forms of liability insurance.* General liability insurance is also needed to cover liability arising out of a hazardous condition on the premises or acts of the insured that are not professional in nature. For example, a patient may trip on a torn carpet in the doctor's office and break an arm. The professional liability policy would not cover this event.

In summary, a professional liability policy for physicians and surgeons provides considerable protection. The insurance is expensive, however. Malpractice insurance covering certain high-risk specialties can cost $100,000 or more each year in certain parts of the country. Physicians have responded to the medical malpractice problem by practicing defensive medicine, by abandoning high-risk specialties such as obstetrics and neurosurgery, and by pushing for legislation to limit malpractice awards. As a practical matter, however, a relatively large percentage of medical malpractice claims are groundless. Nevertheless, insurers must still defend the claims, which is expensive and increases the cost of malpractice insurance.

Errors and Omissions Insurance

Some types of professional liability policies are referred to as "error and omissions" policies. **Errors and omissions insurance** provides protection against loss incurred by a client because of negligent acts, errors, or omissions by the insured. Professionals who need errors and omissions insurance include insurance agents and brokers, travel agents, real estate agents, stockbrokers, attorneys, consultants, engineers, architects, and other individuals who give advice to clients. The errors and omissions coverage is designed to meet the needs of each profession.

This type of coverage can be illustrated by the *insurance agents and brokers errors and omissions policy*. The policy has a number of provisions. First, the insurer agrees to pay all sums that the insured is legally obligated to pay because of any negligent act, error, or omission by the insured (or by any other person for whose acts the insured is legally liable) in the conduct of business as general agents, insurance agents, or insurance brokers. For example, assume that Mark is an independent agent who fails to renew a property insurance policy for a client. The policy lapses, and a subsequent loss is not covered. If the client sues for damages, Mark would be covered for the omission. The policy is normally sold with a sizable deductible so that the agent has an incentive to minimize mistakes and errors.

Errors and omissions policies are generally issued on a claims-made basis covering claims made against the agent or broker only because of errors during the current policy period (and after the retroactive date).

Finally, the policy contains relatively few exclusions. However, claims that result from dishonest, fraudulent, criminal, or malicious acts by the insured, libel and slander, bodily injury, and destruction of tangible property are specifically excluded.

DIRECTORS AND OFFICERS LIABILITY INSURANCE

Officers and directors of corporations are increasingly being sued by shareholders, employees, retirees, competing firms, government agencies, and other parties because of alleged mismanagement. **Directors and officers (D&O) liability insurance** provides financial protection for the directors and officers and the corporation if the directors and officers are sued for mismanagement of the company's affairs. Most corporations have bylaws that require the company to bear the financial responsibility of indemnifying directors and officers for claims alleging mismanagement. In addition to covering suits made directly against a company's director and officers, a D&O policy reimburses the company for its costs in indemnifying directors and officers for such suits.

D&O policies are not uniform, but they have certain common features. The following discussion summarizes the major characteristics of D&O policies.

Insuring Agreements Most policies contain the following insuring agreements:

- *Personal liability of directors and officers.* The first agreement covers the personal liability of directors and officers. The policy agrees to pay damages on behalf of insured persons because of a wrongful act. Insured persons include directors and officers and employees.

  The definition of a wrongful act varies among insurers. One policy defines a wrongful act broadly as any employment practices wrongful act; errors and omissions by a director or officer; any matter against an insured person solely because the person is a director or officer; errors and omissions by insured persons in their capacity as a director or officer of an outside entity; and any other errors and omissions by the corporation.

- *Corporate reimbursement coverage.* The second insuring agreement pays on behalf of the corporation. This coverage reimburses the corporation for loss resulting from the company's obligation to reimburse directors and officers to the extent required or permitted by law for suits alleging wrongful acts by such directors and officers.

- *Entity coverage.* Some D&O policies offer a third insuring agreement that covers the legal liability of a corporation arising out of the wrongful acts of directors and officers. *Entity coverage* covers the corporation if it is named as a defendant in a covered suit alleging wrongful acts by directors and officers. The insurer will defend the corporation and settle claims made directly against the corporation.

D&O policies are written on a claims-made basis. The policies typically have a discovery or extended reporting period in the event the insurer cancels the policy or refuses to renew. The reporting period varies by insurers—such as 90 days to 12 months—and applies only to claims for wrongful acts committed prior to termination of the policy but reported during the reporting period.

Exclusions D&O policies contain numerous exclusions. Common exclusions are as follows:

- Bodily injury and property damage (covered under the CGL policy)

- Libel and slander (covered under the CGL policy)
- Personal profit, such as profit from insider trading
- Certain violations of the Securities Exchange Act of 1934 or similar provisions of state law

- Return of salaries or bonuses illegally received without stockholder approval
- Deliberate dishonesty by an insured
- Failure to procure or maintain insurance
- Violation of ERISA law
- Illegal discrimination

CASE APPLICATION

a. Lastovica Construction is insured under a commercial general liability (CGL) policy. The firm agreed to build a new plant for the Smith Corporation. A heavy machine used by Lastovica Construction accidentally fell from the roof of the partially completed plant. Bill, an employee of the construction firm, was severely injured when the falling machine crushed his foot. Heather, a pedestrian, was also injured by the machine while walking on a public sidewalk in front of the building.

   (1) Heather sued both Lastovica Construction and the Smith Corporation for her injury. Indicate the extent, if any, of the CGL insurer's obligation to provide a legal defense for Lastovica Construction.
   (2) What legal defense could the Smith Corporation use to counter Heather 's claim based on the nature of its relationship with Lastovica Construction? Explain your answer.
   (3) Does Lastovica Construction have any responsibility for Bill's medical expenses and lost wages? Explain.

b. James owns a restaurant that is insured under a claims-made CGL policy. The policy term is January 1, 2006, through December 31, 2006. On December 15, 2006, a customer became violently ill from eating a piece of banana cream pie that had become contaminated. On February 1, 2007, the customer made a claim against James for the illness. James had no prior notice that the customer had become ill. Explain with reasons whether James's policy will cover the loss.

SUMMARY

- General liability refers to the legal liability of business firms arising out of business operations other than liability for auto or aviation accidents or employee injuries. Important general liability loss exposures are as follows:

    Premises and operations

    Products liability

    Completed operations

    Contractual liability

    Contingent liability

- Legal liability can arise out of the *ownership and maintenance of the premises* where the firm does business. *Products liability* means that the firm can be held liable for property damage or bodily injury arising out of a defective product. *Completed operations liability* refers to liability arising out of faulty work performed away from the premises after the work is completed. *Contractual liability* means that the business firm agrees to assume the legal liability of another party by a written or oral contract. *Contingent liability* means that the firm can be held liable for work by independent contractors.

- Other important general liability loss exposures include environmental pollution; property in the insured's care, custody, or control; fire legal liability; liability arising out of a liquor or dramshop law; directors and officers liability; personal and advertising injury; and liability arising out of sexual harassment and employment-related practices.

- The *commercial general liability (CGL) policy* can be used to cover most general liability loss exposures of business firms. The CGL provides coverage for the following:

Bodily injury and property damage liability

Personal and advertising injury liability

Medical payments

Supplementary payments

- An *occurrence policy* covers liability claims arising out of occurrences that take place during the policy period, regardless of when the claim is made.

- A *claims-made policy* covers only claims that are first reported during the policy period or extended reporting period, provided that the event occurred after the retroactive date, if any, stated in the policy.

- Insurers use claims-made policies because of the problem of the *long tail*. The long tail refers to the relatively small number of claims that are reported years after the policy is first written. As a result of these claims, it is difficult to estimate premiums, losses, and loss reserves accurately. A claims-made policy enables an insurer to estimate premiums and losses more accurately.

- *Employment-related practices liability insurance* covers employers against suits arising out of wrongful termination, discrimination against employees, sexual harassment, and other employment-related practices.

- All states have workers compensation laws that require covered employers to provide workers compensation benefits to employees who become disabled because of work-related accidents or occupational disease. The workers compensation insurer pays all benefits that the employer must legally provide to employees who are occupationally disabled.

- The *business auto coverage form* can be used by business firms to insure their liability exposures from automobiles. The employer can select those autos to be covered under the policy.

- The *garage coverage form* is designed to meet the insurance needs of auto dealers. The major coverages include liability insurance, garagekeepers insurance, and physical damage insurance. *Garagekeepers insurance* covers the garage owner's liability for damage to customers' autos while the autos are in the dealer's care for service, repairs, or storage.

- Aircraft insurance covering private business and pleasure aircraft provides physical damage coverage on the aircraft and liability coverage for injury to passengers and people on the ground.

- A *commercial umbrella policy* provides protection to firms against a catastrophic judgment. An umbrella policy is excess insurance over the underlying coverages.

- A *businessowners policy* (BOP) provides business liability coverage and medical expense coverage to small- to medium-sized business firms. The insured's employees are also covered for their negligent acts while acting within the scope of their employment.

- The *physicians, surgeons, and dentists professional liability coverage form* covers acts of malpractice by physicians, surgeons, and dentists. The policy has several important features:

  There are two insuring agreements.

  Liability is not restricted to accidental acts.

  There is a maximum limit for each medical incident and an aggregate limit for each coverage.

  Current forms permit the company to settle a claim without the physician's or surgeon's consent.

  An extended reporting period endorsement can be added.

  Professional liability insurance is not a substitute for other necessary forms of liability insurance.

- *Errors and omissions insurance* provides protection against loss incurred by a client because of negligent acts, errors, or omissions by the insured.

- *Directors and officers (D&O) liability insurance* provides financial protection for the directors and officers and the corporation if the directors and officers are sued for mismanagement of the company's affairs.

KEY CONCEPTS AND TERMS

Advertising injury
Aircraft insurance
Basic extended reporting period
Bodily injury or property damage
Business auto coverage form
Business liability coverage form
Claims-made policy
Commercial general liability (CGL) policy
Commercial umbrella policy
Completed operations
Contingent liability
Contractual liability
Directors and officers (D&O) liability insurance
Each occurrence or per occurrence limit
Employers liability insurance

Employment-related practices liability coverage

Errors and omissions insurance

Fire legal liability

Garage coverage form

General aggregate limit

Liquor liability law (dramshop law)

Long-tail claims

Medical payments

Occurrence

Occurrence policy

Other-states insurance

Personal injury

Physicians, surgeons, and dentists professional liability coverage form

Products-completed operations aggregate limit

Products-completed operations hazard

Products liability

Property damage to impaired property

Property damage to the insured's product

Property damage to the insured's work

Retained limit

Self-insured retention (SIR)

Ultimate net loss

Voluntary compensation endorsement

Workers compensation and employers liability insurance

REVIEW QUESTIONS

1. Identify the major general liability loss exposures of business firms.

2. Define each of the following:
   a. Products liability
   b. Completed operations
   c. Contractual liability
   d. Contingent liability

3. Briefly describe the meaning of "products and completed operations hazard."

4. The commercial general liability policy (CGL) contains several coverages. Briefly explain each of the following coverages:
   a. Bodily injury and property damage liability
   b. Personal and advertising injury liability
   c. Medical payments

5. Explain the difference between an occurrence policy and a claims-made policy.

6. A workers compensation policy contains several coverages. Briefly explain each of the following coverages:
   a. Part one: workers compensation insurance
   b. Part two: employers liability insurance
   c. Part three: other states insurance

7. a. Identify the major coverages in the business auto coverage form.
   b. Describe the major characteristics of the garage coverage form.

8. Briefly describe the following coverages that appear in an aircraft policy:
   a. Physical damage coverage
   b. Liability coverage

9. Explain the following characteristics in a commercial umbrella policy:
   a. Coverages provided
   b. Required underlying coverages
   c. Self-insured retention (SIR)

10. Briefly describe the major characteristics of a physicians, surgeons, and dentists professional liability insurance policy.

11. Explain the insuring agreements that typically appear in a directors & officers (D&O) liability policy.

APPLICATION QUESTIONS

1. Ben owns an appliance and furniture store and is insured under a commercial general liability policy written on an occurrence basis. Explain whether Ben's CGL policy would provide coverage for each of the following situations:
   a. Ben forcibly detained a customer whom he erroneously accused of shoplifting. One month later, after the policy had expired, the customer sued Ben for defamation of character.
   b. Ben's employees were delivering a large desk to a customer's house. The customer's front door was scratched and damaged when the desk hit the door. The customer immediately filed a claim for the damage to the door.
   c. An advertising firm sues Ben for using copyrighted material without permission when the material first appeared in a special holiday ad. Ben maintains that the ad material is original and belongs to him.
   d. Unknown to Ben, an automatic dishwasher had a defective part. One week after the dishwasher was installed in a customer's house, it malfunctioned and caused considerable water damage to the kitchen carpet. The homeowner holds Ben responsible for the damage.

e. An employee accidentally knocked over a heavy lamp that injured a customer's foot. The customer later presents a bill for medical expenses to Ben for payment.

2. Jill operates a sporting goods store in a rented location at a shopping mall. She is insured under a CGL policy with the following limits:

General aggregate limit	$1,000,000
Products-completed operations aggregate limit	1,000,000
Personal and advertising injury limit	250,000
Each-occurrence limit	300,000
Damage to rented premises	100,000
Medical expense limit (any one person)	5,000

A propane tank in the store exploded. Indicate the dollar amount, if any, that Jill's insurer will pay for each of the following losses:

a. Three customers were injured by flying debris from the explosion with medical expenses of $6000, $7500, and $5000, respectively.

b. A fire resulted from the explosion. Damages to the rented building are $50,000.

c. A customer injured by the explosion sues Jill for $200,000 for the bodily injury.

3. Allison owns and operates a small retail food store in a suburban shopping center. The store is insured for liability coverage under a businessowners policy. Explain whether the following situations are covered under Allison 's businessowners policy. Treat each situation separately.

a. A clerk accidentally injures a customer with a shopping cart. Both Allison and the clerk are sued.

b. A customer slips on a wet floor and breaks a leg.

c. Allison has a customer arrested for shoplifting. The customer is innocent and sues for damages.

d. A woman returns a spoiled package of gourmet cheese and demands her money back.

4. A surgeon is insured under a physicians, surgeons, and dentists professional liability policy. Explain whether the following situations are covered by the professional liability policy. Treat each situation separately.

a. An office nurse gives a patient a wrong drug. Both the physician and the nurse are sued.

b. The surgeon sets the broken arm of a patient. The patient sues because the arm becomes deformed and crooked.

c. A patient waiting to see the doctor is injured when the legs of an office chair collapse.

5. Delivery Service purchased a commercial umbrella policy with a $10 million liability limit and a $100,000 self-insured retention. The umbrella insurer required Delivery Service to carry a $1 million per-occurrence limit on its general liability policy and a $1 million per-occurrence limit on its business auto policy. A Delivery Service driver was intoxicated while driving a company van and killed another motorist. The court ruled that Delivery Service must pay damages in the amount of $5 million. How much, if any, of this amount will the umbrella insurer pay? Explain your answer.

6. Electrical Services is an electrical contractor that employs 10 electricians. Electrical Services faces numerous loss exposures. One general liability loss exposure arises out of faulty work that an electrician performs in a customer's home, which can cause property damage to the home. Identify the general liability loss exposure to which this example refers.

7. Fast Pizza hires college students who drive their own cars to deliver pizzas to customers. Fast Pizza is concerned that the company may be liable for damages caused by company employees while they are driving their cars on company business. Identify a liability coverage form that Fast Pizza could purchase to deal with this exposure.

INTERNET RESOURCES

■ The **Defense Research Institute** is a service organization created to improve the administration of justice and the skills of defense attorneys. Visit the site at

http://www.dri.org

■ The **RAND Institute for Civil Justice** is a research unit within the RAND Organization that conducts independent, objective research on the civil justice system. Visit the site at

http://www.rand.org

■ The **Insurance Information Institute** is a primary source of information, analysis, and referral on subjects dealing with property and liability insurance. Visit the site at

http://www.iii.org

- The **Insurance Services Office (ISO)** provides statistical information, actuarial analyses, policy language, and technical information to participants in property and liability insurance markets. ISO drafted the commercial general liability policy discussed in this chapter. Visit the site at

  http://www.iso.com

- The **National Council on Compensation Insurance** develops and administers rating plans and systems for workers compensation insurance. Visit the site at

  http://www.ncci.com

- The **National Safety Council** provides national support and leadership in the field of safety; publishes safety materials of all kinds; and conducts a public information and publicity program to support safety. Visit the site at

  http://www.nsc.org

- The **Risk and Insurance Management Society (RIMS)** is the premier professional organization for corporate risk managers and buyers of insurance. RIMS makes known to insurers the insurance needs of business and industry, supports loss prevention programs, and provides a forum for discussing common risk management objectives and problems. RIMS also publishes *Risk Management Magazine*. Visit the site at

  http://www.rims.org

SELECTED REFERENCES

Commercial Insurance Fact Book 2006. New York: Insurance Information Institute, 2006.

The CPCU Handbook of Insurance Policies, 6th ed. Malvern PA.: American Institute of Chartered Property Casualty Underwriters/Insurance Institute of America, 2005.

Fire, Casualty & Surety Bulletins. Erlanger, KY: National Underwriter Company, Casualty & Surety volume. The bulletins are published monthly. Detailed information on all forms of commercial liability insurance can be found in this volume.

Flitner, Arthur L., and Jerome Trupin. *Commercial Insurance,* 1st ed. 5th printing. Malvern, PA.: American Institute for Property Casualty Underwriters/Insurance of America, March 2005.

Malecki, Donald S., and Arthur L. Flitner. *CGL Commercial General Liability,* 8th ed. Cincinnati, OH: The National Underwriter Company, 2005.

Wells, Alexander T., and Bruce D. Chadbourne. *Introduction to Aviation Insurance and Risk Management,* 2nd ed. Malabar, FL: Krieger Publishing Company, 2000.

NOTES

1. Emmett J. Vaughan, and Therese M. Vaughan, *Fundamentals of Risk and Insurance,* 9th ed. (New York: Wiley, 2003), p. 584.

2. This section is based on *Fire, Casualty & Surety Bulletins,* Casualty and Surety volume, Public Liability section (Erlanger, KY: National Underwriter Company); and Arthur L. Flitner and Jerome Trupin, *Commercial Insurance,* 1st ed., 5th printing (Malvern, PA: American Institute for Chartered Property Casualty Underwriters/Insurance Institute of America, March 2005). The author also drew on the various commercial general liability forms of the Insurance Services Office (copyrighted) that appeared in *The CPCU Handbook of Insurance Policies,* 6th ed. (Malvern, PA: American Institute for CPCU, 2005). The author drew heavily on these sources in the preparation of this chapter.

3. *The I.I.I. Insurance Fact Book, 2006,* p. 145.

4. The workers compensation and employers liability policy is discussed in detail in *Fire, Casualty & Surety Bulletins,* Casualty and Surety volume, Workers Compensation section (Erlanger, KY: National Underwriter Company).

5. This section is based on the *Fire, Casualty & Surety Bulletins,* Casualty and Surety volume, Auto section (Erlanger, KY: National Underwriter Company), and the ISO business auto coverage form and garage coverage form.

6. Flinter and Trupin, *Commercial Insurance,* p. 10.29.

7. Aircraft insurance is discussed in *Fire, Casualty & Surety Bulletins,* Companies & Coverages volume, Aircraft-Marine section (Erlanger, KY: National Underwriter). See also Alexander T. Wells and Bruce D. Chadbourne, *Introduction to Aviation Insurance and Risk Management,* 2nd ed. (Malabar, FL: Krieger Publishing Company, 2000).

8. A detailed discussion of the commercial umbrella policy can be found in *Fire, Casualty & Surety Bulletins,* Casualty and Surety volume, Public Liability section (Erlanger, KY: National Underwriter). See also Flitner and Trupin, *Commercial Insurance,* pp. 13.5–13.12.

9. A detailed discussion of the businessowners policy can be found in *Fire, Casualty & Surety Bulletins,* Fire and Marine volume, Commercial Property section (Erlanger, KY: National Underwriter Company).

10. Professional liability insurance for physicians is discussed in *Fire, Casualty & Surety Bulletins,* Casualty and Surety volume, Public Liability section (Erlanger, KY: National Underwriter Company).

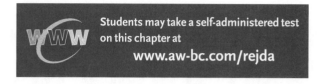

Students may take a self-administered test on this chapter at
www.aw-bc.com/rejda

CHAPTER 27

CRIME INSURANCE AND SURETY BONDS

"Thieves respect property. They merely wish the property to become their property that they may more perfectly respect it."

G. K. Chesterton

After studying this chapter, you should be able to

◆ Define theft, robbery, burglary, and safe burglary.

◆ Identify the insuring agreements in the commercial crime coverage form (loss-sustained form).

◆ Explain the difference between the discovery form and the loss-sustained form.

◆ Identify the basic insuring agreements in a financial institution bond for a commercial bank.

◆ Show how surety bonds differ from insurance.

◆ Identify the major types of surety bonds and give an example of where each can be used.

Carlos, age 28, works as a cashier in a 24-hour supermarket in Detroit, Michigan. Around 2 A.M., a male customer pulled a gun on Carlos and demanded all of the cash in the cash register. As a matter of company policy, all employees are instructed never to resist a holdup but to surrender the cash. Carlos gave the thief an undisclosed amount of cash. The store manager later told Carlos that the company has a crime insurance policy that covers holdups and other crimes.

Most firms need protection against crime loss exposures. Business firms lose billions of dollars annually because of robbery, burglary, larceny, and employee theft. Other crimes are widespread, including fraud, embezzlement, and other illegal activities. Computer crimes are also increasing.

This chapter discusses the Insurance Services Office (ISO) commercial crime insurance program that protects business firms against robbery, burglary, employee theft, and other crime losses. The chapter also discusses financial institution bonds that cover the crime exposures of commercial banks and other financial institutions. It concludes with a discussion of surety bonds that provide indemnification to an injured party if the bonded party fails to perform an agreed upon act.

ISO COMMERCIAL CRIME INSURANCE PROGRAM

Crime insurance coverage can either be added to a package policy or purchased separately as a stand-alone (monoline) policy. There are five basic crime coverage forms and policies: (1) commercial crime coverage form, (2) commercial crime policy, (3) government crime coverage form, (4) government crime policy, and (5) employee theft and forgery policy. Each coverage form or policy is written in two versions—a discovery version and a loss-sustained version (see Exhibit 27.1). The *discovery version* covers a loss that is discovered during the policy period or within 60 days after the policy expires even though the loss may have occurred before the policy's inception date. The *loss-sustained version* covers a loss that occurs during the policy period (or a loss that would have been covered under a prior policy if the insurance had been kept in force), and the loss is discovered during the policy period or within one year after the policy expires. These two versions are discussed in greater detail later in the chapter.

The commercial crime coverage form and the commercial crime policy are designed for most private firms and nonprofit organizations other than financial institutions, such as banks and savings and loan institutions.

The government crime coverage form and government crime policy are designed for governmental entities, such as states, cities, counties, state universities, and public utilities.

The employee theft and forgery policy is designed for business firms that need coverage only for

EXHIBIT 27.1
ISO Commercial Crime Coverage Forms and Policies

- Commercial Crime Coverage Form (discovery version and loss-sustained version)
- Commercial Crime Policy (discovery version and loss-sustained version)
- Government Crime Coverage Form (discovery version and loss-sustained version)
- Government Crime Policy (discovery version and loss-sustained version)
- Employee Theft and Forgery Policy (discovery version and loss-sustained version)

employee theft and forgery losses. With certain exceptions, the crime coverage forms and policies follow a similar format with respect to insuring agreements, exclusions, and policy conditions.

It is beyond the scope of the text to discuss each of the five crime coverage forms and policies in detail. Instead, the fundamentals of commercial crime insurance can be illustrated by a discussion of the ISO commercial crime coverage form (loss-sustained form).[1]

COMMERCIAL CRIME COVERAGE FORM (LOSS-SUSTAINED FORM)

The **commercial crime coverage form (loss-sustained form)** can be added to a package policy to cover the crime exposures of business firms. The following discussion is based on the May 2006 edition of the form.

Basic Definitions

Most property crimes against business firms are due to robbery, burglary, or theft. The commercial crime coverage form has a definitions page that defines key terms. **Robbery** is the unlawful taking of property from the care and custody of a person by someone who (1) has caused or threatens to cause that person with bodily harm, or (2) has committed an obviously unlawful act witnessed by that person.

Burglary is not defined in the ISO commercial crime policy (loss-sustained form). However, **burglary** typically is defined as the unlawful taking of property from inside the premises by a person who unlawfully enters or leaves the premises, as evidenced by marks of forcible entry or exit.

Safe burglary is the unlawful taking of property from within a locked safe or vault by someone who unlawfully enters the safe or vault as evidenced by marks of forcible entry upon the exterior. For coverage to apply, there must be marks of forcible entry upon the exterior of the safe. The definition of safe burglary also includes the unlawful taking of a safe or vault from the premises. Coverage applies if the entire safe is taken from inside the premises, which some burglars may do.

Theft is a broader term and is defined as the unlawful taking of money, securities, or other property

to the deprivation of the insured. It includes robbery and burglary as well as shoplifting, employee theft, and forgery.

Insuring Agreements

The commercial crime coverage form contains several insuring agreements. Firms can select one or more of the following coverages:

- Employee Theft
- Forgery or Alteration
- Inside the Premises—Theft of Money and Securities
- Inside the Premises—Robbery or Safe Burglary of Other Property
- Outside the Premises
- Computer Fraud
- Funds Transfer Fraud
- Money Orders and Counterfeit Currency

Employee Theft This coverage pays for the loss of money, securities, and other property that results directly from theft committed by an employee. The theft is covered even if the employee cannot be identified, or the employee is acting alone or in collusion with other persons. For example, if an employee steals money from a cash register, the loss is covered. Other types of employee theft are common, especially for small business firms (see Insight 27.1).

Coverage of employee theft includes the theft of other property. **Other property** *is any tangible property other than money or securities that has intrinsic value. However, other property does not include computer programs, electronic data, or any property excluded under the policy.* For example, if an employee in an appliance store steals a television set, the loss is covered.

The insuring agreement applies on a *blanket basis* to all persons who meet the definition of an employee—that is, covered employees are not specifically named in the policy. If desired, employers can instead use a *schedule approach,* which identifies covered employees in the policy by name or by position. Most employers prefer to cover employees on a blanket basis.

Forgery or Alteration This coverage pays for a loss that results directly from forgery or from the alter-

INSIGHT 27.1

Taking Home More Than a Paycheck: Employee Theft Costs U.S. Employers $20 Billion–$40 Billion a Year

Jim Lashley has always paid close attention to the behind-the-scenes paperwork needed to keep his landscape company on task. The 36-year-old Orlando, Fla., business owner handles the money, invoices and checks for Landscape Supply Co. Only his accountant is privy to the quarterly records.

For 10 years, Lashley's hands-on management was the ultimate insurance against employee theft or fraud. Or so he thought.

About two years ago, Lashley's secretary at the time began secretly diverting installation orders to her boyfriend. She also went to Lashley's sod provider and opened a line of credit for supplies. Because she had no intention of paying back the sod provider, Lashley said, she was able to secure dozens of sod-installation jobs at a fraction of the going rate.

In the end, her actions cost Lashley roughly 20 jobs and at least $10,000. The sod provider also had to swallow a $5,000 supply bill.

"She'd been with me for two years before all of this started," Lashley said. "I trusted her."

At one time or another, nearly every small business experiences some type of employee theft or fraud. Whether it's a theft of money, incoming business, inventory or intellectual property, small businesses are especially vulnerable to being swindled.

Often, a small company lacks the resources to supervise every employee. For instance, a small business may rely on one person to complete accounting and bookkeeping transactions in addition to opening mail, making deposits, writing checks and overseeing petty cash. This type of unrestricted access lends itself to the possibility of theft.

According to the U.S. Chamber of Commerce, employee theft costs U.S. employers $20 billion to $40 billion annually. Nearly 90% of all businesses report that they have experienced employee theft of some kind. Unfortunately, 75% of employee-related crimes go unnoticed.

To avoid becoming a victim, small-business owners should learn to recognize and avoid potential problems.

Start by dividing responsibilities among two or more employees. If one person writes checks or disburses cash, for example, then another person should be in charge of handling the accounts-payable records, said Judith Dacey, president of Small Business Resources Inc. in Orlando.

Dacey, a certified public accountant, also recommends business owners do extensive background checks before hiring a new employee. Call former employers and ask whether they would rehire the worker.

"Small-business owners tend to skip this step," Dacey said. "But it's one of the most important. Make sure and ask each reference, 'Can I trust this person?'"

Owners also should keep an eye on the vacation schedule, their accounting records and any changes in an employee's personal life.

An employee who takes very brief vacations or no vacation at all should draw your attention. Employee-perpetrated crimes are most often discovered while the employee is away on vacation and other employees are filling in.

Examine accounting records frequently and double-check vendor payments. Keep an eye out for missing or altered documentation or weak and disorganized records. Require employees to file original invoices and contracts—not copies. It's also not a bad idea to have some documents, such as bank statements, mailed directly to your home.

Changes in your employees' personal lives can also cause a trusted employee to go bad. Watch for employees who are under some new stress, such as large medical bills, excessive use of alcohol or large investment losses.

SOURCE: From Sarah Hale, *Sentinel* Staff Writer. "Taking Home More Than a Paycheck: Employee Theft Costs U.S. Employers $20 Billion–$40 Billion a Year," *Orlando Sentinel*, Monday, March 11, 2002.

ation of checks, drafts, promissory notes, or similar instruments made or drawn by the insured or insured's agent. For example, if a thief steals some company checks and forges the insured's name, the resulting loss is covered. Likewise, if a check signed by the insured is altered from $100 to $1000, that loss too is covered.

Note that this coverage applies only to forgery or alteration of the insured's checks or instruments and not to losses that result from the acceptance of forged checks or the instruments of others.[2]

Inside the Premises—Theft of Money and Securities This coverage pays for the loss of money and securities inside the premises or banking premises that result directly from theft committed by a person present inside the premises, or from disappearance, or destruction. Coverage also applies to (1) damage to the premises or its exterior resulting from the actual or attempted theft of money or securities if the insured owns the premises or is liable for damage to it, and (2) damage to a locked safe, vault, cash register, or cash box because of an actual or attempted theft or an unlawful entry into those containers.

Coverage is broad because of the words "theft, disappearance, or destruction." For example, covered losses include losses that occur when a cashier inside a liquor store is held up; money is destroyed in a fire or tornado; or a cash register or safe is damaged in a burglary. In addition, damage to the premises or its exterior is covered if the insured owns the building or is liable for any damage to it.

Inside the Premises——Robbery or Safe Burglary of Other Property This provision complements the previous insuring agreement of money and securities. This coverage pays for the loss or damage to *other property* inside the premises by the actual or attempted robbery of a custodian, or by safe burglary inside the premises. The term "custodian" is defined in the policy and includes the named insured, partners, and employees but not a janitor or watchperson. For example, if the owner of a pawn shop is robbed of several guns, the loss is covered. Likewise, if a cashier in a liquor store sees a customer take a bottle of liquor and then sprint out of the store without paying, that loss too is covered.

Safe burglary of other property inside the premises is also covered. As stated earlier, **safe burglary** *is the unlawful taking of (1) property from within a locked safe or vault by a person unlawfully entering the safe as evidenced by marks of forcible entry upon its exterior, or (2) a safe or vault from inside the premises.* For example, if a burglar breaks into a locked safe and steals a watch and rings owned by the insured, the loss is covered.

Note that the burglary coverage in this insuring agreement applies only to safe burglary of other property inside the premises. For coverage to apply, property classified as other property must be in a locked safe or vault. Thus, if a burglar breaks into a clothing store and steals several suits and dresses off the rack, the burglary loss of other property would not be covered.

If broader coverage of burglary losses is desired, the policy can be endorsed with an optional insur-

ing agreement to cover such losses. One optional agreement is **inside the premises—robbery or burglary of other property.** This agreement covers actual or attempted burglary as well as robbery of a watchperson.

Outside the Premises The **outside the premises** insuring agreement covers the theft, disappearance, or destruction of money and securities outside the premises while in the custody of a messenger or an armored-car company. A "messenger" is someone who has care and custody of the property outside the premises. For example, if an employee is robbed while taking the daily cash receipts to the bank, the loss is covered. Likewise, the loss of money or securities in the custody of an armored-car company is also covered.

In addition, actual or attempted robbery of other property outside the premises in the care of a messenger or armored-car company is covered. For example, if an employee is robbed while taking the insured's diamond ring and other jewelry to a bank, the loss is covered.

Computer Fraud This provision covers the loss of money, securities, and other property if a computer is used to transfer property fraudulently from inside the premises or banking premises to a person or place outside the premises. For example, if a computer hacker breaks into a business computer and a check is issued to a fictitious person and cashed, the loss is covered.

Funds Transfer Fraud The insuring agreement covers the loss of funds that result directly from fraudulent instructions that direct a financial institution to transfer or pay funds from the insured's account. For example, assume that a bank transfers funds from the insured's account to a bank in Switzerland. If the instruction to transfer the funds (such as electronic, cable, or telephone) is fraudulently made without the insured's knowledge or consent, the loss of money or securities is covered.

Computer crime losses and incidents have increased dramatically in recent years. According to a recent FBI survey, nine out of ten organizations in the country have experienced computer security incidents. About two-thirds of the firms and organizations have incurred financial loss (see Insight 27.2).

INSIGHT 27.2

FBI: 90% of Organizations Face Computer Attack; 64% Incur Financial Loss

The FBI reports that 9 out of 10 organizations in the country are victims of some sort of computer security incident, and one-fifth are hit more than 20 times a year.

Almost two-thirds suffer financial loss as a result of the cyber incidents.

The 2005 FBI Computer Crime Survey is based on responses from a cross-section of more than 2000 public and private organizations.

Among its findings:

- **Frequency of attacks.** Nearly nine out of 10 organizations experienced computer security incidents in a year's time; 20% of them indicated they had experienced 20 or more attacks.
- **Types of attacks.** Viruses (83.7%) and spyware (79.5%) headed the list. More than one in five organizations said they experienced port scans and network or data sabotage.
- **Financial impact.** Over 64% of the respondents incurred a loss. Viruses and worms cost the most, accounting for $12 million of the $32 million in total losses.
- **Sources of the attacks.** They came from 36 different countries. The U.S. (26.1%) and China (23.9%) were the source of over half of the intrusion attempts, though masking technologies make it difficult to get an accurate reading.

- **Defenses.** Most said they installed new security updates and software following incidents, but advanced security techniques such as biometrics (4%) and smart cards (7%) were used infrequently. In addition, 44% reported intrusions from within their own organizations, suggesting the need for strong internal controls.
- **Reporting.** Just 9% said they reported incidents to law enforcement, believing the infractions were not illegal or that there was little law enforcement could or would do. Of those reporting, however, 91% were satisfied with law enforcement's response. And 81% said they'd report future incidents to the FBI or other law enforcement agencies. Many also said they were unaware of InfraGard, a joint FBI/private sector initiative that battles computer crimes and other threats through information sharing.

Frank Abagnale, security consultant and subject of the movie *Catch Me If You Can,* echoed those comments, saying: "Every company, both large and small, should study this survey and use the data as the basis for making changes. Those who ignore it do so at their peril."

SOURCE: Excerpted from "FBI: 90% of Organizations Face Computer Attack; 64% Incur Financial Loss," *Insurance Journal,* National News, January 18, 2006.

Money Orders and Counterfeit Paper Currency

This coverage pays for losses resulting directly from the good-faith acceptance of money orders that are not paid upon presentation or from counterfeit currency acquired in the course of business. For example, if a sales clerk accepts a $50 counterfeit bill in exchange for merchandise, the loss is covered.

Exclusions

The commercial crime coverage form contains numerous exclusions. It is beyond the scope of the text to discuss each exclusion. However, certain exclusions merit a brief discussion and are summarized here.

- *Dishonest acts or theft committed by the named insured, partners, or members.* Loss due to dishonest acts or theft by the insured or the insured's partners or members is specifically - excluded.
- *Knowledge of dishonest acts of employees prior to policy period.* Loss caused by an employee is not covered if the employee committed theft or any other dishonest act prior to the effective date of the insurance, and the named insured or any partner, manager, officer, director, or trustee not in collusion with the employee learned of that theft or dishonest act prior to the policy period.
- *Dishonest acts or theft by employees, managers, directors, trustees, or representatives.* With the exception of the employee theft insuring agreement, dishonest acts or theft committed by employees, managers, directors, trustees, or representatives are excluded.

- *Confidential information.* Loss from the unauthorized disclosure of confidential information is excluded. Confidential information includes patents, trade secrets, processing methods, and customer lists. The exclusion also applies to the unauthorized disclosure of information of another person or party, including financial information, personal information, and credit card information.
- *Indirect loss.* An indirect loss that results from a covered loss is excluded. For example, if the business is temporarily closed because of a burglary, the loss of business income under this form is not covered.
- *Inventory shortages.* This exclusion applies only to the employee theft insuring agreement. There is no coverage for any loss if proof of loss depends on an inventory computation or on a profit and loss computation. The intent here is to exclude inventory losses that may be due to errors in record keeping rather than employee dishonesty.
- *Trading losses.* This exclusion applies only to the employee theft insuring agreement. Trading losses whether in the named insured's name or in a fictitious account are specifically excluded. Thus, unauthorized trading in stocks, bonds, futures, and derivatives is not covered. However, unauthorized trading losses can be catastrophic. An endorsement is available to cover trading losses that meet the criteria for employee theft.

Policy Conditions

The policy conditions section in the commercial crime coverage form contains numerous conditions. Four important policy conditions are discussed here.

Discovery Form   As stated earlier, the crime coverage forms and policies are written in two versions—a discovery version and a loss-sustained version.

The **discovery form** *covers losses that are discovered during the policy period or within 60 days after the policy's expiration date, regardless of when the loss occurred.* Thus, losses that occur prior to a policy's inception date are covered if they are discovered within the policy period or within 60 days after termination or cancellation of the policy. In the case of employee benefit plans, the discovery period extends to one year after the policy's expiration date.

Employee theft can go undetected for years. The discovery form can be especially valuable for a business firm that has been in business for several years but is uninsured for employee theft losses. If the new insurance were written on a discovery basis, it would cover any losses that occurred years earlier but were only discovered during the current policy period (or within 60 days after expiration of the policy).

However, an underwriter may have reason to believe that large undiscovered losses might exist prior to the policy's inception date. To deal with adverse selection, a **retroactive date endorsement** could be added to the policy, which covers losses that occur only after the retroactive date and are discovered during the current policy period. If the retroactive date is the same as the policy's inception date, losses that occurred prior to the policy's inception date would not be covered.[3]

Loss-Sustained Form   The **loss-sustained form** *covers losses that occur during the policy period and are discovered during the policy period or within one year after the policy expires.* For example, if an employee steals $25,000 in cash during the policy period, the loss is covered if it is discovered during the current policy period or within one year after the policy's expiration date.

Loss Sustained During Prior Insurance Not Issued By Us or Any Affiliate   Under this provision, the current policy provides coverage for a loss that occurred during the term of the prior policy but was discovered only after the discovery period under the prior policy had expired. This provision enables an insurer to change insurers without penalty. This provision applies only if there is no break in the continuity of coverage under both policies; that is, the present insurance became effective at the time of cancellation of the prior insurance. Another requirement is that the loss is one that would have been covered by the current policy if it had been in force when the loss occurred.

The maximum amount paid is the policy limit under the previous policy, or the limit of insurance under the current policy, whichever is less. For example, assume that the policy limit under the previous policy is $10,000, and the policy limit under the current policy is $50,000. The current policy will pay only a maximum of $10,000 for any covered loss that occurred while the previous policy was in force.

Termination as to Any Employee This provision states that the employee theft insuring agreement terminates as to any employee once the insured has knowledge that the employee has committed a theft or dishonest act. Once the insured becomes aware of the theft or dishonest act committed by the employee either before or after the worker is employed, employee theft coverage on that worker is terminated.

FINANCIAL INSTITUTION BONDS

Commercial banks, savings and loan institutions, credit unions, stock brokerage firms, and other financial institutions are faced with crime loss exposures that can result in enormous financial losses. These exposures include bank holdups, employee dishonesty, forgery and alteration of checks, acceptance of counterfeit money, theft of securities, armored-car exposures, and numerous additional crime exposures. Because of the size and complexity of their crime exposures, financial institutions use some type of financial institution bond to deal with these exposures. In its application to financial institutions, the word "bond" is synonymous with "insurance policy" and should not be confused with surety bonds discussed later.

The Surety Association of America makes available a number of financial institution bonds that banks and other financial institutions can use. One widely used form is **Financial Institution Bond, Standard Form No. 24 (Revised to April 1, 2004)**, which is designed for commercial banks, savings banks, and savings and loan institutions. The following discussion is based on this form.

The financial institution bond contains a number of insuring agreements. Agreements A, B, C, and F are part of the basic bond coverage. Agreements D, E, and F are optional.[4]

- Insuring Agreement A—Fidelity
- Insuring Agreement B—On Premises
- Insuring Agreement C—In Transit
- Insuring Agreement D—Forgery or Alteration

- Insuring Agreement E—Securities
- Insuring Agreement F—Counterfeit Currency
- Insuring Agreement G—Fraudulent Mortgages

Fidelity Coverage

Financial institutions frequently experience fidelity losses due to employee dishonesty. **Fidelity coverage** *covers losses that result directly from the dishonest or fraudulent acts of employees acting alone or in collusion with others, with the active and conscious purpose of causing the insured to sustain such loss.* For example, if a bank teller steals cash from a cash register or vault, the loss is covered. However, an exclusion applies to losses due to trading or loan transactions. If part or all of the insured's loss results from trading or loan transactions, that portion of the loss is not covered unless the employee has received an improper financial benefit.

On Premises Coverage

This provision covers the loss of property on the premises from robbery, burglary, misplacement, mysterious unexplainable disappearance, theft, and a number of additional perils. For example, if a bank robber threatens a bank teller with bodily harm and escapes with $25,000, the loss is covered. Loss or damage to furnishings, fixtures, and office equipment as a result of burglary, robbery, vandalism, or malicious mischief is also covered.

In-Transit Coverage

This provision covers in-transit losses, which include losses from robbery, larceny, theft, misplacement, mysterious unexplainable disappearance, and other specified perils. The property must be in the custody of a messenger or in the custody of a transportation company. For example, if a bank loses money in an armored car robbery, the loss is covered.

Forgery or Alteration Coverage

This optional provision covers loss from forgery or alteration of most negotiable instruments and certain financial instruments specified in the bond. For example, if a bank officer's name is forged on a check payable to a fictitious person, the loss is covered.

Securities Coverage

This optional provision covers losses to the insured because securities accepted in good faith have been forged, altered, lost, or stolen. For example, if a bank in good faith accepts some stolen stock certificates as collateral for a loan and the bank later tries to sell the certificates when the borrower defaults, any resulting loss is covered.

Counterfeit Money

This provision covers loss to the insured from counterfeit money. For example, if a bank teller accepts a fake $100 bill, the loss to the bank is covered.

Fraudulent Mortgages

This optional provision covers loss that results directly from having accepted or acted upon any mortgage on real property that proves defective because of a fraudulent signature. For example, if a bank accepts a mortgage on a building as collateral for a loan, and the mortgage is defective because the mortgagee's signature on the document is a forgery, any resulting loss would be covered.

SURETY BONDS

A **surety bond** *is a bond that usually provides monetary compensation if the bonded party fails to perform certain promised acts.* For example, a contractor may be financially overextended and unable to complete a building project. A public official may embezzle public funds, or the executor of an estate may illegally convert part of the estate assets to his or her own use. Surety bonds can be used to meet these loss exposures.

Parties to a Surety Bond

There are always three parties to a surety bond:

- Principal
- Obligee
- Surety (obligor)

The **principal** *is the party who agrees to perform certain acts or fulfill certain obligations.* For example, a construction company may agree to build an office building for a commercial bank. The construction company may be required to obtain a performance bond before the contract is awarded. The construction company would be known as the principal.

The **obligee** *is the party who receives the proceeds of the bond if the principal fails to perform.* In the previous example, the bank would be reimbursed for any loss that resulted from failure of the construction company to complete the building on time or according to contract specifications.

The surety is the final party to the bond. The **surety (obligor)** *is the party who agrees to answer for the debt, default, or obligation of another.* For example, the construction company may have purchased a performance bond from a commercial insurer. If the construction company (principal) fails to perform, the bank (obligee) would be reimbursed for any loss by the commercial insurer (surety).

Comparison of Surety Bonds and Insurance

Surety bonds are similar to insurance contracts in that both provide protection against specified losses. However, there are some important differences between them, as listed in Exhibit 27.2.

Types of Surety Bonds

Different types of surety bonds can be used to meet specific needs and situations. Although surety bonds are not uniform and have different characteristics, they can generally be grouped into the following categories:[5]

- Contract bonds
    Bid bond
    Performance bond
    Payment bond
    Maintenance bond
    Completion bond
- License and permit bonds
- Public official bonds
- Judicial bonds
    Fiduciary bond
    Court bond
- Federal surety bonds
- Miscellaneous surety bonds

Exhibit 27.2
Comparison of Insurance and Surety Bonds

Insurance

1. There are two parties to an insurance contract.

2. The insurer expects to pay losses. The premium reflects expected loss costs.

3. The insurer normally does not have the right to recover a loss payment from the insured.

4. Insurance is designed to cover unintentional losses that ideally are outside of the insured's control.

Surety Bonds

1. There are three parties to a surety bond.

2. The surety theoretically expects no losses to occur. The premium is viewed as a service fee, by which the surety's credit is substituted for that of the principal.

3. The surety has the legal right to recover a loss payment from the defaulting principal.

4. The surety guarantees the principal's character, honesty, integrity, and ability to perform. These qualities are within the principal's control.

Contract Bonds Contract bonds are used in connection with construction contracts. A **contract bond** *guarantees that the principal will fulfill all contractual obligations.* There are several types of contract bonds. Under a *bid bond,* the owner (obligee) is guaranteed that the party awarded a bid on a project will sign a contract and furnish a performance bond.

Under a **performance bond,** the owner is guaranteed that work will be completed according to the contract specifications. For example, if a building is not completed, the surety is responsible for completion of the project and the extra expense in hiring another contractor. Performance bonds are especially important in the construction industry where a large number of construction firms fail each year.

A *payment bond* guarantees that the bills for labor and materials used in building the project will be paid by the contractor when the bills are due.

A *maintenance bond* guarantees that poor workmanship by the principal will be corrected, or defective materials will be replaced. This maintenance guarantee is often included in a performance bond for one year without additional charge.

A *completion bond* deals with contracts that involve the financing and design of projects. The completion bond guarantees the completion of a building or project. It is designed to protect lending institutions and lessors of property.

Exhibit 27.3 compares the various types of contract bonds.

License and Permit Bonds These types of bonds are commonly required of persons who must obtain a license or permit from a city or town before they can engage in certain activities. A **license and permit**

Exhibit 27.3
Comparison of Five Contract Bonds

Type of Bond	Obligee	Principal	Guarantee
1. Bid Bond	Property owner or party requesting bids	Firm or party submitting the bid	Party whose bid is accepted will sign a contract and furnish a performance bond
2. Performance Bond	Property owner or party having work done	Contractor doing the work	Work will be completed according to contract specifications
3. Payment Bond	Property owner or party having work done	Contractor doing the work	Bills for labor and materials will be paid when due
4. Maintenance Bond	Party having work done	Contractor doing the work	Faulty work of principal will be corrected, or defective materials replaced
5. Completion Bond	Lending institution or lessor	Contractor doing the work	Guarantees completion of the building or improvement

bond *guarantees that the person bonded will comply with all laws and regulations that govern his or her activities.* For example, a liquor store owner may post a bond guaranteeing that liquor will be sold according to the law. A plumber or electrician may post a bond guaranteeing that the work performed will comply with the local building code.

Public Official Bonds

This type of bond is usually required by law for public officials who are elected or appointed to public office. A **public official bond** *guarantees that public officials will faithfully perform their duties for the protection of the public.* For example, a state treasurer must comply with state law governing the deposit of public funds.

Judicial Bonds

Judicial bonds *guarantee that the party bonded will fulfill certain obligations specified by law.* There are several types of judicial bonds. A **fiduciary bond** guarantees that the person who is responsible for the property of another will faithfully perform all required duties, give an accounting of all property, and make up any deficiency for which the courts hold the fiduciary liable. For example, administrators of estates, receivers or liquidators, or guardians of minor children may be required to post a bond guaranteeing their performance.

A **court bond** is designed to protect one person (obligee) against loss in the event that the person bonded does not prove that he or she is legally entitled to the remedy sought against the obligee. For example, an **attachment bond** guarantees that if the court rules against the plaintiff who has attached the property of the defendant in a lawsuit, the defendant will be reimbursed for damages as a result of having the property attached.

Finally, a **bail bond** is another type of court bond. If the bonded person fails to appear in court at the appointed time, the entire bond is forfeited.

Federal Surety Bonds

These bonds are required by federal agencies that regulate the actions of business firms such as manufacturers, wholesalers, and large import firms. A **federal surety bond** *guarantees that the bonded party will comply with federal standards.* The bond also guarantees the payment of taxes or duties that accrue if the bonded party fails to pay.

Miscellaneous Surety Bonds

This category consists of bonds that cannot be classified in any other group. For example, an *auctioneer's bond* guarantees the accounting of sales proceeds by an auctioneer; a *lost-instrument bond* guarantees the obligee against loss if the original instrument (such as a lost stock certificate) shows up later in the possession of another party; and an *insurance agent bond* indemnifies an insurer for any penalties that result from the unlawful acts of agents.

CASE APPLICATION

The ISO commercial crime coverage form can be used to insure specific crime exposures of most business firms. Assume that you are a risk management consultant. For each of the following losses, identify an appropriate insuring agreement that would have covered the loss.

a. Jennifer owns a restaurant and is taking the daily cash receipts to the bank. While walking to her car, she is confronted by a person with a gun and is told to hand over the cash. Fearing for her life, she surrenders the money.

b. Travis owns a large supermarket. When the store was closed, a burglar broke into a locked safe and stole several thousand dollars.

c. Rebecca is a cashier at a 24-hour convenience store. In the early morning, a drug addict confronts her with a knife and threatens her with bodily harm if she does not give him all the cash in the cash drawer.

d. Kevin is the manager of a retail store that sells lamps and lighting accessories. A company audit revealed that a longtime accountant had embezzled several thousands of dollars. The loss was discovered when the accountant was on vacation.

e. Josh sells merchandise over the Internet. Josh is concerned that a thief might break into his business computer and transfer company funds to a fictitious person.

SUMMARY

- *Theft* is the unlawful taking of money, securities, or other property to the deprivation of the insured. Robbery and burglary are forms of theft.

- *Robbery* is the unlawful taking of property from the care and custody of a person by one who has (1) caused or threatened to cause that person bodily harm or (2) committed an obviously unlawful act witnessed by that person.

- *Burglary* is defined as the unlawful taking of property from inside the premises by a person who unlawfully enters or leaves the premises, as evidenced by marks of forcible entry or exit.

- *Safe burglary* is the unlawful taking of property from within a locked safe or vault by someone who unlawfully enters the safe or vault as evidenced by marks of forcible entry upon the exterior. The definition of safe burglary also includes the unlawful taking of a safe or vault from the premises.

- There are five basic ISO crime coverage forms and policies:

  Commercial Crime Coverage Form

  Commercial Crime Policy

  Government Crime Coverage Form

  Government Crime Policy

  Employee Theft and Forgery Policy

  Each crime coverage form or policy is written in two versions—a discovery version and a loss-sustained version.

- The *discovery form* covers losses that are discovered during the policy period or within 60 days after the policy's expiration date, regardless of when the loss occurred.

- The *loss-sustained form* covers losses that occur during the policy period and are discovered during the policy period or within one year after the policy expires.

- The commercial crime coverage form (loss-sustained form) contains several insuring agreements. Firms can select one or more of the following coverages:

  Employee Theft

  Forgery or Alteration

  Inside the Premises—Theft of Money and Securities

  Inside the Premises—Robbery or Safe Burglary of Other Property

  Outside the Premises

  Computer Fraud

  Funds Transfer Fraud

  Money Orders and Counterfeit Currency

- *Loss Sustained During Prior Insurance Not Issued By Us or Any Affiliate* is a provision by which the current policy provides coverage for a loss that occurred during the term of the prior policy but was not discovered until after the discovery period under the prior policy had expired. The purpose is to enable an insured to change insurers without penalty. The provision applies only if there is no break in the continuity of coverage under both policies, and the loss is one that would have been covered by the current policy if it had been in force when the loss occurred.

- A financial institution bond is designed for banks and similar institutions. The following coverages are available:

  Insuring Agreement A—Fidelity

  Insuring Agreement B—On Premises

  Insuring Agreement C—In Transit

  Insuring Agreement D—Forgery or Alteration

  Insuring Agreement E—Securities

  Insuring Agreement F—Counterfeit Currency

  Insuring Agreement G—Fraudulent Mortgages

- There are three parties to a surety bond. The *principal* is the party who agrees to perform certain obligations. The *obligee* is the party who receives the proceeds of the bond if the principal fails to perform. The *surety* (obligor) is the party who agrees to answer for the debt, default, or obligation of another.

- Surety bonds are similar to insurance contracts in that losses are expected. However, there are several major differences between surety bonds and insurance.

  There are two parties to an insurance contract; there are three parties to a surety bond.

  The insurer expects to pay losses; the surety theoretically expects no losses to occur.

  The insurer normally does not have the right to recover a loss payment from an insured; the surety has the right to recover from a defaulting principal.

  Insurance covers unintentional losses outside of the insured's control; the surety guarantees the principal's character and ability to perform, which are within the principal's control.

- Surety bonds guarantee the performance of the principal. They include various contract bonds, license and permit bonds, public official bonds, judicial bonds, federal surety bonds, and miscellaneous surety bonds.

KEY CONCEPTS AND TERMS

Attachment bond	License and permit bonds
Bail bond	Loss-sustained form
Burglary	Loss sustained during
Cancellation as to any	prior insurance not
employee	issued by us or any
Commercial crime	affiliate
coverage form (loss-	Obligee
sustained form)	Other property
Contract bond	Outside the premises
Court bond	Performance bond
Discovery form	Principal
Federal surety bond	Public official bond
Fidelity coverage	Retroactive date
Fiduciary bond	endorsement
Financial institution bond	Robbery
Inside the premises—theft	Safe burglary
of money and securities	Surety bonds
Inside the premises—	Surety (obligor)
robbery or burglary of	Termination as to any
other property	employee
Judicial bonds	Theft

REVIEW QUESTIONS

1. Define robbery, burglary, safe burglary, and theft.

2. Briefly describe the following insuring agreements in the commercial crime coverage form (loss-sustained form):
   a. Employee Theft
   b. Forgery or Alteration
   c. Inside the Premises—Theft of Money and Securities
   d. Inside the Premises—Robbery or Safe Burglary of Other Property
   e. Outside the Premises

3. a. Explain the difference between a discovery form and a loss-sustained form.
   b. What is the purpose of the retroactive date endorsement that might be attached to a policy written on a discovery basis?

4. Identify the major exclusions in the commercial crime coverage form (loss-sustained form).

5. An important policy provision is called *termination as to any employee*. Explain the meaning of this provision.

6. When commercial crime insurance is written on a loss-sustained basis, the policy contains a provision called *loss sustained during prior insurance not issued by us or any affiliate*. Explain the meaning of this provision.

7. Briefly describe the following insuring agreements that appear in a financial institutions bond.
   a. Fidelity coverage
   b. On premises coverage
   c. In transit coverage
   d. Forgery or alteration

8. Identify the three parties to a surety bond.

9. How do surety bonds differ from insurance contracts?

10. Identify three types of surety bonds and give an example where each can be used.

APPLICATION QUESTIONS

1. Patrick is the owner of a liquor store that is insured under an ISO commercial crime coverage form (loss-sustained form) with the following insuring agreements:
   - Employee Theft
   - Inside the Premises—Theft of Money and Securities
   - Inside the Premises—Robbery or Safe Burglary of Other Property
   - Outside the Premises

   For each of the following losses, indicate whether any of the above insuring agreements would cover the loss. Explain your answer.
   a. Patrick withdrew money from a bank on a Friday afternoon to cash the payroll checks of customers over the weekend. He drove back to the liquor store and parked his car in the store's parking lot. As he was walking toward the liquor store, he was robbed of the cash at gunpoint.
   b. A television surveillance tape revealed that a newly hired employee was stealing money from the cash register.
   c. Patrick suspected that one employee was taking liquor from the stock of inventory without paying.

A physical inventory revealed a shortage of five cases of Kentucky whiskey.

d. A burglar forced open a locked safe and money inside the safe was taken. Also, the interior of the store was badly damaged in the burglary.

e. Because of the burglary, the business was closed for two days. Patrick's sales receipts for the week were substantially reduced.

f. A robber threatened a cashier with a knife and demanded the cash receipts. The cashier resisted paying and was severely cut and injured. The thief escaped with a substantial amount of cash.

g. A customer paid for merchandise by giving the cashier a $50 money order drawn on a commercial bank. When the money order was presented to the bank for payment, the bank refused to pay because the money order had been stolen.

2. Kathy owns a large retail electrical store that sells light fixtures, lamps, and electrical equipment. The firm is not insured for employee theft. A risk management consultant recommended adding an ISO commercial crime coverage form to the firm's package policy, including coverage for employee theft. The crime form was issued on a *discovery basis* on July 1, 2006, without a retroactive date endorsement. The coverage amount for employee theft is $25,000. A routine audit in December 2006 by an accounting firm revealed that one of the bookkeepers had embezzled $20,000 over a three-month period in 2004.

a. What dollar amount, if any, will the insurer pay for the loss?

b. Would your answer to part (a) be the same or different if the crime coverage form were issued on a loss-sustained basis? Explain.

3. Richard owns several retail stores. The employees are insured for employee theft under a commercial crime coverage form (loss-sustained form) with an insurance limit of $10,000. Richard discovered that Vera, a long-time accountant, had embezzled $5000 during the current policy period to pay the gambling debts of her son, who had been threatened with bodily harm. What is the liability of the insurer, if any, for the preceding loss? Explain your answer.

4. Vasquez Construction has been awarded a contract by a local school board to build a new public school and must provide a performance bond.

a. With respect to the performance bond, identify the principal, surety, and obligee.

b. If Vasquez Construction fails to complete the building according to the terms of the contract, what would be the surety's obligation?

c. Does the surety have any recourse against Vasquez Construction in this example? Explain your answer.

INTERNET RESOURCES

- The **Coalition Against Insurance Fraud** is an alliance of consumer, law enforcement, and insurance industry groups that attempts to reduce all types of insurance fraud by public advocacy and education. Visit the site at

  http://www.insurancefraud.org

- The **Insurance Committee for Arson Control** is an industry group that works to increase public awareness of arson and what can be done to reduce the arson problem. The organization also helps insurers recognize arson-prone risks and resist payment of fraudulent arson claims. Visit the site at

  http://www.arsoncontrol.org

- The **National Association of Surety Bond Producers** is a trade association of surety bond producers. Visit the site at

  http://www.nasbp.org

- The **National Insurance Crime Bureau** is a nonprofit organization dedicated to combating crime and vehicle theft. Visit the site at

  http://www.nicb.org

- The **Surety Association of America** is a statistical, rating, development, and advisory organization for surety companies. Visit the site at

  http://www.surety.org

- The **Surety Information Office** is a source of information about contract surety bonds. Visit the site at

  http://www.sio.org

SELECTED REFERENCES

Fire, Casualty & Surety Bulletins. Casualty and Surety volume, Crime section and Surety section. Erlanger, KY: National Underwriter Company. The bulletins are updated monthly. Detailed information on commercial crime insurance and surety bonds can be found in this volume.

Flinter, Arthur L., and Jerome Trupin. *Commercial Insurance,* 1st ed., 5th printing. Malvern, PA: American Institute for Chartered Property Casualty Underwriters/Insurance Institute of America, March 2005, ch. 5.

Trupin, Jerome, and Arthur L. Flitner. *Commercial Property Risk Management and Insurance,* 6th ed., vol. 2. Malvern, PA: American Institute for Chartered Property Casualty Underwriters/Insurance Institute of America, 2001, chs. 11, 12, 15.

Trupin, Jerome and Arthur L. Flitner. *Commercial Property Risk Management and Insurance,* 7th ed. Malvern, PA.: American Institute for CPCU/Insurance of America, 2003.

NOTES

1. The commercial crime coverages discussed in this chapter are based on Arthur L. Flitner and Jerome Trupin, *Commercial Insurance,* 1st ed., 5th printing (Malvern, PA: American Institute for Chartered Property Casualty Underwriters/Insurance Institute of America, March 2005), ch. 5; Jerome Trupin and Arthur L. Flitner, *Commercial Property Risk Management and Insurance,* 6th ed., vol. 2 (Malvern, PA: American Institute for Chartered Property Casualty Underwriters/Insurance Institute of America, 2001), chs. 11, 12; and *Fire, Casualty & Surety Bulletins,* Casualty and Surety volume, Crime section and Surety section (Erlanger, KY: National Underwriter Company). The author also drew on the copyrighted commercial crime coverage forms and contractual provisions of the Insurance Services Office (ISO). The material is used with the permission of the Insurance Services Office.

2. Flitner and Trupin, *Commercial Insurance,* p. 5.10.

3. Trupin and Flitner, *Commercial Property Risk Management and Insurance,* pp. 11.39, 11.40.

4. The discussion of financial institution bonds is based on *Fire, Casualty & Surety Bulletins,* Casualty and Surety volume, Financial Institutions section (Erlanger, KY: National Underwriter Company). The author also drew on the Financial Institution Bond, Standard Form No. 24 (Revised to April 1, 2004), the Surety Association of America, for purposes of discussing relevant contractual provisions.

5. Discussion of surety bonds is based on *Fire, Casualty & Surety Bulletins,* Casualty and Surety volume, Surety section (Erlanger, KY: National Underwriter Company).

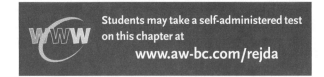

Students may take a self-administered test on this chapter at
www.aw-bc.com/rejda

HOMEOWNERS 3 (SPECIAL FORM)

Homeowners Policy Declarations

POLICYHOLDER: Chris and Karen Swift
(Named Insured) 8110 Lake Street
Lincoln, Nebraska 68506

POLICY NUMBER: 296 H 578661

POLICY PERIOD: **Inception:** June 1, 2007
Expiration: June 1, 2008

Policy period begins 12:01 A.M. standard time at the residence premises.

FIRST MORTGAGEE AND MAILING ADDRESS:

First National Bank of Lincoln
7000 Pioneer Blvd.
Lincoln, NE 68506

We will provide the insurance described in this policy in return for the premium and compliance with all applicable policy provisions.

SECTION I COVERAGES	LIMIT	
A—Dwelling	$ 250,000	**SECTION I DEDUCTIBLE:** $ 1000
B—Other Structures	$ 25,000	**(In case of loss under Section I, we cover**
C—Personal Property	$ 125,000	**only that part of the loss over the**
D—Loss of Use	$ 75,000	**deductible amount shown above.)**

SECTION II COVERAGES	LIMIT	
E—Personal Liability	$ 300,000	Each Occurrence
F—Medical Payments to Others	$ 1,000	Each Person

CONSTRUCTION: Masonry Veneer **NO. FAMILIES:** One **TYPE ROOF:** Approved

YEAR BUILT: 1985 **PROTECTION CLASS:** 7 **FIRE DISTRICT:** City of Lincoln

NOT MORE THAN 1000 FEET FROM HYDRANT

NOT MORE THAN 5 MILES FROM FIRE DEPT.

FORMS AND ENDORSEMENTS IN POLICY: HO 00 03 10 00

POLICY PREMIUM: $710.00 **COUNTERSIGNATURE DATE:** May 1, 2007 **AGENT:** Alex Rejda

SAMPLE

HOMEOWNERS 3 – SPECIAL FORM

AGREEMENT

We will provide the insurance described in this policy in return for the premium and compliance with all applicable provisions of this policy.

DEFINITIONS

A. In this policy, "you" and "your" refer to the "named insured" shown in the Declarations and the spouse if a resident of the same household. "We", "us" and "our" refer to the Company providing this insurance.

B. In addition, certain words and phrases are defined as follows:

1. "Aircraft Liability", "Hovercraft Liability", "Motor Vehicle Liability" and "Watercraft Liability", subject to the provisions in **b.** below, mean the following:

a. Liability for "bodily injury" or "property damage" arising out of the:

(1) Ownership of such vehicle or craft by an "insured";

(2) Maintenance, occupancy, operation, use, loading or unloading of such vehicle or craft by any person;

(3) Entrustment of such vehicle or craft by an "insured" to any person;

(4) Failure to supervise or negligent supervision of any person involving such vehicle or craft by an "insured"; and

(5) Vicarious liability, whether or not imposed by law, for the actions of a child or minor involving such vehicle or craft.

b. For the purpose of this definition:

(1) Aircraft means any contrivance used or designed for flight except model or hobby aircraft not used or designed to carry people or cargo;

(2) Hovercraft means a self-propelled motorized ground effect vehicle and includes, but is not limited to, flarecraft and air cushion vehicles; and

(3) Watercraft means a craft principally designed to be propelled on or in water by wind, engine power or electric motor.

(4) Motor vehicle means a "motor vehicle" as defined in **7.** below.

2. "Bodily injury" means bodily harm, sickness or disease, including required care, loss of services and death that results.

3. "Business" means:

a. A trade, profession or occupation engaged in on a full-time, part-time or occasional basis; or

b. Any other activity engaged in for money or other compensation, except the following:

(1) One or more activities, not described in **(2)** through **(4)** below, for which no "insured" receives more than $2,000 in total compensation for the 12 months before the inception date of the policy;

(2) Volunteer activities for which no money is received other than payment for expenses incurred to perform the activity;

(3) Providing home day care services for which no compensation is received, other than the mutual exchange of such services; or

(4) The rendering of home day care services to a relative of an "insured".

4. "Employee" means an employee of an "insured", or an employee leased to an "insured" by a labor leasing firm under an agreement between an "insured" and the labor leasing firm, whose duties are other than those performed by a "residence employee".

5. "Insured" means:

a. You and residents of your household who are:

(1) Your relatives; or

(2) Other persons under the age of 21 and in the care of any person named above;

b. A student enrolled in school full time, as defined by the school, who was a resident of your household before moving out to attend school, provided the student is under the age of:

(1) 24 and your relative; or

(2) 21 and in your care or the care of a person described in **a.(1)** above; or

SAMPLE

c. Under Section **II:**

(1) With respect to animals or watercraft to which this policy applies, any person or organization legally responsible for these animals or watercraft which are owned by you or any person included in **a.** or **b.** above. "Insured" does not mean a person or organization using or having custody of these animals or watercraft in the course of any "business" or without consent of the owner; or

(2) With respect to a "motor vehicle" to which this policy applies:

(a) Persons while engaged in your employ or that of any person included in **a.** or **b.** above; or

(b) Other persons using the vehicle on an "insured location" with your consent.

Under both Sections **I** and **II,** when the word an immediately precedes the word "insured", the words an "insured" together mean one or more "insureds".

6. "Insured location" means:

a. The "residence premises";

b. The part of other premises, other structures and grounds used by you as a residence; and

(1) Which is shown in the Declarations; or

(2) Which is acquired by you during the policy period for your use as a residence;

c. Any premises used by you in connection with a premises described in **a.** and **b.** above;

d. Any part of a premises:

(1) Not owned by an "insured"; and

(2) Where an "insured" is temporarily residing;

e. Vacant land, other than farm land, owned by or rented to an "insured";

f. Land owned by or rented to an "insured" on which a one, two, three or four family dwelling is being built as a residence for an "insured";

g. Individual or family cemetery plots or burial vaults of an "insured"; or

h. Any part of a premises occasionally rented to an "insured" for other than "business" use.

7. "Motor vehicle" means:

a. A self-propelled land or amphibious vehicle; or

b. Any trailer or semitrailer which is being carried on, towed by or hitched for towing by a vehicle described in **a.** above.

8. "Occurrence" means an accident, including continuous or repeated exposure to substantially the same general harmful conditions, which results, during the policy period, in:

a. "Bodily injury"; or

b. "Property damage".

9. "Property damage" means physical injury to, destruction of, or loss of use of tangible property.

10. "Residence employee" means:

a. An employee of an "insured", or an employee leased to an "insured" by a labor leasing firm, under an agreement between an "insured" and the labor leasing firm, whose duties are related to the maintenance or use of the "residence premises", including household or domestic services; or

b. One who performs similar duties elsewhere not related to the "business" of an "insured".

A "residence employee" does not include a temporary employee who is furnished to an "insured" to substitute for a permanent "residence employee" on leave or to meet seasonal or short-term workload conditions.

11. "Residence premises" means:

a. The one family dwelling where you reside;

b. The two, three or four family dwelling where you reside in at least one of the family units; or

c. That part of any other building where you reside;

and which is shown as the "residence premises" in the Declarations.

"Residence premises" also includes other structures and grounds at that location.

         HO 00 03 10 00

SAMPLE

DEDUCTIBLE

Unless otherwise noted in this policy, the following deductible provision applies:

Subject to the policy limits that apply, we will pay only that part of the total of all loss payable under Section I that exceeds the deductible amount shown in the Declarations.

SECTION I – PROPERTY COVERAGES

A. Coverage A – Dwelling

1. We cover:

    a. The dwelling on the "residence premises" shown in the Declarations, including structures attached to the dwelling; and

    b. Materials and supplies located on or next to the "residence premises" used to construct, alter or repair the dwelling or other structures on the "residence premises".

2. We do not cover land, including land on which the dwelling is located.

B. Coverage B – Other Structures

1. We cover other structures on the "residence premises" set apart from the dwelling by clear space. This includes structures connected to the dwelling by only a fence, utility line, or similar connection.

2. We do not cover:

    a. Land, including land on which the other structures are located;

    b. Other structures rented or held for rental to any person not a tenant of the dwelling, unless used solely as a private garage;

    c. Other structures from which any "business" is conducted; or

    d. Other structures used to store "business" property. However, we do cover a structure that contains "business" property solely owned by an "insured" or a tenant of the dwelling provided that "business" property does not include gaseous or liquid fuel, other than fuel in a permanently installed fuel tank of a vehicle or craft parked or stored in the structure.

3. The limit of liability for this coverage will not be more than 10% of the limit of liability that applies to Coverage **A**. Use of this coverage does not reduce the Coverage **A** limit of liability.

C. Coverage C – Personal Property

1. **Covered Property**

    We cover personal property owned or used by an "insured" while it is anywhere in the world. After a loss and at your request, we will cover personal property owned by:

    a. Others while the property is on the part of the "residence premises" occupied by an "insured"; or

    b. A guest or a "residence employee", while the property is in any residence occupied by an "insured".

2. **Limit For Property At Other Residences**

    Our limit of liability for personal property usually located at an "insured's" residence, other than the "residence premises", is 10% of the limit of liability for Coverage **C**, or $1,000, whichever is greater. However, this limitation does not apply to personal property:

    a. Moved from the "residence premises" because it is being repaired, renovated or rebuilt and is not fit to live in or store property in; or

    b. In a newly acquired principal residence for 30 days from the time you begin to move the property there.

3. **Special Limits Of Liability**

    The special limit for each category shown below is the total limit for each loss for all property in that category. These special limits do not increase the Coverage **C** limit of liability.

    a. $200 on money, bank notes, bullion, gold other than goldware, silver other than silverware, platinum other than platinumware, coins, medals, scrip, stored value cards and smart cards.

    b. $1,500 on securities, accounts, deeds, evidences of debt, letters of credit, notes other than bank notes, manuscripts, personal records, passports, tickets and stamps. This dollar limit applies to these categories regardless of the medium (such as paper or computer software) on which the material exists.

    This limit includes the cost to research, replace or restore the information from the lost or damaged material.

SAMPLE

c. $1,500 on watercraft of all types, including their trailers, furnishings, equipment and outboard engines or motors.

d. $1,500 on trailers or semitrailers not used with watercraft of all types.

e. $1,500 for loss by theft of jewelry, watches, furs, precious and semiprecious stones.

f. $2,500 for loss by theft of firearms and related equipment.

g. $2,500 for loss by theft of silverware, silver-plated ware, goldware, gold-plated ware, platinumware, platinum-plated ware and pewterware. This includes flatware, hollowware, tea sets, trays and trophies made of or including silver, gold or pewter.

h. $2,500 on property, on the "residence premises", used primarily for "business" purposes.

i. $500 on property, away from the "residence premises", used primarily for "business" purposes. However, this limit does not apply to loss to electronic apparatus and other property described in Categories j. and k. below.

j. $1,500 on electronic apparatus and accessories, while in or upon a "motor vehicle", but only if the apparatus is equipped to be operated by power from the "motor vehicle's" electrical system while still capable of being operated by other power sources.

Accessories include antennas, tapes, wires, records, discs or other media that can be used with any apparatus described in this Category j.

k. $1,500 on electronic apparatus and accessories used primarily for "business" while away from the "residence premises" and not in or upon a "motor vehicle". The apparatus must be equipped to be operated by power from the "motor vehicle's" electrical system while still capable of being operated by other power sources.

Accessories include antennas, tapes, wires, records, discs or other media that can be used with any apparatus described in this Category k.

4. Property Not Covered

We do not cover:

a. Articles separately described and specifically insured, regardless of the limit for which they are insured, in this or other insurance;

b. Animals, birds or fish;

c. "Motor vehicles".

   (1) This includes:

      (a) Their accessories, equipment and parts; or

      (b) Electronic apparatus and accessories designed to be operated solely by power from the electrical system of the "motor vehicle", but only while such property is in or upon the "motor vehicle". Accessories include antennas, tapes, wires, records, discs or other media that can be used with any apparatus described above, but only while such property is in or upon the "motor vehicle".

   (2) We do cover "motor vehicles" not required to be registered for use on public roads or property which are:

      (a) Used solely to service an "insured's" residence; or

      (b) Designed to assist the handicapped;

d. Aircraft meaning any contrivance used or designed for flight including any parts whether or not attached to the aircraft;

   We do cover model or hobby aircraft not used or designed to carry people or cargo;

e. Hovercraft and parts. Hovercraft means a self-propelled motorized ground effect vehicle and includes, but is not limited to, flarecraft and air cushion vehicles;

f. Property of roomers, boarders and other tenants, except property of roomers and boarders related to an "insured";

g. Property in an apartment regularly rented or held for rental to others by an "insured", except as provided in E.10. Landlord's Furnishings under Section I – Property Coverages;

h. Property rented or held for rental to others off the "residence premises";

i. "Business" data, including such data stored in:

   (1) Books of account, drawings or other paper records; or

   (2) Computers and related equipment.

   We do cover the cost of blank recording or storage media, and of prerecorded computer programs available on the retail market;

SAMPLE

j. Credit cards, electronic fund transfer cards or access devices used solely for deposit, withdrawal or transfer of funds except as provided in **E.6.** Credit Card, Electronic Fund Transfer Card Or Access Device, Forgery And Counterfeit Money under Section **I** – Property Coverages; or

k. Water or steam.

D. Coverage D – Loss Of Use

The limit of liability for Coverage **D** is the total limit for the coverages in **1.** Additional Living Expense, **2.** Fair Rental Value and **3.** Civil Authority Prohibits Use below.

1. Additional Living Expense

If a loss covered under Section **I** makes that part of the "residence premises" where you reside not fit to live in, we cover any necessary increase in living expenses incurred by you so that your household can maintain its normal standard of living.

Payment will be for the shortest time required to repair or replace the damage or, if you permanently relocate, the shortest time required for your household to settle elsewhere.

2. Fair Rental Value

If a loss covered under Section **I** makes that part of the "residence premises" rented to others or held for rental by you not fit to live in, we cover the fair rental value of such premises less any expenses that do not continue while it is not fit to live in.

Payment will be for the shortest time required to repair or replace that part of the premises rented or held for rental.

3. Civil Authority Prohibits Use

If a civil authority prohibits you from use of the "residence premises" as a result of direct damage to neighboring premises by a Peril Insured Against, we cover the loss as provided in **1.** Additional Living Expense and **2.** Fair Rental Value above for no more than two weeks.

4. Loss Or Expense Not Covered

We do not cover loss or expense due to cancellation of a lease or agreement.

The periods of time under **1.** Additional Living Expense, **2.** Fair Rental Value and **3.** Civil Authority Prohibits Use above are not limited by expiration of this policy.

E. Additional Coverages

1. Debris Removal

a. We will pay your reasonable expense for the removal of:

(1) Debris of covered property if a Peril Insured Against that applies to the damaged property causes the loss; or

(2) Ash, dust or particles from a volcanic eruption that has caused direct loss to a building or property contained in a building.

This expense is included in the limit of liability that applies to the damaged property. If the amount to be paid for the actual damage to the property plus the debris removal expense is more than the limit of liability for the damaged property, an additional 5% of that limit is available for such expense.

b. We will also pay your reasonable expense, up to $1,000, for the removal from the "residence premises" of:

(1) Your tree(s) felled by the peril of Windstorm or Hail or Weight of Ice, Snow or Sleet; or

(2) A neighbor's tree(s) felled by a Peril Insured Against under Coverage **C**;

provided the tree(s):

(3) Damage(s) a covered structure; or

(4) Does not damage a covered structure, but:

(a) Block(s) a driveway on the "residence premises" which prevent(s) a "motor vehicle", that is registered for use on public roads or property, from entering or leaving the "residence premises"; or

(b) Block(s) a ramp or other fixture designed to assist a handicapped person to enter or leave the dwelling building.

The $1,000 limit is the most we will pay in any one loss regardless of the number of fallen trees. No more than $500 of this limit will be paid for the removal of any one tree.

This coverage is additional insurance.

2. Reasonable Repairs

a. We will pay the reasonable cost incurred by you for the necessary measures taken solely to protect covered property that is damaged by a Peril Insured Against from further damage.

SAMPLE

b. If the measures taken involve repair to other damaged property, we will only pay if that property is covered under this policy and the damage is caused by a Peril Insured Against. This coverage does not:

(1) Increase the limit of liability that applies to the covered property; or

(2) Relieve you of your duties, in case of a loss to covered property, described in **B.4.** under Section I – Conditions.

3. Trees, Shrubs And Other Plants

We cover trees, shrubs, plants or lawns, on the "residence premises", for loss caused by the following Perils Insured Against:

a. Fire or Lightning;

b. Explosion;

c. Riot or Civil Commotion;

d. Aircraft;

e. Vehicles not owned or operated by a resident of the "residence premises";

f. Vandalism or Malicious Mischief; or

g. Theft.

We will pay up to 5% of the limit of liability that applies to the dwelling for all trees, shrubs, plants or lawns. No more than $500 of this limit will be paid for any one tree, shrub or plant. We do not cover property grown for "business" purposes.

This coverage is additional insurance.

4. Fire Department Service Charge

We will pay up to $500 for your liability assumed by contract or agreement for fire department charges incurred when the fire department is called to save or protect covered property from a Peril Insured Against. We do not cover fire department service charges if the property is located within the limits of the city, municipality or protection district furnishing the fire department response.

This coverage is additional insurance. No deductible applies to this coverage.

5. Property Removed

We insure covered property against direct loss from any cause while being removed from a premises endangered by a Peril Insured Against and for no more than 30 days while removed.

This coverage does not change the limit of liability that applies to the property being removed.

6. Credit Card, Electronic Fund Transfer Card Or Access Device, Forgery And Counterfeit Money

a. We will pay up to $500 for:

(1) The legal obligation of an "insured" to pay because of the theft or unauthorized use of credit cards issued to or registered in an "insured's" name;

(2) Loss resulting from theft or unauthorized use of an electronic fund transfer card or access device used for deposit, withdrawal or transfer of funds, issued to or registered in an "insured's" name;

(3) Loss to an "insured" caused by forgery or alteration of any check or negotiable instrument; and

(4) Loss to an "insured" through acceptance in good faith of counterfeit United States or Canadian paper currency.

All loss resulting from a series of acts committed by any one person or in which any one person is concerned or implicated is considered to be one loss.

This coverage is additional insurance. No deductible applies to this coverage.

b. We do not cover:

(1) Use of a credit card, electronic fund transfer card or access device:

(a) By a resident of your household;

(b) By a person who has been entrusted with either type of card or access device; or

(c) If an "insured" has not complied with all terms and conditions under which the cards are issued or the devices accessed; or

(2) Loss arising out of "business" use or dishonesty of an "insured".

c. If the coverage in **a.** above applies, the following defense provisions also apply:

(1) We may investigate and settle any claim or suit that we decide is appropriate. Our duty to defend a claim or suit ends when the amount we pay for the loss equals our limit of liability.

(2) If a suit is brought against an "insured" for liability under **a.(1)** or **(2)** above, we will provide a defense at our expense by counsel of our choice.

(3) We have the option to defend at our expense an "insured" or an "insured's" bank against any suit for the enforcement of payment under **a.(3)** above.

Copyright, Insurance Services Office, Inc., 1999 HO 00 03 10 00

SAMPLE

7. Loss Assessment

a. We will pay up to $1,000 for your share of loss assessment charged during the policy period against you, as owner or tenant of the "residence premises", by a corporation or association of property owners. The assessment must be made as a result of direct loss to property, owned by all members collectively, of the type that would be covered by this policy if owned by you, caused by a Peril Insured Against under Coverage **A**, other than:

(1) Earthquake; or

(2) Land shock waves or tremors before, during or after a volcanic eruption.

The limit of $1,000 is the most we will pay with respect to any one loss, regardless of the number of assessments. We will only apply one deductible, per unit, to the total amount of any one loss to the property described above, regardless of the number of assessments.

b. We do not cover assessments charged against you or a corporation or association of property owners by any governmental body.

c. Paragraph **P**. Policy Period under Section **I** – Conditions does not apply to this coverage.

This coverage is additional insurance.

8. Collapse

a. With respect to this Additional Coverage:

(1) Collapse means an abrupt falling down or caving in of a building or any part of a building with the result that the building or part of the building cannot be occupied for its current intended purpose.

(2) A building or any part of a building that is in danger of falling down or caving in is not considered to be in a state of collapse.

(3) A part of a building that is standing is not considered to be in a state of collapse even if it has separated from another part of the building.

(4) A building or any part of a building that is standing is not considered to be in a state of collapse even if it shows evidence of cracking, bulging, sagging, bending, leaning, settling, shrinkage or expansion.

b. We insure for direct physical loss to covered property involving collapse of a building or any part of a building if the collapse was caused by one or more of the following:

(1) The Perils Insured Against named under Coverage **C**;

(2) Decay that is hidden from view, unless the presence of such decay is known to an "insured" prior to collapse;

(3) Insect or vermin damage that is hidden from view, unless the presence of such damage is known to an "insured" prior to collapse;

(4) Weight of contents, equipment, animals or people;

(5) Weight of rain which collects on a roof; or

(6) Use of defective material or methods in construction, remodeling or renovation if the collapse occurs during the course of the construction, remodeling or renovation.

c. Loss to an awning, fence, patio, deck, pavement, swimming pool, underground pipe, flue, drain, cesspool, septic tank, foundation, retaining wall, bulkhead, pier, wharf or dock is not included under **b.(2)** through **(6)** above, unless the loss is a direct result of the collapse of a building or any part of a building.

d. This coverage does not increase the limit of liability that applies to the damaged covered property.

9. Glass Or Safety Glazing Material

a. We cover:

(1) The breakage of glass or safety glazing material which is part of a covered building, storm door or storm window;

(2) The breakage of glass or safety glazing material which is part of a covered building, storm door or storm window when caused directly by earth movement; and

(3) The direct physical loss to covered property caused solely by the pieces, fragments or splinters of broken glass or safety glazing material which is part of a building, storm door or storm window.

SAMPLE

b. This coverage does not include loss:

   (1) To covered property which results because the glass or safety glazing material has been broken, except as provided in **a.(3)** above; or

   (2) On the "residence premises" if the dwelling has been vacant for more than 60 consecutive days immediately before the loss, except when the breakage results directly from earth movement as provided in **a.(2)** above. A dwelling being constructed is not considered vacant.

c. This coverage does not increase the limit of liability that applies to the damaged property.

10. **Landlord's Furnishings**

We will pay up to $2,500 for your appliances, carpeting and other household furnishings, in each apartment on the "residence premises" regularly rented or held for rental to others by an "insured", for loss caused by a Peril Insured Against in Coverage **C**, other than Theft.

This limit is the most we will pay in any one loss regardless of the number of appliances, carpeting or other household furnishings involved in the loss.

This coverage does not increase the limit of liability applying to the damaged property.

11. **Ordinance Or Law**

   a. You may use up to 10% of the limit of liability that applies to Coverage **A** for the increased costs you incur due to the enforcement of any ordinance or law which requires or regulates:

      (1) The construction, demolition, remodeling, renovation or repair of that part of a covered building or other structure damaged by a Peril Insured Against;

      (2) The demolition and reconstruction of the undamaged part of a covered building or other structure, when that building or other structure must be totally demolished because of damage by a Peril Insured Against to another part of that covered building or other structure; or

      (3) The remodeling, removal or replacement of the portion of the undamaged part of a covered building or other structure necessary to complete the remodeling, repair or replacement of that part of the covered building or other structure damaged by a Peril Insured Against.

   b. You may use all or part of this ordinance or law coverage to pay for the increased costs you incur to remove debris resulting from the construction, demolition, remodeling, renovation, repair or replacement of property as stated in **a.** above.

   c. We do not cover:

      (1) The loss in value to any covered building or other structure due to the requirements of any ordinance or law; or

      (2) The costs to comply with any ordinance or law which requires any "insured" or others to test for, monitor, clean up, remove, contain, treat, detoxify or neutralize, or in any way respond to, or assess the effects of, pollutants in or on any covered building or other structure.

      Pollutants means any solid, liquid, gaseous or thermal irritant or contaminant, including smoke, vapor, soot, fumes, acids, alkalis, chemicals and waste. Waste includes materials to be recycled, reconditioned or reclaimed.

   This coverage is additional insurance.

12. **Grave Markers**

We will pay up to $5,000 for grave markers, including mausoleums, on or away from the "residence premises" for loss caused by a Peril Insured Against under Coverage **C**.

This coverage does not increase the limits of liability that apply to the damaged covered property.

SECTION I – PERILS INSURED AGAINST

A. Coverage A – Dwelling And Coverage B – Other Structures

1. We insure against risk of direct physical loss to property described in Coverages **A** and **B**.

2. We do not insure, however, for loss:

   a. Excluded under Section I – Exclusions;

   b. Involving collapse, except as provided in **E.8.** Collapse under Section I – Property Coverages; and

   c. Caused by:

      (1) Freezing of a plumbing, heating, air conditioning or automatic fire protective sprinkler system or of a household appliance, or by discharge, leakage or overflow from within the system or appliance caused by freezing. This provision does not apply if you have used reasonable care to:

         (a) Maintain heat in the building; or

SAMPLE

(b) Shut off the water supply and drain all systems and appliances of water.

However, if the building is protected by an automatic fire protective sprinkler system, you must use reasonable care to continue the water supply and maintain heat in the building for coverage to apply.

For purposes of this provision a plumbing system or household appliance does not include a sump, sump pump or related equipment or a roof drain, gutter, downspout or similar fixtures or equipment;

(2) Freezing, thawing, pressure or weight of water or ice, whether driven by wind or not, to a:

(a) Fence, pavement, patio or swimming pool;

(b) Footing, foundation, bulkhead, wall, or any other structure or device that supports all or part of a building, or other structure;

(c) Retaining wall or bulkhead that does not support all or part of a building or other structure; or

(d) Pier, wharf or dock;

(3) Theft in or to a dwelling under construction, or of materials and supplies for use in the construction until the dwelling is finished and occupied;

(4) Vandalism and malicious mischief, and any ensuing loss caused by any intentional and wrongful act committed in the course of the vandalism or malicious mischief, if the dwelling has been vacant for more than 60 consecutive days immediately before the loss. A dwelling being constructed is not considered vacant;

(5) Mold, fungus or wet rot. However, we do insure for loss caused by mold, fungus or wet rot that is hidden within the walls or ceilings or beneath the floors or above the ceilings of a structure if such loss results from the accidental discharge or overflow of water or steam from within:

(a) A plumbing, heating, air conditioning or automatic fire protective sprinkler system, or a household appliance, on the "residence premises"; or

(b) A storm drain, or water, steam or sewer pipes, off the "residence premises".

For purposes of this provision, a plumbing system or household appliance does not include a sump, sump pump or related equipment or a roof drain, gutter, downspout or similar fixtures or equipment; or

(6) Any of the following:

(a) Wear and tear, marring, deterioration;

(b) Mechanical breakdown, latent defect, inherent vice, or any quality in property that causes it to damage or destroy itself;

(c) Smog, rust or other corrosion, or dry rot;

(d) Smoke from agricultural smudging or industrial operations;

(e) Discharge, dispersal, seepage, migration, release or escape of pollutants unless the discharge, dispersal, seepage, migration, release or escape is itself caused by a Peril Insured Against named under Coverage **C**.

Pollutants means any solid, liquid, gaseous or thermal irritant or contaminant, including smoke, vapor, soot, fumes, acids, alkalis, chemicals and waste. Waste includes materials to be recycled, reconditioned or reclaimed;

(f) Settling, shrinking, bulging or expansion, including resultant cracking, of bulkheads, pavements, patios, footings, foundations, walls, floors, roofs or ceilings;

(g) Birds, vermin, rodents, or insects; or

(h) Animals owned or kept by an "insured".

Exception To c.(6)

Unless the loss is otherwise excluded, we cover loss to property covered under Coverage **A** or **B** resulting from an accidental discharge or overflow of water or steam from within a:

(i) Storm drain, or water, steam or sewer pipe, off the "residence premises"; or

SAMPLE

    (ii) Plumbing, heating, air conditioning or automatic fire protective sprinkler system or household appliance on the "residence premises". This includes the cost to tear out and replace any part of a building, or other structure, on the "residence premises", but only when necessary to repair the system or appliance. However, such tear out and replacement coverage only applies to other structures if the water or steam causes actual damage to a building on the "residence premises".

    We do not cover loss to the system or appliance from which this water or steam escaped.

    For purposes of this provision, a plumbing system or household appliance does not include a sump, sump pump or related equipment or a roof drain, gutter, down spout or similar fixtures or equipment.

    Section I – Exclusion **A.3.** Water Damage, Paragraphs **a.** and **c.** that apply to surface water and water below the surface of the ground do not apply to loss by water covered under **c.(5)** and **(6)** above.

    Under **2.b.** and **c.** above, any ensuing loss to property described in Coverages **A** and **B** not precluded by any other provision in this policy is covered.

B. Coverage C – Personal Property

We insure for direct physical loss to the property described in Coverage **C** caused by any of the following perils unless the loss is excluded in Section I – Exclusions.

1. Fire Or Lightning

2. Windstorm Or Hail

This peril includes loss to watercraft of all types and their trailers, furnishings, equipment, and outboard engines or motors, only while inside a fully enclosed building.

This peril does not include loss to the property contained in a building caused by rain, snow, sleet, sand or dust unless the direct force of wind or hail damages the building causing an opening in a roof or wall and the rain, snow, sleet, sand or dust enters through this opening.

3. Explosion

4. Riot Or Civil Commotion

5. Aircraft

This peril includes self-propelled missiles and spacecraft.

6. Vehicles

7. Smoke

This peril means sudden and accidental damage from smoke, including the emission or puffback of smoke, soot, fumes or vapors from a boiler, furnace or related equipment.

This peril does not include loss caused by smoke from agricultural smudging or industrial operations.

8. Vandalism Or Malicious Mischief

9. Theft

    a. This peril includes attempted theft and loss of property from a known place when it is likely that the property has been stolen.

    b. This peril does not include loss caused by theft:

        (1) Committed by an "insured";

        (2) In or to a dwelling under construction, or of materials and supplies for use in the construction until the dwelling is finished and occupied;

        (3) From that part of a "residence premises" rented by an "insured" to someone other than another "insured"; or

        (4) That occurs off the "residence premises" of:

           (a) Trailers, semitrailers and campers;

           (b) Watercraft of all types, and their furnishings, equipment and outboard engines or motors; or

           (c) Property while at any other residence owned by, rented to, or occupied by an "insured", except while an "insured" is temporarily living there. Property of an "insured" who is a student is covered while at the residence the student occupies to attend school as long as the student has been there at any time during the 60 days immediately before the loss.

10. Falling Objects

This peril does not include loss to property contained in a building unless the roof or an outside wall of the building is first damaged by a falling object. Damage to the falling object itself is not included.

11. Weight Of Ice, Snow Or Sleet

This peril means weight of ice, snow or sleet which causes damage to property contained in a building.

SAMPLE

12. **Accidental Discharge Or Overflow Of Water Or Steam**

   a. This peril means accidental discharge or overflow of water or steam from within a plumbing, heating, air conditioning or automatic fire protective sprinkler system or from within a household appliance.

   b. This peril does not include loss:

      (1) To the system or appliance from which the water or steam escaped;

      (2) Caused by or resulting from freezing except as provided in Peril Insured Against 14. Freezing;

      (3) On the "residence premises" caused by accidental discharge or overflow which occurs off the "residence premises"; or

      (4) Caused by mold, fungus or wet rot unless hidden within the walls or ceilings or beneath the floors or above the ceilings of a structure.

   c. In this peril, a plumbing system or household appliance does not include a sump, sump pump or related equipment or a roof drain, gutter, downspout or similar fixtures or equipment.

   d. Section I – Exclusion **A.3.** Water Damage, Paragraphs **a.** and **c.** that apply to surface water and water below the surface of the ground do not apply to loss by water covered under this peril.

13. **Sudden And Accidental Tearing Apart, Cracking, Burning Or Bulging**

   This peril means sudden and accidental tearing apart, cracking, burning or bulging of a steam or hot water heating system, an air conditioning or automatic fire protective sprinkler system, or an appliance for heating water.

   We do not cover loss caused by or resulting from freezing under this peril.

14. **Freezing**

   a. This peril means freezing of a plumbing, heating, air conditioning or automatic fire protective sprinkler system or of a household appliance but only if you have used reasonable care to:

      (1) Maintain heat in the building; or

      (2) Shut off the water supply and drain all systems and appliances of water.

   However, if the building is protected by an automatic fire protective sprinkler system, you must use reasonable care to continue the water supply and maintain heat in the building for coverage to apply.

   b. In this peril, a plumbing system or household appliance does not include a sump, sump pump or related equipment or a roof drain, gutter, downspout or similar fixtures or equipment.

15. **Sudden And Accidental Damage From Artificially Generated Electrical Current**

   This peril does not include loss to tubes, transistors, electronic components or circuitry that are a part of appliances, fixtures, computers, home entertainment units or other types of electronic apparatus.

16. **Volcanic Eruption**

   This peril does not include loss caused by earthquake, land shock waves or tremors.

SECTION I – EXCLUSIONS

A. We do not insure for loss caused directly or indirectly by any of the following. Such loss is excluded regardless of any other cause or event contributing concurrently or in any sequence to the loss. These exclusions apply whether or not the loss event results in widespread damage or affects a substantial area.

   1. **Ordinance Or Law**

      Ordinance Or Law means any ordinance or law:

      a. Requiring or regulating the construction, demolition, remodeling, renovation or repair of property, including removal of any resulting debris. This Exclusion **A.1.a.** does not apply to the amount of coverage that may be provided for in **E.11.** Ordinance Or Law under Section I – Property Coverages;

      b. The requirements of which result in a loss in value to property; or

      c. Requiring any "insured" or others to test for, monitor, clean up, remove, contain, treat, detoxify or neutralize, or in any way respond to, or assess the effects of, pollutants.

      Pollutants means any solid, liquid, gaseous or thermal irritant or contaminant, including smoke, vapor, soot, fumes, acids, alkalis, chemicals and waste. Waste includes materials to be recycled, reconditioned or reclaimed.

      This Exclusion **1.** applies whether or not the property has been physically damaged.

   2. **Earth Movement**

      Earth Movement means:

      a. Earthquake, including land shock waves or tremors before, during or after a volcanic eruption;

SAMPLE

b. Landslide, mudslide or mudflow;

c. Subsidence or sinkhole; or

d. Any other earth movement including earth sinking, rising or shifting;

caused by or resulting from human or animal forces or any act of nature unless direct loss by fire or explosion ensues and then we will pay only for the ensuing loss.

This Exclusion **2.** does not apply to loss by theft.

3. Water Damage

Water Damage means:

a. Flood, surface water, waves, tidal water, overflow of a body of water, or spray from any of these, whether or not driven by wind;

b. Water or water-borne material which backs up through sewers or drains or which overflows or is discharged from a sump, sump pump or related equipment; or

c. Water or water-borne material below the surface of the ground, including water which exerts pressure on or seeps or leaks through a building, sidewalk, driveway, foundation, swimming pool or other structure;

caused by or resulting from human or animal forces or any act of nature.

Direct loss by fire, explosion or theft resulting from water damage is covered.

4. Power Failure

Power Failure means the failure of power or other utility service if the failure takes place off the "residence premises". But if the failure results in a loss, from a Peril Insured Against on the "residence premises", we will pay for the loss caused by that peril.

5. Neglect

Neglect means neglect of an "insured" to use all reasonable means to save and preserve property at and after the time of a loss.

6. War

War includes the following and any consequence of any of the following:

a. Undeclared war, civil war, insurrection, rebellion or revolution;

b. Warlike act by a military force or military personnel; or

c. Destruction, seizure or use for a military purpose.

Discharge of a nuclear weapon will be deemed a warlike act even if accidental.

7. Nuclear Hazard

This Exclusion **7.** pertains to Nuclear Hazard to the extent set forth in **M.** Nuclear Hazard Clause under Section **I** – Conditions.

8. Intentional Loss

Intentional Loss means any loss arising out of any act an "insured" commits or conspires to commit with the intent to cause a loss.

In the event of such loss, no "insured" is entitled to coverage, even "insureds" who did not commit or conspire to commit the act causing the loss.

9. Governmental Action

Governmental Action means the destruction, confiscation or seizure of property described in Coverage **A, B** or **C** by order of any governmental or public authority.

This exclusion does not apply to such acts ordered by any governmental or public authority that are taken at the time of a fire to prevent its spread, if the loss caused by fire would be covered under this policy.

B. We do not insure for loss to property described in Coverages **A** and **B** caused by any of the following. However, any ensuing loss to property described in Coverages **A** and **B** not precluded by any other provision in this policy is covered.

1. Weather conditions. However, this exclusion only applies if weather conditions contribute in any way with a cause or event excluded in **A.** above to produce the loss.

2. Acts or decisions, including the failure to act or decide, of any person, group, organization or governmental body.

3. Faulty, inadequate or defective:

   a. Planning, zoning, development, surveying, siting;

   b. Design, specifications, workmanship, repair, construction, renovation, remodeling, grading, compaction;

   c. Materials used in repair, construction, renovation or remodeling; or

   d. Maintenance;

   of part or all of any property whether on or off the "residence premises".

SAMPLE

SECTION I – CONDITIONS

A. Insurable Interest And Limit Of Liability

Even if more than one person has an insurable interest in the property covered, we will not be liable in any one loss:

1. To an "insured" for more than the amount of such "insured's" interest at the time of loss; or

2. For more than the applicable limit of liability.

B. Duties After Loss

In case of a loss to covered property, we have no duty to provide coverage under this policy if the failure to comply with the following duties is prejudicial to us. These duties must be performed either by you, an "insured" seeking coverage, or a representative of either:

1. Give prompt notice to us or our agent;

2. Notify the police in case of loss by theft;

3. Notify the credit card or electronic fund transfer card or access device company in case of loss as provided for in E.6. Credit Card, Electronic Fund Transfer Card Or Access Device, Forgery And Counterfeit Money under Section I – Property Coverages;

4. Protect the property from further damage. If repairs to the property are required, you must:

   a. Make reasonable and necessary repairs to protect the property; and

   b. Keep an accurate record of repair expenses;

5. Cooperate with us in the investigation of a claim;

6. Prepare an inventory of damaged personal property showing the quantity, description, actual cash value and amount of loss. Attach all bills, receipts and related documents that justify the figures in the inventory;

7. As often as we reasonably require:

   a. Show the damaged property;

   b. Provide us with records and documents we request and permit us to make copies; and

   c. Submit to examination under oath, while not in the presence of another "insured", and sign the same;

8. Send to us, within 60 days after our request, your signed, sworn proof of loss which sets forth, to the best of your knowledge and belief:

   a. The time and cause of loss;

   b. The interests of all "insureds" and all others in the property involved and all liens on the property;

   c. Other insurance which may cover the loss;

   d. Changes in title or occupancy of the property during the term of the policy;

   e. Specifications of damaged buildings and detailed repair estimates;

   f. The inventory of damaged personal property described in 6. above;

   g. Receipts for additional living expenses incurred and records that support the fair rental value loss; and

   h. Evidence or affidavit that supports a claim under E.6. Credit Card, Electronic Fund Transfer Card Or Access Device, Forgery And Counterfeit Money under Section I – Property Coverages, stating the amount and cause of loss.

C. Loss Settlement

In this Condition C., the terms "cost to repair or replace" and "replacement cost" do not include the increased costs incurred to comply with the enforcement of any ordinance or law, except to the extent that coverage for these increased costs is provided in E.11. Ordinance Or Law under Section I – Property Coverages. Covered property losses are settled as follows:

1. Property of the following types:

   a. Personal property;

   b. Awnings, carpeting, household appliances, outdoor antennas and outdoor equipment, whether or not attached to buildings;

   c. Structures that are not buildings; and

   d. Grave markers, including mausoleums;

   at actual cash value at the time of loss but not more than the amount required to repair or replace.

2. Buildings covered under Coverage A or B at replacement cost without deduction for depreciation, subject to the following:

   a. If, at the time of loss, the amount of insurance in this policy on the damaged building is 80% or more of the full replacement cost of the building immediately before the loss, we will pay the cost to repair or replace, after application of any deductible and without deduction for depreciation, but not more than the least of the following amounts:

      (1) The limit of liability under this policy that applies to the building;

      (2) The replacement cost of that part of the building damaged with material of like kind and quality and for like use; or

      (3) The necessary amount actually spent to repair or replace the damaged building.

SAMPLE

If the building is rebuilt at a new premises, the cost described in **(2)** above is limited to the cost which would have been incurred if the building had been built at the original premises.

b. If, at the time of loss, the amount of insurance in this policy on the damaged building is less than 80% of the full replacement cost of the building immediately before the loss, we will pay the greater of the following amounts, but not more than the limit of liability under this policy that applies to the building:

   (1) The actual cash value of that part of the building damaged; or

   (2) That proportion of the cost to repair or replace, after application of any deductible and without deduction for depreciation, that part of the building damaged, which the total amount of insurance in this policy on the damaged building bears to 80% of the replacement cost of the building.

c. To determine the amount of insurance required to equal 80% of the full replacement cost of the building immediately before the loss, do not include the value of:

   (1) Excavations, footings, foundations, piers, or any other structures or devices that support all or part of the building, which are below the undersurface of the lowest basement floor;

   (2) Those supports described in **(1)** above which are below the surface of the ground inside the foundation walls, if there is no basement; and

   (3) Underground flues, pipes, wiring and drains.

d. We will pay no more than the actual cash value of the damage until actual repair or replacement is complete. Once actual repair or replacement is complete, we will settle the loss as noted in **2.a.** and **b.** above.

However, if the cost to repair or replace the damage is both:

   (1) Less than 5% of the amount of insurance in this policy on the building; and

   (2) Less than $2,500;

we will settle the loss as noted in **2.a.** and **b.** above whether or not actual repair or replacement is complete.

   e. You may disregard the replacement cost loss settlement provisions and make claim under this policy for loss to buildings on an actual cash value basis. You may then make claim for any additional liability according to the provisions of this Condition **C. Loss Settlement**, provided you notify us of your intent to do so within 180 days after the date of loss.

D. Loss To A Pair Or Set

In case of loss to a pair or set we may elect to:

1. Repair or replace any part to restore the pair or set to its value before the loss; or

2. Pay the difference between actual cash value of the property before and after the loss.

E. Appraisal

If you and we fail to agree on the amount of loss, either may demand an appraisal of the loss. In this event, each party will choose a competent and impartial appraiser within 20 days after receiving a written request from the other. The two appraisers will choose an umpire. If they cannot agree upon an umpire within 15 days, you or we may request that the choice be made by a judge of a court of record in the state where the "residence premises" is located. The appraisers will separately set the amount of loss. If the appraisers submit a written report of an agreement to us, the amount agreed upon will be the amount of loss. If they fail to agree, they will submit their differences to the umpire. A decision agreed to by any two will set the amount of loss.

Each party will:

1. Pay its own appraiser; and

2. Bear the other expenses of the appraisal and umpire equally.

F. Other Insurance And Service Agreement

If a loss covered by this policy is also covered by:

1. Other insurance, we will pay only the proportion of the loss that the limit of liability that applies under this policy bears to the total amount of insurance covering the loss; or

2. A service agreement, this insurance is excess over any amounts payable under any such agreement. Service agreement means a service plan, property restoration plan, home warranty or other similar service warranty agreement, even if it is characterized as insurance.

G. Suit Against Us

No action can be brought against us unless there has been full compliance with all of the terms under Section I of this policy and the action is started within two years after the date of loss.

HO 00 03 10 00

SAMPLE

H. Our Option

If we give you written notice within 30 days after we receive your signed, sworn proof of loss, we may repair or replace any part of the damaged property with material or property of like kind and quality.

I. Loss Payment

We will adjust all losses with you. We will pay you unless some other person is named in the policy or is legally entitled to receive payment. Loss will be payable 60 days after we receive your proof of loss and:

1. Reach an agreement with you;
2. There is an entry of a final judgment; or
3. There is a filing of an appraisal award with us.

J. Abandonment Of Property

We need not accept any property abandoned by an "insured".

K. Mortgage Clause

1. If a mortgagee is named in this policy, any loss payable under Coverage **A** or **B** will be paid to the mortgagee and you, as interests appear. If more than one mortgagee is named, the order of payment will be the same as the order of precedence of the mortgages.
2. If we deny your claim, that denial will not apply to a valid claim of the mortgagee, if the mortgagee:
   a. Notifies us of any change in ownership, occupancy or substantial change in risk of which the mortgagee is aware;
   b. Pays any premium due under this policy on demand if you have neglected to pay the premium; and
   c. Submits a signed, sworn statement of loss within 60 days after receiving notice from us of your failure to do so. Paragraphs **E.** Appraisal, **G.** Suit Against Us and **I.** Loss Payment under Section I – Conditions also apply to the mortgagee.
3. If we decide to cancel or not to renew this policy, the mortgagee will be notified at least 10 days before the date cancellation or nonrenewal takes effect.
4. If we pay the mortgagee for any loss and deny payment to you:
   a. We are subrogated to all the rights of the mortgagee granted under the mortgage on the property; or

   b. At our option, we may pay to the mortgagee the whole principal on the mortgage plus any accrued interest. In this event, we will receive a full assignment and transfer of the mortgage and all securities held as collateral to the mortgage debt.
5. Subrogation will not impair the right of the mortgagee to recover the full amount of the mortgagee's claim.

L. No Benefit To Bailee

We will not recognize any assignment or grant any coverage that benefits a person or organization holding, storing or moving property for a fee regardless of any other provision of this policy.

M. Nuclear Hazard Clause

1. "Nuclear Hazard" means any nuclear reaction, radiation, or radioactive contamination, all whether controlled or uncontrolled or however caused, or any consequence of any of these.
2. Loss caused by the nuclear hazard will not be considered loss caused by fire, explosion, or smoke, whether these perils are specifically named in or otherwise included within the Perils Insured Against.
3. This policy does not apply under Section I to loss caused directly or indirectly by nuclear hazard, except that direct loss by fire resulting from the nuclear hazard is covered.

N. Recovered Property

If you or we recover any property for which we have made payment under this policy, you or we will notify the other of the recovery. At your option, the property will be returned to or retained by you or it will become our property. If the recovered property is returned to or retained by you, the loss payment will be adjusted based on the amount you received for the recovered property.

O. Volcanic Eruption Period

One or more volcanic eruptions that occur within a 72 hour period will be considered as one volcanic eruption.

P. Policy Period

This policy applies only to loss which occurs during the policy period.

Q. Concealment Or Fraud

We provide coverage to no "insureds" under this policy if, whether before or after a loss, an "insured" has:

1. Intentionally concealed or misrepresented any material fact or circumstance;

SAMPLE

2. Engaged in fraudulent conduct; or

3. Made false statements;

relating to this insurance.

R. Loss Payable Clause

If the Declarations show a loss payee for certain listed insured personal property, the definition of "insured" is changed to include that loss payee with respect to that property.

If we decide to cancel or not renew this policy, that loss payee will be notified in writing.

SECTION II – LIABILITY COVERAGES

A. Coverage E – Personal Liability

If a claim is made or a suit is brought against an "insured" for damages because of "bodily injury" or "property damage" caused by an "occurrence" to which this coverage applies, we will:

1. Pay up to our limit of liability for the damages for which an "insured" is legally liable. Damages include prejudgment interest awarded against an "insured"; and

2. Provide a defense at our expense by counsel of our choice, even if the suit is groundless, false or fraudulent. We may investigate and settle any claim or suit that we decide is appropriate. Our duty to settle or defend ends when our limit of liability for the "occurrence" has been exhausted by payment of a judgment or settlement.

B. Coverage F – Medical Payments To Others

We will pay the necessary medical expenses that are incurred or medically ascertained within three years from the date of an accident causing "bodily injury". Medical expenses means reasonable charges for medical, surgical, x-ray, dental, ambulance, hospital, professional nursing, prosthetic devices and funeral services. This coverage does not apply to you or regular residents of your household except "residence employees". As to others, this coverage applies only:

1. To a person on the "insured location" with the permission of an "insured"; or

2. To a person off the "insured location", if the "bodily injury":

a. Arises out of a condition on the "insured location" or the ways immediately adjoining;

b. Is caused by the activities of an "insured";

c. Is caused by a "residence employee" in the course of the "residence employee's" employment by an "insured"; or

d. Is caused by an animal owned by or in the care of an "insured".

SECTION II – EXCLUSIONS

A. "Motor Vehicle Liability"

1. Coverages **E** and **F** do not apply to any "motor vehicle liability" if, at the time and place of an "occurrence", the involved "motor vehicle":

a. Is registered for use on public roads or property;

b. Is not registered for use on public roads or property, but such registration is required by a law, or regulation issued by a government agency, for it to be used at the place of the "occurrence"; or

c. Is being:

(1) Operated in, or practicing for, any prearranged or organized race, speed contest or other competition;

(2) Rented to others;

(3) Used to carry persons or cargo for a charge; or

(4) Used for any "business" purpose except for a motorized golf cart while on a golfing facility.

2. If Exclusion **A.1.** does not apply, there is still no coverage for "motor vehicle liability" unless the "motor vehicle" is:

a. In dead storage on an "insured location";

b. Used solely to service an "insured's" residence;

c. Designed to assist the handicapped and, at the time of an "occurrence", it is:

(1) Being used to assist a handicapped person; or

(2) Parked on an "insured location";

d. Designed for recreational use off public roads and:

(1) Not owned by an "insured"; or

(2) Owned by an "insured" provided the "occurrence" takes place on an "insured location" as defined in Definitions **B. 6.a., b., d., e.** or **h.**; or

e. A motorized golf cart that is owned by an "insured", designed to carry up to 4 persons, not built or modified after manufacture to exceed a speed of 25 miles per hour on level ground and, at the time of an "occurrence", is within the legal boundaries of:

(1) A golfing facility and is parked or stored there, or being used by an "insured" to:

(a) Play the game of golf or for other recreational or leisure activity allowed by the facility;

 HO 00 03 10 00

SAMPLE

(b) Travel to or from an area where "motor vehicles" or golf carts are parked or stored; or

(c) Cross public roads at designated points to access other parts of the golfing facility; or

(2) A private residential community, including its public roads upon which a motorized golf cart can legally travel, which is subject to the authority of a property owners association and contains an "insured's" residence.

B. **"Watercraft Liability"**

1. Coverages **E** and **F** do not apply to any "watercraft liability" if, at the time of an "occurrence", the involved watercraft is being:

a. Operated in, or practicing for, any prearranged or organized race, speed contest or other competition. This exclusion does not apply to a sailing vessel or a predicted log cruise;

b. Rented to others;

c. Used to carry persons or cargo for a charge; or

d. Used for any "business" purpose.

2. If Exclusion **B.1.** does not apply, there is still no coverage for "watercraft liability" unless, at the time of the "occurrence", the watercraft:

a. Is stored;

b. Is a sailing vessel, with or without auxiliary power that is:

(1) Less than 26 feet in overall length; or

(2) 26 feet or more in overall length and not owned by or rented to an "insured"; or

c. Is not a sailing vessel and is powered by:

(1) An inboard or inboard-outdrive engine or motor, including those that power a water jet pump, of:

(a) 50 horsepower or less and not owned by an "insured"; or

(b) More than 50 horsepower and not owned by or rented to an "insured"; or

(2) One or more outboard engines or motors with:

(a) 25 total horsepower or less;

(b) More than 25 horsepower if the outboard engine or motor is not owned by an "insured";

(c) More than 25 horsepower if the outboard engine or motor is owned by an "insured" who acquired it during the policy period; or

(d) More than 25 horsepower if the outboard engine or motor is owned by an "insured" who acquired it before the policy period, but only if:

(i) You declare them at policy inception; or

(ii) Your intent to insure them is reported to us in writing within 45 days after you acquire them.

The coverages in **(c)** and **(d)** above apply for the policy period.

Horsepower means the maximum power rating assigned to the engine or motor by the manufacturer.

C. **"Aircraft Liability"**

This policy does not cover "aircraft liability".

D. **"Hovercraft Liability"**

This policy does not cover "hovercraft liability".

E. **Coverage E – Personal Liability And Coverage F – Medical Payments To Others**

Coverages **E** and **F** do not apply to the following:

1. **Expected Or Intended Injury**

"Bodily injury" or "property damage" which is expected or intended by an "insured" even if the resulting "bodily injury" or "property damage":

a. Is of a different kind, quality or degree than initially expected or intended; or

b. Is sustained by a different person, entity, real or personal property, than initially expected or intended.

However, this Exclusion **E.1.** does not apply to "bodily injury" resulting from the use of reasonable force by an "insured" to protect persons or property;

2. **"Business"**

a. "Bodily injury" or "property damage" arising out of or in connection with a "business" conducted from an "insured location" or engaged in by an "insured", whether or not the "business" is owned or operated by an "insured" or employs an "insured".

This Exclusion **E.2.** applies but is not limited to an act or omission, regardless of its nature or circumstance, involving a service or duty rendered, promised, owed, or implied to be provided because of the nature of the "business".

b. This Exclusion **E.2.** does not apply to:

(1) The rental or holding for rental of an "insured location";

SAMPLE

(a) On an occasional basis if used only as a residence;

(b) In part for use only as a residence, unless a single family unit is intended for use by the occupying family to lodge more than two roomers or boarders; or

(c) In part, as an office, school, studio or private garage; and

(2) An "insured" under the age of 21 years involved in a part-time or occasional, self-employed "business" with no employees;

3. Professional Services

"Bodily injury" or "property damage" arising out of the rendering of or failure to render professional services;

4. "Insured's" Premises Not An "Insured Location"

"Bodily injury" or "property damage" arising out of a premises:

a. Owned by an "insured";

b. Rented to an "insured"; or

c. Rented to others by an "insured";

that is not an "insured location";

5. War

"Bodily injury" or "property damage" caused directly or indirectly by war, including the following and any consequence of any of the following:

a. Undeclared war, civil war, insurrection, rebellion or revolution;

b. Warlike act by a military force or military personnel; or

c. Destruction, seizure or use for a military purpose.

Discharge of a nuclear weapon will be deemed a warlike act even if accidental;

6. Communicable Disease

"Bodily injury" or "property damage" which arises out of the transmission of a communicable disease by an "insured";

7. Sexual Molestation, Corporal Punishment Or Physical Or Mental Abuse

"Bodily injury" or "property damage" arising out of sexual molestation, corporal punishment or physical or mental abuse; or

8. Controlled Substance

"Bodily injury" or "property damage" arising out of the use, sale, manufacture, delivery, transfer or possession by any person of a Controlled Substance as defined by the Federal Food and Drug Law at 21 U.S.C.A. Sections 811 and 812. Controlled Substances include but are not limited to cocaine, LSD, marijuana and all narcotic drugs. However, this exclusion does not apply to the legitimate use of prescription drugs by a person following the orders of a licensed physician.

Exclusions **A.** "Motor Vehicle Liability", **B.** "Watercraft Liability", **C.** "Aircraft Liability", **D.** "Hovercraft Liability", and **E.4.** "Insured's" Premises Not An "Insured Location" do not apply to "bodily injury" to a "residence employee" arising out of and in the course of the "residence employee's" employment by an "insured".

F. Coverage E – Personal Liability

Coverage E does not apply to:

1. Liability:

a. For any loss assessment charged against you as a member of an association, corporation or community of property owners, except as provided in **D.** Loss Assessment under Section II – Additional Coverages;

b. Under any contract or agreement entered into by an "insured". However, this exclusion does not apply to written contracts:

(1) That directly relate to the ownership, maintenance or use of an "insured location"; or

(2) Where the liability of others is assumed by you prior to an "occurrence";

unless excluded in **a.** above or elsewhere in this policy;

2. "Property damage" to property owned by an "insured". This includes costs or expenses incurred by an "insured" or others to repair, replace, enhance, restore or maintain such property to prevent injury to a person or damage to property of others, whether on or away from an "insured location";

3. "Property damage" to property rented to, occupied or used by or in the care of an "insured". This exclusion does not apply to "property damage" caused by fire, smoke or explosion;

4. "Bodily injury" to any person eligible to receive any benefits voluntarily provided or required to be provided by an "insured" under any:

a. Workers' compensation law;

Copyright, Insurance Services Office, Inc., 1999 HO 00 03 10 00

SAMPLE

b. Non-occupational disability law; or

c. Occupational disease law;

5. "Bodily injury" or "property damage" for which an "insured" under this policy:

a. Is also an insured under a nuclear energy liability policy issued by the:

(1) Nuclear Energy Liability Insurance Association;

(2) Mutual Atomic Energy Liability Underwriters;

(3) Nuclear Insurance Association of Canada;

or any of their successors; or

b. Would be an insured under such a policy but for the exhaustion of its limit of liability; or

6. "Bodily injury" to you or an "insured" as defined under Definitions 5.a. or b.

This exclusion also applies to any claim made or suit brought against you or an "insured":

(1) To repay; or

(2) Share damages with;

another person who may be obligated to pay damages because of "bodily injury" to an "insured".

G. **Coverage F – Medical Payments To Others**

Coverage F does not apply to "bodily injury":

1. To a "residence employee" if the "bodily injury":

a. Occurs off the "insured location"; and

b. Does not arise out of or in the course of the "residence employee's" employment by an "insured";

2. To any person eligible to receive benefits voluntarily provided or required to be provided under any:

a. Workers' compensation law;

b. Non-occupational disability law; or

c. Occupational disease law;

3. From any:

a. Nuclear reaction;

b. Nuclear radiation; or

c. Radioactive contamination;

all whether controlled or uncontrolled or however caused; or

d. Any consequence of any of these; or

4. To any person, other than a "residence employee" of an "insured", regularly residing on any part of the "insured location".

SECTION II – ADDITIONAL COVERAGES

We cover the following in addition to the limits of liability:

A. **Claim Expenses**

We pay:

1. Expenses we incur and costs taxed against an "insured" in any suit we defend;

2. Premiums on bonds required in a suit we defend, but not for bond amounts more than the Coverage E limit of liability. We need not apply for or furnish any bond;

3. Reasonable expenses incurred by an "insured" at our request, including actual loss of earnings (but not loss of other income) up to $250 per day, for assisting us in the investigation or defense of a claim or suit; and

4. Interest on the entire judgment which accrues after entry of the judgment and before we pay or tender, or deposit in court that part of the judgment which does not exceed the limit of liability that applies.

B. **First Aid Expenses**

We will pay expenses for first aid to others incurred by an "insured" for "bodily injury" covered under this policy. We will not pay for first aid to an "insured".

C. **Damage To Property Of Others**

1. We will pay, at replacement cost, up to $1,000 per "occurrence" for "property damage" to property of others caused by an "insured".

2. We will not pay for "property damage":

a. To the extent of any amount recoverable under Section I;

b. Caused intentionally by an "insured" who is 13 years of age or older;

c. To property owned by an "insured";

d. To property owned by or rented to a tenant of an "insured" or a resident in your household; or

e. Arising out of:

(1) A "business" engaged in by an "insured";

(2) Any act or omission in connection with a premises owned, rented or controlled by an "insured", other than the "insured location"; or

(3) The ownership, maintenance, occupancy, operation, use, loading or unloading of aircraft, hovercraft, watercraft or "motor vehicles".

SAMPLE

This exclusion **e.(3)** does not apply to a "motor vehicle" that:

(a) Is designed for recreational use off public roads;

(b) Is not owned by an "insured"; and

(c) At the time of the "occurrence", is not required by law, or regulation issued by a government agency, to have been registered for it to be used on public roads or property.

D. Loss Assessment

1. We will pay up to $1,000 for your share of loss assessment charged against you, as owner or tenant of the "residence premises", during the policy period by a corporation or association of property owners, when the assessment is made as a result of:

   a. "Bodily injury" or "property damage" not excluded from coverage under Section II – Exclusions; or

   b. Liability for an act of a director, officer or trustee in the capacity as a director, officer or trustee, provided such person:

      (1) Is elected by the members of a corporation or association of property owners; and

      (2) Serves without deriving any income from the exercise of duties which are solely on behalf of a corporation or association of property owners.

2. Paragraph I. Policy Period under Section II – Conditions does not apply to this Loss Assessment Coverage.

3. Regardless of the number of assessments, the limit of $1,000 is the most we will pay for loss arising out of:

   a. One accident, including continuous or repeated exposure to substantially the same general harmful condition; or

   b. A covered act of a director, officer or trustee. An act involving more than one director, officer or trustee is considered to be a single act.

4. We do not cover assessments charged against you or a corporation or association of property owners by any governmental body.

SECTION II – CONDITIONS

A. Limit Of Liability

Our total liability under Coverage **E** for all damages resulting from any one "occurrence" will not be more than the Coverage **E** limit of liability shown in the Declarations. This limit is the same regardless of the number of "insureds", claims made or persons injured. All "bodily injury" and "property damage" resulting from any one accident or from continuous or repeated exposure to substantially the same general harmful conditions shall be considered to be the result of one "occurrence".

Our total liability under Coverage **F** for all medical expense payable for "bodily injury" to one person as the result of one accident will not be more than the Coverage **F** limit of liability shown in the Declarations.

B. Severability Of Insurance

This insurance applies separately to each "insured". This condition will not increase our limit of liability for any one "occurrence".

C. Duties After "Occurrence"

In case of an "occurrence", you or another "insured" will perform the following duties that apply. We have no duty to provide coverage under this policy if your failure to comply with the following duties is prejudicial to us. You will help us by seeing that these duties are performed:

1. Give written notice to us or our agent as soon as is practical, which sets forth:

   a. The identity of the policy and the "named insured" shown in the Declarations;

   b. Reasonably available information on the time, place and circumstances of the "occurrence"; and

   c. Names and addresses of any claimants and witnesses;

2. Cooperate with us in the investigation, settlement or defense of any claim or suit;

3. Promptly forward to us every notice, demand, summons or other process relating to the "occurrence";

4. At our request, help us:

   a. To make settlement;

   b. To enforce any right of contribution or indemnity against any person or organization who may be liable to an "insured";

Copyright, Insurance Services Office, Inc., 1999   HO 00 03 10 00

SAMPLE

c. With the conduct of suits and attend hearings and trials; and

d. To secure and give evidence and obtain the attendance of witnesses;

5. With respect to **C. Damage To Property Of Others** under Section **II** – Additional Coverages, submit to us within 60 days after the loss, a sworn statement of loss and show the damaged property, if in an "insured's" control;

6. No "insured" shall, except at such "insured's" own cost, voluntarily make payment, assume obligation or incur expense other than for first aid to others at the time of the "bodily injury".

D. Duties Of An Injured Person – Coverage F – Medical Payments To Others

1. The injured person or someone acting for the injured person will:

    a. Give us written proof of claim, under oath if required, as soon as is practical; and

    b. Authorize us to obtain copies of medical reports and records.

2. The injured person will submit to a physical exam by a doctor of our choice when and as often as we reasonably require.

E. Payment Of Claim – Coverage F – Medical Payments To Others

Payment under this coverage is not an admission of liability by an "insured" or us.

F. Suit Against Us

1. No action can be brought against us unless there has been full compliance with all of the terms under this Section **II**.

2. No one will have the right to join us as a party to any action against an "insured".

3. Also, no action with respect to Coverage **E** can be brought against us until the obligation of such "insured" has been determined by final judgment or agreement signed by us.

G. Bankruptcy Of An "Insured"

Bankruptcy or insolvency of an "insured" will not relieve us of our obligations under this policy.

H. Other Insurance

This insurance is excess over other valid and collectible insurance except insurance written specifically to cover as excess over the limits of liability that apply in this policy.

I. Policy Period

This policy applies only to "bodily injury" or "property damage" which occurs during the policy period.

J. Concealment Or Fraud

We do not provide coverage to an "insured" who, whether before or after a loss, has:

1. Intentionally concealed or misrepresented any material fact or circumstance;

2. Engaged in fraudulent conduct; or

3. Made false statements;

relating to this insurance.

SECTIONS I AND II – CONDITIONS

A. Liberalization Clause

If we make a change which broadens coverage under this edition of our policy without additional premium charge, that change will automatically apply to your insurance as of the date we implement the change in your state, provided that this implementation date falls within 60 days prior to or during the policy period stated in the Declarations.

This Liberalization Clause does not apply to changes implemented with a general program revision that includes both broadenings and restrictions in coverage, whether that general program revision is implemented through introduction of:

1. A subsequent edition of this policy; or

2. An amendatory endorsement.

B. Waiver Or Change Of Policy Provisions

A waiver or change of a provision of this policy must be in writing by us to be valid. Our request for an appraisal or examination will not waive any of our rights.

C. Cancellation

1. You may cancel this policy at any time by returning it to us or by letting us know in writing of the date cancellation is to take effect.

2. We may cancel this policy only for the reasons stated below by letting you know in writing of the date cancellation takes effect. This cancellation notice may be delivered to you, or mailed to you at your mailing address shown in the Declarations. Proof of mailing will be sufficient proof of notice.

    a. When you have not paid the premium, we may cancel at any time by letting you know at least 10 days before the date cancellation takes effect.

    b. When this policy has been in effect for less than 60 days and is not a renewal with us, we may cancel for any reason by letting you know at least 10 days before the date cancellation takes effect.

SAMPLE

c. When this policy has been in effect for 60 days or more, or at any time if it is a renewal with us, we may cancel:

   (1) If there has been a material misrepresentation of fact which if known to us would have caused us not to issue the policy; or

   (2) If the risk has changed substantially since the policy was issued.

   This can be done by letting you know at least 30 days before the date cancellation takes effect.

d. When this policy is written for a period of more than one year, we may cancel for any reason at anniversary by letting you know at least 30 days before the date cancellation takes effect.

3. When this policy is canceled, the premium for the period from the date of cancellation to the expiration date will be refunded pro rata.

4. If the return premium is not refunded with the notice of cancellation or when this policy is returned to us, we will refund it within a reasonable time after the date cancellation takes effect.

D. Nonrenewal

We may elect not to renew this policy. We may do so by delivering to you, or mailing to you at your mailing address shown in the Declarations, written notice at least 30 days before the expiration date of this policy. Proof of mailing will be sufficient proof of notice.

E. Assignment

Assignment of this policy will not be valid unless we give our written consent.

F. Subrogation

An "insured" may waive in writing before a loss all rights of recovery against any person. If not waived, we may require an assignment of rights of recovery for a loss to the extent that payment is made by us.

If an assignment is sought, an "insured" must sign and deliver all related papers and cooperate with us.

Subrogation does not apply to Coverage F or Paragraph C. Damage To Property Of Others under Section II – Additional Coverages.

G. Death

If any person named in the Declarations or the spouse, if a resident of the same household, dies, the following apply:

1. We insure the legal representative of the deceased but only with respect to the premises and property of the deceased covered under the policy at the time of death; and

2. "Insured" includes:

   a. An "insured" who is a member of your household at the time of your death, but only while a resident of the "residence premises"; and

   b. With respect to your property, the person having proper temporary custody of the property until appointment and qualification of a legal representative.

Personal Auto Policy Declarations

POLICYHOLDER:
(Named Insured)
Chris and Karen Swift
8110 Lake Street
Lincoln, Nebraska 68506

POLICY NUMBER: 296 S 468211

POLICY PERIOD: **FROM:**   August 1, 2007
TO: February 1, 2008

But only if the required premium for this period has been paid, and for six-month renewal periods if renewal premiums are paid as required. Each period begins and ends at 12:01 A.M. standard time at the address of the policy-holder.

INSURED VEHICLES AND SCHEDULE OF COVERAGES

VEHICLE	COVERAGES	LIMITS OF INSURANCE	PREMIUM
1	2000 Toyota Corolla	ID #JT2AL21E8B3306553	
	Coverage A—Liability:		
	Bodily Injury Liability	$100,000 **Each Person**	$110.00
		$300,000 **Each Accident**	
	Property Damage Liability	$ 50,000 **Each Accident**	$ 40.00
	Coverage B—Medical Payments	$ 5,000 **Each Person**	$ 36.00
	Coverage C—Uninsured Motorists:		
	Bodily Injury	$100,000 **Each Person**	$ 40.00
		$300,000 **Each Accident**	
		TOTAL	$226.00
2	2007 Ford Five Hundred	ID #1FABP3OU7GG212619	
	Coverage A—Liability:		
	Bodily Injury Liability	$100,000 **Each Person**	$145.00
		$300,000 **Each Accident**	
	Property Damage Liability	$ 50,000 **Each Accident**	$ 60.00
	Coverage B—Medical Payments	$ 5,000 **Each Person**	$ 36.00
	Coverage C—Uninsured Motorists:		
	Bodily Injury	$100,000 **Each Person**	$ 40.00
		$300,000 **Each Accident**	
	Coverage D—Other Than Collision	**Actual Cash Value Less** $250	$ 50.00
	—Collision	**Actual Cash Value Less** $500	$130.00
		TOTAL	$461.00

POLICY FORM AND ENDORSEMENTS: PP 00 01 01 05
COUNTERSIGNATURE DATE: July 1, 2007
AGENT: Alex Rejda

SAMPLE

PERSONAL AUTO
PP 00 01 01 05

PERSONAL AUTO POLICY

AGREEMENT

In return for payment of the premium and subject to all the terms of this policy, we agree with you as follows:

DEFINITIONS

A. Throughout this policy, "you" and "your" refer to:

  1. The "named insured" shown in the Declarations; and

  2. The spouse if a resident of the same household.

If the spouse ceases to be a resident of the same household during the policy period or prior to the inception of this policy, the spouse will be considered "you" and "your" under this policy but only until the earlier of:

  1. The end of 90 days following the spouse's change of residency;

  2. The effective date of another policy listing the spouse as a named insured; or

  3. The end of the policy period.

B. "We", "us" and "our" refer to the Company providing this insurance.

C. For purposes of this policy, a private passenger type auto, pickup or van shall be deemed to be owned by a person if leased:

  1. Under a written agreement to that person; and

  2. For a continuous period of at least 6 months.

Other words and phrases are defined. They are in quotation marks when used.

D. "Bodily injury" means bodily harm, sickness or disease, including death that results.

E. "Business" includes trade, profession or occupation.

F. "Family member" means a person related to you by blood, marriage or adoption who is a resident of your household. This includes a ward or foster child.

G. "Occupying" means:

  1. In;

  2. Upon; or

  3. Getting in, on, out or off.

H. "Property damage" means physical injury to, destruction of or loss of use of tangible property.

I. "Trailer" means a vehicle designed to be pulled by a:

  1. Private passenger auto; or

  2. Pickup or van.

It also means a farm wagon or farm implement while towed by a vehicle listed in **1.** or **2.** above.

J. "Your covered auto" means:

  1. Any vehicle shown in the Declarations.

  2. A "newly acquired auto".

  3. Any "trailer" you own.

  4. Any auto or "trailer" you do not own while used as a temporary substitute for any other vehicle described in this definition which is out of normal use because of its:

    a. Breakdown;

    b. Repair;

    c. Servicing;

    d. Loss; or

    e. Destruction.

   This Provision (**J.4.**) does not apply to Coverage For Damage To Your Auto.

K. "Newly acquired auto":

  1. "Newly acquired auto" means any of the following types of vehicles you become the owner of during the policy period:

    a. A private passenger auto; or

    b. A pickup or van, for which no other insurance policy provides coverage, that:

      (1) Has a Gross Vehicle Weight Rating of 10,000 lbs. or less; and

      (2) Is not used for the delivery or transportation of goods and materials unless such use is:

        (a) Incidental to your "business" of installing, maintaining or repairing furnishings or equipment; or

        (b) For farming or ranching.

  2. Coverage for a "newly acquired auto" is provided as described below. If you ask us to insure a "newly acquired auto" after a specified time period described below has elapsed, any coverage we provide for a "newly acquired auto" will begin at the time you request the coverage.

SAMPLE

a. For any coverage provided in this policy except Coverage For Damage To Your Auto, a "newly acquired auto" will have the broadest coverage we now provide for any vehicle shown in the Declarations. Coverage begins on the date you become the owner. However, for this coverage to apply to a "newly acquired auto" which is in addition to any vehicle shown in the Declarations, you must ask us to insure it within 14 days after you become the owner.

If a "newly acquired auto" replaces a vehicle shown in the Declarations, coverage is provided for this vehicle without your having to ask us to insure it.

b. Collision Coverage for a "newly acquired auto" begins on the date you become the owner. However, for this coverage to apply, you must ask us to insure it within:

(1) 14 days after you become the owner if the Declarations indicate that Collision Coverage applies to at least one auto. In this case, the "newly acquired auto" will have the broadest coverage we now provide for any auto shown in the Declarations.

(2) Four days after you become the owner if the Declarations do not indicate that Collision Coverage applies to at least one auto. If you comply with the 4 day requirement and a loss occurred before you asked us to insure the "newly acquired auto", a Collision deductible of $500 will apply.

c. Other Than Collision Coverage for a "newly acquired auto" begins on the date you become the owner. However, for this coverage to apply, you must ask us to insure it within:

(1) 14 days after you become the owner if the Declarations indicate that Other Than Collision Coverage applies to at least one auto. In this case, the "newly acquired auto" will have the broadest coverage we now provide for any auto shown in the Declarations.

(2) Four days after you become the owner if the Declarations do not indicate that Other Than Collision Coverage applies to at least one auto. If you comply with the 4 day requirement and a loss occurred before you asked us to insure the "newly acquired auto", an Other Than Collision deductible of $500 will apply.

PART A – LIABILITY COVERAGE

INSURING AGREEMENT

A. We will pay damages for "bodily injury" or "property damage" for which any "insured" becomes legally responsible because of an auto accident. Damages include prejudgment interest awarded against the "insured". We will settle or defend, as we consider appropriate, any claim or suit asking for these damages. In addition to our limit of liability, we will pay all defense costs we incur. Our duty to settle or defend ends when our limit of liability for this coverage has been exhausted by payment of judgments or settlements. We have no duty to defend any suit or settle any claim for "bodily injury" or "property damage" not covered under this policy.

B. "Insured" as used in this Part means:

1. You or any "family member" for the ownership, maintenance or use of any auto or "trailer".

2. Any person using "your covered auto".

3. For "your covered auto", any person or organization but only with respect to legal responsibility for acts or omissions of a person for whom coverage is afforded under this Part.

4. For any auto or "trailer", other than "your covered auto", any other person or organization but only with respect to legal responsibility for acts or omissions of you or any "family member" for whom coverage is afforded under this Part. This Provision (B.4.) applies only if the person or organization does not own or hire the auto or "trailer".

SUPPLEMENTARY PAYMENTS

We will pay on behalf of an "insured":

1. Up to $250 for the cost of bail bonds required because of an accident, including related traffic law violations. The accident must result in "bodily injury" or "property damage" covered under this policy.

2. Premiums on appeal bonds and bonds to release attachments in any suit we defend.

3. Interest accruing after a judgment is entered in any suit we defend. Our duty to pay interest ends when we offer to pay that part of the judgment which does not exceed our limit of liability for this coverage.

SAMPLE

4. Up to $200 a day for loss of earnings, but not other income, because of attendance at hearings or trials at our request.

5. Other reasonable expenses incurred at our request.

These payments will not reduce the limit of liability.

EXCLUSIONS

A. We do not provide Liability Coverage for any "insured":

1. Who intentionally causes "bodily injury" or "property damage".

2. For "property damage" to property owned or being transported by that "insured".

3. For "property damage" to property:

    a. Rented to;

    b. Used by; or

    c. In the care of;

    that "insured".

    This Exclusion (**A.3.**) does not apply to "property damage" to a residence or private garage.

4. For "bodily injury" to an employee of that "insured" during the course of employment. This Exclusion (**A.4.**) does not apply to "bodily injury" to a domestic employee unless workers' compensation benefits are required or available for that domestic employee.

5. For that "insured's" liability arising out of the ownership or operation of a vehicle while it is being used as a public or livery conveyance. This Exclusion (**A.5.**) does not apply to a share-the-expense car pool.

6. While employed or otherwise engaged in the "business" of:

    a. Selling;

    b. Repairing;

    c. Servicing;

    d. Storing; or

    e. Parking;

    vehicles designed for use mainly on public highways. This includes road testing and delivery. This Exclusion (**A.6.**) does not apply to the ownership, maintenance or use of "your covered auto" by:

    a. You;

    b. Any "family member"; or

    c. Any partner, agent or employee of you or any "family member".

7. Maintaining or using any vehicle while that "insured" is employed or otherwise engaged in any "business" (other than farming or ranching) not described in Exclusion **A.6.**

    This Exclusion (**A.7.**) does not apply to the maintenance or use of a:

    a. Private passenger auto;

    b. Pickup or van; or

    c. "Trailer" used with a vehicle described in **a.** or **b.** above.

8. Using a vehicle without a reasonable belief that that "insured" is entitled to do so. This Exclusion (**A.8.**) does not apply to a "family member" using "your covered auto" which is owned by you.

9. For "bodily injury" or "property damage" for which that "insured":

    a. Is an insured under a nuclear energy liability policy; or

    b. Would be an insured under a nuclear energy liability policy but for its termination upon exhaustion of its limit of liability.

    A nuclear energy liability policy is a policy issued by any of the following or their successors:

    a. Nuclear Energy Liability Insurance Association;

    b. Mutual Atomic Energy Liability Underwriters; or

    c. Nuclear Insurance Association of Canada.

B. We do not provide Liability Coverage for the ownership, maintenance or use of:

1. Any vehicle which:

    a. Has fewer than four wheels; or

    b. Is designed mainly for use off public roads.

    This Exclusion (**B.1.**) does not apply:

    a. While such vehicle is being used by an "insured" in a medical emergency;

    b. To any "trailer"; or

    c. To any non-owned golf cart.

2. Any vehicle, other than "your covered auto", which is:

    a. Owned by you; or

    b. Furnished or available for your regular use.

3. Any vehicle, other than "your covered auto", which is:

    a. Owned by any "family member"; or

    b. Furnished or available for the regular use of any "family member".

SAMPLE

However, this Exclusion (**B.3.**) does not apply to you while you are maintaining or "occupying" any vehicle which is:

a. Owned by a "family member"; or

b. Furnished or available for the regular use of a "family member".

4. Any vehicle, located inside a facility designed for racing, for the purpose of:

a. Competing in; or

b. Practicing or preparing for;

any prearranged or organized racing or speed contest.

LIMIT OF LIABILITY

A. The limit of liability shown in the Declarations for each person for Bodily Injury Liability is our maximum limit of liability for all damages, including damages for care, loss of services or death, arising out of "bodily injury" sustained by any one person in any one auto accident. Subject to this limit for each person, the limit of liability shown in the Declarations for each accident for Bodily Injury Liability is our maximum limit of liability for all damages for "bodily injury" resulting from any one auto accident.

The limit of liability shown in the Declarations for each accident for Property Damage Liability is our maximum limit of liability for all "property damage" resulting from any one auto accident.

This is the most we will pay regardless of the number of:

1. "Insureds";

2. Claims made;

3. Vehicles or premiums shown in the Declarations; or

4. Vehicles involved in the auto accident.

B. No one will be entitled to receive duplicate payments for the same elements of loss under this coverage and:

1. Part **B** or Part **C** of this policy; or

2. Any Underinsured Motorists Coverage provided by this policy.

OUT OF STATE COVERAGE

If an auto accident to which this policy applies occurs in any state or province other than the one in which "your covered auto" is principally garaged, we will interpret your policy for that accident as follows:

A. If the state or province has:

1. A financial responsibility or similar law specifying limits of liability for "bodily injury" or "property damage" higher than the limit shown in the Declarations, your policy will provide the higher specified limit.

2. A compulsory insurance or similar law requiring a nonresident to maintain insurance whenever the nonresident uses a vehicle in that state or province, your policy will provide at least the required minimum amounts and types of coverage.

B. No one will be entitled to duplicate payments for the same elements of loss.

FINANCIAL RESPONSIBILITY

When this policy is certified as future proof of financial responsibility, this policy shall comply with the law to the extent required.

OTHER INSURANCE

If there is other applicable liability insurance we will pay only our share of the loss. Our share is the proportion that our limit of liability bears to the total of all applicable limits. However, any insurance we provide for a vehicle you do not own, including any vehicle while used as a temporary substitute for "your covered auto", shall be excess over any other collectible insurance.

PART B – MEDICAL PAYMENTS COVERAGE

INSURING AGREEMENT

A. We will pay reasonable expenses incurred for necessary medical and funeral services because of "bodily injury":

1. Caused by accident; and

2. Sustained by an "insured".

We will pay only those expenses incurred for services rendered within 3 years from the date of the accident.

B. "Insured" as used in this Part means:

1. You or any "family member":

a. While "occupying"; or

b. As a pedestrian when struck by;

a motor vehicle designed for use mainly on public roads or a trailer of any type.

2. Any other person while "occupying" "your covered auto".

SAMPLE

EXCLUSIONS

We do not provide Medical Payments Coverage for any "insured" for "bodily injury":

1. Sustained while "occupying" any motorized vehicle having fewer than four wheels.
2. Sustained while "occupying" "your covered auto" when it is being used as a public or livery conveyance. This Exclusion **(2.)** does not apply to a share-the-expense car pool.
3. Sustained while "occupying" any vehicle located for use as a residence or premises.
4. Occurring during the course of employment if workers' compensation benefits are required or available for the "bodily injury".
5. Sustained while "occupying", or when struck by, any vehicle (other than "your covered auto") which is:
   a. Owned by you; or
   b. Furnished or available for your regular use.
6. Sustained while "occupying", or when struck by, any vehicle (other than "your covered auto") which is:
   a. Owned by any "family member"; or
   b. Furnished or available for the regular use of any "family member".
   However, this Exclusion **(6.)** does not apply to you.
7. Sustained while "occupying" a vehicle without a reasonable belief that that "insured" is entitled to do so. This Exclusion **(7.)** does not apply to a "family member" using "your covered auto" which is owned by you.
8. Sustained while "occupying" a vehicle when it is being used in the "business" of an "insured". This Exclusion **(8.)** does not apply to "bodily injury" sustained while "occupying" a:
   a. Private passenger auto;
   b. Pickup or van; or
   c. "Trailer" used with a vehicle described in **a.** or **b.** above.
9. Caused by or as a consequence of:
   a. Discharge of a nuclear weapon (even if accidental);
   b. War (declared or undeclared);
   c. Civil war;
   d. Insurrection; or
   e. Rebellion or revolution.
10. From or as a consequence of the following, whether controlled or uncontrolled or however caused:
    a. Nuclear reaction;
    b. Radiation; or
    c. Radioactive contamination.
11. Sustained while "occupying" any vehicle located inside a facility designed for racing, for the purpose of:
    a. Competing in; or
    b. Practicing or preparing for;
    any prearranged or organized racing or speed contest.

LIMIT OF LIABILITY

A. The limit of liability shown in the Declarations for this coverage is our maximum limit of liability for each person injured in any one accident. This is the most we will pay regardless of the number of:
   1. "Insureds";
   2. Claims made;
   3. Vehicles or premiums shown in the Declarations; or
   4. Vehicles involved in the accident.
B. No one will be entitled to receive duplicate payments for the same elements of loss under this coverage and:
   1. Part **A** or Part **C** of this policy; or
   2. Any Underinsured Motorists Coverage provided by this policy.

OTHER INSURANCE

If there is other applicable auto medical payments insurance we will pay only our share of the loss. Our share is the proportion that our limit of liability bears to the total of all applicable limits. However, any insurance we provide with respect to a vehicle you do not own, including any vehicle while used as a temporary substitute for "your covered auto", shall be excess over any other collectible auto insurance providing payments for medical or funeral expenses.

SAMPLE

PART C – UNINSURED MOTORISTS COVERAGE

INSURING AGREEMENT

A. We will pay compensatory damages which an "insured" is legally entitled to recover from the owner or operator of an "uninsured motor vehicle" because of "bodily injury":

1. Sustained by an "insured"; and

2. Caused by an accident.

The owner's or operator's liability for these damages must arise out of the ownership, maintenance or use of the "uninsured motor vehicle".

Any judgment for damages arising out of a suit brought without our written consent is not binding on us.

B. "Insured" as used in this Part means:

1. You or any "family member".

2. Any other person "occupying" "your covered auto".

3. Any person for damages that person is entitled to recover because of "bodily injury" to which this coverage applies sustained by a person described in **1.** or **2.** above.

C. "Uninsured motor vehicle" means a land motor vehicle or trailer of any type:

1. To which no bodily injury liability bond or policy applies at the time of the accident.

2. To which a bodily injury liability bond or policy applies at the time of the accident. In this case its limit for bodily injury liability must be less than the minimum limit for bodily injury liability specified by the financial responsibility law of the state in which "your covered auto" is principally garaged.

3. Which is a hit-and-run vehicle whose operator or owner cannot be identified and which hits:

   a. You or any "family member";

   b. A vehicle which you or any "family member" are "occupying"; or

   c. "Your covered auto".

4. To which a bodily injury liability bond or policy applies at the time of the accident but the bonding or insuring company:

   a. Denies coverage; or

   b. Is or becomes insolvent.

However, "uninsured motor vehicle" does not include any vehicle or equipment:

1. Owned by or furnished or available for the regular use of you or any "family member".

2. Owned or operated by a self-insurer under any applicable motor vehicle law, except a self-insurer which is or becomes insolvent.

3. Owned by any governmental unit or agency.

4. Operated on rails or crawler treads.

5. Designed mainly for use off public roads while not on public roads.

6. While located for use as a residence or premises.

EXCLUSIONS

A. We do not provide Uninsured Motorists Coverage for "bodily injury" sustained:

1. By an "insured" while "occupying", or when struck by, any motor vehicle owned by that "insured" which is not insured for this coverage under this policy. This includes a trailer of any type used with that vehicle.

2. By any "family member" while "occupying", or when struck by, any motor vehicle you own which is insured for this coverage on a primary basis under any other policy.

B. We do not provide Uninsured Motorists Coverage for "bodily injury" sustained by any "insured":

1. If that "insured" or the legal representative settles the "bodily injury" claim and such settlement prejudices our right to recover payment.

2. While "occupying" "your covered auto" when it is being used as a public or livery conveyance. This Exclusion (**B.2.**) does not apply to a share-the-expense car pool.

3. Using a vehicle without a reasonable belief that that "insured" is entitled to do so. This Exclusion (**B.3.**) does not apply to a "family member" using "your covered auto" which is owned by you.

C. This coverage shall not apply directly or indirectly to benefit any insurer or self-insurer under any of the following or similar law:

1. Workers' compensation law; or

2. Disability benefits law.

D. We do not provide Uninsured Motorists Coverage for punitive or exemplary damages.

PP 00 01 01 05

SAMPLE

LIMIT OF LIABILITY

A. The limit of liability shown in the Declarations for each person for Uninsured Motorists Coverage is our maximum limit of liability for all damages, including damages for care, loss of services or death, arising out of "bodily injury" sustained by any one person in any one accident. Subject to this limit for each person, the limit of liability shown in the Declarations for each accident for Uninsured Motorists Coverage is our maximum limit of liability for all damages for "bodily injury" resulting from any one accident.

This is the most we will pay regardless of the number of:

1. "Insureds";
2. Claims made;
3. Vehicles or premiums shown in the Declarations; or
4. Vehicles involved in the accident.

B. No one will be entitled to receive duplicate payments for the same elements of loss under this coverage and:

1. Part **A** or Part **B** of this policy; or
2. Any Underinsured Motorists Coverage provided by this policy.

C. We will not make a duplicate payment under this coverage for any element of loss for which payment has been made by or on behalf of persons or organizations who may be legally responsible.

D. We will not pay for any element of loss if a person is entitled to receive payment for the same element of loss under any of the following or similar law:

1. Workers' compensation law; or
2. Disability benefits law.

OTHER INSURANCE

If there is other applicable insurance available under one or more policies or provisions of coverage that is similar to the insurance provided under this Part of the policy:

1. Any recovery for damages under all such policies or provisions of coverage may equal but not exceed the highest applicable limit for any one vehicle under any insurance providing coverage on either a primary or excess basis.
2. Any insurance we provide with respect to a vehicle you do not own, including any vehicle while used as a temporary substitute for "your covered auto", shall be excess over any collectible insurance providing such coverage on a primary basis.

3. If the coverage under this policy is provided:

   a. On a primary basis, we will pay only our share of the loss that must be paid under insurance providing coverage on a primary basis. Our share is the proportion that our limit of liability bears to the total of all applicable limits of liability for coverage provided on a primary basis.

   b. On an excess basis, we will pay only our share of the loss that must be paid under insurance providing coverage on an excess basis. Our share is the proportion that our limit of liability bears to the total of all applicable limits of liability for coverage provided on an excess basis.

ARBITRATION

A. If we and an "insured" do not agree:

1. Whether that "insured" is legally entitled to recover damages; or
2. As to the amount of damages which are recoverable by that "insured";

from the owner or operator of an "uninsured motor vehicle", then the matter may be arbitrated. However, disputes concerning coverage under this Part may not be arbitrated.

Both parties must agree to arbitration. If so agreed, each party will select an arbitrator. The two arbitrators will select a third. If they cannot agree within 30 days, either may request that selection be made by a judge of a court having jurisdiction.

B. Each party will:

1. Pay the expenses it incurs; and
2. Bear the expenses of the third arbitrator equally.

C. Unless both parties agree otherwise, arbitration will take place in the county in which the "insured" lives. Local rules of law as to procedure and evidence will apply. A decision agreed to by at least two of the arbitrators will be binding as to:

1. Whether the "insured" is legally entitled to recover damages; and
2. The amount of damages. This applies only if the amount does not exceed the minimum limit for bodily injury liability specified by the financial responsibility law of the state in which "your covered auto" is principally garaged. If the amount exceeds that limit, either party may demand the right to a trial. This demand must be made within 60 days of the arbitrators' decision. If this demand is not made, the amount of damages agreed to by the arbitrators will be binding.

SAMPLE

PART D – COVERAGE FOR DAMAGE TO YOUR AUTO

INSURING AGREEMENT

A. We will pay for direct and accidental loss to "your covered auto" or any "non-owned auto", including their equipment, minus any applicable deductible shown in the Declarations. If loss to more than one "your covered auto" or "non-owned auto" results from the same "collision", only the highest applicable deductible will apply. We will pay for loss to "your covered auto" caused by:

1. Other than "collision" only if the Declarations indicate that Other Than Collision Coverage is provided for that auto.

2. "Collision" only if the Declarations indicate that Collision Coverage is provided for that auto.

If there is a loss to a "non-owned auto", we will provide the broadest coverage applicable to any "your covered auto" shown in the Declarations.

B. "Collision" means the upset of "your covered auto" or a "non-owned auto" or their impact with another vehicle or object.

Loss caused by the following is considered other than "collision":

1. Missiles or falling objects;

2. Fire;

3. Theft or larceny;

4. Explosion or earthquake;

5. Windstorm;

6. Hail, water or flood;

7. Malicious mischief or vandalism;

8. Riot or civil commotion;

9. Contact with bird or animal; or

10. Breakage of glass.

If breakage of glass is caused by a "collision", you may elect to have it considered a loss caused by "collision".

C. "Non-owned auto" means:

1. Any private passenger auto, pickup, van or "trailer" not owned by or furnished or available for the regular use of you or any "family member" while in the custody of or being operated by you or any "family member"; or

2. Any auto or "trailer" you do not own while used as a temporary substitute for "your covered auto" which is out of normal use because of its:

   a. Breakdown;

   b. Repair;

   c. Servicing;

   d. Loss; or

   e. Destruction.

TRANSPORTATION EXPENSES

A. In addition, we will pay, without application of a deductible, up to a maximum of $600 for:

1. Temporary transportation expenses not exceeding $20 per day incurred by you in the event of a loss to "your covered auto". We will pay for such expenses if the loss is caused by:

   a. Other than "collision" only if the Declarations indicate that Other Than Collision Coverage is provided for that auto.

   b. "Collision" only if the Declarations indicate that Collision Coverage is provided for that auto.

2. Expenses for which you become legally responsible in the event of loss to a "non-owned auto". We will pay for such expenses if the loss is caused by:

   a. Other than "collision" only if the Declarations indicate that Other Than Collision Coverage is provided for any "your covered auto".

   b. "Collision" only if the Declarations indicate that Collision Coverage is provided for any "your covered auto".

However, the most we will pay for any expenses for loss of use is $20 per day.

B. Subject to the provisions of Paragraph A., if the loss is caused by:

1. A total theft of "your covered auto" or a "non-owned auto", we will pay only expenses incurred during the period:

   a. Beginning 48 hours after the theft; and

   b. Ending when "your covered auto" or the "non-owned auto" is returned to use or we pay for its loss.

2. Other than theft of a "your covered auto" or a "non-owned auto", we will pay only expenses beginning when the auto is withdrawn from use for more than 24 hours.

Our payment will be limited to that period of time reasonably required to repair or replace the "your covered auto" or the "non-owned auto".

© ISO Properties, Inc., 2003 **PP 00 01 01 05**

SAMPLE

EXCLUSIONS

We will not pay for:

1. Loss to "your covered auto" or any "non-owned auto" which occurs while it is being used as a public or livery conveyance. This Exclusion **(1.)** does not apply to a share-the-expense car pool.

2. Damage due and confined to:

   a. Wear and tear;

   b. Freezing;

   c. Mechanical or electrical breakdown or failure; or

   d. Road damage to tires.

   This Exclusion **(2.)** does not apply if the damage results from the total theft of "your covered auto" or any "non-owned auto".

3. Loss due to or as a consequence of:

   a. Radioactive contamination;

   b. Discharge of any nuclear weapon (even if accidental);

   c. War (declared or undeclared);

   d. Civil war;

   e. Insurrection; or

   f. Rebellion or revolution.

4. Loss to any electronic equipment that reproduces, receives or transmits audio, visual or data signals. This includes but is not limited to:

   a. Radios and stereos;

   b. Tape decks;

   c. Compact disk systems;

   d. Navigation systems;

   e. Internet access systems;

   f. Personal computers;

   g. Video entertainment systems;

   h. Telephones;

   i. Televisions;

   j. Two-way mobile radios;

   k. Scanners; or

   l. Citizens band radios.

   This Exclusion **(4.)** does not apply to electronic equipment that is permanently installed in "your covered auto" or any "non-owned auto".

5. Loss to tapes, records, disks or other media used with equipment described in Exclusion **4.**

6. A total loss to "your covered auto" or any "non-owned auto" due to destruction or confiscation by governmental or civil authorities.

   This Exclusion **(6.)** does not apply to the interests of Loss Payees in "your covered auto".

7. Loss to:

   a. A "trailer", camper body, or motor home, which is not shown in the Declarations; or

   b. Facilities or equipment used with such "trailer", camper body or motor home. Facilities or equipment include but are not limited to:

      (1) Cooking, dining, plumbing or refrigeration facilities;

      (2) Awnings or cabanas; or

      (3) Any other facilities or equipment used with a "trailer", camper body, or motor home.

   This Exclusion **(7.)** does not apply to a:

   a. "Trailer", and its facilities or equipment, which you do not own; or

   b. "Trailer", camper body, or the facilities or equipment in or attached to the "trailer" or camper body, which you:

      (1) Acquire during the policy period; and

      (2) Ask us to insure within 14 days after you become the owner.

8. Loss to any "non-owned auto" when used by you or any "family member" without a reasonable belief that you or that "family member" are entitled to do so.

9. Loss to equipment designed or used for the detection or location of radar or laser.

10. Loss to any custom furnishings or equipment in or upon any pickup or van. Custom furnishings or equipment include but are not limited to:

    a. Special carpeting or insulation;

    b. Furniture or bars;

    c. Height-extending roofs; or

    d. Custom murals, paintings or other decals or graphics.

    This Exclusion **(10.)** does not apply to a cap, cover or bedliner in or upon any "your covered auto" which is a pickup.

11. Loss to any "non-owned auto" being maintained or used by any person while employed or otherwise engaged in the "business" of:

    a. Selling;

    b. Repairing;

SAMPLE

    c. Servicing;

    d. Storing; or

    e. Parking;

vehicles designed for use on public highways. This includes road testing and delivery.

12. Loss to "your covered auto" or any "non-owned auto", located inside a facility designed for racing, for the purpose of:

    a. Competing in; or

    b. Practicing or preparing for;

any prearranged or organized racing or speed contest.

13. Loss to, or loss of use of, a "non-owned auto" rented by:

    a. You; or

    b. Any "family member";

if a rental vehicle company is precluded from recovering such loss or loss of use, from you or that "family member", pursuant to the provisions of any applicable rental agreement or state law.

LIMIT OF LIABILITY

A. Our limit of liability for loss will be the lesser of the:

    1. Actual cash value of the stolen or damaged property; or

    2. Amount necessary to repair or replace the property with other property of like kind and quality.

However, the most we will pay for loss to:

    1. Any "non-owned auto" which is a trailer is $1500.

    2. Electronic equipment that reproduces, receives or transmits audio, visual or data signals, which is permanently installed in the auto in locations not used by the auto manufacturer for installation of such equipment, is $1,000.

B. An adjustment for depreciation and physical condition will be made in determining actual cash value in the event of a total loss.

C. If a repair or replacement results in better than like kind or quality, we will not pay for the amount of the betterment.

PAYMENT OF LOSS

We may pay for loss in money or repair or replace the damaged or stolen property. We may, at our expense, return any stolen property to:

    1. You; or

    2. The address shown in this policy.

If we return stolen property we will pay for any damage resulting from the theft. We may keep all or part of the property at an agreed or appraised value.

If we pay for loss in money, our payment will include the applicable sales tax for the damaged or stolen property.

NO BENEFIT TO BAILEE

This insurance shall not directly or indirectly benefit any carrier or other bailee for hire.

OTHER SOURCES OF RECOVERY

If other sources of recovery also cover the loss, we will pay only our share of the loss. Our share is the proportion that our limit of liability bears to the total of all applicable limits. However, any insurance we provide with respect to a "non-owned auto" shall be excess over any other collectible source of recovery including, but not limited to:

    1. Any coverage provided by the owner of the "non-owned auto";

    2. Any other applicable physical damage insurance;

    3. Any other source of recovery applicable to the loss.

APPRAISAL

A. If we and you do not agree on the amount of loss, either may demand an appraisal of the loss. In this event, each party will select a competent and impartial appraiser. The two appraisers will select an umpire. The appraisers will state separately the actual cash value and the amount of loss. If they fail to agree, they will submit their differences to the umpire. A decision agreed to by any two will be binding. Each party will:

    1. Pay its chosen appraiser; and

    2. Bear the expenses of the appraisal and umpire equally.

B. We do not waive any of our rights under this policy by agreeing to an appraisal.

SAMPLE

PART E – DUTIES AFTER AN ACCIDENT OR LOSS

We have no duty to provide coverage under this policy if the failure to comply with the following duties is prejudicial to us:

A. We must be notified promptly of how, when and where the accident or loss happened. Notice should also include the names and addresses of any injured persons and of any witnesses.

B. A person seeking any coverage must:

  1. Cooperate with us in the investigation, settlement or defense of any claim or suit.

  2. Promptly send us copies of any notices or legal papers received in connection with the accident or loss.

  3. Submit, as often as we reasonably require:

    a. To physical exams by physicians we select. We will pay for these exams.

    b. To examination under oath and subscribe the same.

  4. Authorize us to obtain:

    a. Medical reports; and

    b. Other pertinent records.

  5. Submit a proof of loss when required by us.

C. A person seeking Uninsured Motorists Coverage must also:

  1. Promptly notify the police if a hit-and-run driver is involved.

  2. Promptly send us copies of the legal papers if a suit is brought.

D. A person seeking Coverage For Damage To Your Auto must also:

  1. Take reasonable steps after loss to protect "your covered auto" or any "non-owned auto" and their equipment from further loss. We will pay reasonable expenses incurred to do this.

  2. Promptly notify the police if "your covered auto" or any "non-owned auto" is stolen.

  3. Permit us to inspect and appraise the damaged property before its repair or disposal.

PART F – GENERAL PROVISIONS

BANKRUPTCY

Bankruptcy or insolvency of the "insured" shall not relieve us of any obligations under this policy.

CHANGES

A. This policy contains all the agreements between you and us. Its terms may not be changed or waived except by endorsement issued by us.

B. If there is a change to the information used to develop the policy premium, we may adjust your premium. Changes during the policy term that may result in a premium increase or decrease include, but are not limited to, changes in:

  1. The number, type or use classification of insured vehicles;

  2. Operators using insured vehicles;

  3. The place of principal garaging of insured vehicles;

  4. Coverage, deductible or limits.

If a change resulting from **A.** or **B.** requires a premium adjustment, we will make the premium adjustment in accordance with our manual rules.

C. If we make a change which broadens coverage under this edition of your policy without additional premium charge, that change will automatically apply to your policy as of the date we implement the change in your state. This Paragraph (**C.**) does not apply to changes implemented with a general program revision that includes both broadenings and restrictions in coverage, whether that general program revision is implemented through introduction of:

  1. A subsequent edition of your policy; or

  2. An Amendatory Endorsement.

FRAUD

We do not provide coverage for any "insured" who has made fraudulent statements or engaged in fraudulent conduct in connection with any accident or loss for which coverage is sought under this policy.

LEGAL ACTION AGAINST US

A. No legal action may be brought against us until there has been full compliance with all the terms of this policy. In addition, under Part **A**, no legal action may be brought against us until:

  1. We agree in writing that the "insured" has an obligation to pay; or

  2. The amount of that obligation has been finally determined by judgment after trial.

SAMPLE

B. No person or organization has any right under this policy to bring us into any action to determine the liability of an "insured".

OUR RIGHT TO RECOVER PAYMENT

A. If we make a payment under this policy and the person to or for whom payment was made has a right to recover damages from another we shall be subrogated to that right. That person shall do:

1. Whatever is necessary to enable us to exercise our rights; and

2. Nothing after loss to prejudice them.

However, our rights in this Paragraph (**A.**) do not apply under Part **D**, against any person using "your covered auto" with a reasonable belief that that person is entitled to do so.

B. If we make a payment under this policy and the person to, or for whom payment is made recovers damages from another, that person shall:

1. Hold in trust for us the proceeds of the recovery; and

2. Reimburse us to the extent of our payment.

POLICY PERIOD AND TERRITORY

A. This policy applies only to accidents and losses which occur:

1. During the policy period as shown in the Declarations; and

2. Within the policy territory.

B. The policy territory is:

1. The United States of America, its territories or possessions;

2. Puerto Rico; or

3. Canada.

This policy also applies to loss to, or accidents involving, "your covered auto" while being transported between their ports.

TERMINATION

A. Cancellation

This policy may be cancelled during the policy period as follows:

1. The named insured shown in the Declarations may cancel by:

   a. Returning this policy to us; or

   b. Giving us advance written notice of the date cancellation is to take effect.

2. We may cancel by mailing to the named insured shown in the Declarations at the address shown in this policy:

   a. At least 10 days notice:

   (1) If cancellation is for nonpayment of premium; or

(2) If notice is mailed during the first 60 days this policy is in effect and this is not a renewal or continuation policy; or

   b. At least 20 days notice in all other cases.

3. After this policy is in effect for 60 days, or if this is a renewal or continuation policy, we will cancel only:

   a. For nonpayment of premium; or

   b. If your driver's license or that of:

   (1) Any driver who lives with you; or

   (2) Any driver who customarily uses "your covered auto";

   has been suspended or revoked. This must have occurred:

   (1) During the policy period; or

   (2) Since the last anniversary of the original effective date if the policy period is other than 1 year; or

   c. If the policy was obtained through material misrepresentation.

B. Nonrenewal

If we decide not to renew or continue this policy, we will mail notice to the named insured shown in the Declarations at the address shown in this policy. Notice will be mailed at least 20 days before the end of the policy period. Subject to this notice requirement, if the policy period is:

1. Less than 6 months, we will have the right not to renew or continue this policy every 6 months, beginning 6 months after its original effective date.

2. 6 months or longer, but less than one year, we will have the right not to renew or continue this policy at the end of the policy period.

3. 1 year or longer, we will have the right not to renew or continue this policy at each anniversary of its original effective date.

C. Automatic Termination

If we offer to renew or continue and you or your representative do not accept, this policy will automatically terminate at the end of the current policy period. Failure to pay the required renewal or continuation premium when due shall mean that you have not accepted our offer.

If you obtain other insurance on "your covered auto", any similar insurance provided by this policy will terminate as to that auto on the effective date of the other insurance.

SAMPLE

D. Other Termination Provisions

1. We may deliver any notice instead of mailing it. Proof of mailing of any notice shall be sufficient proof of notice.

2. If this policy is cancelled, you may be entitled to a premium refund. If so, we will send you the refund. The premium refund, if any, will be computed according to our manuals. However, making or offering to make the refund is not a condition of cancellation.

3. The effective date of cancellation stated in the notice shall become the end of the policy period.

TRANSFER OF YOUR INTEREST IN THIS POLICY

A. Your rights and duties under this policy may not be assigned without our written consent. However, if a named insured shown in the Declarations dies, coverage will be provided for:

1. The surviving spouse if resident in the same household at the time of death. Coverage applies to the spouse as if a named insured shown in the Declarations; and

2. The legal representative of the deceased person as if a named insured shown in the Declarations. This applies only with respect to the representative's legal responsibility to maintain or use "your covered auto".

B. Coverage will only be provided until the end of the policy period.

TWO OR MORE AUTO POLICIES

If this policy and any other auto insurance policy issued to you by us apply to the same accident, the maximum limit of our liability under all the policies shall not exceed the highest applicable limit of liability under any one policy.

WHOLE LIFE INSURANCE POLICY WITH RIDERS

INSURED – JOHN DOE

POLICY NUMBER – 36 000 000

POLICY DATE – AUGUST 8, 1999

ABC Life Insurance Company
123 Main Street, Anytown, USA

ABC Life Insurance Company will pay the benefits of this policy in accordance with its provisions. The pages which follow are also a part of this policy.

10 Day Right To Examine Policy. Please examine your policy. Within 10 days after delivery, you can return it to ABC Life Insurance Company or to the agent through whom it was purchased, with a written request for a full refund of premium. Upon such request, the policy will be void from the start, and a full premium refund will be made.

Premiums. The premiums for this policy are shown in the Premium Schedule on the Policy Data page. They are payable in accordance with the Premiums section.

This policy is executed as of the date of issue shown on the Policy Data page.

John Johnson
President

Mary Smith
Secretary

Whole Life Policy.

Life Insurance Proceeds Payable at Insured's Death.

Premiums Payable During Insured's Lifetime, December 1, 2002 as shown on the Policy Data page.

Policy is Eligible for Dividends.

SAMPLE

INSURED — JOHN DOE   AGE 37   MALE

POLICY NUMBER — 36000000   CLASS OF RISK - STANDARD
                            (NON-SMOKER DISCOUNT)

POLICY DATE — AUGUST 8, 1999   DATE OF ISSUE
                                AUGUST 15,1999

OWNER — INSURED

PLAN   WHOLE LIFE WITH
                OPTION TO PURCHASE PAID-UP ADDITIONS (OPP) AND
                ACCIDENTAL DEATH BENEFIT (ADB) AND
                DISABILITY WAIVER OF PREMIUM (WP) AND
                POLICY PURCHASE OPTION (PPO) - OPTION AMOUNT IS $50,000.00 AND
                ACCELERATION OF DEATH BENEFITS

AMOUNT   FACE AMOUNT $100,000.00
                ACCIDENTAL DEATH BENEFIT $100,000.00
                (ADB, WHEN PAYABLE, IS IN ADDITION TO
                ANY OTHER INSURANCE BENEFIT)

BENEFICIARY
(subject to change) FIRST - ESTATE OF THE INSURED

PREMIUM SCHEDULE
PREMIUMS PAYABLE AT MONTHLY INTERVALS, AS FOLLOWS (SEE ENDORSEMENT HEREON)
    (Premium includes the following amounts for any supplementary benefits)

BEGINNING AS OF			TOTAL			
MO.	DAY	YR.	PREMIUM			
8-	8-	1999	$144.00			
8-	8-	2008	$134.00			
8-	8-	2027	$130.00			
8-	8-	2032	$123.00	PAYABLE FOR REMAINDER OF INSURED'S LIFE.**		
			ADB	WP	PPO	
8-	8-	1999	$7.00	$5.50	$8.50	
8-	8-	2008	$7.00	$4.00		
8-	8-	2027	$7.00			
8-	8-	2032				

PREMIUM PAYING PERIOD MAY BE SHORTENED BY USING DIVIDEND VALUES TO MAKE POLICY FULLY PAID-UP.

THE EXPENSE CHARGE APPLIED TO ALL PAYMENTS MADE UNDER THE OPTION TO PURCHASE PAID-UP ADDITIONS (OPP) RIDER WILL NOT EXCEED 3%.

THE INTEREST RATES, REFERRED TO IN THE BASIS OF COMPUTATION SECTION, ARE AS FOLLOWS:

A) 6.25% PER YEAR FOR THE CALCULATION OF CASH VALUES, EXTENDED INSURANCE AND PAID-UP INSURANCE FOR THE FIRST 20 POLICY YEARS.

B) 5% PER YEAR FOR THE COMPUTATION OF ALL OTHER VALUES.

DIVIDENDS ARE NOT GUARANTEED. WE HAVE THE RIGHT TO CHANGE THE AMOUNT OF DIVIDENDS TO BE CREDITED TO THE POLICY WHICH MAY RESULT IN LOWER DIVIDEND VALUES, OR, IF APPLICABLE, MORE PREMIUMS TO BE PAID, THAN WERE ILLUSTRATED.

GAT111   Page 2

SAMPLE

TABLE OF GUARANTEED VALUES*

Alternatives to Cash Value

End of Policy Year	Cash Value	Paid-Up Insurance	or	Extended Insurance		End of Policy Year
				Years	Days	
1	*****	***		**	***	1
2	*****	***		**	***	2
3	$400.00	$2,400		1	18	3
4	1,400.00	7,900		3	114	4
5	2,400.00	12,900		5	62	5
6	3,500.00	17,900		6	328	6
7	4,500.00	22,000		8	55	7
8	5,600.00	26,200		9	109	8
9	6,800.00	30,400		10	121	9
10	8,000.00	34,300		11	50	10
11	9,300.00	38,100		11	321	11
12	11,000.00	43,200		12	325	12
13	12,900.00	48,500		13	323	13
14	14,800.00	53,300		14	239	14
15	16,700.00	57,700		15	91	15
16	18,700.00	61,900		15	287	16
17	20,700.00	65,800		16	73	17
18	22,700.00	69,300		16	187	18
19	24,800.00	72,800		16	291	19
20	26,900.00	75,900		16	358	20
AGE 60	32,300.00	69,400		14	319	AGE 60
AGE 65	41,700.00	77,300		13	198	AGE 65

*This table assumes premiums have been paid to the end of the policy year shown. These values do not include any dividend accumulations, paid-up additions, or policy loans.

POLICY DATA   ABC LIFE INSURANCE COMPANY

SAMPLE

WE & YOU

In this policy, the words "we," "our" or "us" refer to ABC Life Insurance Company, and the words "you" or "your" refer to the owner of this policy.

When you write to us, please include the policy number, the Insured's full name, and your current address.

CONTENTS

POLICY DATA PAGES
Policy Identification and Specifications; Table of Guaranteed Values / **2–3**

LIFE INSURANCE PROCEEDS
Life Insurance Proceeds / **5**

POLICY OWNERSHIP
Owner; Successor Owner; Change of Ownership / **5**

BENEFICIARY
Naming of Beneficiary; Change of Beneficiary; Death of Beneficiary / **5**

PREMIUMS
Payment of Premiums; Grace Period; Nonpayment of Premium; Options Upon Lapse; Reinstatement; Premium Adjustment at Death / **6–7**

CASH VALUE AND LOANS
Cash Value; Loan Value; Loan Interest; Loan Interest Rate; Automatic Premium Loan (APL); Loan Repayment; When Unpaid Loan Exceeds Loan Value / **7–8**

DIVIDENDS
Annual Dividend; Dividend Options; Automatic Dividend Option; Dividend Values; Fully Paid-up Policy; Dividend at Death / **9**

PAYMENT OF POLICY PROCEEDS
Payment; Election of Optional Method of Payment; Change of Option; Payees; Minimum Payment; Options IAand IB. Proceeds at Interest; Options 2A and 2B. Elected Income; Options 3A, 3B and 3C. Life Income / **9–11**

GENERAL PROVISIONS
Entire Contract; Application; Incontestability; Suicide Exclusion; Dates; Age and Sex; Policy Changes; Assignment; Protection Against Creditors; Payments to Company; Basis of Computation; Conformity with Law; Voting Rights / **12**

APPLICATION
Attached to the Policy.

RIDERS OR ENDORSEMENTS (IF ANY)
Attached to the Policy.

Note: This policy is a legal contract between the policyowner and the Company.
READ YOUR POLICY CAREFULLY FOR FULL DETAILS.

SAMPLE

LIFE INSURANCE PROCEEDS

Life Insurance Proceeds We will pay the life insurance proceeds to the beneficiary promptly when we have proof that the Insured died, if premiums have been paid as called for in the Premiums section. These proceeds will include the face amount and any other benefits from riders or dividends which are payable because of the Insured's death, all as stated in the policy. When we determine these proceeds, there may be an adjustment for the last premium. We will deduct any unpaid loan.

POLICY OWNERSHIP

Owner In this policy, the words "you" and "your" refer to the owner of this policy. As the owner, you have all rights of ownership in this policy while the Insured is living. To exercise these rights, you do not need the consent of any successor owner or beneficiary.

Successor Owner A successor owner can be named in the application, or in a notice you sign which gives us the facts that we need. The successor owner will become the new owner when you die, if you die before the Insured. If no successor owner survives you and you die before the Insured, your estate becomes the new owner.

Change of Ownership You can change the owner of this policy, from yourself to a new owner, in a notice you sign which gives us the facts that we need. When this change takes effect, all rights of ownership in this policy will pass to the new owner.

When we record a change of owner or successor owner, these changes will take effect as of the date you signed the notice, subject to any payment we made or action we took before recording these changes. We may require that these changes be endorsed in the policy. Changing the owner or naming a new successor owner cancels any prior choice of successor owner, but does not change the beneficiary.

BENEFICIARY

Naming of Beneficiary One or more beneficiaries for any life insurance proceeds can be named in the application, or in a notice you sign which gives us the facts that we need. If more than one beneficiary is named, they can be classed as first, second, and so on. If 2 or more are named in a class, their shares in the proceeds can be stated.

The stated shares of the proceeds will be paid to any first beneficiaries who survive the Insured. If no first beneficiaries survive, payment will be made to any beneficiary surviving in the second class, and so on. Beneficiaries who survive in the same class have an equal share in the proceeds, unless the shares are stated otherwise.

Change of Beneficiary While the Insured is living, you can change a beneficiary in a notice you sign which gives us the facts that we need. When we record a change, it will take effect as of the date you signed the notice, subject to any payment we made or action we took before recording the change.

Death of Beneficiary If no beneficiary for the life insurance proceeds, or for a stated share, survives the Insured, the right to these proceeds or this share will pass to you. If you are the Insured, this right will pass to your estate. Unless stated otherwise in the policy or in your signed notice which is in effect at the Insured's death, if any beneficiary dies at the same time as the Insured, or within 15 days after the Insured but before we receive proof of the Insured's death, we will pay the proceeds as though that beneficiary died first.

SAMPLE

PREMIUMS

Payment of Premiums Each premium is payable, while the Insured is living, on or before its due date as shown in the Premium Schedule on the Policy Data page. Premiums are payable at our Home Office or at one of our service offices.

The premium for this policy can be paid at intervals of 3 months or 6 months, or once each year. The method we use to determine the premium rate for each of these intervals is the method that was in effect as of the policy date shown on the Policy Data page. The interval can be changed by paying the correct premium for the new interval. Premiums can be paid by any other method we make available.

Grace Period We allow 31 days from the due date for payment of a premium. All insurance coverage continues during this grace period.

Nonpayment of Premium If a premium is not paid by the end of the grace period, this policy will lapse. All insurance will end at the time of lapse, if the policy has no cash value and no dividend values. If the policy has cash value or dividend values, insurance can be continued only as stated in Options 1 or 2 of the Options Upon Lapse provision, but any insurance or benefits from riders or dividends will end at the time of lapse.

Options Upon Lapse If the policy has cash value or dividend values at the time of lapse, it will continue as extended insurance, if available. It may happen that the amount of extended insurance would be less than or equal to the amount of paid-up insurance available, or the Table of Guaranteed Values on the Policy Data page shows that extended insurance is not available. In these cases, the policy will continue under the paid-up insurance option instead.

Instead of extended insurance, paid-up insurance can be elected or you can surrender the policy for cash. The paid-up insurance option can be elected in the application or in your signed notice. We must receive this notice no later than 3 months after the due date of the overdue premium.

1. **Extended Insurance** Extended insurance is level term insurance for which no more premiums are due. It is payable to the beneficiary when we

have proof that the Insured died after the end of the grace period and before the end of the term period. The amount of extended insurance will equal the face amount of this policy, plus the amount of any paid-up additions and dividend accumulations, less any unpaid loan. No insurance or benefits from riders or dividends will be provided after the end of the grace period.

We calculate the term period as of the due date of the overdue premium. We do this by applying the sum of the cash value and dividend values, less any unpaid loan, at the net single premium rate for term insurance for the Insured's age on that date. The term period is measured from that due date.

This insurance can be surrendered at any time for its cash value, but it has no loan value and is not eligible for dividends. All insurance will end when you send us your signed request for the cash value proceeds.

2. **Paid-up Insurance** Paid-up life insurance begins as of the date we record your notice electing it, or begins at the end of the grace period if later. No more premiums are due for this insurance. It is payable to the beneficiary when we have proof that the Insured died while this paid-up insurance option was in effect.

We calculate the amount of paid-up insurance as of the due date of the overdue premium. We do this by applying the sum of the cash value and dividend values, less any unpaid loan, at the net single premium rate for the Insured's age on that date. In most cases, this amount will be less than the face amount of this policy. No insurance or benefits from riders will be provided after this paid-up insurance option goes into effect.

This insurance can be surrendered at any time. It has cash value and loan value, and is eligible for dividends. All insurance will end when you send us your signed request for the cash value proceeds.

3. **Surrender for Cash** Instead of extended insurance or paid-up insurance, you can surrender this policy for its cash value and dividend values, less any unpaid loan, as stated in the Cash Value provision. All insurance will end when you send us your signed request for the cash value proceeds.

GAT111   Page 6

SAMPLE

PREMIUMS (continued)

Reinstatement Within 5 years after lapse, you may apply to reinstate the policy if you have not surrendered it. We must have evidence of insurability that is acceptable to us. All overdue premiums must be paid, with interest at 6% per year from each of their due dates, unless we declare a policy loan interest rate of less than 6%. In that case, the interest rate for all overdue premiums at the time of reinstatement will be the same as the policy loan interest rate, but not more than 6%. Any unpaid loan, and any loan deducted when we determined the extended or paid-up insurance, must also be repaid. Interest on the loan will be compounded once each year and will be based on the loan interest rate or rates that were in effect since the time of lapse.

All or part of these payments can be charged as a new unpaid loan if there is enough loan value.

We do not need evidence of insurability if we receive the required payment within 31 days after the end of the grace period, but the Insured must be living when we receive it.

Premium Adjustment at Death We will increase the life insurance proceeds by any part of a premium paid for the period after the policy month in which the Insured dies.

If the Insured dies during a grace period, we will reduce the proceeds by an amount equal to the premium for one policy month.

CASH VALUE AND LOANS

Cash Value Cash values for this policy at the end of selected policy years are as shown in the Table of Guaranteed Values on the Policy Data page, if premiums have been paid as called for in the Premiums section. These values do not include dividend values, and they do not reflect any unpaid loan. Cash values at other times depend on the date to which premiums have been paid, and on how much time has passed since the last policy anniversary. When you ask us, we will tell you how much cash value there is.

The cash value on the due date of an unpaid premium will not decrease during the 3 months after that date. Also, the cash value of any extended or paid-up insurance on a policy anniversary will not decrease during the next 31 days after that anniversary.

At any time after the policy has cash value or dividend values, you can surrender it for the sum of these values, less any unpaid loan. All insurance will end when you send us your signed request for these surrender proceeds.

We may defer paying these proceeds for up to 6 months after the date of surrender. Interest will be paid from the date of surrender on any payment deferred more than 10 days. We set the interest rate each year. This rate will be at least 3.5% per year or the rate required by law.

Loan Value You can borrow any amount up to the loan value, using this policy as sole security.

On a policy anniversary, on a premium due date, or during the grace period, the loan value is the cash value, plus any dividend values, less any unpaid loan and accrued interest. At any other time, the loan value is the amount which, with interest, will equal the loan value on the next anniversary or on the next premium due date, if earlier. Extended insurance has no loan value.

We may require that you sign a loan agreement. We may defer a loan, except to pay a premium due us for this policy, for as long as 6 months after we receive your loan request. Interest will be paid on any amount deferred if that amount is not mailed within 10 days after we receive the necessary information to complete the loan transaction. We will set the interest rate to be at least 3.5% per year or the rate required by law.

Loan Interest Loan interest accrues each day. Interest is due on each anniversary, or on the date of death, surrender, a lapse, a loan increase or loan repayment, or on any other date we specify. Interest not paid when due becomes part of the loan and will also bear interest.

Loan Interest Rate The loan interest rate for this policy may go up or down as described in this provision. However, the rate at any given time will apply to the entire amount of an unpaid loan. We will review this rate once every 3 months and, if necessary, adjust it.

SAMPLE

CASH VALUE AND LOANS (continued)

The loan interest rate will not be more than the Monthly Average Corporates yield shown in Moody's Corporate Bond Yield Averages published by Moody's Investors Services, Inc., or any successor to that service (the published monthly average), for the second calendar month prior to the date when we set an interest rate for this policy. If the rate, at this time, as determined by the published monthly average, is 0.5% or more above the current loan interest rate, we have the right to increase the loan interest rate to reflect this. However if the rate, at this time, as determined by the published monthly average, is 0.5% or more below the current loan interest rate, we will reduce the loan interest rate to reflect this. The loan interest rate will never be less than the interest rate shown on the Policy Data page plus 1%.

We will tell you the interest rate in effect when a loan, including an Automatic Premium Loan (APL), is made and when we send you notice of loan interest due. If a loan is outstanding 40 days or more before the effective date of an increase in the interest rate, we will notify you of that increase at least 30 days prior to its effective date. We will notify you of any increase in the interest rate when a loan is made during the 40 days before the effective date of the increase.

It may happen that the published monthly average ceases to be published. In this case, we will use a new basis approved by the insurance supervisory official of the state or district in which the policy is delivered.

Automatic Premium Loan (APL) If elected, APL provides an automatic loan which pays an overdue premium at the end of the grace period, subject to 2 conditions. First, the loan value must be enough to pay that premium.

Second, if premiums have been paid by APL for 2 years in a row, the next premium will not be paid by APL. After a premium is paid other than by APL, before the end of the grace period, premiums can again be paid by APL.

APL can be elected in the application. You can also elect APL in your signed notice which we must receive before the end of the grace period. You can cancel this election for future premiums by telling us in your signed notice.

Loan Repayment All or part of an unpaid loan and accrued interest can be repaid before the Insured's death or before you surrender the policy. We will deduct any unpaid loan when policy proceeds are payable.

If the policy is being continued as extended or paid-up insurance, any loan which we deducted in determining that insurance may be repaid only if the policy is reinstated. If that loan is not repaid, we will not deduct it again when policy proceeds are payable.

When Unpaid Loan Exceeds Loan Value In a given policy year it may happen that an unpaid loan and accrued interest will exceed the sum of the cash value and any dividend values. In this case, we will mail a notice to you at your last known address, and a copy to any assignee on our records. All insurance will end 31 days after the date on which we mail that notice, if the excess of the unpaid loan and accrued interest over the sum of the cash value and any dividend values is not paid within that 31 days.

We will not terminate this policy in a given policy year as the sole result of a change in the loan interest rate during that policy year.

GAT111

SAMPLE

DIVIDENDS

Annual Dividend While this policy is in force, except as extended insurance, it is eligible to share in our divisible surplus. Each year we determine the policy's share, if any. This share is payable as a dividend on the policy anniversary, if all premiums due before then have been paid. We do not expect a dividend to be payable before the second anniversary.

Dividend Options Each dividend can be applied under one of the 4 options listed below. An option can be elected in the application. You can also elect or change the option for future dividends if you tell us in your signed notice.

1. Paid-up Addition Applied to provide paid-up life insurance at the net single premium rate for the Insured's age at that time. No more premiums are due for this insurance. It has cash value and is eligible for dividends. Before the Insured's death, you can surrender paid-up additions for their cash value that has not been borrowed against. The amount of this insurance in force at the Insured's death will be part of the life insurance proceeds.

2. Dividend Accumulation Left with us to accumulate at interest. On each policy anniversary, we credit interest at the rate we set each year. This rate will be at least 3.5% per year. Before the Insured's death, you can withdraw accumulations that have not been borrowed against, with interest to the date of withdrawal. Any accumulations which we still have at the Insured's death will be part of the life insurance proceeds.

3. Premium Payment Applied toward payment of a premium, provided any balance of that premium is also paid when due. Any part of the dividend not needed to pay the premium will be used to pay any loan interest due, unless you have asked to have that part paid in cash. Any part of the dividend not used to pay a premium or loan interest will be paid in cash.

4. Cash Paid in cash.

Automatic Dividend Option If no other option is in effect when a dividend becomes payable, we will apply it as a paid-up addition. If we pay a dividend in cash, and the dividend check is not cashed within one year after that dividend became payable, we will apply the dividend as a paid-up addition instead.

Dividend Values Dividend values are any dividend accumulations plus the cash value of any paid-up additions.

Fully Paid-up Policy You may shorten the premium paying period for this policy by having it made fully paid-up with no more premiums due. This may be done on any premium due date, if the sum of the cash value and dividend values equals the total single premium for the policy and any riders, based on the Insured's age on that date. We must receive your signed notice within 31 days of that date.

Dividend at Death The part of any annual dividend earned from the last policy anniversary to the end of the policy month in which the Insured dies will be part of the life insurance proceeds.

PAYMENT OF POLICY PROCEEDS

Payment We will pay the life insurance proceeds in one sum or, if elected, all or part of these proceeds may be placed under one or more of the options described in this section. If we agree, the proceeds may be placed under some other method of payment instead.

Any life insurance proceeds paid in one sum will bear interest compounded each year from the Insured's death to the date of payment. We set the interest rate each year. This rate will be at least 3.5% per year, and will not be less than required by law.

Election of Optional Method of Payment While the Insured is living, you can elect or change an option. You can also name or change one or more beneficiaries for the life insurance proceeds who will be the payee or payees under that option.

After the Insured dies, any person who is to receive proceeds in one sum (other than an assignee) can elect an option and name payees. The person who elects an option can also name one or more successor payees to receive any unpaid amount we have at the death of a payee. Naming these payees cancels any prior choice of successor payee.

SAMPLE

PAYMENT OF POLICY PROCEEDS (continued)

A payee who did not elect the option does not have the right to advance or assign payments, take the payments in one sum, or make any other change. However, the payee may be given the right to do one or more of these things if the person who elects the option tells us in writing and we agree.

Change of Option If we agree, a payee who elects Option 1A, 1B, 2A or 2B may later elect to have any unpaid amount we still have, or the present value of any elected payments, placed under some other option described in this section.

Payees Only individuals who are to receive payments in their own behalf may be named as payees or successor payees, unless we agree to some other payee. We may require proof of the age or the survival of a payee.

It may happen that when the last surviving payee dies, we still have an unpaid amount, or there are some payments which remain to be made. If so, we will pay the unpaid amount with interest to the date of payment, or pay the present value of the remaining payments, to that payee's estate in one sum. The present value of any remaining payments is based on the interest rate used to compute them, and is always less than their sum.

Minimum Payment When any payment under an option would be less than $20, we may pay any unpaid amount or present value in one sum.

Options 1 A and 1 B. Proceeds at Interest

The policy proceeds may be left with us at interest. We set the interest rate each year. This rate will be at least 3.5% per year.

1A. Interest Accumulation

We credit interest each year on the amount we still have. This amount can be withdrawn at any time in sums of $100 or more. We pay interest to the date of withdrawal on sums withdrawn.

1B. Interest Payment

We pay interest once each month, every 3 months or every 6 months, or once each year, as chosen, based on the amount we still have.

Options 2A and 2B. Elected Income

We make equal payments once each month, every 3 months or every 6 months, or once each year, as chosen, for an elected period of years or for an elected amount. We set the interest rate for these options each year. This rate will be at least 3.5% per year. If the rate is more than 3.5%, we will increase each payment to reflect this.

2A. Income for Elected Period

We make the payments for the number of years elected. Monthly payments based on 3.5% interest are shown in the Option 2A Table.

OPTION 2A TABLE
Minimum Monthly Payment per $1,000 of Proceeds

Years		Years		Years		Years	
1	$84.65	5	$18.12	9	$10.75	15	$7.10
2	43.05	6	15.35	10	9.83	20	5.75
3	29.19	7	13.38	11	9.09	25	4.96
4	22.27	8	11.90	12	8.46	30	4.45

When asked, we will state in writing what each payment would be, if made every 3 months or every 6 months, or once each year.

2B. Income of Elected Amount

We make payments of the elected amount until all proceeds and interest have been paid. The total payments made each year must be at least 5% of the proceeds placed under this option. Each year we credit interest of at least 3.5% on the amount we still have.

Options 3A, 3B, and 3C. Life Income

We make equal payments each month during the lifetime of the named payee or payees. We determine the amount of the monthly payment by applying the policy proceeds to purchase a corresponding single premium life annuity policy which is being issued when the first payment is due. Payments are based on the appropriately adjusted annuity premium rate in effect at that time, but will not be less than the corresponding minimum amount based on the tables for Options 3A, 3B, and 3C in this policy. The minimum amounts are based on the "1983 Table **a**" mortality table with projection, and with interest compounded each year at 4%.

SAMPLE

PAYMENT OF POLICY PROCEEDS (continued)

When asked, we will state in writing what the minimum amount of each monthly payment would be under these options. It is based on the sex and the adjusted age of the payee or payees in the year the first payment is due. To find the adjusted age, we increase or decrease the payee's age at that time, as follows:

1987–91	1992–98	1999–2006	2007–2013	2014–20	2021–28	2029+
+3	+2	+1	0	−1	−2	−3

3A. Life Income–Guaranteed Period

We make a payment each month during the lifetime of the payee. Payments do not change, and are guaranteed for 5, 10, 15, or 20 years, as chosen, even if that payee dies sooner.

OPTION 3A TABLE
Minimum Monthly Payment per $1,000 of Proceeds

Payee's Adjusted Age	MALE Guaranteed Period				FEMALE Guaranteed Period			
	5 Yrs	10 Yrs	15 Yrs	20 Yrs	5 Yrs	10 Yrs	15 Yrs	20 Yrs
60	$5.14	$5.08	$4.98	$4.84	$4.68	$4.85	$4.61	$4.54
61	5.25	5.18	5.07	4.91	4.76	4.73	4.68	4.63
62	5.36	5.28	5.15	4.97	4.84	4.81	4.75	4.67
63	5.48	5.39	5.24	5.04	4.93	4.89	4.83	4.73
64	5.61	5.50	5.33	5.10	5.03	4.99	4.91	4.80
65	5.75	5.62	5.42	5.17	5.13	5.08	5.00	4.87
66	5.89	5.75	5.52	5.23	5.25	5.19	5.09	4.94
67	6.05	5.88	5.62	5.30	5.36	5.30	5.18	5.01
68	6.21	6.02	5.72	5.36	5.49	5.41	5.28	5.08
69	6.39	6.16	5.82	5.42	5.63	5.54	5.38	5.16
70	6.57	6.31	5.92	5.48	5.78	5.67	5.48	5.23
71	6.77	6.46	6.02	5.54	5.94	5.81	5.59	5.30
72	6.97	6.62	6.13	5.60	6.11	5.95	5.70	5.37
73	7.19	6.78	6.23	5.65	6.29	6.11	5.81	5.44
74	7.42	6.95	6.33	5.69	6.49	6.27	5.93	5.50
75	7.66	7.12	6.42	5.74	6.70	6.44	6.04	5.58
76	7.91	7.29	6.52	5.78	6.92	6.61	6.15	5.62
77	8.18	7.46	6.60	5.81	7.16	6.80	6.27	5.67
78	8.47	7.84	6.69	5.84	7.42	6.98	6.37	5.72
79	8.77	7.82	6.77	5.87	7.69	7.18	6.48	5.76
80	9.08	8.00	6.84	5.90	7.98	7.37	6.58	5.80
81	9.41	8.17	6.91	5.92	8.29	7.57	6.67	5.84
82	9.74	8.34	6.97	5.94	8.62	7.77	6.75	5.87
83	10.10	8.51	7.03	5.95	8.96	7.97	6.83	5.89
84	10.46	8.67	7.08	5.96	9.33	8.16	6.91	5.92
85 & over	10.84	8.82	7.13	5.97	9.71	8.34	6.97	5.94

3B. Life Income–Guaranteed Total Amount

We make a payment each month during the lifetime of the payee. Payments do not change, and are guaranteed until the total amount paid equals the amount placed under this option, even if that payee dies sooner.

OPTION 3B TABLE
Minimum Monthly Payment per $1,000 of Proceeds

Payee's Adjusted Age	Male	Female	Payee's Adjusted Age	Male	Female
60	$4.93	$4.57	73	$6.47	$5.87
61	5.02	4.64	74	6.84	6.01
62	5.11	4.71	75	6.81	6.17
63	5.20	4.79	76	7.00	6.34
64	5.30	4.87	77	7.19	6.51
65	5.40	4.96	78	7.40	6.70
66	5.52	5.05	79	7.62	6.90
67	5.63	5.14	80	7.85	7.11
68	5.75	5.25	81	8.09	7.33
69	5.88	5.36	82	8.35	7.57
70	6.02	5.47	83	8.61	7.81
71	6.16	5.60	84	8.89	8.07
72	6.31	5.73	85&over	9.19	8.35

3C. Life Income–Joint and Survivor

We make a payment each month while both or one of the two payees are living. Payments do not change, and are guaranteed for 10 years, even if both payees die sooner.

OPTION 3C TABLE
10 YEAR GUARANTEED PERIOD
Minimum Monthly Payment per $1,000 of Proceeds

Male Payee's Adjusted Age	Female Payee's Adjusted Age				
	60	65	70	75	80
60	$4.32	$4.50	$4.67	$4.82	$4.93
65	4.42	4.66	4.91	5.15	5.34
70	4.81	4.81	5.14	5.49	5.80
75	4.57	4.92	5.34	5.81	6.27
80	4.61	4.99	5.49	6.07	6.69

SAMPLE

GENERAL PROVISIONS

Entire Contract The entire contract consists of this policy, any attached riders or endorsements and the attached copy of the application. Only our Chairman, President, Secretary, or one of our Vice Presidents can change the contract, and then only in writing. No change will be made in the contract without your consent. No agent is authorized to change this contract.

Application In issuing this policy, we have relied on the statements made in the application. All such statements are deemed to be representations and not warranties. We assume these statements are true and complete to the best of the knowledge and belief of those who made them.

No statement made in connection with the application will be used by us to void the policy or to deny a claim unless that statement is a material misrepresentation and is part of the application.

Incontestability We will not contest this policy after it has been in force during the lifetime of the Insured for 2 years from the date of issue.

Please refer to the Incontestability of Rider provision that may be in any rider or riders attached to this policy.

Suicide Exclusion Suicide of the Insured within one year of the date of issue, is not covered by this policy. In that event, this policy will end and the only amount payable will be the premiums paid to us, less any unpaid loan. **(SEE ENDORSEMENT HEREON)**

Dates Policy years, months, and anniversaries are measured from the policy date.

Age and Sex In this policy when we refer to a person's age on any date, we mean his or her age on the birthday which is nearest that date. If a date on the Policy Data page is based on an age that is not correct, we may change the date to reflect the correct age.

If the age or sex of an insured person is not correct as stated, any amount payable under this policy will be what the premiums paid would have purchased at the correct age and sex.

Policy Changes If we agree, you may have riders added to this policy, or have it changed to another plan or to a smaller amount of insurance.

Assignment While the Insured is living, you can assign this policy or any interest in it. If you do this, your interest, and anyone else's is subject to that of the assignee. As owner, you still have the rights of ownership that have not been assigned.

An assignee may not change the owner or the beneficiary, and may not elect or change an optional method of payment of proceeds. Any policy proceeds payable to the assignee will be paid in one sum.

We must have a copy of any assignment. We will not be responsible for the validity of an assignment. It will be subject to any payment we make or other action we take before we record it.

Protection Against Creditors Except as stated in the Assignment provision, payments we make under this policy are, to the extent the law permits, exempt from the claims, attachments, or levies of any creditors.

Payments to Company Any payment made to us by check or money order must be payable to ABC Life Insurance Company. When asked, we will give a counter-signed receipt, signed by our President or Secretary, for any premium paid to us.

Basis of Computation All cash values and net single premium rates referred to in this policy are based on the 1980 CSO Tables of Mortality. All extended insurance rates and cash values are based on the corresponding 1980 CET Insurance Tables. The interest rate is shown on the Policy Data page. Continuous functions are used.

At the end of each policy year not shown in the Table on the Policy Data page, the cash value is the reserve based on the Commissioner's Reserve Valuation Method. At any time, the cash value of any extended or paid-up insurance or paid-up additions is the reserve on each of these.

We have filed a statement with the insurance official in the state or district in which this policy is delivered. It describes, in detail, the method we used to compute these cash values. Each value is at least as much as the law requires.

Conformity with Law This policy is subject to all laws which apply.

Voting Rights Each year there is an election of persons to our Board of Directors. You have the right to vote in person or by mail if your policy is in force, and has been in force for at least one year after the date of issue. To find out more about this, write to the Secretary at our Home Office, 100 Ordinary Avenue, New York, New York 00000.

GAT111

SAMPLE

RIDER

ACCIDENTAL DEATH BENEFIT (ADB)

Benefit We will pay this benefit to the beneficiary when we have proof that the Insured's death was caused directly, and apart from any other cause, by accidental bodily injury, and that death occurred within one year after that injury and while this rider was in effect.

When Benefit Not Payable We will not pay this benefit if death is caused or is contributed to by any of these items.

1. Disease or infirmity of mind or body.

2. Suicide.

3. Travel in or descent from an aircraft, if the Insured at any time during the aircraft's flight acted in any role other than as a passenger.

4. Any kind of war, declared or not, or by any act incident to a war or to an armed conflict involving the armed forces of one or more countries.

We will not pay this benefit if the Insured dies prior to his or her first birthday, or dies after the anniversary on which he or she is age 70.

Values This rider does not have cash or loan values.

Contract This rider, when paid for, is made a part of the policy, based on the application for the rider.

Incontestability of Rider We will not contest this rider after it has been in force during the lifetime of the Insured for 2 years from its date of issue.

Dates and Amounts When this rider is issued at the same time as the policy, we show the amount of ADB and the rider premium amount on the front page of the policy. The rider and the policy have the same date of issue.

When this rider is added to a policy which is already in force, we also put in an add-on rider. The add-on rider shows the date of issue and the amount of ADB. The rider premium amount is shown in a new Premium Schedule for the policy.

When Rider Ends You can cancel this rider as of the due date of a premium. To do this, you must send the policy and your signed notice to us within 31 days of that date. If this rider is still in effect on the anniversary on which the Insured is age 70, it will end on that date.

This rider ends if the policy ends or is surrendered. Also, this rider will not be in effect if the policy lapses or is in force as extended or paid-up insurance.

When this rider is part of an endowment policy, the rider will end on the day just before the endowment date, and will not be in effect if that date is deferred.

ABC LIFE INSURANCE COMPANY

Mary Smith
Secretary

John Johnson
President

THIS PAGE INTENTIONALLY LEFT BLANK

SAMPLE

RIDER

DISABILITY WAIVER OF PREMIUM (WP)

Waiver of Premiums We will start to waive the premiums for this policy when proof is furnished that the Insured's total disability, as defined in this rider, has gone on for at least 6 months in a row.

If a total disability starts on or prior to the anniversary on which the Insured is age 60, we will waive all of the premiums which fall due during that total disability. If it goes on until the anniversary on which the Insured is age 65, we will make the policy fully paid-up as of that date, with no more premiums due.

If a total disability starts after the anniversary on which the Insured is age 60, we will waive only those premiums which fall due during that total disability, and prior to the anniversary on which the Insured is age 65.

Premiums are waived at the interval of payment in effect when the total disability started. While we waive premiums, all insurance goes on as if they had been paid. We will not deduct a waived premium from the policy proceeds.

Definition of Total Disability "Total Disability" means that, because of disease or bodily injury, the Insured can not do any of the essential acts and duties of his or her job, or of any other job for which he or she is suited based on schooling, training, or experience. If the Insured can do some but not all of these acts and duties, disability is not total and premiums will not be waived. If the Insured is a minor and is required by law to go to school, "Total Disability" means that, because of disease or bodily injury, he or she is not able to go to school.

"Total Disability" also means the Insured's total loss, starting while this rider is in effect, of the sight of both eyes or the use of both hands, both feet, or one hand and one foot.

Total Disabilities For Which Premiums Not Waived We will not waive premiums in connection with any of these total disabilities.

1. Those that start prior to the fifth birthday of the Insured, or start at a time when this rider is not in effect.

2. Those that are caused by an injury that is self-inflicted on purpose.

3. Those that are caused by any kind of war, declared or not, or by any act incident to a war or to an armed conflict involving the armed forces of one or more countries while the Insured is a member of those armed forces.

Proof of Total Disability Written notice and proof of this condition must be given to us, while the Insured is living and totally disabled, or as soon as it can reasonably be done. As long as we waive premiums, we may require proof from time to time. After we have waived premiums for 2 years in a row, we will not need to have this proof more than once each year. As part of the proof, we may have the Insured examined by doctors we approve.

Payment of Premiums Premiums must be paid when due, until we approve a claim under this rider. If a total disability starts during a grace period, the overdue premium must be paid before we will approve any claim.

Refund of Premiums If a total disability starts after a premium has been paid, and if it goes on for at least 6 months in a row, we will refund the part of that premium paid for the period after the policy month when that disability started. Any other premium paid and then waived will be refunded in full.

SAMPLE

DISABILITY WAIVER OF PREMIUM (WP)

(continued)

Values This rider does not have cash or loan values.

Contract This rider, when paid for, is made a part of the policy, based on the application for the rider.

Incontestability of Rider We have no right to contest this rider after it has been in force during the lifetime of the Insured for 2 years from its date of issue, unless the Insured is totally disabled at some time within 2 years of the date of issue.

Dates and Amounts When this rider is issued at the same time as the policy, we show the rider premium amount on the front page of the policy. The rider and the policy have the same date of issue.

When this rider is added to a policy which is already in force, we also put in an add-on rider. The add-on rider shows the date of issue. The rider premium amount is shown in a new Premium Schedule for the policy.

When Rider Ends You can cancel this rider as of the due date of a premium. To do this, you must send the policy and your signed notice to us within 31 days of that date. If this rider is still in effect on the anniversary on which the Insured is age 65, it will end on that date.

This rider ends if the policy ends or is surrendered. Also, this rider will not be in effect if the policy lapses or is in force as extended or paid-up insurance.

ABC LIFE INSURANCE COMPANY

Mary Smith
Secretary

John Johnson
President

SAMPLE

RIDER

POLICY PURCHASE OPTION (PPO)

Benefit The Owner can purchase a new policy on the Insured on each Scheduled Option Date or Special Option Date, without proof of insurability. The new policy will take effect as of the option date, with premiums based on the Insured's age and the Company's premium rates on that date. The face amount of the new policy may not be less than $10,000 or more than the Option Amount of the rider, except when a larger amount can be purchased on a Special Option Date.

During the 3 months prior to a Special Option Date, the Company provides term insurance on the Insured. The amount of this insurance is equal to the largest face amount of the new policy that can be purchased under this rider on that date.

Scheduled Option Dates The Scheduled Option Dates are the anniversaries on which the Insured is age 22, 25, 28, 31, 34, 37, 40, 43, and 46, and on which this rider is in effect. No new policy can be purchased on any Scheduled Option Date which has been cancelled by a prior Special Option Date purchase.

Special Option Dates A Special Option Date is the date 3 months after any of the events listed below.

1. The marriage of the Insured.
2. The birth of a living child to the Insured.
3. The legal adoption of a child by the Insured.

This rider must be in effect on the date the marriage, birth, or adoption takes place. Proof acceptable to the Company, that the event took place, may be required.

Each purchase of a new policy as of a Special Option Date cancels the next available Scheduled Option Date, except where 2 or more children are born or adopted on the same date. In this case, an amount of insurance can be purchased which equals the Option Amount times the number of these children.

The number of Scheduled Option Dates cancelled by this amount of purchase is equal to the number of these children.

Savings Allowance The Company provides a savings allowance when a new policy is purchased. The amount of this allowance is on file with the insurance official in the state or district in which the policy is delivered. This allowance is used to reduce premiums that are due during the first policy year of the new policy. At the time of purchase, the Company will tell the Owner how much the total allowance is for the new policy.

Purchase of Policy The Owner's application for the new policy must also be signed by the Insured. The application and the first premium for the new policy, less the savings allowance, may be submifted to the Company during the 60 days before or the 31 days after the option date. However, these must be received by the Company while the Insured is living.

On an option date, if the Owner does not have an insurable interest in the life of the Insured that is acceptable to the Company, the Insured may purchase the new policy instead.

If the Insured dies prior to the option date, any new policy which has been applied for will not take effect, and the Company will refund any premium paid for it.

New Policy The new policy may be on any life, term-life, or endowment plan offered on the option date, for the face amount being purchased.

The new policy may not be on a plan which provides only term insurance or provides an increasing amount of insurance. It will have the same provisions and be subject to the same limitations on the Company's liability as are generally in the series of policies being issued on that date. The Insured's class of risk will be the same as it was for the rider.

SAMPLE

POLICY PURCHASE OPTION (PPO)

(continued)

However, if this rider was issued with a policy in a preferred risk class, the new policy will be on a preferred risk basis only if it meets the Company's minimum amount and age limits for that class.

The time periods of the new policy, which relate to a suicide exclusion or to a contest of that policy, will start on the date of issue of this rider. However, in some cases the new policy may be issued with a rider or an additional amount of insurance which the Owner requested, and which required the Company's agreement. If this happens, the time periods for that rider or amount will start instead on the date of issue of the new policy.

Availability of Riders A waiver of premium rider can be made a part of the new policy if one is in effect under this policy on an option date. However, if the Insured has recovered from a total disability that had gone on for at least 6 months in a row, that rider can only be in a new policy for which premiums are payable for the rest of the Insured's life.

An accidental death benefit rider can be made a part of the new policy if one is in effect under this policy on an option date. The amount of that rider may not be more than the face amount of the new policy.

No other riders can be made a part of the new policy, unless the Company agrees.

Waiver of Premiums for New Policy If, on an option date, this policy has a waiver of premium rider in effect, and if the Insured is totally disabled and all conditions for waiver of premiums in that rider have been met, the Company will waive the premiums

for the new policy which fall due during that disability. The new policy must be on a plan with premiums payable for the rest of the Insured's life, and with the same premium interval as this policy.

Values This rider does not have cash or loan values.

Contract This rider, when paid for, is made a part of the policy, based on the application for the rider.

Incontestability of Rider The Company will not contest this rider after it has been in force during the lifetime of the Insured for 2 years from its date of issue.

Dates and Amounts When this rider is issued at the same time as the policy, the Company shows the Option Amount and the rider premium amount on the front page of the policy. The rider and the policy have the same date of issue.

When this rider is added to a policy which is already in force, the Company also puts in an add-on rider. The add-on rider shows the date of issue and the Option Amount. The rider premium amount is shown in a new Premium Schedule for the policy.

When Rider Ends The Owner can cancel this rider as of the due date of a premium. To do this, the policy and the Owner's signed notice must be sent to the Company within 31 days of that date. If this rider is still in effect on the anniversary on which the Insured is age 46, it will end on that date.

This rider ends if the policy ends or is surrendered. Also, this rider will not be in effect if the policy lapses or is in force as extended or reduced paid-up insurance.

ABC LIFE INSURANCE COMPANY

Mary Smith
Secretary

John Johnson
President

GAR013

Page 18

FLEXIBLE PREMIUM (UNIVERSAL) LIFE INSURANCE POLICY

ABC Life Insurance Company

An XYZ Company

123 Main Street, Anytown, USA 54321   (505) 555-1234   (800) 555-4321

WE PROMISE TO PAY THE Insurance Proceeds to the Beneficiary, subject to the provisions of this Contract, when We receive due proof of the Insured's death. Payment will be made only if this Contract is in force on the date of such Insured's death.

THE CONSIDERATION FOR THIS CONTRACT is the application hereof and the payment in advance of the premiums in accordance with the terms and conditions of this Contract. The first premium is payable on or before delivery of this contract; the amount of and the interval between planned premiums are shown in the Schedule.

Insured: John Q. Doe   Face Amount: $ 75,000.00   **Issue Date: July 3, 1999**

This is a legal Contract. Read Your Contract carefully.

20 DAY RIGHT TO EXAMINE CONTRACT.

It is important to Us that You are satisfied with this Contract. If You are not satisfied You may, within 20 days after this Contract is delivered to You, return it to Us or to Our agent. If You return the Contract within this time period We will refund all of the premium You have paid. The Contract will then be deemed void from the beginning.

SIGNED BY ABC LIFE INSURANCE COMPANY at Anytown, USA, its Home Office, 123 Main Street on the Contract Date of this Contract.

Mary Smith
Secretary

John Johnson
President

FLEXIBLE PREMIUM LIFE INSURANCE TO AGE 100

Life insurance payable if the Insured dies prior to age 100. Coverage continues provided Cash Value less indebtedness is sufficient to cover monthly deduction. Cash Value less indebtedness payable at Final Policy Date. Non-participating.

POLICY CONTENTS

DEFINITIONS.. 5

TABLE OF GUARANTEED MAXIMUM MONTHLY COST OF INSURANCE RATES 6

DEATH BENEFITS.. 7
Insurance Proceeds
Payment of Insurance Proceeds
Effect of Partial Surrender on Insurance Proceeds

PREMIUMS AND REINSTATEMENT 8
Payment of Premiums
Planned Periodic Premiums
Additional Premiums
Grace Period
Reinstatement

CONTRACT VALUES 9
Cash Value
Interest Rate
Monthly Deductions
Continuation of Insurance
Cost of Insurance
Cost of Insurance Rates
Surrender
Partial Surrender

CONTRACT LOANS 11
Contract Loan
Interest Rate Charged on Contract Loan

GENERAL PROVISIONS 11
Contract
Your Rights
Misstatement of Age
Suicide
Incontestability
Beneficiary
Computation of Values
Ownership
Change of Ownership
Collateral Assignment
Annual Report
Nonparticipating
Deferment
Right to Extend Final Policy Date
Tax Considerations
Governing Law

OPTIONAL INCOME PLANS 15

SAMPLE

SCHEDULE FOR CONTRACT NUMBER GA001

Form No.	Type of Coverage	Face Amount	Rate Class Numeral	Years Payable
XYZ-091	Flexible Premium Life Insurance to Attained Age 100	$75,000.00	Standard (1.0000)	65
XYZ-090	Endorsement			

Beneficiary - As stated in the application for this Contract unless changed in accordance with Contract provisions.

Owner .... John Q. Doe
Issue Age 35
Contract Date .... July 3, 1999
Monthly Anniversary Date 3
Additional Initial Lump-Sum Premium .... $ 0.00
Planned Payment Interval .... Annual
Monthly Secondary Guarantee Premium $36.00

Insured .... John Q. Doe
Issue Date .... July 3,1999
Final Policy Date .... July 3, 2064
Minimum Premium Due At Issue .... $ 36.00
Planned Periodic Premium .... $ 1,004.31
Permanent Monthly Flat Extra .... Amount $ 0.00
Guaranteed Date† .... July 3, 2064

Temporary Monthly Flat Extra Amount ... $ 0.00 For all Contract Year(s).

Maximum Contract Loan Interest Rate 7.4% in advance

† The Guaranteed Date is the date to which coverage is guaranteed to continue provided We receive payment of the Additional Initial Lump-Sum Premium, if any, on the Issue Date plus the continuous timely, and uninterrupted monthly payment of a premium equal to the Monthly Secondary Guarantee Premium of $36.00 and no partial surrenders or indebtedness.

XYZ-091   Page 3   Contract GA001

SAMPLE

SCHEDULE FOR CONTRACT NUMBER GA001

PERCENT OF PREMIUM LOAD

A Maximum Premium Load of 10.00% will be deducted from each premium paid. We may from time to time, at Our sole discretion, charge a lesser Premium Load in a uniform manner based upon such factors as the rate class, the amount of cumulative premiums, Cash Value and number of Contract Years expired.

MONTHLY LIFE INSURANCE LOAD

A permanent monthly life insurance load of $2.70 will be included in the monthly deduction deducted from the Cash Value on the Issue Date and on each Monthly Anniversary Date.

A monthly life insurance load will be included in the monthly deduction deducted from the Cash Value on the Issue Date and on each Monthly Anniversary Date. The maximum monthly life insurance load per $1,000 of Face Amount is shown in Table A below. We may from time to time, at Our sole discretion, charge a lesser monthly life insurance load in a uniform manner based upon such factors as the rate class, amount of cumulative premiums paid, Cash Value and number of Contract Years expired.

TABLE A
TABLE OF MAXIMUM MONTHLY LOADS
(Per $1,000 of Face Amount)

Contract Year	Monthly Load	Contract Year	Monthly Load	Contract Year	Monthly Load	Contract Year	Monthly Load
1	0.2274	2	0.2158	3	0.2025	4	0.1875
5	0.1700	6 & Up	0.0000				

ACCELERATION OF FLAT EXTRA AND MONTHLY LOAD

Notwithstanding any other provision of this Contract to the contrary, if the Contract is surrendered during the first Contract Year then We reserve the right to deduct from the surrender value so many of the subsequent Monthly Life Insurance Loads and Permanent Monthly Flat Extra Amounts that otherwise would have been due for the first Contract Year as is equal to the remainder of full months (not less than zero) of (a) minus (b), where: (a) is the smaller of twelve (12), or the total premiums paid to date divided by the Minimum Premium Due At Issue; and, (b) is the number of Contract Months already expired.

SAMPLE

Definitions

To make this Contract easier to read, We have left out many cross-references and conditional statements. Therefore, the provisions of the Contract must be read as a whole.

In this Contract, the following words mean:

Attained Age - The Issue Age shown on page 3 increased by 1 on each succeeding Contract Anniversary Date. For example, if the Issue Age is 35, then the Attained Age on the 5th Contract Anniversary Date is 40 (35 plus 5).

Benchmark Cash Value - On each Monthly Anniverary Date the cash value that would have been produced pursuant to the terms of this Contract assuming: (a) the continuous, timely, and uninterrupted monthly payment of a premium equal to the Minimum Premium Due At Issue shown on page 3; (b) actual interest rates applied and actual cost of insurance rates used; and, (c) no prior Partial Surrenders. The Benchmark Cash Value will never be less than zero.

Beneficiary - The person, persons or entity named in writing by You to receive the Insurance Proceeds at the Insured's death while this Contract is in force

Contract Anniversary Date - The same day and month as the Issue Date shown on page 3 for each succeeding year.

Contract Month - The interval of time from the Issue Date to the Monthly Anniversary Date, and between consecutive Monthly Anniversary Dates.

Contract Year - The interval of time from the Issue Date to the first Contract Anniversary Date, and between consecutive Contract Anniversary Dates.

Cash Value - The amount in this Contract to which We credit interest.

Indebtedness - The sum of any unpaid Contract loans and any accrued and unpaid Contract loan interest.

Insurance Proceeds - The total amount of money We will pay the Beneficiary at the death of the Insured if this Contract is then in force.

Monthly Anniversary Date - The same day of each calendar month as shown on page 3.

Insured - The person whose life is insured under the terms of this Contract. See page 3.

You, Your - The owner of this Contract. The owner may be someone other than the Insured.

We, Our, Us - Texas Life Insurance Company at its Home Office.

Written Request - A writing to exercise any rights under this Contract, appropriately signed and received by Us at Our Home Office in Anytown, USA, on forms that We supply. We may also require that the Contract be sent to Us with any Written Request.

SAMPLE

TABLE OF GUARANTEED MAXIMUM MONTHLY COST
OF INSURANCE RATES PER $1,000

The table below is the guaranteed maximum monthly cost of insurance rates We will charge based on the Insured's Attained Age. These rates must be multiplied times the rate class numeral shown on page 3.

Attained Age	Male	Female	Attained Age	Male	Female
0	0.19417	0.19417	50	0.52083	0.52083
1	0.08000	0.08000	51	0.56417	0.56417
2	0.07667	0.07667	52	0.61333	0.61333
3	0.07417	0.07417	53	0.66833	0.66833
4	0.07167	0.07167	54	0.72833	0.72833
5	0.06917	0.06917	55	0.79083	0.79083
6	0.06583	0.06583	56	0.85667	0.85667
7	0.06250	0.06250	57	0.92417	0.92417
8	0.06083	0.06083	58	0.99500	0.99500
9	0.06000	0.06000	59	1.07333	1.07333
10	0.06000	0.06000	60	1.16000	1.16000
11	0.06417	0.06417	61	1.26083	1.26083
12	0.07000	0.07000	62	1.37833	1.37833
13	0.07917	0.07917	63	1.51250	1.51250
14	0.08917	0.08917	64	1.66167	1.66167
15	0.10000	0.10000	65	1.82083	1.82083
16	0.11000	0.11000	66	1.98833	1.98833
17	0.11833	0.11833	67	2.16333	2.16333
18	0.12417	0.12417	68	2.34667	2.34667
19	0.12833	0.12833	69	2.55000	2.55000
20	0.13083	0.13083	70	2.78250	2.78250
21	0.13167	0.13167	71	3.05083	3.05083
22	0.13083	0.13083	72	3.36583	3.36583
23	0.13000	0.13000	73	3.72833	3.72833
24	0.12833	0.12833	74	4.13083	4.13083
25	0.12750	0.12750	75	4.56667	4.56667
26	0.12667	0.12667	76	5.02707	5.02707
27	0.12667	0.12667	77	5.50750	5.50750
28	0.12750	0.12750	78	6.01333	6.01333
29	0.13000	0.13000	79	6.56167	6.56167
30	0.13333	0.13333	80	7.17417	7.17417
31	0.13750	0.13750	81	7.86917	7.86917
32	0.14250	0.14250	82	8.66333	8.66333
33	0.14917	0.14917	83	9.55250	9.55250
34	0.15667	0.15667	84	10.52000	10.52000
35	0.16500	0.16500	85	11.55167	11.55167
36	0.17667	0.17667	86	12.63583	12.63583
37	0.19000	0.19000	87	13.77083	13.77083
38	0.20500	0.20500	88	14.95917	14.95917
39	0.22250	0.22250	89	16.20917	16.20917
40	0.24167	0.24167	90	17.54000	17.54000
41	0.26333	0.26333	91	18.98667	18.98667
42	0.28500	0.28500	92	20.60917	20.60917
43	0.30833	0.30833	93	22.52417	22.52417
44	0.33250	0.33250	94	25.04500	25.04500
45	0.35917	0.35917	95	28.73917	28.73917
46	0.38667	0.38667	96	34.68083	34.68083
47	0.41583	0.41583	97	44.88917	44.88917
48	0.44750	0.44750	98	62.05500	62.05500
49	0.48250	0.48250	99	83.33333	83.33333

SAMPLE

Death Benefits

Insurance Proceeds

The Insurance Proceeds are the sum of (a) minus (b) where:

(a) is the death benefit as calculated below; and,

(b) is any Indebtedness.

The death benefit is the greater of (a) or (b), where:

(a) is the Face Amount shown on page 3 (or as reduced by the effect of a Partial Surrender); and,

(b) is the applicable percentage from Table B multiplied times the Cash Value on the date the Insured dies. The percentage is based upon the Insured's Attained Age and changes on each Contract Anniversary Date as shown in Table B below.

TABLE B

Attained Age	Percentage	Attained Age	Percentage	Attained Age	Percentage
0–40	250%	54	157%	68	117%
41	243	55	150	69	116
42	236	56	146	70	115
43	229	57	142	71	113
44	222	58	138	72	111
45	215	59	134	73	109
46	209	60	130	74	107
47	203	61	128	75–90	105
48	197	62	126	91	104
49	191	63	124	92	103
50	185	64	122	93	102
51	178	65	120	94 & Later	101
52	171	66	119		
53	164	67	118		

Payment of Insurance Proceeds

Subject to the provisions of this Contract, when the Insured dies We will pay the Insurance Proceeds to the Beneficiary, and this Contract will then terminate. We will pay the Insurance Proceeds to the Beneficiary only after We receive:

(a) this Contract;

(b) due proof that the Insured died while this Contract was in force;

(c) a properly completed claim form on a form which We will provide; and,

(d) an authorization on a form We supply, from the next of kin of the Insured, which allows Us to obtain and disclose information concerning the Insured.

SAMPLE

Effect of Partial Surrender on Insurance Proceeds

A partial surrender will decrease the Insurance Proceeds. If the death benefit is the Face Amount, We will reduce the Face Amount by the amount of the partial surrender. If the death benefit is not the Face Amount in calculating the new death benefit, We will reduce the Face Amount by the larger of zero, or (a) minus (b) plus (c) where:

(a) is the amount of the partial surrender;

(b) is the amount of death benefit prior to the partial surrender; and,

(c) is the Face Amount.

Premiums And Reinstatement

Payment of Premiums

An initial premium equal to or greater than the Minimum Premium Due At Issue shown on page 3 is due on the Issue Date. This Contract is not in force until the initial premium has been paid. If premium payments cease, this Contract will continue in force, subject to the grace period provision. Subject to the provisions of this section, You can choose the amount and the frequency of any further premiums. Premiums are to be paid to Us at Our Home Office. You may request a receipt signed by one of Our officers.

Planned Periodic Premiums

Planned Periodic Premiums are shown on page 3. This is the amount and frequency of premiums You selected on the Issue Date. You may change the amount and frequency. You may choose only intervals of 1 month, 6 months (for a Planned Periodic Premium of $100 or more), or 12 months.

If You choose the monthly interval, payment must be:

(a) by pre-authorized payment from a bank or institution that permits similar payment;

(b) as a part of a billing involving five or more employees of a common employer; or,

(c) by direct payment to Us, but only if premiums for this Contract were previously paid as a part of a billing involving a common employer. For this method of payment We will send You reminder notices each month, and to cover the added handling cost deduct from each premium so received a monthly direct billing fee not to exceed $2.00.

If You choose 6 or 12 month intervals, We will send You reminder notices at the planned payment interval.

Additional Premiums

You may pay additional premiums at any time while this Contract is in force, except that We may refuse to accept a premium if the death benefit is not the Face Amount.

We will not knowingly accept any premium which would result in the Internal Revenue Code not treating any of the Insurance Proceeds as life insurance. If We accept any premium in error, We will refund it to You with interest immediately after the error is discovered. The interest rate will be that credited to the Cash Value attributable to the premium refunded. Any premiums which We accept in error will not be considered premium paid under this Contract.

SAMPLE

Grace Period

On any Monthly Anniversary Date, if the Cash Value minus any Indebtedness is less than the monthly deduction this Contract will terminate 61 days after such date. These 61 days are called the grace period. We will notify You and any assignee recorded on Our records in writing of the Contract entering the grace period.

Reinstatement

Reinstatement means to place this Contract in force after it terminates because it reached the end of a grace period. We will reinstate this Contract if We receive:

(a) Your Written Request within five years after this Contract terminates at the end of a grace period;

(b) Satisfactory proof that the Insured is still insurable at the original rate class;

(c) Payment or reinstatement of any Indebtedness; and

(d) Payment of a premium which is equal to the result of multiplying the Minimum Premium Due At Issue times the sum of the number of Contract Months expired since termination plus three (the Cash Value and Indebtedness will not be less than they would have been had a premium equal to the Minimum Premium Due At Issue been paid each month during the period of termination).

If We approve Your Written Request for reinstatement on a Monthly Anniversary Date this Contract will again be in force on that day. If Our approval occurs on any other day this Contract will again be in force as of the preceding Monthly Anniversary Date.

Contract Values

Cash Value

On each Monthly Anniversary Date the Cash Value is the sum of (a) plus (b) plus (c) minus (d) minus (e), where:

(a) is the Cash Value on the preceding Monthly Anniversary Date;

(b) is the interest for one month on item (a);

(c) is all premiums received since the preceding Monthly Anniversary Date, less a premium load not to exceed the percent of premium load of such premiums, as shown on page 4;

(d) is the monthly deduction for the ensuing month; and
(e) is the sum of all partial surrenders since the preceding Monthly Anniversary Date.

On the Issue Date the Cash Value is (c) minus (d). On any other day the Cash Value is (a) plus (c) minus (e). The Cash Value will never be less than zero.

Interest Rate

We guarantee to credit interest at a rate not less than 0.46698% a month, compounded monthly, on that portion of the Cash Value up to the Benchmark Cash Value. This is equivalent to 5.75% a year, compounded yearly. On the balance of the Cash Value, if any, We guarantee to credit interest at a rate not less than 0.36748% a month, compounded monthly. This is equivalent to 4.50% a year, compounded yearly.

SAMPLE

We may, in Our discretion, use one or more higher interest rate(s) and credit each rate to different portions of Your Cash Value in such a manner as We determine. For example, We may credit a different interest rate to that portion of the Cash Value in excess of the Benchmark Cash Value. The monthly rate We will credit that portion of the Cash Value which equals any Indebtedness will be 0.36748% a month.

Monthly Deductions

The monthly deduction whether or not premium payments are received is (a) plus (b) plus (c) where:

(a) is the cost of insurance for this Contract and any riders attached to it;

(b) is the monthly life insurance load as described on page 4; and,

(c) is the Permanent and Temporary Monthly Flat Extra Amount(s), if any, for this Contract shown on page 3.

Continuation of Insurance

When the Cash Value minus Indebtedness is less than the monthly deduction this Contract will terminate according to the Grace Period provision.

Cost of Insurance

We calculate the cost of insurance for the ensuing month on the Issue Date and on each Monthly Anniversary Date. The cost of insurance is (a) mulitiplied times the quotient resulting from dividing the remainder of (b) minus (c) by 1,000 where:

(a) is the cost of insurance rate;

(b) is the amount of death benefit divided by 1.0036748; and

(c) is the Cash Value.

We calculate the cost of insurance for benefits provided by any riders attached to this Contract as provided in those riders.

Cost of Insurance Rates

The cost of insurance rate depends on the Issue Age, Contract Year and rate class. The guaranteed maximum monthly cost of insurance rates are found by multiplying (a) times (b) where:

(a) is the monthly cost of insurance rates shown on page 6; and

(b) is the rate class numeral shown on page 3. The monthly cost of insurance rates shown on page 6 are based on the 1980 CSO Mortality Table-C, Age Last Birthday. We can use cost of insurance rates that are lower than these guaranteed rates. The cost of insurance rates We will use will apply uniformly to all policies of the same class, Issue Age, and Contract Year. However, the guaranteed maximum cost of insurance rates will apply whenever the Cash Value is less than the Benchmark Cash Value.

Surrender

While the Insured is alive You may surrender this Contract for its Cash Value less any Indebtedness. We will pay You such amount in a lump sum after We receive Your Written Request to do so, subject to the "Deferment" provision. The amount will be determined as of the date the Written Request is received. If You request to surrender this Contract then all of Our obligations under it will end.

SAMPLE

In lieu of a lump sum payment, You may ask that the surrender amount be applied under one of the Optional Income Plans Upon surrender of this Contract during the grace period and within 30 days after a Contract Anniversary Date, the surrender amount will not be less than it would have been on such date. If the Insured is alive on the Final Policy Date shown on page 3 We will pay You the Cash Value minus any Indebtedness and this Contract and all of Our obligations under it will end.

Partial Surrender

On any Monthly Anniversary Date while the Insured is alive, You may make a partial surrender. The amount of the partial surrender must be for at least $500.00 but cannot exceed the amount You would receive if You surrendered this Contract.

Contract Loans

Contract Loan

By Written Request while this Contract is in force You may receive cash from Us by taking a Contract loan upon the assignment of this Contract to Us as sole security. If there is an existing loan You can increase it. The most You can borrow at any time is the Cash Value as of the date We receive Your Written Request. We will deduct the amount of any existing Indebtedness from the amount We send You. All or any part of the Indebtedness may be repaid at any time while this Contract is in force. However, this Contract will terminate when the total Indebtedness equals or exceeds the Cash Value. The effective date this Contract will so terminate will be 62 days after We mail a notice to the last known address of You and any assignee recorded on Our records.

Interest Rate Charged on Contract Loan

The maximum effective annual interest rate We charge on money You borrow under this Contract is shown on page 3. We can charge interest at a lower rate for any period of time. If We change the interest rate We charge We will notify You and any assignee recorded on Our records.

Interest to the next Contract Anniversary Date is due and payable on the date the loan is made. Thereafter interest is due and payable annually on each Contract Anniversary Date. If You do not pay the interest when it is due, any unpaid interest will be added to the amount You borrowed and will be charged the same interest rate.

General Provisions

Contract

This Contract, endorsements if any, and a copy of the application attached to it make up the entire Contract between You and Us. In the absence of fraud, all statements made in the application will be considered representations and not warranties. Also, We will not use any statement to void this Contract or defend against any claim made under it unless such statement is contained in the application. Only Our President or Our Secretary together with one of Our Vice Presidents have the authority to make any changes in this Contract. Any change must be in writing. We are not bound by any promise or representation made by any agent or person other than as specifically contained in this Contract. Any additional benefit rider attached to this Contract will become a part of this Contract and will be subject to all the terms and conditions of this Contract, unless We state otherwise in the rider.

SAMPLE

Your Rights

You can exercise Your rights under this Contract while the Insured is alive by making a Written Request. We will also require a Written Request from the assignee if Your Contract is assigned as collateral. We will also require a Written Request from the Beneficiary if You have not reserved the right to change the Beneficiary.

Misstatement Of Age

If the age of the Insured is misstated in the application, We will adjust the benefits of this Contract. The Face Amount shall be the amount the Minimum Premium Due At Issue would have then purchased if the Insured's age had been correctly stated. The Cash Value will be recalculated using the mortality rates actually charged for the correct age and the interest rates actually paid under this Contract.

Suicide

If the Insured commits suicide, while sane or insane, within two years from the Issue Date, this Contract will immediately terminate, and We will not pay the Insurance Proceeds. The amount We will pay shall be limited to the premiums We actually received for this Contract reduced by the amount of any Contract loan and accrued loan interest then outstanding, and by any prior partial surrenders.

Incontestability

Except for nonpayment of premiums, this Contract will be incontestable after it has been in force during the lifetime of the Insured for two years from the Issue Date. This provision does not apply to any rider providing benefits specifically for disability or death by accident.

If this Contract is reinstated, We will not contest the reinstatement after it is again in force during the lifetime of the Insured for two years from the effective date of the reinstatement. For this purpose, if We contest the reinstatement the contest will be based upon material statement(s) made only in the application for reinstatement.

Beneficiary

Unless You choose otherwise, any payment to beneficiaries will be paid based on the following order of priority. Payment will be made to:

(a) The Beneficiary. If more than one Beneficiary is then living, we will pay them in equal shares unless You specify otherwise.

(b) The contingent Beneficiary, if no Beneficiary is living when a payment is due. If more than one contingent Beneficiary is then living, we will pay them in equal shares unless You specify otherwise.

(c) The estate of the last Beneficiary or contingent Beneficiary to die, if no Beneficiary or contingent Beneficiary is living when payment is due. This payment will be in one sum.

You may change the Beneficiary by Written Request. Unless You specify otherwise, You will not need the permission of the Beneficiary to make another change in the future.

SAMPLE

Computation of Values

We have filed in the state where this Contract is issued a detailed statement showing how Contract benefits and reserves are calculated. All values are at least as great as the values required by that state. We use the 1980 CSO Mortality Table-C, Age Last Birthday, to calculate minimum Cash Value and reserves. The interest rate used to calculate minimum Cash Values is 5.75% per annum on that portion created by the monthly payment of the Minimum Premium Due At Issue multiplied times the number of Contract Months expired and 4.5% per annum on the excess. Reserves are calculated by using a modified preliminary term method, but they are not less than the Commissioners Reserve Valuation Method reserves. Reserves held on this Contract will never be less than the Cash Value.

All computations assume that premiums are paid annually and that deaths during a Contract Year occur immediately. Any benefits provided by attached riders are excluded from these computations.

Ownership

As owner, You may by Written Request exercise all rights under Your Contract while the Insured is alive. You may name a contingent owner should You die before the death of the Insured.

Change of Ownership

By Written Request You may name a new owner at any time. If You designate a new owner, it will not change the Beneficiary or contingent Beneficiary, unless You specify otherwise. The new owner can exercise all the rights of ownership, unless You specify otherwise. No change is binding on Us until We record it. Once recorded, the change binds Us as of the date You signed it. The change will not apply to any payment made by Us before We record Your Written Request.

Collateral Assignment

Your Contract may be collaterally assigned. We are not bound by the assignment unless You make a Written Request. No assignment is binding on Us until We record it. We are not responsible for determining if Your assignment is valid or the extent of the assignee's interest.

Annual Report

We will send You a report shortly after each Contract Anniversary Date. This report will show: (a) premiums paid since the last report; (b) the Cash Value at the beginning of the period; (c) interest credited since the last report; (d) Monthly Deductions from the Cash Value since the last report; (e) Indebtedness activity; (f) the Cash Value at the end of the period; and, (g) Insurance Proceeds at the end of the period. Any time after the first Contract Anniversary Date We will provide a hypothetical illustration of future death benefits and Cash Values upon Written Request. We will charge a reasonable fee for this service not to exceed $25.00. We will make any necessary reasonable assumptions not otherwise prohibited by law.

Nonparticipating

This Contract does not participate in any distribution of surplus. No dividends are payable.

SAMPLE

Deferment

We may delay paying the Cash Value for up to 6 months from the date We receive Your Written Request for payment. If We delay for 30 days or more, interest will be paid from the date We receive the request at the rate We set from time to time. We also may delay making a Contract loan, except for a loan to pay a premium, for up to 6 months from the date We receive Your Written Request for the loan.

Right to Extend Final Policy Date

If the Insured is alive on the Final Policy Date shown on page 3 We will pay You the Cash Value minus any Indebtedness and this Contract and all of Our obligations under it will end. However, You may instead by Written Request extend the Contract during the life of Insured to a later alternative Final Policy Date, but not beyond Attained Age 110. Your Written Request must be received by Us within 60 days prior to the Final Policy Date shown on page 3.

If You elect an alternate Final Policy Date, the Cash Value at Attained Age 100 will therafter be credited interest at 0.36748% a month, compounded monthly. This is equivalent to 4.5% a year, compounded yearly. No monthly deduction will be deducted from the Cash Value after Attained Age 99.

> **NOTE**
>
> 1. **The policy may not qualify as life insurance after Attained Age 99;**
>
> 2. **The policy may be subject to tax consequences; and,**
>
> 3. **A tax advisor should be consulted prior to making any election.**

Tax Considerations

You are encouraged to consult a qualified tax advisor. Neither We nor Our agents are authorized to give tax or legal advice. The following is not intended as tax advice, and it is not a complete statement of what the effect of federal income taxes will be under all circumstances. Rather, it provides information about how We believe the tax law applies in the most common circumstances. There is no guarantee that the current federal income tax laws and regulations or interpretations will remain the same, and this provision should not be construed to mean that the Insurance Proceeds and/or other values will be exempt from the future actions of any tax authority.

We believe that We have taken adequate steps so that this Contract is considered life insurance for tax purposes, and that the Contract is designed to comply with Sections 7702 and 7702A of the Internal Revenue Code of 1986, or any other equivalent section of the Code. Your individual situation, or that of any Beneficiary, will determine the federal estate taxes and state and local estate, inheritance or other taxes due if You or the Insured die.

Governing Law

This Contract is subject to the laws of the state of Georgia. If any provision of the Contract does not conform to these laws, the Contract will be applied to conform to the law.

SAMPLE

Optional Income Plans

Unless otherwise requested, We may pay the Insurance Proceeds in one sum or by placing the amount in an account that earns interest. The payee will have immediate access to all or any part of the account. The Insurance Proceeds, instead of being paid in one sum, may be applied under one or more of the following Income Plans. Also, at any time while the Contract is in force and the Insured is alive, You may by Written Request ask that:

(a) all or a part of the Cash Value less any Indebtedness of this Contract be applied under a non-life income plan (a plan which provides a schedule of payments which is not dependent on the lifetime of the payee); or

(b) all or a part of the Cash Value less any Indebtedness of this Contract be applied under a life income plan (a plan which provides a schedule of payments which depends on the lifetime of one or more payees and which may guarantee that payments will be made for at least a specified number of years).

If only a part of the Cash Value is to be applied the balance of the value will be paid to You in a single sum. If only a part of the Insurance Proceeds is to be applied after the Insured dies, the balance of the Insurance Proceeds will be paid to the Beneficiary.

Non-Life Income Plans

Available with respect to the Insurance Proceeds or Cash Value less Indebtedness.

Option 1. Interest Income - The amount applied will earn interest which will be paid monthly. Withdrawals of at least $500 each may be made at any time by Written Request.

Option 2. Installment Income for a Stated Period - Monthly installment payments will be made so that the amount applied, with interest, will be paid over the period chosen (from 1 to 30 years). See Table 1.

Option 2A. Installment Income of a Stated Amount - Monthly installment payments of a chosen amount will be made until the entire amount applied, with interest, is paid

Life Income Plans

Available with respect to the Insurance Proceeds or Cash Value less Indebtedness.

Option 3. Single Life Income - With Guaranteed Payment Period - Monthly payments will be made during the lifetime of the payee with chosen guaranteed payment period of 10, 15 or 20 years. See Table 2.

Option 3A. Single Life Income - Installment Refund - Monthly payments will be made during the lifetime of the payee. If the payee dies before the total amount applied under this plan has been paid, the remainder will be paid in one sum as a death benefit. See Table 2.

Option 4. Joint and Survivor Life Income - Monthly payments will be made jointly to two persons during their lifetime and will continue during the remaining lifetime of the survivor. See Table 3.

Other Frequencies and Plans

Instead of monthly payments, You may choose to have payments made quarterly, semiannually or annually. Other Income Plans may be arranged which are mutually agreeable to You and Us.

SAMPLE

Choice of Income Plans

A choice of Income Plan for any Insurance Proceeds made by You while the Insured is alive will take effect when the Insured dies. All other choices of Income Plans will take effect when recorded by Us, or later, if requested. When an Income Plan starts, We will issue an agreement which will describe the terms of the plan. We may require that You send Us this Contract. We may also require proof of the payee's age.

Income Plans may be chosen:

(a) By You during the lifetime of the Insured.

(b) By the Beneficiary within one year after the date the Insured dies and before any payment has been made to the Beneficiary, if no election was in effect on the date of death.

A choice of an Income Plan will not become effective unless each payment under the plan would be at least $50.

Limitations

If the payee is not a natural person, the choice of an income plan will be subject to Our approval.

Income plan payments may not be assigned and, to the extent permitted by law, will not be subject to the claims of creditors.

Income Plan Rates

Amounts applied under the non-life income plans will earn interest at a rate We set from time to time. That rate will never be less than 3% a year.

Life income plan payments will be based on a rate set by Us and in effect on the date the Insurance Proceeds become payable or on the date the Cash Value less Indebtedness is applied. The minimum rates are shown in Tables 2 and 3 following, and are based upon the 1983 Table "a" for individual annuities and a guaranteed interest rate of 3.5% per annum.

Minimum Payments under Optional Income Plans

Monthly payments under Options 2, 3, and 4 for each $1,000 applied will not be less than the amount shown in the following Tables. Monthly life income payments will not be less than those that would be provided to a person in the same class as the Insured by a single payment immediate annuity bought with an equal amount at the time monthly payments start.

SAMPLE

TABLES

TABLE 1

Installment Income for a Stated Period
Monthly Payments for each $1,000 Applied

Years Payable	Monthly Payment	Years Payable	Monthly Payment	Years Payable	Monthly Payment
1	$84.47	11	$8.86	21	$5.32
2	42.86	12	8.24	22	5.15
3	28.99	13	7.71	23	4.99
4	22.06	14	7.26	24	4.84
5	17.91	15	6.87	25	4.71
6	15.14	16	6.53	26	4.59
7	13.16	17	6.23	27	4.47
8	11.68	18	5.96	28	4.37
9	10.53	19	5.73	29	4.27
10	9.61	20	5.51	30	4.18

Annual, semi-annual or quarterly payments will be determined by multiplying the monthly payment by 11.838, 5.963 or 2.991, respectively.

SAMPLE

TABLE 2

Single Life Income
Guaranteed Payment Period or Installment Refund

Age	Life Only	Guaranteed Period 10 Years	Guaranteed Period 15 Years	Guaranteed Period 20 Years	Installment Refund
35	3.57	3.56	3.56	3.55	3.54
36	3.60	3.59	3.59	3.58	3.57
37	3.63	3.62	3.62	3.61	3.60
38	3.66	3.65	3.65	3.64	3.63
39	3.69	3.69	3.68	3.67	3.66
40	3.73	3.72	3.71	3.70	3.69
41	3.76	3.76	3.75	3.73	3.72
42	3.80	3.80	3.78	3.77	3.76
43	3.84	3.84	3.82	3.81	3.80
44	3.89	3.88	3.86	3.84	3.83
45	3.93	3.92	3.91	3.88	3.87
46	3.98	3.97	3.95	3.92	3.92
47	4.03	4.02	4.00	3.97	3.96
48	4.08	4.07	4.05	4.01	4.01
49	4.14	4.12	4.10	4.06	4.06
50	4.20	4.18	4.15	4.11	4.11
51	4.26	4.24	4.21	4.16	4.16
52	4.32	4.30	4.26	4.21	4.22
53	4.39	4.36	4.33	4.27	4.27
54	4.46	4.43	4.39	4.32	4.34
55	4.54	4.51	4.46	4.38	4.40
56	4.62	4.58	4.53	4.44	4.47
57	4.71	4.66	4.60	4.51	4.54
58	4.80	4.75	4.68	4.57	4.62
59	4.90	4.84	4.76	4.64	4.70
60	5.00	4.93	4.84	4.70	4.78
61	5.11	5.03	4.93	4.77	4.87
62	5.23	5.14	5.02	4.84	4.96
63	5.36	5.25	5.12	4.91	5.06
64	5.49	5.37	5.21	4.98	5.17
65	5.64	5.50	5.31	5.05	5.28
66	5.79	5.63	5.42	5.12	5.39
67	5.95	5.77	5.53	5.19	5.52
68	6.13	5.91	5.63	5.25	5.65
69	6.32	6.07	5.74	5.32	5.79
70	6.53	6.23	5.86	5.37	5.94
71	6.75	6.40	5.97	5.43	6.09
72	6.99	6.58	6.08	5.48	6.26
73	7.26	6.76	6.18	5.52	6.44
74	7.54	6.95	6.29	5.57	6.63
75	7.85	7.14	6.39	5.60	6.83
76	8.18	7.34	6.48	5.63	7.04
77	8.54	7.54	6.57	5.66	7.26
78	8.94	7.74	6.65	5.68	7.51
79	9.36	7.94	6.72	5.70	7.76
80	9.82	8.13	6.79	5.71	8.03

Values for ages not shown will be furnished upon request.

SAMPLE

TABLE 3

Joint and Survivor Life Income
Minimum Amount of each Monthly Payment for each $1,000 Applied

| Age | - - - - - - - - - - - - - Age of Second Participant - - - - - - - - - - - - - | | | | | | | | |
	40	45	50	55	60	65	70	75	80
40	3.48	3.54	3.59	3.63	3.66	3.68	3.70	3.71	3.72
41	3.49	3.56	3.61	3.65	3.69	3.71	3.73	3.74	3.75
42	3.50	3.57	3.63	3.68	3.72	3.75	3.77	3.78	3.79
43	3.52	3.59	3.66	3.71	3.75	3.78	3.80	3.82	3.83
44	3.53	3.61	3.68	3.74	3.78	3.82	3.84	3.86	3.87
45	3.54	3.62	3.70	3.76	3.81	3.85	3.88	3.90	3.91
46	3.55	3.64	3.72	3.79	3.85	3.89	3.92	3.94	3.96
47	3.56	3.65	3.74	3.82	3.88	3.93	3.97	3.99	4.01
48	3.57	3.67	3.77	3.85	3.92	3.97	4.01	4.04	4.06
49	3.58	3.69	3.79	3.88	3.95	4.01	4.06	4.09	4.11
50	3.59	3.70	3.81	3.91	3.99	4.06	4.11	4.14	4.16
51	3.60	3.71	3.83	3.94	4.03	4.10	4.16	4.20	4.22
52	3.61	3.73	3.85	3.97	4.07	4.15	4.21	4.25	4.28
53	3.61	3.74	3.87	3.99	4.10	4.19	4.26	4.31	4.35
54	3.62	3.75	3.89	4.02	4.14	4.24	4.32	4.37	4.41
55	3.63	3.76	3.91	4.05	4.18	4.29	4.38	4.44	4.48
56	3.64	3.78	3.93	4.08	4.22	4.34	4.44	4.51	4.56
57	3.64	3.79	3.94	4.10	4.26	4.39	4.50	4.58	4.63
58	3.65	3.80	3.96	4.13	4.30	4.44	4.56	4.65	4.71
59	3.65	3.81	3.98	4.16	4.33	4.50	4.63	4.73	4.80
60	3.66	3.81	3.99	4.18	4.37	4.55	4.70	4.81	4.89
61	3.66	3.82	4.01	4.20	4.41	4.60	4.77	4.89	4.98
62	3.67	3.83	4.02	4.23	4.45	4.65	4.84	4.98	5.08
63	3.67	3.84	4.03	4.25	4.48	4.71	4.91	5.07	5.19
64	3.68	3.85	4.05	4.27	4.51	4.76	4.98	5.16	5.29
65	3.68	3.85	4.06	4.29	4.55	4.81	5.05	5.26	5.41
66	3.69	3.86	4.07	4.31	4.58	4.86	5.13	5.36	5.53
67	3.69	3.87	4.08	4.33	4.61	4.91	5.20	5.46	5.65
68	3.69	3.87	4.09	4.35	4.64	4.96	5.28	5.56	5.78
69	3.70	3.88	4.10	4.36	4.67	5.01	5.35	5.67	5.92
70	3.70	3.88	4.11	4.38	4.70	5.05	5.43	5.77	6.06
71	3.70	3.89	4.11	4.39	4.72	5.10	5.50	5.88	6.20
72	3.70	3.89	4.12	4.40	4.75	5.14	5.57	5.99	6.35
73	3.71	3.89	4.13	4.42	4.77	5.18	5.64	6.10	6.50
74	3.71	3.90	4.13	4.43	4.79	5.22	5.71	6.21	6.66
75	3.71	3.90	4.14	4.44	4.81	5.26	5.77	6.32	6.82
76	3.71	3.90	4.15	4.45	4.83	5.29	5.84	6.42	6.99
77	3.71	3.91	4.15	4.46	4.85	5.32	5.90	6.53	7.15
78	3.71	3.91	4.16	4.47	4.86	5.36	5.95	6.63	7.31
79	3.72	3.91	4.16	4.47	4.88	5.38	6.01	6.73	7.48
80	3.72	3.91	4.16	4.48	4.89	5.41	6.06	6.82	7.64

SAMPLE

ABC Life Insurance Company

An XYZ Company

ENDORSEMENT TO CONTRACT NUMBER GA001

Effective on the Issue Date, this endorsement is added to and made a part of the Contract referred to above.

Notwithstanding any other provision in this Contract to the contrary, this Contract will not terminate if for each Contract Month that the Contract has been in force, (a) equals or exceeds the sum of (b) plus (c), where:

(a)   is the total premiums paid less any partial surrenders and indebtedness;

(b)   is the Additional Initial Lump-Sum Premium (shown on page 3); and,

(c)   is the Monthly Secondary Guarantee Premium (shown on page 3) multiplied times the number of Contract Months elapsed since the Issue Date, including the current Contract Month.

Mary Smith
Secretary

John Johnson
President

Form: XYZ-090   Page 20   Contract GA001

GLOSSARY

Absolute liability *See* **Strict liability.**

Accelerated death benefits rider A rider that allows insureds who are terminally ill or who suffer from certain catastrophic diseases to collect part or all of their life insurance benefits before they die, primarily to pay for the care they require.

Accident A loss-causing event that is sudden, unforeseen, and unintentional. *See also* **Occurrence.**

Accidental bodily injury Bodily injury resulting from an act whose result was accidental or unexpected.

Actual cash value Value of property at the time of its damage or loss, determined by subtracting depreciation of the item from its replacement cost.

Add-on plan Pays benefits to an accident victim without regard to fault, but the injured person still has the right to sue the negligent driver who caused the accident.

Adjustment bureau Organization for adjusting insurance claims that is supported by insurers using the bureau's services.

Advance funding Pension-funding method in which the employer systematically and periodically sets aside funds prior to the employee's retirement.

Advance premium mutual Mutual insurance company owned by the policyowners that does not issue assessable policies but charges premiums expected to be sufficient to pay all claims and expenses.

Adverse selection Tendency of persons with a higher-than-average chance of loss to seek insurance at standard (average) rates, which, if not controlled by underwriting, results in higher-than-expected loss levels.

Agency agreement Contract between an insurance agent and insurance company that describes the powers, rights, and duties of the agent.

Agency building system Marketing system in life insurance by which an insurer builds its own agency force by recruiting, financing, training, and supervising new agents.

Agent Someone who legally represents the insurer, has the authority to act on the insurer's behalf, and can bind the principal by expressed authority, by implied authority, and by apparent authority.

Aggregate deductible Deductible in some property and health insurance contracts in which all covered losses during a year are added together and the insurer pays only when the aggregate deductible amount is exceeded.

Aleatory contract One in which the values exchanged may not be equal but depend on an uncertain event.

Alien insurer Insurance company chartered by a foreign country and meeting certain licensing requirements.

"All-risks" policy Coverage by an insurance contract that promises to cover all losses except those losses specifically excluded in the policy. Also called an **open perils policy** and a **special coverage policy.**

Alternative dispute resolution (ADR) techniques Techniques to resolve a legal dispute without litigation.

Annuitant Person who receives the periodic payment from an annuity.

Annuity Periodic payment to an individual that continues for a fixed period or for the duration of a designated life or lives.

Appraisal clause Used when the insured and insurer agree that the loss is covered, but the amount of the loss is in dispute.

Assessment mutual Mutual insurance company that has the right to assess policyowners for losses and expenses.

Assigned risk plan *See* **Automobile insurance plan.**

Assumption-of-risk Defense against a negligence claim that bars recovery for damages if a person understands and recognizes the danger inherent in a particular activity or occupation.

Attractive nuisance Condition that can attract and injure children. Occupants of land on which such a condition exists are liable for injuries to children.

Automatic premium loan Cash borrowed from a life insurance policy's cash value to pay an overdue premium after the grace period for paying the premium has expired.

Automobile insurance plan Formerly called **assigned risk plan.** Method for providing auto insurance to persons considered to be high-risk drivers who cannot obtain protection in the voluntary markets. All auto insurers in the state are assigned their share of such drivers based on the volume of auto insurance business written in the state.

Average indexed monthly earnings (AIME) Under the OASDI program, the person's actual earnings are indexed to determine his or her primary insurance amount (PIA).

Avoidance *See* **Loss avoidance.**

Bailee's customer policy Policy that covers the loss or damage to property of customers regardless of a bailee's legal liability.

Basic form *See* **Dwelling Property 1.**

Benefit period A period of time, typically one to three years, during which major medical benefits are paid after the deductible is satisfied. When the benefit period ends, the insured must then satisfy a new deductible in order to establish a new benefit period.

Binder Authorization of coverage by an agent given before the company has formally approved a policy. Provides evidence that the insurance is in force.

Blackout period The period during which Social Security benefits are not paid to a surviving spouse—between the time the youngest child reaches age 16 and the surviving spouse's sixtieth birthday.

Blue Cross plans Typically nonprofit, community-oriented prepayment plans that provide health insurance coverage primarily for hospital services.

Blue Shield plans Typically nonprofit prepayment plans that provide health insurance coverage mainly for physicians' services.

Boatowners package policy A special package policy for boat owners that combines physical damage insurance, medical expense insurance, liability insurance, and other coverages in one contract.

Broad form *See* **Dwelling Property 2; Homeowners 2 policy.**

Broker Someone who legally represents the insured, soliciting or accepting applications for insurance that are not in force until the company accepts the business.

Burglary The unlawful taking of property from inside the premises by a person who unlawfully enters or leaves the premises, as evidenced by marks of forcible entry or exit.

Business income coverage form Business income form drafted by the Insurance Services Office to cover the loss of business income regardless of whether the income is derived from retail or service operations, manufacturing, or rents.

Businessowners policy Package policy specifically designed to meet the basic property and liability insurance needs of smaller business firms in one contract.

Cafeteria plan Generic term for an employee benefit plan that allows employees to select among the various group life, medical expense, disability, dental, and other plans that best meet their specific needs.

Calendar-year deductible Amount payable by an insured during a calendar year before a group or individual health insurance policy begins to pay for medical expenses.

Capacity Term used in the property and casualty insurance industry that refers to the relative level of surplus; the greater the industry's surplus position, the more willing underwriters will write new business or reduce premiums.

Capital budgeting Method of determining which capital investment projects a company should undertake based on the time value of money.

Capital retention approach A method used to estimate the amount of life insurance to own. Under this method, the insurance proceeds are retained and are not liquidated.

Capitation fee A method of payment in managed care plans by which a physician or hospital receives a fixed annual payment for each plan member regardless of the frequency type or type of service provided.

Captive insurer Insurance company established and owned by a parent firm in order to insure its loss exposures while reducing premium costs, providing easier access to a reinsurer, and perhaps easing tax burdens.

Cargo insurance Type of ocean marine insurance that protects the shipper of the goods against financial loss if the goods are damaged or lost.

Cash refund annuity The balance is paid in one lump sum to the beneficiary after the death of the annuitant, if total payments do not equal the annuity purchase price.

Cash surrender value Amount payable to the owner of a cash-value life insurance policy if he or she decides the insurance is no longer wanted. Calculated separately from the legal reserve.

Casualty insurance Field of insurance that covers whatever is not covered by fire, marine, and life insurance. Includes auto, liability, burglary and theft, workers compensation, glass, and health insurance.

Catastrophe bonds Corporate bonds that permit the issuer of the bond to skip or defer scheduled payments of principal or interest if a catastrophic loss occurs.

Causes-of-loss form Form added to commercial property insurance policy that indicates the causes of loss that are covered. There are three causes-of-loss forms: basic, broad, and special.

Ceding company Insurer that writes the policy initially and later shifts part or all of the coverage to a reinsurer.

Certified Financial Planner (CFP) Professional who has attained a high degree of technical competency in financial planning and has passed a series of professional examinations.

Certified Insurance Counselor (CIC) Professional in property and casualty insurance who has passed a series of examinations sponsored by the Society of Certified Insurance Counselors.

Chance of loss The probability that an event will occur.

Change-of-plan provision Allows life insurance policy-owners to exchange their present policies for different contracts, provides flexibility.

Chartered Financial Consultant (ChFC) An individual who has attained a high degree of technical competency in the fields of financial planning, investments, and life and health insurance and has passed professional examinations administered by The American College.

Chartered Life Underwriter (CLU) An individual who has attained a high degree of technical competency in the fields of life and health insurance and has passed professional examinations administered by The American College.

Chartered Property Casualty Underwriter (CPCU) Professional who has attained a high degree of technical competency in property and liability insurance and has passed professional examinations administered by the American Institute for Chartered Property Casualty Underwriters.

Chief risk officer (CRO) Person responsible for the treatment of pure and speculative risks faced by an organization.

Choice no-fault plans Motorists can elect to be covered under the state's no-fault law with lower premiums or can retain the right to sue under the tort liability system with higher premiums.

Claims adjustor Person who settles claims: an agent, company adjustor, independent adjustor, adjustment bureau, or public adjustor.

Claims-made policy A liability insurance policy that only covers claims that are first reported during the policy period, provided the event occurred after the retroactive date (if any) stated in the policy.

Class rating Rate-making method in which similar insureds are placed in the same underwriting class and each is charged the same rate. Also called manual rating.

CLU See **Chartered Life Underwriter.**

Coinsurance provision Common provision in commercial property insurance contracts that requires the insured to maintain insurance on the property at a stated percentage of its actual cash value or its replacement cost. Payment for a loss is determined by multiplying the amount of the loss by the fraction derived from the amount of insurance required. If the coinsurance requirement is not met at the time of loss, the insured will be penalized. Coinsurance is also used to refer to the percentage participation clause in health insurance. See also **Percentage participation clause.**

Collateral source rule Under this rule, the defendant cannot introduce any evidence that shows the injured party has received compensation from other collateral sources.

Collision loss Damages to an automobile caused by the upset of the automobile or its impact with another vehicle or object. Collision losses are paid by the insurer regardless of fault.

Commercial crime coverage form ISO form that can be added to a package policy to cover crime exposures of business firms.

Commercial general liability policy (CGL) Commercial liability policy drafted by the Insurance Services Office containing two coverage forms—an occurrence form and a claims-made form.

Commercial lines Property and casualty coverages for business firms, nonprofit organizations, and government agencies.

Commercial package policy (CPP) A commercial policy that can be designed to meet the specific insurance needs of business firms. Property and liability coverage forms are combined to form a single policy.

Commodity price risk Risk of losing money if the price of a commodity changes.

Commutative contract One in which the values exchanged by both parties are theoretically even.

Company adjustor Claims adjustor who is a salaried employee representing only one company.

Comparative negligence laws Laws enacted by many jurisdictions permitting an injured person to recover damages even though he or she may have contributed to the accident. The financial burden is shared by both parties according to their respective degrees of fault.

Compensatory damages An award for damages that compensates an injured victim for losses actually incurred. Compensatory damages include both special damages and general damages.

Completed operations Liability arising out of faulty work performed away from the premises after the work or operations are completed; applicable to contractors, plumbers, electricians, repair shops, and similar firms.

Comprehensive major medical insurance Type of group plan combining basic plan benefits and major medical insurance in one policy.

Compulsory insurance law Law protecting accident victims against irresponsible motorists by requiring owners and operators of automobiles to carry certain amounts of liability insurance in order to license the vehicle and drive legally within the state.

Concealment Deliberate failure of an applicant for insurance to reveal a material fact to the insurer.

Conditions Provisions inserted in an insurance contract that qualify or place limitations on the insurer's promise to perform.

Consequential loss Financial loss occurring as the consequence of some other loss. Often called an indirect loss.

Consolidation Combining of business organizations through mergers and acquisitions.

Consumer-driven health plan (CDHP) A generic term for an arrangement that gives employees a choice of health-care plans, which are designed to make employees more sensitive to health-care costs, to provide a financial incentive to avoid unnecessary care, and to seek out low-cost providers.

Contingent beneficiary   Beneficiary of a life insurance policy who is entitled to receive the policy proceeds on the insured's death if the primary beneficiary dies before the insured; or the beneficiary who receives the remaining payments if the primary beneficiary dies before receiving the guaranteed number of payments.

Contingent liability   Liability arising out of work done by independent contractors for a firm. A firm may be liable for the work done by an independent contractor if the activity is illegal, the situation does not permit delegation of authority, or the work is inherently dangerous.

Contract bond   Type of surety bond guaranteeing that the principal will fulfill all contractual obligations.

Contract of adhesion   The insured must accept the entire contract, with all of its terms and conditions.

Contractual liability   Legal liability of another party that the business firm agrees to assume by a written or oral contract.

Contribution by equal shares   Type of other-insurance provision often found in liability insurance contracts that requires each company to share equally in the loss until the share of each insurer equals the lowest limit of liability under any policy or until the full amount of loss is paid.

Contributory negligence   Common law defense blocking an injured person from recovering damages if he or she has contributed in any way to the accident.

Contributory plan   Group life, health, or pension plan in which the employees pay part of the premiums.

Coordination-of-benefits provision   Provision in a group medical expense plan that prevents over-insurance and duplication of benefits when one person is covered under more than one group plan.

Corridor deductible   Major medical plan deductible that integrates a basic plan with a supplemental group major medical expense policy.

Cost-of-living rider   Benefit that can be added to a life insurance policy under which the policyowner can purchase one-year term insurance equal to the cumulative percentage change in the consumer price index with no evidence of insurability.

Cost of risk   A risk management tool that measures certain costs in a risk management program, including premiums paid, retained losses, outside risk management services, financial guarantees, internal administrative costs, taxes and fees, and certain other expenses.

Coverage for damage to your auto   That part of the personal auto policy insuring payment for damage or theft of the insured automobile. This optional coverage can be used to insure both collision and other-than-collision losses.

CPCU   *See* **Chartered Property Casualty Underwriter.**

Currency exchange rate risk   Risk of loss of value caused by changes in exchange rates between countries.

Current assumption whole life insurance   Nonparticipating whole life policy in which the cash values are based on the insurer's current mortality, investment, and expense experience. An accumulation account is credited with a current interest rate that changes over time. Also called interest-sensitive whole life insurance.

Currently insured   Status of a covered person under the Old-Age, Survivors, and Disability Insurance (OASDI) program who has at least six credits out of the last thirteen quarters, ending with the quarter of death, disability, or entitlement to retirement benefits.

Damage to property of others   Damage covered up to $1000 per occurrence for an insured who damages another's property. Payment is made despite the lack of legal liability. Coverage is included in Section II of the homeowners policy.

Declarations   Statements in an insurance contract that provide information about the property to be insured and used for underwriting and rating purposes and identification of the property to be insured.

Deductible   A provision by which a specified amount is subtracted from the total loss payment that would otherwise be paid.

Deferred annuity   A retirement annuity that provides benefits at some future date.

Defined-benefit plan   Type of pension plan in which the retirement benefit is known in advance but the contributions vary depending on the amount necessary to fund the desired benefit.

Defined-contribution plan   Type of pension plan in which the contribution rate is fixed but the retirement benefit is variable.

Defined contribution health plan   A generic term to describe an arrangement in which the employee has a choice of health-care plans, such as an HMO, PPO, or POS, and to which the employer contributes a fixed amount—hence the term, "defined contribution."

Demutualization   A term to describe the conversion of a mutual insurer into a stock insurer.

Dependency period   Period of time following the readjustment period during which the surviving spouse's children are under eighteen and therefore dependent on the parent.

Diagnosis-related groups (DRGs)   Method for reimbursing hospitals under the Medicare program. Under this system, a flat, uniform amount is paid to each hospital for the same type of medical care or treatment.

Difference in conditions insurance (DIC) "All-risks" policy that covers other perils not insured by basic property insurance contracts, supplemental to and excluding the coverage provided by underlying contracts.

Direct loss Financial loss that results directly from an insured peril.

Directors and officer liability (D&O) A commercial liability coverage that provides financial protection for the directors, officers, and the corporation if the directors and officers are sued for mismanagement of the company's affairs.

Direct-response system A marketing method where insurance is sold without the services of an agent. Potential customers are solicited by advertising in the mails, newspapers, magazines, television, radio, and other media.

Direct writer Insurance company in which the salesperson is an employee of the insurer, not an independent contractor, and which pays all selling expenses, including salary.

Disability-insured Status of an individual who is insured for disability benefits under the Old-Age, Survivors, and Disability Insurance (OASDI) program.

Dividend accumulations A dividend option in a participating life insurance policy in which the dividend is retained by the insurer and accumulated at interest.

Domestic insurer Insurance company domiciled and licensed in the state in which it does business.

Double indemnity rider Benefit that can be added to a life insurance policy doubling the face amount of life insurance if death occurs as the result of an accident.

Dram shop law Law that imputes negligence to the owner of a business that sells liquor in the event that an intoxicated customer causes injury or property damage to another person; usually excluded from general liability policies.

Driver education credit Student discount or reduction in premium amount for which young drivers become eligible on completion of a driver education course.

Dwelling Property 1 Property insurance policy that insures the dwelling, structures, personal property, fair rental value, and certain other coverages; covers a limited number of perils.

Dwelling Property 2 Property insurance policy that insures the dwelling and other structures at replacement cost. It adds additional coverages and has a greater number of covered perils than the Dwelling Property 1 policy.

Dwelling Property 3 Property insurance policy that covers the dwelling and other structures against direct physical loss from any peril except for those perils otherwise excluded. However, personal property is covered on a named-perils basis.

Earned premiums Premiums actually earned during the accounting period as contrasted with premiums written. Earned premiums represent the portion of written premiums that can be recognized as income for the portion of the policy period that has already elapsed.

Earnings test (retirement test) Test under the Old-Age, Survivors, and Disability Insurance (OASDI) program that reduces monthly benefits to those persons who have annual earned income in excess of the maximum allowed.

Eligibility period Brief period of time during which an employee can sign up for group insurance without furnishing evidence of insurability.

Elimination period (waiting period) Waiting period in health insurance during which benefits are not paid. Also a period of time that must be met before disability benefits are payable.

Employee Retirement Income Security Act (ERISA) Legislation passed in 1974 applying to most private pension and welfare plans that requires certain standards to protect participating employees.

Employers liability insurance Covers employers against lawsuits by employees who are injured in the course of employment, but whose injuries (or disease) are not compensable under the state's workers compensation law.

Endorsement Written provision that adds to, deletes, or modifies the provisions in the original contract. *See also* **Rider.**

Endowment insurance Type of life insurance that pays the face amount of insurance to the beneficiary if the insured dies within a specified period or to the policyowner if the insured survives to the end of the period.

Enterprise risk A term that encompasses all major risks faced by a business, including pure risk, speculative risk, strategic risk, operational risk, and financial risk.

Enterprise risk management Comprehensive risk management program that considers an organization's pure risks, speculative risks, strategic risks, and operational risks.

Entire-contract clause Provision in life insurance policies stating that the life insurance policy and attached application constitute the entire contract between the parties.

Equipment breakdown insurance Insurance that covers losses due to accidental breakdown of covered equipment; also known as **boiler and machinery insurance.**

Equity in the unearned premium reserve Amount by which an unearned premium reserve is overstated because it is established on the basis of gross premiums rather than net premiums.

Equity indexed annuity A fixed, deferred annuity that allows limited participation in the stock market but guarantees the principal against loss if the contract is held to term.

ERISA *See* **Employee Retirement Income Security Act.**

Errors and omissions insurance   Liability insurance policy that provides protection against loss incurred by a client because of some negligent act, error, or omission by the insured.

Estate planning   Process designed to conserve estate assets before and after death, distribute property according to the individual's wishes, minimize federal estate and state inheritance taxes, provide estate liquidity to meet costs of estate settlement, and provide for the family's financial needs.

Estoppel   Legal doctrine that prevents a person from denying the truth of a previous representation of fact, especially when such representation has been relied on by the one to whom the statement was made.

Excess insurance   Under an excess insurance plan, the insurer does not participate in the loss until the actual loss exceeds a certain amount.

Exclusion ratio   Calculation to determine the taxable and nontaxable portions of annuity payments, which is determined by dividing the investment in the contract by the expected return.

Exclusions   Provisions in an insurance contract that list the perils, losses, and property excluded from coverage.

Exclusive agency system   Type of insurance marketing system under which the agent represents only one company or group of companies under common ownership.

Exclusive provider organization (EPO)   A plan that does not cover medical care received outside of a network of preferred providers.

Exclusive remedy doctrine   Doctrine in workers compensation insurance that states that workers compensation benefits should be the exclusive or sole source of recovery for workers who have a job-related accident or disease; doctrine has been eroded by legal decisions.

Expense loading   *See* **Loading.**

Expense ratio   That proportion of the gross rate available for expenses and profit. Ratio of expenses incurred to premiums written.

Experience rating   (1) Method of rating group life and health insurance plans that uses the loss experience of the group to determine the premiums to be charged. (2) As applied to property and casualty insurance, the class or manual rate is adjusted upward or downward based on past loss experience. (3) As applied to state unemployment insurance programs, firms with favorable employment records pay lower tax rates.

Exposure unit   Unit of measurement used in insurance pricing.

Extended nonowned coverage   Endorsement that can be added to an auto liability insurance policy that covers the insured while driving any nonowned automobile on a regular basis.

Extra expense coverage form   A separate form that can be used to cover the extra expenses incurred by a firm to continue operations during a period of restoration.

Factory mutual   Mutual insurance company insuring only properties that meet high underwriting standards; emphasizes loss prevention.

Facultative reinsurance   Optional, case-by-case method of reinsurance used when the ceding company receives an application for insurance that exceeds its retention limit.

Fair Access to Insurance Requirements (FAIR plan)   Property insurance plan that provides basic property insurance to property owners in areas where they are unable to obtain insurance in the normal markets. Each state with such a plan has a central placement facility.

Fair rental value   Amount payable to an insured homeowner for loss of rental income due to damage that makes the premises uninhabitable.

Family purpose doctrine   Concept that imputes negligence committed by immediate family members while operating a family car to the owner of the car.

Federal crop insurance   Various federal insurance programs that provides coverage for unavoidable crop losses, such as hail, wind, drought, and plant disease.

Federal surety bond   Type of surety bond required by federal agencies that regulates the actions of business firms. It guarantees that the bonded party will comply with federal standards, pay all taxes or duties accrued, or pay any penalty if the bondholder fails to pay.

File-and-use law   Law for regulating insurance rates under which companies are required only to file the rates with the state insurance department before putting them into effect.

Financial institution bond   Bond that covers crime loss exposures of commercial banks, savings and loan institutions, and other financial institutions; used to cover bank holdups, employee dishonesty, forgery, alteration of checks, armored car exposures, and other crime exposures of financial institutions.

Financial Modernization Act of 1999   A federal law that allows banks, insurers, investment firms, and other financial institutions to enter and compete in each other's financial markets.

Financial responsibility law   Law that requires persons involved in automobile accidents to furnish proof of financial responsibility up to a minimum dollar limit or face having driving privileges revoked or suspended.

Financial risk   A risk that business firms face because of adverse changes in commodity prices, interest rates, foreign exchange rates, and the value of money.

Fire legal liability   Liability of a firm or person for fire damage caused by negligence and damage to property of others.

Fixed-amount option   Life insurance settlement option in which the policy proceeds are paid out in fixed amounts.

Fixed annuity   Annuity whose periodic payment is a guaranteed fixed amount.

Fixed-period option   Life insurance settlement option in which the policy proceeds are paid out over a fixed period of time.

Flexible-premium annuity   An annuity contract that permits the owner to vary the size and frequency of premium payments. The amount of retirement income depends on the accumulated sum in the annuity at retirement.

Flexible-spending account   An arrangement by which the employee agrees to a salary reduction, which can be used to pay for plan benefits, unreimbursed medical and dental expenses, and other expenses permitted by the Internal Revenue Code.

Flex-rating law   Type of rating law in which prior approval of the rates is required only if the rates exceed a certain percentage above and below the rates previously filed.

Foreign insurer   Insurance company chartered by one state but licensed to do business in another.

Fortuitous loss   Unforeseen and unexpected loss that occurs as a result of chance.

Franchise deductible   Deductible found in some marine insurance contracts in which the insurer has no liability if the loss is under a certain percentage amount, but once this percentage is exceeded, the entire loss is paid in full.

Fraternal insurer   Mutual insurance company that provides life and health insurance to members of a social organization.

Fully insured   Insured status of a covered person under the Old-Age, Survivors, and Disability Insurance (OASDI) program. To be fully insured for retirement benefits, 40 credits are required.

Fundamental risk   A risk that affects the entire economy or large numbers of persons or groups within the economy.

Funding agency   A financial institution that provides for the accumulation or administration of the contributions that will be used to pay pension benefits.

Funding instrument   An insurance contract or trust agreement that states the terms under which the funding agency will accumulate, administer, and disburse the pension funds.

General agency system   Type of life insurance marketing system in which the general agent is an independent businessperson who represents only one insurer, is in charge of a territory, and is responsible for hiring, training, and motivating new agents.

General aggregate limit   In the commercial general liability policy, it is the maximum amount the insurer will pay for the sum of the following—damages under Coverage A, B, and medical expenses under Coverage C.

General average   In ocean marine insurance, a loss incurred for the common good that is shared by all parties to the venture.

General damages   An award for damages that cannot be specifically measured or itemized, such as compensation for pain and suffering, disfigurement, or loss of companionship of a spouse.

Good student discount   Reduction of automobile premium for a young driver at least sixteen who ranks in the upper 20 percent of his or her class, has a B or 3.0 average, or is on the Dean's list or honor roll. It is based on the premise that good students are better drivers.

Grace period   Period of time during which a policyowner may pay an overdue life insurance premium without causing the policy to lapse.

Gross estate   The value of the property that you own when you die. Also includes value of jointly owned property, life insurance, death proceeds, and certain other items.

Gross premium   Amount paid by the insured, consisting of the gross rate multiplied by the number of exposure units.

Gross rate   The sum of the pure premium and a loading element.

Group deferred annuity   Type of allocated pension plan in which a single-premium deferred annuity is purchased each year and is equal to the retirement benefit for that year.

Group life insurance   Life insurance provided on a number of persons in a single master contract. Physical examinations are not required, and certificates of insurance are issued to members of the group as evidence of insurance.

Group term life insurance   Most common form of group life insurance. Yearly renewable term insurance on employees during their working careers.

Group universal life products (GULP)   Universal life insurance plans sold to members of a group, such as individual employees of an employer. There are some differences between GULP plans and individual universal life plans; for instance, GULP expense charges are generally lower than those assessed against individual policies.

Guaranteed investment contract (GIC)   An arrangement in private pension plans in which the insurer guarantees the interest rate on a lump-sum pension deposit and also guarantees the principal against loss.

Guaranteed purchase option   Benefit that can be added to a life insurance policy permitting the insured to purchase additional amounts of life insurance at specified times in the future without requiring evidence of insurability.

Guaranteed renewable   Continuance provision of a health insurance policy under which the company guarantees to renew the policy to a stated age, and whose renewal is at the insured's option. Premiums can be increased for broad classes of insureds.

Guaranteed replacement cost   In the event of a total loss, the insurer agrees to replace the home exactly as it was before the loss even though the replacement cost exceeds the amount of insurance stated in the policy.

Hard insurance market   A period in the underwriting cycle during which underwriting standards are strict and premiums are high. *See also* **Soft insurance market** and **Underwriting cycle.**

Hazard   Condition that creates or increases the chance of loss.

Health maintenance organization (HMO)   Organized system of health care that provides comprehensive health services to its members for a fixed prepaid fee.

Health savings account (HSA)   A tax-exempt or custodial account established exclusively for the purpose of paying qualified medical expenses of the account beneficiary who is covered under a high-deductible health insurance plan.

Hedging   Technique for transferring the risk of unfavorable price fluctuations to a speculator by purchasing and selling options and futures contracts on an organized exchange.

High-deductible health plan (HDHP)   A consumer-driven health plan that consists of major medical health insurance with a high deductible and a health savings account (HSA).

HMO   See **Health maintenance organization.**

Hold-harmless clause   Clause written into a contract by which one party agrees to release another party from all legal liability, such as a retailer who agrees to release the manufacturer from legal liability if the product injures someone.

Home service life insurance   Industrial life insurance and monthly debit ordinary life insurance contracts that are serviced by agents who earlier called on the policyowners at their homes to collect the premiums.

Homeowners 2 policy (broad form)   Homeowners insurance policy that provides coverage on a named-perils basis on the dwelling, other structures, and personal property. Personal liability insurance is also provided.

Homeowners 3 policy (special form)   Homeowners insurance policy that covers the dwelling and other structures on a risk-of-direct-loss basis and personal property on a named-perils basis. Personal liability insurance is also provided.

Homeowners 4 policy (contents broad form)   Homeowners insurance policy that applies to tenants renting a home or apartment. Covers the tenant's personal property and provides personal liability insurance.

Homeowners 5 policy (comprehensive form)   Homeowners insurance policy that provides open perils coverage ("all risks coverage") on both the building and personal property. The dwelling, other structures, and personal property are insured against the risk of direct physical loss to property; all losses are covered except those losses specifically excluded.

Homeowners 6 policy (unit-owners form)   Homeowners insurance policy that covers personal property of insured owners of condominium units and cooperative apartments on a broad form, named-perils basis. Personal liability insurance is also provided.

Homeowners 8 policy (modified coverage form)   Homeowner policy that is designed for older homes. Dwelling and other structures are indemnified on the basis of repair cost using common construction materials and methods. Personal liability insurance is also provided.

Hospital expense insurance   Individual health insurance that pays for medical expenses incurred while in a hospital.

Hospital Insurance (Part A)   Part A of Medicare that covers inpatient hospital care, skilled nursing facility care, home health-care services, and hospice care for Medicare beneficiaries.

Hospital-surgical insurance   Medical expense plan that provides hospital and surgical benefits and other ancillary benefits.

Hull insurance (1)   Class of ocean marine insurance that covers physical damage to the ship or vessel insured. Typically written on an "all-risks" basis. (2) Physical damage insurance on aircraft—similar to collision insurance in an auto policy.

Human life value   For purposes of life insurance, the present value of the family's share of the deceased breadwinner's future earnings.

Immediate annuity   An annuity where the first payment is due one payment interval from the date of purchase.

Imputed negligence   Case in which responsibility for damage can be transferred from the negligent party to another person, such as an employer.

Incontestable clause   Contractual provision in a life insurance policy stating that the insurer cannot contest the policy after it has been in force two years during the insured's lifetime.

Indemnification   Compensation to the victim of a loss, in whole or in part, by payment, repair, or replacement.

Independent adjustor   Claims adjustor who offers his or her services to insurance companies and is compensated by a fee.

Independent agency system   Type of property and casualty insurance marketing system, sometimes called the American agency system, in which the agent is an independent businessperson representing several insurers. The agency owns the expirations or renewal rights to the business, and the agent is compensated by commissions that vary by line of insurance.

Indeterminate-premium whole life insurance   Nonparticipating whole life policy that permits the insurer to
adjust premiums based on anticipated future experience. Initial premiums are guaranteed for a certain
period. After the initial guaranteed period expires,
the insurer can increase premiums up to some maximum limit.

Indirect loss   *See* **Consequential loss.**

Individual Retirement Account (IRA)   Individual retirement
plan that can be established by a person with earned
income. An IRA plan enjoys favorable income tax
advantages.

Industrial life insurance   Type of life insurance in which
policies are sold in small amounts and the premiums
are collected weekly or monthly by a debit agent at
the policyowner's home. *See also* **Home service life
insurance.**

Inflation-guard endorsement   Endorsement added at the
insured's request to a homeowners policy to increase
periodically the face amount of insurance on the
dwelling and other policy coverages by a specified
percentage.

Initial reserve   In life insurance, the reserve at the beginning of any policy year.

Inland marine insurance   Transportation insurance
that provides protection for goods shipped on
land, including imports, exports, domestic shipments, means of transportation, personal property
floater risks, and commercial property floater
risks.

Installment refund annuity   Pays the annuitant a lifetime
income, but if death occurs before receiving payments equal to the purchase price, the income payments continue to the beneficiary.

Insurance   Pooling of fortuitous losses by transfer of
risks to insurers who agree to indemnify insureds for
such losses, to provide other pecuniary benefits on
their occurrence, or to render services connected with
the risk.

Insurance guaranty funds   State funds that provide for the
payment of unpaid claims of insolvent insurers.

Insurance score   A credit-based score based on an individual's credit record and other factors that is highly
predictive of future claim costs; insureds with low
insurance scores generally file more homeowners and
auto insurance claims than insureds with good credit
and higher insurance scores.

Insurance Services Office (ISO)   Major rating organization in property and casualty insurance that drafts
policy forms for personal and commercial lines of
insurance and provides rate data on loss costs for
property and liability insurance lines.

Insuring agreement   That part of an insurance contract
that states the promises of the insurer.

Integrated risk management   A risk management technique that combines coverage for pure and speculative risks in the same insurance contract.

Interest-adjusted method   Method of determining cost to
an insured of a life insurance policy that considers
the time cost of money by applying an interest factor
to each element of cost. *See also* **Net payment cost
index; Surrender cost index.**

Interest option   Life insurance settlement option in which
the principal is retained by the insurer and interest is
paid periodically.

Interest rate risk   Risk of loss caused by adverse interest
rate movements.

Investment guarantee contract (IG)   Used in group pension plans in which the insurer receives pension
funds over a number of years but the guaranteed
interest rate for later years is only a projected rate; if
actual returns are higher, the pension fund receives
the higher rate.

Invitee   Someone who is invited onto the premises for the
benefit of the occupant.

IRA   *See* **Individual Retirement Account.**

Irrevocable beneficiary   Beneficiary designation allowing
no change to be made in the beneficiary of an insurance policy without the beneficiary's consent.

ISO   *See* **Insurance Services Office.**

Joint and several liability   Rule under which several people
may be responsible for the injury, but a defendant
who is only slightly responsible may be required to
pay the full amount of damages.

Joint-and-survivor annuity   Annuity based on the lives of
two or more annuitants. The annuity income (either
the full amount of the original income or only two-
thirds or one-half of the original income when the
first annuitant dies) is paid until the death of the last
annuitant.

Joint underwriting association (JUA)   Organization of auto
insurers operating in a state that makes auto insurance available to high-risk drivers. All underwriting
losses are proportionately shared by insurers on the
basis of premiums written in the state.

Judgment rating   Rate-making method for which
each exposure is individually evaluated and the
rate is determined largely by the underwriter's judgment.

Judicial bond   Type of surety bond used for court pro-
ceedings and guaranteeing that the party bonded will
fulfill certain obligations specified by law, for
example, fiduciary responsibilities.

Juvenile insurance   Life insurance purchased by parents
for children under a specified age.

Keogh plan for the self-employed   Retirement plan individually adopted by self-employed persons that
allows a tax deductible contribution to a defined-
contribution or defined-benefit plan.

Lapsed policy   One that is not in force because premiums
have not been paid.

Last clear chance rule Statutory modification of the contributory negligence law allowing the claimant endangered by his or her own negligence to recover damages from a defendant if the defendant has a last clear chance to avoid the accident but fails to do so.

Law of large numbers Concept that the greater the number of exposures, the more closely will actual results approach the probable results expected from an infinite number of exposures.

Legal hazard Characteristics of the legal system or regulatory environment that increase the frequency or severity of losses.

Legal reserve Liability item on a life insurer's balance sheet representing the redundant or excessive premiums paid under the level-premium method during the early years. Assets must be accumulated to offset the legal reserve liability. Purpose of the legal reserve is to provide lifetime protection.

Liability coverage That part of the personal auto policy that protects a covered person against a suit or claim for bodily injury or property damage arising out of negligent ownership or operation of an automobile. Liability coverage is also included in the homeowner's policy, which provides coverage for bodily injury and property damage liability.

Liability without fault Principle on which workers compensation is based, holding the employer absolutely liable for occupational injuries or disease suffered by workers, regardless of who is at fault.

License and permit bond Type of surety bond guaranteeing that the person bonded will comply with all laws and regulations that govern his or her activities.

Licensee Someone who enters or remains on the premises with the occupant's expressed or implied permission.

Life annuity with guaranteed payments Pays a life income to the annuitant with a certain number of guaranteed payments.

Life income option Life insurance settlement option in which the policy proceeds are paid during the lifetime of the beneficiary. A certain number of guaranteed payments may also be payable.

Life insurance planning Systematic method of determining the insured's financial goals, which are translated into specific amounts of life insurance, then periodically reviewed for possible changes.

Limited-payment policy Type of whole life insurance providing protection throughout the insured's lifetime and for which relatively high premiums are paid only for a limited period.

Liquor liability law *See* **Dram shop law.**

Loading The amount that must be added to the pure premium for expenses, profit, and a margin for contingencies.

Long-term-care insurance A form of health insurance that pays a daily benefit for medical or custodial care received in a nursing facility or hospital.

Loss control Risk management activities that reduce both the frequency and severity of losses for a firm or organization.

Loss exposure Any situation or circumstance in which a loss is possible, regardless of whether a loss occurs.

Loss frequency The probable number of losses that may occur during some given time period.

Loss ratio The ratio of incurred losses and loss adjustment expenses to earned premiums.

Loss ratio method of rating A rating system in property and casualty insurance by which the actual loss ratio is compared with the expected loss ratio, and the rate is adjusted accordingly.

Loss reserve Amount set aside by property and casualty insurers for claims reported and adjusted but not yet paid, claims reported and filed but not yet adjusted, and claims incurred but not yet reported to the insurer.

Loss severity The probable size of the losses that may occur.

McCarran-Ferguson Act Federal law passed in 1945 stating that continued regulation of the insurance industry by the states is in the public interest and that federal antitrust laws apply to insurance only to the extent that the industry is not regulated by state law.

Major medical insurance Health insurance designed to pay a large proportion of the covered expenses of a catastrophic illness or injury.

Malpractice liability insurance Covers acts of malpractice resulting in harm or injury to patients.

Managed care A generic name for medical expense plans that provide covered services to the members in a cost-effective manner.

Manual rating *See* **Class rating.**

Manuscript policy Policy designed for a firm's specific needs and requirements.

Mass merchandising Plan for insuring individual members of a group, such as employees of firms or members of labor unions, under a single program of insurance at reduced premiums. Property and liability insurance is sold to individual members using group insurance marketing methods.

Master contract Formed between the insurer and group policyowner for the benefit of the individual members.

Maximum possible loss Worst loss that could possibly happen to a firm during its lifetime.

Maximum probable loss Worst loss that is likely to happen to a firm during its lifetime.

Mean reserve In life insurance, the average of the terminal and initial reserves.

Medical Information Bureau (MIB) Bureau whose purpose is to supply underwriting information in life insurance to member companies, which report any health impairments of an applicant for insurance.

Medical payments coverage   That part of the personal auto policy that pays all reasonable medical and funeral expenses incurred by a covered person within three years from the date of an accident.

Medical payments to others   Pays for medical expenses of others under the homeowners policy in the event that a person (not an insured) is accidentally injured on the premises, or by the activities of an insured, resident employee, or animal owned by or in the care of an insured.

Medicare   Part of the total Social Security program that covers the medical expenses of most people age 65 and older and certain disabled people under age 65.

Medicare Advantage plans   Private health plans that are part of Medicare that allow beneficiaries to choose alternates to the Original Medicare Plan, such as Medicare HMOs, Medicare PPOs, Medicare special needs plans, and Medicare private-fee-for-service plans.

Medicare Part B   Part B of the Medicare program that covers physicians' fees and other related medical services. Most eligible Medicare recipients are automatically included unless they voluntarily refuse this coverage.

Medicare prescription drug plans   Plans that provide coverage for prescription drugs under the Medicare program; beneficiaries have a choice of plans.

Merit rating   Rate-making method in which class rates are adjusted upward or downward based on individual loss experience.

MIB   *See* **Medical Information Bureau.**

Minimum coverage requirement   A test that must be met to prevent employers from establishing a qualified pension plan that covers only the highly compensated. *See also* **Ratio test.**

Misstatement of age or sex clause   Contractual provision in a life insurance policy stating that if the insured's age or sex is misstated, the amount payable is the amount that the premium would have purchased at the correct age.

Mobilehome insurance   A package policy that provides property insurance and personal liability insurance to mobilhome owners. A special endorsement is added to HO-2 or HO-3.

Modified life policy   Whole life policy for which premiums are reduced for the first three to five years and are higher thereafter.

Modified no-fault plan   An injured person has the right to sue a negligent driver only if the bodily injury claim exceeds the dollar or verbal threshold.

Modified prior-approval law   A state rating law where rate changes are based solely on loss experience; the rates must be filed with the state insurance department and can be used immediately. However, if the rate change is based on a change in rate classification or expense relationship, prior approval of the rates is necessary.

Monetary threshold   An injured motorist would not be permitted to sue but would collect from his or her insurer, unless the claim exceeded the threshold amount.

Moral hazard   Dishonesty or character defects in an individual that increase the chance of loss.

Morale hazard   Carelessness or indifference to a loss because of the existence of insurance.

Multicar discount   Reduction in auto insurance premiums for an insured who owns two or more automobiles, on the assumption that two such autos owned by the same person will not be driven as frequently as only one.

Multiple distribution systems   Insurance marketing method that refers to the use of several distribution systems by an insurer; for example, a property and casualty insurer may use the independent agency method and direct response system to sell insurance.

Multiple-line insurance   Type of insurance that combines several lines of insurance into one contract, for example, property insurance and casualty insurance.

Mutual insurer   Insurance corporation owned by the policyowners, who elect the board of directors. The board appoints managing executives, and the company may pay a dividend or give a rate reduction in advance to insureds.

NAIC   *See* **National Association of Insurance Commissioners.**

NALP   *See* **Net annual level premium.**

Named insured   The person or persons named in the declarations section of the policy, as opposed to someone who may have an interest in the policy but is not named as an insured.

Named-perils policy   Coverage by an insurance contract that promises to pay only for those losses caused by perils specifically listed in the policy.

National Association of Insurance Commissioners (NAIC)   Group founded in 1871 that meets periodically to discuss industry problems and draft model laws in various areas and recommends adoption of these proposals by state legislatures.

Needs approach   Method for estimating amount of life insurance appropriate for a family by analyzing various family needs that must be met if the family head should die and converting them into specific amounts of life insurance. Financial assets are considered in determining the amount of life insurance needed.

Negligence   Failure to exercise the standard of care required by law to protect others from harm.

Net amount at risk   Concept associated with a level-premium life insurance policy. Calculated as the difference between the face amount of the policy and the legal reserve.

Net annual level premium (NALP)   Annual level premium for a life insurance policy with no expense loading. Mathematically equivalent to the net single premium.

Net payment cost index   Method of measuring the cost of an insurance policy to an insured if death occurs at the end of some specified time period. The time value of money is taken into consideration.

Net present value   Used in capital budgeting and is the sum of the present values of the future cash flows minus the cost of the project. A positive net present value represents an increase in value for the firm.

Net retention   *See* **Retention limit.**

Net single premium (NSP)   Present value of the future death benefit of a life insurance policy.

No-fault insurance   A tort reform proposal in which the injured person would collect benefits from his or her insurer and would not have to sue a negligent third party who caused the accident and prove legal liability.

No-filing law   Rating law where insurers are not required to file their rates with the state insurance department but may be required to furnish rate schedules and supporting data to state officials. Also called an **open competition law.**

Nonbuilding agency system   Life insurance marketing system by which an insurer sells its products through established agents who are already engaged in selling life insurance.

Noncancellable   Continuance provision in a health insurance policy stipulating that the policy cannot be canceled, that the renewal is guaranteed to a stated age, and that the premium rates cannot be increased.

Noncontributory plan   Employer pays the entire cost of a group insurance or private pension plan. All eligible employees are covered.

Nonforfeiture law   State law requiring insurance companies to provide at least a minimum nonforfeiture value to policyowners who surrender their cash-value life insurance policies.

Noninsurance transfers   Various methods other than insurance by which a pure risk and its potential financial consequences can be transferred to another party, for example, contracts, leases, and hold-harmless agreements.

Nonoccupational disability   The accident or illness must occur off the job.

Nonparticipating policy   Term used to describe a life insurance policy that does not pay dividends.

Objective risk   Relative variation of actual loss from expected loss, which varies inversely with the square root of the number of cases under observation.

Obligee   The party to a surety bond who is reimbursed for damages if the principal to the bond fails to perform.

Occurrence   An accident, including continuous or repeated exposure to substantially the same general, harmful conditions, which results in bodily injury or property damage during the policy period. *See also* **Accident.**

Occurrence policy   A liability insurance policy that covers claims arising out of occurrences that take place during the policy period, regardless of when the claim is made. *See also* **Claims-made policy.**

Ocean marine insurance   Type of insurance that provides protection for all types of oceangoing vessels and their cargoes as well as legal liability of owners and shippers.

Open-competition law   Law for regulating insurance rates under which insurers are not required to file rates at all with the state insurance department but may be required to furnish rate schedules and supporting data to state officials.

Open perils policy   *See* **"All-risks policy."**

Optionally renewable policy   The insurer has the right to terminate a policy on any anniversary date, or in some cases, on a premium date.

Ordinary life insurance   Type of whole life insurance providing protection throughout the insured's lifetime and for which premiums are paid throughout the insured's lifetime.

Original Medicare Plan   The traditional plan for beneficiaries run by the federal government that provides Hospital Insurance (Medicare Part A) benefits and Medical Insurance (Medicare Part B) benefits.

Other-insurance provisions   Provisions whose purpose is to prevent profiting from insurance and violation of the principle of indemnity.

Other-than-collision loss   Part of the coverage available under Part D: Coverage for Damage to Your Auto in the personal auto policy. All physical damage losses to an insured vehicle are covered except collision losses and those losses specifically excluded.

Ownership clause   Provision in life insurance policies under which the policyowner possesses all contractual rights in the policy while the insured is living. These rights can generally be exercised without the beneficiary's consent.

P&I Insurance   *See* **Protection and indemnity insurance.**

Package policy   Policy that combines two or more separate contracts of insurance in one policy, for example, homeowners insurance.

Partial disability   Inability of the insured to perform one or more important duties of his or her occupation.

Participating policy   Life insurance policy that pays dividends to the policyowners.

Particular average   An ocean marine loss that falls entirely on a particular interest as contrasted with a general average loss that falls on all parties to the voyage.

Particular risk   A risk that affects only individuals and not the entire community.

Past-service credits   Pension benefits awarded to employees based on service with the employer prior to the inception of the plan.

Paul v. Virginia   Landmark legal decision of 1869 establishing the right of the states, and not the federal government, to regulate insurance. Ruled that insurance was not interstate commerce.

Pension accrual benefit   A disability income benefit that makes a pension contribution so that the disabled employee's pension benefit remains intact.

Pension Benefit Guaranty Corporation (PBGC)   A federal corporation that guarantees the payment of vested or nonforfeitable benefits up to certain limits if a private defined benefit pension plan is terminated.

Percentage participation clause   Provision in a health insurance policy that requires the insured to pay a certain percentage of eligible medical expenses in excess of the deductible. Also called coinsurance.

Peril   Cause or source of loss.

Personal injury   Injury for which legal liability arises (such as for false arrest, detention or imprisonment, malicious prosecution, libel, slander, defamation of character, violation of the right of privacy, and unlawful entry or eviction) and which may be covered by an endorsement to the homeowners policy.

Personal liability insurance   Liability insurance that protects the insured for an amount up to policy limits against a claim or suit for damages because of bodily injury or property damage caused by the insured's negligence. This coverage is provided by Section II of the homeowners policy.

Personal lines   Property and liability insurance coverages that insure the home and personal property of individuals and families or provide protection against legal liability.

Personal-producing general agent   Term used to describe an above-average salesperson with a proven sales record who is hired primarily to sell life insurance under a contract that provides both direct and overriding commissions.

Personal umbrella policy liability   Policy designed to provide protection against a catastrophic lawsuit or judgment, whose coverage ranges generally from $1 million to $10 million and extends to the entire family. Insurance is excess over underlying coverages.

Physical hazard   Physical condition that increases the chance of loss.

PIA   *See* **Primary insurance amount.**

Point-of-service plan (POS)   Establishes a network of preferred providers. If patients see a preferred provider, they pay little or nothing. Outside provider care is covered, but at a substantially higher deductible and coinsurance rate.

Policy loan   Cash value of a life insurance policy that can be borrowed by the policyowner in lieu of surrendering the policy.

Policyowners' surplus   Difference between an insurance company's assets and its liabilities.

Pooling   Spreading of losses incurred by the few over the entire group, so that in the process, average loss is substituted for actual loss.

Preexisting condition   Physical or mental condition of an insured that existed prior to issuance of a policy.

Preexisting-conditions clause   Contractual provision in a health insurance policy stating that preexisting conditions are not covered or are covered only after the policy has been in force for a specified period.

Preferred risks   Individuals whose mortality experience is expected to be lower than average.

Primary and excess insurance   Type of other-insurance provision that requires the primary insurer to pay first in the case of a loss; when the policy limits under the primary policy are exhausted, the excess insurer pays.

Primary beneficiary   Beneficiary of a life insurance policy who is first entitled to receive the policy proceeds on the insured's death.

Primary insurance amount (PIA)   Monthly cash benefit paid to a retired worker at the full retirement age, or to a disabled worker eligible for benefits under the Old-Age, Survivors, and Disability Insurance (OASDI) program.

Principal   The bonded party in the purchase of a surety bond who agrees to perform certain acts or fulfill certain obligations.

Principal of indemnity   States that the insurer agrees to pay no more than the actual amount of the loss. The insured should not profit from a covered loss but should be restored to approximately the same financial position that existed prior to the loss.

Prior-approval law   Law for regulating insurance rates under which the rates must be filed and approved by the state insurance department before they can be used.

Pro rata liability clause   Clause in a property insurance policy that makes each company insuring the same interest in a property liable according to the proportion that its insurance bears to the total amount of insurance on the property.

Probationary period   Waiting period of one to six months required of an employee before he or she is allowed to participate in a group insurance plan.

Products-completed operations hazard   Liability losses that occur away from the premises and arise out of the insured's product or work after the insured has relinquished possession of the product, or the work has been completed.

Products liability   The legal liability of manufacturers, wholesalers, and retailers to persons who are injured or who incur property damage from defective products.

Prospective reserve   In life insurance, the difference between the present value of future benefits and the present value of future net premiums.

Protection and indemnity insurance (P&I)   Coverage that can be added to an ocean marine insurance policy to provide liability insurance for property damage and bodily injury to third parties.

Proximate cause   Factor causing damage to property for which there is an unbroken chain of events between the occurrence of an insured peril and damage or destruction of the property.

Public adjustor   Claims adjustor who represents the insured rather than the insurance company and is paid a fee based on the amount of the claim settlement. A public adjustor may be employed in those cases where the insured and insurer cannot resolve a dispute over a claim, or if the insured needs technical assistance in a complex loss situation.

Public official bond   Type of surety bond guaranteeing that public officials will faithfully perform their duties for the protection of the public.

Punitive damages   An award for damages designed to punish people and organizations so that others are deterred from committing the same wrongful act. Awards for punitive damages are often several times the amount awarded for compensatory damages.

Pure no-fault plan   The injured person cannot sue at all, regardless of the seriousness of the claim, and no payments are made for pain and suffering.

Pure premium   That portion of the insurance rate needed to pay losses and loss-adjustment expenses.

Pure premium method of rating   A rating system in property and casualty insurance. The pure premium is determined by dividing the dollar amount of incurred losses and loss-adjustment expenses by the number of exposure units.

Pure risk   Situation in which there are only the possibilities of loss or no loss.

Rate   Price per unit of insurance.

Rate making   Process by which insurance pricing or premium rates are determined for an insurance company.

Ratio test   A test that a qualified pension plan must meet to receive favorable income-tax treatment. The pension plan must benefit a percentage of employees that is at least 70 percent of the highly compensated employees covered by the plan.

Readjustment period   One- to two-year period immediately following the breadwinner's death during which time the family should receive approximately the same amount of income it received while the breadwinner was alive.

Reasonable and customary charges   Payment of physicians' normal fees if they are reasonable and customary, such as a fee that does not exceed the 80th or 90th percentile for a similar procedure performed by physicians in the area.

Rebating   A practice—illegal in virtually all states—of giving a premium reduction or some other financial advantage to an individual as an inducement to purchase the policy.

Reciprocal exchange   Unincorporated mutual insuring organization in which insurance is exchanged among members and which is managed by an attorney-in-fact.

Regression analysis   Method of characterizing the relationship between two or more variables, and then using this characterization as a predictor.

Reinstatement clause   Contractual provision in a life insurance policy that permits the owner to reinstate a lapsed policy within three or five years if certain requirements are fulfilled; for example, evidence of insurability is required and overdue premiums plus interest must be paid.

Reinstatement provision   Provision of a health insurance policy that allows the insured to reinstate a lapsed policy by payment of premium either without an application or with an application.

Reinsurance   An arrangement by which the primary insurer that initially writes the insurance transfers to another insurer (called the reinsurer) part or all of the potential losses associated with such insurance.

Reinsurance facility   Pool for placing high-risk automobile drivers that arranges for an insurer to accept all applicants for insurance. Underwriting losses are shared by all auto insurers in the state.

Replacement cost insurance   Property insurance by which the insured is indemnified on the basis of replacement cost with no deduction for depreciation.

Reporting form   Coverage for commercial property insurance that requires the insured to report monthly or quarterly the value of the insured inventory, with automatic adjustment of insurance amount to cover the accurately reported inventory.

Representations   Statements made by an applicant for insurance, for example, in life insurance, occupation, state of health, and family history.

Residual disability   Residual disability means that a proportionate disability-income benefit is paid to an insured whose earned income is reduced because of an accident or illness.

Residual market   The residual market refers to plans in which auto insurers participate to make insurance available to high-risk drivers who are unable to obtain coverage in the standard markets. Examples include an automobile insurance plan, joint underwriting association, and reinsurance facility. Also called the **shared market.**

Res ipsa loquitur   Literally, the thing speaks for itself. Under this doctrine, the very fact that the event occurred establishes a presumption of negligence on behalf of the defendant.

Retained limit Term found in an umbrella policy that refers to (1) the total limits of the underlying insurance or any other insurance available to the insured, or (2) the deductible stated in the declarations if the loss is covered by the umbrella policy but not by any underlying insurance or other insurance, whichever is applicable.

Retention Risk management technique in which the firm retains part or all of the losses resulting from a given loss exposure. Used when no other method is available, the worst possible loss is not serious, and losses are highly predictable.

Retention limit Amount of insurance retained by a ceding company for its own account in a reinsurance operation.

Retirement test *See* **Earnings test.**

Retrocession Process by which a reinsurer obtains reinsurance from another company.

Retrospective rating Type of merit-rating method in which the insured's loss experience during the current policy period determines the actual premium paid for that period.

Retrospective reserve In life insurance, the net premiums collected by the insurer for a particular block of policies, plus interest earnings at an assumed rate, less the amounts paid out as death claims.

Revocable beneficiary Beneficiary designation allowing the policyowner the right to change the beneficiary without consent of the beneficiary.

Rider Term used in insurance contracts to describe a document that amends or changes the original policy. *See also* **Endorsement.**

Risk Uncertainty concerning the occurrence of a loss.

Risk-based capital (RBC) Under NAIC standards, insurers are required to have a certain amount of capital that is based on the riskiness of their investments and operations.

Risk control Risk management techniques that reduce the frequency and severity of losses, such as avoidance, loss prevention, and an automatic sprinkler system.

Risk financing Risk management techniques that provide for the funding of losses after they occur, such as retention, noninsurance transfers, and commercial insurance.

Risk management Systematic process for the identification and evaluation of loss exposures faced by an organization or individual, and for the selection and implementation of the most appropriate techniques for treating such exposures.

Risk management information system Computerized data base that permits the risk manager to store and analyze risk management data and to use such data to predict future loss levels.

Risk map Map used in risk management that shows grids detailing the potential frequency and severity of risks faced by the organization.

Robbery Taking of property from a person by someone who has (1) caused or threatens to cause bodily harm to that person, or (2) committed an obviously unlawful act witnessed by that person.

Roth IRA An IRA in which the contributions are not income-tax deductible but distributions are received income-tax free if certain conditions are met.

Roth 401(k) plan A qualified retirement plan in which contributions are made with after-tax dollars and qualified distributions at retirement are received income-tax free; investment earnings also accumulate on a tax-free basis.

Safe driver plan Plan in which the automobile premiums paid are based on the insured's driving record and on the records of those living with the insured.

Savings bank life insurance Life insurance originally sold by mutual savings banks in Massachusetts, New York, and Connecticut. Now sold in other states as well.

Scheduled personal property endorsement Special coverage added at the insured's request to a homeowners policy to insure items specifically listed. Used to insure valuable property such as jewelry, furs, and paintings.

Schedule rating Type of merit-rating method in which each exposure is individually rated and given a basis rate that is then modified by debits or credits for undesirable or desirable physical features.

Second-injury fund State funds paying the excess amount of benefit awarded an employee for a second injury if the disability is greater than that caused by the second injury alone. Its purpose is to encourage employers to hire handicapped workers.

Section 401(k) plan A qualified profit-sharing or thrift plan that allows participants the option of putting money into the plan or receiving the funds as cash. The employee can voluntarily elect to have his or her salary reduced up to some maximum annual limit, which is then invested in the employer's Section 401(k) plan.

Section 403(B) plan A qualified retirement plan designed for employees of public educational systems and tax-exempt organization, such as hospitals, nonprofit groups, and churches. Also known as **tax-sheltered annuities.**

Securitization of risk Term to describe the transfer of an insurable risk to the capital markets through the creation of a financial instrument, such as a catastrophe bond, futures contract, options contract, or other financial instrument.

Self-employed 401(k) plan A qualified retirement plan with significant tax savings for self-employed individuals or businessowners with no employees other than a spouse, which combines a profit-sharing plan with an individual 401(k) plan.

Self-insurance Retention program in which the employer self-funds or pays part or all of its losses.

Self-insured retention   *See* **Retained limit.**

SEP   *See* **Simplified Employee Pension.**

Separate investment account   Used in group pension plans in which the plan administrator has the option to invest in separate accounts offered by the insurer, such as stock funds, bond funds, and similar investments. Assets are segregated from the insurer's general investment account and are not subject to claims by the insurer's creditors.

Service benefits   Health insurance benefits that pay hospital charges or payment for care received by the insured directly to the hospital or providers of care. The plan provides service rather than cash benefits to the insured.

Settlement options   Ways in which life insurance policy proceeds can be paid other than in a lump sum, including interest, fixed period, fixed amount, and life income options.

SEUA case   *See* **South-Eastern Underwriters Association (SEUA) case.**

Shared market   *See* **Residual market.**

SIMPLE retirement plan   A qualified retirement plan for smaller employers who are exempt from most nondiscrimination and administrative rules. Employees can elect to contribute up to certain annual limits.

Simplified Employee Pension (SEP)   An employer-sponsored individual retirement account that meets certain requirements. Paperwork is reduced for employers who wish to cover employees in a retirement plan.

Single limit   The total amount of liability insurance that applies to the entire accident without a separate limit for each person. The total amount of insurance applies to both bodily injury liability and property damage liability.

Single-premium deferred annuity   A retirement annuity that is purchased with a single premium with benefits to start at some future date.

Single-premium whole life insurance   A whole life policy that provides lifetime protection with a single premium payment.

Social insurance   Government insurance programs with certain characteristics that distinguish them from other government insurance programs. Programs are generally compulsory; specific earmarked taxes fund the programs; benefits are heavily weighted in favor of low-income groups; and programs are designed to achieve certain social goals.

Soft insurance market   A period during which underwriting standards are more liberal and premiums are relatively low. *See also* **Hard insurance market** and **Underwriting cycle.**

South-Eastern Underwriters Association (SEUA) case   Legal landmark decision of 1944 overruling the *Paul v. Virginia* ruling and finding that insurance was interstate commerce when conducted across state lines and was subject to federal regulation.

Special coverage policy   *See* **"All-risks policy."**

Special damages   An award for damages that can be determined and documented, such as medical expenses, lost earnings, or property damage.

Speculative risk   Situation in which either profit or loss are clear possibilities.

Split limits   The amounts of insurance for bodily injury liability and property damage liability are stated separately.

Stop-loss limit   Modification of the coinsurance provision in major medical plans that places a dollar limit on the maximum amount that an individual must pay.

Straight deductible   Deductible in an insurance contract by which the insured must pay a certain number of dollars of loss before the insurer is required to make a payment.

Strict liability   Liability for damages even though fault or negligence cannot be proven, for example, in such situations as occupational injury of employees under a workers compensation law. Also known as **absolute liability.**

Subjective risk   Uncertainty based on one's mental condition or state of mind.

Subrogation   Substitution of the insurer in place of the insured for the purpose of claiming indemnity from a negligent third party for a loss covered by insurance.

Suicide clause   Contractual provision in a life insurance policy stating that if the insured commits suicide within two years after the policy is issued, the face amount of insurance will not be paid; only premiums paid will be refunded.

Supplemental major medical insurance   Group health insurance plan that supplements the benefits provided by a basic medical expense plan. It provides more comprehensive benefits with higher limits and is designed for a catastrophic loss.

Surety   Party who agrees to answer for the debt, default, or obligation of another in the purchase of a bond.

Surety bond   Bond that provides monetary compensation if the bonded party fails to perform certain acts.

Surgical expense insurance   Health insurance that provides for payment of physicians' fees for surgical operations performed in a hospital or elsewhere.

Surplus line broker   Specialized insurance broker licensed to place business with a nonadmitted insurer (a company not licensed to do business in the state).

Surrender-cost index   Method of measuring the cost of an insurance policy to an insured if the policy is surrendered at the end of some specified time period. The time value of money is taken into consideration.

Term insurance   Type of life insurance that provides temporary protection for a specified number of years. It is usually renewable and convertible.

Terminal reserve   In life insurance, the reserve at the end of any given policy year.

Theft   Unlawful taking of money, securities, or other property to the deprivation of the insured; includes burglary, robbery. *See also* **Burglary; Robbery.**

Time limit on certain defenses provision   Provision in an individual health insurance policy that prohibits the company from canceling the policy or denying a claim on the basis of a preexisting condition or misstatement in the application after the policy has been in force for two or three years, with the exception of fraudulent misstatement.

Total disability   In many life insurance waiver-of-premium provisions, total disability means that because of disease or bodily injury, the insured cannot do any of the essential duties of his or her job, or of any job for which he or she is suited based on schooling, training, or experience.

Traditional IRA   An IRA that allows workers to deduct part or all of their IRA contributions if taxable compensation is under a certain limit. Distributions are taxed as ordinary income.

Traditional net cost method   Traditional method of determining cost to an insured of a life insurance policy, determined by subtracting the total dividends received and cash value at the end of a period from the total premiums paid during that period.

Treaty reinsurance   Type of reinsurance in which the primary company must cede insurance to the reinsurer and the reinsurer must accept. The ceding company is automatically reinsured according to the terms of the reinsurance contract.

Trespasser   A person who enters or remains on the owner's property without the owner's consent.

Trust   Arrangement in which property is legally transferred to a trustee who manages it for the benefit of named beneficiaries for their security and to insure competent management of estate property.

Trust-fund plan   Type of pension plan in which all pension contributions are deposited with a trustee who invests the funds according to a trust agreement between employer and trustee. Benefits are paid directly out of the trust fund.

Twisting   Illegal practice of inducing a policyowner to drop an existing policy in one company and take out a new policy in another through misrepresentation or incomplete information.

Ultimate net loss   The total amount that the insurer is legally obligated to pay in a commercial umbrella policy.

Underinsured motorists coverage   Coverage that can be added to the personal auto policy. Coverage pays damages for a bodily injury to an insured caused by the ownership or operation of an underinsured vehicle by another driver. The negligent driver may have insurance that meets the state's financial responsibility or compulsory insurance law requirement, but the amount carried is insufficient to cover the loss sustained by the insured.

Underwriting   The selection and classification of applicants for insurance through a clearly stated company policy consistent with company objectives.

Underwriting cycle   A term to describe the cyclical pattern in underwriting standards, premium levels, and profitability. *See also* **Hard insurance market; Soft insurance market.**

Unearned premium reserve   Liability reserve of an insurance company that represents the unearned part of gross premiums on all outstanding policies at the time of valuation.

Unified tax credit   Tax credit that can be used to reduce the amount of the federal estate or gift tax.

Unilateral contract   Only one party makes a legally enforceable promise.

Uninsured motorists coverage   That part of the personal auto policy designed to insure against bodily injury caused by an uninsured motorist, a hit-and-run driver, or a driver whose company is insolvent.

Unisex rating   A rating system in which the pooled loss experience of both sexes is used to determine the rates charged.

Unit-owners form   *See* **Homeowners 6 policy.**

Universal life insurance   A flexible-premium whole life policy that provides lifetime protection under a contract that separates the protection and saving components. The contract is an interest-sensitive product that unbundles the protection, saving, and expense components.

Unsatisfied judgment fund   Fund established by a small number of states to compensate accident victims who have exhausted all other means of recovery.

Use-and-file law   A rating law that is a variation of a file-and-use; insurers can put into effect immediately any rate changes, but the rates must be filed with regulatory authorities within a certain period after first being used.

Utmost good faith   A higher degree of honesty is imposed on both parties to an insurance contract than is imposed on parties to other contracts.

Value at risk (VAR)   The value of the worst probable loss likely to occur in a given time period under regular market conditions at some level of confidence.

Valued policy   Policy that pays the face amount of insurance, regardless of actual cash value, if a total loss occurs.

Valued policy laws   Laws requiring payment to an insured of the face amount of insurance if a total loss to real property occurs from a peril specified in the law, even though the policy may state that only actual cash value will be paid.

Vanishing-premium policy   A whole life policy in which the premium vanishes or disappears after a number of years.

Variable annuity   Annuity whose periodic lifetime payments vary depending on the level of common stock prices (or other investments), based on the assumption that cost of living and common stock prices are correlated in the long run. Its purpose is to provide an inflation hedge.

Variable life insurance   Life insurance policy in which the death benefit and cash surrender values vary according to the investment experience of a separate account maintained by the insurer.

Verbal threshold   A suit for damages is allowed only in serious cases, such as those involving death or dismemberment.

Vesting   Characteristic of pension plans guaranteeing the employee's right to part or all of the employer's contributions if employment terminates prior to retirement.

Vicarious liability   Responsibility for damage done by the driver of an automobile that is imputed to the vehicle's owner.

Waiver   Voluntary relinquishment of a known legal right.

Waiver-of-premium provision   Benefit that can be added to a life insurance policy providing for waiver of all premiums coming due during a period of total disability of the insured.

War clause   Restriction in a life insurance policy that excludes payment if the insured dies as a direct result of war.

Warranty   Statement of fact or a promise made by the insured, which is part of the insurance contract and which must be true if the insurer is to be liable under the contract.

Weather option   Provides a payment if a specified weather contingency (e.g., temperatures higher or lower than normal) occurs.

Workers compensation insurance   Insurance that covers payment of all workers compensation and other benefits that the employer must legally provide to covered employees who are occupationally disabled.

INDEX

A

A. M. Best Company, 166, 241, 590
AAIS. *See* American Association of Insurance Services (AAIS)
AAU. *See* Associated Aviation Underwriters (AAU)
Abagnale, Frank, 623
Abandonment of property, 406
Absolute assignment, 249, 276
Absolute liability, 418
Abuse exclusion, 473
Accelerated death benefits rider, 262–263
Acceptance, and offer, 183
Accidental and unintentional loss, 21
Accidental death and dismemberment insurance (AD&D), group, 338
Accidental death benefit rider, 261
Accidental death benefits, 261, 323
Accident and health insurance, 28
Accident-only policies, 328–329
Accidents by driver age, 533. *See also* Automobile accidents
Accounting department, 124
Accounting practices, questionable, 163–164
Accounts receivable coverage form, 583
Accumulated dividends, 251
Accumulation period, 292
Accumulation units, 295
ACLI. *See* American Council of Life Insurers (ACLI)
ACO Brokerage, 68
Acordia Inc., 68
Acquisitions, 68. *See also* Mergers and acquisitions
Active retention, 13
Active risk retention, 46, 55
Activities of daily living (ADLs), 320
Acts/decisions exclusion, 456
Actual cash value, 175–176, 459
Actual deferral percentage (ADP) test, 371
Actuary, 108

AD&D. *See* Group accidental death and dismemberment insurance (AD&D)
Additional coverages
    under building and personal property coverage form, 570–571
    under business income coverage form, 575
    under businessowners policy, 585–586
Additional insurance purchase option, under disability-income insurance, 324
Additional living expense coverage, 449
Additional vehicle, coverage of, 496
Add-on plan, 527
Adhesion, contract of, 186
Adjustment bureau, 114
ADLs. *See* Activities of daily living (ADLs)
Administration, of group insurance, 336
Administrative charge, 296
Administrative services only contract, 341
Admitted assets, 154
ADP test, 371
ADR. *See* Alternative dispute resolution (ADR) techniques
Adult day care, 319
Advance funding, 367
Advance premium mutual, 93–94
Advance purchase privilege, 260
Adverse selection, 24
Advisory Council on Unemployment Compensation, 403
Age, auto insurance cost and, 532, 534
Age misstatement clause, 247
Agency agreement, 187
Agency building system, 100
Agency department, 112
Agency relationship, 186–187, 422
Agency systems, 100–102
Agents, 98, 101, 113

competent, 279
    as first underwriters, 110
    law and, 186–188
    licensing of, 157–158
Agent's report, 111
Aggregate deductible, 199
Agricultural firms, 402
AHIP. *See* America's Health Insurance Plans (AHIP)
AIA. *See* American Insurance Association (AIA)
AIDS, 262
AIG. *See* American International Group (AIG)
AIME. *See* Average indexed monthly earnings (AIME)
Aircraft, pleasure, 606
Aircraft damage, 453
Aircraft exclusion, 448
    commercial general liability policy, 596
    ISO personal umbrella policy, 559
Aircraft insurance, 27, 606–607
Aircraft liability exclusion, 471
Aleatory contract, 185
Alien insurer, 154
Allen, Woody, 210
Allied lines, 26
All Quotes Insurance.Com, 518, 543
"All-risks" basis, 581
    with aircraft insurance, 607
"All-risks" policy, 195, 607
All-terrain vehicle, 471
Alternative dispute resolution (ADR) techniques, 429
American Academy of Actuaries, 146, 394, 395
American Association of Insurance Services (AAIS), 440, 590
American Bankers Association, 249
American Benefits Council, 381
American College, 104, 127, 241
American Council of Life Insurers (ACLI), 104, 127, 146, 165, 241, 266

American Institute for Chartered Property Casualty Underwriters, 79, 104, 127
American Insurance Association (AIA), 35, 104, 127, 590
American International Group (AIG), 64, 163, 164
American Risk and Insurance Association, 17, 19
American Society of Pension Actuaries, 146
America's Health Insurance Plans (AHIP), 332, 359
Ameritas Direct, 279, 288
Analysis, of insurance contracts, 193–207. *See also* Financial analysis, in risk management decision making
Animals, liability for, 423
Annual pro rata method, 133
Annual rates-of-return, 278
Annual reports, 155–156, 273
Annual reset method, 297
Annual transit policy, 584
Annuitant, 291–292
Annuities, 290–299
    individual, 291–292
    purpose of, 292
    taxation of, 297–299
    types of, 292–297, 298
Annuity.com, 307
Annuity payments, examples of, 295
Annuity principle, 291–292
Annuity settlement options, 294
Annuityshopper.com, 307
Annuity units, 295
Apparent authority, 187
Appraisal clause, 459
Appraisal provision, under auto damage coverage, 512
Arbitration, 429, 432
ARM. *See* "Associate in Risk Management" (ARM) designation
Asbestos lawsuits, increase in, 433
Assessment method, 156
Assessment mutual, 94
Asset risk, 154
Assets, 132, 137–138
Assets, admitted, 154
Asset valuation reserve, 138
Assigned risk plan, 530
Assignment clause, 249
Assisted living care, 319
Associated Aviation Underwriters (AAU), 606

"Associate in Risk Management" (ARM) designation, 79
Association captive, 47
Assumption-of-risk doctrine, 405, 420
Attachment bond, 628
Attained-age method, 219
Attending physician's report, 111
Attorney fees, under no-fault laws, 528
Attractive nuisance doctrine, 421–422
Auctioneer's bond, 628
Authority, 187
Auto accidents
    damage from, 453
    by driver age, 533
    duties after, 512–513
    staged, 31
    victims, compensating, 521–529
Auto business vehicle exclusion, 499, 509
Auto damage coverage, under Personal Auto Policy, 505–512
Auto insurance, 26, 197, 494–519. *See also* Personal auto policy (PAP) 2005
    commercial, 316–319, 604–606
    complaints, 159–160
    cost of, 241–247
    definition of insured person under, 112
    discounts, 248–250
    expenditures, by state, 243–244
    for high-risk drivers, 240–241
    no-fault, 235–240, 252
    premiums, 253
    saving on, 248
    shopping for, 247–252, 253
    society and, 520–544
Auto insurers, specialty, 531
Auto use, insurance cost and, 534
Automatic cost-of-living adjustment, Social Security, 391
Automatic premium loan, 250–251
Automatic reinsurance treaties, 118
Automatic termination, under personal auto policy, 513
Automobile coverage, misrepresentation in application for, 182
Automobile exclusion, commercial general liability policy, 596
Automobile insurance plan, 530
Automobile owners and operators, 422
Average benefits test, 364
Average high-cost multiple, 403, 405

Average indexed monthly earnings (AIME), 389–390
Average value method, 133
Aviation exclusions, 249
Aviation market, 119
Avoidance, 45, 55
    as a method of handling risk, 12

B

Back-end surrender charge, 231
Bail bond, 628
Bailee forms, 584
Bailees, property held by, 582
Bailee's customers policy, 584
Bailee's liability policy, 584
Baker, Rep. Richard, 166
Balance sheet, 131–134, 136–139
Bankruptcies
    asbestos, 433
    medical bills and, 10
Basic extended reporting period, 600
Basic medical expense insurance, 342
Basis, 298
Belth, Joseph M., 274, 279
Benchmark prices, 275
Beneficiary designation, 247–248
Benefit formulas, retirement, 364–365
Benefit period, 315, 394
    under disability-income insurance, 323
Benefits
    earnings-related, 385
    limits on, in retirement plans, 366, 374–375
    prescribed by law, 385
    Social Security, 387–394
    unemployment insurance, 402
    workers compensation, 407–408
Benefit triggers, under long-term-care insurance, 320
Bernstein, Peter L., 2, 41
Betterment, 511
Bid bond, 627
Bid rigging, 163
Bierce, Ambrose, 18
Bilateral contracts, 185
Bill of rights, patients', 350
Binder, 183
Birthday rule, 203
Blackout period, 214
Blanket basis, 549, 620
Blended families, premature death and, 212
"Block" policies, inland marine, 583
Blood, under Medicare B, 397

Blood transfusions, under Medicare A, 396
Blue Cross and Blue Shield plans, 97, 340–341–342, 359
Boards of directors
directors and officers (D&O) liability and, 433, 611
lax governance by, 432–433
Boatowners insurance, 26
Boatowners package policy, 549–550
Bodily injury and property damage liability, commercial umbrella policy exclusions, 608
Bodily injury coverage, commercial general liability policy, 595
Bodily injury exclusion, 474, 499
Boiler and machinery insurance, 578
Boiler insurance, 27
Bonus annuities, 293
BOP. *See* Businessowners policy (BOP)
Brands and labels coverage, 579
Breach of contract, 417
Breadwinner's death, readjustment period after, 214
Breakdown, of equipment, 578
British Medical Journal, 510
Broad coverage
and major medical, 314
under umbrella policy, 556–557
Broad evidence rule, 176
Brochures, state insurance department, 158
Brokers, 68, 99
licensing of, 157
Builders risk insurance, 577
Builders risk coverage form, 577
Builders risk reporting form, 577
Building and personal property coverage form, 563–572
examples of coverage, 570
property covered under, 569–571
Building collapse, coverage for, 450–451
Building construction, 142
Building coverage, under businessowners policy, 585
Bulk reinsurance, 94
Burglary, 620
Burglary, safe, 620, 622
Burglary insurance, 27
Burns, George, 361
Business, aircraft insurance for, 606
Business activities exclusion, 472–473
Business auto coverage form, 604
Business firms, incorporation of, 14
Business floaters, 584

Business income
from dependent properties, 576–577
extended, 575
insurance, 574–577
loss exposures, 44
loss of, 574–575
Business income (and extra expense) coverage form, 574
Business income and extra expense—extra expense only, 578
Business liability exclusion, ISO personal umbrella policy, 558–559
Business liability insurance, 586
Businessowners policy (BOP), 584–586, 609
liability insurance, 586, 609
special form, 585
Business personal property, 569–570
coverage, under businessowners policy, 585
Business records, exclusion of, 449
Business risk, 633
Business vehicle exclusion, 499, 502

C

Cafeteria plans, 355
Calculable chance of loss, 22
Calculators on the Internet, interactive, 218
Calendar-year deductible, 199, 315, 343
California Earthquake Authority (CEA), 477
Camera and musical instrument dealers coverage form, 583
Cameras, 549
Camper exclusion, 455, 509
Cancellation conditions, 461, 569
Cancellation of personal auto policy, 513
Cancer policy, 328
Cap, equity-indexed annuity, 297
Capacity, insurance industry, 67
Capital budgeting, 74
Capital needs analysis, 217–218
Capital-raising transactions, 120–121
Capital retention approach, 217–218
Capitation fee, 344
Captive.com, 59
Captive insurer, 47–48, 98
tax treatment of, 48
Care, custody, and control exclusion, ISO personal umbrella policy, 559
Career-average earnings, 365

Cargo insurance, 580
Car number and type, insurance cost and, 535
Case reserves, 132, 620
Cash-balance plans, 369–371
Cash dividend, 401
Cash flows, analyzing, 72, 74
Cash needs, life insurance and, 216
Cash option (annuities), 294
Cash option (life insurance), 251
Cash or deferred arrangement (CODA), 371
Cash refund option (annuities), 294
Cash settlement option, 255
Cash-surrender value, 222, 225
Cash value(s), 222
actual, 175–176, 459
policy surrender for, 253
Cash value coverage, 457
Cash-value life insurance, 219, 221, 223, 224, 250
Cash-value option, 253
Cash-value policies, rates of return for, 274
Cash withdrawals, 227
Casualty Actuarial Society (CAS), 79, 109, 146
Casualty insurance, 26–27
marketing systems, 101–102
rate making, 139–143
Casualty insurers, financial performance, 131–136
Catastrophe bonds, 69, 120–121
Catastrophe coverage, 400
Catastrophic illness rider, 262
Catastrophic loss, 22, 121, 580
insurance, 326–327
reinsurance and, 117–118
Catch Me If You Can (Abagnale), 623
Causes-of-loss forms, 572–573
basic form, 572
broad form, 572
special form, 572–573
Ceding commission, 118. *See also* Cession
Ceding company, 115
Cell phone use and crash risk, 510
Centers for Disease Control and Prevention (CDC), 211, 360
Centers for Medicare & Medicaid Services (CMS), 311, 412
Central Limit Theorem, 39
Certified Financial Planner (CFP) designation, 113, 280
Certified Insurance Counselor (CIC) designation, 113

Certified Risk Manager (CRM) designation, 79
Cession, 593. *See also* Ceding commission
CFA. *See* Consumer Federation of America (CFA)
CFP. *See* Certified Financial Planner (CFP) designation
CGL. *See* Commercial general liability (CGL) policy
Chance of loss, 4–5
  calculable, 22
  versus risk, 5
Change-of-plan provision, 248–249
Change of policy provisions, 461, 569
Charitable institutions, liability of, 422
Charles Schwab, 307, 381
Charter, optional federal, 165
Chartered Financial Consultant (ChFC), 113, 280
Chartered Life Underwriter (CLU), 112, 279
Chartered Property Casualty Underwriter (CPCU) program, 113
Check alteration, 620–621, 625
CheckPoint, 480
"Cheeseburger bill," 427
Chesterton, G.K., 618
ChFC. *See* Chartered Financial Consultant (ChFC) designation
Chief risk officer (CRO), 65
Choice no-fault plans, 527
ChoicePoint, 536
Chubb Group of Insurance Companies, 479
CIC. *See* Certified Insurance Counselor (CIC) designation
Citibank, 68
Citigroup, 68
Civil commotion damage, 453
Civil Service Retirement System, 28
Claimant, 417
Claim expenses, 475
Claim forms provision, 325
Claims
  fraudulent, 31–32, 33, 528, 529
  inflated, 32–33
  investigation of, 114
Claims adjustors, 113–114
Claim settlement, 113–115
  under no-fault laws, 528–529
  steps in, 114–115
Claims-made policy, 599–600
Clash loss, 67
Class Action Fairness Act, 427

Class beneficiary, 248
Class rating, 140–141
Class underwriting, 110
"Clean risks," 530
Cliff vesting, 365
Clinical laboratory tests, 397
CLU. *See* Chartered Life Underwriter (CLU)
CLUE Report, 480–481
CMS. *See* Centers for Medicare and Medicaid Services (CMS)
Coalition Against Insurance Fraud, 30, 31, 32, 33, 35, 631
COBRA, 352
CODA. *See* Cash or deferred arrangement
Coin collections, 549
Coinsurance, 200–201
  under building and personal property coverage form, 572
  under business income coverage form, 575–576
  clause, 200
  in group dental insurance, 353
  in health insurance, 201
  and health savings account, 317
  in major medical policies, 315–316, 342
  Medicare, 400
  penalty, 572
  problems with, 201
  provision, 315
  purpose of, 200–201
Collapse, losses involving, 450, 451
Collateral assignment, 249
Collateral source rule, 428–429
Collision coverage, 505, 605, 606
  dropping, 537
Collision damage waiver (CDW) on rental cars, 506–507, 508
Collision liability clause, ocean marine insurance, 580
Collision loss, 505
Combined ratio, 66, 135–136, 431
Commencement of employment, 337
Commercial articles coverage form, 583
Commercial auto insurance, 604–606
Commercial coverages, miscellaneous, 577–580
Commercial crime coverage form, 620–625
Commercial crime insurance program, ISO, 619–620
Commercial general liability (CGL) policy, 593, 594–600, 607
  CGL claims-made policy, 599–600

CGL occurrence policy, 595–599
  definitions under, 599
  insurance limits of, 598–599
  insured under, 598
  liability conditions under, 599
Commercial insurance, 46
  risk management program and, 50–51
Commercial insurers, medical expense plans of, 240
Commercial liability insurance, 592–617
Commercial liability umbrella coverage form, 607
Commercial lines, 26–27
Commercial lines deregulation, 157
Commercial multiple peril insurance, 26
Commercial package policy (CPP), 567–569
Commercial property insurance, 142, 566–591
Commercial umbrella policy, 607–608
Commissioners Standard Ordinary 1980 Mortality Table, 288
Commissioners Standard Ordinary 2001 Mortality Table, 221, 222, 284, 285 288
Commission on Insurance Terminology, 19
Commodity price risk, 63, 64
Common-accident provision, 315
Common law of industrial accidents, 405
Common policy conditions page, 569
Common policy declarations page, 569
Communicable disease exclusion, 473
  ISO personal umbrella policy, 559
Commutative contract, 185
Company adjustor, 114
Company mergers, 94
Comparative negligence, 419–420
Compensation awards, 426
Compensatory damages, 419
Competent parties, 184
Competitive state fund, 407
Complaint divisions, 158
Complaint handling, 162
Completed operations liability, 594
Compounding, 73
  tax-deferred, 291
Comprehensive auto coverage, 505, 605, 606
Comprehensive long-term-care policy, 319

Comprehensive Loss Underwriting Exchange (CLUE) reports, 480, 482

Comprehensive major medical insurance, 343

Compulsory insurance laws, 522, 523

Compulsory programs, 384

Compulsory temporary disability insurance, 28

Computer attacks, 623

Computer fraud, 622

Computer security, 623

Concealment, 182, 460

Conditional contract, 185

Conditional premium receipt, 184

Conditions, 185
  in commercial crime policy, 624–625
  in commercial general liability policy, 599
  in commercial package policy, 569
  in Homeowners 3 policy, 457–462
  in insurance contracts, 196

Condominium association coverage form, 577

Condominium commercial unit-owners coverage form, 577–578

Conference of Consulting Actuaries, 146

Confidential information exclusion, 624

Congressional Budget Office (CBO), and tort reform, 429

Consequential loss, 10–11

Consideration, 184

Consolidated Omnibus Budget Reconciliation Act of 1985 (COBRA), 352

Consolidation, 68
  cross-industry, 68
  in financial services industry, 89–90

Construction costs, 479, 571

Construction risk, 627

Consumer-driven health plans (CDHP), 349–350

Consumer Federation of America (CFA), 232, 241, 266, 274, 282

Consumer knowledge, inadequate, 151

Consumer price index (CPI), 261, 320, 408

Consumer protection, 157–158, 162

Consumers Union, 268, 320

Contingent beneficiary, 248

Contingent business income and extra expense—extra expense only coverage, 579–580

Contingent commission, 110

Contingent liability, 594

Contingent nonforfeiture benefits upon lapse, 321

Continuation of group health insurance, 352

Continuous premium whole life, 221

Contract bonds, 627

Contract of adhesion, 186

Contractors equipment floater, 584

Contracts, transfer of risk by, 13. *See also* Insurance contracts

Contractual liability, 473–474, 594

Contractual liability exclusion, commercial general liability policy, 595

Contractual right, 178

Contributing location, 576

Contribution by equal shares, 202

Contribution limits, in retirement plans, 366, 374–375
  IRA, 299, 301

Contributory negligence doctrine, 405

Contributory negligence laws, 419

Contributory plan, 336

Controlled substance exclusion, 473
  ISO personal umbrella policy, 559

Convergence, 90

Convertible term policies, 219

Coordination-of-benefits provision, 203, 352

Co-payments, 400, 601

Corporal punishment exclusion, 473

Corporate directors/officers, liability of, 434–435, 611

Corporate fraud, 432–433

Corporate governance, lax, 432–433

Corporate reimbursement coverage, 611

Corridor deductible, 199, 343

Corridor test, 226

Cost(s)
  of auto insurance, 532–536
  of homeowners insurance, 478–485
  under no-fault system, 528
  of premature death, 211
  of medical costs, rising, 408
  of risk, 53
  third-party sharing of, 336
  tort liability, rising, 423–424, 425
  umbrella policy, 557

Cost controls, group insurance, 349, 353

Cost information, obtaining, 271–272

Cost of doing business, 31

Cost-of-living adjustment, 354, 391

Cost-of-living rider, 261–262, 323–324

Cost sharing, increased, in health insurance, 349

Cost-sharing provisions, Medicare prescription drugs, 400

Counterfeit money coverage, 450, 623, 626

Court bond, 628

Court decisions, 153

Court delays, under no-fault system, 529

Coverage
  under businessowners policy, 585–586
  under commercial general liability policy, 595–598
  under commercial umbrella policy, 607–608
  under equipment breakdown insurance, 578–580
  under Homeowners 3 policy, 441, 445–451
  under mobilehome insurance, 548
  under National Flood Insurance, 551–552
  under unemployment insurance, 402

Coverage E, homeowners policy, 468–469

Coverage extensions, under building and personal property coverage form, 571

Coverage F, homeowners policy, 469–470

Coverage gap ("donut hole"), Medicare prescription drugs, 400

Coverage parts, commercial package policy, 569

Covered auto, your, 495–496

Covered earnings credits, 386

Covered equipment, 578

Covered perils, in ocean marine insurance, 581

Cowper, William, 545

CPCU. *See* Chartered Property Casualty Underwriter (CPCU) program

CPI. *See* Consumer price index (CPI)

CPP. *See* Commercial package policy (CPP)

Crash risk and cell phone use, 510

Credibility factor, 142

Credit-based insurance scores, 167–168
Credit cards, 449, 550
Credit enhancement, as a benefit of insurance, 29
Credit, in Social Security, 386
Credit insurance, 27
  overcharges, 339
Credit life insurance, 338
Credit line, paying losses via, 47
Creditors, secured, 178
Credit record, 485, 535–536, 538
Credit scores, 482, 167–168
  automobile insurance and, 535–536
Crime, 417
Crime coverage forms, 619
Crime insurance, 27, 618–632
Crime loss exposures, 4
CRM. *See* Certified Risk Manager (CRM) designation
CRO. *See* Chief risk officer (CRO)
CSO tables, 221, 222, 284, 285, 288
Currency exchange rate risk, 63
Current assumption whole life insurance, 232–234
Currently insured status, 387
Current net income, paying losses out of, 47
Current rate, 293
Custodial care, 319
Custom furnishings or equipment exclusion, 509

D

Damaged property, exhibiting, 457
Damages, 418–419. *See also* Physical damage insurance; Property damage
  capping noneconomic, 427, 432
Damage to property of others, 475–476
Dealer property, 583
Death
  faked, 30, 31
  insurable interest at time of, 179
  motor vehicle, 533
  of named insured or spouse, 462
  premature, 8, 211–213
Death benefit(s), 226, 229–230, 233
  accidental, 323
  riders, 261–263
  variable annuity, 295–296
  under workers compensation, 408
Debris removal coverage, 449–450, 570, 585

Deceptive sales practices, 273
Declarations, in insurance contract, 194
  in commercial package policy, 569
Declarations page, in PAP, 496
Decreasing term insurance, 219
Deductibles, 50, 198–199, 329, 451
  aggregate, 199
  auto insurance, 507, 536
  building and personal property coverage form, 571–572
  businessowners policy, 586
  calendar-year, 199, 315, 343
  corridor, 199
  elimination period, 199
  flood insurance, 552
  group dental insurance, 353
  health insurance, 199
  health savings account, 316
  homeowners insurance, 480, 483
  major medical insurance, 315
  Medicare B, 397
  Medicare prescription drug plans, 400
  optional, 527
  property insurance, 199
  purposes of, 198–199
  straight, 199
Defendant, 417
Defense costs coverage, 595
Defense Research Institute, 615
Deferred annuity, 293
  group, 527
Deferred retirement age, 364
Deficit Reduction Act of 2005, 366
Defined-benefit formulas, 365
Defined-benefit plans, 365, 366, 369–371, 375
Defined-contribution formulas, 364–365
Defined-contribution health plan, 350
Defined-contribution plans, 366, 368–369, 374
Definitions, in insurance contract, 194–195
Delayed retirement credit, 390–391
Demutualization, 94, 95
Dental insurance, group, 352–353
Department of Health and Human Services, 401
Dependency period, 214
Dependent events, 69–71
Dependent properties, business income from, 576
Derivatives, weather, 70

Determinable and measurable loss, 21–22
Diagnosis-related groups (DRGs), 396–397
Dickens, Charles, 290
Difference in conditions (DIC) insurance, 580
Diminution in value, 511
Direct billing, 101
Direct loss, 10
Directors and officers liability (D&O) insurance, 433, 611–612
Directors exclusion, ISO personal umbrella policy, 559
Direct physical loss, 451
Direct response system, 100, 101–102
Direct writer, 101
Disability
  partial, 322
  probability of, 321
  residual, 322–323
  total, 259–260, 321–322
Disability income, under workers compensation, 407–408
Disability-income benefits, 322–324
  optional, 323–324
  Social Security, 392
Disability-income insurance, 321–324, 326, 327–328
  compulsory temporary disability insurance, 28
  group, 353–355
  statistics on, 321
Disability insured status, 387, 392
Disaster assistance, federal, 545
Discounts, 73
  auto insurance, 537–538
  taking advantage of, 483
Discovery form, 624
Discovery version policy, 619
Discriminatory insurance rates, 139
Disease management programs, 349
Dishonest acts exclusions, 623
Dismemberment benefits, 323
Distributions
  IRA, 299, 300, 301, 302
  limitations on, 371–372
Dividend options, life insurance, 251–253
  selecting, 252
Dividend policy, 155
Dividends, policies that pay, 278
Dog owner's liability, 469
Dollar-a-day auto insurance, 525–526
Domestic employment, 402
Domestic goods in transit, 582

Domestic insurer, 154
Double indemnity, 261
Double-trigger option, 65
Dram shop law, 420
DRGs. *See* Diagnosis-related groups (DRGs)
Driver education, 535
Driving record
  improving, 538
  insurance cost and, 535
Driving under the influence (DUI), 538
Dry rot, losses involving, 452
Duty(ies)
  legal, 418
  after loss, 457
  after motor vehicle accident/loss, 512–513
  of slight care, 421
Dwelling Property 1, 546–547
Dwelling Property 2, 547
Dwelling Property 3, 547
Dwellings
  coverage for, 445–446
  ISO dwelling program, 546–547
  loss settlement for, 457–459
  perils to, 451–452
Dwelling under construction, losses involving, 452

E

Each-occurrence limit, 599
Early distribution penalty, 366–367
Early retirement age, 364, 387
Earned premiums, 135
Earnings test, 391
Earth movement exclusions, 455
Earthquake endorsement, 476–477, 482
Earthquake exclusion, 455
Earthquake loss, 455
EBRI. *See* Employee Benefit Research Institute (EBRI)
Economically feasible premium, 22–23
Educational fund, 214
eHealthInsurance.com, 332
"Elective deferral," 371, 373
Electrical current damage, 455
Electronic data, 571
Electronic data exclusion, under commercial general liability, 597
Electronic data processing (EDP), 124
Electronic equipment exclusion, 507, 509

Electronic fund transfer cards, 449, 450
Eligibility period, 337
Eligibility requirements
  in group insurance, 336–337
  for long-term-care insurance benefits, 320
  for mobilehome insurance, 548
  under National Flood Insurance Program, 551
  for a traditional IRA, 299
  for unemployment insurance, 402
  for workers compensation, 407
Elimination (waiting) periods, 199, 329
  under disability-income insurance, 323
  under long-term-care insurance, 319–320
  under National Flood Insurance Program, 552
Emergency fund, 214
  size of, 11
Emergency program flood insurance coverages, 551, 552
Employee benefit loss exposures, 44
Employee Benefit Research Institute (EBRI), 359, 381
Employee benefits, 99
  group life and health insurance, 335–360
  retirement plans, 361–382
Employee Benefits Security Administration (EBSA), 381
Employee contributions, 364–365
  to SIMPLE retirement plans, 376
Employee injury exclusion, 474
Employee Retirement Income Security Act of 1974 (ERISA), 49, 153, 341, 362, 608, 612
Employee theft, 620, 621
Employer and employee relationships, liability in, 422–423
Employer contributions, 364–365
  to SIMPLE retirement plans, 376–377
Employer–employee relationship, imputed negligence and, 420
Employer liability laws, 405
Employers, self-insured group health plans and, 49
Employers Liability Act, 603
Employers liability exclusion, commercial general liability policy, 596
Employers liability insurance, 602–603

Employment and Training Administration (ETA), 412
Employment-related practices liability coverage form, 600
Employment-related practices liability insurance, 600–601
Endorsements, 198
  to dwelling program, 547
  to homeowners policy, 476–478, 482–483
  in insurance contracts, 198
Endowment insurance, 223, 225, 253
Enhanced earning benefit, 296
Enron, 371, 432
Enterprise risk, 7–8
Enterprise risk management, 8, 65
Entire-contract clause, 245–246
EPO. *See* Exclusive provider organization (EPO)
Equipment breakdown insurance, 27, 578–580
  examples of losses under, 579
Equipment dealers form, 583
Equity-indexed annuity, 296–297
Equity in rating, 200
ERISA, 49, 153, 341, 362, 608, 612
Errors and omissions coverage, 579
Errors and omissions insurance, 610–611
Essential services expenses, 527
Estate clearance fund, 214
Estate tax, federal, 276–277
Estoppel, 187–188
ETA. *See* Employment and Training Administration (ETA)
Excess basis coverage, 504
Excessive claims, under no-fault laws, 528
Excess liability insurance, 556
Excess-of-loss treaty, 119
Excess plan, 367
Excluded losses, 195
Excluded perils, 195
Excluded property, 196
Exclusionary riders, 329
Exclusion ratio, 298–299
Exclusions, 195–196
  under auto damage coverage, 507, 509
  businessowners policy, 609
  commercial crime coverage form, 623–624
  commercial general liability policy, 595–597
  commercial umbrella policy, 608
  directors and officers (D&O) liability policy, 611–612

employment-related practices liability insurance, 601
Homeowners 3 policy, 455–457
ISO personal umbrella policy, 558–559
life insurance policy, 249
under major medical policies, 316
under Medicare Part B, 397
under PAP, 498–500501–502, 503–504
reasons for, 196
Section II, 470–474
Exclusive agency system, 101
Exclusive remedy doctrine, 408–409
Exhaustion rates, 404, 406
Expected injury exclusion, 471, 595
Expected return, 298
Expediting expenses, 578
Expense charges, 226, 296
Expense loading, 31
Expense ratio, 135–136
Expenses
    company's, 135
    extra, 11, 575
    variable annuity, 296
Experience rating, 142, 335, 403
Explosion damage, 453
Exposure units, 21, 140
Express authority, 187
Extended-benefits program, 402
Extended nonowned coverage endorsement, 500
Extended replacement cost endorsement, 459
Extended reporting period endorsement, 610
Extended reporting periods, 600
Extended term insurance, 253–254
Extra expense coverage form, 576
Extra expenses, 11, 575

F

FBI Computer Crime Survey, 623
Facility-only policy, 319
Facultative reinsurance, 118
Fair Isaac Corporation (FICO), 480, 536
FAIR (Fair Access to Insurance Programs) plans, 555
Fair market value, 176
Fair rental value, 449, 546
Falling objects, damage from, 455
Family and Medical Leave Act of 1993, 601
Family deductible provision, 315, 343
Family purpose doctrine, 420, 422

FAST. See Financial Analysis Solvency Tracking (FAST) scores
Faulty planning and design exclusion, 456–457
Federal Deposit Insurance Corporation (FDIC), 28
Federal disaster assistance, 554
Federal Emergency Management Agency (FEMA), 493, 562
Federal Employees Retirement System, 28
Federal estate tax, 276–277
Federal income tax, 276
Federal regulation, 161. See also Insurance regulation
Federal Reserve, 152
Federal surety bonds, 628
Federal tort reform, 427
Federal Trade Commission, 153, 479
Federal Unemployment Trust Fund, 403
Fee-for-service plans, 341, 399, 401
Fees, variable annuity, 296, 298
Fellow-servant doctrine, 405
FEMA. See Federal Emergency Management Agency (FEMA)
Fences, losses involving, 452
FICO. See Fair Isaac Corporation (FICO)
Fidelity bonds, 27
Fidelity coverage, 625
Fidelity Investments, 307, 381
Fiduciary bond, 628
Field examinations, 167
Field underwriting, 110
Fifth dividend option, 252
50 percent rule, 419–420
File-and-use laws, 157
Filed forms, 583
Filed inland marine forms, 583–584
Film coverage form, 583
Final average pay, 365
Financial analysis, in risk management decision making, 72–75
Financial Analysis Solvency Tracking (FAST) scores, 167
Financial guaranty insurance, 27
Financial institution bonds, 625–626
Financial Institution Bond, Standard Form No. 24 (Revised to April 1, 2004), 625
Financial operations of insurers, 130–148
    life insurance companies, 136–139
    property and casualty insurers, 131–136

Financial performance of insurers, measuring, 135–136, 139
Financial Services Modernization Act of 1999, 68, 90, 152,
Financial regulation, 153–156
Financial responsibility laws, 521–522
Financial risk, 7
Financial risk management, 62–65, 76
Financial services, convergence of, 154–157
Financial services industry, private insurance in, 89–91
Financial statements, 44, 167
Fine arts, 549
Finite reinsurance, 163
Finite risk insurance, 163
Fire
    losses involving, 452
    risk of, 23
Fire damage limit, 599
Fire department service coverage, 450, 570
Fire insurance, 25, 26
Fire legal liability, 597
Fire-protection class, 479
Fire protective sprinkler system damage, 455
First-aid expenses, 475
Five-year term insurance, 285–286
Fixed-amount option, 255–256
Fixed annuity, 292–294
Fixed-period option, 255
Flat dollar amount retirement benefit formulas, 365
Flat percentage retirement benefit formula, 365
Flexible-premium annuity, 294
Flexible-premium life insurance, 225
Flexible spending account, 355
Flex-rating laws, 157
Flood, defined, 551
Flood insurance, 483, 485, 550–555
    myths and facts about, 553–554
    critical problems with, 552, 555
Floor of income, 385
Floor plan coverage form, 583
Flowcharts, 44
Forecasting, based on loss distributions, 71–72
Foreign insurer, 154
Foreign loss exposures, 44
Forgery, 620–621
    coverage, 450, 625
Fortuitous losses, payment of, 20
49 percent rule, 419

"Forum shopping," 428, 433
401(k) plans, 371–373, 375, 376
403(b) plans, 373–374
FPA. *See* Free-of-particular-average clause (FPA)
Fraternal insurers, 94
Fraud, 460. *See also* Insurance fraud
computer, 622
corporate, 432–433
funds transfer, 622
lax public attitude toward, 33
Fraudulent claims, 30–31, 33
cost of, 33
no-fault auto, 528, 529
Fraudulent mortgage coverage, 626
FreeAdvice.com, 436
Free-of-particular-average clause (FPA), 581
Freezing, losses involving, 452
Freezing damage, 455
Freight, 581
Freight insurance, 581
Front-end load, 231
Full retirement age, 387, 391
Full-time worker, 337
Fully funded programs, 385
Fully insured status, 387
Fundamental risk, 6–7
Funded reserve, paying losses out of, 47
Funding agency, 377
Funding instruments, 377
Funds transfer fraud, 622
Fungus, losses involving, 452
Furnished vehicle exclusion, 500, 501
Furs, 549

G

GAAP, 602
Gambling, 178
Gambling, insurance versus, 24–25
GAO. *See* Government Accountability Office (GAO)
Gap insurance, 511
Garage coverage form, 605–606
Garagekeepers coverage, 605–606
Garage operations, 605
Garment contractors floater, 584
Gatekeeper physician, 344
GDP. *See* Gross domestic product (GDP)
Geico Direct, 518, 543
Gender, auto insurance cost and, 532–533
General agency system, 100
General aggregate limit, 598

General average, 581–582
General damages, 419
General liability, 593. *See also* Commercial general liability (CGL) policy
insurance, 26–27
loss exposures, 593–594
Generally Accepted Accounting Principles (GAAP), 124, 136
General Re, 164
General Rule, 297–298
GIC. *See* Guaranteed investment contract (GIC)
Glass coverage, 451, 506, 573
Global Crossing, 432
Golf cart, 471, 499, 514
Golfer's equipment, 549
Goods, shipment of, 584
Goods and services, loss of, 11–12
Good student discount, 535
Government Accountability Office (GAO), 120, 149, 161, 164, 552
Governmental action exclusion, 456
Governmental functions, 422
Governmental liability, 422
Government destruction exclusion, 509
Government entities and unemployment, 402
Government insurance, 27–28
Government property insurance programs, 550–551
Government regulation, 149–172
Grace period, 246, 325
Graded rates, 201
Graded vesting, 365
Gramm-Leach-Bliley Act of 1999, 68, 90, 152
Grave marker coverage, 451
Great Depression, 384
Gross domestic product (GDP), 311
Gross estate, 277
Gross premium, 140
Gross rate, 140
Group accidental death and dismemberment insurance (AD&D), 338
Group basic medical expense insurance, 342
Group captive, 47
Group dental insurance, 351–352
Group disability-income insurance, 353–355
Group health insurance, 311, 327, 352
Group health plans, 49

Group indemnity plans, traditional, 341–343
Group insurance, 335–343
eligibility requirements in, 336–337
marketing, 102
Group life insurance, 236, 337–340
types of, 337–340
Group major medical insurance, 342–343
Group medical expense contractual provisions, 351–352
Group medical expense insurance, 340–343
Group model HMO, 344
Group term life insurance, 337–338
Group universal life insurance, 338–340
Guaranteed investment contract (GIC), 377
Guaranteed minimum value, 297
Guaranteed purchase option, 260–261
Guaranteed rate, 293
Guaranteed renewable policies, 320, 324
Guaranteed replacement cost policy, 459
Guaranteed values for life policy, 254
Guaranty funds, 156

H

Hail damage, 452–453
"Hard" insurance market, 66
Harvard School of Public Health, 312
Hazard, 5–6
Health risk assessment (HRA), 349
Health, risk of poor, 9
Health-care expenditures, rising, 311–312
Health-care system, 310
waste and inefficiency in, 313
HealthGrades, 313
Healthgrades.com, 359
Health insurance, 25, 27, 28, 309–333. *See also* Disability-income insurance; Long-term-care insurance; Major medical insurance
coinsurance in, 201
coverages, 313–326
deductibles in, 199
fraud, 30, 31
group, 327, 340–356

reasons for not having, 312–313
for retired workers, 349
shopping for, 326–329
Health insurance pools, state, 28
Health Insurance Portability and
    Accountability Act (HIPPA) of
    1996, 325, 337, 351, 352
Health maintenance organizations
    (HMOs), 97–98, 327, 340, 341,
    343–349, 398, 407
Health savings account (HSA),
    316–318
  contributions, 317
  and controlling health-care costs,
    318
  eligibility, 316
  high deductible, 316–317
  rationale, 317
  tax treatment, 317
Hedging, 8, 14
  of commodity price risk, 64
  versus insurance, 25
  with weather derivatives, 70
Hedging price risks, 14, 63
Hedrick, William B., 593
High-deductible health plan (HDHP),
    350
Higher-premium policy, change to,
    248
Highly compensated employees,
    363
High maximum limits, and major
    medical, 314–315
High-premium products, 234
High-risk drivers, auto insurance for,
    530–531
High-risk pools, 328, 329, 530
High severity of loss, 52
HIPPA, 325, 337, 351
Historical loss data, 44
HMOs. See Health maintenance
    organizations
Hold-harmless clause, 13, 50
Holding company schemes, 94, 95,
    96
Home business insurance coverage
    endorsement, 478
Home construction, 479
Home health-care policy, 319
Home health-care services, 395–396,
    397
Homeowners 2 (HO-2) policy, 441,
    442
Homeowners 3 (HO-3) policy, 441,
    442
  analysis of, 441–442, 445–451
  conditions in, 457–462

exclusions under, 455–457
perils insured against, 451–455
Homeowners 4 (HO-4) policy, 441,
    442
Homeowners 5 (HO-5) policy, 441,
    443
Homeowners 6 (HO-6) policy, 441,
    443
Homeowners 8 (HO-8) policy, 441,
    443
Homeowners Annual Insurance
    Premiums table (2006),
    484–485
Homeowners insurance, 26, 440–441
  comparison of, 442–443
  cost of, 478–486
  Section I, 439–466
  Section II, 467–493
Homeowner's insurer, choice of, 483
Homeowners policies
  eligible dwellings under, 440
  endorsements to, 476–478
  overview of, 440–441
  saving money on, 491–493
  shopping for, 483
  suggestions for buying, 482–486
Home service life insurance, 236
Home warranty, 459
Honeywell, 65
Hospice care, 396
Hospital care, inpatient, 311,
    394–395
Hospital expense insurance, 342
Hospital expenses, 311–312, 314
Hospital indemnity policy, 328
Hospital Insurance (Medicare Part A),
    394–397
Hospital services, outpatient, 397
Hospital-surgical insurance, 314
Household appliance damage, 455
Hovercraft, exclusion of, 448, 471
Hubbard, Kin, 361
Huebner Foundation and Geneva
    Association, 17
Hull insurance, 580
Human life value, 8, 213
Human life value approach, to life
    insurance, 213
Human resources loss exposures, 44
Hurricane Dennis, 136
Hurricane Katrina, 6, 7, 67, 76, 117,
    136, 166, 394, 454, 485, 551
Hurricane Rita, 6, 7, 136
Hurricane Wilma, 6, 7, 136
Hurricanes, 10 most costly in U.S., 7
"Hypothetical accounts," cash bal-
    ance plans, 369

I

IBNR. See Incurred-but-not-reported
    (IBNR) reserve; Incurred but not
    yet reported (IBNR) claims
Ice damage, 455
Identity theft insurance, 478, 479
III. See Insurance Information
    Institute (III)
ImmediateAnnuites.com, 307
Immediate annuity, 293
  advantages of, 293
Impaired property, property damage
    to, 597
Impairment, severe cognitive, 320
Implied authority, 187
Implied warranties, in ocean marine
    insurance, 581
Imputed negligence, 420
Income. See also Business income
  during dependency period, 214,
    216
  floor of, 385
  during readjustment period, 214,
    216
  during retirement, 8–9
Income and expense statement,
    134–136, 138–139
Income annuity payments, 294, 295
Income for elected period option, 255
Income needs, life insurance and, 216
Income of elected amount option,
    255–256
Income payments, fixed annuity,
    437–438, 439. See also
    Individual annuities
Income tax, federal, 276. See also
    Internal Revenue Service (IRS)
Income-tax treatment. See also
    Taxation
  for retirement plans, 362–363
Incontestable clause, 246
Incorporation, as risk transfer, 14
Incurred-but-not-reported (IBNR)
    reserve, 133
Incurred-but-not-yet-reported (IBNR)
    claims, 599
Indemnification for loss, 21, 28
Indemnity payments, 408
Indemnity, principle of, 175–178, 202
  exceptions to, 176–178
Independent adjustor, 114
Independent agency system, 101
Independent events, 69–71
Independent Insurance Agents &
    Brokers of America, 507, 508,
    562, 590

Indeterminate-premium whole life insurance, 234
Indexing method, equity-indexed annuity, 297
Indirect loss, 10–11
Indirect loss exclusion, 624
Individual annuities, 291–292
    taxation of, 297–299
Individual equity, 385
Individual health insurance coverages, 309–333
Individual medical expense contractual provisions, 324–326
Individual practice association plan (IPA), 345
Individual retirement accounts (IRAs), 214, 216, 299–304
    adequacy of funds, 302–304
    contributions, 299, 301
    distributions, taxation of, 300–301
    investments, 301
    rollover account, 301
    Roth IRA, 301–304
    spousal, 300
    tax advantages, 299, 301
    traditional IRA, 299–301
    types of, 299, 301
withdrawal of funds, 300
Individual retirement annuity, 301
Industrial life insurance, 236
Inflated claims, 32
Inflation guard endorsement, 476, 482
Inflation guard option, 572
Inflation-indexed annuity option, 294
Inflation protection, under long-term-care insurance, 320
Inherent vice, 196
Initial reserve, 289
Injury, 424–425, 600–601. See also Personal injury
Inland marine floaters, 548–549
Inland marine forms, 583–584
Inland marine insurance, 26, 27, 580, 582–584
    major classes of, 582–583
Inland Marine Underwriters Association, 590
Innocent misrepresentation, 181
Inpatient hospital care, 314, 394–395
Inpatient hospital expenses, 311–312, 314
Inside the premises insuring agreement, 621–622
Insolvency, protection against, 166–167

Inspection and surveys, 569
Inspection of records and books, 569
Inspection report, 111
Installment refund option, 294
Institute for Civil Justice, 529
Institute of Medicine, 431
Insurable interest, 457
    principle of, 178–179
Insurable risk, 21–23
Insurance. See also Group insurance
    advantages of, 51
    adverse selection and, 24
    basic characteristics of, 19–21
    benefits to society, 28–29
    costs to society, 29–33
    defined, 19
    disadvantages of, 51–52
    gambling versus, 24–25
    hedging versus, 25
    investment returns on, 67–68
    as method for handling risk, 14
    pricing of, 139–143. See also Rate making
    risk and, 18–36
    risk management program and, 50–52
    surety bonds versus, 626, 627
    types of, 25–28
    unemployment, 401
Insurance.com, 282, 465, 489
Insurance agent bond, 628
Insurance agents and brokers errors and omissions policy, 611
Insurance brokerage mergers and acquisitions, 68
Insurance brokers, 68, 99, 157
Insurance claims. See Claims
Insurance commissions, state, 151
Insurance Committee for Arson Control, 631
Insurance companies
    financial reserves of, 132–134, 138, 154
    mergers and acquisitions, 68
    operations of, 130–148
    other functions of, 124
    ratings, 279
Insurance contracts
    analysis of, 193–207
    complaint records, 115
    distinct legal characteristics of, 185–186
    parts of, 194–196
    requirements of, 183–184
Insurance costs, under no-fault system, 528

Insurance coverage, misrepresentation in application for, 181
Insurance coverage bids, analyzing, 73–74
Insurance fraud, 29–33, 592. See also Fraud
Insurance industry
    capacity, 67
    consolidation in, 68
    profitability, 137
    regulation of, 149–172
    September 11 terrorist attack and, 67, 121
    as source of investment funds, 29
Insurance Information Institute (III), 17, 35, 79, 88, 105, 107, 127, 146, 206, 465, 489, 518, 543, 562, 590, 615
Insurance Institute for Highway Safety, 510, 590
Insurance Journal, 35–36, 105, 146
Insurance laws, 631. See also specific laws
    compulsory, 522, 523
Insurance limits, commercial general liability policy, 598–599
Insurance market, dynamics of, 65–69
Insurance rates. See also Rate making
    adequate, 112, 608
    reasonable, 151
Insurance regulation, 149–172
    areas regulated, 153–141
    goal of, 139
    historical development of, 151–152
    modernizing, 165
    problems and issues, 163–168
    reasons for, 150–151
    state vs. federal, 161–163
Insurance Regulatory Examiners Society, 171
Insurance Research Council (IRC), 36, 518, 502, 528, 529, 543, 590
Insurance risk, 154–155
Insurance score, 480, 481, 535–536
Insurance Services Office (ISO), 109, 146, 195, 440, 479, 511, 546, 557, 567, 590, 594, 599, 616
    commercial crime insurance program, 619–620
    commercial liability umbrella coverage policy, 607
    commercial package policy (CPP), 567–569
    crime coverage forms, 619
    dwelling program, 546–547

homeowners coverages, comparison of, 442–443
personal umbrella policy, 485–486, 557–559
Insurance to full value, 200–201
Insurance to half value, 200–201
Insure.com, 35, 105, 241, 266, 282, 307, 332, 465, 489, 518, 543, 562
Insured contract, 595
Insured locations, 470, 473
Insured persons
death of, 462
defined, 197, 445
under PAP, 112, 497–498, 501, 503
Insured's product, property damage to, 596
Insured status, types of, 386–387
Insurer fraud. *See* Fraud
Insurers
cost variation among, 271
financial operations of, 130–148
financial strength of, 279
formation and licensing of, 153–154
growth of assets, 122
insolvency of, 166–167
liquidation of, 156
methods for regulating, 153
private, 92–98
sales and marketing activities of, 112
solvency of, 150, 154–156
suits against, 459
taxation of, 158–161
types of, 92–98
Insurer's option, 460
Insurers Supervision, Rehabilitation, and Liquidation Model Act, 156
Insuring agreements, 195, 468–470
under auto damage coverage, 505
commercial crime coverage form, 620–623
directors and officers (D&O) liability insurance, 611
employment-related practices liability insurance, 600–601
under PAP, 497, 500, 502–503
INSWEB, 36, 105, 191, 241, 266, 282, 332, 465, 489, 518, 543, 562
Integrated risk program, 64
Intentional injury exclusion, 471, 498–499
Intentional loss exclusion, 456
Intentional torts, 417

Interest-adjusted cost method, 270–271
Interest credit, 369
Interest option, 255
Interest rate risk, 155
Interest rates, 226
decline in, 228
Internal limits, 316
Internal rate of return, 74
Internal Revenue Service (IRS), 48, 300, 355, 362, 367. *See also* Taxation
International Financial Risk Institute, 59, 79
International Foundation of Employee Benefit Plans, 359
International Risk Management Institute (IRMI), 465, 489, 518, 543
Interstate Commission of Employment Security Administrators, 403
Intranets, 75–76
In-transit coverage, 625
Inventory shortages exclusion, 624
Investment(s)
insurance industry as source of funds for, 29
regulation of, 155
Investment guarantee contract, 377
Investment income, 123
Investment income ratio, 136
Investment in the contract, 298
Investment management charge, 296
Investment returns, on insurance, 67–68
Invitees, 421, 593
Ionesco, Eugene, 210
IPA. *See* Individual practice association plan (IPA)
IPG. *See* Immediate-participation guarantee (IPG) plan
IRA. *See* Individual retirement accounts (IRAs)
Iraq war, 394
IRC. *See* Insurance Research Council (IRC)
Irrevocable beneficiary, 248
IRS. *See* Internal Revenue Service (IRS)
ISO. *See* Insurance Services Office (ISO)

J

Jewelers block coverage form, 583
Jewelry, personal articles floater, 549

Johnson & Higgins, 68
Joint and several liability rule, 429
Joint-and-survivor annuity option, 294
Joint-and-survivor income option, 256
Joint business venture, imputed negligence and, 420
Joint Economic Committee, 105th Congress, 520
Joint underwriting associations (JUAs), 530
Judgment method, 132
Judgment rating, 140
Judicial bonds, 628
"Judicial hellholes," 428
Junk bonds, 154
Jury awards, higher, 426
Jury Verdict Research, 426, 431
Justice system. *See* Tort liability problems

K

Kaiser Family Foundation, 312
Keogh plans, 374–376
Keyes, Mike, 130

L

Landlord's furnishings, coverage for, 451
Large-loss principle, 198
Large numbers, law of, 4, 6, 14, 20, 37–40
Last clear chance rule, 420
Law
insurance agents and, 186–188
loss due to, 455
Law of large numbers, 4, 6, 14, 20, 37–40
Law of negligence, 418–420
res ipsa loquitur, 420–421
specific applications of, 421–423
Lawsuit Abuse Reduction Act, 427
Lawsuits
asbestos, 433
delays in settling, 426
workers compensation and, 408
Lawyers.com, 191
Leader location, 577
Legal competence, 184
Legal defense, businessowners policy, 609
Legal defense costs, 11
Legal defense, employment-related practices liability insurance, 601

Legal duty, 418
Legal function, of insurance companies, 124
Legal hazard, 6
Legal Information Institute (Cornell Law School), 191, 437
Legal liability, 304, 328, 417–418, 473, 475. *See also* Liability
Legally competent, 184
Legal outcomes, uncertainty of, 425
Legal principles, fundamental, 174–192
Legal purpose, 184
Legal reserves, 221–222, 287
Legal wrong, 417
Level-premium method, 221
Lewis, Joe E., 309
Liabilities, 132–134, 138
Liability. *See also* General liability; Liability limits
  absolute, 418
  contractual, 473–474, 594
  governmental, 422
  legal, 417–418, 473, 475, 593–594
  products, 426, 427–428, 594
  strict, 418
Liability awards, higher, 426
Liability coverage, 545–561. *See also* Liability insurance
  aircraft insurance, 607
  under boatowners package policy, 549–550
  commercial auto insurance, 604
  garage coverage form, 605
  under Personal Auto Policy, 497–500
  under yacht insurance, 550
Liability insurance, 25–27. *See also* Commercial liability insurance; Liability coverage
  adequate, 536
  excess, 556
  general, 26–27
  personal, 468–469
Liability limits, 447–448, 457
  under auto damage coverage, 510–511
  under Personal Auto Policy, 500
  under personal property coverage, 446–447
Liability loss exposures, 44, 55, 594
Liability risks, 11, 55, 416–438. *See also* Tort liability problems
Liability without fault, 405–406, 601
Liberalization clause, 461
License and permit bonds, 627–628
Licensees, 421

Lieberman, Gerald F., 174
Lien, 11
Life annuity due, 286–287
Life annuity (no refund), 294
Life annuity with guaranteed payments option, 294
Life annuity with period certain, 294
Life expectancy, 211–212
Life income options, 256
  with guaranteed period, 256, 257, 258
  with guaranteed total amount, 256, 258
  joint-and survivor, 256
Life insurance, 25, 210–243. *See also* Ordinary life insurance
  additional benefits added to, 259–263
  amount to own, 213–219
  best type of, 278
  buying, 268–269
  calculation of premiums, 284–289
  comparison of policies, 235
  contractual provisions, 244–267
  cost variations in, 271
  determining cost of, 269–273
  determining need for, 212, 277–278
  economic justification of, 212
  factors in replacing, 273
  group, 357–340
  insurable interest and, 178–179
  low-cost, 278–279
  principle of indemnity and, 177–178
  rate making, 143, 157
  shopping for, 277–280
  taxation of, 275–277
  types of, 219–225
Life insurance companies, financial performance, 136–139
Life insurance marketing systems, 100
Life insurance policy reserves, 138
Life Office Management Association (LOMA), 127, 241–242
Life settlement, 262, 263
Lifetime reserve, 395
Lightning, losses involving, 452
Limited-payment life insurance, 223
Limited-payment policy, 223
Limited policies, 328
Limit of liability. *See* Liability limits
Limits, in compulsory auto insurance, 523
LIMRA International, Inc., 105, 128, 218, 242
Line underwriters, 109
Linton, M. Albert, 274

Linton yield, 274
Liquidation of insurers, 156
Liquidation period, 293
Liquor liability exclusion, commercial general liability policy, 592–595
Livery conveyance exclusion, 499, 501, 504, 507
Living expense coverage, 449, 547
Lloyd's of London, 95–97, 105
Loading, 140
Loading allowance expenses, 287
Loan provision, 401(k) plan, 372
Location of home, insurance cost and, 479
LOMA. *See* Life Office Management Association (LOMA)
Long-range deficit, reducing, 393–394, 395
Long-tail claims, 599
Long-term-care insurance, 319–321
Long-term-care rider, 262–263
Long-term plans, 354
Loss(es)
  accidental and unintentional, 21, 22
  calculable chance of, 22
  catastrophic, 22, 580
  determinable and measurable, 21–22
  duties after, 457
  excluded, 195–196, 451–452
  indemnification for, 21, 28–29
  paying, 47
  pooling of, 19–20
  potential, 43–45, 55
  social costs of, 13
  sustained during prior insurance, 624–625
Loss-adjustment expenses, 134
Loss assessment, 476
Loss assessment coverage, 450
Loss control, 12–13, 140
Loss-control investment decisions, 74–75
Loss-control services, 124
Loss damage waiver (LDW), 506
Loss distributions, forecasting based on, 71–72
Loss experience, 141–143
Loss exposures, 42
  analyzing, 44–45, 55
  general liability, 593–594
  identifying, 44, 54–55
  techniques for treating, 45–52, 55–56
Loss forecasting, 69–72
  using normal distribution, 82–83

Loss frequency, 44–45
Loss handling, appropriate methods for, 52, 55–56
Loss of consortium, 603
Loss of earnings, 527
Loss-of-sight benefits, 323
Loss-of-use coverage, 449
Loss payment, 460
Loss prediction, 76
Loss prevention, 12, 19, 46
Loss ratio, 135
Loss ratio method, 133, 141
Loss reduction, 12–13, 46
Loss reserves, 132
Loss settlement, 457–459
Loss severity, 45, 52
Loss-sustained form, 624
Loss-sustained version policy, 619
Lost-instrument bond, 628
Low-cost auto insurance, 525–526
Low-cost life insurance policy, 278–279
Low-cost variable annuities, 296
Lower-premium policy, change to, 249
Low-load life insurance, 278–279
Low-premium products, 233–234
Low severity of loss, 52

M

McCarran-Ferguson Act, 152, 161, 162–163
McCartt, Anne, 510
McEvoy, S., 510
McQuade, Rebecca A., 566
Maintenance bond, 627
Major medical insurance, 314–316, 342–343
Malicious mischief, 452, 453
Managed care, 343
    major medical insurance and, 316
Managed care plans, 341, 343–349
    advantages and disadvantages of, 345–347
    current developments in, 347–349
    declining HMO enrollments, 347–349
    new cost management strategies, 349
Managerial system, 100
Manual rating, 141
Manufacturing location, 576–577
Marine insurance, 26, 27. See also Boat insurance; Boatowners package policy; Watercraft entries

Marital deduction, 277
Marital status, auto insurance cost and, 533
Market conduct examinations, 162
Marketing systems, 99–102
Marsh and McLennan Companies, Inc., 68
Maryland Automobile Insurance Fund, 28, 531
Mass merchandising, 102
Matching option, 376
Material representation, 181, 182
Maximum cap rate or cap, 297
Maximum possible loss, 45
Maximum probable loss, 45
Means of transportation and communication, 583, 584
Means test, 385, 398
Measurable loss, 21–22
Mediation, 429
Medicaid, 313, 319
Medical bills
    bankruptcies caused by, 10
    catastrophic, 54
Medical care
    quality of, 313
    under workers compensation, 407
Medical errors, 430, 431
Medical expense contractual provisions, 324–326
Medical expense coverage
    under boatowners package policy, 550
    under businessowners policy, 609
Medical expense limit, under commercial general liability policy, 599
Medical expenses, under no-fault laws, 527
Medical incident, 609
Medical Information Bureau (MIB), 111
Medical insurance. See Blue Cross and Blue Shield plans; Group medical expense insurance; Health insurance; Managed care plans; Medical expense entries; Medical payments coverage; Medicare; Medigap insurance; Social Security
Medical Insurance (Medicare Part B), 397–398
    amount paid, 397
    exclusions, 397
    monthly premium, 397–398
Medical malpractice, 27, 426, 427, 429–432

Medical necessity trigger, 320
Medical payments coverage
    commercial general liability policy, 597–598
    under Personal Auto Policy, 500–502
    under yacht insurance, 550
Medical payments exclusions, 474
Medical payments to others, 469–470
Medical savings account plans, Medicare, 399
Medicare, 28, 313, 319, 386, 387, 394–401
    defined, 394
    financing of Medicare, 398
    Medicare Advantage Plans (Part C), 398–399
    Medicare Prescription Drug Plans, 399–401
    Medigap insurance, 401
    Original Medicare Plan, 394–398
    other Medicare health plans, 399
Medicare financial crisis, 398
Medicare.gov, 360, 412
Medicare cost plans, 399
Medicare HMOs, 398
Medicare medical savings accounts plans, 399
Medicare Part A (Hospital Insurance), 394–397
Medicare Part B (Medical Insurance), 397–398
    amount paid, 397
    exclusions, 397
    monthly premium, 397–398
Medicare PPOs, 398–399
Medicare Prescription Drug Coverage (Part D), 399
    costs of coverage, 399–400
    financial help, 400–401
    other provisions, 401
Medicare private fee-for-service plans, 399
Medicare special needs plans, 399
Medigap insurance, 401
Mental abuse exclusion, 473
Mercer Human Resource Consulting, 346, 347
Mergers and acquisitions
    company, 94
    insurance brokerage, 68
    insurance industry, 68
Merit rating, 141–143
Messenger, 622
MIB. See Medical Information Bureau (MIB)

Migrant and Seasonal Agricultural Worker Protection Act, 603
Minimum age and service requirements, for retirement plans, 364
Minimum coverage requirements, for retirement plans, 363–364
Minimum distribution requirements, 367
Minimum vesting standards, 365–366
Minor children as beneficiaries, 248
Miscellaneous insurance contract provisions, 196
Miscellaneous surety bonds, 628
Miscellaneous-type vehicle endorsement, 514
Misrepresentation, 181, 182
  innocent, 181
Misstatement of age or sex clause, 247
Mobile equipment and property, in inland marine insurance, 582–583
Mobile equipment exclusion, commercial general liability policy, 596
Mobilehome insurance, 547–548
Modified life insurance, 234
Modified no-fault plan, 527
Modified prior-approval law, 156
Mold, losses involving, 452
Monetary threshold, 526
Money
  theft of, 621–622
  time value of, 72–73, 84
Money order coverage, 623
Money purchase plan, 368
Mono-line policy, 567
Monopoly state fund, 407
Monte Carlo simulation and retirement, 301–302
Monthly retirement benefits, Social Security, 388
Mopeds, 499, 514
Morale hazard, 5, 199
Moral hazard, 5, 110, 175, 178
Morgan, Henry, 494
Mortality and expense (M&E) charges, 231, 340
Mortality and expense (M&E) risk charge, 296
Mortality charge, 226, 228
Mortality table, 221, 222, 284, 285, 288
Mortgage clause, 460
Mortgage redemption fund, 214

Motorcycles, 499, 514
Motor home exclusion, 509
Motor homes, 514
Motorists. *See* Automobile insurance; Uninsured motorists coverage
Motor vehicle liability exclusion, 470–471
Motor vehicles, exclusion of, 448
MRI tests, 408
Multicar discount, 535
Multiple distribution systems, 102
Multiple-line policy, 26, 567
Musical instruments, 549
Mutual holding company, 94–95, 96
Mutual insurers, 93–95, 96
Myers, Robert J., 383

N

NAIC. *See* National Association of Insurance Commissioners (NAIC)
NAII. *See* National Association of Independent Insurers (NAII)
NALP. *See* Net annual level premium (NALP)
Named insured, 197
Named-perils policy, 195, 441
National Academy of Social Insurance, 412
National Alliance for Insurance Education and Research, 79
National Association of Health Underwriters, 332
National Association of Insurance and Financial Advisors, 242
National Association of Insurance Commissioners (NAIC), 115, 128, 153, 154, 156, 157, 164, 166, 167, 171, 203, 242, 250, 267, 270, 272, 319, 332, 339, 352, 465, 518, 562, 582
  Policy Illustration Model Regulation, 272–273
National Association of Mutual Insurance Companies, 36, 105, 128
National Association of Surety Bond Producers, 631
National Center for State Courts, 426
National Committee for Quality Assurance (NCQA), 313, 347, 360
National Conference of Insurance Guaranty Funds, 171
National Conference of Insurance Legislators, 171

National Council on Compensation Insurance Holdings, Inc., 412, 601, 616
National Flood Insurance Program (NFIP), 550–555
  myths and facts about, 553–554
  critical problems with, 552, 555
National Insurance Act of 2006, 166
National Safety Council, 20, 616
National Underwriter Company, 242, 267
National Underwriter Data Services, 431
Nationwide marine definition, 582
NCQA. *See* National Committee for Quality Assurance (NCQA)
Needs approach, to life insurance, 214–217
Neglect exclusion, 456
Negligence, 418, 429–430
  defenses against, 419–420
  elements of, 418–419
  imputed, 420
  law of, 418–423
  specific applications of, 421–423
  res ipsa loquitur and, 420–421
Negligence system, 528
Net amount at risk, 222
Net annual level premium (NALP), 286–287
Net cost method, traditional, 269–270
Net gain from operations (net income), 139
Net payment cost index, 270, 271
Net present value, 74
Net retention, 116
Net single premium (NSP), 143, 284–286
Network model HMO, 344–345
New life insurance, amount needed, 216–217
Newly acquired auto, 496
Newly acquired premises coverage, 571, 579
New York State Insurance Department, 206
NFIP. *See* National Flood Insurance Program (NFIP)
No-fault automobile insurance, 526–529
  arguments for and against, 528–529
No-fault benefits, 527
No-fault laws, evaluation of, 529
No-lapse guarantee, 225
Nolo.com, 191, 437

Nonadmitted insurer, 97, 99
Nonbuilding agency system, 100
Noncancellable policy, 324–325
Noncontributory plan, 336
Nondeductible IRA, 300
Nonelective contribution option, 376
Nonfiled forms, 583
Nonfiled inland marine forms, 584
Nonforfeiture benefits, 320
Nonforfeiture options, 253–254
Noninsurance transfers, 12, 13–14, 50, 55
Nonoccupational disability, 354
Nonowned vehicle, 500, 501, 502, 504, 506, 509
Nonparticipating policy, 251
Nonprofit organizations and unemployment, 402
Nonprofit Risk Management Center, 59, 79
Nonqualified annuity, 297
Nonrenewable for stated reasons only provision, 324
Nonrenewal of personal auto policy, 513
Nonsurgical treatment, 314
"No pay, no play" laws, 526
No reasonable belief exclusion, ISO personal umbrella policy, 559
Normal distribution, 39. *See also* Law of large numbers
Normal retirement age, 364
Notice, 457
Notice of claim provision, 325
Notice of loss, 114
Notice of 10-day right to examine policy, 325
NSP. *See* Net single premium (NSP)
Nuclear energy exclusion, 474, 499
Nuclear hazard exclusion, 165
Nuclear weapon, radiation, war exclusion, 502
Numeric summary, 272
Nursing care, skilled, 395
Nursing home, chance of entering, 319

O

OASDI. *See* Old-age, survivors, and disability insurance (OASDI)
Obesity lawsuits, 427, 429
Objective probability, 4
Objective risk, 3–4
Obligee, 626
Obligor, 626
Occurrence, 468, 595

Occurrence policy, 595, 599
Ocean marine insurance, 27, 580–582
OEM. *See* Original equipment manufacturer (OEM)
Offer and acceptance, 183–184
Office of the Chief Actuary (Social Security Administration), 412–413
Office of the Commissioner of Insurance, State of Wisconsin, 206
Office of Thrift Supervision, 91
Officers exclusion, ISO personal umbrella policy, 559
Off-premises property, 571
Off-premises rental property, exclusion of, 449
Old-Age, Survivors, and Disability Insurance (OASDI), 28, 367, 386–387
  long-range actuarial deficit, 393
  payroll tax for, 367
  personal retirement accounts proposal, pros and cons, 396
On premises coverage, 625
Open-competition laws, 157
Open-perils policy, 195
Operational risks, 65
Opportunity cost of buying life insurance, 218–219
Optional coverages
  under business income coverage form, 576
  under building and personal property coverage form, 572
  under businessowners policy, 586
Optional deductibles, 527
Optional disability-income benefits, 323–324
Optional federal charter, 165
Optionally renewable policy, 324
Optional no-fault benefits, 527
Options, to protect against adverse stock price movements, 63, 64
Ordinance, loss due to, 455
Ordinance or law coverage, 451, 579
Ordinary life insurance, 221–223
  net annual level premium for, 287
  net single premium for, 143, 286
  nonforfeiture options of, 253–254
Oregon Mutual Insurance Company, 130
Original-age method, 219
Original equipment manufacturer (OEM), 511
Original Medicare Plan, 394–398
  competition from private plans, 401

Other insurance and service agreement, 459
Other-insurance provisions, 201–203
Other insurance under PAP, 500
  medical payments coverage, 502
  uninsured motorists coverage, 504
Other property, employee theft of, 620
Other recovery sources, under auto physical damage coverage, 511–512
Other-states insurance, 603
Other-than-collision loss, 505–506
Outdoor property, 571
Out-of-pocket expenses, and health-care savings account, 317
Out-of-state coverage, under Personal Auto Policy, 500
Outpatient hospital services, 311, 314, 397
Outside the premises insuring agreement, 622
Overall operating ratio, 136
Owned vehicle, 500, 502
Ownership clause, 245
Oxley, Michael, 166

P

Package policies, 567–569
PACE (programs of all-inclusive care for the elderly) and Medicare, 399
"Padded" claims, 32
PAF. *See* Personal articles floater (PAF)
Paid-up additions option, 251
Paid-up contract, 252
Pain and suffering payment, under no-fault system, 529
Pair or set, loss to, 459
PAP. *See* Personal auto policy (PAP) 2005
Parental liability, 423
Partial disability, 322
Participating policy, 251
Participation rate, 297
Particular average, 581
Particular risk, 6–7
Passive retention, 13
Passive risk retention, 46
Passenger hazard exclusion, 514
Past-service credits, 365
Patients' bill of rights, 350
Patio, losses involving, 452
Paul v. Virginia, 151–152

Pavement, losses involving, home-owners policy, 452
Pay credit, 369
Payment bond, 627
Payment of fortuitous losses, 20
Payment of loss, under auto damage coverage, 511
Payout period, 293
PBGC. *See* Pension Benefit Guaranty Corporation (PBGC)
Pecuniary interest, 93
Pension accrual benefit, 354
Pension Benefit Guaranty Corporation (PBGC), 366, 381
Pension benefits, funding of, 367
Pension Protection Act of 2006, 362, 366, 371, 372
Pensions. *See* Retirement plans
Percentage deductibles, 451
Percentage participation clause, 201. *See also* Coinsurance
Percentage test, 363
Per diem policy, 319, 321
Performance bond, 627
Perils, 5
  covered, HO-3, 451–455
  of the sea, 581
  imminent, 581
Permitted disparity rules, 367
Personal and advertising injury exclusion, commercial general liability policy, 597
Personal and advertising injury liability, 597
  commercial umbrella policy exclusions, 608
Personal and advertising injury limit, 599
Personal articles floater (PAF), 548–549
Personal auto policy (PAP) 2005, 495–496
  auto physical damage coverage under, 505–512
  duties after accident or loss, 512–513
  general provisions of, 513–514
  liability coverage, 497–500
  medical payments coverage, 500–502
  summary of coverages, 496
  uninsured motorists coverage under, 502–505
Personal balance sheet, 217
Personal contract, 185–186
Personal effects and property of others, 571

Personal injury, 556–557
Personal injury endorsement, 477–478
Personal injury protection (PIP) coverage, 527
Personal liability exclusions, 473–474
Personal liability insurance, 468–469
Personal liability of directors and officers, 611–612
Personal liability supplement, 547
Personal lines, 26
Personal lines market, 102
Personal loss exposures, 54
Personal-producing general agent, 100
Personal property
  loss settlement for, 457–459
  in transit, 573
Personal property coverage, 446–447
  cash value coverage, 457
  under Homeowners 3 policy, 452–455
Personal property of others, under building and personal property coverage form, 570
Personal property replacement cost endorsement, 477, 482
Personal Responsibility in Food Consumption Act ("cheeseburger bill"), 427
Personal retirement accounts proposal, under OASDI, 396
Personal risk management programs, 53–56
Personal risks, 8–10, 54–55
Personal umbrella policy, 26, 485–486, 556–559
Pets, exclusion of, 448
Physical abuse exclusion, 473
Physical damage insurance, 26
  aircraft insurance, 606–607
  under boatowners package policy, 549
  with commercial auto insurance, 604–605
  garage coverage form, 605–606
Physical hazard, 5
Physical inspection, 44, 111
Physicians and surgeons equipment coverage form, 583–584
Physician services, 312
  Medicare B coverage of, 397
  visits, 342
Physician's in-hospital benefit, 314

Physicians professional liability insurance, 609–610
  Coverage A, 609–610
  Coverage B, 610
P&I. *See* Protection and indemnity (P&I) insurance
PIA. *See* Primary insurance amount (PIA)
PIP. *See* Personal injury protection (PIP) coverage
Plaintiff, 417
Planning and design exclusion, 456
Plants, coverage for, 450
Pleasure aircraft, aircraft insurance for, 606
Point-of-service (POS) plan, 345
Policies
  assignment of, 461
Policy cancellation, 461
Policy conditions
  commercial crime coverage form, 624–625
  commercial package policy, 569
Policy declarations, commercial package policy, 569
Policy forms, regulation of, 157–158
Policyholders' surplus, 134, 138, 633
Policy Illustration Model Regulation, 272–273
Policy loan provision, 250
Policy nonrenewal, 461
Policy period, 460
  under Personal Auto Policy, 513
Policy provisions
  waiver or change of, 461
Policy reserves, 287–289
Pollutant cleanup and removal, 570–571
Pollution exclusion, commercial general liability policy, 596
Pooled benefits, 319
Pooling of losses, 19–20
Pooling technique, 14
Poor health, risk of, 9, 10
Portability, 351
POS. *See* Point-of-service (POS) plan
Post-loss risk management objectives, 43
Potential legal liability, 178
Potential losses, 43–45, 55
Power failure exclusion, 456
PPOs. *See* Preferred provider organizations (PPOs)
Predetermination-of-benefits provision, 353
Preexisting-conditions clause, 325
Preexisting-conditions provision, 351

Preferred provider organizations (PPOs), 97, 317, 327, 340, 345, 348, 349, 350, 398–399, 401, 407
Preferred providers, 316, 327
Pre-loss risk management objectives, 4
Premature death, 211–213
    declining problem of, 211–212
    financial impact of, 212–213
    risk of, 8
Premium-conversion plans, 355
Premiums
    automobile insurance, 526, 529, 530, 531, 532–536, 537, 538, 539–540
    commercial package policy, 569
    economically feasible, 22–23
    flood insurance, 552
    level-premium method, 221
    life insurance, 249
    calculating, 284–289
    long-term-care insurance, 320
    Medicare Part B, 397–398
    Medicare prescription drug plans, 399
    reducing, 329
    term insurance, 219, 220, 221, 284–286, 286–287
    universal life insurance, 225–226
Prescription drugs, 312, 349
    importing, 401
    negotiating prices, 401
    under Medicare, 399–401
Present value of a life annuity due (PVLAD), 286
Presumptive disability, 322
Price risks, hedging, 14
Primary and excess insurance, 202–203, 501, 503–504
Primary basis, 504
Primary beneficiary, 248
Primary insurance amount (PIA), 388
Principal, 187, 626
Principal sum, 338
Principle of indemnity, 175
Principle of insurable interest, 178
Principle of reasonable expectations, 186
Principle of subrogation, 179
Principle of utmost good faith, 181
Prior-approval laws, 156
Private business, aircraft insurance for, 606
Aircraft insurance, 606–607
Private fee-for-service plans, Medicare, 399, 401

Private insurance, 25–27
Private insurers, 92–98
Private retirement plans, 362–368
Probability, 4, 37–38
Probability analysis, 69–71
Probability distributions, 38–40
Probationary period, 337
Producers, 112
Production, 112–113
Product recall exclusion, commercial general liability policy, 597
Products-completed operations aggregate limit, 599
Products-completed operations hazard, 599
Products liability, 426, 427–428, 594
Professional liability, 473
    medical malpractice crisis, 429–432
Professional liability insurance, 27, 609–611
Professional services exclusion, 473
    ISO personal umbrella policy, 559
Profits, loss of, 574–575
Profit-sharing commission, 110
Profit-sharing plans, 374
Profit stabilization, reinsurance and, 116
Progressive Casualty Insurance Company, 518, 543
Progressive indexing, 393
Prohibited use losses, coverage of, 449
Prompt notice, 457
Proof of loss, filing, 114, 457
Proof-of-loss provision, 325
Property Casualty Insurers Association of America (PCI), 522, 590
Property Casualty Magazine, 146
Property damage
    under equipment breakdown insurance, 578
    to impaired property, 597
    to the insured's product, 596
    to the insured's work, 596
    under no-fault laws, 527–528
    to property of others, 475–476
    to rented premises, commercial general liability policy, 599
    under yacht insurance, 550
Property damage coverage, commercial general liability policy, 595
Property damage exclusion, 474
    commercial general liability policy, 596

Property exclusion, 499
Property held by bailees, 582
Property insurance, 25–26, 545–561
    commercial, 142, 566–591
    rate making in, 139–143, 156–157
Property insurance investments, 123–124
Property insurance marketing systems, 99–102
Property insurers, financial performance, 131–136
Property inventory, 457
Property loss exposures, 44, 54–55
Property not covered, under Homeowners 3 policy, 448–449
Property owners, law of negligence and, 421
Property, perils to, 450–451
Property preservation, 570
Property protection, 457
Property removal coverage, 450
Property rented exclusion, 499
Property risks, 10–11, 55–56
Pro rata liability, 202
Prospective reserve, 288
Protection and indemnity (P&I) insurance, 580–581
Proximate cause relationship, 419, 452
Public adjustor, 114
Publications, state insurance department, 158
Public conveyance exclusion, 499, 501, 504, 507
Public official bonds, 628
Public Risk Management Association, 59, 79
Punitive damages, 419, 428
Punitive damages exclusion, 504
Pure captive, 47
Pure conversion, 94
Pure no-fault plan, 526
Pure premium, 140
Pure premium method, 141
Pure risks, 6, 8–11, 63–65
Pure rule, 419
PVLAD. *See* Present value of a life annuity due (PVLAD)

Q

Qualified retirement plans, 362–363, 368–377
Quarter of coverage, 386
Quicken.com, 465–466, 489
QuickQuote, 282, 332
Quota-share treaty, 118–119

R

Racing vehicle exclusion, 500, 502, 509
   ISO personal umbrella policy, 559
Radar detection equipment exclusion, 509
Radioactive contamination exclusion, under PAP, 507
Railroad Retirement Act, 28, 386
Railroad Unemployment Insurance Act, 28
RAND Institute for Civil Justice, 437, 518, 543, 615
Ratchet method, 297
Rate, 140
Rate adequacy, 139, 156
   underwriting and, 112
Rate making, 108–109
   definitions in, 140
   in life insurance, 143
   methods, 140–143
   objectives of, 139–140, 156
   in property and casualty insurance, 139–143
   regulation, 151
Rate of return, on saving component, 273–275
Rate regulation, 151
Rating agencies, rating categories of, 279
Rating laws, state, 156
Rating system
   business objectives of, 139–140
   regulatory objectives, 139
Ratio test, 363
Readjustment period, after breadwinner's death, 214
Reasonable and customary charges, 314, 342
Reasonable expectations principle, 186
Reasonable repairs coverage, 450
Rebating, 158
Recipient location, 576
Reciprocal exchange, 97
Recordings exclusion, under PAP, 509
Recreational vehicles exclusion, ISO personal umbrella policy, 559
Reduced paid-up insurance, 253
Reentry term, 220
Regional PPOs, 399
Regression analysis, 71
Regulation, state versus federal, 161–163. *See also* Insurance regulation

Regular program, under National Flood Insurance, 551, 552
Rehabilitation provision, under disability-income insurance, 323
Rehabilitation services, under workers compensation, 408
Reimbursement policy, 319, 321
Reinstatement clause, 246–247
Reinstatement provision, 325
Reinsurance, 22, 115–120
   alternatives to traditional, 120–121
   reasons for, 116–118
   types of, 118–120
   underwriting and, 112
Reinsurance facility (pool), 119–120, 530–531
Reinsurance treaties, automatic, 118
Reinsurer, 116
Released bill of lading, 582
Renewable term policies, 219
Renewal provisions, 324–325
Renewal underwriting, 112
Rental apartment property, exclusion of, 449
Rental car exclusion, 509
Rental cars, collision damage waiver (CDW) on, 506–507, 508
Rental of the residence premises exclusion, ISO personal umbrella policy, 558
Renters insurance, 444–445
Repairs, coverage for, 450
Replacement cost, 457–459
   extended and guaranteed, 459
Replacement cost insurance, 177
Replacement cost less depreciation rule, 176
Replacement cost loss settlement endorsement, personal property, 477
Replacement vehicle, coverage of, 496
Reporting forms, 574
Reporting period, basic extended, 600
Reports, annual, 155–156
Representations, 181–182
Reserve for amounts held on deposit, 138
Reserves, 132–133, 138
   legal, 221–222, 287
   life insurance policy, 287–289
   types of, 288–289
Residence exclusion, 474
Residential vehicle exclusion, 501
Residual disability, 322–323
Residual market, 530
Res ipsa loquitur doctrine, 420–421

Respondeat superior doctrine, 422
Restrictions, life insurance policy, 249
Restrictive policy provisions, 329
Retained limit, 607
Retaliatory tax laws, 160
Retention, 46–47, 55
   advantages and disadvantages of, 49–50
   as a method of handling risk, 13
   self-insured, 607
Retention levels, determining, 46–47
Retention limit, 116, 118
Retired workers, health insurance for, 349
Retirement
   amounts saved for, 9, 303
   Monte Carlo simulation of funds, 303
   personal retirement accounts proposal, under OASDI, 396
risk of insufficient income during, 8–9
Retirement ages, 364, 387, 388
Retirement benefit amount, Social Security, 388–389
Retirement benefit formulas, 364–365
Retirement benefits, Social Security, 387–391
Retirement needs, 214, 303
Retirement plans, 361–382
   integration with Social Security, 367–368
   private, 362–368
   qualified, 368–377
   for the self-employed, 374–376
Retirement test, Social Security, 391
Retroactive date, 599–600
Retrocession, 116
Retrocessionaire, 116
Retrospective rating, 143
Retrospective reserve, 288
Return of premium benefit, under long-term-care insurance, 320
Return of premium rider, under disability-income insurance, 324
Return of premium term insurance, 220
Revenues, 134–135
Revocable beneficiary, 248
Riders, 198
   exclusionary, 329
   in insurance contracts, 198
   types of, 261–263, 323–324
Right to sue, under no-fault laws, 527
RIMS. *See* Risk and Insurance Management Society (RIMS)
Riot damage, 453
Rising-floor death benefit, 295

Risk
  burden on society, 11–12
  categories of, 6–8, 63–65, 154–155
  chance of loss versus, 5
  cost of, 55
  defined, 3
  insurable, 21–23
  insurance and, 18–36
  liability, 11, 55, 416–438
  meaning of, 3–4
  methods of handling, 12–14
  preferred, 234
  pure, 6, 8–11, 63–65
  securitization of, 69, 120
Risk analysis questionnaires, 44
Risk and Insurance Management
  Society (RIMS), 59, 79,
  590–591, 616
Risk-based capital, 154–155
Risk-based capital standards,
  154–155
Risk control, 45–46, 55
Risk financing, 45, 46–52
Risk insurance, builders, 287
Risk management, 41–60. *See also*
  Personal risk management programs
  advanced topics in, 61–81
  application problems, 82–86
  benefits of, 53
  changing scope of, 62–65
  defined, 42
  internal cooperation and, 53
  in medicine, 432
  objectives of, 42–43
  steps in, 43
  Web sites, 75–76
Risk management decision making,
  financial analysis in, 72–75
Risk management information system
  (RMIS), 75
Risk management manual, 52–53
Risk management matrix, 53
Risk management policy statement,
  52
Risk management programs, 52
  implementing and administering,
  52–53
  review and evaluation of, 53
  use of technology in, 75–76
Risk managers, average salary of,
  54
Risk mapping, 76
Risk retention, 55
Risk retention groups, 48–49
Risk Theory Society, 17
Risk transfer, 13, 20–21

RMIS. *See* Risk management informa-
  tion system (RMIS)
Robbery, 620
Rollover account, IRA, 301
Roomer/boarder property, exclusion
  of, 448
Rosenbloom, Jerry S, 334
Roth 401(k) plan, 373
Roth 403(b) plan, 374
Roth IRA, 301–302
Roth IRA Web site, 307
Running down clause, 580

S

Safe burglary, 620, 622
Safe driver plans, 535
Safety glazing material, coverage for,
  451
St. Paul Companies, 68
St. Paul Travelers, 68
Sales practices
  regulation of, 157–158
Sandwiched families, premature death
  and, 212
Sarbanes-Oxley Act (2002), 432
Saving component, rate of return on,
  273–275
Savings bank life insurance (SBLI),
  98, 236
Schedule, 447
Schedule approach, 314, 342,
  620–621
Scheduled personal property endorse-
  ment, 477, 483, 549
Schedule rating, 142
Second-to-die life insurance, 236
Section 401(k) plans, 371–373, 375,
  376
Section 403(b) plans, 373–374
Secured creditors, 178
Securities, theft of, 621–622
Securities and Exchange Commission,
  152, 153, 432
Securities coverage, 626
Securities Exchange Act of 1934,
  612
Securitization of risk, 79, 120
Sedgwick Group, 68
Select Quote, 282
Self-employed 401(k) plan, 375, 376
Self-employed persons, retirement
  plans for, 374–375
Self-funding, 48, 341
Self-insurance, 48, 49, 341, 407
Self-Insurance Institute of America,
  59, 79

Self-insured retention (SIR), 557,
  607–608
Self-supporting social insurance pro-
  grams, 386
Selling, professionalism in, 112–113
Separate investment account, 377
SEP-IRA, 376. *See also* Individual
  retirement accounts (IRAs)
SEPs, 376
September 11 terrorist attacks (2001),
  6, 67, 117, 121
Service benefits, 342
Set or pair, loss to, 459
Settlement options, 254–259
  advantages of, 256–257
  disadvantages of, 257–259
  use of a trust, 259
SEUA. *See* South-Eastern
  Underwriters Association
  (SEUA)
Sexual molestation exclusion, 473
Shakespeare, William, 193
Shared market, 530
Shipment of goods, 584
Shortened benefit period, under long-
  term-care insurance, 320
Short-term involuntary unemploy-
  ment, 401
Short-term plans, 354
Sight, loss of, 323
Signs coverage form, 584
Silverware, 549
SIMPLE (Savings Incentive Match
  Plan for Employees) retirement
  plans, 376–377. *See also*
  Individual retirement accounts
  (IRAs)
Simplified employee pensions (SEPs),
  376
Single limit, 497, 523
Single-parent families, premature
  death and, 212
Single people, premature death and,
  212
Single-premium deferred annuity, 294
Single-premium whole life insurance,
  223
SIR. *See* Self-insured retention (SIR)
Six-year graded vesting, 366
Skilled nursing facility care, 395
Sleet damage, 455
Small Business Resources Inc., 621
SMART Act, 166
Smith Barney, 68
Smoke damage, 453
Snow damage, 455
Snowmobiles, 514

Social adequacy, 385
Social insurance, 27–28, 384–414.
        See also Medicare; Social
        Security; Unemployment insur-
        ance; Workers compensation
    characteristics of, 384–386
    programs, compulsory, 384
    reasons for, 384
Social Security, 28, 214, 384, 385,
        386. *See also* Medicare; Old-
        Age, Survivors, and Disability
        Insurance (OASDI); Social
        Security benefits
    cost-of-living adjustment, 391
    covered occupations, 386
    insured status, determination of,
        386–387
    integration of pension plans with,
        367–368
    personal retirement accounts pro-
        posal, pros and cons, 396
    proposed changes, 395
    retirement ages, 387, 388
    saving, 395
    2006 Board of Trustees Report,
        393
    when to draw, 389
Social Security Act of 1935, 386, 401
Social Security Administration (SSA),
        413
Social Security Advisory Board, 393,
        413
Social Security benefits, 387–394
    disability benefits, 395
    financing, 393–394
    retirement benefits, 387–391
    survivor benefits, 391–392
    taxation of, 392–393
Social Security rider, under disability-
        income insurance, 324
Society
    costs and benefits of insurance to,
        28–33
    risk in, 2–17
Society for Risk Analysis (SRA), 17
Society of Actuaries (SOA), 108, 146
Society of Financial Service
        Professionals, 242
"Soft" insurance market, 66–67
Solvency, methods of ensuring,
        154–156, 167
Solvency regulation, 150, 154–156
South-Eastern Underwriters
        Association (SEUA), 152
Sovereign immunity doctrine, 422
Special agent, 112
Special-causes-of-loss form, 195

Special coverage policy, 195
Special damages, 419
Special needs, life insurance and, 214,
        216
Special needs plans, Medicare, 399
Special purpose reinsurance vehicle
        (SPRV), 120
Specialty auto insurers, 531
Specific beneficiary, 248
Specified causes-of-loss coverage, 605,
        606
Speculative risk, 6, 62–65
Spoilage damage coverage, 497, 523,
        579
Spousal IRA, 300
Spouse
    death of, 462
SSA. *See* Social Security
        Administration (SSA)
Stable value fund, 369
Staff model HMO, 344
Stamp collections, 549
Standard coverage (Medicare pre-
        scription drugs), 399
Standard of care, 418
State health insurance pools, 28
State insurance commissions, 151
State insurance departments, 153,
        158, 162
    complaint divisions, 158
State-of-the-art defense, 427–428
State-made rates, 157
Statement of underwriting policy, 109
State Modernization and Regulatory
        Transparency Act (SMART),
        166
State premium tax, 158, 231
State rating laws, 156
State regulation, 161–162
States, and liability laws, 428
State tort reform, 427–429
    effectiveness of, 429
Statistics, 37–38
Steam, exclusion of, 449
Steam discharge or overflow, damage
        from, 455
Stepped-up benefit, 295
Stock insurers, 92–93
Stop-loss limit, 316, 341, 343
Straight deductible, 199
Straight life insurance, 221
Strategic risk, 65
Strict liability, 418
Structures
    coverage for, 446
    loss settlement for, 457–459
    perils to, 451

Subjective probability, 4–5
Subjective risk, 4
Subrogation, 461–462
    principle of, 179–181
    rights, 180, 460
Suicide, 247
Suicide clause, 246
Suit against insurer condition, 459
Supplemental major medical insur-
        ance, 342–343
Supplementary payments, under
        Personal Auto Policy, 498
Supplementary payments coverage,
        commercial general liability
        policy, 598
Surety Association of America, 631
Surety bonds, 27, 626–628
Surety Information Office, 631
Surety (obligor), 626
Surgery, wrong-site, 430
Surgical expense insurance, 342
Surgical expenses, 314
Surgical insurance, 314
Surplus, insurance industry, 67
Surplus lines, 99
Surplus lines broker, 99
Surplus-share treaty, 119
Surrender charge, 296
Surrender cost index, 270–271
Surviving spouse, life income to, 214
Survivor benefits, Social Security,
        391–392
Survivor income benefits, 354–355
Survivors' loss benefits, 527
Swiss Reinsurance Company, 120

T

Tabular reserve, 133
Tabular value method, 133
"Tails," 600
Target premium, 225
Taxable estate, 277
Taxation
    of individual annuities, 297–299
    of life insurance, 275–277
    of long-term-care insurance, 321
    of Social Security benefits, 392–393
Tax-deferred compounding, 295
Tax-qualified retirement plans,
        362–363
Tax-sheltered annuities (TSA),
        373–374
Temporary life annuity due, 286
Temporary residence exclusion,
        453–454
Temporary substitute vehicle, 496

Term4Sale, 282
Terminal illness rider, 262
Terminal reserve, 289
Termination of personal auto policy, 513–514
Term insurance, 219–221, 284
  extended, 253–254
  fifth dividend option for, 252
  limitations of, 220–221
  premiums for, 219, 220, 221, 284–286, 286–287
  types of, 219–220
  uses of, 220
Term to age 65 policy, 220
Termination as to any employee, 625
Territory, auto insurance cost and, 532
Terrorism
  continued threat of, workers compensation and, 117
Terrorism Risk Insurance Act of 2002, 112
Terrorist attacks, 6, 408
  impact on insurance industry, 67, 112
  reinsurance and, 112
  World Trade Center (WTC), 6, 67
Texas Department of Insurance, 206, 524
Theatrical property coverage form, 584
Theft, 620–623
  identity, 478, 479
Theft coverage, 26, 547
Theft losses, 453–455
Third-party claims, in auto insurance, 522, 524
Third-party over cases, 603
Third-party sharing of cost, 336
Three-tier pricing of prescription drugs, 349
Three-year cliff vesting, 366
TIAA-CREF, 307, 381
Tiered networks, 349
Tillinghast-Towers Perrin, 105, 147, 424, 480, 481
Time limit on certain defenses, 326
Time value of money, 72–73, 84
Title insurance, 28, 555–556
Top-heavy plans, 368
Tortfeasor, 417
Tort liability problems, 423–433
  asbestos lawsuits, increase in, 433
  corporate fraud and lax corporate governance, 432–433
  defective tort liability system, 423–429, 529

delays in settling lawsuits, 426
  higher awards, 426
  inefficiency in compensating injured victims, 424–425
  medical malpractice crisis, 429–432
  rising costs, 423–424, 425
  uncertainty of legal outcomes, 425
Tort reform, 427–429
Torts, 417
  intentional, 417
  negligence, 418
  strict liability, 418
Total adjusted capital, 155
Total disability, 259–260, 321–322
Towers Perrin, 105, 128, 147. See also Tillinghast-Towers Perrin
Towing and labor costs, 507
Trade profit/loss, 158
Trading losses exclusion, 624
Traditional families, premature death and, 212
Traditional indemnity plans, 341–343
Traditional IRA, 299–301
Traditional net cost method, 269–270
Trailer, coverage of, 496, 502
Trailer exclusion, 455, 509
Trailer, nonowned, 571
Transactions costs, under no-fault laws, 528, 529
Transportation expenses, under auto damage coverage, 507
Transportation insurance, 580–584
Travelers Insurance Group, 68
Travelers Property Casualty Company, 68
Treaty reinsurance, 118
Trees, coverage for, 450
Trespassers, 421
Trip transit policy, 584
T. Rowe Price, 303
Trust-fund plan, 377
Twisting, 158
Two-income earners, premature death and, 212

U

Ultimate net loss, 607
Umbrella policy
  commercial, 606–607
  personal, 26, 485–486, 556–559
  protections under, 558
Unauthorized entities selling insurance, 164–165
Underinsured motorists coverage, 504–505
Underwriting, 24, 109–112

Underwriting capacity, reinsurance and, 116
Underwriting cycle, 66–68
Underwriting decisions, 111
Underwriting guide, 109
Underwriting information, 110–111
Underwriting losses, medical malpractice and, 431
Underwriting policy, statement of, 109
Underwriting principles, 109–110, 335–336
Underwriting results, recent, 136
Underwriting risk, 40
Unearned premium reserve, 116–117, 133
Unemployment, risk of, 9–10, 23–24
Unemployment insurance, 28, 401–404
  benefits, 402–403
  coverage, 402
  defined, 401
  eligibility, 402
  financing, 403
  objectives, 401
  problems and issues, 403–404
Unfunded reserve, paying losses out of, 47
Unified credit, 276
Unilateral contract, 185
Uninsured boaters coverage, 550
Uninsured for medical care, large number of persons, 312–313
Uninsured locations exclusion, 473
Uninsured motorists coverage, 525–526
  under Personal Auto Policy, 502–505
Uninsured motorists exclusion, 503
Uninsured vehicles, under PAP uninsured motorists coverage, 503
Unintentional loss, 21
Unit-benefit formula, 365, 369
United States Aircraft Insurance Group (USAIG), 606
Universal life insurance, 225–228
  flexibility of, 226
  forms of, 226
  group, 338–340
  income-tax treatment, 227
  limitations of, 228
  variable, 228–232
Unsatisfied judgment funds, 522–525
Urban Property and Reinsurance Act of 1968, 555
USAA Life, 279
USA Today, 312

and-file law, 157
.e of auto, 534
J.S. Chamber of Commerce, 621
U.S. Longshoremen's and Harbor
    Workers' Compensation Act,
    550, 603
*U.S. v. South-Eastern Underwriters
    Association,* 631
Utility interruption coverage, 579
Utmost good faith, principle of,
    181–183

V

Valuable papers and records coverage
    form, 584
Valuable property, 482
Valued policy, 176–177
Valued policy laws, 177
Value reporting form, 574
Vandalism, 452, 453, 475
Vanguard Group, 307, 381
Variable annuities, 294–296, 298,
    299
Variable life insurance, 225
Variable universal life insurance,
    228–231, 232–233
Vehicle exclusions under PAP,
    498–500, 507, 509
    medical payments coverage,
    501–502
Vehicle permission exclusion, 499,
    501–502
Vehicles
    PAP-eligible, 495
    older, and collision coverage, 537
property damage from, 453
Verbal threshold, 526
Vesting provisions, 365–366
Vesting standards, minimum,
    365–366
Viatical Association of America, 267
Viatical settlement, 263
Vicarious liability law, 420
Volcanic eruption, loss resulting from,
    455
Voltaire, 416
Voluntary accidental death and dis-
    memberment insurance, 338

Voluntary personal retirement
    accounts, 394

W

Waiting period. *See* Elimination
    (waiting) periods
Waiver, 187
    of policy provisions, 461
Waiver-of-premium provision,
    259–260
    under disability-income insurance,
    323
War clause, 249
War exclusion, 456, 473
    commercial general liability policy,
    596
Warranties, 183
    implied, 581
Water, exclusion of, 449
Watercraft endorsement, 478
Watercraft exclusion, 454
    commercial general liability policy,
    596
    ISO personal umbrella policy,
    557–559
Watercraft insurance, 549–550
Watercraft liability exclusion, 471
Water damage exclusion, 456
Water discharge or overflow, damage
    from, 455, 573
Water heater damage, 455
Weather derivatives, 70
Weather exclusion, 456
Weather option, 69
WebAnnuities.com, 454
Web sites, risk management,
    75–76
Wells Fargo, 68
Whole life annuity due, 286, 287
Whole life insurance, 221–223. *See
    also* Current assumption whole
    life insurance
    indeterminate-premium, 234
    variations of, 225–234
Windstorm damage, 452–453
Wisconsin State Life Fund, 28
Work, property damage to the
    insured's, 596

Workers compensation, 26, 27, 28,
    404–409, 601–604
    average claim cost, 409
    basic facts about, 602
    benefits, 407–408
    compulsory laws associated with,
    407
    defined, 404
    development of, 405–406
    eligibility requirements for, 407
    objectives of, 406–407
    occupations covered by, 407
    problems and issues associated
    with, 408–409
Workers compensation and employers
    liability insurance policy, 601
Workers compensation exclusions,
    474
    commercial general liability policy,
    596
Workers compensation insurance, 602
Workers Compensation Research
    Institute, 413
Workman, Millicent W., 61
WorldCom, 432
World Trade Center (WTC) attacks,
    6, 67. *See also* September 11
    terrorist attacks (2001)
Worry and fear, as a burden of risk,
    11, 12
Worry and fear reduction, as a benefit
    of insurance, 29
Write-your-own program, 551
Wrong-site surgery, 430
WTC. *See* World Trade Center
    (WTC) attacks

X

X-ray expenses, 314, 342

Y

Yacht insurance, 550
Yearly rate-of-return method
Yearly renewable term insurance,
    219–220, 284–285, 337–338
Young drivers, insuring, 534